D0207345

An Introduction to Social Psychology

FIFTH EDITION

BPS Textbooks in Psychology

BPS Blackwell presents a comprehensive and authoritative series covering everything a student needs in order to complete an undergraduate degree in psychology. Refreshingly written to consider more than North American research, this series is the first to give a truly international perspective. Written by the very best names in the field, the series offers an extensive range of titles from introductory level through to final year optional modules, and every text fully complies with the BPS syllabus in the topic. No other series bears the BPS seal of approval!

Each book is supported by a companion website, featuring additional resource materials for both instructors and students, designed to encourage critical thinking and providing for all your course lecturing and testing needs.

For other titles in this series, please go to **www.bpsblackwell.co.uk**.

An Introduction
to Social Psychology

FIFTH EDITION

EDITED BY

MILES HEWSTONE
WOLFGANG STROEBE
KLAUS JONAS

 The British Psychological Society | BPS BLACKWELL

This edition first published 2012 by the British Psychological Society and John Wiley & Sons Ltd

Copyright © 2012 the British Psychological Society and John Wiley & Sons Ltd

Reprinted September 2013, April 2014

BPS Blackwell is an imprint of John Wiley & Sons Ltd

All effort has been made to trace and acknowledge ownership of copyright. The publisher would be glad to hear from any copyright holders whom it has not been possible to contact.

Cover image: © Radius Images. Used under licence from Getty Images.

Registered office

John Wiley & Sons Ltd, The Atrium, Southern Gate, Chichester, West Sussex, PO19 8SQ, United Kingdom

For details of our global editorial offices, for customer services and for information about how to apply for permission to reuse the copyright material in this book, please see our website at www.wiley.com.

The right of Miles Hewstone, Wolfgang Stroebe and Klaus Jonas to be identified as the editors of this work has been asserted in accordance with the UK Copyright, Designs and Patents Act 1988.

All rights reserved. No part of this publication may be reproduced, stored in a retrieval system, or transmitted, in any form or by any means, electronic, mechanical, photocopying, recording or otherwise, except as permitted by the UK Copyright, Designs and Patents Act 1988, without the prior permission of the publisher.

Wiley publishes in a variety of print and electronic formats and by print-on-demand. Some material included with standard print versions of this book may not be included in e-books or in print-on-demand. If this book refers to media such as a CD or DVD that is not included in the version you purchased, you may download this material at http://booksupport.wiley.com. For more information about Wiley products, visit www.wiley.com.

Designations used by companies to distinguish their products are often claimed as trademarks. All brand names and product names used in this book are trade names, service marks, trademarks or registered trademarks of their respective owners. The publisher is not associated with any product or vendor mentioned in this book. This publication is designed to provide accurate and authoritative information in regard to the subject matter covered. It is sold on the understanding that the publisher is not engaged in rendering professional services. If professional advice or other expert assistance is required, the services of a competent professional should be sought.

Library of Congress Cataloging-in-Publication Data

An introduction to social psychology / Miles Hewstone, Wolfgang Stroebe, Klaus Jonas. – Fifth edition.
    p.   cm.
    Includes bibliographical references and index.
    ISBN 978-1-4443-3544-6 (pbk.)
      1. Social psychology.   2. Social psychology–Europe.   I. Hewstone, Miles.   II. Stroebe, Wolfgang.   III. Jonas, Klaus.
  HM1033.I59 2012
  302–dc23

                                                                                            2012000110

A catalogue record for this book is available from the British Library.

Set in 11/12.5pt Dante MT by MPS Limited, Chennai, India
Printed in Great Britain by Bell and Bain Ltd, Glasgow

The British Psychological Society's free Research Digest e-mail service rounds up the latest research and relates it to your syllabus in a user-friendly way. To subscribe, go to www.researchdigest.org.uk or send a blank e-mail to subscribe-rd@lists.bps.org.uk.

Senior Commissioning Editor: Andrew McAleer
Assistant Editor: Katharine Earwaker
Marketing Managers: Fran Hunt and Jo Underwood
Project Editor: Juliet Booker

To

The memory of Audrey Cole Hewstone (1929–2010)

Lisa Stroebe

Jessie and Julie Jonas

Brief Contents

Contents

Chapter 6 **Attitudes** 171

Geoffrey Haddock and Gregory R. Maio

Notes on Contributors

Felix C. Brodbeck is Chair of Organizational and Economic Psychology at Ludwig-Maximilians University, Munich, Germany. His main research interests are leadership, group performance, collective information processing, economic decision making, diversity and cross-cultural psychology. He has edited or authored several books, including *Culture and Leadership Across the World,* and numerous research papers.

Catrin Finkenauer is Associate Professor at Clinical Child and Family Studies, VU University Amsterdam, The Netherlands. She is currently associate editor of *Social Psychological and Personality Science*. Her research on interpersonal relationships includes basic research on relationship processes (e.g. trust, understanding) and applied research on interventions targeting children who have been witness to or a target of domestic violence and abuse.

Geoffrey Haddock is a Professor of Social Psychology at Cardiff University, UK. He has published widely on the topics of attitudes and social cognition. His current research focuses on affective and cognitive processes of evaluation.

Miles Hewstone is Professor of Social Psychology and Fellow of New College, Oxford University, UK. His main research topic is intergroup relations and the reduction of intergroup conflict, especially via intergroup contact, and he has edited or authored many books. He is founding co-editor (with Wolfgang Stroebe) of the *European Review of Social Psychology,* and has received numerous awards for his research.

Klaus Jonas has taught social and organizational psychology at universities in Germany, Austria and Switzerland. He is Professor of Social and Business Psychology at the University of Zurich, Switzerland. He has published on attitudes, stereotypes and human resource management. His current interests concern the influence of leadership on performance and satisfaction of subordinates.

Johan C. Karremans is Associate Professor at the Behavioural Science Institute (BSI) at the Radboud University Nijmegen, The Netherlands. His research mainly focuses on the processes that benefit or harm interpersonal relationships, especially in the face of relationship threat (e.g. conflict, attractive alternatives).

Sander L. Koole is Associate Professor of Social Psychology at the VU University, Amsterdam. His main research topics are self-regulation and emotion regulation. He co-edited the *Handbook of experimental existential psychology,* which focuses on a new area of psychology that uses experimental methods to investigate how people are dealing with important life issues.

Barbara Krahé is Professor of Social Psychology at the University of Potsdam, Germany. Her research focuses on aggression and social cognition applied to legal decision-making. She is a member of the International Society for Research on Aggression and associate editor of its journal, *Aggressive Behavior*.

Mark Levine is a Professor of Social Psychology at the University of Exeter, UK. His research focuses on the role of social identity in pro-social and anti-social behaviour. His recent work has examined the role of group processes in the regulation of perpetrator, victim and bystander behaviour during aggressive and violent events.

Andrew G. Livingstone is a Lecturer in Social Psychology at the University of Stirling, UK, having previously held positions at Cardiff University. His research focuses on social identity, emotion, and intergroup relations.

Gregory R. Maio is a Professor of Social Psychology at Cardiff University, UK. He has published widely on the topics of attitudes and social cognition. His current research focuses on the mental structure of social values.

Rachel Manning is a Senior Lecturer in Psychology at Anglia Ruskin University, UK. Her research interests include prosocial behaviours such as intervention in emergencies, charitable giving and volunteering.

Antony S. R. Manstead is Professor of Psychology at Cardiff University, UK, having previously held positions at the Universities of Sussex, Manchester, Amsterdam and Cambridge. He has been Editor or Associate Editor of several journals, the most recent case being *Psychological Science*. His research focuses on emotion, attitudes, and social identity.

Robin Martin is Professor of Social and Organizational Psychology at Aston Business School, Aston University, Birmingham, UK. He has served on the faculties of the Universities of Sheffield, Swansea, Cardiff and Queensland (Brisbane, Australia). He conducts research in the area of social influence processes (especially majority and minority influence), workplace leadership, innovation and team working.

Carolyn C. Morf is Professor of Personality Psychology at the University of Bern, Switzerland. Her research focuses on understanding self-regulatory processes through which individuals construct and maintain their desired self-views. She has published numerous chapters and articles on the self, self-regulatory processes, and their expression in personality (in particular narcissism). Her edited books include the *Handbook of Methods in Social Psychology* (Sage, 2004).

Bernard A. Nijstad is Professor of Decision Making and Organizational Behavior at the University of Groningen, The Netherlands. His main research interests are individual and group creativity and individual and group decision-making.

Brian Parkinson lectures at Oxford University, UK. His research focuses on the interpersonal causes, effects and functions of emotion. His books include *Ideas and Realities of Emotion* (1995) and (with Fischer and Manstead) *Emotion in Social Relations* (2005). He was editor of the *British Journal of Social Psychology* from 2004 to 2009 and is currently associate editor of *IEEE Transactions in Affective Computing*.

Louise Pendry is Senior Lecturer in Psychology at Exeter University, UK. She has published articles on stereotyping and social cognition. More recently, her research focuses on some applications of social cognition and stereotype activation/use (e.g. within the field of diversity training).

Stefan Schulz-Hardt is Professor of Industrial, Economic and Social Psychology at Georg-August-University Göttingen, Germany. He has published on group decision-making, escalation of commitment, stress in the workplace, and other topics. He is currently Associate Editor of the *Journal of Economic Psychology*.

Peter B. Smith is Emeritus Professor of Social Psychology at the University of Sussex, UK. His research has mostly been concerned with cross-cultural aspects of formal and informal influence processes, and with cross-cultural communication. He is author (with Bond and Kagitcibasi) of *Understanding Social Psychology across Cultures*, and a former editor of the *Journal of Cross-Cultural Psychology*.

Russell Spears is Professor of Psychology at the University of Groningen, The Netherlands. His main research interests are in social identity processes with particular focus on the group emotions that play a role in intergroup relations. He has edited the *British Journal of Social Psychology* and (with Anne Maass) the *European Journal of Social Psychology*.

Wolfgang Stroebe has taught social psychology at universities in Great Britain, Germany and the US. He now holds professorial positions at both Utrecht University and the University of Groningen in The Netherlands. He has authored many books, chapters and articles in scientific journals on social and health psychology and is co-editor (with Miles Hewstone) of the *European Review of Social Psychology*.

Nicole Tausch obtained her D.Phil at the University of Oxford in 2006. She is currently lecturer in social psychology at the University of St Andrews, UK. Her research interests lie broadly in the areas of social identity, intergroup relations, prejudice, and collective action. She is a recipient of the British Psychological Society's Award for Outstanding Doctoral Research Contributions to Psychology.

Daan van Knippenberg is Professor of Organizational Behavior at the Rotterdam School of Management, Rotterdam, The Netherlands. His current research focuses on leadership, diversity, team performance, and creativity. Daan is Founding Editor of *Organizational Psychology Review* and an associate editor of *Journal of Organizational Behavior*. He is a Fellow of the Society for Industrial and Organizational Psychology, and of the American Psychological Association.

Preface to Fifth Edition

This is the fifth, and completely revised, edition of this bestselling textbook, designed to teach social psychology to an audience of students at universities throughout Europe and many other parts of the world. When, in 1986, we set out with the aim of publishing such a book, we certainly did not imagine that we would be publishing this fifth edition more than a quarter of a century later. This, and the fact that our book has been translated into nearly a dozen foreign languages (ranging from Croatian to Japanese), confirmed the success of our original concept, to have each chapter written by an internationally renowned scholar with great expertise on this particular topic, while making certain of the integration of these chapters through tight editorial control.

Notwithstanding the success of previous editions, we have not stood still. This new volume represents a most thorough revision, both in terms of *who* the authors are and *what* material is covered. Only 10 of the 15 chapters are by the same authors as in the last edition, and even these chapters have been extensively revised to integrate new theoretical and empirical developments. The volume contains chapters dealing with all the core topics one would expect to find in an introduction to social psychology (methods, social perception and attribution, social cognition, self and social identity, attitudes, social influence, aggression, prosocial behaviour, relationships, group processes and intergroup relations). We have also added an important new chapter on cultural social psychology, showing that social psychology is a global science, but also acknowledging the fact that replications of social psychological studies in other parts of the world often result in somewhat different findings. Drawing on studies that have been discussed in many of the earlier chapters in this book, this new chapter shows that cultural variations can benefit social psychologists rather than handicap them. By identifying the social behaviours that are particularly salient in different parts of the world, we can take account of causal factors that have been given insufficient attention within mainstream social psychology. We can also test which social psychological phenomena are universal and which occur only in some parts of the world.

There are many didactic improvements and pedagogical aids in this new edition. Each chapter focuses on the central *theories, concepts, paradigms, results* and *conclusions*. In terms of structure, each chapter contains the following specific features, designed to improve learning and enhance the enjoyment of the task:

- A short 'route map' written in clear English, providing an overview of the chapter.

- A list of key concepts, consisting of the main terms which a student should know about each topic area. The definitions of each key concept are provided in the text of each chapter, and gathered together in an alphabetical glossary at the end of the book.

- The body of the text in each chapter is broken down into clear sections, and the reader is guided by subheadings throughout the chapter, to prevent long, uninterrupted passages of text. Text is also broken up by figures, tables and occasional photographs, and key theories are depicted in 'theory boxes' to aid understanding of more complex processes.

- Each main section or subsection of the chapter begins with 'learning questions'; these are the major questions that the student should be able to answer having read the chapter.

- Each major section of the chapter ends with a summary, and each chapter ends with a summary and conclusions in the form of bullet points.

- A list of further reading is suggested, with a sentence indicating what the student will find in each source.

- Each chapter includes brief biographies of 'leaders in the field', both classic and contemporary scholars from across the globe who have had a major impact on the research area covered in each chapter.

- Each chapter contains boxed features of three different types:
    - *Research close-up*   Brief summaries of classic and contemporary research studies, explaining clearly why and how the research was done, what it found and what its implications are.
    - *Individual differences*   Illustrative items from scales used to measure variables discussed in the text.

- *Social psychology beyond the lab*   Descriptions of some 'real life application' of theory and research described in the chapter.

Features designed to aid learning and help both instructors and students do not end with the material *inside* the book. Extensive online resources are also provided on the web (www.wiley.com/college/hewstone), including a bank of over 1500 self-study and instructor test-bank questions, links to other useful websites, and PowerPoint presentations and flashcards.

As always when we come to the end of an edition, we are grateful that we are such poor predictors of how much work is involved. Had we known this at the outset, we might not have agreed so willingly to undertake a major new edition. As always in such a major enterprise, there are many others to whom we owe thanks. First and foremost, we thank our authors for their excellent manuscripts and their willingness to go through repeated revisions in response to our editorial feedback. We would also like to thank Juliet Booker for her superb work in this endeavour, and both Zora Schnarwyler and Christian Bucher for their diligence in checking the references in the list compiled at the back of the book, Steve Rickaby for his careful work copy-editing this large volume, and Joanna Tester for her apparently inexhaustible supplies of both attention to detail and patience in dealing with editors and authors; last but not least, we thank Rachel New for patiently implementing endless pedantic edits to the final version.

Miles Hewstone, Oxford
Wolfgang Stroebe, Utrecht
Klaus Jonas, Zürich

Guided Tour

CHAPTER HIGHLIGHTS

Key Terms are listed on each chapter opening page, highlighting the main topic areas for students.

KEY TERMS

- attribution theories
- authoritarian personality
- autokinetic effect
- balance theory
- Bennington study
- consistency theories
- covariation theory
- crisis in social psychology
- demand characteristics
- European Association of Social Psychology
- experiment
- experimenter expectancy effects
- field experiment
- field theory
- laboratory experiment
- methodological individualism
- minimal group paradigm
- priming
- realistic conflict theory
- rebound effect
- scapegoat theory
- social facilitation
- social loafing

Chapter Outline reflects the coverage of each chapter, by main and subsection headings.

CHAPTER OUTLINE

A short outline of each chapter, written in clear English, is presented in the **Route Map of the Chapter**.

ROUTE MAP OF THE CHAPTER

Most textbooks introduce social psychology with examples of everyday experiences of social behaviour or even with a formal definition. We thought that a better way of familiarizing you with our discipline was to present some examples of classic studies. These should give you an impression of the research questions social psychologists address and of the methods they use to tackle these questions. Only then do we present a formal definition of social psychology and discuss the differences between social psychology and related areas. The second part of the chapter is devoted to the history of social psychology, which we trace from its starting years around 1900 until today. As our American colleagues like to point out, much of this history took place in the US. However, as we Europeans like to point out, this development was strongly influenced by European researchers, even before the establishment of social psychology in Europe during the last four decades.

ENHANCED LEARNING TOOLS

Each main section or subsection starts with a '**learning question**' (rendered purple in the printed book), major questions that the student should be able to answer upon completion of the chapter.

Each main section ends with a **Summary** to aid memorizing key segments of the content as students progress through the chapter.

Key Terms listed at the beginning of the chapter are emboldened at the first point of use in the current chapter and appear with their **definition** at the first main point of discussion in the book. All Key Terms and definitions are collated and arranged alphabetically in the **Glossary** at the back of the book.

---

the target that marks the beginning of a new episode and may further escalate or de-escalate the conflict. The general aggression model provides a structure that helps us to understand the complex processes through which particular input variables, such as violent media stimuli or biographical experiences of abuse, can lead to aggressive behaviour as the critical outcome variable.

Summary

This section has presented the most prominent theories of the causes and underlying processes of aggressive behaviour. Biological theories focus on the role of genetic and hormonal factors accounting for differences in aggressive behaviour. In contrast, psychological theories refer to affective and cognitive reactions to aggression-eliciting stimuli and how they pave the way for aggressive responses. These models show that negative affect – caused by a range of adverse stimuli such as frustration, pain or noise – is a powerful trigger of selective information processing that enhances the probability of aggressive behaviour. This information processing draws on aggressive scripts, i.e. abstract representations of how and when aggressive behaviour should be enacted. Another well-supported theoretical position is that aggression is a form of learned behaviour, implemented in the individual's behavioural repertoire through direct reinforcement as well as observational learning. The general aggression model integrates the diverse psychological theories of aggression into a common framework.

PERSONAL AND SITUATIONAL VARIABLES AFFECTING AGGRESSIVE BEHAVIOUR

Do people differ in their propensity to engage in aggressive behaviour, and what are critical factors in the situation or the social environment that make aggressive behaviour more likely?

In this section, we will take a closer look at some of the factors associated with differences between people and between situations in their likelihood of showing or evoking aggression. In terms of the general aggression

model, these are the input variables that are crucial in eliciting cognitive, affective and physiological responses that may or may not lead to an aggressive response. The guiding question for this section is: how can we distinguish between more or less aggressive individuals and groups of individuals; and what situational influences of a transient or persistent nature precipitate aggressive behaviour?

Individual differences in aggressive behaviour

Researchers have suggested several variables as predictors of individual differences in aggressive behaviour. In this section we will focus on three that have received intense research attention: **trait aggressiveness**, **hostile attribution bias**, and gender (cf. Krahé, 2012, Chapter 3, for a coverage of additional person variables related to aggression).

trait aggressiveness denotes stable differences between individuals in the likelihood and intensity of aggressive behaviour.

hostile attribution bias tendency to attribute hostile intentions to a person who has caused damage when it is unclear whether or not the damage was caused accidentally or on purpose.

Trait aggressiveness The concept of trait aggressiveness describes dispositional (i.e. temporally and cross-situationally stable) differences between individuals with respect to the likelihood of showing aggressive behaviour. Whereas some individuals are easy to anger and quickly get 'hot under the collar', others are generally less inclined to respond with aggression. Longitudinal studies following the same research participants over many years from childhood into adulthood have shown that the tendency to engage in aggressive behaviour is remarkably stable over time. Drawing on findings from 16 studies exploring the temporal stability of men's aggressive behaviour, Olweus (1979) found a stability coefficient of $r = .76$ over a one year period, of $r = .69$ over five years and still of $r = .60$ over a period of 10 years. These figures are matched only by the stability of intelligence scores over time, and indicate that aggression in later stages of development may be predicted on the basis of earlier aggression scores. Trait aggressiveness is conceptualized as a multidimensional construct comprising four different components: physical aggression, verbal aggression, anger and hostility. It is typically assessed by self-report questionnaires in which participants indicate the likelihood of showing different forms of physical aggression, verbal aggression, anger and hostility. The most widely used instrument is the Aggression Questionnaire (Buss & Perry, 1992; Buss & Warren, 2000; see Individual Differences 9.1), but there

---

Table 2.2 *How well do some common criticisms levelled at web-based studies stand up to empirical scrutiny?*

Preconceptions about Internet methods	
Preconception	**Finding**
1. Internet samples are not demographically diverse.	*Mixed.* Internet samples are more diverse than traditional samples in many domains (e.g. gender), but they are not completely representative of the population.
2. Internet samples are maladjusted, socially isolated, or depressed.	*Myth.* Internet users do not differ from non-users on markers of adjustment and depression.
3. Internet participants are unmotivated.	*Myth.* Internet methods provide ways of motivating participants (e.g. by providing feedback).
4. Internet data are compromised by the anonymity of respondents.	*Fact.* However, Internet researchers can take steps to eliminate repeat responders.
5. Internet-based findings differ from those obtained using other methods.	*Myth?* Evidence so far suggests that Internet-based findings are consistent with those obtained using traditional methods, but more data are needed.

Gosling and colleagues (2004) compared a large Internet sample ($N = 361,703$) with a set of 510 published traditional samples and were led to the conclusions summarized above.

Source: Adapted from Table 1 of Gosling et al. (2004). *American Psychologist, 59,* 93–104. Adapted with permission of APA.

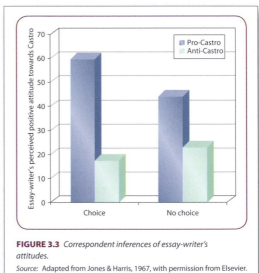

FIGURE 3.3 *Correspondent inferences of essay-writer's attitudes.*

Source: Adapted from Jones & Harris, 1967, with permission from Elsevier.

FIGURE 3.8 *Your behaviour, e.g. being lively at a party, may appear more consistent to others than it really is.*

Source: © Melissa Farlow. Used under licence from Getty Images.

The main chapter text is punctuated by **diagrams, graphs, tables and occasional photographs**, all present to improve the reading and learning experience.

Key theories are made accessible in the text by way of **Theory Box** features to aid the understanding of more complex processes.

THEORY BOX 3.2

FIVE STEPS TO DEPRESSION: THE ATTRIBUTIONAL REFORMULATION OF LEARNED HELPLESSNESS THEORY

Objective non-contingency
Nothing the person does makes a difference to what happens.

Perceived non-contingency
The person notices that nothing she does makes a difference.

Attribution
Non-contingency is attributed to internal, global and stable factors.

Expectations of non-contingency
The person concludes that future actions will make no difference to what happens.

Helplessness symptoms
Depression coupled with motivational deficits.

Source: Based on Abramson, Seligman, & Teasdale (1978). Learned helplessness in humans: Critique and reformulation. *Journal of Abnormal and Social Psychology, 87*, p. 52. Adapted with permission of APA.

Brief biographies of **Leaders in the Field** are included, representing both classic and contemporary scholars from around the world, specific to the research area covered in each chapter.

LEADER IN THE FIELD

Daniel Gilbert (b. 1957) is Professor in Psychology at Harvard University. His academic career started inauspiciously at the age of 19 when his intention of studying creative writing in order to become a science fiction writer was thwarted because the class was full. The only available alternative was an Introduction to Psychology course. He still ended up as a best-selling author, but of non-fiction instead of fiction. The book in question (*Stumbling on Happiness*, 2006) drew on his influential research (with Timothy Wilson) into *affective forecasting*, which concerns people's often inaccurate predictions about their own emotional reactions to events (see Wilson & Gilbert, 2003). Of course, he is also famous for his innovative research on the correspondence bias.

Research Close-Ups provide brief summaries of pertinent research studies, both classic and contemporary, as an aid to explain why and how research was carried out and what the results implied.

ATTITUDE CONTENT AND PERSUASION

RESEARCH CLOSE-UP 6.1

Haddock, G., Maio, G. R., Arnold, K., & Huskinson, T. L. H. (2008). Should persuasion be affective or cognitive? The moderating effects of need for affect and need for cognition. *Personality and Social Psychology Bulletin, 34*, 769–778.

Introduction

In the 1970s a series of famous television advertisements shown in North America featured former professional athletes exalting their preference for a particular brand of beer. While some of the athletes noted that the beer was *less filling* than other beers, others replied that it *tasted great*. The first component of the message highlighted a positive belief about the beverage (i.e. its low caloric intake), whereas the second component highlighted a positive affective response associated with the beverage (i.e. its taste). Which part of the message would you find more persuasive? Perhaps it depends on whether your attitudes tend to be based more upon the content of your beliefs or more upon the content of your feelings.

Haddock and colleagues (2008) tested whether individuals whose attitudes tend to be based more on cognition or affect would be more or less persuaded by an appeal that was either cognitive or affective in nature. Based on previous research, they predicted that individuals with affect-based attitudes would be more persuaded by an affect-based appeal compared to a cognition-based appeal, whereas individuals with cognition-based attitudes would be more persuaded by a cognition-based appeal compared to an affect-based appeal.

Method

Participants

Twenty-four students (16 women and 8 men) took part for psychology course credit.

Design and procedure

The basic design included two factors: whether a person's attitudes were based more on cognition or affect, and whether they received a persuasive appeal that was cognitive or affective. The basis of a person's attitudes as cognitive or affective was determined by their responses on two scales: (1) the need for cognition scale (Cacioppo & Petty, 1982), which measures individuals' tendency to engage in and enjoy effortful processing (see Individual Differences 7.1, Chapter 7); and (2) the need for affect scale (Maio & Esses, 2001), which measures individuals' tendency to seek out emotional experiences. Participants high in need for cognition and low in need for affect were conceptualized as being cognition-based, while participants high in need for affect and low in need for cognition were conceptualized as being affect-based.

In the experiment, participants were informed that they would be evaluating a new beverage called 'Power-Plus'. Half of the participants were randomly assigned to receive an affect-based appeal, and the other half to receive a cognition-based appeal. Participants in the affect-based appeal condition tasted a sample of a pleasant tasting, unfamiliar beverage. The affect within the appeal is derived from the pleasant feeling resulting from having tasted the beverage. Participants in the cognition-based appeal condition read a set of strong and positive attributes about the drink. For instance, they were told that the drink was made from natural ingredients and contained real fruit extracts. Immediately after either tasting or reading about Power-Plus, participants indicated their attitude toward the beverage using a series of nine-point semantic differential scales (good – bad; positive – negative; like – dislike).

Results and discussion

The results of the study provided support for the researchers' hypothesis that the effectiveness of cogent affect- and cognition-based persuasive messages depends on individual differences in need for affect and need for cognition (see Figure 6.6). As expected, an affect-based message was more persuasive among individuals with an affect preference (i.e. individuals high in need for affect and low in need for cognition), whereas a cognition-based message was more persuasive among individuals with a cognition preference (i.e. individuals low in need for affect and high in need for cognition). These results demonstrate how the content of an attitude influences persuasion (see also Mayer & Tormala, 2010).

FIGURE 6.6 *The influence of affective–cognitive preference and appeal type on attitudes.*

Source: Adapted from Haddock et al., 2008. Reproduced with permission from SAGE Publications Ltd.

INDIVIDUAL DIFFERENCES 2.1

MEASURING THE TENDENCY TO RESPOND IN SOCIALLY DESIRABLE WAYS

Paulhus (1984, 1991) has developed a measure known as the Balanced Inventory of Desirable Responding (BIDR). On the basis of detailed pre-testing, and prediction of actual differences in behaviour, Paulhus was able to create two sub-scales, one measuring self-deceptive enhancement and the other measuring impression management. *Self-enhancement* refers to the tendency to think of oneself in a favourable light, whereas *impression management* refers to a deliberate attempt to distort one's responses in order to create a favourable impression with others. Below are example items from each sub-scale.

Self-enhancement
- My first impressions of people usually turn out to be right
- I always know why I like things
- I never regret my decisions
- I am a completely rational person

Respondents who agree with such items are deemed to have positively biased images of themselves (on the grounds that it is unlikely that these statements are true for most people).

Impression management
- I never swear
- I never conceal my mistakes
- I never drop litter in the street
- I never read sexy books or magazines

Respondents who agree with such items are deemed to be motivated to present themselves in positive ways (again, it is unlikely that these statements are true for most people).

Scores on these scales can be used to detect respondents who may be attempting to present themselves in a favourable light. If their scores on self-enhancement or impression management scales are correlated with their responses to other measures, it seems likely that the latter responses have been affected by social desirability, and these effects can be partialled out using statistical techniques.

Individual Differences are illustrative items from scales used to measure variables discussed in the text.

Social Psychology Beyond the Lab are feature boxes that describe various 'real-life applications' of theory and research applicable to the content of the current chapter.

SOCIAL PSYCHOLOGY BEYOND THE LAB 6.1

ATTITUDES AND PUBLIC OPINION SURVEYS

Given the importance of attitudes in understanding behaviour, it is not surprising that they have an enormous impact 'beyond the lab'. One area where attitudes and attitude measurement is very important is in the context of public opinion surveys. The use of public opinion surveys is widespread – across continents and across issues. For instance, public opinion surveys are often used to gauge the public's attitudes toward things like their national government, views on core social issues or policies (such as environmental attitudes or attitudes toward capital punishment), even to assess levels of happiness in a country and how happiness might change over time.

These opinion surveys will usually be carried out by public companies (e.g. the Gallup organization in the United States; IPSOS-MORI or YouGov in the United Kingdom) or through government organizations (e.g. the Office for National Statistics in the United Kingdom). Often, these surveys will be developed by individuals with a background in social psychology, and their methodology will almost certainly have been informed by advances made by social psychologists. Public opinion surveys might be completed over the phone, via post, or more recently, via the Internet.

One particularly interesting development has been the application of response time methodologies to public opinion surveys. Research by John Bassili and colleagues (e.g. Bassili, 1993, 1996; Bassili & Fletcher, 1991) has utilized computer-assisted telephone interviewing (CATI) to integrate contemporary attitudes research with public opinion surveys. The methodology involves the use of a computer clock that can provide millisecond accuracy in the timing of responses and a voice-recognition framework that converts an individual's responses into signals that trigger the clock after the interviewer asks a question. Using the CATI approach in a survey of Canadians' opinions, Bassili (1993) tested how two operationalizations of attitude strength, attitude accessibility and attitude certainty, might predict the discrepancy between an individual's voting intentions and their actual voting behaviour. The results showed that the response-time measure of accessibility was a significant predictor of the discrepancy between people's voting intentions and their actual voting behaviour. For example, the more accessible the attitude, the lower the discrepancy between voting intentions and voting behaviour.

END-OF-CHAPTER RESOURCES

A list of key learning points are presented in the **Chapter Summary** to help students consolidate their knowledge and understanding of the chapter's content.

CHAPTER SUMMARY

- *What is an attitude?* An attitude is an overall evaluation of an attitude object.
- *Can we have attitudes about anything?* Anything that can be evaluated along a dimension of favourability can be conceptualized as an attitude object.
- *What are the bases of attitudes?* Attitudes have affective, cognitive and behavioural antecedents. All three antecedents contribute to our overall evaluation of an object.
- *Is the structure of an attitude best considered to be one-dimensional or two-dimensional?* The two-dimensional perspective is advantageous as it allows for attitude ambivalence.
- *Why do we hold attitudes?* Attitudes serve a variety of functions, the most important of which is the object appraisal function.
- *Why is it useful to know the function of an attitude?* Knowing the function of an attitude is important because attempts to change an attitude are more likely to be successful when the persuasive appeal matches the attitude's function.
- *Does it matter if an attitude is strong or weak?* Yes – strong attitudes are more stable over time, more resistant to change and more likely to guide both information processing and behaviour.
- *What is the difference between explicit and implicit measures of attitude?* Explicit measures directly ask respondents to think about and report their attitude, whereas implicit measures do not.
- *Do explicit and implicit measures predict different types of behaviour?* Research has shown that explicit measures are more effective in predicting deliberative behaviour, whereas implicit measures are more effective in predicting spontaneous behaviour.
- *Do attitudes predict behaviour?* On the whole, attitudes do a reasonable job of predicting behaviour. The degree to which attitudes predict behaviour depends on a number of factors, including correspondence, the domain of behaviour, the strength of an attitude and person variables.
- *How do attitudes predict behaviour?* A number of models have been developed to understand how attitudes predict behaviour. The most influential models are the theory of planned behaviour and the MODE model.

Each chapter ends with a list of **Suggestions for Further Reading** indicating key material found in each resource.

SUGGESTIONS FOR FURTHER READING

Albarracín, D., Johnson, B. T., & Zanna, M. P. (Eds.). (2005). *Handbook of attitudes.* Mahwah, NJ: Erlbaum. This volume offers an advanced review of the field of attitudes research.

Cialdini, R. B. (2008). *Influence: Science and practice (5th ed.).* Boston, MA: Allyn & Bacon. This volume offers an accessible look at research on social influence.

Crano, W., & Prislin, R. (Eds.). (2009). *Attitudes and persuasion.* New York: Psychology Press. This volume reviews different streams of research on attitudes and attitude change.

Eagly, A. H., & Chaiken, S. (1993). *The psychology of attitudes.* Fort Worth, TX: Harcourt Brace Jovanovich. This volume provides a comprehensive review of research that laid the foundation for the progress that has been made in the past two decades.

Fazio, R. H., & Olson, M. A. (2003). Implicit measures in social cognition research: Their meaning and use. *Annual Review of Psychology, 54,* 297–327. This paper reviews advances that have been made concerning implicit measures of attitude.

Fazio, R. H., & Petty, R. E. (Eds.). (2007). *Attitudes: Structure, function, and consequences.* Hove, UK: Psychology Press. This volume comprises a collection of important published papers on attitude structure, attitude content and the attitude–behaviour relation.

Haddock, G., & Maio, G. R. (Eds.). (2004). *Contemporary perspectives on the psychology of attitudes.* Hove, UK: Psychology Press. This volume reviews a number of contemporary research programmes on the psychology of attitudes.

Maio, G. R., & Haddock, G. (2010). *The psychology of attitudes and attitude change.* London: Sage. This volume provides a comprehensive and accessible overview of research and theories relevant to the psychology of attitudes.

Maio, G. R., & Olson, J. M. (Eds.). (2000). *Why we evaluate: Functions of attitudes.* Mahwah, NJ: Erlbaum. This volume is a comprehensive examination of research on attitude functions.

Petty, R. E., & Cacioppo, J. T. (1986). *Communication and persuasion: Central and peripheral routes to attitude change.* New York: Springer. This volume highlights the research that was conducted in the development of the highly influential Elaboration Likelihood Model of persuasion.

Petty, R. E., Fazio, R. H., & Briñol, P. (Eds.). (2009). *Attitudes: Insights from the new implicit measures.* New York: Psychology Press. This volume highlights different research programmes regarding implicit measures of attitude.

Wittenbrink, B., & Schwarz, N. (Eds.). (2007). *Implicit measures of attitudes.* New York: Guilford. This volume provides an overview of different perspectives on the utility of implicit measures of attitude.

Accompanying Online Resources for Instructors and Students

BOOK COMPANION SITE FOR INSTRUCTORS

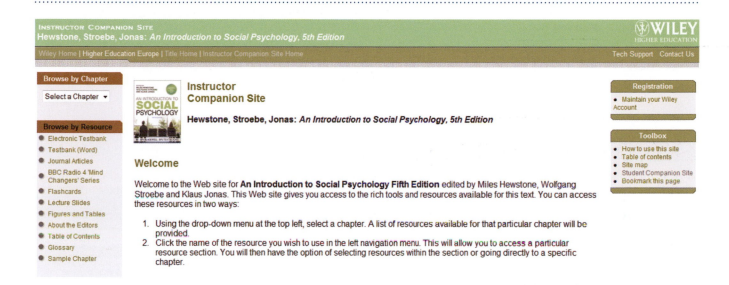

The Book Companion Site contains an extensive support package for instructors and can be found at **www.wiley.com/college/hewstone**.

On the website instructors will find:

- Test bank with over 1000 questions, including true/false, multiple choice and essay questions.
- Computerized test bank allowing instructors to create and print multiple versions of the test bank, as well as allowing users to customize exams by altering or adding new questions.
- PowerPoint presentations containing a combination of key concepts, examples, and figures and tables from the book.
- Flashcards showing key terms and definitions from the glossary.
- Links to the BBC Radio 4 'Mind Changers' series with contributions from the editors.

BOOK COMPANION SITE FOR STUDENTS

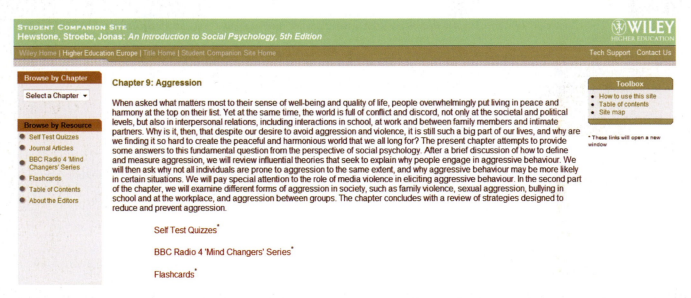

The *Introduction to Social Psychology* student website provides students with support material that will help develop their conceptual understanding of the material. The student website contains:

- Over 500 Self-Study Quizzes including true/false, multiple choice and 'fill in the blank' questions to aid students' learning and self-study.

- Links to relevant journal articles that are referenced in the text to encourage further reading and critical analysis of the material.

- Flashcards showing key terms and definitions from the glossary.

- Links to the BBC Radio 4 'Mind Changers' series with contributions from the editors.

1 Introducing Social Psychology

WOLFGANG STROEBE, MILES HEWSTONE AND KLAUS JONAS

Source: © Action Plus. Used under licence from Getty Images.

KEY TERMS

- attribution theories
- authoritarian personality
- autokinetic effect
- balance theory
- Bennington study
- consistency theories
- covariation theory
- crisis in social psychology

- demand characteristics
- European Association of Social Psychology
- experiment
- experimenter expectancy effects
- field experiment
- field theory
- laboratory experiment

- methodological individualism
- minimal group paradigm
- priming
- realistic conflict theory
- rebound effect
- scapegoat theory
- social facilitation
- social loafing

CHAPTER OUTLINE

ROUTE MAP OF THE CHAPTER

Most textbooks introduce social psychology with examples of everyday experiences of social behaviour or even with a formal definition. We thought that a better way of familiarizing you with our discipline was to present some examples of classic studies. These should give you an impression of the research questions social psychologists address and of the methods they use to tackle these questions. Only then do we present a formal definition of social psychology and discuss the differences between social psychology and related areas. The second part of the chapter is devoted to the history of social psychology, which we trace from its starting years around 1900 until today. As our American colleagues like to point out, much of this history took place in the US. However, as we Europeans like to point out, this development was strongly influenced by European researchers, even before the establishment of social psychology in Europe during the last four decades.

INTRODUCTION: SOME CLASSIC STUDIES

How do social psychologists go about addressing research questions?

In 1954, Muzafer Sherif (see the Leader in the Field, Muzafer Sherif, in Chapter 14), who was then professor of social psychology at the University of Oklahoma (US), conducted one of a series of classic studies with 11–12 year-old boys, who had been sent to a remote summer camp at Robbers Cave State Park, Oklahoma. None of the boys knew each other before the study. They were divided into two groups, who stayed in cabins far apart from each other and did not know of each other's existence. For one week, each of the groups enjoyed the typical summer camp life, engaging in fun activities like camping out, transporting canoes over rough terrain to the water and playing various games. They had a great time. It is therefore not surprising that at the end of the week, group members had grown very fond of one another and the groups had developed strong group identities. Each chose a name for itself (the 'Rattlers' and the 'Eagles'), which they proudly displayed on shirts and flags.

At the end of the week, each of the groups was told that there was another group in the vicinity. As though acceding to the boys' requests, the staff arranged tournaments of games (e.g. touch football, baseball, tug of war) between the groups. The winning team would receive a cup, and members of the winning team would each be given a new penknife. The tournament started in the spirit of good sportsmanship, but as it progressed, hostilities between the groups began to develop. 'Soon members of each group began to call their rivals "stinkers", "sneaks" and "cheats" . . . Near the end of this stage, the members of each group found the other group and its members so distasteful that they expressed strong preferences to have no further contact with them at all' (Sherif, 1967, p. 82).

What was the point of all of this? What can tales about boys in a summer camp tell us about real life? The answer is a great deal. These Robber's cave studies actually mark a turning point in the study of prejudice (i.e. dislike for members of an outgroup), because they challenged the then dominant view of prejudice as either an outflow of a prejudiced personality disposition (**authoritarian personality**; see Chapter 14) or as the result of displaced frustration (**scapegoat theory**). There was no indication that these boys had prejudiced personalities or needed scapegoats to displace their aggression. And yet, they developed strong dislikes for the members of the other group (the 'stinkers' and 'sneaks'), because they were competing with them for some valued good which only one of the two groups could attain. Sherif interpreted these findings as support for his **realistic conflict theory**, which assumed that intergroup hostility and intergroup prejudice are usually the result of a conflict of interest between groups over valued commodities or opportunities. Goals were the central concept in Sherif's theory: he argued that when two groups were competing for the same goal, which only one could achieve, there would be intergroup hostility.

Not surprising, you might say. After all, this is the reason why football supporters beat each other up every so often before and after games between their clubs. And yet, this is not the full story. Nearly two decades later, Henri Tajfel (see Leader in the Field, Henri Tajfel, in Chapter 14), then professor of social psychology at Bristol University (UK), and colleagues conducted a series of studies that called into question the assumption that competitive goals are a necessary condition for the development of intergroup hostility (Tajfel, Billig, Bundy, & Flament, 1971). Participants in these studies were 14- to 15-year-old schoolboys, who all knew each other well and came to the psychology laboratory in groups of eight to participate in an **experiment** (see Chapter 2) on visual perception. Their task was to estimate the number of dots that were flashed onto a screen. After completion of this task, they were told that they would also participate in a second experiment and, for the ease of coding, would be divided on the basis of the dot estimates they had just made. Half the boys were then (randomly) assigned to the 'under-estimators' group, the other half to the 'over-estimators' group. (In later studies, boys were often divided on the basis of their alleged preference for paintings by Klee or Kandinsky, an equally irrelevant criterion for boys of that age.) The boys then had to assign rewards to other individuals in real money. They did not know the identity of the other individuals, but only their code numbers and their group membership.

This experimental procedure became known as **minimal group paradigm**. These groups were minimal, because they were created using arbitrary criteria, involved no interaction between

scapegoat theory the theory that prejudice is due to aggression displaced towards members of an outgroup (scapegoats), because the group (or circumstances) that was the source of frustration is not within reach.

realistic conflict theory a theory developed by Sherif that holds that conflict and competition between groups over valued resources can create intergroup hostility and prejudice.

minimal group paradigm a set of experimental procedures designed to create groups based on essentially arbitrary criteria (with no interaction within or between them, and with no knowledge of who else belongs to each group) whose members show intergroup discrimination.

members of the two groups, and group members had no knowledge of who belonged to the group. And yet Tajfel could show that members of these groups displayed intergroup discrimination. When asked to divide money between a member of their own group and a member of the other group, most boys gave consistently more money to members of their own group than to members of the other group (see Chapter 14). These studies were again quite innovative, because they showed that intergroup conflict was not an essential cause of intergroup discrimination (or at least ingroup favouritism). Apparently, the mere fact of division into groups was sufficient to trigger discriminatory behaviour.

You might now believe that you have some idea of what social psychology is all about and how social psychologists conduct their research. You might also think that the approach of Sherif was more in line with what you had expected, but that the studies by Tajfel, despite their artificiality, led to some interesting results. However, you will be somewhat premature in your confidence. A clearer and more appropriate picture of the field of social psychology will emerge after considering some additional studies, described below.

In 1994, Neil Macrae (then at Cardiff University) and colleagues studied people's ability to suppress their prejudicial thoughts (Macrae, Bodenhausen, Milne, & Jetten, 1994). After all, there is a great deal of evidence that people acquire their prejudices quite early and may not be able to get rid of them later in life, even if these prejudicial thoughts have become inconsistent with their egalitarian values (Wilson, Lindsey, & Schooler, 2000). Thus, if people cannot forget their prejudicial thoughts, it would be good if, at least, they could inhibit them and prevent them from affecting their actions. As the studies by Macrae et al. (1994; see Chapter 4) show, this may be more difficult than one would think.

Participants in these studies were students. When they arrived at the laboratory, they were told that they were to participate in an investigation of people's ability to construct life event details from visual information. They were then presented with a colour photograph of a skinhead and were asked to write a short essay about a typical day in the life of a skinhead (Figure 1.1). Skinheads were chosen here not only because there is widespread prejudice against them, but also because, unlike prejudice towards other minority groups, expressing prejudice towards skinheads is not (yet) politically incorrect. Half of the participants were asked to suppress their prejudice against skinheads in writing this essay. They were told to try to write their essay without being influenced by their stereotypes about skinheads – that is, the beliefs they might have about the characteristics of skinheads in

FIGURE 1.1 *How easy is it for people to suppress their prejudice towards skinheads?*
Source: © BROOKS WALKER. Used under licence from Getty Images.

general. The other half (i.e. the control group) were not given this instruction.

After the participants had finished the first essay, they were given a photo of another skinhead and asked to write another essay. This time, however, they were not given any instructions about suppressing stereotypes. Both essays were then rated by independent raters, who did not know whether a given essay had been written by a participant from either the experimental or the control group and who evaluated the extent to which writers expressed stereotypes about skinheads. With regard to the first essay, results were not very surprising. As one would expect of 'good' (i.e. obedient) participants, individuals who had been instructed to suppress their stereotypes in their first essay did so quite successfully. Their essays were much less stereotypic than the essays of the control group. However, the analysis of their second essays provided a striking finding: there was a **rebound effect** (see Chapter 4). The second essay of these 'suppressors' was more stereotypic than that of the control group. Thus, when people no longer tried to suppress their stereotypes, they showed a higher level of stereotypical thinking than if they had never tried to suppress their thoughts in the first place.

Although these are fascinating results, Macrae and his colleagues were not satisfied with merely showing a rebound effect of stereotype suppression on thinking (see Chapter 4): they also wanted to know whether attempts to suppress one's stereotype would affect people's behaviour. They therefore conducted a second study. The first part of this study was identical to that of their first experiment. However, after having written an essay under either stereotype suppression or no-suppression instructions, participants were told that they would now go next door to meet the person depicted in the photograph (i.e. the skinhead). When they entered the room next door, there was a row of chairs standing next to each other, but no skinhead. However, on the first chair there was a denim jacket and bag. The experimenter told the participant that the other person must just have gone to the toilet and would return shortly and that the participant should sit down on one of the chairs in the meantime. The measure of interest in this case was the seating position, that is, how far the participant would choose to sit away from the skinhead he or she was supposed to meet. We would all acknowledge that the distance we keep from someone is an indication of our liking for that person (Macrae et al., 1994). And in line with the findings of the previous study, participants who had (successfully) suppressed their stereotype on writing the essay now chose a chair that was significantly further away from the skinhead than did individuals in the control group. Thus, the rebound effect of stereotype suppression affected not only thoughts, but also behaviour (but for some constraints on the general effect, see Monteith, Sherman, & Devine, 1998).

As surprising as these findings were, the impact of stereotypes on behaviour was still restricted to the way the individual behaved towards a member of the group towards whom the stereotype was held. As we will see in the next experiment, the impact of stereotypes can be even more pervasive. This study was conducted by John Bargh (see Leader in the Field, John Bargh, in Chapter 4) and his colleagues (Bargh, Chen, & Burrows, 1996) at New York University (US). In the first part of this experiment, participants had to complete a 'scrambled sentence test' in which they had to form sentences from scrambled sets of words. For participants in the experimental group, these sentences contained words that were part of the (American) stereotype of the elderly, such as 'Florida', 'Bingo' and 'grey'. This procedure is known as **priming** (see Chapter 4), because these words will bring the elderly stereotype to participants' minds (i.e. make it more accessible), including characteristics of elderly people that were not even mentioned in the priming procedure.

One such characteristic that is typically attributed to the elderly, but which was not mentioned in the priming procedure, is that elderly people move rather slowly. The researchers assumed that participants who were primed with the stereotype of the elderly would also think of 'moving slowly' as another salient characteristic of the elderly. It was further assumed that this thought would affect the participants' own behaviour. The researchers predicted that participants primed with the elderly stereotype would move more slowly than participants in the control condition who had been exposed to neutral primes. The experimenters then measured the time it

took participants to walk from the experimental room to the nearest lift. In line with the hypothesis, participants who were primed with the elderly stereotype took significantly longer to reach the lift than did participants who had been primed with neutral words. It appears that thinking of the concept 'slow' influenced behaviour, and that consciousness did not play any part in this process, because participants were aware neither that they had been primed nor that they had been led to walk more slowly (see Research Close-Up 4.1 in Chapter 4).

We hope that reading about these studies has stimulated your interest in social psychology. If it has, you can read more about the first two studies in Chapter 14 (Prejudice and Intergroup Relations). The last two studies are discussed in Chapter 4 (Social Cognition). Given that the research we have discussed so far is quite varied in its research questions, scope and methods, we now turn to a more general discussion of the nature of social psychology.

WHAT IS SOCIAL PSYCHOLOGY?

How do social psychologists define their discipline?

When social psychologists are called upon to define their discipline, they usually refer to the definition given by Gordon Allport (1954a) (see Leader in the Field, Gordon Allport, in Chapter 14) in his classic chapter on the history of social psychology, published in the second edition of the Handbook of Social Psychology: 'Social psychology is the attempt to understand and explain how the thoughts, feelings, and behaviours of individuals are influenced by the actual, imagined, or implied presence of other human beings' (p. 5). With 'imagined presence' Allport referred to the influence of reference persons (e.g. our parents) whose expectations might influence our behaviour. With the 'implied presence' he acknowledged the fact that much of our behaviour is shaped by social roles and cultural norms. This is quite a good definition, which can accommodate the studies that we have described earlier.

One characteristic of social psychology, which Allport implied but did not mention specifically, is the use of scientific methods. The scientific method of choice used in the studies we have just described was the experiment. We will discuss this method only briefly, because you will learn more about the experimental method in the chapter on methods (Chapter 2). Experiments are a method in which the researcher deliberately introduces some change into a setting to examine the consequences of that change. The typical procedure used in experiments is that conditions in which a change has been introduced (i.e. an independent variable manipulated) are compared to conditions in which this has not been the case, the so-called control group. By randomly assigning participants to either experimental or control group, the researcher can be reasonably certain that any difference between the two groups was due to the manipulation of the independent variable.

Thus, Macrae and colleagues asked half their participants to suppress their stereotype of skinheads, and compared their thoughts and behaviour to those of a control group of individuals who had not been asked to suppress their stereotype. Bargh and colleagues compared the walking speed of participants who had been primed with the elderly stereotype with that of (control) participants who had not been primed. The study by Sherif is somewhat deficient in this respect, because he did not really have a proper control group. He compared the impact of the introduction of intergroup competition on group members' behaviour over time. The control conditions in the Tajfel experiment are difficult to explain without a more detailed description of the study. You may remember that Tajfel and colleagues assessed how the boys would divide money between a member of their own group and a member of the other group. As a control for ingroup bias, they simply reversed the alleged group membership of the two individuals between whom the money had to be divided.

Another methodological difference between the study by Sherif and those of the other researchers is that Sherif's study was a **field experiment** rather than a **laboratory experiment**: he used a natural setting (summer camp) to test his hypotheses. The other studies were all laboratory experiments which used settings that were specially created by the experimenter. For example, Macrae and colleagues led their participants to believe that they were in a study of people's ability to construct life event details from visual information. This is also an example of a darker aspect of social psychology, namely, that we often have to use deception to test our predictions. But if the participants in the study by Macrae and colleagues (1994) had known the real purpose of the study, this would have

field experiment a true randomized experiment conducted in a natural setting.

laboratory experiment a study, conducted in the laboratory, in which the researcher deliberately introduces some change into a setting, while holding all other factors constant, to examine the consequences of that change.

influenced their thoughts and behaviour and the results of such a study would have been meaningless. (We therefore often disregard the data of participants who guess the purpose of our experiments.) Field and laboratory experiments are not the only scientific methods used by social psychologists to test their hypotheses. You can read about other methods in Chapter 2 (Research Methods in Social Psychology).

Obviously, the use of scientific methods is not a characteristic that allows one to distinguish social psychology from other social sciences, as by definition all social sciences use methods they consider scientific, and for many of them, experiments are the method of choice. A more distinctive characteristic introduced by Allport is the fact that social psychology is concerned with social influence, and that it studies the impact of others on individuals' thoughts, feelings and behaviours. All the studies we described earlier tried to understand and explain how the thoughts, feelings and behaviours of their participants were influenced by the presence of other human beings. In the case of the study by Sherif, these human beings were mainly the members of the other group with whom the boys competed, although the members of their own groups also influenced the behaviour of these boys. In contrast to the Sherif study, where the others were actually present, the presence of others was imagined rather than real in the Tajfel study (recall that Allport's careful definition allowed for the impact of the *imagined* presence of others). Finally, in the studies by Macrae and by Bargh and colleagues, it was not really the presence of others that influenced participants' thoughts or behaviour, but the suppression or activation of their beliefs about other groups.

The studies by Macrae and Bargh are also good examples of an aspect of social psychological research that is less clearly emphasized in Allport's definition, namely, the fact that we are interested not only in the impact others have on our thoughts, feelings and behaviour, but also in the *cognitive processes* by which our thoughts, emotions and goals guide our understanding of the world around us and our actions. You can read more about this in Chapter 4 (Social Cognition).

A final characteristic of social psychology emphasized in Allport's definition is that social psychologists study the impact that the implied or actual presence of others has on the thoughts, feelings and behaviours of *individuals*. Thus, even when we study social groups, we examine the impact groups have on the individual group members. For example, in the classic study of conformity with group majorities, Asch (1956) examined the impact of the majority opinion on the judgements of individual participants (see Chapter 8). Similarly, Tajfel and colleagues (1971) studied the impact of the mere categorization of others into ingroup and outgroup on the way individuals distributed money between them. This emphasis on the individual is actually a very important point which had already been made by the elder brother of Gordon Allport, Floyd Allport, in his classic textbook of social psychology: 'There is no psychology of groups which is not essentially and entirely a psychology of individuals. Social psychology must not be placed in contradistinction to the psychology of the individual; it is a part of the psychology of the individual, whose behaviour it studies in relation to that sector of his environment comprised by his fellows' (F. Allport, 1924, p. 4). The emphasis on the individual does not deny the importance of the social context as a determinant of individual behaviour, but it rejects the existence of a group consciousness or a collective mind as separate from the minds of the individuals who comprise the group.

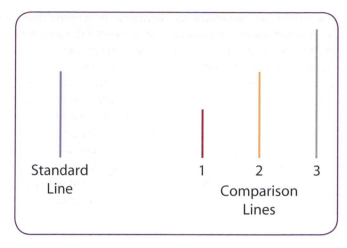

FIGURE 1.2 *Example of the stimulus pattern used in the conformity studies of Asch (1955).*

Source: Original data from Asch (1955), *Scientific American*, 193, 31–35.

HOW DOES SOCIAL PSYCHOLOGY DIFFER FROM OTHER DISCIPLINES?

What differentiates social psychology from related disciplines such as personality psychology and sociology?

In addition to using examples of studies as well as a definition to illuminate the nature of social psychology, it might be helpful to contrast social psychological research to that of research in related disciplines. As in the previous section, we will use the example of an experimental study to clarify these differences. This study was conducted at a small elite college in the United States and was announced as an experiment on perception. The experimental sessions were held in a small classroom and eight participants attended each of the sessions. The participants, who were seated in two rows of four, were presented with sets of four lines of different length, a standard line and three comparison lines. Their task consisted of the comparison of the standard line with the three other lines, one of which was equal to the standard line. The comparison lines were numbered from 1 to 3, and the participants stated their judgements by calling out one of the numbers (see Figure 1.2).

Obviously, this was a simple experiment in visual discrimination in which the experimenter probably wanted to find out how accurately participants could differentiate between lines of different lengths and where the threshold lay at which people would begin to make mistakes. However, there is one feature of the experiment which does not fit with standard procedures in perception experiments – namely that participants judged these lines in groups. This would not have been a problem had the experimenter ensured that judgements were written down, to exclude the possibility that participants would be aware of each others' judgements. But in the present experiment, participants were asked to *call out* their judgements to the experimenter. This appears to be a serious methodological fault. Any determination of a difference threshold based on such data would be flawed, because participants might have been influenced by the earlier judgements that they overheard. Let us assume that the first participant calling out his judgements committed an error. The second participant, who might normally have given a correct response, might now have become uncertain and given the same erroneous response as the first participant. In this way, an experiment on perception might, in fact, have become a study of social influence.

Since we are concerned here with social psychology, it will not come as a surprise that the experimenter, a professor of social psychology at Swarthmore College, Pennsylvania, was not really interested in measuring perceptual thresholds, but in the extent to which individuals would be influenced by a discrepant majority judgement. In fact, only one of the eight participants in each session was a 'naïve' participant; all the others were confederates of the experimenter and were instructed to give unanimous but wrong judgements on 12 out of the 18 trials. These judgements were so easy that participants who judged the stimuli in individual sessions made practically no incorrect judgements. And yet, when participants were exposed to the incorrect judgements of a unanimous majority, 36.8 per cent of their judgements were incorrect (Asch, 1955).

With this experimental setting, Asch created a situation that is familiar to most of us from everyday life. We have probably all had the experience of members of our group disagreeing with us on some issue, then having to decide whether we should go with the group or stick to our own position at the risk of becoming disliked or of looking foolish. Naturally, we do not usually disagree about the length of lines, but about some issue of greater importance, and often the disagreeing majority is not unanimous. However, the setting that was developed by Asch would allow us to manipulate all these variables, and most of them have indeed been investigated in subsequent research (for a review, see Allen, 1966). Our decision to stick to our guns or go with the group will depend very much on how confident we are of the correctness of our own opinion, on how important a correct decision is for us and for the group, and on how well we know the other group members. We are probably also more willing to conform to a majority if we are confronted with a majority that is unanimous rather than divided. If we return to Gordon Allport's definition of social psychology, it is easy to see that the Asch experiment fits all of the characteristics: Asch used a laboratory experiment to study the social influence which a (false) majority judgement would have on the thoughts and behaviours (i.e. judgements) of individuals.

The Asch experiment also allows us to demonstrate the difference between social psychology and 'asocial' *general psychology*. If Asch had been interested in studying perceptual thresholds, he would have varied the difference in the lengths of his standard and comparison stimuli systematically, to assess the extent to which such variations affected perceptual judgements. The (perceptual) judgements would have remained the same, but they would now be investigated in relation to variations in the physical aspects of the stimuli, while keeping the social context constant. In contrast, Asch kept the physical stimulus constellation relatively constant and was interested in the effect that varying the social context (i.e. majority size and unanimity) had on perceptual judgements.

The Asch situation is also useful for demonstrating the difference between social and personality psychology. As a social psychologist, Asch was interested in the impact that characteristics of the social situation had on the thoughts and behaviours of his participants. Does the rate of conformity increase if we increase the number of majority members who give erroneous judgements? Does the conformity rate decrease if participants are

allowed to give their judgements anonymously? Asch's approach is typical of social psychological research, which usually *manipulates* important aspects of the social context in order to assess the impact these changes have on the thoughts, feelings and behaviour of the target person.

Personality psychologists, on the other hand, might be less interested in the impact of the social context on behaviour and, instead, ask themselves why some participants are influenced by the erroneous judgements of the majority while others remain unaffected. Thus, the personality psychologist would be interested in the personality traits that are responsible for the fact that different individuals act differently in what is essentially the same social situation. The personality psychologist might test whether intelligent individuals are less likely than unintelligent ones to conform to majorities, or whether conformity is more prevalent among authoritarian rather than non-authoritarian personalities (see the discussion of the authoritarian personality in Chapter 14; Adorno, Frenkel-Brunswik, Levinson, & Sanford, 1950).

Personality psychologists would not, however, only address the question of individual differences as determinants of conformity; they would also want to know how these individual differences came about. Is it possible to relate differences in authoritarianism to differences in the way parents brought up their children, and what aspects of a person's upbringing determine his or her self-esteem? Thus, one could try to separate the disciplines of social and personality psychology as follows: individual behaviour is determined by three factors: (1) the biological constitution of individuals, (2) their acquired traits, and (3) the social and physical context. Whereas personality psychologists are mainly interested in studying how particular traits are acquired and how these traits influence the individual's behaviour, social psychologists study the impact of the social situation on individual behaviour.

Unfortunately, such a distinction would oversimplify the differences between social and personality psychology (for more details, see Krahé, 1992) because one of the central concepts of social psychology, namely social attitudes, is defined by many social psychologists (e.g. Eagly & Chaiken, 1993) as a tendency (i.e. individual disposition) to evaluate an attitude object positively or negatively (see Chapter 6). Even though social psychologists are mainly interested in studying how attitudes change in response to social influence attempts (see Chapters 7 and 8), they also use attitudes to predict individual behaviour (see Chapter 6). Furthermore, within social psychology, researchers have often been interested in studying individual difference variables, such as the degree to which individuals are prone to prejudice and susceptible to Fascist ideologies ('authoritarianism'; Adorno et al., 1950; see Chapter 14), or the degree to which individuals are oriented to situational cues or reactions of others ('self-monitoring'; Snyder, 1974).

Since there is a great deal of agreement that individual behaviour is influenced by personality traits (see Chapter 9 on aggression) as well as the social context, the two fields of personality psychology and social psychology are, in fact, difficult to separate. It is therefore not surprising that the leading social psychological journal is the *Journal of Personality and Social Psychology*, and that most American social psychologists are members of the Society of Personality and Social Psychology. However, there are subtle differences in focus. Social psychologists are typically interested in personality variables as *moderators*. They look for the extent to which the impact of an independent variable on a dependent variable is qualified by, or depends on, the level of an individual's score on a personality measure. For example, there is a higher correlation between attitudes and behaviour for 'low' than for 'high' self-monitors (Snyder & Kendzierski, 1982). Many of the chapters in this volume refer to such personality influences on social behaviour. Social psychologists also tend to emphasize that the impact of personality variables on social behaviour is weaker in 'strong' compared to 'weak' social situations (Mischel, 1977). Thus, social psychologists emphasize the power of strong social situations to relegate personality influences to the background. This occurs, for example, in experiments investigating helping in emergencies (Latané & Darley, 1976; see Chapter 10) and obeying an authority figure's orders to behave in immoral ways (Milgram, 1974; see Chapter 8).

After the difficulties we experienced in distinguishing social psychology from personality psychology, distinguishing it from neighbouring social sciences such as sociology might seem easy. It would appear that sociology differs from social psychology both in the issues it studies and in the level of analysis at which it addresses these issues. Unfortunately, things are again not that simple. First, there is quite a bit of overlap between the issues studied by social psychologists and those that interest sociologists. Thus, social groups and group norms are topics that are of equal interest to sociologists and social psychologists (see Chapter 12). The sociologist George Homans wrote one of the classic monographs on social groups (Homans, 1950) and the sociologists Hechter and Opp (2001) edited a volume that summarizes the important work of sociologists in the area of social norms.

Although there are sociological approaches that, influenced by the work of Talcott Parsons and Emile Durkheim, emphasize that sociological facts should not be explained through psychological processes (Vanberg, 1975), most sociologists would no longer accept this position. In fact, sociologists have made major contributions to the development of individualistic social psychological

theories. Thus, the sociologists Homans (1961) and Blau (1964) have written monographs on exchange theory, a theory that has become central in social psychology through the classic *Social Psychology of Groups* written by the social psychologists Thibaut and Kelley (1959), but is now more frequently referred to as interdependence theory. The central tenet of this theory is that individuals interact with those others who provide the greatest rewards for the least costs (see Chapter 11). Thus, most sociologists agree with social psychologists in espousing what has been called **methodological individualism**, namely the assumption that even collective behaviour is essentially behaviour of the individuals who form the collective and therefore has to be explained in terms of rewards and costs of this behaviour to the individual (e.g. Klandermans, 1997).

methodological individualism the assumption that collective action must be explained by showing how it results from individual decisions and behaviour; collective behaviour is seen as essentially behaviour of the individuals who form the collective.

Even though there is a great deal of overlap between sociology and social psychology, there are also major differences in the way these areas approach social behaviour. Sociologists are more likely to trace social behaviour upwards to structural variables such as norms, roles or social class, whereas social psychologists will trace it downwards to the individual's goals, motives and cognitions. For example, both sociologists and social psychologists are interested in aggression and violence. Social psychologists have studied the cognitive and affective processes through which anger can, given the right contextual cues, explode in aggressive behaviour – that is, behaviour performed with the express intention of hurting another person (Figure 1.3;

FIGURE 1.3 *How is the way social psychologists study aggression and violence different from the approach of sociologists?*
Source: © Hurricane. Used under licence from Shutterstock.

Chapter 9). Sociologists, on the other hand, have been more interested in why levels of aggression are higher in some societies or groups than in others. Why is the murder rate in the US so much higher than in Canada, even though guns are widely available in both countries? Since a possible difference could be the type of guns that are available in the two countries, with hunting rifles being more prevalent in Canada and hand guns or assault weapons more frequently held in the United States, the potential answer might lie in the aggressive images that will be activated by different types of weapons, leading us back to individual psychological processes. Thus, even though sociologists are more likely to link individual behaviour to social structural variables, while social psychologists are more likely to study individual processes, a combination of the two approaches might often provide a fuller explanation than either discipline can offer on its own.

A BRIEF HISTORY OF SOCIAL PSYCHOLOGY

The beginning

Who conducted the first experiment and who wrote the first textbook?

Authors who write about the history of a scientific discipline usually like to report dates that mark the origin of that discipline. Often these are the years in which the first textbooks or handbooks bearing the name of the discipline were published. In social psychology, 1908 is usually noted as the year when the first two textbooks of social psychology were published, one by a sociologist (Ross, 1908), the other by a psychologist (McDougall, 1908). However, since both texts cover very little material that we would consider social psychological these days, 1908 may not be the best choice for the birth year of social psychology.

One could also argue that using the date of the first textbook to mark the beginning of a discipline is questionable anyway, because it would be difficult to write a textbook about a discipline that did not already exist. There must first be relevant theorizing and research available with which to fill the pages of a textbook. It is probably for this reason that another date has become quite prominent in chapters on the history of social psychology, namely the date of (presumably) the first social psychological experiment, a study published in 1898 by Norman Triplett.

Triplett appeared to have been a fan of bicycle races. He was interested in the phenomenon whereby racing cyclists go faster when racing with others or when being paced than when riding alone, racing against the clock (Figure 1.4). Illustrating the research tool of 'archival analysis' (see Chapter 2), Triplett (1898) used records of the average speed of cyclists under these different conditions; he could indeed demonstrate that cyclists ride faster in competition or with pacers than when riding alone. However, as Triplett recognized, the shortcoming of this kind of quasi-experimental evidence is that different racers participate in different kinds of races and select those in which they do particularly well. The differences in speed between cyclists racing against the clock or racing in competition could therefore have been due to self-selection. To rule out this explanation, Triplett (1898) conducted an experiment in which schoolchildren performed a simple task (turning a fishing reel) either alone or in competition with another participant (see Research Close-Up 1.1). The experiment is usually cited as demonstrating the effects of what later became known as **social facilitation**, the phenomenon whereby the performance of simple tasks is facilitated by the presence of an audience or of others working on the same task (see Chapter 8). However, if you read the Research Close-Up, you will realize that his data do not warrant such a strong conclusion.

Although the study by Triplett (1898) had the elegance and clarity that became the hallmark of

> **social facilitation** an improvement in the performance of well-learned/easy tasks and a worsening of performance of poorly-learned/difficult tasks due to the presence of members of the same species.

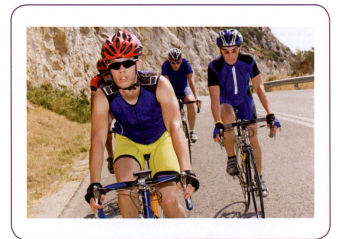

FIGURE 1.4 *It is a well known phenomenon that racing cyclists go faster when racing with others or when being paced than when riding alone, racing against the clock.*
Source: © AISPIX. Used under licence from Shutterstock.

TRIPLETT'S CLASSIC STUDY OF SOCIAL FACILITATION EFFECTS

Triplett, N. (1898). The dynamogenic factors in pacemaking and competition. *American Journal of Psychology, 9,* 507–533.

Introduction

Triplett suggested several theoretical explanations for the superiority of cyclists who are paced or ride in a competition over those who ride alone. For example, there could be aerodynamic or psychological advantages for a racer who was paced or racing in a competition. However, Triplett was most interested in what he called 'dynamogenic factors', namely that 'the presence of another rider is a stimulus to the racer in arousing the competitive instinct; that another can thus be the means of releasing or freeing nervous energy from him that he cannot of himself release' (p. 516). His concept of nervous energy appears to be similar to the modern concept of arousal.

Method

Participants

Forty schoolchildren (14 boys, 26 girls) from 8 to 17 years participated in the study.

Design and procedure

The apparatus consisted of two fishing reels fixed to a wooden frame and placed sufficiently far apart so that two people could turn them side-by-side. A cord was looped from each of the fishing reels through corresponding wheels fixed to the opposite end of the frame, creating two closed circuits (like the circuit formed by the chain on a bicycle). A small white flag was sewn to each of the cords. By winding the fishing reel the flag traversed the course from the fishing reel to the wheel at the opposite end and back again. A trial consisted of four circuits of the course and the time taken for this performance was measured by stopwatch. After an initial practice session, each participant performed six trials. Triplett created a somewhat complicated but quite ingenious design, with the sequence of alone and competition trials differing for Groups A and B in a systematic way (see Table 1.1).

The rationale behind these two sequences was that it eliminated practice as well as fatigue effects. Both effects are related to the number of trials performed by a participant (i.e. trial order). One would expect that during the first few trials performance improves due to practice. In later trials fatigue might set in and begin to slow down participants. Triplett controlled for both of these effects from trial 2 onwards by having the task performed under both conditions during each of the trials.

Results

Triplett categorized his participants into three groups on the basis of their performance during the various trials: those who were stimulated positively by competition and performed faster ($N = 20$), those who were 'overstimulated' and performed more slowly ($N = 10$), and those who were not affected ($N = 10$). From visual inspection of his data, Triplett concluded that his findings showed 'that the bodily presence of another contestant participating simultaneously in the race serves to liberate latent energy not ordinarily available' (p. 533). This conclusion formed the basis of the myth reported in most textbooks that his study provided the first evidence for social facilitation. These days conclusions based on visual inspection of data are no longer accepted and journal editors require that researchers conduct (often extensive) statistical analysis of their results, and test how likely the results are to be due to chance. When Strube (2005) reanalysed Triplett's data more than a century after the publication of the original study using modern statistics, he found very little support for the original conclusion. Only one of several analyses resulted in a significant effect. This effect disappeared, however, when Strube eliminated the data of two left-handed participants, for whom the task would have been more difficult, as they were instructed to turn the wheel with their right hand. As you will learn in

Table 1.1 *Sequence of alone and competition trials for Groups A and B in Triplett's design.*

Group A	alone	competition	alone	competition	alone	competition
Group B	alone	alone	competition	alone	competition	alone

Chapter 8, the presence of others facilitates performance only for easy tasks, but inhibits performance with difficult tasks. Elimination of the left-handed participants should therefore have strengthened rather than weakened the social facilitation effects. Strube concluded that 'the analysis of Triplett's data . . . indicate barely a statistical hint of the social facilitation of performance to which his experiment has been credited' (2005, p. 280). This is quite different from the conclusions usually drawn in textbooks of social psychology.

Discussion

If significance tests had already been available and required by journal editors in 1898, Triplett's study might never have been published and historians of social psychology would have had to look elsewhere for the first experiment (Stroebe, 2012; Strube, 2005). It is nevertheless puzzling that Triplett failed to find clear evidence of social facilitation. After all, turning a fishing reel is a simple mechanical task and competition should clearly have facilitated performance.

experimentation in social psychology, its historical significance has been challenged by scholars who doubted whether it really was the *first* social psychological experiment. For example, Haines and Vaughan (1979) have argued that there were other experiments before 1898 deserving to be called social psychological, such as studies on suggestibility by Binet and Henri (1894; see Stroebe, 2012). But social psychological experiments may have been performed even earlier by the French agricultural engineer Max Ringelmann, who between 1882 and 1887 conducted investigations into the maximum performance of workers pulling a load under different conditions (Kravitz & Martin, 1986). Although the comparison of individual and group performance was of only secondary interest to Ringelmann, he found the first evidence of productivity loss in groups, a phenomenon that was later named **social loafing** (see Chapter 13). Ringelmann found that eight men who pull at a rope together achieve only about 50 per cent of the pulling power that could be expected on the basis of their pulling measured individually. However, since Ringelmann only published this research in 1913, Triplett predates him, certainly as far as publication is concerned.

It is interesting to note that these early experiments were studies of an applied nature in areas which later became known as sports psychology and psychology of work performance. There were other studies of this nature available in other applied areas (e.g. Mayer, 1903; Moede, 1920) and it needed somebody to recognize that the study of the impact of the social context on performance was really a discipline by itself, namely, social psychology. It may then be justifiable to choose the date of the first textbook or handbook about a discipline as its 'origin' insofar as a discipline is characterized not only by its content, but also by its disciplinary identity. Thus, it is not sufficient that research that is vaguely social psychological has been conducted in the area of sports psychology

or even agriculture. There needs to be somebody who pulls all this research together and declares the emergence of a new area (in which, incidentally, this applied research then becomes fundamental).

In our view, this was first achieved by Floyd Allport (1924), who in his textbook made several major contributions towards defining the field of social psychology (see Leader in the Field, Floyd Henry Allport). He declared the study of social behaviour as the subject of social psychology. He defined social behaviour as 'behavior in which the responses either serve as social stimuli or are evoked by social stimuli' (p. 148). As mentioned above, he postulated that social psychology 'is part of the psychology of the individual, whose behavior it studies in relation to that sector of the environment comprised by his fellows' (p. 4). He had noted earlier, in the same volume, 'For . . . only within the individual can we find the behavioral mechanisms and the consciousness which are fundamental in the interactions between individuals' (p. vi). Another contribution, which may be less embraced today, was his emphasis on the experimental method. Although the experimental method is still

 LEADER IN THE FIELD

Floyd Henry Allport (1890–1978), the elder brother of Gordon Allport (see Leader in the Field, Chapter 14), received both his undergraduate degree (1914) and his PhD (1919) from Harvard University. His dissertation was based on his studies on social facilitation, a research area that had been suggested to him by Hugo Münsterberg, then professor of psychology at Harvard. In 1922 Allport obtained a position as Associate Professor of Social Psychology at the University of North Carolina at Chapel Hill. It was here that he began writing his *Social Psychology*, which was widely praised and adopted as a text. This book and his studies on the impact of the group on individual cognitive performance are his major contribution to social psychology. He retired from Syracuse University in 1956.

one of the major research tools of social psychologists, other research methods have become equally accepted these days. However, in Allport's time, the emphasis on experiments was probably essential for establishing the scientific respectability of social psychology. It would also have helped to distinguish it further from sociology, a discipline that still prefers surveys and field studies to conducting experiments. It is interesting, though, that with the exception of his chapter on the 'Response to social stimulation in groups', Allport (1924) did not review a great deal of experimental evidence of a social psychological nature.

Allport's conception of social psychology derived from his research on social facilitation (see Chapter 8). His experimental paradigm, which had the defining characteristics that he attributed to all social psychology research, had been developed 'in Germany by August Mayer, Meumann, Moede and others . . . prior to 1915'; Allport, 1919, p. 304). This strong German influence on his dissertation research is no coincidence, given that his dissertation supervisor was Hugo Münsterberg, a German psychologist who was then head of the psychology department at Harvard. Allport (1924, p. vii) acknowledges Münsterberg's influence in the preface to his book, where he writes 'For the origins of my interest in social psychology I am indebted to the memory of Hugo Münsterberg. It was he who suggested the setting for my first experiment and who foresaw many of the possibilities which have been developed in this book.'

attitudes, that by Dashiell on 'Experimental studies of the influence of social situation on the behaviour of individual human adults', and Cox Miles's chapter on gender differences. But there are also other chapters that could be part of a social psychology curriculum, even though they are not included in most modern handbooks. For example, there is a chapter on language by Esper, on age in human society by Miles, on material culture by Wissler, and on the physical environment by Shelford.

Three other significant events during this early period were the publication by Thurstone (1928) of a paper with the provocative title 'Attitudes can be measured', *The Psychology of Social Norms* by Sherif in 1936, and Newcomb's (1943) *Personality and Social Change*, a study of attitude formation in the student community of Bennington College (see Leader in the Field, Theodore Newcomb). Thurstone's article was remarkable because he described the first psychometrically sound method for the measurement of attitudes. Sherif's study became a classic, because he devised an experimental paradigm that allowed him to study the development of group norms in a laboratory situation (see Chapter 8). Participants in his study were repeatedly exposed to a stationary light source in a darkened room. Sherif made use of the fact that participants perceive this light source as moving (**autokinetic effect**) and that, if asked to judge the movement over repeated trials, they establish relatively stable individual norms. By putting individuals who had developed

autokinetic effect perceptual illusion, whereby, in the absence of reference points, a stationary light appears to move.

The early years

What were the key contributions to social psychology during the first half of the twentieth century?

It would be an exaggeration to claim that the publication of Floyd Allport's textbook stimulated an exponential growth in social psychological research immediately. In fact, not that many milestones are to be reported for the period before World War II. A rather doubtful one is the publication of the first *Handbook of Social Psychology* by Carl Murchison (1935). We call it doubtful because this handbook covers many topics which nobody would consider social psychological today, such as 'Population behavior of bacteria' or the 'Social history of the yellow man'. There are really only three chapters included in this volume that are truly social psychological in the sense that they would still be included in social psychology handbooks today: the chapter by Gordon Allport on

 LEADER IN THE FIELD

Theodore Newcomb (1903–1984) received his undergraduate degree from Oberlin College in 1924 and entered Union Theological Seminary in New York intending to become a Christian Missionary (Converse, 1994). However, more attracted by the psychology courses taught at Columbia University across the road, he switched to psychology and received his PhD from Columbia in 1929. He joined Bennington College in 1934, a newly founded women's college that drew its students from the politically conservative 'upper crust' of Vermont's society, but had a famously liberal atmosphere. His Bennington study of the change in attitudes that these young women underwent during their studies became a classic. Not only was the longitudinal design innovative at that time, but the study captured the interplay between individual and group processes and thus supported one of the central assumptions of social psychology. After a stint of wartime research, he became director of a joint doctoral program of the departments of sociology and social psychology at the University of Michigan, where he stayed for the remainder of his career. Intrigued by the work of Fritz Heider (see Leader in the Field, Chapter 3), Newcomb developed his own interpersonal version of balance theory.

widely differing individual estimates into a group situation, Sherif could demonstrate that individuals in groups develop a joint and stable group norm, which they then maintain even when they continue to make their estimates again in individual situations.

Finally, Newcomb's **Bennington study** became a classic, because it is an ingenious longitudinal field study of social influence on a college campus. It maps out the way in which the political attitudes of students, all women who came from conservative homes, changed over time towards the liberal attitudes that were predominant on this college campus. Thus, it illustrates how individual beliefs and attitudes can be shaped by the group context, and thus supports one of the basic assumptions of social psychology. The study is particularly interesting because these students were followed up for 50 years, allowing researchers to demonstrate the stability of their attitude change over a lifetime (Alwin, Cohen, & Newcomb, 1991).

> **Bennington study**
> a longitudinal field study of social influence showing how political attitudes of initially conservative female students changed over time towards the liberal attitudes that were predominant on this college campus.

The years of expansion

How did Adolf Hitler inadvertently further the development of social psychology in the US?

Somewhat tongue in cheek, Cartwright once wrote that the one person who most furthered the development of social psychology in North America was Adolf Hitler (Cartwright, 1979; Figure 1.5). This observation is correct insofar as Hitler's actions had an important impact on the development of social psychology in the US. World War II greatly stimulated interest in social psychological research. The Information and Education Branch of the US Army initiated surveys and experiments to assess the impact of army propaganda films on the morale of their soldiers. One social psychologist who became heavily involved in this work was Carl Hovland (see Leader in the Field, Carl Iver Hovland). Originally a learning theorist, Hovland became fascinated by the experimental study of the determinants of attitude change. The work he directed during his army years on experiments in mass communication was eventually published as one of the volumes of the *American Soldier* series under the editorship of the sociologist Stouffer (Hovland, Lumsdaine, & Sheffield, 1949).

After the war, Hovland returned to his academic career and founded the Yale Communication and Attitude Change programme. This programme attracted young

LEADER IN THE FIELD

Carl Iver Hovland (1912–1961) received his bachelor's and master's degrees from Northwestern University in 1932 and 1933. He then moved to Yale to work for his PhD under the prominent learning theorist Clark Hull. After finishing his dissertation in 1936, Hovland was invited to join the Yale faculty, of which he remained a member for the rest of his life. Hovland never abandoned his interest in learning theory. Even when he became fascinated by persuasion and attitude change during his wartime leave from Yale in the period from 1942 to 1945, he used learning theory principles as a theoretical perspective. His wartime research was published (with Lumsdaine and Sheffield) in 1949 in *Experiments in Mass Communication*. After returning to Yale, Hovland established the Yale Communication and Attitude Change programme, which he directed until his premature death in 1961. The research conducted there by Hovland and 30 students and co-workers over a 15-year period established the field of attitude change research as we know it today (Shepard, 1998).

FIGURE 1.5 *How did Hitler's actions affect the development of social psychology?*
Source: © Dariush M. Used under licence from Shutterstock.

researchers from a variety of universities and generated a stream of collaborative studies that defined attitude change research for decades to come (see Chapter 7). The programme resulted in the publication of four highly influential volumes on studies of the determinants of persuasion and attitude change. In the first of these volumes, Hovland, Janis, and Kelley (1953) explored the impact of communicator variables (e.g. prestige, credibility and expertise), communication variables (e.g. fear appeals) and context variables (e.g. salience of reference groups). Although the theoretical perspective of the programme was eclectic, Hovland himself was most comfortable with the view that attitude change was a special form of human learning (Jones, 1998).

A second action of the Hitler regime that advanced the development of social psychology in the US was the forced emigration of Jewish (e.g. Koffka, Lewin, Wertheimer) and even some non-Jewish (e.g. Köhler) academics from Germany. The most important of these émigrés for social psychology was undoubtedly Kurt Lewin, considered by many to be the most charismatic psychologist of his generation (Marrow, 1969). Lewin left the Berlin Psychological Institute in 1933 for the Department of Home Economics at Cornell University, to move in 1935 to the Iowa Child Research Station. In 1945 he established the Research Center for Group Dynamics at the Massachusetts Institute of Technology, which, after his premature death in 1947 at the age of 57 years, was moved to the University of Michigan (see Leader in the Field, Kurt Lewin).

It is difficult to understand today how and why Lewin became such a key figure in social psychology. As is the case today, the impact of a researcher in those days was mainly determined by three factors: (1) a great number of publications in top journals; (2) the development of a theory, which stimulated a great deal of research; or (3) training of a stream of outstanding graduate students, who would later continue the work. Lewin did not score all that well on the first two criteria. Although Lewin's students were highly productive, he himself published only a few empirical studies in social psychology, the most well known being the study of autocratic and democratic leadership (Lewin et al., 1939), which initiated interest in the impact of leadership styles on group atmosphere and performance (see Chapter 13). His **field theory** provided a framework for looking at the forces (e.g. positive and negative valences) that influence the individual in a social situation.

field theory a framework adopted by Kurt Lewin which represented the individual as an element in a larger system of social forces.

However, it did not lend itself easily to the derivation of testable hypotheses. Even his own empirical work was only very loosely related to that theory. And as Morton Deutsch (1968), one of Lewin's most eminent students, concluded two decades after Lewin's death: 'It cannot be said that field theory as a specific psychological theory has much current vitality. Nor can it be said that Lewin's specific theoretical constructs . . . are central to research now being carried out in social psychology' (p. 478).

So how could Lewin become so influential? As Deutsch (1968) explains, Lewin's 'impact is reflected instead in his general orientation to psychology, which has left its impression on his colleagues and students.' (Deutsch, 1968, p. 478). Lewin believed that psychological events must be explained in psychological terms and that central processes in the 'life space' or psychological field of the individual such as cognition, motivation and goals are the proper focus of investigation. This theoretical perspective offered an exciting alternative to the behaviouristic theories that dominated psychology at that time. Furthermore, Lewin's approach to social psychology had two characteristics which were novel at the time. For him, a problem was only worth studying if addressing it would make a difference with regard to actual problems in the world (Festinger, 1980). Second, and more importantly, he insisted on studying such problems experimentally and on creating in the laboratory powerful situations that made a big difference (Festinger, 1980). Lewin instilled these ideas in his graduate students, and his impact on social psychology was mainly due to these graduate students, who, as a group, were highly influential during the second half of the twentieth century.

 LEADER IN THE FIELD

Kurt Lewin (1890–1947) studied psychology and philosophy in Berlin. After fulfilling the formal requirements for a PhD in 1914 (a degree he received only in 1916), he volunteered for the army and spent the next four years fighting World War I (Marrow, 1969). He then returned to the University of Berlin to join the Gestalt psychologists Köhler and Wertheimer at the Institute of Psychology, where he stayed until his (permanent) move to the United States in 1933. The time at Berlin University was probably Lewin's most productive period. He attracted an international group of students, developed his field theory, which argued that behaviour is a function of both the person and the environment, and supervised a series of classic studies, mainly conducted by his students as part of their dissertation. These studies addressed fundamental issues of the psychology of motivation. Lewin's interest in social psychology developed only after his move to the United States (Marrow, 1969). In the US he first worked at Cornell University, then moved to the University of Iowa. During his 10 years at the University of Iowa (1935–1945) Lewin conducted some classic experimental studies in social psychology, such as the experiment on the impact of authoritarian and democratic leadership styles on group atmosphere and performance (Lewin, Lippitt, & White, 1939), which later stimulated research on participative leadership to overcome resistance to change (Coch & French, 1948). Lewin became more and more interested in social processes, and in 1944 he moved to the Massachusetts Institute of Technology, where he founded the Research Center for Group Dynamics.

LEADER IN THE FIELD

Leon Festinger (1919–1990) completed his undergraduate studies at City College in New York, and his graduate research at the University of Iowa with Kurt Lewin (see Leader in the Field, Chapter 1). After receiving his PhD in 1942, and a stint of wartime research, he rejoined Lewin and the newly formed Center for Group Dynamics at the Massachusetts Institute of Technology in 1945. In 1948, he moved with the Center to the University of Michigan, from there to the University of Minnesota in 1951, on to Stanford in 1955, and finally, in 1968, to the New School for Social Research in New York, where he stayed until his retirement (Schachter, 1994). During his period at MIT, Festinger, Schachter, and Back (1950) conducted their classic study of friendship patterns and residential proximity (see Chapter 11). Festinger (1950) published his first theoretical paper in social psychology on informal social communication and the process, via social comparison, of establishing the correctness of one's beliefs. These ideas were later elaborated in his paper on social comparison processes (Festinger, 1954). Soon afterwards, Festinger (1957) published the work for which he is best known, his theory of cognitive dissonance (see Chapter 7). It marked the end of his interest in social psychology, which shifted, first to the visual system and perception, then to archaeology and the history of religion.

All these individuals shaped the field of experimental social psychology in the post-war period, but the most illustrious among them was undoubtedly Leon Festinger, whose theory of cognitive dissonance dictated the research agenda in social psychology during the 1960s and 1970s (Festinger, 1957; see also Chapter 7; Leader in the Field, Leon Festinger). The theory of social comparison processes, which he had developed earlier (Festinger, 1954), had less of an immediate impact, but is still influential today (see e.g. Chapters 5, 8, 10 and 12).

Another important émigré was the Austrian, Fritz Heider (see Leader in the Field, Fritz Heider, in Chapter 3), although in this case Hitler cannot be blamed for his emigration. Heider came to the US in 1930 to work with Kurt Koffka, who was then at Smith College in Northampton, Massachusetts. He had initially planned to stay for only one year, but decided to remain when he fell in love with Grace Moore, whom he later married. He moved to the University of Kansas in 1947, where he remained until his retirement. His impact on the field is intriguing, because he was not a prolific writer, attracted few graduate students, and published no experimental research in social psychology. Yet he stimulated two of the theoretical traditions which dominated social psychology during the second half of the last century, namely **consistency theories** and **attribution theories**.

consistency theories a group of theories (see balance theory, cognitive dissonance theory) proposing that people prefer congruence or consistency among their various cognitions, especially among their beliefs, values, and attitudes.

With his paper on **balance theory** in 1946, Heider developed the notion central to consistency theories that inconsistency between our attitudes and beliefs creates tension in our cognitive system and a tendency to establish consistency. Although only a limited amount of research has been conducted to test Heider's balance theory, the theory stimulated the development of other consistency theories, most importantly the theory of cognitive dissonance.

attribution theories a group of theories about how individuals manage to infer the 'causes' underlying the behaviour of others, or even their own behaviour.

balance theory a cognitive consistency theory that assumes that individuals strive to maintain consistency or balance (objects or persons perceived as belonging together are evaluated similarly) in their social perceptions.

With his paper on phenomenal causality, published in 1944, and his monograph *The Psychology of Interpersonal Relations*, published in 1958, Heider initiated another important theoretical perspective, namely attribution theory (see Chapter 3). Attribution theory is a social psychological theory about how individuals manage to infer the 'causes' underlying the behaviour of others, or even their own behaviour. In trying to interpret behaviour, we will typically attempt to disentangle the contribution of internal causes (e.g. personality traits, motivation) from external causes (e.g. situational factors). For example, if a mother learns that her son has received a poor grade in his first maths test, she will wonder whether this poor result is due to lack of ability, lack of motivation or to an overly zealous maths teacher who gave too tough a test. Deciding between these alternatives will be important for her, because it will suggest different strategies to prevent this situation from happening again.

The impact of attribution theory in stimulating a great deal of research in the 1960s and 1970s is intriguing, because neither Heider's (1958) monograph nor his 1944 article was written in a way that would make it accessible or appealing to the average researcher in North America. There was also very little research to back up Heider's ideas. It is generally accepted that attribution theory became influential because three major figures in the field of social psychology – Edward Jones, Harold Kelley and Bernard Weiner – adopted it and translated it into a language that was more accessible to social psychologists and yielded clear, testable hypotheses (Jones & Davis, 1965; Kelley, 1967; Weiner, 1986). Probably most influential was Kelley's (1967) **covariation theory** (see Chapter 3). This model was appealing because Kelley argued that, in inferring causes of behaviour, our inference process would be analogous to conducting an analysis of variance, a statistical procedure highly familiar to social psychologists. Other influential adaptations of attribution theory were Jones and Davis's (1965) correspondent inference theory and Weiner's (1986) application of attribution theory to achievement motivation and emotion.

A final way in which Hitler influenced the development of social psychology is by stimulating interest in topics such as obedience and authoritarianism. Why did the German people accept such an authoritarian regime, and why did so many of them carry out commands they must have perceived as immoral even at the time? These questions stimulated some of the most influential research in social psychology: researchers studied the authoritarian personality (Adorno et al., 1950), the determinants of conformity (Asch, 1955) and obedience (Milgram, 1963). Lewin's interest in the effects of authoritarian and democratic leadership styles can be seen as an attempt to demonstrate the superiority of the democratic style, an attempt that was only partly effective because in his research autocratically led groups outperformed the democratic groups with regard to quantity of production, although democratic leadership produced more creative groups whose performance did not deteriorate so dramatically when the leader was removed (White & Lippitt, 1968).

The crisis years

How and why did the crisis in social psychology develop?

So far the history of social psychology appears to have been one of unmitigated success. Stimulated by World War II, social psychological research expanded enormously and there was soon no single psychology department at a top university that did not also have a strong social psychology unit. But just when social psychology was on the up and up, a **crisis in social psychology** developed that led to years of infighting about the right course one should follow. This crisis was probably initiated by two critical papers published in 1967 and 1973.

crisis in social psychology a short-lived crisis of confidence among social psychologists during the 1960s, when social psychologists questioned the values, the methods and the scientific status of their discipline.

The first of these two papers was a paper by Kenneth Ring entitled 'Experimental social psychology: Some sober questions about some frivolous values', published in the highly respected *Journal of Experimental Social Psychology*. In this paper, Ring contrasted the vision of Kurt Lewin of a social psychology that would contribute to the solution of important social problems with

what he called the 'fun and games' attitude of the social psychology of his days. He argued that: 'Experimental social psychology today seems dominated by values that suggest the following slogan: 'Social psychology ought to be and is a lot of fun . . . Clever experimentation on exotic topics with zany manipulations seems to be the guaranteed formula for success . . . One sometimes gets the impression that an ever-growing coterie of social psychologists is playing (largely for another's benefit) a game of "can you top this?"' (pp. 116–17). Although Ring did not refer to any specific examples of this fun and games approach, his criticism was probably directed at some of the work conducted in tests of dissonance theory.

Ring, although a respected researcher, was not a very central figure in the social psychology of his days. Therefore, the paper stimulated some discussion but did not really have a serious impact on the field. However, in 1973, one of the golden boys of experimental social psychology, Kenneth Gergen, published an article entitled 'Social psychology as history' in the top journal of our discipline, the *Journal of Personality and Social Psychology*. As the title already suggests, Gergen's article was not an attack on the values directing social psychological research. Much more seriously, he questioned its scientific value. His two most important arguments were (1) that knowledge of social psychological principles could change our behaviour in ways which would negate these principles, and (2) that since the basic motives assumed by many of our theories are unlikely to be genetically determined, they might be affected by cultural change.

As an example of the first principle, Gergen argued that once groups were aware of their tendency to make extreme decisions (i.e. group polarization; see Chapter 8), they might consciously counteract this tendency in their decision-making. As an example of the second principle, Gergen used social comparison and dissonance theory. Social comparison theory assumes that people have a desire to evaluate themselves accurately and do this by comparing themselves to others. Gergen argued that one could easily imagine societies in which such a desire would not exist. Similarly, dissonance theory assumes a need for consistency, which not everybody might share. Gergen saw these problems as the main reason why, as he claimed, social psychological research often failed to be replicable, and hence did not result in a body of cumulative knowledge.

Most researchers these days would accept these arguments without questioning the scientific status of social psychology. With regard to Gergen's first point, we would argue that it would be difficult, even for a trained social psychologist, to keep in mind all situations in which our behaviour might be affected by others, to recognize all the relevant cues signalling such situations, and then to counteract the situational pressures. With regard to his second point, the jury is still out. There is increasing evidence that repeating the same social psychology study in different parts of the world often leads to rather different results (see Chapter 15). However, such variation does not necessarily challenge the assumption that there are universal social processes. After all, cultural differences might merely qualify such universal processes. For example, it is hard to imagine societies in which people do not engage in social comparison, because the evaluation of one's own abilities through social comparison is highly functional and essential for effective action. However, we do know that there are individual differences in the need for social comparison (Gibbons & Buunk, 1999), as there are in individual need for consistency (Cialdini, Trost, & Newsom, 1995). Since there are substantial individual differences within cultures, differences between cultures would not necessarily imply that the theories of social comparison or cognitive consistency should not apply to other cultures.

Gergen's (1973) critique would probably have been less effective had it not come at a time when the collective self-esteem of social psychologists had been undermined by other developments. For one, there was an attack on the usefulness of a concept that Allport (1935) had hailed as the most central concept of social psychology. In a review of studies that empirically assessed the value of social attitudes in predicting behaviour, the sociologist Alan Wicker (1969) drew the following conclusion: 'Taken as a whole, these studies suggest that it is considerably more likely that attitudes will be unrelated or only slightly related to overt behavior than that attitudes will be closely related to actions.' (p. 65). This conclusion was highly damaging, since social psychologists were interested in attitudes mainly because they expected them to predict behaviour. Since attitude change in most studies is assessed through an individual's self-rated position on some attitude dimension, the news that such ratings might be unrelated to behaviour was devastating.

A second development with a negative impact on the collective self-esteem of the scientific community of social psychologists was the publication of a series of papers that were highly critical of the experimental method (see Chapter 2). Thus, Martin Orne (1962) had suggested that most experimental situations contained **demand characteristics**, which would help research participants to guess the

demand characteristics cues that are perceived as telling participants how they are expected to behave or respond in a research setting; that is, cues that 'demand' a certain sort of response.

hypothesis to be tested in a given study. Since participants typically tried to be 'good subjects', Orne argued, they would then do their best to support these hypotheses.[1] Even more damaging was the suggestion of Robert Rosenthal (Rosenthal & Fode, 1963) that the expectations of the experimenter might influence the behaviour of research participants, even without their knowledge (**experimenter expectancy effects**). The impact of these expectations on the behaviour of research participants could, for example, be mediated by experimenters' reacting positively to responses that supported their hypotheses and negatively to responses that were inconsistent with expectations.

experimenter expectancy effects effects produced unintentionally by the experimenter that increase the likelihood that participants will confirm the experimenter's hypothesis.

The reaction to these critical voices was the organization of numerous conferences in which the crisis was discussed, sometimes in rather heated language. Although these conferences resulted in a number of crisis books (e.g. Strickland, Aboud, & Gergen, 1976), they failed to bridge the theoretical and methodological chasm that separated the critics from mainstream social psychology. The critics finally founded their own social psychological schools, such as social constructionism in the United States (e.g. Gergen, 1999) and discourse analysis in the United Kingdom (e.g. Potter & Wetherell, 1987), which developed their own methodologies in an attempt to address these problems.

Overcoming the crisis

How was the crisis overcome?

In mainstream social psychology a number of developments were initiated, which over the years helped to alleviate some of the problems highlighted by these critics:

- Social psychologists began to demonstrate their ability to contribute to the solution of real-life problems by developing several applied areas, which contributed to resolving important societal problems. To mention only one such area, health psychology is an application of social psychology. One of the major research areas in health psychology is aimed at changing health-impairing behaviour patterns in our society (e.g. smoking, eating too much, drinking too much alcohol, practising unsafe sex). Social psychologists have helped to understand the reasons why people engage in these behaviours as well as to develop interventions aimed at changing them (Stroebe, 2011). The following chapters in this volume give many additional examples of how social psychology can be, and has been, applied to real social issues.

- The impression that social psychological research did not result in cumulative knowledge may have been the result of improper strategies of reviewing, a problem that was mostly resolved with the development of meta-analytic procedures (see Chapter 2). When reviewing research areas, researchers often erroneously concluded that support for a theory was missing or inconsistent, because few studies supported the theory by yielding significant results, whereas the majority of studies failed to find significant results. In the meantime, we have realized as a discipline (as has science, in general) that the failure to find significant results may simply have been due to conducting a study with an insufficiently large number of participants. If the effects we were looking for were small, this might have resulted in insignificant findings, even though the differences between conditions might all have been in the predicted direction. Since then, meta-analytic procedures have been developed which allow us to integrate statistically the results of independent studies of a given phenomenon, with a view to establishing whether the findings exhibit a pattern of relationships that is reliable across studies (Cooper & Hedges, 1994).

- We now know that attitudes are predictive of behaviour but that this relationship is often obscured in studies which employ inappropriate procedures in measuring the two components (see Chapter 6). As Ajzen and Fishbein (1977) demonstrated in their classic review, attitudes are related to behaviour if both components are assessed with measures that are both reliable and compatible. To be reliable, measures have to consist of multiple items rather than a single item. To be compatible, attitude and behaviour have to be assessed at the same level of specificity. Thus, if we want to predict whether people are likely to engage in physical exercise to improve their health, we should not measure their attitude towards their health, but their attitude towards engaging in physical exercise. The latter attitude is likely to be highly correlated with an aggregate measure of a variety of exercise behaviours (such as jogging, walking, going to the gym). If one wanted to predict specific exercise behaviour, such as whether an individual is likely to jog, one

should measure his or her attitude towards jogging rather than towards physical exercise in general.

- Finally, social psychologists have tried to design their experimental manipulations in ways that would minimize the threat of demand characteristics and experimenter expectancy effects. Furthermore, the fact that many research participants do not even meet experimenters any more (because experiments are often run on the computer by computer programs) should certainly rule out experimenter expectancy effects. The depressing fact that most experiments do not work out the way they were expected to by the experimenter who designed them also appears to suggest that demand characteristics and experimenter expectancy effects cannot be all that powerful. Festinger (1980) most aptly expressed these feelings when he wrote: 'I've always wondered why, if these spurious experimenter effects were so strong, so many of my own experiments did not show the expected results.' (p. 252.)

SOCIAL PSYCHOLOGY IN EUROPE

How did social psychology develop in Europe?

Until the end of World War II, the development of social psychology as a discipline was restricted to the US. However, even before the influx of academic refugees in the 1930s, there had been a great deal of European influence on this development. For example, as mentioned earlier, F. Allport's (1924) work on social facilitation had been stimulated by one of his academic teachers at Harvard, the German Hugo Münsterberg, who in turn was familiar with similar work that had been done in Germany by Moede (1920). The experimental work of Bartlett (1932) in Britain on remembering can be viewed as a major precursor of contemporary research on social cognition. And finally, the theorizing underlying Sherif's (1936) studies of norm development is heavily influenced by Gestalt psychology.

However, even though there were individuals in Europe who conducted research that could be considered social psychological, there was no unitary social psychology. This situation continued into the 1960s, even though social psychology groups had been established at a number of European universities. But while there *was* social psychology in Europe, there was no *European social psychology*: there was no European collaboration, and most European researchers had not met each other, nor were they even aware of each other's work.

Obviously, a European network was not necessary for the development of a strong social psychology in some of the European countries where effective social psychology research groups already existed (e.g. Belgium, Britain, the Netherlands and Germany). However, in some other countries it would probably have taken many decades for social psychology to develop. Furthermore, since most of the European researchers met each other, if at all, only at conferences held in the US, without the foundation of a European association European social psychology would probably have remained a minor appendix of North American social psychology rather than developing its own theoretical perspective. Thus, the foundation of the European Association of Experimental Social Psychology was critical.

Given the dominance of North American social psychology at that time, even in Europe, it is no coincidence that it was again an American, John Lanzetta, who set things in motion in 1963. During a sabbatical year in London, Lanzetta, then Professor of Social Psychology at the University of Delaware, visited various social psychology groups in Europe. He was struck by the fact that many of these colleagues, though well informed about US social psychology, were not really aware of what was going on in the social psychology departments of neighbouring European countries. He decided to change this and raised funds for a first European Conference on Experimental Social Psychology, held in Sorrento, Italy, in 1963 (Nuttin, 1990; Moscovici & Marková, 2006). One of the main initiatives which emerged from this and two follow-up conferences was the foundation of the **European Association of Experimental Social Psychology** (EAESP) in 1966. The European Association engaged in a number of regular activities, which had great impact on the development of social psychology in Europe. These included:

> **European Association of Social Psychology** an association formed by European researchers in 1966 to further social psychology in Europe (originally named the European Association of Experimental Social Psychology).

- Summer schools for advanced students, taught by outstanding researchers.
- Publication of the *European Journal of Social Psychology* from 1970, which included most of the early research thought of (then at least) as typically 'European' (e.g. studies of intergroup relations or minority influence). Other key European publications were, first, the *European Monographs* series and, later, the *European Review of Social Psychology*. The first edition of the textbook you are reading now was published in 1988, in part to counteract the tendency of American textbooks to under-report the work of European social psychologists.
- The regular organization of conferences, including plenary meetings of the whole membership, and special East–West meetings (the latter were particularly effective forums at a time when travel and currency restrictions made it extremely difficult for social psychologists from Eastern and Western Europe to meet).

Membership in the European Association of Social Psychology (EASP), as it is known now after dropping 'experimental' from its name in 2008, has grown at a phenomenal rate, from less than 100 in 1970 to more than 1,000 members in 2010. During this period, scientific development in social psychology also changed from being a one-sided enterprise, with American ideas being adopted in Europe, to a mutual development, with European ideas being taken up enthusiastically in the United States and ever-increasing collaboration leading to scientific growth. It is now accepted practice for prominent North American journals (*Journal of Personality and Social Psychology*, *Journal of Experimental Social Psychology* and *Personality and Social Psychology Bulletin*) to have at least one European editor, and likewise for the *European Journal of Social Psychology* to have non-European editors.

Probably the two most important examples of European ideas influencing social psychology in the United States are research on intergroup behaviour and on minority influence. Although Henri Tajfel was not the first to conduct experimental research on intergroup behaviour (that honour goes to Sherif), he developed the paradigm (the *minimal group paradigm*) that turned intergroup behaviour into a major research area (see Chapter 14). The minimal group paradigm offered an easy and very economical procedure for the study of intergroup behaviour, but Tajfel and Turner (1979, 1986) developed from it a theoretical framework that could account for these findings, social identity theory (see Chapter 14).

The second theoretical innovation that was started in Europe and then accepted in the United States is research on minority influence. Social influence research in North America focused exclusively on conformity, that is, on explaining how majorities influence minorities. It was Moscovici who first pointed out that this type of theorizing could hardly explain social or religious innovations, where powerless minorities influenced powerful majorities (e.g. women's rights, Christianity). After Moscovici and his colleagues in Paris (e.g. Moscovici, Lage, & Naffrechoux, 1969) had published a number of studies demonstrating minority influence, and again with the development of a theory that could account for these effects, research on minority influence became a major research area both in the US and in Europe (Moscovici, 1976; see Chapter 8).

SOCIAL PSYCHOLOGY TODAY

What new theoretical perspectives have emerged during the last few decades?

In the 1980s most of the researchers who had contributed to modern social psychology, and who, as often as not, had come from the research centres directed by either Lewin or Hovland, were still alive and active (Cartwright, 1979). In the meantime, not only have many of these pioneers retired or died, but so also have most of the students whom they, in turn, had trained. The field has grown at an exponential rate. There are now chairs in social psychology at practically all major universities in the United States, in Europe, and in Australasia, and social psychologists number in the thousands rather than a few hundreds. Social psychology has also become an essential part of the psychology curriculum in these countries.

Not surprisingly, social psychology has also changed over these decades. Major scientific perspectives, such as consistency theory or attribution theory, have faded and new perspectives, such as *social cognition, evolutionary social psychology* and *social neuroscience*, have emerged. Jones (1998) colourfully described these changing trends in research as 'band wagons and sinking ships' (p. 54).

Social cognition research is an application of principles of cognitive psychology to the area of social psychology (see Devine, Hamilton, & Ostrom, 1994). Unlike other psychological disciplines, social psychology has always placed a strong emphasis on how individuals internally represent their environment. Many of our theories have been labelled 'cognitive' (e.g. cognitive dissonance), and central concepts of social psychology (e.g. attitudes, beliefs, intentions) are cognitive constructs. It would thus appear a small step for social psychologists to borrow methods from cognitive psychology to study how social information is encoded and how the information is stored and retrieved from memory. This perspective has had a widespread influence across the field of social psychology, but is seen perhaps most clearly in changes to the way we theorize and do research in person perception (see Chapters 3 and 4), attitude

change (Chapter 7), and prejudice and intergroup relations (Chapter 14).

Evolutionary social psychology (e.g. Burnstein & Branigan, 2001; Buss & Kendrick, 1998) is an application of evolutionary theory to social psychology. Evolutionary theory explains human behaviours, including differences in partner preference according to gender, from their reproductive value, that is, their value in producing offspring in our evolutionary past. Evolutionary psychology makes the basic assumption that if a given behaviour is (1) at least partly genetically determined and (2) increases the probability that an individual will produce offspring, the gene that determines this behaviour will become more prevalent in the gene pool of future generations. Evolutionary social psychologists have made important contributions to the study of interpersonal attraction (Chapter 11), helping and cooperation (Chapter 10) and aggression (Chapter 9). The development of evolutionary social psychology as an accepted research area in social psychology is surprising, as talking about genetic determinants of social behaviour was considered heresy in the decades following World War II and the defeat of the race ideology of the Hitler regime. However, modern applications of evolutionary social psychology are less deterministic, less ideological and, most importantly, more solidly based on evolutionary theory than such earlier approaches.

Social neuroscience is the study of the neural correlates of social psychological phenomena (Cacioppo & Berntson, 2005; Ochsner & Lieberman, 2001). Building on huge recent advances in the use of non-invasive techniques for examining the functioning of the human brain, social neuroscience studies participants' brains while they are engaged in processing social information. There are two major approaches used by social neuroscience, namely *brain mapping* and *psychological hypothesis testing* (Amodio, 2010). Brain mapping studies (e.g. by functional magnetic resonance imaging, fMRI; see Figure 1.6a) attempt to identify the neural substrates of specific psychological processes. The hypothesis testing approach uses the results of brain mapping to test hypotheses about psychological variables. 'For example, a social psychologist, who studies intergroup prejudice might hypothesize that implicit racial bias is rooted in mechanisms of basic classical fear conditioning. To test this hypothesis, one might measure brain activity in the amygdala – a structure implicated in fear conditioning in many studies – while a participant completes a behavioural measure of implicit racial bias. In this case, the construct validity of the neural measure of fear conditioning . . . is already reasonably established . . . and the question concerns not the meaning of brain activation, but experimental effects among psychological variables' (Amodio, 2010, pp. 699–700).

FIGURE 1.6(a) *Functional MRI scanning techniques have already been used to further our understanding of issues such as self, altruism and racial prejudice.*

Source: © Levent Konuk. Used under licence from Shutterstock.

FIGURE 1.6(b) *An fMRI scan shows activation of the amygdala processing social, fear-related information.*

Source: © 2000 by the Massachusetts Institute of Technology. (Elizabeth A. Phelps, Kevin J. O'Connor, William A. Cunningham, E. Sumie Funayama, J. Christopher Gatenby, John C. Gore and Mahzarin R. Banaji, 2000. Performance on Indirect Measures of Race Evaluation Predicts Amygdala Activation. *Journal of Cognitive Neuroscience, 12:5,* 729–738.)

Studies have already used such techniques to further our understanding of such disparate issues as the self (see Chapter 5), altruism (see Chapter 10), and racial prejudice (see Chapter 14). Some studies, for example, have examined changes in blood flow within the brain (using fMRI; Figure 1.6b) while people are shown race-relevant stimuli under different conditions. Such research has indicated that there is a link between social categorization and the amygdala. Phelps et al. (2000) showed, for example, that white participants' greater amygdala activation in response to black versus white faces was significantly correlated with their implicit racial prejudice only when the faces were of unknown black people, but not when they were of famous and well-liked black and white individuals. These findings suggest that amygdala activation and behavioural responses of race evaluation are heavily shaped by social learning, and that familiarity with members of these groups can modulate bias. Thus, involvement of biological processes does not imply something fundamental and unchangeable. In fact, social neuroscience emphasizes that *social* variables can *influence* biological processes (Eberhardt, 2005; Phelps & Thomas, 2003). Furthermore, even if the neural correlates of prejudice can be identified, prejudice is a psychological construct and cannot be redefined as the activation of particular brain regions (Sherman, 2010).

Because brain mapping helps neuroscientists to understand the brain, whereas psychological hypotheses can usually be tested without using neural indicators, it can be argued that social psychology is much more useful in helping neuroscientists to understand the brain than neuroscience is in helping us to understand social psychological processes (Kihlstrom, 2010). As Kihlstrom (2010) nicely put it: 'Psychology without neuroscience is still the science of mental life, but neuroscience without psychology is just a science of neurons.' (Kihlstrom, 2010, p. 762.)

Social psychology today is an exhilarating and thriving enterprise. Living up to Lewin's motto that nothing is as practical as a good theory, social psychologists are applying the understanding they have gained from their study of fundamental cognitive, emotional and motivational processes to the solution of real-life problems. As the chapters in this volume illustrate, they have contributed importantly to the development of applied areas ranging from health psychology, to organizational psychology (see Chapters 12 and 13), to resolving intergroup conflict (see Chapter 14). In the absence of systematic and controlled social psychological research in most areas, F. Allport (1924) had to rely heavily on speculation in his ambitious road map for social psychology as an empirical science. We hope that the readers of this textbook will appreciate the progress social psychologists have made in less than a century in replacing speculation with theory-guided empirical research.

CHAPTER SUMMARY

- *How can social psychology be defined?* Social psychology is often defined as the scientific attempt to understand and explain how thoughts, feelings and behaviours of individuals are influenced by the actual, imagined or implied presence of other human beings.

- *How does social psychology differ from other psychological disciplines?* One of the main differences is the focus on the impact of the characteristics of the social situation on thoughts and behaviour of individuals. Although social psychologists might also be interested in individual differences, they are usually concerned with individual differences in responses to characteristics of the social situation.

- *When was the first social psychology experiment conducted?* There are several candidates that could claim to have been the first experiment in social psychology, but all were conducted just before 1900.

- *When did the first textbook of social psychology appear?* The first textbook that covered topics which would still be considered social psychology today was written by Floyd Allport (1924).

- *Was there much social psychological research before World War II?* Although there was some important research conducted before World War II, most theorizing and research considered part of modern social psychology has been published since 1945.

- *What were the unintended effects of Hitler's actions on social psychology?* World War II created interest in social influence and attitude change. But the crimes of the Nazi regime also stimulated interest in issues such as conformity and obedience. Finally, the forced emigration of Jewish academics strongly shaped the development of social psychology in the US.

- *Who were the émigrés with the greatest influence on social psychology?* The most important émigré was Kurt Lewin. He attracted an illustrious group of students who shaped social psychology in the decades following World War II. Another influential émigré was the Austrian Fritz Heider, who left Europe for personal reasons. He stimulated two theoretical traditions, consistency theory and attribution theory, which dominated social psychology in the decades following World War II.

- *What were the causes of the crisis that developed in social psychology?* There were doubts raised about the societal relevance of social psychological research (i.e. frivolous values) as well as scientific nature of our methods (i.e. the influence of demand characteristics, experimenter expectancy effects). These doubts were strengthened by the impression that our research did not result in cumulative knowledge and that attitudes did not predict behaviour. Finally it was questioned whether social psychological theories developed and tested in Western cultures (i.e. mainly in the US) would also apply to other cultures.

- *How was the crisis overcome?* Social psychology emerged from the crisis stronger than it was before. Some of the problems were overcome by theoretical or methodological improvements. Others resulted in the emergence of new research areas. For example, cultural social psychology was developed to assess the extent to which our theories are applicable across cultures (see Chapter 15). A strong applied social psychology was developed to demonstrate the societal relevance of social psychological theories and research.

- *What new theoretical perspectives have emerged during the last few decades?* Major scientific perspectives such as consistency theory or attribution theory have faded and new perspectives, such as social cognition, evolutionary social psychology and social neuroscience have emerged.

NOTE

1. Early research reports referred to those who took part in psychological research as 'subjects'. It is now standard practice to refer to them as 'participants'.

SUGGESTIONS FOR FURTHER READING

Berscheid, E. (1992). A glance back at a quarter century of social psychology. *Journal of Personality and Social Psychology, 63,* 525–533. A personal reflection by a leading scholar on developments in North America in the 25 years up to its publication.
Cartwright, D. (1979). Contemporary social psychology in historical perspective. *Social Psychology Quarterly, 42,* 82–93. A lively attempt to put social psychology into historical perspective, famous for highlighting the 'influence' of Adolf Hitler.

Farr, R. M. (1996). *The roots of modern social psychology: 1872–1954*. Oxford: Blackwell. Scholarly treatment of the background to the modern era, with special reference to the relationship between social psychology and other social sciences.

Jahoda, G. (2007). *A history of social psychology: From the eighteenth-century enlightenment to the Second World War*. Cambridge, UK: Cambridge University Press. Another book that provides great insights into the history of ideas which finally led to the development of modern social psychology.

Kruglanski, A. W., & Stroebe, W. (Eds.). (2012). *Handbook of the history of social psychology*. New York: Psychology Press. Researchers, who have substantially contributed to central areas of social psychology, present their view of the development of their particular research area.

Moscovici, S., & Marková, I. (2006). *The making of modern social psychology: The hidden story of how an international social science was created*. Cambridge, UK: Polity. This book tells the fascinating story of how European Social Psychology was born.

2 Research Methods in Social Psychology

ANTONY S. R. MANSTEAD AND ANDREW G. LIVINGSTONE

Source: © René Hendriks (One of the laboratory rooms of the social psychology laboratory at Utrecht University.)

KEY TERMS

- confederate
- construct
- construct validity
- control group
- convergent validity
- cover story
- debriefing
- demand characteristics
- dependent variable
- discourse analysis
- experiment
- experimental confound
- experimental group
- experimental scenario
- experimenter expectancy effect
- external validity
- factorial experiment

- field experiment
- hypothesis
- implicit measures
- independent variable
- interaction effect
- internal validity
- Internet experiment
- main effect
- manipulation check
- mediating variable
- meta-analysis
- one-shot case study
- operationalization
- participant
- participant observation
- post-experimental enquiry
- post-test only control group design

- quasi-experiment
- quota sample
- random allocation
- reactivity
- reliability
- sampling
- simple random sample
- social desirability
- social neuroscience
- survey research
- theory
- triangulation
- true randomized experiment
- unobtrusive measures
- validity
- variable

CHAPTER OUTLINE

ROUTE MAP OF THE CHAPTER

This chapter provides an overview of research methods in social psychology, from the development of theory to the collection of data. After describing three quantitative research strategies (experiments and quasi-experiments, and survey research), the chapter briefly discusses qualitative approaches, focusing on discourse analysis. There follows a description of the key elements of experimentation, as this is the most popular research method in social psychology. We also consider threats to validity in experimental research, and discuss problems with experimental research in social psychology. The final section of the chapter contains a description of three methods of data collection (observation, self-report and implicit measures).

INTRODUCTION

How do social psychologists go about testing their theories?

Why should a chapter about the technical aspects of research methods come so early in this textbook? Why do we need to study research methods, rather than go directly to the real substance of social psychological phenomena and explanations for those phenomena? To answer these questions, we need to consider an even more fundamental question: Why do psychologists conduct research in the first place?

As social psychologists, we are of course interested in 'big' phenomena. What causes intergroup conflict? Why do people stereotype members of other groups? How do we form impressions of other people? Why do people behave differently when they are in a group? What leads people to change their attitudes? What factors influence whether close relationships succeed or fail? To answer these questions, we develop *theo-*

> **theory** a set of abstract concepts (i.e. constructs) together with propositions about how those constructs are related to one another.

> **construct** an abstract theoretical concept (such as social influence).

> **variable** the term used to refer to the measurable representation of a construct.

ries. For example, we might want to develop a **theory** about the causes of intergroup conflict. In the first instance, this involves identifying **constructs** (abstract concepts, such as 'threat', or 'prejudice') or **variables** (a measurable representation of a construct, such as scores on questionnaire measures of threat perceptions or intergroup hostility) that we think are relevant to the question, and speculating about how these relate to one another. Crucially, our theories typically consist of propositions about *causal relationships* between constructs. In this way, we are not content with simply *describing* these 'big' phenomena; rather, we seek to *explain* them by identifying their antecedents. In developing a theory of intergroup conflict (see Chapter 14), we are not only interested in what conflict is like, but also in what causes it and how it might be reduced. For example, we might theorize that intergroup conflict is caused by feelings that the interests or well-being of one's own group are threatened by another group (see Branscombe, Ellemers, Spears, & Doosje, 1999).

We might initially base our theories on observation of real-life events, on intuition or on existing theories. But coming up with theories is only part of the story. Many other disciplines – such as philosophy, sociology, and anthropology – are concerned with the same issues and phenomena that interest social psychologists.

What helps to distinguish social psychology – and psychology as a whole – from these other disciplines is not simply the *type* of explanation we provide, but also a commitment to the *scientific method*, in which we test our theories against *evidence*. This introduces an essential characteristic of a theory: it must be *testable*. This means that we should be able to derive specific predictions (or **hypotheses**) from the theory concerning the relationship between two or more constructs, and to gather evidence that could support or contradict those predictions.

> **hypothesis** a prediction derived from a theory concerning the relationship between variables.

Consider Janis's (1982) theory about the poor quality of decision-making that is apparent even in groups of competent and experienced persons – a phenomenon he termed 'groupthink' (see Chapter 8). Janis's (1982) theory consists of one set of concepts representing the antecedent conditions of poor group decision-making, another set representing the symptoms of groupthink, a third set representing symptoms of poor decision-making and a final set representing the process linking antecedent conditions to the symptoms of groupthink and poor decision-making (see Theory Box 2.1). One of the *antecedent conditions* is a 'cohesive group', a group whose members are psychologically dependent on the group. Because they are dependent on their group membership, they are more likely to conform to what they believe to be the consensual position in the group. An example *symptom* of groupthink is the presence of 'mind guards', a term Janis used to describe group members who take it on themselves to protect the group from information that questions the correctness or morality of an emerging decision. An example symptom of defective decision-making is failure to examine the risks of the preferred decision. Janis also specified how groupthink is brought about (i.e. the *mediating process*). In this case, the mediating process is a premature 'concurrence-seeking tendency', a powerful preference for agreement with fellow group members, before all these issues have been properly discussed. Thus antecedent conditions are linked to symptoms via a mediating process; we discuss the concept of mediation in more detail later in this chapter.

A prediction that we can derive logically from Janis's theory is that groups that are more cohesive should be more prone to making poor-quality decisions than groups that are less cohesive (see Research Close-Up 2.1). To the extent that the evidence is consistent with the prediction, we can be more confident in the theory from which we derived the prediction. Correspondingly, if the evidence is inconsistent with the prediction, we should be less confident in the underlying theory. Evidence might also reveal limits or

THEORY BOX 2.1

ANTECEDENT CONDITIONS, MEDIATING PROCESS AND SYMPTOMS OF GROUPTHINK IN JANIS'S (1982) THEORETICAL MODEL

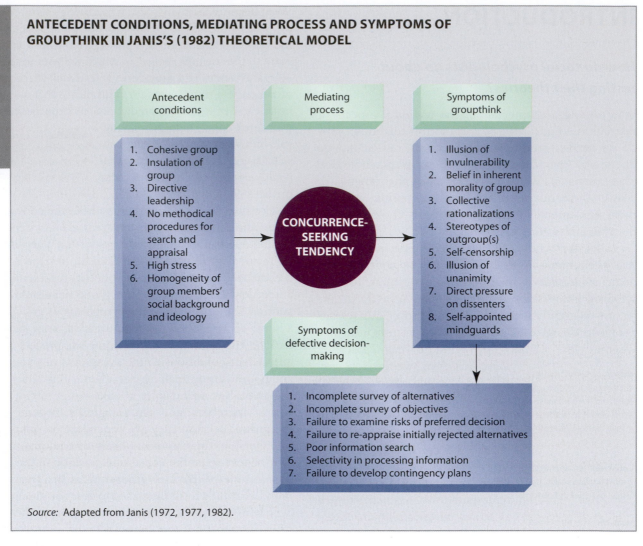

Antecedent conditions

1. Cohesive group
2. Insulation of group
3. Directive leadership
4. No methodical procedures for search and appraisal
5. High stress
6. Homogeneity of group members' social background and ideology

Mediating process

CONCURRENCE-SEEKING TENDENCY

Symptoms of groupthink

1. Illusion of invulnerability
2. Belief in inherent morality of group
3. Collective rationalizations
4. Stereotypes of outgroup(s)
5. Self-censorship
6. Illusion of unanimity
7. Direct pressure on dissenters
8. Self-appointed mindguards

Symptoms of defective decision-making

1. Incomplete survey of alternatives
2. Incomplete survey of objectives
3. Failure to examine risks of preferred decision
4. Failure to re-appraise initially rejected alternatives
5. Poor information search
6. Selectivity in processing information
7. Failure to develop contingency plans

Source: Adapted from Janis (1972, 1977, 1982).

boundary conditions to a predicted effect, showing that it only occurs under specific circumstances. An example of boundary conditions in relation to Janis's theory comes from research conducted by Postmes, Spears, and Cihangir (2001), who found that the effect of group cohesiveness on the quality of a group's decisions depended upon the *norm* of the group. Specifically, the quality of decisions was improved when the group had a norm of critical thinking compared to when it had a norm of maintaining consensus. In the light of this sort of evidence, the original theory may need to be modified, or even rejected entirely in favour of an alternative.

Now we can see why research methods are so important. They are the essential tools of our trade, providing a way of translating our ideas into actions, and of

testing, challenging and improving our theories. The quality of our research depends not only on the quality of our theories, but on the quality of the research methods we use to test those theories.

Summary

Methods are the tools researchers use to test their theoretical ideas. These ideas can come from a variety of sources, but two that are quite common in social psychology are observations of real-life events and inconsistencies between previous research findings. A theory consists of a set of constructs linked together in a system, and specifies when particular phenomena should occur.

ARCHIVAL ANALYSES OF 'GROUPTHINK'

RESEARCH CLOSE-UP 2.1

Janis, I. L. (1972). Victims of groupthink: A psychological study of foreign-policy decisions and fiascoes. Boston: Houghton Mifflin.

Introduction

Janis's research on groupthink provides an excellent example of 'archival research', a research strategy that is not described or discussed elsewhere in the present chapter. In archival research the data come from archives – that is, from stored records of facts. 'Archival data may include such items as personal documents (letters or diaries), creative products (poems, paintings, essays), biographies or autobiographies, and histories or governmental records' (Simonton, 1981, p. 218). Janis (1972) decided to study in detail archival material relating to four major US foreign policy fiascoes: the Bay of Pigs invasion of Cuba in 1961; the decision to escalate the Korean War in 1950; the failure to be prepared for the attack on Pearl Harbor in 1941; and the decision to escalate the Vietnam War in 1964. Janis argues that in the case of each of these disastrous decisions, information was potentially or actually available to the policy-making groups that should have led them to different decisions.

Method

Janis's research took the form of careful scouring of all the documentary sources of information on the circumstances in which these faulty decisions were made. In his 1972 book *Victims of Groupthink*, Janis attempted to show how the archival data on each of these decisions can be regarded as forming a consistent social psychological pattern, the essence of which is shown in Theory Box 2.1. Janis (1982) published a second edition of his book in which he applied the notion of groupthink to the Watergate incident that ultimately led to US President Richard Nixon's resignation in 1974.

Later research

Tetlock (1979) conducted a more quantitative analysis of archival materials. He applied standardized procedures for analysing the content of public statements made by key decision-makers involved in the 'groupthink' and 'non-groupthink' decisions examined by Janis (1972). Tetlock was particularly interested in assessing the extent to which public statements made by key decision-makers reflected 'a tendency to process policy-relevant information in simplistic and biased ways' (p. 1317), and the extent to which these statements reflected 'a tendency to evaluate one's own group highly positively and to evaluate one's . . . opponents highly negatively' (p. 1317).

To assess these two aspects of groupthink, Tetlock identified six key decision-makers who were intimately involved in five different foreign policy decisions, two of which were classified by Janis as 'non-groupthink', while he classified the other three as 'groupthink' decisions. He then randomly selected and analysed 12 paragraph-sized passages from the public statements made by each decision-maker at the time of each crisis. He found that the public statements of decision-makers in groupthink crises were significantly less complex than were the public statements of decision-makers in non-groupthink crises. He also found evidence that decision-makers in the groupthink crises gave more positive evaluations of their own political groups than did decision-makers in crises not characterized by groupthink. However, contrary to predictions, there was no difference between groupthink and non-groupthink decision-makers in terms of the intensity of negative evaluations of their political opponents. With the exception of this last finding, the results of Tetlock's study are consistent with Janis's conclusions, which were based on a more qualitative analysis of historical documents.

Discussion

A key advantage of the archival research strategy is that the evidence gleaned from archives is not distorted by **participants**' knowledge that researchers are investigating their behaviour. The behaviour took place in natural settings at an earlier time than that at which the behaviour was studied.

participant a person who takes part in a psychological study.

There is, therefore, little or no chance that the behaviour could have been 'contaminated' by the research process. As Simonton (1981) put it, 'Because archival research exploits data already collected by others for purposes often very different from the intentions of the researcher, this methodology constitutes a class of "unobtrusive measures"' (p. 218). Offsetting this advantage are some disadvantages. The most obvious of these are (1) that the researcher is dependent on the quality of the archival information, which may not contain a good basis for assessing key variables, and (2) that even when associations between variables (such as the quality of a decision and the complexity of statements made by decision-makers) are found, it is unclear whether or how they are *causally* related.

RESEARCH STRATEGIES

What are the strengths and weaknesses of the principal research strategies available to the social psychologist?

Researchers who want to test their ideas and predictions have a range of different research strategies available to them. In this section we will consider experimental and quasi-experimental research, survey research and qualitative approaches.

Experiments and quasi-experiments

Experimental research is designed to yield causal information. The goal of an **experiment** is to see what happens to a phenomenon when the researcher deliberately modifies some feature of the environment in which the phenomenon occurs ('If I change variable *B*, will there be resulting changes in variable *A*?'). By controlling the variation in *B*, the researcher who finds that there are changes in *A* can draw causal conclusions. Instead of just knowing that more of variable *A* is associated with more of variable *B*, the experimental researcher discovers whether *A* increases when *B* is increased, decreases when *B* is reduced, remains stable when *B* is left unchanged and so on. Such a pattern of results would suggest that changes in *B cause* the changes in *A*.

> **experiment** a method in which the researcher deliberately introduces some change into a setting to examine the consequences of that change.

The experimental method is a theme with many variations. Two common variations are the **quasi-experiment** and the **true randomized experiment**. They differ with respect to the realism of the setting in which the data are collected and the degree of control that the researcher has over that setting. A quasi-experiment is typically conducted in a natural, everyday setting, one over which the researcher does not have complete control. The true randomized experiment, by contrast, is one in which the researcher has complete control over key features of the setting; however, this often involves a loss of realism.

> **quasi-experiment** an experiment in which participants are not randomly allocated to the different experimental conditions (typically because of factors beyond the control of the researcher).

> **true randomized experiment** an experiment in which participants are allocated to the different conditions of the experiment on a random basis.

To grasp the key difference between a quasi-experiment and a true experiment, we need to consider further what is meant by the term *experiment*. Experiments are studies in which the researcher examines the effects of one class of variables (independent, or manipulated, variables) on another class of variables (dependent, or measured, variables). In a true randomized experiment the researcher has control over the independent variable *and* over who is exposed to this variable. Most importantly, the researcher is able to allocate research participants randomly to different conditions of the experiment (**random allocation**). In a quasi-experiment the researcher usually cannot control who is exposed to the independent variable. In a typical quasi-experiment, pre-existing groups of people are either exposed or not exposed to the independent variable.

> **random allocation** (sometimes called *random assignment*) the process of allocating participants to groups (or conditions) in such a way that each participant has an equal chance of being assigned to each group.

Examples of each method may help to bring out the points of difference. Social psychologists interested in aggression have studied whether exposure to violent film

FIGURE 2.1 *What research method might be used to study the impact of viewing violent television on subsequent behaviour?*

Source: © Edouard Berne. Used under licence from Getty Images.

and television material has an impact on the subsequent behaviour of the viewer (see Chapter 9 and Figure 2.1). This can be done using true randomized experiments or quasi-experiments. An example of a true experiment on this issue is the study reported by Liebert and Baron (1972). Male and female children in each of two age groups were randomly allocated to one of two experimental conditions, one in which they viewed an excerpt from a violent television programme and another in which they viewed an exciting athletics race. Later both groups of children were ostensibly given the opportunity to hurt another child. Those who had seen the violent material were more likely to use this opportunity than were those who had seen the non-violent material. Because children had been randomly allocated to the violent and non-violent conditions, the observed difference can be attributed to the difference in type of material seen, rather than any difference in the type of children who saw the material.

An example of a quasi-experimental study of the same issue is the study reported by Black and Bevan (1992). They asked people to complete a questionnaire measure of tendency to engage in aggressive behaviour under one of four conditions: while waiting in line outside a cinema to see a violent movie; while waiting in line to see a non-violent movie; having just seen a violent movie; and having just seen a non-violent movie. As can be seen in Figure 2.2, the researchers found that those waiting to see the violent film had higher aggression scores than those waiting to see the non-violent film; and also that those who had just seen the violent film scored higher than those waiting to see the violent film (although there was no difference in aggression scores between those who had just seen a non-violent movie and those waiting to see a non-violent movie). These findings are consistent with the notion that viewing a violent movie increases the tendency to aggress (Figure 2.3), but the fact that participants were not allocated at random to the different conditions makes it impossible to rule out alternative explanations. For example, it may be that violent movies only increase aggressive tendencies among those who are attracted to view such movies in the first place.

Often the only way in which to conduct an experimental study of a social phenomenon is via a quasi-experiment. Ethical and practical considerations frequently make it impossible to allocate people randomly to different experimental conditions. If, like Stroebe, Stroebe, and

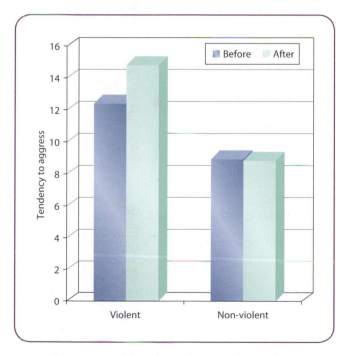

FIGURE 2.2 *Self-reported tendency to aggress, as a function of type of movie, and whether or not the respondent was waiting to see the movie or had just seen the movie.*

Source: Based on data reported by Black and Bevan, 1992. Reproduced with permission from John Wiley & Sons, Inc.

FIGURE 2.3 *Does viewing a violent movie increase the tendency to aggressive behaviour in us all, or simply increase aggressive tendencies only in those who are attracted to viewing such movies in the first place?*

Source: HOSTEL 2 © 2007 Screen Gems, Inc. and Lions Gate Films Inc. All Rights Reserved. COURTESY OF SCREEN GEMS.

LEADER IN THE FIELD

Charles M. Judd (b. 1946) is a leading scholar in the field of social cognition and stereotyping, but also an outstanding methodologist. He took his BA at Yale University, majoring in French, then studied theology at Union Theological Seminary, New York, before discovering a greater calling and pursuing graduate studies in psychology at Columbia University, where he obtained his PhD under Morton Deutsch. He began his teaching career at Harvard University, then moved to the University of Colorado, Boulder, where he has remained since 1986 (with the exception of two years at the University of California, Berkeley), and is now Professor of Distinction, College of Arts and Sciences. He is an expert on experimental design and analysis, and evaluation and quasi-experimental designs. He has contributed numerous highly influential articles on statistics (notably mediation and moderation analysis), has served as editor of many of the leading journals in the field, and received the 1999 Thomas M. Ostrom Award for Lifetime Contributions to Social Cognition Theory and Research. He was awarded the degree of Doctor Honoris Causa, Faculté de Psychologie et des Sciences de l'Education, Université Catholique de Louvain, Louvain-la-Neuve, Belgium, in 2006.

Domittner (1988), you wish to study the effects of bereavement, for example, you obviously cannot randomly allocate research participants to a 'bereaved' and a 'non-bereaved' condition. The same applies in many other fields of research. Thus, the choice of research strategy is often a compromise between what is optimal and what is practicable. Fortunately, the sophistication of some quasi-experimental designs is such that it is possible to draw conclusions about causality with some confidence (Judd & Kenny, 1981a, b; West, Biesanz, & Pitts, 2000; see Leader in the Field, Charles M. Judd).

It is also possible to conduct true experiments in field settings, in which case they are referred to as **field experiments** (see Chapter 1), which attempt to combine the control of a laboratory experiment with the realism of a quasi-experiment. An example of such a field experiment is given in Research Close-Up 2.2.

Survey research

The practical and ethical considerations that can make quasi-experiments a useful strategy also apply more generally to **survey research** (Oppenheim, 1992; Schwarz, Groves, & Schuman, 1998; Visser, Krosnick, & Lavrakas, 2000). Surveys differ from experiments and quasi-experiments in that they focus on measuring existing levels of relevant variables, rather than manipulating them (see Social Psychology Beyond the Lab 2.1). Like experiments, survey designs are typically concerned with associations and/or cause-

survey research
a research strategy that involves interviewing (or administering a questionnaire to) a sample of respondents who are selected so as to be representative of the population from which they are drawn.

and-effect relationships between variables. However, the lack of control over independent – or *predictor* – variables means that it is virtually impossible to be certain about their causal role. For this reason, surveys often also measure other variables that can be taken into account in statistical analyses – that is, *controlled for* – in order to rule out possible alternative explanations for a relationship between a predictor variable and an outcome variable.

An example of this strategy is provided by Pratto, Sidanius, Stallworth, and Malle (1994). They proposed that many different types of intergroup prejudice are predicted by a personality variable which they call *social dominance orientation*, or SDO (see Chapter 14). This variable reflects an individual's preference for unequal status relations between social categories. So, someone who scores high in SDO should be more sexist, and more likely to oppose equal rights for racial minorities. In support of this prediction, Pratto et al. (1994) found that SDO was indeed positively correlated with sexism, and negatively correlated with support for racial equality. However, they were also concerned that the relation between these variables and SDO could actually be due to the influence of another variable, such as political conservatism. If so, the argument that SDO is a unique predictor of prejudice would be greatly undermined. To test this possibility, Pratto et al. re-examined the correlations between prejudice and SDO while controlling for (or *partialling out*) the effect of political conservatism. The correlations remained significant, increasing their confidence that the role of SDO is not simply due to political conservatism.

Another strategy that can increase certainty regarding causal relationships in survey research involves taking measures of relevant variables at several points in time – a *longitudinal* survey design. The logic here is that if variable A at time 1 predicts variable B at time 2 (especially when controlling for differences in variable B at time 1), then we can be more certain that variable A has a causal effect on variable B.

Qualitative approaches

Traditionally, social psychological research – including the overwhelming majority of the research discussed in this book – has involved *quantitative* data analysis. That is, the data we analyse are represented as numbers. This makes our data amenable to statistical analyses, allowing researchers to say something about the *average* score on a variable (e.g. the *mean, median,* and/or *modal* score in a sample); the *range* of scores on a variable (e.g. the *variance* or *standard deviation*); and the *strength* and *reliability* of relations between two or more variables (e.g. through inferential tests such as *t*-tests, analysis of variance or regression). These analyses usually provide

A FIELD EXPERIMENT TO STUDY HELPING BEHAVIOUR

RESEARCH CLOSE-UP 2.2

Darley, J. M. & Batson, C. D. (1973). 'From Jerusalem to Jericho': A study of situational and dispositional variables in helping behavior. *Journal of Personality and Social Psychology, 27*, 100–108.

Introduction

The researchers were interested in testing the idea that one reason why bystanders do not come to the assistance of others, even when these others clearly need help, is that helping is costly. The particular 'cost' they studied in their research was time. To come to a stranger's assistance often involves a departure from your original plan. Such a departure can throw you off your schedule. The researchers also wanted to examine whether reminding people of the parable of the Good Samaritan, in which a passer-by does come to the assistance of a stranger in need of help, would influence willingness to give help. They tested these notions in a field experiment (see also Chapter 10). They also measured individual differences in religiosity, to see whether these would influence helping.

Method

The participants in the study were male seminary students (i.e. trainee priests) who believed that they were taking part in a study on 'religious education and vocations'. Each participant began the study in one building and was then asked to proceed to a second building to complete the study. Before leaving the first building, the participant was led to believe one of three things about the speed with which he should go to the other building: that there was no special hurry, that there was an intermediate degree of hurry, or that he was late for the second part of the study and should hurry up. This was the manipulation of the first variable, time pressure (no versus medium versus high degree of hurry). In the second part of the study, the participant expected to do one of two things: either talk about the parable of the Good Samaritan, or talk about job prospects for seminary students. This constituted the second manipulation: either having or not having the parable of the Good Samaritan made psychologically salient. The design of the study is shown in Figure 2.4.

On his way to the other building, the participant passed through an alley in which a person (the 'victim', but actually an accomplice of the experimenters) was sitting slumped in a doorway, head down, eyes closed. As the participant passed the victim, the latter coughed twice and groaned. The dependent variable in this field experiment was the extent to which the participant did anything to

Message	Degree of hurry		
	No	Medium	High
Good Samaritan			
Job prospects			

FIGURE 2.4 *Design of the Darley and Batson (1973) field experiment.*

Source: Copyright © 1973 by the American Psychological Association. Adapted with permission. *Journal of Personality and Social Psychology, 27*, 100–108. The use of APA information does not imply endorsement by APA.

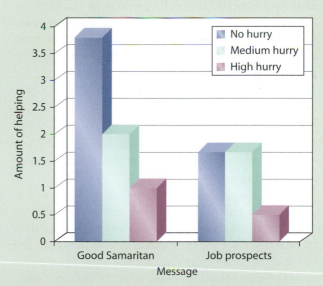

FIGURE 2.5 *Mean helping scores as a function of degree of hurry (no, medium, or high) and anticipated topic of talk (parable of Good Samaritan or job prospects for trainee priests).*

Source: Based on data reported by Darley & Batson (1973). Copyright © 1973 by the American Psychological Association. Adapted with permission. *Journal of Personality and Social Psychology, 27*, 100–108. The use of APA information does not imply endorsement by APA.

help this person apparently in distress. The extent of the participant's helping behaviour was observed and coded.

Results

Helping was significantly influenced by the time pressure manipulation. The results are summarized in Figure 2.5. Those in the 'no hurry' condition were more helpful than those in the 'medium hurry' condition, who in turn were more helpful than those in the 'high hurry' condition. There was also a tendency for being reminded about the parable to have an influence; those who were reminded were more helpful than those who were not. Individual differences in religiosity did not predict whether or not participants stopped to help, although they were related to the nature of the help given.

Discussion

Even those who have chosen to be trained in a vocation in which helping others is supposed to play a central role were affected by the time pressure variable. When they were in a hurry, even those trainee priests who thought that they were on their way to a discussion of the parable of the Good Samaritan were less likely to offer help to a stranger in need than were their counterparts who were in less of a hurry (Figure 2.6). From a methodological perspective, the neat thing about this field experiment is that it was conducted in a natural, everyday setting. Participants were randomly allocated to one of the six conditions of the experiment, so any differences found between these six conditions resulted, in principle, from the experimental manipulations. Thus internal validity was high (i.e. the

FIGURE 2.6 *Would you be more likely to help someone in need after hearing a sermon on the parable of the Good Samaritan?*

Source: © Digital Vision. Used under licence from Getty Images.

researchers could be confident that changes in the independent variable *caused* changes in the dependent variable). But the fact that the setting of the experiment was such an everyday one means that this study also scores quite highly on realism (i.e. it has high external validity too). It is a good example of a field experiment.

clear and interpretable outcomes, and moreover there is broad consensus among researchers about the meaning of these outcomes.

However, the quantitative approach is far from universal in social psychology. An alternative is *qualitative* analysis, in which data are typically textual rather than numerical, focusing on the content and meaning of the words and language used by participants. Qualitative approaches encompass a wide range of analytic techniques. Some of these are perfectly consistent with the philosophical assumptions that underpin quantitative research and the scientific method more generally. Among these assumptions is the belief that the phenomena in which we are interested represent an objective set of 'facts' that exist independently of the researcher's (or anyone else's) perspective on them. According to this view, the fact that many of the phenomena we study – such as an attitude – cannot be directly observed or measured simply means that we require sensitive and sophisticated research methods in order to study them. However, other qualitative approaches are more radical and explicitly reject these assumptions. What unifies qualitative approaches is a concern with the limitations of quantitative research of social phenomena, and the belief that qualitative techniques can provide additional, or even radically different insights (see Henwood, 1996).

The supposed limitations of quantitative techniques relate to the ways in which they potentially misrepresent and/or over-simplify phenomena and participants' perspectives on them. In particular, quantitative measures – especially *self-report* measures, which we discuss later – require the researcher to make assumptions regarding the range and content of possible responses, not to mention their *meaning* to participants. This is important, because a participant's understanding of a task or a questionnaire item may be quite different to that of the researcher.

SOCIAL PSYCHOLOGY BEYOND THE LAB 2.1

SURVEY RESEARCH

Descriptive survey designs focus on describing overall levels of relevant variables, such as the characteristics of one or more groups of people. Examples of descriptive survey designs include political opinion polls, market research and a census (Figure 2.7). Such descriptions can range from the simple (e.g. describing the percentage of people eligible to vote in a particular constituency who say that they intend to vote for a particular political candidate) to the more complex (e.g. describing the personal and social characteristics associated with use of recreational drugs among school-age children and teenagers).

Descriptive survey research is often concerned with large populations, such as all adults living in a particular community, region or country. To ensure that responses are *representative,* one could interview or collect completed questionnaires from the entire population in question (as is done in a census). In most cases, however, collecting data from all members of a population is simply not possible; even where it is possible, it is typically

FIGURE 2.7 *One strategy for gathering research evidence is to survey public opinion by interview.*
Source: © pixsooz. Used under licence from Shutterstock.

not cost-effective. The result is that the researcher has to choose which members of that population to survey. The process of selecting a subset of members is known as **sampling**.

Two main types of sampling are used in survey research: probabilistic and non-probabilistic. The most basic form of probabilistic sampling is the **simple random sample**. A simple random sample is one which satisfies two conditions: first, each member of the population has an equal chance of being selected; second, the selection of every possible combination of the desired number of members is equally likely. To explain the second condition, imagine that the population size is 10 (consisting of persons labelled A to J) and the sample size is two. There are 45 possible combinations of two members of the population (A + B, A + C, A + D, and so on, to I + J). In simple random sampling, each of these 45 possible combinations of two members has to be equally likely. In practice, of course, the sample size of a random sample (e.g. of the whole population of a country) is much larger than two and the process is much more complex.

> **sampling** the process of selecting a subset of members of a population with a view to describing the population from which they are taken.

> **simple random sample** a sample in which each member of the population has an equal chance of being selected and in which the selection of every possible combination of the desired number of members is equally likely.

Researchers achieve random sampling by allocating numbers to each member of the population and using computer-generated random numbers to select a sample of the required size, a feature available on the web.

Because probability sampling is expensive and time-consuming, non-probability sampling is frequently used. The most common form of a non-probability sample is the **quota sample**. Here the objective is to select a sample that reflects basic attributes of the population. Such attributes might be age and sex. If you know the age and sex composition of the population concerned, you then ensure that the age and sex composition of the sample reflects that of the population. The term 'quota' refers to the number of people of a given type (e.g. females between the ages of 55 and 60) who have to be interviewed. The major advantage of quota sampling is that the interviewer can approach potential respondents until the quotas are filled without needing to recruit a specifically identified respondent. Some disadvantages of quota sampling are (1) that it is usually left to the interviewer to decide whom to approach in order to fill a quota, with the result that bias can enter into the selection process, and (2) that it is impossible to provide an accurate estimate of sampling error.

> **quota sample** a sample that fills certain prespecified quotas and thereby reflects certain attributes of the population (such as age and sex) that are thought to be important to the issue being researched.

Moreover, the range of possible responses may not allow participants to communicate responses or perspectives that the researcher did not anticipate.

Several qualitative approaches help to address these concerns. At an early, exploratory stage of a research project, *content analysis* or *thematic analysis* of open-ended oral or written responses can shed light on potentially relevant factors. This approach can also be used to follow up quantitative analyses by exploring unexpected or ambiguous findings (see Livingstone & Haslam, 2008, for an example of the latter). Indeed, content analysis often ultimately produces *quantitative* outcomes, because it allows the researcher to count occurrences of particular words, phrases or themes and conduct statistical analyses on the results. Alternatively, *grounded theory* focuses on systematically *generating* theory about a specific phenomenon in an inductive or 'bottom-up' manner, for example on the basis of exploratory interview data. Other techniques (e.g. *interpretative phenomenological analysis*) focus on revealing and interpreting the subjective meaning that participants attach to particular issues or events.

All of these techniques can complement or extend quantitative research. By contrast, other qualitative approaches such as forms of **discourse analysis** involve a more fundamental rejection of the assumptions that underlie quantitative and much qualitative research.

discourse analysis
a family of methods for analysing talk and texts, with the goal of revealing how people make sense of their everyday worlds.

Rather than searching for an objective, knowable set of 'facts' about social psychological phenomena, advocates of these approaches instead assume that there is no unique, valid interpretation of the world. Consequently, the focus of their research is on fine-grained features of everyday talk and interaction to explore how people actively construct particular interpretations of events. They might seek to show how, for example, racist or sexist attitudes arise not because of the beliefs or biases of the individual who expresses them, but rather as evaluations that emerge in the context of particular social interactions. Rather than being relatively fixed products of individual cognitive systems, such evaluations arise in the context of conversations and vary according to the particular cultural setting.

An example of the use of discourse analysis is the study reported by Wetherell, Stiven, and Potter (1987). These researchers were interested in male and female university students' views about employment opportunities for women. They reasoned that analysing how a group of 17 students talk about these issues would reveal the practical ideologies that are used to reproduce gender inequalities. The students were interviewed in a semistructured way and their responses were transcribed and analysed. A benefit of this approach is that it enabled the researchers to identify contradictions in the way ordinary people talk about issues like gender inequality. Rather than having a single attitude, the students tended to endorse different positions at different points during the interview. Some of these positions were inconsistent with each other, but served specific ideological and strategic purposes at the particular point at which they were adopted.

This sort of qualitative approach is not represented in the present volume, where the emphasis is on the strengths of approaches that assume the objective existence of the phenomena we study. The role played by qualitative research methods in social psychology largely reflects differences in philosophical belief about the causation of social behaviour. From the standpoint of the research represented in the present volume, qualitative research seems to be more focused on description than explanation, and more concerned with how behaviour is constructed than with how it is caused.

One of the most important decisions to be made during the research process is which of the strategies outlined above to adopt. It is worth pointing out that although some research strategies will be better suited than others to studying a given phenomenon, each and every strategy, however sophisticated its implementation, has its limitations. It is for this reason that one of the great pioneers of research methodology in the social sciences, Donald Campbell (see Leader in the Field, Donald T. Campbell), argued for **triangulation**. By this he meant that using multiple methods to study a given issue provides a better basis for drawing conclusions than does any single

triangulation the use of multiple methods and measures to research a given issue.

 LEADER IN THE FIELD

Donald T. Campbell (1917–1996) is regarded as having been a master research methodologist. Campbell completed his undergraduate education at the University of California, Berkeley. After serving in the US Naval Reserve during World War II, he earned his doctorate from Berkeley and subsequently served on the faculties at Ohio State University, the University of Chicago, Northwestern, and Lehigh. He made lasting contributions in a wide range of disciplines, including psychology, sociology, anthropology, biology and philosophy. In social psychology he is best known for co-authoring two of the most influential research methodology texts ever published, *Experimental and Quasi-Experimental Designs for Research* (1966, with Julian C. Stanley) and *Quasi-Experimentation: Design and Analysis Issues for Field Settings* (1979, with Thomas D. Cook). Campbell argued that the sophisticated use of many approaches, each with its own distinct but measurable flaws, was required to design reliable research projects. The paper he wrote with Donald W. Fiske to present this thesis, 'Convergent and discriminant validation by the multitrait–multimethod matrix' (1959), is one of the most frequently cited papers in the social science literature.

method. Because each method has its own strengths and weaknesses, using different methods helps the strengths of one method to compensate for the weaknesses of another (e.g. Fine & Elsbach, 2000).

Summary

Research strategies are broad categories of research methods that are available to study social psychological phenomena. We began by noting that it often makes sense to study a phenomenon using more than one strategy. We identified three quantitative strategies (experiments and quasi-experiments, and survey research) before discussing qualitative research strategies.

A CLOSER LOOK AT EXPERIMENTATION IN SOCIAL PSYCHOLOGY

What are the main elements of a social psychological experiment?

Experimentation has been the dominant research method in social psychology, mainly because it is unrivalled as a method for testing theories that predict causal relationships between variables. Standard guides to research in social psychology (e.g. Aronson, Ellsworth, Carlsmith, & Gonzales, 1990; Aronson, Wilson, & Brewer, 1998) treat experimentation as the preferred research method. In fact there are some grounds for questioning the extent to which experimental studies provide unambiguous evidence about causation, as we shall see later.

We will first describe the principal features of the experimental approach to social psychological research. To assist this process of description, we will use Milgram's (1965; see Chapter 8) well-known study of obedience as an illustrative example.

Features of the social psychological experiment

The **experimental scenario** is the context in which the study is presented. In laboratory

experimental scenario the 'package' within which an experiment is presented to participants.

settings it is important to devise a scenario for which there is a convincing and well-integrated rationale, because the situation

should strike participants as realistic and involving, and the experimental manipulations and the measurement process should not 'leap out' at the participant. In Milgram's study, participants were told that the study was an investigation of the effects of punishment on learning. The participant was given, apparently at random, the role of 'teacher', while an accomplice of the experimenter posing as another participant (known as a **confederate**) took the role of 'learner'. The learner's task was to memorize a list of word pairs. The teacher's task was to read out the first word of each pair, to see whether the learner could correctly remember the second

confederate an accomplice or assistant of the experimenter who is ostensibly another participant but who in fact plays a prescribed role in the experiment.

word, and to administer a graded series of punishments, in the form of electric shocks of increasing severity, if the learner failed to recall the correct word (which he had been instructed to do from time to time). This scenario was devised with a view to convincing the participant that the shocks were genuine (which they were not), and that the learner was actually receiving the shocks.

The **independent variable** is the one that is deliberately manipulated by the experimenter. All other aspects of the scenario are held constant, and the independent variable is changed systematically.

independent variable the variable that an experimenter manipulates or modifies in order to examine the effect on one or more dependent variables.

Operationalization refers to the way in which the variable is measured or manipulated in practice. In Milgram's research a key independent variable was the proximity of the 'learner' to the 'teacher'. In one condition, learner and teacher were in separate rooms; in a second

operationalization the way in which a theoretical construct is turned into a measurable dependent variable or a manipulable independent variable in a particular study.

condition, the teacher could hear the learner but could not see him; in a third condition, the teacher could both see and hear the learner's reactions; in a fourth condition, the teacher had to hold the learner's hand down on a metal plate in order for the shock to be delivered. All other aspects of the experimental setting were held constant, so that any variations in the teacher's behaviour in these four conditions should be attributable to the change in proximity between teacher and learner.

The success of an experiment often hinges on the effectiveness of manipulations of the independent variable. By *effectiveness* we mean (1) the extent to which changes in the independent variable capture the essential qualities of the construct that is theoretically expected to have a causal influence on behaviour, and (2) the size of the changes that are introduced. For example, in Milgram's study, we should consider how well the four proximity conditions capture the construct of proximity. What is being manipulated, clearly, is *physical* proximity. Then there is the question of whether the changes between the four conditions are sufficiently large to produce an effect. In this case it is hard to see how the proximity variable could have been manipulated more powerfully; an investigator who adopts weaker manipulations runs the risk of failing to find the predicted effects simply because the variations across levels of the independent variable are too subtle to have an impact. It has become standard practice in social psychological experiments to include among the

manipulation check a measure of the effectiveness of the independent variable.

measured variables one or more measures of the effectiveness of the manipulation; these are known as **manipulation checks**.

Assessing whether an independent variable has had an effect requires the measurement of the participant's behaviour or internal state. This measured variable is known as the **dependent variable**, so called because systematic changes in this measured variable *depend upon*

dependent variable the variable that is expected to change as a function of changes in the independent variable. Measured changes in the dependent variable are seen as 'dependent on' manipulated changes in the independent variable.

the impact of the independent variable. In Milgram's study, the dependent variable was the intensity of shocks in a 30-step sequence that the teacher was prepared to deliver. The results of Milgram's experiments are often expressed in terms of the percentage of participants who gave the maximum shock level (corresponding

to 450 volts). The results of the Milgram (1965) study are shown in these terms in Figure 2.8. A key question to ask of any dependent variable is the extent to which it is a good measure of the underlying theoretical construct. In addition to this question of the 'fit' between a theoretical construct and the measured or dependent variable, the most important issue involved in designing dependent variables is what type of measure to use. We will discuss this in more detail below.

Laboratory experiments often involve deception, in the sense that the participant is misled about some aspect of the research. The extent of this deception can range from withholding information about the purpose of the research to misleading participants into thinking that the research is concerned with something other than its real purpose. The main reason for using deception is that participants would act differently if they were aware of the true objective of the study. If Milgram's participants had known that his was a study of obedience, we can be sure that the rate of disobedience would have been higher: the participants would have wanted to demonstrate their ability to resist orders to harm a fellow human.

Attitudes to the use of deception in social psychological research have changed during the past 45 years: misleading participants about the nature of an experiment is now viewed more negatively. The reason for this change is partly moral (i.e. where possible one should avoid deceiving someone else, whether or not in the context of an experiment) and partly practical (if participants are routinely misled about research, they will enter any future research in the expectation that they are going to be misled, which may influence their behaviour). Striking an appropriate balance between being completely honest with participants and wanting to study them free of the influence of their knowledge of the nature of the experiment is difficult. Psychological research conducted in universities in Europe, North America and Australasia is typically subject to prior approval by an ethics committee that evaluates and monitors research involving human participants, and national bodies such as the American Psychological Association (APA) and the British Psychological Society (BPS) have published guidelines concerning research using human participants that should be followed by researchers (see Table 2.1).

One way to address the ethical issues that arise from the use of deception is by carefully **debriefing** participants. This is done at the end of the experimental session and involves informing the participant as fully as possible about the nature and purpose of the experiment, and the reason for any deception. In Milgram's study, for

debriefing the practice of explaining to participants the purpose of the experiment in which they have just participated and answering any questions the participant may have.

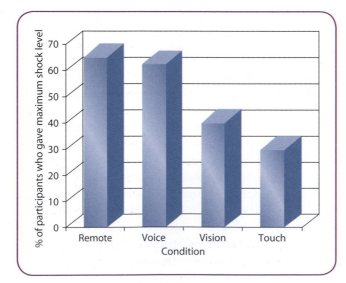

FIGURE 2.8 *Percentage of participants who administered the maximum shock level, and who were therefore deemed to be fully obedient.*

Source: Based on data reported by Milgram, 1965. Reproduction with permission from SAGE Publications.

Table 2.1 *Summary of ethical principles governing psychological research.*

8.01 Institutional approval

When institutional approval is required, psychologists provide accurate information about their research proposals and obtain approval prior to conducting the research. They conduct the research in accordance with the approved research protocol.

8.02 Informed consent to research

(a) When obtaining informed consent, psychologists inform participants about (1) the purpose of the research, expected duration and procedures; (2) their right to decline to participate and to withdraw from the research once participation has begun; (3) the foreseeable consequences of declining or withdrawing; (4) reasonably foreseeable factors that may be expected to influence their willingness to participate such as potential risks, discomfort, or adverse effects; (5) any prospective research benefits; (6) limits of confidentiality; (7) incentives for participation; and (8) whom to contact for questions about the research and research participants' rights. They provide opportunity for the prospective participants to ask questions and receive answers.

8.03 Informed consent for recording voices and images in research

Psychologists obtain informed consent from research participants prior to recording their voices or images for data collection unless (1) the research consists solely of naturalistic observations in public places, and it is not anticipated that the recording will be used in a manner that could cause personal identification or harm, or (2) the research design includes deception, and consent for the use of the recording is obtained during debriefing.

8.04 Client/patient, student and subordinate research participants

(a) When psychologists conduct research with clients/patients, students, or subordinates as participants, psychologists take steps to protect the prospective participants from adverse consequences of declining or withdrawing from participation.

(b) When research participation is a course requirement or an opportunity for extra credit, the prospective participant is given the choice of equitable alternative activities.

8.05 Dispensing with informed consent for research

Psychologists may dispense with informed consent only (1) where research would not reasonably be assumed to create distress or harm and involves (a) the study of normal educational practices, curricula, or classroom management methods conducted in educational settings; (b) only anonymous questionnaires, naturalistic observations, or archival research for which disclosure of responses would not place participants at risk of criminal or civil liability or damage their financial standing, employability, or reputation, and confidentiality is protected; or (c) the study of factors related to job or organization effectiveness conducted in organizational settings for which there is no risk to participants' employability, and confidentiality is protected or (2) where otherwise permitted by law or federal or institutional regulations.

8.06 Offering inducements for research participation

(a) Psychologists make reasonable efforts to avoid offering excessive or inappropriate financial or other inducements for research participation when such inducements are likely to coerce participation.

(b) When offering professional services as an inducement for research participation, psychologists clarify the nature of the services, as well as the risks, obligations, and limitations.

8.07 Deception in research

(a) Psychologists do not conduct a study involving deception unless they have determined that the use of deceptive techniques is justified by the study's significant prospective scientific, educational, or applied value and that effective non-deceptive alternative procedures are not feasible.

(b) Psychologists do not deceive prospective participants about research that is reasonably expected to cause physical pain or severe emotional distress.

(c) Psychologists explain any deception that is an integral feature of the design and conduct of an experiment to participants as early as is feasible, preferably at the conclusion of their participation, but no later than at the conclusion of the data collection, and permit participants to withdraw their data.

(Continued)

Table 2.1 (*Continued*)

8.08 Debriefing

(a) Psychologists provide a prompt opportunity for participants to obtain appropriate information about the nature, results, and conclusions of the research, and they take reasonable steps to correct any misconceptions that participants may have of which the psychologists are aware.
(b) If scientific or humane values justify delaying or withholding this information, psychologists take reasonable measures to reduce the risk of harm.
(c) When psychologists become aware that research procedures have harmed a participant, they take reasonable steps to minimize the harm.

8.10 Reporting research results

(a) Psychologists do not fabricate data.
(b) If psychologists discover significant errors in their published data, they take reasonable steps to correct such errors in a correction, retraction, erratum, or other appropriate publication means.

Source: Copyright © 2010 by the American Psychological Association. (2010a). *Ethical principles of psychologists and code of conduct* (2002, amended June 1, 2010). Reproduced with permission. No further reproduction or distribution is permitted without written permission from the American Psychological Association.

example, care was taken to assure participants that the 'shocks' they had administered were in fact bogus, and that the learner had not been harmed in any way; the reason for the deception was also carefully explained. The debriefing process should leave participants understanding the purpose of the research, satisfied with their role in the experiment, and with as much self-respect as they had before participating in the study.

Experimental designs

When and why is it important to have a control condition in an experiment?

As we have seen, it is important that participants are allocated randomly to the different conditions of an experiment. Failure to achieve this goal constrains the researcher from concluding that observed differences between conditions in the dependent variable result from changes in the independent variable. We shall now examine more closely the issue of designing experiments in order to rule out alternative inferences as far as possible.

First consider a study that may *appear* to be an experiment but cannot properly be described as experimental. This is the **one-shot case study** (Cook & Campbell, 1979). To take a concrete example, imagine that a researcher wanted to know the effect of a new teaching method on learning. The researcher takes a class of students, introduces the new

method, and measures the students' comprehension of the taught material. What conclusions can be drawn from such a design? Strictly speaking, none, for there is nothing with which the students' comprehension can be compared, so the researcher cannot infer whether the observed comprehension is good, poor or indifferent.

A simple extension of the one-shot design provides the *minimal* requirements for a true experimental study and is known as the **post-test only control group design**. Here there are two conditions. In the experimental condition participants are exposed to the manipulation (participants in this condition are known as the **experimental group**), and possible effects of the manipulation are measured. In the control condition there is no manipulation (here the participants are known as the **control group**), but these participants are also assessed on the same dependent variable and at the same time point as the experimental group. Now the observation made in the experimental condition *can* be compared with something: the observation made in the control condition. So the researcher might compare one group of students who have been exposed to the new teaching method with another group who continued to receive the normal method, with respect to their comprehension of the course material.

one-shot case study a research design in which observations are made on a group after some event has occurred or some manipulation has been introduced.

post-test only control group design an experimental design in which participants are randomly allocated to one of two groups; one group is exposed to the independent variable, another (the control group) is not.

experimental group a group of participants allocated to the 'experimental' condition of the experiment.

control group a group of participants who are typically not exposed to the independent variable(s) used in experimental research.

An important point is that participants are randomly allocated to the two conditions, ruling out the possibility that differences between the conditions are due to differences between the two groups of participants that were present before the new teaching method was implemented. So if the measure of students' comprehension differs markedly between the two conditions, it is reasonable to infer that the new teaching method caused this difference.

There are several other more sophisticated and complex designs, each representing a more complete attempt to rule out the possibility that observed differences between conditions result from something other than the manipulation of the independent variable (see Cook & Campbell, 1979). A very common design in social psychological experiments is the **factorial experiment**, in which two or more independent variables are manipulated within the same study. The simplest case that can be represented is that in which there are two independent variables, each with two levels. Combining these, you have the design shown in Figure 2.9. A factorial design contains all possible combinations of the independent variables. In the design shown in Figure 2.9, each independent variable has two levels, resulting in four conditions. The main benefit of a factorial design is that it allows the researcher to examine the separate *and combined* effects of two or more independent variables. The separate effects of each independent variable are known as **main effects**. If the combined effect of two independent variables differs from the sum of their two main effects, this is known as an **interaction effect**.

factorial experiment an experiment in which two or more independent variables are manipulated within the same design.

main effect a term used to refer to the separate effects of each independent variable in a factorial experiment.

interaction effect a term used when the combination of two (or more) independent variables in a factorial experiment yields an effect that differs from the sum of the main effects.

To illustrate an interaction effect, let us consider Petty, Cacioppo, and Goldman's (1981) study of the effects of persuasive communications on attitude change. To test Petty and Cacioppo's (1986a) 'elaboration likelihood model', a theory of persuasion (see Chapter 7), these researchers manipulated two variables. The first was argument quality, i.e. whether the persuasive communication the participants read consisted of strong or weak arguments in favour of making the university examination system tougher. The second variable was involvement, i.e. whether the participants, who were students, thought that the university would introduce the tougher exam system next year, such that it would affect them personally (high involvement), or in the next decade, such that it would not affect them personally (low involvement).

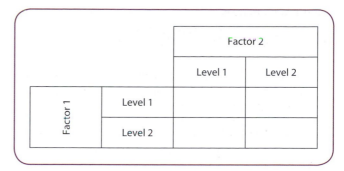

FIGURE 2.9 *Factorial experimental design involving two factors, each with two levels.*

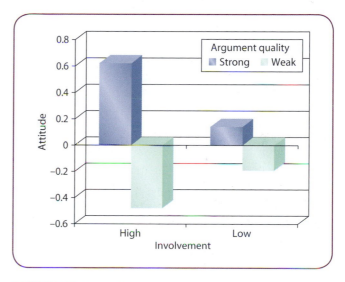

FIGURE 2.10 *Interaction between argument quality and involvement, showing that argument quality had a much stronger effect on attitudes when involvement was high.*
Source: Based on data reported by Petty, Cacioppo & Goldman, 1981.

According to the elaboration likelihood model, argument quality should have a stronger impact on attitudes when participants are involved with the message topic than when they are not. Figure 2.10 shows some of the key findings from the study by Petty et al. (1981). It can be seen that the effect of argument quality on attitudes was indeed much greater when involvement was high than when it was low. Because the predicted effect is an interaction, testing this prediction requires a factorial design.

An interaction effect is an instance of what is known more generally as *moderation*, in which the effect of one variable on another varies in strength depending on the level of a third variable. In other words, the role of the third variable is in determining *when* (under what conditions) the independent variable influences the dependent variable. In Figure 2.11, for example, the effect of variable X on variable O is moderated by variable Z. Specifically,

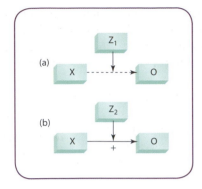

FIGURE 2.11(a) and (b) *Diagram to illustrate the moderating influence of variable Z on the relationship between variables X and O. X only has an effect on O when Z has the value 2 (b). When Z has the value 1 (a), there is no effect of X on O.*

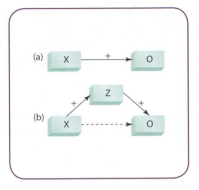

FIGURE 2.12(a) and (b) *Diagram to illustrate that the effect of variable X on variable O is mediated by variable Z. When Z is not taken into account, X has a significant effect on O (a). Here X has a direct effect on O. When Z is taken into account (b), the effect of X on O is non-significant. Here X has an indirect effect on O, via Z.*

X has an effect on O, but only when $Z = 2$ (Figure 2.11b). When $Z = 1$, X does not affect O (Figure 2.11a). It is important to distinguish moderation from another type of statistical relationship between three or more variables: namely, *mediation*.

To understand the concept of mediation, consider that the phenomena of interest to social psychologists often entail *chains* of events. If we strip this issue down to its bare essentials, we can ask whether variable X influences variable O *directly*, or whether the relation between X and O is mediated by another variable, Z. In other words, X may have an effect on O, but this is not a direct effect. Instead, X affects Z – the *mediating* variable – which in turn affects O (so, X affects O *via Z*). Researchers are therefore not only concerned with *if* or *when* X affects O: they are also concerned with *how* (through what process) X affects O.

In modern social psychological research, researchers therefore often attempt to measure **mediating variables** and then to conduct mediational analysis, for which there are well-established procedures (see Judd & Kenny, 1981a, b; Kenny, Kashy, & Bolger, 1998; Preacher & Hayes, 2004). By conducting an experiment we may establish that there is a causal relation between X and O; but we also measure Z, and find that the relation between X and Z is also very high, as is the relation between Z and O. We can then examine whether, once the X–Z and Z–O relationships are statistically taken into account, the originally established relationship between X and O becomes smaller, or disappears. This is the type of situation in which one can infer that the relationship between X and O is mediated by Z (Baron & Kenny, 1986; see Leader in the Field, David A. Kenny). This type of relationship is illustrated in

> **mediating variable**
> a variable that mediates the relation between two other variables.

🌐 **LEADER IN THE FIELD**

David A. Kenny (b. 1946) took his undergraduate degree at the University of California, Davis, followed by both his MA and PhD at Northwestern University, where his adviser was the methodological pioneer, Donald T. Campbell (see previous Leader in the Field). He then taught at Harvard University, before moving to the University of Connecticut, where he is now Board of Trustees Distinguished Professor. He has published many influential methodological papers and books, and is interested in the study of naturalistic social behaviour and models of such behaviour. He has specialized in the analysis of dyadic processes (where each person's behaviour affects the other person's, with the result that they have to be treated as inter-dependent, rather than independent, pieces of data). His paper on moderation and mediation (co-authored with Reuben Baron; Baron & Kenny, 1986) is one of the most-cited articles in the field. He was honoured with the Donald T. Campbell Award by the Society of Personality and Social Psychology in 2006, and is a Fellow of the American Academy of Arts and Sciences.

Figure 2.12. In part (a), X has a direct, positive effect on O. In part (b), when the relationships between X and Z, and between Z and O, are taken into account, the direct effect of X on O becomes non-significant. Instead, the indirect effect of X on O via Z is positive and significant.

Threats to validity in experimental research

What is the difference between internal and external validity?

In a research context, **validity** refers to the extent to which one is justified in drawing inferences from one's findings. Experimental research attempts to maximize

> **validity** a measure is valid to the extent that it measures precisely what it is supposed to measure.

each of three types of validity: internal validity, construct validity and external validity.

Internal validity refers to the validity of the conclusion that an observed relationship between independent and dependent variables reflects a *causal* relationship,

> **internal validity** refers to the validity of the inference that changes in the independent variable result in changes in the dependent variable.

and is promoted by the use of a sound experimental design. We have already seen that the use of a control group greatly enhances internal validity, but even if one uses a control group there remain many potential threats to internal validity (Brewer, 2000; Cook & Campbell, 1979). Chief among these is the possibility that the groups being compared differ with respect to more than the independent variable of interest.

For example, let's assume that in Milgram's obedience research a different experimenter had been used for each of the four conditions described earlier, such that experimenter 1 ran all participants in one condition, experimenter 2 ran all participants in another condition, and so on. It might seem efficient to divide the work among different experimenters, but to do so in this way poses a major threat to the internal validity of the experiment. This is because the four conditions would no longer differ *solely* in terms of the proximity of the 'victim'; they would also have different experimenters running them. Thus the differing amounts of obedience observed in the four conditions *might* reflect the impact of the proximity variable, *or* the influence of the different experimenters (or, indeed, some combination of these two factors). The problem is that there would be an **experimental confound** between the physical proximity variable and a second variable, namely experimenter identity. It is impossible to disentangle the effects of confounded variables.

> **experimental confound** when an independent variable incorporates two or more potentially separable components it is a confounded variable. When an independent variable is confounded, the researcher's ability to draw causal inferences is seriously compromised.

> **construct validity** the validity of the assumption that independent and dependent variables adequately capture the abstract variables (constructs) they are supposed to represent.

Even when we are confident that the relationship between X and O *is* a causal one, in the sense that internal validity is high, we need to consider carefully the nature of the constructs involved in this relationship. **Construct validity** refers to the validity of the assumption that independent or dependent variables adequately capture the variables (or 'constructs') they are supposed to represent. Even if the researcher has reason to feel satisfied with the construct validity of the independent variable, there remains the question of whether the dependent variables actually

assess what they were intended to assess. There are three main types of threat to the construct validity of dependent variables in social psychological experimentation: social desirability, demand characteristics and experimenter expectancy.

Social desirability refers to the fact that participants are usually keen to be seen in a positive light, and may therefore be reluctant to provide honest reports of anything which they think would be regarded negatively. Equally, participants may 'censor' some of their behaviours so as to avoid being evaluated negatively. To the extent that a researcher's measures are affected by social desirability, they fail to

> **social desirability** refers to the fact that research participants are likely to want to be seen in a positive light and may therefore adjust their responses or behaviour in order to avoid being negatively evaluated.

capture the theoretical construct of interest. An obvious way to reduce social desirability effects is to make the measurement process unobtrusive: if participants do not know what it is that is being measured, they will be unable to modify their behaviour.

An alternative strategy is to measure individual differences in the tendency to make socially desirable responses, and then to control for this statistically. Paulhus (1984, 1991) has developed a measure known as the Balanced Inventory of Desirable Responding (BIDR). This is a 40-item self-report questionnaire designed to measure the tendency to give socially acceptable or desirable responses. It consists of two sub-scales, one measuring *self-deceptive enhancement* and the other measuring *impression management*. Examples of items from each sub-scale are shown in Individual Differences 2.1. If scores on a self-report measure (like attitudes to an ethnic minority group) are correlated with BIDR scores, this suggests that self-reports are being biased in a socially desirable direction.

We should note, however, that it is better to try to eliminate completely the tendency to make socially desirable responses (rather than measuring it, and controlling for it statistically), simply because we do not know precisely what scales such as the BIDR measure.

Demand characteristics (see Chapter 1) are cues that unintentionally convey the experimenter's hypothesis to the participant. Individuals who know that they are being studied will often have hunches about what the experimenter is expecting to find. They may then attempt to provide the expected responses. When behaviour is enacted with the intention of fulfilling the experimenter's hypotheses, it is said to be a response to the demand characteristics of the experiment. Orne (1962, 1969) suggested ways of pinpointing the role demand characteristics play in any given experimental situation.

MEASURING THE TENDENCY TO RESPOND IN SOCIALLY DESIRABLE WAYS

Paulhus (1984, 1991) has developed a measure known as the Balanced Inventory of Desirable Responding (BIDR). On the basis of detailed pre-testing, and prediction of actual differences in behaviour, Paulhus was able to create two sub-scales, one measuring self-deceptive enhancement and the other measuring impression management. *Self-enhancement* refers to the tendency to think of oneself in a favourable light, whereas *impression management* refers to a deliberate attempt to distort one's responses in order to create a favourable impression with others. Below are example items from each sub-scale.

Self-enhancement

- My first impressions of people usually turn out to be right
- I always know why I like things
- I never regret my decisions
- I am a completely rational person

Respondents who agree with such items are deemed to have positively biased images of themselves (on the grounds that it is unlikely that these statements are true for most people).

Impression management

- I never swear
- I never conceal my mistakes
- I never drop litter in the street
- I never read sexy books or magazines

Respondents who agree with such items are deemed to be motivated to present themselves in positive ways (again, it is unlikely that these statements are true for most people).

Scores on these scales can be used to detect respondents who may be attempting to present themselves in a favourable light. If their scores on self-enhancement or impression management scales are correlated with their responses to other measures, it seems likely that the latter responses have been affected by social desirability, and these effects can be partialled out using statistical techniques.

---

post-experimental enquiry a technique advocated by Orne (1962) for detecting the operation of demand characteristics. The participant is carefully interviewed after participation in an experiment, the object being to assess perceptions of the purpose of the experiment.

unobtrusive measures (also called **non-reactive measures**) measures that the participant is not aware of, and which therefore cannot influence his or her behaviour.

cover story a false but supposedly plausible explanation of the purpose of an experiment; the intention is to limit the operation of demand characteristics.

For example, he advocated the use of **post-experimental enquiry**, in the form of an interview, preferably conducted by someone other than the experimenter, the object being to elicit from participants what they believed to be the aim of the experiment and the extent to which this affected their behaviour. Clearly, researchers should do all they can to minimize the operation of demand characteristics, for example by using **unobtrusive measures**, that is, measures that are so subtle that participants are unaware of the fact that they are being taken, or by telling participants that the purpose of the experiment cannot be revealed until the end of the study and that in the meantime it is important that they do *not* attempt to guess the hypothesis. A **cover story** that leads participants to believe that the purpose of the study is something other than the real purpose is a widely used means of lessening the impact of demand characteristics.

Experimenter expectancy refers to the experimenter's own hypothesis or expectations about the outcome of the research. This expectancy can unintentionally influence the experimenter's behaviour towards participants in a way that increases the likelihood that they will confirm the experimenter's hypothesis. Rosenthal (1966) called this type of influence the **experimenter expectancy effect** (see Chapter 1). The processes mediating experimenter expectancy effects are complex, but non-verbal communication is centrally involved. An obvious way of reducing these effects is to keep experimenters 'blind' to the hypothesis under test, or at least blind to the condition to which a given participant has been allocated; other possibilities include minimizing the interaction between experimenter and participant, and automating the experiment as far as possible. Indeed, in much current social psychological research, the entire experiment, including all instructions to the participants, is presented via a computer. This obviously limits the opportunity for experimenters to communicate their expectancies (either verbally or non-verbally).

Even if the experimenter manages to avoid all these threats to internal and construct validity, an important question remains: to what extent can the causal relationship between X and O be generalized beyond the circumstances of the experiment? **External validity** refers to the generalizability of a finding beyond the circumstances in which it was observed by the researcher. One important feature of the experimental circumstances, of course, is the type of person who participates in the experiment. In many cases participants volunteer their participation, and to establish external validity it is important to consider whether results obtained using volunteers can be generalized to other populations. There is a good deal of research on differences between volunteers and non-volunteers in psychological studies (see Rosenthal & Rosnow, 1975). The general conclusion is that there *are* systematic personality differences between volunteers and non-volunteers. Such findings are explained in terms of volunteers' supposedly greater sensitivity to and willingness to comply with demand characteristics. The external validity of studies based only on volunteers' behaviour is therefore open to question, and the solution to this problem is to use a 'captive' population, preferably in a field setting. One factor that limits the influence of this problem is the use of 'participant pools' in many psychology departments at large universities. Typically, these pools consist of first- and (sometimes) second-year undergraduate students who have to accumulate a set number of participant credits as part of their course. Thus, participants in studies that recruit from these pools are not, strictly speaking, volunteers.

> **external validity** refers to the generalizability of research findings to settings and populations other than those involved in the research.

Another criticism of social (and indeed other) psychological experiments is that the participants are often university students. Sears (1986) examined research articles published in major social psychology journals in 1985 and found that 74 per cent were conducted with student participants. Although students are certainly unrepresentative of the general population, being younger, more intelligent and more highly educated than the average citizen, this in itself is *not* a threat to the validity of the research. This is because the goal of much social psychological research is to understand the process(es) underlying a phenomenon (such as attitude change or stereotyping), rather than to describe the general population (a goal for which survey research is much better suited). In any case, there is often little reason to suppose that the processes underlying a phenomenon such as attitude change or stereotyping differ in some fundamental way between students and non-students.

Social psychological experiments on the Internet

What are the advantages and disadvantages of web-based experiments?

A relatively new development in psychological research is the use of the Internet to recruit and conduct experiments (**Internet experiments**). People are invited to participate in the research by visiting a website where the server runs the whole study, from allocating participants to an experimental condition to debriefing them about the nature and purpose of the study once they have completed the experimental task. Birnbaum (2000) noted that the number of experiments listed on sites such as the one maintained by the American Psychological Society has grown very rapidly, by around 100 per cent per year, and that many of these studies are social psychological.

> **Internet experiment** an experiment that is accessed via the Internet; participants access the experiment via the web, receive instructions and questions on their computer screen and provide responses via their keyboard or touch screen.

What are the primary advantages and disadvantages of such web-based experiments? A major advantage is the ease with which quite large amounts of data can be collected in a relatively short time. Other advantages are that participants are recruited from different countries, from different age groups and – now that access to the Internet is more widespread – from different socioeconomic backgrounds. An obvious disadvantage is that the researcher loses a degree of control over the running of the experiment. Participants complete the study in different physical settings, at different times of the day and night, and probably with differing levels of motivation and seriousness.

There are three further issues that arise. The first concerns the representativeness of those who choose to participate in an Internet study (they tend to be white, to live in the US or Europe, and to be relatively young – but not as young as those who take part in laboratory experiments). The second issue concerns the effect of linguistic competence on the reliability and validity of responses (most studies posted on the web are in English, and although the majority of respondents tend to be from the US or other English-speaking countries, some are not). The third issue is that those who choose to participate in such studies are of course volunteers, raising the possibility that they differ systematically from

Table 2.2 *How well do some common criticisms levelled at web-based studies stand up to empirical scrutiny?*

Preconceptions about Internet methods	
Preconception	**Finding**
1. Internet samples are not demographically diverse.	*Mixed.* Internet samples are more diverse than traditional samples in many domains (e.g. gender), but they are not completely representative of the population.
2. Internet samples are maladjusted, socially isolated, or depressed.	*Myth.* Internet users do not differ from non-users on markers of adjustment and depression.
3. Internet participants are unmotivated.	*Myth.* Internet methods provide ways of motivating participants (e.g. by providing feedback).
4. Internet data are compromised by the anonymity of respondents.	*Fact.* However, Internet researchers can take steps to eliminate repeat responders.
5. Internet-based findings differ from those obtained using other methods.	*Myth?* Evidence so far suggests that Internet-based findings are consistent with those obtained using traditional methods, but more data are needed.

Gosling and colleagues (2004) compared a large Internet sample ($N = 361,703$) with a set of 510 published traditional samples and were led to the conclusions summarized above.

Source: Adapted from Table 1 of Gosling et al. (2004). *American Psychologist, 59*, 93–104. Adapted with permission of APA.

the general population with respect to certain personality attributes. However, it is worth noting that Gosling, Vazire, Srivastava, and John (2004) examined several preconceptions about web-based studies and concluded that most of them were myths, without empirical foundation (see Table 2.2).

Despite the potential problems associated with running experiments on the web, the evidence suggests that Internet studies yield results that parallel those of conventional experiments (see Gosling et al., 2004). It is clear that this way of conducting experiments is going to continue to expand very rapidly. Before embarking on such research it is important to consult sources such as Nosek, Banaji, and Greenwald (2002) and Reips (2002), who offer advice about how to avoid the potential pitfalls.

Problems with experimentation

What are the main criticisms that have been levelled at the use of experiments in social psychology?

The experimental method is central to social psychology's status as an empirical science, largely because it provides the 'royal road' to causal inference (Aronson et al., 1998). Nevertheless, there are numerous critiques of experimentation in social psychology, some of which

relate to the knowledge that experiments provide, and some that question the assumptions that underlie experimentation. These assumptions – shared with other disciplines that employ the scientific method – include that the subject or object under study exists independently of the researcher, and that the researcher occupies an 'objective' and 'neutral' stance when it comes to theory and analysis of the subject. Indeed, some radical critiques of experimentation – such as those that inform discourse analysis, as discussed above – reject these assumptions entirely, questioning the extent to which there is an objective, knowable reality that can be studied scientifically (e.g. Potter & Wetherell, 1987). Other critiques take a less radical stance, but nevertheless question the role of the researcher in experimental settings, and emphasize how the broader social context can shape the meaning and value of experimental findings.

One problem concerns what Gergen (1978) has called the *cultural embeddedness* of social events, by which he means that a laboratory experimental demonstration that independent variable X has an impact on dependent variable O needs to be qualified by adding that the wider social circumstances in which X was manipulated may have played a role in producing the effects on O. Smith, Bond, and Kağitçibaşi (2006) review many social psychological experiments, including the Milgram obedience experiment, that have been conducted in different countries. It is not unusual for these experiments to produce different findings in different cultural settings (see Chapter 15). More generally, cross-cultural research often highlights how supposedly universal psychological tendencies are actually linked to cultural norms and values. For example, Miller (1984) studied the tendency to attribute other people's behavior to dispositional factors rather than contextual factors – known as the fundamental attribution error – among Americans and Indian Hindus. She found that while American adults did tend to explain others' behaviour in terms of dispositional factors rather than situational or contextual factors, Indian adults in contrast offered contextual explanations more frequently than dispositional explanations. These differences were attributed to cultural differences in how the self is conceptualized in everyday life.

A second issue is that although the ostensible goal of social psychological experimentation is the accumulation of scientific knowledge, in the form of laws or principles of social behaviour that are valid across time, there is some reason to doubt whether experimentation (or, indeed, any other method) is capable of generating evidence that could be the basis of such laws. To understand why this is the case in social sciences but not in natural sciences, bear in mind that the relationship between researcher and the object of study is radically different in these two types of science. In contrast to the natural sciences, the objects of investigation in social sciences are people, who of course attribute meaning and significance to their own actions. Social psychology cannot therefore be neatly separated from what it studies. Laypeople are able to acquire social psychological knowledge and use it to modify their actions in a way that atoms, elements and particles cannot.

One implication of this fact is that even well-supported social psychological theories should not be regarded as embodying 'laws' that hold good across time: if learning about a theory leads people to modify the behaviour that the theory tries to explain, the theory has limited temporal validity. It is also worth noting, however, that some of the problems of accumulation of knowledge in social psychology can be addressed through the use of

meta-analysis a set of techniques for statistically integrating the results of independent studies of a given phenomenon, with a view to establishing whether the findings exhibit a pattern of relationships that is reliable across studies.

meta-analysis. Meta-analysis is a technique for statistically integrating the results of independent studies of the same phenomenon in order to establish whether findings are reliable across a number of independent investigations (see Cooper, 1989; Hedges & Olkin, 1985; Johnson & Eagly, 2000). The increasing use of meta-analysis in social psychology (where relevant, one is cited in every chapter of this book) has shown, without doubt, that many social

psychological claims have, in fact, been confirmed over multiple experiments, often conducted over many decades.

A third controversy concerns the extent to which the values, motives and behaviour of experimenters influence the research process. This goes beyond our earlier discussion of validity, demand characteristics and suchlike. Some critiques suggest that a researcher can *never* be truly 'objective' and detached, and that every aspect of the research process – including topics, theory and hypotheses, and the interpretation of research findings – is informed by the researchers' value system. Even within a social psychology experiment, a researcher is rarely uninvolved or detached. Rather, researchers exist in a power relationship with participants, in which they instruct participants what to do, and in turn the participant actively interprets the researcher's actions and infers and reacts to their intentions, often in complex ways that the researcher may not recognize, or simply choose to ignore (Spears & Smith, 2001).

What are the implications of these problems for the status of experimentation in social psychological research? It is important to note that defences of the experimental method have been every bit as staunch as its critiques (e.g. Tetlock, 1994). Moreover, many critics of the experimental approach do not advocate the abandonment of experimentation. For example, Gergen (1973) acknowledged that experiments would continue to play an important role in explaining the relationship between biological processes (such as physiological arousal) and social behaviour; that studies such as the Milgram experiment are useful for raising consciousness about the insidious nature of social influence; that experiments can increase the impact of theories by providing vivid demonstrations of conditions under which a theory makes successful predictions; and that experimentation can be useful to evaluate social reforms, such as the effectiveness of measures designed to conserve energy. Others (e.g. Spears & Smith, 2001) point out that recognizing the subjective, involved role of an experimenter – and the nuanced ways in which participants react – does not invalidate the experimental method; rather it can actually provide us with a richer and more complete understanding of the findings that emerge.

Summary

In this section we examined different aspects of the use of experimentation in social psychology. We began by describing the principal features of the social psychological experiment, before going on to discuss some common experimental designs. We then considered the main threats to validity in experimental research, such as demand characteristics and experimenter expectancy effects, before going on to describe how researchers are making increasing use of the Internet to conduct experiments. Finally, we considered some possible problems with the use of experiments in social psychological research.

DATA COLLECTION TECHNIQUES

What are the strengths and weaknesses of the principal data collection techniques used in social psychological research?

Assuming that an investigator is conducting quantitative research, he or she will need to measure one or more variables, regardless of which research strategy has been adopted. In correlational designs the researcher has to measure each of the variables that are expected to correlate. In experimental designs the researcher needs to measure the dependent variable. In either case, the investigator is confronted with the task of translating a theoretical construct (for example, aggression) into a measurable variable (for example, willingness to harm someone). Any psychological measure should be both reliable and valid. **Reliability** here refers to the stability of the measure. If you measure an adult's height, the measurement will be highly stable from one day to the next and will also be independent of who is doing the measuring. A reliable measure is one that is not dependent on the time of measurement or on the person taking the measurement. However, a measure can be highly reliable yet low in validity. To pursue the height example, let us imagine that what you *really* want to measure is a person's weight. In the absence of a proper weighing scale you decide to measure height instead, because you do have a tape measure. Of course, height and weight are correlated with each other, so height may be a better estimate of weight than simple guesswork. But clearly, height is not especially valid as a measure of weight. So validity in this context refers to the extent to which the measured variable captures the construct you want to measure.

In social psychological research the investigator typically chooses to measure a variable using one or more of

reliability the degree to which a measure is free from measurement error; a measure is reliable if it yields the same result on more than one occasion or when used by different individuals.

the following: observational measures, self-report measures or (a more recent development) implicit measures.

Observational measures

If the object of one's research is to collect information about social *behaviour*, an obvious means of doing so is by observation. Many behaviours of interest to social psychologists are detectable without sophisticated equipment and take place in public settings, which makes them suitable for observation. Although observational methods vary in kind from the informal and unstructured to the highly formal and structured, the object in each case is the same: to extract from the complex flux of social behaviour those actions that are of potential significance to the research question, and to record each instance of such actions over some period (Weick, 1985).

Sometimes the nature of the research setting or topic dictates that observation is conducted in a relatively informal and unstructured manner, with the researcher posing as a member of the group being observed. A classic example of research employing this method is Festinger, Riecken, and Schachter's (1956) study of the consequences of blatant disconfirmation of strongly held beliefs. The investigators identified a religious sect that predicted that the northern hemisphere would be destroyed by flood on a certain date. By joining that sect, members of the research team were able to observe what happened when the predicted events failed to materialize. Under such circumstances, observation clearly has to be covert and informal: if other sect members suspected that the researchers were not *bona fide* believers, the opportunity for observation would be removed. This type of observation is known as **participant observation**, and typically yields qualitative data.

More formal methods of observation can be used when it is possible to record actions relevant to the research question without disrupting the occurrence of the behaviour. An example is Dixon and Durrheim's (2003) study of informal segregation on racial lines on a beach in post-apartheid South Africa. Their observational study charted the nature and extent of informal segregation by plotting the distribution of members of different racial categories in different areas of a Durban beach over time (Figure 2.13). In observing human spatial distribution on the beach, they noted that pairs and small groups of people tend to cluster together in areas the researchers termed 'umbrella spaces'. These spaces were typically marked by personal possessions and acted as regions in which typical beach activities took place. They coded the racial composition

participant observation a method of observation in which the researcher studies the target group or community from within, making careful records of what he or she observes.

FIGURE 2.13 *Racial distribution on Scottburgh's beachfront at 12.30 p.m. on 25 December 1999.*

Note: Each red circle = one 'black' person; each blue circle = one 'white' person; each yellow circle = one Indian person.

Source: From Dixon and Durrheim (2003), with permission from John Wiley & Sons. Photograph courtesy of Professor Durrheim.

of a total of 2654 umbrella spaces during a defined time period. Over 99.9 per cent of these spaces were racially homogeneous, either exclusively 'white' ($N = 1949$; 73.4 per cent) or exclusively 'black' ($N = 705$; 26.6 per cent). The pattern was stable across time; during the entire observation period the researchers located only one integrated grouping on the beachfront. In this instance the failure to inform people that they were unwittingly participating in a research project is covered by the ethical code shown earlier (see reference in APA guidelines to 'naturalistic observations').

What these two examples have in common is the fact that the targets of the researchers' observations were unaware that they were being observed. Such observation overcomes a problem peculiar to any research that uses humans as participants, namely the tendency for the measurement process itself to have an impact on participants' behaviour, a phenomenon known as **reactivity**. It is well established that the knowledge that one is being observed can influence behaviour (see research

reactivity a measurement procedure is reactive if it alters the nature of what is being measured.

on social facilitation effects, discussed in Chapter 8). Awareness of this problem has led many researchers to develop unobtrusive methods of observing and measuring behaviour. Webb, Campbell, Schwartz, and Sechrest (2000) compiled a useful sourcebook of methods of unobtrusive measurement.

The most formal type of observational method is one in which the researcher uses a predetermined category system for scoring social behaviour. A well-known example of such a system is Bales's (1950) interaction process analysis (IPA), developed to study interaction in small social groups. Here the verbal exchanges between group members are coded in terms of 12 predetermined categories (e.g. 'requests information'; see Chapter 12). The scores of group members can then be used to determine (among other things) who is the leader of the group (see Bales & Slater, 1955). Further examples of observational coding schemes can be found in Bakeman (2000).

Observational methods of data collection have two main advantages over the self-report methods we shall consider below: first, they can often be made unobtrusively; second, even where the participant knows that his or her behaviour is being observed, enacting the behaviour is typically quite engrossing, with the result that participants have less opportunity to modify their behaviour than they would when completing a questionnaire. Nevertheless, there are some types of behaviour that are either difficult to observe directly (because they are normally enacted in private) or impossible to observe directly (because they took place in the past). Moreover, social psychologists are often interested in measuring people's *perceptions, cognitions* or *evaluations*, none of which can be directly assessed simply through observation. For these reasons, researchers often make use of self-report measures.

Self-report measures

The essential feature of data collection using self-report measures is that questions about issues such as the participant's beliefs, attitudes and behaviour are put directly to the participant. The responses are self-report data. Self-report measurement is usually quicker, cheaper and easier to use than observational measurement. The researcher does not have to contrive a laboratory setting or find a natural setting in which to observe a behavioural response; furthermore, there is typically no need to train observers or to use recording equipment, because self-reports are usually recorded by the participant. Finally, as noted above, some of the variables that are of most significance to social psychologists are not directly observable. For these reasons, self-report measurement is very common in social psychological research, and it is not unusual for studies to depend exclusively on self-report data.

There are two principal methods of collecting self-report data: the questionnaire and the interview. In the *questionnaire* method, participants are given a set of questions, along with instructions on how to record their answers (nowadays, this is often done by means of web-based surveys too). In the *interview* method, questions are put to the participant by an interviewer, who then records the participant's responses. Interviewing is particularly useful when there is reason to believe that the questions might be difficult to understand without clarification. A tactful and sensitive interviewer should be able to establish rapport and ensure that the respondent fully comprehends a question before answering. Another advantage of interviewing is that interviews can be 'semi-structured', meaning that although the interviewer has a set series of topics to be covered in the interview, he or she is able to vary the specific questions that are asked so that they are relevant to the unfolding discussion. However, interviewing is costly in terms of time and money, and a poorly trained interviewer can easily bias the respondent's answers by hinting at a desired or socially acceptable response. Questionnaires are especially useful for gathering data from large numbers of participants with minimal expense, and the comparative anonymity of the process is preferable when the questions touch on sensitive issues. On the other hand, many people who are given questionnaires fail to complete and/or return them. Response rates for questionnaires sent by mail to randomly selected names and addresses vary between 10 and 50 per cent. Because there is always the danger that non-respondents differ systematically from respondents in some respect, low response rates are undesirable.

Devising a good questionnaire or interview schedule is a harder task than you might imagine. As with any psychological measure, the goal is to produce questions that are reliable and valid. Although there are many potential sources of unreliability in the construction of questionnaires, the most serious threat to reliability is *ambiguity*: if a question is ambiguous, different respondents may interpret it differently and therefore provide answers to what is in effect a different question. The most serious threat to question validity is failure on the part of the investigator to have *specific objectives* for each question: the hazier the intent of the researcher in posing a particular question, the greater are the chances that it will fail to elicit information relevant to his or her objectives. However, there are other sources of unreliability and invalidity that cannot easily be controlled. A simple rule-of-thumb is never to assume that answers to a single question will reliably or validly measure a construct. If two or more items are used to measure that construct, the factors that decrease reliability and validity of responses to any single question should cancel each other out, so a measure based on the average of the responses to the different items will be a more reliable measure of the underlying construct.

Because it is difficult to envisage all the potential pitfalls in questionnaire construction, there is no substitute for pilot work in which drafts of the final questionnaire are administered to participants whose answers and comments provide a basis for revision. Constructing an entirely fresh questionnaire can therefore be a time-consuming and painstaking process. Fortunately, there are collections of previously developed and pre-tested questionnaires, such as the one edited by Robinson, Shaver, Wrightsman, and Andrews (1991). It is worth checking such a source before setting out to construct an original questionnaire. If no suitable questionnaire already exists, the researcher should consult a text on questionnaire design such as the one by Oppenheim (1992) before devising a fresh questionnaire.

Self-report measures have several advantages. What are their drawbacks? Obviously it is not possible to collect self-report data completely unobtrusively: participants are aware that they are under investigation, and may modify their responses as a result of this awareness. In particular, there is ample opportunity for the respondent's answers to be influenced by motivational factors, such as social desirability. There is no simple solution to this difficulty, although there are steps that can be taken which reduce the scale of the problem. First, it is worth emphasizing to participants whenever possible that their responses are anonymous. Second, it is worth stressing the point that there are no right or wrong answers. Third, it is often possible to increase participants' motivation to respond truthfully by treating them as research accomplices rather than 'guinea-pigs'. Fourth, one could measure individual differences in the tendency to make socially desirable responses, and then control for these statistically. Fifth, one can validate self-report measures by checking them against reports provided by observers, who are unlikely to share the same biases as those making the self-reports (see Hewstone, Judd, & Sharp, 2011).

Implicit measures

A recent development in social psychological research methods has been the increasing use of techniques for measuring perceptions, cognitions and evaluations that do not rely on the usual type of self-report measure, thereby avoiding the disadvantages of the latter. These techniques are often referred to as **implicit measures** (Greenwald & Banaji, 1995). Although not previously widely used, implicit measures have a long history in social psychology: Campbell (1950) published a classic paper on the indirect assessment of attitudes more than half a century ago.

> **implicit measures** measures of constructs such as attitudes that are unobtrusively assessed (e.g. by reaction times) so that participants are unaware of what is being assessed.

What is different about the modern use of implicit measures is that they usually take advantage of computer technology (Figure 2.14). Here computers are used not only for the presentation of experimental materials but also (and more importantly) for the precise measurement of various aspects of the participants' responses to these materials. An example of an implicit measure is the use of response latencies (i.e. how long it takes a participant to answer a particular question). Such measures can provide fresh insights into cognitive structures and processes.

For example, Mussweiler (2006) reported a series of studies in which he investigated whether behaving in a stereotyped way activates the corresponding stereotype. It is known that activating the stereotype of the elderly induces people to walk more slowly (Bargh, Chen, & Burrows, 1996). Mussweiler wanted to examine whether the reverse is also true. Would walking more slowly activate the stereotype of the elderly? In one of his studies participants were instructed to walk at a speed determined by a metronome while listening to a story presented through headphones. The pace of walking was manipulated to be 30 paces per minute (slow) or 90 paces per minute (control). Participants then performed a lexical decision task, in which they had to judge as quickly and as accurately as possible whether strings of letters presented on a computer screen were words or non-words. Some of the real words were elderly-stereotypical (e.g. *forgetful, wise*) and others were not (e.g. *right, unclear*). Participants in the slow walking condition were faster to judge the elderly-stereotypical words than their counterparts in the control walking condition; however, they were no faster to make judgments about the non-stereotypical words. The advantage of using an implicit measure in this context is that participants simply are unaware of what it is that is being assessed in the lexical decision task, so the findings cannot be explained in terms of demand characteristics. Examples of the use of implicit measures to assess attitudes can be found in Chapter 6.

A major advantage of implicit measures is that they are not reactive. That is, implicit measures are not subject to biases such as social desirability and demand characteristics, because they tap processes that the respondent cannot control (and sometimes even operate outside awareness). However, it does not follow automatically that such measures have high validity. How does one know, for example, whether a fast reaction time reflects automatic stereotyping, as opposed to individual or group differences in lexical knowledge? To address questions such as this, one ideally needs to have other measures (e.g. observational) that provide evidence that converges with the evidence provided by implicit measures. In principle such evidence helps to establish the **convergent validity** of both types of measure. Convergent

> **convergent validity** established by showing that different measures of the same construct (e.g. self-report, implicit, observation) are significantly associated with each other.

FIGURE 2.14 *Implicit measures usually take advantage of computer technology.*

Source: © Konvex/Franziska Pilz. www.konvex.net. Used with permission.

validity is established when different operationalizations of the same construct produce the same results.

Another key advantage of implicit measures is that they can assess constructs and processes that may be outside the awareness of the individual. If people are not aware of having certain thoughts or feelings, they will by definition be unable to report them, even if they are highly motivated to be honest. The study of 'automatic' processes has become a key theme in social cognition research (see Bargh & Chartrand, 2000). Given that one of the attributes of an automatic process is that the individual is unaware of it, studying such a process requires the use of implicit measurement.

Choosing a measure

All three types of measure considered here have certain advantages and disadvantages. Although there are no hard-and-fast rules for choosing one type of measure over another, two points should be borne in mind when judging the appropriateness of a measure. First, the three types of measure – observational, self-report and implicit – can be used in conjunction with each other in many types of research. Second, the three types of measure differ in terms of the type of information they yield. If observational, self-report and implicit measures of the same conceptual variable point to the same conclusion, this clearly enhances confidence in that conclusion. Furthermore, self-report measures often assess the outcome of a process; by using observational and implicit measures as well, the researcher can gain insight into the processes responsible for that outcome. A special quality of implicit measures is that they enable researchers to capture aspects of the individual's thoughts, feelings and behaviour that are beyond conscious control and therefore not susceptible to feigning.

Social neuroscience

Strictly speaking, **social neuroscience** is an interdisciplinary field of enquiry rather than a data collection technique, but we include it here because researchers who adopt a social neuroscience approach to studying social behaviour typically measure neural activity, in addition to observational, self-report, or implicit measures. So although social neuroscience involves much more than the use of measures of biological processes, it is the measurement of such processes that is the most distinctive characteristic of the social neuroscience approach. As Cacioppo and

social neuroscience an interdisciplinary field devoted to understanding how biological systems implement social processes and behaviour.

colleagues (2007, p. 101) put it, 'An assumption underlying social neuroscience is that all human social behavior is implemented biologically.' This assumption leads researchers who adopt this approach to study the 'social brain'. The most popular way to do this is by using functional magnetic resonance imaging (fMRI), a technique for studying the regions of the brain that are activated while people engage in tasks such as perceiving self and others, regulating their emotions, and thinking about social groups. The technique works by measuring the changes in blood flow that relate to neural activity.

Although the use of fMRI to study social behaviour is a new endeavour and remains expensive in terms of equipment costs and training time, there is no doubt that its popularity will grow, as social psychologists become more familiar with the opportunities it affords and neuroscientists become increasingly motivated to study human social behaviour. To illustrate the potential for using fMRI to gain a better understanding of social psychological phenomena, consider a study by Harris and Fiske (2006). These researchers studied neural responses to 'extreme' outgroups, such as drug addicts and homeless people, groups who in terms of the stereotype content model (see Chapter 14) are seen as low in both warmth and competence (in contrast, for example, to the elderly, who are seen as high in warmth but low in competence, or rich people, who are seen as high in competence but low in warmth). It is known that there is an area of the brain, the medial prefrontal cortex (mPFC), which is activated during social cognition. Harris and Fiske found that the mPFC was activated by photographs depicting people belonging to all kinds of groups *except* those scoring low on both warmth and competence. Instead, viewing photographs of these groups activated the insula, a brain area associated with disgust. So the neural evidence from this study is consistent with the view that extreme outgroups are not thought about in the same way as members of other social groups (indeed, they may be seen as less than human; see Chapter 14).

Summary

This section examined the main data collection techniques available to the social psychological researcher. Three such techniques were identified: observational, self-report and implicit measurement. We noted that each technique has its own advantages and disadvantages, and that there is often a case for using more than one type of measure in a piece of research. We also noted the emergence of social neuroscience as a new interdisciplinary field of enquiry in which researchers use techniques such as brain imaging to study the neural bases of human social behaviour.

CHAPTER SUMMARY

- *What are research methods, and what is meant by methodology?* Research methods are the procedures a researcher uses to gather information, and *methodology* is a term used to refer to all aspects of the implementation of methods.

- *How do researchers test their theoretical predictions, and where do these predictions come from?* Information gathered using research methods is used to test the researcher's theoretical predictions. These predictions are derived from a theory. The theory is often generated through observation of real-life events or by trying to make sense of puzzling findings from previous research.

- *What research strategies are available?* We described three quantitative research strategies: quasi-experiments, true randomized experiments and survey research. Two key ways in which these strategies differ are in terms of (1) the degree to which one is able to generalize to a population and (2) the degree to which one can draw inferences about causality.

- *What are qualitative research methods?* These are methods that do not aim to provide, and indeed cannot provide, numerical data. They tend to focus on textual and interpretative analysis, and are often used by researchers who believe that quantitative methods are unsuited to studying the phenomenon under investigation. Discourse analysis was identified as a popular qualitative approach. Discourse analysis emphasizes the importance of how social phenomena are constructed through discourse.

- *What are the main features of social psychological experiments?* We singled out the experiment for detailed discussion because of its prominence as a research strategy in social psychology during the last six decades. The main features of experimentation are the experimental scenario; the independent variable; the dependent variable; the manipulation check; and debriefing.

- *What is a true experimental design?* It is one that enables the researcher to infer that changes in the independent variable produce changes in the dependent variable. Such a design must therefore incorporate more than one condition, allowing the researcher to compare observations made under different conditions.

- *What is the minimal true experimental design?* It is the post-test only control group design, in which participants are randomly allocated to one of two conditions, only one of which involves being exposed to the manipulation. Several more complex designs are available, and of these the factorial design is very commonly used, mainly because of its ability to test predictions concerning interaction effects.

- *What is 'validity' in the context of research methods?* Drawing strong inferences from social psychological research depends on three types of validity: internal, construct and external. We identified confounding as a threat to internal validity; social desirability effects, demand characteristics and experimenter effects as threats to construct validity; and volunteer/non-volunteer differences as a threat to external validity.

- *Can the Internet be used as a way of collecting research?* The Internet has provided social (and other) psychologists with a new arena in which to conduct experiments, enabling them to reach larger and more diverse groups of participants. The evidence to date suggests that, despite the potential problems of web-based experiments, their results tend to parallel those obtained using conventional methods.

- *What are the possible disadvantages of experiments?* Some social psychologists have questioned the usefulness of experiments. We identified the cultural embeddedness of social behaviour, the fact that social behaviour is determined by multiple factors, and the ability of humans to modify their behaviour in the light of social psychological theories as grounds for questioning the assumption that experimentation generates cumulative knowledge of the laws governing social behaviour.

- *What are the principal ways in which data can be collected in social psychological research?* We identified three principal methods: observational measurement, self-report measurement and implicit measures. Observational and implicit measures have the advantage of being less susceptible to social desirability effects, and can be made completely unobtrusive. However, observational measures are obviously limited to phenomena that can be observed and are not suited to the assessment of covert cognitive phenomena such as attitudes, causal attributions and stereotypes (see Chapters 3, 6, 7 and 14).

- *How can the 'covert' phenomena that are often of interest to social psychologists be studied?* To study such covert phenomena, researchers have traditionally relied on self-report measures, although there has been an increasing tendency to make use of implicit measures, the goal of which is to reveal phenomena that may either be outside the awareness of the individual or be misreported in conventional self-report measures due to social desirability concerns.

- *Can the different ways of collecting data be used in conjunction?* There are obvious advantages in using these different types of measure in conjunction with each other.

- *Do new ways of imaging brain activity have anything to offer social psychology?* Social psychologists and neuroscientists will make increasing use of techniques such as brain imaging in the search for a better understanding of the neural underpinnings of human social behaviour.

SUGGESTIONS FOR FURTHER READING

Aronson, E., Ellsworth, P. C., Carlsmith, J. M., & Gonzales, M. H. (1990). *Methods of research in social psychology* (2nd ed.). New York: McGraw-Hill. A comprehensive introduction to research methods in social psychology, with an emphasis on experimentation.

Cook, T. D., & Campbell, D. T. (1979). *Quasi-experimentation: Design and analysis issues for field settings.* Chicago: Rand McNally. An authoritative account of how to minimize threats to validity by careful research design.

Fiske, S. T., Gilbert, D. T., & Lindzey, G. (Eds.). (2010). *Handbook of Social Psychology* (5th ed., Vol. 1). Hoboken, NJ: Wiley. The most recent edition of this essential handbook, containing contributions on experimentation (Chapter 2), non-experimental methods (Chapter 3), and data analysis (Chapter 4).

Greenberg, J., & Folger, R. (1988). *Controversial issues in social research methods.* New York: Springer. This book does a good job of presenting the debates surrounding key issues in research.

Greenwood, J. D. (1989). *Explanation and experiment in social psychological science: Realism and the social constitution of action.* New York: Springer. An interesting, critical treatment of the philosophical background to research methods.

Haslam, S. A., & McGarty, C. (2003). *Research methods and statistics in psychology.* London: Sage. A highly accessible book written by social psychologists who believe that you cannot understand psychology unless you understand the process of conducting and interpreting psychological research.

Reis, H. T., & Judd, C. M. (Eds.). (2000). *Handbook of research methods in social and personality psychology.* New York: Cambridge University Press. State-of-the-art coverage of the key methodological issues in social and personality psychology.

3 Social Perception and Attribution

Brian Parkinson

Source: © Ron Chapple. Used under licence from Getty Images.

KEY TERMS

- actor–observer difference
- analysis of non-common effects
- attributional biases
- augmenting principle
- averaging
- causal attribution
- causal power
- causal schema
- central trait
- cognitive algebra
- configural model
- consensus information
- consistency information
- correspondence bias
- correspondent inference theory
- covariation theory
- depressive realism
- discounting principle
- distinctiveness information
- false consensus bias
- implicit personality theory
- learned helplessness theory
- naïve scientist model
- peripheral trait
- primacy effect
- probabilistic contrast
- salience
- self-fulfilling prophecy
- self-serving attributional biases
- social perception
- summation

CHAPTER OUTLINE

ROUTE MAP OF THE CHAPTER

Other people are so much part of our everyday lives that we take our understanding of them for granted. We are so familiar with their characteristics and activities that we rarely think about how we manage to make sense of their similarities and differences, and the puzzling or complicated things they sometimes do. This chapter describes research designed to address these processes. Studies of how we perceive information about the social world show that impressions of what others are like depend on what information is provided and when. Our assumptions about how personality characteristics fit together also make a difference. Research into how people explain events shows that people do not see all possible explanations of behaviour as equally likely. For example, systematic biases occur when we attach disproportionate importance to personalities and abilities as causes (especially in individualistic Western societies). Impressions and explanations also depend on current motivations and goals. Indeed, we may describe and explain social events in different ways to different people and under different circumstances. Therefore, both communication and private interpretation seem to play a role in social perception and attribution.

INTRODUCTION

Can you remember first meeting your closest friend? How quickly did you get a sense of what he or she was like, and of how you would get on together? Did your impression turn out to be correct, and if not, where and why did you go wrong?

Now imagine someone *telling* you about another person instead of you meeting them face to face. Although you might usually expect to receive information about appearance, age, occupation and a whole range of other things, let's assume that this time (strange as it might seem) you are only told about the person's personality characteristics (trait information). Let's also assume that you receive the information in the form of single words rather than complete sentences, and that you are given no opportunity to ask further questions. Try it now. What kind of person is described by these adjectives?

intelligent – skilful – industrious – warm – determined – practical – cautious

How easy was it to form your impression this time? Did you reach your conclusions in the same way as when you first met your friend? Are you as confident that your judgement is correct?

Even when meeting someone for the first time, you usually know something about what to expect. Even if you haven't heard anything about the person, the place you meet (a bar, lecture theatre or supermarket) tells you something about them. You already know that they must be the kind of person who goes somewhere like this, and this category information may provide sufficient evidence for your purposes (see Chapter 4, and Fiske & Neuberg, 1990). However, it can happen that we start with very few clues and need to construct impressions from scratch. And we often make up our minds about whom we like and dislike before any conversation begins.

But people we dislike at first can later become great friends, and people we think we will like may ultimately prove less congenial. In any enduring relationship, we get to see how the other person acts in different situations and may use these observations to draw conclusions about their feelings and personality. It is rare indeed that all this subsequent information perfectly matches first impressions.

This chapter is about how we make sense of other people. Because we draw conclusions about someone else's personality so readily, and because we usually have little trouble understanding the meaning of their actions, it may seem that our social perceptions are straightforward and direct. However, the fact that we often have to correct initial impressions suggests that matters may be more complicated. Most social psychologists believe that we piece together and weigh up available information before arriving at any conclusion, even when we are not explicitly aware of going through the stages of such a process. And each additional stage brings another opportunity for bias to creep in.

It is important to understand both how we perceive other people and how we explain their behaviour, because both these processes make a difference to the way we act. A teacher who explains poor performance in terms of a pupil's lack of ability may devote less effort to coaching that pupil. On a broader scale, prejudice may lead us to see economic disadvantage as arising from a person or group's negative characteristics rather than deeper structural problems in society (see also Chapter 14). Knowing what biases shape our understanding of others helps us to guard against their potentially negative influence.

The next section of this chapter will review research into social perception, focusing on how information is combined when forming impressions of others. The rest of the chapter concerns attribution theory, which focuses on people's causal explanations. After describing general models of how information is processed in order to infer the causes of behaviour, we consider how attributions influence our motivations and emotions, and examine evidence for various attributional biases. Next, we discuss the role of language and conversation in the attribution process. Finally, we consider how data-driven perceptual processes might combine with conversational processes in social perception and attribution.

> **social perception** the process of collecting and interpreting information about another person's individual characteristics.

SOCIAL PERCEPTION

How do we form impressions of what other people are like?

Pioneering research conducted by Asch (1946) shaped the way social psychologists investigate and understand perceptions of other people. What struck Asch was how quickly we seem to arrive at impressions, despite the diversity of information that needs to be combined. To investigate this process, Asch read out personality adjectives to students and instructed them to form an impression of the person (*target*) described by these words (just as you were asked to do at the beginning of this chapter).

One of Asch's first studies compared two lists of adjectives that were identical except for a single word. The first list contained the same words that you read earlier (intelligent, skilful, industrious, warm, determined, practical, cautious). Think about these words again. Which do you think gave you the most useful information?

The second list simply replaced the word 'warm' with the word 'cold'. Asch found that this single change made a big difference. Participants hearing the 'warm' list were far more likely to describe the target as generous, wise, and good-natured. Effects even extended to perception of physical characteristics concerning whether the target was short, thin, or pale (see Figure 3.1). A typical description was 'A person who believes certain things to be right, wants others to see his point, would be sincere in an argument and would like to see his point won' (Asch, 1946, p. 263). By contrast, a typical description of the 'cold personality' was 'A rather snobbish person who feels that his success and intelligence set him apart from the run-of-the-mill individual. Calculating and unsympathetic . . .' (p. 263).

In the next experiment, Asch assessed the effect of replacing 'polite' with 'blunt' instead of 'warm' with 'cold' (as used in the lists above) and found that these new words did not yield such different impressions. This suggests that warmth is seen as a **central trait** that alters the meaning of the target's whole personality, whereas politeness is a more **peripheral trait** that has only specific and delimited effects. However, Asch found that trait centrality also depends on what other words are presented, and that no word is central across all possible contexts (see Zanna & Hamilton, 1972).

Other experiments showed that the sequencing of adjectives also made a difference. In particular, earlier information exerted a disproportionate impact on impressions. For example, a target described as intelligent, industrious, impulsive, critical, stubborn, and envious was

central trait a dispositional characteristic viewed by social perceivers as integral to the organization of personality.

peripheral trait a trait whose perceived presence does not significantly change the overall interpretation of a person's personality.

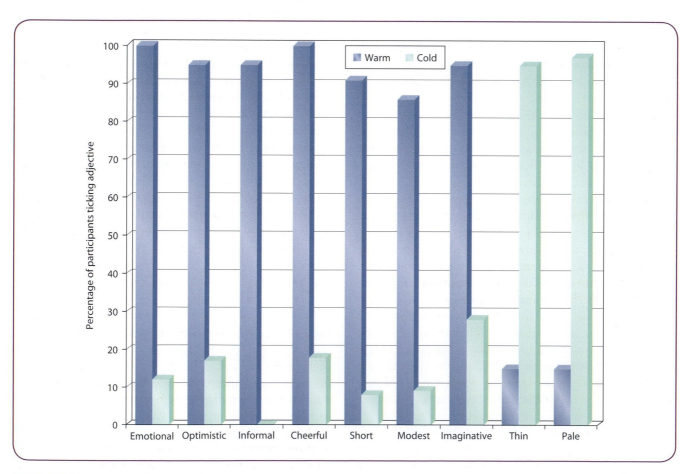

FIGURE 3.1 *Impressions of 'warm' and 'cold' targets.*

Source: Based on Asch, 1946. Copyright © 1946 by the American Psychological Association. Adapted with permission. *Journal of Abnormal and Social Psychology, 41*, 258–290. The use of APA information does not imply endorsement by APA.

seen as competent and ambitious, but when exactly the same words were presented in the opposite order (so that 'envious' came first), the target was thought to be overly emotional and socially maladjusted. This greater influence of initial information is generally known as a **primacy effect**. Evidently, people do not wait until all evidence is in before starting to integrate it. Primacy effects can be stronger when perceivers are under time pressure and motivated to arrive at a conclusion quickly and accurately (i.e. when their *need for closure* is higher; see Kruglanski & Freund, 1983).

primacy effect the tendency for earlier information to be more influential in social perception and interpretation.

Early information can also have strong effects on judgements of people actually confronted in person (rather than described in words). In Kelley's (1950) study, students rated a guest lecturer's teaching more positively and asked more questions when he had been introduced as a 'warm' person than when he had been introduced as a 'cold' person. In this study, the first thing that students learned about the target was that he was either warm or cold, so the results can be explained by either primacy or trait centrality. It is also worth noting that most introductions focus on a speaker's positive rather than negative qualities, and thus the unexpectedness of the 'cold' description of the lecturer may have given it more impact on ratings and behaviour than under other circumstances.

summation perceivers add together pieces of information about a person; when other information is strongly positive, additional mildly positive information yields a more positive impression.

implicit personality theory an integrated set of ideas held by a social perceiver about how different traits tend to be organized within a person.

configural model a holistic approach to impression formation, implying that social perceivers actively construct deeper meanings out of the bits of information that they receive about other people.

The results presented so far suggest that people do not simply add together the bits of information they receive about a target (**summation**), but instead actively construct meaning based on their ideas about how different personality characteristics hang together. As later theorists concluded, these ideas are organized in **implicit personality theories** that help social perceivers make sense of other people (e.g. Bruner & Tagiuri, 1954). More generally, the notion that people integrate social information by trying to discern its overall pattern is referred to as the **configural model**.

The alternative **cognitive algebra** model suggests that separate pieces of information are simply averaged (**averaging**, e.g. Anderson, 1981). For example, if a person is described as 'warm' and 'boring', the overall impression would be less positive than if he or she were described as 'warm' and 'interesting', but more positive than if he or she were described as 'cold' and 'boring'. According to this view, disproportionate effects of 'central' adjectives depend on them conveying comparatively more evaluative information than the other words that are presented. Further, the impact of a word may depend on its relevance to the judgement being made. For example, we care more about whether someone is 'warm' when selecting a potential friend than a plumber, and therefore attach more weight to its connotations. Asch's (1946) configural model, by contrast, implies that central adjectives change the interpretation of other words rather than simply attracting greater emphasis.

cognitive algebra a proposed process for averaging or summing trait information when forming impressions of other people.

averaging perceivers compute the (weighted or unweighted) mean value of pieces of information about a person; when other information is strongly positive, additional mildly positive information yields a less positive impression.

But do social perceivers always make sense of personality information in either of these ways? In Asch's (1946) experiments, participants heard a list of separate personality adjectives and were explicitly told to construct an impression based on these words (as in the task at the start of this chapter). As Asch acknowledged, this is unlike what normally happens when we meet someone face to face (e.g. getting to know your best friend for the first time). How then might this particular way of presenting information have affected processes of impression formation?

Some people get acquainted by e-mail before ever physically meeting (see Chapter 11). It may take months or even years before they so much as exchange photographs (not necessarily genuine ones: see Ben-Ze'ev, 2004), assuming that they ever do (see Joinson, 2003). What happens when these people finally confront one another in the flesh? Are they surprised by what they see?

Considerations such as this suggest that transmitting information in words rather than raw sensory data (sights, sounds, and smells) makes a difference to the content of our impressions. Further, sensory information can carry direct implications about personality. For example, people with large, round eyes, short noses, high foreheads, and/or small chins (*baby-faced* individuals) are typically perceived as less dominant, more naïve and warmer than people with mature-seeming features (e.g. Berry & McArthur, 1986; Figure 3.2), and people with louder or higher-pitched voices are often perceived as more extraverted (e.g. Scherer & Scherer, 1981). The way that patterns of sensory information change over time can also carry important information. For example, we are quite good at judging which of two people is older by observing the way that they both walk,

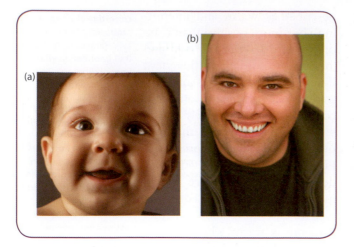

(a)
(b)

FIGURE 3.2(a) and (b) *Adults who possess facial features common in babies, such as large, round eyes, short noses, high foreheads and/or small chins are typically perceived as less dominant, more naïve and warmer than people with mature-seeming features.*

Source: (a) © Chepko Danil Vitalevich; (b) © CURAphotography. Both images used under licence from Shutterstock.

even when all other evidence is removed. Adults with a younger-seeming gait are also perceived as more energetic (Montepare & Zebrowitz-McArthur, 1988).

Asch's procedure also differs from most everyday interactions because it provides no opportunity for the other person to respond to participants' judgements of them (or for participants to respond to these responses). Interpersonal exchange of this kind may make a big difference to the process of impression formation. For example, when you meet someone, you don't simply draw private conclusions and keep them to yourself. Instead, you adjust how you behave on the basis of what you think the person is like, and they correspondingly adjust their conduct to their impression of you (which is partly based on how you are responding to them, and so on). If you think someone is friendly, you may be more friendly back, leading them in turn to reciprocate your friendly response (and so on). Thus, our impressions of others can lead to self-fulfilling prophecies (e.g. Snyder, 1984). However, people are also able to adjust their impressions when expectations are disconfirmed. Indeed, if you know that someone has the wrong idea about you, you may deliberately act in ways that show them that they are mistaken (a *self-verification effect*, Swann, 1984, and see Chapter 5).

self-fulfilling prophecy when an originally false expectation leads to its own confirmation. The social perceiver's initially incorrect beliefs about a target cause that target to act in ways that objectively confirm those beliefs.

Summary

The study of social perception focuses on how social perceivers form impressions of other people, and how they combine information into a coherent overall picture. Pioneering studies revealed the importance of the nature and order of presented information, and how perceivers actively construct meaning, rather than simply adding information together. But how specific pieces of information are weighted, integrated and used depends on a variety of factors, including the nature of the current situation and the form in which information is presented.

ATTRIBUTION THEORY

What are the main theories of causal attribution, and what do they say about processing of causal information?

The familiar logo of the Pixar® animation studio refers to one of their earliest short films (*Luxo Jr.*), in which the movements of two Anglepoise® desk lamps – one large, one small – are accompanied by voice-like sounds containing no discernible words. Although items of office equipment do not usually have social relationships, viewers quickly conclude that the larger lamp is the smaller lamp's parent, and that the smaller lamp is a rather boisterous child. The lamps' contractions and extensions soon appear to be goal-oriented actions, and the noises start sounding like communications or expressions of emotion. A micro-drama of conflicting desires and thwarted impulses seems to unfold on the screen, even though we know that every movement has been computer-generated.   *Also the circle (two triangles)*

How is this impression of animate personality and intention achieved? Part of the answer is that our tendency to see motives and dispositions behind human actions may be so automatic that we sometimes find it hard to override it even in situations where motives and dispositions don't really apply. However, the illusion of human-like agency also depends on the way that the movements of objects unfold over time, without being rigid, and how one object's movements relate to another object's movements (e.g. Michotte, 1963; Rochat, Morgan, & Carpenter, 1997). Indeed, neuroscientific research suggests that there may be a specialized brain region (in the temporo-parietal junction or TPJ) that detects the movement patterns that typically indicate animate activity or intentional behaviour

(Pavlova, Guerreschi, Lutzenberger, & Krägeloh-Mann, 2010; Puce & Perrett, 2003).

Attribution theory (e.g. Försterling, 2001; Heider, 1958; Kelley, 1972) provides a set of ideas about how these kinds of inferences about the causes of action are made in more usual situations of observing or hearing about a human being's actions (rather than those of a desk lamp); this process is termed causal attribution. It addresses our explanations of our own as well as other people's behaviour (see also Chapter 5, which addresses more general questions of self-perception).

causal attribution the process whereby social perceivers arrive at conclusions about the causes of another person's behaviour.

Most of the phenomena investigated by attribution researchers involve an *observer* explaining an *actor's* behaviour towards a human or non-human object (or *entity*), but sometimes the actor and observer can be the same person (*self-attribution*). Unlike much of psychology, attribution research is not directly concerned with why actors do what they do, but focuses instead on what observers conclude about why actors do what they do (e.g. whether they *attribute* behaviour to an actor's or object's characteristics or 'attributes'). In the parlance of the theory, to make an *attribution* is to assign causality to some person, object or situation. According to attribution theory, we are all amateur psychologists trying to explain each other's behaviour.

For example, imagine a friend (*actor*) has just spent a substantial proportion of her student loan on an expensive digital camera with all the latest features (*entity*). This might lead you (as *observer*) to think about what provoked such a purchase. Was it an 'impulse buy' reflecting a failure of your friend's self-control? Was she talked into it by a canny sales assistant? Or did her deep-seated interest in photography motivate her spending? Was the camera so special that she just had to have it? Or had other friends persuaded her that she couldn't do without it? Our answers to these causal questions shape our reactions and our expectations about her future behaviour.

Heider (1958) is usually credited with inventing attribution theory. He argued that people are most concerned with identifying the personal *dispositions* (enduring characteristics such as ability and personality traits) that account for other people's behaviour. In other words, observers want to know what it is about actors that leads them to act the way they do. Drawing conclusions about a person's dispositions helps the social perceiver in two ways. First, it permits integration of a variety of otherwise disorganized information about others, just as working out that a larger lamp has a maternal attitude to a smaller lamp makes sense of an otherwise baffling piece of animation (see also Heider & Simmel, 1944; Michotte, 1963; Leader in the Field, Fritz Heider).

LEADER IN THE FIELD

Fritz Heider (1896–1988), the 'founding father' of attribution theory, was born in Vienna, Austria. He was invited to the US in 1930 to join the Gestalt psychologist Koffka's laboratory at Smith College, then worked at the University of Kansas from 1947, where his most influential work on attribution was conducted. Heider is famous for two theories in different areas of social psychology: attribution theory and 'balance theory' (a consistency theory about how relationships between more than two people are kept in equilibrium). He was awarded the American Psychological Association's Distinguished Scientific Contribution Award in 1965.

Second, it permits prediction (and, to some extent, control) of future behaviour. For example, knowing that you are a friendly person means that I can expect a friendly reaction from you when we meet again.

Correspondent inference theory

How do we work out why someone chooses one action rather than another?

Jones and Davis (1965) tried to make Heider's ideas about dispositional attribution more systematic. Like Heider, they argued that observers learn most from actors' behaviour when it provides information concerning personal characteristics. For example, you would probably attribute your friend's camera purchase to her specific intention (buying the camera did not just happen to your friend, she decided to do it), and may in turn attribute this intention to an underlying disposition, such as enthusiasm for photography. Jones and Davis called this process of inferring dispositions from behaviour **correspondent inference**, because observers infer intentions and dispositions that *correspond* to the behaviour's characteristics.

correspondent inference theory proposes that observers infer correspondent intentions and dispositions for observed intentional behaviour under certain circumstances.

Correspondent inference theory proposes that observers consider the range of behavioural options that were available to the actor at the time of making a decision in order to work out the actor's intention. Each of these behavioural options would have brought a number of different effects if selected. Some of these effects are desirable (your friend's camera has lots of useful features) and some undesirable (the camera cost a great deal of money). According to Jones and Davis, observers work out *why* actions are performed by comparing the effects of the selected action with those of alternative unselected actions (taking into account their perceived desirability). In particular, actors are assumed to have selected their action on the basis of the effects that this action produced, but alternative actions would not have produced.

For example, think back to when you chose to go to the particular university or college where you are currently studying. The theory suggests that we could infer your original intention by comparing the features of your chosen university and a university you rejected and working out what distinguishes them. For example, the chosen university might be located in a large city and the rejected one in a quieter, more rural setting. If the rejected university also had several advantages over the one you chose (e.g. a higher reputation, a stronger psychology department, better accommodation), then we might well conclude that living in a city is important enough to you to outweigh these other

analysis of non-common effects
observers infer intentions behind actions by comparing the consequences of the behavioural options that were open to the actor and identifying distinctive outcomes.

considerations. More generally, correspondent inference theory argues that people try to work out what it was about a chosen course of action that made it seem preferable to alternative courses of action. Jones and Davis call this process the analysis of non-common effects (see Table 3.1).

In reality, our analysis may be more complex than implied by this example. For instance, we might focus on why you chose to go to university at all rather than why you selected this particular one. How then do observers know what alternatives to compare when trying to explain a course of action? Research suggests that people are more interested in explaining unusual than predictable events, and that they explain them by comparing what actually happened with what they think would *normally* have happened (Hilton & Slugoski, 1986). For example, if a close friend walks past you in the street without saying hello, you think about what is different this time from the usual times when she stops to chat. Perhaps she forgot to put on her glasses this morning, or perhaps you have had such a radical change of hairstyle that you are now almost unrecognizable.

Although correspondent inference theory was only intended to apply when actors are free to *choose* their behaviour, an experiment conducted by Jones and Harris (1967) cast doubt on this assumption. Students at an American university were asked to assess another student's opinion about Fidel Castro's communist regime in Cuba after reading a pro-Castro essay that the other student had supposedly written (see Figure 3.3). One group of participants was told that the writer had *freely chosen* what position to adopt in the essay,

Table 3.1 *Analysis of non-common effects after observed selection of University X.*

Features of University X (chosen)	Features of University Y (not chosen)	Are features common or non-common?	Implication about intention
Comfortable accommodation	Comfortable accommodation	Common	None
Sports facilities	Sports facilities	Common	None
Good reputation	Good reputation	Common	None
Friends applying	Friends applying	Common	None
Urban location	Rural location	Non-common	University X chosen because candidate wanted to live in an urban location
Poor reputation	Good reputation	Non-common	University X chosen despite inferior reputation, so candidate's desire for an urban location must have been strong enough to outweigh this negative feature

Source: After Jones & Davis, 1965.

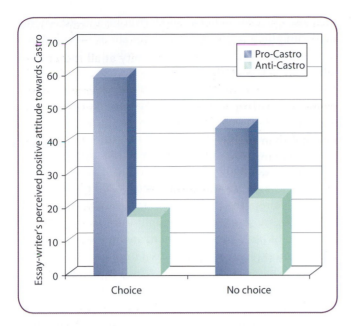

FIGURE 3.3 *Correspondent inferences of essay-writer's attitudes.*

Source: Adapted from Jones & Harris, 1967, with permission from Elsevier.

whereas another group was told that the essay title had *explicitly requested* pro-Castro arguments (no-choice condition). According to correspondent inference theory, participants in the no-choice condition should have ignored the essay's content when estimating the writer's attitudes. However, participants tended to conclude that the essay-writer had pro-Castro attitudes even when they knew that the essay's stance could be explained by the situation, and even though most American students were strongly anti-Castro at the time when the study was conducted.

The investigators concluded that people tend to overestimate personal causes of behaviour but underestimate situational ones, an important phenomenon later termed the **correspondence bias**. However, this bias has some limiting conditions, which we will discuss later.

> **correspondence bias** the proposed tendency to infer a personal disposition corresponding to observed behaviour even when the behaviour was determined by the situation.

Correspondent inference theory describes a set of generally valid principles for working out someone's intentions and dispositions when they have deliberately performed a certain action with prior knowledge of its possible consequences. However, it is not designed to identify the causes of other kinds of behaviour, such as impulsive or habitual acts, or of people's experiences such as emotions and other feelings. A more general model of attribution that accounts for how people arrive at conclusions about which aspects of a behavioural episode caused an observed effect is described in the next section.

Covariation theory

How do we weigh up different possible causes of behaviour?

Imagine that you know a very conscientious student (Hermione) who always goes through everything on reading lists well in advance of classes. Before you had a chance to look at this chapter, she already told you what it was about and expressed the opinion that attribution theory was a really boring topic. Clearly, you want to know why she said this. Is it because attribution theory actually is tedious? Is it because Hermione is rarely excited by anything? Or was her showy lack of enthusiasm designed to impress your jaundiced roommate Ron, who happened to be listening in on this particular conversation? Jones and Davis's (1965) model would help you to identify Hermione's possible intentions (assuming that you knew what alternative actions she was choosing between). However, it would not lead you directly to a conclusion about the causal role played by the situation or the object toward which action is directed.

Kelley's (1967) **covariation theory** provides a more general account of how people weigh up different possible causes of an observed action or experience. In all these cases, an actor (e.g. Hermione) has responded in some way to an object (e.g. attribution theory) in a particular situation (e.g. while Ron was listening). The observer wants to know whether what happened was caused by something about the actor, something about the object or something about the situation (or some combination of these three factors). According to Kelley, observers work this out by systematically collecting and processing additional data. The aim is to discover what factors need to be in place for the effect to happen.

> **covariation theory** proposes that observers work out the causes of behaviour by collecting data about comparison cases. Causality is attributed to the person, entity or situation depending on which of these factors covaries with the observed effect.

As its name suggests, Kelley's covariation theory argues that observers make their judgements on the basis of covariations or correlations between effects and their possible causes. In simpler terms, 'the effect is attributed to that condition which is present when the effect is present and which is absent when the effect is absent' (p. 194). The idea, then, is that we work out what caused an effect by observing which factors are, and

LEADER IN THE FIELD

Harold Kelley (1921–2003) was one of two pioneering attribution theorists working at the University of California at Los Angeles (the other was Bernard Weiner; see Leader in the Field, this chapter). His covariation theory of attribution stands as the most influential general approach to lay causation, although from the start he acknowledged that it did not apply across all possible situations. His second, causal schema theory was specifically intended to explain how people arrive at causal explanations when they are unable to carry out the systematic collection of data implied by covariation theory. In addition to these two influential theories, Kelley also worked on person perception, attitude change and relationships.

are not, consistently associated with its occurrence (see Leader in the Field, Harold Kelley).

Why then did Hermione say that attribution theory was boring? Kelley argues that you need to consider three kinds of evidence, each corresponding to one of the possible causes (the object, situation or person). First, you need to know whether Hermione expresses boredom only about attribution theory (high distinctiveness) or whether she says that a lot of things are boring (low distinctiveness). In other words, you collect **distinctiveness information** by sampling across objects. Second, you need to know whether Hermione only says attribution theory is boring in public situations when people she wants to impress may be listening (low consistency), or makes similar comments across a range of situations and at different times regardless of who might be listening (high consistency). In other words, you collect **consistency information** by sampling across situations. Third, you need to know whether it is only Hermione who finds attribution theory boring (low consensus) or if other students on your course say the same thing (high consensus). In other words, you collect **consensus information** by sampling across actors.

distinctiveness information evidence relating to how an actor responds to different objects (or 'entities') under similar circumstances.

consistency information evidence relating to how an actor's behaviour towards an object varies across different situations and times.

consensus information evidence relating to how different actors behave towards the same object.

Having collected all the relevant data, you are now in a position to make your attribution. For example, if Hermione says lots of things are boring (low distinctiveness), says that attribution theory is boring regardless of circumstances (high consistency) and none of your other friends says it is boring (low consensus), you may conclude that it is something about Hermione that makes her bored (a 'person attribution'). You infer this from

the close correlation between Hermione and statements that something is boring (whenever she is included in a sampled episode, something is described as boring, but whenever she is absent, nothing is described as boring). Interestingly, Harris, Todorov, and Fiske (2005) found that presenting participants with covariation information following this particular pattern (low distinctiveness, high consistency and low consensus) not only encouraged person attributions (replicating research by McArthur, 1972 described below), but also produced greater activation of the superior temporal sulcus (STS) region in the brain. This region is part of the temporo-parietal junction (TPJ), and is generally thought to be involved in the detection of biological movement and intentional behaviour (as mentioned above). Causal implications of some other possible combinations of consensus, consistency and distinctiveness (CCD) information are presented in Table 3.2.

Covariation theory's proposals about the implications of different patterns of CCD information seem generally logical and consistent. However, in some cases, they lead to conclusions that are not necessarily correct (see Försterling, 2001; Hilton, 1988). For example, knowing that other people don't find attribution theory boring (low consensus), that Hermione only says attribution theory is boring in front of Ron (low consistency), and that she doesn't say other things are boring (high distinctiveness) is certainly consistent with a context attribution (something about Ron is making Hermione say attribution theory is boring). However, the same pattern of information would also be observed if something about the specific *relationship* between Hermione and Ron led to the effect (a person-context interaction). The only way of being sure which of these alternative explanations is correct is to collect even more information, this time relating to how other people behave in front of Ron. If other people behave like Hermione does in Ron's presence, then a context attribution is supported. But if not, that conclusion oversimplifies matters. Setting aside this problem, there is good evidence that people provided with information specifically relating to consensus, consistency and distinctiveness can infer many of the predicted implications (e.g. McArthur, 1972; see Hewstone, 1989, and Kassin, 1979, for reviews).

Although Kelley's theory provides a logical basis for attribution, it is difficult to imagine that people collect evidence so systematically and engage in such detached processes of analysis every time they make sense of an event's causes. *That* certainly *would* get boring. Many more recent developments in attribution theory have therefore involved correcting this limitation of the covariation approach.

Table 3.2 *Four patterns of consensus, consistency and distinctiveness information, and their perceived implications.*

Consensus (across people)	Consistency (across situations)	Distinctiveness (across objects)	Attribution
Low No one else says that attribution theory is boring	**High** Hermione says attribution theory is boring in many different contexts	**Low** Hermione says that lots of things are boring	**Person attribution** Effect covaries with person: something about Hermione causes her to say that attribution theory is boring
Low No one else says that attribution theory is boring	**Low** Hermione only says attribution theory is boring in public situations	**High** Hermione doesn't say that other things are boring	**Context attribution** Effect covaries with situation: something about public situations causes Hermione to say that attribution theory is boring
High Everyone else says attribution theory is boring	**High** Hermione says attribution theory is boring in many different contexts	**High** Hermione doesn't say that other things are boring	**Entity attribution** Effect covaries with object: something about attribution theory makes Hermione say that it is boring
Low No one else says that attribution theory is boring	**High** Hermione says attribution theory is boring in many different contexts	**High** Hermione doesn't say that other things are boring	**Person–entity interaction** Effect covaries with Hermione together with attribution theory: something about their combination causes her to say attribution theory is boring

Source: After Kelley (1967). Reprinted from the Nebraska Symposium on Motivation Vol. 15 by permission of the University of Nebraska Press. Copyright 1967 by the University of Nebraska Press.

Access to covariation information

How do we make causal attributions when full covariation information is not available?

One obvious problem for the covariation approach was soon recognized by Kelley (1972) himself: often we want to make causal inferences about events under circumstances when CCD information is either unavailable or too time-consuming to collect. On these occasions, Kelley argued that we fill in missing information by reference to our existing ideas about how effects are produced (**causal schemas**). In particular, we rule out certain explanations and make assumptions about the presence of unobserved causal factors on the basis of single observations.

> **causal schema** knowledge structure shaping attributions: causal schemas may be either abstract representations of general causal principles (e.g. multiple necessary and multiple sufficient causes schemas), or domain-specific ideas about cause and effect.

For example, imagine that you see a cyclist going very fast down a steep hill. Because you know that the slope is enough to explain her speed, you are unlikely to draw strong conclusions about the cyclist's strength or ability to cycle fast (see Theory Box 3.1). More generally,

Kelley argued that observers rule out alternative causes when they already know of factors working towards an observed effect (the **discounting principle**). However this only happens when explaining outcomes that may be reached by a variety of alternative possible routes, each of which would be enough to yield the effect (easily produced effects). Our ideas about causation under these circumstances are represented by what Kelley terms a *multiple sufficient causes schema*. In cases where outcomes depend on the simultaneous presence of more than one condition (outcomes that are difficult to produce), observers instead use a *multiple necessary causes schema*, which encourages them to continue searching for causes even when they have found one.

The converse of the discounting principle is the **augmenting principle**. Here, knowledge of factors working *against* an effect leads people to conclude that plausible causes must be stronger than otherwise. For example, if you saw a cyclist going very fast *up* a steep hill, you would need to

> **discounting principle** the presence of a causal factor working towards an observed effect implies that other potential factors are less influential. The converse of the augmenting principle.

> **augmenting principle** the assumption that causal factors need to be stronger if an inhibitory influence on an observed effect is present. The converse of the discounting principle.

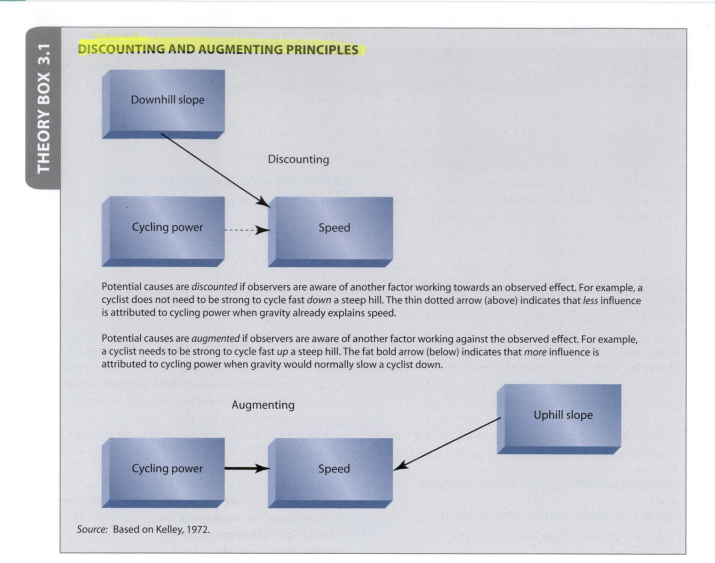

THEORY BOX 3.1

DISCOUNTING AND AUGMENTING PRINCIPLES

Potential causes are *discounted* if observers are aware of another factor working towards an observed effect. For example, a cyclist does not need to be strong to cycle fast *down* a steep hill. The thin dotted arrow (above) indicates that *less* influence is attributed to cycling power when gravity already explains speed.

Potential causes are *augmented* if observers are aware of another factor working against the observed effect. For example, a cyclist needs to be strong to cycle fast *up* a steep hill. The fat bold arrow (below) indicates that *more* influence is attributed to cycling power when gravity would normally slow a cyclist down.

Source: Based on Kelley, 1972.

conclude that she was able to pedal strongly enough to override the slope's power to slow her down. Of course, augmenting and discounting also work when the factors working towards or against the observed effect are psychological rather than physical forces. Thus, we would be less likely to infer that Hermione's attitude to attribution theory was really negative if she said it was boring knowing that Ron also found it boring, than if she said it was boring despite Ron's fascination with the topic.

Knowledge, expectation and covariation

How do we use domain-specific knowledge to guide our attributions?

Kelley's causal schema theory suggests that people take shortcuts to inferential conclusions when information or resources are limited (as in other contemporary dual-process models of social cognition; see Chapter 4).

However, Kelley still believed that observers engaged in more systematic analysis of covariation whenever possible. Partial support for this conclusion is provided by studies in which participants are explicitly presented with information packaged in terms of consensus, consistency and distinctiveness. For example, McArthur (1972) asked participants to explain why John laughed at the comedian, after telling them whether other people laughed at the comedian, whether John always laughed at this comedian, and whether John laughed at other comedians. Participants' attributions broadly followed covariation theory's predictions, except that participants made less use of consensus information than expected (see Fiske, 2004, for a review). However, these findings only tell us that people are able to use CCD information sensibly when it is presented to them (and when it is the only information available); they do not tell us whether people normally seek out and use CCD information when making attributions in other situations.

In fact, there is little evidence that people spontaneously collect CCD information even when it is readily available. Lalljee, Lamb, Furnham, and Jaspars (1984) presented participants with descriptions of events that required explanation (e.g. 'John did well on his history essay'; 'John lied to Mary'). Participants were asked to write down the questions that they wanted to ask in order to explain these events. Fewer than 20 per cent of their questions were specifically related to CCD. Instead, most were designed to evaluate participants' specific hypotheses about why the events had occurred (e.g. 'Did John try especially hard on this occasion?').

On reflection, this may not be particularly surprising. A problem with CCD information is that it can only tell us whether the actor, object, or situation (or some combination of these) caused the event, and not what it is about the actor, object, or situation that caused it. As Lalljee and Abelson (1983) pointed out, knowing that John lied to Mary because of something about Mary begs the question of what this something might be that makes people want to lie to her. To work this out, we would need to refer to prior knowledge about why people might deceive one another based on our experiences of lying and being lied to (e.g. knowledge that people lie to conceal secrets, to protect other people from the truth, to escape censure, and so on). But then why not just start by consulting this useful knowledge instead of first conducting a time-consuming covariation analysis? If we need to rely on ready-made explanations anyway, and these can tell us what we really want to know, then there is little point in going through the preliminary step of collecting and sifting through all possible combinations of CCD information.

It is now generally accepted that people don't usually engage in a systematic data-collection process every time they make an attribution. Because we already have expectations that events will unfold in a certain way, these can be used as a reference point for our attributions.

In effect, Kelley's theory implies that lay perceivers approach explanation without prior assumptions and ask themselves: 'why did this happen instead of not happening?' (a question that would lead them to weigh up all possible factors that might have led to the event). By contrast, Hilton and Slugoski (1986) suggest that people usually want to know the answer to a more specific question: 'why did this happen *instead of what usually happens* (under these circumstances)?' They call their model the *abnormal conditions focus* model because it focuses on identifying the condition that 'makes a difference' to what normally happens (e.g. the bent rail that makes a train come off its track and causes an accident). Thus, people look for causes among the differences between actual and anticipated event sequences rather than exhaustively sifting through all available evidence. Observers know where to look for relevant causes not only because they understand general principles of causality (as implied by Kelley's causal schema model), but also because they

have access to cognitive scripts telling them how particular kinds of event (e.g. conversations, parties, restaurant visits) ordinarily unfold in the social world (e.g. Cheng & Novick, 1990; Read, 1987). For example, the cognitive script for a restaurant visit follows a set sequence: a waiter takes you to your seat; gives you the menu; you order; you eat; you ask for the bill; you pay; you leave.

Learning about causation using covariation and causal power

How is causal knowledge originally acquired?

A final limitation of covariation theory is captured by a slogan familiar from statistics classes: 'correlation is not causation'. Establishing that factor X covaries with effect Y can never prove that X caused Y for at least two reasons. First, it may be that Y caused X rather than vice versa. Second, a third variable (Z) may have caused both X and Y. For example, covariation between revision for examinations and fine weather does not show that studying hard can make the sun shine.

Again, prior knowledge can help us disentangle causal relations of this kind. Because we are already aware what kinds of factors are likely causes of particular effects, we can reject certain factors as irrelevant and focus down our causal search. We know, for instance, that energy is required to induce movement, pressure to bend or break something, that people sometimes say things in order to impress others, and that people's actions don't immediately change the weather. However, because much of this specific knowledge needs to be learned from observation, the question of how people work out what typically causes what in the first place still remains.

It is not possible to acquire accurate knowledge about causal relations simply by observing covariations between events for the reasons stated above (correlation does not imply causation). Cheng (1997) argues, therefore, that something else needs to supplement covariation learning. According to her, this extra something is an innate predisposition to attribute observed effects to the unobservable **causal powers** (see also White, 1989) of objects or events. In other words, we naturally assume that associations between perceived occurrences reflect deeper hidden processes, and seek out the nature of those processes rather than staying at the level of objective observation. We try to work out what it is about something that gives it the capacity to influence other things (i.e. its causal power). For example, seeing a magnet attract metallic objects makes us want to know

> **causal power** an intrinsic property of an object or event that enables it to exert influence on some other object or event.

what quality (causal power) it possesses that allows it to exert these effects (its magnetism).

Attempting to uncover causal powers rather than record observable regularities for their own sake allows us to be more focused in our sampling of covariation data. According to Cheng (1997), we identify potential causes on the basis of prior beliefs about causal powers, and then assess their actual causal influence using a form of covariation analysis termed **probabilistic contrast** (Cheng & Novick, 1990). This involves comparing the probability of the effect occurring when the potential cause is present with the probability of the effect occurring when the potential cause is absent. For example, a child might find out that pointing at something can cause parents to bring this object near for closer inspection; she may do this by comparing what happens when she points, with what happens when she does not point. Importantly, even infants do not need to sample from the full range of possible causes in order to work out the effects of pointing, because they already have implicit awareness of the causal power of pointing. They know from an early age that activities such as pointing (and staring intently) are the kind of things that might direct another person's attention to something, whereas looking away or lying still are not. This prior knowledge limits the range of probabilistic contrasts that are required before arriving at useful conclusions about what causes what. These conclusions in turn shape subsequent causal reasoning over the course of development.

> **probabilistic contrast** comparison of the frequency of an effect in the presence of a potential cause with its frequency in the absence of that cause.

Attributions and achievement

What are the consequences of different attributions for success and failure?

Some of the events that we are most motivated to explain are our successes and failures. For example, you may wonder if a high exam mark was due to your particular affinity for the topics covered, your thorough exam revision, or the fact that exactly the right questions happened to come up. Depending on your conclusion, you will be more or less confident about maintaining this level of performance.

The most influential theory of achievement-related attribution was developed by Weiner (1979, 1985), who argued that inferences about the causes of our success and failure directly affect future expectations, motivations and emotions. According to Weiner, perceived causes of success and failure may be classified as: (1) internal or external (*locus*); (2) stable or variable (*stability*); and (3) controllable or uncontrollable (*controllability*, see Table 3.3; Leader in the Field, Bernard Weiner).

Attributing your exam success to an internal factor means that you believe that something relating to you as a person determined the outcome, whereas attributing performance to an external factor means that something to do with the situation was responsible. Both internal and external factors can be either variable or stable. For example, attributing your performance to intelligence means that you think something internal and relatively unchanging about you led you to do well.

 LEADER IN THE FIELD

Bernard Weiner (b. 1935) is Professor of Psychology at the University of California, Los Angeles, where he has worked since 1965. He received his undergraduate degree from the University of Chicago and his doctorate from the University of Michigan in 1963. In 1965, following two years at the University of Minnesota, he went to UCLA. He is most famous for his influential research into attributions for success and failure, identifying the main types of attribution, their underlying dimensions and their effects on motivation and emotion. His classification of perceived causes of behaviour has had an even greater impact. He received the Distinguished Scientist Award from the Society for Experimental Social Psychology in 2010.

Table 3.3 *Possible causes of success and failure.*

	Internal		External	
	Stable	**Unstable**	**Stable**	**Unstable**
Controllable	Mastery (e.g. knowledge, skill)	Effort	Enduring situational and social resources (e.g. contacts, wealth)	Temporarily available situational and social resources (e.g. advice, assistance)
Uncontrollable	Aptitude (e.g. intelligence, height and physical build, motor coordination)	Energy	Task ease or difficulty	Luck/chance

Source: Based on material in Weiner, 1979, 1985.

Weiner also distinguished between causal factors perceived as either controllable or uncontrollable. For example, if you believe that your exam success was due to an internal, stable and uncontrollable factor (your innate aptitude for this kind of material), then you may feel that there is no need to try hard in order to repeat your success. On the other hand, if you think that your good grade was due to an internal, variable and controllable factor (e.g. effort), you will probably conclude that you need to stay motivated in order to succeed in future. Thus, attributions about success and failure are not simply intellectual conclusions about performance, they also make a real difference to our expectations and motivation (Figure 3.4).

Mueller and Dweck (1998) showed that receiving different kinds of praise from other people can affect attributions about the stability and controllability of the personal causes of success, with consequences for subsequent motivation and task enjoyment. These investigators found that schoolchildren congratulated for being smart after correctly answering questions from an intelligence test were subsequently less likely to choose difficult tasks and less likely to enjoy solving problems than children congratulated for trying hard.

Continuing exposure to these different kinds of praise from parents and teachers while growing up may lead to more general mindsets about the causes of success. Dweck (2006) argues that attributing your own

FIGURE 3.4 *Do our conclusions about the causes of success and failure, e.g. in an exam, directly affect future expectations, motivations and emotions?*

Source: © Sally and Richard Greenhill. Used under licence from Alamy.

success to internal, stable and uncontrollable factors is part of a *fixed mindset* that brings far-reaching negative consequences for life-long development. By contrast, a *growth mindset* that sees abilities and skills as variable and controllable encourages people to extend themselves and develop their talents (see also Individual Differences 3.1, and Chapter 5).

If told smart - won't try harder. If praised for trying hard - will work hard and stay motivated.

INDIVIDUAL DIFFERENCES 3.1

ASSESSING YOUR IMPLICIT THEORY OF INTELLIGENCE

Read each sentence below and then choose the one number that shows how much you agree with it. There are no right or wrong answers.

1	2	3	4	5	6
Strongly agree	Agree	Mostly Agree	Mostly disagree	Disagree	Strongly Disagree

- You have a certain amount of intelligence, and you really can't do much to change it.
- Your intelligence is something about you that you can't change very much.
- You can learn new things, but you can't really change your basic intelligence.

Add together the three numbers you chose. The lower your overall score, the more you subscribe to an 'entity' view of intelligence as something that you either have or don't have (part of a 'fixed' mindset). The higher your overall score, the more you subscribe to an 'incremental' view of intelligence as something that may be cultivated and developed (part of a 'growth' mindset). A score of 3 means that you wholly subscribe to an entity theory, and a score of 18 means that you wholly subscribe to an incremental theory. Scores between 4 and 10 indicate a less extreme entity theory. Scores between 11 and 17 indicate a less extreme incremental theory.

Source: Dweck, Chiu, & Hong, 1995.

Attribution and depression

Can certain patterns of attribution lead to clinical depression?

Weiner's ideas about the consequences of achievement-related attributions have broader implications for understanding clinical disorders. One influential application has been the attributional reformulation of the learned helplessness theory of depression. Learned helplessness theory (Seligman, 1975) originally argued that depression results from learning that nothing you do makes any difference to outcomes. The idea was that if rewards and punishments do not depend on your actions, you soon learn to give up trying to attain the former and avoid the latter. However, many uncontrollable situations in everyday life don't make people depressed. For example, some people enjoy betting on games of chance, where the outcomes are completely beyond their influence. Gambling does not always make people depressed, even when they lose money.

This observation suggests that helplessness alone does not automatically lead to depression; other factors must also be in place. One clue to what these other factors might be comes from the observation that clinically depressed people usually have an exaggerated sense of personal responsibility for negative outcomes. If uncontrollable events cause depression, why should depressed people think that they have personally brought about these events? Abramson, Seligman, and Teasdale's (1978) answer is that helplessness only makes people feel chronically depressed if it is attributed to intrinsic features of the self. In other words, a specific pattern of attribution for uncontrollability may determine clinical depression (see Theory Box 3.2).

In defining this pattern, Abramson and colleagues extended Weiner's classification (shown in Table 3.3) to include another distinction between specific and global causes. Global causes apply across a wide variety of situations, whereas specific factors relate only to the particular situation at hand. The quality and persistence of depression depends on whether the cause of uncontrollability is perceived as internal or external, stable or variable, and global or specific.

By way of illustration, Abramson and colleagues used the example of a woman who has been rejected by a man in whom she is romantically interested. Nothing she does makes any difference to the way he feels about her. According to the model, the way this woman reacts to this experience of helplessness depends on her conclusions about the causes of rejection (see Table 3.4).

The least-threatening interpretation would be that her rejection was caused by something external, unstable, and specific. This man in particular was not attracted to her at this moment and in this particular situation (e.g. he may simply not have been in the mood for romance at the time). The consequences of this conclusion are not too serious for the woman, because she is still able to anticipate greater success with this man (or other men) in future. Consider, however, the contrasting attribution to internal, stable, and global causes: the man finds her unattractive not out of any passing whim, but because of the kind of person she is. His dislike is permanent and applies across all situations. Because being disliked is seen as reflecting something about her, other men will dislike her too and her future chances of romantic happiness are non-existent. Further, because the causal factors are global, they apply not only to romantic attraction but to other areas of her life as well. She can only look forward to consistent and universal bad outcomes that she can do nothing about. Unsurprisingly, such negative expectations are likely to make her depressed.

The theory proposed by Abramson and colleagues argues that people who have developed a tendency to attribute uncontrollable events to internal, stable, and global attributions have a greater risk of subsequently developing chronic and generalized depression (see

> **learned helplessness theory** the proposal that depression results from learning that outcomes are not contingent on one's behaviour.

Table 3.4 *Possible causes of romantic rejection.*

	Internal		External	
	Stable	**Unstable**	**Stable**	**Unstable**
Global	I'm unattractive to men	My conversation sometimes bores men	Men are overly competitive with intelligent women	Men get into rejecting moods
Specific	I'm unattractive to him	My conversation sometimes bores him	He's overly competitive with intelligent women	He was in a rejecting mood

Source: Based on Abramson, Seligman, & Teasdale (1978). Learned helplessness in humans: Critique and reformulation. *Journal of Abnormal and Social Psychology, 87*, p. 57. Adapted with permission of APA.

Social Psychology Beyond the Lab 3.1 and 3.2 for other applications of attribution theory to clinical disorders). Although some researchers have suggested that changes in attribution are consequences rather than causes of depression (Lewinsohn, Steinmetz, Larson, & Franklin, 1981), most of the subsequent evidence confirms that measures of negative thinking style (including attribution) help to predict subsequent depressive episodes (e.g. Rude, Durham-Fowler, Baum, Rooney, & Maestas, 2010).

Having established that depressed and non-depressed people interpret negative events in different ways, we may wonder whose interpretations are more accurate. Although it is tempting to assume that depression causes people to lose touch with reality, some theorists have argued that it is in fact non-depressed people who protect themselves from unpleasant truths by seeing things in an unduly positive light (the 'illusory glow';

depressive realism the idea that depressed people's interpretations of reality are more accurate than those of non-depressed people.

Taylor & Brown, 1988). This so-called depressive realism would mean that depressed people are 'sadder but wiser'. In support of this idea, Lewinsohn, Mischel, Chaplin, and Barton (1980) showed that depressed participants' ratings of their own social functioning during a group discussion were more similar to ratings of them made by external observers than were non-depressed participants' ratings. Although observers rated the performance of non-depressed participants more positively than that of depressed participants, they did not rate it as positively as the non-depressed participants themselves did.

However, Campbell and Fehr (1990) found that ratings of own social functioning made by participants with low self-esteem (a typical feature of depression) were more different from ratings of them made by their *conversation partners* than were ratings made by participants with high self-esteem. The apparent greater accuracy among depressed participants shown in the study by Lewinsohn et al. may have been a consequence of using observers who did not participate in the interaction to provide 'objective' ratings of behaviour. In fact, outside observers are often unduly harsh judges because they think that their task is to be critical. On balance, it seems that depressed people's negative outlook may only seem realistic when they are exposed to situations in which other people's judgements are also negatively biased. However, it is also worth bearing in mind that depressives' negative judgements can easily turn into self-fulfilling prophecies. If someone doesn't even try because they are sure they will fail regardless of effort, this makes it more likely that they will in fact fail (thus making their negative prediction more accurate).

Whether the attributional pattern associated with depression is realistic or unrealistic, reformulated learned helplessness theory suggests that therapy should focus on changing it in order to alleviate the symptoms of depression. In practice, current cognitive and psychodynamic therapies for depression attempt to modify a wide range of negative interpretations, only some of which specifically relate to attributions. Nevertheless, it seems likely that at least part of their effectiveness depends on attributional retraining (e.g. Barber et al., 2005).

Misattribution of arousal

How do we ascertain what we are feeling?

The previous section suggested that we feel more depressed about unpleasant events if we conclude that their causes are internal, stable and global. But how do we then recognize our reaction to this attributional pattern as depression rather than something else? This may sound a silly question because it usually seems that we know that depression is depression because of what it feels like (depressing). More generally, emotions are often assumed to be unambiguous private states that are available for direct introspection: we just know what we are feeling without having to think about it. By contrast, misattribution theories imply that we sometimes need

---

THEORY BOX 3.2

FIVE STEPS TO DEPRESSION: THE ATTRIBUTIONAL REFORMULATION OF LEARNED HELPLESSNESS THEORY

Objective non-contingency	Perceived non-contingency	Attribution	Expectations of non-contingency	Helplessness symptoms
Nothing the person does makes a difference to what happens.	The person notices that nothing she does makes a difference.	Non-contingency is attributed to internal, global and stable factors.	The person concludes that future actions will make no difference to what happens.	Depression coupled with motivational deficits.

Source: Based on Abramson, Seligman, & Teasdale (1978). Learned helplessness in humans: Critique and reformulation. *Journal of Abnormal and Social Psychology, 87,* p. 52. Adapted with permission of APA.

SOCIAL PSYCHOLOGY BEYOND THE LAB 3.1

PERSECUTORY DELUSIONS AND ATTRIBUTIONAL STYLE

Bentall and Fernyhough (2008) and Bentall, Kinderman, and Kaney (1994) argue that complex and variable clinical syndromes such as schizophrenia and psychotic depression are best understood by investigating their separate components. One common set of symptoms experienced across a range of psychotic disorders involves persecutory delusion, where sufferers believe that other people are deliberately acting against them. Clearly, such a delusion involves a pattern of attribution in which negative events are seen as caused by external agents (external-personalizing attributions) rather than by internal factors as in the attributional style characterizing 'hopelessness' depression (Abramson, Metalsky, & Alloy, 1989). Bentall and colleagues' influential theory proposes that experiences of victimization during childhood lead to negative views of the self and a tendency to attribute bad outcomes to the intentional activities of powerful other people (Bentall & Fernyhough, 2008). When a negative event threatens to activate uncomfortable thoughts about personal inadequacy, sufferers defend themselves by diverting blame to an outside agent (Bentall et al., 1994). An additional risk factor is a tendency to jump to conclusions, meaning that sufferers do not check on the validity of their external-personalizing attributions by considering evidence that might otherwise refute them (Merrin, Kinderman, & Bentall, 2007). One direct clinical implication of this analysis is that a range of cognitive beliefs and processes including those relating to attributions need to be targeted during therapy. More generally, therapy may alleviate suffering best if each specific component of a complex mental disorder is treated separately.

to work out what emotion we are experiencing and that this inference process is susceptible to social influence.

One of the earliest psychological theories of emotion was devised by William James (1884). He argued that each emotion has its own distinctive profile of bodily changes and that we directly sense our emotion by registering this profile. However, Cannon (1927) pointed out that the patterns of internal physiological activity associated with very different emotions are actually rather similar. For example, both fear and anger involve increases in heart rate, blood pressure, and other kinds of metabolic activity designed to release energy to the muscles in preparation for vigorous activity (*arousal* of the autonomic nervous system, ANS). This means that we cannot tell these emotions apart simply by checking what is happening inside our bodies.

Schachter (1964) therefore argued that emotions depend upon the attributions we make for our internal feelings, rather than directly reflecting these feelings themselves. Thus, perceptions of arousal (the physiological factor) tell us *that* we may be experiencing an emotion, but not *what* emotion it is. We therefore try to work out why our bodies are aroused (the cognitive factor) in order to answer this second question (see Theory Box 3.3; Leader in the Field, Stanley Schachter). If we conclude that our arousal is caused by the attractive person we are

 LEADER IN THE FIELD

Stanley Schachter (1922–1997) worked with Kurt Lewin (see Leader in the Field, Chapter 1) at MIT before moving to the University of Michigan, where Lewin's ex-student Leon Festinger (see Leader in the Field, Chapter 1) supervised his dissertation. Most of his career was spent at Columbia University, where his colleagues and collaborators included Bibb Latané (see Leader in the Field, Chapter 10), Richard Nisbett (see Leader in the Field, this chapter), and Lee Ross. Schachter is probably best remembered for his two-factor theory, which inspired many cognitive approaches to emotion, and for his clever experiment with Jerome Singer. His earlier work on affiliation also provided a forerunner of contemporary interpersonal approaches to emotion, showing that people seek out other people in order to make sense of their own feelings. Throughout his career, Schachter pursued the important idea that external cues (including social cues) can shape the interpretation of supposedly internal states such as emotions and feelings of pain and hunger. He was elected to the US National Academy of Sciences in 1983.

having coffee with, we may interpret it as a symptom of love (or at least lust; see Chapter 11). However, if we think our arousal is due to the fact that someone else keeps butting into our private conversation, we may conclude that it reflects anger. Finally, if we attribute our symptoms to the caffeine in the strong cup of coffee we are drinking, we may conclude that our arousal is non-emotional.

SOCIAL PSYCHOLOGY BEYOND THE LAB 3.2

ATTRIBUTIONS FOR MENTAL SYMPTOMS

Ideas based on attribution theory have been applied not only to the explanation of depression and anxiety, but also to other clinical conditions. Some of the most exotic of these include Capgras Syndrome and Cotard's delusion. People suffering from Capgras Syndrome believe that family and close friends have been replaced by impostors who look exactly like the people they used to know but are not really them (a scenario uncomfortably reminiscent of the plot of *Invasion of the Body Snatchers*, a book and frequently remade film in which extra-terrestrial plant pods infiltrate humanity by growing replica people and killing off the originals). People suffering from Cotard's delusion believe that they have died or do not really exist while they carry on their normal lives and interact with other people. Both disorders are associated with brain damage to similar regions of the right cerebral cortex that are thought to be associated with the sense of familiarity attached to faces and other familiar objects. Lesions in these areas can leave face and object recognition intact but take away the more emotional feelings that usually go together with recognition. According to Young and Leafhead (1996), Capgras and Cotard's sufferers may all experience this same experience of recognition without familiarity, but make different attributions for it. Capgras sufferers attribute their symptoms externally, concluding that something about other people is making them seem different. By contrast, Cotard's sufferers attribute the symptoms internally, concluding that it is they themselves who have lost contact with others rather than the other way around. Whether or not this turns out to be the correct explanation for these unusual conditions, it seems clear that attributions can make dramatic differences to our relations with other people and the external world.

In a famous experiment, Schachter and Singer (1962) tried to determine whether an identical physiological state could be perceived as anger or euphoria (or in non-emotional terms) depending on how participants interpreted its causes (see Theory Box 3.4). Schachter and Singer manipulated autonomic arousal by administering an adrenaline injection to some participants and a placebo injection to others under the guise that the syringe contained a new vitamin compound ('Suproxin') that the experimenters were testing.

The experimenters told one group of adrenaline-injected participants that Suproxin might lead to side effects such as a pounding heart and shaking hands (genuine symptoms of arousal). These participants were therefore able to interpret their bodily symptoms correctly as non-emotional responses to the injection. However, another group of adrenaline-injected participants received incorrect information about the effects of Suproxin (i.e. that there would be no side effects, or that there would be side-effects unrelated to arousal). Participants in this condition should therefore experience arousal symptoms without knowing their cause, and consequently seek an emotional explanation.

Schachter and Singer stage-managed the situation to encourage specific attributions for any unexplained arousal. Each participant was left in a waiting room with an accomplice of the experimenter posing as another participant who behaved in one of two ways. In one condition, the accomplice improvised a basketball game using scrap paper and a wastebasket, and encouraged the other participant to join in. In the other condition, the accomplice became increasingly irate while working through an insulting questionnaire that the participant also had to complete. Its final item read: 'With how many men (other than your father) has your mother had extra-marital relationships?' The only response alternatives provided were: '10 and over', '5–9' and '4 and under'.

According to Schachter's theory, emotion only occurs when arousal is attributed to an emotional cause. In other words, emotion should not have been experienced

THEORY BOX 3.3

SCHACHTER'S (1964) TWO-FACTOR THEORY OF EMOTION

THEORY BOX 3.4

MANIPULATIONS AND PREDICTIONS OF SCHACHTER AND SINGER'S (1962) EXPERIMENT

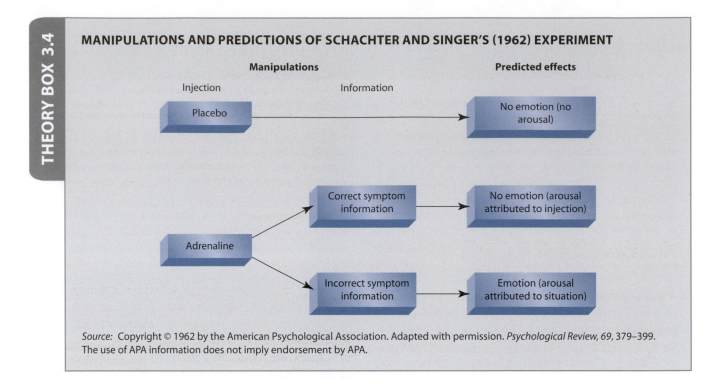

Source: Copyright © 1962 by the American Psychological Association. Adapted with permission. *Psychological Review, 69,* 379–399. The use of APA information does not imply endorsement by APA.

by either placebo-injected participants (because they were not aroused) or participants who had been correctly informed about the adrenaline injection's effects (because they should attribute arousal symptoms to the non-emotional injection). However, adrenaline-injected participants who were unaware that their symptoms were caused by this injection should have attributed their arousal to euphoric aspects of the situation when with the playful confederate, but to irritating aspects of the situation when completing the insulting questionnaire. These two groups, therefore, should have experienced widely divergent emotional reactions of euphoria and anger respectively.

In fact, results were less clear-cut (see Reisenzein, 1983). For example, placebo-injected participants did not report significantly less emotion than participants who were injected with adrenaline but who were not informed about the injection's genuine side effects. Further, emotion reports of misinformed adrenaline-injected participants did not differ substantially between euphoria and anger conditions (participants reported themselves to be mildly happy in both conditions; see Zimbardo, Ebbesen, & Maslach, 1977). Observations of participants' emotional *behaviour* (from behind one-way glass) provided some support for the hypotheses, but the reported behavioural effects may have partly depended on direct effects of arousal on activity levels (producing apparently more euphoric behaviour when playing,

and apparently more angry behaviour when filling out an annoying questionnaire).

One significant result obtained by Schachter and Singer (1962) clearly did accord with predictions, however. Participants injected with adrenaline and correctly warned of the effects consistently reported less positive emotion in the euphoria condition, and less negative emotion in the anger condition than participants misled about side effects. Schachter and Singer's explanation was that the informed group correctly attributed their arousal to the injection and labelled it in non-emotional terms.

Subsequent experiments have suggested that arousal that is actually caused by emotional events may also be misattributed to non-emotional sources; this insight has proved useful to clinicians who are trying to minimize otherwise maladaptive reactions in their clients' behaviour (e.g. Ross, Rodin, & Zimbardo, 1969). For example, Storms and Nisbett (1970) reported that students with mild insomnia fell asleep *more quickly* after taking a placebo that they believed was an arousal-inducing pill (*reverse placebo effect*) (see Leader in the Field, Richard Nisbett). The investigators argued that misattribution of arousal symptoms to the pill neutralized the mild-insomniac participants' usual interpretation in terms of anxiety (see Social Psychology Beyond the Lab 3.1 for another application of attribution theory to clinical disorders). However, Calvert-Boyanowsky and Leventhal (1975) demonstrated that supposed misattribution effects may

LEADER IN THE FIELD

Richard Nisbett (b. 1941) obtained his first degree from Tufts University, and his PhD from Columbia University, where his advisor was Stanley Schachter (see previous Leader in the Field). His wide-ranging research not only addresses several topics relating to attribution (as described in this chapter) but also touches on more general issues relating to human judgement (e.g. Nisbett & Ross, 1980; see Chapter 4) and cultural differences (Nisbett, 2003; see Chapter 15). One of his most influential papers argued that, contrary to intuition, people do not normally have awareness of the causal processes that lead to their own judgements or behaviour, and rely on naïve theories to infer what they must have been after the fact (Nisbett & Wilson, 1977). He is also a vociferous critic of the idea that racial differences in IQ have any genetic basis (Nisbett, 2009). He is currently Theodore M. Newcomb Distinguished Professor of Psychology at the University of Michigan.

LEADER IN THE FIELD

Daniel Gilbert (b. 1957) is Professor in Psychology at Harvard University. His academic career started inauspiciously at the age of 19 when his intention of studying creative writing in order to become a science fiction writer was thwarted because the class was full. The only available alternative was an Introduction to Psychology course. He still ended up as a best-selling author, but of non-fiction instead of fiction. The book in question (*Stumbling on Happiness*, 2006) drew on his influential research (with Timothy Wilson) into *affective forecasting*, which concerns people's often inaccurate predictions about their own emotional reactions to events (see Wilson & Gilbert, 2003). Of course, he is also famous for his innovative research on the correspondence bias.

instead be explained by the correct anticipations set up by symptom warnings. For example, knowing what is about to happen to your body means that symptoms are less surprising and less emotionally upsetting when they arrive.

In sum, Schachter and Singer's clever experiment does not offer conclusive support for all aspects of two-factor theory. This may be partly because it is difficult to manipulate arousal and emotional cognitions independently when the two usually go hand in hand. Subsequent studies have been similarly inconclusive (e.g. Erdmann & Janke, 1978; Marshall & Zimbardo, 1979; Maslach, 1979), and many theorists now believe that Schachter overstated how easily interpretations of own emotion can be modified. Because our attributions about, and appraisals of, emotional situations usually determine our autonomic as well as emotional reactions in the first place (e.g. Lazarus, 1991), arousal symptoms mostly arrive with an unambiguous ready-made emotional explanation.

Attributional biases

What are the main types of attributional bias, and how can they be explained?

According to covariation theory and the correspondent inference model, observers systematically process all potentially relevant information when making attributions. However, as we have seen, subsequent research suggests that causal inferences are shaped by prior knowledge and expectations (e.g. Hilton & Slugoski, 1986; Read, 1987), or by learned attributional styles (e.g. Abramson et al., 1978), and that they may be redirected by

deceptive manipulations (e.g. Schachter & Singer, 1962). In general, people seem to attach more weight to some causes at the expense of others when drawing causal conclusions. Precisely what kinds of causes are typically favoured under different circumstances has been the focus of research into various **attributional biases**.

attributional biases systematic distortions in the sampling or processing of information about the causes of behaviour.

The correspondence bias In their professional lives, psychologists sometimes disagree about whether internal or external explanations of human behaviour deserve more emphasis. For example, most experimental social psychologists focus on situational influences and often downplay the influence of people's characteristic dispositions. By contrast, personality psychologists attach more weight to personal traits, usually without taking as much account of environmental influences (see Chapter 1). The correspondence bias suggests that the naïve psychology practised by laypeople is closer to personality psychology than to experimental social psychology. Behaviour is often seen as a reflection of an actor's corresponding internal disposition (e.g. aggressive behaviour reflects aggressive personality) even when it is actually caused by situational factors (e.g. severe provocation). Research Close-Up 3.1 presents a famous example of this effect (see also Jones & Harris, 1967, described earlier).

Why do people underestimate situational influences? According to Gilbert and Malone (1995), a number of different processes are involved (see Leader in the Field, Daniel Gilbert). First, some situational forces are subtle and difficult to detect. If observers are not aware of these influences in the first place, they can hardly be expected to factor them into their explanations. Second, our *expectations* about how other people will behave may distort our interpretations. For example, we may mistakenly assume that the prospect of public speaking

THE CORRESPONDENCE BIAS IN ATTRIBUTING KNOWLEDGE TO QUESTIONER OR CONTESTANT

RESEARCH CLOSE-UP 3.1

Ross, L. D., Amabile, T. M. & Steinmetz, J. L. (1977). Social roles, social control, and biases in social-perception processes. *Journal of Personality and Social Psychology, 35*, 485–494.

Introduction

People's social roles shape their interactions with one another. These influences are most obvious in situations in which one person has relatively greater control over an interaction. An oral examination, for example, permits examiners to decide what topics should be discussed, while the student cannot choose which questions to answer and which not to. One consequence is that examiners have greater opportunity to display their specialized knowledge. In accordance with the correspondence bias, Ross and colleagues argue that people pay too little attention to these role-conferred advantages when arriving at attributions for behaviour. As a consequence, people with relatively greater social control appear wiser and more able than they really are (and their social position therefore seems more justified). To test this hypothesis, the investigators simulated a quiz game in which participants were arbitrarily allocated the role of either questioner or contestant. Questioners were given the opportunity to devise their own questions, thereby giving them a clear advantage in demonstrating their own specialized knowledge. The prediction was that questioners would be viewed as higher in general knowledge.

Method

Participants

Twelve pairs of male students and 12 pairs of female students from an introductory psychology class were recruited for a study into processes whereby 'people form impressions about general knowledge'.

Design and procedure

The role of questioner or contestant was allocated to one person in each pair using an explicitly random procedure. Questioners were told to devise 10 'challenging but not impossible' general knowledge questions, which they then asked contestants in a quiz. For example, one question was: 'What is the longest glacier in the world?' As soon as the quiz was over, questioners and contestants separately rated their own and each other's general knowledge

compared to the average student at the same university, using a 100-point scale.

Results

On average, contestants got only 4 out of 10 questions right in the quiz. General knowledge ratings of questioners and contestants were analysed. Contestants rated questioners' general knowledge as significantly better than their own, but questioners did not rate their own general knowledge as better than that of contestants. An additional group of observers subsequently watched simulations of some of the original quizzes and, like the contestants, rated questioners as significantly higher in general knowledge than contestants (see Figure 3.5 for the mean ratings of general knowledge made by all three groups of participants).

Discussion

The findings demonstrate that the situational advantage conferred by being allowed to devise your own questions led to higher general knowledge ratings from both contestants and observers (who probably attempted to answer the questions privately). This seems to provide a

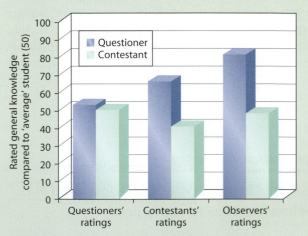

FIGURE 3.5 *Mean ratings of general knowledge after quiz game.*

Source: Copyright © 1977 by the American Psychological Association. Adapted with permission. Ross et al., *Journal of Personality and Social Psychology, 35*, 485–494. The use of APA information does not imply endorsement by APA.

clear example of the correspondence bias. Because participants' roles were allocated randomly in this study, it is statistically unlikely that one group (the questioners) should happen to be genuinely higher in general knowledge. Indeed, Ross and colleagues administered brief tests of general knowledge to all participants after the quiz and found no differences in performance.

Although some of the contestants' and observers' general knowledge ratings must have been *inaccurate*, there still remains the issue of whether they were *irrational* too (see Hilton, 1990, on the distinction between accuracy and rationality in attribution). Given only a limited sample of the questioners' knowledge, how could contestants make accurate inferences about other areas? Does it not make sense for them to give questioners the benefit of any doubt and rate their general knowledge as superior? How else might they have acknowledged questioners' apparently superior performance in this particular context? After all, assessing their own general knowledge as equal or superior might be seen as being a bad loser.

In a later study, Sumpton and Gregson (1981) asked observers to estimate questioners' knowledge of the specific areas covered by the quiz. They found that observers' ratings were higher only for these particular topics, and not for general knowledge. Similarly, Johnson, Jemmott, and Pettigrew (1984) found that observers believed that contestants would perform as well as questioners if their roles were reversed. Thus, bias in this setting depends partly on what information is requested by experimenters, and what these questions imply about their intentions (e.g. Schwarz, 1994). Participants evidently try to make sense of what is required of them in the study in addition to the performance exhibited by questioners and contestants.

The study also carries implications about the limits of the correspondence bias. Questioners did not conclude that contestants' inability to answer their questions meant that they must be inferior in general knowledge, presumably because their own role-conferred advantage was extremely salient to them.

THEORY BOX 3.5

PROCESS LEADING TO CORRESPONDENCE BIASES

Source: Adapted from Gilbert & Malone (1995). Copyright © 1995 by the American Psychological Association. Adapted with permission. *Psychological Bulletin, 117*, 21–38. The use of APA information does not imply endorsement by APA.

---

false consensus bias the assumption that other people generally share one's own personal attitudes and opinions.

terrifies others just as much as it terrifies us (an example of the **false consensus bias**). Therefore, when someone appears calm before their turn to speak, we may conclude that their confident personality must be overriding an otherwise anxiety-provoking situation.

Finally, Gilbert and Malone suggest that people sometimes fail to correct their initial inferences about the causes of behaviour, especially when processing demands are high. The idea here is that people's automatic reaction to observed behaviour is to conclude that it reflects an actor's disposition. Any relevant situational influences are then factored in using a more deliberate reasoning process. Because the initial dispositional inference is effortless, it happens regardless of current circumstances. However, other demands on cognitive resources may interfere with the situational correction process, leading us to underestimate the power of external factors. (The different stages at which these sources of bias may intrude are shown in Theory Box 3.5.)

An experiment conducted by Gilbert, Pelham, and Krull (1988) provides support for this last explanation. Participants observed a silent videotape (i.e. the sound was turned right down) of a woman talking nervously to a stranger, and then rated how anxious she was as a person. Subtitles indicating current conversation topics informed some participants that the woman was discussing her sexual fantasies (offering a situational explanation for her nervousness), but others that she was talking about gardening. Further, some participants were told to memorize the subtitles, imposing an additional cognitive demand that should interfere with any situational correction process. As predicted, participants under higher cognitive demand tended to believe that the woman had an anxious personality regardless of conversation topic, whereas participants under low cognitive demand rated her as less dispositionally anxious when they believed she was discussing sex rather than gardening. Presumably low-demand participants had sufficient cognitive resources left over to correct for their initial automatic dispositional inference.

Gilbert and colleagues' theory suggests that attribution *always* involves automatic processes, but only *sometimes* involves controlled processes as well (e.g. Shiffrin & Schneider, 1977). It is therefore another example of the dual-process models that are currently popular in research on social perception and cognition (see Chapter 4).

The argument that we spontaneously and automatically make inferences about people's traits is supported by research conducted by Smith and Miller (1983). In two studies, these investigators demonstrated that participants presented with sentences describing an actor's behaviour (e.g. 'Ted breaks a friend's expensive camera that he borrowed') made judgements about the actor's traits more quickly than they made inferences about the specific causes of the action. Indeed, it may be that we only go to the effort of engaging in a deliberate causal analysis and check the validity of our automatic trait attributions when we are specifically motivated to think about why a particular behaviour occurred (e.g. when the behaviour affects us negatively, or when it is unexpected), and when we have sufficient cognitive resources to engage in the necessary controlled processing.

The correspondence bias was once believed to be so pervasive and inescapable that it was dubbed 'the fundamental attribution error' (Ross, 1977). However, subsequent research suggests that it is more context-dependent than this name implies (see Gawronski, 2004, for a review). For example, Krull (1993) showed that asking people to interpret the situation rather than the person led them to make automatic situational rather than dispositional inferences. Participants were again exposed to a silent videotape showing a woman talking, and

were told that she was discussing sensitive topics with her therapist. When the task was to assess how anxiety-provoking the conversation was (rather than how anxious the woman was), high cognitive load led participants to rate the woman as *less* dispositionally anxious, but the situation as *more* anxiety-provoking. Krull concluded that automatic dispositional inferences only occur if the inferential goal is to understand the person rather than the situation that person is in.

An alternative account of this evidence is provided by Trope and Gaunt (2000), who do not believe that people are predisposed to make automatic dispositional inferences that are subsequently corrected by more controlled processing. Their two-stage model instead argues that the initial automatic stage of behaviour identification already integrates both situational and dispositional information. According to Trope and Gaunt, behaviour identification is followed by a controlled and resource-demanding process of hypothesis evaluation in which possible explanations for the identified behaviour are assessed. For example, in Krull's (1993) study described above, participants may have evaluated the hypothesis that it was the anxiety-provoking nature of the situation that caused the observed anxiety in the interviewee. When cognitive load is high, this hypothesis-evaluation process is more cursory and tends to be biased towards information that is easily available or salient.

In many attribution studies, the most salient information relates to the actor, and participants are directed (implicitly or explicitly) to make sense of the actor's behaviour, making dispositional inference more likely under cognitive load. However, studies such as Krull's (1993) that orient participants towards the situation lead to more situational attributions when cognitive load is high. Thus, according to Trope and Gaunt (2000), cognitive load does not disrupt correction of an initial automatic inference, but limits the range of information used to evaluate hypotheses about the cause of the identified behaviour. If situational information is salient (as it was for the questioners in the quiz-game study of Ross et al. (1977), reported in Research Close-Up 3.1), then there may be no automatic dispositional inference and no correspondence bias.

Trope and Gaunt's (2000) model may also account for Smith and Miller's (1983) apparent demonstration of automatic dispositional inference. Like all other sentences presented in this study, 'Ted breaks a friend's expensive camera that he borrowed' begins with the name of the actor performing the behaviour, and uses this name as the subject of the sentence's main verb. Such sentences may activate trait information more directly than they

salience attention-grabbing property of objects or events depending on perceptual features such as vividness, perceiver sensitivity or some combination of the two.

activate situational information (see also Brown & Fish, 1983, discussed later).

Another reason why the correspondence bias is no longer considered 'fundamental' is that it varies across cultures (see Chapter 15 for a more extended discussion of cultural influences). For example, Miller (1984) compared explanations offered for deviant and prosocial behaviours by children (aged 8, 11 and 15) and adults from the US and Southern India. She found that US adults attributed events to dispositional causes significantly more than Indian adults or children from either country did, suggesting that North Americans but not Indian Hindus learn over the course of development to favour dispositional explanations (see Figure 3.6).

Why should members of some societies develop a stronger preference for dispositional explanations? Many western societies such as the US and most countries in Europe are said to be characterized by a culture of *individualism* in which personal effort and ability combine to produce deserved outcomes. People socialized into such cultures may learn to be more attuned to actors rather than their circumstances in a wide range of contexts, so that information relating to actors tends to be more salient and accessible. However, in some other societies (e.g. India, Japan), children are socialized to see themselves more as part of groups that must work together to attain valued outcomes (*collectivistic culture*; see Chapter 15). This cultural emphasis may make situations (especially social situations) rather than individual actors more salient (Figure 3.7).

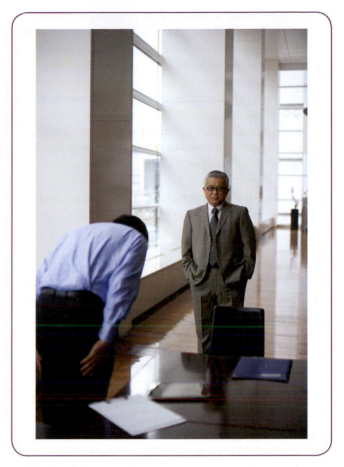

FIGURE 3.7 *Members of collectivistic cultures are more sensitive than members of individualistic cultures to the power of situations.*

Source: © Ryouchin. Used under licence from Getty Images.

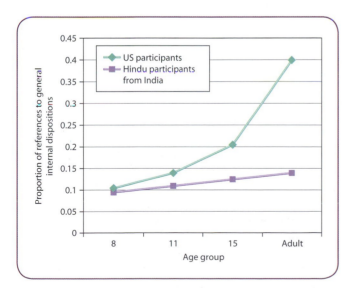

FIGURE 3.6 *Dispositional attributions in two cultural settings across four age groups.*

Source: From Miller (1984). Copyright © 1984 by the American Psychological Association. Reproduced with permission. *Journal of Personality and Social Psychology, 46,* 961–978. The use of APA information does not imply endorsement by APA.

Despite their relatively greater use of situational explanations, even collectivists frequently assume that actors have dispositions corresponding to their behaviour. For example, Korean participants (like US participants) assumed that a controversial essay reflected the writer's opinions even when they believed that the writer had been told what point of view to defend (Choi & Nisbett, 1998). However, when the salience of the situational constraint was increased, Korean participants were better able than American participants to take its influence into account. Choi, Nisbett, and Norenzayan (1999) argue that members of collectivistic cultures are more sensitive to the power of situations than are members of individualistic cultures, enabling them to correct their initial dispositional inferences more easily under many circumstances.

Cultural differences in dispositional attribution may reflect differences in automatic or controlled processing (or both). For example, Easterners may be more motivated to correct initial dispositional inferences and engage in more controlled processing to achieve this.

Alternatively, they may be so well-practised at correction using situational information that they do it automatically. Mason and Morris (2010) suggest that cross-cultural comparison of brain activity during attributional tasks may allow us to determine the relative degree of involvement of neurological processes underlying automatic and controlled processing of social information. Preliminary evidence suggests that at least some of the differences depend on automatic processes (e.g. Kobayashi, Glover, & Temple, 2006).

The actor–observer difference   The actor–observer difference (or self–other difference) compares attributions people make about other people with those that they make about themselves. Although Westerners' default assumption is often that other people's behaviour reflects a corresponding disposition, Jones and Nisbett (1972) argued that, when explaining our own behaviour, we tend instead to emphasize external, situational factors.

> **actor–observer difference** proposed general tendency for people to explain their own behaviour in more situational terms, but other people's behaviour in more dispositional terms.

Why should there be a difference between these two kinds of attribution? Two main reasons have been proposed. First, people have access to a wider range of information about the factors leading to their own actions (Jones & Nisbett, 1972). For example, when explaining your liveliness at a party, you are able to consider other situations in which you have acted in a less extroverted manner (e.g. when meeting someone for the first time, or being interviewed), and may therefore conclude that you are not a consistently lively person (Figure 3.8). By contrast, most other people only know how you have acted in a restricted range of situations, and may therefore think that your behaviour is more consistent than it really is.

A second possible reason for actor–observer differences concerns direction of attention. When observing someone else's behaviour, we tend to focus on that person rather than their situation. Conversely, our attention tends to be directed outwards when we are performing behaviours ourselves. Perhaps we simply assume that whatever is occupying our attention is exerting the most causal influence (e.g. Taylor & Fiske, 1978; see Research Close-Up 3.2 on Storms, 1973).

Of course, direction of attention can only explain preferences for dispositional explanations of other people's behaviour when we are directly observing those other people acting. However, observers also often attribute behaviour to actors' dispositions when it is described to them in words. For example, when told that 'John went to the cinema', most people tend to think that this behaviour reflects something about John rather than something

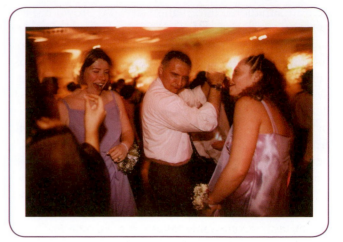

FIGURE 3.8   *Your behaviour, e.g. being lively at a party, may appear more consistent to others than it really is.*
Source: © Melissa Farlow. Used under licence from Getty Images.

about the cinema. According to Brown and Fish (1983), this is because the English language implies that *subjects* of *action verbs* are responsible for the action described. By contrast, for *experience verbs* it is the *objects*, and not the subjects, that are usually seen as causal (e.g. we tend to interpret the sentence *John liked Angela* as John's liking for Angela being caused by something about Angela).

Evidence reviewed by Malle (2006) suggests that actor–observer differences (like correspondence biases) are not consistently found across all contexts. They are especially likely in studies that imply that the other person whose behaviour is to be explained is idiosyncratic in some way (thus drawing attention to distinctive personal characteristics), and when the outcome of the action is negative (because there are obvious personal advantages to blaming bad things that happen to you on situational factors, as discussed in the next section).

Self-serving attributional biases   What pushes or pulls our attributions in particular directions? Most of the examples presented so far in this chapter suggest either that we are drawn towards salient factors or that we follow generally valid rules of explanation (e.g. people cause effects) in circumstances where they happen to be less appropriate (see Nisbett & Ross, 1980). The basic idea is that people's attributions are occasionally imperfect approximations of the causal structure of reality, but at least aim to represent that reality accurately. However, some kinds of bias are harder to explain in these terms. Self-serving attributional biases seem to represent a *motivated* distortion of what has happened in order to serve personal interests. Instead of being neutral observers

> **self-serving attributional biases** motivated distortions of attribution that function to maintain or increase self-esteem.

REVERSING THE ACTOR–OBSERVER EFFECT BY MANIPULATING PERSPECTIVE

Storms, M. D. (1973). Videotape and the attribution process: Reversing actors' and observers' points of view. *Journal of Personality and Social Psychology, 27*, 165–175.

Introduction

Storms (1973) proposed that differences between actors' and observers' attributions depend partly on their different physical points of view: actors' attention is typically directed outwards towards the situation (including other actors), whereas observers' attention focuses on the observed person (i.e. the actor). Indeed, one explanation for the related correspondence bias is that actors are often the most dynamic and interesting objects in the environment and therefore attract observers' attention (and deflect it from other aspects of the situation; see Heider, 1958; Taylor & Fiske, 1978). The increasing availability of video technology in the early 1970s allowed Storms to manipulate actors' and observers' perspectives in order to assess the influence of this factor on situational and dispositional attributions.

Method

Participants

Thirty groups of four male students took part in this study. Two members of each group were randomly assigned the role of observer and the other two were assigned the role of actor.

Design and procedure

Stage 1. Actors were told to have a conversation to get to know each other while facing each other across a table. Each observer was seated next to one of the actors and told to observe the actor opposite him across the table. Two video cameras were positioned so that each pointed at one of the actors (see Figure 3.9, Stage 1).

   Stage 2. Participants in the video condition were shown the videotape of the recorded interaction, but told that because only one camera had functioned correctly, they would only be able to see the visual image of one of the actors (coupled with audio of both sides of the conversation). Thus, one actor and one observer from each group saw a replay of the conversation from the same perspective as before, while the other actor and observer saw the reversed perspective (i.e. the actor now saw his own face instead of the face of his interaction partner, and the observer saw the face of the actor that he had not originally observed; see Figure 3.9, Stage 2). In the no-video

Stage 1 Bird's-eye view of get acquainted session (arrows indicate direction of attention)

Stage 2 Bird's-eye view of video replay

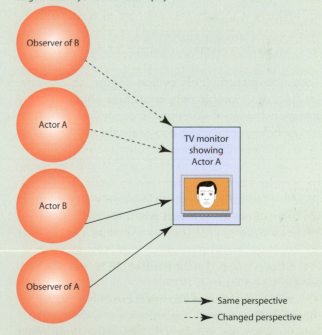

FIGURE 3.9 *The two stages of Storms's (1973) procedure.*

Source: Copyright © 1973 by the American Psychological Association. Reproduced with permission. *Journal of Personality and Social Psychology, 27,* 165–175. The use of APA information does not imply endorsement by APA.

condition, participants were told that none of the video equipment had worked and that the planned video replay would therefore not take place.

Measures

After Stage 2, actors rated their own friendliness, nervousness, talkativeness and dominance during the conversation, then rated the extent to which each of these behaviours had been caused by personal characteristics and by characteristics of the situation. Observers made corresponding ratings of the actors they had originally observed at Stage 1.

Results

Storms calculated difference scores by subtracting summed ratings of situational attribution for the four key behaviours from summed ratings of dispositional attribution. These difference scores were then analysed. In the no-video and same-perspective conditions, actors' attributions were less dispositional (more situational) than observers' (see Figure 3.10). But in the reversed-perspective condition, observers' attributions were *less* dispositional (more situational) than actors'.

Discussion

This study demonstrates that actor–observer differences can be reversed by showing actors their own behaviour and showing observers the situation that actors are responding to (in this case, the other actor). A more general conclusion is also possible: that actors and observers tend to attribute greater causality wherever they pay attention. Indeed, later studies (e.g. Taylor & Fiske, 1978) have shown that salient (attention-grabbing) factors tend to be seen as exerting more influence than non-salient factors.

One criticism of this study is that the usual actor–observer difference was not demonstrated (e.g. Gilbert &

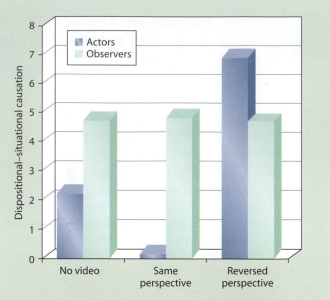

FIGURE 3.10 *Reversing the actor–observer difference following video replay.*

Source: Adapted from Storms (1973). Copyright © 1973 by the American Psychological Association. Adapted with permission. *Journal of Personality and Social Psychology, 27*, 165–175. The use of APA information does not imply endorsement by APA.

Malone, 1995). For example, analysis of the original ratings (separately assessing dispositional and situational attribution) rather than difference scores shows that actors were rated in equally dispositional terms by themselves and their observers across all conditions. However, the reported effect on situational attribution is theoretically interesting even if dispositional attribution is unaffected. The general implication is that we can correct for inattention to situational factors by manipulating attention.

of social events, we may sometimes interpret them in ways that suit us (or suit our ingroup more generally; Islam & Hewstone, 1993b, and see Chapter 14), allowing us to feel better about what has happened.

Let's assume that you have just done well in an exam. Your tendency may be to conclude that this reflects your innate ability (*self-enhancing bias*). However, if you do badly, perhaps you will decide that the questions were unfair or unusually difficult, or that the person sitting next to you in the examination hall was distracting you by sharpening his pencils so noisily (*self-protective bias*). More generally, you may be inclined to arrive at conclusions that maintain your positive self-image (e.g. Alicke & Sedikides, 2009, and see Chapter 5).

Johnson, Feigenbaum, and Weiby (1964) provided one of the earliest demonstrations of self-serving bias. Participants in their study were educational psychology students and their task was to teach two children how to multiply numbers via a one-way intercom system (which meant that they never actually saw or heard their pupils). The first phase involved explaining how to multiply by 10 and the second phase involved explaining how to multiply by 20. After each phase, the pupils' worksheets were returned to participants, allowing them to assess how successfully the concepts had been conveyed. In fact, the worksheets were concocted by the experimenters to manipulate whether or not the answers were correct. In both conditions, pupil A answered the questions on both take rather than disown responsibility for failure). Indeed, research suggests that simply being in a bad mood can reverse self-serving biases (e.g. Forgas, Bower, & Moylan, 1990), perhaps by removing the illusory glow that preserves our sense of well-being in happier times (Taylor & Brown, 1988). There is evidence that self-serving biases are weaker for depressed participants (see review by Mezulis, Abramson, Hyde, & Hankin, 2004), and also for members of collectivist cultures (Heine, Lehman, Markus, & Kitayama, 1999; but see Sedikides, Gaertner, & Toguchi, 2003, for a dissenting opinion), but they are commonly observed across a wide variety of other contexts.

Motivational or cognitive effect? In the 1970s, a debate arose about whether so-called self-serving biases were genuinely self-serving. Miller and Ross (1975) proposed that some personally advantageous attributions were entirely rational, while others simply reflected the application of explanatory principles that would normally be valid. According to this view, people do not distort their thinking to protect self-esteem (*motivational explanation*) but rather use rules of thumb that happen to lead to faulty conclusions on some occasions (*cognitive explanation*). Take the educational psychology students in the study by Johnson and colleagues (1964) described earlier. It would be illogical for them to attribute pupil B's improvement on the second exercise to the pupil's abilities, because the pupil had done badly on the first sheet. Further, improvement, when it occurred, followed the teacher's careful attempt to explain multiplication after the pupil had done badly at the first attempt. Under these circumstances, it makes perfect sense to conclude that one's teaching skills led to success. In the failure condition, by contrast, the pupil did not improve *despite* renewed efforts at explanation, and was consistently worse than pupil A on both exercise sheets. Thus, failure is associated with pupil B but not with pupil A, or with the person doing the teaching. According to Kelley's (1967) covariation principle, even a detached observer should attribute bad performance to pupil B rather than the teacher when these conditions hold.

More generally, Miller and Ross (1975) argued that apparently self-serving biases arise because effort covaries with success but not with failure. If trying harder does not improve performance, then it is reasonable to conclude that something about the task is presenting an obstacle. However, if trying harder does improve performance, then it is logical to attribute one's success to trying hard.

Although these are valid points, few contemporary psychologists would deny that thinking can also be distorted by motivations and emotions (see Alicke & Sedikides, 2009). Indeed, Miller and Ross's idea that we adjust our inferences to match existing positive expectations already

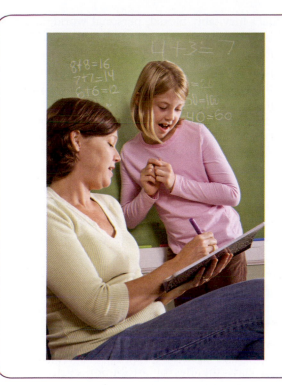

FIGURE 3.11 *Teacher's explanation of pupils' success and failure can show self-serving bias.*
Source: © Golden Pixels LLC. Used under licence from Shutterstock.

worksheets correctly. However, pupil B either did badly on both tasks or did badly on the first but improved on the second. In other words, participants either failed or succeeded in teaching pupil B how to multiply. In the condition where pupil B's performance improved, participants explained this improvement in terms of their own teaching abilities. But when pupil B failed to improve, they attributed this negative outcome to his lack of ability rather than their own ineffective teaching (Figure 3.11).

Zuckerman (1979) reviewed a number of apparent demonstrations of self-serving bias, and concluded that the effect depends on the desire to maintain self-esteem. However, competing motivations can also reduce self-serving attributions. For example, self-presentation may not be served by taking undue credit for positive outcomes in public settings, either because we don't want to be seen to show off, or in order to avoid any embarrassment at failing to live up to the unduly favourable image that this would imply (e.g. Weary et al., 1982). Further, some situations require accurate self-assessment in order to identify ways in which performance may be improved in future (e.g. Sedikides & Strube, 1997).

Abramson and colleagues' (1978) attributional reformulation of learned helplessness theory discussed earlier implies that depressed people adopt an attributional style that is the precise opposite of the self-serving pattern (they sounds rather like an acknowledgement that we want to make ourselves look good under certain circumstances (Tetlock & Levi, 1982). Thus, many apparently cognitive explanations can be translated into motivational terms, and many apparently motivational explanations can be translated into cognitive terms. Nevertheless, the fact that brain regions associated with reward and motivation are activated in association with self-serving biases is consistent with the argument that non-cognitive motivational factors contribute to the effect (see Blackwood et al., 2003; Seidel et al., 2010).

Accuracy of attribution The preceding sections may have given the impression that people's judgements about the causes of behaviour are seriously prone to error. Perceivers seem to distort their processing to suit personal goals and to attach undue importance to factors that really do not play as much of a role as they believe. However, it is important to emphasize that people would not be able to function adequately in the social and practical world if they continually drew wildly incorrect conclusions about causal processes. The point of finding the cause of something is to be able to predict and prepare for what will happen when that cause is present in future, and inaccurate attributions would not help in this regard. Indeed, Nisbett and Ross (1980) argue that many examples of bias are caused by the application of cognitive shortcuts which typically lead to valid conclusions, but can lead perceivers astray under certain special circumstances, such as those investigated in studies of attributional bias (see discussion of cognitive heuristics in Chapter 4).

Some theorists (e.g. Funder, 1987) have also argued that the standards against which lay perceivers are judged when assessing accuracy of attribution may often be inappropriate, and that attributions are more attuned to reality than the bias account suggests. In many studies there is no correct answer in the first place, because causal judgements are applied to fictitious events, so accuracy assessments ultimately boil down to matters of opinion or belief. Often, different answers are justifiable on different grounds. In other cases, however, it is clearer that some error of judgement has occurred. For example, although contestants rated questioners as higher than them in general knowledge in the quiz-game study conducted by Ross et al. (1977), described earlier, random allocation of participants to the different experimental roles made it statistically improbable that these differences were genuine. Further, the fact that different groups of participants disagree about attributional conclusions in this and other studies logically implies that at least one group must be incorrect.

Even when attributions are inaccurate according to valid scientific criteria, they may still correspond to an individual's inevitably partial, personal world, and thus lead to conclusions that are useful for them specifically. For example, believing that other people's behaviour is more consistent and caused more by internal dispositions than it really is may not be disadvantageous in practical terms. We are only likely to encounter any particular other person in a limited range of situations (ones in which we too are also present) and these situations may constrain the range of behaviours that this other person performs (Jones & Nisbett, 1972). Thus, even if Harry is not really an extravert in all possible contexts, if we only meet him at times and in places where he is outgoing and excited, attributing his behaviour to an extraverted disposition is unlikely to be too problematic.

Explaining intentional behaviour

Are intentions perceived as special kinds of causes?

Although early theories of attribution such as correspondent inference theory focused on uncovering the motives behind intentional behaviour, much of the subsequent research was more concerned with dispositional attributions, and often focused on involuntary effects on behaviour (e.g. symptoms of anxiety in the silent videotape procedure described earlier, inability to answer questions in quiz-games, etc.). Indeed, apparent differences between intentional and unintentional behaviour were often downplayed.

Reeder (2009) argues that principles of 'mindreading' need to be applied when explaining intentional, motive-driven behaviour, and that these are distinct from the more simple process of weighing up the relative impact of situational and dispositional explanations for non-intentional behaviour (as suggested by many models of trait inference dating back to Heider (1958), and by more recent theories implying that automatic trait inferences may be corrected after factoring in alternative situational explanations, e.g. Gilbert and Malone, 1995). Situational information may be used as the basis for inferring an actor's motive (perhaps corresponding to an underlying disposition) rather than as the basis for discounting dispositional explanations.

For example, participants in Reeder, Kumar, Hesson-McInnis, and Trafimow's (2002) experiment were told about an incident in a football match when one player intentionally dug his boot-studs into the leg of a player from the other team after a tumble. In one condition, the player had previously been insulted by the injured player. In another condition, the player believed that the opposing player's performance was so good that his own team stood no chance of winning unless the opposing player was forced to leave the pitch due to injury. In both scenarios, a strong situational factor encouraged an attack on the other player. If perceivers only used situational information to discount automatic dispositional inferences, then both conditions should have discouraged perceivers from concluding that the actor had a trait of low morality causing his immoral behaviour. In fact, dispositional low morality was attributed to the offending player only in the condition in which injuring the other player helped his team win the game (instrumental condition), and not in the condition in which the other player had provoked him (reactive condition). This pattern can be explained by the fact that participants inferred that the player was motivated by personal gain in the instrumental condition, but by retaliation or self-defence in the reactive condition. Because the self-defence motive is seen as less immoral than the personal gain motive, dispositional inferences to low morality were weaker in the reactive condition. Thus, situational pressures do not necessarily lead to discounting of dispositional causes when the observed behaviour is intentional.

The research by Reeder and colleagues suggests that intentional behaviours are explained according to different principles from non-intentional behaviours. A separate line of evidence also shows that actors' intentions are seen as particularly important when observers are weighing up a variety of possible causes. In one of the studies in question, Hilton, McClure, and Sutton (2010) asked participants to state their preferred explanation for effects arising as outcomes of extended causal chains, in which a sequence of events unfolds with each event leading to the next. For example, leakage from a water pipe was described as producing corrosion in a wire to an electricity generator powering railway signals, whose failure led to a train crash that resulted in injury to the train driver. In most cases, participants preferred not to attribute outcomes to the initial event that set off the causal sequence in the first place (i.e. water leakage). However, when this initial event was produced by the voluntary action of a person (e.g. a saboteur had damaged the water pipe) it was consistently selected as the cause. In short, the availability of an actor's intentional action overrides other factors in determining attributions for observed events.

The naïve scientist metaphor

Do lay perceivers always act like scientists when making causal attributions?

Most of the theory and research considered above assumes that people seek to understand the social world

in a detached, scientific manner, but sometimes get it wrong. This assumption is generally known as the naïve scientist model (e.g. Fiske & Taylor, 2008), and, like all metaphors, it has its limits. Perhaps some of our everyday explanations are not designed to provide a neutral characterization of reality in the first place. In this case, evaluating attributions against abstract rules of inference such as Kelley's (1967) covariation principle is rather like complaining that someone playing draughts is not following the rules of chess properly.

> **naïve scientist model** a metaphor for how social information is processed that likens social perceivers to academic researchers who formulate theories and use data to test hypotheses in order to predict and control behaviour.

If people are not trying to be scientific when making attributions, what are they trying to do? One possibility is that explanations are generated to solve specific practical problems (White, 1989). For example, if you have to explain why you have done well in an examination, you probably don't weigh up all possible contributory factors. Instead, you look specifically for those causes that will further your ends in the current situation. If the explanation is formulated while talking with a friend who is disappointed by his or her own performance, you might search your memory for any bits of good luck that aided your success. If, on the other hand, you are trying to score a point against the other person, you might try to think of some particularly clever things that you wrote.

Hilton (1990) argues that our explanations are specifically designed to provide information that is useful to the person we are talking to. For example, when explaining to a close friend why I got upset during our conversation, I will refer to the particular thing she said that sparked off my reaction. This is because I assume that my friend wants to know what topics are more and less likely to make me distressed. However, if my distress is serious enough, the explanation I give to my therapist will probably emphasize my personal sensitivity rather than the emotional content of what was said to me. This is because I know that the therapist will be interested in what my particular problem is and how it differs from those of other clients.

Note that these two explanations are mutually compatible and may both be true, despite the fact that one refers to an external cause (what my friend said) and the other to an internal cause (my sensitivity to that topic). Typically, a number of factors need to be in place to cause a given event, and the task of explanation involves selecting which of these factors should be emphasized in a particular context. To look at this another way, a number of changes in prior events could have averted the observed effect of my getting upset (my friend and I could have been discussing something different, I could have been a less sensitive person, and so on) and each of these possible changes reflects one of the causal factors contributing to my outburst (my friend's remark, my sensitivity, the existence of our relationship, etc.). Deciding which of these causes to use in explanation depends on what you think the person to whom you are explaining the event already knows about its causes, and what you think they expected would happen.

On some occasions, another person's expectations about what would normally happen are not entirely obvious, leading to ambiguity about how to approach the explanatory task. However, the precise phrasing of the causal question often helps to clarify matters. For example, if someone asks you 'Does discussing work make you upset?', the question's implicit emphasis (i.e. 'discussing work' as the subject of the action verb) may suggest that the questioner wants to know about the effects of this topic. By contrast, the question 'Do you get upset when discussing work?' implies an interest in your own causal role in events.

According to Hilton (1990), some apparent cases of bias can be explained by applying these conversational principles. For example, Nisbett, Caputo, Legant, and Marecek (1973) found that students explained their own choice of university course in more situational terms than their best friend's choice of course, consistent with their proposed actor–observer difference. However, the emphasis of the question 'Why did you choose this university course?' naturally falls on the course as the topic about which information is required. By contrast, the question 'Why did your best friend choose this course?' implies that the investigators want to know about the friend rather than the course (otherwise, why not directly ask for the participant's own reasons?). In this study, then, the reported actor–observer difference may simply reflect a rationally motivated attempt to provide the kind of information that was implicitly requested.

An experiment by McGill (1989) supports this reasoning. She found that a simple change in wording reversed the effect found by Nisbett et al. When participants were asked 'Why did you *in particular* choose this course?' they tended to offer less situational explanations than when they were asked 'Why did your friend choose this course *in particular*?'

More generally, attribution experiments may be viewed as 'conversations' taking place between experimenters and participants in which the participants are trying to work out what information the experimenter is seeking (Schwarz, 1994). Making sense of questionnaire items often depends on thinking about who is asking these questions and for what purposes. Adopting this kind of conversational approach also allows a reinterpretation of other supposed illustrations of attributional bias. For

example, in Jones and Harris's (1967) original demonstration of the correspondence bias discussed earlier, participants were told to gauge another student's attitudes towards Castro. In order to do this, they were provided with an excerpt from an essay that this other student had (supposedly) written. Should participants simply ignore this essay if its writer had no choice about what position to take on this issue? Surely the experimenter wouldn't have gone to the trouble of showing it to them if it provided no information about the writer's opinions. Participants probably assumed, therefore, that the experimenter believed that the essay was relevant and concluded that they were meant to infer the writer's opinion on the basis of its content. Indeed, in another study in which participants were explicitly warned that some of the material they would see might not be relevant, the correspondence bias was reduced (Wright & Wells, 1988).

Attributions as discourse

Are attributions always produced for cooperative reasons?

Hilton's (1990) working assumption was that people try to provide other people with information that helps to complete their understanding of events (Grice, 1975). However, conversations are not always cooperative processes in which information is generously exchanged for mutual benefit. Often, our aim is not to help someone else understand what has happened, but rather to argue against them or defend our own point of view against their attack. According to Edwards and Potter (1993), attributions may be formulated rather differently in these more antagonistic contexts. As an example, these investigators presented an excerpt from a transcript of a rape trial (Figure 3.12). In this excerpt, the defence barrister is cross-examining the victim and trying to imply that she was partly culpable for the alleged rape:

> *Barrister: (referring to a club where the defendant and the victim met)* It's where girls and fellas meet isn't it?
> *Victim:* People go there.
> (Edwards & Potter, 1993, p. 30)

Note that the barrister's description of events on the night in question implies certain motives and intentions on the part of the victim: that she had gone to this place specifically to meet members of the opposite sex. Her response is designed specifically to neutralize this inference. Although neither party is explicitly presenting

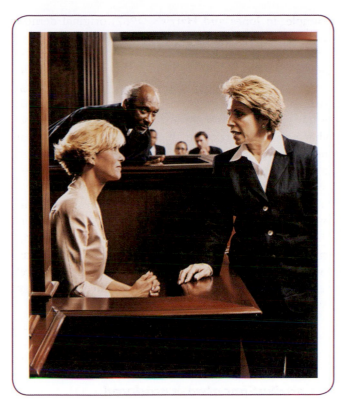

FIGURE 3.12 *Attributions do not always function as part of a cooperative process between people.*
Source: © Jim Arbogast. Used under licence from Getty Images.

explanations, the way that events are formulated already carries implications for what caused what and who is to blame. Clearly, this isn't a cooperative process, but rather one in which attributions are actively contested.

Like White (1984), Edwards and Potter (1993) believe that attributions are formulated for particular purposes, but these purposes specifically reflect conversational goals such as persuading, undermining, blaming, or accusing. Further, a range of alternative tactics and strategies may be improvised online in response to the other person's formulations. In this view, attributions do not function as attempts to explain a separately existing social reality, but instead to *construct* a version of reality suited to the current conversational business. Attributions are not descriptive representations, but rhetorical moves in an ongoing dialogue.

Summary

This central part of the chapter has covered a great deal of ground. We reviewed the major theories of attribution and identified some of their limitations, including the need to explain how general and specific knowledge

is used as part of the attribution process. We also considered applications of attribution theory, notably to the understanding and treatment of clinical depression. Next we considered the key role of attributions in emotion and the misattribution of arousal, and summarized evidence for the main types of attributional bias. Finally, we evaluated whether lay perceivers do, in fact, function as naïve scientists, and the role of causal attributions within the study of conversations and everyday discourse.

SOCIAL PERCEPTION AND SOCIAL REALITY

What are the reality checks on perceivers' perceptions and attributions?

Conversational and discursive models of attribution take us some distance from the classic work of Asch (1946) and Heider (1958) that was designed to find out how people privately make sense of other people and what they do. More generally, they unsettle the notion that people are simply naïve scientists trying to uncover the structure of an independent social reality. Subsequent models have seen social perceivers as lawyers (Hamilton, 1980), tacticians (Fiske & Taylor, 2008), pragmatists (White, 1984) or politicians (Tetlock, 2002). Although there is some truth in each of these characterizations, the bottom line seems to be that a variety of strategies are available for dealing with social information, which may be deployed selectively depending on circumstances.

But does this mean that social perceivers are free to construct whatever formulation suits their current purposes? There are three reasons why not. The first is that biology and culture do not equip people with infinitely flexible cognitive resources for understanding other people. At the biological level, we are innately attuned to certain kinds of social information at the expense of others (e.g. Fantz, 1963; Johnson & Morton, 1991) and automatically detect intentionality from certain patterns of observed movement (e.g. Pavlova et al., 2010). At the cultural level, socialization leads us to interpret the interpersonal world in ways that are compatible with the ideas of our parents, teachers, and, more generally, the society to which we belong (e.g. Markus & Kitayama, 1991). Attribution and social perception always take place against the backdrop of norms of understanding that make some inferences more likely than others. A related point is that other people often contest any formulation of social reality that doesn't match their own (just as their own formulation may be contested in turn). The upshot is that some degree of consensus tends to emerge among people who have regular contact with one another.

A final constraint on formulations relates to the content of the social information itself. Social perception research tends to focus on the interpretation of verbally represented information or static, sensory stimuli. However, when people confront each other in everyday life, they often have access to a dynamic multimodal presentation that is responsive to their own conduct. Some characteristics of others can be read directly from the available information (Baron & Boudreau, 1987; Gibson, 1979). For example, we can register where someone else's attention is focused from the orientation of their sensory organs. The dynamic features of some actions even allow us to detect intentions directly. For example, Morris and Lewis (2010) showed that observers of videotaped football tackles could reliably and accurately detect when a player was deliberately diving (in order to get the referee to award a free kick or penalty). Their judgements were based on the disproportionate momentum of the player's fall, its temporal discontinuity with the moment of contact, or the adoption of an 'archer's bow' posture (see Figure 3.13) designed to draw attention to the supposed loss of control. A final example of directly perceptible causation occurs in some examples of 'property transmission' (White, 2009), where characteristics corresponding to some features of the causal agent are clearly visible in the observed effect. For example, pressing a hand into wet concrete, as film stars are often asked to do, leaves a trace that shows exactly how it was produced.

Many of these data-driven forms of social perception and attribution do not seem to depend on explicit verbally mediated processes, but instead involve direct registration of sensory information. An important challenge facing future research is to specify how these two kinds of process – verbal representation as shaped by conversational pragmatics and rhetoric, and direct perception determined by active pick-up of social information – might relate to, or interact with, one another.

Some of the distinctions between different kinds of attributional process may also be clarified by evidence derived from brain-scanning. For example, Van Overwalle (2009) reviewed studies using fMRI to detect neural correlates of various kinds of social cognition and found that inferences about other people's goals, desires and intention were associated with activation of the TPJ brain region, mentioned earlier, while inferences about longer-term dispositions were more likely to be associated with medial prefrontal cortex (mPFC) activation. Van Overwalle concluded that goal detection can utilize

FIGURE 3.13 *A football player adopting the 'archer's bow' posture, which is commonly used following a tackle.*
Source: From Morris & Lewis, 2010. © Paul Morris.

a 'where-to system' (a mechanism designed to pinpoint the direction taken by an observed action) that operates at a more perceptual, less abstract level than judgements about disposition which require integration of information.

AUTOMATIC AND CONTROLLED SOCIAL PERCEPTION

How much thought is involved in social perception and attribution?

Early theories of social perception (e.g. Asch, 1946) and attribution (e.g. Heider, 1958; Kelley, 1967) seemed to imply that people think long and hard before arriving at conclusions about other people and their behaviour. They apply best to those occasions when we treat other people's personalities and behaviours as puzzles that need to be solved carefully, for instance when actors do something unexpected or highly consequential. Most everyday encounters with other people simply do not involve such a great deal of thought, and we often reach conclusions without really thinking about it. Recent theories correspondingly emphasize the automaticity and effortlessness of the cognitive processes that are involved. For example, Gilbert and Malone's (1995) ideas about automatic dispositional inference have parallels in accounts of stereotyping that suggest social categories relating to ethnic or minority groups may be directly activated in response to simple perceptual cues (e.g. Bargh, 1999, and see Chapter 4).

The idea that initial automatic attributions may subsequently be corrected using more controlled and effortful processing also relates to research into self-regulation of prejudice (see Monteith & Mark, 2005, and Chapter 4). Evidence suggests that stopping ourselves from applying unwarranted prejudices may face similar problems to adjusting dispositional inferences in response to situational information. For example, Fiske and Neuberg (1990) argue that automatic stereotyping is only followed by individuated impression formation when participants are sufficiently motivated to expend the additional cognitive effort. Further, Macrae, Bodenhausen, Milne, and Jetten (1994) showed that participants who had deliberately avoided thinking about a skinhead in prejudiced terms reverted to even more strongly stereotypical views once the requirement for self-control was removed (see Chapter 4). Evidently social perception and stereotyping depend on interactions and conflicts between controlled, systematic thinking and more automatic processes. Learning to detect unwanted effects of automatically activated conclusions is certainly possible if conditions are right (Monteith & Mark, 2005), but depends on systematic intervention and cooperative participants. Arriving at accurate and constructive social perceptions is not always a straightforward matter.

CHAPTER SUMMARY

- *How do we form impressions of what other people are like?* Information presented early in a sequence tends to be more influential (*primacy effect*), especially under time pressure. Information regarding 'central' personality traits, such as warmth, is given more weight, especially when it provides new and distinctive information.

- *Do the same processes of person perception operate when people meet face to face?* Information transmitted nonverbally can have more direct effects on impressions. We sometimes behave in ways that encourage other people to conform to our impressions of them (*self-fulfilling prophecies*).

- *What is attribution theory?* Attribution theory tries to explain how people work out the causes of events, particularly events involving other people.

- *How do people draw conclusions about the motives and dispositions guiding deliberate behaviour?* According to correspondent inference theory, observers compare the effects of a chosen option with those of a rejected option. Non-common effects reveal the actor's motivation and corresponding disposition.

- *How do people weigh up different possible causes?* According to *covariation theory*, lay perceivers conduct an informal statistical analysis to work out whether an observed effect correlates with the person, entity, or context.

- *What happens when there is insufficient information for covariation analysis?* People make use of prior knowledge about general principles of causation (*causal schemas*) or about specific people, objects, and events when deciding between possible causes.

- *How do people explain their successes and failures?* Weiner classified perceived causes of success and failure using three dimensions: locus (whether the cause is internal to the person or external), stability (whether the cause is stable or variable over time), and controllability (whether the person can influence the cause). Attributing failure to internal, stable, and uncontrollable causes reduces achievement motivation.

- *Are certain patterns of attribution associated with clinical depression?* Clinically depressed people often attribute negative outcomes to internal, stable and global (widely applicable) factors.

- *Do attributions shape our own emotions?* Schachter believed that emotions depend on attributing experienced physiological arousal to emotional situations. Although this is probably not true, the way that we interpret our emotions may be influenced by manipulating our explanations for bodily symptoms.

- *Are people more likely to attribute behaviour to internal or external causes?* In many situations, people from individualistic cultures underestimate the impact of situational causes of another person's behaviour (*correspondence bias*).

- *Why do people fall victim to correspondence biases?* Situational information may not be noticed, expectations about behaviour may distort interpretations, and people may not have the motivation and opportunity to correct automatic dispositional inferences.

- *Are correspondence biases inevitable?* Asking people to interpret the situation rather than the person may reverse correspondence biases under cognitive load. People from collectivistic cultures seem less susceptible to correspondence biases.

- *Do people favour internal attributions for their own behaviour?* According to the actor–observer difference, people are more likely to use external attributions for their own behaviour but internal attributions for other people's behaviour.

- *Are attributions motivated by self-interest?* Self-serving biases occur when people attribute positive outcomes to internal factors and negative outcomes to external factors.

- *Are attributions usually inaccurate?* Attributions usually lead to practically useful conclusions. Bias and error are probably restricted to special situations.

- *Do people try to be good scientists when making attributions?* Attributions are often motivated by practical concerns or conversational demands. Scientifically valid conclusions may not always suit our purposes.

- *How hard do people typically think about the causes of behaviour?* Many attributions are made automatically. Controlled processing is only involved when what needs explaining is unexpected and important, and when there is sufficient motivation and opportunity to think about why something happened.

SUGGESTIONS FOR FURTHER READING

Dweck, C. S. (2006). *Mindset: The new psychology of success*. New York: Random House. Combines accessible descriptions of research findings from studies of attributions for success with relevant case studies to make a readable self-help book.

Fiske, S. T., & Taylor, S. E. (2008). *Social cognition: From brains to culture* (3rd ed.). New York: McGraw-Hill. Includes treatment of attribution theory within an overarching perspective on social cognition.

Försterling, F. (2001). *Attribution: An introduction to theories, research, and applications*. Hove, UK: Psychology Press. An accessible overview of attribution models and findings from Heider to the early twenty-first century.

Gladwell, M. (2005). *Blink: The power of thinking without thinking*. London: Penguin. A popular account of how quickly and automatically people reach conclusions about objects, events, and, of course, other people.

Hewstone, M. (1989). *Causal attribution: From cognitive processes to collective beliefs*. Oxford: Blackwell. A wide-ranging view of the field, including intrapersonal, interpersonal, intergroup and societal aspects of attribution.

Ross, L., & Nisbett, R. E. (1991). *The person and the situation: Perspectives of social psychology*. New York: McGraw-Hill. Highly readable introduction to the cognitive perspective on attributional bias and other aspects of social perception and inference.

Sloman, S. A. (2005). *Causal models: How people think about the world and its alternatives*. New York: Oxford University Press. A (mostly) non-technical introduction to some sophisticated ideas about causation, intentionality and how people reason using these concepts.

Weiner, B. (2006). *Social motivation, justice, and the moral emotions: An attributional approach*. Mahwah, NJ: Erlbaum. Weiner's latest book applies his ideas about attribution and motivation to issues relating to justice and to legal settings.

Zebrowitz, L. A. (1990). *Social perception*. Belmont, CA: Brooks. A thorough review of research into social perception that attempts to integrate ecological and cognitive approaches.

4 Social Cognition

LOUISE PENDRY

Source: © siamionau pavel. Used under licence from Shutterstock.

KEY TERMS

- accessibility
- accountability
- anchoring/adjustment heuristic
- automatic process
- availability heuristic
- base rate information
- categorization
- cognitive miser
- continuum model of impression formation

- controlled process
- dissociation model
- encoding
- goal
- goal dependent
- heuristic
- implicit goal operation
- individuating information
- lexical decision task
- outcome dependency

- priming
- probe reaction task
- rebound effect
- representativeness heuristic
- schema
- social cognition
- stereotype
- stereotype suppression

CHAPTER OUTLINE

ROUTE MAP OF THE CHAPTER

We inhabit a hectic social world. In any one day we can expect to deal with many other people. We may meet people for the first time, go out with old friends, find ourselves in a job interview trying to make a good impression on our prospective employer, or else queuing in a supermarket to pay for groceries, or waiting for a train on a busy platform. Even for those of us professing to live ordinary lives, no two days are exactly alike. So, precisely how do we navigate this complex social life? What social information grabs our attention? How do we organize and use it in our interactions with and judgements about others? These are some of the questions that interest social cognition researchers, and providing answers to them strikes at the very heart of understanding human mental life. In this chapter we investigate some of the ways in which we process social information in situations such as these. The chapter focuses especially on the distinction between the social processes and judgements we make that are often speedy and automatic 'gut reactions', such as categorization and heuristic processing, and those which may require more effort, deliberation and control (for example, forming more careful impressions of others and avoiding stereotyping).

INTRODUCTION

What is social cognition?

A core topic in social psychology is the study of social cognition, which is concerned with how we make sense of ourselves and others in our social world. Understanding how we select, store, remember and use social information can tell us a great deal about how we are able to successfully navigate what is a very complex social environment.

social cognition a large topic within social psychology concerned with understanding how we think about ourselves and other people and how the processes involved impact upon our judgements and behaviour in social contexts.

As we go about our daily schedules, we are busy 'doing' social cognition for real. So, just what is it? Essentially, the study of social cognition promotes a deeper understanding of the mental processes that underlie human social behaviour (Fiske & Taylor, 1991). It sheds light on the steps people go through when thinking about others (Fiske, 2004).

If we think about it for just a moment, this has implications for a very broad range of human social phenomena and domains. What is especially intriguing about social cognition is that it taps into the kinds of questions we find ourselves asking. Questions such as:

- Why did I assume that the man at the coffee machine in the boardroom was the company director when he was in fact the secretary?
- Why did I assume that Dr Alex James would be male/white?
- Why is it that I expected Albert to be elderly?
- Why did it surprise me to discover that Hilda, my elderly neighbour, had a passion for car maintenance?
- Why did I take the time to talk to my new female work colleague and find myself subsequently re-evaluating my initially stereotypic impression of her?

The aim of this chapter is to pass on to you a little of what we have learned thus far about some of the main theoretical issues in the field (for more detail, see Bless, Fiedler, & Strack, 2004; Fiske & Taylor, 1991, 2008; Kunda, 1999; Moskowitz, 2005). This chapter will give you a flavour of some of the more established theories in the field, and consider both the classic and more contemporary research that such theories have generated in their quest to understand better the workings of the social mind.

JUMPING TO CONCLUSIONS OR WORKING THINGS OUT SLOWLY

Why is it so easy to jump to conclusions when making judgements about others?

Although the field of social cognition is extremely broad and vibrant, few researchers would deny that one recurring, overarching theme is the distinction between social thinking that is *fast and furious* and social thinking that is more *measured and precise*. Since the 1970s, significant developments in theory and methodology have meant that it is possible for us to now focus independently on these different types of thinking, that is, the influence of *unintentional* (i.e. unconscious) and *intentional* (i.e. conscious) processes in human thought and behaviour (Posner & Snyder, 1975). You might see this distinction encompassed in the term *dual-processing theories*. Or, to put it yet another way (and the way we will mainly refer to it hereafter), it refers to the contrast between automatic and controlled processes.

In this chapter, we focus primarily upon this distinction. Do we process information about others carefully and rationally, or do we instead make rash judgements on the spur of the moment? Understanding when and why we engage in automatic or controlled processing can tell us a lot about how we view our social world.

automatic process a process that occurs without intention, effort or awareness and does not interfere with other concurrent cognitive processes.

controlled process a process that is intentional, under the individual's volitional control, effortful and entailing conscious awareness.

To make this kind of distinction a little clearer, consider the following passage:

> Simon tried to put nationalities to faces, according to stereotype. The group of brawny, over-tanned and over-jewelled men and women who had ordered Bordeaux rather than local wine should be German – prosperous, large and loud. Any table giving off a cloud of cigarette smoke should be French, just as a table of non-smokers, with more water than wine being drunk, should be Americans. The English loaded butter onto their bread and ordered the heaviest desserts. The Swiss ate neatly and kept their elbows off the table, alternating sips of wine and sips of water like clockwork. (Mayle, 1993, p. 234)

Simon's observations, taken from Peter Mayle's amusing book *Hotel Pastis*, may not strike us as particularly unusual. We may not endorse the national stereotypes conveyed in the passage quoted above, or we may at least question their accuracy, but somehow, we know exactly what Simon is talking about. Despite the perils of stereotypical thinking, it is something that we are apt to find irresistible (e.g. Brewer, 1988; Devine, 1989; Fiske & Neuberg, 1990).

Did Simon pause for even a moment to consider if his snap decisions were accurate? Did he stop to consider that in fact several of the French contingent were not actually smoking? Or that at least two of the English group were nibbling abstemiously on fruit salad (no cream)? No. The questions for social cognition researchers are: how and why did Simon respond in this manner? What processes led him to these conclusions? In social cognitive terms, the above illustration demonstrates several steps in a process that will be the focus of the next sections. Simon has:

- *Categorized* each of the people in the restaurant in terms of nationality (grouped them into discrete sets – here, nationalities – based upon perceived shared characteristics).
- *Activated* the *content* of these categories (what we term **schemas**: our expectancies about members of a category, here people belonging to such groups).

> **schema** a cognitive structure or mental representation comprising pre-digested information or knowledge about objects or people from specific categories, our expectancies about objects or groups, what defines them.

- Used a mental shortcut (rule of thumb) to pigeonhole individuals according to how similar they are to typical members of a particular group (in line with the common stereotype that a large percentage of the British population eat unhealthily).

Much of this occurred fairly spontaneously. Simon did not stop to deliberate more carefully. As we shall see, it is a fundamental tenet of social cognition research that we often process information in precisely this way, only moving beyond the obvious stereotype if motivated and able to do so (e.g. Fiske & Neuberg, 1990). Schemas such as those outlined above have a functional role to play in facilitating person perception. They are, as Bodenhausen (1990) has noted, a kind of cognitive shortcut, a simpli-

> **heuristic** a well-used, non-optimal rule of thumb used to arrive at a judgement that is effective in many but not all cases; stereotypes are often said to function as heuristics.

fying rule of thumb or **heuristic** that serves us well a lot of the time, but not always (for more on heuristics, see later in this chapter, and also Chapter 7).

In this chapter, we will consider some of the research that speaks to the distinction between automatic and controlled

processes: when, why and how do we engage in automatic versus controlled processing in person perception? By the end of this chapter you will be well equipped to provide preliminary answers to these questions.

THE AUTOMATIC PILOT WITHIN

Read the following passage:

> A father and his son were involved in a car accident in which the father was killed and the son was seriously injured. The father was pronounced dead at the scene of the accident and his body taken to a local morgue. The son was taken by ambulance to a nearby hospital and was immediately wheeled into an emergency operating room. A surgeon was called. Upon arrival, and seeing the patient, the attending surgeon exclaimed, 'Oh my God, it's my son!'
> Can you explain this?

So, how did you do? Many people find this question impossible to answer (based on lab class demonstrations

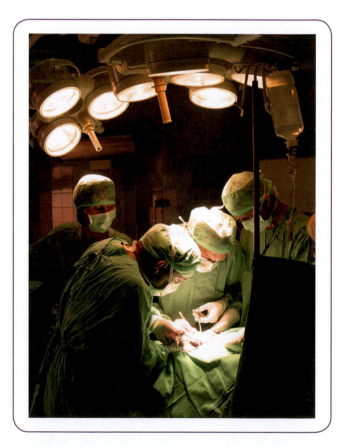

FIGURE 4.1 *Did you assume that these surgeons were men?*
Source: © Brasiliao. Used under licence from Shutterstock.

over a number of years, often more than 40 per cent of students simply cannot do it). Moreover, they are apt to generate a wide range of convoluted explanations (for example, the 'father' who was killed is a Catholic priest and the term 'son' is therefore being used rather loosely) other than the most obvious one (the surgeon is the boy's mother). Why do people have so much trouble and why do they generate such complex rationalizations?

> **stereotype** a cognitive structure that contains our knowledge, beliefs and expectancies about some human social group.

Essentially, they find it hard to overcome the automatically activated **stereotype** (i.e. surgeons are generally men).

As we shall see, this tendency to activate stereotypes automatically happens an awful lot (Figure 4.1). We will now pay some closer attention to why this occurs.

What makes a process automatic?

For a process to be considered automatic, several criteria are deemed necessary (e.g. Posner & Snyder, 1975): the process needs to occur without *intention, effort* or *awareness* and is *not expected to interfere with other concurrent cognitive processes*. For those of us who have been behind the wheel of a car for a few years, the act of changing gear would possibly meet these criteria. A controlled process, on the other hand, is one that is: *intentional, under the individual's volitional control, effortful* and *entails conscious awareness*. To continue the driving analogy, deciding whether it is safe to overtake on a busy motorway should (one would hope!) fulfill these criteria. Let us now consider how this automatic versus controlled distinction contributes to our understanding of the process of person perception. We will start by looking at social categorization.

The pervasive nature of social categorization

Almost every doctor who saw and examined me, labelled me a very interesting but also a hopeless case. Many told my mother very gently that I was mentally defective and would remain so… nothing could be done for me.

(Christy Brown, 1955, p. 10)

Christy Brown suffered from cerebral palsy and was considered mentally disabled until one day he snatched a piece of chalk from his sister and wrote some words

with it. He went on to astound and defy the medical profession by becoming a widely acclaimed author, whose autobiography was made into a successful film, *My Left Foot*. Branded from birth as 'retarded and useless', he fought to overcome prejudice and ignorance. The consequences of **categorization** can, then, sometimes be rather unpalatable. Once we assign others to particular social categories, associated stereotypic information can dominate our judgements to a worrying degree. Nonetheless, it does seem unlikely that

> **categorization** the tendency to group objects (including people) into discrete groups based upon shared characteristics common to them.

we can view others in total isolation from their obvious physical and social categories. This is the view adopted by many theorists who work in the area (e.g. Brewer, 1988; Fiske & Neuberg, 1990; Macrae & Bodenhausen, 2000), and we will now turn our attention to why they endorse such a position.

Categorization refers to the tendency we have to group objects (including people) into discrete groups, based upon shared characteristics. There are object categories for furniture, takeaway food and musical instruments, but also social categories for women, refuse collectors, children, rock stars and so on. It is a fundamental premise of the social cognition approach that such categories serve a very useful function (e.g. Allport, 1954b; Macrae, Milne, & Bodenhausen, 1994). Why do you think this is?

Consider the following thought experiment. Imagine a far-off planet, Zygon, a place where perceptual mechanisms and inferential strategies have evolved in a decidedly unearthly manner. One day, an inhabitant from Zygon lands her spaceship somewhere on planet Earth and begins her journey into the unknown. She will doubtless be faced with many new objects and life forms that we human beings would, effortlessly, be able to sort into people, buildings, animals, trees and so on. Not so the Zygonian. Devoid of the cognitive know-how to parse this new and complex social landscape into something more intelligible, she would eventually experience information overload. There would simply be too many stimuli to process, at least in any meaningful manner.

This ability to separate our social world into discrete social categories is therefore a vital adaptation that ensures we don't find ourselves in a similarly daunting position. Without it, each person we meet (or each object) would be unique and need to be treated accordingly. Imagine how much time and effort that would take. Stated simply, *categorization favours simplification*, which in turn renders the world a more orderly, predictable and controllable place.

So, having established why categorization is so useful, let's look in more detail at the evidence that it is an *automatic* process. In 1989, Devine published an influential article in which she argued that (1) knowledge about racial stereotypes is culturally shared, even by people who do not endorse such stereotypes, and (2) activation of this knowledge (i.e. stereotype activation) is an automatic process (see Leader in the Field, Patricia Devine). Recall that the criteria for a process to be automatic include that it is unconscious and does not require intention, attention or effort. If stereotype activation is truly automatic, this should mean that any time the appropriate cues are present (e.g. age, race or gender), stereotype activation should *invariably* result. So, how might this be tested empirically? Devine (1989, Study 2) used what is known as

> **priming** activating one stimulus (e.g. bird) facilitates the subsequent processing of another related stimulus (e.g. wing, feather).

a **priming** paradigm (see Bargh & Pietromonaco, 1982). We need to dwell a moment on what priming is and why the priming paradigm is such a useful research tool to enable us to test Devine's hypothesis (and indeed, many other related research questions within social cognition).

When a construct is triggered in memory and made *temporarily accessible*, this is called priming and the stimulus that leads to this construct being triggered is called the prime (Moskowitz, 2005). In concrete terms, priming or activating one stimulus (e.g. horse) facilitates the way in which we subsequently process another related stimulus (e.g. mane, tail) via a process known as *spreading activation* (e.g. Neely, 1977; see Figure 4.2 for a schematic representation of this process).

Once a construct is activated, associated concepts are also triggered and attain a state of heightened **accessibil-**

> **accessibility** the extent to which information is easily located and retrieved.

ity, even if they were not directly primed initially. Such concepts therefore require some kind of cue to render them momentar-

LEADER IN THE FIELD

Patricia Devine (b. 1959) spent her undergraduate years at the State University of New York, graduating in 1981, *summa cum laude*. This was followed by an MA (in 1983) and a PhD (in 1986) from Ohio State University. Devine's research centres around the intrapersonal and interpersonal challenges associated with prejudice in contemporary society. Her early work on the automatic and controlled components of stereotyping (1989) has been extremely influential in the field. Recent research concerns include the relation between explicit and implicit prejudice and the processes that regulate the use of stereotypes.

ily accessible. To use an analogy proposed by Higgins, Bargh, and Lombardi (1985), these concepts are like a battery that is running low but can be recharged in certain circumstances (i.e. when the appropriate environmental trigger is present). It should be noted that other concepts, such as strongly held political beliefs, are often perpetually well charged (aided, for example, by repeated exposure to political arguments in the press, or political debates with like-minded friends). Being in a state of permanently high charge, they are routinely more accessible. These are termed *chronically accessible* concepts (for a detailed review, see Moskowitz, 2005). Here, though, we focus primarily on how priming makes concepts temporarily accessible.

In one measure of accessibility, known as a **lexical decision task**, priming stimuli (e.g. words or pictures) are often presented on a computer, usually very quickly. Participants are then shown a letter string that may or may not be associated with the prime (and may or may not be a real word), and asked to decide if

> **lexical decision task** cognitive measure of how quickly people classify stimuli as real words or nonsense words; quicker responses to certain word categories indicate increased accessibility.

it is a real word or a non-word by pressing one of two computer keys. A priming effect is obtained when participants are shown to respond significantly faster to real words preceded by an associated prime (i.e. are quicker to respond to *wing* after being primed with *bird* than when not primed). The advantage of priming paradigms is that they usually indicate uncontrolled automatic processing. Participants' subsequent reaction times are not influenced by self-presentational strategies (i.e. wanting to show themselves in a certain, often socially desirable, light), as might be the case, say, with paper and pencil measures of stereotyping.

Now that we are clearer about how priming paradigms work and why they are so suited to the study of automatic processes within social cognition, let's return to Devine's work. In her experiment, primes related to a

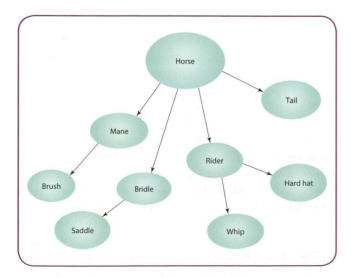

FIGURE 4.2 *Example of spreading activation.*

stereotype were presented outside of participants' conscious awareness. In order to do this, she presented the primes outside of participants' parafoveal field (i.e. out of their direct line of vision). The primes Devine used were terms related to the stereotype associated with black people (i.e. labels such as *blacks*, *niggers*, and physical or trait characteristics including *poor*, *lazy*). The participants had been pre-tested for prejudice level: half were high in prejudice towards black people, whereas half were low. This distinction forms an important part of Devine's experimental hypotheses, as we shall see later. Devine presented some participants with a high proportion (80 per cent) of ethnically associated words, and other participants with a much lower proportion (20 per cent).

Following the prime, in an ostensibly unrelated second experiment, participants read a brief scenario and were asked to form an impression of a target person who engaged in ambiguously hostile behaviours (after a paradigm originally developed by Srull & Wyer, 1980). Why hostile? Because pre-testing had indicated that hostility was a very strong feature of the black stereotype (see also Duncan, 1976). None of the words used in the priming phase, however, were directly related to hostility. This is important, because it suggests that if the prime exerts the predicted effects upon interpretation of the ambiguous behaviour, it is due to automatic stereotype activation rather than simple priming of the hostile construct.

Let's consider what Devine predicted and found. Devine reported that those participants who received the high proportion of ethnic primes rated the target person in the story significantly more negatively (e.g. as more hostile and unfriendly) than did participants who received the low proportion of ethnic primes. Recall that Devine's view is that stereotypes are activated automatically. If this is so, then we should find that participants activate the black stereotype in the priming phase of the study (unconsciously) and go on to use it (without awareness) in the second part of the study (when forming an impression of the target). This should translate into higher ratings of the target as hostile, following a black prime.

What about the differing levels of prejudice among participants? This was a very neat twist: if these results are found in both high- and low-prejudice individuals, it is stronger evidence still that stereotype knowledge is culturally shared and that activation is indeed automatic. If the priming effect can be demonstrated even among individuals who do not endorse the stereotype, this is pretty good evidence that it happened automatically. If low-prejudice participants could have found some way of controlling this rather undesirable response, they surely would have done so, since it is clearly at odds with their beliefs. In fact, Devine found that participants' prior level of prejudice made little difference to how susceptible they were to the ethnic primes (for more on the studies in this paper, see Research Close-Up 4.3).

This study is one of a number that have investigated the so-called automaticity of stereotype activation (see also Banaji & Hardin, 1996; Perdue & Gurtman, 1990). The results seem to provide quite compelling evidence. Moreover, during the 1990s research in this area blossomed and the literature is now replete with evidence of the seeming automaticity of stereotype activation (for recent reviews see Bargh, 1999; Bodenhausen, Todd, & Richeson, 2009; Devine & Monteith, 1999).

So should we conclude that the case for the automaticity of stereotype activation is established beyond question? Perhaps not just yet. The situation regarding automaticity is actually rather complex, and researchers themselves are divided in terms of how it is best interpreted (see Bargh, 1999; Bodenhausen et al., 2009; Devine & Monteith, 1999). Moreover, recent research has provided some important qualifications to the debate, as we shall see later in this chapter. For now, we will note that stereotypes are often automatically activated. The question we now consider is this: once a stereotype category has been activated, what can happen next?

Schemas: The next step in the process?

Several years ago a British national daily newspaper ran an advertising campaign on television. The advertisements featured a skinhead running at speed towards a businessman. Figures 4.3a and 4.3b show two shots in the sequence; what do you think happened next?

Most people, when asked, assumed the next shot showed the skinhead mugging the businessman. He was instead rushing to save him from a large pile of falling bricks (see Figure 4.4).

The newspaper (*The Guardian*) used this example to illustrate its commitment to impartial reporting – the need to get the full picture. Here it serves a useful educational purpose: it potently depicts what can happen once a category has been activated. Why did people jump to this conclusion? The answer lies in the spontaneous **encoding** of the situation. People see the skinhead, readily activate the pertinent skinhead schema (e.g. anarchic, violent) and arrive at the mistaken conclusion that he is probably about to behave aggressively. Encoding refers to how we translate what we see into a suitable format that can be readily stored in our mind (Fiske & Taylor, 1991).

encoding the way in which we translate what we see into a digestible format to be stored in the mind.

This example illustrates that while it may be a useful strategy to leap to the first obvious conclusions when perceiving others, it is not always a sound one. The

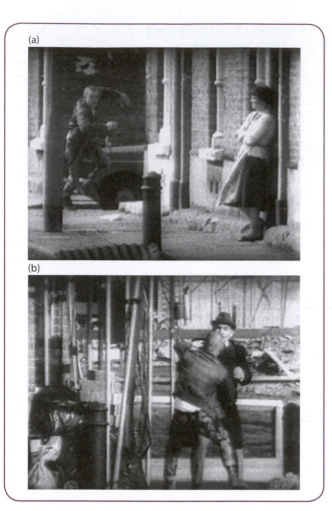

(a)

(b)

FIGURE 4.3(a) and (b) *Two stills of a skinhead in the Guardian advertising campaign.*

Source: © Guardian News & Media Ltd 1986. Reproduced with permission.

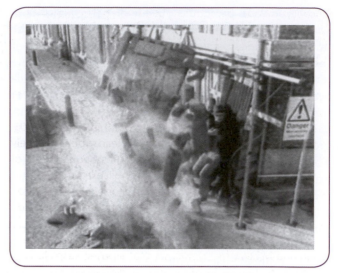

FIGURE 4.4 *Final still of the skinhead in the Guardian campaign.*

Source: © Guardian News & Media Ltd 1986. Reproduced with permission.

behaviour was somewhat *ambiguous*: there are many reasons why a person may be running in the direction of another. The important point is that, in this case, the activated schema *biased the interpretation of the behaviour* in line with the skinhead stereotype.

This tendency has been demonstrated in a number of laboratory experiments (e.g. Correll, Park, Judd, & Wittenbrink, 2002; Duncan, 1976; Payne, 2001). In an example reminiscent of the above real-world scenario, Correll et al. (2002) had participants play a video game in which they were shown photographs of young men in a range of settings (at a train station, in a park). Half were black, half were white. Additionally, half were holding a gun, whereas the other half were holding harmless objects (mobile phone, camera). In the so-called 'Shooter Task' or 'Weapons-Identification Task,' participants had to press a button labelled 'Shoot' if the man in the photo was carrying a gun, or press another button labelled

'Don't shoot' if he was not. They had just half a second to make each decision, so it really was a gut-reaction judgement. Points were awarded or deducted based upon whether participants made the correct judgements. Results showed that participants were most likely to hit 'Shoot' when the person was black, regardless of whether they were holding a gun. This 'Shooter Bias' reveals how accessible schemas can bias the interpretation given to social events, especially when time (and processing capacity) are in short supply. (We now suggest you read Social Psychology Beyond the Lab 4.1 to see how this bias has been demonstrated beyond the laboratory setting.)

Let's now consider the schema topic in more detail. Once we have activated a category stereotype, we bring into play the *knowledge* contained within these structures: our schemas or stereotypes (Brewer, 1988; Fiske & Neuberg, 1990). Schemas are – stated simply – packets of pre-digested information we hold in our heads about objects or people from specific categories: our expectancies about objects or groups. As an illustration, consider the kinds of information that come to mind when the category 'woman' is activated. Such a person might be readily described as kind, gentle, nurturing and home-loving. Or perhaps one might instead consider a subcategory of this broad category, such as 'business woman' (ambitious, assertive, motivated, ruthless, wears designer suits, unpopular with colleagues). Clearly, several different types of information may be discerned, including, for example, knowledge about 'business women' (what they typically do and don't do) and value judgements about them (their likeability, popularity, etc.). However,

SOCIAL PSYCHOLOGY BEYOND THE LAB 4.1

IF THE FACE FITS… HOW JEAN CHARLES DE MENEZES CAME TO BE SHOT DEAD IN ERROR

In the wake of the London terrorist bombings of July 2005, police were following up a number of leads about the likely whereabouts of the bombers. An address found in one of the unexploded bags recovered by police led to close surveillance of a block of flats near to Stockwell tube station in London. At 9.30 a.m., Brazilian-born Jean Charles de Menezes, an electrician, left the building following a call to fix a broken fire alarm. Believing him to be wearing clothing and behaving in a manner that aroused suspicions of his being a suicide bomber, and wanting to avert a further terrorist episode, the police followed him to Stockwell tube station, where he was shot dead. It was subsequently discovered that Menezes was not carrying explosives and indeed was not connected in any way to the terrorist attack. The facts of the case have been the subject of ongoing debate, and inconsistencies in police statements have never been entirely resolved. Subsequent information suggests that the police may have jumped to conclusions based on the potential match between Menezes and the Muslim terrorists. The Menezes shooting highlights how schema use (here based upon physical appearance, clothing and behaviour) can have tragic consequences.

a schema should not be misconstrued as a long list of separate unrelated items and attributes. Rather, it is a cognitive structure within which attributes are organized and relations between them perceived. Thus, we might perceive a relationship between the fact that 'business women' are ambitious and assertive, or perhaps between the observation that they are ruthless and not very popular (see Figure 4.5 for an illustration of such a schema).

So, a schema contains many different kinds of knowledge about a particular category. Armed with this knowledge, the process of impression formation is greatly facilitated, because schemas affect how quickly we perceive, notice and interpret available information (Fiske & Taylor, 1991; Kunda, 1999). We are apt to rely upon schemas for a number of reasons. Table 4.1 summarizes some of the main ones (from Fiske and Taylor, 1991).

In the following section we broaden the topic of cognitive shortcuts still further to see how other kinds of heuristic schematic processing can affect the judgements and decisions we make about others when there may be demands on our information processing capacities.

Table 4.1 *When do we rely upon schemas?*

Role schemas (that imply jobs or tasks people do) may dominate over traits (role schemas are more informative because they are richer and imply more associations)

Subtype schemas (business woman) may be used more than superordinate ones (woman) because they allow us to reconcile information that contradicts the broader superordinate level schema (women at work whose assertive behaviour contradicts their gender role may be viewed as business women)

Information presented early on can cue schemas (primacy) that help organize subsequent information

We use schemas that attract our attention (salience) because they set a person apart such as a male nurse in a ward with otherwise all female staff

We use schemas that have previously been primed (accessibility) because such information comes to mind easily and is readily available to us

We use schemas consistent with our current feelings (mood) because in most cases, our moods seem to cue mood-consistent schemas

We use schemas relevant to controlling our outcomes (power) because status hierarchies affect us whether we are high (leader) or low (minority group) in status

Source: Adapted from Fiske and Taylor (1991) *Social Cognition*, 2nd Edition © The McGraw-Hill Companies, with permission.

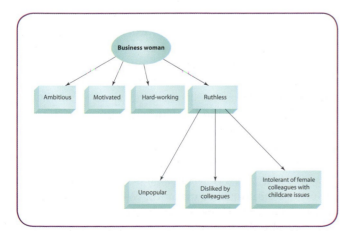

FIGURE 4.5 *Example of business woman schema.*

Making judgements when you don't have all the data: cognitive heuristics

Imagine that you have just started your degree course at a large London University. In your first tutorial meeting with your professor, you are introduced to the other students in your tutor group. One of them, Jez, has a deep tan, sun-bleached tousled locks, and is asking the tutor what facilities there are to store large surfing equipment in his hall of residence. Keen to get to know your fellow students and engage in friendly conversation, you say "Hi Jez. Let me guess . . . Are you maybe from Newquay or some other surfy place in the South West of England?" You base this hypothesis upon your knowledge of the common stereotype for surfers, which Jez seems to fit perfectly. This illustrates what is called the

representativeness heuristic a mental shortcut whereby instances are assigned to categories on the basis of how similar they are to the category in general.

representativeness heuristic, a mental shortcut (rule of thumb) that we use in order to pigeonhole something/someone according to how similar it is to (or how representative it is of) a typical exemplar (here, the surfer stereotype; Kahneman & Tversky, 1972). It is one of several *judgemental heuristics* that allow us to make sense of large amounts of information in a relatively easy way.

Yet, if you had access to the profile of students at this particular university, you would see that students from the South West are not very well represented: most students are drawn from the counties around London. If you were then told this, would you revise your initial opinion of Jez's likely origins? After all, you now know there are probably not that many students from the South West at this university. This information about the frequency of certain categories in the general popu-

base rate information information that gives us an idea about how frequent certain categories are in the general population.

lation is called **base rate information**. If you were to give it due weight in your decision-making process, you might conclude that your original assumption was perhaps a bit hasty. The trouble is, and as decades of research have shown (see Gilovich and Savitsky, 2002), when we are faced with base rate information and seemingly conflicting exemplars, we often fail to take account of base rate information and are more influenced by representativeness information.

We don't only rely upon the representativeness heuristic when taking judgemental shortcuts. Say you are asked to estimate how many famous celebrities have succumbed to plastic surgery in the past few years. How would you go about calculating this? Would you, say, look at some comprehensive list compiled of the top one hundred celebrities and then systematically search for

evidence about whether each of them had undergone plastic surgery before you made a cautious estimate? Or would you instead bring to mind (probably with very little trouble) the instances of celebrities whose faces are regularly splashed across the pages of the popular press who are well-known to have gone under the knife (Katie Price, Victoria Beckham, Angelina Jolie, Tom Cruise, Britney Spears, Cher, Tom Jones). And from this would you deduce that it is probably fairly commonplace for celebrities to indulge their desires for cosmetic self-enhancement? If you think you would probably have opted for this second 'quick and dirty' method, then you have just demonstrated for yourself the lure of the **availability heuristic**: you have based your judgement on how easily information comes to mind (Schwarz et al., 1991).

availability heuristic a cognitive shortcut that allows us to draw upon information about how quickly information comes to mind about a particular event, to deduce the frequency or likelihood of that event.

Sometimes it works to our advantage, but at times it can let us down. Say for example that you are asked to guess how many high school students of your daughter's age prefer a particular, popular designer brand of clothing. Without really trying, you bring to mind numerous examples of male and female pre-teens you have seen hanging around in town, or friends of your daughter, all kitted out in hooded tops and sweatpants by this designer. It seems every young person is wearing this gear. From this mental exercise, you may infer that the entire year group is equally addicted to the brand. And when you read in the press how over three quarters of this age group own at least one item of clothing by this designer, you will feel your reliance on the availability heuristic was justified. Students of this age do clearly love this brand!

On the other hand, say you are asked how many women in their twenties are currently having babies. Without hesitation, you bring to mind numerous examples in your workplace of female colleagues in that age bracket who are either pregnant or off on maternity leave. From this you deduce that a high percentage of twenty-something women are reproducing right now. In fact, the higher numbers of women in your workplace are something of a blip that does not correlate that well with a falling birth-rate among this age group in the more general population. On this occasion, then, the availability heuristic has not provided an accurate estimate.

As a final illustration of another cognitive heuristic, imagine you are a judge deciding upon a prison sentence for a defendant who has been accused of rape. Obviously your decision ought to be made based upon a systematic review of the available evidence. What might surprise you, however, is that your decision about how many years the sentence should run for could be very easily influenced by seemingly trivial factors. Say on your journey to the courtroom that day you had passed through roadworks with a series of 20mph speed restrictions punctuating your journey. Could something as random as the temporary accessibility of an arbitrary number affect your decision? Might this number act as some kind of anchor, providing a numerical start point that you will probably not stray too far from when making your sentencing decision?

Englich, Mussweiler, and Strack (2006) tested this idea in a real-life legal setting involving sentencing decisions made by experienced legal professionals. Participating legal experts were shown realistic case materials involving an alleged case of rape and asked to provide their sentencing decision based on their appraisal of the situation. Participants received one of three anchors: in one condition the anchor came from an irrelevant source (a journalist asking about the appropriateness of a certain sentencing decision); in a second condition they were told the anchor had been randomly chosen; and in a third condition, participants themselves randomly decided upon the anchor by the toss of dice. In each case, the anchor was either high (three years) or low (one year). In all three conditions, the anchor constrained sentencing decisions, with participants assimilating their answer in the direction provided by the anchor. For example, in Study 1, participants provided with a high (three years) anchor reached a mean decision length of 33.38 months, whereas those provided with a low (one year) anchor suggested a mean decision length of 25.43 months (see Figure 4.6). Although one might expect

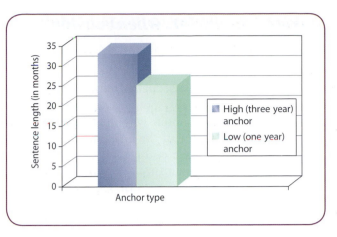

FIGURE 4.6 *Mean sentencing decisions (in months) as a function of different anchors.*

Source: From Englich et al. (2006) with permission from SAGE publications.

(and indeed, hope) that experience and practice would reduce this tendency to be affected by arbitrary anchors, this was not the case. This result neatly illustrates what is known as the **anchoring/adjustment heuristic**. We now suggest you read Social Psychology Beyond the Lab 4.2 to see another demonstration of this cognitive heuristic.

anchoring/adjustment heuristic a cognitive heuristic that makes us place weight upon initial standards/schemas (anchors) and as a result means we may not always adjust sufficiently far from these anchors to provide accurate judgements.

SOCIAL PSYCHOLOGY BEYOND THE LAB 4.2

ANCHORING AND ADJUSTMENT AT WORK IN THE PROPERTY MARKET: MORE THAN JUST A PARLOUR TRICK?

Some researchers have suggested that the anchoring/adjustment heuristic is more likely to occur in lab settings where the information available is impoverished and not terribly realistic (Hogarth, 1981). Anxious to see if the lab findings generalized to more information-rich real-world settings, Northcraft and Neale (1987) asked experts (estate agents) and, for comparison, amateurs (students) to tour real properties that were for sale at the time and make judgements about their fair market value (FMV). As in the lab studies, and indeed reflecting common estate agent practice, all participants received an 'anchor' value in their information packs – here in the form of a guide price – which varied (low, moderately low, moderately high and high). As expected, participants' FMV estimates varied as a function of the guide price they received. For example, if provided with a guide price of $65,900,

estimates were $63,571 for students and $67,811 for estate agents. If the anchor value was higher ($83,900) estimates were $72,196 and $75,190 respectively. This was the case for both the 'experts' and 'amateurs' (although one might comment that the experts' valuations tended to be a little more optimistic and the students' a little more cautious!). The authors concluded that 'decision biases and heuristics are more than just parlour tricks and that they should play an important role in our understanding of everyday decision behaviour' (Northcraft & Neale, 1987, p. 96). Although a more realistic example, this research still provides an anchor, as opposed to letting people generate one for themselves. As we see in the next section, this distinction can have important implications for the prevalence of the anchoring/adjustment heuristic.

Why do we fall prey to judgemental heuristics?

Judgemental heuristics such as these show us how cognitive shortcuts can exert a seductive influence upon our decision-making processes. Social cognition research can tell us a good deal about why they occur, and we will briefly consider some of the main findings here (for detailed reviews, see Fiske & Taylor, 2008; Moskowitz, 2005; Tversky & Kahneman 1974). We will consider each of the three main heuristics in turn: representativeness, availability and anchoring.

The representativeness heuristic is often used because we are unwilling to engage in the kind of effortful processing required to properly factor in base rate information, as noted above. We rely upon a fairly simple similarity judgement (e.g. Jez is more similar to the typical surfing dude than to the typical computer nerd). In addition, we may neglect to take proper account of sample size. In statistics it is well known that estimates drawn from large samples are more reliable than those drawn from small ones, yet we are often happy to make judgements via representativeness even if we base them on just a few exemplars. A third factor that may affect use of the representativeness heuristic is predictive value. When we hear information about a person second-hand, we should really pay heed to the source of that information in terms of its credibility. Imagine you hear a student describe a male housemate she has only just met as 'a bit antisocial', based solely upon his reclusive behaviour during Fresher's Week. Are you less inclined to believe this description is accurate than if you had heard a similar characterization from the housemate's best school friend who had garnered rather more evidence of her male friend's behaviours over several years? Ideally, we would give the second source more weight, but a lot of the time we do not (Fiske & Taylor, 2008). In sum, like much of the material in the first part of this chapter, the representativeness heuristic is another example of our tendency to prefer simple over more complex cognitive deliberations (that is, to behave as **cognitive misers;** Fiske & Taylor, 1991; 2008).

cognitive miser a view of people as being often limited in processing capacity and apt to take shortcuts where possible to make life simple.

Turning to the availability heuristic, it is perhaps best understood by thinking about how easily information springs to mind. If information about the many instances of celebrities choosing plastic surgery pops into our heads with consummate ease, then we may conclude it is probably something that happens an awful lot. That is, we assume that volume of exemplars (*content*) correlates with its *ease of retrieval* (Schwarz et al., 1991). Another possibility is that we simply *feel* that

if information comes to mind easily (or not) then it must say something about how frequent it actually is.

These two explanations (content versus feel) were considered in a study by Schwarz et al. (1991). People were first asked to recall six or twelve assertive behaviours they themselves had engaged in, and then had to judge their own assertiveness. Who do you think rated themselves as more assertive: those who had recalled six behaviours that confirmed this, or those who had to recall twelve behaviours? You might think the answer is easy, and that of course, those who provided more instances of their own assertiveness rated themselves as more assertive, but in fact this was not what was found. Those recalling only six assertive examples rated themselves as more assertive than those recalling twelve examples (by the way, these researchers also collected data on unassertiveness, and found the same pattern of results, such that those providing fewer examples of unassertive behaviour rated themselves as less assertive).

So, what is going on? Well, try this for yourself – how easy do you find listing twelve examples of your own assertive behaviour? The answer is probably 'not very'. You might easily come up with a few at first ('I said no to the extra workload my boss was trying to make me agree to', 'I stood up for a female colleague who was being bullied', 'I intervened when a group of youths were hassling an old lady in the shopping mall'), but you are likely to falter soon after. So, what Schwarz et al. concluded was that it was the difficulty of retrieving examples that drove these effects. If you are struggling to get even four examples of assertive behaviour when you've been instructed to come up with twelve, you may be left thinking you are a pretty unassertive kind of person. What this study neatly shows, therefore, is that the feeling of difficulty/ ease of retrieval can matter as much as absolute numbers (content).

Finally, the anchoring/adjustment heuristic is traditionally thought to occur because of a failure to properly adjust from an irrelevant value that provides an anchor (Tversky & Kahneman, 1974). More recently, though, the debate has broadened out to better understand why adjustments tend to be insufficient (Epley & Gilovich, 2006). Such research looks more closely at the processes that underpin the adjustment phase. Epley and Gilovich (Study 1a) asked participants a series of questions (e.g. "When was Washington elected president?"). Half of the questions were considered to produce self-generated anchors (based on previous research). This means that participants themselves would seek to generate an anchor to help them work out an appropriate answer. For most American citizens, for example, it is possible to provide a reasonable estimate of Washington's election date by adjusting from the date (i.e. anchor) of the

Declaration of Independence in 1776. For the remaining half of the questions, anchors were provided by the experimenter. After providing their answers, participants were told that the questions were intentionally difficult, and to look again at their answers and provide a range that specified what they considered their lowest and highest plausible estimate to be. To clarify this, for the question about Washington, participants had to provide what they felt was the earliest or latest feasible date on which he would have been elected. By comparing initial answers with the ranges subsequently provided, the researchers were able to establish how far participants adjusted from either self-generated or experimenter-provided anchors. Overall, participants faced with a self-generated anchor appeared to search for a plausible estimate, and as soon as they felt it has been reached, they then terminated the adjustment process.

In later studies, Epley and Gilovich went on to show how several different variables influence this adjustment process. Study 2a compared participants who were either high or low in need for cognition (NFC). This individual difference measure assesses the extent to which people are inclined to engage in effortful thinking (see Individual Differences 7.1 in Chapter 7 for further details of the items in this scale). In Study 2b, the researchers compared participants who had or had not consumed alcohol. This variable was of interest because some studies have found that alcohol impairs our ability to process information carefully (e.g. Cunningham, Milne, & Crawford, 2007). Finally, Study 2c looked at the adjustment processes of participants who were or were not cognitively busy (cognitively busy participants were required to rehearse an eight letter string before each question was posed, a task that we know uses up cognitive resources and makes it hard for people to process information systematically; Pendry & Macrae, 1994). Epley and Gilovich (2006) predicted and found that participants would be more reliant on (less inclined to adjust from) self-generated anchors when they were low in NFC, or under the influence of alcohol, or cognitively busy (see Table 4.2 for results from the study that compared participants who were high or low in NFC).

In sum, these results demonstrate that the degree of adjustment-based anchoring biases is influenced by participants' motivation (Study 2a) and ability (Studies 2b and 2c) to continue adjusting from an anchor. The authors conclude that the adjustment process is effortful, and so anything that affects the ability or motivation to expend cognitive effort is likely to reduce the degree of adjustment that occurs (Epley & Gilovich, 2006).

Overall, then, we can see how a range of judgemental heuristics serve to make the job of social information processing a good deal easier. Next we consider some

Table 4.2 *Mean responses to self-generated-anchoring items among participants low and high in need for cognition.*

Question	Anchor	Need for cognition	
		Low	High
Washington elected president	1776	1779.74	1786.36
Second explorer after Columbus	1492	1501.13	1507.37
Boiling point on Mt. Everest (deg F)	212	177.99	171.04
Freezing point of vodka (deg F)	32	14.31	6.09

Note: In each case, those low in need for cognition (that is, those not inclined to engage in more effortful thought) provided estimates closer to self-generated anchors than those high in need for cognition (who were more inclined to think harder and reach a more accurate estimate).

Source: Epley & Gilovich, *Psychological Science*, 17, 311–318, copyright © 2006 Sage. Reprinted by permission of SAGE Publications.

of the consequences of schematic processing for our behaviour.

Schema activation and behaviour

Can we be primed to think, feel or behave in a certain way without even knowing it?

In the late 1990s, a number of articles appeared that demonstrated a very intriguing phenomenon: behavioural responses (e.g. walking slowly) can be automatically activated in response to an activated schema-relevant word (e.g. 'wrinkle'). (We now suggest that you read Research Close-Up 4.1; see also Figure 4.8.)

This same basic effect was subsequently demonstrated using a range of category stereotypes and trait concepts, and showed several behavioural consequences (e.g. performance on intelligence tasks, interpersonal behaviour, memory performance; for a review, see Dijksterhuis & Bargh, 2001; Leader in the Field, John Bargh). The priming methods can vary. For example, Bargh, Chen and Burrows (1996) used a scrambled sentence task to activate the elderly stereotype. Others have used subliminal word priming methods (Dijksterhuis, Aarts, Bargh, & Van Knippenberg, 2000), or have asked people to think/write about typical people of the categories (e.g. professors or secretaries; Dijksterhuis & Van Knippenberg, 1998),

HOW DOES PRIMING AFFECT BEHAVIOUR?

Bargh, J. A., Chen, M., & Burrows, L. (1996). Automaticity of social behavior: Direct effects of trait construct and stereotype activation on action. *Journal of Personality and Social Psychology, 71,* 230–244.

This set of studies builds upon past priming research that demonstrates how a recently activated trait construct or stereotype, in an apparently unrelated context, can persist and exert an unintended effect upon the *interpretation of behaviour*. Here, the authors argue that *behavioural responses* to situations can also occur in response to an activated trait or stereotype prime. This rather disquieting suggestion is somewhat at odds with the prevailing assumption that behavioural responses to the social world are under conscious control. However, the authors reason that behavioural responses can be represented internally, just as are trait concepts and attitudes, and as such they should be capable of being activated automatically when triggering responses from the environment are present.

In three studies, the authors set out to put this hypothesis to the test. Here we focus on Study 2a: *Behavioural effects of activating the elderly stereotype*, in which participants were primed either with the elderly stereotype or with a neutral prime, and their subsequent walking speed was assessed. The authors hypothesized that elderly-primed participants would demonstrate significantly slower walking speeds in comparison to neutral-primed participants.

Design

Thirty male and female students participated in the study, which had a single factor (prime: elderly versus neutral) between-participants design.

Procedure

Participants were first asked to work on a scrambled sentence task under the guise of a language proficiency experiment. For each of 30 items, participants had to use the five words listed to construct a grammatically correct four-word sentence as quickly as possible. This task formed the priming phase, serving to activate (or not) the appropriate stereotype. Hidden within the scrambled sentences were words either relevant to the elderly stereotype (e.g. *grey, bingo, wrinkle*) or neutral, non-age-specific words. Importantly, elderly words associated with slowness (a common elderly stereotypic trait) were excluded from the elderly prime condition. After completing the task, participants were partially debriefed. A second experimenter then covertly recorded the amount of time participants took to walk down the corridor after leaving the laboratory. Finally, participants were fully debriefed.

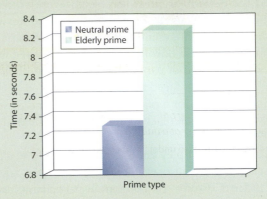

FIGURE 4.7 *Mean time (in seconds) needed to walk down a hallway as a function of prime type.*

Source: From Bargh et al., 1996, Study 2a. Copyright © 1996 by the American Psychological Association. Reproduced with permission. *Journal of Personality and Social Psychology, 71,* 230–244. The use of APA information does not imply endorsement by APA.

Results

After the conclusion of the experiment, participants in the elderly priming condition walked down a hallway more slowly than neutral prime control participants (see Figure 4.7).

Implications

These results, together with data from other studies reported in this article, provided compelling initial evidence in support of the authors' hypothesis. After participants were exposed to an elderly prime, they demonstrated motor behaviour in line with the activated stereotype (i.e. slower walking speeds). Importantly, the authors took care to exclude any references to time or speed in the stimulus materials, so the effect is not simply a result of trait priming. This suggests that the elderly-prime stimulus words instead activated the elderly stereotype in memory.

The take-home message is that social behaviour can be triggered automatically by relevant features of the stimulus environment and can occur without awareness. This finding is qualified somewhat by the observation that such effects only occur if participants have 'walking slowly' as part of their stereotype. It is further constrained by factors such as whether the prime generates behaviour that is relevant/possible in a particular situation (here, walking speed upon leaving the laboratory), and of course, whether a person is actually able to engage in the behaviour (a person with a broken leg and on crutches, for example, may be less affected by such a prime).

This paper spawned a great deal of interest and subsequent research and it remains a classic in this field.

FIGURE 4.8 *Could being primed with a photo of a 'professor' make you perform better at a quiz?*

Source: © Trevor Lush. Used under licence from Getty Images.

LEADER IN THE FIELD

John Bargh (b. 1955) attended the University of Illinois as an undergraduate. He attended graduate school at the University of Michigan, with Robert Zajonc (see Leader in the Field, Chapter 7) as his adviser. In 1981 he was awarded his PhD, and he then worked for several years at New York University. Currently he is at Yale University. He has received many prestigious awards, including the SESP Dissertation Award in 1982 and the APA Early Career Award for contributions to psychology in 1989. His research interests centre on the topic of automaticity and analysis of the unconscious nature of a wide range of psychological phenomena such as attitudes, emotions, motivations and social behaviour.

FIGURE 4.9 *Primes associated with the elderly appear to cue the activation of the elderly stereotype (e.g. walking more slowly).*

Source: © Monkey Business Images. Used under licence from Shutterstock.

or have used photographs of target group members (e.g. punks or accountants; Pendry & Carrick, 2001; Figure 4.8). Moreover, the effect is not confined to stereotype activation. It has been shown to affect trait activation (Macrae & Johnston, 1998; see later in this chapter) and goal activation, as we shall now see (e.g. Holland, Hendriks, & Aarts, 2005; for a recent review, see Dijksterhuis, Chartrand, & Aarts, 2007).

For example, Holland et al. (2005) exposed participants to the recognizable scent of a cleaning product (although they did not know this was happening). The researchers hypothesized that the cleaner smell would increase the accessibility of the concept of cleaning, and that this would guide participants' descriptions of future home activities (goal setting). Participants were asked to list five activities they wanted to do later that day. In the scent condition, 36 per cent listed cleaning as a goal, in comparison to only 11 per cent in the control (no smell) group. The authors suggest that this finding demonstrates that people use accessible representations of behavioural concepts to help them develop an appropriate **goal** (Holland et al., 2005; for a review see Custers & Aarts, 2005). In other words, the cleaner prime promoted the goal of cleaning.

goal a positively valued behavioural end-state that encompasses the purposeful drive/ motivation to engage in a behaviour/action/ judgement.

So, why does it happen? According to Dijksterhuis et al. (2007), a number of concepts may be involved (see Figure 4.5). Initially, we need to either *think* or *perceive* something (e.g. the smell of a cleaning product, reading words associated with elderly; Figure 4.9). This is the *'input'* bit of their model. At the *output* end are what are termed motor programmes (which are what make us walk more slowly). In between input and output are three key elements that are ultimately responsible for the enactment of behaviour: traits, goals and behaviour representations. Nearly all social behaviour is said to be *mediated* by at least one (usually two) of these three variables, which means they are needed for the link between perception and behaviour to occur.

Traits are adjectival terms we use to describe general classes of behaviour. Often they are learned while we are young (Bargh, 2005). Most of us can recall instances where we have been praised by our parents (e.g. for being 'polite' when we remembered to say please and thank you) or chastised by them for rather less positive behaviour (e.g. being called 'naughty' when we drew on the walls of their newly painted bedroom). We are actually extremely quick to infer a trait from an observed behaviour (Winter & Uleman, 1984). As such, traits exert a very strong effect upon social behaviour, much of the time without our being aware of it (Dijksterhuis & Bargh, 2001).

Goals are what make our actions have an enduring purpose and can be described as positively valued behavioural end-states (Custers & Aarts, 2005). We may learn goals from experiencing the consequences of our behaviour (not submitting homework on time and getting a detention can lead us to develop a goal to schedule our work more carefully) or from liking the feeling that accompanies a behavioural endstate ('I like how it feels when I jump on the scales and have lost a few kilos, I'll keep on with my goal of dieting'; for more on goals, see Chapter 6).

The effect of both traits and goals on actual behaviour is mediated by behaviour representations (Dijksterhuis et al., 2007). In the Holland, Hendricks, and Aarts (2005) study, participants primed with the scent of a cleaning product activated the means to achieve the goal: the behaviour representation of cleaning the house. In the Bargh et al. (1996) study, trait concepts probably activated behaviour representations. For example, activating the trait 'slow' probably results in activation of a behaviour representation such as 'linger' or 'dawdle'. Theory Box 4.1 provides a schematic representation of these routes.

The above findings on priming of behaviours and goals may at first seem somewhat surprising, but there is quite a lot of evidence accumulating in support of these results (for recent reviews see Bargh, 2005; Dijksterhuis & Bargh, 2001; Dijksterhuis et al., 2007). Research of this kind provides more evidence for the idea that much of our behaviour can occur without conscious awareness. Later in this chapter, though, we shall see that such effects are not inevitable.

Summary

Thus far we have considered how social information can be activated automatically, and explored some of the consequences of this, in terms of stereotype activation, schemas and reliance on cognitive shortcuts such as heuristics. Taken to an extreme, such research can generate some seemingly pessimistic conclusions about how much we are in control of our person-perception faculties. If so much goes on without our awareness, are we forever at the mercy of our processing frailties? That is certainly one interpretation of this literature, although as we will see, such a view is far from the whole story.

GOING THE EXTRA MILE: REGAINING COGNITIVE CONTROL

What factors allow us to make more careful, considered judgements?

Recently a colleague recounted the following story. He had been introduced at a party to a staff member from another department, Computer Science. He recounted his tale thus: 'When I first saw him I thought, computer nerd! The geeky 70s clothes, the old-fashioned specs, the terrible hairstyle. The kind of guy who drives a Skoda and watches endless episodes of *Star Trek*. But after a few minutes of talking to him, I had to think again. This guy was wild. A real party animal, who drove an Audi TT and enjoyed bungee jumping in his spare time. I couldn't have been more wrong.' This illustration hints at the yawning gap that can exist between our initial category-driven impressions and the reality of what lies beyond. The colleague took the time to get beyond his initial impression. In this section we'll look at when and why, like this colleague, we may go this extra mile.

THEORY BOX 4.1

HOW TRAITS AND GOALS MEDIATE BEHAVIOUR

Perception/ Thought

Traits

Goals

Behaviour representation

Motor programs

Behaviour

Source: Adapted from Dijksterhuis et al., 2007.

Stereotype? What stereotype? How goals can stop the stereotype being activated in the first place

In the wake of early research implying the inevitability of stereotype activation, researchers have documented a number of qualifications to this view. Let's consider an illustration of **implicit goal operation**, whereby implicit goals (linked to perceivers' individual motivation to behave in a certain way) can affect stereotype activation. (We now suggest that you read Research Close-Up 4.2.)

> **implicit goal operation** the process whereby a goal that enables people to regulate responses (e.g. to overcome stereotyping) is engaged without conscious awareness.

The research of Moskowitz et al. (1999) demonstrates how stereotype activation is affected by participants' implicit goals to behave in a certain way that may direct cognitive processing so as to prevent stereotype activation. Further research corroborates this viewpoint. Sassenberg and Moskowitz (2005) approached the notion of implicit goals from a different angle. Rather than looking at how people's chronic goals can effectively eliminate stereotype activation, they illustrated the generality of the 'implicit goals' argument by simply priming goal states. They found that priming participants with implicit goals to be creative disrupted typical stereotypic associations (conventional routes of thinking) and thereby implicitly controlled stereotypic responses.

These and several other studies temper the initially extreme conclusions reached about the inevitability and automaticity of stereotype activation. We now know that a wide range of target and perceiver-related factors can work to moderate stereotype activation. These include processing goals, individual beliefs about prejudice/egalitarianism, and attentional capacity (Lepore & Brown, 1997; Macrae, Bodenhausen, Milne, Thorn, & Castelli, 1997; Moskowitz et al., 1999). Hence, category activation would appear to be **goal dependent** (Bargh, 1994), arising from the interplay of a range of cognitive, motivational and biological factors. In sum, evidence is accumulating that suggests it is sometimes possible to prevent stereotype activation (for more detail see Bargh, 1999; Bodenhausen et al., 2009; Devine & Monteith, 1999; Research Close-Up 4.3).

> **goal dependent** where an outcome is conditional upon a specific goal being in place (e.g. goal-dependent automatic stereotype activation).

Quashing the effects of stereotype activation once it has occurred

Can we prevent automatically activated stereotypes from affecting our judgements?

What happens, though, in those situations in which it is not possible to prevent activation? If stereotype activation happens, and we would really rather it hadn't, what can we do? Most researchers agree that perceivers are able to exercise some degree of choice in their responses towards others (Fiske, 1989), provided they are *aware* of the potential influence of the stereotype, have sufficient *cognitive resources* available to exert control, and are in some way *motivated* not to respond in a stereotypic fashion (Devine & Monteith, 1999). If we fulfil these important criteria, then there are a number of strategies at our disposal.

In this section we consider several theoretical approaches that have furthered our understanding of the processes that may intervene following stereotype activation: Fiske and Neuberg's (1990) continuum model of impression formation; Devine's (1989) dissociation model of stereotyping; research on stereotype suppression (e.g. Macrae, Bodenhausen, Milne, & Jetten, 1994); and moderators of the perception–behaviour link (Dijksterhuis & Bargh, 2001).

Impression formation: the rocky road from category-based to individuated processing When forming impressions of others, we commonly rely upon two sources of information: (1) knowledge of a person's category membership (e.g. female, elderly, as we saw in the work reviewed earlier) and (2) **individuating information**, i.e. details of his or her personal characteristics (e.g. honest, forgetful). The persistent problem facing researchers has been to determine which of these contrasting sources of information contribute to the impressions derived (e.g. Brewer, 1988; Fiske & Neuberg, 1990).

> **individuating information** information about a person's personal characteristics (not normally derived from a particular category membership).

Fiske and Neuberg's (1990) **continuum model of impression formation** provides one detailed answer to this puzzle. This model proposes that perceivers' evaluations of others fall somewhere along a continuum of impression formation, with category-based evaluations anchoring one end of the continuum and individuated responses the other. Constructed upon a number of theoretical premises, the model asserts that: (1) category-based responses have priority, and (2) movement along the continuum, from category-based to individuated responses, is a function of interpretational, motivational and attentional factors (see Leader in the Field, Susan T. Fiske).

> **continuum model of impression formation** views impression formation as a process going from category-based evaluations at one end of the continuum to individuated responses at the other, dependent on the interplay of motivational and attentional factors.

According to the model (and in line with much of the work we have already considered in this chapter), perceivers initially encounter a target and readily categorize him or her as a member of a particular social group. They then consider the personal relevance of the categorized

CAN IMPLICIT GOALS OVERRIDE STEREOTYPE ACTIVATION?

RESEARCH CLOSE-UP 4.2

Moskowitz, G. B., Gollwitzer, P. M., Wasel. W., & Schaal, B. (1999; Study 3). Preconscious control of stereotype activation through chronic egalitarian goals. *Journal of Personality and Social Psychology, 77*, 167–184.

In earlier studies in this paper, Moskowitz et al. demonstrated that there may be an effortless, preconscious form of cognitive control that in certain individuals prevents stereotype activation. Consider two people, Jack and Joe. Both would say they are low-prejudice, but whereas Jack would experience a feeling of incompleteness and self-disappointment upon learning that he had inadvertently acted in a stereotypic manner (and may want to do something about it), for Joe this realization would not be too troubling. Moskowitz et al. (1999) would view Jack as someone who chronically pursues egalitarian goals to be egalitarian, fair, tolerant and open-minded. Joe, on the other hand, would be more of a 'non-chronic egalitarian' in this respect. Do such differences in implicit goal states impact upon stereotype activation? Moskowitz et al. (1999, Study 3) investigated this very question. Methodologically, their design manipulated the length of time between a prime and the presentation of attributes; this is known as Stimulus Onset Asynchrony, or SOA.

Method

Participants

Seventy-eight male students participated in the study, which had a 2 (SOA: short versus long) x 2 (chronicity: chronic versus non-chronic egalitarians) x 2 (prime: men or women in photographs) x 2 (target attributes: stereotype-relevant versus irrelevant). The first two factors were between-participants, the last two were within-participants.

Design and procedure

Participants were classified as chronic or non-chronic based upon responses to measures designed to assess commitment to egalitarian goals (here, with respect to fair treatment for women). In a second phase, participants saw photographs of men or women followed by an attribute, and were asked to pronounce this attribute as fast as possible. The attributes were either relevant to (e.g. 'loving') or irrelevant to (e.g. 'lonely') the stereotype of women, and they were presented either 200ms (short SOA) or 1,500ms (long SOA) after the prime.

Results

Stereotype activation was demonstrated if participants were quicker to respond to stereotype-relevant attributes

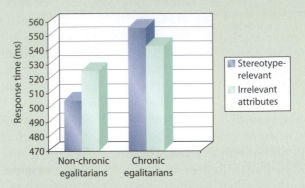

FIGURE 4.10 *Response times (ms) to target attributes at short (200ms) Stimulus Onset Asynchrony.*

Source: From Moskowitz et al., 1999, Study 3. Copyright © 1999 by the American Psychological Association. Reproduced with permission. *Journal of Personality and Social Psychology, 77*, 167–184. The use of APA information does not imply endorsement by APA.

(e.g. loving) following stereotype-relevant primes (e.g. woman). Importantly, only non-chronics showed evidence of such stereotype activation (see extreme left-hand bar in Figure 4.10, which shows faster reaction times to stereotypic words – 504ms – for non-chronics following exposure to stereotypical primes). Participants with chronic goals failed to show this effect (see second bar from right in Figure 4.10, which shows slower reaction times to stereotype-relevant words – 554ms – for chronic egalitarians following exposure to stereotypical primes).

Discussion

These results show that stereotype activation is goal-dependent, because participants who were chronic egalitarians did not show the usual effect of faster responses to category-relevant items after a category relevant prime, whereas non-chronics did show this effect. This lack of activation could not, however, be due to conscious goals exerted on the part of chronics, because the difference between chronics and non-chronics was found even when attributes were presented 200ms after the prime (conscious control is possible only after 600ms have elapsed between the presentation of a prime and a stimulus). This led Moskowitz et al. (1999) to conclude that stereotype activation is not inevitable. For more on how goals affect stereotype control, see Moskowitz and Ignarri (2009).

Table 4.3 *Fiske and Neuberg's (1990) continuum model of impression formation: an illustration of how processing can stop at different stages.*

	Example	Example	Example
Initial categorization	Woman encountered in busy supermarket with a clutch of kids trailing behind: probably a mother *Processing stops here*, target is of no further interest/ perceiver is in a hurry	Person overheard in next office, has high-pitched voice: probably female Perceiver needs to know more (could be new work colleague), looks for more clues	Elderly person who is female called Hilda. Perceiver needs to know more (it's his prospective mother-in-law)
Confirmatory categorization		Person is applying make-up: definitely female Perceiver still not satisfied, processing continues	Hilda enjoys listening to *The Darkness* and visiting her grandchildren: not your average elderly woman; hard to confirm initial categorization as sufficient, perceiver carries on
Recategorization		Wait a minute, she is also carrying a briefcase and a palmtop organizer, so actually she is probably a *business* woman *Processing stops here*, perceiver is satisfied (realizes he will not be working with this business woman); recategorization will suffice	Hilda services her own car and likes spicy curries and flower arranging: defies an obvious recategorization, perceiver probes deeper
Piecemeal integration			This family-loving, elderly woman called Hilda enjoys loud modern music, calmer creative activities, is mechanically minded and thrives on a diet of chicken vindaloo and Bombay potatoes *Processing stops here:* target is not amenable to a categorical impression; perceiver satisfied with impression, although he has an extremely atypical mother-in-law

Source: Reprinted from *Advances in Experimental Social Psychology*, Vol. 23, Fiske & Neuberg, A continuum of impression formation, from category-based to individuating processes, pp. 1–74, Copyright 1990, with permission from Elsevier.

target in the context of currently active concerns and goals. If the target is of little interest (e.g. the perceiver is merely passing a person in a street), then the impression formation process is short-circuited and resulting evaluations are predominantly category-based. If, however, the target is of at least minimal relevance (e.g. the target is an interviewer and the perceiver an interviewee hopeful of securing a new job), attentional resources are allocated to an appraisal of his or her personal attributes, and the protracted journey towards a more individuated impression begins. There are several stages at which processing can stop. An illustration of how this might work in practice in different situations is provided in Table 4.3.

Thus, initial categorization is relatively spontaneous, but the social perceiver will only stop here if the motivation to go further is lacking or if there are pressures (e.g. scarcity of time) conspiring against a more systematic appraisal of the evidence. Research on perceiver motivation and its effects on the impression formation

LEADER IN THE FIELD

Susan T. Fiske (b. 1952) obtained her PhD from Harvard in 1978. After a number of years, first at Carnegie Mellon and then at the University of Massachusetts (Amherst), she moved to Princeton. In the course of her career she has amassed many prestigious awards, including (with Shelley Taylor; see Leader in the Field, Chapter 5) the 2003 Thomas Ostrom Award from the Person Memory Interest Group for work in social cognition. A past president of the American Psychological Society (2002–2003), she has published numerous articles, book chapters and books. Her current research focuses upon how stereotyping, prejudice and discrimination are encouraged or discouraged by social relationships, such as cooperation, competition and power.

process have resulted in the identification of several goals and task objectives that reliably elicit more individuated processing. Among the most important are: (1) **outcome dependency** on a target (participants believe they will later meet the target and work together on a jointly judged task; Neuberg & Fiske, 1987; Pendry & Macrae, 1994); (2) perceiver **accountability** (perceivers believe they will have to justify their responses to a third party, and be held responsible for their impressions; Pendry, 1998; Tetlock, 1983); and (3) accuracy-set instructions (perceivers are instructed to be as accurate as possible; Kruglanski & Freund, 1983).

outcome dependency a motivational objective in which participants believe they will later meet a target and work together on a jointly judged task; shown to lead to less stereotypical target impressions.

accountability a processing goal whereby perceivers believe they will have to justify their responses to a third party and be held responsible for their impressions; this typically leads to less stereotypical impressions.

While differing on a number of counts, these motivational factors all share a common feature: they increase perceiver involvement with the target and encourage more individuated impressions. However, motivation to engage in controlled processing may on its own be insufficient if cognitive resources are depleted. For example, Pendry and Macrae (1994, Study 1) led participants to believe they would meet and interact with Hilda, an elderly female. Half the participants were also made outcome-dependent: they stood to gain £20 for their joint performance with Hilda on a word-puzzle task. The remaining participants would work with Hilda, but their outcome would not depend on her performance. All participants received the same information about Hilda, half of which (12 items) was stereotypic, half of which was counter-stereotypic.

While reading the profile, half the participants performed a resource-depleting concurrent mental task (digit rehearsal); the others simply read the profile. To assess their impressions, all participants were asked to rate six personality traits (three pre-tested as stereotypic and three as counter-stereotypic with respect to elderly females) for how characteristic they were of Hilda. Pendry and Macrae predicted and found that the formation of an individuated impression was contingent upon participants being both motivated (here, by being outcome-dependent) and having full processing capacity (i.e. not being required to rehearse the digits while forming the impression).

In a second study, Pendry and Macrae (1994) sought to establish whether participants who are outcome-dependent rather than outcome-independent devote a greater proportion of their attentional capacity when forming an impression of a target. The idea that motivated perceivers allocate more attention to processing information is a fundamental premise of Fiske and Neuberg's model, although support for it at that time was somewhat limited.

To test this hypothesis, Pendry and Macrae (1994, Study 2) used what is called a **probe reaction task** (PRT; see Bargh, 1982). Participants were instructed to optimize their performance on the impression formation task and to use their remaining attentional capacity to respond to a probe stimulus that was presented

probe reaction task a simple reaction-time task that assesses attention left over from performing the primary task; does not take away attention from the primary task (i.e. is not resource-depleting).

in addition to the main task (i.e. turning off a randomly illuminated light bulb icon that appeared several times on a computer screen while the impression task was being performed). Importantly, this probe reaction task was not a method of resource depletion (like the digit rehearsal task). That is, its purpose was not to divert attentional resources away from the primary impression formation task and make the process harder. Rather, it assessed what attention was not being used in the primary task (i.e. how much attention was left over). If more involving motivational goals do entail greater attention to the target, then we should expect that participants under these conditions would have less attention left over to switch off the light bulb quickly. This translates into slower reaction times on this measure for outcome-dependent participants. This is indeed what the study found (see Figure 4.11).

This research provides evidence for the view that motivated involvement with a target can lead to more controlled processing (and hence less stereotypic impressions; Neuberg & Fiske, 1987). More than this, it suggests that the extent to which we are able to go beyond initial, category-based impressions will be dependent upon the interplay between motivational and attentional factors. In sum, once attention is depleted, our ability to systematically process information about others, even if we are motivated to do so, may be diminished (for more on this topic, see Fiske, Lin, & Neuberg, 1999; Gawronski, Ehrenberg, Banse, Zukova, & Klauer, 2003).

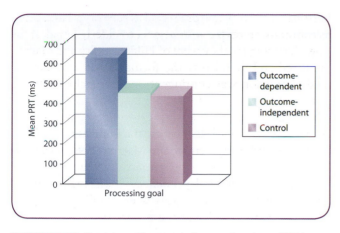

FIGURE 4.11 *Participants' mean probe reaction times (PRTs) (milliseconds) as a function of processing goal.*

Source: From Pendry & Macrae (1994), Study 2, with permission from Elsevier.

Replacing stereotypic thoughts with egalitarian responses As we saw earlier, Devine's (1989) paper provided some initial evidence for the automaticity of stereotype activation. Devine's thesis did not, however, stop there. In her **dissociation model** of stereotyping, she argued that automatic and controlled processes may be dissociated. What this means is that automatic activation of a stereotype does not inevitably lead to stereotypic responding. We now suggest that you read Research Close-Up 4.3, and look at Theory Box 4.2 for a schematic overview of Devine's model.

Later research echoes this general sentiment. For example, Monteith (1993) has shown that

dissociation model proposes that two different processes can occur independently and that one does not inevitably follow from the other (e.g. Devine's proposed dissociation between automatic and controlled processes in stereotyping).

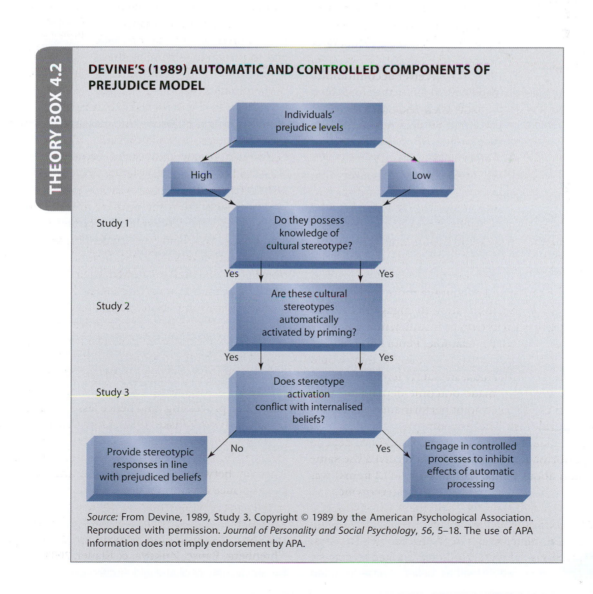

THEORY BOX 4.2

DEVINE'S (1989) AUTOMATIC AND CONTROLLED COMPONENTS OF PREJUDICE MODEL

Individuals' prejudice levels

High   Low

Study 1: Do they possess knowledge of cultural stereotype?   Yes / Yes

Study 2: Are these cultural stereotypes automatically activated by priming?   Yes / Yes

Study 3: Does stereotype activation conflict with internalised beliefs?

No → Provide stereotypic responses in line with prejudiced beliefs

Yes → Engage in controlled processes to inhibit effects of automatic processing

Source: From Devine, 1989, Study 3. Copyright © 1989 by the American Psychological Association. Reproduced with permission. *Journal of Personality and Social Psychology, 56,* 5–18. The use of APA information does not imply endorsement by APA.

WHAT ARE THE AUTOMATIC AND CONTROLLED COMPONENTS OF STEREOTYPES AND PREJUDICE?

RESEARCH CLOSE-UP 4.3

Devine, P. G. (1989, Study 3). Stereotypes and prejudice: Their automatic and controlled components. *Journal of Personality and Social Psychology, 56,* 5–18.

In her first study in this series, Devine demonstrated that all participants, whether high or low in prejudice, were equally knowledgeable of the cultural stereotype of black individuals. The second study demonstrated that when participants' ability to consciously monitor stereotype activation was prevented, all participants responded in line with the activated stereotype (as we saw earlier). However, Devine's theoretical model proposes a dissociation between automatic and controlled processes. In essence, this means that once a stereotype has been activated automatically, a stereotypic response is not inevitable. When participants have time and motivation to correct for initially stereotypic thoughts, they will do so. Later in the paper (Study 3) she set out to demonstrate this.

Method

Participants

The design involved a simple one-way comparison between participants low versus high on prejudice. Sixty-seven white students took part in the study. Participants were divided into high-prejudice ($N = 34$) and low-prejudice ($N = 33$) groups based on a median split of scores on the Modern Racism Scale (MRS; McConahay et al., 1981).

Design and procedure

Participants were run in small groups. First, they were asked to list as many alternative labels as possible for the social group black Americans (to include slang terms). This served to activate participants' cognitive representations of black people. Following the label-generation task, they were asked to list their honest thoughts about the racial group of black people, under anonymous conditions. Afterwards, they completed the seven-item MRS.

Results

The proportion of pejorative and non-pejorative labels arising from the label-generation task was computed for each participant. A comparison between high- and low-prejudice participants revealed no significant differences in terms of the proportion of pejorative labels generated in the first phase. Then the researchers coded participants' responses to the thought-listing task in terms of valence (positive or negative) and whether the thought concerned a belief about the group or was instead a trait description. Thus, four different kinds of thoughts were coded (positive trait, negative trait, positive belief, negative belief). Examples of positive traits included 'brothers' and 'Afro Americans', whereas negative traits covered terms such as 'coons' and 'spear-chuckers'. For responses coded instead as 'beliefs', these included

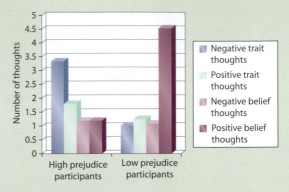

FIGURE 4.12 *Thought listing (labels used to describe African Americans) by High and Low prejudice participants.*

Source: From Devine, 1989, Study 3. Copyright © 1989 by the American Psychological Association. Reproduced with permission. *Journal of Personality and Social Psychology, 56,* 5–18. The use of APA information does not imply endorsement by APA.

'Affirmative action will restore historical inequalities' (positive) and 'Blacks are free loaders' (negative).

Analyses of the frequencies of different types of thoughts listed by participants revealed that high-prejudice participants more often listed negative traits than each of the other three types of thoughts (which did not differ from each other). However, low-prejudice participants listed positive belief thoughts more often than the other three types of thoughts (which did not differ from each other). These results can be seen in Figure 4.12.

Discussion

This study demonstrated that low-prejudice participants were able to provide non-stereotypic and egalitarian descriptions about black people, because in this more deliberate thought-listing paradigm, participants were more inclined to think carefully about what they said, and how this would fit with their prejudice-relevant self-concepts. As such, they produced very few pejorative thoughts. Devine would argue that this shows that these participants overcame the automatically activated stereotype and replaced it with thoughts more in keeping with their nonprejudiced beliefs. As such, Study 3 appears to qualify the rather pessimistic conclusions highlighted by the first two studies in the paper.

It should be noted, though, that subsequent research has questioned some of the conclusions drawn from this research (see Lepore & Brown, 1997). Whilst later research has qualified some of the original findings, this remains an extremely influential and widely cited paper in the field.

when people are committed to being non-prejudiced and their behaviour appears to violate these standards, they feel guilty, become self-focused (direct attention towards the self) and direct their efforts at reducing this discrepancy to ensure it does not happen again. Hence, Monteith (1993) found that low-prejudice participants provided unfavourable (i.e. non-stereotypic) evaluations of jokes about gay people, but only if they had been made to realize that in an earlier phase of the experiment they had (without realizing it) acted in a prejudiced fashion. Research of this nature relies upon classifying participants based upon their scores on a prejudice scale which is constructed so as to minimize social desirability effects (e.g. Modern Racism Scale: McConahay, Hardee, & Batts, 1981).

What research of this kind demonstrates is that it is possible to regulate stereotypic responding if (1) we are aware of the possibility of unconscious prejudicial influence, (2) we are sufficiently motivated (here, by virtue of a desire to appear unprejudiced), and (3) we have the required time available to do so (see Macrae & Bodenhausen, 2000). There are several issues of note here. For example, we may not always be aware of the unfelt influence of the stereotype (Bargh, 1999; Wilson & Brekke, 1994). Also, as we have seen, time or processing capacity limitations can impede even the most motivated perceiver (Pendry & Macrae, 1994). It is possible, too, that even if we are motivated to control stereotypic reactions, attempts at control can backfire for an altogether different reason, as we shall now see.

Stereotype suppression: pushing the unwanted thought out of mind (if not always out of sight)

Imagine you have just encountered an elderly woman in the supermarket. She looms large as you enter the fruit and vegetable aisle, thwarting your speedy passage to secure an aubergine by inconveniently standing right in front of you, consulting her shopping list. 'Dithery old biddy, it must be pension day!', you catch yourself thinking, and then you chastise yourself. You think, 'I really must stop this, she is no more in my way than anyone else, she is just rather older than most'. You try to banish such stereotypic thoughts and proceed to the dairy aisle. There, you encounter another elderly female. She is also in your way, but this time she's carefully weighing up the prices of different cheeses as you wait to extricate the last packet of Parmesan from the depleted shelf above her. How do you react to this second elderly female? Are you successfully able to suppress the elderly stereotype?

There has been a great deal of interest in precisely this topic: does **stereotype suppression** work? The research was

stereotype suppression the act of trying to prevent an activated stereotype from impacting upon one's judgements about a person from a stereotyped group.

stimulated by Wegner's (1994) ironic processes of mental control model. Wegner termed these processes *ironic* because they result in exactly the opposite of what the suppression instructions were intended to achieve (e.g. instructions to suppress stereotyping actually *increase* stereotyping). According to Wegner, when we try to suppress unwanted thoughts, two mental processes result. First, the intentional operating process (IOP) begins to search for thoughts that can serve as distractors (to distract us from thinking about the thing we don't want to think about). Let's use the example of trying not to think about an ex-partner to illustrate these processes, and then relate these to the process of stereotype suppression. What Wegner suggests is that the IOP looks for evidence that you are thinking, not about your ex-partner (unwanted thought), but about other things (the essay that is due in next week, the party invite you have received). At the same time, a second, ironic monitoring process (IMP) kicks in, searching for evidence of the unwanted thoughts (the romantic meals you used to enjoy with your ex, the gifts you received from him or her, the beach holiday you'd planned to take together in the Seychelles). In order to identify these unwanted thoughts, the IMP has to hold at some preconscious level the very thoughts one wants to suppress. Here's the important point: the IOP is a cognitively demanding process. To use the terminology we employed earlier, it entails controlled thinking. However, the IMP is thought to operate in an automatic manner.

So what happens next? Because the IMP (the process that spots signs of suppression failure) can operate in the absence of cognitive resources, it is free to run mental riot even when resources are depleted, constantly searching for signs of failure. To continue the above example, this means it can very easily and repeatedly locate instances of your thinking about the unwanted thought (i.e. your ex-partner, all the good times you had). Recall earlier we learned that constructs that were frequently activated (primed) become more accessible. Well, that is pretty much what is hypothesized to happen here. The unwanted thoughts on which the IMP is focusing receive a healthy dose of priming and, without the IOP, become even more accessible. In other words, a **rebound effect** is demonstrated. Essentially, we end up thinking even *more* about our ex-partner than we would have done had we not been trying

rebound effect where suppression attempts fail; used here to demonstrate how a suppressed stereotype returns to have an even greater impact upon one's judgements about a person from a stereotyped group.

to suppress such thoughts in the first place! The implication for stereotype suppression is that, under certain circumstances, the more people try to suppress stereotypes, the less successful they will be. See Theory Box 4.3 for a summary of this process.

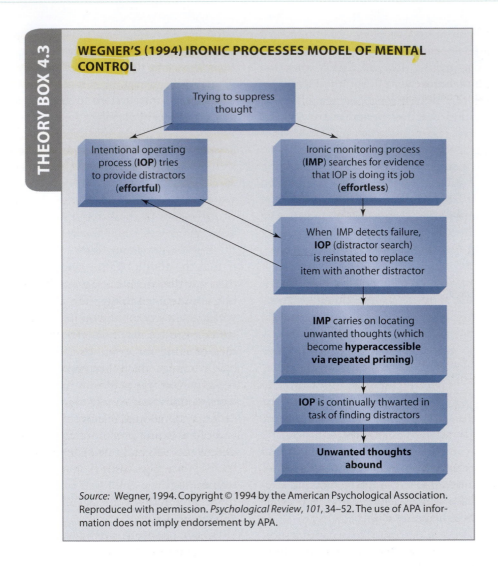

THEORY BOX 4.3

WEGNER'S (1994) IRONIC PROCESSES MODEL OF MENTAL CONTROL

Trying to suppress thought

Intentional operating process (**IOP**) tries to provide distractors (**effortful**)

Ironic monitoring process (**IMP**) searches for evidence that IOP is doing its job (**effortless**)

When IMP detects failure, **IOP** (distractor search) is reinstated to replace item with another distractor

IMP carries on locating unwanted thoughts (which become **hyperaccessible via repeated priming**)

IOP is continually thwarted in task of finding distractors

Unwanted thoughts abound

Source: Wegner, 1994. Copyright © 1994 by the American Psychological Association. Reproduced with permission. *Psychological Review, 101*, 34–52. The use of APA information does not imply endorsement by APA.

Macrae and colleagues (1994) reported a series of experiments that demonstrate this rebound effect. In their first study, participants were asked to write about a day in the life of a skinhead, with a photo as a prompt (the study purportedly investigated people's ability to construct life event details from visual information). Half were told to avoid stereotypic thoughts about skinheads (i.e. suppress stereotype) while writing the passage, half were not. Later, they were shown another skinhead photograph and asked to write a second passage. This time no 'skinhead suppression' instructions were given. The researchers hypothesized that if the 'suppression' participants experienced repeated stereotype priming in the first phase, then they might show evidence of a rebound effect in the second phase. As a result, their passages should be more stereotypic in the second phase. This is indeed what Macrae et al. found (see Figure 4.13).

Two additional studies provide further support for this finding. In a second study, the rebound effect was demonstrated in a different way (behavioural reactions). After participants had initially suppressed (or not) the stereotype of skinheads, they were taken to an adjacent room where they were to meet the skinhead depicted in the photograph. They were led to believe that the skinhead had just stepped out of the room for a moment, and that he had left his belongings on one of the chairs. The authors reasoned that if rebound effects are revealed in overt behaviour, this would manifest itself in 'suppress' participants seeking to maintain a greater social distance from the skinhead. This would result in these participants electing to sit further away from a skinhead's belongings in the second phase than participants who were not instructed to suppress. Results confirmed these predictions.

The final study used a lexical decision task to demonstrate that participants who were suppressing a stereotype about a skinhead later showed faster responses to traits related to the skinhead stereotype. This finding suggests that the initial suppression phase resulted in

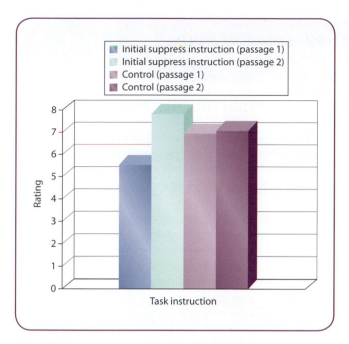

FIGURE 4.13 *Ratings of passage stereotypicality as a function of task instruction.*

Source: From Macrae et al., 1994, Study 1. Copyright © 1994 by the American Psychological Association. Reproduced with permission. *Journal of Personality and Social Psychology, 67,* 808–817. The use of APA information does not imply endorsement by APA.

the stereotype becoming hyperaccessible. Later research developed these preliminary findings, in particular by showing that heightened self-focus (being made aware of oneself, for example by being visible in a mirror or on video camera) can cause suppression to occur in a spontaneous fashion (e.g. Macrae, Bodenhausen, & Milne, 1998; see Leader in the Field, Neil Macrae).

This tendency for suppressed thoughts to return later with greater ferocity is not confined to stereotyping. It has also been demonstrated in other domains, such as the legal setting. For example, in mock juror settings, participants may not appropriately discount a defendant's confession when deciding upon a verdict, even when they have been informed that the confession was coerced, the judge ruled the evidence inadmissible, and, importantly, even when participants report that the evidence has not swayed their decisions (Kassin & Sukel, 1997; for a review, see Steblay, Hosch, Culhane, & McWethy, 2006; for a further example, we now suggest that you read Social Psychology Beyond the Lab 4.3).

Although these results paint a fairly convincing picture, several years and a handful of studies later some caveats are in order that pertain to methodological issues and concerns about external validity (for a review, see Monteith, Sherman, & Devine, 1998). Consider the stereotypes used in these early studies. Skinheads (and in other studies, hairdressers, supermodels and

LEADER IN THE FIELD

Neil Macrae (b. 1963) gained all his qualifications at the University of Aberdeen [BSc (1987), PhD (1990), DSc (2006)]. After working in several universities in the UK and US, he returned to Scotland in 2005, where he is currently Professor of Social Cognition at the University of Aberdeen. Macrae has published widely in the fields of social cognition and social cognitive neuroscience. He has received several prestigious career awards over the years (BPS Spearman Medal, APA Early Career Award, EAESP Jaspars Award, SESP Career Trajectory Award, EAESP Kurt Lewin Award, Royal Society-Wolfson Fellowship) and is a Fellow of the Royal Society of Edinburgh (FRSE). His current research interests focus upon person perception and mental time travel.

construction workers) may not be groups for whom we feel a great need to suppress stereotypes (in comparison to, say, black people, gay people or women). Stereotyping certain groups may not carry the same potential penalties or condemnation. Also, people differ in terms of the extent to which they endorse or avoid stereotyping. Where stereotypes refer to more stigmatized groups about whom people are likely to be less openly prejudiced (e.g. gays), rebound effects are weakened among participants low in prejudice towards this group (e.g. Monteith, Spicer, & Tooman, 1998). However, participants high in prejudice demonstrate the same rebound effects we saw earlier.

Several reasons are advanced for these differences (see Monteith et al., 1998). It may be that people low in prejudice are more motivated to avoid prejudiced reactions (Dunton & Fazio, 1997; see Individual Differences 4.1 for more details on the scale used; Wyer, 2007); or that they are more practised in trying to rid themselves of stereotypic thoughts (Kawakami, Dovidio, Moll, Hermsen, & Russin, 2000). Perhaps they have faster access to replacement (i.e. non-stereotypic) thoughts (e.g. Blair & Banaji, 1996); or they may be more motivated to form individuated impressions of others (e.g. Fiske & Neuberg's, 1990, continuum model mentioned previously). Finally, they may possess a goal state that encourages them to create a particular desirable state of mind (e.g. chronic egalitarian goals, as in the research by Moskowitz et al., 1999, we saw earlier) as opposed to suppressing an unfavourable one (stereotypes).

There is also a cultural qualification that is worth noting. For example, Zhang and Hunt (2008) demonstrated how stereotype rebound effects are less pervasive among Chinese participants, because collectivist cultures such as the Chinese place greater emphasis on inhibiting personal beliefs and on maintaining group harmony, and so are better practised in inhibition (see Chapter 15 for more on cultural influences on social psychology). In sum, the

SOCIAL PSYCHOLOGY BEYOND THE LAB 4.3

STEREOTYPE SUPPRESSION AND REBOUND EFFECTS IN THE COURTROOM

In the courtroom jurors are often instructed to disregard inadmissible evidence, but what impact does this have upon their later judgements? In a study by Peters, Jelicic, and Merckelbach (2006) this question was addressed with respect to stereotype suppression. Dutch participants played the role of mock jurors and were first shown a photo of either a group of immigrant (negative prime) or Dutch (neutral prime) individuals, and under the guise of an unrelated experiment, were asked to rate each face on a sympathy scale. Next they were told that they would be reading a crime story, and half were told they ought not to think of specific stereotypes such as age, race and gender when reading the story (thought suppression condition), whereas the other half were simply told they would be reading a crime story. The story was an article about a group of young people who had acted in a violent manner towards a victim. Their race was never specified. Later, participants had to decide whether statements were either *old*

(they had been in the original article) or *new* (they were not present in the original story). The researchers then looked at the errors in participants' recollections. Peters et al. found that participants who had been primed with the immigrant photograph and instructed to suppress stereotypes made more stereotype consistent recognition errors (that is, they 'remembered' more information in line with the racial stereotype) in comparison to the other conditions. The researchers conclude that forget/suppress instructions can actually foster the creation of false memories. In this case, it seemed to create a rebound effect, such that stereotypical memories were more likely to be found. Although this is still a lab-based study, the implications of this research for real-life legal settings are important. It is often the case that jurors are instructed to disregard statements as 'inadmissible evidence', and this type of research shows quite powerfully how the very instruction to do so can backfire when that information is related to stereotypes.

---

extent to which rebound effects occur is dependent upon a variety of factors – of which only a few could be illustrated here.

The link between social perception and social behaviour is not inevitable Earlier we saw some intriguing demonstrations of the link between stereotype activation (e.g. priming participants with elderly traits) and behaviour (e.g. participants walking more slowly). This seems quite compelling evidence for the inevitability of stereotype activation (and as we saw, the effect extends to trait and goal activation also). Subsequent research has, however, enabled us to paint a more balanced picture. It appears that while this effect does often occur, there are several factors which, when present, modify the typical pattern of results.

Many of the studies demonstrating the automatic effects of schema activation upon behaviour fail to take into account the potentially moderating effect of both factors inside the person (perceivers' motivations and goals) and factors outside the person (characteristics of the environment). Macrae and Johnston's (1998) paper neatly fills this gap. In the first study, participants were either primed (or not) with the construct of helpfulness by means of a scrambled sentence task. That is, for those in the 'helpfulness' prime condition, two thirds of the scrambled sentences contained words associated with helpfulness (e.g. aided,

provided, encouraging). For those in the control condition, these critical 'helpfulness' words were replaced with words that were not associated with helping in any way.

As they were preparing to leave the experimental room to move to an adjacent laboratory, the experimenter dropped her belongings on the floor, including a number of pens. Importantly, in one condition the pens were leaking badly, but in the other condition they were not. What Macrae and Johnston predicted and found was that participants were more likely overall to help following the helpful prime, but only when the pens were normal (helping was high in both help prime and control prime conditions: 93.7 per cent and 68.7 per cent, respectively). But the prime had no effect when the pens were leaky. Apparently, the thought of helping to pick up the pens and getting covered in ink was a strong disincentive to help in both priming conditions (help prime: 6.2 per cent and control prime: 12.5 per cent). In the second study, participants were again primed with the construct of helpfulness. In addition, they were told they were either on time or late. Again, as they got up to leave, the experimenter dropped her belongings, including some pens (none of which was leaking). While participants primed with helpfulness were more inclined to help, this tendency was notably decreased for participants led to believe they were running late. (For additional studies on helping behaviour, see Chapter 10.)

MOTIVATION TO CONTROL PREJUDICED REACTIONS SCALE

Researchers have noted that direct, self-report measures of racial attitudes (such as the Modern Racism Scale, MRS) may not always be a valid assessment of true attitudes. Fazio, Jackson, Dunton, and Williams (1995) noted that for some people completing the MRS, there may exist a motivation to control prejudiced reactions, and that this can affect responses. Dunton and Fazio's (1997) Motivation to Control Prejudiced Reactions Scale sought to isolate and assess the factors that explain such a motivation. The scale items were developed to assess different kinds of motivation. Responses to items are given on a scale of -3 (*strongly disagree*) to +3 (*strongly agree*) with a higher score indicative of a stronger motivation to control prejudice. (Note that items followed by (R) are reverse-scored).

After administering the scale to several samples of undergraduate students, the researchers isolated certain distinct motivational factors. First, some items provided checks on whether participants' reluctance to reveal negative reactions to black individuals was related to a desire to conform to societal norms to not appear prejudiced (see items 1, 6, 12, and 14). Second, some items assessed an internal motivation to control prejudice (that is, a concern with appearing prejudiced to oneself; see items 3, 10, 11, 13, and 15); taken together, these two motivations (whether reflecting a private or public concern with not appearing prejudiced) reflect *'concern with acting prejudiced'*. Finally, since either of the above motivations could be linked to an individual's sensitivity regarding whether certain verbal expressions or behaviour may offend others, several items also assessed one's willingness to refrain from showing thoughts, feelings or behaviour that might offend or lead to dispute (see items 2, 4, 9, and 16). This latter factor therefore reflects *'restraint to avoid dispute'*.

The authors found that the extent to which people are prepared to express racial prejudice was moderated by the extent to which they reported being motivated to avoid prejudiced reactions. As such, this measure provides a useful insight into how prejudicial judgements and behaviours may be controlled.

1. In today's society it is important that one not be perceived as prejudiced in any manner.
2. I always express my thoughts and feelings, regardless of how controversial they might be. (R)
3. I get angry with myself when I have a thought or feeling that might be considered prejudiced.
4. If I were participating in a class discussion and a Black student expressed an opinion with which I disagreed, I would be hesitant to express my own viewpoint.
5. Going through life worrying about whether you might offend someone is just more trouble than it's worth. (R)
6. It's important to me that other people not think I'm prejudiced.
7. I feel it's important to behave according to society's standards.
8. I'm careful not to offend my friends, but I don't worry about offending people I don't know or don't like. (R)
9. I think that it is important to speak one's mind rather than to worry about offending someone. (R)
10. It's never acceptable to express one's prejudices.
11. I feel guilty when I have a negative thought or feeling about a Black person.
12. When speaking to a Black person, it's important to me that he/she not think I'm prejudiced.
13. It bothers me a great deal when I think I've offended someone, so I'm always careful to consider other people's feelings.
14. If I have a prejudiced thought or feeling, I keep it to myself.
15. I would never tell jokes that might offend others.
16. I'm not afraid to tell others what I think, even when I know they disagree with me. (R)
17. If someone who made me uncomfortable sat next to me on a bus, I would not hesitate to move to another seat. (R)

Source: Dunton & Fazio, 1997, with permission from SAGE Publications.

These findings imply that the typical effects of perception upon behaviour are dominated by current processing goals, when the behaviours needed to attain the goals are at odds with those implied perceptually (i.e. even though primed with helpfulness, the costs of being helpful in terms of getting covered in ink or being late serve to override the effects of the prime). Hence, behavioural control is viewed as a battle between activated schemas and various environmental cues and internal goal states either promoting or inhibiting the occurrence of certain action patterns (Shallice, 1988).

The effects of priming on automatic social behaviour seem also to be eliminated when participants' self-focus is increased (for more on effects of self-focus, see Chapter 5). Dijksterhuis, Bargh and Miedema (2000) primed participants with the politician stereotype (or did not). Half were seated in front of a mirror (high self-focus), half were not. Later they were all asked to write an essay about nuclear testing. Pre-testing had established that an aspect of the politician stereotype is that they are notoriously long-winded. Hence, the researchers hypothesized that the politician prime would result in longer essays. This was true, but only for participants in the low self-focus condition. Participants seated in front of a mirror did not show the effect.

So why does self-focus diminish the effects of the prime? The researchers argue that self-focus has been shown to activate what are termed *action tendencies* (Carver & Scheier, 1981). The action tendencies that self-focus can make more salient and accessible are certain norms, behavioural standards and goals. Here self-focus effectively serves to prevent the execution of an undesirable behaviour (being long-winded). Under conditions of self-focus, usual effects of perception on behaviour can be eliminated.

So, the situation regarding the seemingly automatic effects of schema activation upon behaviour is rather more elaborate than was first thought. In many cases, though, the effects of stereotypes and other schemas upon behaviour are far from inevitable (for more on this topic, see Dijksterhuis & Bargh, 2001; Dijksterhuis et al., 2007).

Summary

In this section, we have seen how implicit goals can exert control over stereotype activation. Moreover, we may still be able to rescue the situation even if stereotypes have been activated, provided we are aware of the potential influence of the activated stereotype, are motivated not to stereotype and are cognitively able to do so. So, the picture may be less bleak than we might have feared.

CHAPTER SUMMARY

In this chapter we have given a broad overview of what social cognition research is like, what questions it asks, and what methods it uses to understand how we process social information, and why we sometimes do so quite superficially, and at other times in greater detail.

- *Why is social cognition research important?* Social cognition research has provided us with some important theoretical clues about how we process and organize social information and how we use it in our interactions with and judgements about others.

- *What is the difference between automatic and controlled processes?* Automatic processes are those that occur without intention, effort or awareness and are not expected to interfere with other concurrent cognitive processes. Controlled processes are intentional, under an individual's volitional control, effortful and entail conscious awareness.

- *What are schemas and how do they affect our judgements and behaviour?* Often, stereotype activation can occur automatically. Once a category is activated, we can bring into play the knowledge contained within these structures (schemas). Schemas affect how quickly we perceive and interpret available information, and impact on subsequent processes of judgement and memory. They can also impact upon our behaviour, as shown by research into the perception–behaviour link.

- *What are cognitive heuristics and when do we rely on them in our judgements?* Cognitive heuristics are mental shortcuts that enable us readily to process large amounts of information. Some of the main cognitive heuristics include representativeness (judging something based on how good a fit it is to our expectations about how it should look), availability (judging something based upon how easily information comes to mind) and anchoring/adjustment (generating an initial start point for a judgement and failing to correct appropriately from it). We rely upon such heuristics because they provide speedy and often good enough decisions and thus avoid more effortful processing.

- *Why are goals important in the study of social cognition?* Researchers have demonstrated that perceivers' goals can impact greatly upon the way social information is processed and equally, can be affected by subtle primes that unconsciously activate goal pursuit. For example, implicit goal activation has been shown to affect the degree to which stereotypes are activated, and priming methods (e.g. priming participants with a cleaner smell) can lead participants to activate implicit goals in line with such primes (e.g. to tidy their homes).

- *When and why do we process social information more systematically?* We may, under certain circumstances and if certain goals are in place, process information more systematically. If we do engage in automatic processing, we may nonetheless engage in several strategies to overcome automatically activated constructs (such as stereotypes). For example, we may engage in a more complex appraisal of the available information (individuated impression formation), replace stereotypic thoughts with more egalitarian ones or attempt to suppress the stereotype.

- *What does the field conclude about the automatic/controlled distinction in stereotyping?* Some researchers, such as Bargh (1999), consider that stereotype activation is more inevitable than we might like. Others, like Devine and Monteith (1999), take a more cautious view, arguing that control appears to be possible, at least some of the time. Over time, evidence is accumulating to suggest this latter view is a more appropriate position.

NOTE

Now that you have reached the end of this chapter, you are in a better position to provide answers to some of the questions posed at the beginning. Let's revisit them and then recap on what we have covered.

- Why did I assume that the man at the coffee machine in the boardroom was the company director when he was in fact the secretary?
- Why did I assume that Dr Alex James would be male and white?
- Why is it that I expected Albert to be elderly?

Answers   Automatic stereotype activation or representativeness heuristic. Categories like gender, race and age are readily activated in the presence of a person from or a name associated with these groups; equally, the person in each example possessed characteristics that made you think he or she was representative of a particular category (e.g. the man in the boardroom was wearing a suit, Albert is a name typically associated with older men).

- Why did it surprise me to discover that Hilda, my elderly neighbour, had a passion for car maintenance?

Answer   We used the representativeness heuristic. Other aspects of Hilda's character seemed representative of how most old ladies behave. We expect, and often seek out, information that is consistent with our stereotypes. An elderly female's penchant for wielding the spanner violates our well-established expectancies of what little old ladies typically do.

- Why did I take the time to talk to my new female work colleague and find myself subsequently re-evaluating my initially stereotypic impression of her?

Answer   When we are motivated by a particular goal – for example we need to get along with someone, or because we are low in prejudice towards members of that group – and have the cognitive resources available – we are able to move beyond initial category-based impressions to form more individuated ones.

SUGGESTIONS FOR FURTHER READING

Bargh, J. A. (1999). The cognitive monster: The case against the controllability of automatic stereotype effects. In S. Chaiken & Y. Trope (Eds.), *Dual-process theories in social psychology* (pp. 361–382). New York: Guilford. A spirited and utterly engaging defence of the inevitability of stereotype activation.

Bodenhausen, G. V., Todd, A. R., & Richeson, J. A. (2009). Controlling prejudice and stereotyping: Antecedents, mechanisms, and contexts. In T. D. Nelson (Ed.), *Handbook of prejudice, stereotyping, and discrimination* (pp. 111–135). New York: Psychology Press. A fascinating, engaging and up to date review of the literature surrounding stereotype control.

Custers, R., & Aarts, H. (2005). Beyond priming effects: The role of positive affect and discrepancies in implicit processes of motivation and goal pursuit. In W. Stroebe & M. Hewstone (Eds.), *European review of social psychology* (Vol. 16, pp. 257–300). Hove, UK: Psychology Press. This article develops and considers an interesting framework for understanding the non-conscious activation of goal-directed behaviour.

Devine, P. G., & Monteith, M. J. (1999). Automaticity and control in stereotyping. In S. Chaiken & Y. Trope (Eds.), *Dual-process theories in social psychology* (pp. 339–360). New York: Guilford. A slightly more even-handed debate on the same topic.

Dijksterhuis, A., & Bargh, J. A. (2001). The perception–behavior expressway: Automatic effects of social perception on social behavior. In M. P. Zanna (Ed.), *Advances in experimental social psychology* (Vol. 33, pp. 1–40). San Diego, CA: Academic Press. This chapter brings together much of the recent literature on this topic and attempts to deepen our understanding of the mechanisms that may underlie the effects.

Dijksterhuis, A., Chartrand, T. L., & Aarts, H. (2007). Effects of priming and perception on social behavior and goal pursuit. In J. A. Bargh (Ed.), *Social Psychology and the Unconscious: The Automaticity of Higher Mental Processes* (pp. 51–131). New York: Psychology Press. This chapter develops the ideas outlined in Dijksterhuis and Bargh's (2001) earlier chapter and incorporates more recent work on goal pursuit.

Fiske, S. T., & Taylor, S. E. (1991). *Social cognition* (2nd ed.). New York: McGraw-Hill. This is the classic text on the topic, with extensive coverage of a wide range of issues within the discipline.

Fiske, S. T., & Taylor, S. E. (2008). *Social cognition: From brains to culture* (3rd ed.). New York: McGraw-Hill. An updated version of the above, this text incorporates both the classic ideas and the more contemporary ones that have emerged in the last decade or so.

Kahneman, D. (2011). *Thinking, fast and slow*. New York: Farrar, Straus and Giroux. A readable overview of the Nobel laureate's ground-breaking research on human decision-making, especially the use of cognitive heuristics.

Macrae, C. N., & Bodenhausen, G. V. (2000). Social cognition: Thinking categorically about others. *Annual Review of Psychology, 51*, 93–120. A thorough, readable overview of the literature.

Monteith, M. J., Sherman, J. W., & Devine, P. G. (1998). Suppression as a stereotype control strategy. *Personality and Social Psychology Review, 2*, 63–82. A clear, considered and interesting review of the literature.

Moskowitz, G. B. (2005). *Social cognition: Understanding self and others*. New York: Guilford. Engagingly written and comprehensive in scope.

Moskowitz, G. B. & Ignarri, C. (2009). Implicit volition and stereotype control. In W. Stroebe & M. Hewstone (Eds.), *European Review of Social Psychology* (Vol. 20, pp. 97–145). Hove, UK: Psychology Press. This article reviews work that looks at how the pursuit of goals can elicit control of stereotyping.

5 The Self

CAROLYN C. MORF AND SANDER L. KOOLE

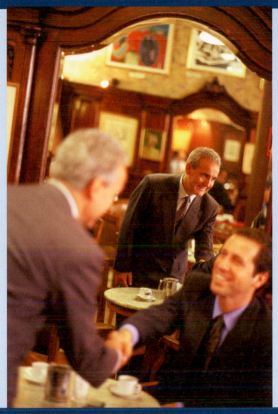

Source: © Terry Vine. Used under licence with Getty Images.

KEY TERMS

- desired selves
- ego depletion
- identity negotiation
- implicit egotism
- implicit self-esteem
- independent versus interdependent self
- introspection
- reflected appraisals
- self-assessment motive

- self-awareness
- self-concept
- self-construals
- self-determination theory
- self-enhancement
- self-esteem
- self-handicapping
- self-perception theory
- self-presentation
- self-reference effect

- self-regulation
- self-schemas
- self-verification
- self-worth contingencies
- social comparison
- sociometer theory
- terror management theory
- working self-concept

CHAPTER OUTLINE

ROUTE MAP OF THE CHAPTER

In this chapter we elaborate theory and research findings regarding the key aspects of the self. Throughout, we focus on the social nature of the self. First, we consider where self-knowledge comes from and explore both its personal and social sources. In tandem, we reflect on the accuracy (or lack thereof) of this self-knowledge. Second, we discuss the organization and content of the self in terms of self-concept and self-esteem and consider how these structures guide our processing of social information – both in general and in the cultural arena in which they transpire. In the third section, we expand on the motives that drive the self to achieve the selves we desire. Fourth, we look at the regulatory functions of the self and how it enables us to pursue our goals and aspirations. The chapter closes by discussing identity negotiation processes and by considering to what extent the self can change.

THE SELF AND ITS SOCIAL NATURE

What makes the self social?

In May 2002 the 13-year-old Christina Long was strangled inside a car in a mall parking lot in Westchester County (Connecticut, US) after having sex with a man nearly twice her age, whom she had met on the Internet. Who was Christina Long? By most outward signs she was a virtuous and well-adjusted person: at her Catholic girls' school, Christina was an honour student, making good grades, and she was popular, serving as co-captain of the cheerleading squad, in addition to being an altar girl. What her family and friends did not know, however, was that Christina also had another life. At night she logged onto the Internet, where she used a provocative screen name (LongToohot4u), flirting and routinely having sex with partners she met in chat rooms. Which was Christina's real self then? The one that came out at night or the one she was during the day? Or, were both selves different sides of her? And if so, how do they fit together?

These are intriguing questions that probably all of us face at one time or another. And even if for most of us the divergences between our self-experiences are not as great as they were for Christina, we are all aware of different aspects of our self in different social contexts (with best friend, with mother, with new date), different moods, and at different times. This highlights a key aspect of the self: the self that is expressed and experienced is highly variable and socially contextualized. The latter means that you develop a sense of who you are through your interactions with others – from your experiences in these interactions, from how others react and respond to you, the values and attitudes you acquire in these interactions, and the meanings you bestow on these experiences.

Thus the self is shaped through an active social construal process. We do not just passively absorb and integrate social feedback, but rather we actively interpret and might even create it. We create our social realities by choosing whom we interact with, the behaviours and demeanour we portray, the clothes and make-up we wear, what we post on Facebook and by selecting the groups we belong to. Although in adolescents there may be some more active experimenting with who one is (deliberately 'trying on' different identities with different people), this construal process is usually subtle and we are not highly cognizant of it most of the time.

Another central theme throughout this chapter is that these self-construals are motivated. We have certain goals for how we want to be and for how we want to be seen by others. Do you want others to think of you as generous, smart and fun-loving? Then you will behave accordingly. You will also avoid doing things that do not fit with how you see yourself and you will feel bad if you slip up and nevertheless do something that clashes with your self-views (such as being nasty to a friend). Nevertheless, you are not unlimited in the self or identity that you can construct – you are limited on the one hand by your biology (e.g. your temperament), and on the other hand by your social experiences (e.g. your early attachment histories, your culture) and the skills and abilities you bring to bear on these experiences.

The self and its diverse expressions thus evolve through 'doing' (behaving and interpreting) in the social world. This is the *agentic* aspect of the self, or what William James (1890, 1950) long ago referred to as the 'I' (see Leader in the Field, William James). It is the active part of the self; the power we have to shape our functioning and life circumstances. But the self is not just a doer; the self also has a 'being' aspect, what James labelled the

> **self-construals** a person's views and knowledge about him- or herself is shaped through an active construal process that plays out in interaction with the social environment. This process is motivated by how one would like to see oneself.

LEADER IN THE FIELD

William James (1842–1910) was an American psychology pioneer and philosopher. Brother of the novelist Henry James, he was born in New York City and received his education from tutors and private schools in the US and Europe. After studying painting and then switching to scientific studies, he finally changed to the Harvard School of Medicine and received his MD in 1869. He never started to practise medicine, but travelled to Germany after finishing his studies in search of a cure for his severe depression. There he got inspired by psychologists and philosophers and decided to become a psychologist. Back at Harvard he started teaching psychology and established the first American psychology laboratory in 1874. He later wrote, 'I never had any philosophic instruction, the first lecture on psychology I ever heard being the first I ever gave' (Perry, R. B., 1948, 1996, p.78). James published his masterwork *The Principles of Psychology* in 1890. His chapter entitled 'The Consciousness of Self', is typically considered the beginning of the modern account of the self in psychology. James foreshadowed in this chapter much of how we conceive of the self today, and the topics he defined still set much of the contemporary research agenda, including the feelings and emotions of the self, the diverse aspects of self, self-esteem, the self-as-knower and known – the I and the Me, and how these two come to work together to create a sense of continuity in the stream of consciousness.

'me'. 'Being' refers to the descriptive or object aspect of the self. These are your beliefs and feelings about yourself – the things you would list, when asked to describe yourself – and your self-esteem. Therefore, another key aspect of the self is that it is an elaborate knowledge and feeling structure – an intricate organized system of beliefs, values, feelings, expectations and goals. This ever-evolving dynamic system emerges through the doing aspect of the self, but it also guides and constrains the construal process (see Morf & Mischel, 2012, for a more detailed discussion). As a result, as James argued, the agent and object, the 'I' and 'me', are inseparable – they come to be known together in the same stream of consciousness. Hence, although we see ourselves as distinct entities and perhaps think of the self as something highly personal, the self is a social construct – formed through our interactions with other people (see Theory Box 5.1).

In this chapter, we elaborate on these key aspects of the self and examine the research findings that support them. We first consider where self-knowledge comes from. We explore both personal (e.g. self-reflection) and social (e.g. social comparisons) sources and reflect on the accuracy of this self-knowledge. Second, we discuss the organization and content of the self – the self as a knowledge and feeling structure – and how this structure guides our processing of social information. In the third section, we expand on the motivational operations in our efforts to construct and maintain our desired selves (e.g. self-enhancement, self-verification). Fourth, we examine the regulatory functions of the self: how the self enables us to plan our actions and pursue our goals and aspirations. Throughout, we also look at cross-cultural differences. The chapter closes with a discussion of identity negotiation processes and by contemplating the question to what degree we are 'hostage' to our selves, or that change may be possible.

WHERE SELF-KNOWLEDGE COMES FROM

How do we know ourselves?

If I ask you who you are, you readily start describing yourself. You probably feel you know who you are and know it better than anyone else. You experience a stable sense of yourself as a distinct being, a person with an identity. But: how do we know ourselves? Where do our selves come from? How accurate is our self-knowledge? This section examines the various forces that shape one's self-knowledge and contribute to our sense of self. These forces can be highly personal; for example, when you self-reflect, observe your own behaviour, or put together your life experiences in meaningful autobiographical stories. But as you will see, to a large extent our selves are shaped interpersonally through experience interacting with others: their judgements about us, the social roles we play, how we compare to other people, and the relationships and cultures we live in. We also examine throughout how well we actually know ourselves. The section ends with a discussion about how we come to experience a unified and coherent sense of self.

Through our own observation: personal sources

Introspection and self-reflection One way to know yourself is to look inward: you reflect on and try to inspect your internal states, both mental and emotional. While this kind of **introspection** perhaps seems like the simplest and most obvious way to achieve self-knowledge – after all, you have access to this information like no

> **introspection** the process by which one observes and examines one's internal states (mental and emotional) for behaving in a certain way.

THEORY BOX 5.1

SELF AND SOCIAL ENVIRONMENT

The self is formed through its interactions with other individuals and groups within the social world, which also contains cultural rules and norms.

Social World

Other System

Other System

Self-System

Source: Adapted and simplified from Morf, Torchetti, & Schürch, 2011.

one else – it turns out to be quite problematic. When people introspect about the reasons for their internal states or behaviours, the information produced is often inaccurate (Wilson & Dunn, 2004). There are a number of reasons for this. One is that, because people are constantly processing lots of information simultaneously, and much of it automatically without conscious awareness, they often are not aware of the most immediate causes of their thoughts or behaviours.

In a now classic study, Wilson and Nisbett (1978) asked female shoppers in a large shopping centre to rate the quality of nylon stockings displayed on a rack – unbeknownst to the participants, the nylons were in fact all identical. The results showed that although female shoppers claimed to have picked which stockings to buy based on softness or workmanship, they in fact simply chose the ones they saw last (see Figure 5.1). Interestingly, people not only do not know how their mind works, they are also rather unaware of being unaware. People seem to make up reasons on the spot for their preferences and actions that simply fit the situation, without realizing that they do not correspond to an internal personal state. For example, in one study participants were shown photograph pairs of women and asked in each to choose the one they found more attractive. Later, when asked to explain the reasons for their choices, they readily gave plausible causes ('she's radiant'; 'I like her earrings'), even though they were on some trials presented with inaccurate information about their choices (i.e. they were shown their less preferred choice) (Johansson, Hall, Sikström, & Olsson, 2005).

Introspection can sometimes even reduce the accuracy of self-knowledge. Many studies show that the more people analyse the reasons for how they feel, the less their attitudes correspond to their behaviours (Wilson, 2002). When it comes to complex choices, such as which room to rent or which plane ticket or car to buy, those who deliberated less during the purchase were later on more satisfied with their purchase, than those who were more analytical (Dijksterhuis, Bos, Nordgren, & Van Baaren, 2006). These findings imply that perhaps those who analysed less had more intuitive access to what they really like or care about – a process that got disrupted by conscious thought.

A second reason why introspection is limited is because people are commonly motivated to keep unwanted thoughts and experiences out of memory or consciousness. These thoughts, however, nevertheless affect their behaviours (see also Chapter 4). Macrae and colleagues (Macrae, Bodenhausen, Milne, & Jetten, 1994) asked participants to avoid stereotypical thinking while writing about a 'skinhead'. Although this thought suppression was successful (the written descriptions contained less stereotypical thoughts, compared to a control group without instructions to suppress), participants' stereotypes still influenced their behaviours in the end. When expecting to meet such an individual, those in the suppression condition sat significantly further away from the seat the 'skinhead' had evidently occupied moments earlier (as seen by the fact that he had left some of his clothes on the chair). This study thus highlights that we have very limited self-insight about those aspects of the self we wish were not true about us.

A third problem, which we will return to later, when discussing the motivational functions of the self, is that people tend to overestimate their positive aspects (Dunning, 2005). Most people think they are better than average – be it on attractiveness, their personality traits, skills or competence, although that is obviously statistically impossible (Alicke & Govorun, 2005). Moreover, a landmark review by Taylor and Brown (1988) concluded that most psychologically healthy individuals harbour a number of positive illusions about the self (see Leader in the Field, Shelley E. Taylor). People entertain not only positive self-illusions of control, of their prospects for success, and of their judgments (Armor & Taylor, 1998; Roese & Olson, 2007). These illusions may be a good thing to some degree, as they help us feel better and thus engage in more active coping (Taylor et al., 1992). However, they will also get in our way, when a more accurate self-view would be helpful, for example when choosing the job or partner that best suits our inclinations, or when self-improvement or self-change would be advantageous (Dunning, Johnson, Ehrlinger, & Kruger, 2003; Robins & Beer, 2001).

Does introspection help us understand our self then? Yes, to some degree: We know what we feel and think, and we can potentially learn more about ourselves that way. Writing about our life experiences seems to help us

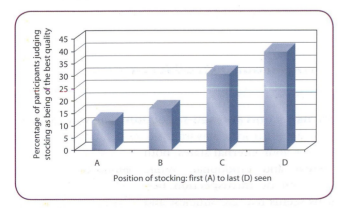

FIGURE 5.1 *Position effects on judgements of the quality of consumer goods (stockings).*

Source: Data from Wilson & Nisbett, 1978; Expt. 2.

LEADER IN THE FIELD

Shelley E. Taylor (b. 1946) received her BA from Connecticut College in 1968 and her PhD from Yale University in 1972. She was Associate Professor at Harvard University until 1979 and then moved to the University of California, Los Angeles, where she is currently Distinguished Professor of Social Psychology. Shelley Taylor's research has made important contributions to several different areas in social psychology. Besides health psychology, social support research and social neuroscience, her work also focuses on social cognition, especially on social comparisons, 'positive illusions' and self-enhancement. Examples of 'positive illusions' are overly positive self-perceptions, illusion of personal control and unrealistic optimism about the future. These illusory beliefs are commonly understood as effects of self-enhancement (i.e. a desire to maximize the positivity of one's self-views) and have been found to be largely beneficial (however, see the section on the *Pros and Cons of Pursuing Self-Esteem* in this chapter for a somewhat contrasting view). Overall her work, for which she has received numerous awards from varied areas in psychology (including the Distinguished Scientist Award of the American Psychological Association), has been dedicated to exploring the socioemotional resources and protective processes that have biological and/or psychological benefits, especially when people have to face stress. Taylor was elected to the American Academy of Arts and Sciences in 2003.

gain better understanding (see Pennebaker & Chung, in press, for a review), as does imagining ourselves in a situation and trying to simulate the emotions we might experience then (e.g. Carver & Scheier, 1981; Fazio, Chen, McDonel, & Sherman, 1982). On the other hand, as we saw, because we tend to try to push certain experiences away, and because we cannot consciously attend to everything we process, introspection provides very limited self-knowledge, especially when it comes to *why* we think or feel something.

Self-perception theory To the extent that internal states are ambiguous or difficult to interpret, Bem's

self-perception theory the theory assumes that when inner states are ambiguous, people can infer these states by observing their own behaviour.

self-perception theory (1972) suggests that people can infer these states by observing their own behaviour – just as we would as outside observers. Have you ever noticed after the fact, for example, that you suddenly started doing something you previously thought was not really of interest to you, like going to the gym or watching football on TV? And you then concluded that it must be more important and more enjoyable to you after all. Or, you may suddenly find yourself smiling and whistling to yourself after a big presentation in a seminar class, only to conclude that you are very relieved and therefore must have been much more stressed by it than you had previously realized. When making these inferences, we also take into account the conditions under which the

behaviour occurs, and we only attribute behaviour to internal states if the situation alone seems insufficient to have caused the behaviour (see also Chapter 3). For example, you will not assume you love cleaning your room if your roommate obliges you to do it. The fact that we take account of situational pressures, including rewards and punishments, points to a very important application of self-perception theory, when it comes to motivation.

People can engage in activities for either extrinsic (praise, esteem, money) or intrinsic (interest, challenge, enjoyment) reasons. Extrinsically motivated activities are ones we do as a means to an end – in order to obtain tangible rewards or to avoid punishment (like cleaning your room). In contrast, intrinsically motivated activities are things like hobbies, where we do them for the sake of the activity itself – for the fun of it. For example, if you are a student who is intrinsically motivated, you will write day and night on your term paper, and on weekends, just because you are interested in the topic, even when you know the paper already fulfils the minimum requirements. But the question now is: what happens if you get very high marks or your term paper is highly praised by your professor? Common sense might suggest that this should enhance your motivation. Self-perception theory, however, predicts the danger of an overjustification effect: The intrinsic motivation may diminish, because the activity has become associated with an external reward (see also Chapter 7). You may stop writing on weekends, or entirely stop working more than necessary. The reward has undermined your motivation. Many studies have confirmed this overjustification effect in both children and adults and in many settings (Deci & Ryan, 1985; Lepper & Greene, 1978).

This creates a serious dilemma: how do we – as teachers, parents, employers – manage this trade-off between intrinsic and extrinsic rewards in order to keep people motivated? A crucial factor seems to be how the reward is perceived. A key issue is that it is perceived as sincere and non-coercive. As such, rewards tend to work better if they are in the form of verbal praise, are unexpected, come as a surprise afterwards, and are seen as a special 'bonus' for superior performance (Covington, 2000; Eisenberger & Cameron, 1996; Henderlong & Lepper, 2002). Trying to foster intrinsic motivation is important not only because it makes activities more enjoyable and people are more likely to perform them, but also because it tends to increase the quality of the work. A study by Amabile (1996) had art experts rate art works and found that artists' commissioned work was judged to be of lesser quality than their non-commissioned work. An implication of this research is that paying children for good grades, although it is widely practised by some parents, may be quite problematic, at least for those who are already highly intrinsically motivated. This is because the financial reward risks replacing intrinsic motivation (doing things for the pleasure of doing them) with extrinsic motivation (doing things to get concrete rewards).

In sum, just like introspection, self-perception has its limits also and for some of the same reasons. Many factors contribute to our behaviour, and it is easy to become confused about which are the most important. We sometimes underestimate less obvious situational factors and other times overestimate them. As noted previously, lots of information processing is done automatically without conscious awareness, thus it makes sense that we often misattribute the causes to that information that most readily springs to mind (see Chapter 4 on the availability heuristic).

Through the help of others: social sources

A primary source of self-knowledge comes from other people. We learn a great deal about ourselves through observing how other people react toward us or from what they directly tell us, as well as from comparing ourselves and our views with those of others.

Attachment processes and social appraisal The first relationship we have in life is with our primary caregiver, usually our mother. Our very first sense of who we are begins to develop through these earliest interactions in infancy. According to attachment theory (see also Chapter 11), we come to learn about our lovability and worth, as we experience how our mother cares for us and responds to our needs (Bowlby, 1969). Caregiving that is consistent and appropriately responsive to the infants' needs plants the seeds for a positive self-concept; whereas caregiving that is neglectful and unresponsive, or even abusive, teaches children that they are not worthy and that others cannot be trusted (Hazan & Shaver, 1994). This can be the foundation for a negative self-concept and low self-esteem. These early so-called 'working models' of both self and others (our expectations about how they are likely to behave toward us) become a lens through which we interpret and react to other people's responses throughout our lives (Hazan & Shaver, 1987).

The rudiments of the self thus develop through these early attachment processes even before we have conscious self-awareness. Later in life, we internalize other people's appraisals of us through more cognitively reflected processes. The sociologist Charles Horton Cooley (1902) suggested that other people's reactions to us serve as a mirror in which we see ourselves. He called this the 'looking-glass self': Through observing others' reactions, you imagine how they perceive and judge you. These reflected appraisals are then internalized into your self-concept and guide future behaviour. If you think others think well of you, you too will have a positive view of yourself and act accordingly. Mead (1934) added that most of what we know about the self comes from taking on the perspective of what he called the 'generalized other' – a combination of perspectives of all others involved in the activity. This idea that we learn who we are through seeing ourselves through the eyes of others has been tested in many studies, but has been found to be only partially correct (see Tice & Wallace, 2003, for a review). While it is true that people see themselves the way they *believe* that other people see them, research shows that there is usually not a good match with others' *actual* evaluations (Shrauger & Schoeneman, 1979).

Why is it that our own self-views are often quite different from the views our family members or friends have of us? Apparently, this is because we have limited ability to detect accurately how other people view us – especially when these views differ from our own (see Kenny & DePaulo, 1993, for a review). One reason for this is that others are not always straightforward: they will often hide their negative assessments so as not to hurt someone's feelings. Another reason is that, as with any theory, we have a confirmation bias. We are more likely to pay attention to instances in which others share and agree with our views, as opposed to when they do not (White, Brockett, & Overstreet, 1993). And finally, even if we do sometimes pick up on discrepant or even negative reactions from others, we are not always receptive to such feedback (Greenwald, 1988). Who wants to know, for example, that others think they are socially inept – lacking in social competences and graces. In general, although we do incorporate some of other people's feedback into our self-views, we are also biased in how we process information about ourselves – hearing what we like and what fits with our own self-conception, while ignoring or rejecting what does not fit. Thus, feedback from others is rarely adopted one-to-one.

Social comparison Another influential source through which the self is actively shaped is through comparing our traits, abilities, or opinions with those of others (see also Chapter 8). If you race down a ski slope in 23 seconds, you have no idea what that means, until you know how it compares with other racers' times. In his theory of **social comparison**, Festinger

reflected appraisals inferences regarding others' appraisals of us that we gain by observing other peoples' reactions towards us.

social comparison a process of comparing oneself with others in order to evaluate one's own abilities and opinions.

(1954) proposed that when people are uncertain of their abilities or opinions – when objective standards are missing – then they evaluate themselves through comparisons with similar others. You will not obtain very useful information about your tennis ability if you compare yourself with Roger Federer (unless you are yourself a pro). Instead, you need to compare yourself with people of the same general ability, or those with similar training and background (Suls, Martin, & Wheeler, 2002; Suls & Wheeler, 2000). Social comparison processes are pervasive, because many facts about the self are such that they carry little information until you use others as a benchmark (Mussweiler, Rüter, & Epstude, 2006).

Indeed, social comparisons seem to be so important that we will use this information even when objective standards are available. We judge our ability to be better if we have a low score that is above average than when we have a high score that is below average (Klein, 1997). We make these comparisons automatically, without thinking and often without being aware of it (Gilbert, Price, & Allan, 1995). Social comparisons sometimes also serve motivational purposes. In this case, we often compare ourselves with others who are better or worse, instead of similar to us. If you want to get better at tennis, then you will compare upward to someone just better enough to inspire you and show you how to reach the next level (Blanton, Buunk, Gibbons, & Kuyper, 1999). Alternatively, if you are feeling really low, because things are not going well for you, you might remind yourself of people who are worse off than you – a downward social comparison, to make yourself feel better (Taylor & Lobel, 1989).

Maintaining, regulating and expanding the self in interpersonal relationships Our sense of who we are is also shaped in more subtle ways through our ongoing interactions with significant relationship partners. This is true even when the other person is not around – we imagine what the other person might say or do, how they would see us. They act like a 'private audience', with whom we carry on internal conversations, or for whom we put on performances (Baldwin & Holmes, 1987). Sometimes we do this explicitly, maybe even arguing with and trying to convince the other person in our minds. But at other times we might not even be aware that these audiences are influencing us. In a study by Baldwin and colleagues (Baldwin, Carrell, & Lopez, 1990), for example, Catholic women were exposed to a subliminal priming procedure. They saw brief flashes of light that, unbeknownst to them, contained images of a disapproving face either of the Pope or of a – to them unknown – psychologist (Robert Zajonc). Subsequently, they evaluated themselves as less moral and more anxious, if they had been exposed to the Pope, as opposed to the unknown

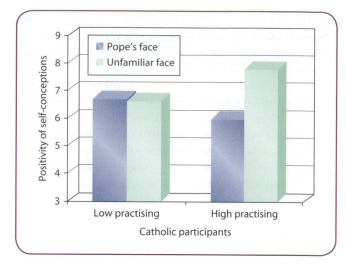

FIGURE 5.2 *Overall self-conceptions as a function of subliminal primed faces.*

Source: Data from Baldwin, Carrell, & Lopez, 1990; Study 2. Reproduced with permission.

psychologist, but *only* if they were practising Catholics (see Figure 5.2). Personally significant others thus shape who we are and our sense of appropriate behaviour.

In interacting with our significant others we develop and store in memory relational schemas – mental models that contain typical interaction and feeling patterns we have, when interacting with the other person (see Baldwin, 1992, for a review). These mental models have far-reaching implications, because they are triggered not only by the specific other person, but also by any feature that reminds one of that person (Andersen & Chen, 2002). So, if a new acquaintance has some resemblance to an earlier important relationship figure in your life like your father, you may start behaving and feeling towards that new person in a similar (positive or negative) way as you did towards your father.

New close relationships not only 'reactivate' old behavioural patterns, they can also contribute to growth by introducing novel features into one's self-knowledge. In a prospective longitudinal study Aron, Paris, and Aron (1995) asked students five times over ten weeks to indicate if they had fallen in love and to make open ended lists of self-descriptive terms (e.g. athletic, outgoing, studious). Students who had recently fallen in love showed increased diversity in their self-descriptions – they literally expanded the self to include features of their new relationship partner in their own self-concepts. Such changes are sustained over time, with people becoming more confused about which traits belong to them and which to their partners (Mashek, Aron, & Boncimino, 2003). In short, together our past and new relationships with significant others in our lives are an important source of who we are.

Social identity People's social identities (see Chapter 14) are an extension of the relational self. We incorporate not only significant others into our self-concepts, but also the social groups we identify with – our gender, ethnicity, religion, profession, political membership and so on. Do you get upset if someone makes a derogatory comment regarding members or practices of your ethnic group? Or do you feel proud when a member of your country wins an international competition? Then these are your social identities. People derive feelings of worth and who they are both from their personal qualities, as well as from associations with the groups they value and to which they attach emotional significance. The focus on social identity emerged in post-World War II Europe driven primarily by the desire to understand the psychological basis of intergroup discrimination (see Tajfel, Jaspars, & Fraser, 1984), but its scope and influence have since reached much beyond that (e.g. Hogg, 2012).

Social identity theory formulated by Tajfel and Turner (1979, 1986) provides a framework about how people connect to their wider social network and derive self-knowledge and meaning from their group memberships. A key assumption is that people have a need for positive social identity and are thus strongly motivated toward contrasting their ingroups (groups to which they feel they belong) favourably with any outgroups (Tajfel & Turner, 1979, 1986). This can have the negative consequence of intergroup discrimination and conflict. On the positive side, however, this raises an ingroup member's self-esteem and can positively shield one from external discrimination if one is of a low-status or otherwise disadvantaged group (Abrams & Hogg, 1988; Rubin & Hewstone, 1998). This may at least partially explain the perhaps surprising finding that many members of low status groups do not display low self-esteem or a negative self-concept (Branscombe, Schmitt, & Harvey, 1999).

Self-categorization theory, which emerged from social identity theory, also divides the world into 'us' and 'them', but does not assume that this is a motivated process, rather simply a fact of life that happens automatically at the perceptual level (Turner, 1985; Turner & Reynolds, 2011). Self-categorization theory is, in a sense, a broader framework than social identity theory, in that it focuses on the shifting between and interplay of both personal and social identity. Personal identity refers to individual trait-like self-attributes which define the individual as a unique person different from other (ingroup) persons (e.g. 'I am generous'). Social identity refers to self-views that define the individual in terms of shared similarities with members of the social groups they care about in contrast to other social groups (e.g. 'we psychologists understand people better than physicists

do') (see also Chapter 14). Sometimes your personal identity is more important, and at other times your social identity is. Self-categorization theory suggests that when your group identity becomes focal, your personal identity decreases in importance – indeed you undergo a 'depersonalization' process, such that you see yourself as highly similar to, in effect as interchangeable with, other group members (Klein, Spears, & Reicher, 2007). When this shift occurs, you will act more in line with your social than your personal identity (e.g. when participating in a group demonstration).

In conclusion, social sources crucially contribute to our self-knowledge – be that from direct feedback in dyadic interactions, our interpretations of how others see us, or our group identifications. Which of his or her many identities is most salient for an individual at any time will vary according to the social context and according to the extent to which a person values each self-view.

Experiencing a coherent self: autobiographical memories and the self as narrative

Has the preceding section left you wondering how it is even possible that we can come to experience a unitary and coherent self, given that it is so diverse in different contexts and highly dependent on social relations? How is it that, despite the fact that we realize that we can be quite a different person in different situations and with different people, we still know it is 'me' and always the same me? There are several mechanisms that allow us to experience a subjectively unified self; they all involve our private thoughts and feelings, and our phenomenological sense of self (i.e. the self we experience).

Autobiographical memories Our autobiographical memories are the recollections of the sequences of events in our lives and how we experienced them (Williams, Conway, & Cohen, 2008). These include lifetime periods, such as your school time, the time you lived at your parents' home, or more specific events, like when you lost an important person in your life, or when you won a competition. These memories shape who we are by connecting the past to the present and giving us a sense of continuity. You may even engage in a kind of 'mental time travel' by imagining the self in the past and experiencing sensory-perceptual details of what it was like then (Conway, 2005). Some memories are more vivid than others, and those are remembered more readily. For example, many 'first-time' experiences are vivid – your first kiss, the first time you travelled to a foreign country on your own, or when you moved into your

FIGURE 5.3 *Many people can remember where they were, what they did and felt, when Princess Diana died.*

Source: © Pictures of London. Used under licence from Alamy.

own apartment. We also have so-called 'flash-bulb' memories, like a vivid snapshot of a moment or circumstance in which something highly emotional happened (Brown & Kulik, 1977), when we remember where we were and what exactly we were doing at the time. Many people, for example, can remember where they were, what they did and felt, when Princess Diana died (Figure 5.3); most of us have similar memories for when we heard about 9/11, or saw it on TV.

Autobiographical memories may be more or less accurate, most likely containing a little of both: objective accuracy as well as biased reconstruction (Ross & Sicoly, 1979). Just like any other information about the self, we revise it in line with our self-concept and often to reflect favourably on us. The more vivid the memory, the more resistant it is to forgetting. The good news is that for most of us our positive memories in general are more vivid and thus more resistant to forgetting; while negative memories fade faster (D'Argembeau, Comblain, & Van der Linden, 2003). This is even more true for people with high self-esteem, although the reverse is true for depressives (Blaney, 1986).

Self as narrative People weave together these autobiographical memories in stories they tell about themselves and their lives. They construct these self-narratives to make meaning out of the events they experience, to integrate their goals, make sense of conflict, and to explain how and why they change over time (McAdams, 2008a). Like any story, these life narratives have *settings, scenes, characters, plots* and *dominant themes*. Perhaps unlike a story though, they have no predetermined storyline or ending; they are ever evolving – being changed and/or redirected as we move through life. As such, they are very subjective and highly selective, as the meanings and values attributed to scenes are dependent on the individual him- or herself and the culture in which he or she lives. Although two stories are never alike, there are some common dominant themes. McAdams's research finds that American narratives often involve redemption – successfully overcoming a negative event in one's life (McAdams, 2008b). A typical example would be the redemptive life story of Oprah Winfrey: 'I grew up a little Negro child who felt so unloved and so isolated – the emotion I felt most as a child was loneliness – and now the exact opposite has occurred for me in adulthood' (p. 24). Stories such as these in general enable people to feel satisfied and content with their lives.

Across cultures, stories take on somewhat different 'flavours'. Asian narratives, for example, tend to be less self-focused. In one study, when asked to recall 20 autobiographical memories, stories of European American adults turned out to be more those of individual experiences – their own role and emotions in the events. In contrast, the Chinese participants reported more social and historical events and they focused on the social interactions and significant others in the stories (Wang & Conway, 2004). This difference is not surprising, as it reflects the differences between the cultural norms of both societies (see also Chapter 15). We can conclude that autobiographical narratives are shaped by the cultural norms in which individuals' lives are situated and from which they derive meaning for their lives.

Together, both autobiographical memories and self-narratives show the role of construal in the social self: the stories we create about ourselves are ultimately who we are – a point we will come back to throughout this chapter. In constructing this self-knowledge, we rely both on self-reflection processes and also on our more subjective experiences of self. The latter may be particularly important in gaining a sense of coherence and continuity in our selves (Conway, Singer, & Tagini, 2004).

Summary

The self is shaped and known through multiple sources: personal, relational, and social. Introspection and self-perception both are personal sources that involve reflecting on the self. Introspection entails trying to look inward to gain access to your inner thoughts and feelings, whereas self-perception involves observing and drawing inferences from your behaviours. But information gained through personal sources is often highly inaccurate due to both errors in information processing and motivational biases. Interpersonally we learn about ourselves by observing how other people, especially our significant others, react toward us. We use these reactions like a mirror in which we can see ourselves. This mirror too, however, is distorted – our perceptions of others' views of us, and how they really view us, do not match up very well. Another important source of self-knowledge comes through social comparisons and through our belonging to social groups. Of course, the results of these evaluations depend on the people we compare or associate ourselves with – thus this knowledge too is biased.

Together, all these sources highlight the active construal aspect of the self. Self-processes are highly subjective (and not always very accurate). In this sense, the self is neither fictional, nor true, but rather constructed within constraints. It is also highly variable and context dependent. But there exists a phenomenological sense of continuity.

THE ORGANIZATIONAL FUNCTION OF THE SELF: THE SELF AS MENTAL REPRESENTATION

How is the self represented in the mind?

So far we have spoken about where self-knowledge comes from and how we come to know who we are. But what is the nature of this self-knowledge? Where and what is the raw material of our self-knowledge? What kind of information does it contain and how is it organized? In essence, whereas the development and expressions of our selves take place mostly in the social arena, the raw material of the self is represented and organized in our minds. In this section, we discuss two types of represented self-knowledge: the cognitive representation in the self-concept, and the affective evaluation of the self – our self-esteem. We also consider cultural differences in content and organization of self-knowledge, and current work by neuroscientists examining the brain activities that underlie self-related processing of information.

The nature of the self-concept

Our **self-concept** involves a network of beliefs we have about ourselves. It is a collection of the content of our self-experiences, including our characteristics, our social roles, our values, goals, and even our fears – everything we use when asked to describe who we are.

> **self-concept** the cognitive representation of our self-knowledge consisting of a sum total of all beliefs we have about ourselves. It gives coherence and meaning to one's experience, including one's relations to other people.

Self-schemas and information processing The elements of our self-concept, the specific beliefs by which we define ourselves, are our **self-schemas**. Self-schemas are mental structures that help us organize past experiences and guide the processing of new self-relevant information. The concept was introduced in a landmark paper by Markus (1977), in which she showed that having a particular self-schema in some domain (e.g. extraversion, independence) will affect how we deal with information in important ways (see Leader in the Field, Hazel R. Markus). In one study she had people rate themselves on a number of attributes related to the dimensions of independence–dependence (e.g. individualistic–conforming, assertive–submissive) and also state how important each aspect was to their self-definition. She identified participants as being 'schematic' (i.e. having a self-schema) on independence or dependence if they considered the related terms as highly descriptive and important to their self-concept. People who rated

> **self-schemas** mental structures that help us organize and guide the processing of self-related information.

 LEADER IN THE FIELD

Hazel R. Markus (b. 1949) was born in London, England and received her BA in Psychology from California State University at San Diego in 1970 and a PhD in Psychology from the University of Michigan (Ann Arbor) in 1975, where she then worked as Assistant Professor, Associate Professor and Professor of Psychology until 1994. Currently she is the Davis-Brack Professor in the Behavioral Sciences at Stanford University. Her research focuses on the socio-cultural shaping of self. A significant contribution of Hazel Markus to social psychology was the introduction of the concept of 'self-schema' that she describes as the cognitive representation of the self that organizes self-knowledge and guides self-relevant information-processing. She is also a pioneer in the research on how cultural contexts (e.g. ethnicity, race, gender, social class) shape and reflect emotions, cognitions and motivations of individuals, with a particular interest in self-relevant processes (see the section on *Cultural Influences on Self-Knowledge* later in this chapter). She has received numerous awards for her work, including the Distinguished Scientist Award of the American Psychological Association. Markus was elected to the American Academy of Arts and Sciences in 1994.

the terms as not particularly descriptive or unimportant to their self-concepts were considered 'aschematic'. The latter people appear to lack a self-schema on that dimension.

In another laboratory session a few weeks later, Markus found that schematic participants judged schema-congruent traits as true or not true of themselves much more quickly and more confidently than did aschematics. Schematics also more easily remembered past behaviours consistent with the trait, and were more likely to reject new information that contradicted their self-view. So, if being sociable is central to your self-concept, you are quick to decide that going out with lots of people describes you and staying home reading a book does not; you will also easily recall many instances when you were the centre of attention, and you will not believe someone who tells you that you are shy. Thus we process information that is relevant to our self-concept quickly and we remember it well.

The reason for this is one of the most basic and widely researched phenomena in the self-concept literature: the **self-reference effect** (Higgins & Bargh, 1987; Klein & Kihlstrom, 1986; Kuiper & Rogers, 1979). This refers to the fact that information related to the self is processed more thoroughly and more deeply, and thus recalled better, than other information. Initial studies on the effect (Rogers, Kuiper, & Kirker, 1977) asked participants to make different types of judgements about trait adjectives, for example their structural properties (small or large font?), their semantic meaning (does x mean the same as y?), or their self-descriptiveness (does it describe you?). Later on, participants were given a surprise recall test asking them to remember as many of the original words as possible. As you probably guessed, findings showed the self-reference effect (see Figure 5.4): participants remembered best those adjectives for which they had rated their self-descriptiveness relative to those for which they had made other types of judgements. The implication is that to the extent that you personalize how you understand or memorize things and events around you, the more you will elaborate on them and the easier they will be to remember. This is true even if you do not agree with them. Even if participants denied the trait-descriptiveness of an adjective (i.e. said 'no' to the question whether the trait described them), they recalled it better later on.

The self-reference effect illustrates that the self is, so to speak, your home base from the position of which everything else is assessed and classified. Not surprisingly then, our self-schemas also play an important role in how we process information about other people. When judging someone else's performance, we often

> **self-reference effect** the tendency to process and remember self-related information better than other information.

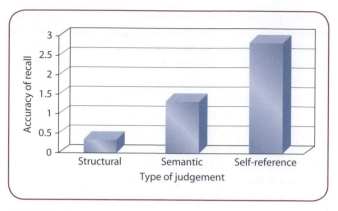

FIGURE 5.4 *Accuracy of recall as a function of type of judgement task.*

Source: Data from Rogers, Kuiper, & Kirker, 1977; Exp 1. Copyright © 1977 by the American Psychological Association. Reproduced with permission. *Journal of Personality and Social Psychology, 35,* 677–688. The use of APA information does not imply endorsement by APA.

spontaneously compare it with our own (Dunning & Hayes, 1996). Or in judging other people's personalities, we do so according to their similarity or dissimilarity to our own (Dunning & McElwee, 1995; Dunning, Perie, & Story, 1991). How do you decide how studious or how athletic someone else is? By comparing them with your own studiousness or athleticism (Dunning & Cohen, 1992). Moreover, your most valued traits are also the most important in judging other people (Lewicki, 1983). If generosity and open-mindedness are aspects you value highly in yourself, you will also notice and pay attention to these dimensions (or lack thereof) in others and judge them accordingly.

Active versus stored self-schemas No doubt then, our self-concept is at the centre of how we process everything that transpires around us. But not all of our mass of self-knowledge is active all of the time. In any situation, only a smaller subset is directly relevant and thus activated to guide our behaviour. This is called the **working self-concept** (Markus & Kunda, 1986). When you are at a party, for example, your easy-going, jolly and maybe wild side of the self may be activated; whereas when meeting with your professor, your intellectual, conscientious and more restrained self comes out. This is similar to when you Google information on the web – only a subset of information becomes available for use, that which is relevant to your current search term. This highlights the importance of the working self-concept, because, once activated, it is what determines your behaviour, rather than the full self-concept, or any other aspect of yourself, even an

> **working self-concept** subset of relevant self-knowledge that is activated and guides our behaviour in a given situation.

important one, if it is not currently 'turned on'. A crucial question therefore, to which a great deal of current research is devoted, is what turns on certain aspects of the self for different people at different times and in different situations.

Some factors are determined by the situational context and are similar for most people. For example, if someone has a religious side, it is more likely to be activated in church than in an amusement park. Another important general situational factor is distinctiveness: if something sets you apart, or makes you unique, in your immediate environment, then this aspect of yourself is more likely to become activated. For example, a friend recently went to what she thought was a mixed gender sauna (Figure 5.5), only to discover one man after another coming in (she had mistakenly gone into the men's sauna). She became acutely aware of herself as a woman, and her gender became more important to her self-concept than it usually would (and certainly more than if she had been in a group of all women). McGuire and colleagues' (McGuire & McGuire, 1988; McGuire, McGuire, & Cheever, 1986) research programme testing distinctiveness theory showed that the spontaneous self-concepts of children typically consist of attributes which are uncommon or unique in

their social environment. For example, age is more salient for children who are younger than their classmates, or ethnicity if they are from a minority group within the school.

In addition to these more general aspects of situations, there are also large individual differences, as to which parts of the self-concept are activated in response to which situational cues. This depends on which domains are especially important to an individual. Imagine, for example, the following scenario in an experiment conducted by Downey and Feldman (1996). After a short initial task with another participant, you are informed by the experimenter that the other participant does not want to continue with the second part. How do you react to this event? In the study, some participants simply assumed the other must have run out of time; others, however, felt upset and assumed they were the reason for the other person's departure. These latter participants were individuals high on rejection sensitivity – people for whom fear of being rejected is a highly salient theme in their self-concept, and this aspect thus became activated in the current ambiguous situation (see Figure 5.6). Their rejection sensitivity, however, did not become activated when the situation was unambiguous; for example, when the experimenter informed participants that they had run out of time to complete the second half of the study (control condition). Altogether, what these studies on the power of the working self-concept show is that our sense of who we are is dramatically shaped by the current situation, but also influences our interpretation of it.

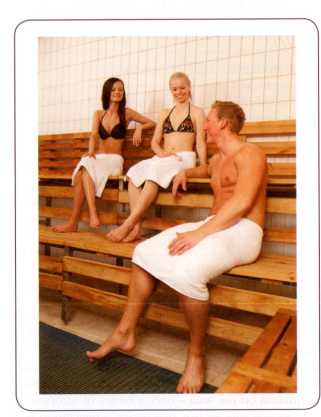

FIGURE 5.5 *In some situations, for example finding yourself in an opposite-gender-only sauna, your gender may become more important to your self-concept than it usually would.*

Source: © Tyler Olson. Used under licence from Shutterstock.

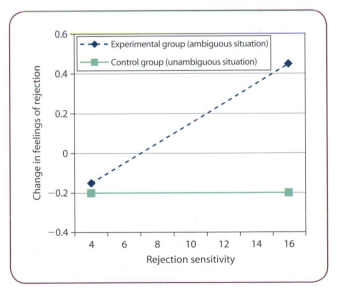

FIGURE 5.6 *Change in feelings of rejection from pre-interaction to post-manipulation as a function of rejection sensitivity and experimental condition.*

Source: From Downey & Feldman, 1996; Expt. 2. Copyright © 1996 by the American Psychological Association. Reproduced with permission. *Journal of Personality and Social Psychology, 70,* 1327–1343. The use of APA information does not imply endorsement by APA.

Actual, ideal and possible selves Thus far we have talked only about self-beliefs that we hold about ourselves in the present. Our self-concepts also include, however, our **desired selves**: our goals, our hopes and fears, our ideals and standards. What are the selves you imagine for yourself in the future? What are your ideas for what you would like to become, or are afraid of becoming and want to avoid? These are your possible selves (Markus & Nurius, 1986). They exert a motivational function – perhaps you are studying, because you have a future image of yourself as a career counsellor, or perhaps you watch your diet to avoid becoming fat. Other types of desired self-schemas are ideal and ought selves (Higgins, 1987; Higgins, Klein, & Strauman, 1985). In contrast to your actual self – who you truly believe you currently are – the ideal self represents your (or your significant others') wishes and hopes for how you would like to be. Our ought selves refer to those aspects we (or our significant others) feel it is our duty or obligation to meet. Discrepancies between our actual and our ideal or ought selves have been shown to have implications for a person's emotional and motivational experiences (Higgins, Bond, Klein, & Strauman, 1986; Strauman, 1992; Strauman & Higgins, 1988; see Theory Box 5.2). Ideal selves motivate us to work actively to attain our aspirations, and when we fall short of achieving them, we experience sadness, disappointment and depression. When we, for example, fail an examination which we had very much hoped to pass, we might feel disappointed and depressed. By contrast,

> **desired selves** contain our potential (possible selves), as well as the wishes and aspirations (ideal self), and the duties and obligations (ought self) that we, or significant others, hold for us.

our ought selves motivate us to avoid negative outcomes (e.g. punishment), and we feel anxiety, guilt and worry to the extent that we fail to meet our duties and obligations. When we, for example, did not help a friend or stranger in a situation in which we think we ought to have helped morally, we might feel guilty about that.

Implicit and explicit self-knowledge A final important distinction is that while some of the knowledge in our self-concept is explicit or conscious, a lot of it is implicit – that means, outside of awareness. Explicit self-beliefs come about through reflection or deliberate thought process, and these beliefs are thus controllable. Implicit aspects of the self, in contrast, are beliefs about ourselves that are below our awareness. As a result, they are much less controllable and more automatic than explicit self-beliefs (Devos, Huynh, & Banaji, 2012). Despite this automaticity, however, implicit self-knowledge is neither necessarily more accurate nor more authentic (Nosek, Greenwald, & Banaji, 2007). The two are different aspects of the same self-system that conjointly influence our thoughts, emotions and behaviours.

Together, our actual, our possible, and our desired (ideal or ought) selves – be they implicit or explicit – as well as the discrepancies between them, affect how we evaluate and feel about our 'now' selves. This is expressed in our self-esteem – the topic to which we turn next.

The nature of self-esteem

In addition to these more cognitive representations of who we are, or have the potential to become, our self-knowledge also contains an overall evaluation or

THEORY BOX 5.2

SELF AND SOCIAL ENVIRONMENT

Affective consequences of discrepancies between actual and ideal or ought self-guides.

Source: Based on Vieth et al., 2003.

appraisal of ourselves. How good a person do you think you are? How proud or embarrassed are you about some of your characteristics? This overall evaluation about how we feel about our qualities and self-worth is our

self-esteem the overall evaluation that we have of ourselves along a positive–negative dimension.

self-esteem. Some people are higher in self-esteem than others, which means that they see themselves in more strongly positive terms and have fewer negative self-views (e.g. see Leary & MacDonald, 2003, for a review). They also are more confident that they will be able to succeed at their goals and are more optimistic that things will generally go their way. In contrast, people with low self-esteem see themselves in less positive ways and are more doubtful about their abilities and qualities. On one hand these overall general self-evaluations are the sum total of how you feel about yourself in a variety of domains – from appearance to particular accomplishments (e.g. in school or athleticism), to social abilities (e.g. Marsh, 1990). At the same time, and equally important, our global feelings of self-esteem direct 'top down' how we feel about our more specific self-views (Brown, Dutton, & Cook, 2001). Thus, a person with high global self-esteem is more likely to see themselves as intelligent, competent, likeable and good looking than someone with lower self-esteem, even when objective evidence suggests they are both equal on those dimensions.

Trait and state self-esteem Trait self-esteem captures how you feel about yourself generally overall and typically most of the time – and, it is what we refer to when we say someone has high or low self-esteem. Individual Differences 5.1 presents a commonly used self-esteem scale to measure these differences between people, both at a trait and state level.

Studies have shown that trait self-esteem remains fairly stable across the life course, despite some general age shifts during stages of development. On average, self-esteem is relatively high in childhood, drops during adolescence (particularly for girls), rises gradually throughout adulthood, then declines again in old age (Robins & Trzesniewski, 2005). These developmental changes notwithstanding, individuals tend to maintain their ordering relative to one another: Individuals who have relatively high self-esteem at one point in time tend to have relatively high self-esteem years later. However, despite the overall long-term stability, just like our self-schemas that are not all always activated at any one time, so too does our momentary experienced self-esteem fluctuate from time to time depending on contextual factors.

State self-esteem refers to these variable self-evaluations that change in response to temporary experiences – successes and failures, interpersonal praise or criticism.

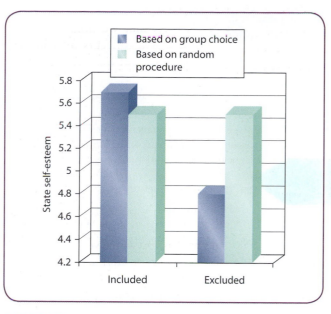

FIGURE 5.7 *Level of state self-esteem as a function of group choice vs. random procedure.*
Source: Data from Leary, Tambor, Terdal, & Downs, 1995; Expt. 3. Reproduced with permission.

Thus, similar to the self-concept more broadly, there are temporary contextual shifts in self-esteem. In an experiment by Leary, Tambor, Terdal, and Downs (1995), for example, some participants learned that they were being excluded from a group task based on personal preferences of the other group members, who had ranked all potential participants based on personal essays. Not surprisingly, these participants experienced decreased state self-esteem in contrast to other participants who had been excluded based on a random procedure justified by the experimenter as needed by the experimental design (see Figure 5.7). In contrast, those who were included for the same reasons showed the opposite pattern: state self-esteem for those included based on group preferences was comparatively somewhat higher than for those who were randomly selected (even if this difference was not statistically significant).

In addition, some people's self-esteem is overall less stable and as a result fluctuates more highly in response to daily experiences (Kernis, Cornell, Sun, Berry, & Harlow, 1993). Self-esteem instability reflects fragile self-esteem and sets people up to experience diminished psychological well-being in a number of ways. People with unstable self-esteem are especially sensitive to and concerned about potential self-esteem threats: they will, for example, react to negative performance feedback with elevated anger, hostility and defensiveness. They also feel less autonomous and less self-determined, and are more likely to experience depressive symptoms in response to hassles (see Kernis & Goldman, 2003, for a review).

INDIVIDUAL DIFFERENCES 5.1

Self-esteem refers to one's overall evaluation of oneself as a person, i.e. more specific assessments concerning one's adequacy in different areas of life are blended into a global judgement. The Rosenberg Self-Esteem Scale (RSES, Rosenberg, 1965), which is characterized by being easy and quick to administer, and having high face-validity (Blascovich & Tomaka, 1991), presents one of the most widely used self-report instruments for measuring self-esteem.

Instruction

Using the scale below, indicate your agreement with each of the following statements.

1 *Strongly disagree*   2 *Disagree*   3 *Agree*   4 *Strongly agree*

1. I feel that I am a person of worth, at least on an equal plane with others.
2. I feel that I have a number of good qualities.
3. All in all, I am inclined to feel that I am a failure.*
4. I am able to do things as well as most other people.
5. I feel I do not have much to be proud of.*
6. I take a positive attitude toward myself.
7. On the whole, I am satisfied with myself.
8. I wish I could have more respect for myself.*
9. I certainly feel useless at times.*
10. At times I think I am no good at all.*

Note: * indicates a reverse-scored item.

The RSES is typically scored using a 4-point format (as shown above), with answers usually coded 1–4, thus resulting in a scale range of 10–40, with higher scores representing higher self-esteem (Blascovich & Tomaka, 1991; although some authors use different scales).

The RSES contains an equal number of positively and negatively worded items. Thus, to determine your score, first reverse the scoring for the five negatively worded items (3, 5, 8, 9 & 10) as follows: 1 = 4, 2 = 3, 3 = 2, 4 = 1. Then add up your scores across the 10 items to see where your total score falls between 10 and 40. There are no discrete cut-off points to delineate high and low self-esteem, but as has been shown in various adolescent and adult samples, mean scores on the RSES are typically somewhat above the midpoint, converging at around 30 (e.g. in an intercultural study, Schmitt & Allik, 2005, obtained a mean value of 30.85, $SD = 4.82$ across 53 nations).

The wording of the RSES as presented above is appropriate when self-esteem is measured as a trait, i.e. a characteristic of one's personality that remains relatively stable over time. However, self-esteem can also be construed as a state, in this case referring to how individuals feel about themselves at a given moment, which must be specified in the item wording. Thus, when self-esteem is conceived of as dynamic and changeable, as opposed to something more constant, question phrasing needs to be adjusted to indicate the point of time referred to ('at the moment', 'right now').

Contingencies of self-worth Which situations matter? Just as individuals differ in which situations activate certain aspects of their self-concepts, they also differ in which life domains are important to their self-esteem. Crocker and colleagues have shown, for example, that for some people their looks are more important, whereas for others their self-esteem hinges more on their academic achievements, and for yet others it may be the approval from others or the relationships with their family members, or alternatively their cultural or religious values (Crocker & Wolfe, 2001). Think for a moment about which setbacks and successes most affect your self-esteem. Your state self-esteem will rise and fall depending on the domains in which you are psychologically most invested – or in other words, those upon which your self-esteem is contingent. Thus, to the degree that you can structure your life such that you can excel in those domains that matter to you, your self-esteem will benefit. Turn to Research close-up 5.1 however, to learn how this was examined in an interesting field study by Crocker, Sommers, and Luhtanen (2002).

Another way to aid your self-esteem may be to try to modify the importance of some of your **self-worth contingencies**. It turns out that more internal contingencies, such as virtue, are associated with less distress than more external contingencies, such as physical appearance or approval from others (Crocker & Luhtanen, 2003). In general, the less your self-esteem depends on attaining specific external outcomes (approval, grades) and the more it can rely on internal reinforcers (interest, autonomy), the more genuine is your self-esteem and the more you will be buffered against setbacks (Deci & Ryan, 1995; Kernis, Lakey, & Heppner, 2008). A final point is that it is best not to stake one's self-worth exclusively on one domain (Linville, 1987). The more one derives one's sense of self-worth from multiple areas, the less one's self-esteem suffers when things are not going well in one domain. For example, in a study on recent relationship break-up, individuals with

> **self-worth contingencies** domains – both internal (e.g. virtue) and external (e.g. power) – on which we stake our self-worth.

CONTINGENCIES OF SELF-WORTH: SELF-WORTH RISES AND FALLS IN RESPONSE TO IMPORTANT LIFE EVENTS

RESEARCH CLOSE-UP 5.1

Crocker, J., Sommers, S. R., & Luhtanen, R. K. (2002). Hopes dashed and dreams fulfilled: Contingencies of self-worth and graduate school admissions. *Personality and Social Psychology Bulletin, 28,* 1275–1286.

Introduction

William James (1890, 1950) proposed that global state self-esteem – our general evaluation of self-worth -- fluctuates around a typical level depending on positive or negative events in domains on which one's self-worth is based. Crocker and colleagues (2002) set out to test this hypothesis in a naturalistic setting involving significant life events that could objectively be classified as successes or failures as they unfolded over time. Specifically, they addressed what this would mean for the self-esteem of senior college students applying for master's and doctoral programmes. Would their self-esteem increase on days they received an acceptance to a graduate school? And would their self-esteem decrease in turn after receiving a rejection, compared to their global self-esteem on days without receiving any decision? And is the boost or decline in self-esteem greater for those students who base their self-esteem more strongly on academic competence? In other words, they assessed the degree to which within-person changes in self-esteem can be linked to specific events in the person's life. They hypothesized that the magnitude of these changes would depend on the importance of the academic domain to the person's self-esteem.

Method

Participants

The participants were 37 college seniors, applying to master's and doctoral programmes. They were recruited through advertisements in the campus newspapers and through electronic mail to the college honours under-graduate mailing list. Participants were paid $50 for their participation.

Design and procedure

At the beginning of the study, participants completed the Rosenberg trait Self-Esteem Scale (Rosenberg, 1965) and the contingency of self-worth measure (Crocker & Wolfe, 2001). The latter distinguishes between eight domains on which people can base their self-esteem (e.g. academic competence, appearance, others' approval, or virtue). An example from the academic domain is: 'My self-esteem gets a boost when I get a good grade on an exam or paper'. Then, for a two-month period, participants completed a web-based questionnaire twice a week on a regular schedule of their own choosing, as well as on any day when they received official notifications from graduate schools. The web-based questionnaire also contained an adapted state version of the Rosenberg Self-Esteem Scale (see Individual Differences 5.1), consisting of 10 items rated on a scale from 1 (*strongly disagree*) to 7 (*strongly agree*), and asking for their self-worth feelings on that day.

This field study had a quasi-experimental design, as there was no random assignment to conditions. It involved a natural manipulation: acceptances versus rejections from graduate schools, which were compared to baseline days (no decision letters). Contingency of self-worth was analysed as a continuous variable from low to high.

Results

Figures 5.8a and 5.8b show the main results. As predicted, students with highly academic contingent self-worth showed a boost of self-esteem on days of acceptance, compared to baseline days (days without a decision), while the self-esteem of students with low academic contingency remained unchanged. Also, as expected, on days of rejection the self-esteem of students with highly academic contingent self-worth decreased more than that of students with low contingency of self-esteem on academics. These fluctuations within people occurred above and beyond large differences between people in overall stable self-esteem.

Discussion

These results show that for those senior students who based their self-esteem strongly on academics, acceptance at or rejection from a graduate school had a stronger impact on their daily self-esteem than for those students whose self-worth was not contingent on academics. Crocker and colleagues (2002) therefore conclude that fluctuations in self-esteem are due, at least in part, to positive and negative events in domains on which people stake their self-worth. Thus, more than a century after William James published his work about the nature of self-esteem, this study provides support for one of his key predictions: while trait self-esteem may remain relatively stable over the life span, there are fluctuations around this typical level reflecting those domains on which one has staked one's self-worth.

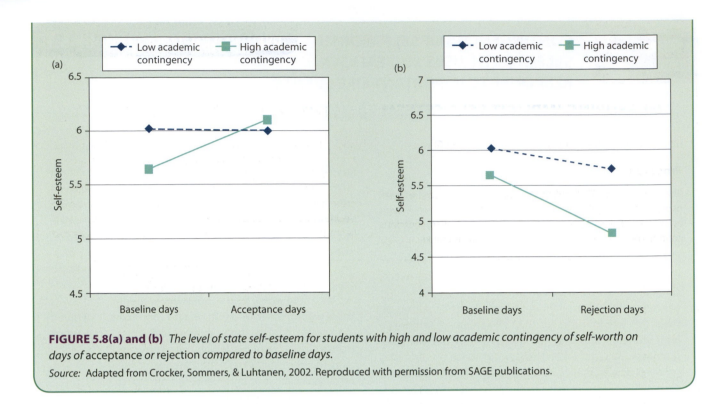

FIGURE 5.8(a) and (b) *The level of state self-esteem for students with high and low academic contingency of self-worth on days of* acceptance *or* rejection *compared to baseline days.*

Source: Adapted from Crocker, Sommers, & Luhtanen, 2002. Reproduced with permission from SAGE publications.

a high number of interrelated self-aspects (self-complexity) experienced much less distress and fewer coping problems than individuals low on self-complexity (Smith & Cohen, 1993).

Implicit and explicit self-esteem Just as self-beliefs come in both explicit and implicit forms, so does self-esteem. We have both conscious and unconscious feelings of positivity or negativity toward ourselves. This is particularly tricky to measure – how does one get information about something that people do not know themselves? This requires rather ingenious methods. One of these is the name-letter effect (Koole, Dijksterhuis, & Van Knippenberg, 2001; Koole & Pelham, 2003; Nuttin, 1985, 1987): To the extent that people have a greater preference for the letters of their own name, more than other people like these letters, the higher is their **implicit**

implicit self-esteem
the positivity of a person's automatic or noncon-scious evaluation of him- or herself.

self-esteem. Another commonly used measure is the implicit asso-ciation test (IAT; Greenwald & Farnham, 2000). See Individual Differences 5.2, which describes this clever method that enables one to measure implicit self-esteem by a timed word-association without the person's awareness.

Some people are consistent in their explicit and implicit self-esteem, others discrepant, such that they have high explicit, but low implicit self-esteem, or vice versa. The case of coexistence of positive explicit and negative implicit feelings about the self is a rather interesting combination, in that it leads people to behave in a 'defensive' manner in order to fend off these negative feelings about the self (e.g. Jordan, Spencer, Zanna, Hoshino-Browne, & Correll, 2003). Individuals with this kind of discrepancy are easily threatened by negative feedback and they will do anything to reduce its impact on the self (Epstein & Morling, 1995). For instance, they might blame the test writer for writing a bad test; they will put down or even aggress against people who outperform them (Bushman & Baumeister, 1998; Morf & Rhodewalt, 1993). Individuals with consist-ent explicit and implicit self-esteem, in contrast, are more secure and have less need to be defensive (Kernis, 2003).

Cultural and gender influences on self-knowledge

In the section on the origins of self-knowledge, we saw how strongly our selves are shaped by our interper-sonal experiences and environments. It will come as no surprise therefore that culture and gender also exert their influence. If you are a person who by heritage or through migration identifies with two (or more) cul-tures yourself, then you know immediately what we mean. Are you one kind of person when with your fam-ily and another when with your friends or at school? Are your two 'selves' compatible, or do they confuse you at

INDIVIDUAL DIFFERENCES 5.2

MEASURING IMPLICIT SELF-ESTEEM WITH THE IMPLICIT ASSOCIATION TEST

(IAT: a full description of the IAT is given in Chapter 6).

Procedure

The self-esteem IAT (Implicit Association Test) measures self-esteem at an implicit level; that is, the test does not require awareness of one's self-esteem and is not subject to conscious control. The basic idea behind the IAT technique is that knowledge about the self has an associative structure. The IAT measures implicit associations between categories of items by assessing how easily those categories are mapped onto each other.

The IAT involves several steps (see Figure 5.9). Participants are presented with words on a computer screen one at a time and must decide as quickly as possible to which of four categories each word belongs by hitting a key on the keyboard. Latencies are measured

Example Step 1

Example Step 2

Example Step 3

Example monitor for Step 4 not shown.

Example Step 5

Step	Category labels	Sample items	Category labels
Step 1: practice block (20 trials)	not me		me
	○	self	●
	●	other	○
Step 2: practice block (20 trials)	unpleasant		pleasant
	○	joy	●
	●	vomit	○
Step 3: practice block (20 trials) critical block (40 trials)	unpleasant or not me		pleasant or me
	○	self	●
	○	joy	●
	●	other	○
	●	vomit	○
Step 4: practice block (20 trials)	me		not me
	●	self	○
	○	other	●
Step 5: practice block (20 trials) critical block (40 trials)	unpleasant or me		pleasant or not me
	●	self	○
	○	joy	●
	○	other	●
	●	vomit	○

FIGURE 5.9 *Categorization tasks for five steps of the self-esteem Implicit Association Test (IAT). Black dots indicate the correct response. The IAT effect is the difference in response times between Steps 3 and 5.*

Source: Copyright © 2000 by the American Psychological Association. Adapted with permission. Greenwald & Farnham (2000). Using the Implicit Association Test to measure self-esteem and self-concept. *Journal of Personality and Social Psychology, 79*, 1022–1038. No further reproduction or distribution is permitted without written permission from the American Psychological Association.

and averaged for each task variation. In the first two steps, participants practise how to categorize two different target concepts ('me' or 'not me' and 'pleasant' or 'unpleasant' attributes) using specific keys. Thus, for example, when the word presented below is 'other', the participant has to press the left key ('not me'), but when the word is 'self' the participant has to press the right key ('me'). The procedure is analogous for unpleasant/pleasant attributes (see Step 2).

Step 3 is the first critical trial. Here participants are asked to map the four categories ('me' and 'not me' targets, 'pleasant' and 'unpleasant' attributes) onto just two responses (these are same keys as they were assigned to in the practice steps: for example 'me + pleasant' to the right key and 'not me + unpleasant' to the left key). Thus, for example, when the word presented below is 'other', the participant has to press the left key ('not me'), but when the word is 'joy', the participant has to press the right key ('pleasant'). The forth step provides practice that reverses the assignments of either the target or attribute concepts learned on Steps 1 and 2 (here shown for 'me' and 'not me' targets). This is followed by the next critical step (Step 5), in which pairings of the categories from Step 3 are switched (e.g. 'me + unpleasant' to the left key and 'not me + pleasant' to the right key). Thus, for example, when the word presented below is 'self', the participant

has to press the left key ('me'), and when the word is 'vomit', the participant also has to press the left key ('unpleasant').

Implicit self-esteem is measured in the form of an IAT effect, computed as the average speed difference between the two critical steps (Step 3 and Step 5). The IAT effect measures how much easier it is for participants to categorize self items with pleasant attributes than self items with unpleasant attributes. Due to the implicit assessment of automatic associations, the IAT makes it extremely difficult, if not impossible, for participants to intentionally control or conceal their self-evaluations.

To try out the IAT for implicit self-esteem (and other implicit measures) for yourself, visit the IAT Project Implicit® homepage, where links to online tests as well as detailed information are provided.

After taking the test, you will be provided with your test score and short feedback labelling your automatic tendency to associate certain categories (e.g. yourself with 'good' versus 'bad') as 'light' 'moderate' or 'strong'. These evaluations are based on speed differences in reaction times to the relevant pairings of categories you exhibited when taking the IAT (see description above). To find out more concerning the interpretation of IAT-results, you may find it helpful to refer to the 'Background and FAQ' section on the Project Implicit homepage.

THEORY BOX 5.3

INDEPENDENT VERSUS INTERDEPENDENT CONCEPTUAL REPRESENTATIONS OF THE SELF

Core concepts (bold **Xs**) are representations of the self that are most elaborated in memory and most accessible when thinking about the self. For those with interdependent self-construals these core concepts are at the intersection between the self and others, whereas for those with independent construals of the self the inner attributes are most important. Xs not shown in bold represent non-core concepts.

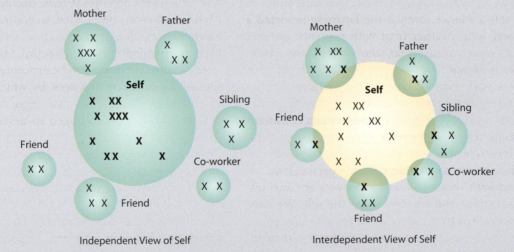

Source: From Markus & Kitayama, 1991. Reproduced with permission from Taylor and Francis.

times, or even seem in conflict with one another? Cultures vary in how similar or different they are in their conceptualizations of the individual and his or her role in society, and thus in the social selves that they encourage (see Chapter 15). These different conceptions of self in turn shape our perceptions of the world, our motivations and our emotional reactions to events (Triandis, 1989, 1995).

Independent versus interdependent selves The most studied contrasting dimension in self-construal first put forward by Markus and Kitayama (1991) involves independence versus interdependence (see Theory Box 5.3, and also Chapter 15). The **independent self**, widespread in the Western world, in particular northwestern Europe and North America, emphasizes autonomy,

independent versus interdependent self while the independent self emphasizes autonomy and individualism and defines the self via internal attributes like traits, an interdependent self stresses the connection to others and defines the self in terms of relationships with others.

individualism, and uniqueness – what makes the self distinct from others. In contrast, the **interdependent self**, more prevalent among East Asians (or other more collectivistic cultures – see Chapter 15) construes the self as fundamentally connected to others and embedded in society, and thus emphasizes relationship harmony and what connects the self to others and groups. When Westerners are asked to describe themselves, they are more likely to use abstract trait adjectives (e.g. smart), whereas East Asians are more likely to describe social relationships or group identities (e.g. college student) (see Trafimow, Triandis, & Goto, 1991).

As you might imagine, self-views for someone with an independent self are more consistent across social contexts than they are for someone with an interdependent self who sees the self in more relational terms (e.g. Choi & Choi, 2002; Tafarodi, Lo, Yamaguchi, Lee, & Katsura, 2004). In one study, Japanese and Americans were asked to fill out twenty sentences beginning with 'I am....' within different contexts (e.g. peer, higher-status partner). This study found that Japanese were less consistent across contexts in their self-descriptions than were Americans (Kanagawa, Cross, & Markus, 2001). Nevertheless, interdependent selves are consistent within specific relationships and highly stable over time (English & Chen, 2007). Hence, even if the Japanese reported a different self with mother than with romantic partner within the same relationship, they stayed the same. Therefore, it is not that interdependents' selves shift willy-nilly across contexts, nor do they lack authenticity; but rather, they have a different kind of self-concept consistency – one in which their selves remain consistent within specific relational contexts. To see such cultural differences, researchers have to adjust their 'cultural glasses' to open their minds to another culture's perspective.

Coupled with these different self-views are also different motivations and feelings about the self. We have already mentioned that most people like to think about themselves as better than average (Alicke & Govorun, 2005) and to entertain positive self-illusions of probable success (Taylor & Brown, 1988). This is, however, primarily true of those with an independent self-view; whereas individuals with interdependent self-views value modesty and self-criticism (Heine, Lehman, Markus, & Kitayama, 1999). As a result, East Asians tend to score lower than Westerners on traditional self-esteem scales. This difference, however likely, does not reflect that individuals with an interdependent self feel worse about themselves, but rather, as we will see later in the chapter, that what

contributes to positive self-regard and how **self-enhancement** is expressed varies across these cultural groups.

To the extent that cultural differences in self-esteem are due to differences in modesty, these cultural differences should be stronger for reports of self-competence than for reports of affective self-regard. Consistent with this, East Asians report equally positive self-feelings toward themselves (lack of shame, pride) as do North Americans, even though East Asians report less positive self-competence (Cai, Brown, Deng, & Oakes, 2007). Moreover, members of East-Asian cultures score as high as Westerners on positivity towards the self on implicit measures (Cai et al., 2011; Kitayama & Uchida, 2003; Yamaguchi et al., 2007). For instance, Japanese individuals show enhanced liking for their own name letters (Kitayama & Karasawa, 1997), and are faster to pair self-related words with positive rather than negative words (Yamaguchi et al., 2007). In short, although there are differences in reported explicit self-esteem across cultures, these do not seem to reflect real differences in underlying self-esteem.

Gender Similar differences in the self can also be found between genders: women tend to develop more interdependent selves and link their self-esteem more to interdependent qualities (Cross, Bacon, & Morris, 2000; Cross & Madson, 1997). Men, in contrast, develop more independent selves and link their self-esteem more to their independent qualities (Josephs, Markus, & Tafarodi, 1992). These differences can be explained through gender-specific socialization practices, by which girls are taught to prioritize the qualities that align them with others, whereas boys get encouraged to develop qualities that distinguish them from others (e.g. Spence, Deaux, & Helmreich, 1985). To answer the question whether men and women also differ in global self-esteem, Kling and colleagues analysed the data of 216 studies and two nationally representative American data sets (Kling, Hyde, Showers, & Buswell, 1999). They found only small differences between genders, wherein men reported slightly higher self-esteem than women.

self-enhancement motivation to enhance the positivity of our self-conceptions, often over what would be objectively warranted; achieved by various strategies (e.g. self-serving attributions, basking in reflected glory, positive self-presentations).

Individual differences and contextual variability
Although culture (of which gender can perhaps be thought of as a special case) has a pervasive impact on the self, it is important to highlight that there are still individual differences, even within cultures. In any culture (or within gender), there are individuals who are more or less independent or interdependent than others (Oyserman, Coon, & Kemmelmeier, 2002). That is, there are interdependent

men or Westerners, just as there are independent women or East-Asians. In addition, no one is just independent or just interdependent, but a bit of both. In fact the degree of independence, or interdependence respectively, can be influenced by the context. For example, a study by Trafimow and colleagues (Trafimow, Silverman, Fan, & Law, 1997) with Chinese students from Hong Kong (who spoke English as a second language), found that filling out a 'Who am I?' test either in English or in Chinese importantly influenced the outcome. Students who took the test in English reported more personal traits, whereas students who took the test in Chinese focused more on social relations. This phenomenon of changing the self in response to situational cues is called *cultural frame switching*. Individuals who live with (at least) two cultures are experts in both of them. They have more than one set of cultural tools to interpret the world, or in other words two cultural meaning systems (DiMaggio, 1997; Shore, 1996) and will switch between them depending on the situational demands (e.g. Hong, Benet-Martínez, Chiu, & Morris, 2003).

The neural underpinnings of self-knowledge

Is there something special about how the brain processes and represents information relevant to the self? With the recent advance of neuroimaging techniques, the past two decades have seen a surge of research trying to identify the neurological correlates of self-knowledge (Figure 5.10). The hope is to be able to understand the mechanisms through which people develop representations of self (versus others), how we come to feel a sense of agentic action, and what processes give rise to experiencing a unitary self. Although our understanding of the neural basis of the self is just beginning, progress has been made on the neural correlates of various aspects of self-processing – both from studying the impaired, injured brain and from imaging the healthy brain.

The bulk of the initial neuroscience research on the self was directed at understanding whether encoding information about the self is carried out by different brain regions than encoding information about other people. Many studies now converge to show that the medial prefrontal cortex (MPFC) is involved in self-referential processing (see Beer, 2012, for a review). For example, there is increased activation in the MPFC related to the self-reference effect described earlier, where we encode information in relation to the self more deeply compared to information related to political figures or syllabic structure (e.g. Craik et al., 1999; Kelley et al., 2002). The MPFC also plays a role when making self-descriptiveness judgements of personality characteristics (Macrae, Moran, Heatherton, Banfield, & Kelley,

(a)

(b)

FIGURE 5.10(a) and (b) *Due to the recent advance of neuroimaging techniques, the past two decades have seen a surge of research trying to identify the neurological correlates of self-knowledge.*

Source: (a) © Charles Thatcher. Used under licence from Getty Images; (b) © Stewart Cohen. Used under licence from Getty Images.

2004), when people observe their own face (Keenan, Wheeler, Gallup, & Pascual-Leone, 2000), or when they determine self-ownership of objects (Kim & Johnson, 2010). Interestingly, the MPFC has also been shown to be sensitive to the cultural differences in self-construal we talked about earlier. One study asked both Japanese and American participants to rate the self-descriptiveness of trait adjectives either in general, or in a particular context (e.g. 'How casual are you when you talk to your mother') (Chiao et al., 2009). Participants who identified with individualistic values showed greater MPFC activation for self-descriptiveness judgements made in general, whereas those for whom collectivistic values were more important had heightened MPFC activation for self-judgements in a particular context.

Does this mean, then, that the MPFC is the 'self' component in the brain? The answer is a firm 'no'. For one thing, a number of regions other than the MPFC have also been shown to be involved in self-related processing (e.g. Klein, 2004). And with regard to the MPFC, the problem is that in other studies the MPFC has also been shown to be activated when processing information about other people, especially close others (e.g. Ochsner et al., 2005), or when we try to take on another person's perspective (Pfeifer et al., 2009), or try to infer their mental state (Mitchell, Banaji, & Macrae, 2005). It appears then that the MPFC is more broadly involved in general social cognition processes and is not unique to the self. In fact, it may be that when we make inferences about the self as an object this may be no different from when we process information about other things. In synthesizing neuroimaging results from a large number of studies, Legrand and Ruby (2009) argue that self-relatedness information processing involves a wide cerebral network, the activity of which can be explained by basic cognitive processes common to all tasks.

As already hinted at by William James, however, there is more to the self than its objective aspect. The self also encompasses a sense of personal agency: the experience that we are the cause and origin of our own thoughts and action. This perspective is unique to the self. Legrand and Ruby (2009) argue that self-specificity may be found here and will come in the form of making the relation between one's own actions and their consequences in the social world. Consistent with this idea, a recent brain imaging study showed that the brain mechanisms involved in experiencing a sense of agency are those responsible for comparing predicted and actual action-effects (Spengler, Von Cramon, & Brass, 2009). In this study, participants first learned an arbitrary action–effect pairing: they had to press a button as quickly as possible when a white square appeared alternating between the use of either their index or middle finger. Immediately

thereafter either a red or blue box appeared, and these colours were systematically mapped on to either of the two fingers. Later on, in the scanner, participants again had to press a button as soon as a white square appeared, and were then presented on some trials with matching and on other trials with non-matching action–effects (i.e. the finger–colour combination they had learned or the opposite).

Following each event, participants had to judge whether they themselves had produced the effects (i.e. the squares), or whether these had been computer-generated. Results revealed that participants showed a decreased sense of agency for mismatched trials, or in other words, when previously learned action–effects were altered and did not meet the internal prediction. These same trials also mapped on to increased neural activation of the temporal parietal junction (TPJ), a brain area responsible for integrating various inputs and monitoring the correspondence of these signals with one's body. Self-specificity may thus derive from integration of (motor) command of one's actions and the sensory consequences we experience in the social world. Further experiments will be required, however, to confirm this interpretation of the somatosensory cortex activation for the first-person perspective.

In conclusion, the important point to be made is that there is no specific 'self' region in the brain. The self cannot be localized as a neural entity, but rather is informed by a set of interrelated, functionally independent systems interacting in complex ways (e.g. Klein, Lax, & Gangi, 2010).

Summary

The self-concept can be described as the collection of the content of all our self-experiences, including our characteristics, our social roles, our values, our goals, our fears and so on. This self-knowledge can be categorized into two types: the cognitive representation in the self-concept – our self-schema – and the affective evaluation of the self – our self-esteem. The self-schemas help organize and guide the information processing of self-relevant contents and often function as a reference for judging others. These schemas exert their influence both at the explicit and at the implicit level, and they contain a range of actual, desired (ideal and ought), and possible self-beliefs. At any one time, it is not the entire self-concept that is driving our feelings, thoughts and behaviours, but rather the active or working self-concept – whatever aspect of the self-concept is applicable to the current situation. Self-esteem can be considered a feeling toward oneself based on an overall evaluation about our qualities and worth. It can be described at the trait or at the state level and – as with the self-schemas – it can influence us explicitly or implicitly. In addition, different domains can be differentially important for the self-esteem of different people. Culture and gender shape both our self-concept and our self-esteem. Finally, there is no specific 'self' region in the brain.

THE MOTIVATIONAL FUNCTIONS OF THE SELF

To what extent are we motivated to find out the truth about ourselves versus preferring positive distortions?

The beginning of the twenty-first century has seen an unprecedented rise of talent shows as a popular genre of reality TV. Popstars, the Idols series, The X-Factor and the Got Talent series and the like have drawn hundreds of millions of viewers around the world (Figure 5.11). Although there are many variations to the theme, talent shows inevitably feature a jury of experts who provide feedback to the contestants about their performance. Indeed, a major part of what is shown on TV focuses on contestants' reactions to the jury's feedback, which are typically highly emotional. Positive feedback makes contestants act euphorically, by jumping up and down, shouting, crying with joy and so on. Negative feedback often shatters contestants, bringing to them tears of sadness, or making them lash out in anger.

FIGURE 5.11 *Talent shows such as Britain's Got Talent have attracted millions of viewers around the UK.*

Source: Press Association Images.

Modern talent shows exploit something that social psychologists have long known, namely, the fact that people care deeply about information that pertains to the self. Indeed, most of us are all too eager to find out what kind of traits, talents and abilities we possess. This basic curiosity may explain the widespread appeal of horoscopes, popular magazines, psychological tests and training programmes that are designed to help us on the road to self-discovery. But how sincere are we in our quest for self-knowledge? Are we genuinely motivated to find out the truth about who we are? Or do we merely seek to confirm our pre-conceived ideas about ourselves?

Know thyself: the self-assessment motive

According to Socrates, a Greek philosopher who lived between 470 and 399 BC, accurate self-knowledge represents the highest human virtue. From this perspective, most of us should try to reach an understanding of the self that is as accurate and objective as possible. This striving is also known as the self-assessment motive. To the extent that we are driven by self-assessment motives, we should be eager to perform tests or tasks that provide us with a maximum amount of objective information about ourselves. For instance, if we truly want to know how smart (or dumb) we are, we should prefer a scientifically validated IQ test over our own subjective impression of our intelligence. In line with the self-assessment perspective, several studies have shown that people prefer high diagnostic tasks, that is, tasks that can clearly tell them whether they have a certain trait or ability, over low diagnostic tasks (Trope, 1983, 1986).

> **self-assessment motive** striving to reach an accurate and objective understanding of the self.

However, there is a catch here. If we were purely interested in developing an accurate understanding of the self, we should be equally motivated to learn about our desirable and undesirable qualities. Most of us are indeed eager to learn about our desirable traits and abilities, which make us look good (Sedikides, 1993). But what about our undesirable traits and weaknesses? Here, research findings are mixed. Some studies have shown that people are equally interested to hear about their desirable and undesirable qualities (Strube, Lott, Lê-Xuân-Hy, Oxenberg, & Deichmann, 1986; Trope, 1980). However, other studies have found that people are primarily interested in obtaining accurate information about their strengths rather than about their weaknesses (Brown, 1990; Strube & Roemmele, 1985). It thus appears that our motivation to learn about our weaknesses is not as reliable as our motivation to learn about our strengths. Although the self-assessment motive seems intuitively plausible, this motive is of only limited use in explaining how most of us process information about the self (Sedikides, 1993).

Bigger, better, faster, stronger: the self-enhancement motive

Our refusal to learn about our weaknesses is readily understandable in terms of the *self-enhancement motive*, which refers to our desire to enhance the positivity of our self-conceptions or protect the self from negative information (Sedikides & Strube, 1997). The self-enhancement motive is central to classic and contemporary psychological theories that assume that people have a basic need to view themselves positively, or a need for self-esteem (e.g. James, 1890, 1950; Rogers, 1951; Steele, 1988). According to the self-enhancement view, our need for self-esteem leads us to focus on information that has favourable implications for the self and to avoid information that has unfavourable implications for the self.

Self-enhancing illusions   One important way in which we self-enhance is revealed through the kinds of beliefs that we adopt. As noted earlier, Taylor and Brown (1988) concluded that most psychologically healthy individuals entertain many positive illusions about the self. The most obvious kind of positive illusion is the superiority bias, which means that we tend to hold unrealistically positive views of the self. For instance, we display a pervasive tendency to see the self as better than others. We judge positive personality attributes to be more descriptive of ourselves than of the average person, but regard negative personality attributes as less descriptive of ourselves than of the average person (Alicke, 1985; Brown, 1986). We further judge ourselves more favourably compared to more objective standards, such as external observers (Lewinsohn, Mischel, Chaplin, & Barton, 1980). One particularly striking demonstration of this self-enhancing illusion was provided by Epley and Whitchurch (2008). These researchers took a facial photograph of each person in a group of participants and used a computerized morphing procedure to make the photographs look more or less attractive (see Figure 5.12). Participants

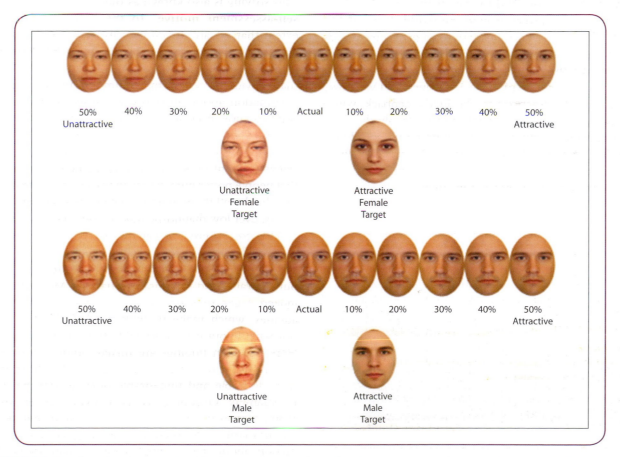

FIGURE 5.12 *Stimuli used to demonstrate self-enhancing illusions: faces of participants were made more or less attractive than the actual photograph using a computer program.*

Source: From Epley & Whitchurch, 2008; Expt. 1. Reproduced with permission from SAGE publications.

THEORY BOX 5.4

THREE STEPS OF THE SELF AS INTUITIVE LAWYER

Selective collection of evidence favourable to the self	Consideration of the implication of self-relevant information. Reassessment of threatening information to the self	Assembly of all information into a coherent account and weight more heavily whatever evidence that makes one look good
Step 1	Step 2	Step 3

Source: Based on Baumeister & Newman, 1994. Reproduced with permission from SAGE publications.

were found to identify the attractively enhanced photo of themselves more readily as their own face than the photo of their actual face. Thus, it appears that we are prone to regard our own facial image as being more desirable than it actually is.

Self-enhancement biases can be found in many other beliefs that we hold about ourselves (Roese & Olson, 2007). For instance, we often display unrealistic optimism, holding overly positive expectations of what the future might bring (Armor & Taylor, 1998). Those of us who are romantically involved further display couple-serving bias, believing that our own romantic relationship is superior to that of others (Buunk, 2001; Rusbult, Van Lange, Wildschut, Yovetich, & Verette, 2000). Likewise, we are prone to ingroup favouritism, believing that our own group is superior to other groups (Hewstone, Rubin, & Willis, 2002; Mullen, Brown, & Smith, 1992). Self-enhancement may also take on less obvious forms. For instance, consider the false consensus effect (Ross, Greene, & House, 1977), which refers to our beliefs that others' opinions are more similar to ours than is actually the case. This effect can be seen as a subtle form of self-enhancement, in that it allows us to think that our own opinions enjoy more popular support than they actually do (McGregor, Nail, Marigold, & Kang, 2005).

Self-enhancing information processing How can we sustain self-enhancing beliefs even when they are contradicted by reality? An underlying reason is that the ways in which we process information are also self-enhancing. Indeed, there is much evidence that our reasoning processes are biased to support conclusions that are favourable to the self. This process is an example of motivated reasoning (Kunda, 1990). Importantly, we are not at liberty to believe whatever we want merely because we want to. Instead, we maintain an 'illusion of objectivity' (Pyszczynski & Greenberg, 1987) by selectively searching for and combining information that supports our desired conclusions. We thus act as if we are intuitive lawyers who are trying to make the best

case for a particular, preselected conclusion (Baumeister & Newman, 1994).

The first step that we take as intuitive lawyers is to collect evidence that reflects favourably on the self (see Theory Box 5.4 for the three steps of the self as intuitive lawyer). We are highly selective in the kinds of self-relevant information we attend to and in what we choose to ignore. For instance, we spend more time reading positive rather than negative self-relevant information (Baumeister & Cairns, 1992). In addition, we are selective in the kinds of self-relevant information that we remember. For instance, when we believe that extraversion is favourable, we quickly recall memories of situations in which we acted in an extraverted manner. By contrast, when we believe that introversion is beneficial, we quickly recall memories of situations in which we acted in an introverted manner (Sanitioso, Kunda, & Fong, 1990). Likewise, when we receive negative feedback about the self, we hardly attend to this information (Green, Sedikides, & Gregg, 2008; Sedikides & Green, 2004), so that we easily forget negative self-relevant information. Conversely, we spend much time reflecting on positive feedback about the self, so that we recall positive self-relevant information very well.

The second step that we take as intuitive lawyers is to consider the implications of self-relevant information and to reassess them, if these implications are threatening to the self. For instance, Liberman and Chaiken (1992) found that regular coffee drinkers were more critical than other individuals of research reports suggesting a link between caffeine consumption and a potentially fatal disease. In a related vein, studies have shown that people become more critical of the validity of psychological tests when the test results are disagreeable to them personally (Pyszczynski, Greenberg, & Holt, 1985; Wyer & Frey, 1983). Our tendency to explain away information that threatens the self may also explain why we tend to assign different causes to successes and failures. Many studies have observed such self-serving attributional biases (see Chapter 3): we take credit for our triumphs, while blaming the circumstances for our personal failures (Miller & Ross, 1975; see also Campbell & Sedikides, 1999). This effect is illustrated by the tendency among athletes to attribute their successes to their personal qualities and their failures to bad luck (Mullen & Riordan, 1988).

The third step that we take as intuitive lawyers consists of combining all the information into a coherent account. If we were truly objective, we would determine our decision rules first and then start collecting the evidence. However, as intuitive lawyers, we prefer to see the evidence first and then give more weight to whatever evidence makes us look good. Indeed, Dunning and associates found that people attach the most weight to those criteria that make them look best (Dunning, Meyerowitz, & Holzberg, 1989). For instance, a student who is good at maths is likely to define competence in terms of maths abilities, whereas a student who is socially skilled may place more emphasis on social abilities. An unfortunate consequence of our idiosyncratic definitions of our abilities is that we tend to remain unaware of our incompetence (Dunning et al., 2003). Self-enhancement motives may thus be an important barrier to self-improvement.

Implicit self-enhancement More generally, we seem to be mostly unaware of the extent to which our thinking is influenced by self-enhancement motives (Baumeister & Newman, 1994; Kunda, 1990; Tesser, 2000). One reason for this lack of awareness may be self-deception. If we openly acknowledge that we are self-enhancing, this may undermine our very efforts to convince ourselves that we are endowed with favourable qualities. Another reason why self-enhancement motives may operate outside of awareness is that these motives are driven by basic affective processes. Successful self-enhancement leads to positive affect and failed self-enhancement leads to negative affect (Roese & Olson, 2007; Tesser, 2000). This affective feedback may guide how we are considering information about the self, even when we have little or no awareness of this process. For instance, learning that we just made an embarrassing mistake may trigger a brief bout of negative feelings, which prompts us to look for a circumstance that could excuse our incompetent behaviour. It is well-established that much of our affective lives occurs outside of awareness (Berridge & Winkielman, 2003; Chartrand, Van Baaren, & Bargh, 2006; Zajonc, 1998). For this reason, self-enhancement processes may similarly be driven by unconscious processes.

In a groundbreaking article, Greenwald and Banaji (1995) observed that persons or objects that are associated with the self are often evaluated more positively. For instance, we evaluate mundane objects like pens and mugs

FIGURE 5.13 *We evaluate people more favourably when they share their date of birth with us.*

Source: © wavebreakmedia Ltd. Used under licence from Shutterstock.

more favourably when we happen to own them (Beggan, 1992). Likewise, we evaluate people more favourably when they share their date of birth with us (Miller, Downs, & Prentice, 1998; see Figure 5.13) or when we are photographed together with them (Burgess, Enzle, & Morry, 2000). As noted earlier, we even like the letters of our name more than other people like these letters (Koole & Pelham, 2003; Nuttin, 1985, 1987). These examples illustrate that we evaluate self-associated objects more positively, even when this association is purely arbitrary. As such, it appears that we are not fully aware of how the self enhances our evaluations of self-associated objects. This tendency to gravitate toward people, places and things that resemble the self is referred to as **implicit egotism** (Pelham, Carvallo, & Jones, 2005).

implicit egotism nonconscious or automatic positive evaluation of self-associated objects.

Self-presentation and self-enhancement So far we have portrayed self-enhancement as a process that largely takes place between the ears. However, it is important to recognize that self-enhancement has

THEORY BOX 5.5

SELF-PRESENTATION STRATEGIES

	Attributions sought	Emotion to be aroused	Prototypical actions
Self-Promotion	Competent (effective, 'a winner')	Respect (awe, deference)	• Talk proudly about your experience or education. • Make people aware of your accomplishments.
Ingratiation	Likeable	Affection	• Take an interest in your colleague's personal lives to show them that you are friendly. • Use flattery and favours to make your colleagues like you more.
Exemplification	Worthy (suffers, dedicated)	Guilt (shame, emulation)	• Try to appear like a hard-working, dedicated employee to make others feel less worthy than you. • Stay at work late so people will know you are hard-working.
Intimidation	Dangerous (ruthless, volatile)	Fear	• Be intimidating with coworkers when it will help you get your job done. • Let others know that you can make things difficult for them if they push you too far.
Supplication	Helpless (handicapped, unfortunate)	Nurturance (obligation)	• Act like you know less than you do so people will help you out. • Pretend not to understand something to gain someone's help.

Source: Bolino & Turnley (1999) table adapted with permission from SAGE Publications Ltd. Also adapted from Jones & Pittman (1982) with permission from Taylor and Francis.

widespread influence on our interactions with other people. Anthropologists like Joseph Campbell (1949) and Ernest Becker (1973) observed that all cultures around the world and throughout history have developed some kind of value system that allows people to gain a feeling that they are a person of worth. If this is correct, then self-enhancement motives may explain why most of us are striving hard every day to live up to the norms of our society by, for instance, dressing according to the latest fashion, getting a university degree, acting as responsible citizens and so on.

The importance of self-enhancement motives for our everyday behaviour is highlighted by research on self-presentation. **Self-presentation** refers to the ways in which we try strategically to manage the impressions we are communicating to an audience (Jones & Pittman, 1982). The audience can be either imagined or real. We present ourselves in many different ways to different people and for many different reasons (Jones & Pittman, 1982). Study Theory Box 5.5 to learn about different types of self-presentational strategies people use when trying to evoke specific attributions and emotions in their

self-presentation a range of strategies that we adopt in order to shape what others think of us.

audience. As you can see, these are quite varied and can run from acting helpless ('supplication') to obtain nurturance and help, to excessive flattery ('ingratiation') to get others to like one. Nevertheless, our primary objective in self-presentation is to convey a favourable image of the self to others. Some of the more direct ways in which we may self-present are by dressing smartly, smiling, and telling others about our important achievements (Wicklund & Gollwitzer, 1982). Self-presentation may also be directed at covering up our inadequacies. For instance, we may make excuses for socially unskilled behaviour (Snyder & Higgins, 1988).

Another tactic is **self-handicapping** (Jones & Berglas, 1978). In this sophisticated form of self-presentation, we create an impediment that makes good performance unlikely, but that will allow a positive interpretation of the performance outcome regardless. For instance, in one study, participants were given the opportunity to practise more, or less, for an upcoming battery of intelligence tests (Tice & Baumeister, 1990). If participants did not engage in much practice, they would have an

self-handicapping the tendency to engage in self-defeating behaviours in order to provide a subsequent excuse for failure and augment ability attributions in the case of success.

external explanation for not performing well. If participants then did poorly, this would not mean that they had to infer that they were incompetent. However, if participants then did well, they succeeded in spite of suboptimal circumstances. The inference therefore is that one must have really high ability. Augmenting ability attributions after success has been shown to be characteristic primarily of individuals high in self-esteem (Rhodewalt, Morf, Hazlett, & Fairfield, 1991).

In other words, through these and other forms of self-handicapping, our self-image is always well off. However, self-handicapping comes at the expense of a lower chance of succeeding, and of finding out just how good we really are. Research suggests that we indeed use various kinds of self-handicapping tactics, such as alcohol use, drug use, test anxiety and procrastination (Tice, 1991; Tucker, Vuchinich, & Sobell, 1981; Zuckerman, Kieffer, & Knee, 1998). Turn to Research close-up 5.2 now to learn about an important gender difference in self-handicapping behaviour.

Notably, we do not always self-present by speaking favourably about ourselves. Indeed, direct self-praise is often frowned upon and invites negative reactions from our social environment (Paulhus, 1998). We therefore self-present in a tactical manner, in ways that elude direct disapproval from others. For instance, we may strengthen our ties with successful others, a strategy known as 'basking in reflected glory' ('BIRGing', Cialdini et al., 1976). For example, you may wear the scarf or shirt of your local sports team after they won a match (Figure 5.14). Through this association you get a boost to your self-esteem. We further make sure that we present ourselves in a more modest fashion when we

are among friends (Tice, Butler, Muraven, & Stillwell, 1995). We will have future interactions with our friends, so that they are better able to verify our claims about ourselves. Furthermore, we do not self-enhance as much when doing so comes at the expense of close others. For instance, self-serving bias in attributions becomes attenuated when we are among close others.

Sedikides and colleagues (Sedikides, Campbell, Reeder, & Elliot, 1998), induced closeness experimentally in one study by having participants engage in a structured self-disclosure task (they were asked to discuss questions that became progressively more personal – for example, from 'How old are you' to 'Tell me one thing that most people do not know about you'). Next, they engaged in a creativity task – either with the person they had become close to, or they were switched to a new person (distant) – and were then provided with success versus failure feedback on the creativity test. Following this feedback, participants were asked to attribute the outcome (success or failure) to themselves or the partner along a continuum. Findings revealed that participants took more credit for the dyad's success and less responsibility for failure if they were with a distant other participant (this is the typical self-serving attribution effect). However, close participants took neither greater responsibility for the dyad's success, nor lower responsibility for failure – they self-attributed responsibility for either outcome somewhere in-between the distant other conditions (see Figure 5.15).

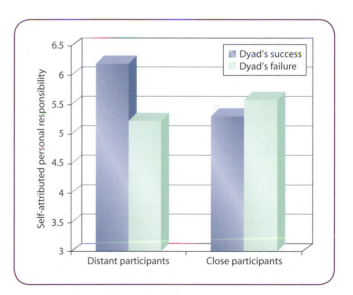

FIGURE 5.15 *Self-attributed personal responsibility as a function of closeness to other participants and success versus failure feedback.*

Source: Adapted from Sedikides, Campbell, Reeder, & Elliot, 1998; Expt. 1. Copyright © 1998 by the American Psychological Association. Adapted with permission. *Journal of Personality and Social Psychology, 74,* 378–386. The use of APA information does not imply endorsement by APA.

FIGURE 5.14 *By wearing the shirt of a local sports team, after they have won a match, people may strengthen their ties with successful others ('basking in reflected glory'), and boost their own self-esteem.*

Source: © Reza Estakhrian. Used under licence from Getty Images.

WOMEN ARE LESS LIKELY TO USE EFFORT WITHDRAWAL AS A SELF-HANDICAP

RESEARCH CLOSE-UP 5.2

McCrea, S. M., Hirt, E. R., & Milner, B. J. (2008). She works hard for the money: Valuing effort underlies gender differences in behavioral self-handicapping. *Journal of Experimental Social Psychology, 44*, 292-311.

Introduction

If individuals worry about failing on a specific task, they sometimes create or claim obstacles in order to have an excuse for possible failing. Hereby they can protect their self-esteem and preserve an impression of ability. This strategy is called self-handicapping. Claimed self-handicaps, in which individuals only state that an obstacle exists (e.g. stress), can be distinguished from behavioural self-handicaps, in which individuals actually create obstacles (e.g. withdraw practice effort). This distinction is important, as it is related to a gender difference in self-handicapping: both men and women have been found to use claimed self-handicaps, but only men engage in behavioural self-handicapping (Hirt, Deppe, & Gordon, 1991). In their study, McCrea and colleagues further analysed this gender difference and tested a possible explanation for it. They hypothesized that, compared to men, women might place more value on exerting effort and thus would be less likely to curtail it. Only the results of Study 3 are reported here.

Method

Participants

The participants were 188 introductory psychology students (92 male and 96 female). They received research credits in return for their participation.

Design and procedure

Before starting the actual experiment, participants completed two questionnaires: (1) a 'worker scale', which measured how hard the students reported that they work (e.g. 'I work hard to be successful at whatever I do.'); (2) a 'prescriptive effort norm scale', which measured how highly they value effort (e.g. 'I admire people who work hard.').

Participants first completed a computerized 15-item multiple-choice analogy test that they believed to be a traditional test for verbal intelligence. The items chosen were particularly difficult. After completing this task, the computer displayed a message informing participants

that they had scored 12 out of 15 items correct, and that this score placed them in the top 10% of college students. They were further told that they would be expected to score highly on a subsequent nonverbal test as well, and that the researchers would compare their two scores to see if they matched this high expectation. These instructions were given in order to make participants feel uncertain of their ability to perform well on the second test, as well as to heighten the impression that the experimenter would be closely observing their performance.

The experimental manipulation followed next. Participants were assigned to one of two practice instruction conditions: Those in the 'practice matters' condition were told that past research had shown that scores on the nonverbal test were not diagnostic, unless individuals had some prior experience with the items; moreover, that without such practice they would score lower than their actual intelligence would warrant. Those in the 'practice doesn't matter' condition were told that past research had shown that practice had no effect on scores on the test. Participants in both conditions were then given a chance to practise prior to the test. All participants received a practice booklet with 18 items and were allowed to practise for as long (or as little) as they liked. The time participants spent practising was surreptitiously recorded, along with the number of practice items completed. Afterwards, they completed the 15-item test.

The experiment thus had a 2-factor design: 2 (gender: male versus female) × 2 (degree to which effort withdrawal could serve as a self-handicap: low/'practice doesn't matter' versus high/'practice matters').

Results

The results provided support for the hypothesis. Figure 5.16 shows the gender differences in behavioural self-handicapping: only men reduced their effort in the 'practice matters' condition, whereas women practised significantly more. In the 'practice doesn't matter'

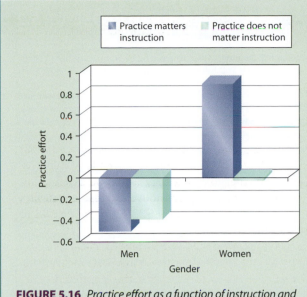

FIGURE 5.16 *Practice effort as a function of instruction and gender.*

Note: Practice effort was computed as an index of time spent practising and number of items completed.

Source: From McCrea, Hirt, & Milner, 2008; Expt. 3.

condition, there was no significant gender difference. Further analyses revealed that the gender difference was due in part to women's reporting being harder workers, as well as their placing more value on effort.

Discussion

The results of this study confirmed the gender difference in behavioural self-handicapping found in earlier studies. Moreover, the authors also provided an explanation for that effect. Women value effort more highly and reported that they invested more in working harder than men did. Therefore, women do not engage in effort withdrawal as a self-handicapping behaviour – the costs of this behavioural self-handicapping would be too high for women. The authors speculate that the difference between men and women in their evaluation of work and effort could be an expression of a greater pressure to adhere to norms. Future studies are needed to further explicate this gender difference, as it was not completely explained by the scales measured in this study.

We display this gracious attributional pattern because we have a positive impression of close others and expect them to reciprocate our self-effacing response. Indeed, when close others display more self-serving responses, our responses become as self-enhancing as with non-close others (Sedikides et al., 1998). In sum, our self-presentations are highly tactical and sensitive to the specific requirements of the social context.

Pancultural self-enhancement Although Western cultures emphasize individualistic values such as personal freedom and self-expression, many non-Western cultures emphasize more collectivistic values such as conformity and fitting in with the group (Triandis, 1989; see Chapter 15). Heine and associates have suggested that self-enhancement motives are only applicable to individuals who have been socialized within individualistic societies (Heine et al., 1999). As discussed earlier in the chapter, in collectivistic cultures individuals are more likely to have an interdependent conception of the self, which may render them less motivated to affirm positive views of the self. Research has confirmed that East Asians, as representatives of collectivistic cultures, typically have self-views that are only moderately positive, and much weaker self-enhancement biases than North Americans, at least in their self-reports. Indeed, several studies have found evidence for a self-critical bias among Japanese individuals. For instance, one experiment found that Japanese students were more easily convinced that their performance was below average than were Canadian students (Heine, Takata, & Lehman, 2000).

Cultural psychologists have thus challenged the universality of the self-enhancement motive. But this challenge has itself been challenged. First, people may be most likely to self-enhance on dimensions that are consistent with our cultural roles (Sedikides, Gaertner, & Toguchi, 2003). Accordingly, a number of studies have found that members of individualistic cultures self-enhance mostly on individualistic traits indicating personal effectiveness (e.g. independent, unique, leader). Members of collectivistic cultures, in contrast, self-enhance mostly on collectivistic traits signifying social connectedness (e.g. respectful, compliant, loyal) (Gaertner, Sedikides, & Chang, 2008; Sedikides et al., 2003). Second, self-evaluations by members of collectivistic cultures may be more influenced by norms that emphasize modesty. Norms towards modesty appear to be stronger in East Asia than in the West (Cai et al., 2007). Such modesty norms typically prohibit boasts about one's accomplishments.

Third, as mentioned earlier, members of East-Asian cultures do show significant positivity towards the self on implicit measures (Cai et al., 2011; Kitayama & Uchida, 2003; Yamaguchi et al., 2007). At first glance, the co-existence of explicit self-criticism and implicit self-regard seems paradoxical. However, various theorists have suggested that one's own self-critical remarks are usually met with sympathy and compassion in interdependent cultures (Cai et al., 2011; Kitayama & Uchida, 2003). Consequently, self-critical East Asians are likely to develop positive associations towards the self, even when (or paradoxically, because) their explicit comments about the self are negative. Consistent with this, explicit modesty is positively associated with implicit self-esteem among members of Eastern cultures, but not among members of Western cultures (Cai et al., 2011). Cai and colleagues (2011) showed this using the 'implicit association test' (IAT) described earlier as an implicit measure of self-esteem. With this method, the researchers found the expected association between enacting modest behaviour and high implicit self-esteem for Asian participants, but not for American participants. Moreover, this was despite Asians reporting low explicit self-esteem. In short, within different cultural contexts, different 'roads' may lead to positive self-regard.

To summarize, there are important differences between cultures that shape both norms for self-presentation and the kinds of qualities people aspire to. These cultural differences lead to striking differences in how East Asians present themselves relative to Westerners. Nevertheless, when appropriately measured, self-enhancement tendencies can be observed equally among members of both Eastern and Western cultures. Self-enhancement thus appears to be a universal human motive.

The puzzle of low self-regard: self-verification

Most of us view the self in largely positive terms. Most, but not all, of us. A small but distinct number of individuals are inclined to view the self in more neutral, if not negative terms. These individuals represent an intriguing psychological puzzle. Are these individuals somehow immune to self-enhancement needs? Or do these individuals still have the desire to self-enhance, but does something keep them from doing so?

A research programme led by Swann and associates (Swann & Buhrmester, 2012) goes a long way towards resolving the puzzle of individuals with low self-regard (see Leader in the Field, William B. Swann). According to these researchers, our stable self-views are tied to feelings that the world is meaningful and coherent.

 LEADER IN THE FIELD

William B. Swann (b. 1952) received his BA from Gettysburg College in 1974 and his PhD from the University of Minnesota in 1978. Since then he has worked at the University of Texas at Austin, where he is Professor of Social and Personality Psychology. He is best known for his research on self-verification: the theory assumes that people prefer others to see them consistent with their own firmly held beliefs and feelings about themselves (both negative and positive). Another focus of Swann's work is on the process of identity negotiation: the processes through which people in relationships reach mutual agreements regarding 'who' each person is. Once these agreements have been reached, people are expected to remain faithful to their identities. These agreements establish what people expect of one another, and thus determine the way they relate and, in turn, keep the relationship together. In a 2004 survey, Professor Swann was listed among the top 30 most-cited authors published in *Journal of Personality and Social Psychology*, and in a 2006 survey in *Dialogue*, among the top 30 most-cited authors in Social Psychology textbooks.

A stable and coherent view of ourselves and the world is crucial, because it allows us to organize our experience, predict future events, and guide social interaction. Our desire for stable and coherent self-views gives rise to the self-verification motive, a motivation to affirm our firmly held beliefs about ourselves. For those of us with positive self-views (who are in the majority), affirming positive self-views jointly serves self-verification and self-enhancement motives. However, for those of us with negative self-views (a sizable minority), there is a fundamental conflict between self-verification and self-enhancement motives. Affirming positive self-views feels good on one level, because it fulfils self-enhancement needs. However, doing so does not feel right, because it compromises the feelings of coherence that drive our self-verification motives (Swann & Buhrmester, 2012).

> **self-verification**
> motivation to affirm firmly held self-beliefs, arising from a desire for stable and coherent self-views.

The self-verification perspective holds that people will fight to maintain stable self-views even when these self-views are negative, so that maintaining them is psychologically painful (Swann & Buhrmester, 2012). In line with this provocative idea, studies have shown that people gravitate towards self-verifying interaction partners (e.g. Hixon & Swann, 1993; Robinson & Smith-Lovin, 1992; Swann, Stein-Seroussi, & Giesler, 1992). For instance, one study asked participants with positive and negative self-views to pick one of two potential partners to get to know better over an interaction of two to three hours (Swann et al., 1992). These potential partners had allegedly provided their evaluations of participants' personality profiles. One partner expressed a very favourable impression of the participant; the other

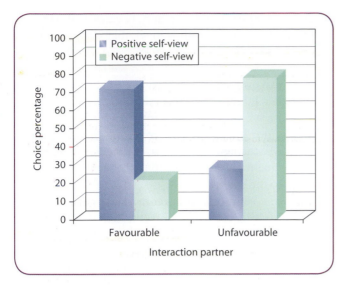

FIGURE 5.17 *Percentage of participants who chose favourable versus unfavourable interaction partners depending on positivity of participants' own self-view.*

Source: Data from Swann, Stein-Seroussi, & Giesler, 1992; Expt. 1. Reproduced with permission.

FIGURE 5.18 *The Babe Ruth room at the Baseball Hall of Fame. Self-enhancement tendencies in members of the Baseball Hall of Fame from 1900 to 1950 were positively associated with increased life expectancy (Peterson & Seligman, 1987).*

Source: Milo Stewart, Jr/National Baseball Hall of Fame and Museum, Cooperstown, N.Y. Reprinted with permission.

expressed a somewhat negative impression. As it turned out, most participants chose a partner whose evaluation of them matched their own self-views (see Figure 5.17). This means that participants with positive self-views preferred interaction partners who had favourable impressions of them. However, perhaps more surprisingly, participants with negative self-views preferred interaction partners who had unfavourable impressions of them. Importantly, these self-verification tendencies occur not just in the laboratory, but have also emerged in real-life relationships, such as marriage, friendships and work teams (see Swann & Buhrmester, 2012). Self-verification strivings occur equally for men and women and both for specific self-views (e.g. intelligence, sociability) and global self-worth. People are particularly likely to seek self-verifying feedback for self-views that are confidently held, important or extreme (see Swann & Buhrmester, 2012, for a review).

Do people with negative self-views relish negative feedback about the self? Or have they simply stopped caring about the self? The answer to both questions is negative. Instead, individuals with a negative self-view feel deeply torn upon receiving negative evaluations. On the one hand, these individuals like to hear others say good things about them. This positive reaction to self-enhancing feedback is characteristic for the first, automatic reaction of individuals with negative self-views (Swann, Hixon, Stein-Seroussi, & Gilbert, 1990).

On the other hand, however, individuals feel that self-enhancing feedback does not describe them very accurately. Consequently, individuals with negative self-views feel more understood by interaction partners who evaluate them negatively. This preference for negative but self-verifying feedback only emerges when people have sufficient time and attentional resources to think about their decision, otherwise people prefer positive feedback, regardless of how self-verifying it is (Swann et al., 1990). In sum, individuals with negative self-views still have self-enhancement tendencies, but these tendencies may be overruled by more deliberate strivings for self-verification.

Why do we self-enhance?

In a classic study, Peterson and Seligman (1987) examined how members of the Baseball Hall of Fame from 1900–1950 explained their successes and failures (Figure 5.18). The results showed that players lived significantly longer to the extent that they provided self-serving explanations of good and bad events (i.e. attributed success to themselves and failure to specific circumstances). This striking finding is consistent with other studies showing that self-enhancement tendencies are positively associated with mental and physical health (Taylor, Kemeny, Reed, Bower, & Gruenewald, 2000). This pattern is not only observed in the West, but also in Eastern cultures, which promote modesty and self-criticism among their members (Gaertner et al., 2008). Moreover, although these findings are correlational, there is also evidence that affirming positive self-views can directly cause health benefits (Creswell et al., 2005, 2007).

Sociometer theory In what way is self-enhancement beneficial to our health? This question relates to the deeper reasons why we are driven to self-enhance. Why is it so important to us to think well of ourselves? In addressing these questions, Leary and associates have emphasized the interpersonal functions of having positive feelings towards the self (Leary et al., 1995). According to Leary, our feelings of self-esteem signal the degree to which we feel acceptance or rejection by other members of our social group. When we experience rejections from others, our self-esteem drops, which motivates us to restore our social standing through various self-enhancing behaviours. When we feel accepted, we maintain our positive sense of self-esteem. Feelings of self-esteem may thus act as a 'sociometer' (a kind of social barometer) that helps us to keep track of our social status.

sociometer theory a theory that posits that our self-esteem functions as a signal of the degree to which we feel accepted or rejected by other people.

The **sociometer theory** has inspired a great deal of research on the effects of social exclusion on self-esteem. However, its assumptions have proven surprisingly difficult to confirm. A recent meta-analysis that combined almost 200 relevant studies found no evidence that social exclusion has a negative impact on self-esteem (Blackhart, Nelson, Knowles, & Baumeister, 2009). Moreover, the same exclusion manipulations that failed to influence self-esteem did have effects on other variables, such as impairing one's ability to self-regulate (Baumeister, DeWall, Ciarocco, & Twenge, 2005) or producing a substantial reduction in prosocial behaviour (Twenge, Baumeister, DeWall, Ciarocco, & Bartels, 2007). These findings call into question whether self-esteem is directly linked to our perceived level of belongingness. More generally, the absence of effects of exclusion on self-esteem poses a major challenge to the sociometer model.

Terror management theory An alternative perspective on the psychological functions of self-esteem is provided by **terror management theory** (Greenberg, Solomon, & Pyszczynski, 1997). Inspired by existential thinkers like Otto Rank and Ernest Becker, terror management theory proposes that our human self-awareness greatly

terror management theory a theory that assumes that people cope with the fear of their own death by constructing worldviews that help to preserve their self-esteem.

magnifies our potential for anxiety, because it allows us to realize that our own death is inevitable. To manage this existential anxiety, we become invested in our culture, which provides our existence with meaning and order. Culture also provides us with ways of achieving immortality, either literally through religious beliefs about an afterlife, or symbolically by identifying with values that transcend our individual existence (e.g. justice, love or science). To achieve literal or symbolic immortality, we must maintain the values that are proscribed by our culture. To the extent that we are effective at this, we will experience a sense of self-esteem. Terror management theory thus suggests that the ultimate reason why we self-enhance is because having a positive self helps us to overcome our deepest existential fears.

Research has provided strong evidence for the basic tenets of terror management theory (see Pyszczynski, Greenberg, Solomon, Arndt, & Schimel, 2004, for an overview). First, affirming positive beliefs about the self reduces death anxiety (Greenberg et al., 1993) and helps to put thoughts about death out of the mind (Schmeichel & Martens, 2005). Second, reminding people of death (i.e. increasing mortality salience) leads to stronger self-enhancement strivings. For instance, in one study, Israeli soldiers were reminded of either death or of a neutral topic (Taubman Ben-Ari, Florian, & Mikulincer, 1999). Risky driving is for many people a means to show off, test their limits, or compete with other drivers (Taubman Ben-Ari, 2000). According to terror management theory, concerns with death should motivate the individuals reminded of their death to engage in more risky driving. In line with this prediction, the results showed that reminders of death led to more dangerous driving manoeuvres (as assessed through self-report and on a driving simulator), particularly among soldiers who took pride in their driving ability.

Likewise, death reminders increase the appeal of high-status items (e.g. a Lexus car) and materialism among people living in capitalist cultures, which emphasize financial success as a source of self-worth (Rindfleisch, Burroughs, & Wong, 2009). Notably, these effects are not paralleled by reminders of other aversive topics, such as failing an important exam, or uncertainty. Third, suggesting to people that there is scientific proof for an afterlife reduces the impact of mortality salience on self-enhancement strivings (Dechesne et al., 2003). After being asked to write down the first thing that came to mind when thinking about death or a control topic (watching television), participants read an article presenting scientific arguments for or against the existence of an afterlife. When reading an article arguing for no life after death, participants showed the typical mortality salience effect of more positive self-ratings when reminded

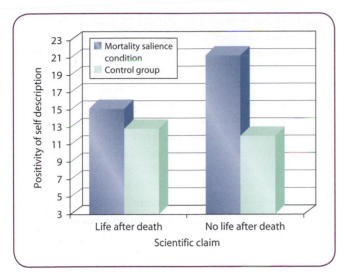

FIGURE 5.19 *Self-enhancement striving (positivity of self description) as a function of mortality salience condition and scientific claim about the existence of life after death.*

Source: Data from Dechesne et al., 2003; Expt. 1. Reproduced with permission.

FIGURE 5.20 *Narcissists display grossly inflated self-views yet have a fragile self-esteem.*

about death relative to the control group. However, when participants read an article containing scientific arguments for a life after death, this self-enhancement following death reminders disappeared (see Figure 5.19).

Taken together, there is impressive support for the terror management functions of self-enhancement. Although self-enhancement is logically unrelated to the problem of death, self-enhancement psychologically protects us against death anxiety. Consequently, one major reason why we self-enhance is that doing so helps us to cope more effectively with existential concerns.

The pros and cons of pursuing self-esteem

People self-enhance in order to support and bolster their self-esteem and to squelch existential fears. But to what degree are self-enhancement and high self-esteem a good thing? On one hand, high self-esteem is linked to many positive outcomes: people with high self-esteem are more resilient to stress, setbacks and depression; they are more optimistic about their futures and have more self-confidence; all round, they feel good about themselves (Baumeister, Campbell, Krueger, & Vohs, 2003; Bonanno, Rennicke, & Dekel, 2005; Taylor, Lerner, Sherman, Sage, & McDowell, 2003). However, this is not the whole story. People with high self-esteem also often take large and inappropriate risks, ranging from unsafe sexual behaviour to substance abuse or even delinquency (Baumeister et al., 2003). High self-esteem is also

associated with stronger ingroup bias and more prejudice (Aberson, Healy, & Romero, 2000; Crocker & Schwartz, 1985). Moreover, when people feel their self-esteem is threatened, they often react by lashing out – putting others down or aggressing against them (Bushman & Baumeister, 1998; Bushman et al., 2009; Morf & Rhodewalt, 1993). In this light, unjustifiably inflated self-esteem is particularly problematic, as it is capricious, and thus easily challenged or threatened.

A special case of grossly inflated self-views yet fragile self-esteem comes in the form of narcissism (Akhtar & Thomson, 1982; Morf & Rhodewalt, 2001; Morf, Torchetti, & Schürch, 2011; see Figure 5.20). The syndrome of narcissism was originally developed by psychiatrists to describe a personality disorder that they observed in some of their clients who displayed a pervasive pattern of a grandiose sense of self and a lack of empathy for others (American Psychiatric Association, 1994). But social psychologists too have been interested in narcissism and have studied weaker forms of this personality trait in nonclinical samples (see Morf, Torchetti, & Schürch, 2011, for a review). Their more controlled research has confirmed that narcissists in the nonclinical range similarly hold sky-high opinions of themselves, yet simultaneously have disparaging views of others. Others are of interest to them not for their own sake, but merely as vehicles for the narcissists' own self-enhancement. Narcissists brag, show off, want others to admire them; they also compete with others and exert power over them in order to assert their superiority (Buss & Chiodo, 1991; Campbell & Foster, 2007; Wallace & Baumeister, 2002). While these behaviours sometimes get narcissists what they want, they also backfire at times and undermine the narcissists' self-enhancement efforts (see Morf, Horvath, & Torchetti, 2011, for a review).

For example, in new groups, narcissists' self-enhancement brings them admiration and they are often chosen as leaders, but once their bluff has been discovered, the admiration turns into dislike and rejection (Brunell et al., 2008; Judge, LePine, & Rich, 2006; Paulhus, 1998). Some studies have questioned whether a hidden negative self-view (Bosson et al., 2008) underlies narcissists' self-enhancement efforts. However, some recent studies using implicit measures (see the section on implicit self-esteem of this chapter) have indeed confirmed the role of latent worthlessness in narcissistic responding (Horvath & Morf, 2009; Morf, Horvath, & Zimmermann, 2011). Thus, narcissistic individuals might harbour latent feelings of self-doubt, despite their highly favourable reported self-views at the explicit level (e.g. Horvath & Morf, 2009; Jordan et al., 2003; also see Gregg & Sedikides, 2010, for an in-depth discussion). It appears then that easily activated latent feelings of worthlessness are part of the psychological makeup of narcissists. As a result, narcissists show the types of defensive behaviours talked about earlier, when explicit and implicit self-beliefs are at odds. They cannot help themselves, it seems, from constantly pushing their self-esteem (Baumeister & Vohs, 2001).

Turn now to Social Psychology Beyond the Lab 5.1 to learn about the link between threatened egotism and violence.

Hence there clearly are risks to raising self-esteem, especially if it is not based on actual deeds and thus unwarranted. Moreover, when we should take these risks depends on the context. Although there clearly are many interpersonal advantages to modesty and humility (Sedikides, Gregg, & Hart, 2007), both modesty and self-enhancement must always be seen in the context in which they transpire. Being excessively modest in a job interview is unlikely to get one an executive position; correspondingly, being overly self-enhancing when a friend just failed a test is not going to seal the friendship. All told, then, pursuing self-esteem is a mixed bag, and one has to take into account that there are many different kinds of high self-esteem. When high self-esteem is genuine, people feel secure and thus are less angered by or reactive to criticism (Kernis, 2003). They also do not care about being the centre of attention, or overtrumping others. Secure self-esteem is rooted in feeling good about who one is, and is not contingent on external sources (Crocker & Park, 2004; Kernis et al., 2008). Importantly, the upshot is that the less one's focus is on self-image, and the more it is on developing one's competence, relationships and autonomy, the more likely it is that one will build a solid base for genuine self-esteem (see Deci & Ryan, 1995).

Summary

We care deeply about any information that pertains to the self. Intuitively, one might expect that we are driven by a self-assessment motive and therefore mainly want to develop an accurate understanding of the kind of person we are. However, the available evidence indicates that we usually prefer to self-enhance, by seeking positive information about the self and by processing it in a self-serving way. Self-enhancement mainly operates implicitly and is found in culturally-appropriate forms in many different parts of the world. Besides presenting oneself toward others in a favourable way, self-enhancement helps in coping with existential anxieties. Nevertheless, we are also inclined to self-verify, by seeking information that supports our pre-existing ideas about the self. Given that most of our self-views are positive, self-enhancement and self-verification motives push us in the same direction most of the time, although people with low self-regard prefer to self-verify their negative self-beliefs. Finally, although high self-esteem is associated with a range of positive outcomes, it also can come with costs – especially when self-esteem is inflated and contingent upon external sources.

THE REGULATORY FUNCTIONS OF THE SELF: THE SELF IN CONTROL

How does the self regulate our behaviour so that we can plan effectively and pursue our goals and aspirations?

Before you read any further, take a look at yourself in the mirror. What goes through your mind as you are doing this? Perhaps your thoughts initially turn to your outward appearance, such as whether your shirt makes you look slimmer, the urgency with which you need a new haircut, or if you have blackheads on your nose. But if you are like most people, your thoughts may quickly turn inwards, to your personal goals and the expectations that others have of you, and whether you are living up to those expectations. Indeed, many scholars of the self have observed that self-reflection often leads people to think about their goals and aspirations. The self thus enables people to plan their actions more effectively,

SOCIAL PSYCHOLOGY BEYOND THE LAB 5.1

THREATENED EGOTISM AND VIOLENCE

On July 22, 2011, the 32-year-old Norwegian Anders Breivik detonated a car bomb in downtown Oslo, killing eight people and critically wounding 10 others. Two hours later, Breivik appeared dressed as a police officer at a Labour Party of Norway youth camp. Here, Breivik shot 69 attendees and injured 66 before he surrendered to the police and was taken into custody. Subsequent investigations suggest that Breivik had acted alone, meticulously planning his attacks years in advance (Figure 5.21).

What could drive an individual like Breivik to plan and commit acts of unspeakable violence towards other human beings? Traditionally, many psychologists have believed that violence and aggression are caused by low self-esteem (e.g. Levin & McDevitt, 1993; Staub, 1989 ; see Chapter 9 on aggression). In the last decade or so however, this view has been challenged. An influential review by Baumeister, Smart, and Boden (1996) found little evidence that individuals with low self-esteem are particularly aggressive. In fact, these researchers found more support for the opposite pattern, such that individuals with high self-esteem tend to be the aggressors. For instance, murderers, rapists, wife beaters, violent youth gangs and aggressive nations

FIGURE 5.21 *The 2011 Norway Massacre: what could drive an individual like Breivik to plan and commit acts of unspeakable violence towards other human beings?*
Source: © Press Association Images.

are all characterized by strongly held views of their own superiority. Moreover, aggressive tendencies increase when people's self-esteem has recently been boosted (e.g. by drinking alcohol), and decrease after people experienced a drop in self-esteem (e.g. by decreases in social status). Baumeister and associates referred to these patterns as the 'dark side' of high self-esteem.

The notion of a dark and violent side of high self-esteem fits with what is currently known about the Breivik case. Just a few hours before his attacks, Breivik uploaded a document on the Internet that disclosed many details about himself. Among other things, he stated that he was 'very proud' of his Viking heritage, boasted of his business ventures as 'successful' and described his personality as 'optimistic, pragmatic, ambitious, creative and hard-working'. As such, Breivik obviously possessed very favourable views of himself.

Should we now embrace the theory that high self-esteem causes aggression? No, that would be too simple. A groundbreaking study by Kernis and associates showed that individuals with high self-esteem display considerable variability in aggressive behaviour (Kernis, Grannemann, & Barclay, 1989). These researchers measured self-esteem at different points in time so that they could simultaneously consider both the level and the stability of self-esteem. The results showed that individuals with unstable high self-esteem had the highest levels of anger and aggressive behaviour. By contrast, individuals with stable high self-esteem had the lowest levels of anger and aggression. Individuals with stable and unstable low self-esteem fell between these extremes. These findings suggest that there are two types of individuals with high self-esteem: some are hot-tempered and aggressive, while others are slow to anger and non-aggressive.

The puzzling mix of people that profess to have high self-esteem has led researchers to search for constructs that might separate the aggressive and non-aggressive subtypes. One construct that has proven useful in this regard is narcissism. As previously noted, narcissists distinguish themselves by exaggerated self-importance; they demand admiration and are prone to exhibitionistic behaviour. Furthermore, they expect special treatment and are inclined to exploit others. At the same time, they are highly reactive to threats to self-esteem, and respond to such threats with feelings of rage, defiance, shame and humiliation (see Morf & Rhodewalt, 2001; Morf, Torchetti, & Schürch, 2011 for reviews). Several pieces of information about Anders Breivik indeed seem to fit with a narcissistic personality.

First, note that his Internet manifesto disclosed many details about his personal life, including his family background, education, employment history and even his hobbies and favourite sports. Breivik's apparent eagerness to publicize a slew of rather trivial personal facts is consistent with a narcissistic preoccupation with the self. The manifesto indicates further that Breivik thought of himself in highly elevated and heroic terms, as he identified himself with an order of knights that was linked to the old Christian crusaders. In addition, Breivik appeared to be fascinated by his own physical appearance, as his manifesto ended with a series of pictures of him posing in several fancy and outlandish outfits (e.g. a Masonic formal outfit, a diving suit). Finally, it is worth noting that Breivik conveyed some awareness of his self-preoccupation, acknowledging that his chief character flaw was 'a relatively inflated ego' and that others generally perceived him as arrogant.

Narcissistic tendencies have similarly been observed among other perpetrators of mass violence, such as the widely publicized shootings at Columbine and Virginia Tech (Twenge & Campbell, 2003). No doubt these cases are extreme and might be considered pathological. But research has shown that narcissists, even in the normal range, display aggressive tendencies, particularly when their positive self-views are threatened. For instance, in two laboratory studies, participants were either praised or insulted by a confederate posing as another participant (Bushman & Baumeister, 1998). Later on, participants received an opportunity to aggress against the confederate (or another person) by subjecting him or her to an aversive blast of loud noise. Both studies showed that participants who had high narcissism scores and had been insulted displayed the greatest aggression – in other words, when their ego was threatened. Notably, narcissists did not aggress when they had received praise, and only aggressed against the person who had insulted them. Narcissists are thus not generally or indiscriminately aggressive.

A number of field studies have investigated the link between narcissism and violent behaviour under more naturalistic conditions. For instance, narcissism scores predicted aggressive behaviour and conduct problems among children at an elementary school (Barry, Frick, Adler, & Grafeman, 2007). In a related vein, narcissistic men are more favourable towards sexual coercion and are more likely to use violence against a woman who has refused to have sex with them (Baumeister, Catanese, & Wallace, 2002; Bushman, Bonacci, Van Dijk, & Baumeister, 2003). These field studies are consistent with laboratory evidence for threatened egotism as a cause of aggression.

Hence, although narcissists endorse highly positive views about themselves, these self-views seem to be rather fragile and easily challenged. Accordingly, the egotism of narcissists might be a surface layer that conceals more basic insecurities – a notion that has been confirmed in some recent studies (e.g. Horvath & Morf, 2009; Jordan et al., 2003; also see Gregg & Sedikides, 2010, for an in-depth discussion). Do latent self-doubts then explain the aggressive outbursts among narcissists? On the nonbehavioural level, Morf and colleagues showed that after subliminal activation of worthlessness, narcissistic men reacted faster to aggression-related words, while the accessibility of aggression decreased even for less narcissistic participants (Morf, Horvath, & Zimmermann, 2011). This indicates that in narcissists the concept of aggression is directly triggered by the concept of worthlessness. Research on aggressive behaviour of individuals with high explicit and low implicit self-esteem provides similar results. For instance, relative to others, individuals with high explicit and low implicit self-esteem are more prone to discriminate against outgroup members (Jordan, Spencer, & Zanna, 2005) and are less forgiving towards someone who has offended them (Eaton, Struthers, Shomrony, & Santelli, 2007). Furthermore, one study showed that teachers rated teenagers with high explicit and low implicit self-esteem as significantly more aggressive than their fellow-students (Sandstrom & Jordan, 2008). Taken together, this work suggests important parallels in aggressive responding among narcissists and individuals with high explicit and low implicit self-esteem.

At this point we want to emphasize the importance of distinguishing between extreme and pathological cases of narcissism and more common subclinical varieties of narcissism and threatened egotism. Most everyday narcissists do not display extreme violence and do not lash out against innocent others. Even though they tend to be interpersonally exploitative and abrasive, many narcissists are nonetheless successful and psychologically healthy (Kernberg, 1975; Morf, Horvath, & Torchetti, 2011; Sedikides, Rudich, Gregg, Kumashiro, & Rusbult, 2004). The latest progress and current ongoing scientific efforts to unravel the links between having an inflated ego, threatened egotism and aggression may eventually bring us closer to understanding what leads to the actions of individuals like Anders Breivik, and, even more important, to ways of preventing such disasters.

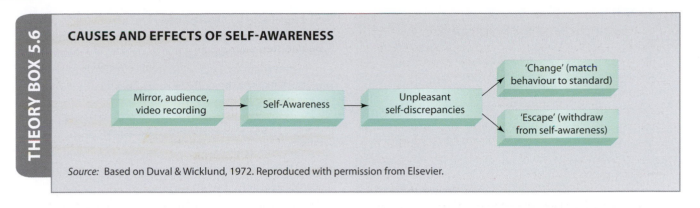

CAUSES AND EFFECTS OF SELF-AWARENESS

Mirror, audience, video recording → Self-Awareness → Unpleasant self-discrepancies → 'Change' (match behaviour to standard) / 'Escape' (withdraw from self-awareness)

Source: Based on Duval & Wicklund, 1972. Reproduced with permission from Elsevier.

and this is among the major adaptive advantages of having a self (Higgins, 1996; Pyszczynski, Greenberg, & Solomon, 1999; Sedikides & Skowronski, 1997).

Self-awareness theory

When you are turning your attention inward, you become the object of your own consciousness. This intriguing state of self-focus may arise when you are looking at yourself in a mirror (Hass & Eisenstadt, 1990). However, self-focus may also be increased by other factors that lead you to pay more attention to yourself. For instance, you are likely to become more self-focused when you see a video recording of yourself, hear an audio recording of your own voice, when your name is mentioned, when you somehow experience yourself as different from the people around you, or when you are writing about yourself (Macrae, Bodenhausen, & Milne, 1998; Silvia & Duval, 2001; Silvia & Eichstaedt, 2004). Self-focus also tends to become increased in public situations, when you realize that your actions are being monitored by an audience (Baumeister, 1984).

So how does self-focus influence behaviour? According to Duval and Wicklund's (1972) classic theory of objective **self-awareness**, focusing attention on the self motivates people to assess how well they are living up to norms for appropriate behaviour and to act

self-awareness a psychological state in which one's attention is directed at the self.

more in accordance with these norms. For instance, as you become self-focused, you may think of the hours of reading that you still have to do in order to prepare for your Social Psychology class. If this assessment reveals that you are falling short of the norm, self-focus will give rise to negative feelings (e.g. feeling guilty for not having done enough reading). These negative feelings, in turn, will motivate you to change your behaviour – you may go to the library in order to complete your readings (see Theory Box 5.6).

This notion has been confirmed in over a hundred empirical studies (for a review, see Silvia & Duval, 2001). One study, for example, showed that self-focus can make people work harder at a difficult task, especially when their attention is directed at their performance (Dana, Lalwani, & Duval, 1997). Other studies have shown that self-focus can lead people to offer more assistance to a person with a legitimate request for help (Gibbons & Wicklund, 1982; see Chapter 10 on helping). Yet other studies found that self-focus leads people to suppress socially undesirable stereotypes (Macrae et al., 1998). Notably, the effects of self-focus also depend upon your self-efficacy, or your beliefs about whether you are capable of acting in a certain manner to achieve certain goals (Bandura, 1977). For instance, imagine that your parents expect you to do well in maths at school. If your self-efficacy is high, you believe that you are capable of mastering your maths lessons. In this case, high self-focus will lead you to invest more time and effort in studying maths. By contrast, if your self-efficacy is low, you believe that you are unable to master maths no matter how hard you try. In the latter case, self-focus will lead you to invest less time and effort in studying maths (see Carver, Blaney, & Scheier, 1979). The effects of self-focus are therefore quite flexible, and depend upon your beliefs about what you can realistically accomplish.

Self-regulation theory

Self-focus makes us more inclined to regulate our behaviour. In this sense, self-focus is closely connected with **self-regulation**, or the control 'of the self by the self' (Baumeister, Schmeichel, & Vohs, 2007). But what does this mean? Should we think of the self as a 'homunculus' or little man in our head that takes charge of what we do or feel?

self-regulation the process of controlling and directing one's behaviour in order to achieve desired thoughts, feelings, and goals.

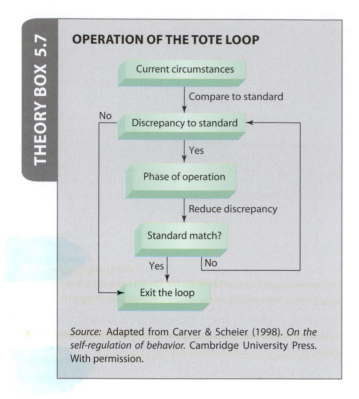

THEORY BOX 5.7

OPERATION OF THE TOTE LOOP

Current circumstances

↓ Compare to standard

No → Discrepancy to standard

↓ Yes

Phase of operation

↓ Reduce discrepancy

Standard match?

Yes ↓   No

Exit the loop

Source: Adapted from Carver & Scheier (1998). *On the self-regulation of behavior.* Cambridge University Press. With permission.

Or is it possible to understand self-regulation in terms of a concrete mechanism or psychological process? Carver and Scheier (1981, 1998) developed a compelling answer to these questions by relating self-focus to a more general understanding of self-regulation. Their approach builds on the notion of a cybernetic system (Miller, Galanter, & Pribram, 1960). An everyday example of such a system is the room thermostat, which turns the heating on or off whenever the local temperature passes a preset value. In its simplest form, a cybernetic system consists of a TOTE loop, an acronym for 'test-operate-test-exit' (see Theory Box 5.7). In the initial test phase, you compare current circumstances to a standard. For instance, you may wonder whether you have been generous enough to your friends. If there is a discrepancy, you enter a phase of operation and take steps to reduce the discrepancy. For instance, if you fear you have been too much of a tightwad, you may decide to throw a party for your friends. Then comes another test, to see whether you have met the standard or not. Can you now say that you are a generous person? If not, the system continues to operate until you have reached the standard. Perhaps you find that generosity is not just about material things, so you really should spend more time with your friends. Finally, when you meet the standard, the system exits the TOTE loop and the cycle ends. The cybernetic theory of self-regulation thus proposes that we self-regulate by monitoring how we live up to standards, and, when we fall short, by taking action to bring us closer to these standards.

Self-regulatory standards The first part of self-regulation means that we adopt some kind of standard, which may be a personal goal, social norm, expectations of others and the like. Self-regulatory standards may be formulated relatively broadly or more specifically. According to Carver and Scheier (1981, 1998) self-regulatory standards may operate on four different levels. At the highest level are system concepts, which consist of the personal characteristics that describe the kind of person we want to be (including the ideal and ought selves discussed earlier). For example, most of us want to be generous, responsible and honest individuals. System concepts give rise to the next lower level – principles, which consist of global behavioural aspirations. For instance, we can become a generous person by adhering to the principle that we should give and share what we have with other people. Principles state values, and are still free of behavioural content, in that they are applicable to many kinds of behaviour. The specific behaviours that we perform are prescribed by programmes or scripts (the next lower level). For example, to adhere to one's principle of sharing with others, one might donate money to charity or leave a large tip at a restaurant. Finally, programmes such as donating money to charity lead to even more specific goals or sequences at the lowest level. Sequences consist of motor control goals that are typically executed without conscious supervision. For instance, the behavioural programme of leaving a tip might be enacted by the sequence of opening one's wallet and taking out a five Euro note.

In most situations we like to think of our goals in abstract, high-level terms (what Carver and Scheier would call system concepts and principles). For example, most individuals reading this chapter will think of it as 'studying psychology' rather than 'staring at letters'. Linking our behaviour to abstract goals renders what we are doing more meaningful (Vallacher & Wegner, 1987). Because the self is closely associated with higher-level meanings, more abstract goals are more strongly connected with the self. Indeed, research suggests that self-regulation improves when we think more abstractly about our goals (Fujita, Trope, Liberman, & Levin-Sagi, 2006; Schmeichel & Vohs, 2009). For instance, relative to those who are thinking of their lower-level goals, people who are thinking of their higher-level goals are more willing to delay immediate gratification to obtain a larger reward, display greater physical endurance, and are better able to resist temptation (Fujita et al., 2006). Specifically, when induced to engage in higher level thinking (think 'why I try to maintain my health', versus 'how'), participants chose to forgo temptation by committing to a healthy food regimen in advance, at least if their goal to improve their health was high

FIGURE 5.22 *Probability of choice to forgo temptation as a function of goal importance and construal level.*

Source: Data from Fujita & Roberts, 2010; Expt. 1. Reprinted with permission from SAGE publications.

LEADER IN THE FIELD

Roy F. Baumeister (b. 1953) is currently the Eppes Eminent Professor of Psychology at Florida State University. He completed his PhD in social psychology from Princeton in 1978, under the supervision of Ned Jones, a social psychologist renowned for his research on attribution and self-presentation. After a postdoctoral fellowship at the University of California at Berkeley, Baumeister worked at Case Western Reserve University from 1982 to 2003. Baumeister's research spans a wide range of topics in self and identity. His early research focused on the nature of self-presentational behaviour when someone is constrained by a reputation. He also examined the question of why people underperform in public situations, a phenomenon known as 'choking under pressure'. His subsequent work explored how the desire to escape self-awareness explains many paradoxical and seemingly self-destructive behaviours such as suicide, masochism and binge eating. Baumeister has further investigated self-esteem, which led him to conclude that the benefits of high self-esteem are often exaggerated (see Social Psychology Beyond the Lab 5.1). Since the mid 1990s, Baumeister and associates have developed the model of ego depletion, which proposes that self-regulation draws upon limited energy resources (see Research Close-Up 5.3). Baumeister has received many honours, and the Institute for Scientific Information lists Baumeister among the handful of most cited psychologists in the world.

(see Figure 5.22; Fujita & Roberts, 2010). In this way they were able to protect their goals from anticipated temptations. Conversely, individuals who fail at self-regulation often tend to think of their goals in more low-level, concrete terms (Schmeichel & Vohs, 2009; Twenge, Catanese, & Baumeister, 2003). Thus, when you are reading this text, you would do better to think of it as 'learning about human nature' instead of 'looking at letters'.

Monitoring The second part of self-regulation is that we start monitoring our behaviour. According to Carver and Scheier (1981, 1998) this monitoring function is facilitated by self-awareness, which leads us to assess the self's standing with regard to relevant standards. To test this notion, these researchers asked participants to copy complex figures from a photograph, while their self-focus was either experimentally heightened (by a mirror or the presence of an experimenter) or not. In the self-focus conditions, participants more often checked whether their drawing matched the standard of the photograph. Related experiments have shown that self-focus led individuals to seek out information about performance norms. Directing attention to the self thus leads us to monitor more closely whether our behaviour is in accordance with standards. The role of monitoring in self-regulation is further supported by neuroscience findings. Specific brain regions – like the anterior cingulate cortex – monitor whether we should step up our self-regulatory efforts (Amodio, Devine, & Harmon-Jones,

2008; Botvinick, Braver, Barch, Carter, & Cohen, 2001; Inzlicht & Gutsell, 2007).

Self-regulatory strength If you have ever followed a diet or tried to give up smoking, you can verify how hard self-regulation can be. Translating our self-regulatory standards into actual behaviour is thus the third important aspect of self-regulation. Common sense relates self-regulation to 'willpower' or 'strength of character'. Research by Baumeister and associates indicates that such notions may actually have a kernel of truth (see Leader in the Field, Roy F. Baumeister). These researchers suggest that self-regulation functions like a strength or a muscle that draws upon limited energy resources (Muraven & Baumeister, 2000). Our capacity for self-regulation may thus become depleted after sustained use. In line with this idea, studies have shown that performing a demanding self-regulation task in one domain often impairs self-regulation in another ostensibly unrelated domain. For instance, dieters who suppressed their facial expressions during a funny movie (a task that uses self-regulatory resources) were subsequently more inclined to indulge in tasty but fattening foods (Vohs & Heatherton, 2000).

Turn now to Research close-up 5.3 to learn more about how this experiment was conducted and to see a figure of its results.

DIETING IS DISRUPTED AFTER HAVING RESISTED EARLIER FOOD TEMPTATIONS

Vohs, K. D., & Heatherton, T. F. (2000). Self-regulatory failure: A resource depletion approach. *Psychological Science*, *11*, 249–254.

Introduction

Ego depletion theory holds that self-regulation draws upon a limited energy resource that allows people to control unwanted impulses and desires (Muraven & Baumeister, 2000). According to this perspective, an active effort to control behaviour in one domain depletes regulatory resources and hence leads to diminished capacity for self-regulation in other domains. Vohs and Heatherton (2000) investigated whether this ego depletion model can be applied to chronic dieters. Prior research on ego depletion had only examined artificial self-regulatory tasks that were implemented during an experimental session (e.g. squeezing a handgrip). Dieting is a more naturalistic and very common form of self-regulation in everyday life. At the same time, dieting is a very challenging task, given that long-term weight loss is extremely difficult to achieve. We summarize only the first study of this paper, and briefly refer to the results of the other two studies in the discussion below.

Method

Participants

One hundred female students participated in the experiment. They were labelled as either chronic dieters ($N = 36$) or nondieters ($N = 64$) on the basis of their scores on a scale designed to measure tendencies for restrained eating (Herman & Polivy, 1980).

Design and procedure

To ensure that participants' eating behaviour was not influenced by their prior food consumption, they were instructed not to eat for two hours before the experiment. Participants arrived individually and were asked to watch a neutral video about the daily activities of Bighorn sheep. The experimental manipulations took place while participants were watching the video.

The experiment had two manipulations. The first manipulation was meant to create differences in temptation level. An array of tasty snacks (Doritos, Skittles, M&Ms and salted peanuts) was placed either within arm's reach of the participants or across the room (approximately 3 meters away). Pilot research had shown that being seated next to tasty snacks is highly tempting for chronic dieters, but does not influence their mood or self-esteem. The second manipulation was meant to create differences in the need for self-regulation. Half of the participants were told that they could help themselves to the snack. This 'help yourself' instruction placed the burden of responsibility on the participants themselves, and hence placed greater demands on their capacity for self-regulation. The other participants were told that the snacks were being used in a different experiment later that day and asked not to touch them. The 'don't touch' instruction placed constraints on participants' behaviour, so that the level of temptation should not matter in this group, as self-regulatory demands were low. Thus, this experiment had a 3-factor design: 2 (type of dieters: chronic versus nondieters) $\times$ 2 (level of temptation: low versus high) $\times$ 2 (self-regulatory demand: low versus high).

After watching the video, participants rated their mood and were taken to another room to taste and rate ice cream flavours for 10 minutes. For this task, participants were seated in front of three flavours of ice cream. The ice cream was presented in very large containers that prevented the experimenter from seeing how much the participants ate. As the experimenter left the room, she added, 'By the way, help yourself to any ice cream you want; we have tons in the freezers.' The measure of self-regulatory ability was the amount of ice cream eaten by the participants. The latter was assessed by weighing the ice cream containers before and after participants had tasted and rated the ice cream.

Results

The results showed that the eating behaviour of chronic dieters was significantly influenced by the experimental manipulations (see Figure 5.23). Dieters in the high temptation condition ate more ice cream than dieters in the low temptation condition. However, this effect only occurred in the 'help yourself' group (high self-regulatory demand) when participants were responsible themselves for their snacking behaviour. In the 'don't touch' group (low self-regulatory demand), temptation level had no effect on eating behaviour of dieters.

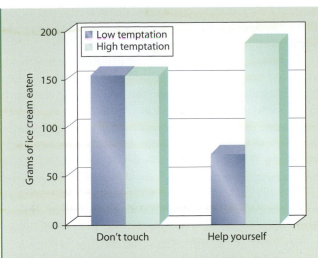

FIGURE 5.23 *Effects of temptation level and availability condition on eating behaviour of chronic dieters.*

Note: Data for nondieters are not shown in this graph.

Source: Data from Vohs & Heatherton, 2000; Expt. 1. Reprinted with permission from SAGE publications.

The eating behaviour of nondieters was not influenced by the experimental manipulations. In addition, the experimental manipulations had no effects on mood.

Discussion

These results demonstrate that resisting food temptations can make it harder for chronic dieters to restrain their eating behaviour in another, subsequent context. This effect fits very well with the model of ego depletion (Muraven & Baumeister, 2000). The ego depletion model is a general model of self-regulation that extends far beyond the domain of eating behaviour. Consequently, the model would predict that the depleting effects of dieting might carry over, not just to eating behaviour, but also to other forms of behaviour that require self-regulation. In line with this, the second study by Vohs and Heatherton (2000) showed that resisting food temptations also leads chronic dieters to display poorer self-regulation on a task that was unrelated to food intake, namely persistence on word puzzles. The ego depletion model further predicts that chronic dieters might suffer from depletion by other activities that require self-regulation. This prediction was tested in a third study by Vohs and Heatherton, which asked chronic dieters either to suppress their emotions or to let their emotions flow naturally during an emotion-eliciting film clip. The results showed that emotion suppression led chronic dieters to eat more ice cream during the taste-rating test. Taken together, the research by Vohs and Heatherton sheds important new light on the dynamics of self-regulation. Their research helps us to understand better why many of us often find it difficult to control our impulses in everyday life.

Similar breakdowns of self-regulation have been observed in many other domains, including health behaviour, aggression, close relationships, academic performance, spending behaviour, and stereotyping (for an extensive overview, see Hagger, Wood, Stiff, & Chatzisarantis, 2010).

The notion of regulatory depletion, also referred to as '**ego depletion**' (Muraven & Baumeister, 2000) is intuitively appealing and potentially explains many instances of self-regulatory failure. However, the effects of regulatory depletion are often hard to distinguish from a lack of monitoring. Indeed, several studies have found that so-called 'regulatory depletion' effects disappear when people are encouraged to monitor their actions more closely. Such monitoring may be promoted by providing people with regular performance feedback (Wan & Sternthal, 2008) and increasing self-awareness (Alberts, Martijn, & De Vries, 2011). These findings are difficult to explain in terms of energy depletion, because increased monitoring might be expected to use up even more energy. Many of the effects in regulatory depletion studies may thus be due to poor monitoring rather than energy depletion. Increasing monitoring therefore may be a promising route to increase self-regulatory capacity.

> **ego depletion** a temporary reduction of one's self-regulatory capacities due to restricted energy resources after sustained self-control efforts.

Are self-regulatory breakdowns inevitable when we have to self-regulate for extended periods of time? Although the strength model (Muraven & Baumeister, 2000) suggests a pessimistic answer to this question, other models leave room for optimism. In the 1980s, Billy Ocean wrote a hit song with the lines, 'When the going gets tough, the tough get going'. In line with this idea, performing an initial self-regulatory task can sometimes lead to increases in self-regulatory performance (Converse & DeShon, 2009; Dewitte, Bruyneel, & Geyskens, 2009; Jostmann & Koole, 2006, 2007). For instance, when a dieting person has to resist a tasty but fattening food on one occasion, this person tends to be better at declining a sugar snack on a subsequent occasion (Dewitte et al., 2009). This is because we can adapt better to a series of self-regulatory tasks when these are all in the same domain (Dewitte et al., 2009). Similarly, providing people with more time to adjust themselves to increases in self-regulatory demands leads to enhanced self-regulation, rather than the deteriorations predicted by the depletion model (Converse & DeShon, 2009). The impact of additional self-regulatory demands may thus depend on how well we can adapt to changes in self-regulatory demands (Koole, Jostmann, & Baumann, 2011). As long as we can adapt to the situation, we can respond to more demanding situations by stepping up our self-regulatory efficiency. It is only when we are no longer capable of such adaptive responding that our self-regulation breaks down.

The dark side of self-regulation

Our capacity for self-regulation is associated with a wide range of desirable outcomes, including higher grades in college, fewer reports of psychopathology, higher self-esteem, less binge eating and alcohol abuse, better relationships and interpersonal skills, secure attachment and more optimal emotional responses (Tangney, Baumeister, & Boone, 2004). Given these benefits, we may wonder if we can ever engage in too much self-regulation. The answer appears to be 'yes'. There are at least two ways in which even our best attempts to self-regulate may backfire.

In high-pressure sports settings, such as during penalty kicks or championship games, well-trained athletes often perform much more poorly than usual (e.g. Dohmen, 2008; Jordet, 2009; Wright, Voyer, Wright, & Roney, 1995; see Figure 5.24). This pattern of *choking under pressure* tends to occur when those athletes are highly self-focused (Baumeister, 1984; Baumeister & Showers, 1986). It appears that self-focus leads people to pay increased attention to their behaviour and to control their behaviour in a step-by-step fashion. Attention at this step-by-step level disrupts the execution of well-

FIGURE 5.24 *In high-pressured sports settings, such as during penalty kicks, well-trained athletes often perform much more poorly than usual.*

Source: © Press Association Images.

learned or proceduralized skills (Beilock & Carr, 2001). Thus, self-regulation may backfire when we engage in skilful, well-learned behaviour.

A second drawback of self-regulation is that it leads us to get stuck in negative emotions. Recall that when we self-regulate, we compare the self against standards for appropriate behaviour. Most of the time, we do not completely live up to these standards. Consequently, the self-regulation of behaviour inevitably evokes negative affect (Higgins, 1987; see Fejfar & Hoyle, 2000, for a meta-analytic overview). When we experience a series of setbacks and failures, focusing on our shortcomings will contribute to the onset and maintenance of depression (Pyszczynski & Greenberg, 1987). In such cases, it may well be adaptive to cease further attempts at self-regulation. Indeed, longitudinal studies have found that people who can disengage from unattainable goals display fewer depressive symptoms (Wrosch & Miller, 2009) and improved immune functioning (Miller & Wrosch, 2007). Thus, despite the many advantages that self-regulation brings, it is healthy to abandon further attempts at self-regulation when our goals turn out to be unrealistic.

Escaping the self

In view of the dark side of self-regulation, we may sometimes be motivated to avoid self-aware states. The desire to avoid self-awareness may underlie a number of seemingly paradoxical and self-destructive behaviours. For instance, this desire may foster alcohol abuse. Experiments have shown that consuming alcohol lowers self-awareness (Hull, Levenson, Young, & Sher, 1983). See Figure 5.25, which shows the relative frequency of self-focus statements while delivering a speech ('what I like and dislike about my body and physical appearance'), relative to other-focused (external) or 'other' (non-focused) statements following alcohol consumption, as compared to a placebo (tonic). Alcohol clearly reduced the frequency of self-statements. Moreover, individuals with chronically high self-awareness are at greater risk of developing drinking problems (Hull & Young, 1983). Another behaviour that may be driven by escapist motives is binge eating (Heatherton & Baumeister, 1991). Dieting individuals frequently engage in periods of disinhibited eating, or eating binges. Such eating binges may be an unintended effect of these individuals' ambitious dieting goals, which may give rise to the need to escape self-awareness. Escapist needs may be met by eating binges, which lead awareness to shift towards the immediate present by invoking strong physical sensations. Finally, the need to escape self-awareness may lead people to commit the ultimate form of self-destructive behaviour, namely suicide.

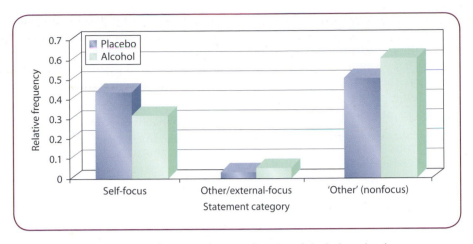

FIGURE 5.25   *Frequency of self-focus statements relative to others as a function of alcohol vs. placebo.*

Source: Data from Hull, Levenson, Young, & Sher, 1983; Expt. 1. Reproduced with permission from APA. The use of APA information does not imply endorsement by APA.

Suicidal individuals are often highly self-focused and tend to hold unrealistically high expectations of themselves (Baumeister, 1990). Moreover, experimental studies have shown that thoughts of suicide automatically spring to mind when people realize they are falling short of their goals (Chatard & Selimbegović, 2011).

Autonomous self-regulation as a resource

In the foregoing paragraphs, we have characterized self-regulation in highly ambivalent terms. On the one hand, self-regulation is an adaptive process that allows us to strive for meaningful goals and act in accordance with social norms. On the other hand, self-regulation (and the self-awareness that supports it) may deplete our energies, and an excessive emphasis on controlling our natural impulses may lead to anxiety, depression, binge eating, and even suicide. This mixture of findings seems puzzling. How can self-regulation be at once adaptive and associated with severe psychological problems?

One way to resolve this paradox is suggested by Ryan and Deci (2008; see also Deci & Ryan, 1985, 2000). According to their **self-determination theory,** people's

> **self-determination theory** accounts for people's reasons for self-regulation: if self-regulation is motivated by external pressure it is effortful; if it is freely chosen it is much more efficient without being depleting.

reasons for regulating their behaviour shape how they go about the self-regulation process. In some situations, people engage in self-regulation because they feel pressured to do so by others, like their peers or authorities. Because such external pressures are often at odds with what people truly want, this type of self-regulation tends to be effortful, energy-depleting and laden with psychological conflict.

At other times, however, people may choose to engage in self-regulation on their own accord, because regulating their behaviour is fully compatible with their own needs and interests. When self-regulation is thus freely chosen and autonomous, it is likely to be more harmonious and efficient.

Studies indeed suggest that self-regulation demands more energy when it is externally motivated rather than driven by intrinsic, autonomous motivations (Muraven, Gagné, & Rosman, 2008, Experiment 1). Ryan and Deci (2008) have gone even further, by suggesting that autonomous self-regulation may boost the overall energy available to the self. This notion was partly inspired by observations that people's reported energy levels and vitality increase markedly over the weekend (Sheldon, Ryan, & Reis, 1996). Follow-up studies in which participants were paged multiple times a day and asked to report on their feelings showed that this 'weekend effect' was statistically explained by the enhanced autonomy that people experienced over the weekend (Ryan, Bernstein, & Brown, 2010). Thus the enhanced freedom that comes with weekends may allow people to replenish their energies. Similar results have been observed for their recreational activities such as playing video games and skilled sports (see Ryan & Deci, 2008, for a review). In addition, the pursuit of intrinsic life goals, such as relationships, personal growth and serving the community is associated with greater self-reported vitality across different cultures, including the US and South Korea (Kasser & Ryan, 1996; Kim, Kasser, & Lee, 2003). By contrast, people who adopt many extrinsic life goals, such as money, fame or image display reduced vitality relative to people who adopt fewer extrinsic life goals. Taken together, it appears that freely chosen autonomous self-regulation may maintain or even enhance people's energies and vitality.

Summary

The self is an active agent that guides and regulates our actions. According to self-awareness theory, when our attention is focused on the self, we monitor our behaviour more closely. Self-focus thus promotes self-regulation, by leading us to act more in accordance with our personal goals and prevailing social norms. Self-regulation generally promotes adaptive and socially responsible behaviour. Nevertheless, self-regulation can deplete our limited energy resources when it has to be sustained over a longer period. In addition, increased self-focus can interfere with well-practised routines and lead us to get stuck in negative emotions. To prevent these problems, we may relax our efforts at self-regulation by avoiding self-aware states. Escapist behaviours may range from alcohol consumption to binge eating and even suicide. Alternatively, we may reduce the negative sides of self-regulation when we engage in autonomous self-regulation – when we, in accord with self-determination theory, self-regulate in the service of intrinsic life goals, such as relationships or personal growth.

SELF STABILITY AND CHANGE

To what degree can the self change, and through what process(es)?

We have seen in this chapter that the self is our 'home base' that guides all of our actions – it colours how we interpret the world, the interaction partners we choose and how we present ourselves. Are we hostage to this self then? Or alternatively: to what degree can the self change, and how? The answer to this question can be found in another fact that also has been amply demonstrated throughout the chapter: the self is a social product (e.g. Stryker & Vryan, 2003). We learn who we are through our interactions with others, but at the same time we influence how these others react to us by behaving toward them in certain ways – ways that are driven by how we view (or would like to view) ourselves, our goals for ourselves, our values. In other words, there is a continual reciprocal interaction between what William James (1890, 1950) called the 'doing' (behaving and interpreting) and the 'being' (descriptive) aspects of the self – the agent and the object (or what we would nowadays call the mental representation of the self). And,

because the agent is acting in the social world and being met by other similarly acting selves of other individuals, there is room for change.

We engage in what Swann and colleagues refer to as an **identity negotiation** process (e.g. Swann & Bosson, 2008; Swann, Johnson, & Bosson, 2009). We establish who we are through ongoing mutual give-and-take interactions with other individuals, and eventually come to a 'working agreed-upon consensus' between both (or multiple) people (see also Goffman, 1959). This negotiation process allows for shifts in the self. These shifts can be more minor, as occurs when people enter new jobs or new relationships, or they can be more dramatic, as when people move to entirely new and foreign environments, or experience a serious illness. A lot of the time, these shifts occur subtly due to factors out of our control, simply due to the fact that other individuals do not always respond to us in ways that are fully commensurate with our self-views. For example, if you just started a new higher status job and people begin treating you with much more respect, with time your self-views and self-esteem may adjust upward. At other times we deliberately influence the process and try to produce change in ourselves. As dramatically illustrated in our introductory example of Christina Long, people can – and do – put on different identities. Someone may also enter therapy to effect a specific desired change.

> **identity negotiation**
> a process by which we establish who we are through mutual give-and-take interactions with others.

What are the processes through which this change comes about? Although any one of these aspects can set off the process, in essence, three things have to come together: we have to change our behaviour, others have to come to consistently respond differently toward us, and we have to come to believe the new self-view(s). Many studies underscore the paramount importance of the social environment in constructing and supporting a new self-view (Schlenker, 2012). Harter (1993) for example has shown that a child's self-esteem is most likely to change when the child's social network changes through a move to a new school or new town. In an important study, Tice (1992) showed that self-presentational behaviour has the biggest impact on private self-views if performed in front of an audience. In this study, she asked students to portray themselves in a specific way (either as extraverted or introverted, randomly assigned). Half of them were being watched by another person (public condition), the other half spoke in a private room into a tape recorder. Later, students were asked to rate their own personalities on trait adjectives. As predicted, those who had self-presented in front of an audience endorsed the self-view they had previously enacted more strongly than those who self-presented in an anonymous

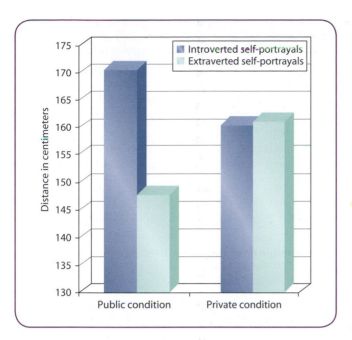

FIGURE 5.26 *Mean distance participants sat from the confederate as a function of prior self-portrayal (introverted versus extraverted) and publicity of self-presentation (audience versus private).*

Source: Data from Tice, 1992; Expt. 2. Reproduced with permission from APA. The use of APA information does not imply endorsement by APA.

condition. Importantly, this private self-view showed up not only in self-report, but also in behaviour. Participants were later asked to wait in a waiting room, in which there was another person. Figure 5.26 shows the distance at which participants seated themselves relative to the other person. As can be seen, those who had previously been in the public condition acted in line with the self-view presented earlier, whereas there was no effect for those in the private condition. Participants who had

self-presented as being extraverted in public sat much closer to the other person than anyone else, and they were also significantly more likely to initiate a conversation.

Many processes contribute to these internalizations of public behaviours. First, we engage in biased scanning – retrieving evidence from memory that fits the self-view (Jones, Rhodewalt, Berglas, & Skelton, 1981). Second, we engage in the self-perception process (Bem, 1972) discussed earlier: We observe our behaviour and assume it accurately reflects who we are. Third, we get 'caught up' in the role we are enacting (Gergen, 1971). Fourth, making a public commitment to a behaviour enlists future action to back it up (e.g. Schlenker & Wowra, 2003). That is, people will match their self-presentations to their performances when these are publicly known (although they will present themselves positively regardless of prior performance if these are unknown to others). Finally, if behaviour is widely discrepant from original self-views, then a cognitive dissonance process may set in (see Chapter 7 on attitude change), requiring us to adjust our self-views to reduce the discomfort experienced from behaving in an inconsistent manner (Aronson, 1969).

In conclusion, for any major change to take hold, an internalization process needs to take place – there has to be a genuine change of your own views of your self. For these to remain permanent, they also have to become integrated into your self-narratives – you have to revise your self-story to fit the new version – and importantly, you have to enlist the social environment to support them. Any one of these factors alone does not suffice. We are neither at the mercy of our self-views, nor of our social environment: The self is constructed, maintained and changed through a transactional process both in the mind and within a social reality.

CHAPTER SUMMARY

- *Why is the self 'social'?* The self we experience and express is highly variable and dependent on social circumstances. The self is constructed, maintained and changed through our interactions with others.

- *What are the personal sources of self-knowledge and how accurate are they?* Reflecting and observing ourselves is a means to gain insight into ourselves. However, these sources of self-knowledge may be inaccurate, as we cannot consciously attend to automatic processes, and we tend to push away unwanted information.

- *What are the interpersonal sources of self-knowledge and how accurate are they?* The things that others tell us about ourselves, their reactions toward us, as well as the comparisons we draw between others and ourselves, permit us to learn much about our self. Furthermore, interactions with significant others as well as belonging to social groups shape our views of ourselves. These sources too, however, can be biased.

- *How do we gain a coherent self?* Autobiographical memories as well as self-narratives – that we construe in line with our self-concept – help create a coherent and continuous sense of the self.

- *What is meant by self-concept?* The self-concept is the cognitive representation of our self-knowledge, and consists of characteristics that we use for describing us. These self-beliefs are stored in self-schemas that organize and guide the processing of self-relevant information. They encompass actual, ideal and possible selves, and they come in both explicit and implicit forms.

- *What is self-esteem?* Self-esteem is the evaluative component of self-knowledge and consists of an overall appraisal of our self. It is conceived as either a trait or a state, and people can differ in which life domains are important to their self-esteem. As with the self-concept, self-esteem too can come in both the explicit and the implicit form.

- *What is the influence of culture on the self?* Cultures differ in their conceptualization of the individual and of his or her role in society. Therefore, cultural differences, as for example between independent and interdependent self-construals, shape our perceptions, motivations and emotional reactions.

- *Do we prefer true or positively distorted self-information?* Although there is evidence for the self-assessment motive (i.e. the desire to learn objective information), we are primarily driven by the self-enhancement motive (i.e. the desire to enhance the positivity of the self and to protect it from negative information).

- *What strategies do we adopt when we self-enhance?* There are intrapersonal strategies, like the superiority bias and the self-serving attributional bias. But self-enhancement also influences our interpersonal self-presentation and encompasses, among other strategies, dressing smartly, talking about achievements, self-handicapping or basking in reflected glory.

- *What is self-verification?* Self-verification is the desire to affirm our firmly held self-views. As long as these self-views are positive, self-enhancement and self-verification go in the same direction. But people with low self-regard prefer to self-verify their negative self-beliefs instead of self-enhancing.

- *Why do we self-enhance?* Self-enhancement is beneficial for our physical and mental health. Sociometer theory suggests that positive self-feelings are desirable because our self-esteem signals the degree of social belongingness. Terror management theory has received more empirical support – it proposes that self-enhancement helps us cope with existential fears.

- *Is high self-esteem good?* High self-esteem is associated with many positive things, such as, for example, higher resiliency to stress and depression. At the same time, it is linked with undesirable outcomes like more risky behaviour of various types and – in the case where someone feels threatened – aggression. High self-esteem seems desirable to the extent that it is genuine and not contingent on external sources.

- *How does the self regulate our behaviour?* Self-regulation can be thought of as a cybernetic system, where actual circumstances are monitored and compared to self-regulatory standards. When these are not met, actions are taken to reduce the discrepancy between desired and actual states.

- *Can the self change?* As the self is a social product, changing it is also socially determined. In the process of negotiating our identity in mutual interactions with others, for changes to take hold we need to change our behaviour, believe the new self-views and enlist others to consistently respond towards us differently.

SUGGESTIONS FOR FURTHER READING

Baer, J., Kaufman, J. C., & Baumeister, R. F. (2008). *Are we free? Psychology and free will.* New York: Oxford University Press. This book reviews experimental and theoretical work by researchers from all branches of psychology interested in investigating humans' free will.

Baumeister, R. F. (1991). *Escaping the self: Alcoholism, spirituality, masochism, and other flights from the burden of selfhood.* New York: Basic Books. This book takes a rather provocative view on the self by exploring the notion that problematic behaviours, such as masochism and suicide, may be understood as resulting from a need to escape self-consciousness.

Dunning, D. (2005). *Self-insight. Roadblocks and detours on the path to knowing thyself.* New York: Psychology Press. An accessibly written book, dealing with frequently encountered human shortcomings in trying to evaluate and know oneself.

Feinberg, T. E., & Keenan, J. P. (Eds.). (2005). *The lost self. Pathologies of the brain and identity.* New York: Oxford University Press. A compilation of contributions from acknowledged experts in the fields of philosophy, cognitive neuroscience, neurology and psychology, grouped to provide an exploration of the neurobiology of the self.

Harter, S. (1999). *The construction of the self. A developmental perspective.* New York: Guilford. This book analyses the emergence of individuals' unique sense of self as a result of cognitive and social construction processes, and provides a theoretical background for this development.

Heatherton, T. F. (2011). Neuroscience of self and self-regulation. *Annual Review of Psychology, 62*, 363–390. This article reviews recent social neuroscience research on the psychological components that support the human capacity for self-regulation.

James, W. (1961). The Self. In G. Allport (Ed.), *Psychology: The briefer course* (pp. 159–191). Cambridge, MA: Harvard University Press. (Original work published 1892.) James's original chapter on the self is a classic – a 'must-read', as James's notions of the self have proven fundamental to modern conceptualizations and continue to influence our present understandings of the construct. It is a captivating read too!

Kernis, M. H. (Ed.). (2006). *Self-esteem issues and answers. A sourcebook of current perspectives.* New York: Psychology Press. This volume summarizes the current status of knowledge on the topic in an engaging and readable format, shedding light on what is known about the functioning of self-esteem, while simultaneously giving the reader a sense of the complexities involved in the concept.

Leary, M. R. (2004). *The curse of the self: Self-awareness, egotism, and the quality of human life.* New York: Oxford University Press. The author illustrates the idea that human sufferings (e.g. depression, anxiety and other negative emotions) in part could be seen as emerging from the human capacity of self-reflection and egocentrism.

Morf, C. C., & Mischel, W. (2012). The self as a psycho-social dynamic processing system: Toward a converging science of self-hood. In M. R. Leary & J. P. Tangney (Eds.), *Handbook of self and identity* (2nd ed., pp. 21–49). New York: Guilford. This chapter expands on the ideas of the self as a coherent, organized, yet dynamic system and elaborates on the self-construction process presented in this chapter.

Sedikides, C., & Skowronski, J. J. (1997). The symbolic self in evolutionary context. *Personality and Social Psychology Review, 1,* 80–102. The authors take an interesting perspective on the symbolic self by evaluating the adaptive value of this human capacity and tracing its emergence back to evolutionary pressures.

Wilson, T. D. (2002). *Strangers to ourselves: Discovering the adaptive unconscious.* Cambridge, MA: Harvard University Press. This book examines the evolution of the idea of the unconscious, the ways in which it operates, and how our actions – rather than our thoughts – help us to know ourselves.

6 Attitudes

GEOFFREY HADDOCK AND GREGORY R. MAIO

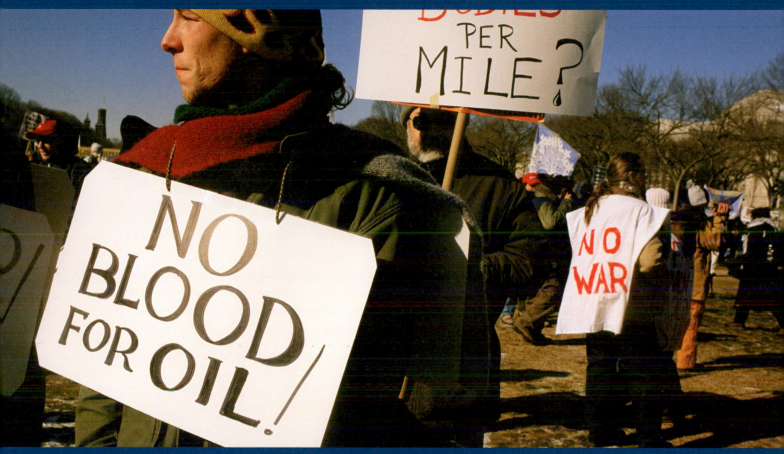

Source: © Sarah Leen. Used under licence from Getty Images.

KEY TERMS

- affective component of attitude
- attitude
- attitude functions
- attitude–behaviour relation
- attitudinal ambivalence
- behavioural component of attitude
- cognitive component of attitude
- cognitive dissonance
- ego-defensive function
- evaluative conditioning
- explicit measures of attitude
- implementation intentions
- implicit measures of attitude
- mere exposure effect
- MODE model
- multicomponent model of attitude
- object appraisal function
- one-dimensional perspective of attitudes
- perceived behavioural control
- self-efficacy
- self-monitoring
- self-perception theory
- social adjustment function
- theory of planned behaviour
- theory of reasoned action
- two-dimensional perspective on attitudes
- utilitarian function
- value-expressive function

CHAPTER OUTLINE

ROUTE MAP OF THE CHAPTER

The study of attitudes is at the core of social psychology. Attitudes refer to our evaluations of issues, people, groups and other types of objects in our social world. Attitudes are important, because they impact both the way we perceive the world and how we behave. For example, a questionable penalty during the World Cup football final is likely to be perceived differently depending upon which team you support. Further, our voting behaviour very much depends on the extent to which we like the different candidates. In this chapter, we introduce the attitude concept. We consider how attitudes are formed and organized and discuss theories explaining why we hold attitudes. We also address how social psychologists measure attitudes, as well as examining how our attitudes help predict our behaviour.

INTRODUCTION

All of us like some things and dislike others. For instance, one person may like the Welsh national rugby team and another person may dislike liver. A social psychologist would say that we possess a positive **attitude** towards the Welsh rugby team and a negative *attitude* towards liver. Understanding differences in attitudes across people and uncovering the reasons why people like and dislike different things has long interested social psychologists. Indeed, over 70 years ago, Gordon Allport (1935, p. 798) asserted that the attitude concept is 'the most distinctive and indispensable concept in . . . social psychology'. That statement remains equally valid today; the study of attitudes remains at the forefront of social psychological research and theory.

> **attitude** an overall evaluation of a stimulus object.

In this chapter, we introduce a number of important issues regarding the attitude concept. First, we define the term 'attitude'. We will show that expressing an attitude involves making an evaluative judgement about an attitude object. Second, we devote attention to the content of attitudes. We will show that attitudes have cognitive, affective and behavioural components; that is, attitudes can be *based* on beliefs, feelings and behaviours, while also *shaping* beliefs, feelings and behaviours. In discussing the content of attitudes, we focus on these components as *antecedents* of an attitude. Third, we consider the structure of attitudes. We will show that attitudes can be organized and structured in different ways. Fourth, we consider the psychological functions or needs that are served by attitudes. We will show that people hold attitudes for a number of reasons. Fifth, we introduce how attitudes are measured, concentrating on direct and indirect strategies that psychologists have developed to measure attitudes. We will show that attitudes can be measured in many ways. Finally, we review research that has addressed a key question for attitude researchers: under what circumstances do attitudes predict behaviour? We will show that our attitudes and opinions are quite effective in predicting how we behave.

Given the importance of attitudes in understanding how we think, feel and behave, it is not surprising that there are numerous links between attitudes and many of the other topics covered in this textbook. For example, self-esteem can be conceptualized as one's attitude toward the self (see Chapter 5), and attitudes have obvious links to the study of persuasion and behaviour change, advertising (Chapter 7), social influence (Chapter 8), and the study of prejudice (Chapter 14).

WHAT IS AN ATTITUDE?

How can we best define an attitude?

A logical starting point is to define what we mean by the term *attitude*. We define an attitude as 'an overall evaluation of an object that is based on cognitive, affective and behavioural information' (Maio & Haddock, 2010, p. 4). Inherent in this definition is the idea that reporting an attitude involves the expression of an *evaluative judgement* about a stimulus object. In other words, reporting an attitude involves making a decision concerning liking versus disliking, approving versus disapproving, or favouring versus disfavouring a particular issue, object or person.

An attitude, when conceptualized as an evaluative judgement, can vary in two important ways (see Eagly & Chaiken, 1993; Maio & Haddock, 2010). First, attitudes can differ in *valence*, or direction. Some attitudes that a person possesses are positive (e.g. 'I like ice-cream'), others are negative (e.g. 'I dislike liver'; Figure 6.1), and

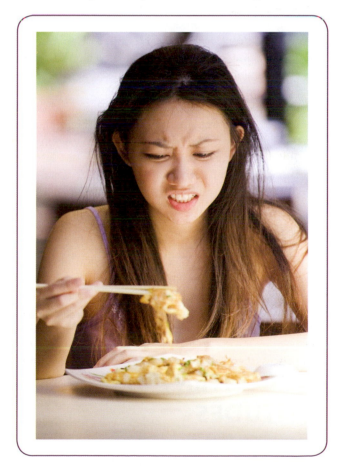

FIGURE 6.1 *Some people are certain of a strong dislike and will express this spontaneously.*

Source: © koh szi kiat. Used under licence from Shutterstock.

LEADER IN THE FIELD

Alice Eagly (b. 1938) completed her undergraduate degree at Radcliffe College before pursuing a PhD at the University of Michigan (1965). Her research on attitude change (with Shelly Chaiken; see Leader in the Field, Chapter 7) led to the development of the heuristic–systematic model of persuasion (see Chapter 7). Together, Eagly and Chaiken (1993) wrote *The Psychology of Attitudes*, arguably the most comprehensive volume written on the attitude concept. In addition to her research on the psychology of attitudes, Eagly has made enormous contributions to our understanding of the psychology of gender.

LEADER IN THE FIELD

Mark Zanna, FRSC (b. 1944) completed his undergraduate and PhD degrees at Yale University. He started his academic career at Princeton University, before moving (in 1975) to the University of Waterloo, where he is currently University Professor of Psychology. In over 200 publications, his research on topics such as attitude content, attitude structure and attitude–behaviour relations have had an enormous impact on the field. Further, Zanna and colleagues have applied conceptualizations of attitude to increase our understanding of concepts such as prejudice, discrimination and how attitude models can be used to influence health-related behaviour.

yet others are neutral ('I neither like nor dislike eating fried foods'). Second, attitudes can differ in *strength*. For example, two people (Geoff and Greg) may both have a negative attitude to liver, but one, Geoff, is rather uncertain about his attitude, and his view comes to mind quite slowly, while the other, Greg, is certain of his strong dislike, and his view is expressed spontaneously when anyone mentions liver ("Yuck!"). You will learn more about different aspects of attitude strength later in this chapter.

Until now, we have used different examples when describing our own attitudes. This leads to an important question – can *anything* be the object of an attitude? Basically, any stimulus that can be evaluated along a dimension of favourability can be conceptualized as an attitude object. As noted by Eagly and Chaiken (1993), some attitude objects are abstract concepts (e.g. 'liberalism'), and others are concrete (e.g. a computer) (see Leader in the Field, Alice Eagly). Furthermore, one's own self (e.g. self-esteem) and other individuals (e.g. a particular politician) can serve as attitude objects, as can social policy issues (e.g. capital punishment) and social groups (e.g. people from Canada).

Summary

Reporting an attitude involves the expression of an evaluative judgement about a stimulus object. Attitudes differ in valence and strength, and any stimulus that can be evaluated along a dimension of favourability can be conceptualized as an attitude object.

THE CONTENT OF ATTITUDES

What are the bases of attitudes?

So far we have seen that attitudes can be thought of as an overall evaluation (e.g. like–dislike) of an attitude object. This perspective has generated a number of conceptual models of the attitude concept. Historically,

one of the most influential models of attitude has been the multicomponent model (Zanna & Rempel, 1988; see Maio & Haddock, 2010, for a review; also Leader in the Field, Mark Zanna). According to this perspective (see Theory Box 6.1 and Figure 6.2), attitudes are summary evaluations

multicomponent model of attitude a model of attitude that conceptualizes attitudes as summary evaluations that have cognitive, affective and behavioural antecedents.

THEORY BOX 6.1

THE MULTICOMPONENT MODEL OF ATTITUDE

The multicomponent model of attitudes (Zanna & Rempel, 1988) proposes that attitudes are overall evaluations of an attitude object that are derived from cognitive, affective and behavioural information. *Cognitions* refer to thoughts and beliefs about an attitude object (e.g. a particular politician is intelligent and values individual freedom). *Affective* information refers to feelings associated with an attitude object (e.g. blood donation may make an individual feel anxious and scared). *Behavioural* information refers to behaviours we have performed (or might perform in the future) with respect to an attitude object (e.g. signing a petition against the practice of factory farming).

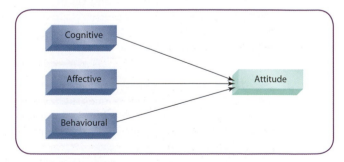

FIGURE 6.2 *The multicomponent model of attitude.*

Source: Reproduced by permission of SAGE Publications, London, Los Angeles, New Delhi and Singapore, from Maio and Haddock, *The psychology of attitudes and attitude change* (© SAGE, 2010).

of an object that have *cognitive*, *affective* and *behavioural* antecedents. A number of researchers have considered how these three antecedents contribute to the formation and expression of attitudes.

The cognitive component of attitudes

Expenctancy-Valence

cognitive component of attitude beliefs, thoughts and attributes associated with an attitude object.

The **cognitive component of attitudes** refers to beliefs, thoughts and attributes we associate with a particular object. In many cases, a person's attitude might be based primarily upon a consideration of the positive and negative attributes of the attitude object (Figure 6.3). For example, when one of us bought a new car a few years ago, he devoted considerable attention to factors such as different vehicles' safety records, fuel economy, resale value and repair costs. In this example, he formed attitudes towards the different cars via a conscious consideration of the positive and negative attributes of each car. Cognitions have an impact on many types of attitudes. Within the study of intergroup attitudes (see Chapters 4 and 14), stereotypes are usually considered as beliefs about the attributes possessed by a particular social group. Further, many studies have revealed that possessing negative stereotypes about a group of people is associated with having a prejudicial attitude towards the group (e.g. Esses, Haddock, & Zanna, 1993; Kawakami, Dion, & Dovidio, 1998; see Maio, Haddock, Manstead, & Spears, 2010).

Cognitions, in the form of beliefs, are a key part of one approach to attitudes, which argues that attitudes are derived from more elementary cognitions about the attitude object. Specifically, Fishbein and Ajzen's (1975) expectancy–value approach describes an attitude towards an object as the sum of 'expectancy × value' products. Expectancies are beliefs or subjective probabilities that the object possesses a certain attribute; these beliefs may range from 0 to 1 in strength. Values, or evaluations, are ratings of the attributes, normally from −3 to +3. An attitude object will be evaluated positively if it is seen as leading to, or associated with, positive things and as helping to avoid negative things. Only salient beliefs count towards the overall attitudes; these are beliefs that a person considers most relevant. We can illustrate the model by computing a person's attitude towards the game of golf. This person might think that golf is (1) a valuable form of exercise, (2) a good way to see friends, and (3) frustrating. Each of these beliefs will have both an expectancy and a value. For example, exercise might have a high expectancy (.9) and positive evaluation (+3); seeing friends might

FIGURE 6.3(a) and (b) *Attitudes towards different cars might be based on the positive and negative characteristics of each car.*
Source: (a) © Juice Images. Used under licence from Getty Images; (b) © Goodluz. Used under licence from Shutterstock.

be perceived as having a lower expected outcome (.7) that is somewhat positive (+2); while frustration is (thankfully!) somewhat infrequent (.3) but very negative (−3). The individual's overall attitude towards golf is computed by summing the belief–evaluation products (e.g. 2.7 + 1.4 − .9 = 3.2).

The affective component of attitudes

affective component of attitude the feelings or emotions associated with an attitude object.

The **affective component of attitudes** refers to feelings or emotions associated with an attitude object. Affective responses influence attitudes in a number of ways. A primary way in which feelings influence attitudes is due to affective reactions that are aroused in the individual after exposure to the attitude object. For instance, many people indicate that spiders make them feel scared. These negative affective responses are likely to produce a negative attitude towards spiders.

evaluative conditioning changes the liking for a stimulus by repeatedly pairing it with another more polarized positive or negative stimulus.

Feelings can become associated with attitude objects in several ways. A number of researchers have used **evaluative conditioning** paradigms to assess how pairing affective information with an attitude object can produce a positive or negative attitude. For example, Krosnick, Betz, Jussim, and Lynn (1992) conducted a study in which they presented participants with a series of pictures of an unfamiliar person. Importantly, each picture was preceded by an affect-arousing image that was presented at a subliminal level, that is, at very brief exposure below the threshold necessary for conscious encoding (see Chapter 4). For some participants, these images were negative (e.g. a bucket of snakes, a bloody shark), while for other participants these images were positive (e.g. a pair of kittens, a couple getting married). After seeing the pictures of the unfamiliar person, participants indicated their overall attitude toward this individual, as well as their evaluation of the target's personality characteristics and physical attractiveness. As can be seen in Figure 6.4, Krosnick et al. found that participants who received subliminal presentations of the positive images liked the individual more compared with participants who received subliminal presentations of the negative images. Not only were participants' attitudes affected by the subliminal presentations, so too were their perceptions of the target person's attributes and physical attractiveness.

In addition to evaluative conditioning and subliminal priming, another way in which affect guides

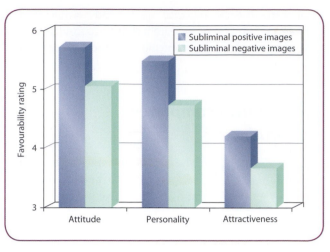

FIGURE 6.4 *The influence of subliminal priming on social perceptions.*

Source: Adapted from Krosnick et al., 1992. Reproduced with permission from SAGE Publications Ltd.

attitudes comes from research by Zajonc and colleagues (e.g. Kunst-Wilson & Zajonc, 1980; Monahan, Murphy, & Zajonc, 2000; Murphy & Zajonc, 1993; Zajonc, 1968; see also Leader in the Field, Robert Zajonc). These researchers argue that attitudes are formed on the basis of affective responses that precede conscious thought. To test this hypothesis, studies have examined how **mere exposure** to stimuli can influence an attitude. In these studies, different types of unfamiliar stimuli

mere exposure effect increase in liking for an object as a result of being repeatedly exposed to it.

(e.g. various Chinese characters) are presented to participants a certain number of times. The stimuli are then shown again to participants along with other, novel stimuli (e.g. new characters), and participants' attitudes towards the familiar and unfamiliar stimuli are measured. A large number of studies have revealed that stimuli that have been presented many times are liked more than stimuli that have not been seen before. For instance, in one study by Zajonc (1968), participants were initially shown 12 different Chinese characters. During this exposure phase, each character was shown either 25 times, 10 times, five times, twice, once or not at all. Later, participants were asked to indicate how much they liked each character. The results of this study are presented in Figure 6.5. As can be seen, participants' attitudes towards the characters became more positive the more times the character had been seen at the exposure phase. Researchers have replicated these findings in many domains (see Maio & Haddock, 2010; see also Chapter 11). The mere exposure

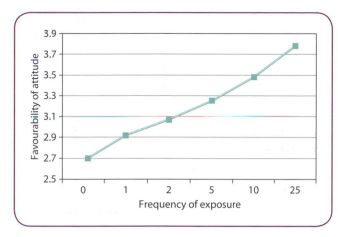

FIGURE 6.5 *The influence of repeated exposure on attitudes.*
Source: Adapted from Zajonc, 1968. Copyright © 1968 by the American Psychological Association. Adapted with permission. *Journal of Personality and Social Psychology, 9*, 1–27. The use of APA information does not imply endorsement by APA.

LEADER IN THE FIELD

Robert Zajonc (1923–2008) was born in Lodz, Poland. After the Nazis invaded Poland he was dispatched to a labour camp in Germany. He escaped, twice, joined the French Resistance and studied at the University of Paris. When the war ended, he worked for the United Nations Relief and Rehabilitation Administration in Paris. He completed his PhD at the University of Michigan (1955), where he remained until 1994. Zajonc's research covered many areas relevant to the psychology of attitudes. His work on the mere exposure effect led to the development of an influential programme of study exploring how affective processes influence attitudes and actions. This research led Zajonc to consider the role of unconscious processes in determining preferences and behaviour.

phenomenon helps explain why we sometimes come to like classical music melodies that we hear repeatedly, even when we are unable to recall the artist who composed the music or any details of our prior experiences hearing it.

More recent research has demonstrated that mere exposure can increase positive affect and that the effects can transfer to novel stimuli that have not been encountered. For example, in one experiment, Monahan et al. (2000) found that repeated subliminal exposure of one set of stimuli elicited more positive mood during a subsequent presentation of similar stimuli. In another experiment, these researchers found that repeated subliminal exposure caused more liking for new stimuli that were similar to the old ones (e.g. both were Chinese ideographs) than for new stimuli that were of a different

category (e.g. different shapes). This result suggests that repeated exposure can create *general* positive affect, which can then be attached to new objects that are similar to the old ones.

The behavioural component of attitudes

The **behavioural component of attitudes** refers to behaviours we have performed (or might perform in the future) with respect to an attitude object. The role of behavioural processes in relation to attitudes can take on different forms. As a starting point, behaviours can serve as an antecedent of attitudes. For instance, people might infer that they have a negative attitude towards nuclear power plants if they recall having previously signed a petition against having a nuclear power plant built near their neighbourhood.

behavioural component of attitude past behaviours (also present and future anticipated behaviours) associated with an attitude object.

The idea that people might infer their attitudes on the basis of their previous actions was developed by Bem. According to Bem's (1972) **self-perception theory**, individuals do not always have access to their opinions about different objects (see also Nisbett & Wilson,

self-perception theory the theory assumes that when inner states are ambiguous, people can infer these states by observing their own behaviour.

1977). Bem argued that this is especially likely when the person's attitude is particularly weak or ambiguous. Many studies have shown results consistent with this reasoning. For example, Chaiken and Baldwin (1981) asked participants to complete a questionnaire containing items that were framed in a way to suggest to people that they did perform pro-environment behaviours (e.g. picking up the garbage of others) with either high or low frequency. After completing this task, participants indicated their attitude towards the environment. The results were consistent with self-perception theory. Participants who were led to infer that they performed pro-environmental behaviours with great frequency reported more favourable attitudes than did participants who were led to infer that they performed pro-environmental behaviours less frequently. Furthermore, this effect was obtained only among those individuals who, prior to the experiment, had weak attitudes about environmental matters.

Research has shown that the mere *belief* in having performed a behaviour is sufficient to shape attitudes. Albarracín and Wyer (2000) tested the effects of beliefs about past behaviour by leading participants to believe that, without being aware of it, they had expressed

- Pinpoint underlying process
- Mechanism
- We like what is familiar

either support for a particular position or opposition to it. Because participants had not actually engaged in such behaviour, the research tested directly the effects of merely *believing* that one has behaved in a certain way. As expected, participants reported attitudes that were consistent with the alleged past behaviour.

Behaviours may also influence strongly held attitudes, but in a different way. Festinger (1954) proposed that people can change their attitudes in order to be consistent with behaviours that they have performed. For example, people might convince themselves that they like several boring tasks if they have just been given a small (rather than large) payment to tell others that the tasks are great (i.e. to engage in counter-attitudinal behaviour; Festinger & Carlsmith, 1959). Many experiments support Festinger's hypothesis that this effect occurs because the counter-attitudinal behaviour induces **cognitive dissonance**.

cognitive dissonance
an aversive state which motivates individuals to reduce it.

Cognitive dissonance is an aversive state, which motivates individuals to reduce it (e.g. Zanna & Cooper, 1974; Zanna, Higgins & Taves, 1976). This motivation will be stronger the greater the dissonance. One way to reduce dissonance is to change one's attitude towards the behaviour. This will be discussed in more detail in Chapter 7, which focuses on how attitudes can be changed.

Behaviours can also serve as an antecedent of attitudes in a more direct way. Research has demonstrated that performing a behaviour that has evaluative implications or connotations influences the favourability of attitudes. For example, Briñol and Petty (2003) conducted a study in which participants believed they were participating in a consumer research study on the quality of headphones. Participants were informed that a headphone manufacturer was interested in determining how headphones performed when listeners were engaged in various movements such as dancing and jogging. Briñol and Petty (2003) had participants move their heads in either an up-and-down motion (nodding the head) or a side-to-side motion (shaking the head) as they listened to an editorial played over the headphones. When the arguments contained in the editorial were strong, it was expected that moving one's head in an up-and-down motion would lead participants to be more positive about the position being advocated in the message, because nodding is a motion that is commonly associated with agreement. The results revealed that participants were more likely to agree with the content of a highly persuasive appeal when they moved their heads up and down as compared to side to side (see also Briñol & Petty, 2008; Wells & Petty, 1980).

The enactment of other types of behaviour also affects the favourability of individuals' attitudes. For example, Cacioppo, Priester and Berntson (1993) asked participants to engage in either arm flexion (moving one's hand towards the body – a behaviour associated with approach) or arm extension (moving one's hand away from the body – a behaviour associated with avoidance) while viewing a variety of unfamiliar Chinese characters. Later in the experiment, when asked to rate the characters, Cacioppo et al. (1993) found that characters viewed during arm flexion were rated more positively than those viewed during arm extension. Taken together, in both the Briñol and Petty (2003) and Cacioppo et al. (1993) studies, a direct physical behaviour initiated by individuals influenced the favourability of their attitude.

Of course, in addition to serving as an antecedent of attitudes, behaviours can also reflect or express a person's attitude (see e.g. Bohner & Wänke, 2002; Eagly & Chaiken, 1993). For instance, an individual's positive attitude toward a particular politician might be reflected in their decision to vote for that candidate. Similarly, intending to write to your local member of parliament stating your opposition to an increase in university tuition fees can express your negative attitude toward this issue. Later in the chapter we will discuss in more detail how attitudes are often reflected in behaviour.

How related are the components of attitudes?

Usually, if you possess positive beliefs about an object, your feelings about the object and behaviours relevant to the object are also likely to be positive. At the same time, there is plenty of evidence suggesting that these antecedents are unique. For example, research has shown that people's attitudes toward some issues or objects (e.g. blood donation) tend to be based on affect, whereas people's attitudes toward other issues or objects (e.g. a new printer) tend to be based on cognitive and behavioural information. More recent research has revealed that some people are more likely to possess cognition-based attitudes, whereas other people are more likely to have affect-based attitudes (see Huskinson & Haddock, 2004; see later in the chapter for a discussion of the role of behaviour). Furthermore, whether someone forms their attitudes on the basis of their beliefs or their feelings has important implications (see Research Close-Up 6.1).

ATTITUDE CONTENT AND PERSUASION

Haddock, G., Maio, G. R., Arnold, K., & Huskinson, T. L. H. (2008). Should persuasion be affective or cognitive? The moderating effects of need for affect and need for cognition. *Personality and Social Psychology Bulletin, 34*, 769–778.

Introduction

In the 1970s a series of famous television advertisements shown in North America featured former professional athletes exalting their preference for a particular brand of beer. While some of the athletes noted that the beer was *less filling* than other beers, others replied that it *tasted great*. The first component of the message highlighted a positive belief about the beverage (i.e. its low caloric intake), whereas the second component highlighted a positive affective response associated with the beverage (i.e. its taste). Which part of the message would you find more persuasive? Perhaps it depends on whether your attitudes tend to be based more upon the content of your beliefs or more upon the content of your feelings.

Haddock and colleagues (2008) tested whether individuals whose attitudes tend to be based more on cognition or affect would be more or less persuaded by an appeal that was either cognitive or affective in nature. Based on previous research, they predicted that individuals with affect-based attitudes would be more persuaded by an affect-based appeal compared to a cognition-based appeal, whereas individuals with cognition-based attitudes would be more persuaded by a cognition-based appeal compared to an affect-based appeal.

Method

Participants

Twenty-four students (16 women and 8 men) took part for psychology course credit.

Design and procedure

The basic design included two factors: whether a person's attitudes were based more on cognition or affect, and whether they received a persuasive appeal that was cognitive or affective. The basis of a person's attitudes as cognitive or affective was determined by their responses on two scales: (1) the need for cognition scale (Cacioppo & Petty, 1982), which measures individuals' tendency to engage in and enjoy effortful processing (see Individual Differences 7.1, Chapter 7); and (2) the need for affect scale (Maio & Esses, 2001), which measures individuals' tendency to seek out emotional experiences. Participants high in need for cognition and low in need for affect were conceptualized as being cognition-based, while participants high in need for affect and low in need for cognition were conceptualized as being affect-based.

In the experiment, participants were informed that they would be evaluating a new beverage called 'Power-Plus'. Half of the participants were randomly assigned to receive an affect-based appeal, and the other half to receive a cognition-based appeal. Participants in the affect-based appeal condition tasted a sample of a pleasant tasting, unfamiliar beverage. The affect within the appeal is derived from the pleasant feeling resulting from having tasted the beverage. Participants in the cognition-based appeal condition read a set of strong and positive attributes about the drink. For instance, they were told that the drink was made from natural ingredients and contained real fruit extracts. Immediately after either tasting or reading about Power-Plus, participants indicated their attitude toward the beverage using a series of nine-point semantic differential scales (*good – bad*; *positive – negative*; *like – dislike*).

Results and discussion

The results of the study provided support for the researchers' hypothesis that the effectiveness of cogent affect- and cognition-based persuasive messages depends on individual differences in need for affect and need for cognition (see Figure 6.6). As expected, an affect-based message was more persuasive among individuals with an affect preference (i.e. individuals high in need for affect and low in need for cognition), whereas a cognition-based message was more persuasive among individuals with a cognition preference (i.e. individuals low in need for affect and high in need for cognition). These results demonstrate how the content of an attitude influences persuasion (see also Mayer & Tormala, 2010).

FIGURE 6.6 *The influence of affective–cognitive preference and appeal type on attitudes.*

Source: Adapted from Haddock et al., 2008. Reproduced with permission from SAGE Publications Ltd.

Summary

Attitudes have cognitive, affective and behavioural components. The cognitive component refers to beliefs, thoughts and attributes associated with an attitude object. The affective component refers to feelings or emotions associated with an attitude object. The behavioural component refers to past behaviours with respect to an attitude object.

THE STRUCTURE OF ATTITUDES

What are the two basic perspectives on attitude structure?

In addition to considering the content of attitudes, another important issue concerns how positive and negative evaluations are organized within and among the cognitive, affective and behavioural antecedents of attitudes. It is typically assumed that the existence of positive beliefs, feelings and behaviours inhibits the occurrence of negative beliefs, feelings and behaviours. For example, this framework suggests that an individual with positive beliefs, feelings and behaviours about the Welsh rugby team is unlikely to have negative beliefs, feelings and behaviours about this team. In other words, according to this **one-dimensional perspective on attitudes**, the positive and negative elements are stored in memory at opposite ends of a single dimension, and people tend to experience either end of the dimension or a location in-between.

This one-dimensional view is opposed by a **two-dimensional perspective on attitudes**, which suggests that positive and negative elements are stored along two separate dimensions (Cacioppo, Gardner, & Berntson, 1997; see Leader in the Field, John Cacioppo). One dimension reflects whether the attitude has few or many positive elements, and the other dimension reflects whether the attitude has few or many negative elements. This view proposes that people can possess any combination of positivity or negativity in their attitudes. Consistent with the one-dimensional view, attitudes may consist of

one-dimensional perspective on attitudes a perspective that perceives positive and negative elements as stored along a single dimension.

two-dimensional perspective on attitudes a perspective that perceives positive and negative elements as stored along separate dimensions.

LEADER IN THE FIELD

John Cacioppo (b. 1951) obtained his PhD from the renowned social psychology programme at the Ohio State University in 1977. He held academic posts at Notre Dame University and the University of Iowa before returning to the Ohio State University as Professor of Psychology. His research (much of it in a highly productive collaboration with Richard Petty, see Leader in the Field, Richard E. Petty, in Chapter 7) has had an enormous impact on different areas of the study of attitudes, such as attitude structure, attitude content and attitude change. He is currently Tiffany and Margaret Blake Distinguished Service Professor of Psychology and Director of the Center for Cognitive and Social Neuroscience at the University of Chicago. His numerous awards include the Scientific Impact Award from the Society for Experimental Social Psychology (2009), the Distinguished Scientific Contribution Award from the American Psychological Association (2002), and the Campbell Award (for Distinguished Scientific Contributions to Personality and Social Psychology) from the Society for Personality and Social Psychology (2000).

few positive and many negative elements, few negative and many positive, or few positive and few negative (i.e. a neutral position). Inconsistent with the one-dimensional view, attitudes might occasionally subsume both positive *and* negative elements, leading to **attitudinal ambivalence**. Ambivalence occurs when a person both likes and dislikes an attitude object. For example, someone might love the taste of chocolate cake, but dislike its effects on their waistline. The two-dimensional perspective explicitly allows for this ambivalence to occur, whereas the one-dimensional perspective does not.

attitudinal ambivalence a state that occurs when an individual both likes and dislikes an attitude object.

The one-dimensional and two-dimensional perspectives are presented in Figure 6.7. The top panel shows the one-dimensional view of attitudes. Person X, who is plotted on an axis depicting the one-dimensional view, would be slightly negative. The single axis does not permit one to mark Person X as being both negative and positive. The bottom panel of Figure 6.7 shows the two-dimensional view of attitudes, with one axis (vertical) representing variability in negative evaluations, and the other axis (horizontal) depicting variability in positive evaluations. From this perspective, a person can possess high amounts of both negativity and positivity towards an object. For example, Person Y could be considered highly ambivalent.

Which perspective is superior? In one important way, the two-dimensional perspective is advantageous, because it allows for the same patterns of positivity and negativity as the one-dimensional view, while also allowing for ambivalence. For instance, it is difficult to interpret the meaning of the neutral point in one-dimensional

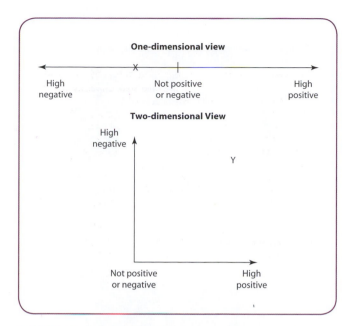

FIGURE 6.7 *The one-dimensional and two-dimensional perspectives on attitudes.*

Source: Reproduced by permission of SAGE Publications, London, Los Angeles, New Delhi and Singapore, from Haddock and Maio, 2009, The Psychology of Attitudes and Attitude Change (© SAGE, 2009).

scales for assessing attitudes (Kaplan, 1972). Imagine that people were asked to report their attitude towards eating fried foods on a nine-point scale that ranged from '1 – *extremely unfavourable*' to '9 – *extremely favourable*' as the end points, with '5 – *neither unfavourable nor favourable*' in the middle. If someone indicated that their attitude was neutral (e.g. '*neither favourable nor unfavourable*'), it is halfway between the most extreme positive response option (e.g. '*extremely favourable*') and the most extreme negative response option (e.g. '*extremely unfavourable*'). People could choose this option because it is a compromise between many positive and negative elements of their attitude (e.g. they have many positive and negative feelings, thoughts and behaviours regarding eating fried foods) *or* because they have no positive or negative elements whatsoever (e.g. they have never eaten fried foods).

Summary

An important issue related to attitudes concerns how positive and negative evaluations are organized within and among the cognitive, affective and behavioural antecedents of attitude. The one-dimensional view postulates that the positive and negative elements are stored as opposite ends of a single dimension. The two-dimensional view postulates that positive and negative elements are stored along two separate dimensions.

WHY DO WE HOLD ATTITUDES?

What are the most basic psychological needs served by attitudes?

Individuals hold attitudes for a variety of reasons. For example, our attitudes towards the Welsh rugby team developed from many of our friends and colleagues supporting the same team (Figure 6.8). In contrast, our attitudes towards abortion are based on the value we place on an individual's freedom of choice and the sanctity of human life (Figure 6.9). Over the years, attitude researchers have devoted considerable attention to understanding the needs or functions that are fulfilled by attitudes.

The most prominent models of **attitude functions** were developed almost 50 years ago (Katz, 1960; Smith, Bruner, & White, 1956). Based on the empirical evidence, we see five functions as particularly important. The **object appraisal function** refers to the ability of attitudes to serve as energy-saving devices by allowing us to summarize the positive and negative attributes of objects in our social world. For example, knowing that you like a certain brand of cereal helps you make a decision when entering the supermarket aisle packed with dozens of choices. Further, attitudes can help people to

attitude functions the psychological needs fulfilled by an attitude.

object appraisal function when attitudes help serve as an energy-saving device.

Attitudes are heuristics

FIGURE 6.8 *Attitudes towards, e.g., the Welsh rugby team may be developed from friends supporting the same team.*
Source: © mitzy. Used under licence from Shutterstock.

(a)

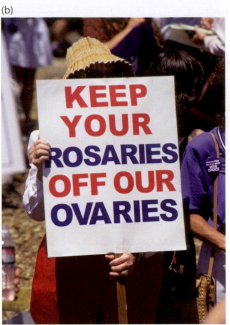

(b)

FIGURE 6.9(a) and (b)   *Attitudes towards abortion might be based on freedom of choice and sanctity of human life.*

Source: (a) © Robert E Daemmrich. Used under licence from Getty Images; (b) Jonathan Nourok. Used under licence from Getty Images.

approach things that are beneficial for them and avoid things that are harmful to them (Maio, Esses, Arnold, & Olson, 2004). Related to the object appraisal function is the **utilitarian function**. This function exists in attitudes that maximize rewards and minimize punishments obtained from attitude objects. **Social adjustment** is fulfilled by attitudes that help us to identify with people we like and to dissociate from people we dislike. For example, individuals may buy a certain soft drink because it is endorsed by their favourite singer. The **ego-defensive function** exists in attitudes that serve to protect an individual's self-esteem. For example, bad golfers might develop an intense dislike for the game because their poor performance threatens their self-esteem. Finally, attitudes may serve a **value-expressive function**, such that an attitude may express an individual's self-concept and central values. For example, a person might cycle to work because she values health and wishes to preserve the environment (Figure 6.10).

utilitarian function when attitudes help us maximize rewards and minimise costs.

social adjustment function when attitudes help us identify with liked others.

ego-defensive function when attitudes help to protect our self-esteem.

value-expressive function when attitudes help express our values.

FIGURE 6.10   *A person might cycle to work because she values health and wishes to preserve the environment.*

Source: © PhotoAlto/Teo Lannie. Used under licence from Getty Images.

A number of themes have developed from research on attitude functions since the emergence of these theoretical perspectives. Here, we focus on two important developments. First, evidence implies that strongly held attitudes fulfil an object-appraisal function. Second, evidence reveals an important distinction between attitudes fulfilling a utilitarian function and those fulfilling a value-expressive function. In the following sections we describe some research behind these observations.

Object appraisal

The object-appraisal function of Smith et al. (1956) perhaps best explains why people form attitudes in the first place. This function suggests that attitudes classify objects in the environment for the purposes of action. In their description of the object-appraisal function, Smith et al. suggested that attitudes are *energy-saving devices*, because attitudes make attitude-relevant judgements faster and easier to perform. Two programmes of research have directly supported this line of reasoning, while suggesting important caveats. First, Fazio (1995, 2000) argued that the object-appraisal function should be more strongly served by attitudes that are high in accessibility. This prediction is based on the assumption that strong attitudes guide relevant judgements and behaviour, whereas weak attitudes will have little effect during judgement and behaviour processes. Consistent with this hypothesis, research has shown that highly accessible attitudes increase the ease with which people make attitude-relevant judgements (Figure 6.11). For example, people who have accessible attitudes towards an abstract

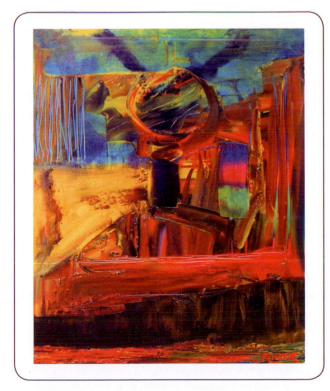

FIGURE 6.11 *How accessible is your attitude towards an abstract painting?*
Source: © Laurin Rinder. Used under licence from Shutterstock.

painting have been shown to be subsequently faster at deciding whether they prefer the painting over another painting (see Fazio, 2000).

A second programme of research has revealed that the strength of the object-appraisal motivation is influenced by differences across people in the need for closure (Kruglanski, 1989). People high in the need for closure like to have a definite answer on some topic, while people low in the need for closure are comfortable with ambiguity. As applied to the study of attitudes, object-appraisal reflects the notion that attitudes can provide such 'answers', because attitudes help people to make decisions about attitude objects. As a result, a high need for closure should increase the desire to form and maintain attitudes. Kruglanski and colleagues have found support for this hypothesis in a number of studies (e.g. Kruglanski, Webster, & Klem, 1993).

Utilitarian versus value-expressive attitudes

Several researchers have argued for a distinction between utilitarian (or instrumental) and value-expressive attitudes (e.g. Herek, 1986; Prentice, 1987; Sears, 1988). Utilitarian attitudes can be thought of as instrumental in helping people achieve positive outcomes and avoiding negative outcomes, whereas value-expressive attitudes express concerns about self-image and personal values. Many lines of research support the distinction between utilitarian and value-expressive attitudes; we will consider just two. First, some attitude objects elicit attitudes that are associated primarily with one or the other of these functions. For example, Shavitt (1990) found that people's thoughts about air conditioners and coffee focus on the utility of the objects, whereas thoughts about greeting cards and national flags tend to focus on the objects' capacity to symbolize the self and social values.

Second, evidence indicates that people are more persuaded by messages containing arguments that match the primary function of their attitudes than by messages containing arguments that do not match the primary function of their attitudes (see Research Close-Up 6.1, P. 179). For example, Shavitt (1990) found that utilitarian advertisements for products about which people held utilitarian attitudes (e.g. an air conditioner) were more persuasive than symbolic advertisements for such instrumental products. Similarly, Snyder and DeBono (1985) found that individual differences in **self-monitoring** affected

self-monitoring an individual difference variable measuring the extent to which people vary their behaviour across social situations (low self-monitors) versus behaving consistently (high self-monitors).

the persuasiveness of different types of advertisements. *Self-monitoring* (Snyder, 1974, 1987) refers to differences in how people vary their behaviour across social situations (see Individual Differences 6.1). ==While high self-monitors are oriented to situational cues and finely tune their behaviour to the situation in which they find themselves, low self-monitors tend to behave in ways that are consistent with their core values and tend not to adapt their behaviour to the situation in which they find themselves.== As applied to advertising, Snyder and DeBono predicted that high self-monitors might be more influenced by advertisements that convey the positive images associated with using a partic-

ular product, while low self-monitors might be more influenced by advertisements that feature the quality of a product.

To test this hypothesis, ==Snyder and DeBono (1985)== presented participants with ==one of two versions of an advertisement== for a particular brand of whisky. In both versions of the advertisement, there was a picture of a whisky bottle resting on a set of architects' plans for a house. In one version of the advertisement (image-based), the picture was accompanied by the phrase 'You're not just moving in, you're moving up'. In the second version of the advertisement (quality-based), the same photo was accompanied by the phrase 'When it comes to great taste, everyone

INDIVIDUAL DIFFERENCES 6.1

SELF-MONITORING

Self-monitoring refers to differences in how people vary their behaviour across social situations (Snyder, 1974). High self-monitors are oriented to situational cues and tune their behaviour to the social situation, whereas low self-monitors tend to behave in ways that are consistent with their values and tend not to mould their behaviour to the social situation. Self-monitoring is assessed by a scale developed by Snyder (1974). For each item, respondents are asked whether the statement is true or false as applied to them. Try it yourself, scoring instructions are below.

1 I find it hard to imitate the behaviour of other people.
2 My behaviour is usually an expression of my true inner feelings, attitudes and beliefs.
3 At parties and social gatherings, I do not attempt to do or say things that others will like.
4 I can only argue for ideas in which I already believe.
5 I can make impromptu speeches even on topics about which I have almost no information.
6 I guess I put on a show to impress or entertain people.
7 When I am uncertain how to act in a social situation, I look to the behaviour of the others for cues.
8 I would probably make a good actor.
9 I rarely seek the advice of my friends to choose movies, books, or music.
10 I sometimes appear to others to be experiencing deeper emotions than I actually am.
11 I laugh more when I watch a comedy with others than when alone.
12 In a group of people I am rarely the centre of attention.
13 In different situations and with different people, I often act like a very different person.

14 I am not particularly good at making other people like me.
15 Even if I am not enjoying myself, I often pretend to be having a good time.
16 I'm not always the person I appear to be.
17 I would not change my opinions in order to please someone or to win their favour.
18 I have considered being an entertainer.
19 In order to get along and be liked, I tend to be what people expect me to be rather than anything else.
20 I have never been good at games like charades or improvisational acting.
21 I have trouble changing my behaviour to suit different people and different situations.
22 At a party I let others keep the jokes and stories going.
23 I feel a bit awkward in company and do not show up quite as I feel I should.
24 I can look anyone in the eye and tell a lie with a straight face (if for a right end).
25 I may deceive people by being friendly when I really dislike them.

Give yourself one point (a) every time you said true to statements 5, 6, 7, 8, 10, 11, 13, 15, 16, 18, 19, 24, and 25, and (b) every time you said false to items 1, 2, 3, 4, 9, 12, 14, 17, 20, 21, 22, and 23. Add these values to calculate your self-monitoring score.

Snyder (1987) reported that across a range of samples, the mean score was approximately 12.5. Put differently, after reverse scoring, low self-monitors score between 0 and 12, while high self-monitors score between 13 and 25.

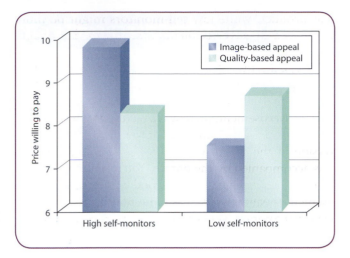

FIGURE 6.12 *The influence of self-monitoring and appeal type on willingness to pay for a consumer product.*

Source: Adapted from Snyder and DeBono, 1985. Copyright © 1985 by the American Psychological Association. Adapted with permission. *Journal of Personality and Social Psychology, 49,* 586–597. The use of APA information does not imply endorsement by APA.

LINKING ATTITUDE CONTENT, STRUCTURE AND FUNCTION

Content, structure, function and attitude strength

One important question that is relevant to the content, structure and function of attitudes is the extent to which attitudes differ in their strength. As mentioned at the beginning of the chapter, we feel more strongly about some topics than about others. *Attitude strength* has been conceptualized in many different ways (see Individual Differences 6.2). For example, individuals can simply be asked how *certain* they are of their attitude, as well as how *important* their attitude is to them personally (see Haddock, Rothman, Reber, & Schwarz, 1999). The strength of an attitude can also be measured by assessing its distance from the middle of a scale. This type of index, known as attitude *extremity*, has been found to have many important outcomes (see Abelson, 1995). Finally, we can conceive of attitude strength in terms of how easy it is to retrieve an attitude from memory; easily retrievable attitudes are referred to as being highly *accessible* (Fazio, 1995).

Strong attitudes differ from weak attitudes in a number of ways. Krosnick and Petty (1995) argue that there are four key manifestations of strong attitudes. First, strong attitudes are *more persistent*. That is, they are more stable over time (Visser & Krosnick, 1998). Second, strong attitudes are *more resistant to change.* When faced with a persuasive appeal, strong attitudes are less likely to change than weak attitudes (Petty, Haugtvedt, & Smith, 1995). Third, strong attitudes are *more likely to influence information processing.* Research has revealed that people devote greater attention to information that is relevant to strong versus weak attitudes (Houston & Fazio, 1989). Finally, strong attitudes are *more likely to guide behaviour.* Put simply, we are more likely to act upon strong versus weak attitudes. We return to this last issue later in the chapter.

draws the same conclusion'. Researchers predicted that high self-monitors would be more persuaded by the image-based appeal, while low self-monitors would be more persuaded by the quality-based appeal. The results of the study are shown in Figure 6.12. As predicted, Snyder and DeBono (1985) found that high self-monitors were willing to pay more for the whisky when presented with the image-based appeal, whereas low self-monitors were willing to pay more when presented with the quality-based appeal. Further research has demonstrated that these 'match the message to the function' effects occur because people devote more attention to convincing arguments that match the function of their attitude than to convincing arguments that do not match the function of their attitude (Petty & Wegener, 1998).

Summary

Individuals hold attitudes for a variety of reasons. Among the functions, the object-appraisal function is especially important, as it suggests that attitudes serve as energy-saving devices that make judgements easier and faster to perform. There is also an important distinction between instrumental and value-expressive attitudes. Knowing the primary function of an attitude is important, because attempts at attitude change are more likely to be successful when the persuasive appeal matches the function of the attitude.

Summary

Attitude content, attitude structure and attitude function are inexorably linked. Centrally relevant to these concepts is attitude strength. Attitudes vary in the degree to which they are persistent over time, resistant to change, influential in guiding information processing and influential in predicting behaviour.

INDIVIDUAL DIFFERENCES 6.2

ATTITUDE STRENGTH

The strength of an attitude can be conceptualized and measured in different ways (see Petty & Krosnick, 1995). Some of the most prominent conceptualizations include attitude accessibility, attitude certainty, attitude extremity, attitude importance, attitude intensity and knowledge. While these conceptualizations are related to each other, they are usually seen as different properties of attitude strength, as they sometimes have different antecedents and consequences (see Maio & Haddock, 2010). Listed below are examples of how these concepts (and the strength of an attitude) were used to assess the strength of a person's attitude toward gay men (from Vonofakou, Hewstone, & Voci, 2007). For each item, respondents indicate an answer using a scale that might range from zero ('not at all') to six ('extremely'). Try it yourself.

1   How certain are you about your feelings towards gay men?
2   How sure are you that your opinion about gay men is correct?
3   How definite are your views about gay men?
4   How important are gay men to you personally?
5   How much do you personally care about gay men?
6   How often do you discuss gay men with others?
7   How often do gay men come up during informal conversations?
8   How often in the past year have you talked about gay men?
9   How often do you think about gay men?
10 How often have you thought about gay men in the past year?

In a sample of 85 British undergraduates, Vonofakou et al. (2007) found a mean score of 2.85 (SD = .89).

THE MEASUREMENT OF ATTITUDES

What are explicit and implicit measures of attitude?

Attitudes, like most constructs in psychology, are not directly observable. For instance, we cannot see that a person holds a positive attitude towards red sports cars. Rather, attitudes have to be inferred from the individual's responses to questions about these vehicles (Fazio & Olson, 2003). As a result, social psychologists have needed to develop different methods to measure attitudes. In this section of the chapter, we describe some of the most commonly used techniques that have been developed. For forms of attitude measurement other than those discussed here (e.g. psychophysical measures, behavioural measures), see Eagly and Chaiken (1993) and Fazio and Olson (2003).

In introducing different types of attitude measures, we have differentiated them on the basis of whether they are **explicit** or **implicit**. Psychologists usually think of explicit measures as those that require respondents' conscious attention to the construct being measured, whereas implicit measures are those that do not require this conscious attention. At a basic level, explicit measures of attitude are those that *directly* ask respondents to think about and report their attitude, whereas implicit measures of attitude are those that assess attitudes *without* directly asking respondents for a verbal report of their attitude (Fazio & Olson, 2003).

Explicit measures of attitudes

The majority of attitude measures can be conceptualized as explicit indicators. Most often, these measures have been self-report questionnaires, in which participants are asked to respond to direct questions about their opinions towards the object in question. For example, if a group of researchers was interested in knowing a respondent's attitude towards abortion, they might ask the question 'What is your attitude towards abortion?' In the following section, we describe two explicit measures of attitude: Likert scales and the semantic differential.

Likert scales Likert (1932) introduced a measure of attitude based upon summated ratings. In this approach, statements are written in such a way that responses indicate either a favourable or unfavourable attitude. An example of a Likert scale to assess attitudes towards euthanasia is presented in Figure 6.13. For each item, respondents are asked to indicate their degree of agreement or disagreement. As you read the items presented in Figure 6.13, you will notice that items can be written such that a strong positive attitude towards euthanasia will

explicit measures of attitude measures that directly ask respondents to think about and report an attitude.

implicit measures of attitude measures that assess spontaneous evaluative associations with an object, without relying on a verbal report.

The following statements are part of a survey on public attitudes. There are no right or wrong answers, only opinions. For each statement, indicate the number that best represents your personal opinion by using the following scale:

If you *strongly disagree* with the statement, indicate 1
If you *disagree* with the statement, indicate 2
If you *neither disagree nor agree* with the statement, indicate 3
If you *agree* with the statement, indicate 4
If you *strongly agree* with the statement, indicate 5

(1) I think euthanasia should be made legal.   _____

(2) I would support a referendum for the institution of euthanasia. _____

(3) Euthanasia should never be used.   _____

(4) Euthanasia is appropriate when someone wants to die.   _____

(5) I am against the use of euthanasia in all circumstances.   _____

FIGURE 6.13 *An example of a Likert scale to access attitudes towards euthanasia.*

Source: Adapted from Haddock et al. (2008) with permission from SAGE Publications Ltd.

Please respond to each scale by placing an 'x' in the space that best represents your opinion.

EUTHANASIA

BAD:__:__:__:__:__:__:__:GOOD
NEGATIVE:__:__:__:__:__:__:__:POSITIVE
DISLIKE:__:__:__:__:__:__:__:LIKE

FIGURE 6.14 *A semantic differential scale to measure attitudes towards euthanasia.*

Source: Adapted from Haddock et al. (2008) with permission from SAGE Publications Ltd.

produce either a '*strongly agree*' response (e.g. to item 1) or a '*strongly disagree*' response (e.g. to item 3). Researchers create items that are worded in opposite directions in order to help avoid response sets (i.e. the tendency for a respondent to agree or disagree with all items on a scale).

How are Likert scales scored? In a questionnaire like the one shown in Figure 6.13, each response alternative is allocated a score (in this case from 1 to 5). Usually, a low score is taken to indicate a strong negative attitude and a high score is taken to indicate a strong positive attitude. Thus, for item 1, an individual who strongly disagrees with the statement would be allocated a score of 1, while a person who strongly agrees would be given a score of 5. For item 3 the procedure is reversed because the item is worded in the opposite direction to item 1. Scores for this item are recoded such that an individual who strongly disagrees with the statement is expressing a positive attitude (and hence is allocated a score of 5 for that item), whereas an individual who strongly agrees with that item is expressing a negative attitude (and thus is allocated a score of 1). To the extent that the items assess the same construct (i.e. a respondent's attitude), correlations among responses to each item should be high. If they are sufficiently high, scores on the individual items are averaged to form a single attitude score.

Semantic differential scales A large amount of research is aimed at testing whether people hold more positive attitudes towards some attitude objects (e.g. abortion) than others (e.g. capital punishment). To address questions concerning the attitudes that people hold about a variety of attitude objects, it was necessary to develop

methodologies that would allow researchers to measure attitudes towards many attitude objects along a common scale. Among the efforts to develop such a technique, the method that has been the most influential is the semantic differential approach (Osgood, Suci, & Tannenbaum, 1957). An example of a semantic differential scale is presented in Figure 6.14. In this technique, participants are given a set of bipolar adjective scales, each of which is separated into a number of categories (typically 5, 7 or 9, with the middle category representing the neutral point). Participants are asked to rate the attitude object by indicating the response that best represents their opinion. The bipolar adjectives typically include general evaluative terms such as 'favourable–unfavourable', 'good–bad' and 'like–dislike'. Similar to Likert scales, correlations among the items should be positive (to the extent that they measure the same attitude). If they are sufficiently high, they can be combined to form a single attitude score.

Issues relevant to the explicit measurement of attitudes

Historically, explicit measures of attitudes have dominated empirical research on the psychology of attitudes. Despite their wide appeal, however, a number of concerns have been raised over their use. For example, individuals might sometimes be unaware of their attitude towards an object (Fazio, Jackson, Dunton, & Williams, 1995; Greenwald & Banaji, 1995; Nisbett & Wilson, 1977). Further, research has demonstrated that subtle differences in the way in which items are presented can influence responses to direct measures of attitude (see Haddock & Carrick, 1999; Schwarz, 1999).

Probably the most important criticism of direct measures of attitude is that they can be affected by people's motivation to give socially desirable responses (see Chapter 2). This refers to deliberate attempts to misrepresent (or fake) responses in a way that allows respondents to present themselves in a favourable way (Paulhus & John, 1998). To the extent that the researcher is interested in studying attitudes towards sensitive issues and/or issues that highlight norms of political or social appropriateness, people's responses might not necessarily reflect their true opinion, but instead may reflect a desire to present themselves in a positive manner. For example, in many cultures it is considered socially inappropriate to express a prejudicial attitude towards ethnic minorities. The use of explicit, direct measures of attitude in such contexts may not provide an accurate report of attitude, as respondents may be reluctant to be perceived as prejudiced.

Implicit measures of attitudes

In an attempt to minimize problems associated with direct measures of attitude, social psychologists have developed a number of indirect or implicit response strategies. We describe here two of the most common measures, the evaluative priming technique (see Fazio et al., 1995) and the Implicit Association Test (IAT; Greenwald, McGhee & Schwartz, 1998).

Evaluative priming Fazio (1995) defines an attitude as an association in memory between an attitude object and a summary evaluation. According to Fazio, these associations vary in strength, and the strength of the association determines the accessibility of an attitude. Let us describe this perspective more concretely by using an example. One of us *really* hates Brussels sprouts. Even thinking about Brussels sprouts sets off an immediate and strong negative reaction within him. He also *really* dislikes rice cakes, but his reaction is not as automatic. Fazio's model would suggest that the negative attitude towards Brussels sprouts is more accessible than the negative attitude towards rice cakes, because the association in memory between 'Brussels sprouts' and 'dislike' is stronger than the association between 'rice cakes' and 'dislike'.

According to Fazio, the strength of these associations should affect how quickly an individual responds to an evaluative word after having been briefly presented with the attitude object. In a typical study of this process, a participant is seated in front of a computer. The attitude object is briefly presented on the computer screen (e.g. the term 'Brussels sprouts') and then replaced by an

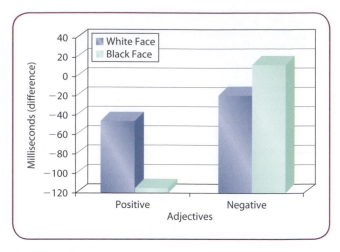

FIGURE 6.15 *Mean scores for positive and negative adjectives preceded by Black and White faces. A positive score represents facilitation, a negative score represents inhibition.*
Source: Adapted from Fazio et al., 1995. Copyright © 1995 by the American Psychological Association. Adapted with permission. *Journal of Personality and Social Psychology, 69,* 1013–1027. The use of APA information does not imply endorsement by APA.

evaluative adjective (e.g. 'disgusting'). The participant's task is to indicate the valence of the adjective as quickly as possible. That is, the participant indicates whether the *adjective* means something positive or negative, *not* whether the attitude object itself is good or bad. Of primary interest is the speed with which the participant makes this response. In our example, the presentation of 'Brussels sprouts' should produce faster responses to negative adjectives and slower responses to positive adjectives. Furthermore, if the person hates Brussels sprouts more than rice cakes, this facilitation/inhibition should be more pronounced when the person is presented with 'Brussels sprouts' than with 'rice cakes'.

Researchers have used this approach in studies of numerous attitude objects, including attitude objects that might elicit social desirability concerns on explicit measures. For example, Fazio et al. (1995) adapted the evaluative priming paradigm to study prejudicial attitudes. In this study, participants were instructed that their task was to indicate the meaning of positive and negative adjectives (see Leader in the Field, Russell Fazio). However, prior to the presentation of each individual adjective, participants were briefly shown a photo of a black or white person. As shown in Figure 6.15, Fazio et al. (1995) found facilitation of positive adjectives by prior presentation of a white versus black person, but facilitation of negative adjectives by prior presentation of a black versus white person, Thus, in this study, a negative attitude towards black people was represented by differences in the time required by white participants to categorize positive and negative adjectives after the presentation

LEADER IN THE FIELD

Russell Fazio (b. 1952) completed his undergraduate degree at Cornell University before completing a PhD at Princeton University in 1978. He started his academic career at Indiana University, where he worked until 2001. He currently holds the Harold E. Burtt Chair in Psychology at the Ohio State University. In over 130 publications, his research on topics such as attitude accessibility, attitude-behaviour relations and attitude measurement has been highly influential in the field.

Not on test

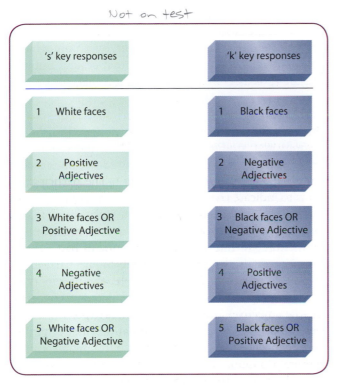

FIGURE 6.16 *The procedure of the five block Implicit Association Test.*

Source: Adapted from Haddock et al. (2008) with permission from SAGE Publications Ltd.

of images of the black versus white individuals (black participants did not show this tendency). Further, white participants who showed the pattern most strongly were more likely to show more negative behaviour towards a black experimenter in the study. Thus, these differences in response times were easily interpretable as reflecting a negative attitude towards black individuals.

The Implicit Association Test Another important indirect procedure is the Implicit Association Test (IAT; Greenwald et al., 1998). For ease of presentation, we will work through an example of procedures that would use the IAT to assess racial attitudes. This example is shown in Figure 6.16. In a typical IAT study, participants are

seated at a computer and asked to classify attitude objects and adjectives. As originally designed, an IAT study generally involves five separate blocks. In *block 1* of a racial attitude IAT, participants are presented with a variety of pictures of white and black individuals. Participants would be instructed to make one response (e.g. press the 's' key on a keyboard) when they see a white face and make a different response (e.g. press the 'k' key) when they see a black face. They are asked to perform this task (and all others in the test) as quickly as possible. There might be anywhere from 20–40 trials within this block (and subsequent blocks).

In *block 2*, participants are presented with a variety of positive and negative adjectives. Again, they would be asked to make one response (press the 's' key) when a positive adjective appears on the screen and a different response (press the 'k' key) when a negative adjective appears on the screen. The purpose of these blocks is to train participants to link a category (e.g. a picture of a white face or a positive adjective) with a response (pressing the 's' key). In *block 3*, participants are instructed that they will see faces or adjectives and that they are to press the 's' key when they see a white face *or* a positive adjective, and press the 'k' key when they see a black face *or* a negative adjective. *Block 4* is similar to block 2, but this time the responses are reversed, such that a participant now presses the 's' key when a negative word appears and the 'k' key when a positive word appears. This block is necessary to train participants to make the opposite link to that already measured. *Block 5* is similar to block 3, but this time participants are to press the 's' key when a white face or a negative adjective appears, and the 'k' key when a black face or a positive adjective appears. The key blocks are 3 and 5 – they measure the strength of association between an attitude object (in this case racial groups) and evaluations.

How does research yield an attitude score from the two key blocks of the IAT (3 and 5)? Imagine an individual who is racially prejudiced. For this individual, the task in block 3 should be quite simple. If the person favours white individuals to black individuals, trials in which white faces are associated with positive adjectives and black faces are associated with negative adjectives should be relatively easy, and hence produce faster responses, because the links between these categories and the evaluations are congruent. Let's imagine that our participant's mean response time to trials in this block is 700 ms. In contrast, responses in block 5 should take longer for this participant. Given the person's preference for white individuals over black individuals, trials that associate black faces with positivity and white faces with negativity should be relatively difficult, and hence require more time to elicit a response.

Let's imagine that the individual's mean response time for this block is 1200 ms. Thus, our participant's mean response time for block 3 is shorter than that for block 5 by 500 ms. This difference is referred to as the 'IAT effect' (see Greenwald, Nosek & Banaji, 2003; Greenwald et al., 1998, for additional details about computing IAT effects).

The IAT and other implicit measures have become increasingly popular among attitude researchers (see Fazio & Olson, 2003). These types of measures have gained popularity because they assess attitudes without the necessity of asking the participant for a direct verbal report. As noted earlier, part of their appeal is due to the belief that responses on these measures are less likely to be affected by socially desirable responding (see Fazio & Olson, 2003). That said, implicit measures of attitude have also been the source of some criticism.

For example, a number of researchers have argued that the (sometimes) low correlation found between implicit and explicit measures of attitude implies that they assess different constructs (see Karpinski & Hilton, 2001). Other criticisms have focused on *how* implicit measures assess attitudes. For instance, Olson and Fazio (2004) argue that a personalized version of the IAT (one in which the positive and negative judgements are personalized; for example, using 'I like' and 'I don't like' versus 'pleasant' and 'unpleasant') is better than a version that can be influenced by factors such as cultural norms (e.g. if most people prefer one category over another, this might be reflected in a general IAT). As research on implicit measures of attitude continues to progress, the debate around implicit measures will surely continue. Our own view is that implicit measures of attitude have much to offer, in that they have allowed social psychologists to generate novel and important questions about the underlying causes of human behaviour. They have also been especially useful in providing researchers with a tool for carrying out research on socially sensitive attitudes, where research participants might not always be willing to give their true explicit attitudes (e.g. prejudice). Later in the chapter we will show how explicit and implicit measures of attitude are important for predicting different types of behaviour.

Are attitude measures reliable and valid?

A sound measure must be both reliable and valid (see Chapter 2). In the context of attitude measurement, reliability has two important meanings. First, reliability in the sense of *internal consistency* refers to whether the individual items are assessing the same psychological construct. Items that assess the same construct should be

positively correlated. Second, *test–retest reliability* refers to consistency in scores across time. A sound attitude measure should produce similar scores across repeated testing (in the absence of any true attitude change).

A number of studies have investigated the reliability of explicit and implicit measures of attitude. Explicit measures have been shown to exhibit high reliability. For example, semantic differential scales using the evaluative dimensions of 'good–bad', 'positive–negative' and 'favourable–unfavourable' exhibit high internal consistency (Huskinson & Haddock, 2004) and test–retest reliability (see Lord, 2004, for a more detailed discussion). Given their more recent introduction, less research has been conducted assessing the reliability of implicit measures of attitude. However, a paper by Cunningham, Preacher, and Banaji (2001) found that several implicit measures possessed reasonably high internal consistency and test–retest correlations.

The *validity* of a measure refers to the degree to which it assesses the construct it is designed to assess. A number of studies have investigated the validity of explicit and implicit measures of attitude. Explicit measures of attitude have been shown to be valid. For example, Haddock, Zanna, and Esses (1993) demonstrated that a semantic differential measure of attitudes towards gay men was highly predictive of a subsequent measure of anti-gay discrimination (see Eagly & Chaiken, 1993, for more examples). Regarding implicit measures, researchers have found that implicit measures possess (1) convergent validity (i.e. scores on different measures are related to each other) and (2) predictive validity (i.e. implicit measures predict other scores that they ought to; see Cunningham et al., 2001; Fazio & Olson, 2003). For example, Cunningham et al. (2001) found that scores on evaluative priming and IAT measures of racial prejudice were highly related to each other and formed a single latent construct. Also, one particularly compelling study used functional magnetic resonance imaging (fMRI) technology to assess brain activity in response to different stimuli. Phelps et al. (2000) found that an IAT measure of white participants' racial prejudice was highly predictive of amygdala activation when they viewed pictures of unknown black individuals (the amygdala is an area of the brain associated with emotional processing). In this research, pronounced amygdala activation in response to black faces was associated with strong implicit prejudice towards African Americans.

Summary

Attitudes can be measured in a number of ways. Attitude measures can be distinguished on the basis of whether they are *explicit* (i.e. direct) or *implicit* (i.e. indirect). Explicit measures of attitude directly ask respondents to think about and report an attitude, whereas implicit measures of attitude are those that assess attitudes *without* directly asking respondents for a verbal report of their attitude. Explicit and implicit measures are both useful tools in attempts to understand and predict human behaviour (see Social Psychology Beyond the Lab 6.1).

DO ATTITUDES PREDICT BEHAVIOUR?

What factors influence the degree to which attitudes predict behaviour?

Common sense would dictate that attitudes should predict behaviour. For example, one would expect that an individual who possesses a positive attitude towards the environment would engage in recycling behaviour. Similarly, it seems sensible to predict that a student who strongly supports saving endangered animals will make an annual donation to the World Wildlife Fund. However, is the link between attitudes and behaviour this simple?

In addressing this question, we wish to start by turning back time and visiting the United States of America in the early 1930s. A college professor named Richard LaPiere was travelling across America with a young Chinese couple. At the time, there was widespread anti-Asian prejudice in the United States. As a result of this prejudice, LaPiere was concerned that he and his travelling companions would be refused service in hotels and restaurants. Much to his surprise, only once (in over 250 establishments) were they not served. A few months after the completion of the journey, LaPiere sent a letter to each of the visited establishments and asked whether they would serve Chinese visitors. Of the establishments that replied, only one indicated that it would serve such a customer, with over 90 per cent stating that they definitely would not (the rest were undecided). While there are a number of methodological problems with LaPiere's (1934) study (e.g. there was no way of ensuring that the individual who answered the letter was the same person who served LaPiere and his friends), it is a reminder that people's behaviour might not necessarily follow from their attitudes.

Let us now move ahead 30 years on from this study. By the late 1960s, a number of studies had examined the relation between attitudes and behaviour. In 1969,

Wicker reviewed the findings of these studies. He reached a rather sobering conclusion: attitudes were a relatively poor predictor of behaviour. Across almost 40 studies that were conducted before 1969, Wicker found that the average correlation between attitudes and behaviour was a modest .15. This finding led a number of social psychologists to question the value of the attitude concept. It was argued that if attitudes do not guide actions, then the construct is of limited use.

Attitude researchers responded to this criticism by devoting greater attention to the study of *when* and *how* attitudes predict behaviour. In the last 30 years, research findings have led to a more optimistic conclusion – attitudes do predict behaviour, under certain conditions. In a meta-analytic review of the literature, Kraus (1995) compared the results of over 100 studies on the **attitude–behaviour relation.** He found that the average correlation between opinions and actions was .38, a value much higher than that obtained by Wicker (1969). This difference in correlations could be explained in various ways. First, more modern research might be using better measures of attitudes and/or behaviours. For example, some measures from early initial studies lacked reliability and validity. Second, modern researchers might be using better techniques for testing their predictions. Returning to LaPiere's (1934) study, it is possible that the measures of attitudes and behaviour did not come from the same individual. Third, contemporary researchers might be doing a better job of examining situations *when* attitudes are highly predictive of behaviour. In this section of the chapter, we first consider a number of variables that influence *when* attitudes predict behaviour, and then introduce models that have been developed to understand *how* attitudes predict behaviour.

> **attitude–behaviour relation** the degree to which an attitude predicts behaviour.

When do attitudes predict behaviour?

(1) When there is correspondence between attitudinal and behavioural measures A number of early attempts to assess the attitude–behaviour relation (included in Wicker's, 1969, review) were plagued by methodological problems. Specifically, in many of these studies there was a low degree of *correspondence* between the measures of attitude and behaviour. Returning to LaPiere's (1934) research, his measure of attitude asked respondents to indicate whether they would serve 'members of the Chinese race'. This statement is quite broad in comparison to the measure of behaviour, which involved service being offered to a highly educated, well-dressed Chinese couple accompanied by an American

Strong when elements are more specific

college professor. Had the attitude measure been more specific (e.g. 'Would you serve a highly educated, well-dressed Chinese couple accompanied by an American college professor?'), the relation between attitudes and behaviour in LaPiere's (1934) study might have been more pronounced.

Ajzen and Fishbein (1977) proposed the idea that there needs to be high correspondence between measures of attitude and behaviour. They stated that measures of attitude and behaviour need to correspond in four key ways: action, target, context and time. The *action* element refers to the behaviour being performed (e.g. recycling glass). The *target* element refers to the target of the behaviour (e.g. a particular brand of coffee, a political candidate). The *context* element refers to the environment in which the behaviour is performed (e.g. whether the behaviour is performed alone or in the presence of others). Finally, the *time* element refers to the time frame in which the behaviour is performed (e.g. whether the behaviour is to be performed immediately or in one year's time). Ajzen and Fishbein (1977) argued that a measure of attitude will be most effective in predicting behaviour when both measures correspond on these four elements. Correspondence can also be achieved when a broad attitude measure is used to predict an aggregated index of behaviour (see Weigel & Newman, 1976).

The importance of correspondence between measures of attitude and behaviour was also demonstrated in a study by Davidson and Jaccard (1979). These researchers were interested in predicting women's use of birth control pills. In this study, women were asked a number of questions about their attitudes, ranging from questions that were very general (their attitude towards birth control) through somewhat specific (their attitude towards birth-control pills) to very specific (their attitude towards using birth-control pills during the next two years). Two years after participants responded to these attitude questions, they were contacted by the researchers and asked to indicate if they had used birth-control pills in the previous two years. The researchers predicted that the correlation between attitudes and behaviour would increase as the measures became more correspondent. The results of this study supported these authors' predictions. To start with, the general attitude measure did not predict behaviour ($r = .08$), probably because this measure was too general in relation to the measure of behaviour. The question that was somewhat specific did a better job of predicting behaviour ($r = .32$); this item had the advantage of matching the behavioural measure with respect to the target. Finally, the most specific question was very effective in predicting behaviour ($r = .57$), because the attitude measure was highly correspondent with the measure of behaviour with respect to two key elements: target and time. Consistent with the results of this study, the meta-analysis by Kraus (1995), noted

earlier, found that the attitude–behaviour correlation was higher when there was greater correspondence between measures.

(2) It depends upon the domain of behaviour Research has also demonstrated that the relation between attitudes and behaviour differs as a function of the topic under investigation. In his review of the literature, Kraus (1995) found that topics varied in the degree to which opinions predicted actions. At one extreme, the relation between political party attitudes and voting behaviour tends to be very high. For example, in an investigation conducted during the 1984 American presidential election, Fazio and Williams (1986) measured attitudes towards the President of the United States at that time, Ronald Reagan. Approximately five months later, they measured whether participants voted for Reagan or his opponent. Despite the time lag between measures, the correlation between voters' initial attitude towards Reagan and their subsequent voting behaviour was an impressive .78. At the other extreme, Kraus (1995) noted that there was a low correlation between individuals' attitudes towards blood donation and the act of donating blood. At first glance, it is perhaps not surprising that this is a behavioural domain where one might expect a low attitude–behaviour relation. It may be that a low relation arises because the behaviour of donating blood is much more difficult to enact than the simple expression of one's attitude through a behaviour like voting.

(3) It depends upon the strength of the attitude As mentioned earlier in the chapter, attitudes differ in their strength. For instance, one person may absolutely love the music of Bruce Springsteen; another may feel less strongly. As we already know, attitude researchers would say that one person has a very strong positive attitude towards the music of Bruce Springsteen, while the other has a weak attitude. Which person once drove all night to see Bruce Springsteen perform live – for the eighth time? Not surprisingly, it is the one with the strong attitude.

A number of studies have demonstrated that strong attitudes are more likely than weak attitudes to predict behaviour. For instance, returning to the study of Fazio and Williams (1986), recall that they found a very high correlation between political attitudes and voting behaviour (Figure 6.17). This study also contained a measure of attitude strength – the accessibility of the participants' initial attitude. Some participants had very accessible (i.e. strong) attitudes towards Reagan, whereas other participants' attitudes were less accessible (i.e. weak). Fazio and Williams (1986) found that the correlation between attitudes and behaviour was significantly greater among those individuals whose attitudes towards Reagan were high in accessibility. Similar results have been found in

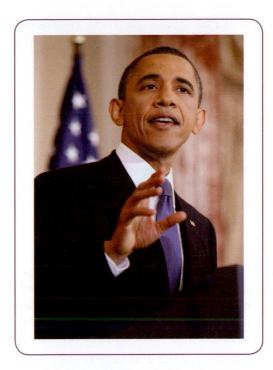

FIGURE 6.17 *Do attitudes towards politicians predict voting behaviour?*

Source: © Chip Somodevilla/Pool/ABACAUSA.COM. Used under licence from Press Association Images.

many other studies using different operationalizations of attitude strength (see Eagly & Chaiken, 1993; Holland, Verplanken, & Van Knippenberg, 2002; Kraus, 1995; see also Research Close-Up 6.2), leading to the conclusion that strong attitudes are more likely than weak attitudes to predict behaviour.

(4) The role of person variables   The final set of variables we wish to consider concerns differences across people in the tendency to behave in line with their actions. In addition to examining how situations influence behaviour, social psychologists are interested in understanding how personality differences help account for our actions, and how the attitude–behaviour link may vary in different samples of people (see Chapter 1).

With respect to the attitude–behaviour relation, a number of researchers have examined how various personality constructs moderate the degree to which opinions influence actions. The personality construct most frequently tested as a moderator of the attitude–behaviour relation is *self-monitoring* (Snyder, 1974, 1987). As discussed earlier in the chapter, self-monitoring refers to differences across people in how they vary their behaviour across social situations. A number of studies have investigated whether the relation between attitudes and

SOCIAL PSYCHOLOGY BEYOND THE LAB 6.1

ATTITUDES AND PUBLIC OPINION SURVEYS

Given the importance of attitudes in understanding behaviour, it is not surprising that they have an enormous impact 'beyond the lab'. One area where attitudes and attitude measurement is very important is in the context of public opinion surveys. The use of public opinion surveys is widespread – across continents and across issues. For instance, public opinion surveys are often used to gauge the public's attitudes toward things like their national government, views on core social issues or policies (such as environmental attitudes or attitudes toward capital punishment), even to assess levels of happiness in a country and how happiness might change over time.

These opinion surveys will usually be carried out by public companies (e.g. the Gallup organization in the United States; IPSOS-MORI or YouGov in the United Kingdom) or through government organizations (e.g. the Office for National Statistics in the United Kingdom). Often, these surveys will be developed by individuals with a background in social psychology, and their methodology will almost certainly have been informed by advances made by social psychologists. Public opinion surveys might be completed over the phone, via post, or more recently, via the Internet.

One particularly interesting development has been the application of response time methodologies to public opinion surveys. Research by John Bassili and colleagues (e.g. Bassili, 1993, 1996; Bassili & Fletcher, 1991) has utilized computer-assisted telephone interviewing (CATI) to integrate contemporary attitudes research with public opinion surveys. The methodology involves the use of a computer clock that can provide millisecond accuracy in the timing of responses and a voice-recognition framework that converts an individual's responses into signals that trigger the clock after the interviewer asks a question. Using the CATI approach in a survey of Canadians' opinions, Bassili (1993) tested how two operationalizations of attitude strength, attitude accessibility and attitude certainty, might predict the discrepancy between an individual's voting intentions and their actual voting behaviour. The results showed that the response-time measure of accessibility was a significant predictor of the discrepancy between people's voting intentions and their actual voting behaviour. For example, the more accessible the attitude, the lower the discrepancy between voting intentions and voting behaviour.

ATTITUDES CAN PREDICT AND FOLLOW BEHAVIOUR

Holland, R.W., Verplanken, B., & Van Knippenberg, A. (2002). On the nature of attitude–behavior relations: The strong guide, the weak follow. *European Journal of Social Psychology*, *32*, 869–876.

Introduction

This study considers the circumstances under which (1) attitudes predict behaviour and (2) behaviour predicts attitudes. The authors review evidence demonstrating both causal pathways. First, they review a number of studies demonstrating that attitudes influence behaviour (some of these studies are discussed in this chapter). Second, they review a number of studies derived from self-perception theory and dissonance theory (see Chapter 7) demonstrating that attitudes can sometimes be inferred from past behaviour. Holland et al. suggest that the concept of attitude strength is crucial to understanding when attitudes predict behaviour (as opposed to behaviour predicting attitudes). Specifically, Holland et al. postulate that strong attitudes are more likely than weak attitudes to predict behaviour, whereas weak attitudes are more likely than strong attitudes to follow from behaviour.

Method

Participants

One hundred and six students participated in the study.

Design and procedure

The study had a correlational design and was split into two sessions, with an interval of one week. In session 1, participants completed measures assessing the favourability and the strength of their attitudes towards Greenpeace. Attitude favourability was measured by the question 'How positive or negative is your attitude towards Greenpeace?'; one of the attitude strength items was 'How certain are you about your attitude towards Greenpeace?' One week later, participants returned for an unrelated study. At the end of this unrelated study, they were paid the equivalent of about £3. Immediately after being paid, participants were told that the experimenter was also conducting a small study for Greenpeace. Importantly, participants were also informed that they could choose to donate money to Greenpeace. After making their decision whether or not to donate money, the experimenter asked participants to complete a short questionnaire, which included an assessment of their attitude towards Greenpeace (also in session 2).

The *attitude–behaviour* relation was derived by comparing the favourability of participants' attitude at time 1 with the amount of money they donated at time 2. The *behaviour–attitude* relation was derived by comparing the amount of money participants donated at time 2 with the measure of attitude that was taken immediately after the donation behaviour.

Results and discussion

As expected, the researchers found that attitude strength was crucial for understanding when attitudes predict behaviour, as opposed to when behaviour predicts attitudes. The results are shown in Figure 6.18. First, participants were split at the median score on attitude strength, to form two equal-sized groups of those with 'strong' versus 'weak' attitudes (this procedure is known as a 'median split'). With respect to the *attitude–behaviour* relation, strong attitudes at time 1 predicted behaviour at time 2; weak attitudes did not. On the other hand, with respect to the *behaviour–attitude* relation, weak attitudes were greatly influenced by behaviour; strong attitudes were not.

The findings of Holland et al. (2002) provided support for their main hypotheses. When participants held strong attitudes about Greenpeace, the favourability of their attitude predicted whether or not they subsequently donated to the organization. When participants held weak attitudes about Greenpeace, their attitude was shaped by (i.e. inferred from) their donation behaviour. This study makes an important contribution to our understanding of the bi-dimensional causal relations between attitudes and behaviour.

FIGURE 6.18 *Regression coefficients showing the effects of weak and strong attitudes on the attitude–behaviour and behaviour–attitude relations.*

Source: Adapted from Holland et al., 2002. Reproduced with permission from John Wiley & Sons Ltd.

behaviour is more pronounced for low self-monitors than for high self-monitors. In one study testing this proposal, Snyder and Kendzierski (1982) investigated attitudes towards affirmative action (policies that give special advantages to members of disadvantaged groups, such as women and ethnic minorities). These researchers gave students who favoured or opposed affirmative action the opportunity to participate in a social situation that supported the behavioural expression of a positive attitude towards this issue. The results revealed that, among low self-monitors, people's attitude towards affirmative action predicted their decisions to participate, or not. However, among high self-monitors, the behavioural decision was unrelated to the favourability of their attitude.

Another relevant variable that affects the size of the attitude–behaviour relation is the nature of the participants involved in the research. Research has found that students show lower attitude–behaviour relations compared to non-students. For example, Kraus (1995) observed that the average correlation between attitudes and behaviour was .34 in studies that used student samples; the correlation was .48 in studies with non-student samples. This difference might be attributable to the observation that university students tend to have less crystallized attitudes compared to older individuals (see Sears, 1986; Visser & Krosnick, 1998).

Do explicit and implicit measures of attitude predict different types of behaviour?

Explicit and implicit measures of attitude are both useful tools in attempts to predict human behaviour. Indeed, a number of researchers have explored whether explicit and implicit measures of attitude predict different types of behaviour. It has been suggested that explicit measures of attitude should be more likely to predict a deliberative (i.e. thoughtful) behaviour, whereas implicit measures of attitude should be more likely to predict more spontaneous (i.e. automatic) behaviour. For example, Dovidio, Kawakami, Johnson, Johnson, and Howard (1997) examined how explicit and implicit measures of prejudice predict deliberative and spontaneous discriminatory behaviours. In one experiment, participants completed explicit and implicit measures of their attitudes toward African Americans (Dovidio et al., 1997). The explicit measure was a questionnaire consisting of items such as 'Discrimination against black people is no longer a problem in the United States', whereas the implicit measure consisted of a response latency task. After completing these measures, participants were met by a second experimenter who asked participants to complete an ostensibly unrelated study. In this other study, participants were asked a series of questions by a black female and white female. The interviews were programmed, such that both interviewers' questions were posed in a well-rehearsed manner.

After completing the interview, participants evaluated both interviewers. Their response to these questions served as the deliberative measure of behaviour. The spontaneous measure of behaviour was derived from participants' non-verbal behaviour during the interaction, which had been videotaped. Two non-verbal measures were considered – participants' eye contact with the experimenters and the frequency with which participants blinked. Less eye contact and more frequent blinking are indicators of less favourable behaviour. Further, these behaviours are seen as spontaneous, because they are difficult to consciously monitor and control.

Dovidio et al. (1997) expected that the explicit measure of prejudice would best predict participants' deliberative evaluations of their interactions with the black and white experimenters, while the implicit measure of prejudice would best predict participants' spontaneous behaviours toward the black and white experimenters. The results were consistent with predictions. Only the explicit measure of prejudice was correlated with participants' conscious assessment of their interaction, while only the implicit measure of prejudice was correlated with participants' non-verbal behaviour.

Models of attitude–behaviour relations

In addition to understanding *when* attitudes predict behaviour, social psychologists have developed a number of models to explain *how* attitudes predict behaviour. In this section of the chapter, we describe three models: Fishbein and Azjen's (1975) *theory of reasoned action* (as well as its extension, the theory of planned behaviour), Fazio's (1990) *MODE model* and Strack and Deutsch's (2004) *RIM model*.

The theory of reasoned action and theory of planned behaviour
As its name suggests, the **theory of reasoned action** (Fishbein & Ajzen, 1975) is a model that was developed to predict deliberative (i.e. planned) behaviour. According to this model (see Theory Box 6.2 and Figure 6.19), the immediate predictor (or determinant) of individuals' behaviour is their *intention*.

> **theory of reasoned action** a model in which behaviour is predicted by behavioural intentions, which are determined by attitudes and subjective norms.

Put simply, if you *intend* to recycle glass bottles, you are likely to engage in this behaviour. Within the original conceptualization of the model, Fishbein and Ajzen proposed that there were two determinants of intentions: attitudes and subjective norms. The *attitude* component refers to the individual's attitude towards the behaviour – whether the person thinks that performing the behaviour is good or bad. A person's attitude towards a behaviour (e.g. recycling glass) is a function of the expectancy that the behaviour will produce a desired consequence (helping the environment) *and the value attached to this consequence* (it is good to help the environment). According to the model, an individual's attitude is derived by multiplying the expectancy and value for each consequence and summing these values (see explanation of expectancy–value models of attitude in the earlier section on the cognitive component of attitudes).

Subjective norms refer to an individual's beliefs about how significant others view the relevant behaviour. Like the attitude component, subjective norms are perceived to be derived from two factors that are multiplied and then summed. Specifically, the subjective norm component is a function of normative beliefs (how important others expect the individual to act) and the individual's motivation to comply with these expectations. Returning to our example, subjective norms will be high if your family and close friends have positive expectations towards recycling glass and you are motivated to comply with these expectations.

While the theory of reasoned action did a commendable job in predicting behaviour, it soon became clear that individuals' actions were also influenced by whether or not they felt they *could* perform the relevant behaviour. For example, if an individual wanted to change his dietary habits by eating a healthier diet, a positive attitude and positive subjective norms are unlikely to produce the desired behaviour change if he is unable to restrain himself from eating sweets, chocolates and fish and chips. Social psychologists use the term self-efficacy to refer to

self-efficacy beliefs about one's ability to carry out certain actions required to attain a specific goal (e.g. that one is capable of following a diet, or to help someone).

perceived behavioural control the notion that behavioural prediction is affected by whether people believe that they can perform the relevant behaviour.

beliefs about one's ability to carry out certain actions required to attain a specific goal.

In light of how these types of self-efficacy factors can influence our actions (see Bandura, 1977), the theory of reasoned action was revised to include the notion that behavioural prediction is affected by whether people believe that they can perform the relevant behaviour. This revision is captured by the concept of perceived behavioural control. The inclusion of

this concept led Ajzen (1991; see also Ajzen & Madden, 1986) to name the revised model the theory of planned behaviour. According to this model (see Theory Box 6.2 and Figure 6.20), perceived behavioural control, in addition to attitudes and subjective norms, determines behavioural intentions. Perceived behavioural control itself is determined by control beliefs (individuals' perceptions about whether they have the resources and opportunities required to perform the behaviour).

theory of planned behaviour an extension to the theory of reasoned action that includes the concept of perceived behavioural control.

Perceived behavioural control influences behaviour in two ways. First, it is postulated to have a direct causal influence on behavioural intentions. This implies that individuals' intention to engage in a particular behaviour is affected by their perceived confidence in their ability to perform the action. Second, perceived behavioural control can also have a direct effect on behaviour. This relationship is dependent upon actual control of the relevant action, that is, whether the behaviour can, in reality, be performed. Put simply, while individuals may believe that they can perform the relevant behaviour, their perception may not be accurate.

The theory of reasoned action and theory of planned behaviour are the most frequently tested models of attitude–behaviour relations. The predictions derived from the models have received strong empirical support. For example, a review by Albarracín, Johnson, Fishbein, and Muellerleile (2001) compared the results of over 90 studies

LEADERS IN THE FIELD

Martin Fishbein (1936–1997) and **Icek Ajzen** (b. 1942). Martin Fishbein received his undergraduate degree in psychology and economics at Reed College and his PhD in 1961 at UCLA. He then accepted a position in social psychology and communication at the University of Illinois, where he stayed until 1997 to become distinguished university professor at the Annenberg School for Communication. In 1963 he published his important expectancy-value theory of attitudes, and in a 1967 article on attitudes and the prediction of behaviour he first described what later became known as the 'theory of reasoned action'. Also in 1966, Icek Ajzen, who had completed his undergraduate degree at the Hebrew University of Jerusalem, joined Fishbein at Illinois to pursue a PhD, which he finished in 1969. Their collaboration continued after Ajzen accepted a position at the University of Massachusetts (Amherst), where he remained throughout his career. In 1975 they published their landmark volume *Belief, Attitude, Intention and Behavior*, in which the theory of reasoned action appeared in its present form. Another landmark publication was their article on the relationship between attitude and behaviour, published in 1977. Ajzen later extended the theory of reasoned action into the theory of planned behaviour, which has now replaced the theory of reasoned action as the dominant social psychological model for the prediction of behaviour.

THEORY BOX 6.2

THE THEORY OF REASONED ACTION

The theory of reasoned action (Fishbein & Ajzen, 1975; see Leaders in the Field, Martin Fishbein and Icek Ajzen) and the theory of planned behaviour (Ajzen, 1991) were developed to predict reasoned, deliberative behaviour. According to the theory of reasoned action, the immediate predictor (or determinant) of individuals' behaviour is their *intention*. As the model was originally conceived, intentions were determined by two factors, attitudes and subjective norms. The *attitude* component refers to the individual's attitude toward the behaviour – whether the person thinks that performing the behaviour is good or bad, while *subjective norms* refer to an individual's beliefs about how significant others view the relevant behaviour (see Figure 6.19).

The theory of planned behaviour (see Figure 6.20) extends the theory of reasoned action by including the idea that individuals' actions are also influenced by whether they feel they can perform the relevant behaviour. Accordingly, the theory of planned behaviour added the concept of *perceived behavioural control*. This concept is conceptualized as influencing behaviour in two possible ways, by having a direct effect on behavioural intentions, and by directly influencing behaviour.

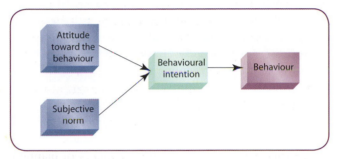

FIGURE 6.19 *The theory of reasoned action.*

Source: Adapted from Haddock et al. (2008) with permission from SAGE Publications Ltd.

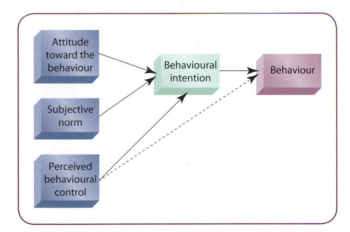

FIGURE 6.20 *The theory of planned behaviour.*

Source: Adapted from Haddock et al. (2008) with permission from SAGE Publications Ltd.

and demonstrated that the models are effective in predicting condom use. Similar findings supporting the models have been found in reviews of other behavioural domains (see e.g. Armitage & Conner, 2001).

A large number of research programmes have used the reasoned action/planned behaviour framework to help understand how additional types of environmental cues influence behaviour. One key issue pertinent to the reasoned action/planned behaviour approach that has received considerable attention concerns *how* behavioural intentions are translated into behaviour. An important development relevant to this issue is the concept of **implementation intentions** (Gollwitzer, 1999; Gollwitzer & Sheeran, 2006). Implementation intentions are conceptualized as 'if–then' plans that specify a behaviour that one will need to perform in order to achieve a goal and the context in which the behaviour will occur (Sheeran, 2002). That is, implementation intentions take the form of mindsets in which an individual attempts to specify where and when a behaviour will be enacted, in the form of 'When I encounter the situational context A, I will perform behaviour B' (Gollwitzer & Brandstätter, 1997). For example, a student might say to herself 'On the first day of the new semester, when I return from Christmas holidays, I will start revising for my exams'.

> **implementation intentions** 'if–then' plans that specify a behaviour that one will need to perform in order to achieve a goal, and the context in which the behaviour will occur.

Numerous studies have demonstrated that forming an implementation intention increases the likelihood that an individual will perform a desired behaviour. In one study, Orbell, Hodgkins, and Sheeran (1997) considered whether the formation of an implementation intention would increase the likelihood that women would perform breast self-examination (BSE). Participants in an intervention group were asked to indicate where and when they would perform BSE, whereas participants in a control group did not receive these instructions. The results of the study revealed that the formation of an implementation intention was effective in eliciting the desired behaviour. For example, one month after the intervention, 64 per cent of participants in the intervention group reported having performed BSE, compared to 14 per cent in the control group (see Gollwitzer & Sheeran, 2006; Sheeran, Milne, Webb, & Gollwitzer, 2005, for extensive reviews of implementation intentions).

Relevant to research on implementation intentions is work that has studied the role of habits in predicting behaviour. Research has demonstrated that habitual behaviours are behaviours that are linked to situational cues (see Aarts & Dijksterhuis, 2000). From a social psychological perspective, habits are more than just behaviours that we perform frequently. Of greater relevance is the idea that habits are *automatic* behaviours, in the sense that they occur without awareness and are difficult to control (see Verplanken, 2006; Verplanken & Orbell, 2003; see also Chapter 4). Many studies have found that habits can play an important role in predicting future behaviour. For example, a field study in the Netherlands considered the degree to which habits and other variables from the theory of planned behaviour predicted travel behaviour (Verplanken, Aarts, Van Knippenberg, & Moonen, 1998). The travel behaviour included decisions about whether to take a bicycle, bus, car or train to work. At the start of the study, participants completed measures of habit strength (e.g. frequency of past behaviour), attitudes, subjective norms, and behavioural intentions about their travel choice. For the next week, participants kept a diary that recorded how often they drove their car and used other forms of transport. The results revealed that habits were highly predictive of behaviour, even predicting behaviour after behavioural intentions and perceived behavioural control were taken into account. Further, the study found that behavioural intentions were uniquely predictive of behaviour only when participants' habits were weak. This suggests that when habits were strong, they were enough to be the main predictor of future behaviour.

Finally, we wish to highlight yet another interesting way in which automatic processes may be important in evaluative judgements: the operation of motives or goals. Goals are linked to the idea of intentions. Goals can be considered cognitive representations that can be primed by environmental cues, and then influence behaviour without the person realizing it. In the last two decades, researchers have addressed how automatically triggered goals influence evaluations and behaviour. There is now a large volume of research that has demonstrated how evaluations and behaviour are influenced by cues and primes without people being aware of them (for reviews, see Custers & Aarts, 2005; Veltkamp, Aarts, & Custers, 2009). For example, in one particularly interesting study, Bargh, Gollwitzer, Lee-Chai, Barndollar, and Trötschel (2001) activated the goal of achievement by unobtrusively priming some participants with words such as 'succeed' and 'achieve'. This was done by having participants complete a word-search puzzle task that contained a number of achievement-relevant words. Subsequent to this task, participants completed another puzzle task in which participants had to find words that were hidden within the puzzle. The researchers were interested in determining whether the unobtrusive priming of the goal of achievement would lead participants to perform better (i.e. achieve more) compared to participants who had not been previously primed with the goal of achievement. Bargh and colleagues (2001) found that participants who had been unobtrusively primed with achievement performed better in locating hidden words than control participants.

The MODE model Not all behaviour is deliberative and planned. Quite often we act spontaneously without consciously thinking of what we intend to do. When our behaviour is spontaneous, the theory of planned behaviour may not provide a proper conceptualization of behavioural prediction (see Fazio, 1990). In an attempt to uncover how attitudes influence spontaneous behaviour, Fazio (1990) developed the *MODE model* of attitude–behaviour relations. MODE refers to Motivation and Opportunity as DEterminants of behaviour.

> **MODE model** a model of attitude–behaviour relations in which motivation and opportunity are necessary to make a deliberative consideration of available information.

At a basic level, the MODE model suggests that, if individuals have *both* sufficient motivation *and* opportunity, they may base their behaviour on a deliberative consideration of the available information. However, when either the motivation or the opportunity to make a reasoned decision is low, only attitudes that are highly accessible will predict spontaneous behaviour. A number of studies by Fazio and colleagues have supported the MODE model (see e.g. Sanbonmatsu & Fazio, 1990; Schuette & Fazio, 1995). For example, Schuette and Fazio (1995) considered how attitude accessibility and motivation influence the extent to which people process information in a biased way. Schuette and Fazio asked university students to evaluate two research studies on the effectiveness of the death penalty as a crime deterrent. One study supported the idea that capital punishment is an effective crime deterrent; the second study reached the opposite conclusion. Before participants looked at the studies, Schuette and Fazio manipulated the accessibility of each participant's attitude toward the death penalty. Some participants expressed their attitude once (low accessibility), whereas others expressed their attitude six times (high accessibility). To manipulate motivation, some participants were told that their conclusions would be compared to those made by an expert panel. Participants in the low motivation condition did not receive this information.

The results revealed that the relation between individuals' prior attitude and their judgement about the study depended on both the accessibility of the participants' attitude and their level of motivation. Participants evaluated the articles in line with their own attitude when their attitude was highly accessible and their motivation was low. In this case, their highly accessible attitude served as a cue that biased their perceptions. However, when participants were highly motivated, or when they had expressed their attitude only one time, attitudes were not correlated with evaluations of the studies. In these conditions, being motivated can lead individuals to overcome the potential biases of their attitude, even if it is accessible. When respondents are not motivated, expressing an attitude just once does not make it sufficiently accessible for it to influence their perceptions.

The RIM model A recent model relevant to the link between attitudes and behaviour has been developed by Strack and Deutsch (2004). Their *reflective–impulsive model* (RIM) proposes that behaviour is controlled by two interacting systems: a reflective system that guides and elicits behaviour via a reasoned consideration of available information, and an impulsive system that guides and elicits behaviour through more automatic associative links. The reflective system can be seen as involving processes that resemble how people respond to explicit measures of attitude, whereas the impulsive system involves processes that bear greater resemblance to implicit measures of attitude. Indeed, Strack and Deutsch suggest that the reflective system should have a greater influence on deliberative behaviour, while the impulsive system should have a greater influence on spontaneous behaviour. Consistent with the ideas proposed in the RIM model, studies have demonstrated that explicit and implicit measures of attitude predict different types of behaviour (as discussed earlier in the chapter).

Summary

On the whole, attitudes do a reasonable job of predicting behaviour. The degree to which attitudes predict behaviour depends upon factors such as the level of correspondence across measures, the domain of behaviour, attitude strength and personality factors. The theory of reasoned action and its extension, the theory of planned behaviour, have received strong support as models for predicting deliberate behaviour. The MODE model suggests that motivation and opportunity are necessary to make a deliberative consideration of available information. The RIM model proposes that behaviour is controlled by two interacting systems: a reflective system and an impulsive system.

CHAPTER SUMMARY

- *What is an attitude?* An attitude is an overall evaluation of an attitude object.

- *Can we have attitudes about anything?* Anything that can be evaluated along a dimension of favourability can be conceptualized as an attitude object.

- *What are the bases of attitudes?* Attitudes have affective, cognitive and behavioural antecedents. All three antecedents contribute to our overall evaluation of an object.

- *Is the structure of an attitude best considered to be one-dimensional or two-dimensional?* The two-dimensional perspective is advantageous as it allows for attitude ambivalence.

- *Why do we hold attitudes?* Attitudes serve a variety of functions, the most important of which is the object appraisal function.

- *Why is it useful to know the function of an attitude?* Knowing the function of an attitude is important because attempts to change an attitude are more likely to be successful when the persuasive appeal matches the attitude's function.

- *Does it matter if an attitude is strong or weak?* Yes – strong attitudes are more stable over time, more resistant to change and more likely to guide both information processing and behaviour.

- *What is the difference between explicit and implicit measures of attitude?* Explicit measures directly ask respondents to think about and report their attitude, whereas implicit measures do not.

- *Do explicit and implicit measures predict different types of behaviour?* Research has shown that explicit measures are more effective in predicting deliberative behaviour, whereas implicit measures are more effective in predicting spontaneous behaviour.

- *Do attitudes predict behaviour?* On the whole, attitudes do a reasonable job of predicting behaviour. The degree to which attitudes predict behaviour depends on a number of factors, including correspondence, the domain of behaviour, the strength of an attitude and person variables.

- *How do attitudes predict behaviour?* A number of models have been developed to understand how attitudes predict behaviour. The most influential models are the theory of planned behaviour and the MODE model.

SUGGESTIONS FOR FURTHER READING

Albarracín, D., Johnson, B. T., & Zanna, M. P. (Eds.). (2005). *Handbook of attitudes*. Mahwah, NJ: Erlbaum. This volume offers an advanced review of the field of attitudes research.

Cialdini, R. B. (2008). *Influence: Science and practice (5th ed.)*. Boston, MA: Allyn & Bacon. This volume offers an accessible look at research on social influence.

Crano, W., & Prislin, R. (Eds.). (2009). *Attitudes and persuasion*. New York: Psychology Press. This volume reviews different streams of research on attitudes and attitude change.

Eagly, A. H., & Chaiken, S. (1993). *The psychology of attitudes*. Fort Worth, TX: Harcourt Brace Jovanovich. This volume provides a comprehensive review of research that laid the foundation for the progress that has been made in the past two decades.

Fazio, R. H., & Olson, M. A. (2003). Implicit measures in social cognition research: Their meaning and use. *Annual Review of Psychology, 54*, 297–327. This paper reviews advances that have been made concerning implicit measures of attitude.

Fazio, R. H., & Petty, R. E. (Eds.). (2007). *Attitudes: Structure, function, and consequences*. Hove, UK: Psychology Press. This volume comprises a collection of important published papers on attitude structure, attitude content and the attitude–behaviour relation.

Haddock, G., & Maio, G. R. (Eds.). (2004). *Contemporary perspectives on the pychology of attitudes*. Hove, UK: Psychology Press. This volume reviews a number of contemporary research programmes on the psychology of attitudes.

Maio, G. R., & Haddock, G. (2010). *The psychology of attitudes and attitude change*. London: Sage. This volume provides a comprehensive and accessible overview of research and theories relevant to the psychology of attitudes.

Maio, G. R., & Olson, J. M. (Eds.). (2000). *Why we evaluate: Functions of attitudes*. Mahwah, NJ: Erlbaum. This volume is a comprehensive examination of research on attitude functions.

Petty, R. E., & Cacioppo, J. T. (1986). *Communication and persuasion: Central and peripheral routes to attitude change*. New York: Springer. This volume highlights the research that was conducted in the development of the highly influential Elaboration Likelihood Model of persuasion.

Petty, R. E., Fazio, R. H., & Briñol, P. (Eds.). (2009). *Attitudes: Insights from the new implicit measures*. New York: Psychology Press. This volume highlights different research programmes regarding implicit measures of attitude.

Wittenbrink, B., & Schwarz, N. (Eds.). (2007). *Implicit measures of attitudes*. New York: Guilford. This volume provides an overview of different perspectives on the utility of implicit measures of attitude.

7 Strategies of Attitude and Behaviour Change

Wolfgang Stroebe

DANGER: SMOKING CAUSES CANCER

Source: © Stuart Hepburn. Used under licence from Shutterstock.

KEY TERMS

- central route to persuasion
- cognitive dissonance theory
- cognitive response model
- counterattitudinal behaviour
- distraction
- dual-process theories of persuasion
- elaboration
- elaboration likelihood model (ELM)
- heuristic processing
- heuristic–systematic model (HSM)
- intrinsic motivation
- need for cognition
- need for cognitive closure
- over-justification effect
- peripheral route to persuasion
- reactance theory
- subliminal advertising
- systematic processing
- thought-listing

CHAPTER OUTLINE

ROUTE MAP OF THE CHAPTER

This chapter discusses two strategies of attitude and behaviour change, namely persuasion and the use of incentives (e.g. taxation, legal sanctions). We will discuss when, how and why persuasion results in attitude and behaviour change and review empirical studies that have been conducted to assess the validity of these theoretical interpretations. Finally, we will apply these theories to the area of advertising. The second part of the chapter will focus on the use of incentives. Instead of relying on the uncertain effects of persuasion to induce people to use seatbelts or give up smoking, governments often employ legal sanctions or taxation to influence behaviour directly. These strategies are quite effective in influencing behaviour, but it is much less clear whether they can also result in attitude change.

INTRODUCTION

The notion of using social psychological knowledge to change attitudes and to influence behaviour conjures up visions of advertising executives planning mass media campaigns to sell cars, refrigerators, alcoholic drinks or margarine. And this vision is certainly not incorrect. However, social psychology is equally useful in persuading people to change unhealthy behaviour patterns such as smoking, drinking or engaging in unsafe sex. In fact, one of the most effective campaigns in recent times, achieving substantial changes in attitudes and behaviour, has probably been the war against smoking. It began in 1964 with the publication of the report of the United States Surgeon General's Advisory Committee on Smoking and Health (USDHEW, 1964). The persuasive information on the substantial health impairment suffered by smokers was quickly adopted by the news media and thus reached a wide audience. The material not only persuaded many smokers to stop, it also convinced politicians that it was time to act and, some years later, compulsory health warnings were introduced on tobacco advertisements and cigarette packets. Finally, in the 1980s, Federal cigarette tax was doubled and various states introduced additional excise taxes on cigarettes. Largely as a result of this anti-smoking campaign, smoking is now generally recognized as a health risk and an addiction. Moreover, especially in the US, smoking has declined substantially. (See Figures 7.1 & 7.2.)

This chapter focuses on the two major strategies of attitude and behaviour change, namely (1) the use of *persuasion*, and (2) the use of *incentives* or *sanctions*. In each section, we will discuss the effectiveness of these strategies and use the major theories in the literature to analyse the psychological processes that are responsible for their impact.

PERSUASION

Persuasion involves the use of communications to change the beliefs, attitudes and behaviour of others. Research on persuasion received a big boost during World War II when the American army looked for strategies to counteract enemy propaganda and to boost the morale of their own troops (Hovland, Lumsdaine, & Sheffield, 1949). After the war, Carl Hovland, the director of the mass communication programme within the US Army's information and education division, assembled a group of eminent researchers at Yale University (e.g. Abelson, Janis, Kelley, McGuire, Rosenberg) and this group was instrumental in making the study of persuasion and attitude change one of the central areas of social psychology.

Theories of systematic processing

Is attitude change determined by how well we understand and remember persuasive arguments?

Before 1980, most of the theories of persuasion and attitude change emphasized systematic processing. They assumed that attitude change was mediated by the message recipient's detailed processing of the persuasive arguments contained in the communication; that is to say, processing of the message arguments was the means by which persuasive arguments had their effect on attitudes (see Chapter 2 for discussion of mediating variables). The two most influential theories of systematic processing have been the information processing model (McGuire, 1969, 1985) and the cognitive response model (e.g. Greenwald, 1968; Petty, Ostrom & Brock, 1981).

> **systematic processing** thorough, detailed processing of information (e.g. attention to the arguments contained in a persuasive communication); this kind of processing relies on ability and effort.

The information processing model of persuasion The paradigm proposed by McGuire (1969, 1985) provides a useful framework for thinking about the stages involved in the processing of persuasive communications. According to this model, the persuasive impact of a message is the product of at least five steps: (1) attention;

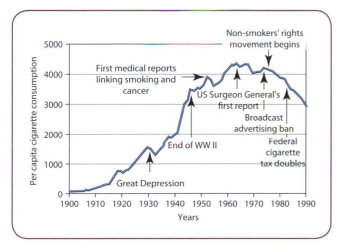

FIGURE 7.1 *Per capita cigarette consumption per year among adults, and major smoking and health events in the US, 1900–1990.*

Source: Based on Novotny, Romano, Davis, & Mills, 1992.

FIGURE 7.2(a), (b), (c) and (d) *Thanks to effective anti-tobacco campaigns, smoking is now generally recognized as a health risk and an addiction.*

Source: (a) © FuzzBones; (b) © STILLFX; (c) © michaeljung; (d) © Jeroen van den Broek. All images used under licence from Shutterstock.

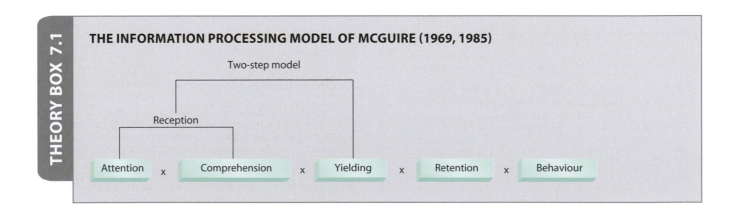

THEORY BOX 7.1

THE INFORMATION PROCESSING MODEL OF MCGUIRE (1969, 1985)

Two-step model

Reception

Attention x Comprehension x Yielding x Retention x Behaviour

(2) comprehension; (3) yielding; (4) retention; and (5) behaviour (see Theory Box 7.1). For example, the ultimate objective of speeches given on television by politicians is to get the members of the audience to vote for their party. If viewers use the break between programmes to go to the bathroom (failure to attend) the appeal will not result in attitude change. Even if viewers attend to the communication, it will have little impact if they find the arguments too complex (failure to comprehend) or if they do not accept the communicator's conclusions and as a result, do not change their beliefs and attitudes (failure to yield). But even if the candidate

manages to persuade the audience, this will be of no use if viewers change their attitudes again before election day (failure to retain) or if bad weather keeps them away from the ballot box (failure to act). Since the message receiver must go through each of these steps if the communication is to have the ultimate persuasive impact, and since it is unlikely that the probability of any given step will be maximal, McGuire's framework offers one explanation of why it is often difficult to induce behaviour change through information campaigns.

In social psychological studies, the impact of a communication is typically assessed immediately following exposure to the message. Thus, our analysis is restricted to the first three steps of the chain. Moreover, attention and comprehension have usually been combined into a single step of reception of the message content in order to simplify measurement. Thus McGuire's model can be reduced to a two-step version, which states that the probability of a communication resulting in change of beliefs and attitudes is the joint product of reception and acceptance (yielding) (see Leader in the Field, William J. McGuire).

Few studies have supported the claim that the reception of message arguments determines attitude change. In general, message reception, when measured by the recall of message arguments, is not found to correlate significantly with attitude change (see Eagly & Chaiken, 1993). This failure to find correlations between argument recall and attitude change raised doubts about McGuire's two-step model, in particular the role of attention to and comprehension of the arguments presented in persuasive communications. Even more critical for the model was the fact that it lacked specific

theoretical principles that would allow one to predict the factors that affect acceptance and to understand the processes that mediate the relationship between acceptance and attitude change. The cognitive response model provides such a theory.

The cognitive response model: a theory of yielding

The cognitive response model of persuasion was developed by Greenwald and his colleagues at Ohio State University, partly to explain the absence of a correlation between argument recall and attitude change (Greenwald, 1968; Petty, Ostrom & Brock, 1981; see Leader in the Field, Anthony Greenwald). According to this model, it is not the reception of arguments that mediates attitude change, but the thoughts (cognitive responses) stimulated in the recipient by those arguments. Listening to a communication is like a mental discussion. Listeners are active participants who relate the communication to their own knowledge. In doing this, the person may consider much cognitive material that is not contained in the communication itself to generate thoughts for or against the arguments presented in the communication. It is these self-generated thoughts and not the presented arguments *per se* which mediate attitude change. Messages persuade if they evoke predominantly favourable thoughts, and they fail to persuade if they evoke predominantly unfavourable thoughts. Thus, the impact of persuasion variables on attitude change does not depend on the extent to which they facilitate argument reception, but on the extent to which they

> **cognitive response model** assumes that attitude change is mediated by the thoughts, or 'cognitive responses', which recipients generate as they receive and reflect upon persuasive communications.

*on exam

LEADER IN THE FIELD

William J. McGuire (1925–2008) was born in New York City, US. After a brief stint in the army, he studied psychology at Fordham University, where he received his BA (1949) and MA (1950). He then spent a year as a Research Fellow at the University of Minnesota at the time Festinger was there (see Leader in the Field, Chapter 1). In 1951 he went to Yale University for his PhD, which he received in 1954. He stayed on at Yale for four more years, and after holding positions at various other universities (Illinois, Columbia and San Diego) he returned to Yale as Professor of Psychology in 1971, remaining there until his retirement in 1999. Bill McGuire dominated research on attitudes and attitude change until the 1980s. During his early time at Yale, he was a member of the famous Yale Communication and Attitude Change Program headed by Carl Hovland (see Leader in the Field, Chapter 1). When he returned to Yale ten years after the death of Hovland, he continued the research tradition of the Yale program. He made numerous empirical and theoretical contributions to the area, and also authored the highly influential chapters on attitudes and attitude change in the second and third edition of the *Handbook of Social Psychology* (McGuire, 1969, 1985).

LEADER IN THE FIELD

Anthony Greenwald (b. 1939) received his BA from Yale University in 1959 and his MA from Harvard University in 1961. In 1963 he completed his PhD, also at Harvard, under the supervision of Gordon Allport (see Leader in the Field, Chapter 14). After a two year Postdoctoral Fellowship at the Educational Testing Service, he moved to the Psychology Department at Ohio State University, where he remained until 1986. During this time he developed the cognitive response approach that revolutionized attitude change theory. The cognitive response model assumed that all persuasion was basically self-persuasion, in that external messages triggered favourable or unfavourable thoughts that were ultimately responsible for persuasion or resistance. After more than 20 years on the faculty of Ohio State University, Greenwald moved to the University of Washington in 1986, where he worked on such topics as subliminal persuasion and the self. Perhaps his second most important contribution to attitudes was the introduction of the *implicit association test* or IAT as a means of assessing automatic evaluations.

stimulate individuals to generate their own favourable or unfavourable thoughts about the information presented.

On first reading, this does not appear to be a very impressive theory. It is also not terribly new. Writing in 1949, Hovland, Lumsdaine, and Sheffield had already suggested that audiences may resist persuasion by going over their own arguments against the position during exposure to the communication. Hovland and Weiss (1951) later emphasized that the best way to study internal processes of attitude change was to have respondents verbalize their thoughts as they responded to the communication. However, although cognitive responses were everybody's favourite concept to be invoked when non-obvious findings of persuasion studies had to be explained (e.g. Festinger & Maccoby, 1964), research on the role of cognitive responses as mediators of persuasion had been hampered by the absence of accepted measures of self-generated thinking.

One major methodological contribution of the Ohio State researchers to the study of persuasion was therefore the development of a measure of cognitive responses: **thought-listing** (Greenwald, 1968; Osterhouse & Brock, 1970). This enabled them to assess the processes assumed to mediate attitude change. With this thought-listing task recipients of a message are asked to list the thoughts they had while listening. These thoughts are later categorized into those that are favourable or unfavourable to the position advocated by the message. Thoughts that do not fit either of these categories (e.g. neutral or irrelevant thoughts) are not considered.

thought-listing
a measure of cognitive responses; message recipients are asked to list all the thoughts that occurred to them while being exposed to a persuasive message.

The second major contribution of the Ohio State researchers was theoretical. Previous conceptualizations of cognitive responses had focused only on the production of counterarguments that *reduce* persuasion (e.g. Festinger & Maccoby, 1964). In an important theoretical contribution, Petty, Wells, and Brock (1976) broadened the concept of cognitive responses by arguing that strong and well-argued messages are likely to produce predominantly favourable thoughts which should *enhance* persuasion.

This extended cognitive response model accounts for a number of inconsistent findings in the attitude change literature. Thus, it helps to explain why there is often no correlation between argument recall and attitude change. If it is the thoughts stimulated by arguments and not the arguments themselves that are responsible for attitude change, then the message arguments that a recipient remembers could not be expected to be related to attitude change. What one would expect, however, is a correlation between the extent to which these thoughts are favourable or unfavourable towards the arguments presented by the communicator and the amount of attitude change. The newly developed thought-listing measure enabled researchers to test (and to support) this assumption (e.g. Osterhouse & Brock, 1970).

Another inconsistency resolved by the cognitive response approach related to findings of research on the impact of **distraction** on attitude change. We have probably all had the experience of being distracted while listening to some communication. The station on our car radio might have faded in the middle of a broadcast, or the people next to us might have started a loud conversation. Since being distracted whilst listening to a communication should impair reception, one would expect distraction to reduce the persuasive impact of a communication. Although some studies reported findings consistent with this prediction (e.g. Haaland & Venkatesan, 1968), others found distraction to strengthen the persuasive impact of a communication (e.g. Festinger & Maccoby, 1964).

distraction while listening to a persuasive communication, individuals are distracted by having to perform an irrelevant activity or by experiencing sensory stimulation irrelevant to the message.

According to the cognitive response model, such discrepant results are to be expected. Distraction reduces the recipient's ability to generate cognitive responses to a message. The impact of distraction on attitude change should therefore depend on the favourability of the thoughts produced by a message (Petty et al., 1976). If these dominant thoughts are mainly unfavourable, distraction should enhance persuasion. However, for messages that elicit predominantly favourable thoughts, distraction should work to inhibit persuasion.

But how can we manipulate the favourability of a listener's dominant thoughts? Since we have put so much emphasis on self-generated thoughts as a mediator of persuasion in this section, it is easy to forget that these thoughts are cognitive responses to persuasive arguments and are therefore likely to be influenced by the quality of these arguments. Thus, communications which present several strong arguments (e.g. arguments which are coherent, logical and compelling) are likely to elicit cognitive responses which are predominantly favourable to the position argued, whereas messages consisting mainly of weak arguments should elicit predominantly unfavourable responses. This process is illustrated in Theory Box 7.2.

Petty and colleagues (1976, Experiment 1) exposed students to messages arguing for an increase in tuition fees at their university. These communications consisted of either very strong or very weak arguments. Distraction was manipulated by having participants

THEORY BOX 7.2

THE COGNITIVE RESPONSE MODEL OF PERSUASION

Persuasive message	Cognitive responses	Attitude
Strong arguments	Predominantly favourable thoughts	Change
Weak arguments	Predominantly unfavourable thoughts	No change

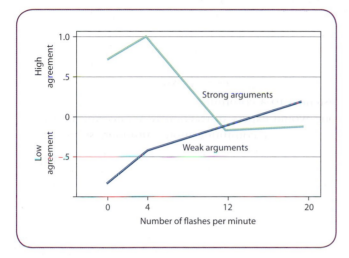

FIGURE 7.3 *Mean level of agreement (shown as z-scores) in relation to argument quality and level of distraction.*

Source: Adapted from Petty et al., 1976. Copyright © 1976 by the American Psychological Association. Adapted with permission. *Journal of Personality and Social Psychology, 34*, 874–884. The use of APA information does not imply endorsement by APA.

record visual stimuli (briefly flashed on a screen at a rate of 0, 4, 12 or 20 flashes per minute) while listening to the message. In line with predictions, increases in distraction enhanced persuasion for the message that consisted of weak arguments, but reduced persuasion for the message containing strong arguments (Figure 7.3). The participants' thought-listing data provided support for the assumption that both the increase and the decrease in persuasion were due to thought disruption. In the case of weak arguments, the distraction manipulation decreased recipients' ability to generate counterarguments to the weak message; in the case of strong arguments, distraction reduced the number of favourable thoughts they were able to generate to that version of the message.

Summary

McGuire's information processing theory shares with the cognitive response model of Greenwald (1968)

the assumption that persuasive arguments have to be processed systematically in order to influence beliefs and attitudes. However, whereas McGuire assumed further that change of beliefs and attitudes was a function of how well we understood and remembered the persuasive arguments, the cognitive response model assumes that it is not the arguments, but the respondents' thoughts generated in response to arguments, which determine change.

Dual-process theories of persuasion

Do people sometimes change their attitudes without systematic processing of persuasive arguments, and what factors determine depth of processing?

That attitude change is mediated by detailed processing of the arguments may strike one as a plausible way to analyse the psychological processes that mediate persuasion. After all, is there any other way to be persuaded, if not through the arguments contained in a persuasive communication? However, if we think of the hundreds of advertisements we are exposed to every day, we might become doubtful. Does anybody really think about the arguments contained in advertisements about soft drinks or toothpaste? Do these advertisements even contain arguments? And yet if people were not influenced by them, these companies would not spend millions on their advertising budgets.

The answer to these questions is that advertisements often work through processes of evaluative conditioning or mere exposure, which we discussed in Chapter 6. Evaluative conditioning changes the liking for a stimulus by repeatedly pairing it with another more polarized positive or negative stimulus. With relatively unfamiliar stimuli liking can even be increased by mere exposure. But how are evaluative conditioning and mere exposure related to systematic processing? Under which conditions does each of these processes operate? These are the types of questions which we will address in our discussion of **dual-process theories of persuasion**. Dual-process theories integrate both theories of systematic processing and persuasion processes that are not based on systematic analysis of message arguments (e.g. evaluative conditioning, mere exposure, heuristic processing). Dual-process theories also specify the conditions under which people will engage in each of these processes. There are two dual-process

> **dual-process theories of persuasion** theories of persuasion postulating two modes of information processing, systematic and non-systematic. Modes differ in the extent to which individuals engage in content-relevant thoughts and critical evaluation of the arguments contained in a message.

LEADER IN THE FIELD

Shelly Chaiken (b. 1949) studied mathematics at the University of Maryland (College Park) and received her BA in 1971. She then became a graduate student in social psychology at the University of Massachusetts (Amherst), where she received her MS in 1975 and her PhD in 1978. After brief spells at the University of Toronto and Vanderbilt University, she moved to New York University as Professor of Psychology in 1985, where she stayed until 2005. She is now associated with the University of Wisconsin (Madison). At the University of Massachusetts, she did her graduate studies with Alice Eagly (see Leader in the Field, Chapter 6) and developed the idea for the heuristic systematic model during her work for her PhD. She continued her close collaboration with Eagly even after her PhD and co-authored *The Psychology of Attitudes* with her in 1993, which has been the defining book on that topic for many years. She has published numerous empirical articles testing and extending her heuristic–systematic model. In 1999 she also edited (jointly with Yaacov Trope) an important volume on *Dual-process theories in social psychology*.

LEADER IN THE FIELD

Richard E. Petty (b. 1951) received his BA in political science and psychology from the University of Virginia in 1973. He then moved to Ohio State University for his graduate studies, where he received his PhD in 1977. He began his academic career the same year at the University of Missouri, from where, after a sabbatical at Yale in 1986, he returned to Ohio State in 1987. Since 1998 he has been Distinguished University Professor at Ohio State University. At Ohio State he began a fruitful collaboration with fellow PhD student John Cacioppo (see Leader in the Field, Chapter 6). At that time persuasion research was plagued by inconsistencies in empirical findings, which could not be explained by available theoretical models. In their attempt to reconcile these conflicting findings and to integrate different theoretical approaches ranging from cognitive response theory to theories based on evaluative conditioning, Petty and Cacioppo developed the idea of the two routes to persuasion which formed the basis for their general theory of attitude change, the elaboration likelihood model (ELM). It is probably fair to say that Petty has taken over the mantle of Bill McGuire (see Leader in the Field, this chapter) as the dominant figure in the area of attitude and attitude change research.

---

elaboration likelihood model (ELM) attitude change to persuasive communications is mediated by either central or peripheral processing; elaboration denotes the extent to which a person thinks about the issue-relevant arguments contained in a message.

heuristic–systematic model (HSM) attitude change to persuasive communications is mediated by heuristic and/or systematic processing: when motivation and ability are high, systematic processing is likely; when they are low, individuals rely on heuristic cues.

theories of persuasion, the **elaboration likelihood model** (Petty & Cacioppo, 1986a, b; Petty & Wegener, 1999; see Leader in the Field, Richard E. Petty) and the **heuristic–systematic model** (e.g. Chaiken, Lieberman & Eagly, 1989; Chen & Chaiken, 1999; see Leader in the Field, Shelly Chaiken). There is, however, so much overlap between these theories in their core assumptions that we will focus mainly on the elaboration likelihood model. After having presented the elaboration likelihood model, we will briefly discuss the major aspects in which this theory differs from the heuristic–systematic model of Chaiken and her colleagues.

The elaboration likelihood model (ELM) When people receive a communication and are faced with the decision whether to accept or reject the position advocated, they will try to form an opinion of its validity. This assessment may be arrived at by two routes of information processing, namely a *central* and a *peripheral* route to persuasion. These two routes mark the endpoints of a continuum that ranges from thoughtful to very non-thoughtful strategies (i.e. the elaboration likelihood continuum). Petty and Cacioppo (1986a, b) use the term **elaboration** to denote the extent

elaboration refers to the extent to which a person thinks about the issue-relevant arguments contained in a message.

to which a person thinks about the issue-relevant arguments contained in a message.

The probability that a recipient will critically evaluate arguments contained in a message (i.e. elaboration likelihood) is determined by both *processing motivation* and *processing ability*. Processing motivation is important because such elaboration requires time and effort. Processing ability is important because, in order to be able to scrutinize arguments, a person needs both issue-relevant knowledge and sufficient time. For example, if a computer salesperson gives us a highly technical speech about the advantages of a computer they are trying to sell us, we will not be able to evaluate these arguments if we lack the necessary computer knowledge. But even if we have the necessary knowledge, we might not be able to think about these arguments if we have no time to do so, because we have to come to a decision immediately. If, however, individuals are motivated and able to think about the arguments contained in a communication, they will engage in systematic processing and follow the **central route to persuasion** (Theory Box 7.3a). This mode of information processing is identical to the processes assumed by the cognitive response model. However, sometimes recipients may not be motivated (e.g. the issue is trivial) or able (e.g. they have no time or lack the knowledge) to engage in an extensive process of message evaluation. Under these conditions attitudes will be formed according to the **peripheral route to persuasion**

central route to persuasion a person's careful and thoughtful consideration of the arguments presented in support of a position.

peripheral route to persuasion subsumes those persuasion processes that are not based on issue-relevant thinking (e.g. evaluative conditioning, heuristic processing).

(see Theory Box 7.3b). This type of persuasion refers to any attitude change mechanism that does not involve systematic processing. The peripheral route thus encompasses cognitive processes such as the use of heuristic decision rules (e.g. 'experts can be trusted'), affective processes such as evaluative conditioning and mere exposure (see Chapter 6), and use of information about the attitudes held by relevant others (see Chapter 8).

The peripheral process that has been most extensively examined in studies of dual-process theories of persuasion has been **heuristic processing** (Theory Box 7.3b), which focuses on the simple decision rules which people use to judge the validity of messages. For example, people may have learned from previous experience that statements by experts tend to be more accurate than statements by non-experts. They may therefore apply the rule 'experts can be trusted' in response to indications that the communicator is an expert (Eagly & Chaiken, 1993). Or they may have learned to trust people they like and, on finding a communicator likeable, they

> **heuristic processing** assessing the validity of a communication through reliance on heuristics; that is, simple rules like 'statistics don't lie', 'experts can be trusted', 'consensus implies correctness', rather than through evaluation of arguments.

will apply the 'liking–agreement' heuristic, such as 'people agree with people they like' or 'people I like usually have correct opinions' (Eagly & Chaiken, 1993).

Assessing elaboration. Petty, Cacioppo and their colleagues developed two strategies that allowed an assessment of the extent to which recipients of a message engage in message processing. One method, which was mentioned earlier, is the thought-listing technique. This technique gives some indication of the number of supportive or unsupportive thoughts stimulated by a message. If attitude change is due to central processing, then (1) recipients of a message should have generated several positive thoughts about the arguments contained in the message, and (2) the relative favourability or unfavourability of these thoughts to the advocated position should be correlated with the extent of attitude change. More specifically, a favourability index based on thought-listing (e.g. ratio of favourable thoughts to total number of relevant thoughts) should act as a mediator of attitude change under central processing, but not under peripheral processing.

An even more powerful tool to assess the degree to which message recipients engage in systematic processing is the systematic variation of argument quality.

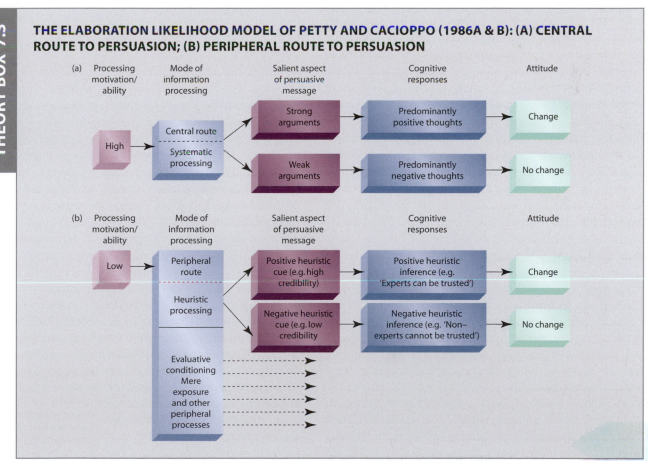

THEORY BOX 7.3

THE ELABORATION LIKELIHOOD MODEL OF PETTY AND CACIOPPO (1986A & B): (A) CENTRAL ROUTE TO PERSUASION; (B) PERIPHERAL ROUTE TO PERSUASION

With this technique, recipients are exposed to communications that consist of either strong or weak arguments. (The categorization of arguments as strong or weak is decided beforehand on the basis of a pilot study.) Exposure to strong arguments should stimulate predominantly favourable thoughts about the message in recipients who engage in central route processing. As a result, there should also be significant attitude change. On the other hand, if arguments are weak, central route processing should produce predominantly unfavourable thoughts about the message, and therefore very little attitude change. The less recipients are motivated and able to engage in central route (i.e. systematic) processing of a message, the weaker should be the effect of a manipulation of argument quality on cognitive responses and attitude change. The combined use of both thought-listing (as one of the dependent measures) and manipulation of argument quality (as one of the independent variables) therefore provides a valid tool for diagnosing the extent to which individuals engage in central processing of the content of a message.

Processing ability, elaboration and attitude change. Variation in processing ability should affect information processing mainly when individuals are motivated to process a message. Thus, studies of variables that influence processing ability have typically used issues which were highly relevant to the students who were the recipients of these communications (e.g. a planned increase in tuition fees, or a proposed change in the college exam system). Among the most important variables influencing a person's ability to systematically process persuasive arguments are distraction and message repetition. Since we have considered research on distraction earlier, we will focus here on message repetition. In contrast to distraction, which reduces processing ability, (moderate) argument repetition should provide recipients with more opportunity for cognitively elaborating a communication. Thus, repetition should enhance attitude change for messages consisting of strong arguments and reduce attitude change for weak messages. Cacioppo and Petty (1989) tested this hypothesis by exposing respondents either one or three times to a message that contained either strong or weak persuasive arguments. Consistent with their predictions, increasing exposure to the same message led to higher agreement with high-quality messages, but led to decreased agreement with low-quality messages. However, the positive impact of repetition on high-quality messages will only occur if recipients are motivated to think about the communication (Claypool, Mackie, Garcia-Marques, McIntosh, & Udal, 2004). Furthermore, when messages are repeated too often, boredom sets in, which can result in rejection

of even high-quality arguments in high-relevance messages (Cacioppo & Petty, 1979).

Processing motivation, elaboration and attitude change. The most influential determinant of a person's motivation to think about the argument contained in a message is the perceived *personal relevance* of the communication. Only if the issue is important to them personally should recipients of a communication be motivated to critically evaluate the arguments contained in a message. With low involvement, when the issue of the communication is of little relevance, recipients are likely to rely on peripheral cues to assess the validity of the position advocated by the communication.

Petty, Cacioppo, and Goldman (1981) tested these predictions experimentally. They exposed college students to an attitude-discrepant communication advocating major changes to the college examination system. This communication, on a topic of great importance to students, contained either strong or weak arguments and was attributed either to a source with high expertise (the Carnegie Commission on Higher Education) or to one with low expertise (a class at a local high school). The researchers manipulated personal relevance by informing students either that these changes were going to be instituted the following year and would thus affect them, or that they would take effect only in ten years' time. Petty and colleagues (1981) predicted that when students believed that the changes would affect their own fate (high personal relevance), they should be motivated to scrutinize the arguments and to engage in issue-relevant thinking. For these highly involved students, argument quality would be a major factor in persuasion. Students who believed that these changes would only be instituted long after they had left the university (low personal relevance) would not be motivated to think a great deal about the communication. Instead, they would use heuristic rules such as 'experts can be trusted' to assess the validity of the advocated position. The results strongly supported these predictions (Figure 7.4). As Figure 7.4a shows, the nature of the source was a significant determinant of attitudes only for the low-involvement participants. But, as Figure 7.4b shows, argument quality was a significant factor only for the high-involvement participants.

The extent to which individuals scrutinize message arguments is affected not only by situational factors but also by individual differences in their motivation to think about persuasive communications. For example, people who frequently engage in and enjoy effortful cognitive activity (high **need for cognition**) should be more likely to form attitudes on the basis of the arguments contained in a communication than are people who are low in need for cognition. Cacioppo and

need for cognition
an individual difference variable which differentiates people according to the extent to which they enjoy thinking about arguments contained in a communication.

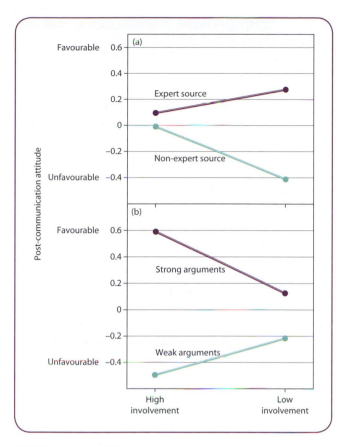

FIGURE 7.4(a) and (b)   *(a) interactive effect of involvement and source expertise on post-communication attitudes; (b) interactive effect of involvement and argument quality on post-communication attitudes.*

Source: Petty, Cacioppo & Goldman, 1981. Copyright © 1981 by the American Psychological Association. Adapted with permission. *Journal of Personality and Social Psychology, 41,* 847–855. The use of APA information does not imply endorsement by APA.

Petty (1982) constructed a scale to measure need for cognition (see Individual Differences 7.1). Since need for cognition reflects a cognitive motivation rather than an intellectual ability, it correlates only moderately with verbal intelligence ($r = .24$; Cacioppo, Petty, Feinstein, & Jarvis, 1996). Consistent with expectations, argument quality affected attitude change mainly for individuals with high rather than low need for cognition. A study by Haugtvedt and Petty (1992) further demonstrated that attitude change in respondents with a high need for cognition was more persistent and more resistant against counterargumentation than in individuals with low need for cognition.

The **need for cognitive closure** is another individual difference variable that has been shown to influence the intensity with which individuals process information (Klein & Webster, 2000; Kruglanski & Webster, 1996;

> **need for cognitive closure** refers to the desire of individuals for a definite answer to a question – any answer, as opposed to uncertainty; the need reflects an individual difference variable, but can also be situationally induced.

Webster & Kruglanski, 1994). It refers to the individual's need for a definite answer to a question, any answer as opposed to confusion and ambiguity. Two highly related tendencies are assumed to underlie this need, namely 'urgency', that is the need to arrive at closure quickly, and 'permanency', that is the need to remain at closure once it has been achieved. These two tendencies are assumed to be separated by a demarcation point, namely the point, when a belief 'crystallizes' and turns from a conjecture to a firm 'fact' (Kruglanski & Webster, 1996). During the 'urgency' phase, before a belief crystallizes, individuals will be relatively open to persuasion attempts, because such attempts should accelerate closure. Once a belief has crystallized, the 'permanency' tendency kicks in, and individuals will be reluctant to engage in further information processing and will be resistant to persuasive arguments (Kruglanski & Webster, 1996). The need for cognitive closure is assumed to reflect a stable individual difference that is mostly measured with the Need for Closure Scale, a 42-item scale developed by Webster and Kruglanski (1994). (A shortened version of this scale has recently been proposed and validated by Roets and Van Hiel, 2011; see Individual Differences 7.2.) These scales show a moderately negative correlation with need for cognition (e.g. $r = -.28$; Webster & Kruglanski, 1994).

A study by Klein and Webster (2000) provides some support for these assumptions. Participants in their study were given promotional material about a new telephone answering machine. The information varied both in length (three versus nine arguments) and in the quality of the arguments that were presented. Results showed that attitudes of individuals high in need for closure were more affected by the number of arguments than by argument quality, whereas low need for closure individuals were more likely to be affected by argument quality. Since the length of a communication can be considered a heuristic cue (Chaiken, 1980), these findings are consistent with the assumption that individuals high in need for closure rely on heuristic cues rather than scrutiny of arguments. In contrast, the fact that argument quality influenced attitudes of individuals who are low in need for cognitive closure suggests that they formed their attitude based on scrutiny of the content of the communication.

The existence of stable individual differences between people in their need for cognitive closure does not preclude the possibility that this need is also influenced by situational factors. One of the situational factors known to heighten need for closure is time pressure. Suppose you are going on a vacation and you decide to buy a camera at the airport, because your old camera has just been stolen on the train. If you have ample time before your plane leaves, you will look at a range of different cameras, have all their advantages and disadvantages explained and then select one, which promises to be most

THE NEED FOR COGNITION

This scale (short version by Cacioppo, Petty, & Kao, 1984) assesses need for cognition, the tendency of individuals to engage in and enjoy effortful cognitive endeavours (Cacioppo et al., 1996). When exposed to a persuasive message, people high in need for cognition are assumed to engage in more content-relevant thinking (i.e. systematic processing) than individuals low in need for cognition.

Instructions: Indicate to what extent each statement is characteristic of you, using the following response alternatives:

1 = *extremely uncharacteristic of me (not at all like me)*
2 = *somewhat uncharacteristic of me*
3 = *neither uncharacteristic nor characteristic of me*
4 = *somewhat characteristic of me*
5 = *extremely characteristic of me*

1. I would prefer complex to simple problems.
2. I like to have the responsibility of handling a situation that requires a lot of thinking.
3. Thinking is not my idea of fun.
4. I would rather do something that requires little thought than something that is sure to challenge my thinking ability.
5. I try to anticipate and avoid situations where there is a likely chance I will have to think in depth about something.
6. I find satisfaction in deliberating hard and for long hours.
7. I only think as hard as I have to.
8. I prefer to think about small, daily projects to long-term ones.

9. I like tasks that require little thought once I've learned them.
10. The idea of relying on thought to make my way to the top appeals to me.
11. I really enjoy a task that involves coming up with new solutions to problems.
12. Learning new ways to think doesn't excite me very much.
13. I prefer my life to be filled with puzzles that I must solve.
14. The notion of thinking abstractly is appealing to me.
15. I would prefer a task that is intellectual, difficult and important to one that is somewhat important but does not require much thought.
16. I feel relief rather than satisfaction after completing a task that required a lot of mental effort.
17. It's enough for me that something gets the job done; I don't care how or why it works.
18. I usually end up deliberating about issues even when they do not affect me personally.

Scoring: First, reverse your scores on items 3, 4, 5, 7, 8, 9, 12, 16 and 17. On any of these items, if you gave a 1 to the question, change it into a 5. If you gave a 2, change it into a 4; if you gave a 4, change it into a 2; and if you gave a 5, change it into a 1. If you gave a 3, leave it as a 3. Scores are added, and the higher your score, the higher your need for cognition. The median score in student samples was 60 (e.g. Petty, Schumann, Richman, & Strathman, 1993).

suitable for your needs. In contrast, if you have only 10 minutes before boarding starts, you have to rely on heuristic cues to reach your decision. You might choose the camera recommended by the salesperson (experts know what is good), you might rely on the price-quality heuristic and buy their most expensive camera, or the camera of a brand that is familiar to you (i.e. if I have heard of this brand, it must be good).

Multiple roles by which variables can influence persuasion. Thus far we have contrasted peripheral cues with content information and argued that peripheral processing is determined by peripheral cues, whereas systematic processing is determined by the content of the message. In doing so, we have given a somewhat oversimplified presentation of the elaboration likelihood model. One of the unique features of this model, but also a feature which complicates predictions, is the assumption that persuasion variables can influence persuasion in multiple ways, depending on the elaboration likelihood. Specifically, the model states that at a low level of

elaboration, a peripheral variable (e.g. communicator credibility, mood) will influence persuasion through heuristic processing or other non-thoughtful means. When elaboration is at a medium level, the same variable might influence persuasion by influencing the extent of the elaboration. And finally, when elaboration is high, a peripheral variable may have no impact at all, may bias processing or may even act as an argument.

We will use the message recipient's *mood* as an example of how a factor can influence persuasion in different ways depending on the level of elaboration likelihood (Petty & Wegener, 1999). Under conditions of *low elaboration* mood might be linked to attitude objects via evaluative conditioning. There is evidence that conditioning of attitudes appears to work best when prior knowledge of the stimulus is low (Cacioppo, Marshall-Goodell, Tassinary, & Petty, 1992). Another way mood can influence attitudes under conditions of low elaboration is by acting as a heuristic cue. According to the 'feelings-as-information' hypothesis (e.g. Bless, Bohner,

INDIVIDUAL DIFFERENCES 7.2

THE NEED FOR COGNITIVE CLOSURE

The need for cognitive closure refers to people's wish for a definite answer to a question – any answer, as opposed to uncertainty. The scale shown here is a brief 15-item version (Roets & Van Hiel, 2011) of the original 42-item Need for Closure Scale (Webster & Kruglanski,1994). Try the scale yourself. You have to indicate the extent to which you endorse each item by responding to a 6-point Likert scale, ranging from 1 (*completely disagree*) to 6 (*completely agree*). If you score 57 or above, your need for cognitive closure is above average.

1. I don't like situations that are uncertain.
2. I dislike questions that could be answered in many different ways.
3. I find that a well-ordered life with regular hours suits my temperament.
4. I feel uncomfortable when I don't understand the reason why an event occurred in my life.
5. I feel irritated when one person disagrees with what everyone else in the group believes.
6. I don't like to go into a situation without knowing what I can expect from it.
7. When I have made a decision, I feel relieved.
8. When I am confronted with a problem, I'm dying to reach a solution very quickly.
9. I would quickly become impatient and irritated if I could not find a solution to a problem immediately.
10. I don't like to be with people who are capable of unexpected actions.
11. I dislike it when a person's statement could mean many different things.
12. I find that establishing a consistent routine enables me to enjoy life more.
13. I enjoy having a clear and structured mode of life.
14. I do not usually consult many different opinions before forming my own view.
15. I dislike unpredictable situations.

Schwarz, & Strack, 1990), people might use the 'how do I feel about it heuristic' to infer their attitude from their present mood. In line with this assumption, Schwarz and Clore (1983) found that people interviewed about their life satisfaction on a sunny day reported more satisfaction than people interviewed on cloudy days (Figure 7.5). The 'feelings-as-information' hypothesis further suggests that this type of misattribution should be eliminated when individuals are given reason to discount their mood state as information about the issue to be evaluated. In support of this assumption, the impact of weather conditions on life satisfaction disappeared when the interviewers (during the phone interview) casually asked about the local weather conditions. Presumably, this made people attribute their mood to the weather. Clore, Schwarz and Conway (1994) argued that the 'how do I feel about it heuristic' is most likely to be used when the evaluation task is affective in nature, when there are time constraints and when there is not much other information available.

Under moderate elaboration, mood can influence the recipient's motivation to elaborate on the content of a message. When in a good mood, individuals seem to be more likely to engage in simplified heuristic processing, whereas in a bad mood they may engage in more effortful systematic processing strategies. There is a great deal of support for this assumption (for a review, see Bless, 2001). For example, Bless et al. (1990) induced good or

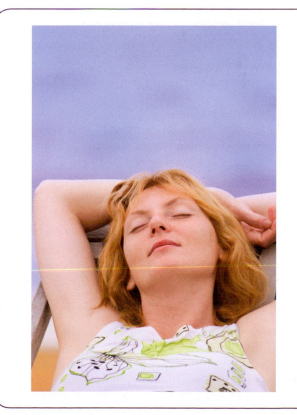

FIGURE 7.5 *How does the weather affect your life satisfaction?*
Source: © Igor Stepovik. Used under licence from Shutterstock.

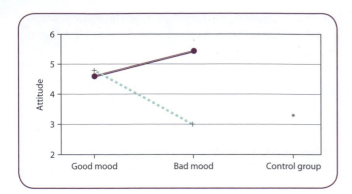

FIGURE 7.6 *Attitude change as function of mood and message quality (●——● strong message quality; +‑‑‑+ weak message quality).*

Source: Adapted from Bless et al., 1990, Expt. 1. Reproduced with permission from SAGE Publications.

bad mood in participants in a laboratory experiment by having them dwell on either a positive or a negative life event. When the participants were subsequently exposed to an attitude-discrepant communication (arguing for an increase in student service fees), consisting of high-quality or low-quality arguments, argument quality affected attitude change only for participants who were in a bad mood (Figure 7.6).

There are a number of different explanations for this effect. According to the 'feelings-as-information' hypothesis, individuals use their feelings as information about the state of their environment. Thus, happy moods inform people that their environment is safe, thereby reducing their motivation to scrutinize information in the environment (Bless et al., 1990). An alternative interpretation in terms of mood maintenance has been suggested by Wegener, Petty, and Smith (1995). Wegener et al. noted that the messages used in these studies have been either counter-attitudinal or on depressing topics such as fee increases or acid rain. Individuals who were happy might then have avoided processing these messages either because their positive mood led them to process the information only superficially, or because they did not want to disrupt their current pleasant state. Wegener et al. (1995) provided some evidence that with messages which could be expected to be uplifting, both sad and happy individuals engaged in equally high levels of elaboration. With a message that could clearly be expected to be depressing, however, the pattern observed by Bless et al. (1990) was replicated.

At very high levels of elaboration, when people are already processing message arguments systematically, mood can influence information processing by affecting

the material that is brought to mind when the merits of an attitude object are being considered (Petty & Wegener, 1999). There is some evidence that positive moods activate positive material in memory, whereas negative moods activate negative material (e.g. Bower, 1981). Thus, when individuals engage in effortful processing and elaboration of message arguments, positive moods might encourage positive interpretation of the information more than do negative moods. This bias in information processing is most likely when the information is relatively ambiguous.

The consequences of elaboration. The elaboration likelihood model predicts that persuasion induced by systematic processing (i.e. central route) is more persistent than persuasion induced by peripheral or heuristic processing. High levels of issue-relevant cognitive activity are likely to require frequent accessing of the attitude and the related knowledge structure. This activity should therefore increase the number of linkages between structural elements, making the attitude schema more internally consistent, enduring and also more resistant to counterarguments. Attitude formation or change that is based on systematic processing should therefore result in stronger attitudes (Krosnick, Boninger, Chuang, Berent, & Carnot, 1993). There are four key manifestations of strong attitudes (Krosnick & Petty, 1995; see also Chapters 6 and 8): strong attitudes are more persistent over time (e.g. Haugvedt & Petty, 1992; Petty & Cacioppo, 1986a, b); they are more resistant to counter-attitudinal appeal (Petty, Haugvedt & Smith, 1995); they are more likely to influence information processing (Houston & Fazio, 1989; Lord, Ross & Lepper, 1979); and they are more likely to guide behaviour (Holland, Verplanken, & Van Knippenberg, 2002; Martin, Martin, Smith, & Hewstone, 2007).

In contrast, attitudes formed via non-systematic processing tend to be relatively weak. This means they do not persist over time, are unlikely to resist counter-persuasion, do not guide information processing and do not predict behaviour. However, as Eagly and Chaiken (1993) pointed out, heuristic processing could also result in enduring attitude change if the cue became associated with the attitude and remained salient over time (for example, I might persistently recall that my drinking two glasses of wine a day was recommended by my trusted physician). Nonetheless, such an attitude would be vulnerable to counter-propaganda, because it lacks elaborate cognitive support. Beyond the fact that my physician recommended it, I would have no rationale for supporting the habit.

The heuristic–systematic model: how does it differ from the ELM? As we noted above, the ELM and the

HSM are similar both with regard to their core assumptions about determinants of persuasion and in their predictions about the impact these variables will have on persuasion. And yet, there are some differences between the two theories in the processes that they assume to mediate these effects. In our discussion of these differences, we will focus on three issues: (1) the unidimensionality of the processing continuum; (2) the interplay of processing modes; and (3) the multiple motive assumption of the HSM.

The unidimensionality of the processing continuum. Like the ELM, the HSM assumes two modes of processing, namely, an effortful systematic mode that is identical to central route processing of the ELM, and an effortless heuristic mode. Since heuristic processing is also one of the low-effort processes subsumed under the broad category of peripheral route processes by the ELM, we have already discussed it in the section on the ELM. However, in contrast to the ELM, where heuristic processing is only one of a variety of central route processes, it is the *only* low-effort process assumed by the HSM. Thus, according to the HSM, information processing ranges from heuristic processing at the low-effort end of the continuum to systematic processing at the high-effort end.

The interplay of processing modes. Like the ELM, the HSM assumes that individuals need to have high processing motivation and ability to engage in systematic processing. When people are unmotivated or unable to scrutinize the arguments contained in a persuasive message, they base their decision on whether to accept or reject the position advocated in the persuasive communication on heuristic cues only. In contrast, when they are motivated to scrutinize message arguments and are able to do so, they base their decision on their evaluation of these arguments, but not exclusively so. The HSM does not assume that individuals necessarily disregard the informational value of heuristic cues once they have begun to engage in systematic processing. Thus, at high levels of motivation and ability, *both* processing modes are likely to affect persuasion. The HSM makes several theoretical assumptions specifying the conditions of such interplay of processing modes (Bohner, Moskowitz, & Chaiken, 1995).

According to the *additivity hypothesis* both heuristic cues and content information exert independent main effects on persuasion. This is most likely to happen when heuristic and systematic processing lead to the same conclusion; for example, if an expert communicator also presents strong arguments. However, the greater the number of strong arguments presented by the expert communicator, the greater the probability that the independent effect of the heuristic cue will be submerged under this wealth of content information. As a result, the effect of the heuristic cue on persuasion may no longer be detectable (*attenuation hypothesis*). Most interesting is the *bias hypothesis* of the HSM, which predicts an interaction between the two processing modes. Such biasing is most likely to occur when the persuasive information is ambiguous and thus amenable to differential interpretations. Recipients might then give more weight to arguments which are consistent with the recommendation made by a source which is credible than by a source which is not credible. A study by Chaiken and Maheswaran (1994; Research Close-Up 7.1) provides support for the bias hypothesis.

Multiple motives. So far we have described the information processing underlying attitude change as a relatively objective and unbiased activity. The ELM, as well as the original version of the HSM, postulates a single motive: people are motivated to hold correct attitudes. This accuracy motivation determines the processing goal, namely to assess the validity of persuasive messages.

Chaiken and her colleagues (1989; Bohner et al., 1995) have extended the HSM and incorporated two further motives or goals for heuristic and systematic processing. Whereas accuracy motivation encourages objective and unbiased information processing, the other two motives are assumed to bias the processing of persuasive information; that is, to induce individuals to hold particular preferred attitude positions. One class of motives likely to bias information processing has been labelled *defence motivation*. The processing goal of defence-motivated individuals is to confirm the validity of preferred attitude positions and to disconfirm the validity of positions that are not preferred (Eagly & Chaiken, 1993). A number of conditions can motivate individuals to defend their present attitudinal position, such as vested interest or a need for consistency. For example, a person who had just spent a great deal of money on buying a camera of brand X would not like to hear that brand X cameras are unreliable and overpriced. Similarly, if a position being argued is inconsistent with other beliefs a person holds quite firmly, accepting this new position would violate that person's need for consistency. Defence-motivated processing can be either heuristic or systematic. The defence-motivated message recipient is assumed to use the same heuristics as somebody who is accuracy-motivated, but to use them selectively so as to support preferred attitude positions. Defence-motivated systematic processing is similarly selective. Attitude-relevant information that supports favoured positions or opposes non-favoured ones should receive more attention and be more positively interpreted than information that supports positions which are not favoured by the recipient (e.g. Das, De Wit, & Stroebe, 2003; De Hoog, Stroebe, & De Wit, 2005).

A second class of motives likely to bias information processing has been termed *impression motivation*. This motive refers to the desire to express attitudes that are socially acceptable. It is assumed to be aroused in influence settings, in which the identities of significant audiences are salient or when people must communicate their attitudes to others who may have the power to reward or punish them. The processing goal of impression-motivated recipients is to assess the social acceptability of alternative positions in order to accept attitudinal positions that will please or appease potential evaluators. Like accuracy- and defence-motivated processing, impression-motivated processing can be both heuristic and systematic. Impression-motivated heuristic processing is assumed to involve the use of simple rules to guide one's selection of socially acceptable attitude positions (for example, 'moderate positions minimize disagreement'). In impression-motivated systematic processing the same goal is reached through scrutinizing the available information in terms of its acceptability in the social influence context (e.g. Chen, Shechter, & Chaiken, 1996).

The incorporation of impression motivation links the HSM to theories of social influence such as the model of Deutsch and Gerard (1955) discussed in Chapter 8. This model postulates that group members may accept opinions from other members either because they believe them to be valid (informational social influence), or because they think that acceptance of these beliefs will make them more accepted as group members (normative social influence). Informational social influence should predominate in settings that arouse accuracy motivation, whereas normative social influence should occur under conditions that arouse impression motivation.

Summary

Dual-process theories of persuasion assume that attitude change does not have to be a result of a critical evaluation of the arguments contained in a message, but can also be determined by attitude change processes that do not require systematic message processing such as heuristic processing or evaluative conditioning. The extent of message processing depends on processing motivation and ability. More systematic processing is assumed to result in stronger attitudes.

Changing implicit attitudes

The theories of attitude change that we have discussed so far make no distinction between implicit and explicit attitudes yet, as we saw in Chapter 6, there is extensive evidence for these two types of attitudes. Furthermore, practically all research conducted to test these theories

assessed attitude change with self-report measures, which would reflect explicit attitudes. Thus, we know a great deal about how to change attitudes reflected by explicit measures, but very little about achieving change on implicit measures.

Dual process models contrast attitude change based on systematic processing of arguments with low effort processes that are not based on argument scrutiny (e.g. evaluative conditioning, mere exposure). It would therefore be tempting to assume that systematic processing – as a process based on extensive deliberation – should result in change of explicit but not implicit attitudes. Evaluative conditioning and mere exposure, on the other hand, should produce changes in implicit but not in explicit attitudes. As appealingly elegant as such a 'matching hypothesis' would be, we already know that it cannot be correct. After all, studies demonstrating the effectiveness of mere exposure (e.g. Zajonc, 1968) and evaluative conditioning (e.g. Staats & Staats, 1958) as methods of attitude change were published years before the first measures of implicit attitudes appeared in print (e.g. Fazio, Jackson, Dunton, & Williams, 1995; Greenwald, McGhee, & Schwartz, 1998). Thus, until recently all demonstrations of attitude change resulting from these procedures were based on explicit measures of attitudes.

In the meantime, there is ample evidence to indicate that evaluative conditioning can change implicit attitudes. For example, in a conditioning study in which one of two cartoon characters was consistently paired with positively valenced words and images, the other with words and images of negative valence, Olson and Fazio (2001) demonstrated that this conditioning did not only influence self-reports of attitudes towards these cartoons, but also attitudes assessed with an implicit measure (IAT). Similarly, Dijksterhuis (2004) reported that repeated association of the word 'I' with either positive or negative trait terms resulted in a change of implicitly measured self-esteem, even when the stimuli were presented subliminally. Finally, Houben, Havermans, and Wiers (2010) used an evaluative conditioning paradigm to unobtrusively change alcohol-related attitudes and drinking behaviour of their participants. The repeated association of alcohol-related words with negative pictures resulted in a change in alcohol-related implicit attitudes (measured with an IAT) in the experimental compared to the control condition. Furthermore, participants in the experimental condition also reported less alcohol consumption in the following week, compared to their drinking at baseline.

Most surprising, however, from a matching perspective, is evidence that implicit attitudes can also be changed by systematic processing of persuasive communications.

HOW HEURISTIC PROCESSING CAN BIAS SYSTEMATIC PROCESSING

RESEARCH CLOSE-UP 7.1

Chaiken, S. & Maheswaran, D. (1994). Heuristic processing can bias systematic processing: Effects of source credibility, argument ambiguity, and task importance on attitude judgment. *Journal of Personality and Social Psychology*, 66, 460–473.

Introduction

Dual-process theories regard systematic processing as more effortful and capacity limited than heuristic processing. They therefore assume that heuristic processing predominates when processing ability and motivation are low, whereas systematic processing becomes the dominant mode when processing ability and motivation are high. The heuristic–systematic model does not assume a trade-off between these processing modes. Instead, it assumes that both processing modes affect persuasion at the high-effort end of the processing continuum, whereas only heuristic processing dominates at the low-effort end. Since systematic processing usually provides much more information than heuristic processing, the effect of heuristic processing on persuasion will often be obscured (*attenuation hypothesis*). However, there are conditions under which this will not be the case. For example, when the persuasion information is ambiguous and thus amenable to differential interpretations, the expectancies established by the individual's processing of heuristic cues can bias the interpretation of the message content (*bias hypothesis*). The present experiment manipulated task importance, source credibility and message ambiguity to test this hypothesis. With an ambiguous message and high task importance, source credibility was expected to positively bias systematic processing when credibility was high and to negatively bias systematic processing when credibility was low.

Method

Participants

Three hundred and sixty-seven students participated in this study.

Design and procedure

Participants were told that they would read and give their opinions about a new telephone answering machine, the 'XT-100'. They then read a 4-page booklet that contained the manipulations of source credibility, message type and task importance. A questionnaire that assessed participants' attitudes and other dependent measures followed.

Independent variables

Source credibility. The information was attributed either to the sales staff of a supermarket chain (low credibility) or to a respected consumer report magazine (high credibility).

Message type. The product description compared the XT-100 with two competing brands on six product attributes, and asserted that the XT-100 was superior to those brands. The recommendation was based either on strong arguments (superior on important attributes), weak arguments (superior on unimportant attributes) or, in the ambiguous condition, on some arguments in favour and some against the XT-100.

Task importance. Participants were told either that they were part of a small selected group being canvassed by the producers of the XT-100 to decide whether the machine should be sold in their area (high task importance), or that they were part of a very large group to be canvassed and that the machine would only be sold outside the state in which the respondent lived (low task importance).

Dependent variables

Attitudes. Participants rated the extent to which they would consider buying the XT-100, their favourability towards it and the extent to which they regarded it a good product.

Cognitive responses. Participants were given three minutes to list their thoughts about the product or product description. Two independent raters then coded these thoughts according to whether (a) they related to the source or to the product attributes, and (b) whether they expressed positive, negative or neutral evaluations of source or product.

Manipulation checks. Participants were asked to indicate their level of motivation to read the product description, their perception of the credibility of the source, and the extent to which the product description contained positive or negative features.

Results

Results supported predictions. Under low task importance, attitudes were mainly determined by source credibility (Figure 7.7a). Under high task importance and

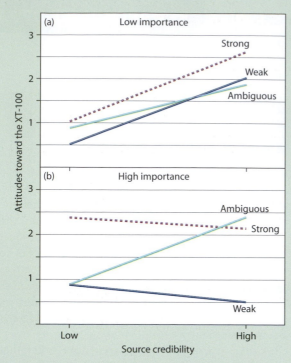

FIGURE 7.7(a) and (b) *Attitudes towards the XT-100 as a function of task importance (low versus high), source credibility (low versus high) and message type (strong versus ambiguous versus weak). Theoretical and actual range of attitude scores was –4 to 4, where higher numbers imply more positive attitudes.*

Source: Adapted from Chaiken & Maheswaran (1994). Copyright © 1994 by the American Psychological Association. Adapted with permission. *Journal of Personality and Social Psychology, 66,* 460–473. The use of APA information does not imply endorsement by APA.

unambiguously strong or weak messages, attitudes were mainly determined by argument quality, an effect mediated by systematic processing. However, respondents under high task importance who had received an ambiguous message showed a strong source credibility effect, despite high levels of systematic processing (Figure 7.7b). Under these conditions, source credibility influenced the valence of the thoughts: Participants thought more positively about the attributes of the XT-100 when source credibility was high rather than low. No such bias occurred when the message was unambiguous. Thus, source credibility exerted a direct influence through heuristic processing when the task was unimportant. When the task was important, but the message ambiguous, source credibility exerted an indirect effect on attitudes by biasing systematic processing.

Discussion

Results under low task importance as well as under high task importance with an unambiguously strong or weak message replicated previous research. Evidence for the bias hypothesis comes from respondents in the high task importance condition, who were exposed to an ambiguous message. Although these motivated participants displayed evidence for systematic processing, their attitudes were mainly affected by source credibility. Analysis of their cognitive responses revealed that source credibility exerted an indirect effect by positively biasing systematic processing when credibility was high and negatively biasing systematic processing when credibility was low.

This was demonstrated in a set of studies conducted by Briñol, Petty, and McCoslin (2009). In one of these studies, participants received strong or weak persuasive arguments in favour of a new policy to integrate more African-American professors into the university. In addition, personal relevance was manipulated by informing students that this policy would either be implemented next year in their own university or in 10 years in a different university. Implicit attitudes were assessed with a race IAT. Consistent with earlier findings on explicit measures (e.g. Petty et al., 1981), argument quality had greater impact on implicit attitudes when personal relevance was high.

In a second study, participants were exposed to strong or weak arguments in favour of including more vegetables in their diet (Briñol et al., 2009). To manipulate personal relevance, the information was either included in

an article about health behaviour that (presumably) had consequences for academic performance or formed part of an article about plant properties. In addition, participants had to list their thoughts about the communications. As in the previous study, argument quality affected implicit attitudes (IAT) mainly under high personal relevance. More importantly, however, under conditions of high relevance, the impact of argument quality on implicit attitudes was mediated by the valence of the thoughts. Thus, the extent to which attitudes are systematically processed influences the magnitude of attitude change on implicit as well explicit measures.

Several theoretical models have been proposed that offer explanations of how implicit and explicit attitudes are changed (Fazio, 1990, 2007; Petty, Briñol, & DeMarree, 2007; Wilson, Lindsey, & Schooler, 2000). The earliest of these models, the MODE model (see Chapter 6) offers an elegant explanation that is well supported by empirical evidence (for reviews, see Fazio, 1990, 2007). We will use this model for explaining change of implicit and explicit attitudes.

According to the MODE model, attitudes are *associations* between a given attitude object and a given summary evaluation of the object. These evaluations can be based on appraisals of the attributes of the attitude object, as assumed by expectancy-value theories. They can also reflect emotional reactions evoked by the attitude object and associated with it through evaluative conditioning. Finally, they can derive from one's past behaviour. Thus, attitudes are one form of knowledge, namely evaluative knowledge and are as such represented in memory. 'Just as we associate "bread" with "butter" and "doctor" with "nurse", we can associate "yuck" with cockroaches, or a sense of ecstatic delight with chocolate or single-malt scotch' (Fazio, 2007, p. 609). This conception of the attitude construct is largely consistent with the attitude definition offered in Chapter 6.

The associations between the attitude object and the evaluative response can vary in strength and therefore also in their accessibility in memory. At the weak end of the continuum from weak to strong associations, people have to construct an attitude when exposed to the attitude object. Moving along this strength dimension, attitudes become sufficiently accessible for the mere perception of the attitude object to *automatically* trigger the evaluative response. It is these automatic evaluative responses that are captured by implicit measures of attitudes. Because these object-evaluation associations can be based on beliefs as well as on conditioned responses, they can be influenced by deliberative as well as automatic processes. The MODE model can therefore explain why explicitly as well as implicitly measured attitudes can be influenced by persuasive communications, as well as evaluative conditioning or frequency of exposure.

But if implicit and explicit measures are influenced by the same processes, why are such measures often hardly related? The reason for such discrepancies according to the MODE model is that implicit measures only (or mainly) reflect the automatically triggered evaluative response (i.e. the object-evaluation association), whereas self-reports of attitudes are often affected by additional factors (e.g. social desirability; political correctness). If individuals are not motivated to misrepresent their attitude, or if they are unable to do so (e.g. because they have to respond quickly), their attitudes measured with implicit measures should be highly correlated with attitudes assessed with explicit measures. And indeed when evaluative priming methods were used to assess attitudes towards puppies or cockroaches, both attitude objects where people should see no reason to misrepresent their true attitude, there

was a close association between explicit and implicit measures (Fazio & Williams, 1986).

Summary

Because most early research on persuasion used explicit measures of attitudes, this section discussed strategies of change that influence implicit attitudes. There is no support for a 'matching hypothesis' (see p. 218). Research shows that implicit attitudes can be changed by processes based on extensive deliberation, as well as processes that do not require deliberation (e.g. evaluative conditioning, mere exposure). These findings are interpreted in terms of the MODE model.

Advertising as applied persuasion

Is subliminal advertising possible?

In the course of this chapter, we have already related some of the findings of persuasion studies to advertising. However, those of you who think of advertising as a powerful force that creates consumer needs and shapes the competition in markets today might have been slightly disappointed by our discussion of persuasion techniques. After all, it is hard to imagine that the processes we discussed here can have powerful effects like creating the image of the Marlboro Man, or helping to propel Absolut Vodka in the United States from an inconsequential brand with fewer than 100,000 bottles sold in 1980 to become America's leading premium vodka brand with a sales volume of 40 million litres in 2006 (Figure 7.8). You might suspect that other factors have been at work (e.g. marketing, pricing strategy) or that there is some secret ingredient, a 'silver bullet' persuasion strategy that we have not discussed so far.

Subliminal advertising One candidate for such a weapon, albeit not a very secret one, is **subliminal advertising**. The term subliminal refers to the presentation of a message so briefly (or faintly) that it is below the threshold of awareness. Subliminal advertising was made notorious in 1957 through publicity surrounding James Vicary's claim (see Social Psychology Beyond the Lab 7.1). People became so upset by the idea that they could be manipulated without their awareness that subliminal advertising has subsequently been legally banned in Australia and Britain. In the United States it was forbidden by the broadcasting

subliminal advertising advertising slogans that are presented so briefly (or faintly) that they are below the threshold of awareness.

SOCIAL PSYCHOLOGY BEYOND THE LAB 7.1

THE BIRTH OF SUBLIMINAL ADVERTISING

On September 12, 1957, James Vicary, a market researcher, gave a press conference that became known around the world. He announced the formation of a new corporation, the *Subliminal Projection Company*, formed to exploit a major break-through in advertising, namely subliminal advertising. Vicary described the results of a six-week test conducted in a New Jersey cinema. Two slogans were flashed over the film at the speed of 3ms at five second intervals, urging viewers to 'drink Coke' and to 'eat popcorn'. Vicary claimed that this subliminal advertising resulted in increases of 57.5 per cent in popcorn and of 18.1 per cent in Coke sales over the six-week period.

Vicary's announcement was reported by the press around the world and triggered waves of protest about this subliminal brainwashing. People became so upset by

the idea that they could be manipulated without their awareness that laws banning subliminal advertising were subsequently introduced in Australia and Britain, with severe penalties for those who disobeyed. In the US subliminal advertising was not legally banned, but the Federal Communication Commission will revoke a company's broadcasting license if the use of subliminal messages is proven (Pratkanis & Aronson, 2001).

At first Vicary refused to release any of his data, or even the location of the cinema where the tests had been conducted. However, when the uproar continued, Vicary admitted in an interview to Advertising Age in 1962 that his claim had been a hoax, he had never done the study (Pratkanis & Aronson, 2001). The irony is that under certain conditions, this type of manipulation could have had an effect, as we will show below.

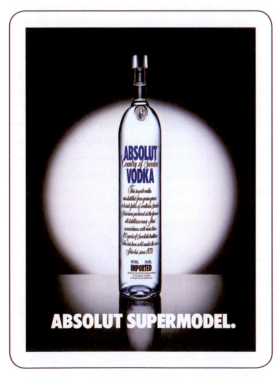

FIGURE 7.8 *Advertising helped propel Absolut Vodka from an inconsequential brand to become America's leading premium vodka.*

Source: © The Absolut Company AB. Used under permission from The Absolut Company AB. ABSOLUT® VODKA ABSOLUT COUNTRY OF SWEDEN VODKA & LOGO, ABSOLUT, ABSOLUT BOTTLE DESIGN AND ABSOLUT CALLIGRAPHY ARE TRADEMARKS OWNED BY THE ABSOLUT COMPANY AB.

authority (Pratkanis & Aronson, 2001). The fear of subliminal advertising was fuelled by the great powers people attributed to this procedure. People seemed to believe that being unaware of an influence attempt also meant that they could be induced to act in ways that were against their own interest. This kind of assumption must have led the police department of the town of Wichita, Kansas in 1978 to try to catch a serial killer by inserting the subliminal message 'contact the chief' into a news broadcast (Gibson, 2005). Since the killer was only apprehended in 2005, and not because of self-incrimination, the subliminal commands appear to have been ineffective.

While the presentation of visual messages is subliminal due to the brief exposure time, back-masking has been used to produce auditory messages assumed to be subliminal. With back-masking messages are recorded backwards on a tape that is otherwise recorded forwards. The method was allegedly first used by the Beatles in 1966, but then taken over by many other rock bands. In another example of irrational beliefs about the effects of subliminal messages, there were court cases against rock bands accused of having inserted subliminal messages into their songs. In one trial against the rock band Judas Priest, the subliminal message 'do it' was considered responsible for two suicides. Fortunately for the rock group, the judge did not accept this argument.

While people do not want to be manipulated against their will, they quite like the idea of their willpower being buttressed by subliminal suggestion. American consumers appear to spend more than $50 million annually on audiotapes that contain subliminal messages to help them to improve their self-esteem, their memory and their study habits, or to help them to lose weight and stop smoking (Pratkanis & Aronson, 2001).

Studies of the effectiveness of self-help tapes have found no evidence of any effects. Greenwald, Spangenberg, Pratkanis, and Eskenazi (1991) conducted a study in which they measured participants' self-esteem and memory and then presented them with tapes that, according to the manufacturers, contained subliminal messages that should either improve self-esteem ('I have high self-worth and high self-esteem') or memory ('My ability to remember and to recall is increasing daily'). Crosscutting the manipulation of the subliminal content of the tapes, half the respondents were led to believe that they listened to the memory tape, the other half that they listened to the self-esteem tape. Respondents took the tapes home and listened to them daily for five weeks. When their self-esteem and their memory were reassessed on their return to the laboratory, no improvements could be detected. It is interesting, though, that those participants who thought that they had received the memory tape (regardless of whether they really had been given the memory tape or had been given the self-esteem tape) believed that their memory had improved. Similarly, respondents who believed that they had received the self-esteem tape reported substantial improvements in their self-esteem. Thus, whereas the actual content of the tapes had no effect whatsoever, the *assumed* content resulted in a 'placebo effect'. Participants believed that their memory (or their self-esteem) had improved, even though, objectively, there had been no improvements at all. Obviously, such beliefs guarantee satisfied customers and the continued sales of self-help tapes.

That these subliminal messages were ineffective is hardly surprising (see Chapter 4 on Social Cognition). First, subliminal verbal primes have to consist of one or perhaps two (very short) words to be effective, and not of whole sentences. Second, while there is support for effects of subliminal visual priming, there is no evidence for priming effects of backward messages (e.g. Kreiner, Altis, & Voss, 2003). Third, successful priming does nothing more than increase the accessibility of the primed concept and of thoughts related to that concept. Thus, even if it were possible to subliminally prime sentences like 'My ability to remember is increasing daily' or 'I have high self-worth', they would be unlikely to improve our memory or our self-esteem.

Coca-Cola is a relatively short brand name and thus meets the first condition for a subliminal prime. Thus, if clever advertising technicians developed a technique that enabled them to successfully prime movie or TV audiences, could Coca-Cola sales be improved through subliminal priming? This would depend on a number of conditions. First, it would depend on the thoughts members of the audience associate with Coca-Cola. If they find it too sweet a drink, priming will not change their opinion. On the other hand, if they associate it with great taste and great thirst-quenching qualities, then priming might make them want to have a Coke, but only if they are thirsty at that particular moment. Finally, as we will discuss, priming effects would depend on the mood induced by the film into which the primes are embedded. You should now stop and read Research Close-Up 7.2, which describes an experiment by Karremans, Stroebe, and Claus (2006) that investigates these issues.

More recently, Bermeitinger et al. (2009) conceptually replicated the findings of Karremans and colleagues. Participants in their study had to play a computer game, which required a great deal of concentration. They were told that the experiment assessed the extent to which dextrose pills helped people to concentrate. During the game they were subliminally primed with one of two logos for brands of dextrose pills. During breaks in the game participants could take pills from two bowls, each clearly labelled with one of the two brand logos. Findings showed that subliminally priming a logo of energy pills increased choice for that brand, but only if participants were tired. Because one can assume that people who were tired felt a greater need for pills that were supposed to help them to concentrate, these findings replicate the pattern observed by Karremans et al. (2006). A further important contribution of the study by Bermeitinger et al. was to demonstrate the effect of subliminal advertising on actual consumption behaviour.

It is interesting to note that in the Karremans et al. study, the prime × thirstiness interaction was strongest for participants who only drank Lipton Ice infrequently. We did not report this third-order interaction, because it was not significant. However, some years later, Verwijmeren, Karremans, Stroebe, and Wigboldus (2011) demonstrated in a replication of the Karremans et al. study that the interaction between priming and thirst was moderated by the extent to which participants were habitual drinkers of Lipton Ice. Priming worked only for thirsty individuals who did not drink Lipton Ice regularly: it had no effect on habitual consumers of Lipton Ice. This finding supports our assumption that subliminal advertising will mainly be effective for brands that are not highly cognitively accessible. For brands like Coca-Cola, which are, for most consumers, already at the 'top of the head', subliminal advertising is unlikely to have an effect.

In the studies reported so far, the subliminal primes were embedded in either a letter search task or a computer game. With both these tasks, the experimenter can determine beforehand which point of the monitor

SUBLIMINAL ADVERTISING

Karremans, J. C., Stroebe, W. & Claus, J. (2006). Beyond Vicary's fantasies: The impact of subliminal priming on brand choice. *Journal of Experimental Social Psychology, 42*, 792–798.

Introduction

Because short brand names can be primed subliminally, it should be possible to influence the choice of different brands with subliminal messages. However, Karremans and colleagues reasoned that certain conditions had to be met for subliminal priming to affect choice. First, because priming merely increases the cognitive accessibility of the primed concept, product priming will only be effective if people really like the product. For example, subliminal advertising is unlikely to induce people to drink Coca-Cola if they do not like its taste. Second, brand priming will only be influential if people really have a need for the advertised product. Thus, even if they like the taste of Coca-Cola, priming will not induce them to choose it if they are not thirsty. And finally, since the Coca-Cola company spends millions each year on advertising and thus on keeping the brand cognitively highly accessible, subliminal advertising of this brand might not be very effective, because it is already at the forefront of most people's minds.

Based on pretesting, Karremans et al. selected Lipton Ice (a type of iced tea) as a brand that is liked, considered thirst-quenching and yet is not highly cognitively accessible. They conducted two experiments to test the hypothesis that subliminally priming the brand name of Lipton Ice (rather than the brand of a popular mineral water) would increase choice of Lipton Ice, but only in participants who are thirsty. Since the only difference between the two experiments was that thirst was rated in the first, but manipulated in the second experiment, and since both studies confirmed the hypothesis, only Experiment 2 will be presented here.

Method

Participants and design

One hundred and five male and female students participated and were randomly assigned to one of the conditions of the 2 (thirst: thirsty versus non-thirsty) × 2 (prime: Lipton Ice versus control) between participants design.

Procedure

Participants were seated in a cubicle behind a computer and were told that they would be participating in a number of unrelated experiments. The first task for half of the participants was a 'tongue detection' task, with which thirst was manipulated. These participants were given a very salty sweet that had a letter on one side, and had to detect the letter with their tongue. They were given one minute for this task. It was assumed that the salty taste and the post-ingestive effect of the salt would increase thirst. Next, participants had to perform a visual detection task, in which they were presented with letter sequences and had to detect small letters interspersed in sequences of capital letters. In fact this task was designed to subliminally prime half of the participants with Lipton Ice and the other half with a control nonsense letter string (e.g. 'Npeic Tol'). The primes were presented 25 times, but each time for only 23ms, so that participants were not aware of them. The letter sequence was preceded and followed by a string of X's ('XXXXXX'), supposedly to help participants to focus on the task. In fact, the string of Xs served as pre- and post-masks. The post-mask is particularly important, because it blocks the visual memory of the prime through visual stimulation. Next, participants were asked to take part in a study on consumer behaviour. First, they were asked which brand of soft drink they would prefer, if they were offered a drink now. Two brand names (Lipton Ice and the control brand) appeared, one on the left and one on the right of the screen, and participants had to push a key on the left or right to indicate their preferred brand. Lipton Ice appeared half of the time on the right, the other half on the left. Next, participants had to rate their intention to drink Lipton Ice, using two rating scales (e.g. 'If you were sitting on a terrace now, how likely would you be to drink Lipton Ice?': 1 — *not at all likely*, to 7 — *very likely*).

Results and discussion

The experiment resulted in a significant main effect for the Lipton Ice prime on choice. Participants in the Lipton

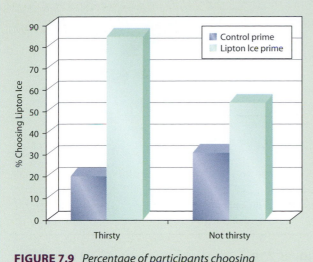

FIGURE 7.9 *Percentage of participants choosing Lipton Ice as a function of thirst and prime*

Source: Karremans et al., 2006, Study 2.

Ice prime condition were significantly more likely (69 per cent) to choose Lipton Ice than participants in the control prime condition (25 per cent). However, this main effect was moderated by a significant prime × thirstiness interaction, with thirsty participants being more strongly affected by the Lipton Ice prime than non-thirsty participants. The equivalent interaction was significant for the measure of intention to drink Lipton Ice. Thus, when offered a choice between a brand of mineral water or Lipton Ice, participants who had been primed with Lipton Ice were significantly more likely to choose it over the mineral water, but mainly if they were thirsty (Figure 7.9). Under these conditions they also expressed greater intentions to choose Lipton Ice in a hypothetical situation (if they were now sitting on a terrace and ordering a drink).

viewers will be focussing on. This is not the case when subliminal primes are embedded in a film. Although a study by Cooper and Cooper (2002) demonstrated the effectiveness of subliminally presenting product primes in a film, they could only show an effect on thirst ratings and not on product choice.

A further complication when embedding brand primes in a film is that the emotions evoked by the film might 'rub off' on the brand name. From what we know about evaluative conditioning, we could expect that repeated subliminal exposure to a brand name would only increase choice of that brand if the brand is presented in a positive context (i.e. in a film that evokes positive emotions). When presented in the context of a film that evokes negative emotions, the negative affect should become attached to the brand. Thus, embedding subliminal brand primes in a film that evokes negative emotions might even decrease the likelihood that the primed brand would be chosen afterwards.

These hypotheses were confirmed by Verwijmeren, Karremans, Stroebe, Wigboldus, and Van Ooijen (2010), in a study in which the Lipton Ice prime was embedded in either a positive or a negative movie. To simulate real-life conditions, participants in this study were seated individually and in a room that was decorated as a living room. They were watching the film on a regular TV set, and afterwards were given a choice of drinks. As in all previous studies, the priming effects were moderated by thirst. As predicted, subliminally advertising Lipton Ice

in a positive film increased the likelihood of Lipton Ice being chosen, but only for thirsty participants. Similarly, subliminally priming Lipton Ice in a negative context reduced choice, but only for thirsty participants.

Would Vicary have succeeded with his subliminal messages to increase Coca-Cola sales in the New Jersey movie theatre if he had tried? It is not impossible. But he would certainly have had a greater chance if he had used a less widely advertised brand. It would also have depended on the film that was shown in that theatre. If it had been a comedy, it might have worked. If it had been a sad film, however, it might even have had adverse effects. What we do know, however, is that subliminal advertising will not induce people to act against their will. It will not even help them to buttress their sagging willpower.

A dual-process analysis of advertising Social psychological research on message processing and persuasion has focused mainly on the processing of verbal information. In contrast, advertising uses pictures, fonts, colours, music and sound effects to draw attention, evoke associations and convey meaning. All of these non-verbal modalities may affect evaluative judgements directly or through their impact on message processing. Despite these differences, the insights into persuasion processes we have gained from social psychological research can be very helpful in understanding advertising.

Advertisements can adopt a variety of appeals. The three most common are arguments, emotions and endorsements (Tellis, 2004). The effectiveness of each of these strategies will depend mainly on two factors, namely the *type of product* being advertised, and the *involvement of the audience*. Products can be classified as either feeling or thinking products (Tellis, 2004). Feeling products such as wine, paintings or soft drinks are evaluated primarily by personal preference. Examples of preference attributes are taste, flavour, style and design. In contrast, thinking products, such as washing machines, computers and most cars, are purchased because of reason attributes such as performance, reliability, quality or fit (Tellis, 2004). Obviously, some products combine aspects of both types (e.g. sports cars).

Since the attitudes towards feeling products will be mainly based on affect and will have very little cognitive content, emotional appeals are preferable for feeling products. It would be difficult to make an argument-based appeal for a particular brand of cola, given that different brands are not all that different and that purchasing decisions for soft drinks are rarely based on objective qualities. Soft drink ads therefore play on people's emotions, trying to associate these products with feelings of youth, energy and sexual attractiveness.

In contrast, the advertising strategies for thinking products usually rely on arguments praising such attributes as the performance characteristics, reliability and quality of the service. As we have discussed earlier, the problem with using argumentative appeals is that even strong arguments are only effective with audiences that are motivated and able to process the information. This may be less of a problem with ads for dishwashers or hair dryers. Although they are not objects of great interest to most people, advertisements for these household appliances are mainly directed at those who want to buy such an appliance and would therefore be motivated to think about the arguments in an advertisement.

But what strategy should one use to advertise products such as toothpaste, washing powder or mouthwash, which neither arouse a great deal of emotion nor are considered to be of sufficient importance by most people to devote a great deal of effort to processing arguments? One possibility is to use endorsements by celebrities or experts (Figure 7.10). We have all seen the actor who, dressed like a dentist (i.e. expert), praises the qualities of a particular toothpaste or toothbrush. Another possibility is to use emotional appeals to increase the perceived importance of a product. One could try to induce guilt feelings in parents who neglect their children's welfare by not making them brush their teeth with toothpaste X.

Alternatively, one could use fear appeals (Das et al., 2003; De Hoog et al., 2005). This approach was taken by Gerald Lambert, who in 1922 hired an advertising agency to improve the sluggish sales of Listerine, at the time

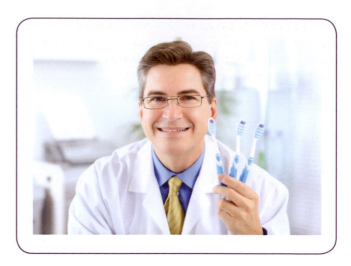

FIGURE 7.10 *In this advertisement endorsement by an expert is used as an advertising strategy.*
Source: © kurhan. Used under licence from Shutterstock.

a product used as an antiseptic in surgery and to fight throat infections (Pratkanis & Aronson, 2001). Seeking a wider market, Lambert decided to promote it as a mouthwash. The problem was that nobody in those days really used a mouthwash. Furthermore, accusing people of having 'bad breath' would not have been a popular message. Thus, the ads for Listerine used the obscure medical term 'halitosis' instead of 'bad breath'. The slogans of this famous campaign played on people's fear of being rejected by their social environment. 'Even your best friend won't tell you. Listerine is good for halitosis.' Or, 'Often a bridesmaid . . . never a bride.' The campaign was extremely effective, turning Listerine into a household name.

But such brilliant campaigns are the exception rather than the rule, as studies of advertising effectiveness indicate (Tellis, 2004). So how can advertising contribute to such dramatic sales increases as in the example of Absolut Vodka mentioned earlier? The answer is simple: through the accumulation of small effects over a long period of time. In the case of Absolut Vodka, it took 19 years and an immense advertising budget to achieve this result.

Summary

In this section we discussed, first, the feasibility of subliminal advertising. There is by now substantial evidence that subliminal messages can influence brand choice, but only under specific conditions, namely for products that are not highly accessible and which are needed to satisfy an active goal. We then discussed the relationship between the type of product advertised and the type of appeal most effective for such products. We introduced the distinction between feeling and thinking products, and argued that for feeling products emotional appeals are most appropriate, whereas persuasive arguments are most effective with thinking products.

INCENTIVE-INDUCED ATTITUDE CHANGE

Does the use of incentives (e.g. taxation, legal sanctions) constitute an effective strategy of attitude and behaviour change?

Powerful institutions often influence behaviour directly through incentives or legal sanctions rather than relying on the uncertain effects of persuasion. For example, when Swedish drivers could not be persuaded to use their seatbelts, the government introduced a law that made seatbelt use compulsory for front-seat passengers in private cars in 1975. The introduction of this law increased the frequency of seatbelt use from 30 per cent to 85 per cent within a few months (Fhanér & Hane, 1979; Figure 7.11).

FIGURE 7.11 *The introduction of compulsory seatbelt laws has increased seatbelt use and reduced deaths of vehicle occupants.*
Source: © l i g h t p o e t. Used under licence from Shutterstock.

Similarly, in New York, where seatbelt use ranged from 10 to 20 per cent prior to the introduction of a seatbelt law in 1984, it increased to 45–70 per cent after the law came into force in early 1985. The introduction of these laws also resulted in substantial reductions in the deaths of vehicle occupants (Robertson, 1986).

Governments can also use taxation to reduce the occurrence of undesirable behaviour patterns. There is ample evidence that the demand for alcoholic drinks and cigarettes, like the demand for most commodities, responds to changes in price and income (see Stroebe, 2011). A review of available research from several countries concluded that, all other things being equal, a rise in alcohol prices generally led to a drop in the consumption of alcohol, whereas an increase in the income of consumers generally led to a rise in alcohol consumption. There is similar evidence for smoking (Stroebe, 2011).

Thus, there is ample evidence that use of incentives is an effective strategy of behaviour change. It is also likely that incentive-induced behaviour change results in a change in attitudes towards the behaviour. According to the value-expectancy models discussed in the previous chapter, one's attitude towards a given behaviour reflects the perceived consequences of engaging in that behaviour. Therefore, changes in the price of, for example, alcoholic drinks should influence one's attitude towards buying alcoholic drinks. It should have no effect, however, on one's attitude towards drinking them. Consequently, although a marked increase in the price of alcoholic drinks is likely to induce people to buy fewer of them, they might drink at their old level of consumption when not constrained by price (e.g. at a party where drinks are freely available). Furthermore, should alcohol prices come down again, people's attitude towards buying alcoholic drinks would again become more positive.

With regard to the effectiveness of legal sanctions, governments have the added problem that, to be effective, these sanctions may require continuous monitoring. It would therefore be desirable if the behaviour change induced by legal sanctions resulted in a change in attitudes. In the following sections we will discuss conditions under which incentive-induced behaviour change might lead to attitude change.

Counterattitudinal behaviour and attitude change

One condition for attitude change following **counterattitudinal behaviour** could be that individuals find performing that behaviour much less aversive than they had

counterattitudinal behaviour behaviour (usually induced by monetary incentives or threats) which is inconsistent with the actor's attitude or beliefs.

anticipated. For example, seatbelt users in the 1980s, who reluctantly used their belts because of the sanctions threatened by the law, may have found them much less restrictive than they anticipated. Thus, they may have realized that their negative attitude towards seatbelt use was unjustified. This attitude change is likely to have been accompanied by a process of habit formation. Over time, putting on their seatbelts may have become habitual for most people. Thus, what was originally a conscious action, requiring cognitive resources and performed purely to avoid being sanctioned, may have turned into effortless and automatic behaviour. There is evidence that behaviour becomes habitual if it is performed frequently and in contexts that are likely to be stable (Ouellette & Wood, 1998). We would further argue that behaviour is unlikely to become habitual if it is effortful and associated with negative consequences. However, all is not lost if performing the behaviour is

> **cognitive dissonance theory** assumes that dissonance is an aversive state which motivates individuals to reduce it (e.g. by changing beliefs, attitudes or behaviour, and searching for consonant, or avoiding dissonant, information).

really as unpleasant as they anticipated, because **cognitive dissonance theory** (Festinger, 1957) would still lead us to expect that people will change their attitudes in the direction of greater consistency with their behaviour, at least under certain well-specified conditions.

Cognitive dissonance theory According to cognitive dissonance theory, individuals who are induced to behave in a way that is discrepant with their attitude will experience cognitive dissonance (Festinger, 1957). Dissonance is an aversive state, which motivates individuals to reduce it. This motivation will be stronger the greater the dissonance. One way to reduce dissonance is to change one's attitude towards the behaviour.

To explain this prediction, we will have to describe cognitive dissonance theory in more detail. Whenever an individual chooses between alternative courses of action, there have to be reasons that justify the chosen action (consonant cognitions), otherwise the person would not have made that particular choice. However, there are usually also reasons that would have argued for choosing the rejected alternative (dissonant cognitions). The more reasons there are that would have justified choosing the rejected alternative, and the more important these reasons are, the greater will be the dissonance the person experiences and the greater the pressure to reduce it. For example, if Susan buys a car and decides on a Mini over a Golf, the good looks of the Mini and the sporty feel of the car would be consonant cognitions. However, the Golf would probably have cost less, had a larger luggage compartment and a more comfortable ride. These

qualities of the Golf, which Susan gave up by choosing the Mini, will contribute to her cognitive dissonance (i.e. dissonant cognitions). Since, once made, choices are difficult to reverse, the most likely means for her to reduce dissonance is to persuade herself that the Mini is even more fun and the Golf more bourgeois than she always thought. There is empirical evidence that people's evaluations of two objects are more discrepant some time after a choice between them than before the choice took place (e.g. Brehm, 1956; Figure 7.12).

If drivers use seatbelts to avoid paying a fine, their behaviour is not completely voluntary. And yet, since

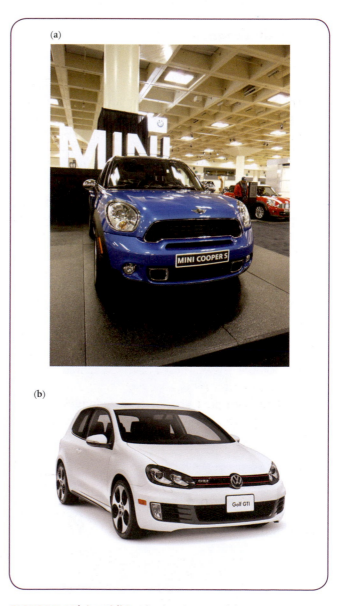

FIGURE 7.12(a) and (b) *After buying one of these two cars, how are you likely to view the other?*

Source: (a) © Eric Broder Van Dyke. Used under licence from Shutterstock; (b) © Oleksiy Maksymenko Photography. Used under licence from Alamy.

they could have decided to risk the fine, it is still a free decision. It is in this situation where dissonance theory makes its most counterintuitive prediction. Since the threatened sanctions are consonant cognitions for those who comply with the law, dissonance would be greater the less severe these sanctions. If death was the penalty for not using one's seatbelt, few seatbelt users would feel dissonance. On the other hand, if the penalty was $1, people who comply would probably feel considerable dissonance. After all, a fine of $1 is not a very substantial justification to engage in behaviour that one did not really want to engage in. Thus, if an individual behaves counterattitudinally to avoid a penalty or gain some benefit, dissonance will be greater if the penalty or the benefits are small rather than large.

Festinger and Carlsmith (1959) tested these predictions in their classic experiment. Participants had to perform two dull motor tasks for an hour and were then asked, under some pretext, whether they would be willing to tell the next participant that the experimental task was really interesting. They were offered either $20 or $1 for agreeing to do this (in effect, telling a lie, although the experimenters did not present it in those terms). According to cognitive dissonance theory, participants who had been offered $20 should have less difficulty in justifying their behaviour than individuals who received only $1; after all, $20 was then (and still is) a large sum of money. Participants in the $20 condition should therefore experience less cognitive dissonance and less need to reduce it than those who had only been offered $1 for telling a lie (see Theory Box 7.4). In line with these predictions, Festinger and Carlsmith found that, when asked afterwards to indicate how enjoyable they had found the two motor tasks, participants in the $1 condition rated it more enjoyable than did individuals who had been paid $20, or than individuals in the control group who had merely rated the motor tasks

without having been asked to describe it as interesting (Figure 7.13).

Festinger and Carlsmith intuitively built two features into their experimental situation that, though not specified by the original version of the theory, turned out to be essential for dissonance arousal. First, since the experimenter's request was not ostensibly part of the experiment, participants were free to refuse the request and thus experienced high freedom of choice. However, since most people are absolute suckers when it comes to refusing requests made in face-to-face situations (see Chapter 8), Festinger and Carlsmith did not have to worry that many participants would refuse, even in the $1 condition. Second, since the target of the lie (actually a confederate of the experimenters) had indicated that she had originally not intended to participate in the experiment because of an exam, the participants'

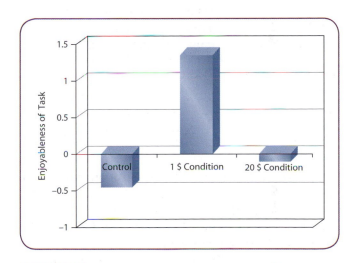

FIGURE 7.13 *Ratings of task enjoyableness by condition.*

Source: Adapted from Festinger & Carlsmith, 1959. Copyright © 1959 by the American Psychological Association. Adapted with permission. *Journal of Abnormal and Social Psychology, 58,* 203–210. The use of APA information does not imply endorsement by APA.

THEORY BOX 7.4

DISSONANCE INTERPRETATION OF THE FESTINGER & CARLSMITH (1959) EXPERIMENT

behaviour led to aversive consequences. Both freedom of choice (Linder, Cooper, & Jones, 1967) and negative consequences (Cooper & Worchel, 1970) are necessary for counterattitudinal behaviour to arouse dissonance.

Self-perception theory Dissonance theory provoked some controversy in its heyday. The major challenge to the dissonance interpretation came from *self-perception theory* (Bem, 1965, 1972). This theory assumes that people often do not know their own attitudes and, when asked about them, are in the same position as an outside observer (see Chapters 5 and 6). As we have learned in the discussion of attribution theory (see Chapter 3), people usually infer attitudes of others from relevant instances of past behaviour. Thus, when asked to state their attitude towards the motor task, participants in Festinger and Carlsmith's experiment would have remembered that they told another participant that the task was interesting. They would have used this knowledge as information about their own attitude towards the task, unless there were reasons to *discount* their own behaviour as a source of information. Being paid a large sum of money to behave in a certain way is a good reason to discount one's behaviour as a source of information about one's attitude. Thus, when paid $20, they would probably discount their own behaviour as source of information and evaluate the experimental task merely on the basis of how they remembered it (i.e. as boring). Self-perception theory can thus account for Festinger and Carlsmith's findings without referring to aversive states and clashing cognitions (see Theory Box 7.5).

It is now generally accepted that the two theories should be regarded as complementary formulations, with each theory being applicable to its own specialized domain. According to Fazio, Zanna, and Cooper (1977),

self-perception theory accurately characterizes attitude change in the context of less discrepant behaviour where the individual argues for a position close to his or her own initial attitude. Fazio and colleagues term such behaviour *attitude-congruent*, and define it as any position that is still acceptable to an individual, even though it may not be in accordance with his or her actual attitude. For example, people who believe that all atomic power stations should be closed down immediately would probably also find acceptable the position that no new atomic power stations should be built and the existing ones should be phased out within 10 years. However, these opponents of atomic power stations would find completely unacceptable the argument that we need new atomic power stations to ensure future energy needs. Since it can be assumed that individuals are motivated to put considerably more cognitive effort into justifying their action if it is counterattitudinal rather than attitude-congruent, this integration is consistent with expectations from dual-process theories: low-involvement individuals (those still behaving in an attitude-congruent manner, hence exerting little effort in justification) should rely predominantly on peripheral processes (i.e. they will take their own behaviour as a source of information).

Stroebe and Diehl (1981, 1988) extended this argument. They demonstrated that self-perception can also account for attitude change following highly attitude-discrepant behaviour, provided it is performed under conditions unlikely to arouse dissonance (e.g. low choice, minimal consequences). In these studies, participants were asked to write counterattitudinal essays in the presence of a second participant (actually a confederate of the experimenter), who either agreed or refused the task (after the real participant had agreed). Since the knowledge that another person also agreed to perform the task (and thus provided

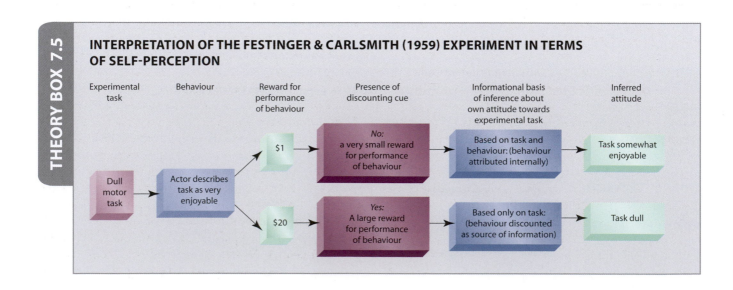

THEORY BOX 7.5

INTERPRETATION OF THE FESTINGER & CARLSMITH (1959) EXPERIMENT IN TERMS OF SELF-PERCEPTION

Experimental task	Behaviour	Reward for performance of behaviour	Presence of discounting cue	Informational basis of inference about own attitude towards experimental task	Inferred attitude
Dull motor task	Actor describes task as very enjoyable	$1	*No:* a very small reward for performance of behaviour	Based on task and behaviour: (behaviour attributed internally)	Task somewhat enjoyable
		$20	*Yes:* A large reward for performance of behaviour	Based only on task: (behaviour discounted as source of information)	Task dull

social support for the participant) would be a consonant cognition, it should reduce dissonance. Stroebe and Diehl (1981) therefore predicted that participants should show less attitude change when the confederate agreed to write the counterattitudinal essay than when he or she refused. These predictions were supported under conditions expected to arouse dissonance (high choice and severe negative consequences). However, under conditions that should not arouse dissonance (i.e. low choice and minimal consequences), the opposite pattern emerged: participants changed their attitude more when the confederate agreed rather than refused to write the essay.

At the time, Stroebe and Diehl (1981) did not have a good explanation for the pattern of findings under low dissonance conditions. But some years later, influenced by the then novel dual-process theories, they suggested an interpretation in terms of motivational influences on depth of processing (Stroebe & Diehl, 1988): individuals engage in the cognitive effort of self-justification only when motivated to do so because they feel responsible for a negative act. In the absence of such responsibility, individuals engage in heuristic processing and use the behaviour of the other participant as a cue for inferring their own position. To test this interpretation, Stroebe and Diehl (1988) used the same paradigm as in their earlier studies. They asked female participants to write an essay in favour of the introduction of a compulsory community service for women, a proposal to which most women were strongly opposed. Again social support was manipulated by having a confederate comply with or not comply with the request. The consequences of writing the essay were described as either serious (essay would be used to persuade other women) or as minimal (the essay would be discarded unread). As an additional variable, attitude similarity between the real participant and the confederate was manipulated. Participants were asked their opinion on a number of attitude issues at the beginning of the study, allegedly to help with a different study. The confederate (answering second) either consistently agreed or disagreed with the real participant.

Stroebe and Diehl (1988) predicted that attitude similarity would moderate the effect of the social support manipulation. When the essay writing was expected to lead to severe consequences, both the dissonance reducing effect of social support, as well as the dissonance increasing effect of non-support, should be less marked if the other participant was perceived as holding dissimilar rather than similar attitudes. Under minimal consequences, when participants would use the behaviour of the confederate as a cue to infer their own attitudes, the pattern of change should be the mirror image of that observed with severe consequences. Thus, if a similar other also agreed to write the essay, participants should

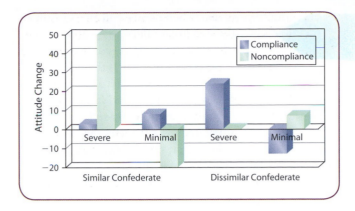

FIGURE 7.14 *Mean differences in female students' attitudes towards the introduction of a compulsory civil service for women.*

Source: Adapted from Stroebe & Diehl, 1988. Reproduced with permission from SAGE Publications.

conclude that the compulsory community service could not be all that bad and move in the positive direction. On the other hand, if a similar other refused the request, they would conclude that it must be quite bad and become more negative. In contrast, with a dissimilar other, her willingness to write the essay would signal that one should be quite negative about the compulsory community service, whereas her disagreement would suggest that the community service was not all that bad. As we can see from Figure 7.14, which illustrates the mean differences in participants' attitudes towards the introduction of compulsory civil service from weeks before the essay writing to directly afterwards, results fully support these predictions.

Dissonance, self-perception and the use of incentives Will people who smoke less or drink less because of taxation-induced price increases also change their attitudes towards smoking or drinking? Individuals who smoke less because cigarette prices have increased, or drink less because alcohol prices have gone up, may experience some dissonance. After all, their decision to reduce their consumption of cigarettes or alcohol will be the result of a decision about how to allocate their income. They would have been able to consume at the old level if they had decided to reduce *other* expenses (on food, vacations, etc.). Like all freely chosen decisions, such a decision is likely to result in cognitive dissonance, and one of the ways to reduce dissonance would be to persuade oneself that one was better off by smoking and drinking less.

It is more doubtful whether dissonance or self-perception processes play an important role in mediating attitude change in the context of behaviour change induced by legal sanctions. According to dissonance theory, counterattitudinal behaviour will only result in attitude change if the incentive offers an insufficient justification for the behaviour change. A similar prerequisite according to self-perception theory is that individuals do not attribute their behaviour change to the incentive. Since legal sanctions only work if individuals are aware of the sanction and if these sanctions are *sufficiently severe* to persuade individuals to abstain from the prohibited behaviour, it is unlikely that individuals who comply will experience a great deal of dissonance or attribute their behaviour to internal causes. Support for the assumption that this type of behaviour change is rarely accompanied by attitude change comes from studies of the use of motorcycle helmets in American states that changed their helmet laws. For example, when Texas and Arkansas changed their law requiring all motorcyclists to wear helmets in 1997 to one requiring this only for riders under the age of 21, helmet use decreased from 97 per cent to 66 per cent in Texas and from 97 per cent to 51 per cent in Arkansas (Waller, 2002). This suggests that helmet use also failed to become habitual, probably because wearing a helmet is effortful and cumbersome.

Some paradoxical effects of incentives and sanctions

Unfortunately, some evidence suggests that legal sanctions or positive incentives can have paradoxical effects on attitudes, with sanctions making the behaviour seem more attractive and positive incentives decreasing the attractiveness of the behaviour they stimulate. There seems to be some truth in the old saying that forbidden fruits are the sweetest, at least for those fruits that had originally been freely available. According to **reactance theory** (Brehm, 1966), the elimination of behavioural freedom should result in reactance, a motivational state directed towards the re-establishment of this behavioural freedom. Obviously, the most direct form of the threatened or lost freedom would be to exercise it. Reactance will therefore frequently result in an intensified form of the behaviour that has been sanctioned. However, regardless of whether or not one violates the sanctions, reactance will increase the motivation to engage in the sanctioned behaviour and thus make it appear more desirable. According to this perspective, introducing a law which forbids smoking could not only induce smokers to smoke whenever they think they can get away with it – it could also make smoking an even more desirable activity for them.

> **reactance theory** reactance is an aversive state caused by restriction of an individual's freedom of choice over important behavioural outcomes. Reactance is assumed to motivate the individual to re-establish the restricted freedom.

There are also reasons to expect that the introduction of positive incentives to motivate individuals to engage in a particular behaviour could have negative consequences on their attitudes (e.g. Deci, Koestner, & Ryan, 1999; Lepper & Greene, 1978). Paradoxically, this is most likely to happen when individuals already engaged in the behaviour before the introduction of the law because they enjoy the behaviour. Imagine that health insurance companies became persuaded by evidence that physical exercise extends life expectancy, reduces illness risk and saves health costs. They therefore decided to offer financial rewards (i.e. reduced premiums) for individuals who jogged regularly. This might induce many people to jog who would not have done so otherwise. But at the same time, it might also undermine the motivation of people who enjoy jogging and are already jogging regularly. At least, this is the prediction one would derive from research on the effects of external (e.g. monetary) rewards on **intrinsic motivation** and performance. Intrinsically motivated behaviours are performed out of interest and because they are enjoyed. This research has demonstrated that both enjoyment and performance of an intrinsically enjoyable task can decrease once people have been given some reward for performing that task (e.g. Deci et al., 1999; Lepper & Greene, 1978).

> **intrinsic motivation** behaviour is said to be intrinsically motivated if people perform it simply because they enjoy it: external reward (e.g. money) is not required, and can reduce intrinsic motivation.

Lepper, Greene, and Nisbett (1973) conducted one of the early investigations of this hypothesis. They introduced an attractive drawing activity during the free-play time of nursery school children. After they had observed the baseline interest of children during free play, children who showed an initial interest in the activity were chosen as participants and asked to perform the activity under one of three conditions: in the *expected reward* condition, children were promised a reward for their performance (and later, given it); in the *unexpected reward* condition, children were unexpectedly given a reward afterwards; in the *no reward* condition, children were neither promised nor given a reward. Two weeks later the material was again provided in the classroom in a free play situation (without either instruction or expectation of a reward) and interest in the activity was unobtrusively observed. As predicted by the researchers, participants who expected a reward showed a significant decrease in interest in the activity from the baseline to post-experimental observation, whereas participants in the *no reward or unexpected reward* conditions showed no significant change in overall interest. Lepper and colleagues (1973) interpreted these findings in terms of Bem's self-perception theory as

over-justification effect providing external rewards for performance of a task, which individuals previously performed because they found it enjoyable, reduces individuals' liking for, and enjoyment of, the task.

an **over-justification effect**. They argued that when people are rewarded for engaging in what is already an enjoyable activity, they are likely to attribute their behaviour to the reward (i.e. discounting cue), and thus discount their interest in the activity as a cause of their behaviour. As a consequence, they will enjoy the behaviour less and, once the rewards are discontinued, they will be less likely to perform it.

The findings reported by Lepper and his colleagues (1973) have subsequently been replicated in numerous studies. Based on a meta-analysis of over a hundred studies conducted with participants ranging from preschool children to college students, Deci and colleagues (1999) concluded that tangible (but not verbal) rewards have a significant negative effect on intrinsic motivation for interesting tasks. Thus, although an offer of reduced insurance premiums to people who jog regularly might persuade people who never jogged to take it up, it would also spoil the enjoyment regular joggers may have had in engaging in this activity.

Further limitations of the effectiveness of incentive-induced change

Since people are rarely interested in attitude change as an end in itself, but rather as a means to changing behaviour, influencing behaviour through monetary incentives or legal sanctions would seem to be the most effective of the strategies discussed in this chapter. As we have seen, there is ample evidence to support this notion. Seatbelt laws succeeded not only in substantially increasing seatbelt use, they also resulted in a change in attitudes towards seatbelt use, at least among those who complied (Fhanér & Hane, 1979). In view of the apparent effectiveness of incentive-induced behaviour change, one wonders why people still bother with persuasion.

There are actually a number of considerations to be taken into account. The most obvious is lack of power. Only governments have the power to enact laws, and even they are constrained in the use of this power. For example, although the behavioural factors that are detrimental to people's health (e.g. smoking, overuse of alcohol) are well known, governments rely on persuasion as well as legal action to change behaviour.

An additional constraint on strategies of influence based on the use of monetary incentives or legal sanctions is that these strategies can only be used for behaviour that can be monitored. Thus, while efficient for publicly identifiable behaviour such as seatbelt use or

speeding, positive or negative incentives are difficult to apply if the behaviour that one wishes to influence is difficult to monitor objectively. For example, in the area of race relations, governments can eliminate some of the objective and observable instances of discrimination (e.g. by introducing quotas for employment of members of racial minorities), but they cannot force people to be nice to members of outgroups, to invite them to their homes or let their children marry one of them. This is one of the reasons why the American Supreme Court mandated the end of segregated schooling. Since they could not outlaw prejudice, they attempted to reduce it by increasing interracial contact (see Chapter 14).

Finally, the effectiveness of legal sanctions is likely to depend on the acceptance of the law and on individual perception that violation of the law is associated with a high risk of sanction. For example, it is quite likely that the introduction of the law making seatbelt use compulsory would not have been effective had people not accepted that such a law was in their own best interest. In fact, without the persuasion campaigns that made it widely known that the wearing of seatbelts substantially reduced the risk of injuries in traffic accidents, it is unlikely that such a law would have been introduced. Similarly, the increases in Federal cigarette tax that occurred in the US during the 1970s and 1980s would not have been possible without the anti-smoking campaign. The anti-smoking campaign in the US also illustrates the fact that persuasion and incentive-related strategies do not preclude each other and are probably most effective when used in combination. Thus, the anti-smoking campaign resulted in a non-smoking ethos that was probably responsible for the legislative successes of the non-smokers' rights movements during the 1970s and 1980s.

Summary

Powerful institutions often use incentives or legal sanctions rather than persuasion to influence behaviour. There is evidence that such strategies are often effective in changing behaviour. It is less clear, however, whether these strategies also achieve a change in relevant attitudes. For incentive-induced counterattitudinal behaviour to induce dissonance, the incentive has to be relatively small and not sufficient to justify the behaviour. Because large incentives would justify the behaviour, there would be no need to reduce dissonance through attitude change. Similarly, self-perception theory would require that individuals do not attribute their behaviour change to the incentive. Since governmental institutions and other powerful organizations usually choose their incentives to be sufficiently powerful to persuade everybody (or nearly everybody) to change their behaviour, these incentives are not only likely to offer sufficient justification for behaviour change, but it is also likely that compliance will be attributed to these incentives. Whereas the magnitude of these incentives makes attitude change (i.e. finding the dull task enjoyable) due to dissonance or self-perception processes unlikely in the case of counterattitudinal behaviour, it increases the likelihood of attitude change (i.e. finding the previously enjoyable task less enjoyable) in the case of pro-attitudinal behaviour. This somewhat paradoxical effect is due to the fact that the presence of a discounting cue (e.g. large payment or expected reward) leads individuals to discount their counterattitudinal behaviour (i.e. describing the dull task as interesting) as well as the pro-attitudinal behaviour (performing an enjoyable drawing task) as information about their attitude.

CHAPTER SUMMARY

- *What are the major strategies of attitude and behaviour change?* This chapter discussed two major strategies, namely persuasion and the use of incentives (e.g. taxation, legal sanctions).

- *What is the difference between the early theories of persuasion and the more recent dual-process theories?* Early theories of persuasion (information processing model, cognitive response theory) focused on persuasion resulting from the systematic processing of the semantic content of persuasive messages. More recently, dual-process theories (elaboration likelihood model, heuristic–systematic model) have accepted that people often adopt attitudes on bases other than their systematic processing of arguments. Dual-process theories integrate theories of systematic processing and persuasion processes that are based on low-effort processes (e.g. evaluative conditioning, self-perception, heuristic processing) and they specify the conditions under which people engage in each of these processes.

- *When do people engage in systematic processing of message arguments?* According to dual-process theories, individuals will engage in systematic processing of message arguments only if they are *motivated* and *able* to do so.

- *What are the factors that determine processing motivation?* Processing motivation is determined by situational factors such as personal relevance of the attitude issue and by individual difference variables such as need for cognition.

- *What are the factors that determine processing ability?* Processing ability is determined by factors such as time, absence of distraction or message repetition. Whenever individuals are unmotivated or unable to engage in systematic processing of message content, they base their decision of whether to accept or reject a persuasive communication on low-effort processing.

- *Does subliminal advertising work?* The effectiveness of subliminal advertising depends on the product and the need state of the target of the advertising. Subliminally advertising Lipton Ice was effective for participants, for whom it was not their habitual drink and who were thirsty.

- *Can dual-process models be applied to advertising?* Applying dual-process theories to advertising, we argued that the effectiveness of the most common appeals used in advertising (arguments, emotions, endorsements) depends on the type of product being advertised (i.e. thinking products or feeling products) and the involvement of the audience.

- *Are incentives useful for influencing attitudes and behaviour?* Governments may use taxation or legal sanctions to make certain behaviours like smoking, drinking alcohol or the non-use of seatbelts more costly to individuals. Such strategies have been effective in promoting the targeted behaviour, but less successful in also inducing attitude change.

- *Can incentives and persuasion be used jointly?* Since private acceptance of these government strategies is likely to aid compliance, we argued that the use of incentives *and* of persuasive appeals should be considered as complementary rather than competing strategies.

SUGGESTIONS FOR FURTHER READING

Bohner, G., & Dickel, N. (2011). Attitudes and attitude change. *Annual Review of Psychology, 62,* 391–417. A state-of-the-art review of the field of attitude research.

Chen, S., & Chaiken, S. (1999). The heuristic–systematic model in its broader context. In S. Chaiken & Y. Trope (Eds.), *Dual-process theories in social psychology* (pp. 73–96). New York: Guilford. This chapter presents the most recent version of the heuristic–systematic model and reviews research conducted to test the theory.

Fennis, B. M., & Stroebe, W. (2010). *The psychology of advertising*. Hove, UK: Psychology Press. A comprehensive, state-of-the-art review of the psychological findings on the impact of advertising. It discusses this research in the context of recent developments in the fields of social and consumer psychology.

Maio, G., & Haddock, G. (2010). *The psychology of attitudes and attitude change*. London: Sage. A well-written introduction. It provides students with a comprehensive and accessible overview of theories and empirical findings in the area of attitude change.

Petty, R. E., Fazio, R. H., & Briñol, P. (Eds.). (2009). *Attitudes: Insights from the new implicit measures*. New York: Psychology Press. The book contains chapters by leading researchers reviewing theorizing and research on the topic of implicit measures of attitudes.

Petty, R. E., & Wegener, D. T. (1999). The elaboration likelihood model: Current status and controversies. In S. Chaiken & Y. Trope (Eds.), *Dual-process theories in social psychology* (pp. 37–72). New York: Guilford. This chapter presents the most recent version of the elaboration likelihood model and reviews research conducted to test the theory.

8 Social Influence

MILES HEWSTONE AND ROBIN MARTIN

Source: © Photos 12. Used under licence from Alamy.

KEY TERMS

- autokinetic effect
- compliance
- conformity
- consistency
- conversion
- deindividuation
- door-in-the-face technique
- evaluation apprehension
- foot-in-the-door technique
- group polarization
- groupthink
- informational influence
- innovation
- lowballing technique
- majority influence
- minority influence
- normative influence
- norms
- obedience to authority
- referent informational influence
- self-categorization theory
- social comparison
- social facilitation
- social influence
- whistle blowing

CHAPTER OUTLINE

ROUTE MAP OF THE CHAPTER

This chapter considers social influence broadly, and how it can be understood in terms of fundamental motives. First, we discuss 'incidental' social influence, where people are influenced by the presence or implied presence of others, although there has been no explicit attempt to influence them. We consider the impact of the mere presence of other people on task performance, and the impact of social norms. In the second part of the chapter, we ask why people succumb to social influence, highlighting types of social influence and motives underlying influence on the part of the target of influence. In the third part of the chapter, we turn to 'deliberate' social influence. We introduce theory and research on induced compliance, the influence of numerical majorities and minorities, group decision-making and obedience. Throughout, we will see that social influence is an ambivalent concept. On the one hand, it is the glue of society; it makes things work, and society would be utterly chaotic without it. But on the other hand it can be a dark force, responsible for some of the most extreme, even immoral, forms of human social behaviour.

INTRODUCTION

On a typical day most of us will be exposed to a large variety of social influences. You might be on your way to a lecture, when you see three of your friends turning away from the psychology department, towards town. Although no one has tried to persuade you, you are influenced to follow them, and drink coffee instead of attending the lecture. Why? As you later sit sipping your cappuccino, the topic turns to the use of animals in experimentation, and you find yourself out of line with your three friends, who all try to convince you that such studies are unnecessary and unethical. You try to counter-argue them, doing your best to offer 'strong' persuasive counter-arguments. Then you head back to the university and run into the lecturer whom you failed to meet yesterday as agreed; she tells you to come and see her that afternoon; meekly, you obey.

As we noted when introducing the field of social psychology (see Chapter 1), one of the pioneers of the field, Gordon Allport (1954a), actually defined the field of social psychology as 'the attempt to understand and explain how the thoughts, feelings, and behaviours of individuals are influenced by the actual, imagined, or implied presence of other human beings' (p. 5). So at one level, the study of social influence is as broad and diverse as the study of social psychology itself.

This chapter focuses on both 'incidental' and 'deliberate' influence. We begin by looking at how the presence or implied presence of others can affect performance, although there has been no explicit attempt at influence. We then review the impact of social norms on social behaviour, where it is more the implied presence, rather than the actual presence, of others that is influential. We show how norms are transmitted, and how they can influence a wide variety of human social behaviour, including our perceptions of physical phenomena and our behaviour towards other people.

Linking the two broad categories of influence, in the second part of the chapter we ask why social influence occurs. We consider group functions that social influence serves, and the key distinction between normative and informational types of social influence. Finally, we integrate different approaches by highlighting four major motives for social influence: 'effective action'; 'building and maintaining relationships'; 'managing the self concept'; and 'understanding'.

In the third part of the chapter we turn to deliberate influence, what might be considered the core of social influence. We introduce theory and research on induced compliance, the influence of numerical majorities and minorities, group decision-making and obedience. There are, obviously, close links between these instances of deliberate social influence and the area of persuasive communication and attitude change, described in the previous chapter (see Chapter 7). We will highlight these links, in particular, when discussing majority and minority influence, where we will draw parallels with the elaboration likelihood model of persuasion (Petty & Cacioppo, 1986a, b; Petty & Wegener, 1999). Social influence is also involved in leadership (see Chapter 13), and it is an aspect of social behaviour that shows some interesting cross-cultural variation (see Chapter 15).

What, then, is the difference between the phenomena considered in this chapter and those covered in Chapter 7 on attitude change? Social influence deals, broadly, with change of attitudes, beliefs, opinions, values and behaviour as a result of being exposed to other individuals' attitudes, beliefs, opinions, values and behaviour. Clearly, research in both areas deals, in part, with similar phenomena concerning change in attitudes and beliefs as a result of being exposed to evidence about how other people think or behave. The main difference between Chapter 7 and Chapter 8 is in the *strategies of influence* that are considered. In Chapter 7 we dealt with persuasive communications, which contain sets of persuasive arguments, and with changes in incentive structure as the two major strategies of influence. In this chapter, when we consider deliberate influence, we focus on the strategies of inducing compliance, majority and minority influence, group decision-making and obedience.

INCIDENTAL SOCIAL INFLUENCE

Social facilitation

What effect does the presence of other people have on task performance?

The most obvious example of incidental influence is that the presence of one or more other people, even though they are not *trying* in any way to influence us, has an impact on our behaviour. We have already referred to Triplett's (1898) classic observation that cyclists rode faster when racing together than when racing alone (see Chapter 1). This is claimed to be the first demonstration of the phenomenon of **social facilitation** (see Chapter 1) (Allport, 1924), whereby the presence of others leads to improved performance. However, neither the phenomenon nor its explanation has turned out to be straightforward (and as we showed in Research Close Up 1.1 in Chapter 1, Triplett's research did not, in fact, find clear evidence for social facilitation). Following the initial demonstration, researchers conducted numerous studies using a variety of tasks, yielding mixed results. Some studies showed improved performance as a result of the presence of others, while other studies showed impaired performance. Three main explanations have been proposed, but it is now widely accepted that no single explanation accounts for all the findings, and a multi-faceted approach is needed.

Mere presence and drive theory Zajonc (1965) highlighted the importance of the task people actually performed in the presence of others. He suggested that mere presence of others leads to improved performance on well-learned or easy tasks (*social facilitation*), but to impaired performance on tasks which are not (yet) well-learned and which may therefore be perceived as difficult or complex (*social inhibition*). The mere presence of others facilitates responses that take precedence in an individual's behavioural repertoire (so-called dominant responses, such as pedalling when on a bicycle, which have a higher likelihood of elicitation than other responses). But the mere presence of other people inhibits novel and complicated responses that the individual has never or only infrequently performed before (so-called non-dominant responses). People will, then, perform better when others are present than when they are working alone, *if* the facilitation of well-learned responses and the inhibition of novel responses are appropriate for successful task completion. Thus, performing well-learned physical motor skills or simple tasks should result in higher performance in the presence of others than when working alone. In contrast, in complex reasoning or problem-solving tasks, requiring concentration and complex cognitive activity, the presence of others interferes with successful task completion (see Theory Box 8.1).

Why does the mere presence of others enhance the emission of dominant responses? Zajonc (1980) used *Hull–Spence drive theory* (see Spence, 1956) to argue that the physical presence of others of the same species leads to an innate increase in arousal: that is, a readiness to respond to whatever unexpected action the others might undertake. According to the Hull–Spence theory, increased drive increases the probability of dominant responses at the expense of non-dominant responses. In order to emphasize that the effect was based on simple drive, rather than high-level information processing, Zajonc even demonstrated social facilitation with cockroaches as well as with undergraduates! (see Zajonc, Heingartner, & Herman, 1969).

Evaluation apprehension Cottrell (1968, 1972) challenged Zajonc's explanation, by suggesting that increased arousal constitutes a learned response to the presence of others, rather than an innate response. According to Cottrell, task performers have learned to associate the presence of other people with performance *evaluation* which, in turn, is linked to the anticipation of positive or negative outcomes. The presence of others will only elicit arousal and the accompanying facilitation of dominant responses (and inhibition of nondominant responses) *if* task performers anticipate being evaluated by these others.

Of course, we would have difficulty in applying Cottrell's concept of **evaluation apprehension** to cockroaches, ants and chickens, which have also shown social facilitation/inhibition (SFI) effects, or to tasks that involve little threat of evaluation, such as putting on or removing items of clothing, on which researchers have also demonstrated SFI effects (Markus, 1978). Yet, there is some experimental support for Cottrell's

> **evaluation apprehension** a learned response to the presence of others when performing a task, whereby the performer experiences arousal when anticipating evaluation by these others (can affect social facilitation, and also helping behaviour; see Chapter 10).

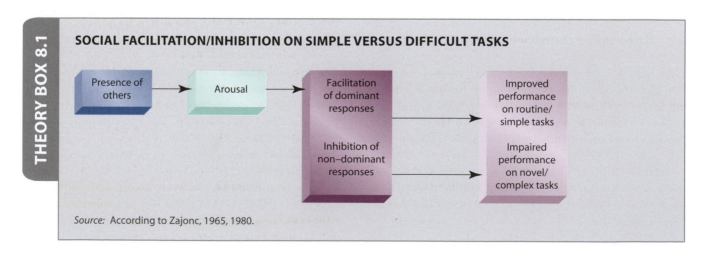

THEORY BOX 8.1

SOCIAL FACILITATION/INHIBITION ON SIMPLE VERSUS DIFFICULT TASKS

Presence of others → Arousal → Facilitation of dominant responses / Inhibition of non-dominant responses → Improved performance on routine/simple tasks / Impaired performance on novel/complex tasks

Source: According to Zajonc, 1965, 1980.

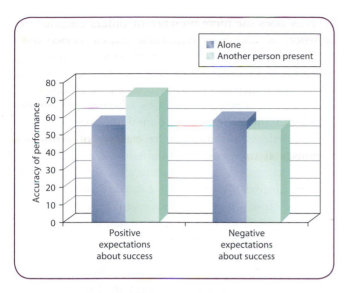

FIGURE 8.1 *Social facilitation as a function of task expectations and the presence of others.*

Source: Data from Robinson-Staveley & Cooper, 1990. Reproduced with permission.

explanation. Research has shown that SFI effects are often eliminated when the salience of evaluation apprehension is decreased, by allowing task performers to give their responses privately rather than publicly, or by having non-evaluative audiences (Henchy & Glass, 1968; Sasfy & Okun, 1974). Further evidence comes from research showing that it is not task difficulty *per se*, but the subjective expectation that one will perform well (or poorly), and that one will receive positive (or negative) outcomes, that improves (or interferes with) task performance (Sanna, 1992; Sanna & Shotland, 1990). Robinson-Staveley and Cooper (1990) provided a clever demonstration of the role of expectation, in a study in which participants performed a computer task alone or in the presence of another person. When participants held positive expectations about success on the task, the accuracy of their performance improved in the presence of another person; but when they held negative expectations, the reverse occurred (see Figure 8.1).

Attention conflict Sanders and his colleagues (Sanders, 1981; Sanders, Baron, & Moore, 1978) proposed that the presence of others may produce a response conflict between attending to the task itself, on the one hand, and attending to others, on the other hand. Others' presence may be distracting because of noises or gestures, anticipated reactions of approval or disapproval, and people's tendency to make social comparisons. Since some of the attention needed to meet the task demands will be directed at the other people, one may expect a general impairment of task performance on all kinds of

tasks, either well-learned or not well-learned. This distraction interferes with the attention given to the task and creates an internal response conflict, which can only be overcome with greater effort. The attention conflict enhances arousal, resulting in the pattern of results noted above – facilitation of dominant responses and inhibition of non-dominant responses.

Integration There is now general acceptance that we need to adopt a multifaceted approach to explain why the presence of others on individual task performance moves from benign to harmful as the perceived complexity of the task increases (Guerin, 1993). The presence of others may interfere with our ability to learn tasks, since learning implies that the most likely (dominant) responses are not yet the correct ones. However, once the required responses have become well learned and routine, the presence of others may improve performance. Given that most tasks in everyday life involve routine as well as non-routine activities, how important are social facilitation effects? A comprehensive meta-analysis by Bond and Titus (1983) concluded that the mere presence of others accounts for only a very small proportion of the variance in individual productivity (for other significant influences on group productivity, see Chapter 13). Nonetheless, we have seen that the presence of others can be a significant, albeit unintended, influence on task performance. As we will now see, that influence is much more significant when those others constitute a source of information about which norms should guide our behaviour in social situations.

The impact of social norms

What are social norms, and how are they formed and transmitted?

The most fundamental concept in the study of **social influence** is that of social **norms**. Social norms are rules and standards that are understood by members of a group; they constitute belief systems about how (not) to behave, thus they guide behaviour but without the force of laws, and they reflect group members' shared expectations about typical or desirable activities (Cialdini & Trost, 1998; Levine & Moreland, 1998; Prislin & Wood, 2005). Norms have a number of

social influence change of attitudes, beliefs, opinions, values and behaviour as a result of being exposed to other individuals' attitudes, beliefs, opinions, values, and behaviour.

norms belief systems about how (not) to behave, that guide behaviour but without the force of laws, and reflect group members' shared expectations about typical or desirable activities.

FIGURE 8.2 *Norms constrain everyone to some degree (e.g. even when you are in a hurry, you have to join the back of the queue to use a cash machine).*

Source: © wavebreakmedia ltd. Used under licence from Shutterstock.

key functions. First, they help to reduce uncertainty about how to behave appropriately (see Van den Bos & Lind, 2002). For example, we know how to behave in some situations (e.g. a mosque) because we have seen how people behave in similar situations (e.g. a church). Second, norms help to coordinate individual behaviour. For example, punctuality reduces coordination losses for other group members – a meeting cannot start until all members are present, so it is important to be punctual so that others do not waste their time. Third, norms help with the distribution of outcomes. If three people are co-writing a chapter, norms help to decide the order in which the names should appear. Norms typically constrain us all, to some degree (e.g. even when you are in a hurry, you have to join the back of the queue to buy a ticket; Figure 8.2); but we each also benefit from the structure and order they provide (e.g. in the UK, at least, people waiting for some service typically form an orderly queue, and you are likely to be served when it is your turn, without having to protest).

Norms also include an evaluative component. Merely complying with a norm (e.g. waiting in line) will rarely earn you praise (or even comment). But violating a norm often generates negative responses (see Milgram, Liberty, Toledo, & Wackenhut's, 1986, research on responses to queue-violators). Indeed, Forsyth (1995) points out that a norm often becomes salient only after it has been violated, and people who fail to comply with situationally-relevant norms without an acceptable explanation are generally subjected to negative evaluation, ranging from pressure to change, through hostility, to punishment (see Schachter's, 1951, classic study on the pressure that is exerted on deviates, discussed in more detail in Chapter 12).

There are two types of norms: *descriptive* norms inform us about how others will act in similar situations (e.g. most English people throw off layers of clothing as soon as the sun comes out in summer), whereas *injunctive* norms specify what behaviour *should* be performed (e.g. when visiting a place of religious worship, one should keep quiet and be respectful) (see Cialdini, Kallgren, & Reno, 1991). Both kinds of norms emerge out of interaction with others, especially members of the same formal or informal group, or social network. The norms may, or may not, be stated explicitly, and any sanctions for deviating from them come not from the legal system, but from social networks. Norms appear in several other chapters of this book (e.g. subjective norms are central to the 'theory of reasoned action' which links attitudes to behaviour, see Chapter 6; norms of reciprocity and social responsibility affect helping, see Chapter 10; and norms are central to understanding group processes, see Chapter 12). On one hand, norms make our lives as social beings simpler and more predictable, and we look to others for guidance in many situations. On the other hand, however, our social lives are made more complex by the fact that in many social situations multiple norms may apply, and some may even be incompatible; in such circumstances, we are all the more likely to turn to other people as sources of information concerning how we should behave.

Norm formation and transmission Since some norms may appear to be arbitrary or random (e.g. rituals to which new group members are subjected) researchers have naturally questioned how norms are formed and transmitted. The three main modes of transmission appear to be (1) through deliberate instruction, demonstrations, rituals and so on (e.g. we are taught how to behave in places of religious worship), (2) more passively, via nonverbal behaviours and implicit activation of normative standards (e.g. you are visiting a church on holiday and realize from people's frowns and gestures that you are immodestly dressed and should cover up), and (3) by inferring the norm from the behaviour of others around us (e.g. you are visiting a mosque and you see that everyone else has removed their shoes, so you remove yours). As Cialdini and Trost (1998) point out, whatever their origin, norms must be communicated to have any effect on behaviour. How is that done? Surprisingly, the social-psychological literature on norm transmission is still very small, and one set of studies still towers above all others – Muzafer Sherif's (1935, 1936) classic research on the **autokinetic effect** (see Chapter 1). This phenomenon has long been known to astronomers, who find that when fixating on a bright stationary star in a dark sky, the star appears to move (this effect is brought about by the fact that our eyes actually move about in small jumps, saccadic movements, and without a frame of reference objects appear to move when they are in fact stationary). Indeed, you may already have experienced yourself that, in the absence of reference points, a stationary light appears to move rather erratically in all directions.

Sherif (1935, 1936) placed participants alone or in groups of two or three in a completely darkened room. He presented participants with a single and small stationary light at a distance of about five metres. Sherif asked his participants to give an oral estimate of the extent of movement of the light, obviously without informing them of the autokinetic effect. Half of the participants made their first 100 judgements alone. On three subsequent days they went through three more sets of trials, but this time in groups of two or three. For the other half of the participants the procedure was reversed: they underwent the three group sessions first and ended with a session alone.

Participants who first made their judgements alone developed a standard estimate (a *personal* norm) around which their judgements fluctuated. This personal norm was stable, but it varied highly between individuals (by as much as 7 inches [17.78 cm]). In the group phases of the experiment, which brought together people with different personal norms and had them call out their answers aloud, participants' judgements converged towards a more or less common position – a *group* norm – within the first group session. Within groups, participants gave essentially the same estimates of movement, even

though the range of movement varied by group on average 1 to 5 inches (2.54 to 12.70 cm). With the reverse procedure this group norm developed in the first session and it persisted in the later session alone. Figure 8.3 illustrates both kinds of findings. The funnel effect in the left-hand panel reveals the convergence in the (median) judgements of three participants who first judged alone (I) and later in each other's presence (II, III, IV). The right-hand panel shows the judgements of a group of three participants who went through the procedure in the reverse order. Here the convergence is already present in the first group session and the slight evidence of funnelling out in the alone-last session is much weaker than in the corresponding alone-first condition.

This famous experiment shows that, where confronted with an unstructured and ambiguous stimulus, people nevertheless develop a stable internal frame of reference against which to judge the stimulus. However, as soon as they are confronted with the different judgements of others, they quickly abandon this personal frame of reference so as to adjust it to that of others. Thus the apparent truth about the environment, whether social or physical, can emerge as people exchange their independent views. Although Sherif's autokinetic study may seem artificial, we can see similar processes at work in real social settings: for example, when we judge someone's physical attractiveness. This judgement is, first, a social topic and, second, one that is often communicated within a social context ('she's beautiful/he's handsome'). Hassebrauck (1993) found that when attractiveness ratings were made in a group there was a

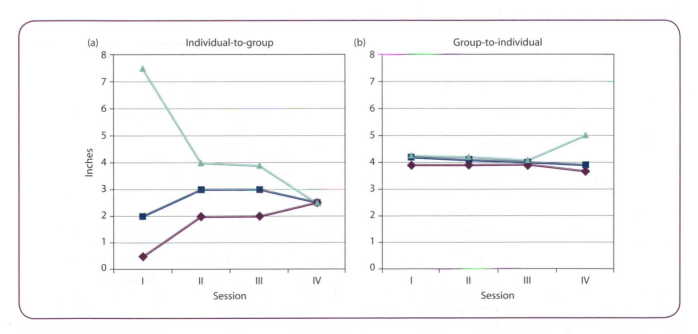

FIGURE 8.3(a) and (b) *Median judgements of movement under alone (I) or group (II, III, IV) conditions (a), and under group (I, II, III) or alone (IV) conditions (b) in Sherif's (1935) study on norm formation.*

convergence in the judges' ratings. Moreover, the judgement convergence continued in a later setting when individual judgements were made after the group session. These findings are in line with Sherif's results, and it appears that participants established a standard during the group sessions that served as a frame of reference for later judgements.

There are two obvious motives for participants' responses in Sherif's study – relating to others and understanding the social world. Sherif himself proposed that this norm formation reflected a rational, accuracy-motivated assessment of the situation (Hood & Sherif, 1962). He concluded that, under unstable conditions, where participants were confused about how to respond, they assumed that 'the group must be right' (Sherif, 1936, p. 111). Interestingly, the joint frame of reference formed in the presence of others endured when the source of influence was no longer present, over considerable time, and it transferred to new settings – including when participants joined a new group, and when they were re-tested individually, even up to a year after their initial exposure to others' estimates (Hood & Sherif, 1962; Rohrer, Baron, Hoffman, & Swander, 1954).

In subsequent studies Sherif (1935, 1936) placed a single individual who made extreme judgements in each of several groups. This one person influenced the remaining group members, whereby a more extreme norm guided their judgements. Then, once this arbitrary standard was established, Sherif removed the extreme individual from the group, replacing him with a new member. Intriguingly, the remaining group members retained as their norm the higher estimate, and the new group member gradually adapted to the higher standard. Research has even shown that old members can be gradually removed from the group and replaced with new members (naïve participants), and the old norm continues to impact on

estimates for a long time until, in fact, the group members have been changed five times (see Jacobs & Campbell, 1961). But there is a finite limit to arbitrary norms, and they tend to decay more rapidly across generations the more contrived they are (MacNeil & Sherif, 1976).

What kind of social influence does Sherif's study demonstrate? It is incidental, rather than deliberate, influence because there were no explicit attempts to influence others. Sherif's work is important precisely because it shows how, at least for an ambiguous stimulus, norms can be adopted implicitly, how they develop through reciprocal influence, and how they become internalized.

Influence via social norms in more social settings

Sherif's autokinetic studies demonstrated the emergence of arbitrary social norms in response to ambiguous stimuli presented in a stark experimental context. But social norms have the power to influence our behaviour in many more realistic situations outside the laboratory. Often we are guided by norms without even being aware of the fact, as Cialdini and his colleagues demonstrated in a series of field experiments to determine the effects of descriptive norms on behaviour (Cialdini, Reno, & Kallgren, 1990). Cialdini and colleagues manipulated the descriptive norm for littering behaviour by controlling the amount of litter in a variety of settings (e.g. a parking garage); the setting was either clean (anti-littering norm) or littered (pro-littering norm). The researchers also helpfully provided a leaflet for the participant to discard (e.g. they placed a reminder to 'drive carefully' under the windscreen wipers of the car parked in the garage). In general, the studies showed that people were more likely to drop litter into a littered environment than into a clean environment (Figure 8.4). Somehow, the presence of litter on the ground seems to send the message that

(a)

(b)

FIGURE 8.4(a) and (b) *The power of social norms: people are more likely to drop litter into a littered environment than into a clean one.*
Source: (a) © DelicatePhoto; (b) © slavcic. Both images used under licence from Shutterstock.

it is not forbidden to litter here (i.e. that the anti-litter norm that applies generally to the environment does not apply in this space), while the clean environment sends the message that it is normative to take your litter home with you. This tendency was especially strong when the researchers directed the participants' attention to the descriptive norm in the setting. For example, when a confederate dropped litter in an already-dirty setting, this focused attention on the littered environment, and people were most likely themselves to litter. When the confederate dropped litter into a clean environment, however, this highlighted the lack of litter; people then littered *less* than they did when there was a clean environment with no confederate who littered. A clever series of studies by Keizer, Lindenberg, and Steg (2008) developed these ideas further, and showed that subtle violation of one norm (e.g. clear evidence of spray-painting on a wall, despite a sign forbidding graffiti) also facilitated violation of a completely different norm (e.g. no littering; Figure 8.5).

Now turn to Research Close-Up 8.1 to read about some of these studies.

Perhaps the most dramatic social-psychological study of norms is the renowned 'Stanford Prison Experiment' (Haney, Banks, & Zimbardo, 1973). These researchers demonstrated that normal people could be brought to behave in extremely anti-social ways, in part at least, by assigning them to specific roles and allowing them to develop norms in line with these roles. These researchers randomly assigned 24 'normal, average, and healthy' (Zimbardo, Maslach, & Haney, 2000, p. 199) students to play the roles of mock prisoners or mock guards in a simulated prison established in the basement of the psychology department at Stanford University, California. The study was intended to last two weeks, but had to be halted after six days, due to the guards 'sadistic' (Zimbardo et al., 2000, p. 202) punishment of the prisoners, whose psychological suffering was deemed unacceptably great. This study was recently replicated for a BBC television programme, yielding different results (Reicher & Haslam, 2006) and fierce controversy (Zimbardo, 2006), and appears also to have been quite strongly influenced by demand characteristics (see Chapter 2).

The extreme forms of behaviour observed by Zimbardo and his colleagues – stripping prisoners naked, depriving them of food, humiliating them, and subjecting them to solitary confinement – were partly a result of the **deindividuation** of both guards and prisoners (who each wore role-consistent clothing), depriving them of their sense of individual identity and responsibility (Figure 8.6). But the power of the

deindividuation a state in which individuals are deprived of their sense of individual identity, and are more likely to behave in an extreme manner, often anti-socially and violating norms.

FIGURE 8.5(a) and (b) *Do more people litter in a setting where the anti-graffiti norm (an injunctive norm) is in conflict with the descriptive norm (i.e., a setting in which it is common for people to spray the walls with graffiti)?*

Source: From Keizer, K., Lindenberg, S., & Steg, L. (2008). The spreading of disorder. *Science, 322*, 1681–1685. © Science publishers, AAAS, with permission.

FIGURE 8.6 *Extreme forms of behaviour, such as the mistreatment of prisoners, result from deindividuation and the development of new behavioural norms that disinhibit traditionally disapproved ways of treating others.*

Source: © Ojo Images. Used under licence from Getty Images.

HOW NORM VIOLATION PROMOTES ANTISOCIAL BEHAVIOUR

RESEARCH CLOSE-UP 8.1

Keizer, K., Lindenberg, S., & Steg, L. (2008). The spreading of disorder. *Science, 322*, 1681–1685.

Introduction

The so-called 'broken windows theory' of crime (Kelling & Wilson, 1982) emphasizes the role of norms in causing petty crime. This criminological theory argues that by removing signs of disorder such as broken windows, litter, and graffiti, we could simultaneously remove triggers of disorderly and petty criminal behaviour. Keizer, Lindenberg, and Steg (2008) conducted six elegant field experiments that provided the first causal evidence in support of this theory.

Theoretically, their studies build on the earlier work of Cialdini and colleagues (Cialdini, Reno, & Kallgren, 1990), which had shown the importance of injunctive norms (which refer to the approval or disapproval of a particular kind of behaviour) and descriptive norms (which simply describe a particular behaviour common in a setting). Whereas injunctive norms provide information about which behaviour is most appropriate in a given situation (e.g. the 'don't litter' norm), descriptive norms affect behaviour simply because they provide information about which behaviour is most common in that situation. Thus, injunctive norms concern what one *should* do in a certain situation, whereas descriptive norms concern what *is* the case in that situation.

The studies by Keizer et al. cleverly addressed what happens when injunctive and descriptive norms are in conflict. For example, do more people litter in a setting where the anti-graffiti norm (an injunctive norm) is in conflict with the descriptive norm (i.e. a setting in which it is common for people to spray the walls with graffiti)? We will summarize only the first study in this paper, but refer briefly to the results of some of the other studies in the discussion, below. All the studies were controlled field experiments, conducted in common public places in the town of Groningen, in The Netherlands.

Method

Participants

One hundred and fifty-four members of the public ($N = 77$ in each of the two conditions) were observed when they came to collect their parked bicycles.

Design and procedure

The experiment compared two conditions, both staged in the same alley located in a shopping area, where people commonly parked their bicycles. A conventional sign clearly indicated that graffiti was prohibited (i.e. injunctive norm disapproving of graffiti). In an 'order' condition, the walls of the alley were clean, whereas in a 'disorder' condition they were sprayed with graffiti. Participants in the study (who were unaware that they were being observed) were people who came to collect their parked bicycles. However, prior to collecting their bicycle, the experimenters had, unobserved, attached a fake advertising flyer to the handlebars of their bicycle in such a way that the participants had to remove it before they could easily use their handlebars. There were, however, no litter bins in the alley, thus the cyclists could only follow the 'no littering' norm by taking the flyer with them. The experimenters simply counted how many cyclists littered (counted as either throwing the flyer on the ground, or hanging it on another bicycle) in the two conditions.

Results

The effect of violating the graffiti norm on the extent of littering was substantial and highly significant. Of the participants in the order (no graffiti) condition, 33 per cent littered, compared with 69 per cent of the participants in the disorder (graffiti) condition (see Figure 8.7).

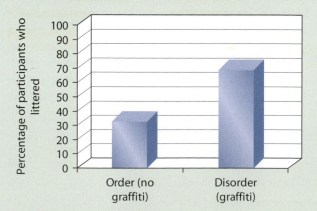

FIGURE 8.7 *Percentage of participants littering as a function of order versus disorder.*

Source: Keizer, Lindenberg, & Steg, 2008; Study 1. Reproduced with permission from AAAS.

Discussion

This study showed very clearly that violating the anti-graffiti norm doubled the extent of littering. Studies 2–6 confirmed these findings, using a variety of norms and behaviours. Studies 5 and 6 even showed that the presence of graffiti (whether on a public post box, or in the area around the post box) substantially increased the proportion of participants who *stole* an envelope clearly containing a five Euro note (which the experimenters had left dangling tantalizingly in the opening of the post box!), compared with a 'clean' control condition. The researchers also ruled out alternative explanations (e.g. it was unlikely that people littered more in some conditions simply because they calculated that they were less likely to be arrested for this, because police in the town generally turned a blind eye to littering).

Based on this impressive evidence the researchers concluded that the most likely explanation for this overall set of results was that one form of 'disorder' (e.g. graffiti) actually encouraged a different form of 'disorder' (e.g. littering, or stealing), because the violation of one norm (e.g. not to spray graffiti) weakened conformity to the other norm (not to litter, not to steal). The researchers conclude by referring to the policy implications of their findings, including the need for early detection of signs of disorder, and prompt intervention to prevent the spread of other forms of disorder as norms for appropriate behaviour are inhibited.

---

contrived situation also encouraged the development of new norms of behaviour, disinhibiting traditionally disapproved ways of treating others, even though there had been no explicit influence from the experimenters to encourage these forms of behaviour. If this all sounds too contrived to be true, or at least to have any consequences beyond the boundaries of this study, consider the treatment by some personnel of the United States Army of their Iraqi prisoners in Abu Ghraib prison, in 2003 (see Hersh, 2004). Norms within that real prison sanctioned terrorizing the prisoners with dogs, making them simulate sex acts with each other, and degrading them in various other ways that violated the Geneva Conventions on the treatment of prisoners of war (for an extended social psychological analysis of such phenomena, see Zimbardo, 2007).

Summary

We have presented social facilitation and norms as examples of incidental influence. The mere presence of others can improve or worsen performance, depending on task complexity. Norms guide our social behaviour in most settings, helping to reduce uncertainty about how to behave appropriately, but typically have a limited domain of application. Norms can be transmitted in various ways, and often have 'carry over' effects, across time and settings. Often social influence takes the form of our being influenced by the norm that we infer from other people's behaviour.

WHY DOES SOCIAL INFLUENCE OCCUR?

What is meant by normative and informational social influence?

Having illustrated some forms of social influence (incidental influence) and before introducing alternative forms (deliberate influence), this is a good place to ask why people are influenced by others. As we have indicated, some forms of influence are low-level, rather trivial effects (e.g. social facilitation), which do not appear to be driven by motives. Other forms of influence are much more interesting, because they illustrate some of the fundamental goals that guide human social behaviour, and their underlying motives.

One of the earliest theoretical analyses of this question was that of Festinger (1950). Focusing on task-oriented groups with face-to-face communication, he argued that norm-formation as well as norm-following were outcomes of pressures towards uniformity within the group. Uniformity itself serves two functions of group membership, *social reality testing* and *group locomotion*. When we follow established social norms, we are confident that our behaviour is appropriate, correct and socially desirable – we have subjective validity (Turner, 1991). Although we can test the subjective validity of some beliefs against physical reality ('Is this water hot? I will put a thermometer in it to check'), other beliefs can only be tested against social reality ('What is my opinion towards euthanasia? I will see what my friends believe'). Agreement with other members of the relevant group (be it immediate task group or wider reference group) by comparing our views with theirs (Festinger, 1954) provides us with subjective validity for our beliefs (see also Chapters 5 and 12 on social comparison theory). (See Individual Differences 8.1 for a scale that assesses the tendency to make social comparisons.)

Social comparison (see Chapter 5) is most likely to occur in situations that are novel, ambiguous or objectively unclear (Sherif, 1936; Tesser, Campbell, & Mickler, 1983), and when people are unsure, they are most likely to look to, and be guided by, the beliefs and behaviours of *similar* others. Thus, social reality testing is the consensual validation of beliefs through social comparison. This is seen as necessary for the group to reach its desired goals, what Festinger (1950) called *group locomotion*. Coordination of goals and activities among group members is necessary for the group to move, as a group, effectively and efficiently in the direction it wants or needs to go. Consider conformity, going along with the group (which we introduced in Chapter 1 and will return to in more detail below). Even though it tends to have negative connotations in Western, individual societies (Markus & Kitayama, 1994), conformity can help us to achieve group goals quickly and easily (Cialdini & Trost, 1998). Think for a few seconds how chaotic society would be in the complete absence of conformity.

Festinger suggested that opinion discrepancies within groups elicit pressures towards uniformity, which produces communication between members of the group. Uniformity is achieved by group members convincing others to move towards their position, by themselves shifting towards the position held by others, or by redefining the group by rejecting those members who disagree (see Levine, 1989; Turner, 1991).

Deutsch and Gerard (1955) proposed a simple but highly influential analysis of motives for social influence. They argued that people agree with others for *normative* or *informational* reasons. **Normative influence** presumes a need for social approval or harmony with others, and occurs when people conform to the positive expectations of others – they avoid behaving in ways that will lead to social punishment or disapproval. The main goal, then, is to build and maintain satisfactory relationships with others, and accuracy becomes correspondingly less important (Prislin & Wood, 2005). **Informational influence**

normative influence influence based on conforming to the positive expectations of others: people avoid behaving in ways that will lead to social punishment or disapproval.

informational influence influence based on accepting the information obtained from others as evidence about reality.

presumes a need to reduce uncertainty, and involves accepting the information obtained from others as evidence about reality. The main goal in this case is to make accurate and valid judgements.

Notwithstanding the impact Deutsch and Gerard's framework has had on the whole social influence literature, Prislin and Wood (2005) have criticized the interpretation of it, which emphasizes only whether people are (public settings) or are not (private settings) under *surveillance*. According to a simplistic application of the normative–informational distinction, social influence based on normative influence is temporary, and evidenced in public settings, but not maintained in private settings in which judgements do not have social consequences; whereas informational influence yields enduring change in judgements, and holds in both private and public settings. In contrast to this view, Prislin and Wood emphasize that normative motives can, in fact, have informational consequences that hold up later in time, and in private settings.

One way to integrate these different approaches to understanding *why* social influence occurs is to highlight four major motives (Cialdini & Trost, 1998; see also Prislin & Wood, 2005): 'effective action', 'building and maintaining relationships', 'managing the self concept' and 'understanding'. This approach emphasizes the goals of both the *target* of influence and the influencing *agent*. Thus, for example, a participant in Sherif's autokinetic studies could have shifted his or her estimate of how much the point of light appeared to move, in the direction of the group norm, in order to facilitate the group working effectively, to gain approval and acceptance from others in the group, to avoid a self-conception as someone who is different or deviant, and to believe that he or she now sees things more accurately. But the target also yields to informational social influence, because he or she takes the behaviour of others as information about reality or wants to be accepted by the group.

We will return to these goals throughout the remainder of this chapter. We emphasize, here, that individuals will process the information available in social situations so as to meet whatever goal is salient. Thus, depending on whether the focus is on action, relationships, the self concept or understanding, the target of social influence will focus information processing on its implications for behavioural effectiveness, social relations, the desired view of the self or the validity of the available information. Each of these goals can also be addressed in various ways (see Lundgren & Prislin, 1998; Prislin & Wood, 2005). When the implications are important, people can address the relevant goal(s) through careful thought and systematic analysis, yielding change that endures across time and settings. Or, when the goals are less compelling, and people have less need to be confident

INDIVIDUAL DIFFERENCES 8.1

MEASURING THE TENDENCY TO COMPARE OURSELVES WITH OTHERS

Social comparison refers to the use of others as points of reference to evaluate our abilities, or to show us what we should be thinking or feeling. This comparison may be considered relatively automatic (Gilbert, Giesler, & Morris, 1995), but occurs most often when we are uncertain about what to think or feel, during periods of stress, novelty or change and in situations that foster competition. Gibbons and Buunk (1999) developed a scale to measure the tendency to make social comparisons as an individual difference variable. The scale addresses the three specific underlying motives for comparison that have been generally accepted in the literature on social comparison: self-evaluation, self-improvement and self-enhancement (Taylor, Wayment, & Carrillo, 1996; Wood, 1989). The scale's eleven items capture the tendency to compare with others concerning life accomplishments, how well one has done at something, social skills, popularity, how one approaches a task, mutual opinions, experiences, problems and situations, or to learn more about something.

You can assess your own tendency to make social comparisons by completing the 11-item scale, below, which is preceded by the instructions:

'Most people compare themselves from time to time with others. For example, they may compare the way they feel, their opinions, their abilities, and/or their situations with those of other people. There is nothing particularly "good" or "bad" about this type of comparison, and some people do it more often than others. We would like to find out how often you compare yourself with other people. To do that we would like to ask you to indicate how much you agree with each statement below, by using the following scale.

'The scale ranges from *I disagree strongly* (1) to *I agree strongly* (5).'

1. I often compare how my loved ones (boy or girlfriend, family members, etc.) are doing with how others are doing.
2. I always pay a lot of attention to how I do things compared with how others do things.
3. If I want to find out how well I have done something, I compare what I have done with how others have done.
4. I often compare how I am doing socially (e.g. social skills, popularity) with other people.
5. I am not the type of person who compares often with others. (reversed)
6. I often compare myself with others with respect to what I have accomplished in life.
7. I often like to talk with others about mutual opinions and experiences.
8. I often try to find out what others think who face similar problems as I face.
9. I always like to know what others in a similar situation would do.
10. If I want to learn more about something, I try to find out what others think about it.
11. I *never* consider my situation in life relative to that of other people. (reversed)

Gibbons and Buunk (1999) reported data on various samples, including five samples of students in The Netherlands ($N = 3200$ total). The mean score (after reverse-scoring items 5 and 11) was 37.93, so if you score clearly lower than this score your tendency to make social comparisons is lower than average, whereas if you score clearly higher than this score your tendency to make social comparisons is higher than average.

---

in their judgements, they can meet them through less systematic, more heuristic strategies (see Chapter 7 on dual-route models of attitude change).

Summary

When we look at why social influence occurs, we see some of the fundamental motives that direct human social behaviour. Pressures toward uniformity and agreement among group members help us to validate social beliefs and guide the group towards its goals. We can also agree with others because we wish to be liked (or to avoid being disliked), or because we accept information from others as evidence about how things 'really are'. Ultimately, we are influenced by others so that we behave effectively, build and maintain relationships with others, manage our own self-concept and understand the social world more effectively.

DELIBERATE SOCIAL INFLUENCE

Inducing compliance

What are the main techniques of inducing compliance, and how and when do they work?

Compliance refers to a particular kind of response whereby the target of influence acquiesces to a request from the source of influence (Cialdini & Trost, 1998), but typically 'gives in' to the request without a true change of attitude. The request may be explicit or implicit, but

compliance a response whereby the target of influence acquiesces to a request from the influence source (also refers to change in behaviour to match a norm without change on a private level).

the target recognizes that he or she is being pressured to respond in a desired way. We emphasize that even though these forms of influence may appear relatively mild, all are based on *requests*, they are also all quite manipulative, and you are likely to encounter them in your interactions with skilled professional salespeople – so beware! But they can also be used for positive ends, as in eliciting donations to charity. (As you will see later, the term *compliance* is also used more generally in the research on conformity, to refer to change in public behaviour to match a norm, but without corresponding change on a private level.) We consider, below, the three main techniques of inducing compliance.

The door-in-the-face technique

In the **door-in-the-face technique** (also known as a 'reciprocal concessions' procedure), the requester begins with an extreme request that is almost always refused (e.g. 'Can you lend me £20?'). The requester, upon the initial request being declined, then retreats to a more moderate request, in fact the one that the requester had in mind all along (e.g. 'Can you lend me £5?'). By acting in this way, the requester hopes that the concession from an extreme to a moderate request will encourage the target of the request to make a similar, reciprocal, concession and move from initial refusal of the larger request to acceptance of the smaller one (e.g. Cialdini et al., 1975).

> **door-in-the-face technique** compliance technique in which the requester begins with an extreme request that is almost always refused, then retreats to a more moderate request, which he or she had in mind all along (also known as a 'reciprocal concessions' procedure).

This technique works effectively in commercial settings (e.g. Fennis, 2008), and is widely used in fundraising. For example, after refusing a larger request for a donation, people are much more likely than before to give any contribution (Reingen, 1978). It has also been used to solicit blood donors (Cialdini & Ascani, 1976). Researchers first asked people to take part in a long-term donor programme. When that request was declined, the requester asked for a one-time donation. Again, compliance with the small request was significantly greater after refusal of the large request (50 per cent), than in a control condition, in which people were asked only to perform the smaller favour (32 per cent). You can even use this technique on your lecturers! Harari, Mohr, and Hosey (1980) found that if students asked faculty members to spend 15 to 20 minutes talking to them about an issue of interest, some 59 per cent of the faculty agreed. But as many as 78 per cent acquiesced if they had first been asked for a much bigger favour (giving 2 hours a week of help to the student for the rest of the semester), which they had of course refused.

The success of this technique relies on two interlinked explanations. First, when the salesperson makes a concession, it is normative for the consumer to *reciprocate*, at least to some extent, which he or she does by accepting the concession. The tactic is much less effective if the time between the two requests is perceived as too long (Cann, Sherman, & Elkes, 1975), if the two requests are made by two different people (Snyder & Cunningham, 1975), and if the first request is excessive (Schwarzwald, Raz, & Zvibel, 1979). Second, when the target (e.g. the consumer, faced with a salesperson) makes a concession, he or she has re-established *equity* with the salesperson. The motives underlying compliance of this sort include our desire to build and maintain social relationships, but also our wish to view ourselves as, for example, generous (Brown & Smart, 1991) or consistent (Cialdini, Trost, & Newsom, 1995).

The foot-in-the-door technique

The **foot-in-the-door technique** adopts the reverse strategy, with the requester first asking for a small favour that is almost certain to be granted, and then following this up with a request for a larger, related favour (Freedman & Fraser, 1966). For example, a car salesperson may ask a potential buyer to test drive a car. Compliance to the critical request (buying the car) will be enhanced if the customer can first be made to comply with the initial, smaller request. The requester uses initial compliance as a means of committing the target to behave in a way that is consistent with it, and there is plentiful evidence that people are suckers for this approach (see Beaman, Cole, Preston, Klentz, & Steblay, 1983, for a review), which is frequently used by telemarketers (see Fennis & Stroebe, 2010). It can also be used for charitable donations: respondents who had agreed to accept and wear a small lapel pin promoting a local charity were also more likely to give money to that charity when approached at a later point in time (Pliner, Hart, Kohl, & Saari, 1974).

> **foot-in-the-door technique** compliance technique in which the requester first asks for a small favour that is almost certain to be granted, then follows this up with a request for a larger, related favour.

The success of this technique relies on the general idea of consistency (Cialdini & Trost, 1998; Cialdini et al., 1995). Thus, the person who agreed to wear the lapel pin will wish to behave consistently when contacted later. This is closely linked to an explanation in terms of self-perception theory (see Chapter 7). For example, the car-buying customer may infer from his or her behaviour that he or she is the kind of person who drives that sort of car.

Lowballing In the **lowballing technique**, which Cialdini and Trost (1998, p. 178) refer to as one of the 'more unsavoury' techniques, compliance to an initial

lowballing technique compliance to an initial attempt is followed by a more costly and less beneficial version of the same request.

attempt is followed by a more costly and less beneficial version of the same request (Cialdini, Cacioppo, Bassett, & Miller, 1978). For example, a car dealer may induce the customer to decide on a particular model of car by offering a low price for it, or an attractive trade-in deal on the customer's old vehicle. Then, after the decision has been made, the dealer goes back on the deal, giving some reason why the car is no longer available at the originally agreed price. Really unscrupulous dealers may even strengthen the customer's commitment, by allowing him or her to arrange financing, or even take the car home overnight (Joule, 1987).

This technique seems to rely on the target, even though he or she has been duped, feeling an unfulfilled obligation to the requester. The target is also already psychologically committed to the purchase, and so proceeds anyway. The technique is primarily effective when used by a single requester (Burger & Petty, 1981), and when the target freely makes the initial commitment (Cialdini et al., 1978; see Chapter 7 on cognitive dissonance theory). Although we have thus far treated low-balling as a rather negative technique, we should also note that it has been used successfully for more noble causes, such as getting people to give more money to a charitable cause (Fennis, Janssen, & Vohs, 2009).

Integration These techniques of inducing compliance rely on general principles such as equity, reciprocity and self-consistency (for further principles, and an application of these techniques to advertising, see Fennis & Stroebe, 2010, Chapter 7). One other general principle guiding induced compliance concerns perceived rewards and costs. People are not quite the suckers that these phenomena may imply, and in general they are likely to comply with a request for help if the costs are low, but not if costs are high (Cialdini & Goldstein, 2004). Under low costs they may display relative 'mindlessness' (Langer, Blank, & Chanowitz, 1978), for example not listening carefully to the exact words of a requester who asks to jump ahead of them in the queue for the photocopier machine, with the lame excuse that they 'have to make some copies'. However, when the requester asks to copy a larger number of pages (implying costs for the target, who will have to hang around and wait), then the requester's words are listened to carefully, and compliance only follows a convincing justification (e.g. 'I have to visit my sick mother in hospital').

The influence of numerical majorities and minorities

How and when do numerical majorities and minorities exert influence?

Whereas strategies for inducing compliance involve interpersonal influence, social influence is also a key phenomenon in small groups. The first studies to examine the conditions under which an individual yields or conforms to a numerical majority were conducted by Solomon Asch (e.g. Asch, 1951, 1956; see Levine, 1999, and Leyens & Corneille, 1999, for commentaries on the impact of Asch's research). The 'Asch experiments' have become a classic in the literature, and we have already described the basic paradigm (see Chapter 1). In this section we will, first, review the main findings from the Asch paradigm, and then consider when and why people conform. Next, we introduce minority influence and **innovation**, the situation in which either an individual or a group in a numerical minority can influence the majority. Finally, we review the major theoretical approaches to explain both **majority influence** and **minority influence**.

innovation see minority influence.

majority influence (conformity) social influence resulting from exposure to the opinions of a majority, or the majority of one's group.

minority influence (innovation) situation in which either an individual or a group in a numerical minority can influence the majority.

Majority influence: the Asch paradigm and beyond

Asch (1956) began his famous work expecting to show that people were *not* as suggestible as was generally believed at that time (see Leader in the Field, Solomon E. Asch). He also believed that the norm-following behaviour shown in Sherif's (1936) studies could be attributed to the ambiguous nature of the autokinetic stimulus. He contended that when unambiguous stimuli were used, and where there was a clearly correct answer, people would remain independent of the group's inaccurate judgements. As you will see, the results turned out rather differently.

Asch used a task in which groups of participants were shown two cards. On one card were three lines of different lengths, with each line having a number. The second card contained just one line (the standard line) that was of the same length as one of the three lines on the first card. The participant's task was simply to state publicly which of the three lines was the same length as the standard line. This task was repeated eighteen times, and on each trial different cards were shown, using different lengths of lines. In a control condition, in which participants

LEADER IN THE FIELD

Solomon E. Asch (1907–1996) was born in Warsaw, Poland and received his BS from the College of the City of New York in 1928, and his MA and PhD from Columbia University in 1930 and 1932, respectively. He taught at Brooklyn College, the New School for Social Research and Swarthmore College, and held visiting posts at Harvard and MIT. He was Distinguished Professor of Psychology and Director of the Institute for Cognitive Studies at Rutgers University from 1966 to 1972, when he joined the University of Pennsylvania. He is best known for his famous experiments on conformity (or 'group forces in the modification and distortion of judgments'). These studies deliberately opposed physical and social reality, and showed that most people succumb to the pressure to conform to majority opinion, even when stimuli are unambiguous. Asch also contributed classic research on impression formation (see Chapter 3), and he influenced many subsequent social psychologists (Stanley Milgram was greatly influenced by, and worked for, him; see Leader in the Field, this chapter). He wrote a distinctive and authoritative textbook on *Social Psychology*, first published in 1952.

performed alone with no group influence, over 99 per cent of the responses were correct, showing that the task was simple and unambiguous.

What Asch did next was very interesting. He had participants perform the task publically, answering aloud, in groups of 6–9. He arranged that all the participants (all were male), except one, would be confederates of the experimenter – that is, they were instructed by the experimenter to give a set pattern of answers, some of which were clearly incorrect. In some studies, the confederates all gave the wrong answer to the task. In addition, the seating arrangement was such that the naïve participant always gave his answers last-but-one. In other words, the naïve participant heard several people give the same wrong answer before he was required to give his own response. Asch's research question was, how would the naïve participant respond when faced with a consistent majority giving an (obviously) incorrect response? In fact, Asch found that the naïve participants gave the same incorrect response as the majority on 36.8 per cent of occasions.

It might be easy to brush aside these findings and assert that participants were just publicly agreeing with the majority. In one variation of the study (Asch, 1956) a situation was arranged so that the naïve participant believed he had arrived too late and so could write down his responses while the other group members (the confederates) still gave their responses aloud. The rate of conforming to the majority fell to 12.5 per cent, but this is still much higher than when no confederates were present (0.7 per cent).

Subsequent studies on **conformity** tended to move away from Asch's paradigm, which was costly and time-consuming, because each naïve participant had to be tested

conformity see majority influence.

alongside a group of confederates. Instead, using the Crutchfield (1955) paradigm, there are no confederates and the numerical majority is implied through feedback about other people's responses. Each participant sits in a separate cubicle (with no visual or verbal contact) and they all respond to the task via response switches. In addition, the response of each other group member is displayed on each participant's consol. Each participant believes that they are receiving the responses of the group members but, in fact, they are not; the response pattern can be programmed by the experimenter to show either agreement or disagreement with other participants. More recently still, most studies of conformity have abandoned the group context completely, and participants receive feedback concerning other people's responses in summary form (e.g. being told that 82 per cent of the population hold a particular attitude). Comparison between different paradigms shows reliable differences, with conformity rates being highest in face-to-face situations (e.g. Levy, 1960). This is not surprising, as literally facing the majority increases normative pressures to conform.

In a clever recent study Mori and Arai (2010) replicated Asch's paradigm without the use of confederates, by colouring the tops of the stimulus lines in either green or magenta. The participants, Japanese students, wore one of two types of polarizing sunglasses to view the stimuli which, unknown to them, filtered either green or magenta, to make the lines appear longer or shorter (so the majority was created simply by having the larger number of participants wearing glasses with the same-coloured filter). Results from this paradigm showed that women conformed to the majority, but men did not. Future replications will be needed, however, to ascertain whether this difference from Asch's results is due to a change of paradigm, cultural differences (see Chapter 15), or both.

When do people conform? Asch's first studies were followed by many variants. Among the most important factors found to influence the level of conformity are group size, unanimity and social support, and culture.

In terms of the numerical size of the majority, conformity increased quite dramatically as the number of majority members (faced with a minority of one) increased from one to three, but the influence of additional members was minimal (Asch, 1951; see Figure 8.8). However, results are rather inconsistent (see Gerard, Wilhelmy, & Conolley, 1968; Reis, Earing, Kent, & Nezlek, 1976). A crucial factor for the levelling off of conformity after the third participant seems to be that the members of the majority must be seen to be independent, and not simply 'sheep' (Wilder, 1977); once

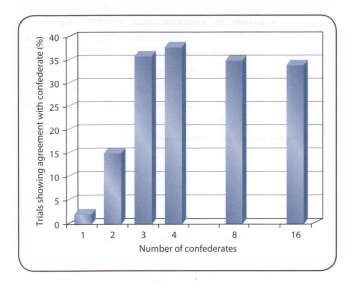

FIGURE 8.8 *Percentage of errors as a function of number of confederates.*

Source: Based on Asch, 1951.

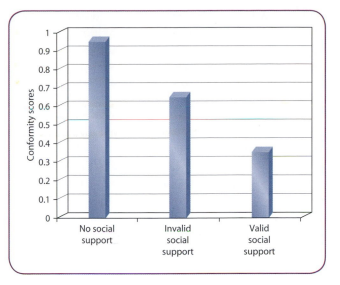

FIGURE 8.9 *Conformity in the absence and in the presence of social support.*

Source: Based on Allen & Levine, 1971. Reproduced with permission.

that is the case, there is a linear increase in conformity as group size increases (Gerard et al., 1968).

In one study Asch arranged for one of the confederates, who responded before the naïve participant, to give the correct answer. The level of conformity by the naïve participant dropped dramatically – but was this due to the correct respondent breaking the majority's unanimity, or his giving the naïve participant 'social support' for the correct answer? Another of Asch's studies was designed to answer this question, and showed that breaking the majority's unanimity was most important. When he had one of the confederates deviate from the majority, but by giving a different incorrect answer, this broke unanimity, but did not give the naïve participant a supporter. The results showed that the rates of conformity by the naïve participant reduced to nearly the same level as when there had been a social supporter. Genuine social support does, however, have a value over and above breaking unanimity when social influence concerns attitudes and opinions rather than unambiguous stimuli (see Allen, 1975, for a review). The true value of the social supporter is in providing a valid and independent assessment of reality (see Allen, 1975). Using the Asch task, Allen and Levine (1971) varied whether the participant had social support, and what type of support. In one of their two support conditions the social support was 'invalid', because the supporter was wearing spectacles with thick lenses. Although giving correct answers, this supporter could not possibly be perceived as a valid source of information on a visual-discrimination task. The results, shown in Figure 8.9, indicate that, although invalid support

was better than none, valid social support was clearly most effective.

Finally, Bond and Smith (1996) conducted a meta-analysis on the Asch conformity paradigm, and found greater acceptance of others' judgements in collectivistic cultures (which tend to subordinate individual goals to group goals) than in individualistic cultures (which tend to place an emphasis on individual goals and achievement; see Chapter 15). Indeed, the impact of culture was much greater than any other moderator of group influence, including the size of the majority.

Why do people conform? In post-experimental interviews conducted by Asch (see Asch, 1987) participants gave a number of reasons why they yielded to the majority. Some thought the majority was wrong, but went along with them simply to feel they belonged to the group and to avoid being ostracized. Others thought that the majority must be right, as they were the only person to see the task differently, i.e. 'several pairs of eyes' are more likely to be correct than the one pair of the naïve participant.

These different reasons given for yielding to the majority map closely onto theoretical accounts of conformity. The most popular explanation for conformity is based upon the dependency perspective on small group behaviour, which we described earlier in this chapter. Group members are cognitively and socially dependent on each other (Festinger, 1950), because opinion uniformity helps them to validate their opinions (social reality) and to move the group towards its goals (group locomotion). Explanations for the Asch studies also relied on Deutsch and Gerard's (1955) distinction between normative and informational social influence, introduced earlier. If conformity is related to the desire to be liked (normative influence) and the desire to be right (informational influence) then factors that affect these desires should increase the likelihood of conformity. In terms of normative social influence, conformity should be greater when people believe they are part of a group than when they do not. Making the group salient will increase people's desire to be part of the group and therefore increase conformity. This was shown in the study by Deutsch and Gerard (1955) that used the Asch lines. They found that conformity increased when participants were told they were part of a group, and that the best-performing groups in the study would win a prize, compared to a condition in which no such information was given. On the other hand, conformity decreased when participants' responses were anonymous (via the Crutchfield apparatus discussed earlier). In terms of informational influence, factors that increase the credibility of the majority as a valid source of reality (e.g. status and expertise) lead to more conformity (Kiesler & Kiesler, 1969). Also, factors that weaken the credibility of the majority as a valid source of information reduce conformity (e.g. breaking the majority consensus as shown above; Allen & Levine, 1971).

More generally, we can understand conformity by considering three main goals that it can serve (Cialdini & Trost, 1998). A shift towards a group consensus can allow the individual (1) to believe that he or she now sees things more accurately; (2) to gain the approval and acceptance of positively-viewed others; and (3) to avoid a self-concept as different, deviant or as refusing to compromise for the good of the group.

Minority influence and innovation Research on conformity focused on the ability of the majority to influence the individual, and therefore neglected the possibility that the individual (or minority) could influence the majority. According to the dependency account, that was the dominant early explanation of conformity, minorities lack the resources to make majority members dependent on them. Minorities, by definition, lack power, status and numerical size, and therefore do not have the means to enforce normative or informational influence.

Yet history is replete with examples of individuals and minorities who, through their actions, have had a tremendous impact upon the majority in society. It was this observation by the French social psychologist, Serge Moscovici (1976, 1980), that led to a theoretical re-shaping of the area. Moscovici argued that if social influence only relied upon conformity to the majority, then it would be difficult to see how groups would change, new ideas develop and innovation might occur.

Moscovici argued that minorities are distinctive – they stand out from the crowd – and from this distinctiveness they can create conflict within the majority by challenging the dominant majority view, and in so doing offer a new and different perspective. Since people wish to avoid conflict, they will often dismiss the minority position by attributing its deviancy to some underlying, undesirable psychological dimension (Papastamou, 1986). For example, the minority might be seen as 'crazy', 'biased' or 'provocative' in an attempt to explain its deviant view. Indeed, if one considers many 'successful' minorities (such as, Galileo, Freud and Copernicus or, more recently, politicians representing the Green Party, who have moved from the margins to the mainstream of politics), they often suffered ridicule and rejection by the majority before their views became accepted.

In order to overcome people's inclination to reject the deviant minority, the minority must adopt a particular style of behaviour that communicates to the majority that the minority is sure of, and committed, to its position. Moscovici termed this the minority's behavioural style and he emphasized, above all, **consistency**: the need for the minority to respond with the same response to the same issue over time. Moscovici, Lage, and Naffrechoux (1969) demonstrated these ideas experimentally. They presented groups of six female participants with a series of slides that were unambiguously blue and differed only in their light intensity. To each slide, every participant was required to say aloud the colour of the slide. In a control condition, participants not exposed to influence named the colour of the slide as 'blue' on almost all trials (99.75 per cent). However, in one condition the group contained two confederates (a numerical minority), who were seated such that they gave their responses, aloud, before the naïve participants, and were instructed to call the blue slides 'green' on every trial. When this occurred the naïve participants also called the slide green on 8.42 per cent of occasions, and this was significantly higher than in the control condition (0.25 per cent) that had no confederates. The importance of the minority responding consistently was shown in a third condition of the experiment, where the confederates were inconsistent (they responded randomly green to only some of the slides, and blue to others). When the minority was inconsistent, the percentage of green responses from the naïve participants fell to 1.25 per cent, which was not different from the control condition (see Figure 8.10). It is clear that for a minority to be successful it must respond consistently (see also Nemeth, Swedlund, & Kanki, 1974).

> **consistency** a behavioural style indicating that the same position is maintained across time; seen as central to minority influence.

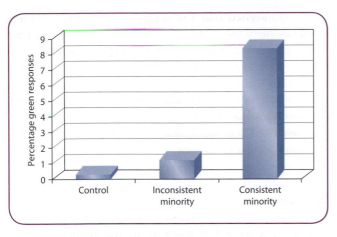

FIGURE 8.10 *Percentage green responses given by majority participants in the experiment by Moscovici, Lage, and Naffrechoux (1969).*

THEORY BOX 8.2

MOSCOVICI'S (1980) CONVERSION THEORY

- **Majority influence**
  - generates **comparison** process (focus on relationship between source and target)
  - conflict is resolved by overt compliance to majority position
    - in **public**, and/or
    - on **direct** measures
  - without further consideration of the issue
- **Minority influence**
  - triggers **validation** process (closer attention to the issue)
  - target is unlikely to agree with minority in public, for fear of being labelled 'deviant'
  - but cognitive processing of minority message can lead to conversion
    - **private** and/or **indirect** attitude change

Theoretical approaches to majority and minority influence There are currently two broad explanations for majority–minority influence phenomena, each of which subsumes several theories (Levine & Moreland, 1998). We term these the 'conflict' and 'social categorization' approaches.

Moscovici (1976, 1980) argued that conflict was the critical factor underlying influence. According to him, all forms of influence, whether from a majority or minority, result in conflict and individuals are motivated to reduce that conflict. However, Moscovici's (1980) dual-process 'conversion theory' argues that people employ different processes, with different outcomes, depending on whether the source of the conflict is a majority or a minority (see Theory Box 8.2). Moscovici proposed a contrast between two types of process, *comparison* and *validation*, which has some similarities to Deutsch

and Gerard's (1955) distinction between normative and informational influence. Moscovici argued that majorities induce a comparison process, in which the target of influence focuses on the discrepancy between his or her position and that advocated by the majority. The minority targets, because they wish to gain the majority's acceptance, show compliance (public influence) towards the majority position, but not a significant change in their original position (private influence). In contrast, minorities induce a validation process, in which majority members focus on the content of the minority's position, to try to understand it. Since people do not wish to publicly agree with a minority (to avoid identifying with a deviant group, Mugny, 1982), the quest to understand the minority's position can lead to **conversion** on a private level.

> **conversion** a change in private response after exposure to influence by others; internalized change; a change in the way one structures an aspect of reality.

The most provocative claim was made by Moscovici and Personnaz (1980). Using the blue-green slide paradigm, they claimed that if a minority consistently responded that a blue slide was 'green', then even though they could not bring that participant to accept that direct influence, they would exert influence on an indirect and private level. In this case the indirect level was the chromatic complementary after-image of the slide. The after-image is what one sees when one views a white screen after viewing a coloured slide; the after-image of blue is yellow-orange, and of green it is red-purple. Of course, the experimenters did not tell participants that different colours were linked to different after-images, and it is assumed that participants were ignorant of this too.

Moscovici and Personnaz did indeed find that when minority-influenced participants reported what colour after-image they saw on a white screen, they tended to see the after-image of a blue slide as more red-purple (complementary colour for green) than did majority-influenced and no-influence control participants, consistent with the idea that they had begun to see the slide as the minority saw it, as 'green'. However, despite the novelty of the study, the claim that a minority can cause a perceptual conversion is implausible, given what we know about the physiology of after-images. There have also been failures to replicate, and the study has been criticized on methodological grounds (see Martin & Hewstone, 2001a, in press, for a discussion).

A much less contentious way of measuring indirect influence is to measure influence on a target attitude, and on an indirectly-related attitude. For example, Pérez and Mugny (1987) exposed participants to a counter-attitudinal pro-abortion message that was attributed to either a majority or minority source. The researchers then measured participants' attitudes towards both the target issue, abortion, and an indirectly-related issue, birth control. Although the issue of birth control had not been mentioned in the source's message, it is related to it at a superordinate level (i.e. someone who is pro-abortion would also tend to be pro-birth control). While the minority had little impact on the direct abortion issue, it had a large impact on the birth control issue – participants had become more favourable to birth control. This was not found when the source was a majority. This result shows that the impact of the minority was low on direct attitudes (presumably because participants did not want to identify publicly with the minority) but the minority had a 'hidden impact' (Maass & Clark, 1984) on a related indirect attitude (see also Alvaro & Crano, 1997).

Moscovici's theory has received partial support from an extensive meta-analysis by Wood, Lundgren, Ouellette, Busceme, and Blackstone (1994). Overall, they reported that majorities had greater influence than minorities on both public measures and direct measures responded to in private. Minorities were, however, equally or more influential than majorities on indirect measures responded to in private.

An important recent development in this area has been the increased use of theory and methodology derived from the persuasion literature (see Chapter 7) to understand majority and minority influence. Specifically, researchers have drawn a parallel between Moscovici's concepts of comparison and validation and the distinction between non-systematic and systematic processing made in models of persuasion (the elaboration likelihood model and the heuristic–systematic model) (see Maass & Clark, 1983; Martin & Hewstone, 2001b). Thus, studies have manipulated source status (majority versus minority) and argument quality (strong versus weak arguments). This design allows the researcher to investigate which source is associated with systematic processing; if processing is systematic, there should be greater persuasion by the strong than the weak message, as well as more message-congruent thoughts, and these thoughts should mediate attitude change. There is, however, disagreement amongst researchers concerning which source condition (minority or majority) should elicit the most cognitive scrutiny of the message, with some advocating superior message processing associated with a minority (e.g. Moscovici, 1980), others advocating this for the majority (e.g. Mackie, 1987), and still others proposing that both a majority and minority can lead to message processing under different circumstances (e.g. Baker & Petty, 1994).

Martin and Hewstone (2008) have developed a theoretical framework that accounts for these inconsistent results; based on Petty and Cacioppo's (1986a, b) elaboration likelihood model, it is termed the 'source context

elaboration model' (see also Crano & Chen, 1998; De Dreu & De Vries, 1993; De Vries, De Dreu, Gordijn, & Schuurman, 1996), and now has extensive empirical support (see Martin & Hewstone, 2008, for a review). Essentially this approach makes two broad sets of predictions concerning (a) the types of processes underlying majority and minority influence and when they occur, and (b) the consequences for attitudes following majority and minority influence.

The first set of predictions states that the effects of source status (majority versus minority) vary along an elaboration continuum (the extent to which the situation allows or encourages elaboration of the source's message). When the elaboration demands are low (e.g. the topic is low in personal relevance), message recipients do not process the source's arguments, and attitudes can be guided through simple heuristics (such as the consensus heuristic, 'the majority is more likely to be right than the minority'). When elaboration demands are high (e.g. the topic is high in personal relevance), then people will attend to, and process, arguments from both the majority and the minority source, and there should be attitude change in each case. However, most influence situations to which people are exposed are not characterized by either very low or high processing demands but, rather, are located at an intermediate level. In this situation, Martin and Hewstone proposed that Moscovici's (1980) conversion theory should apply – that is, systematic processing of only the minority arguments.

Martin, Hewstone, and Martin (2007, Experiment 2) presented participants with a set of typed strong or weak anti-voluntary euthanasia arguments, and assessed both thoughts generated and attitudes. Portions of the arguments were repeated alongside the original message (the selected text). The level of message elaboration was manipulated by asking participants to conduct one of three tasks on the selected text. In the low elaboration condition participants were asked simply to check whether the selected text was written in the same font type and size as the original message. This task should result in only shallow message processing, and therefore there should be no effect of argument quality. However, the majority source, operating via a consensus heuristic, should have greater impact on attitudes than the minority source. In the intermediate elaboration condition participants were asked to check the spelling of words in the selected text. This task requires semantic processing of single words, and Martin et al. predicted message processing only for the minority source, due to its distinctiveness leading to message validation (cf. Moscovici, 1980). Finally, in the high elaboration condition participants were asked to paraphrase some highlighted portions of the presented texts in different words but to

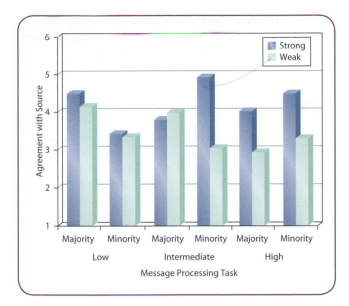

FIGURE 8.11 *Agreement as a function of numerical size of source, argument quality and level of message processing task.*
Source: Martin et al., 2007; Expt. 2.

convey the same meaning as the original text. This task requires semantic processing of sentences, and Martin et al. therefore predicted that strong arguments (regardless of majority/minority support) would have greater impact on the reported attitudes than weak arguments.

Results confirmed the authors' hypotheses (see Figure 8.11). In the low elaboration condition, the only reliable effect was for source status, with the majority having more influence than the minority. The lack of an argument quality effect suggests the source status main effect was due to non-elaborative processing. In the intermediate elaboration condition, there was a reliable interaction between source status and argument quality, showing a difference between strong and weak messages for the minority but not majority source. Finally, in the high elaboration condition there was an argument quality effect for *both* majority and minority sources, showing participants had engaged in elaborative processing for both sources.

The pattern of results for message-congruent thoughts complemented the attitude data. In the low elaboration condition there were no reliable effects, consistent with the claim that attitudes were guided by heuristic cues and not by elaboration of the source's arguments. In the intermediate elaboration condition there was a reliable interaction between source status and argument quality that mirrored the pattern found for attitudes. Finally, in the high elaboration condition, the only reliable finding was for argument quality. Further evidence that the argument quality effect was due to elaborative processing comes from the finding that the proportion of message-congruent thinking in both the intermediate

and high elaboration conditions mediated the effects found on attitude scores.

The second set of predictions concerns the nature of the attitudes that are formed following majority and minority influence. According to the persuasion literature, attitudes formed through systematic processing are 'strong' (Krosnick, Boninger, Chuang, Berent, & Carnot, 1993) in terms of being more resistant to counter-persuasion, more persistent over time, and more predictive of behaviour than attitudes formed via non-systematic processing. Martin and Hewstone have published consistent evidence showing that minorities lead to 'strong' attitudes, in that attitudes following minority influence were more resistant to counter-persuasion (Martin, Hewstone, & Martin, 2003), more persistent over time (Martin, Hewstone, & Martin, 2008) and better predictors of behaviour (Martin, Martin, Smith, & Hewstone, 2007) compared to attitudes formed following majority influence. Turn now to Research Close-Up 8.2, which summarizes the evidence that minority-instigated attitudes are more resistant to counter-persuasion.

There is stronger support for the conflict explanation of majority–minority influence from Nemeth's (1986, 1995) research and her convergent–divergent theory (see Leader in the Field, Charlan Jeanne Nemeth). According to Nemeth, majority versus minority status does not affect the *amount* of thinking about the message, but the *type* of thinking and the focus of thoughts. She has consistently found that majorities produce a narrow focus on the message they present, whereas minorities produce a broader focus on new information and attitudinal positions. Her explanation for this effect is that learning that the majority has a different position to oneself creates stress, particularly if the majority is physically present, and stress is known to narrow the focus of attention. Specifically,

 LEADER IN THE FIELD

Charlan Jeanne Nemeth (b. 1941) was born in St. Louis, Missouri. She received her BA in Mathematics from Washington University in St. Louis in 1963, an MA in Social Psychology from the University of Wisconsin-Madison in 1965, and a PhD in Psychology from Cornell University in 1968 (where her advisors were Len Berkowitz (see Leader in the Field, Chapter 9) and Steve Jones). One year after her PhD, she spent a year working with two of the founding fathers of European Social Psychology, Henri Tajfel (Bristol; see Leader in the Field, Chapter 14) and Serge Moscovici (Paris; see Leader in the Field, this chapter). She is currently professor in the Department of Psychology, University of California, Berkeley. For most of her professional career she has studied small group decision-making with an emphasis on the ways in which such decisions can be made 'better', more correct and more creative. Her work on the value of dissent has been broadly applied in the law as it pertains to jury decision-making, and in business as it pertains to corporate cultures of innovation.

MINORITY SOURCES INDUCE STRONGER ATTITUDES

Martin, R., Hewstone, M., & Martin, P. Y. (2003). Resistance to persuasive messages as a function of majority and minority source status. *Journal of Experimental Social Psychology, 39,* 585-593.

Introduction

As the main text of the chapter explains, Moscovici's (1980) conversion theory predicts that minority influence leads to greater message processing than does majority influence. This paper reports three studies that take a different, and novel, approach to examining this hypothesis. We describe one study here. In this study the participants were exposed to two messages that argued different positions in relation to the same topic. The messages were delayed in time, and participants completed attitude measures after each message. The first message (initial message) argued a counter-attitudinal position, while the second argued the opposite, pro-attitudinal position (counter-message).

If attitudes following the initial message had been formed from processing the message in detail, then these attitudes should resist the second counter-message. Active processing of the arguments in the initial message (i.e. thinking of issues in agreement with the message) should provide individuals with arguments to resist the attack from the second counter-message. If, however, the attitudes formed following the first message were *not* based upon detailed message processing, then these attitudes should be influenced by (or yield to) the second message.

The authors predicted that if minority influence leads to greater message processing, as proposed by Moscovici (1980), then attitudes formed following exposure to a minority should be more resistant to a second counter-message than are attitudes formed following majority influence.

Method

Participants and design.

The participants were 69 undergraduate students at a British university (25 males and 44 females) who were randomly assigned to one of two conditions (majority versus minority support of initial message).

Stimulus materials.

The topic of the message was the legalization of voluntary euthanasia (i.e. the right to end life if suffering from a terminal illness). Pre-testing had shown that the participants were moderately in favour of voluntary euthanasia. Two messages were employed which used strong and persuasive arguments that were either in favour (initial message) or against (counter-message) voluntary euthanasia.

Procedure

Participants were tested in groups of between two and five. The study had five stages. First, participants rated their attitude towards voluntary euthanasia on a 9-point scale from 1 – *totally disagree* to 9 – *totally agree* (pre-test). Second, they were informed that a recent survey at their university showed that either 82 per cent (majority) or 18 per cent (minority) of students were in favour of legalizing voluntary euthanasia. They then read several arguments that summarized the majority or minority position in favour of voluntary euthanasia (initial message) (note, the researchers presented the same arguments in each condition, only the majority/minority label changed). Third, participants' attitudes towards voluntary euthanasia were measured again on the same 9-point scale employed in the first booklet (post-test I: initial message). Fourth, participants were then shown arguments that conveyed the opposite perspective to the initial message; that is, against voluntary euthanasia (counter-message). Fifth, participants rated their attitude towards voluntary euthanasia for a third time on the 9-point scale (post-test II: counter-message).

Results

Scores on the attitude scale were reverse-coded so that high scores indicated greater influence to the initial message while low scores indicated greater influence to the counter-message. As can be seen from Figure 8.12, the participants were influenced by both the majority and minority, as there was a significant change in attitudes between pre-test and post-test I: initial message, in the direction of the source of influence. The amount of change in the majority and minority conditions was the same. At this stage, it appears that the majority and minority led to the same amount of influence, but the results for the counter-message show this was derived from different processes.

The prediction was that attitudes following majority influence would result from compliance, without thinking about the message arguments in detail and, therefore,

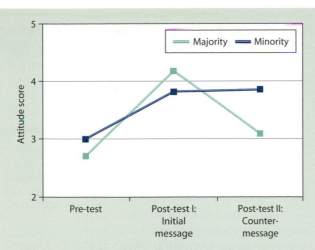

FIGURE 8.12 *Mean attitudes as a function of majority versus minority source and pre-test, post-test 1 (initial message) and post-test 2 (counter-message).*

Note: Greater agreement with the source is reflected by *high* scores on the initial message and *low* scores on the counter-message. The difference between initial message and counter-message reflects the degree of resistance – the smaller the difference, the greater the resistance.

Source: Data from Martin, Hewstone, & Martin, 2003.

these attitudes should yield to a counter-message. This is what happened in the majority condition, as the scores following the counter-message (post-test II) were significantly lower than scores following the initial message (post-test I). In fact, in the majority condition, attitudes following the counter-message reduced to the same level as the pre-test attitude; this suggests that the attitude change to the initial message was only superficial, as attitudes returned to their pre-test level when exposed to the counter-message.

By contrast, the prediction was that attitudes following minority influence would be due to detailed evaluation of the minority's arguments, and this should enable participants to resist the counter-message. Again, this is what happened. There was no difference in attitude scores between the initial message (post-test I) and the counter-message (post-test II), showing that participants had not changed their attitude (i.e. had resisted) when exposed to the second message.

Discussion

This is the first investigation of resistance to persuasion in the context of majority and minority influence and it offers a new demonstration, consistent with Moscovici's (1980) conversion theory, of greater message processing induced by a minority, compared with a majority, source. However, the authors acknowledge that majorities can, and often do, encourage systematic message processing but in situations that encourage message elaboration. This was shown in another study where participants were told, before they read the majority message, that they would later be asked to recall the arguments contained in it (this procedure should encourage message processing). With these instructions, attitudes following majority influence also resisted the counter-message (Martin, Hewstone, & Martin, 2008).

exposure to majority influence leads to message-relevant, convergent thinking, which yields uncreative solutions to problems. In contrast, exposure to minority influence leads to issue-relevant, divergent thinking, producing creative problem-solving solutions (e.g. Maass & Volpato, 1994; Mucchi-Faina, Maass, & Volpato, 1991; Nemeth & Kwan, 1985). Consistent with this view, exposure to majority dissent is more helpful than exposure to minority dissent when a task requires convergent thinking, while minority dissent is more effective on tasks requiring divergent thinking (Nemeth, Mosier, & Chiles, 1992).

In an illustrative study of how minorities lead to more creative task performance Nemeth and Wachtler (1983) conducted a study involving an embedded figures test (see Figure 8.13). Participants had to identify if a standard figure was contained (or embedded) within a set of comparisons. The participants were led to believe that either a numerical majority (four out of six group members) or a numerical

minority (only two out of six members) supported a particular answer. When people were exposed to a majority view, they followed that majority answer exactly (i.e. they identified the standard figure in other figures, but in the same orientation as the majority source had, for example stimulus U in Figure 8.13), or they performed as they would alone. However, when people were exposed to a minority view, they detected more instances of the standard figure, including correct answers that were not proposed by the minority (i.e. they identified the standard figure in more other figures, and both in the same orientation as the minority source had done, and when inverted, or rotated; e.g. stimuli I and R in Figure 8.13). These results show improved task performance as a result of exposure to minority rather than majority dissent.

Research has recently investigated the nature of the arguments *generated by* individuals who find themselves in either a numerical majority or minority (Kenworthy,

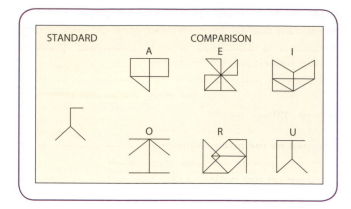

STANDARD   COMPARISON

FIGURE 8.13 *Stimuli used by Nemeth and Wachtler (1983).*

Source: Nemeth & Wachtler, 1983. Reproduced with permission of John Wiley & Sons, Ltd.

Hewstone, Levine, Martin, & Willis, 2008). Because they are outnumbered, numerical minorities must necessarily take multiple perspectives – both their own as well as that of the numerical majority – in order to reduce the threat of invalidation. By contrast, numerical majorities will be less motivated to adopt others' perspective and to think in novel and creative ways to defend their position, because their opinion has the weight of consensus (see Levine & Russo, 1995). In three studies Kenworthy et al. (2008) showed that being in a numerical minority led to the generation of arguments that were rated more original and convincing (by judges blind to experimental condition and hypotheses of the experiment) than those produced by participants in the numerical majority condition. For a broader analysis of how minority status affects how people think, feel, and relate to others, see Butera and Levine (2009). We will return to the value of dissent within groups later, in the section on group decision-making. There we see that an over-emphasis on harmony and consensus, and a failure to encourage and attend to diverse viewpoints, can lead to disastrous decision-making.

Whereas the dependence and conflict approaches focus on intragroup processes, the social categorization account focuses on intergroup *and* intragroup processes (Mugny, 1982; Mugny & Pérez, 1991; Turner, Hogg, Oakes, Reicher, & Wetherell, 1987). Mugny and Pérez argue that minority influence occurs if identification with the source is compatible with a positive social identity (essentially, the extent to which one feels positive about membership of a group; see Chapter 14). According to this view, minorities categorized as outgroups have little direct influence, but can have indirect influence if they induce a validation process (see also Mugny, Butera, Sanchez-Mazas, & Pérez, 1995; Pérez & Mugny, 1996; Quiamzade, Mugny, Falomir-Pichastor, & Butera, 2010). Whereas minorities categorized as ingroups can produce

direct influence, because the target of influence identifies with the source of influence. (See also research by Crano and colleagues suggesting that ingroup minorities are evaluated in a more open-minded way, e.g. Alvaro & Crano, 1997; Crano & Alvaro, 1997; Crano & Chen, 1998).

The impact of group identification on social influence also lies at the heart of the **self-categorization theory** analysis of majority and minority influence (see Turner, 1991). According to self-categorization theory (for a fuller account see Chapters 5 and 14), individuals identify with a particular group and conform to a prototypical group position. This form of social influence is termed **referent informational influence**. The prototypical position maximizes both similarities between ingroup members and differences between ingroup and outgroup (Hogg, Turner, & Davidson, 1990; Mackie, 1986). Self-categorization theory predicts that social influence will occur only if three conditions are met: (1) the target perceives that the source disagrees with his or her position; (2) the source and target are perceived as members of the same group; and (3) the source's position is prototypical of the group norm (i.e. it is most typical of the ingroup, and least typical of the outgroup; Van Knippenberg, Lossie, & Wilke, 1994).

People have a need to hold attitudes consistent with their social identities, and according to self-categorization theory people adopt ingroup positions to reduce subjective uncertainty about their responses. Disagreement with others categorized as similar to the self, however, conveys subjective uncertainty, and motivates people to resolve the discrepancy by means of mutual social influence. David and Turner (1996, 1999) provided evidence for self-categorization theory. They found majority compliance and minority conversion only when the source of influence was categorized as similar to the target of influence; when the source was characterized as being dissimilar to the target of influence there was no direct or indirect influence (see also Gordijn, Postmes, & De Vries, 2001).

To summarize, there is clear support for Moscovici's (1980) proposal that we should study the influence of minorities as well as majorities. However, there is mixed support for his theory, as there is for self-categorization theory's prediction that only ingroup minorities will have an impact. There is evidence that both majorities and minorities can instigate detailed processing of their messages, under specific circumstances, and that both

self-categorization theory explains how the process of categorizing oneself as a group member forms social identity and brings about various forms of both group (e.g. polarization, influence) and intergroup (e.g. discrimination) behaviours.

referent informational influence individuals identify with a particular group and conform to a prototypical group position.

ingroup and outgroup minorities can exert influence; typically, however, the influence of ingroup minorities will be greater, and it will be shown primarily on indirect private measures of influence and on measures of divergent thinking.

One final observation we make about research on minority influence is that how and where we do research may have underestimated the impact of minorities (Hewstone & Martin, 2010). For example, while the meta-analysis carried out by Wood et al. (1994) found that minority influence is more likely to be indirect rather than direct, is more frequently found in private rather than public contexts, and tends to be delayed rather than immediate, this may not be the case when we study influence processes in freely-interacting groups, which allow for reciprocal exchange between minority and majority members, and especially when consensus must be reached (see Smith & Tindale, 2010). Research conducted using freely-interacting groups has shown that the presence of a minority source of influence brings about a change in how the group considers and treats the evidence before it (see Schulz-Hardt, Frey, Lüthgens, & Moscovici, 2000), and, generally, this is associated with an improvement in the group's products or decisions (e.g. Brodbeck, Kerschreiter, Mojzisch, Frey, & Schulz-Hardt, 2002; see Chapter 13). Minorities may also have more impact outside the laboratory, in organizations for example. Whereas empirical studies in our laboratories show that minorities, compared with majorities, are rarely able to exert direct influence in changing the views of others, Aime and Van Dyne (2010) argue that the study of groups in organizations provides a more balanced view of the impact of minorities and majorities on issues that are important to group functioning. For example, research by De Dreu and colleagues (e.g. De Dreu & West, 2001), using diverse work groups, has shown that minority dissent stimulates the consideration of multiple perspectives in a decision-making task and enhances group creativity (see also Park & DeShon, 2010).

Group decision making

Why do groups make more extreme decisions than individuals?

Group polarization Imagine that you get together with a group of friends and discuss your favourite lectures. If you reach a group decision on, say, your evaluation of the social-psychology course, is it likely to be the average of your individual views? In fact, although this was originally thought to be how groups made decisions, through research on norm formation such

as the work of Sherif (1936) discussed earlier, research has shown that far from an 'averaging' process, group discussion is associated with a 'polarizing' process. **Group polarization** refers to the tendency to make decisions that are more extreme than the average of group members' initial positions, in the direction already favoured by the group. Individual members' private opinions then converge on this polarized decision. Although many of the relevant studies demonstrate *attitude* polarization we emphasize that, consistent with our description of the field of social influence in general, the same phenomenon has been demonstrated for many kinds of judgements and decision, including stereotypes, interpersonal impressions and jury decisions (see Lamm & Myers, 1978, and Social Psychology Beyond the Lab 8.1). There is plentiful empirical evidence for group polarization, and it has a broad impact on social and political life (see Sunstein, 2009).

The phenomenon of group polarization was first demonstrated by Moscovici and Zavalloni (1969) (see Leader in the Field, Serge Moscovici). They had small groups of French high-school students first write down in private their attitudes towards two topics, one on which they were initially somewhat positive (their attitude to the then-President, Charles De Gaulle) and one on which they were initially somewhat negative (their attitude towards Americans). Then, they had to reach consensus, as a group, on each item; finally, they made another private attitude rating. As a result of the discussion, participants became more extreme in the same direction as their initial attitudes tended. As Figure 8.15

> **group polarization** tendency to make decisions that are more extreme than the average of group members' initial positions, in the direction already favoured by the group.

LEADER IN THE FIELD

Serge Moscovici (b. 1925) was born in Romania to Jewish parents. Following systematic discrimination, including exclusion from high school, he was a victim of the 1941 Bucharest pogrom, and was interned in a Nazi forced labour camp. He made his way secretly to France, where he studied psychology at the Sorbonne. His professional career has been spent at the Ecole des Hautes Etudes en Sciences Sociales, Paris, with visiting appointments in Princeton, and at the New School for Social Research, New York. He became director of the Laboratoire Européen de Psychologie Sociale (European Laboratory of Social Psychology) at the Maison des Sciences de l'Homme, Paris. His ground-breaking contributions to the study of social influence comprise the very first experimental studies of both group polarization and minority influence. He is one of the giants of European social psychology, as well as one of its founding fathers, whose impact on the discipline would be hard to exaggerate.

SOCIAL PSYCHOLOGY BEYOND THE LAB 8.1

JURY DECISION-MAKING

Although we have focused on experimental studies of social influence in this chapter, there is no shortage of examples of these phenomena in the real world, nor of applications of the relevant theory and research. One prime example is the work of juries, a group of twelve laypeople who, primarily in countries with English common-law traditions, decide on culpability in criminal trials or liability in civil trials. These groups make important, sometimes literally life-and-death, decisions. But they are often quite homogeneous – famously described by British Judge, Lord Devlin, as 'middle aged, middle minded and middle class' – and illustrate several of the phenomena discussed in this chapter.

Social psychologists have studied juries for many years, typically using an experimental trial-simulation methodology (because, for legal reasons, researchers are not permitted direct access to jurors' decisions). While this may appear to be a fundamental weakness of the relevant research, because the laboratory analogue cannot exactly reproduce the pressures and responsibilities of a real jury, Kerr (1995) notes that laboratory and jury groups are similar in that they are both *ad hoc* collections of people who, initially, do not know each other.

Although some key aspects of how juries operate involve individual decision-making tendencies and biases (involving the *juror*, rather than the *jury*, see Hastie, 1993), social psychologists have focused on jury deliberation processes (e.g. Hastie, Penrod, & Pennington, 1983; Stasser, Kerr, & Bray, 1982). Many of the phenomena considered in this chapter (and the two chapters in this volume that deal with group dynamics, Chapters 12 and 13) can be seen at work in juries. Here we will highlight some of those relating to social influence, focusing on group polarization, majority influence and minority influence.

Juries clearly show group polarization. A classic legal source noted that verdicts handed down are more extreme than the individual jury members' initial judgements, but always in the same direction as the initial judgements (Kalven & Zeisel, 1966). Moreover, bias found in individual jurors' judgements (e.g. attention paid to pre-trial publicity) tends to be accentuated by deliberating juries (Stasser et al., 1982). Myers and Kaplan (1976) studied this issue experimentally, by forming mock juries that had to determine the guilt of defendants. Via a manipulation of the strength of the evidence, some groups already initially favoured conviction, while other groups initially favoured

acquittal. Discussions within each of these kinds of groups led to a polarization of these initial tendencies (see also Hastie et al., 1983). Subdividing the group of twelve into smaller groups for part of the deliberation process might be one way to weaken this tendency to polarize. Waller, Hope, Burrowes, and Morrison (2011) compared decision-making in mock juries that were and were not subdivided, and found that individuals in the subdivided groups reported more equal contribution of group members and less inhibition about contribution to the group discussion.

Juries also illustrate majority influence, because initial, pre-deliberation majorities nearly always prevail in the criminal courts (Kalven & Zeisel, 1966). Moreover, social psychologists studying juries emphasize that jury deliberation involves more than simple persuasion (i.e. informational influence) and, in fact, there is a strong normative component (Kerr, 1995).

Smith and Tindale (2010) demonstrate that once it achieves a two-thirds majority, the majority view tends to determine the outcome of the jury decision process (Davis, 1980; Tindale & Davis, 1983). They note, however, that, overall, jurors who support acquittal tend to be more influential than those who support conviction (Davis, Kerr, Stasser, Meek, & Holt, 1977; Kerr & MacCoun, 1985; Tindale,

FIGURE 8.14 *Henry Fonda wins over a previously unanimous majority of other jurors in the film Twelve Angry Men.*

Source: © Photos 12. Used under licence from Alamy.

Davis, Vollrath, Nagao, & Hinsz, 1990), most likely because the not-guilty verdict is in keeping with social norms. Therefore, even if seven members of a twelve-person jury favour guilty at the beginning of their deliberation, the final verdict is more likely than not to be defined by the five-person minority favouring not guilty; thus minority influence is at work too.

The 'reasonable doubt' criterion used in law requires that jurors vote for conviction only in the event that they cannot generate any reasonable doubts concerning the defendant's guilt. Therefore, arguing in favour of acquittal is often much easier than is arguing in favour of conviction, because only one reasonable doubt needs to be generated in order to validate the acquittal position. Consistent with this notion, Kerr and MacCoun (1985) found that minority factions favouring acquittal were not influential when the reasonable doubt criterion was replaced by a 'preponderance of the evidence' criterion. Under this latter criterion, neither verdict is inherently easier to validate, and, therefore, majority factions tend to prevail.

Banned, as you are, from ever actually observing a jury deliberate, you could at least take a well-justified break from your studies of social influence to watch the classic film *Twelve Angry Men* (directed by Sidney Lumet, 1957). This film illustrates the strong normative component within juries, as the majority attempts to coerce opposed and undecided jurors. But, most famously, it demonstrates minority influence, as the main protagonist (played by Henry Fonda) succeeds in overturning an 11-to-1 jury favouring a guilty judgement (Figure 8.14). Or you could read Grove's (1998) interesting account of what it is like to serve on a jury, *The Juryman's Tale*.

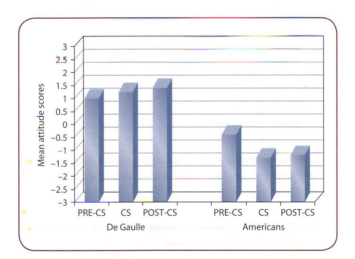

FIGURE 8.15 *Group polarization: attitudes towards De Gaulle and towards Americans in pre-consensus, consensus and post-consensus conditions.*
Source: Data from Moscovici & Zavalloni, 1969.

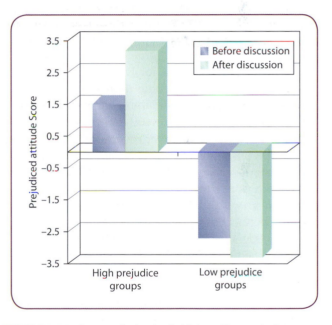

FIGURE 8.16 *Group polarization in high and low prejudice groups as a function of discussion.*
Source: Myers & Bishop, 1970. Reproduced with permission from AAAS.

shows, attitudes towards De Gaulle became more positive, and attitudes towards Americans became more negative after the discussion, and the new attitudes remained at these levels at the post-consensus phase. Myers and Bishop (1970) showed how this process can polarize racial attitudes, as those who discuss their attitudes with like-minded others become more prejudiced if they are already inclined in that direction, but less prejudiced if they are inclined to be more liberal (see Figure 8.16). This provides a neat demonstration of a process that promotes extremism (see Sunstein, 2009).

There are three main explanations for this effect – persuasive arguments, social comparison, and self-categorization – which we will, first, review and then integrate (see Theory Box 8.3).

Persuasive arguments As the discussion in a group unfolds, individuals typically learn something from each other; the discussion allows for an exchange of knowledge, opinions, and, above all, *arguments*, as group members try to convince one another (Burnstein & Vinokur, 1977).

THEORY BOX 8.3

WHAT PRODUCES GROUP POLARIZATION? THREE MAIN THEORIES

A group member:

- Hears *arguments* from other group members
  1. Persuasive arguments theory
- Learns the *position* of other group members
  2. Social comparison theory
- Is more influenced by ingroup than outgroup members
  3. Self-categorization theory
- Together, these 3 processes lead to:
  4. More polarized attitudes following group discussion (more extreme, in the same direction)

Vinokur and Burnstein (1974) highlighted three kinds of information that circulate among members of a group: information that (1) expresses a view pro or contra the issue; (2) contains some novelty (which is intrinsically persuasive); and (3) has cogency (the ability to persuade). During the exchange of arguments, each individual is likely to learn novel reasons for holding the consensual view, whereby attitudes become more extreme; indeed, arguments consistent with the dominant tendency are rated more persuasive than those that contradict it, and the greater the number of arguments related to their initial position, the more group members polarize (Burnstein, Vinokur, & Trope, 1973). Discussion also provides an opportunity for individuals both to repeat their own views and to hear those views repeated by others; repetition contributes to the shift towards more extreme judgements (Brauer & Judd, 1996; Brauer, Judd, & Gliner, 1995).

Three lines of evidence support the persuasive arguments approach, also called the informational approach, because it argues that polarization is based on informational social influence (Deutsch & Gerard, 1955). First, polarization is correlated with the ratio of pro versus con arguments available to group members; second, polarization can be produced by manipulating this ratio; and third, polarization increases with the novelty and validity of the arguments that group members hear (Kaplan & Miller, 1977; Vinokur & Burnstein, 1978). Thus, this explanation is essentially parallel to that offered by cognitive theories of persuasion (see Chapter 7): a group member's attitude is a function of the number and persuasiveness of pro and contra arguments recalled from memory when he or she formulates this position (Eagly & Chaiken, 1993).

Social comparison   An alternative account of group polarization is based on social comparison theory (Festinger, 1954). It is also known as the normative explanation for polarization, because it contends that polarization is due to normative influence (Deutsch & Gerard, 1955; see above). According to this view, group members tend to compare themselves with others, and have a need to view themselves positively and gain approval from others (Goethals & Zanna, 1979; Myers & Lamm, 1976). Moreover, they wish to be different from other group members, but in a socially desirable direction; so, after learning others' positions, they shift to an even more extreme position themselves (Myers, 1978).

The main line of support for this explanation is that group polarization can be brought about, quite simply, by learning of other group members' attitudinal *positions*. Participants who received information about the distribution of other group members' positions before they made their own decisions took more extreme positions than those unaware of other group members' positions (Myers, Bach, & Schreiber, 1974). They did so, moreover, without ever hearing others' arguments, and only when they were informed about the distribution of opinions held by all other members of the group, not simply when they were informed of the group average (Myers & Kaplan, 1976).

Self-categorization   A more recent normative account of group polarization acknowledges the importance of both persuasive arguments *and* members' positions, but in addition emphasizes that group membership is essential to group polarization (Turner, 1991). Polarization arises from tendencies to accentuate similarities within members of one's own group, but to differentiate from members of outgroups. Consistent with this view, polarization is enhanced by reference to an outside group (Doise, 1969), which emphasizes the ingroup–outgroup division. Indeed, even in the absence of actual discussion between members of the same group, members' attitudes shift towards a perceived ingroup norm that best defines the group in contrast to the relevant outgroup (Hogg, Turner, & Davidson, 1990).

Whereas the earlier accounts define the group norm as the *average* position of all the group's members, and view polarization as movement beyond that norm, the self-categorization account argues that the group norm can be more extreme than the average position, and polarization can reflect movement *towards* that norm. For example, a group of conservative students may share the view that taxes should be reduced, but when they think of a comparison group (such as socialist students) who do not share this view, then they may polarize even further in their support for taxation. According to self-categorization theory (which we introduced earlier in the section on majority–minority influence), individuals identify with a particular group and conform to a prototypical group position, a position that defines views held in their group. Prototypes are individual representations of group norms, and they are formed by making comparisons, both within the group and between groups, which maximize the perceived difference between the two groups (see earlier section on minority influence). Thus, group members perceive the group's position to be more extreme than it actually is, based on the average of the group members' responses. This referent informational influence helps to define the ingroup as different from the outgroup (Hogg et al., 1990; Mackie, 1986). Interestingly, group members are more comfortable and more vocal when their opinions differ from the average group member's opinion in the direction of the group prototype, than if their opinions differ in the opposite direction (Miller & Morrison, 2009; Morrison & Miller, 2008).

There are three main lines of empirical support for the self-categorization account of group polarization. First, polarization produced by listening to a group discussion, or learning others' positions, depends on participants believing that they are members of the *same* group (i.e. ingroup members), and not a competing group (i.e. outgroup members) (Mackie & Cooper, 1984; Turner et al., 1987; Turner, Wetherell, & Hogg, 1989). Listeners also perceive the content of the discussion to be more polarized when they think the discussants are ingroup members than when they do not (Mackie, 1986). Second, polarization is mediated by group members' perceptions of the ingroup's position (Turner et al., 1989). Third, intergroup attitudinal polarization is more extreme (ingroup and outgroup positions are further apart) when group membership is more salient or members identify more strongly with their group (e.g. Mackie, 1986; Mackie & Cooper, 1984; Turner et al., 1989).

Integration   It has long been acknowledged that informational and normative approaches appear to work together to produce group polarization (Kaplan & Miller, 1987). Can we say which theory best accounts for the data? In fact, they each contribute something distinctive. Isenberg's (1986) meta-analysis, which predates the self-categorization account, reported significant effect sizes for both the normative account and, especially, the persuasive-arguments account. Which kind of influence is more important depends on the context. Kaplan (1987) concluded that normative influence was more likely with judgemental issues, a group goal of harmony, person-oriented group members and public responses, whereas informational influence was more likely with intellectual issues, a group goal of making a correct decision, task-oriented group members and private responses. The self-categorization account builds

on the other two approaches, because it contends that *arguments* from other ingroup members will be more persuasive than those of outgroup members, and that learning the *positions* held by different ingroup members will be more persuasive than learning about the positions of outgroup members.

Groupthink   Part of the explanation for research activity on group polarization is the potentially serious implications of polarization for decision-making in natural settings (Eagly & Chaiken, 1993). Such decisions are typically made by groups composed of like-minded participants (e.g. councils, committees, juries, the cabinets of ruling governments), and the processes involved may lead the groups to make decisions which are incorrect, unwise or, in the worst case, disastrous (Figure 8.17). This is most evident in the case of **groupthink**, a syndrome of poor group decision-making in which members of a cohesive ingroup strive for unanimity at the expense of a realistic appraisal of alternative courses of action (Janis, 1982; see Theory Box 8.4). Groupthink does not necessarily arise from group polarization, but it is an extreme form of problems associated with the failure to exchange information (or, at least, different views) among group members (Levine & Moreland, 1998). In essence, groupthink constitutes an extreme form of normative influence, where the norm to reach and maintain consensus and harmony within the group completely eliminates any

> **groupthink** a syndrome of poor group decision-making in which members of a cohesive ingroup strive for unanimity at the expense of a realistic appraisal of alternative courses of action.

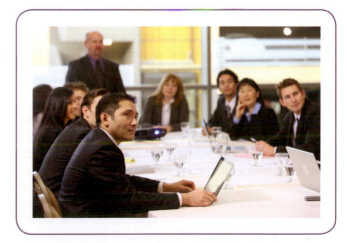

FIGURE 8.17 *Group polarization can have potentially serious implications for decision-making in natural settings such as committee meetings.*

Source: © Morgan Lane Photography. Used under licence from Shutterstock.

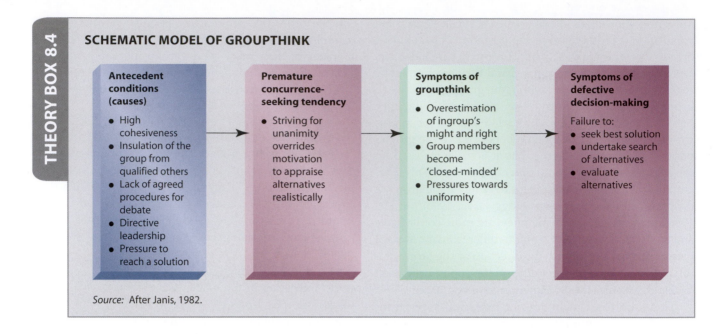

THEORY BOX 8.4

SCHEMATIC MODEL OF GROUPTHINK

Antecedent conditions (causes)
- High cohesiveness
- Insulation of the group from qualified others
- Lack of agreed procedures for debate
- Directive leadership
- Pressure to reach a solution

Premature concurrence-seeking tendency
- Striving for unanimity overrides motivation to appraise alternatives realistically

Symptoms of groupthink
- Overestimation of ingroup's might and right
- Group members become 'closed-minded'
- Pressures towards uniformity

Symptoms of defective decision-making
Failure to:
- seek best solution
- undertake search of alternatives
- evaluate alternatives

Source: After Janis, 1982.

informational influence that could show how disastrous the group's intended decision is likely to be.

The concept of groupthink (which alludes to 'Big Brother's' attempt to control the way people think, in George Orwell's 1949 novel, *Nineteen Eighty-Four*) has received a great deal of popular attention, because it claims to explain a series of US foreign-policy fiascos, including the calamitous Bay of Pigs invasion of Cuba (1961) and the escalation of the Vietnam War (1964–67). Janis applied work on group decisions to elite political settings by carrying out a series of case studies, in which he researched government records, political diaries and politicians' accounts of these turbulent periods (see also Raven, 1974; 't Hart, 1990). According to Janis, the main causes of groupthink include high cohesiveness, insulation of the group from external critics, opinionated leadership, lack of agreed procedures for debate and pressure to reach a solution. Specifically, Janis (1982) claimed that high cohesiveness in interaction with a stressful situation leads to groupthink; this outcome will be more likely the more structural weaknesses are present in the group (e.g. insulation, directive leadership and lack of agreed decision-making procedures).

In turn, some of the main characteristics of groupthink decision-makers are that they are more prone to jump to premature conclusions, dismiss contradictory information, bolster preferred options, suppress dissent within the group and display excessive optimism about the outcomes (Tetlock, 1998). Such decision-making is, moreover, not restricted to foreign-policy issues. Esser and Lindoerfer (1989) argued that the ill-fated decision to launch the *Challenger* space shuttle in 1986 (in which seven astronauts died, as the shuttle exploded 58 seconds after lift-off) had many of the hallmarks of groupthink (see also Starbuck & Farjoun, 2005).

Popular as the notion of groupthink is, its empirical support is rather weak. Analysis of case studies, often based on content analysis of available records, does show increased rigidity and more simplistic thinking among decision makers involved in groupthink decisions, compared to more favourable outcomes (Tetlock, 1979). Herek, Janis, and Huth (1987) also reported a negative association between the number of symptoms of groupthink and the quality of the decision. But there is little evidence that cohesiveness alone, or in combination with other supposed antecedents, contributes to defective decision-making. As Tetlock (1998) also points out, one can quite easily find successful political decisions in cases with evidence of groupthink (e.g. Churchill suppressed dissent in cabinet meetings in 1940–41 when some group members advocated a negotiated peace with Hitler), but also instances in which vigilant decision-making failed to prevent disastrous outcomes (e.g. President Jimmy Carter's failed mission to rescue hostages from Iran in 1980, despite his encouragement of open debate).

Laboratory studies are even less supportive, perhaps because it is difficult, if not impossible, to create in the laboratory true analogues of highly-cohesive, insulated groups, working under high pressure to make decisions with massive political consequences (Esser, 1998; Mullen, Anthony, Salas, & Driskell, 1994). Manipulations of groupthink have generally not produced poor-quality discussions and decisions (Flowers, 1977; Leana, 1985), and groupthink has been found in groups with either high- or low-cohesiveness (see Aldag & Fuller, 1993; Turner, Pratkanis, Probasco, & Leve, 1992).

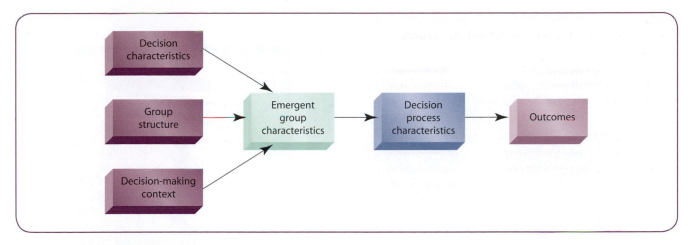

FIGURE 8.18 *Simplified general problem-solving model .*

Source: After Aldag & Fuller, 1993. Copyright © 1993 by the American Psychological Association. Adapted with permission. *Psychological Bulletin, 113,* 533–552. The use of APA information does not imply endorsement by APA.

There are, also, fundamental weaknesses of the groupthink model. It does not allow precise predictions, it is difficult to operationalize the concept (must all the characteristics of groupthink be present to define it as such?), and it is often only applied after-the-fact. Thus, Aldag and Fuller (1993) proposed a more general, but also more complex, group problem-solving model (see also 't Hart, Stern, & Sundelius, 1997). It includes many of the features discussed by Janis, but includes others. For example, it allows for cohesiveness to play a role, but it is seen as just one aspect of *group structure* (see Chapter 12) which, along with *decision characteristics* and *decision-making context*, determine *emergent group characteristics* (e.g. perceptions that the ingroup is moral and unanimous in its opinions); these characteristics, in turn, affect *decision process characteristics* (e.g. how carefully objectives are surveyed, and whether alternatives are generated), leading ultimately to *outcomes*. We present a simplified version of this model in Figure 8.18.

obedience to a source who is not an equal, but an authority figure (see Leader in the Field, Stanley Milgram). Obedience, here, is defined as complying with orders from a person of higher social status within a defined hierarchy or chain of command (Miller, 1995). It is often an example of the functioning of legitimate power, whereby an internalized framework of norms, values, customs and procedures specifies that such influence is appropriate (Turner, 1991; e.g. we are told to 'do as your parents/teachers/ senior officers tell you'). The motives underlying obedience are diverse, including respect for the expertise of authority and fear of the consequences of disobedience. In the following sections we will (1) outline Milgram's paradigm and initial results; (2) review some of the findings on the situational determinants of obedience; (3) evaluate the theoretical analysis of obedience; (4) consider ethical issues and alternatives to the Milgram paradigm for studying obedience; and (5) introduce the phenomenon of disobedience.

Obedience to authority

What are the main situational determinants of obedience to authority?

As we have seen in this chapter, social influence emanates from many sources, often group members of equal status to the target of influence. Research on **obedience to authority**, which began with Stanley Milgram's (1963) famous research, addresses a different form of influence, namely

obedience to authority complying with orders from a person of higher social status within a defined hierarchy or chain of command.

 LEADER IN THE FIELD

Stanley Milgram (1933–1984) earned his Bachelor's degree at Queens College, New York in 1954, but in political science: he never took a psychology course as an undergraduate. He completed his PhD at Harvard University, and taught at Yale University and the New School for Social Research, New York. Although best known for his research on obedience, Milgram also studied conformity, life in cities, and did pioneering work on nonreactive measures. His research across many diverse fields is characterized by its phenomenological approach, the salience of moral issues and the importance he attached to situational determinants of social behaviour. Milgram has recently received the honour of a full-length biography, entitled *The Man who Shocked the World: The Life and Legacy of Stanley Milgram* (Blass, 2004).

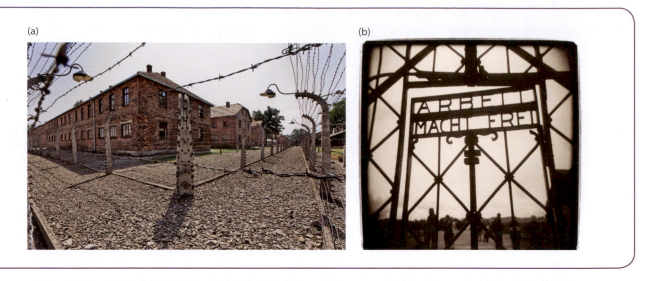

FIGURE 8.19(a) and (b) *Milgram's research into obedience was originally intended to help us to understand how the Nazi Holocaust could have taken place.*

Source: (a) © Bruno De Hogues. Used under licence from Getty Images; (b) © Robert Holmgren. Used under licence from Getty Images.

Milgram's obedience paradigm The classic research was conducted by Milgram (1963, 1974), who intended that his experimental research should help to understand better how the Nazi Holocaust (and all the individual acts of obedience involved in that systematic annihilation) could have taken place (Figure 8.19). Milgram was, specifically, fascinated with the trial in Jerusalem of the arch-architect of the 'final solution', Adolf Eichmann, as reported by the philosopher Hannah Arendt (1965) in her book *Eichmann in Jerusalem: A Report on the Banality of Evil*. If such evil were 'banal', or unexceptional, then would most people show destructive obedience? Prior to his research Milgram doubted it, and indeed his first study was intended to be the 'baseline', a situation in which few people would obey. Later research was then to manipulate key variables and investigate their impact on rates of obedience (see Milgram, 1963, 1974; see also Blass, 1999, 2000; Miller, Collins, & Brief, 1995).

We have already referred to some details of this notorious research to lay out principles of research methodology (see Chapter 2). Now we go into more detail, highlighting crucial aspects of the research, and referring to some of the 18 studies reported by Milgram in his 1974 book. For his first study Milgram recruited 40 male participants via newspaper advertisements (for a study on memory, with no mention made of obedience) to take part in a study at Yale University. At the laboratory, the investigator explained that a teacher–learner scenario would be used, and participants were led to believe that roles had been determined by chance. In fact, it was always arranged such that the 'learner' was the experimental confederate, and he was instructed to make

errors on the task in a pre-determined way. The experimenter explained that, by means of a simulated shock generator, the participant (as 'teacher') was to deliver increasingly more intense electric shocks to the 'learner' each time he made a mistake on the learning task (participants were informed that the shocks were extremely painful, but that they would cause no permanent damage; Milgram, 1963). In fact, no shocks were delivered, but the impact of the experimental scenario was so high that all participants believed that they were shocking the learner.

The learner was strapped into a chair and electrodes were fixed to his wrists. The teacher was taken to a different room, where he was instructed to punish the learner's first mistake with a shock of 15 volts, increasing in intensity by a further 15 volts with every new mistake. A shock generator in front of him showed the teacher 30 buttons, and clear verbal labels, ranging from '15V', through '60V' ('slight shock'), to '120V' ('moderate shock'), and finally to '450V' ('danger: severe shock XXX'). In a clever touch, at the onset of the study Milgram ensured that all participants experienced the reality of a relatively low-intensity electric shock (45 volts), so that they could not later claim that they had not believed they were really shocking the victim.

Milgram, a dramatist as much as an experimenter (see Blass, 1992), carefully *scripted* the whole scenario, down to the detail of having the experimenter wear a *grey* lab coat (indicating that he was a mere technician, rather than, as is frequently *mis*reported, a white coat, which might have signified that he was a higher-status physician or scientist). The victim's responses followed a predetermined series, rising in intensity with the level of shock: 'Ugh' (75, 90, 105 volts); 'Hey, this really hurts' (120 volts); 'Experimenter, get me out of here! I won't be in the experiment any more! I refuse to go on' (150 volts); screams of agony (270 volts); screams and refusal to answer (300, 315 volts); intense and prolonged agonized scream (330 volts). Likewise, the experimenter used a graded set of commands ('prods') to keep the teacher going: 'Please continue'; 'The experiment requires that you continue'; 'It is absolutely essential that you continue'; and 'You have no other choice, you *must* go on'. In this way Milgram ensured that his experimental scenario had a very high impact on participants without sacrificing control over the situation.

The results of this baseline study were staggering. Far from the minimal level of obedience expected, no participant stopped before administering a 300 volt shock. Across the sample, maximal obedience was shown by 26 of 40 respondents: 65 per cent. By comparison, in a later study, when participants were free to choose any shock level, only 2 out of 40 participants exceeded the 150 volts level, and 28 never went beyond 75 volts. Rather surprisingly, when Milgram moved the location of the study from a laboratory at a prestigious university to a room in a run-down building located in a nearby city, away from the university, he still found evidence for obedience (although the rate dropped from 65 per cent to 48 per cent).

Situational determinants of obedience The main thrust of Milgram's subsequent studies was to explore variation in the rate of obedience across different social situations. In various conditions, for example, Milgram manipulated the proximity of the victim, the authority of the experimenter and the behaviour of peers.

Four conditions varied the physical (and emotional) proximity of the victim. In one condition he pounded heavily on the wall separating his room from the teacher's; in another the participant heard his crying and shouting (as described earlier). In two other conditions the teacher and the victim were actually in the same room; in one condition, the teacher not only heard but also saw the victim; in the other condition, the teacher had to hold the victim's hand down on a shock plate. The obedience rates corresponding to these four conditions of increasing proximity are shown in Figure 8.20. Maximal obedience fell from 65 per cent of the participants to 30 per cent. Milgram also found that the duration of the shock given decreased with increasing proximity.

Milgram also varied the authority of the experimenter and how much control he exerted. This was hugely influential. When the experimenter was absent from the participant's room and gave his orders over the telephone, maximal obedience dropped to 21 per cent (a number of participants said over the phone that they were giving

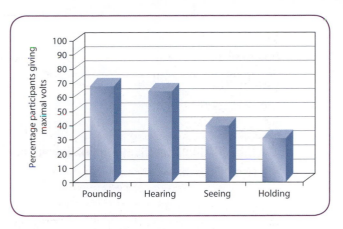

FIGURE 8.20 *Obedience as a function of physical proximity.*
Source: Data from Milgram, 1974.

higher shocks than they in fact did!). In another variation, the experimenter had to leave the room before instructing the participant to increase shock levels. He handed over his authority to a second participant who was present, and who would only have to record the learner's reaction times. This second participant then came up with the idea of increasing the shock level with every error and, throughout the learning session, he insisted that the teacher applied his rules. Only 20 per cent of the participants obeyed the equal-status authority to the end. In addition, when a participant refused to obey and the 'authority' decided that he would administer the shocks himself, a number of participants physically attacked the experimenter or tried to unplug the shock generator. Participants did not, however, show such heroism when the authority was the scientist in a lab coat.

Two experimental variations investigated the role of peer pressure. In the first there were three co-teachers, the participant and two confederates. The first confederate presented the task, the second recorded the learner's responses, and the participant administered the shocks. The first confederate refused to continue at 150 volts, and was joined by the second confederate at 210 volts. Their refusal had a dramatic effect on the participants: only 10 per cent were maximally obedient, compared with 65 per cent when no peer was present (see Figure 8.21). In contrast, if the teacher, who administered the learning task, was accompanied by a co-teacher who gave the shocks, 92 per cent of the participants participated in the experiment to the end.

Why do people obey? It is not convincing to argue that the participants (a majority of whom obeyed to high levels across most studies) were sadists. In one study by Milgram participants *chose* their own level of shock, and they opted for very low-level shocks. Surely sadists would have seized their opportunity here? Participants

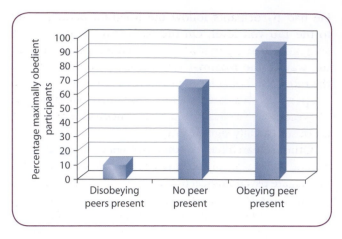

FIGURE 8.21 *Obedience as a function of peer behaviour.*
Source: Data from Milgram, 1974.

THEORY BOX 8.5

WHY DO WE OBEY?

- **Sociocultural perspective**
  - We learn to obey authority and expect to encounter legitimate, trustworthy authority
- **Binding factors**
  - Subtle creation of psychological barriers to disobedience; gradual increase in punishment levels in Milgram's research is a means of 'entrapment'
- **Responsibility**
  - **The agentic shift**: The subordinate in a hierarchical system does not accept personal responsibility for his or her actions but allocates responsibility to an individual higher in the organization
- **Situational factors**
  - Some situations are so 'strong' that they dominate individual differences in personality, and make us behave in extreme ways

Source: Based on data in Milgram, 1974.

also appeared to be distressed by the experience, often appearing tense, displaying nervous laughter, sweating profusely and even begging the experimenter to stop. This evidence tends to rule out both the possibility that participants were sadists, and the claim that they did not believe Milgram's cover story. Milgram's own theoretical analysis of obedience included four factors, which have received varying levels of support (see Theory Box 8.5).

First, and rather descriptively, Milgram argued for the importance of socio-cultural factors. We grow up in a society in which we learn (indeed, we are taught) to obey authorities, beginning with parents and school teachers, and ending with police officers. Moreover, we expect those authority figures to be legitimate and trustworthy.

Second, and more persuasively, Milgram pointed to 'binding factors', the subtle creation of psychological barriers to disobedience. He used the notion of 'entrapment' to refer to the experimenter's gradual increase in punishment levels ordered, rather than beginning with an outrageous demand which most participants would probably have refused. This approach can be seen as an instance of the 'foot-in-the-door' technique for obtaining compliance (Freedman & Fraser, 1966) discussed earlier, and this subtle progression towards destructive obedience may be crucial in helping us to understand how ordinary individuals can ultimately commit acts of evil (see Browning, 1992; Darley, 1992; Kelman & Hamilton, 1990; Miller, 1986).

Third, Milgram argued that the subordinate in a hierarchical system does not accept personal responsibility for his or her actions, but allocates this responsibility to someone higher up in the organization. He referred to this as an 'agentic shift', where the obedient participants switch off their own conscience and see themselves as *agents* for carrying out a more senior person's wishes. This, of course, is a convenient, self-serving account used by many perpetrators of evil, such as the former Iraqi

torturer's statement that 'I was following orders. Saddam [Hussein] is responsible' (reported in *The Observer*, 14 May 2006). Empirical support for this notion is, however, weak (see Nissani, 1990; Waller, 2002). Mantell and Panzarella (1976), in a replication of Milgram's research conducted in Germany, reported no relationship between participants' degree of obedience and their post-experimental assignment of responsibility. In his own post-experimental interviews Milgram asked participants to use a 'responsibility clock' to divide up responsibility between the experimenter, themselves and the victim. He did not, however, find that obedient participants assigned more responsibility to the experimenter. In fact, both obedient and disobedient participants attributed almost equal responsibility to the experimenter, which contradicts the claim that obedient participants somehow pass responsibility up the 'chain of command'. However, disobedient participants saw themselves as more responsible (and the learner-victim as less responsible) than did the obedient participants, whereas obedient participants assigned relatively less responsibility to themselves and relatively more responsibility to the learner-victim than did disobedient participants (see Milgram, 1974, Appendix II).

Fourth, and finally, Milgram's whole research programme placed huge emphasis on the power of the situation, something that is fundamental to the study of social psychology (see Chapter 1). His findings suggest that destructive obedience is well within the behavioural repertoire of most people (Miller, 1986), and he emphasized the power of the situation rather than personality factors. There is, in fact, some evidence of influential personality variables. Individuals who hold authoritarian beliefs are more likely to obey authorities (Elms & Milgram, 1966; Kelman & Hamilton, 1990), and participants high in empathic concern expressed a reluctance to continue with the procedure earlier than did participants lower on this trait, although they were not actually more likely to refuse to continue (in a study that stopped at the 150 volt level; Burger, 2009). Notwithstanding some evidence for personality variables, Milgram's paradigm highlights the power of the situation. To acknowledge this fact, however, is not to exonerate the perpetrators of evil deeds and adopt a morally condoning attitude towards them (Miller, Gordon, & Buddie, 1999). Harm-doing, which may well have been instigated by situational factors initially, demands self-regulation processes that definitely involve the actor-person himself (see Bandura, 1999). Hence Blass (1991) underlined the complexities of predicting obedience, arguing for both personality and situational factors, which should be studied in interaction.

Ethical issues and alternatives to the Milgram paradigm Milgram's research has become the most famous of all experiments in social psychology (it spawned TV programmes, films, a play, and even a song by Peter Gabriel, *We do what we're told*). It speaks to the darkest side of human nature, and has been used in attempts to understand better phenomena such as genocide (Staub, 1989) and war crimes (Bourke, 1999). But it also became infamous, generating controversy, centred on ethical issues (see Baumrind, 1964; Miller, 1986; see also Chapter 2). Milgram was severely criticized for inducing suffering in his participants. Using a procedure that would be impossible to replicate today given ethical guidelines for research, he induced stress and anxiety in his participants and, among those who did obey, guilt about how they had behaved. No contemporary study could inform participants that, although blatantly untrue, 'It is absolutely essential that you continue', or 'You have no other choice, you *must* go on'. Indeed, the furore caused by this research is credited with generating regulations that control the use of human participants in psychological research. More generally, some of the questions you may care to consider are: could the participants' psychological suffering be dealt with in normal debriefing? How would participants react, on learning that they were – apparently – capable of heinous acts in response to orders? Should the experiment have ever been carried out? Is the research sufficiently important to justify such deception of, and stress experienced by, participants? To what extent was the criticism triggered by the results, rather than the research itself?

It is, of course, because of the ethical issues that research using the Milgram paradigm can no longer be conducted. However, other milder forms of obedience can be, and have been, researched. Burger (2009) did actually conduct a partial replication of Milgram's paradigm in 2006, in which he protected the wellbeing of participants (in accordance with ethical guidelines).

He had participants follow the Milgram paradigm up to the 150 volt level. On the basis that 79 per cent of Milgram's participants who exceeded this point went all the way to the maximal shock level, he estimated that the rate of full obedience at 150 volts in his 2006 sample (70 per cent) was only slightly lower than Milgram's at 150 volts, 45 years earlier (82.5 per cent), a difference that is not statistically significantly.

Other research has explored obedience in less damaging and more ethically acceptable contexts, which can still investigate psychological processes in obedience, but simply not in the Milgram paradigm. The first alternative may strike you, in fact, as just as ethically dubious as Milgram's study. Sheridan and King (1972) conducted a conceptual replication of Milgram in which, rather than have participants ordered to give imagined shocks to a fake human victim, they gave actual shocks to a real canine victim, 'a cute, fluffy puppy' (p. 165) when it made errors on a discrimination task. The levels of actual shocks (ranging from 15-75 volts to 300-450 volts) were designed to create 'responses such as running, howling, and yelping, without, however, doing the [puppy] any serious harm' (p. 165). At the highest level (the shock indicator showed 300-450 volts, but the puppy actually received 800 volts at 1 milliamps) the actual voltage level was sufficient to produce 'continuous barking and howling' (p. 165). Under these conditions male and female participants showed maximal levels of obedience of comparable and higher levels, respectively, than in Milgram's paradigm.

Obedience has also been studied in the context of asking a participant to disrupt a job interview in the name of scientific research (Meeus & Raaijmakers, 1986, 1995). Another fascinating field study (Gamson, Fireman, & Rytina, 1982) telephoned volunteers to ask if they were willing to take part in various kinds of research, including research in which they would be misled about its purpose until later. Having agreed, participants were asked to go to a nearby hotel, in which they were asked to act in an unethical and damaging way towards an innocent victim in order to help a legal case on behalf of a large oil company against an individual. Under these conditions 25 per cent of participants fully complied with the request.

Finally, Slater et al. (2006) conducted a conceptual replication of Milgram's paradigm in an immersive virtual environment, in which a virtual human was to be shocked, with increasing voltage, for her mistakes in a series of memory tests. The virtual victim responded in comparable ways to Milgram's actual learner-victim, and participants responded – even at the physiological level (assessed by their galvanic skin responses) – as if she were actually real; they also responded with high levels of obedience. Two conditions were compared: 'visible' (in which the learner was seen and heard throughout, and responded to shocks with increasing signs of discomfort); and 'hidden' (in which the learner was only seen and heard briefly, at the start of the study, and thereafter responded through text). There was some evidence that participants showed a stronger desire to stop in the visible condition. These promising initial results suggest that virtual reality might provide a methodology by which future research on obedience could be conducted in a more ethically acceptable manner.

Disobedience Another valuable perspective on Milgram's research is whether the results are, in fact, so surprising. Later critics suggested that the experimenter may have played a more active role in instigating obedience than is evident from Milgram's (1965) early report (perhaps inducing obedience through demand characteristics; see Chapter 2), and that the evidence of *dis*obedience is itself remarkable (35 per cent of the participants defied the experiment at some point, and disobedient participants gave shocks of shorter duration). Early resistance seems crucial (only 17 per cent of those showing early signs of protest delivered shocks of more than 150 volts), a claim substantiated by re-analysis of some of Milgram's data.

Packer (2008) conducted a meta-analysis of data from eight of Milgram's obedience experiments, and reported that disobedience was most likely at 150 volts. This was the point at which the learner-victim supposedly receiving the shocks first asked to be released. Packer further reports that, across the studies, as obedience decreased, disobedience at 150 volts (but at no other level) increased. He concludes his analysis by proposing that disobedience is not simply associated with increasing expressions of pain on the part of the learner-victim. Rather, the 150 volt point is a 'critical decision point' (p. 301) at which participants acknowledged that the learner's right to terminate the experiment should override their obedience to the experimenter. Bocchiaro and Zimbardo (2010), using an administrative obedience paradigm based on Meeus and Raaijmakers (1986), also reported that disobedience at the victim's first request to be released was crucial. Interestingly, this evidence highlighting the importance of early resistance is consistent with Rochat and Modigliani's (1995) historical study of French citizens who, under Nazi rule during World War II, refused to persecute war refugees in the village of Le Chambon. Those who resisted, resisted early.

Whistle blowing is a specific form of disobedience, occurring when people report corruption or unethical practice within an organization (Miceli, Near, & Dworkin, 2008; Near & Miceli, 1985). Such behaviour is, however, relatively rare, not least because a significant proportion of whistle blowers

> **whistle blowing** a specific form of disobedience in which people report corruption or unethical practice within an organization.

are subjected to harassment from senior members of the organization, ostracism from peers (Glazer & Glazer, 1989; MacNamara, 1991; Miceli & Near, 1992) and are very likely to lose their jobs (Alford, 2001). Whistle blowers are, in effect, critics of the ingroup, who are generally damned for their temerity (see Hornsey, 2005). There is evidence from the medical domain suggesting that willingness to blow the whistle declines with time in training (Goldie, Schwartz, McConnachie, & Morrison, 2003). Apparently medical students learn to keep quiet by seeing the retaliation meted out to whistle blowers (Bolsin, 2003). Yet such courageous action is necessary, whether to stop medical malpractice (as in the case of the junior doctor who blew the whistle on a senior surgeon responsible for abnormally high mortality rates in paediatric heart surgery at a hospital in Bristol, UK during the 1990s) or mistreatment of prisoners of war (as in the case of the Navy dog handler who refused to be drawn into the abuse of Iraqi prisoners in Abu Ghraib prison; see Greenberg & Dratel, 2005). Yet as a rule such 'moral rebels' rarely receive the respect and support they deserve (Monin, Sawyer, & Marquez, 2008).

Research on obedience in perspective Whatever your view of Milgram's experiments (ethically acceptable – or not?; due to demand characteristics – or not?), every social psychologist should read and have an opinion about Milgram's research on obedience (see Blass, 1992). Subsequent studies in different countries and with various paradigms have demonstrated the generality of the effect he first demonstrated (e.g. Mantell, 1971; Meeus & Raaijmakers, 1986, 1995; Shanab & Yahya, 1978), and highlighted the importance of obedience in a range of settings, including military, medical and organizational contexts (see Brief, Dukerich, & Doran, 1991), and financial scandals that clearly involved an element of obedience or 'wilful blindness' (Heffernan, 2011; Swartz & Watkins, 2003; Toffler & Reingold, 2003). For example, in medical settings blind obedience of nurses to physicians' orders can lead to medication errors and even fatal consequences (Hofling, Brotzman, Dalrymple, Graves, & Pierce, 1966; Lesar, Briceland, & Stein, 1997; Rank & Jacobson, 1977).

Milgram specifically sought to extend Asch's conformity experiment to 'something more consequential than judging lengths of lines' (Blass, 1992, p. 286). In this he was hugely successful; destructive obedience is more widespread than most of us would ever have imagined. This research can, however, provide only part of the explanation for the excesses of the Third Reich, which Milgram set out to understand (see Miller, 2004). The Nazi Holocaust included many acts that were not simply acts of obedience to authority (see Browning, 1992;

Johnson & Reuband, 2005; Newman & Erber, 2002). As Berkowitz (1999) argued, the slaughter of millions of Jews and other 'undesirables' in the Holocaust cannot be reduced to the 'central dynamic' of obedience alone. Milgram's research does not represent many significant features of the Holocaust, including well-documented sadism and the individual psychology of those who initiated the barbaric policy, thus questioning his 'banality of evil' thesis (Haslam & Reicher, 2007, 2008).

Summary

The study of deliberate social influence introduces some of the most celebrated experiments ever carried out by social psychologists. We began by considering three main techniques of inducing compliance, based on requests – the door-in-the-face, the foot-in-the-door, and lowballing. Next, we reviewed the literature on majority versus minority social influence, showing how the field has moved from a narrow focus on majority influence only, to an understanding that both majorities and minorities can be influential and in various ways. We then reported on the tendency of groups to polarize individual members' views, and linked this to some of the extreme consequences of social influence in groups, as seen in groupthink. Finally, we reviewed research on obedience to authority, including Milgram's classic research, the ethical issues it raises and the phenomenon of whistle blowing.

CHAPTER SUMMARY

- *What are the main types of influence, and how can they be best understood?* This chapter discussed two main types of social influence, 'incidental' and 'deliberate,' and sought to understand them in terms of fundamental motives.

- *What is meant by social influence?* Social influence refers to change of attitudes, beliefs, opinions, values and behaviour, as a result of being exposed to other individuals' attitudes, beliefs, opinions, values and behaviour.

- *What is meant by incidental social influence?* Incidental social influence refers to situations in which people are influenced, although there has been no explicit attempt to influence them (e.g. social facilitation and inhibition effects).

- *How does the presence of other people affect task performance?* People are influenced by the presence or implied presence of others, which tends to improve performance on simple/well-learned tasks, but worsen performance on complex/novel tasks.

- *What are social norms, and why are they important?* Social norms are rules and standards that guide behaviour. They can be descriptive or injunctive; we can infer them from other people's behaviour, and they can be easily established and transmitted.

- *What drives social influence?* Social influence is driven by some of the fundamental motives directing human social behaviour. Ultimately, we are influenced by others so that we behave effectively, build and maintain relationships with others, manage our own self-concept, and understand the social world more effectively.

- *What are the main types of deliberate social influence?* Deliberate social influence includes inducing compliance with requests, the influence of numerical majorities and minorities, group decision-making and obedience to authority.

- *What are the main strategies for inducing compliance, and how do they work?* There is evidence for three main strategies of inducing compliance – door-in-the-face, foot-in-the-door, and lowballing – that rely greatly on general principles such as equity, reciprocity and self-consistency.

- *Are we only influenced by majorities, or can minorities also have an impact?* Both numerical majorities and minorities can exert influence, and the major explanations concern conflict and social categorization. Majorities tend to have greater influence on public and direct measures, but minorities can be more effective on indirect, private measures.

- *Overall, is conformity a 'good' or a 'bad' thing?* Conformity is a rather ambivalent concept. The very existence of a society depends on it, but it can be a force for good (e.g. encouraging donations to charity) as well as for bad (e.g. tyranny of the majority), and even evil (e.g. following others and behaving immorally).

- *What impact do groups have on decision-making?* Groups tend to polarize decisions, due to normative, informational and referent influence. Groupthink is proposed as an extreme form of poor decision-making, but its empirical and theoretical basis is rather weak.

- *When and why do we obey?* Obedience to authority is primarily driven by situational factors, but we still lack a clear explanation of why it occurs. Research on this topic poses important ethical questions, and more recent work on whistle blowing underlines the moral importance of disobedience.

SUGGESTIONS FOR FURTHER READING

Allen, V. L. (1975). Social support for nonconformity. In L. Berkowitz (Ed.), *Advances in experimental social psychology* (Vol. 8, pp. 1–43). New York: Academic Press. A detailed account of theory and research with respect to the factors leading to a reduction in conformity to a majority.

Anderson, N. B. (Ed.). (2009). Obedience – then and now [Special issue]. *American Psychologist, 64*(1), whole issue. A special issue on obedience, including a 2006 replication of Milgram and critical commentaries on what this later study does, and does not, actually tell us.

Asch, S. E. (1956). Studies of independence and conformity: A minority of one against a unanimous majority. *Psychological Monographs, 70*, 70. This text presents Asch's own account of his famous conformity experiments. The best way to learn about these studies is to read them firsthand.

Baron, R. S., & Kerr, N. L. (2003). *Group process, group decision, group action* (2nd ed.). Buckingham, UK: Open University Press. Extends the material presented in this chapter on social facilitation, majority and minority influence, and group decision-making.

Cialdini, R. B., & Trost, M. R. (1998). Social influence: Social norms, conformity, and compliance. In D. T. Gilbert, S. T. Fiske, & G. Lindzey (Eds.), *Handbook of social psychology* (4th ed., Vol. 2, pp. 151–192). Boston, MA: McGraw-Hill. Authoritative source, especially good on norms and compliance strategies.

Janis, I. L. (1972). *Victims of groupthink: A psychological study of foreign-policy decisions and fiascoes*. Boston, MA: Houghton Mifflin. Janis's original presentation of groupthink, illustrated with case materials showing disastrous decision-making in the area of foreign policy.

Martin, R., & Hewstone, M. (Eds.). (2010). *Minority influence and innovation: Antecedents, processes and consequences*. Hove, UK: Psychology Press (Taylor & Francis). An overview of contemporary theoretical approaches to and applications of minority influence.

Milgram, S. (1974). *Obedience to authority: An experimental view*. New York: Harper & Row. Compelling and readable overview of Milgram's own programme of 18 experiments, and the furore they unleashed.

Miller, A. G., Collins, B. E., & Brief, D. E. (1995). Perspectives on obedience to authority: The legacy of the Milgram experiments. *Journal of Social Issues, 51*, 1–19. A journal special issue on reactions to Milgram's obedience research and subsequent theory and research on obedient and defiant behaviour.

Sunstein, C. R. (2009). *Going to extremes: How like minds unite and divide*. New York: Oxford University Press. A readable guide to how group polarization impacts on social and political life, encouraging people to adopt extremism in their attitudes and behaviour.

Turner, J. C. (1991). *Social influence*. Buckingham, UK: Open University Press. A scholarly overview of the whole field, with a sophisticated theoretical analysis from the perspective of self-categorization theory.

9 Aggression

Barbara Krahé

Source: © Cesar Lucas Abreu. Used under licence from Getty Images.

KEY TERMS

- aggression
- Aggression Questionnaire (AQ)
- aggressive cues
- aggressive scripts
- bullying
- catharsis
- cognitive neo-associationist model
- collective violence
- Conflict Tactics Scales (CTS)
- cyberbullying
- direct aggression
- direct reinforcement
- displaced aggression
- excitation transfer theory
- frustration–aggression hypothesis
- general aggression model (GAM)
- geographic regions approach
- habituation
- heat hypothesis
- hormones
- hostile aggression
- hostile attribution bias
- indirect aggression
- instrumental aggression
- intergroup aggression
- interpersonal aggression
- intimate partner violence
- media violence–aggression link
- mobbing
- modelling
- peer nominations
- physical aggression
- post-traumatic stress disorder (PTSD)
- relational aggression
- sexual aggression
- staircase model
- steam boiler model
- terrorism
- time periods approach
- trait aggressiveness
- violence
- weapons effect

CHAPTER OUTLINE

ROUTE MAP OF THE CHAPTER

When asked what matters most to their sense of well-being and quality of life, people overwhelmingly put living in peace and harmony at the top on their list. Yet, at the same time, the world is full of conflict and discord, not only at the societal and political levels, but also in interpersonal relations, including interactions in school, at work and between family members and intimate partners. Why is it, then, that despite our desire to avoid aggression and violence, it is still such a big part of our lives, and why are we finding it so hard to create the peaceful and harmonious world that we all long for? The present chapter attempts to provide some answers to this fundamental question from the perspective of social psychology. After a brief discussion of how to define and measure aggression, we will review influential theories that seek to explain why people engage in aggressive behaviour. We will then ask why not all individuals are prone to aggression to the same extent, and why aggressive behaviour may be more likely in certain situations. We will pay special attention to the role of media violence in eliciting aggressive behaviour. In the second part of the chapter, we will examine different forms of aggression in society, such as family violence, sexual aggression, bullying in school and at the workplace, and aggression between groups. The chapter concludes with a review of strategies designed to reduce and prevent aggression.

INTRODUCTION

In 2008, the case of 'Baby P' shocked a nation. Tracey Connelly, 28, and her sadistic boyfriend Steven Barker, 33, were jailed for causing or allowing the death of 17-month-old Peter Connelly in his blood-spattered room in Haringey, North London. He had suffered dozens of injuries after months of abuse at the time of his death, including a broken back and fractured ribs.

In March 2009, the small town of Winnenden in Germany was the scene of a school massacre in which a 17-year-old killed nine students and three teachers at his former school, shooting three further people during his flight from police before turning his gun against himself. A news magazine reported at the time: 'Tim K. was by all accounts a quiet but friendly boy, say those who knew him – then he became a mass murderer. Police are trying to find out what made him kill 15 people and finally himself.' (*Der Spiegel*, March 12 2009).

aggression any form of behaviour intended to harm or injure another living being who is motivated to avoid such treatment.

intimate partner violence perpetration or threat of an act of physical violence within the context of a dating or marital relationship.

bullying denotes aggressive behaviour directed at victims who cannot easily defend themselves, typically in schools and at the workplace.

terrorism politically motivated violence, intended to spread fear and terror among members of a society in order to influence the decision-making or behaviour of political agents.

These two examples highlight the disturbing but undeniable fact that **aggression** as a destructive form of social behaviour is prevalent in human interactions on a large scale. Aggression permeates close relationships (e.g. child abuse and **intimate partner violence**), workplace interactions (e.g. **bullying**), intergroup relationships (e.g. football hooliganism and gang violence) and contacts between ethnic or political groups (e.g. **terrorism** and international warfare). Therefore, social psychologists' concern with understanding the processes that trigger, intensify or pre-empt aggressive behaviour is by no means a purely scientific one. Instead, it is motivated by the aim to create a knowledge base from which we can develop interventions to reduce and prevent aggression to make the world a more peaceful place.

The review of social psychological theory and research on aggression offered in this chapter is guided by five key questions:

1. How do social psychologists define aggressive behaviour and what are their main methods for studying it?

2. How can we explain why individuals show aggressive behaviour and what are the processes that lead from an aggression-eliciting stimulus to an aggressive response?

3. Do people differ in their propensity to engage in aggressive behaviour, and what are critical factors in the situation or the social environment that make aggressive behaviour more likely?

4. What do we know about the prevalence and the risk factors of intimate partner violence, sexual aggression, bullying and violence between groups?

5. What can be done to prevent or reduce aggression?

DEFINITION AND MEASUREMENT OF AGGRESSIVE BEHAVIOUR

How do social psychologists define aggressive behaviour and what are their main methods for studying it?

When social psychologists talk about aggression, they look at it as a form of social behaviour, that is, behaviour shown by one person or group towards another individual or group. In a widely accepted definition, Baron and Richardson (1994, p. 7) characterized aggression as 'any form of behavior directed toward the goal of harming or injuring another living being who is motivated to avoid such treatment.' Broadly speaking, 'harm' denotes any form of treatment unwanted by the target person, such as causing physical injury, hurting their feelings, damaging their social relationships by spreading rumours or taking away or destroying cherished possessions. It is important to add that, of course, individuals may act aggressively against themselves up to the point of taking their own life. However, this form of self-inflicted harm does not represent a form of interpersonal behaviour, and is therefore outside the focus of the social psychological perspective on aggression adopted in this chapter. In terms of distinguishing aggression from other forms of social behaviour, Baron and Richardson's (1994) definition has three important implications:

(1) Aggressive behaviour is characterized by its underlying motivation (to harm or injure another

living being), *not* by its consequences (whether or not harm or injury actually occurs). This means that a behaviour is regarded as aggressive if it was guided by the intention to harm, even if no damage was done to the target. A shot fired from a gun may miss its target, but if the shot was intended to hit the target, it is nonetheless an instance of aggression. On the other hand, your dentist may cause you pain, but it is incidental or accidental, and not intended; hence it is not aggression.

(2) A necessary feature of the intention to harm is the actor's understanding that the behaviour in question has the potential to cause harm or injury to the target. If one person's actions lead to harm or injury of another, but the actor could not have expected or been aware that the behaviour could lead to those adverse effects, they do not represent instances of aggression. They could be due to carelessness or incompetence, but do not actually reflect an intention to harm.

(3) Defining aggression as behaviour that the target would want to avoid means that harmful actions performed at the target's request, such as painful medical procedures carried out with the consent of the patient, or sadomasochistic sexual practices, do not represent instances of aggression.

> **violence** behaviours carried out with intention to cause serious harm that involve the use or threat of *physical force*.

The term **violence** is more narrow in meaning and restricted to behaviours carried out with intention to cause serious harm that involve the use or threat of *physical force*, such as hitting someone over the head. Thus, not all instances of aggression are violence (e.g. shouting at someone would be aggressive, but not violent), but all acts of violence qualify as aggression.

Aggressive behaviour may be divided into more specific subcategories, such as physical and verbal aggression, spontaneous (unprovoked) and reactive (provoked) aggression, individual and group aggression. It is also important to distinguish between direct aggression that involves a face-to-face confrontation between the aggressor and the target, and indirect aggression, which is aimed at harming other people by spreading rumours or otherwise damaging their peer relationships behind their back (Björkqvist, Lagerspetz, & Kaukiainen, 1992). Indirect aggression overlaps with another term, **relational aggression**, used by some authors to denote aggression aimed at damaging the target person's social relationships (Crick & Grotpeter, 1995; see Archer & Coyne, 2005, for

> **relational aggression** behaviour that is intended to harm the target person through damaging his or her social relationships, for example negative comments behind the person's back.

more detailed definitions). Because indirect/relational aggression can be inflicted covertly, without the target being aware of the aggressor's identity, it represents an alternative strategy for harming another person when the costs of engaging in direct forms of aggression would be high.

Aggression, whether expressed in physical or verbal, direct or indirect forms, can be linked to different underlying motives captured by the distinction between instrumental and hostile (also called *angry* or *affective*) aggression. People carry out acts of **instrumental aggression** for the purpose of achieving a particular goal, such as taking a hostage in order to secure a ransom, or committing a terrorist act in pursuit of a political goal. Here, the behaviour is driven by the ultimate goal the actor wants to achieve (obtaining a large sum of money or overthrowing a government). Aggression is selected as one of several possible means towards reaching that end, and harm is accepted as a side effect of reaching the goal by means of aggression. In contrast, **hostile aggression** is motivated by the actor's desire to express negative feelings, such as anger, and the primary motive is to harm the target person or group.

> **instrumental aggression** aggressive behaviour performed to reach a particular goal, as a means to an end.

> **hostile aggression** aggressive behaviour motivated by the desire to express anger and hostile feelings.

The *measurement of aggressive behaviour* creates particular challenges for researchers due to its potentially harmful nature. When studying prosocial behaviour, creating situations in which research participants may give help to others is not problematic from an ethical point of view (see Chapter 2 on ethics in research and Chapter 10 on prosocial behaviour). By contrast, it would be unethical to set up experimental situations in which research participants are given the chance to inflict genuine harm on another person or to expose them to treatments expected to increase the likelihood of subsequent aggression. In addition, except for unusual circumstances such as war or civil unrest, acts of severe aggression are relatively rare in everyday life, and therefore hard to measure in natural contexts. Therefore, aggression researchers' methodological toolbox is limited. The available strategies for measuring aggressive behaviour can be organized under two broad headings: *observation* – data collected by the researcher; and *reporting* – data obtained from other sources, such as the research participants or independent observers. In addition, aggression researchers can draw upon archival data collected for other purposes, such as crime statistics, newspaper reports and records of historical events, for example lynchings.

Observation of aggressive behaviour

The most common method for studying aggressive behaviour by observation is the *laboratory experiment* in which aggressive behaviour is observed as a function of experimental conditions created by the researcher (see Chapter 2 for a discussion of experimental methods). Experimental studies of aggression need to resort to paradigms in which participants can show behaviour *intended* to harm another person without actually allowing any harm to be inflicted on the target. Several experimental paradigms have been developed to address this challenge (see Krahé, 2012, for a comprehensive discussion). They create situations in which participants are given the opportunity to deliver aversive stimuli to another person, in the form of electric shocks (Giancola & Parrott, 2008), loud noise (Bartholow & Anderson, 2002), cold water (Vasquez, Denson, Pedersen, Stenstrom, & Miller, 2005) or unpleasantly hot spicy sauce (the 'hot sauce' paradigm; Lieberman, Solomon, Greenberg, & McGregor, 1999). Using the extent to which research participants deliver aversive stimuli to another person as a measure of aggression, researchers can study the effects of various independent variables – such as frustration, alcohol consumption, or exposure to media violence – on aggression (**media violence–aggression link**) as the dependent variable.

> **media violence– aggression link** hypothesis that exposure to violent media contents makes media users more aggressive.

Despite their artificial nature, these experimental procedures for measuring aggressive behaviour do have construct validity; that is, correspondence amongst each other and with other indicators, such as aggressive behaviour observed in natural settings (Anderson & Bushman, 1997; see Chapter 2 on types of validity). Because they allow researchers to observe variations in aggressive behaviour as a result of their experimental manipulations, such as creating a high versus low level of frustration, experimental procedures facilitate the testing of hypotheses about why, when and on what scale aggressive behaviour is shown.

Obtaining reports of aggressive behaviour

An important source of information about the occurrence of aggression in natural contexts is provided by *behavioural self-reports* in which individuals describe their own aggressive tendencies. A range of measures has been developed to assess self-reported dispositional aggression; that is, individual differences in how aggressive people are in general. A widely used instrument is the **Aggression Questionnaire** (known as the AQ) by Buss and Perry (1992). Individual Differences 9.1 presents the items from the Aggression Questionnaire. Take a look at it now to find out how high you score on trait aggression.

> **Aggression Questionnaire (AQ)** self-report instrument to measure stable individual differences in trait aggressiveness.

Self-report questionnaires have also been developed to assess aggression in particular domains, such as the 'Sexual Experiences Survey' (known as the SES) by Koss et al. (2007) eliciting men's reports of **sexual aggression** (see Leader in the Field, Mary Koss). The problem with using self-reports to measure aggression is that it is a socially undesirable behaviour. People may be unwilling to disclose their aggressive behaviour in an effort to provide socially desirable answers, resulting in an underestimation of the true scale of aggression.

> **sexual aggression** forcing another person into sexual activities through a range of coercive strategies, such as threat or use of physical force, exploitation of the victim's inability to resist, or verbal pressure.

Given these limitations of self-report measures of aggression, an alternative is to use peer/other nominations; that is, reports by informed others, such as parents, teachers or class-mates, about the aggressive behaviour of a target person. These reports by others are less susceptible to the problem of social desirability. For example, Lefkowitz, Eron, Walder, and Huesmann (1977) showed that peer-rated aggression was linked to the level of violence in 8-year-old boys' favourite and most frequently watched TV programmes (see Research Close-Up 9.1, p. 292–293). Boys who were rated more aggressive by their peers tended to watch more violent TV. **Peer nominations**

> **peer nominations** method for measuring (aggressive) behaviour by asking other people (e.g. classmates) to rate the aggressiveness of an individual.

LEADER IN THE FIELD

Mary Koss completed a PhD in Clinical Psychology at the University of Minnesota in 1972 and is currently Professor of Public Health, Psychiatry and Psychology in the Mel and Enid Zuckerman Arizona College of Public Health at the University of Arizona. Mary Koss established the study of sexual aggression against women on the international research agenda, and developed the 'sexual experiences survey' as the most widely used research tool to measure women's victimization by and men's perpetration of sexual aggression. She received the 2000 Award for Distinguished Contributions to Research in Public Policy from the American Psychological Association, and served as a member of the Coordinating Committee of the Sexual Violence Research Initiative begun under the auspices of the World Health Organization. Important publications include a two-volume co-edited collection of chapters in 2011 on violence against women and children.

can be used to validate self-reports or to identify differences between actors and observers in the perception of aggressive behaviour.

A final source of data on aggressive behaviour is provided by *archival records*, most notably crime statistics, such as the Uniform Crime Reports in the US or the Criminal Statistics in England and Wales (see Chapter 2 for other uses of archival records). These data sources are not compiled for research purposes, and therefore researchers are limited to whatever information is available in the data base. However, crime statistics are informative about the incidence of particular forms of aggression, such as intimate partner violence, child sexual abuse or homicide. They can also be used for hypothesis testing, for example about the link between high temperature and violent crime (e.g. Anderson, Anderson, Dorr, DeNeve, & Flanagan, 2000; see Social Psychology Beyond the Lab 9.1, p. 291). Another example of archival records is provided by newspaper reports that have been used, for example, to analyse violent behaviour by lynch mobs. Based on newspaper reports of 60 lynchings in the United States between 1899 and 1946, Mullen (1986) demonstrated that lynch mobs were more savage in their atrocities the larger the mob relative to the number of

INDIVIDUAL DIFFERENCES 9.1

WHERE DO YOU STAND ON TRAIT AGGRESSION?

Items of the Aggression Questionnaire (AQ) by Buss and Perry (1992)

Response scale:

1	2	3	4	5
extremely uncharacteristic of me				extremely characteristic of me

Physical aggression

1. Once in a while I can't control the urge to strike another person.
2. Given enough provocation, I may hit another person.
3. If somebody hits me, I hit back.
4. I get into fights a little more than the average person.
5. If I have to resort to violence to protect my rights, I will.
6. There are people who pushed me so far we came to blows.
7. I can think of no good reason for ever hitting a person.*
8. I have threatened people I know.
9. I have become so mad that I have broken things.

Verbal aggression

10. I tell my friends openly when I disagree with them.
11. I often find myself disagreeing with people.
12. When people annoy me, I may tell them what I think of them.
13. I can't help getting into arguments when people disagree with me.
14. My friends say that I'm somewhat argumentative.

Anger

15. I flare up quickly but get over it quickly.
16. When frustrated, I let my irritation show.
17. I sometimes feel like a powder keg ready to explode.
18. I am an even-tempered person.*
19. Some of my friends think I'm a hothead.
20. Sometimes I fly off the handle for no good reason.
21. I have trouble controlling my temper.

Hostility

22. I am sometimes eaten up with jealousy.
23. At times I feel I have gotten a raw deal out of life.
24. Other people always seem to get the breaks.
25. I wonder why sometimes I feel so bitter about things.
26. I know that 'friends' talk about me behind my back.
27. I am suspicious of overly friendly strangers.
28. I sometimes feel that people are laughing at me behind my back.
29. When people are especially nice, I wonder what they want.

Please give each item a number from 1 to 5 depending on how characteristic it is of you.

Reverse the coding on the items marked with * so that high scores always mean high aggressiveness. Then compute the mean of the items for each scale.

In the Buss and Perry (1992) study, men had significantly higher scores on physical aggression, verbal aggression, and hostility, but not on anger. The sex difference was largest on the physical aggression scale.

You can compare your mean score on each scale to the following mean scores derived from Buss and Perry (1992, Table 3), based on US college students:

Scale	Men (N = 612)	Women (N = 641)
Physical aggression	2.70	1.98
Verbal aggression	3.04	2.70
Anger	2.42	2.38
Hostility	2.66	2.52

Source: Copyright ©1992 by the American Psychological Association. Adapted from Buss & Perry, with permission.

victims. Mullen used these data to argue that the larger the mob, the more difficult it is for members to retain self-focused attention that is important for inhibiting violent behaviour. We will return to this issue in our discussion of intergroup aggression later in the chapter.

Summary

Aggression is defined in social psychology as behaviour carried out with the *intention* to harm another person. The range of methods available for studying aggression is limited by the essentially harmful nature of this behaviour. For ethical reasons, researchers cannot create situations in which harm is inflicted on another person. The main methods for studying aggressive behaviour include observations of aggressive behaviour in laboratory experiments that provide an opportunity for behavioural analogues of real-life aggression (such as administering electric shocks or aversive noise), and the collection of reports of aggressive behaviour in the form of self-reports, reports from peers, parents or teachers, or archival records, such as statistical data on violent crime.

THEORIES OF AGGRESSION

How can we explain why individuals show aggressive behaviour and what are the processes that lead from an aggression-eliciting stimulus to an aggressive response?

Developing theories to explain why people engage in aggressive behaviour has been a prime objective for researchers from different disciplines, not least because understanding the factors that promote aggressive behaviour is a first step towards prevention. Table 9.1

Table 9.1 *Major theories of aggression.*

	Aggression conceptualized as ...	Data base	Empirical evidence
Biological Approaches			
Ethology	... internal energy released by external cues; steam boiler model	Animal studies	No support as a model for human aggression, but still popular in lay discourse
Behaviour genetics	... transmitted as part of genetic makeup	Twin + adoption studies	Support for the predictive value of genetic similarity
Hormonal explanations	... influenced by male sex hormones and cortisol	Comparisons of violent and non-violent individuals	Some empirical support
Psychological approaches			
Frustration–aggression hypothesis	... as a likely response to frustration, likelihood enhanced by aggressive cues	Experimental studies	Supported by empirical evidence
Cognitive neo-associationist model and excitation transfer	... as a result of affect elicited by aversive stimulation that is interpreted as anger	Experimental studies	Supported by empirical evidence
Learning theory	... as a result of reinforcement, either direct or indirect (observed)	Experimental + observational studies	Supported by empirical evidence
Social information processing models	... as a result of social information processing, enactment of learned scripts	Experimental + longitudinal studies	Supported by empirical evidence

provides a summary of the major theoretical models discussed in this section.

Biological approaches

Biological explanations of aggression refer to evolutionary and genetic principles as well as the role of hormones to explain why individuals differ in their tendency to engage in aggressive behaviour.

(1) The *ethological perspective*, represented most prominently by Konrad Lorenz (1966), looks at aggressive behaviour of animals and humans as driven by an internal energy which is released by aggression-related stimuli. In his well-known **steam boiler model**, Lorenz assumed that aggressive energy is produced continuously within the organism until it is released by an external cue, such as the appearance of a rival in the contest for a mating partner. If the amount of energy rises beyond a certain level without being released by an external stimulus, it will overflow, leading to spontaneous aggression. According to this view, aggressive behaviour is the inevitable consequence of a continuous production of aggressive energy. Even if it were possible to remove all instigating stimuli, this would not resolve the problem. As Lorenz (1966, p. 269) put it, such an attempt would be 'as judicious as trying to counteract the increasing pressure in a continuously heated boiler by screwing down the safety valve more tightly'.

> **steam boiler model**
> part of Konrad Lorenz's theory of aggression, assuming that aggressive energy is produced continuously within the organism and will burst out spontaneously unless released by an external stimulus.

Psychologists have challenged Lorenz's application of his findings from animal studies to human aggression (e.g. Lore & Schultz, 1993). An important criticism is directed at the assumption that once the internal reservoir of aggressive energy has been used up by an aggressive act, it is impossible to trigger another aggressive response for as long as it takes the organism to rebuild a sufficient energy level. There is ample evidence from school shootings and other instances of multiple killings that humans can, tragically, perform several aggressive behaviours in quick succession, and that one aggressive act often serves to precipitate rather than suppress further aggressive acts.

(2) Researchers in the field of *behaviour genetics* examine the extent to which individual differences in aggressive behaviour can be linked to differences in genetic make-up (Plomin, Nitz, & Rowe, 1990). Specifically, behaviour geneticists have used twin and adoption studies to demonstrate that genetically related individuals are more similar in terms of their aggressive tendencies than individuals who are not genetically related (Figure 9.1). *Adoption studies* are capable of separating the influence

FIGURE 9.1 *Our genes partly determine how aggressive we are, but so too does the social environment.*
Source: © Irena Rogona. Used under licence from Shutterstock.

of genetic and environmental studies by comparing individuals to their biological parents (shared genes) and to their adoptive parents (shared environment). *Twin studies* compare identical and fraternal twins in terms of the similarity of their aggressive tendencies. Identical twins share 100 per cent of their genetic make-up, while fraternal twins only have 50 per cent genetic similarity. Therefore, evidence that identical twins are more similar than fraternal twins in their aggressive behaviour would support the idea that aggression is to some extent genetically transmitted. A meta-analysis of twin and adoption studies by Miles and Carey (1997) concluded that on the basis of self- and other-reports of aggression, shared genetic makeup accounted to a substantial degree for similarities between identical twins as well as between adopted children and their biological parents, explaining up to 50 per cent of the variance. However, an important qualification comes from the two studies in the meta-analysis that used behavioural observation as a measure of aggression. In these studies, the impact of shared environment was substantially greater than that of genetic similarity. A later meta-analysis by Rhee and Waldman (2002) also found substantial effects of genetic similarity, explaining 41 per cent of the variance, but environmental influences were even stronger with 59 per cent. Thus, the evidence from a broad range of studies suggests that aggressive behaviour is affected both by genetic dispositions and by socialization experiences in the course of individual development. An individual's genetic make-up may dispose him or her towards becoming an aggressive person, but environmental factors play a crucial role in determining whether or not that disposition will actually be expressed in aggressive behaviour.

hormones higher levels of testosterone and lower levels of cortisol have been linked to aggression, but they need to be considered in combination with environmental influences.

(3) Another line of biological research on aggression is concerned with the role of hormones in relation to aggressive behaviour (see Van Goozen, 2005, for a review). An obvious candidate to examine in this context is the male sex hormone testosterone, both to account for individual differences among men in their aggressive tendencies and to explain the widely demonstrated gender differences in physical aggression. Testosterone is related to the activation of fight impulses and the inhibition of flight or avoidance behaviour, thereby increasing the likelihood of an aggressive response. A meta-analysis of 18 studies conducted by Archer, Birring, and Wu (1998) found that highly aggressive men had higher levels of testosterone than non-aggressive men. In terms of situational variations of testosterone levels, Klinesmith, Kasser, and McAndrew (2006) conducted an interesting experimental study. They asked male participants to handle a gun or a children's toy for 15 minutes and measured testosterone levels before and after. Men who had handled the gun showed a significant increase in testosterone, whereas those who had handled the toy did not. Those who handled the gun also showed more aggressive behaviour in a subsequent phase, as measured by the 'hot sauce' paradigm, and this effect could be explained at least partly by the increase in testosterone levels shown in the group that handled the gun. Nonetheless, Van Goozen (2005, p. 287) concluded that the link between male sex hormones and aggression is much weaker in humans than in animals.

physical aggression behaviour that is intended to inflict physical harm on the target person.

Cortisol has been examined as another hormonal correlate of aggression as it is related to the experience and management of stress. Low cortisol levels have been linked to fearlessness, risk taking and insensitivity to punishment. Longitudinal studies have shown that low levels of resting cortisol in boys predict aggressive behaviour over time (e.g. Shoal, Giancola, & Kirillova, 2003; see also McBurnett, Lahey, Rathouz, & Loeber, 2000). Psychological under-reactivity, as indicated by low cortisol, seems to be a characteristic feature of aggressive and antisocial behaviour and plays a role in disinhibiting aggressive behaviour. By way of explanation, it has been argued that individuals with low levels of cortisol are less susceptible to fear of punishment that would stop them from engaging in aggressive behaviour (Raine, 1996). It is clear, however, that hormones do not shape aggressive behaviour in a deterministic fashion. They work together with a wide range of factors in the social environment that may reinforce or attenuate the impact of biological influences on aggression.

Psychological approaches

Early psychological models also assumed aggression to be an innate response tendency. Freud's (1920) view of aggression as an instinct in the service of the pleasure principle inspired the **frustration–aggression hypothesis**, which regards aggression as driven by the goal of overcoming frustration. Subsequent psychological approaches widened the frustration–aggression link into a more general model of negative affect and highlighted the role of cognitive factors, learning experiences and social information processing in predicting aggressive responses.

frustration–aggression hypothesis assumes that frustration – that is, blockage of a goal-directed activity – increases the likelihood of aggressive behaviour.

The frustration–aggression hypothesis One of the earliest empirically-tested theories about the origins of aggressive behaviour is the frustration–aggression hypothesis (Dollard, Doob, Miller, Mowrer, & Sears 1939; Miller, 1941). It states that 'frustration produces instigations to a number of different types of response, one of which is an instigation of some form of aggression' (Miller, 1941, p. 338; see Leader in the Field, Neal E. Miller). In this view, aggression is not the only, but a possible response to frustration. Whether or not frustration will result in an aggressive response depends on the influence of additional variables in the individual or the environment. Fear of punishment for overt aggression or unavailability of the frustrator are factors that inhibit aggression. Frustration that cannot be expressed

LEADER IN THE FIELD

Neal E. Miller (1909–2002) received his PhD in Psychology from Yale University in 1935 and held professorial posts at Yale University and Rockefeller University in New York. He was the architect of the frustration–aggression hypothesis that laid the groundwork for subsequent socio-cognitive and neo-associationist models of aggression. He stressed that aggression is not an inevitable, but a likely response to frustration, and drew attention to the need to specify conditions under which frustration is likely to lead to aggression. Berkowitz's (see Leader in the Field, Leonard Berkowitz, this chapter) model of aggressive cues and subsequent cognitive neo-associationist view built upon his ideas. His views on displaced aggression were recently revitalized and elaborated by Norman Miller and colleagues in their 'triggered displaced aggression model' (Miller, Pedersen, Earleywine, & Pollock, 2003).

displaced aggression
tendency to respond to frustration with an aggressive response directed not at the original source of the frustration but at an unrelated, more easily accessible target.

in retaliation against the original source is often **displaced**; that is, directed at an innocent target person who is more easily accessible or less threatening. In a meta-analysis including 49 studies, Marcus-Newhall, Pedersen, Carlson, and Miller (2000) found consistent evidence that frustrated individuals show displacement of aggression from the source of the frustration onto a less powerful or more accessible target.

If aggression is one of several potential consequences of frustration, it is important to identify the conditions under which individuals are likely to show aggressive behaviour when frustrated. One variable shown to enhance the probability of an aggressive response to a frustration is the presence of **aggressive cues**.

aggressive cues
situational cues with an aggressive meaning that increase the accessibility of aggressive cognitions.

Aggressive cues are aspects of the situation that draw the actor's attention to the possibility of an aggressive response (Figure 9.2), such as seeing pictures of people fighting, or being presented with the names of famous boxing champions. In a much-cited study, Berkowitz and LePage (1967) demonstrated that participants who had previously been angered by receiving negative feedback administered more electric shocks (as a measure of aggression) in the presence of weapons – that is, aggressive cues – than in the presence of a badminton racket (i.e. a neutral object) or in a no-object control condition (Figure 9.3). They were told that the object (the weapon or the badminton racket) had been left behind in the lab room by a previous experimenter unassociated with the frustration situation, or by the confederate who had delivered the negative feedback. It made no difference whether the weapon was associated or unassociated with the person who was the source of the frustration. The number of shocks administered by the frustrated participants is shown in Figure 9.3.

weapons effect
finding that individuals who were previously frustrated showed more aggressive behaviour in the presence of weapons than in the presence of neutral objects.

Although subsequent studies have not always replicated the effect – some failing to find a **weapons effect**, and others finding an effect in nonfrustrated participants as well – overall support for the role of aggression-related cues in facilitating aggressive behaviour is impressive. From their meta-analysis of 57 studies, Carlson, Marcus-Newhall, and Miller (1990, p. 632) concluded that 'aggression-related cues present in experimental settings act to increase aggressive responding'. The effect was particularly pronounced among participants who were first angered, but the authors also found an effect, albeit weaker, of aggressive cues on participants in a neutral

FIGURE 9.2 *Does seeing a gun make us more likely to behave aggressively?*

Source: © Gregory James Van Raalte. Used under licence from Shutterstock.

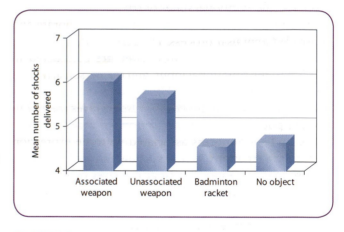

FIGURE 9.3 *Angered participants delivered more electric shocks to the frustrator in the presence of a weapon.*

Note: The means between the associated and unassociated weapons conditions and between the badminton racket and the no object conditions were not significantly different.

Source: Adapted from Berkowitz & LePage, 1967, Table 2. Copyright © 1967 by the American Psychological Association. Adapted with permission. *Journal of Personality and Social Psychology, 7,* 202–207. The use of APA information does not imply endorsement by APA.

mood state. The finding that the impact of aggressive cues is not limited to situations in which the person is already in an angry mood suggests that aggressive cues have a wide-ranging potential to activate ('prime') cognitive schemata related to aggression and thus increase the salience of aggressive response options.

Cognitive neo-associationism and excitation transfer Berkowitz (1993) extended the frustration–aggression hypothesis into a more general conceptualization of the role of negative affect as a trigger for

cognitive neo-associationist model explains aggressive behaviour as the result of negative affect that is subjected to cognitive processing and activates a network of aggression-related thoughts and feelings.

aggressive behaviour (see Leader in the Field, Leonard Berkowitz). He termed his model the **cognitive neo-associationist model**, and argued that frustration is just one type of stimulus that elicits negative affective arousal. Other aversive stimuli, such as pain or loud noise, may in the same way lead to aggressive responses via eliciting anger. He proposed that aversive (unpleasant) stimuli give rise to unspecific negative feelings that evoke two immediate reactions, fight and flight. In a swift and automatic appraisal process that occurs with little or no conscious awareness, the fight impulse is associated with aggression-related thoughts, memories and behavioural responses, whereas flight is associated with escape-related responses. These responses serve to quickly channel the initially undifferentiated negative affect into the more specific emotional states of (rudimentary) anger or (rudimentary) fear. In a subsequent more elaborate and controlled appraisal process, the person *interprets* these basic or rudimentary feelings. They are considered in relation to the situational input, and the person arrives at a more specific and consolidated emotional state: anger *or* fear. This cognitive processing also involves the evaluation of potential outcomes, memories of similar experiences, and social norms associated with the expression of different emotions. Figure 9.4 illustrates this process.

Although the model stops at the level of emotional responses, it is assumed that when the evaluation gives rise to feelings of anger, irritation or annoyance, an aggressive response becomes likely. For example, when a child is hit by a stone thrown by a classmate, he will immediately experience pain, associated with negative affect (probably a combination of anger, inducing the

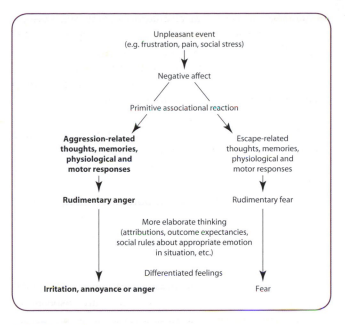

FIGURE 9.4 *The cognitive neo-associationist model of aggression.*

Source: Adapted from Berkowitz, 1993, p. 57. Reprinted with permission.

urge to fight, and fear, inducing the urge to run away). Depending on the context and the child's past experience, either the anger or the fear response is likely to dominate and guide his further analysis of the situation. Before deciding how to respond, the child will engage in a more careful appraisal process, including an assessment of his classmate's motives. If he concludes that his classmate threw the stone on purpose, the immediate feeling of anger will be consolidated, and retaliation (i.e. aggression) will be considered as an appropriate response. Because all the components of the emotional experience are associated with each other, activating one component is assumed to trigger other components relative to the strength of their association, hence the term 'associationism'. The weapons effect described earlier can be explained in the context of this model as a result of aggression-related associations elicited by the presentation of a weapon, which then activate other, connected, aggressive thoughts, feelings and behaviours.

The cognitive appraisal of physiological arousal is also at the core of another influential theory of aggression, the **excitation transfer theory** proposed by Zillmann (1978). Zillmann argued that the effects of frustration as a trigger for aggressive behaviour can be augmented by physiological arousal from a neutral or non-aggression-related source. If physiological

excitation transfer theory transfer of neutral physiological arousal onto arousal resulting from frustration, thus augmenting negative affect and enhancing the strength of an aggressive response.

 LEADER IN THE FIELD

Leonard Berkowitz (b. 1926) obtained his PhD in Psychology from the University of Michigan in 1951 and is still active as Vilas Research Professor Emeritus at the University of Wisconsin. He is a key figure in aggression research who has promoted both theoretical development and empirical evidence with respect to the role of negative affect and cognitive appraisal in aggressive behaviour. His study on the 'weapons effect' (Berkowitz & LePage, 1967) became a classic in social psychology; it showed that people who were previously frustrated were more likely to show aggressive behaviour if aggressive cues, such as guns, were present in the situation. Subsequently, Berkowitz developed his ideas into the cognitive neo-associationist model of aggressive behaviour described in this chapter. He also studied the other side of human nature, helping behaviour. His book *Aggression: Its causes, consequences, and control*, published in 1993, provides a comprehensive and authoritative review of aggression research.

arousal from a neutral activity, such as climbing up a flight of stairs or riding a bike, is still present when the person encounters an anger-eliciting situation, such as being verbally attacked, the earlier neutral arousal (excitation) is transferred onto the anger-related arousal and falsely attributed as anger. As a result, the strength of the subsequent aggressive response is increased. However, this misattribution will only happen if the person is no longer aware of the source of the neutral arousal. For example, a football player may have sprinted 70 metres across the pitch towards the goal when he is tackled unfairly by a member of the opposite team and loses the ball. As he picks himself up, the anger-related arousal based on the foul is magnified by the arousal that is left from the sprint, leading him to lash out at the opponent rather than, perhaps, just complaining to the referee (Figure 9.5).

To support this line of reasoning, Zillmann and Bryant (1974) conducted an experiment in which participants had to perform either a physically nonarousing task (threading disks on a wire) or an arousing task (pedalling a bicycle ergometer for one minute). Two minutes later, they received a provocation in the form of an aversive noise; another six minutes later, they were given the opportunity to administer aversive noise blasts to the person who had provoked them. In line with the excitation transfer model and as shown in Figure 9.6, participants in the bicycle condition, who were still aroused from the physical exercise at the time of the provocation, administered louder noise blasts than did participants in the low-arousal condition.

In combination, the cognitive neo-associationist model and the excitation transfer model highlight the role of negative affect as a powerful stimulant of aggression. It activates a network of affective and cognitive responses that enhance the salience of aggressive responses and thus increase the likelihood that aggressive intentions will be formed and translated into action.

Learning and aggression Studies within the behaviour genetic approach described above suggest that an individual's genetic make-up plays a role in his or her disposition towards aggressive behaviour. However, there is no doubt that learning experiences in the course of the socialization process are as, if not more, important in affecting the development of aggressive behaviour patterns (Bandura, 1983). Learning is defined as behaviour change through experience, and two mechanisms in particular affect the acquisition of aggressive behaviour: **direct reinforcement** and *observational learning* (vicarious reinforcement). Direct reinforcement involves the experience of being rewarded for aggressive behaviour, either

direct reinforcement experience of positive consequences of aggressive behaviour (e.g. status gain among peers) that increases the probability of future aggressive acts.

FIGURE 9.5 *Angry arousal may be augmented by arousal resulting from physical activity.*

Source: © Hepp. Used under licence from Getty Images.

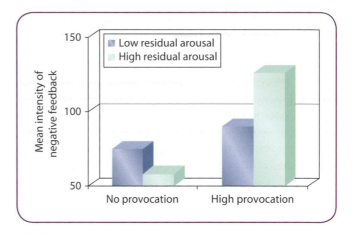

FIGURE 9.6 *High residual arousal at the time of provocation intensifies aggressive responses.*

Note: The means in the no provocation conditions are significantly different from the high provocation/high residual arousal condition. In the high provocation condition, the means of low and high residual arousal are also significantly different.

Source: Adapted from Zillmann & Bryant, 1974, Table 2. Copyright © 1974 by the American Psychological Association. Adapted with permission. *Journal of Personality and Social Psychology, 30,* 782–791. The use of APA information does not imply endorsement by APA.

by achieving a desired goal through the aggressive act or by winning social approval for showing aggressive behaviour. Children who are praised by their parents for 'standing up for themselves' after being provoked, or who succeed in getting hold of a desired toy by grabbing it from another child learn that aggressive behaviour pays off, and they are encouraged by the positive effects of their behaviour to perform similar aggressive acts in the future. Observational learning refers to learning

FIGURE 9.7 *The Bobo Doll paradigm.*

Source: From Albert Bandura et al. (1961). Transmission of aggression through imitation of aggressive models, *Journal of Abnormal and Social Psychology*, 63, 575–582. Published by American Psychological Association. Photograph reprinted with kind permission of Professor Bandura.

by imitation. Watching others being rewarded for their aggressive behaviour also increases the likelihood of aggressive behaviour among the observers.

In a classic study, Bandura, Ross, and Ross (1961) pioneered the Bobo Doll paradigm in which children are exposed to adult models behaving either in an aggressive or in a non-aggressive way towards a large, inflatable clown figure called Bobo (Figure 9.7). When the children were subsequently given the opportunity to play with the doll, those who had watched the aggressive model showed more aggressive behaviour towards the doll than did children who had watched the non-aggressive model. A video of the original experiment, including an interview with Albert Bandura, can be found on YouTube. In a later study, an aggressive model instigated more imitative aggression when he was praised for his aggressive behaviour than when he was punished; that is, beaten up by the target of the aggression (Bandura, Ross, & Ross, 1963).

The social learning perspective is a major theoretical approach for understanding the effects of media violence on aggressive behaviour that can be regarded as a paradigmatic case of observational learning (see the section on violent media contents below).

Social information processing models The theoretical approaches discussed so far stressed the role of affect and cognition as antecedents of aggressive behaviour, and highlighted the importance of learning experiences in understanding aggressive behaviour. Social information processing models of aggression refer to these lines of thinking and elaborate them by focusing on the role of cognitive representations, or 'scripts', in the prediction of aggressive behaviour. Huesmann (1998) proposed that social behaviour in general, and aggressive behaviour in particular, is shaped by abstract representations of appropriate behaviours in different situational contexts (see Leader in the Field, L. Rowell Huesmann). These abstract representations are called **aggressive scripts**: blueprints for behaviour and guidelines for deciding in favour of or against acting aggressively in specific situations. For example, if children have repeatedly responded (or seen others responding) to provocations by showing physical aggression, they will develop a generalized cognitive representation in which provocation and physical aggression are closely linked. When encountering a provocation, they are likely to activate their scripted knowledge, which then prompts them to enact the behaviour specified by the script. The script also contains normative beliefs that tell the person when it is appropriate to show aggressive behaviour and which of various variants of the script to enact. These normative beliefs may specify that it is acceptable to respond with physical aggression when angered or provoked by a peer, but not when angered by an adult, and the likelihood of showing an aggressive response towards a peer or an adult will vary accordingly (Huesmann & Guerra, 1997).

aggressive scripts cognitive representation of when and how to show aggressive behaviour.

 LEADER IN THE FIELD

L. Rowell Huesmann (b. 1943) gained his PhD at Carnegie-Mellon University in 1969, then held positions at Yale University and the University of Illinois at Chicago, before moving in 1992 to the University of Michigan, Ann Arbor, where he is Amos N. Tversky Collegiate Professor of Communication Studies and Psychology and Director of the Research Center for Group Dynamics at the Institute for Social Research. He is past president of ISRA, the International Society for Research on Aggression, and has been editor-in-chief of its journal, *Aggressive Behavior*, since 2004. He was the recipient in 2005 of the American Psychological Association's award for Distinguished Lifetime Contributions to Media Psychology. He has made key theoretical and empirical contributions to understanding the development of aggressive behaviour, focusing on aggressive scripts and social learning processes. He is also a leading scholar on long-term effects of media violence on aggression, and has been a principal researcher in the famous Columbia County Longitudinal Study that began in 1960, and the Cross National Television Study that began in 1977 (Huesmann, Moise-Titus, Podolski, & Eron, 2003).

Each of the psychological explanations of aggression highlights particular aspects of the processes that give rise to aggressive behaviour. Rather than competing against each other, they are best seen as pieces of a jigsaw that – when put together – create a clearer picture of the phenomenon called aggression. The **general aggression model** (also known as the GAM) by Anderson and colleagues (Anderson & Dill, 2000; Lindsay & Anderson, 2000; see Leader in the Field, Craig A. Anderson) combines the different pieces of knowledge into a comprehensive framework, as shown in Figure 9.8.

According to the general aggression model, individual dispositions, such as trait anger, and external stimuli, such as aggressive cues in the environment, come together in a particular situation to create an internal state in the person that is characterized by specific cognitions, feelings and arousal symptoms. For example, someone who is easy to anger may only need a small provocation from a stranger to enter into a state of fury, characterized by aggressive thoughts ('this person is an idiot'), negative feelings ('this person makes me mad'), and bodily symptoms ('I can feel my blood pressure rising'). This internal state, in turn, gives rise to a quick, automatic appraisal

general aggression model (GAM)
integrative framework explaining how personal and situational input variables lead to aggressive behaviour via cognitive appraisal and negative affective arousal.

 LEADER IN THE FIELD

Craig A. Anderson (b. 1952) obtained his PhD from Stanford University in 1980. After holding positions at Rice University in Texas and the University of Missouri, Columbia, he moved to Iowa State University in Ames in 1999, where he is Distinguished Professor of Liberal Arts and Sciences and Director of the Center for the Study of Violence. Since 2010, Craig Anderson has been president of ISRA, the International Society for Research on Aggression. He developed the *general aggression model* that is currently the most prominent conceptual framework for the study of aggression in a wide range of domains. He has pioneered research on the heat hypothesis, combining archival and experimental analyses, and is one of the most prominent researchers of media violence effects on aggressive behaviour. His recent publications include a co-authored book in 2007 on violent video game effects on children and adolescents (Anderson, Gentile, & Buckley, 2007).

of the situation, for example 'this person's behaviour is totally unacceptable'. In the subsequent reappraisal stage, the initial evaluation of the situation is considered in a more controlled and elaborate way, leading to a behavioural response. Depending on the reappraisal, this response will either be aggressive ('this person annoyed me on purpose and therefore I will shout abuse at him') or non-aggressive ('let's try and calm down, everybody'). The behavioural decision may trigger a response from

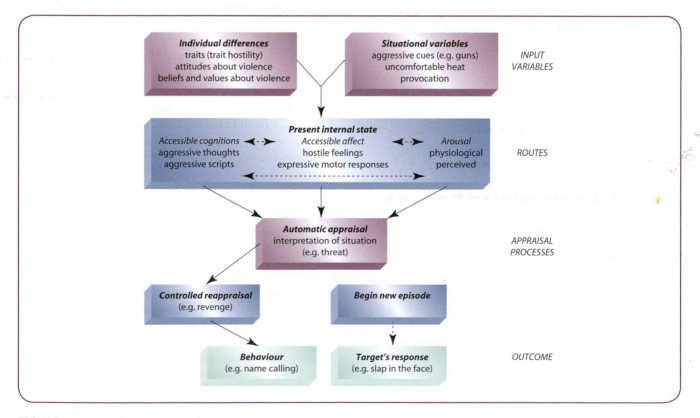

FIGURE 9.8 *General Aggression Model (GAM).*

Source: Based on Anderson & Dill, 2000, and Lindsay & Anderson, 2000, with permission from SAGE Publications Ltd.

the target that marks the beginning of a new episode and may further escalate or de-escalate the conflict. The general aggression model provides a structure that helps us to understand the complex processes through which particular input variables, such as violent media stimuli or biographical experiences of abuse, can lead to aggressive behaviour as the critical outcome variable.

Summary

This section has presented the most prominent theories of the causes and underlying processes of aggressive behaviour. Biological theories focus on the role of genetic and hormonal factors accounting for differences in aggressive behaviour. In contrast, psychological theories refer to affective and cognitive reactions to aggression-eliciting stimuli and how they pave the way for aggressive responses. These models show that negative affect – caused by a range of adverse stimuli such as frustration, pain or noise – is a powerful trigger of selective information processing that enhances the probability of aggressive behaviour. This information processing draws on aggressive scripts, i.e. abstract representations of how and when aggressive behaviour should be enacted. Another well-supported theoretical position is that aggression is a form of learned behaviour, implemented in the individual's behavioural repertoire through direct reinforcement as well as observational learning. The general aggression model integrates the diverse psychological theories of aggression into a common framework.

PERSONAL AND SITUATIONAL VARIABLES AFFECTING AGGRESSIVE BEHAVIOUR

Do people differ in their propensity to engage in aggressive behaviour, and what are critical factors in the situation or the social environment that make aggressive behaviour more likely?

In this section, we will take a closer look at some of the factors associated with differences between people and between situations in their likelihood of showing or evoking aggression. In terms of the general aggression model, these are the input variables that are crucial in eliciting cognitive, affective and physiological responses that may or may not lead to an aggressive response. The guiding question for this section is: how can we distinguish between more or less aggressive individuals and groups of individuals; and what situational influences of a transient or persistent nature precipitate aggressive behaviour?

Individual differences in aggressive behaviour

Researchers have suggested several variables as predictors of individual differences in aggressive behaviour. In this section we will focus on three that have received intense research attention: trait aggressiveness, hostile attribution bias, and gender (cf. Krahé, 2012, Chapter 3, for a coverage of additional person variables related to aggression).

> **trait aggressiveness** denotes stable differences between individuals in the likelihood and intensity of aggressive behaviour.

> **hostile attribution bias** tendency to attribute hostile intentions to a person who has caused damage when it is unclear whether or not the damage was caused accidentally or on purpose.

Trait aggressiveness The concept of trait aggressiveness describes dispositional (i.e. temporally and cross-situationally stable) differences between individuals with respect to the likelihood of showing aggressive behaviour. Whereas some individuals are easy to anger and quickly get 'hot under the collar', others are generally less inclined to respond with aggression. Longitudinal studies following the same research participants over many years from childhood into adulthood have shown that the tendency to engage in aggressive behaviour is remarkably stable over time. Drawing on findings from 16 studies exploring the temporal stability of men's aggressive behaviour, Olweus (1979) found a stability coefficient of $r = .76$ over a one year period, of $r = .69$ over five years and still of $r = .60$ over a period of 10 years. These figures are matched only by the stability of intelligence scores over time, and indicate that aggression in later stages of development may be predicted on the basis of earlier aggression scores. Trait aggressiveness is conceptualized as a multidimensional construct comprising four different components: physical aggression, verbal aggression, anger and hostility. It is typically assessed by self-report questionnaires in which participants indicate the likelihood of showing different forms of physical aggression, verbal aggression, anger and hostility. The most widely used instrument is the Aggression Questionnaire (Buss & Perry, 1992; Buss & Warren, 2000; see Individual Differences 9.1), but there are also instruments specially designed for adolescents (e.g. Orpinas & Frankowski, 2001).

Hostile attribution bias Another variable linked to stable differences in the tendency to show aggressive behaviour is the 'hostile attribution bias' (see Chapter 3 on how we attribute or explain behaviour). This construct refers to the tendency to interpret ambiguous behaviour by another person as an expression of the actor's hostile intent. For example, in deciding whether or not another person causes harm accidentally or on purpose, individuals with a hostile attributional style prefer an attribution to hostile intent rather than seeing the actor's behaviour as unintentional or caused by carelessness. The hostile attribution bias is typically measured by presenting short films or written scenarios in which one actor causes harm to another person, but the stimulus material is unclear as to whether the harm was caused by accident or on purpose (e.g. Dodge, 1980). For example, children are shown a video in which two boys build a tower of bricks. One boy then knocks down the tower, and the film is ambiguous as to whether he did so intentionally. The participants are asked to indicate if they think the child knocked down the tower by mistake or on purpose. Respondents who consistently prefer explanations that attribute the damage to the actor's intent are seen as having a hostile attribution bias.

A meta-analysis including 41 studies with more than 6000 participants yielded a significant association between the attribution of hostile intent and aggressive behaviour in children and adolescents (Orobio de Castro, Veerman, Koops, Bosch, & Monshouwer, 2002). Studies with adults demonstrated that individuals with a hostile attributional style are more likely to show aggressive behaviour, and that differences in trait aggressiveness are predictive of the hostile attribution bias (Dill, Anderson, Anderson, & Deuser, 1997). A longitudinal study by Burks, Laird, Dodge, Pettit, and Bates (1999) followed participants from kindergarten to Grade 8. These researchers found that aggressive behaviour at kindergarten age predicted hostile information processing in Grade 8, which, in turn, predicted aggressive behaviour at the same grade level. These findings suggest that hostile information processing contributes to the stability of aggression over time. From this perspective, individual differences in aggression may to some extent be the result of schematic, habitual ways of processing information which highlight the hostile nature of social interactions and thereby lower the threshold for aggressive responses.

To explain the development of the hostile attribution bias, several studies point to the role of exposure

FIGURE 9.9 *Mothers' and daughters' hostile attributional styles are significantly correlated.*
Source: © Gladskikh Tatiana. Used under licence from Shutterstock.

to violent media contents. Correlational studies found a relationship between attraction to media violence and hostile attribution bias (Krahé & Möller, 2004). Other studies investigated whether hostile attributional styles are transmitted from mothers to their children. MacBrayer, Milich, and Hundley (2003) found that mothers of aggressive children perceived more hostile intent and were more likely to report an intention to respond aggressively in interactions with an adult peer or their own child than were mothers of non-aggressive children. However, mothers' and children's hostile attributions and aggressive behavioural intentions were found to be significantly correlated only for the girls, but not for the boys (Figure 9.9). The authors explain this sex-specific effect with reference to the principle of learning by **modelling**, which predicts that children are more likely to imitate similar models (here: models of the same sex) than dissimilar models. Unfortunately, no studies have yet examined the correspondence between fathers' and sons' hostile attribution biases to substantiate this explanation.

> **modelling** learning by imitation, observing a model being rewarded or punished for his or her behaviour.

Gender differences A final variable associated with individual differences in aggression is gender, with the underlying assumption that men are more aggressive than women. Support for this assumption comes from the analysis of crime statistics across a range of countries, which show that men are overrepresented as perpetrators of violent crime at a ratio of about 8 to 1 (Archer & Lloyd, 2002). Meta-analyses of the psychological literature also found significant gender differences in aggression, with boys and men showing more physical and verbal aggression (Archer, 2004; Eagly & Steffen, 1986). However, despite being significant, the size of the effects is moderate at best, and smaller for verbal than for physical aggression. Cross-cultural analyses suggest that this is a general pattern across different societies (Archer & McDaniel, 1995). It appears that situational factors play an important role in this context. In their meta-analysis of 64 studies, Bettencourt and Miller (1996) found that men scored higher than women on unprovoked aggression, but the gender difference was markedly smaller on provoked aggression (Figure 9.10). Looking at indirect aggression, defined as harming others through purposeful manipulation and damage of their peer relationships, some authors have suggested that women may be as involved as, if not more involved than, men in this type of aggression (e.g. Österman et al., 1998). However, Archer and Coyne (2005) point out that the empirical evidence is mixed. Girls showed more indirect aggression than boys in studies using behavioural observation, whereas research using peer nominations typically failed to find gender differences. In studies with adults, there is also no evidence of gender differences in indirect aggression, which may be explained by the fact that the social costs of direct aggression are high for both men and women, levelling out gender differences in indirect aggression. We will return to the issue of gender differences in aggression in our discussion of intimate partner violence later in the chapter, where it has been argued by some researchers that women feature more prominently than men as perpetrators of physical aggression.

Situational influences on aggressive behaviour

Just as it is clear that not all individuals respond with aggression in a given situation, it is obvious that not all situations elicit aggressive responses to the same extent. In this section, we examine evidence concerning the role of three situational input variables that affect the occurrence of aggressive behaviour: alcohol consumption, high temperatures and exposure to violent media contents.

Alcohol From the evidence available to date, it seems safe to conclude that even moderate amounts of alcohol lead to increased aggressive behaviour (Figure 9.11). Alcohol plays an important role in the perpetration of violent crime, including homicide (Parker & Auerhahn, 1999), domestic violence, such as the physical and sexual abuse of children, sexual aggression and wife battering (Barnett, Miller-Perrin, & Perrin, 2011), and many forms of group violence, such as sports violence, rioting and vandalism (Russell, 2004). Epidemiological studies have established that more than 80 per cent of violent offenders had been drinking prior to committing their crimes (Murdoch, Phil, & Ross, 1990). Experimental research has established that alcohol has a causal effect on aggressive behaviour. These studies compared the aggressive responses of individuals who were given alcohol to those of individuals in a control condition who did not receive alcohol. Two meta-analyses examined evidence from a wide range of studies comparing alcohol versus control groups and found that alcohol was a significant predictor of aggressive behaviour (Bushman & Cooper, 1990;

FIGURE 9.10 *Are women really less aggressive than men?*
Source: © Digital Vision. Used under licence from Getty Images.

FIGURE 9.11 *Even moderate amounts of alcohol lead to increased aggressive behaviour.*
Source: © Paul Bradbury. Used under licence from Getty Images.

Ito, Miller, & Pollock, 1996). A more recent review by Exum (2006, p. 131), focusing on evidence from experimental studies, also concluded that the findings affirmed the 'popular belief that alcohol consumption increases aggressive behavior'.

It is important to note, however, that general measures of the strength of the alcohol-aggression link mask the fact that the effects of alcohol may be strong for some people, but weak for others. Consider individual differences in empathy (i.e. the ease with which people can imagine how another person perceives a situation and might feel as a result). A study by Giancola (2003) showed that alcohol dramatically increased the administration of (supposedly) painful electric shocks to an opponent for individuals low in dispositional empathy, but failed to affect the behaviour of participants high in dispositional empathy (see Chapter 10 for more detail on empathy).

In terms of explaining the effects of alcohol on aggression, the *attentional hypothesis* suggests that alcohol has an indirect effect on aggression by reducing the attentional capacity of the individual, preventing a comprehensive appraisal of situational cues (Giancola & Corman, 2007). The resulting 'alcohol myopia' prevents people from engaging in a thorough processing of situational information. Instead, they only pay attention to the most salient features of the situation. For example, imagine a young man on his way home one night who overhears another man making a lewd comment about his girlfriend. The man whose girlfriend has been insulted is more likely to respond aggressively if he is drunk, because he lacks the cognitive capacity to engage in a full appraisal of the situation, for example to consider the possibility that the other man is equally drunk and did not really mean to be offensive. Alcohol myopia also impairs people's awareness of social norms that normally inhibit aggressive behaviour, for example the norm that men should not hit women. Finally, by limiting attention to salient situational stimuli, alcohol makes people more responsive to aggressive cues present in the situation (see the earlier discussion about the weapons effect).

High temperature Another situational input variable affecting aggressive behaviour is high temperature. The **heat hypothesis** predicts that aggression should increase as temperature goes up (Anderson, 2001). Two paradigms were developed to test this hypothesis under natural conditions. The first paradigm is the **geographic regions approach** comparing

heat hypothesis hypothesis that aggression increases with higher temperatures.

geographic regions approach method for testing the heat hypothesis by comparing violence rates in cooler and hotter climates.

violent crime rates in hotter versus cooler regions, finding support for a link between hotter climates and higher violence rates in archival data (Anderson et al., 2000). However, the regions included in the comparison, typically the North versus the South of the United States, differed in aspects other than temperature, such as unemployment rates or normative beliefs condoning violence, that could be relevant to aggression (and these variables were not always controlled in the relevant research). Nisbett (1993) has argued that there is a special culture of honour that makes Southerners more accepting of violence in response to threat and insults (see Chapter 15 for a discussion of the 'culture of honour' theory). He argues that this normative endorsement of aggression grew out of the traditional way of making a living through the herding of animals, which required farmers to be highly sensitive to possible attacks on their herds, lowering their threshold for aggression. Thus, regional traditions could account at least to some extent for temperature-related variations in violent crime, but as Anderson et al. (2000) argue, they do not fully explain away the heat effect.

To address this potential alternative explanation, a second paradigm was developed, the **time periods approach**, that compares changes in violent crime rates within the same region as a function of fluctuations in temperature, for example between winter and summer months, or between hotter and cooler summers (the 'hot year effect'). This approach also supports the heat hypothesis, by showing that violent crime rates were higher in the summer months than during the winter period as well as in hotter as compared to cooler summers (Anderson, 2001). Critics of the time periods approach have argued that, rather than reflecting a causal effect of the aversive effects of high temperatures, the increase in violence could be explained by differences in people's routine activities (Cohen & Felson, 1979). People tend to spend more time outdoors in the summer months and in years with hotter as opposed to cooler summers, and this may create more opportunities for aggressive encounters, leading to higher rates of violent crime. Anderson (1989) argues against this interpretation by pointing out that rates of domestic violence are also higher in the summer months, although families most probably spend more time at home together in the winter months.

Laboratory studies, in which ambient temperature can be manipulated with other factors being held constant, provide a third approach to the study of heat and aggression. Unfortunately, lab studies on the effect of high temperatures have produced divergent results.

time periods approach method for testing the heat hypothesis by comparing violence rates in the same region during cooler and hotter periods.

SOCIAL PSYCHOLOGY BEYOND THE LAB 9.1

THE HEAT HYPOTHESIS AND THE EFFECTS OF GLOBAL WARMING

The 'heat hypothesis' states that high temperature increases the likelihood of violent behaviour. The implications of studies supporting the heat hypothesis are worrying in the face of global warming. If increases in temperature are systematically related to increases in violent crime, then the continuous rise in global temperature presents a risk factor for the rise of violent crime. Based on archival data on the link between temperature and violent crime in the United States over 48 years from 1950 to 1997, Anderson et al. (2000) estimated the magnitude of this danger, as shown in Figure 9.12.

Their analysis predicts that an increase in temperature by 2 degrees Fahrenheit increases the murder and assault rate by 9 cases per 100,000 citizens. For a US population of 270 million, this increase translates into 24,000 additional murder/assault cases per year. For readers more familiar with Celsius than Fahrenheit, with an increase in average temperature of just 1.1°C, the murder and assault rate is projected to go up by 24,000 cases in the US. It is important to bear in mind that temperature is only one of many factors affecting violent crime rates. However, it remains significant when other contributory factors, such as poverty, are controlled for (Anderson, Bushman, & Groom, 1997). Research on the heat hypothesis alerts both policy makers and the general public to the fact that the dangers of global

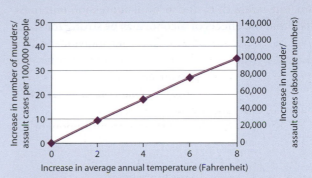

FIGURE 9.12 *Estimates of global warming effect on murders and assaults per year in the United States with a population of 270 million.*

Source: Based on Anderson et al., 2000, p. 124. With permission from Elsevier.

warming are not restricted to our natural environment, but also pose a threat to the social functioning of human communities. At the same time, this line of research has important implications for preventing violence. As noted by Anderson et al. (2000), keeping temperatures at a comfortable level through air-conditioning may help to bring down violence rates and may be particularly useful in settings such as prisons, factories and schools, where temperature-related violence is likely to pose a specific problem.

While some studies supported the conclusions drawn from naturalistic analyses of the temperature-aggression link, other studies found a decrease in aggression when temperatures rose beyond a certain level. On the basis of a meta-analysis of 11 studies, Anderson et al. (2000) concluded that so far the results of laboratory studies on the heat hypothesis have remained inconsistent. You can study the effects of global warming on the rate of murder and assault by looking at Social Psychology Beyond the Lab 9.1.

The effect of high temperature on aggression found under natural conditions can be explained with reference to the General Aggression Model. Heat gives rise to feelings of discomfort, which are proposed as input variables that trigger negative affective arousal; these, in turn, affect the cognitive processing of social stimuli and thereby enhance the likelihood of aggressive behaviour.

Interestingly, no corresponding effect has been found for uncomfortably cold temperatures in natural settings. The explanation offered by Anderson et al. (2000) is that people are generally better equipped to protect themselves against the cold than they are to escape the heat, enabling them to reduce coldness-related discomfort more easily than heat-related discomfort.

Violent media contents Evidence concerning the potentially harmful effect of exposure to media violence comes from three sources: (1) experimental studies exposing participants to either violent or non-violent media contents and exploring the effects of this manipulation on subsequent aggressive thoughts, feelings and behaviours (e.g. Kirsh, 1998); (2) correlational studies collecting self-reports of violent media usage and relating them to measures of aggression obtained at the same time

SUMMARY OF THE 'NEW YORK STATE STUDIES' ON THE LONG-TERM EFFECTS OF TV VIOLENCE

Lefkowitz, M. M., Eron, L. D., Walder, L. O., & Huesmann, L. R. (1977). *Growing up to be violent*. New York: Pergamon.

Introduction

This study explored the long-term effects of exposure to television violence on aggression. Correlational evidence showing that viewing television violence and behaving aggressively are linked if both constructs are measured at the same time are open to two competing explanations of the relationship between TV violence and aggression: (1) that viewing TV violence makes viewers more aggressive (i.e. violent TV causes aggression); or (2) that more aggressive individuals are more strongly attracted by violent TV programmes (i.e. a selection bias). By using a longitudinal design in which the same participants were studied three times over a period of 22 years, the authors were able to examine which of the two hypotheses is more likely to be correct: if the link from viewing TV violence at the beginning of the study (time 1) to aggressive behaviour 10 years on (time 2) is stronger than the link from aggression at time 1 to the viewing of violent TV programmes at time 2, this speaks in favour of the first hypothesis, that TV violence is a causal factor in the development of aggressive behaviour patterns.

Method

The study started in 1960 with a sample of 875 children that comprised the entire population of third-graders in a community in Columbia County, New York. Ten years later, 427 of the original participants, who were then 18, were re-interviewed. Another 12 years later, in 1982, data were collected from 409 of the original participants, who by then had reached the age of 30. At the first assessment, measures of aggressive behaviour were obtained for each child on the basis of peer nominations. Exposure to TV violence was assessed by asking the mothers to name their child's most-watched TV programmes, which were then rated by experts for level of violent content. Aggressive behaviour and exposure to TV violence were measured again at the subsequent two data points, and additional data about criminal offences were collected at the last data point.

Results

First, concurrent correlations between exposure to TV violence and aggression were computed for each data point. At time 1, there was a significant correlation for boys, but not for girls; at time 2, there was no relationship for

either sex. More important, however, are the correlations over time. Cross-lagged panel analyses were conducted in which the correlations between time 1 aggression and time 2 exposure to violent TV programmes were compared against time 1 TV violence exposure and time 2 aggression. No evidence was found for a longitudinal link between TV violence and aggression in girls. However, for boys exposure to TV violence at time 1 was significantly correlated with aggression at time 2, whereas aggression at time 1 was unrelated to TV violence exposure at time 2. The path model that presents the relationships for the sample of 184 boys for whom complete data were available from both time 1 and time 2 is shown in Figure 9.13a. For the 162 male participants still in the

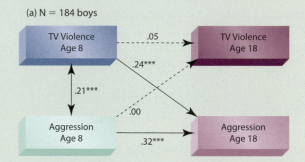

(a) N = 184 boys

Note. Dashed lines indicate non-significant links.

(b) N = 162 boys

FIGURE 9.13(a) and (b) *Longitudinal links between exposure to television violence and aggression in a sample of boys followed over 22 years.*

Source: Based on Huesmann, L. R., & Miller, L. S. (1994). Long-term effects of the repeated exposure to media violence in childhood. In L. R. Huesmann (Ed.), *Aggressive behavior: Current perspectives* (pp. 153–186). New York: Plenum © Springer. With kind permission from Springer Science & Business Media B. V.

sample at time 3, 22 years after the start of the study, a significant path (.18**) was found from exposure to TV violence at age 8 and conviction for violent crime at the age of 30, as shown in Figure 9.13b.

Discussion

The study provides an impressive longitudinal data base from which long-term relationships between media violence and aggression can be inferred. For boys, there was clear evidence that early exposure to TV violence predicted aggressive behaviour over a period as long as 22 years. The magnitude of the link was not dramatic, which is unsurprising given the host of other factors that affected participants in the course of that period, but it suggests that the potential long-term effects of exposure to TV violence in childhood give cause for concern. Subsequent studies, including cross-national comparisons, confirmed this finding (Huesmann & Eron, 1986). For girls, the evidence remains inconclusive. A subsequent longitudinal study by Huesmann, Moise-Titus, Podolski, and Eron (2003) found parallel links among men and women between exposure to TV violence in childhood and aggression in adulthood, but studies into the impact of violent computer games also showed stronger effects for male than for female players (e.g. Bartholow & Anderson, 2002).

(e.g. Krahé & Möller, 2004); and (3) longitudinal studies which measure media violence usage and aggression at different points in time to test the hypothesis that earlier exposure to media violence predicts aggression at a later stage (e.g. Huesmann & Miller, 1994; Möller & Krahé, 2009). Even though violent media contents are discussed here in the context of situational input variables for aggressive behaviour, it is important to note that researchers and the general public are not concerned primarily with the effects of a single or short-term presentation, but with the cumulative effects of repeated exposure over time. Therefore, studying the pathways from habitual exposure to media violence to aggression over substantial periods of time is critical to establish the potentially harmful effects of exposure to violent media. An impressive study that started with a sample of eight-year-olds in 1960 and followed them over a period of 22 years is presented in Research Close-Up 9.1.

Anderson et al. (2003) assessed the state of knowledge derived from each of these approaches in an authoritative review. They concluded that 'Research on violent television and films, video games, and music reveals unequivocal evidence that media violence increases the likelihood of aggressive and violent behavior in both immediate and long-term contexts'. (p. 81). Integrating the findings from almost 300 individual studies, Anderson and Bushman (2002) reported significant effect sizes (correlations weighted by sample size) for the link between exposure to media violence and aggression. The effect sizes vary between .17 and .23 across different methodologies (cross-sectional versus longitudinal studies, laboratory versus field experiments). Focusing on violent video games, a recent meta-analysis by Anderson et al. (2010), including 136 studies, found an overall effect size of $r = .19$ between violent video game play and aggressive behaviour across a range of methodologies.

Critics have, however, disputed the claim that using violent media increases aggressive thoughts, feeling and behaviour. They argue that, due to methodological problems with some of the available evidence, the strength of the link between media violence exposure and aggression is overestimated (e.g. Ferguson 2007). To address this criticism, Anderson et al. (2010) identified a list of 'best practice' criteria that allowed them to separate good and poor quality studies. For example, studies were classified as 'good practice' if they compared violent games with games that did not contain violence, rather than using comparison games that did include some violence, or if they used measures of violent game play rather than total time spent playing video games regardless of their content. When considering only those studies that met the 'best practice' criteria, the average effect size increased to $r = .24$, effectively rebutting the criticism that the potential risk of violent video game usage may be overestimated due to the poor quality of the studies in which a link was found. The real-life implications of these effect sizes are put into perspective in Social Psychology Beyond the Lab 9.2.

Anderson et al. (2010) also found a significant, albeit smaller link between violent video game usage and *prosocial behaviour* ($r = -.10$). The negative correlation indicates that the higher the amount of time spent playing violent video games, the lower the willingness to engage in prosocial behaviour (see also Chapter 10 on situational determinants of prosocial behaviour).

The observed effect sizes are relatively small in magnitude, explaining no more than 10 per cent of the variance. This means that while some of the variability in aggressive behaviour can be accounted for by differences

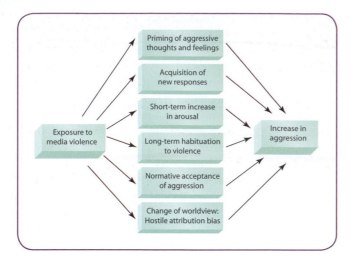

FIGURE 9.14 *Psychological processes linking media violence exposure to aggression.*

Source: Adapted from Krahé (2001). *The social psychology of aggression.* Copyright © 2001 by the American Psychological Association. Adapted with permission. The use of APA information does not imply endorsement by APA.

in exposure to violent media contents, a much larger proportion of the variance is attributable to other factors. However, even small effect sizes can have practical importance considering the huge number of media users across the world. As Sparks and Sparks (2002) pointed out, if only one person in several hundred thousand viewers was inspired by a violent movie to commit a violent act, the consequences of several million people watching that movie would be dramatic. Beyond demonstrating that media violence has a causal effect on aggressive behaviour, it is important to understand *how* this effect is produced. Several interlocking mechanisms have been identified that link violent media contents as input variables and aggressive behaviour as outcome variable (Figure 9.14; see Krahé, 2012, Chapter 5, for a comprehensive discussion):

1. Watching media depictions of aggressive interactions increases the *accessibility of aggressive thoughts and feelings*. Asking participants to list their thoughts when exposed to a violent or non-violent videotape, Bushman and Geen (1990) found that participants who had watched the violent videotape listed more aggressive thoughts than participants who had watched a non-violent tape.

2. Exposure to aggression may *instigate social learning processes* that result in the acquisition of new behaviours through direct reinforcement and imitation (Gentile & Gentile, 2008). Much of the aggression portrayed in the media is rewarded (e.g. winning extra points for running

over a blind pedestrian in reverse gear, as in the racing game Carmageddon II) or at least goes unpunished (e.g. when a cartoon character is blown to pieces and quickly reassembled a moment later; Figure 9.15). Moreover, it is often shown by attractive characters with whom viewers identify. As social learning theory suggests, learning through modelling is particularly likely under these conditions (Bandura, 1983).

3. In terms of affective and physiological responses to violent media stimuli, it is necessary to distinguish between short-term and long-term effects. In the short term, violent media stimuli elicit more hostile affect (Bushman & Geen, 1990). They also produce an *increase in arousal* that may intensify angry arousal from other sources, such as provocation, by means of excitation transfer, as described earlier. Over time, however, habitual exposure to media violence leads to **habituation** that, in turn, reduces

habituation process whereby the ability of a stimulus to elicit arousal become weaker with each consecutive presentation.

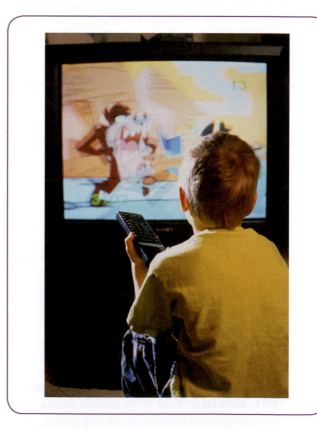

FIGURE 9.15 *Cartoon violence – an example of how aggression portrayed in the media often goes unpunished.*

Source: © Donna Day. Used under licence from Getty Images.

SOCIAL PSYCHOLOGY BEYOND THE LAB 9.2

PUTTING MEDIA VIOLENCE IN THE CONTEXT OF OTHER RISK FACTORS FOR AGGRESSION

Critics of the media violence literature often claim that effects sizes found in media violence studies are too low to be practically meaningful (Ferguson, 2002). To address this claim, Anderson, Gentile, and Buckley (2007) brought together data from several sources to place the typical effect sizes for the link between media violence and aggression in the context of other established risk factors. Drawing on evidence from longitudinal studies, they compiled a list of empirically established risk factors that were associated with a higher probability of aggressive and violent behaviour over time. By comparing the strength of the link between these other risk factors and aggression to the link between media violence usage and aggression, it is possible to gauge how serious a problem the widespread usage of violent media may be for society. Table 9.2 presents some candidates from their list.

With the exception of gang membership, no other risk factor accounts for more variation in aggressive behaviour than violent video game usage. This is an impressive finding, because most people would think that being a member of a gang would be a far greater risk factor for engaging in aggression and violence than sitting in front of a computer screen and acting aggressively in a virtual reality. The data further show that violent video games are more closely related to aggression than violence in other media, because the aggregated index of media violence, including non-interactive media such as movies, has a lower effect size of .17 compared to .30 for violent games. However, overall media violence usage still ranks

Table 9.2 *Risk factors for aggression in adolescence.*

Risk factor	Effect size (r)	% Variance explained
Gang membership	.31	9.6
Violent video game usage	.30	8.8
Poor parent–child relations	.19	3.6
Media violence usage (all media)	.17	2.9
Low IQ	.11	1.2
Broken home	.10	1.0
Abusive parents	.09	0.8

Note: The measure of effect size reported here is the average correlation (*r*). According to Cohen's (1988) benchmarks, *r* = .10 denotes a small effect, *r* = .30 a medium-sized effect, and *r* = .50 or above a large effect.

Source: Adapted from Anderson, Gentile, & Buckley, 2007, p. 143, with permission from Oxford University Press. Includes data reported in U.S. Department of Health & Services (2001) Youth Violence: A Report of the Surgeon General. Rockville, M.D: U.S. Government Printing Office.

well above variables that most people would believe to be far more important in predicting the risk of aggression, such as coming from a broken home or having abusive parents.

empathy with victims of real-life violence. Habituation describes the process whereby the ability of a stimulus to elicit arousal becomes weaker with each consecutive presentation. The person gets used to it, and the stimulus loses its impact. The decline in physiological arousal in the course of prolonged exposure to violence is well documented (e.g. Averill, Malmstrom, Koriat, & Lazarus, 1972). A study by Krahé, Möller, Huesmann, Kirwil, Felber, and Berger (2011) showed that the more violent media participants used habitually, the less anxiety and the more pleasant arousal they reported when shown a violent film clip. No such habituation was found for sad or funny clips, indicating that

habituation is specific to the violent content of the media diet.

4. Habitual exposure to violent media content also affects the readiness to engage in aggressive behaviour through promoting the *normative acceptance of aggression* and the development of a hostile attribution bias. The more people see aggression presented as a way of resolving conflicts of interests and expressing anger, the more they come to think of it as common and acceptable. A longitudinal study with Grade 7 and 8 pupils in Germany by Möller and Krahé (2009) showed that violent video game-playing predicted higher normative acceptance of aggression thirty months later which, in turn,

was a significant predictor of self-reported physical aggression. Media portrayals of violence also create a view of the world as a hostile place, thereby promoting the development of a hostile attribution bias (Krahé & Möller, 2004).

In addition to violence in films and video games, recent research has examined violent lyrics in music as triggers of aggressive responses. In research by Fischer and Greitemeyer (2006), men exposed to songs with lyrics that derogate women (such as 'Superman' by Eminem and 'Self-Esteem' by Offspring), recalled more negative attributes about women and behaved more aggressively toward a female experimenter than men exposed to neutral lyrics. In a second study, women who had listened to songs with men-hating lyrics (such as 'You Oughta Know' by Alanis Morrisette and 'Can't Hold Us Down' by Christina Aguilera) displayed more aggression towards a male confederate.

Finally, it is worth noting that even reading the Bible can make you more aggressive. Bushman, Ridge, Das, Key, and Busath (2007) gave students a text from the Book of Judges from the Old Testament describing an act of violent retaliation by an Israelite tribe. Half were told the text was taken from the Bible, the other half were told it came from an ancient scroll. For half of the participants, a section was added to the text stating that God had sanctioned the killing ('. . . the LORD commanded Israel to take arms against their brothers and chasten them before the LORD'). Participants who thought the text came from the bible subsequently administered more aversive noise blasts to a confederate than those who believed the text was from an ancient scroll, and those who had read that God sanctioned the killing behaved more aggressively than those not hearing about God. In a second study, belief in God was added as an individual difference variable, and a significant interaction between belief in God and God sanctioning the violent actions was found: whether or not God had sanctioned the killing only made a difference to those who believed in God. Believers showed significantly more aggression when they thought that God sanctioned the killing than when God was not mentioned. For the nonbelievers, mentioning that God had sanctioned the killing had no effect on the level of noise delivered to the other person.

Summary

The research reviewed in this section shows that aggressive behaviour varies both as a function of person variables and as a function of situational context. Stable individual differences in the propensity to act aggressively (trait aggressiveness) and to interpret others' actions as an expression of hostile intent (hostile attribution bias) predict differences in the ease with which aggressive responses are triggered in a particular situation. Research has also identified gender differences, with men showing more physical aggression than do women. So far, the evidence is less clear-cut for indirect aggression, such as spreading rumours. Among the situational variables affecting the likelihood of aggressive behaviour, research has consistently shown that alcohol consumption, high temperature and exposure to media violence lower the threshold for aggressive behaviour. In the case of media violence, longitudinal studies have demonstrated that negative effects can be found over extended periods of time.

AGGRESSION AS A SOCIAL PROBLEM

What do we know about the prevalence and the risk factors of intimate partner violence, sexual aggression, bullying and violence between groups?

The theoretical and empirical contributions discussed so far identified critical input variables as well as cognitive, affective and arousal processes that explain the occurrence of aggressive behaviour. In this section we will look at specific forms of aggressive behaviour between individuals and between groups and discuss how the theories and findings examined earlier can contribute to a better understanding of these social problems.

Intimate partner violence

'Intimate partner violence' is defined as the perpetration or threat of an act of physical violence, by one partner on the other, in the context of a dating/marital relationship. It is a serious problem across the world, even though the prevalence rates vary enormously, not only between, but also within countries (see reviews of the international evidence by Krahé, Bieneck, & Möller, 2005; Krug, Dahlberg, Mercy, Zwi, & Lozano, 2002). One of the most contentious issues in this field of research refers to the question of whether men and women are involved in intimate partner violence to the same or a different degree. Two main data sources are available to address the scale of intimate partner violence and the question of men's and women's involvement as perpetrators: (a) official crime statistics and crime victimization surveys using representative samples; and (b) research collecting self-reports of perpetration of, or victimization by,

Conflict Tactics Scales (CTS) instrument for measuring intimate partner violence by collecting self-reports of perpetration and/or victimization.

relationship aggression, using the **Conflict Tactics Scales** (originally called the CTS, Straus, 1979; and revised as CTS2, Straus, Hamby, Boney-McCoy, & Sugarman, 1996).

Official crime victimization figures show that women outnumber men by a wide margin as victims of partner violence and are more likely to suffer injuries as a result of the partner's actions (e.g. Rennison & Welchans, 2000). Figure 9.16 presents the gender imbalance for three forms of intimate partner violence, namely simple assault, aggravated assault and robbery, in data from the National Crime Victimization Survey (NCVS) in the US for the period 2001 to 2005.

For the UK, findings from the British Crime Survey (BCS) 2007–08 revealed that 18 per cent of the women and 10 per cent of the men surveyed had experienced physical abuse by an intimate partner at least once since the age of 16 (Povey, Coleman, Kaiza, & Roe, 2009). For incidents in the last 12 months, the gender ratio was more balanced, with 2 per cent of men and 2.2 per cent of women reporting physical abuse by an intimate partner (Figure 9.17).

Studies using the **Conflict Tactics Scales**, however, portray a different picture. In this measure, participants are presented with a list of minor and severe acts of physical aggression and asked to indicate whether and how many times they have shown the behaviour in question towards an intimate partner. Parallel items are included to measure experiences of victimization by an intimate

FIGURE 9.17 *Intimate partner violence is a serious problem across the world. Research looks at whether men and women are involved as perpetrators to the same or a different degree.*
Source: © Purestock. Used under licence from Getty Images.

partner. In addition, the scale measures injuries suffered by or inflicted on a partner. Individual Differences 9.2 presents the items of the physical assault scale and the injury scale, and shows you how to use it to assess gender differences in the perpetration of physical aggression towards a partner amongst your fellow students.

In addition to the items presented in the table, the CTS2 contains three further scales, measuring *psychological aggression* (defined as communications intended to cause psychological pain to a partner, such as insults or

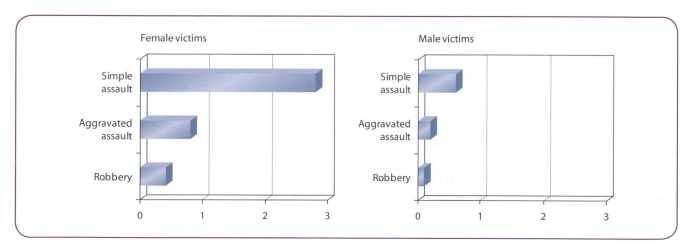

FIGURE 9.16 *Average annual rate of nonfatal intimate partner victimization in the United States, by type of crime, 2001–2005. Rate per 1000 people of age 12 or older.*

Note: **Simple assault:** an attack without a weapon resulting either in no injury, minor injury (for example, bruises, black eyes, cuts) or in undetermined injury requiring less than 2 days of hospitalization. Also includes attempted assault without weapon. **Aggravated assault:** the attack or attempted attack with a weapon, regardless of whether or not an injury occurred and attack without a weapon when serious injury results. **Robbery:** completed or attempted theft, directly from a person, of property or cash by force or threat of force, with or without a weapon, and with or without injury.

Source: Bureau of Justice Statistics. *National Crime Victimization Survey.* Retrieved from http://bjs.ojp.usdoj.gov/content/pub/pdf/ipvus.pdf

IS THERE A GENDER DIFFERENCE IN THE PERPETRATION OF AGGRESSION AGAINST AN INTIMATE PARTNER AND THE RISK OF INJURY?

Items of the Physical Assault Scale and the Injury Scale of the Revised Conflict Tactics Scales (CTS2; based on Straus et al., 1996).

Task

Ask ten male and ten female students from your year to complete (anonymously) the list of items displayed below. Do not ask for any additional information except respondents' gender. Then collect the responses in a sealed envelope and calculate the mean score on each item for the male and female participants, using the scores from 1 to 6. Can you replicate the findings that (a) women score higher on the physical assault scale of the CTS2 and (b) men score higher on the injury scale?

Instruction

No matter how well a couple gets along, there are times when they disagree, get annoyed with the other person, want different things from each other, or just have spats or fights because they are in a bad mood, are tired or for some other reason. Couples also have many different ways to settle their differences. This is a list of things that might happen when you have differences. Please circle how many times you did each of the things in the past year.

How often did this happen:

1	2	3	4	5	6	B	N								
Once in the past year	Twice in the past year	3–5 times in the past year	6–10 times in the past year	11–20 times in the past year	More than 20 times in the past year	Not in the past year, but happened before	This has never happened								
1. I threw something at my partner that could hurt.								1	2	3	4	5	6	B	N
2. I twisted my partner's arm or hair.															
3. I pushed or shoved my partner.															
4. I grabbed my partner.															
5. I slapped my partner.															
6. I used a knife or gun on my partner.															
7. I punched or hit my partner with something that could hurt.															
8. I choked my partner.															
9. I slammed my partner against a wall.															
10. I beat up my partner.															
11. I burned or scalded my partner on purpose.															
12. I kicked my partner.															
13. My partner had a sprain, bruise or small cut because of a fight with me.															
14. My partner still felt physical pain the next day because of a fight we had.															
15. My partner passed out from being hit on the head in a fight with me.															
16. My partner went to a doctor because of a fight with me.															
17. My partner needed to see a doctor because of a fight with me, but didn't.															
18. My partner had a broken bone from a fight with me.															

Source: Based on Straus et al., 1996, with permission from SAGE Publications, Inc.

Note: Items 1–5 describe behaviours classified by Straus et al. as 'minor physical assault', Items 6–12 represent 'severe physical assault' and Items 13–18 form the 'injury' scale. These labels should not be communicated to your participants.

verbal abuse), *sexual aggression, and negotiation* as a non-aggressive form of conflict resolution in relationships. A large body of evidence has shown that on the CTS women feature as much as or even more than men do in the perpetration of physical aggression toward a partner. In a German study with young adults, all gender differences that were found on the items of the CTS2 were in the direction of women scoring higher than men on the perpetration of, and men scoring higher than women on victimization by, physical aggression by a partner (Krahé & Berger, 2005). In a meta-analysis including 82 studies, Archer (2000) also found that women were slightly more likely than men to show physical aggression towards a partner. At the same time, however, he concluded that men were more likely to inflict injury on their partner, a finding that may explain, at least to some extent, why men feature more prominently as perpetrators of interpersonal violence in crime statistics. If their actions are more likely to lead to injuries, the odds are increased that they will be reported to the police and find their way into official records.

Critics have argued that the overrepresentation of women as perpetrators of intimate partner violence portrayed by studies using the CTS is distorted, because this instrument records acts of violence without considering their context. In particular, it does not consider whether the behaviour shown is an act of unprovoked aggression or a response to a previous attack, so that an act of self-defence by a woman is counted in the same way as the initial assault by her male partner. It is now widely acknowledged by researchers that intimate partner violence is not a unitary phenomenon, but comprises different forms, contexts and underlying dynamics. Kelly and Johnson (2008) distinguish coercive controlling violence as a stable feature of a relationship (more often shown by men), violent resistance in response to a coercive controlling partner (more often shown by women), and situational couple violence, arising out of everyday conflict situations (which is largely gender-symmetrical). Therefore, to make progress in the understanding of the dynamics of intimate partner violence, greater attention needs to be paid to the specific forms and contexts in which assaults on intimate partners take place (Frieze, 2000).

Sexual aggression

Sexual aggression includes a range of forced sexual activities, such as sexual intercourse, oral sex, kissing and petting, using a range of coercive strategies, such as threat or use of physical force, exploitation of the victim's inability to resist or verbal pressure. It also includes unwanted sexual attention in the form of sexual harassment, stalking

and obscene phone calls (Belknap, Fisher, & Cullen, 1999; Frieze & Davis, 2002). In contrast to intimate partner violence, it is undisputed that sexual violence is gender-asymmetrical, with the vast majority of sexual assaults committed by male perpetrators against female victims, and this is reflected both in rapes recorded by the police and in large-scale victimization surveys. Of the 7314 cases of completed and attempted rape and sexual assault recorded by the police in Germany in 2009, 99 per cent involved a male perpetrator (Polizeiliche Kriminalstatistik, 2009, p. 134 and 136). Of the victims, 96.1 per cent were female and 3.9 per cent were male. Although the figures do not show the sex of the perpetrator for male victims, it is clear from the very low overall perpetration rate for women that the majority of male rapes must have been committed by a male perpetrator. UK crime statistics revealed that 7778 rapes of a female aged 16 and over were reported to the police in 2008–9, compared to 316 rapes of a male aged 16 or over (Walker, Flatley, Kershaw, & Moon, 2009). Complementing crime statistics that only reflect cases actually reported to the police, large-scale studies have been conducted to record sexual victimization of women by men. An example of the data generated by this approach is presented in Table 9.3.

Although less widely studied, it should be noted that sexual violence is also a problem in same-sex relationships

Table 9.3 *Prevalence of men's sexual aggression against women.*

Form of sexual victimization/ aggression	Women's victimization reports in %	Men's perpetration reports in %	N of studies
Rape[a]	12.9	4.7	63
Attempted rape	18.3	10.8	35
Sexual assault[b]	22.0	8.9	40
Sexual contact[c]	24.0	13.4	28
Sexual coercion[d]	24.9	24.0	39

[a] Completed sexual intercourse through threat or use of force.

[b] Penetration of the body through threat or use of force.

[c] Sexual acts without penetration of the body through continued arguments, authority, force or threat of force.

[d] Sexual intercourse through verbal pressure or abuse of position of authority.

Source: Adapted from Spitzberg (1999), with permission from Springer Publishing Company.

(e.g. Krahé, Schütze, Fritsche, & Waizenhöfer, 2000) and that women do show sexual aggression against men (Krahé, Waizenhöfer, & Möller, 2003; Schatzel-Murphy, Harris, Knight, & Milburn, 2009). The majority of sexual assaults are committed by a perpetrator known to the victim, either as an acquaintance or as an intimate partner. Despite the persistence of the 'real rape stereotype' that pictures rape as a violent surprise attack in a dark alleyway, sexual assaults by strangers are the exception rather than the rule. Childhood abuse has been identified as an important biographical risk factor for perpetrating sexual aggression in both men and women (Schatzel-Murphy et al., 2009). As a situational risk factor, alcohol use has also been found consistently to increase the risk of sexual aggression (Abbey, Zawacki, Buck, Clinton, & McAuslan, 2004).

The consequences of a sexual assault for the victim are severe. A substantial number of rape victims develop the clinical symptomatology of **post-traumatic stress disorder** (PTSD). Victims re-experience the assault in dreams, images and intrusive memories, they try to avoid cues reminding them of the assault, and experience a general emotional numbness (Koss, Bailey, Yuan, Herrera, & Lichter, 2003). Contrary to a widely held public belief, assaults by partners and acquaintances are as traumatizing for the victim as are assaults by strangers (Culbertson & Dehle, 2001).

> **post-traumatic stress disorder (PTSD)** characteristic patterns of symptoms observed in survivors of traumatic experiences such as rape.

Victims of sexual aggression not only have to come to terms with the emotional trauma of the assault itself, they also have to cope with the reactions of others who learn about their fate. There is a widespread tendency to blame the victim of a sexual assault, unparalleled in judgements of victims of other criminal offences (Bieneck & Krahé, 2011). A large body of evidence has shown that certain victim characteristics, such as low social status, higher number of sexual partners and pre-rape behaviour that is at odds with female role requirements (e.g. drinking alone in a bar) are linked to higher attributions of responsibility to the victim, and often correspondingly lower responsibility attributed to the attacker. The tendency to shift blame from the perpetrator to the victim is seen as a major factor in the low conviction rates for rape that have plagued the legal systems of many Western countries (Temkin & Krahé, 2008).

Bullying in school and the workplace

The last 30 years have seen a growing concern about aggressive behaviour in school and work settings (Olweus, 1994; Randall, 1997). Referred to by different terms, such as **bullying, mobbing,** or workplace aggression, this phenomenon denotes aggressive behaviour directed at victims who cannot easily defend themselves within an institutional setting (Smith, Ananiadou, & Cowie, 2003; Figure 9.18). Forms of bullying include physical, verbal and relational aggression; that is, behaviour directed at damaging the victim's peer relationships.

> **bullying** (also known as *mobbing*) denotes aggressive behaviour directed at victims who cannot easily defend themselves, typically in schools and at the workplace.

With the advent of modern communication technology a new mode of bullying, **cyberbullying,** has appeared on the scene. Cyberbullying is not limited to a relatively small face-to-face audience, but can humiliate and intimidate others on a large scale and under the cloak of anonymity (Dooley, Pyzalski, & Cross, 2009). Cyberbullying involves the use of modern technology, such as computers, mobile phones or other electronic devices to inflict intentional harm on others. Sending threatening e-mails, posting derogatory comments about a classmate on Internet platforms, or circulating photos designed to embarrass or humiliate another person are examples of cyberbullying.

> **cyberbullying** involves the use of modern technology, such as computers, mobile phones or other electronic devices to inflict intentional harm on others.

In an international survey of 11- to 15-year-olds in 40 countries conducted on behalf of the World Health Organization, 12.6 per cent of participants were identified as victims of bullying, 10.7 per cent were identified as bullies, and 3.6 per cent were both bullies and victims (Craig et al., 2009). Bullying typically takes place over

FIGURE 9.18 *Bullying, either in schools or in the workplace, denotes aggressive behaviour directed at victims who cannot easily defend themselves.*

Source: © Weston Colton. Used under licence from Getty Images.

extended periods of time and involves a power differential between bully and victim based on physical strength or superior status that undermines the victim's ability to defend him or herself, or to retaliate.

The typical victim is an anxious, socially withdrawn child or adolescent, isolated from his or her peer group and likely to be physically weaker than most peers. In contrast, bullies are typically strong, dominant and assertive, showing aggressive behaviour not just towards their victims, but also towards parents, teachers and other adults (see Griffin & Gross, 2004, for a comprehensive review). Boys feature more prominently than girls as victims as well as perpetrators of bullying (Olweus, 1994). They are also more likely to use physical aggression than are girls, who rely more on verbal and relational forms of aggression, as shown in a cross-national comparison involving 21 countries (Smith et al., 1999). Salmivalli (2010) points out that bullying needs to be examined in a group context, looking not only at the roles of bullies and victims, but also at those of peer witnesses who may assist or encourage the bullies, intervene on behalf of the victim, or remain passive bystanders. Being able to dominate and intimidate others is associated with status gain in one's peer group, which makes it hard for others to intervene and take sides with the weaker victim. Being the target of bullying can bring long-term misery to the victims, including an increased risk of suicide (see Social Psychology Beyond the Lab 9.3). Being a bully may also have long-term negative consequences (Hawker & Boulton, 2000). Social Psychology Beyond the Lab 9.3 presents some relevant data from a large-scale study.

Harassing weaker members of the peer group is not limited to the school context, but also happens to people at work. Workplace bullying refers to behaviours intended to make another person feel miserable at work over longer periods of time, with the targets being unable to defend themselves due to an imbalance of power between perpetrator and victim, either because the bully has a higher status (e.g. as a boss bullying a subordinate) or a stronger position among peers (e.g. as a man bullying an equal-status woman in a male-dominated workgroup). According to Hoel, Rayner, and Cooper (1999), both the prevalence and the nature of bullying experienced in the workplace are similar for men and women. However, women appear to be more negatively affected by bullying than are men. A large-scale study by Smith, Singer, Hoel, and Cooper (2003) explored potential links between individuals' experience of bullying at school and in the workplace and found a significant association between school and workplace bullying: respondents who had been victimized at school were more likely to have been bullied at work in the last five years than respondents who had not been bullied at school. It is important to note, however, that the relationship was inferred on the basis of retrospective reports of school bullying that may have been inaccurately recalled or distorted in the light of subsequent experiences of bullying in the workplace. A meta-analysis including data from 90 samples showed that workplace bullying was more likely to occur in work environments where other stressors were present, such as role conflict and ambiguity, and that it was associated with significant impairments of victims' well-being, such as increased levels of anxiety, depression and physical symptoms (Bowling & Beehr, 2006).

Intergroup violence

The forms of aggression discussed so far have referred to confrontations between individuals, that is, they were manifestations of **interpersonal aggression**. In this section, we will turn to **intergroup aggression**, that is aggression originating in the context of encounters between groups (Goldstein, 2002). Groups may get into violent conflict because they compete for goals, such as power or material profit, that only one party can obtain, as postulated by Sherif's (1966) theory of realistic group conflict (see Chapter 14 for a more detailed account of Sherif's theorizing). However, even in the absence of realistic conflicts of interest, the mere categorization of people into groups may produce feelings of intergroup hostility in an attempt to make the ingroup appear superior and promote a positive view of their own group (see discussion of social identity theory in Chapter 14). From this perspective, examined in more detail below, intergroup aggression is closely linked to the group membership and affiliation of the actors. For example, Van Hiel, Hautman, Cornelis, and De Clercq (2007) showed that the more football fans identified with their favourite team, the higher their self-reported physical and verbal aggression in the context of football matches. Intergroup aggression can be both hostile (e.g. letting off steam after a defeat of one's favoured sports team) and instrumental (e.g. attacks by terrorist groups in pursuit of a political cause).

In the *World Report on Violence and Health* compiled by the World Health Organization, the term **collective violence** is used to refer to 'the instrumental use of violence by people who identify themselves

interpersonal aggression aggressive behaviour between individuals rather than groups.

intergroup aggression aggressive encounters between groups or aggression based on group membership rather than individual characteristics, such as football hooliganism.

collective violence instrumental use of violence by people who identify themselves as members of a group against another group in order to achieve political, economic or social objectives.

SOCIAL PSYCHOLOGY BEYOND THE LAB 9.3

BULLIED TO DEATH? BULLYING AND THE RISK OF SUICIDE

From *The Times*, August 22 2009, 'Cyberbullying was believed to be the cause of the suicide of 15-year-old Megan Gillan, from Macclesfield, Cheshire, who took an overdose of painkillers after receiving abusive messages on networking site Bebo'.

Systematic research shows that victims of traditional as well as cyberbullying are at increased risk of suicidal thoughts and self-killings. A survey of about 2000 randomly selected middle-school students in the US revealed that victims of traditional bullying were 1.7 times more likely than non-victims to attempt suicide, and victims of cyberbullying were 1.9 times more likely than non-victims (Hinduja & Patchin, 2010). A Finnish study examining the link between bullying and victimization at the age of 8 with attempted and completed suicides before the age of 25 (in a sample of more than 5300 children born in 1981) also yielded troubling results, as shown in Table 9.4.

Both being a bully and being a victim was associated with an increased suicidal risk. Among girls, the odds ratio shows that those who were frequently bullied at age 8 were 6.3 times more likely to have attempted or completed suicide before the age of 25 than those not bullied at age 8. This figure is adjusted for conduct disorders and depression assessed at age 8 which would be additional risk factors of suicide.

Table 9.4 *Percentage of boys and girls who attempted or committed suicide before the age of 25 in relation to their status as bullies or victims at the age of 8.*

	Victims			Bullies		
	Never	**Sometimes**	**Frequently**	**Never**	**Sometimes**	**Frequently**
Boys						
%	0.5	1.2	2.9	0.5	1.0	3.9
OR*		1.9	3.8		1.3	1.8
Girls						
%	0.8	1.0	3.3	1.1	0.7	0.0
OR*		1.5	6.3		0.7	–

*OR (odds ratios) adjusted for conduct disorders and depression at age 8. ORs indicate the increased probability of attempted or completed suicide in the bully and victim groups compared to the non-bully or non-victim groups.

Source: Based on Klomek et al., 2009, with permission from Elsevier.

as members of a group . . . against another group or set of individuals, in order to achieve political, economic, or social objectives' (Krug et al., 2002, p. 215). It comprises (1) political conflicts within and between states, such as war and terrorism; (2) state-perpetrated violence, such as genocide and torture; and (3) organized violent crime, such as banditry and gang warfare. The report identifies a range of risk factors at the societal level that make collective violence more likely. The main factors are summarized in Table 9.5.

While these risk factors may not be sufficient on their own to explain collective violence, in combination they create conditions that precipitate aggressive confrontations between groups. Collective violence has dramatic

Table 9.5 *Risk factors of collective violence.*

Political factors	- Lack of democratic processes - Unequal access to political power and to natural resources of different regions, social classes, religions or ethnic groups
Societal and community factors	- Inequality between groups in the allocation of goods and services - Fuelling of group fanaticism along ethnic, national or religious lines - Ready availability of weapons
Demographic factors	- Rapid demographic change, particularly increases in population density and in the proportion of young people

Source: Based on data reported in the WHO World Report on Violence and Health, Krug et al., 2002, Chapter 8.

consequences on people directly or indirectly involved in the conflict, in terms of physical and mental health, as well as their socioeconomic welfare.

Whereas the risk factors shown in Table 9.5 operate at the level of society, it is equally important to understand what happens to individuals to make them more prone to act aggressively as members of a group. Social psychologists have addressed this question from different angles, and there are two lines of research that are particularly relevant here. The first line of research is concerned with short-term, situational changes in the individual as a result of being part of a group, focusing on the construct of deindividuation (see Chapter 8). The second line of research looks at more long-term processes of identification and affiliation with a group and their impact on aggression towards outgroups, based on the construct of social identity. We will consider both approaches in turn.

Following LeBon's (1896) early work on crowd behaviour, Zimbardo (1969) proposed in his theory of deindividuation that individuals acting in a large group lose their sense of personal identity and responsibility and may show aggressive behaviour that would be suppressed by their internal standards if they were more aware of their identity as individuals. He investigated this phenomenon, most dramatically, in his famous 'Stanford Prison Experiment' (see Chapter 8; Figure 9.19), in which he randomly allocated a group of mentally healthy young men to the roles of prisoners or prison guards and then asked them to enact their respective roles in a mock prison established in his laboratory at Stanford University. The guards engaged in increasingly cruel treatments of their prisoners, and the prisoners developed symptoms of severe trauma.

In order to explain why ordinary people engage in behaviours totally out of their character as individuals, Zimbardo proposed three input variables that promote deindividuation: anonymity, diffusion of responsibility

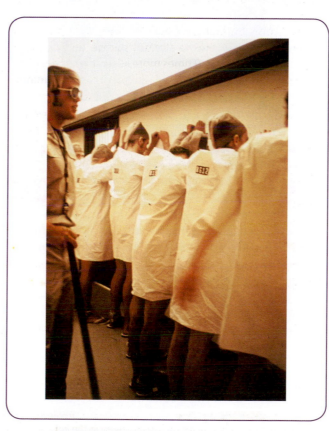

FIGURE 9.19 *The Stanford Prison Experiment.*
Source: © Philip G. Zimbardo, Inc. Reprinted with permission.

and large group size. Under these conditions, people are thought to engage in actions characterized by impulsiveness, irrationality and regression to primitive forms of behaviour. A change in attentional focus has been proposed as a key mechanism explaining aggression by members of a crowd (Diener, 1980). When people are on their own, their attention is typically focused on the self, and they monitor their own behaviour against the standard of their personal norms and values. By contrast, being

(a)

(b)

FIGURE 9.20(a) and (b) *Perceived group norms are critical in making individuals' behaviour either more or less aggressive when they are part of a group.*

Source: (a) © Danita Delimont. Used under licence from Getty Images; (b) © michaeljung. Used under licence from Shutterstock.

part of a larger group shifts attention away from the self onto the situation, reducing people's ability to regulate their behaviour in accordance with their personal norms and increasing their attention to the situational cues, e.g. the aggressive behaviour of other group members. We earlier referred to the work by Mullen (1986), who analysed newspaper reports of lynchings by violent mobs, which also emphasized the lack of self-focused attention as an explanation for violent group behaviour.

If being in a large group involves a shift from individual norms to norms prevailing in the group, it follows that group behaviour should only be more violent than individual behaviour if the group norms are seen as promoting or at least condoning aggression. This is exactly what the research showed. For example, when people were deindividuated by wearing uniforms, they behaved more aggressively when dressed in outfits of the Ku Klux Klan, a group associated with aggressive norms, than when dressed as nurses, a group associated with prosocial values (Johnson & Downing, 1979; Figure 9.20). Thus, perceived group norms are critical in making individuals' behaviour either more or less aggressive when they are part of a group.

From the perspective of social identity theory (Tajfel, 1981), intergroup aggression is seen as the result of the psychological need to establish and maintain a positive identity. In addition to a positive sense of personal identity based on their individual qualities, people seek to establish a sense of self-worth through the social groups to which they belong. For example, being a member of a national group is a source of personal pride for many people, and they are keen to stress the positive qualities of their group (Figure 9.21). At the same time, they may also seek to minimize the positive qualities and stress the shortcomings of other groups, thereby achieving positive distinctiveness for their own group (Brown, 1999). Feeling close to ingroup members and distancing oneself from outgroups gives rise to ingroup favouritism, i.e. preferential treatment and evaluations of ingroup members solely on the basis of their group membership. The conflict between Protestants and Catholics in Northern Ireland is a case in point. As shown by Cairns, Kenworthy, Campbell, and Hewstone (2006), members of each religious group had more positive feelings for their own community than for the respective other community, and this pattern was particularly evident for those who identified strongly with their religious group.

Devaluing the outgroup is a stronger form of intergroup bias than merely favouring the ingroup (see Chapter 14). Outgroup derogation promotes feelings of hostility that may lower the threshold for aggressive

FIGURE 9.21 *Being a member of a national group is a source of personal pride for many people.*

Source: © Michael Blann. Used under licence from Getty Images.

behaviour towards outgroup members, even when there is no material conflict of interest between the groups. As Lickel, Miller, Stenstrom, Denson, and Schmader (2006) have shown, there is even a tendency for ingroup members to engage in 'vicarious retribution' against outgroups; that is, to show an aggressive response to an outgroup member after a member of their own group had been the target of aggression from another person in that outgroup. For example, if a German boy sees a member of his national group being verbally abused by a Turk, he may retaliate by yelling abuse next time he meets another Turk, even though neither he nor the other Turk had anything to do with the initial confrontation. According to a recent analysis of displaced aggression and gang violence by Vasquez, Lickel, and Hennigan (2010), the motivation to retaliate vicariously against outgroup members is stronger the more people identify with their respective ingroup. This line of research underlines the importance of social identity concerns in understanding aggression between groups.

As we have seen from the preceding discussion, there are societal-level, group-level and individual-level factors that promote aggression and violence between groups, and they need to be considered in conjunction for a full understanding of when and why intergroup aggression occurs. We will illustrate how to integrate these different levels for a better understanding of intergroup aggression using the case of terrorism, and applying Moghaddam's (2005) so-called **staircase model**. Terrorism refers

staircase model describes the pathway to terrorism as a succession of steps explaining why out of large numbers of disaffected people in a society only very few end up committing terrorist acts.

to politically motivated violence, intended to spread fear and terror among members of a society in order to influence the decision making or behaviour of political agents. Understanding the processes that lead to the carrying out of terrorist attacks is of critical importance in addressing this worldwide problem. In his analysis, Moghaddam started off with the observation that societal-level variables, such as those listed in Table 9.5, cannot explain why, out of all the people living under the same adverse conditions, only very few end up as terrorists. Similarly, individual-level variables cannot explain why, out of all people to which particular individual characteristics apply, only very few turn to terrorism. In his model, shown in Figure 9.22, he describes the pathway to becoming a terrorist as a narrowing staircase that only very few people climb to the top.

The *ground floor* is occupied by all members of society who evaluate their living conditions in terms of fairness and justice. Those who perceive their conditions to be fair and just remain on the ground floor, those who see them as unjust move on to the first floor. On the *first floor*, they evaluate the options for improving conditions. Those who conclude that there are options for them to improve their individual position and influence decision-makers leave the staircase to terrorism at this level and pursue non-violent paths. Those who are dissatisfied with available options for redressing injustices move on to the *second floor*. On the second floor, feelings of anger and frustration over not being able to improve their situation predominate, triggering the search for a target to blame for their misfortune. This enemy can either be a direct opponent, such as a central government denying autonomy to an ethnic group or region, or a third party to whom aggression is displaced, such as reflected in the widespread anti-Americanism in the Middle East.

People on this level, who are persuaded that there is an enemy towards whom they can direct their aggressive tendencies, will then climb up to the next floor. By the time they arrive on the *third floor*, individuals have developed a certain readiness towards violence that can now be exploited by terrorist organizations by offering a sense of 'moral engagement' to their potential new recruits. Violent actions against the 'enemy' are presented as morally acceptable or even imperative, and recruits are offered a new and appealing social identity as members of a highly selective ingroup aiming to bring justice to the world. Those for whom this offer is attractive climb up to the next floor. On the *fourth floor*, categorical thinking in terms of 'we' versus 'them' is promoted, by isolating new recruits from their families and friends, imposing strict secrecy and emphasizing the legitimacy of the terrorist organization. There is

Review: Selective Moral disengagement by Bandura

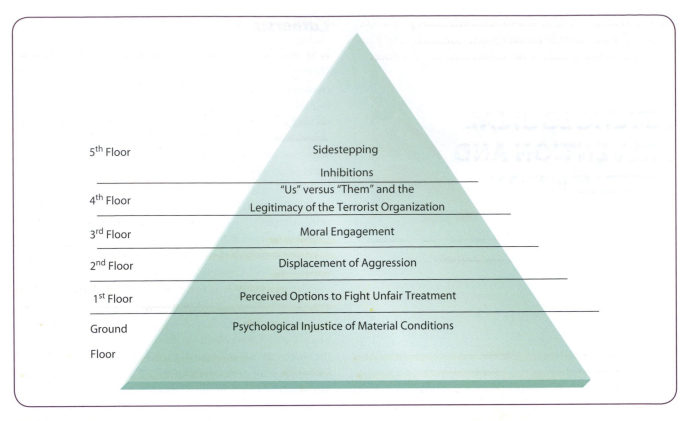

5th Floor	Sidestepping
	Inhibitions
4th Floor	"Us" versus "Them" and the
	Legitimacy of the Terrorist Organization
3rd Floor	Moral Engagement
2nd Floor	Displacement of Aggression
1st Floor	Perceived Options to Fight Unfair Treatment
Ground Floor	Psychological Injustice of Material Conditions

FIGURE 9.22   *The 'staircase model' of terrorism.*

Source: Based on information in Moghaddam, 2005.

virtually no chance for people who have climbed up to this floor to withdraw and exit alive. Therefore, they move on to the *fifth floor,* which involves carrying out the terrorist act. In order to operate effectively on this floor, inhibitions against killing innocent people must be overcome, and this is achieved by two well-established psychological mechanisms: *categorization,* stressing the differentiation between ingroup and out-group, and *distancing,* exaggerating the differences between the ingroup and the targets that are seen as the 'enemy'.

The staircase metaphor is useful for conceptualiz-ing the process by which a small number of individu-als from large groups of disaffected people living under adverse conditions end up committing acts of violence against innocent targets. At the same time, it provides some clues regarding the prevention of terrorism. Moghaddam (2005) points out that it is not enough to try and identify the individuals prepared to carry out terrorist acts before they get a chance to do so, because that would only make room for new people to step for-ward. Instead, terrorism can only be ended by reform-ing the conditions on the ground floor so that they are no longer perceived as unjust and hopeless by large parts of the population.

Summary

Intimate partner violence, sexual aggression, bullying and intergroup violence are widespread forms of aggres-sion in everyday life. They can lead to lasting negative effects on the victims' psychological functioning and well-being. In research on intimate partner violence, the issue of whether men or women feature more promi-nently as perpetrators is controversial, but there is con-sistent evidence that women are more likely to be injured by an intimate partner than are men. Sexual aggression is perpetrated mostly by men against women. Bullying in school and the workplace is typically characterized by a power differential between perpetrator and victim. Some studies suggest that the experience of being bul-lied in school makes victims vulnerable to long-term psy-chological problems. In explaining aggression between groups, societal factors, such as perceived injustice, group factors, such as common norms, and individual factors, such as a lack of self-focused attention play a role. The 'staircase model' of terrorism considers the joint influence of these factors to explain terrorist violence.

PSYCHOLOGICAL PREVENTION AND INTERVENTION

What are effective strategies for preventing or reducing aggression?

It has become clear that aggression poses a serious threat to the health and well-being of individuals and the functioning of societies. Although the present chapter has focused on physical and psychological effects of aggression on the individual, it should also be remembered that the economic costs of interpersonal violence for a society as a whole are enormous. A report by the World Health Organization shows the financial consequences of different forms of violence (Waters et al., 2004). For example, it quotes data by Miller, Cohen, and Rossman (1993) who estimated the costs of rape in the United States in terms of medical treatment as well as impairment of mental health, productivity and quality of life at $47,000 per case. In a survey of over 3000 women in the United States, Rivara et al. (2007) found that annual health care costs were 19 per cent higher among victims of intimate partner violence than among nonvictimized women. Based on a victimization rate of 44 per cent in their sample, they extrapolated that for every 100,000 women in the health care system, excess health care costs of $19.3 million are incurred each year as a result of intimate partner violence.

Given the dramatic effects of aggression and violence on individuals, social groups and communities at large, psychologists not only have to deal with the task of investigating how, when, and why aggressive behaviour is shown, they are also expected to propose ways of counteracting and preventing its occurrence. Aggressive behaviour is ultimately performed by individual actors. Therefore, an important aim of intervention efforts is to reduce the probability that a person will show aggressive behaviour, either in a specific situation or over time. Three main mechanisms have been discussed by which aggressive behaviour might, in principle, be prevented: catharsis, punishment, and the elicitation of incompatible responses.

catharsis release of aggressive tension through symbolic engagement in aggressive behaviour.

Catharsis

It is widely believed that releasing aggressive tension through physical activity in sport or in symbolic ways, such as through sarcastic humour or acting aggressively in the virtual reality of a videogame, is a successful strategy for 'letting off steam' and reducing aggression (Bushman & Whitaker, 2010). The idea that aggressive urges can be channelled into harmless forms of expression, which is also part of Lorenz's (1966) steam boiler model of aggression discussed earlier, is captured in the *catharsis hypothesis*. Catharsis refers to the idea of Greek tragedy that watching tragic conflict unfold and be resolved on stage leads to a purification or 'cleansing' of emotions (pity and fear) and brings about spiritual renewal or release from tension in the spectators. However, empirical evidence shows that symbolic engagement in aggressive thoughts or actions is not just ineffective, but even counterproductive for reducing aggression (Schaefer & Mattei, 2005). Several studies indicate that the imaginary performance of aggressive behaviour, such as in pretend play or watching media violence, is more likely to enhance aggression than to reduce it (Bushman, 2002; Bushman, Baumeister, & Stack, 1999). These findings are explained with reference to the role of aggressive cues in enhancing the likelihood of aggressive behaviour: symbolic acts of aggression can be regarded as aggressive cues that prime hostile thoughts and feelings, and thereby pave the way for aggressive behaviour. Focusing on the arousal component of catharsis, Verona and Sullivan (2008) conducted a study in which they made participants engage in aggressive behaviour by delivering unpleasant air blasts to a confederate, and recorded the participants' heart rate before and after they engaged in aggressive behaviour. They found that those participants who showed the greatest reduction in heart rate after performing the aggressive behaviour, that is, those who could be thought to have experienced most catharsis, were most aggressive in the next phase of the experiment. This finding suggests that the reduction in arousal experienced after an aggressive act makes people more rather than less aggressive in a subsequent situation. Thus, it can be said that the idea of catharsis is a popular myth that is not supported by empirical evidence.

Punishment

Explanations of aggression as a result of learning processes suggest that we should look at punishment as an effective mechanism to suppress the performance of aggressive behaviour. Indeed, punishment can work to suppress aggression provided that several conditions are met (e.g. Berkowitz, 1993): (1) anticipated punishment must be sufficiently adverse; (2) it must have a high probability of being imposed; (3) punishment can only exert a deterrent effect if the individual's negative arousal is not too strong to prevent him or her from calculating the costs of an aggressive response in advance in a rational manner; (4) punishment will only be effective if acceptable or attractive behavioural alternatives are available to the actor in the situation; and (5) punishment must follow immediately upon the transgression so that it is perceived as contingent upon the aggressive behaviour. If these conditions are present, punishment may be an effective strategy for stopping people from behaving aggressively on future occasions. However, the probability that these necessary conditions will co-occur in a given situation is relatively low, limiting the scope of punishment as a strategy for controlling aggression. In addition to this practical limitation, a more fundamental criticism must be raised against punishment: punitive responses may in themselves instigate aggression by functioning as aggressive cues and may reinforce beliefs about the normative acceptability of aggressive behaviour. Punishment may also convey the message that the use of aggression is a viable strategy of conflict resolution. If it is to produce desirable consequences, punishment needs to be embedded into a more general approach towards instrumental learning in which the primary aim is to reward desirable rather than penalize undesirable behaviour (Coie & Dodge, 1998).

De-escalation through eliciting incompatible responses

As posited by the theoretical models reviewed earlier, aggressive affect and cognition are important antecedents of aggressive behaviour. Therefore, eliciting positive affect and cognition may be a successful way of buffering these negative responses, resulting in a reduction of aggressive behaviour. In support of this idea, Greitemeyer and Osswald (2009) asked participants to play either a prosocial video game (Lemmings) or a neutral game (Tetris) before administering a measure of aggressive cognitions. This measure consisted of three story stems of situations that could or could not end in an aggressive interaction (e.g. a friend turning up 30 minutes late for an appointment to watch a movie without giving an apology). The participants' task was to write down what was likely to happen next and what the main character would do, think or feel. These responses were then coded for aggressive content by independent raters to yield a measure of aggressive cognitions. The data showed that participants who had played the prosocial game generated fewer aggressive cognitions than those in the neutral game condition, suggesting that aggressive thoughts may be reduced by engaging people in prosocial activities.

Using music to elicit positive affect, Krahé and Bieneck (2012) showed that participants who were provoked whilst listening to pleasant music (a range of classical pieces, such as Grieg's Peer Gynt Suite) subsequently reported less anger (see Figure 9.23a) and took longer to recognize aggression-related words in a lexical decision-task (see Figure 9.23b) than did participants

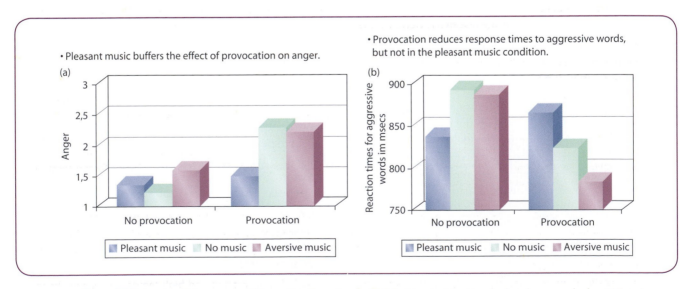

FIGURE 9.23(a) and (b) *Levels of (a) anger and (b) reaction times in a lexical decision task in provoked and unprovoked participants as a function of exposure to pleasant music, aversive music, or no music.*

Note: Shorter response times indicate higher accessibility of aggressive cognitions.

Source: From Krahé & Bieneck (2012) with permission from John Wiley & Sons.

listening to aversive music (a mix of Hardcore and Techno, such as King Deuce) or those in a no-music control condition. On the lexical decision task, they were presented with aggressive words (e.g. 'cannons'), non-aggressive words (e.g. 'flower'), and non-words (e.g. 'rahmin'), and had to indicate as fast as possible whether the stimulus represented a meaningful word or a non-word. The speed with which participants correctly identified aggressive words as words was taken as a measure of accessibility of aggressive cognitions.

The results show that among provoked participants, anger was reduced to the level of the non-provoked comparison group when they were exposed to the pleasant music. Provoked participants in the pleasant music group also took significantly longer to recognize the aggressive words in the lexical decision task than did participants in the other two music conditions, indicating that aggressive cognitions were less salient under the influence of the pleasant music.

Addressing the buffering role of music in a real-life context, Wiesenthal, Hennessy, and Totten (2000) assigned a sample of commuters to a group listening to self-selected music while driving to work, or to a no-music group. Depending on their routes, participants were classified as experiencing low versus high traffic congestion, representing different stress levels. Self-reported driver stress was the dependent variable. Under low congestion conditions, music made no difference, but under high congestion, participants in the music group reported significantly lower levels of stress than those in the no-music condition. Overall, this research suggests that eliciting positive affect may be an effective strategy for buffering the effects of frustration and provocation in triggering aggressive responses.

Summary

Compared to the wealth of research into the causes and precipitating factors of aggressive behaviour, evidence on how to reduce it is limited. Contrary to popular wisdom, catharsis, i.e. acting out aggressive impulses in a symbolic or innocuous way, is counterproductive in reducing aggression. It leads to an increase rather than a decrease in aggressive responses. Punishment may be a potentially effective control strategy, but only if it is imposed swiftly after a transgression. However, a disadvantage is that punishment also involves inflicting harm on the target person, making aggression appear as an acceptable way of resolving conflicts. Eliciting prosocial behaviour or using pleasant music to buffer stress and anger illustrate ways of reducing aggression by influencing affective and cognitive antecedents of aggressive behaviour.

*Kruglanski et al.

CHAPTER SUMMARY

This chapter has looked at some of the most important domains in which aggression is part and parcel of everyday life. The main conclusions suggested by the research reviewed in the course of the chapter can be summarized as follows:

- *What is aggression and why does it occur?* Aggressive behaviour is defined as behaviour carried out with the intention of harming another person. It can be a means to an end (instrumental aggression) or an expression of negative affect (affective or hostile aggression).

- *What methods do social psychologists use to study aggression?* Methods for studying aggressive behaviour include laboratory experiments, reports of aggressive behaviour from actors and observers and the analysis of archival records.

- *What are the main theoretical approaches used in social psychological research on aggression?* Theoretical approaches aimed at explaining aggressive behaviour include both biological and psychological lines of thinking and research. They share the assumption that the likelihood of aggressive behaviour depends on the operation of facilitating or inhibiting factors located both within the person and the environment.

- *Is aggression a stable characteristic over the life course and do men and women differ in their tendency to show aggressive behaviour?* Individual differences in aggression show considerable stability from childhood to early adulthood. Dispositional aggressiveness and the hostile attribution bias have been linked to individual differences in aggressive behaviour. Research on gender differences in aggression has found that men are more physically aggressive than women, even though the difference is only moderate in size.

- *In what situations does aggressive behaviour become more likely?* Alcohol consumption and high temperatures have been identified as situational variables that exert a significant influence on the manifestation of aggressive behaviour. Alcohol impairs the ability to process situational information and reduces the awareness of social norms inhibiting aggressive responses.

- *Is there a link between using violent media and aggression?* Studies examining the effect of violent media contents have provided overall support for the proposed aggression-enhancing effect of media violence, including violent computer games. Learning by imitation, emotional desensitization and a change in worldview (seeing the world as a hostile place) are important underlying processes.

- *How common is domestic violence and is there a gender difference?* Intimate partner violence is a widespread problem across the world. Studies using frequency counts of aggressive acts that ignore the context in which they take place show that men and women are equally likely to show aggressive behaviour against a partner. In contrast, crime statistics and studies taking context and consequences of aggressive acts into account show that men dominate as perpetrators and women as victims of intimate partner violence.

- *How common is sexual aggression and what are the psychological consequences?* Sexual violence is committed mostly by men against women, even though a few studies have documented same-sex sexual aggression and women's sexual aggression towards men. In the majority of cases the assailant is someone previously known to the victim. The consequences of sexual victimization are severe, including negative reactions from others.

- *What is bullying and how harmful is it?* School and workplace bullying are forms of aggressive behaviour characterized by an imbalance of power between aggressor and victim, and often take place over extended periods of time. Cyberbullying is a new form of harassment using electronic devices that makes it easy for perpetrators to remain anonymous.

- *What are the processes triggering aggression between groups?* Intergroup aggression occurs not only as a result of conflicts between groups over material resources, but also as a result of changes in self-focused attention and social identity concerns. People shift attention from their individual norms to the norms of the group when they are in a crowd, and they prefer members of their own group over those of outgroups to secure a positive social identity. The staircase model of terrorism illustrates the interplay between social conditions of injustice and individual characteristics in explaining why people commit terrorist acts.

- *How can aggressive behaviour be prevented or reduced?* The popular notion of catharsis has been disconfirmed as a strategy for reducing aggression. Punishment may be effective if imposed swiftly and reliably, but it conveys the message that aggression is an accepted means of conflict resolution. Inducing responses incompatible with aggression, such as prosocial behaviour or positive affect, may reduce aggressive cognitions, anger and aggressive behaviour.

SUGGESTIONS FOR FURTHER READING

Anderson, C. A. (2001). Heat and violence. *Current Directions in Psychological Science, 10*, 33–38. Concise summary of the evidence and theoretical explanations of the link between hot temperatures and aggression.

Anderson, C. A., Berkowitz, L., Donnerstein, E., Huesmann, L. R., Johnson, J. D., Linz, D., Malamuth, N. M., & Wartella, E. (2003). The influence of media violence on youth. *Psychological Science in the Public Interest, 4*, 81–110. A comprehensive and critical review of the evidence on the influence of media violence on aggression, particularly among young media users.

Anderson, C. A., & Bushman, B. J. (1997). External validity of 'trivial' experiments: The case of laboratory aggression. *Review of General Psychology, 1*, 19–41. A thought-provoking analysis of the way in which different measurement strategies in aggression research complement and cross-validate each other.

Archer, J. (2000). Sex differences in aggression between heterosexual partners: A meta-analytic review. *Psychological Bulletin, 126*, 651–680. A comprehensive review of the evidence based on the Conflict Tactics Scales (CTS) to address gender differences in intimate partner violence.

Flannery, D. J., Vazsonyi, A. T., & Waldman, I. D. (Eds.). (2007). *Cambridge handbook of violent behavior and aggression*. New York: Cambridge University Press. A comprehensive and up-to-date collection of papers with a focus on criminality and violence.

Geen, R. G. (2001*). Human aggression* (2nd ed.). Buckingham, UK: Open University Press. An introductory text providing an overview of definitions, theories and forms of aggression.

Goldstein, A. P. (2002). *The psychology of group aggression*. Chichester, UK: Wiley. Examines different forms and dynamics of aggression between social groups.

Horvath, M., & Brown, J. (Eds.). (2009). *Rape: Challenging contemporary thinking*. Cullompton, UK: Willan. A collection of topical papers examining sexual violence from an interdisciplinary perspective.

Johnson, M. P., & Ferraro, K. J. (2000). Research on domestic violence in the 1990s: Making distinctions. *Journal of Marriage and the Family, 62*, 948–963. Provides a conceptual analysis of different forms and patterns of intimate partner violence and shows how this differentiation may be useful for understanding gender differences.

Kirsh, S. J. (2011). *Children, adolescents, and media violence* (2nd ed.). Thousand Oaks, CA: Sage. Fun to read. Addresses all the facets of young people's attraction to violent media and the potential risks involved.

Krahé, B. (2012). *The social psychology of aggression* (2nd ed.). Hove, UK: Psychology Press. Textbook that provides an introduction to theories, methods and topics in social psychological aggression research.

Moghaddam, F. M. (2006). *From the terrorists' point of view*. Westport, CT: Praeger. The book provides a more elaborate account of the staircase model described in this chapter and outlines possible ways of diminishing the threat of terrorism.

Ruback, R. B., & Thompson, M. P. (2001). *Social and psychological consequences of violent victimization*. Thousand Oaks, CA: Sage. A clear and comprehensive review of the impact of violence from the victims' perspective.

Victoroff, J., & Kruglanski, A. W. (Eds.). (2009). *Psychology of terrorism*. New York: Psychology Press. Up-to-date collection of papers addressing many facets of this pressing worldwide problem.

MARK LEVINE AND RACHEL MANNING

Source: © Gina Sanders. Used under licence from Shutterstock.

KEY TERMS

- altruism
- arousal: cost–reward model
- audience inhibition
- bystander effect
- coefficient of relatedness
- common ingroup identity model
- diffusion of responsibility
- empathic concern

- empathy
- evaluation apprehension
- helping behaviour
- impulsive helping
- kin selection
- negative-state-relief model
- pluralistic ignorance
- proportion of shared genes

- prosocial behaviour
- prosocial personality
- public goods game
- reciprocal altruism
- self-efficacy
- strong reciprocity
- volunteerism

CHAPTER OUTLINE

ROUTE MAP OF THE CHAPTER

The topic of prosocial behaviour covers a wide range of phenomena and can be studied in a variety of ways. In this chapter we consider different kinds of prosocial behaviour, and explore theories of why people help (and who they help) at several different levels. We consider prosocial behaviour at the intra-individual level (are there biological mechanisms which affect helping?), the interpersonal level (how does the relationship between helper and recipient affect helping?), and the group level (what do we know about helping within and between groups?). We also explore how situational factors affect helping, and reveal how the social context is key to the understanding of many forms of helping behaviours. In addition we explore a range of different prosocial behaviours, from instant acts of physical courage in emergency situations to long-term commitments to a particular cause or a specific person. In the course of exploring these topics we reveal the wide range of inventive and creative research methods used by researchers in this area. The chapter also looks at some of the key 'big picture' questions about prosocial behaviour. For example, we ask whether helping can ever be truly selfless. We also ask if prosocial behaviour necessarily has positive effects. In the course of the chapter we consider some amazing examples of human prosocial behaviour. We discover that human cooperative behaviour is something of an evolutionary puzzle. Unlike other creatures, humans frequently cooperate with strangers, often in large groups and even in the absence of personal or reputational gain. By studying prosocial behaviour we have the opportunity to explore some of the things that make us uniquely human.

INTRODUCTION

The study of prosocial behaviour allows psychologists to explore basic questions about human nature, the kinds of questions that philosophers have been asking for centuries. These include questions of whether humans are fundamentally selfish or selfless by nature, or whether humans are ultimately good or bad. Take for example the way in which ordinary people have responded to natural disasters and emergencies over the last decade. Unfortunately there have been many such events to choose from, including the Japanese earthquake and tsunami (2011), the Haiti earthquake (2010; Figure 10.1), the Asian tsunami (2005), Hurricane Katrina in the US (2005), the Kashmir earthquake (2005) or the Iran earthquake (2003).

The first thing to note is that many ordinary people donated huge amounts of money to the relief funds set up after these disasters. People donated money to help strangers they will never meet, strangers who would never be able to thank them for the help they had given. This kind of behaviour is a puzzle to those who think that humans are only concerned with their own self-interest, and to those who believe that humans only feel ties to a small band of close family and kin. By giving money in this way, humans demonstrate the capacity to feel a sense of empathy with others in distress and a willingness to help others, even when it is not clear that they will benefit in return. All of this suggests that we possess a powerful capacity for good.

empathy the experience of understanding or sharing the emotional state of another person.

And yet . . . not all of us help and, even when we do, we don't help everybody equally or all the time. For example, according to figures from the Centre for Research on the Epidemiology of Disasters (CRED) at the Catholic University of Louvain (in Belgium), more than a hundred times as many people died in the Haiti earthquake (222,570 deaths) than as a result of Hurricane Katrina (1833 deaths). However, despite the huge difference in death tolls and the vast disparity in the wealth of the respective countries, researchers at the Centre on Philanthropy at Indiana University discovered that Americans gave much more to the American disaster ($5.3 billion) than they did to Haiti ($1.45 billion). Compare both of these with responses to the earthquake in the Pakistan controlled area of Kashmir. Here 73,338 people lost their lives, but Americans gave much less – $630 million – to the appeal. Of course, it is not only in America that these kinds of patterns can be found. In 2000, people in Switzerland gave their (relatively) wealthy fellow citizens 74 million Swiss Francs following a landslide in the canton of Wallis in which 13 people died, but gave less – 9 million Swiss Francs – to Iranian victims of the 2003 earthquake in the city of Bam, in which 26,796 people died.

How do we explain the differences? Why do we seem more willing to help some people than others? Is it simply to do with the relative publicity that the different disasters get? Or are important psychological processes at work?

In his book *The Life You Can Save*, the philosopher and ethicist Peter Singer (2009) poses the following conundrum: if you saw a small child drowning in a pond, you would leap in to save them; it wouldn't be an acceptable excuse to say that you did not save the child because you did not want to ruin a new pair of shoes, or couldn't afford to have your clothes cleaned. Everybody would save the child. And yet, UNICEF, the United Nations International Children's Emergency Fund, estimates that about 24,000 children die every day from preventable, poverty-related causes. They could be saved if the billion people in the world that live very comfortable lives could be persuaded to give; Singer argues that if you have ever spent money on buying a drink when water is freely available from a tap, then you are one of those people with money to spare. It sounds easy, but in practice, people can always think of reasons not to do it. Even when we have the means, and it wouldn't cost us much to do it, we can be reluctant to help.

Contrast this with the workers who volunteered to stay behind at the stricken Fukushima nuclear reactor after the Japanese earthquake and tsunami. With the radiation at potentially lethal levels, and the reactor in danger of meltdown, 50 workers volunteered to

FIGURE 10.1 *Haitian people standing amongst the ruins of collapsed buildings after the 2010 earthquake.*

Source: © Design Pics/Reynold Mainse. Used under licence from Getty Images.

remain when conditions became so dangerous that most workers were evacuated. Dubbed the 'Fukushima 50', they fought to bring the reactor under control in life-threatening conditions. Some workers said they volunteered because they were single men with no children, and thus were more able to face the risks than those who had dependents relying on them. Others said they did so because they felt a sense of responsibility to their fellow workers. Yet others felt a duty to protect their fellow citizens and to preserve the reputation of Japan. Whatever the reasons, conditions at the Fukushima plant meant that people were putting their lives in danger to protect others.

In these few examples we see some of the key questions, conundrums and dilemmas that animate research on prosocial behaviour. The aim of this chapter will be to explore the wide range of psychological research that touches on prosocial behaviour in all its forms. In doing so we will encounter the key social psychological theories of helping, the methods used to explore these theories, and examine work at the cutting edge of contemporary research on prosocial behaviour.

PROSOCIAL BEHAVIOUR, HELPING AND ALTRUISM

Does pure altruism exist?

As the examples above demonstrate, we are seemingly surrounded with opportunities for helping. However, before we look at the various social psychological accounts of these phenomena, it is useful to begin by thinking about the nature of the phenomena themselves. What do we mean by the terms 'prosocial behaviour' or 'helping'? Examples of the contrasting reactions to the emergency/disaster situations noted above highlight some of the different situations that seemingly require the help of others. There is, evidently, a vast range of situations that may elicit helping. Clearly this raises an additional challenge to social psychologists. Therefore, before we begin to work through the various ways in which social psychologists have approached the issue of understanding prosocial behaviour, we might firstly consider what we mean by prosocial behaviour itself. As we will see, much of the thinking about what constitutes prosocial behaviour focuses either on particular forms or types of behaviours, or on the motivations behind such behaviours. At a more general level, we might also begin to consider whether it is possible to develop a

single theory, model or approach which can account for all the different behaviours that might be encapsulated by the term 'prosocial behaviour'.

Definitions

As Bierhoff (2002) has pointed out, the terms **helping behaviour, prosocial behaviour** and **altruism** are frequently used interchangeably. However, distinct definitions for each are available. Piliavin (see Leader in the Field, Jane Allyn Piliavin, later in this chapter) and her colleagues have defined helping behaviour as 'an action that has the consequence of providing some benefit to or improving the well-being of another person' (Dovidio, Piliavin, Schroeder, & Penner, 2006, p. 22).

This definition makes helping behaviour the most inclusive term. Bierhoff (2002) argues that the definition of prosocial behaviour is narrower because 'helping' is not considered as 'prosocial behaviour' if the act is motivated by professional obligations. An example of helping behaviour that would not be considered prosocial behaviour would be a nurse caring for a patient, as this behaviour is performed as part of their job. Furthermore, Piliavin, Dovidio, Gaertner, and Clark (1981) point to the fact that what is considered to be prosocial behaviour is culturally dependent. They therefore suggest that prosocial behaviour is 'defined by society as behaviour generally beneficial to other people and to the ongoing social system', and go on to state that 'a great deal of disagreement regarding what is really prosocial action can occur depending on where one stands' (p. 4).

This point has been highlighted by a number of different researchers. For example, Grzelak and Derlega (1982) have suggested that there may be some positive aspects to social behaviour that we might ordinarily consider 'negative': for example, although social conflict may involve some injury, or even loss of life, it may also help to improve the living conditions of many people; see Chapter 14. Similarly, Huston and Korte (1976) have challenged the seemingly unproblematic subscription of many social psychologists to the moral tradition represented by the parable of the Good Samaritan. They point to cross-cultural variation to suggest that in some contexts, endangering oneself and thereby one's

> **helping behaviour** actions that are intended to provide some benefit to or improve the well-being of others.

> **prosocial behaviour** defined by society as beneficial to other people; it excludes behaviour motivated by professional obligations; it may be driven by more selfish (egoistic) and/or more selfless (altruistic) motivations.

> **altruism** refers to behaviour carried out to benefit others without anticipation of external rewards; it is driven by exclusively empathic motivation.

'kin' is in itself a transgression. Thus, giving help may not necessarily be experienced as positive from the position of the person giving help. In parallel to this, Grzelak and Derlega (1982) have also questioned the notion of prosocial behaviour in terms of whether these assumed positive forms of behaviour are indeed experienced as positive by the recipient. In line with this suggestion, Nadler (see Leader in the Field, Arie Nadler, later in this chapter) has conducted a programme of research that empirically demonstrates the potential negative impact of helping on the recipient of the help. We will return to Nadler's work towards the end of this chapter.

Finally, the term altruism is the most constrained – and the most contested. Altruism is usually reserved for cases in which the helper tries to improve the welfare of the other person *as an end in itself*. In other words, altruism should normally refer to acts that in no way benefit the help-giver (for example, acts which might bring social approval or reduce personal distress at witnessing pain in others). Piliavin (2009) defines altruism as behaviour that is carried out in order to benefit others without anticipation of rewards from external sources.

What is most contentious about the definition of altruism is the problem of defining the motivations that are believed to lie behind it. The definition of altruism implies a clear separation between self and other. Actions must be 'selfless' to qualify as altruistic. However, as we have seen from psychological research on the self (see Chapter 5) the concept of the self is contested. There is no clear agreement on how we might separate self from other, and there is a body of research on the idea of self–other overlap (see Chapter 11). This has contributed to debates on whether 'pure' (or selfless) altruistic behaviour can ever exist. More specifically, it has lead to an intense debate about the motivations that may (or may not) lie behind helping behaviour. As we will see, researchers have argued over the degree to which helping can be explained by altruistic or egoistic concerns.

The altruism–egoism debate

Obviously, if it's help you're after, you may not be concerned with why you are helped, only that you are (or not, as the case may be). Moreover, as others have pointed out (Piliavin et al., 1981), the final outcome of a particular helping situation might be reached from a number of different starting points, and in a number of different ways. But the question of what motivates helping is one that has concerned a range of psychologists. Is the goal of helping to benefit others, or to benefit ourselves? In social psychology, one of the main distinctions is between egoistically motivated helping and altruistically motivated helping – although, as Batson (1994) has suggested, there are other motives for prosocial action, which he calls *principlism* (acting to uphold a principle), and *collectivism* (acting to benefit a group).

A considerable amount of research has highlighted the contrast between egoistic and altruistic helping. For example, using data from the World Values Survey – a survey of 13,584 voluntary workers in 33 countries – Van de Vliert, Huang and Levine (2004) conducted a factor analysis that revealed a two-factor structure in motivations for doing unpaid voluntary work. Items loading on an 'egoistic' motivations factor were: 'time on my hands, wanted something worthwhile to do'; 'purely for personal satisfaction'; 'for social reasons, to meet people'; and 'to gain new skills and useful experience'. The five items loading on an altruistic motivations factor were: 'a sense of solidarity with the poor and disadvantaged'; 'compassion for those in need'; 'identifying with people who were suffering'; 'religious beliefs'; and 'to help give disadvantaged people hope and dignity'. When checking the cross-national equivalence of the two constructs, egoistic motivations and altruistic motivations, these researchers reported fairly consistent findings cross-nationally.

Demonstrating whether behaviours are motivated egoistically or altruistically is both a theoretical and methodological challenge. Research addressing this issue has utilized ingeniously designed experiments that have required the careful consideration of how to distinguish egoistic from altruistic helping (see Research Close-Up 10.1). One of the key researchers in this field is Batson (see Leader in the Field, C. Daniel Batson). Batson and his colleagues have developed the empathy-altruism hypothesis in their attempts to demonstrate the existence of helping that is motivated by altruistic rather than egoistic concerns. This is not to suggest that we can claim that all helping is motivated altruistically. Rather, altruism is a possible underlying motivation. According to the empathy-altruism hypothesis, it is the feeling of empathy, specifically, that evokes altruistic motivation.

LEADER IN THE FIELD

C. Daniel Batson (b. 1943) obtained his PhD in Psychology from Princeton in 1972 (he also holds a PhD in Theology). He has spent most of his career at the University of Kansas, where he is currently Emeritus Professor; he is also Adjunct Professor at the University of Tennessee. Batson famously developed the empathy-altruism hypothesis during his sustained attempt to experimentally test for the existence of true altruistic motivation for helping. Using a range of ingenious experimental procedures, Batson has sought to distinguish the egoistic and altruistic motivational systems, and has highlighted empathy as a possible source of the altruistic motivation systems. More recently, Batson and his colleagues have begun to examine the alternative motivations of principlism and collectivism in more detail.

EMPATHY LEADS TO ALTRUISTIC HELPING

Batson, C. D., Duncan, B. D., Ackerman, P., Buckley, T., & Birch, K. (1981). Is empathic emotion a source of altruistic motivation? *Journal of Personality and Social Psychology*, 40, 290–302.

Introduction

There are real difficulties in identifying underlying motivations, or being able to say precisely why someone acted as they did. Seemingly altruistic motives might sometimes be ultimately interpreted as egoistic ones. For example, you may have helped someone in order to relieve their distress, but this was, in turn, in order to alleviate the unpleasant feelings you experienced through knowing someone was in need, because you yourself would feel bad if you did nothing. This study began by dealing with the issue of how to differentiate between behaviours that are egoistically motivated and behaviours that are altruistically motivated. Egoistic helping is conceptually distinguished from altruistic helping in terms of the 'end state goal' of each: for egoistic helping it is increasing the helper's own welfare; for altruistic helping it is increasing the other's welfare. In order to distinguish empirically between egoistic and altruistic helping, the behavioural correlates of these two forms of helping are considered. The egoistically motivated bystander can alleviate their personal distress in seeing another person suffer by either helping, or by leaving: both achieve the same end state goal. If leaving is made harder (or the 'costs' of leaving are increased), then the egoistically motivated bystander is more likely to help. If leaving is easier, the egoistically motivated bystander is less likely to help (and more likely to leave). In contrast, for the altruistically motivated bystander, the end state goal can only be achieved by helping, therefore making leaving harder will have no impact on their likelihood of helping.

Method

Participants

In their first study, forty-four female students at the University of Kansas took part in the study. Eleven participants were assigned to each of four conditions (four additional participants were excluded from the analysis because they did not believe that the scenario used in the experiment was real). Participants had previously completed a personal values and interest questionnaire.

Design and procedure

In the study, participants observed a confederate, Elaine, taking part in what they were told was a learning experiment. Participants were also told that Elaine would receive electric shocks at random intervals during the experiment.

A 2 (difficulty of escape: easy versus difficult) × 2 (similarity of victim: similar versus dissimilar) between-groups design was used. Difficulty of escape was manipulated by telling participants that they needed to observe either the first two or all ten of the trials. Similarity of victim was manipulated by giving participants a copy of a 'personal values and interests' questionnaire and telling them that it was Elaine's. By creating two versions of the questionnaire, Elaine could be presented as having either similar or dissimilar values and interests to the participant. Based on the work of Stotland (1969) and Krebs (1975), this similarity manipulation was used as an indirect manipulation of empathic emotion – more similar victims would elicit greater empathy. As the experiment took place, Elaine was seen to be having considerable difficulty in taking part, and went on to explain that she had experienced difficulty in reaction to electric shocks in the past. The experimenter then asked the participant if she would be willing to take over Elaine's role. The dependent measure was the willingness (or not) of the participant to trade places with Elaine.

Results

There was a significant escape × similarity interaction: the proportion of participants willing to take Elaine's place in the easy-escape, dissimilar-victim condition was much lower than in the other three conditions (see Figure 10.2).

FIGURE 10.2 *Percentage of participants who helped Elaine depending on similarity to victim and ease or difficulty of escape*

Source: From Batson, 1991.

Discussion

As the manipulation of empathic emotion in this study was indirect, a second experiment was conducted in order to manipulate it more directly. This second study replaced the similarity manipulation with a manipulation of arousal attribution. Participants were given a placebo drug that they were told would (depending on the experimental condition) induce feelings similar to **empathic concern** or to personal distress. Researchers argued that participants who could attribute their feelings of personal distress to the drug were more likely to act out of empathic concern, while those who could attribute their feelings of empathic concern to the drug were more likely to act out of personal

> **empathic concern** an emotional state consisting of emotions such as compassion, warmth and concern for another person.

distress. After receiving the placebo and the instructions, participants watched Elaine receiving electric shocks. The results of both studies supported the predictions of the empathy-altruism hypothesis (see Theory Box 10.1): when participants believed that Elaine was similar to them (and therefore empathized with her, as in study 1), or when they believed they were acting out of feelings of empathic concern (as in study 2), they helped her regardless of whether escape was easy or difficult. Participants who believed that Elaine was dissimilar to themselves (and therefore did not empathize with her, as in study 1), or who perceived their response to Elaine receiving shocks as personal distress (as in study 2), helped more often if it was difficult to leave the experiment.

We are dealing with a fairly fundamental issue here – is it possible to demonstrate definitively the existence of helping that is not motivated by egoistic concerns? There are also difficult challenges posed in trying to demonstrate which motivations (singly, or together) ultimately drive behaviour. It is therefore perhaps not surprising that other scholars have challenged Batson's position that altruistically motivated helping does exist. One of the leaders of this challenge has been Cialdini, with whom Batson had a lengthy debate throughout the 1970s and 1980s. Cialdini's alternative position was based on the **negative-state-relief model** of helping behaviour. This approach suggests that witnessing someone in need creates an unpleasant mood in the observer, who is thus motivated to act to relieve this unpleasant mood. Helping will occur in reaction to the suffering or need of another person, but is motivated on the basis of alleviating one's own negative mood. Therefore actions are based on self-interest, with no possibility for truly altruistically motivated helping.

Cialdini and his colleagues have argued, therefore, that seeing a victim suffering causes participants to feel sadness, and that it is this sadness that leads people to help (see Theory Box 10.2). Research in support of the negative-state-relief model has suggested, for example, that participants in the 'high-empathy' conditions of experiments such as Batson et al., (1981), also feel increased sadness, and that it is this sadness, and

> **negative-state-relief model** argues that human beings have an innate drive to reduce their own negative moods. Helping behaviour can elevate mood – thus people help for egoistic rather than altruistic reasons.

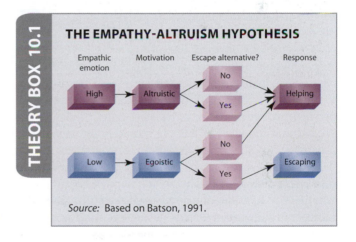

THEORY BOX 10.1

THE EMPATHY-ALTRUISM HYPOTHESIS

Source: Based on Batson, 1991.

not empathy, that predicts helping (Cialdini et al., 1987). Although a meta-analysis by Carlson and Miller (1987) suggested that there was no support for the negative-state-relief model, this has in turn been disputed by Cialdini and colleagues (Cialdini & Fultz, 1990).

While there may be no straightforward resolution to these seemingly diametrically opposed positions, Piliavin (2009) suggests that the 'coup de grace to Cialdini's position' (p. 213) came when its supporters, Dovidio and colleagues, carried out an experiment anticipating that they would find support for purely egoistically motivated helping. In Dovidio, Allen, and Schroeder's (1990) study, participants watched a video of an interview in which a student explained either that she was having problems recruiting students for her project, or that she was having problems collecting information for a university committee. Participants in an 'imagine' condition were instructed to

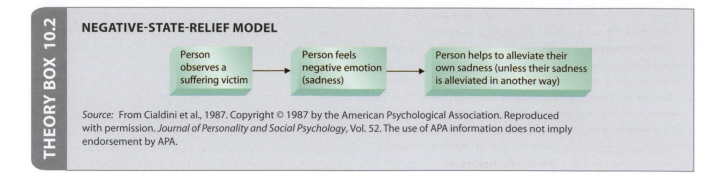

Source: From Cialdini et al., 1987. Copyright © 1987 by the American Psychological Association. Reproduced with permission. *Journal of Personality and Social Psychology*, Vol. 52. The use of APA information does not imply endorsement by APA.

think about how the student in need felt as they watched the video, whereas participants in an 'observe' condition were instructed to just watch and listen to the student. The participants then read a newspaper report of the same student explaining either the same problem or a different problem, and were subsequently given the chance to help the student on the problem explained in the newspaper report. The primary dependent variable was how many participants indicated that they would be willing to distribute notices for the student in need.

The empathy-altruism hypothesis would predict that helping would be greater in the 'imagine' condition only when participants are presented with the same problem, as the goal of altruistic motivation is to alleviate the other person's problem. The negative-state-relief model would predict that the level of helping would be greater in the 'imagine' condition than the 'observe' condition, as participants in the 'imagine' condition would experience more personal sadness. This would happen regardless of whether the subsequent helping opportunity involved the same or a different problem as the one that produced the sadness. However, the researchers found only one statistically significant effect in relation to rates of helping. Participants instructed to think about how the person in need felt when they watched the video (the 'imagine' condition) were significantly more likely to subsequently help that person – but only when empathic concern was related to the same problem. Empathic concern related to a different problem and general feelings of empathic concern did not predict helping behaviour (see Figure 10.3). Thus, participants did not simply help in order to alleviate their own negative feelings, they helped because their goal was to relieve the other person's problem. Thus, in some cases at least, altruistically motivated helping does occur, as a result of empathizing with the person in need.

Prosocial behaviours

So far we have noted a number of core concepts that are used in the field of prosocial behaviour. We have noted the importance of distinguishing 'prosocial behaviour' from 'helping behaviour' and 'altruism', and highlighted

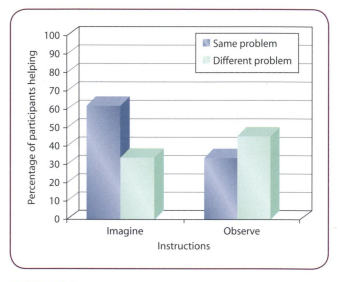

FIGURE 10.3 *Percentage of participants helping as a function of instructions (imagine or observe) and problem type (same or different)*

Source: From Dovidio et al., 1990. Copyright © 1990 by the American Psychological Association. Reproduced with permission. *Journal of Personality and Social Psychology*, Vol. 59. The use of APA information does not imply endorsement by APA.

additional problems with these terms: is 'prosocial behaviour' necessarily positive? Is there even such a thing as altruism? Researchers have pointed to how we might organize our understandings of prosocial behaviour by classifying them into different levels of analysis. Penner, Dovidio, Piliavin, and Schroeder (2005) have suggested three distinct but related levels of prosocial behaviour: micro, meso and macro. Research in the field of prosocial behaviour has traditionally been focused on the meso level: helper–recipient dyads in specific situations. Thus, much of the work that we will cover looks at the motivations for different forms of prosocial behaviours, and the contribution of individual and situational factors. Micro-level analysis, on the other hand, refers to research that is concerned with the 'origins of prosocial tendencies' (Penner et al., 2005, p. 221), whereas macro-level analyses examine prosocial behaviours in the context of groups and large organizations. The latter two levels of analysis have received relatively less attention, although we will present some examples in this chapter.

This suggestion of the different levels of analysis involved in the study of prosocial behaviour additionally points us to a range of terms that characterize research in this area. These terms include *cooperation* (whereby helping is not a one-way process: people act together, and each may expect to benefit; Argyle, 1991), *courageous resistance* (suggested to be a subset of altruistic), *selfless* (in which there is high risk to the helper, and where the behaviour is sustained over time; Shepela et al., 1999), *volunteering* (any activity in which time is given freely to benefit another person, group, or organization; Wilson, 2000), *emergency intervention* (taking action in response to an urgent, unpredictable, risky situation; Piliavin et al., 1981), and *bystander intervention* (helping in an emergency which one observes; Latané & Darley, 1970), to name just a few. We examine bystander intervention in more detail in the next section, and return to the different forms of prosocial behaviours towards the end of this chapter.

Summary

We have noted how, just as there are many different situations that may require various forms of prosocial behaviours, there are also different perspectives on what constitutes prosocial behaviour itself. We have seen how three common terms in this field – prosocial behaviour, helping behaviour and altruism – are often used interchangeably, although they are distinct. Moreover, we have seen how the existence of altruistically motivated helping in itself has been a point of considerable debate within social psychology, which has required the use of some carefully designed and choreographed research. We will continue this theme of the ingenuity of social psychologists in examining prosocial behaviours as we turn to some of the different ways that social psychologists have developed research in this area.

WHY DON'T PEOPLE HELP?

To what extent does the situation determine the behaviour of bystanders in an emergency?

As we saw in the introduction, various different features of potential helping situations – as well as features of the potential helper – may come together to motivate, facilitate, inhibit or prevent helping. In contrast to the

concerns with motivation highlighted in the previous section, we now turn to a highly influential body of work that has been primarily focused on the situational determinants of helping behaviour.

Just as there may be different motivations for prosocial behaviours, social psychologists are motivated to study particular phenomena for many different reasons. Social psychologists have often been motivated to study such phenomena in response to hearing about incidents or stories of negative behaviour in the mass media. Thus, social psychological research and theorizing on prosocial behaviours has often been in response to events or stories of incidents that seemingly required helping behaviour, yet in which this behaviour did not occur. For example, in 2009 in Germany, Dominik Brunner tried to help children being attacked by two 18-year-olds and was subsequently murdered by them. However, unlike Dominik, fellow passers-by did not physically intervene to help him. It is in such situations that people often look to psychology for answers, and ways of attempting to ensure that such situations do not arise in future.

Counter-examples of spontaneous helping or helping in dangerous circumstances thankfully also feature both in media outlets and as the inspiration for academic research, although it has been pointed out that research that looks at why people do help is less common than why they do not (Piliavin et al., 1981). However, there is one story in particular which has played an important role in the development of the social psychological study of helping behaviour: the story of the 38 witnesses to the murder of Kitty Genovese in New York in 1964 – see Social Psychology Beyond the Lab 10.1. Many researchers have pointed to the fact that social psychologists have been interested in helping behaviour for as long as social psychology has been a distinct field (e.g. Dovidio, 1995). However, it is the story of the 38 witnesses that inspired a wealth of research in this area.

As social psychologists Latané and Darley have themselves explained, a few days after the *New York Times* story ran, they began to analyse the story in social psychological terms over dinner. They were unconvinced by claims that bystander behaviour in the Kitty Genovese case reflected modern processes of social breakdown. Instead they argued that more generic social psychological factors might be at work. To test some of their ideas, they devised a series of choreographed experiments in which they systematically controlled and varied different aspects of emergency situations. Latané and Darley (1970) demonstrated the bystander effect – the observation that an increasing number of bystanders to an emergency reduces the likelihood that witnesses to that emergency will intervene – and formulated their influential decision-making model of bystander behaviour (see Leaders in the Field, Bibb Latané and John M. Darley).

THE IMPACT OF BYSTANDERS ON HELPING IN AN EMERGENCY

RESEARCH CLOSE-UP 10.2

Darley, J. M., & Latané, B. (1968). Bystander intervention in emergencies: Diffusion of responsibility. *Journal of Personality and Social Psychology*, 8, 377–383.

Introduction

When other people are present in an emergency, the norms that favour the helping of a victim can be weakened, as each individual bystander is aware that there are others present who could help. Although each bystander may not know what the others are doing, the responsibility for helping – as well as the potential blame for not helping – is shared amongst those present. No single person is solely responsible for helping, and therefore each person is less likely to help. When only one bystander is present in an emergency situation, the full responsibility for helping rests with that individual. In addition, when a bystander knows that other people are present in an emergency situation, but cannot see them, he or she might reasonably assume that someone else has already helped the person in need. This leads to the hypothesis that the more bystanders present in an emergency, the less likely (or less quickly) any individual bystander will intervene to help.

Method

Participants

Thirteen male and 59 female students at New York University took part in the experiment as part of a class requirement.

Design and procedure

Participants arrived at the experiment in a long corridor containing doors that opened off into several small rooms. Each participant was shown into one of these rooms, seated at a table and told that they would take part in a discussion about personal problems experienced by college students in a high-pressure, urban environment. Participants were told that the discussion would take place via an intercom system in order to guarantee the anonymity of participants (although this was in fact to allow a tape recorded simulation of the other participants and the emergency). Moreover, participants were told that in order to ensure that the discussion was not inhibited by the presence of outside listeners, the experimenter would not be listening to the discussion (whereas the true purpose of this instruction was to ensure that the experimenter, who would be perceived as responsible, was not considered to be present in the emergency situation).

As the experimenter would not be present as far as the participants understood, they were told that each person would take turns to talk, presenting their problem to the group. Each person would then comment in turn on what had been talked about, and then there would be a free discussion. Only one participant could be heard at any one time, as each participant's microphone would only be switched on for two minutes, and at the same time all other microphones would be switched off (so that, when an emergency arose, participants could not hear what other people present were doing or saying, or discuss the emergency with them). Once the instructions had been given, the discussion began.

The first person to speak was the future 'victim'. He talked about the difficulty he had in adjusting to his studies and to life in New York City. He also mentioned that he was prone to seizures. The discussion then moved round the other people, including the real participant who spoke last in each cycle. When it was the future victim's next turn, his speech became louder and incoherent, he began to choke and then went quiet. Judges who listened to the tape estimated that it was evident that the victim had collapsed 70 seconds after the signal for his turn in the discussion. The victim's turn was cut off 125 seconds after the signal for him to speak. The time between the beginning of the victim's apparent seizure and when the participant left the cubicle to help was recorded by the experimenter, which constituted the main dependent variable. If the participant did not leave their room within six minutes, the experimenter terminated the experiment. The participant was then told the true nature of the experiment, at which point any emotions aroused in the emergency situation were dealt with. Participants then filled out a questionnaire on their thoughts and feelings during the experiment, along with several measures of personality.

The main independent variable was the number of other people that the participant was told were also part of the discussion group – who the real participant could also hear as part of the discussion. There were three main conditions: a two-person group (which contained only the real participant and the future victim), a three-person group (which contained the real participant, the future victim and the sound of one additional confederate), and a six-person group (which contained the real participant, the future victim and the sound of four additional confederates).

Results

The data from two participants who did not perceive the seizure as real were excluded from the study. The number of bystanders perceived by the participant to be present in the emergency situation had a strong effect on the level of participants leaving their room and reporting the emergency. Eighty-five per cent of participants who thought that they were the only person witnessing the victim's seizure reported it before the victim's turn was cut off on the intercom, compared to 62 per cent of participants who thought that one other person was present, and 31 per cent of those who thought that there were four other witnesses to the emergency (see Figure 10.4). Every participant in the two-person condition, versus 62 per cent of the participants in the six-person conditions, reported the emergency at some point. At every point in time over the duration of the emergency situation, more participants in the two-person condition had responded than in the three-person condition, and more in the three-person conditions had responded compared to the six-person condition. All participants who reported the emergency to the experimenter did so within three minutes of the seizure. No significant correlations were found between speed of reporting and any of the personality measures.

Discussion

The results support the authors' hypothesis that the presence of other bystanders in an emergency situation would reduce feelings of personal responsibility and reduce the speed with which the participants reported the emergency,

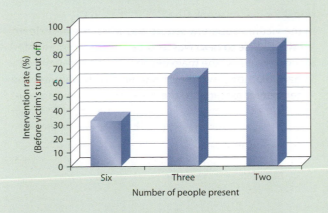

FIGURE 10.4 *Helping as a function of number of people present.*

Note: Criterion of helping shown is reporting before victim's turn is cut off.

Source: From Darley & Latané, 1968. Copyright © 1968 by the American Psychological Association. Reproduced with permission. *Journal of Personality and Social Psychology*, Vol. 8. The use of APA information does not imply endorsement by APA.

a social psychological process they termed the *diffusion of responsibility*. An awareness of four other bystanders who could help the victim (in the six-person condition) led to less helping than an awareness of no or one other bystander. Those participants who did not report the emergency did not appear apathetic at the end of the experiment. They often showed concern for the victim, and physical signs of nervousness suggesting they were in a state of indecision and conflict regarding what they should do, rather than having decided not to help.

In a second experiment Latané and Darley (1968) identified additional ways in which the presence of others had an impact on bystanders' reactions to an emergency. In this experiment, they examined participants' reactions to an emergency that unfolded as they sat in a room filling in a questionnaire. Participants were all male students at Columbia University in New York City who had been recruited to take part in a study on 'problems involved in life at an urban university'. When they arrived they were directed to a waiting room and asked to complete a preliminary questionnaire. However, as they were doing this, the room began to fill with a visible (but harmless) white smoke. The researchers then noted whether participants left the room to report the smoke, and measured the length of time that it took them to do so. The experiment was terminated after six minutes if participants had still failed to raise the alarm.

In different experimental conditions, participants were either on their own in the room or there with two others. Moreover, sometimes the others were naïve participants and sometimes they were confederates who had been instructed to ignore the smoke and remain passive. The results indicated that when people were on their own most of them (75 per cent) raised the alarm, but that when they were with others only 38 per cent did so. Participants also responded much more quickly in the former condition. For example, after two minutes, 55 per cent of the participants in the alone condition had reported the smoke, but only 12 per cent of the three-person groups had done so. After four minutes, 75 per cent of the participants in the alone condition had reported the smoke, but the reporting rate in the 3-person groups was still at 12 per cent (the reporting rate for 3-person groups rose to 38 per cent in the final two minutes). Moreover, when the other people in the room were confederates who remained passive throughout the unfolding drama, then participants were also likely to be passive, with only 10 per cent raising the alarm in this condition (a small minority helped immediately while the rest remained passive throughout).

Latané and Darley proposed that social influence processes could account for the inaction of bystanders in emergencies such as this. The presence of other bystanders was, they suggested, a key feature of understanding bystander behaviour.

LEADER IN THE FIELD

Bibb Latané (b. 1937) obtained his PhD from the University of Minnesota in 1963, and later taught at Ohio State University, the University of North Carolina and Florida Atlantic University. He is one of the most frequently cited psychologists in social psychology textbooks, and coined terms such as 'bystander intervention' and 'social loafing'. Together with John Darley (see Leader in the Field, this chapter) he carried out research on bystander behaviour in the wake of the murder of Kitty Genovese, proposing the term 'diffusion of responsibility' as an explanation of reduced rates of helping in groups of bystanders. Latané subsequently developed *social impact theory*, which uses mathematical equations to predict how people affect one another in social situations. He has twice won the Behavioural Science Award given by the American Association for the Advancement of Science, for work on bystander intervention and on social loafing. He has also been the recipient of career research awards given by the Society of Experimental Psychology and the Society for Personality and Social Psychology.

LEADER IN THE FIELD

John M. Darley (b. 1938) obtained his PhD from Harvard University in 1965 and has been based at Princeton University for much of his academic career. Some of his earliest publications focused on fear, affiliation and social comparison. Working with Bibb Latané (see Leader in the Field, this chapter) he developed a decision-making model of bystander behaviour that explains the social psychological processes behind the inaction of bystanders. Darley and Latané's (1968) article 'Bystander intervention in emergencies: Diffusion of responsibility' became one of the most-cited articles in social psychology. His later research focused on ordinary people's moral judgements and their beliefs about crime and the criminal justice system. Darley has been a recipient of the Society of Experimental Social Psychology's Distinguished Scientist Award and the American Psychological Foundation Media Award for Distinguished Contributions in Communicating Psychology to the Public.

Darley and Latané (1968) demonstrated this phenomenon in one of their first experiments looking at bystander behaviour (see Research Close-Up 10.2). In this experiment they varied the number of other bystanders perceived to be present in an emergency situation, to show that the level of reporting an emergency is lower when an individual bystander believes there are numerous others present.

A decision-making model of bystander behaviour

Based on a careful programme of research, Latané and Darley formulated a five-step decision-making model of

bystander behaviour, focusing on the situational factors involved in the intervention situation; this has become one of the most influential approaches to bystander behaviour. The sequential decision-making model that Latané and Darley proposed consists of the following stages: (1) noticing the event; (2) deciding if it is an emergency; (3) deciding on the degree of personal responsibility; (4) deciding on the specific mode of intervention; and (5) implementing the chosen intervention (Latané & Darley, 1970; see Theory Box 10.3). Latané and Darley propose that a negative decision at any stage of this series will result in help not being given. Crucially, it is the presence or absence of others that is key to the individual's response to an emergency. Thus, Latané and Darley suggest that bystander intervention can be inhibited by three social psychological processes: diffusion of responsibility, pluralistic ignorance and audience inhibition.

Diffusion of responsibility On your own, you feel the focus of responsibility for helping is on you – there is no one else present who can help, therefore you are

THEORY BOX 10.3

FIVE-STEP DECISION-MAKING MODEL OF BYSTANDER INTERVENTION

External event

Step 1	High awareness of the event	Low awareness of the event
Step 2	Interpretation of the event as emergency	No emergency
Step 3	Personal responsibility	No personal responsibility
Step 4	Mode of assistance available	No mode of assistance available
Step 5	Implementing the intervention	No intervention

Source: Based on Latané & Darley, 1970.

SOCIAL PSYCHOLOGY BEYOND THE LAB 10.1

THE ORIGINS OF RESEARCH ON BYSTANDER INTERVENTION

Catherine 'Kitty' Genovese was a young woman who worked as a barmaid in New York. Returning to her home in the area of Kew Gardens, Queens, after work in the early hours of 13 March 1964, Kitty was attacked and murdered by Winston Moseley. Moseley was subsequently convicted of her murder and remains in prison to this day. However, it is not Kitty's life, or her death, that has been the focus of social psychological investigations. Rather, it was the story that appeared in the *New York Times* two weeks after her death (Gansberg, 1964) that inspired a new paradigm of social psychological investigation. The story reported how 38 witnesses who lived close to Kitty's apartment saw her being attacked and murdered, but did nothing to help until after she was dead. Rosenthal (1964), then editor of the *New York Times*, subsequently suggested that some of the 38 witnesses *heard* rather than *saw* the attack.

Appalled by the apparently heartless behaviour (or inaction) of the bystanders, public figures, social commentators and academics all offered explanations of why this event may have occurred. Most of these stories suggested that moral decay, social alienation or the state of contemporary urban life were to blame. However, two young social psychologists, Bibb Latané and John Darley used social psychological ideas to explain the behaviour of the bystanders in a different way. They focused on the number of people present who witnessed the murder – and conducted experiments that showed how this could lead to psychological processes like **diffusion of responsibility**, **pluralistic ignorance** or **audience inhibition**. They used this work to develop a 5-step model of decision-making that shapes bystander behaviour (this model is described in more detail below). The **bystander effect** is one of the most robust and well-replicated findings in social psychology.

More recently, however, the number of witnesses suggested by the original *New York Times* story has been questioned (e.g. Manning, Levine, & Collins, 2007). There is considerable evidence that challenges the existence of 38 witnesses, and shows that some people did phone the police as the attack was occurring. In addition, Winston Moseley's second, lethal attack on Kitty took place inside a stairwell of an apartment building that could be seen by very few people. The idea that 38 witnesses watched from their windows for half an hour in awed fascination as the murder unfolded is not supported by the evidence. This suggests that, in the Genovese murder at least, the bystander effect may not have played a part.

Regardless of the details of the number of witnesses to the attack on Kitty Genovese, and what they could or couldn't see, the fact remains that Winston Moseley effectively stalked and killed her with no one intervening in the series of events that led to her death. Manning et al. (2007) suggest that a potential danger of the continued popularity of the story of the 38 witnesses is that it narrows the focus of psychological enquiry. Researchers have concentrated on the potential dangers of the presence of others for helping behaviour, and have neglected the study of when and how the presence of others could promote bystander intervention.

diffusion of responsibility the process by which responsibility is divided between bystanders; with more people present in an emergency, responsibility is diffused and bystanders feel less responsible than if they were alone.

pluralistic ignorance emergency bystanders look to others in reacting to the event; as each person fails to react, they look at non-reacting bystanders, and interpret the event as not requiring a response.

audience inhibition the experience of individual bystanders whose behaviour can be seen by other bystanders. In an emergency bystanders may fear embarrassment by their actions, resulting in lower likelihood of them helping.

bystander effect refers to the phenomenon whereby the likelihood of any one person helping in an emergency situation decreases as the number of other bystanders increases.

responsible for helping. If, however, you are with other people, friends or strangers, each individual bystander feels less responsibility, as the responsibility for helping is spread or 'diffused' across all those who are present. This leads to each person being less likely to provide help themselves. This process may occur at step 3 of the decision-making model, where the bystander decides on the level of personal responsibility to take.

Pluralistic ignorance Most of us do not witness emergencies on a regular basis. Due to their very nature, emergencies tend to be unpredictable, potentially risky, sudden events that we generally are neither prepared for nor expect in our everyday lives. Because of this, when confronted with an emergency we may well hesitate and try to work out what is going on and what should be done. If other people are present while we are doing this, we often look at them, and they look at us, as each of us tries to work out what to do. In doing so, we inadvertently become models of inaction for each other (see discussion of modelling in Chapter 9). This process suggests that the appropriate response to the emergency is therefore to do nothing. The situation has become socially defined as a non-emergency, which lessens the likelihood of helping, thereby inaction becomes normative for the situation. This process may occur at step 2 of the decision-making model, where the bystander decides if the event is an emergency or not. He or she may look to others to define the situation, in which case pluralistic ignorance may occur if there are other people present.

Audience inhibition This third social psychological process also decreases the likelihood of bystanders helping. When other bystanders are present, individuals become aware that the other people present would see their intervention attempt. This results in anxiety, which decreases the individual likelihood of intervention, particularly in unfamiliar situations in which the individual bystander is unsure of what to do or of whether their intervention attempt will be successful. This may be due to a belief that they lack the ability to intervene successfully. There is also a chance that the bystander has misinterpreted the situation as an emergency when, in fact, it is not one – intervention would therefore risk additional embarrassment in front of an audience. As such, this process can be seen as a form of **evaluation apprehension** (see Chapter 8), whereby people become concerned that, as they perform a task, they are being evaluated by others present. This process may occur at step 5 of the model, where the bystander decides whether or not to implement the intervention. At this stage you may be concerned with how others might perceive you, and anticipate possible embarrassment as a result – in other words, the process of audience inhibition may lead to you not helping.

The more that these inhibitory processes are activated, the less likely it is that helping will occur. Latané and Darley (1976) demonstrated this in an experiment using five different conditions. Each condition varied according to whether the participant believed there were other bystanders present or not, and which communication channels were available between the

bystanders. In the condition with the lowest number of inhibitory factors (condition 1), participants were alone in a room watching (via a monitor) a person receiving electric shocks and falling on the floor. In the condition with the highest number of inhibitory factors (condition 5), participants could see, and be seen by, another bystander. The other bystander was a confederate who, in the relevant conditions, could be seen by the participant responding passively to the emergency. Thus, in the condition with the largest number of inhibitory factors, the participant was aware of the presence of others, could see another inactive bystander, and also knew that their own actions would be seen by the other bystander. As expected, those participants in the alone condition helped the most. Those who knew of another bystander but couldn't see or be seen by them (condition 2) helped slightly less. This was followed by the one-way communication conditions (seeing but not being seen, or not seeing but being seen; conditions 3 and 4), with those people who could see the other bystander and be seen by them helping the least. The greater number of channels of communication led to more social inhibition, suggesting that the three processes identified are independent and operate additively.

The bystander effect is robust and has been replicated many times (see meta-analysis of 53 articles by Fischer et al., 2011), although researchers have also demonstrated some of the limitations of the effect, suggesting, for example, that the effect does not hold in situations of high potential danger for both victim and bystanders (Fischer, Greitemeyer, Pollozek & Frey, 2006). One of the key challenges for this research, which demonstrates the power of situational factors in bystander behaviour, is how the bystander effect might be overcome in order to ensure that victims obtain the help that they need in emergencies where there is more than one bystander. As Latané and Nida (1981) have highlighted, in spite of a wealth of research, using this research to ensure that people in need receive help has been a significant challenge. In their meta-analysis, Fischer et al. (2011) suggest that the bystander effect has lessened in size over time, and that this may be due to the use of less realistic bystander situations than in older studies. Alternatively, it has also been suggested that knowledge of the bystander effect may militate against its occurrence. In an experiment by Beaman, Barnes, Klentz, and McQuirk (1978) students were told about the bystander effect, including the three inhibition processes, in a lecture. In a seemingly unrelated subsequent study, when confronted with an emergency in the presence of a passive confederate, students who had learned about the bystander effect were more likely to offer help to a victim than students who had not learned about the bystander effect. This might suggest that providing people with more information about the bystander effect might help to lessen its impact.

Alternatively, given that the audience inhibition process is particularly strong when bystanders feel that they lack competence to provide help, it has been suggested that various forms of training may help to overcome the bystander effect – in fact, the presence of others may facilitate helping when a bystander feels that they are competent to provide help (Schwartz & Gottlieb, 1976). This highlights the role of **self-efficacy** (see Chapter 6) in helping: if a bystander feels that they are able to help, then helping is more likely. However, it has been pointed out that a feeling of responsibility is a more important predictor of helpfulness, although a sense of competence can contribute to feelings of responsibility (Bierhoff, 2002).

Summary

The bystander effect is one of the most robust in social psychology: one of the key reasons why people don't help is because of the presence of others. As the number of fellow bystanders to an emergency increases, so responsibility for helping is diffused amongst all those present: individual bystanders therefore feel less personally responsible and are less likely to intervene. Bystanders appear to react passively to emergencies, inadvertently creating a passive model for others. And fear of negative evaluation of one's own potential helping behaviour is an additional barrier to helping. The challenge remains in terms of understanding what makes people help, as opposed to not help.

WHY DO PEOPLE HELP?

What are the underlying motivations of prosocial behaviour?

In the previous section we looked at some of the factors that inhibit or prevent people from helping. This approach tends to focus on the disruptions to individual cognitive decision-making. In this section we will look at a range of different approaches that have attempted to explain why people *do* help. These approaches take a different kind of focus. Rather than emphasizing individual cognitive processes, they explore the role of physiology, emotion and group processes.

The costs and rewards of helping

In contrast to Latané and Darley's focus on explaining why people *do not* help, Piliavin and colleagues, contemporaries of Latané and Darley, set out to explain why people *do* help. Their 'subway train studies' (e.g. Piliavin, Rodin, & Piliavin, 1969), which involved the researchers staging emergency incidents on the subway trains of New York and then observing rates of intervention, provided some of the earliest bystander intervention studies that challenge the bystander effect. In one of the studies of Piliavin et al. a 'victim' (one member of a team of students who ran the field experiments) would stagger and collapse on a subway car while other members of the team recorded how many people helped. The trials were run with either black or white 'victims', all of whom were male. In some of the trials the 'victim' smelled of alcohol and carried a bottle wrapped tightly in a brown bag ('drunk' condition), while on other trials the 'victim' appeared sober and carried a black cane ('cane' condition).

The researchers recorded the number of people who came to the victims' assistance, and were surprised to find that helping was often at ceiling level, regardless of the number of other people present. Piliavin et al. (1969) reported that helping was offered by at least one bystander in 100 per cent of trials for all victims in the 'cane' condition, and for white victims in the 'drunk' condition; helping was shown in 73 per cent of trials for black victims in the 'drunk' condition. None of the bystanders left the subway car on any of the trials, but some people did leave the area in the immediate vicinity of the victim, particularly on the 'drunk' trials. Piliavin et al. concluded that, in their real-life 'laboratory on wheels', there was no strong relationship between number of bystanders and speed or likelihood of help. There was, however, a greater tendency for black individuals to help black victims, and for white individuals to help white victims, especially when the victim was drunk rather than ill; the longer the emergency went on without any intervention, the more people were likely to move away.

Inspired by numerous stories of emergency intervention where bystanders put themselves in considerable personal danger, Piliavin and colleagues developed a model of emergency intervention

arousal: cost–reward model suggests that observing an emergency creates a sense of arousal in the bystander which becomes increasingly unpleasant. Bystander responds by considering costs and rewards of helping or not helping.

called the **arousal: cost–reward model**. In part this model addressed the suggestion that the decision-making model of bystander intervention proposed by Latané and Darley did not incorporate a specific motivational construct in order to explain the movement of people through the suggested decisions. The model developed by Piliavin et al. has two main components: a central motivational construct, that of *vicarious arousal*, and a cognitive, decision-making component regarding the calculation of *costs and rewards of actions* (Piliavin et al., 1981, p. 6; see Leader in the Field, Jane Allyn Piliavin).

The original formulation of the arousal: cost–reward model proposes that observing an emergency creates a state of arousal in the bystander. This arousal becomes more unpleasant as it increases, but can be reduced by a response that is selected on the basis of cost and reward considerations (see Theory Box 10.4, panel (a)). Costs and rewards are comprised of two different categories, depending on whether the bystander helps or whether the victim receives no help (Piliavin et al., 1981; Piliavin, Piliavin, & Rodin, 1975). The costs associated with the bystander helping come in forms such as of loss of time, physical danger and effort expenditure. The potential rewards for helping include raised self-esteem, thanks from the victim, praise, honour and glory. The costs associated with the victim not receiving any help include continued unpleasant empathic arousal, self-blame, public censure and loss of rewards that would have followed had the bystander helped (Piliavin et al., 1981). The potential rewards associated with not helping relate primarily to the continuation of activities (Piliavin

et al., 1969). In the original model, situational factors in an emergency situation were proposed to either stimulate or not stimulate arousal in the bystander; severe, clear emergencies, where the bystander witnesses the distress of another person and which happen close to a bystander were proposed to stimulate the most arousal. If they do not stimulate arousal, then no response is given. If they do stimulate arousal, this will be interpreted differently in different situations. Cost/reward calculations will subsequently occur and lead to a response that might include direct or indirect intervention, escape or a reinterpretation of the situation (see Theory Box 10.4).

One study illustrating how costs can impact on helping behaviour comes from the work of Darley and Batson (1973), and has already been discussed in Chapter 2 (see Research Close-Up 2.2, Chapter 2). Participants who were told that they were in a hurry offered less help than participants who were not in a hurry, thus the personal cost of being late led to less helping.

Piliavin and colleagues went on to develop their original model further to include a range of additional constructs (see Theory Box 10.4, panel (b)). Rather than a sequence of processes, they suggested that different processes can occur simultaneously, allowing for cyclical effects. In the revised model, the researchers added bystander characteristics (trait factors such as competence and personal norms; state factors such as mood and attention) and victim characteristics (such as their similarity to the victim) as factors that contribute to the emergency intervention process. They also emphasized the importance of the attribution of the cause and nature of the arousal felt by the bystander in an emergency situation, the role of empathy felt towards victims as a possible form of arousal, and the point that in extreme emergencies costs may only be attended to partly, or not at all (Piliavin et al., 1981). Thus, in some emergency situations – characterized in terms of their clarity, reality, prior knowledge of the victim and physical orientation of the bystander to the emergency – a response consisting of **impulsive helping** may occur, when the bystander's attention is completely focused on the victim. Such situational, bystander and victim characteristics can lead to high levels of arousal, which can lead directly to a response that does not rely on the consideration of potential costs and rewards.

impulsive helping immediate, non-deliberative form of helping that does not appear to involve a conscious decision-making process, and in which the helper does not attend to the presence of other bystanders.

 LEADER IN THE FIELD

Jane Allyn Piliavin obtained her PhD from Stanford University in 1962, and is currently Conway-Bascom Professor Emerita of Sociology and Women's Studies at the University of Wisconsin-Madison. Together with Irving Piliavin, she developed the influential arousal: cost–reward model of helping behaviour in emergency situations. Her interest in helping behaviour subsequently led her to shift focus from isolated incidents of helping towards the study of long-term, repeated help-giving. This work has highlighted the importance of roles, and the development of an altruistic identity. Various aspects of her work, particularly in the area of blood donation, have fed into public policy.

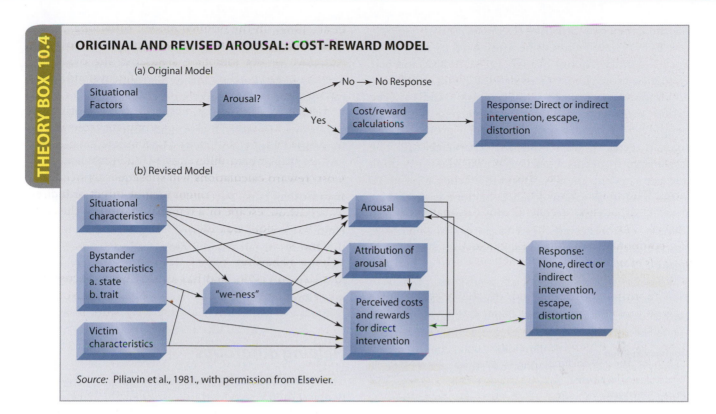

THEORY BOX 10.4

ORIGINAL AND REVISED AROUSAL: COST-REWARD MODEL

(a) Original Model

(b) Revised Model

Source: Piliavin et al., 1981., with permission from Elsevier.

The general expansion of the arousal: cost–reward model additionally includes the concept of 'we-ness' as it relates to the bystander–victim relationship. Piliavin et al. (1981) suggest that a sense of 'we-ness' between the bystander and victim increases the likelihood of intervention, as it differentially impacts on the associated costs and rewards of helping. They suggest that helping responses towards victims perceived as 'we-group' are innate in human beings, whereas socialization seeks to eliminate these forms of impulsive or immediate helping. In clear emergency situations this innate response can happen very quickly, and therefore 'beat' the slower, socialized response that attempts to eliminate them. 'We-ness' is proposed to increase the likelihood of intervention, as it increases the benefits and reduces the costs of helping: a bystander may be more confident of the consequences of helping a victim with whom she or he felt a sense of 'we-ness', and therefore the relative costs of helping would be reduced. 'We-ness' is also proposed to increase the arousal felt by the bystander, and increase the costs of the victim receiving no help. Subsequently, these researchers have begun to draw on social identity approaches in order to consider the group-based features of helping (e.g. Dovidio, Piliavin, Gaertner, Schroeder, & Clark, 1991). It is to this aspect of helping – the role of group level explanations of behaviour – that we now turn.

Groups, identity and prosocial behaviour

The traditional focus of the social psychology of prosocial behaviour has been on how people relate to each other as individuals rather than as members of social groups. Thus, researchers have considered *individual* decision-making processes (Latané & Darley, 1970), *individual* emotions (Batson et al., 1981), or the characteristics of relationships between *individual* helpers and the recipients of help (Clark, Mills, & Corcoran, 1989). Until recently there had been very little focus on the role of group processes in early helping research (but see Hornstein, 1976, for an exception). In fact, if groups were considered at all, they were usually assumed to have a negative effect on people's willingness to help. The classic concepts of *diffusion of responsibility* or *pluralistic ignorance* both seem to suggest that groups impact negatively on an individual's ability to behave prosocially at the appropriate time.

In recent years, however, researchers have begun to move away from seeing the influence of the group in a wholly negative light. This shift in focus has been the result of collaborations between researchers interested in helping behaviour, on the one hand, and researchers interested in group processes and intergroup relations on the other (see Stürmer & Snyder, 2010). Helping researchers have begun to be influenced by ideas from Social Identity Theory (Tajfel, 1978a, 1982a) and Self Categorization Theory (Turner, Hogg, Oakes, Reicher, & Wetherell, 1987) (see also Chapters 5 and 14). The group processes literature is concerned with how people act as members of their social groups, rather than in terms of their individual characteristics. The key insight from this work is that individuals can think and act as group members, and that when a group or social identity is salient, then behaviour is shaped by the norms and the values of the group. This group identity can sometimes lead to antisocial behaviour, but it can also lead to prosocial behaviour (Postmes & Spears, 1998).

Dovidio and colleagues, using insights from both Social Identity Theory and Self Categorization Theory, have shown how groups can shape willingness to help. Using the **common ingroup identity model** (Gaertner & Dovidio, 2000, 2008; see also Chapter 14) they show that if members of different groups can be made to see themselves as members of a common group, then hostility and bias between groups can be reduced and prosocial behaviour towards others can be increased. For example, Dovidio et al. (1997) conducted an experiment in which students were divided into two arbitrary groups: they were told that they had the kind of personality that 'overestimates' or 'underestimates'. They then spent some time in a group of three 'underestimators' or a group of three 'overestimators'. Having done this they were then placed in one of two conditions: a 'common superordinate identity' condition, or a 'two-group' condition. In the common superordinate identity condition groups of underestimators and overestimators were put together, but all participants were asked to wear the same colour university sweatshirt, and to sit around a table with a member of the other group on either side of them (i.e. in an A, B, A, B pattern). In the two-group (separate identity) condition, overestimators wore a sweatshirt of one colour and sat on one side of the table, while understimators wore a sweatshirt of another colour and sat on the other side of the table. All participants then worked together on a decision-making task. After the task had been completed, participants were separated, and when they were on their own, they were given an opportunity to help an ingroup or an outgroup member. The help request was in the form of an appeal to help with recruitment of participants for a study, and to help put up posters around

common ingroup identity model this model seeks to reduce bias between groups by changing the nature of categorization from ingroups versus outgroups to a single, more inclusive identity. The model harnesses the forces of ingroup favouritism to reduce bias and promote helping.

the university campus. Participants were much more likely to help an outgroup person if they had been in the common ingroup identity condition (see also Chapter 14 for how re-categorizing former ingroups and outgroups can promote better intergroup relations).

Similar group processes can be seen in the study by Levine, Prosser, Evans, and Reicher (2005) (see Research Close-Up 10.3) in which football fans were primed to see themselves in terms of their team identity (Manchester United fans) or a superordinate identity (football fans). Participants failed to help a stranger identified as a Liverpool FC fan when a Manchester United identity was salient, but extended help to the Liverpool fan when a more inclusive football fan identity was salient. However, strangers who could not be identified as football fans were not helped to the same degree.

Helping outgroups

Thus far we have seen that there is good evidence that people are likely to help others when they are seen as ingroup members. However, it would be a mistake to assume that there is a single social identity mechanism – a simple 'ingroup favouritism' – which underlies helping behaviour at the group level. Take, for example, the extensive literature which uses helping as a non-reactive measure of prejudice (Saucier, Miller, & Doucet, 2005): some studies find that white participants show ingroup favouritism, while others find no differences (Bickman & Kamzan, 1973), or even outgroup favouritism (Dutton & Lake, 1973). Saucier et al. (2005) reveal a complex picture of the way white participants offer help to white and black victims. They argue that white people are less likely to help black people in situations where failure to help can clearly be attributed to something other than race, or in situations of high emergency where interventions are potentially very costly. Outgroup helping is most likely as an attempt to avoid appearing prejudiced, or to avoid aversive internal states.

Faced with this rich complexity of ingroup and outgroup helping, a social identity approach does not imply that the salience of social identity always results in ingroup favouritism. Rather, the suggestion is that when social identity is salient, people will act in terms of the norms and values of the group. Some identities may contain norms to 'look after your own'. Other identities (like some religious identities, for example) might have norms that encourage members to help outgroup members even more than ingroup members. When thinking about groups and helping, it is important to distinguish between helping based on ingroup inclusion and helping based on ingroup

THE IMPACT OF SOCIAL IDENTITY ON EMERGENCY HELPING

RESEARCH CLOSE-UP 10.3

Levine, M., Prosser, A., Evans, D., & Reicher, S. D. (2005). Identity and emergency intervention: How social group membership and inclusiveness of group boundaries shape helping behavior. *Personality and Social Psychology Bulletin, 31*, 443–453.

Introduction

This research uses football fans to study the effect of social identity on helping behaviour in 'real life' emergencies. The paper explores the hypothesis that bystanders are more likely to help victims of an emergency when the victims are seen as fellow ingroup members. However, the paper also acknowledges that group boundaries are not fixed. It seeks to demonstrate that, by changing the way people think about their own social identity, we can extend the boundaries of the ingroup. By extending the boundaries of the ingroup it becomes possible to increase the range of people who are helped.

Two experiments were conducted. Manchester United football fans were recruited to take part in both experiments. In Study 1 they were primed to think about themselves in terms of their Manchester United social identity. However, in Study 2 they were primed to think about themselves in terms of a more inclusive social identity – as a football fan (rather than a Manchester United fan).

In both experiments, participants were exposed to an accident. While they were walking across a university campus, a stranger came jogging along, then tripped and fell, and appeared to be hurt. The stranger was sometimes wearing a Manchester United football shirt, sometimes a Liverpool FC football shirt, and sometimes an ordinary unbranded sports shirt. It was predicted that, when Manchester United identity was salient (Study 1), participants would help the stranger wearing a Manchester United shirt more often than when the stranger wore a Liverpool or plain shirt. However, when football fan identity was salient (Study 2) they were expected to help as much when the stranger wore either a Manchester United or a Liverpool shirt, but not when the stranger wore a plain shirt.

Method

Participants

Thirty-five male participants aged between 18 and 21 (who were self-identified Manchester United fans) participated in Study 1. Twenty-nine male Manchester United fans (aged between 18 and 21) participated in Study 2.

Design and procedure

In both studies, participants came to the psychology department of an English university and were placed in a small cubicle. In Study 1 they completed a questionnaire and wrote an essay about how much they loved being a Manchester United fan. In Study 2 they completed a questionnaire and wrote an essay about how much they loved being a football fan. After this first stage, they left the cubicle and were asked to walk on their own to another building to watch a video about football fans. While they were walking an accident was staged in front of them. A confederate, who was a stranger to the participants, came running along, tripped, fell, and cried out in pain while holding on to his ankle. The confederate was sometimes wearing a Manchester United shirt, sometimes a Liverpool FC shirt, and sometimes an ordinary unbranded sports shirt. Three hidden observers (who were blind to the hypothesis of the study) watched the behaviour of each participant and rated his behaviour independently. They rated the amount and form of helping using measures adapted from Darley and Batson's (1973) 'Good Samaritan' study explained above. Participants were also questioned by a member of the research team when they reached their destination (but before they were debriefed) about anything they may have witnessed on their journey. This was to ensure that they had witnessed the event and that they had recognized the appropriate football shirt in the appropriate condition.

Results

In Study 1, when the Manchester United social identity was salient, participants were significantly more likely to help when the victim wore a Manchester United shirt than either a Liverpool or a plain shirt; see Figure 10.5. In Study 2, when football fan social identity was salient, participants were equally likely to help when the victim wore either a Liverpool shirt or a Manchester United shirt, but not when he wore a plain shirt.

Discussion

The results confirm the hypothesis that people are more likely to help strangers when they see some signs

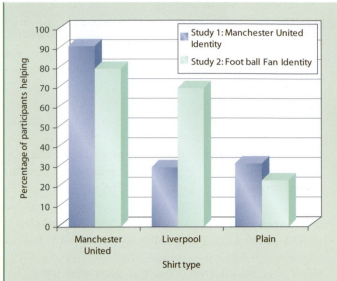

FIGURE 10.5 *Effects of inclusivity of social identities on rates of helping.*

of common group membership in the person in need. However, the study also shows that group boundaries are not fixed, and by getting people to think about themselves in terms of more inclusive social identities we can increase the range of people who are helped. The findings are particularly interesting because Manchester United and Liverpool fans have a strong historical rivalry. This rivalry has been known to result in intergroup violence (Figure 10.6). And yet, simply by changing the level at which people identify, Manchester United fans can be encouraged to extend a helping hand to those they might otherwise feel antagonistic towards. This suggests that a way to increase feelings of responsibility for the welfare of others is to promote social identities that are as inclusive as possible.

(a)   (b)

FIGURE 10.6(a) and (b) *Manchester United and Liverpool fans have a strong historical rivalry, which has been known to result in intergroup violence.*

Source: (a) © Jon Super. Used under licence from Press Association Images; (b) © Press Association Images.

norms. Take, for example, the work of Reicher and colleagues on holocaust rescue – in particular the rescue of Bulgarian Jews. Reicher, Cassidy, Wolpert, Hopkins, and Levine (2006) show that, unlike most countries in Europe under the influence of the Nazis during the Second World War, Bulgaria managed to resist German demands to deport Jews to the concentration camps (Denmark was the only other country to do so successfully).

Reicher et al. analysed key documents (including political speeches, open letters and official statements) from influential people and organizations (including politicians, lawyers, and the church). By conducting a systematic qualitative analysis of the way arguments were constructed and deployed in the texts, they showed that the Bulgarian political elite based their resistance to German demands on two main strategies. The first strategy was to argue that Jews were Bulgarians, and thus to deport a Jew was to deport a Bulgarian. They termed this an 'ingroup inclusion' strategy, and it could be achieved because the nature of Bulgarian identity was constructed in civic rather than racial terms. The second strategy was to argue that it violated the values of Bulgarian identity to allow Jews to be deported. Reicher et al. termed this an 'ingroup norm' strategy. The argument here was that it was fundamentally '*un*Bulgarian' to allow such a fate to befall any group, and so to stand back and allow the deportation to happen would be a threat to the core values of the group. Reicher et al. demonstrate that these strategies were not mutually exclusive, and that ingroup inclusion and ingroup norm strategies could appear in the same document. However, they argue that speakers tended to emphasize one strategy over another to maximize the likelihood of influence given the particular context in which the appeal was being made. They conclude that this kind of qualitative analysis can usefully be combined with experimental methods to explore the relationship between the choice of strategy and the effectiveness of the influence.

Social identity and the bystander effect

The social identity tradition has also been applied to the behaviour of bystanders in emergencies. Levine and colleagues have argued that the bystander effect (the idea that bystanders are more likely to intervene when alone than when in the presence of others) is a partial story. Using insights from the social identity and self-categorization theories, they suggest that the key to bystander behaviour in the presence of others is not simply the number of other bystanders, but rather the psychological relationship between the bystanders. For example, Levine, Cassidy, and Jentzsch (2010) conducted experiments in which they asked (university student) participants to imagine they were with one other person, or many other people, in a public place. The public places were settings like a restaurant or a cinema. The experiment followed the design of Garcia, Weaver, Moskowitz, and Darley (2002) who had shown that simply imagining the presence of others led to a decrease in willingness to donate money – something they called the 'implicit bystander effect'. However, Levine et al. varied who the others were imagined to be. Depending on the experimental condition, the others were imagined as strangers, friends or group members (i.e. students). As part of the experiment, participants were asked about willingness to donate money to charity and willingness to volunteer time to take part in further psychology experiments.

Results showed that when the others were imagined as friends, increasing group size resulted in a reduction in the amount people were willing to donate to charity, or the hours they were prepared to volunteer to help the psychology department. This was the same finding as in Garcia et al. However, when the others were imagined as strangers, increasing group size resulted in an increase in donation intention and an increase in willingness to volunteer for experiments. When the others were imagined as students, increasing group size did not affect willingness to donate money, but did lead to an increase in volunteering for the experiments. Levine et al. (2010) argue that this pattern of results suggests something more complex than the traditional bystander effect. It is the combination of who the others are believed to be (i.e. the psychological relationship between bystanders),

the context in which the presence of others is imagined, and the kind of helping behaviour which is proposed, that shapes the nature of bystander behaviour.

Levine, Cassidy, Brazier, and Reicher (2002) have also shown that the social identity relationships between bystander and fellow bystander can shape willingness to intervene in an emergency. Fellow bystanders are more influential when they are seen as ingroup members rather than outgroup members. Moreover, social identity and group size can interact to promote as well as inhibit helping in emergencies. For example, Levine and Crowther (2008) showed that, when gender identities were salient, and men and women witnessed an incident of public domestic violence, group size could have different effects. In this experiment, participants watched CCTV footage of an attack by a man on a woman (on a public street) while they sat on their own, or in groups of three. The group conditions were comprised of either three men, or three women, or were groups with a male majority or a female majority. After they watched the footage, participants were asked to say how likely they would be to intervene if they saw an incident like this in real life. Men were more likely to say they would intervene when they had watched the footage on their own rather than in the presence of other men. This is the classic bystander effect. However, for women, the presence of other women led to an increased readiness to help. They were more likely to express an intention to intervene when in an all-female group than when on their own. This runs contrary to the traditional bystander effect. When groups contained both men and women, then co-presence had different effects for the men and the women. When men were in the minority, they were more likely to say they would intervene. However, when women were in the minority, they were significantly less likely to say they would intervene.

Taken together, these studies suggest that it is the way people understand the psychological relationships between bystanders, rather than the simple presence of others, that is key to understanding bystander behaviour.

Social identity, emotion and bystander intervention

In addition to the work on how the salience, boundaries and contents of social identities shape helping behaviour, recent research has also explored the role of identity processes at the intersection of emotion and helping. For example, Stürmer and colleagues (Stürmer, Snyder, Kropp, & Siem, 2006; Stürmer, Snyder, & Omoto, 2005) argue that much of the literature on emotion and helping is limited by an individualistic or interpersonal focus. By introducing insights from the social identity tradition, they were able to demonstrate that social identity relationships moderate empathy-motivated helping. Stürmer and colleagues conducted research on longer-term helping and volunteering (for example volunteers in community-based HIV/AIDS service organizations) and argued that it is not that people are more likely to help ingroup members than outgroup members, but rather that ingroup and outgroup helping can be explained by different psychological pathways.

Using data from a large-scale project on the psychological aspects of volunteerism in a community-based AIDS service organization, they compared a sample of (male and female) heterosexual and homosexual volunteers who were all serving as 'buddies' or 'home-helps' to male homosexual HIV/AIDS patients. Using self-defined sexual orientation as a proxy measure of ingroup/outgroup status, they looked at the behaviours, motivations and emotions that volunteers expressed in their relationship to the person they were volunteering to help. Results showed that empathy with the client tended to be a strong predictor of helping in homosexual volunteers, while liking or attraction was a strong predictor of help when volunteers were heterosexual.

Summary

There are several levels at which the motivation to help others can be understood. Evidence shows that people help as a way of dealing with the emotional and physiological costs of being in an emergency situation. People also help because of their psychological connections to others. When we see people as members of a common ingroup then we are more likely to help them. Outgroup members can be helped too. However, when ingroup members are helped it is based on feelings of empathy. When outgroup members are helped, feelings of liking or warmth towards the outgroup member are usually the key. Finally, when social identities are salient, then the presence of other people does not always lead to inhibition of helping (the traditional bystander effect). When the norms and values of an identity promote helping, then having other group members around can enhance the expression of the identity and thus lead to greater helping.

ISSUES IN RESEARCHING PROSOCIAL BEHAVIOUR

What effect do violence and gender have on willingness to help?

Thus far we have seen a range of work focusing on why people help and why they don't help. One of the most

impressive features of this work is the attempt to study *actual helping behaviour* – as opposed to methods that ask about hypothetical helping situations, or ask about intentions to act. The inventive and cleverly choreographed behavioural studies that established the bystander effect are good examples of this. Despite the achievements of laboratory research on helping behaviour, Cherry (1995), in her critique of the bystander tradition, makes an important observation. She argues that when Latané and Darley went into the lab to study bystander behaviour in the light of the story of the 38 witnesses, they neglected two key features of the original event – violence and gender. By concentrating only on the number of bystanders they ignored much of what was socially meaningful about the behaviour of the bystanders. Cherry argues that this neglect was a result of 'culturally embedded theorizing' (p. 16.). Latané and Darley were working at a time when society in general was not sensitized to the problem of male violence (see Chapter 9) or the gendered nature of helping behaviour.

A contributing factor to this omission must also have been the practical and ethical difficulties associated with researching violence. It is logistically very difficult to create a violent incident in a laboratory context that is both believable to participants and can be reproduced with the degree of consistency required for experimental designs. At the same time, exposing participants to violence in experimental settings raises a number of ethical challenges. These include considerations of the deception and distress that participants might be exposed to (see the discussion of ethical issues in Chapter 2). Some researchers have, however, managed to overcome these difficulties to the satisfaction of the ethical review committees in their universities, and the research they have produced has suggested some important new directions for research on prosocial behaviour.

Violence and helping

In research that does explore the behaviour of bystanders to violent (rather than non-violent) emergencies, the bystander-effect explanation seems to work less well. While the presence of others can sometimes inhibit intervention, more often than not, the presence of others tends to enhance the likelihood of intervention in violent emergencies. This research tends not to be traditional laboratory research, given the difficulties of simulating violence in a laboratory. For example, Harari, Harari, and White (1985) conducted a field experiment in which they staged an 'attempted rape' on the grounds of a university campus. Participants were divided into those in groups (defined as students walking close together,

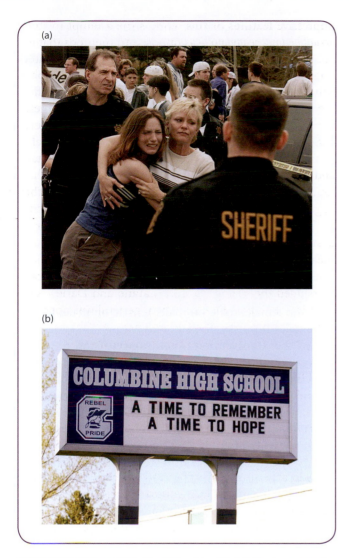

(a)

(b)

FIGURE 10.7(a) and (b) *The Columbine High School massacre in 1999 left 12 students and one teacher dead and many more injured.*

Source: (a) © Ed Andrieski; (b) © Ed Andrieski. Both images used under licence from Press Association Images.

rather than being in intact groups in order to 'reduce experimental contamination', p. 635), and those who were alone. While they were walking along, they saw a female student (a confederate of the experimenters) being grabbed by a male confederate who jumped out from behind a bush and attempted to drag the female student away while she struggled and called for help. Harari et al. found that 85 per cent of participants in groups intervened, whereas 65 per cent of participants who were alone intervened. Moreover, 80 per cent of interventions were direct (an indirect intervention route was offered via a campus security officer in the distance).

In similar fashion, Schreiber (1979) also set up a violent emergency outside of the lab, using a procedure that would be unlikely to receive ethical approval today (not least given the number of high-profile school shootings;

see Figure 10.7). Schreiber used his own lecture class to simulate a shooting incident on campus. Every year for six years, Schreiber had a confederate intruder rush into his lecture room, shout at, scuffle with and then shoot a 'victim' in the class. The victim then fell on the floor 'covered in blood', while the instructor 'simulated an emotional state of intense fear and yelled' (p. 245). In the six years, only two people intervened directly, and both of these had some expertise in dealing with violence (one was a probation officer, the other an American football player). However, fourteen people did try to get help, and these indirect interveners came from the larger lecture classes rather than the smaller lecture classes.

Using a less ethically controversial method, Wells and Graham (1999) explored the reactions of bystanders to aggressive bar-room incidents. They conducted systematic observations of 12 bars, then conducted a series of telephone interviews in which people talked about violent incidents in bars. In addition to their observation that third parties became involved in almost 50 per cent of incidents, they found that aggressive interventions served to increase the violence, while non-aggressive interventions decreased it. Their research showed that the nature and form of third-party behaviour is important to the outcome of violent incidents. In other words, understanding the nature of the violence requires more than just the study of the perpetrator and the victim.

In contrast to these examples that make use of direct observations of people's behaviour in violent situations, Christy and Voigt (1994) extended the study of bystanders and violence to consider responses to public episodes of child abuse. They gave an 80-item questionnaire to 269 people who self-reported that they had witnessed an event of child abuse. Almost half the sample reported having witnessed child abuse in a public rather than a private place. However, of those who were bystanders to public violence towards children, only one out of four witnesses acted to intervene. Of those who did intervene, direct interveners, in addition to feeling greater certainty about taking action, had more often witnessed abuse and were themselves more likely to have been abused as children, compared to indirect interveners.

Levine (1999) used yet another method to study bystander responses to violence towards children. He examined the court transcripts of the trial of two 12-year old boys (Jon Venables and Robert Thompson) for the abduction and murder of two-year-old James Bulger in Liverpool in 1993. In an echo of the Kitty Genovese case, 38 witnesses were called at the trial, all of whom had encountered James and his abductors on the walk around Liverpool before his eventual murder. Levine argues that the traditional five-step cognitive decision-making model did not fit with the witnesses' accounts of why they

Table 10.1 *Percentage of men and women intervening as a function of victim and perpetrator gender.*

Perpetrator gender	Victim gender	Participant Gender	
		Male	**Female**
Male	Male	80%	0%
	Female	0%	25%
Female	Male	67%	0%
	Female	57%	20%

Source: From Borofsky et al., 1971.

FIGURE 10.8 *Levine (1999) argues that witnesses in the James Bulger murder case did not intervene because they assumed, or were told by the older boys, that James was their brother, and it is a widely held belief that strangers are not supposed to approach or become involved with children from other families.*

Source: © Press Association Images

failed to intervene. Witnesses *did* notice that James was injured and in distress, they *did* think that some kind of intervention might be warranted, and they *did not* explain their failure to act in terms of diffusion of responsibility or pluralistic ignorance. Instead, they did not intervene because they assumed, or were told by the older boys, that James was their brother (Figure 10.8). Levine argues that invoking 'the family' as a way of making sense of the relationship between the bystanders and the boys made it psychologically difficult for bystanders to act. Strangers are not supposed to approach or become involved with children from other families. This is particularly true for men, given current scares over the risk posed to children by 'predatory paedophiles'. However, Levine argues that it was not inevitable that the category of 'the family' should have come to dominate the interactions between bystanders and the boys. If the bystanders had constructed their encounter as one between adults and children (rather than family and non-family members) – and acted as though adults have responsibility for the welfare of all children – then they might have been more likely to intervene. (See the previous section on groups, identity and prosocial behaviour for other examples of how changing the group identity can change willingness to intervene.)

Gender and helping

Some studies have specifically looked at the role of gender in violent situations. Using simulated 'attacks'

(male on female; male on male; female on male; female on female) Borofsky, Stollak, and Messé (1971) demonstrated that intervention (attempting to stop the fight, or speaking directly to those involved) was at its lowest for male bystander participants when a man attacked a woman (see Table 10.1). Female participants showed low rates of intervention overall, with only two out of twenty-one female participants intervening during the whole experiment (although less than half – 10 – of the twenty-one male participants intervened). Shotland and Straw (1976) also reported a series of experiments that involved a staged fight between a man and a woman in the presence of a bystander. The incident was characterized as involving either a husband-and-wife couple, or two strangers. In the 'married' condition, the woman was overheard shouting 'I don't know why I ever married you'; in the 'strangers' condition, the woman was overheard shouting 'I don't know you'. Shotland and Straw's experiments showed that bystanders were more likely to intervene in an attack on a woman by a man if they believed the couple were strangers than if they were married. If the bystanders were unsure of the nature of the relationship between the man and the woman, they were more likely to infer an intimate connection, and were therefore less likely to intervene.

While Cherry's (1995) analysis points to the importance of gender in the analysis of bystander intervention, and notes that gendered violence generally shows a different pattern of results from the classic research on bystander intervention, gender often manifests itself in the analysis of differential rates of helping for men and women. Eagly and Crowley (1986), for example, provided a meta-analysis of gender differences in helping behaviour research. While they found, in general, that men helped more than women in the range of studies that they reviewed, they pointed out that this was due to the focus in the literature on short-term encounters between strangers, highlighting the way in which a large proportion of the research in the area has focused on particular forms of helping behaviour. Thus, Eagly and Crowley argued that the differential rates of helping by men and women were a product of the form of the studies themselves and the specific helping behaviours that they have studied. In particular, they argued that behaviours prescribed by the female gender role are more often shown in long-term close relationships that do not tend to feature in the bystander literature. They suggest that such behaviours include caring for the personal and emotional needs of others, delivering routine forms of personal service, and facilitating the progress of others toward their goals (Eagly & Crowley, p. 284). Behaviours that are prescribed by the male gender role, on the other hand, consist of the type of non-routine, risky acts of rescuing others that often feature in bystander experiments.

In a questionnaire study of intervention in drunk driving situations, Rabow, Newcomb, Monto, and Hernandez (1990) asked participants about their past experiences of seeing and reacting to someone they thought was too drunk to drive. Rabow et al. found that rates of intervention (doing something to stop the person from driving) reported by men and women did not differ significantly; although more women than men reported intervening: 57 per cent compared to 43 per cent, this difference was not statistically significant. Rabow et al. used Eagly and Crowley's (1986) analysis to suggest that, when bystanders have had no prior training and when the relationships between those present are not strangers (laboratory studies typically involve strangers), women are as likely to intervene as men, perhaps even more so.

Eagly and Crowley (1986) suggested that this bias towards the kinds of helping behaviours prescribed by the male gender role was due to the dominance of the experimental paradigm in social psychological research, particularly during the 1970s. They argued that manipulating independent variables and assigning participants randomly to conditions, which are defining features of experimentation (see Chapter 2) can generally only be accomplished in the context of short-term encounters with strangers. The difficulty of using the experimental method to explore long-term helping behaviours has meant that there has been relatively less interest in them. There is now, however, a growing body of research that has looked at longer-term helping, to which we now turn.

Long-term, sustained helping behaviours

As the study of helping behaviour has developed in the years following its original impetus in the 1960s, various forms of helping behaviours have been studied. For example, Piliavin and her colleagues have shifted focus from the arousal: cost–reward model of helping towards a consideration of roles and the longer-term context of helping behaviour (e.g. Callero, Howard, & Piliavin, 1987; Grube & Piliavin, 2000; Lee, Piliavin, & Call, 1999). This more recent work draws from Identity Theory (Stryker, 1980), a sociological theory which suggests that we have different role identities which, taken together, make up the self (see also Chapter 5). Note that Identity Theory is a distinct approach from Social Identity Theory, which is covered in Chapter 14. While Social Identity Theory focuses on intergroup relations and group processes, and their implications for identity, Identity Theory focuses on the notion of roles and their relationship to behaviour. These role identities are related to social structure, and influence behaviour as different roles relate to different expectations. Moreover, the more a person voluntarily performs a particular role, the more likely it is that their identity will develop in relation to the behaviours involved in that performance. Piliavin and her colleagues have used this perspective to look at a series of long-term helping behaviours in order to examine how such behaviours come to be sustained. Lee et al. (1999), for example, demonstrated how their model of blood donation, based on identity theory, was also applicable to volunteering and charitable donation (Figure 10.9). The model, developed on the basis of longitudinal studies of the antecedents and consequences of role-identity as a blood donor, suggests that perceived expectations,

FIGURE 10.9 *Lee, Piliavin, and Call's (1999) model of blood donation, based on identity theory, suggests that perceived expectations, parental modelling, personal norms, past behaviour, and role-identity as a donor can predict the intention to donate.*

Source: © Gina Sanders. Used under licence from Shutterstock.

parental modelling, personal norms, past behaviour and role-identity as a donor predict the intention to donate (time, money and blood).

The research of Lee et al. (1999) was based on the National Charity Survey, a telephone interview survey based in New York City involving 1002 respondents. They asked questions about participants' perceptions of others' expectations concerning donating blood, money and time. For each of the different helping behaviours – donating blood, money and time – the participants were asked about: (1) others' expectations (whether other people expected them to donate); (2) modelling (whether their parents donated); (3) past receipt of help (whether they or someone close to them had previously received help); (4) personal norms (how often they thought other people should donate); (5) past behaviour (i.e. how many times they had donated blood, money or time over the past year); (6) role identity (whether the behaviour was an important part of who they are); and (7) behavioural intention (how likely it was that they would donate each of the goods in the next 12 months). The researchers tested the model that they had developed with blood donation and found that, while there were some differences, the model was applicable to all three forms of donation. The authors noted some differences, however, between the different types of helping: for example, in comparison to other forms of donation, past behaviour was more important to blood donation and role identity was more important to donating time (i.e.

volunteering). This work usefully highlights both the precursors to helping and the longer term effects of helping on the helper, beyond the specific helping situation, and also demonstrates how a model developed in one area of helping can be applied to different areas.

An alternative approach that looks at long-term helping behaviour, and specifically **volunteerism**, comes from the work of Omoto and Snyder (2010). These researchers have developed the volunteer process model, which examines the antecedents, experiences and consequences of volunteer behaviour. This model proposes that these antecedents, experiences and consequences of volunteer activity operate at different levels of analysis: *individual* (e.g. individual decisions regarding involvement in volunteering, and associated individual level psychological processes); *interpersonal* (e.g. the dynamics of relationships between volunteers and the various other people they come into contact with as a result of their volunteering); *organizational* (e.g. the issues faced by volunteer-related organizations in recruiting and retaining volunteers); and *societal* (e.g. the relationships between volunteers and broader social structures and collective dynamics); see Figure 10.10. This growing body of work has largely examined volunteering for AIDS-related organizations in the US.

The volunteer process model emphasizes how volunteerism is a process that develops over time, and

> **volunteerism** when individuals give time and effort willingly without expecting rewards.

	Volunteer Process		
Level of analysis	Antecedents	Experiences	Consequences
Individual	Prior experiences Personality differences	Volunteer's performance and choice of role	Changes in knowledge, attitude, behaviour, motivation
Interpersonal	Existing social support networks	Relationships with other volunteers and with recipients of their services	Recruitment of other volunteers
Organizational	Recruitment of volunteers	Tracking of volunteers	Quantity and quality of services
Societal	Community resources Cultural context	Recipients of services	Public education Systems of service delivery

Community Context

FIGURE 10.10 *Volunteer process model in a community context (from Omoto & Snyder, 2002; 2010).*

Source: From Omoto & Snyder, 2002, 2010.

involves the decision to get involved in volunteering, seeking out volunteering opportunities, undertaking volunteer activities, and ultimately ceasing volunteer activities. Antecedents of volunteering have been identified in a range of studies. Personality and dispositional factors, such as empathic concern, and motivational factors, such as a concern for community, together with particular life circumstances, such as levels of social support, have been found to predict involvement in volunteering (e.g. Omoto & Snyder, 1993; Omoto, Snyder, & Martino, 2000). In terms of volunteer experiences, researchers have found that volunteers become increasingly connected to the people in receipt of their volunteering work ('clients'). In one study, after six months of volunteers working in a buddy programme in an AIDS service organization, 76 per cent of volunteers had been introduced to the members of their clients' social network, and 52 per cent of clients had been introduced to volunteers' own social networks (Omoto & Snyder, 2010). The consequences of volunteering have been illustrated, for example, in a study that found that 28 per cent of volunteers had recruited another volunteer after six months of volunteering. In addition, as volunteers become increasingly connected to a 'community of shared concerns' (Omoto & Snyder, 2010, p. 233), so too does their participation in other forms of prosocial action increase (e.g. charitable giving and social activism). While this work has thus far been primarily focused on individual level processes, it has also begun to look at community processes, and how the concern about and connections to community can help to both motivate and sustain volunteer behaviours. Thus, a psychological sense of community – for example, a community of people concerned with HIV – has been found to motivate volunteerism, to be an important feature of volunteers' experiences, and to be enhanced through volunteering. Those people reporting a stronger psychological sense of community have been found to undertake prosocial behaviours more frequently, feel psychologically healthier, and to be intent on undertaking more prosocial action in the future.

Another area of research that has focused specifically on longer term forms of helping – and in particular those which carry a significant amount of risk for the helper – is the study of those individuals who helped Jews during World War II. Some researchers have referred to this as 'courageous resistance' (Shepela et al., 1999), whereas others have attempted to isolate an 'altruistic personality' through the study of those involved (e.g. Oliner & Oliner, 1992); we return to the issue of personality below. While there is no clear consensus regarding the explanation of these acts of helping, research suggests that all such helpers tended to share a world view in which victims were seen as part of a common moral community with themselves (e.g. all human beings), and felt obliged to help members of that community who were in need (Reicher et al., 2006). This suggestion illustrates how research in this particular area of prosocial behaviour shows some theoretical and conceptual similarities to research in other areas of helping, which have begun to highlight the role of a sense of shared group membership in the helping process, and also illustrates a possible link between explanations of different forms of helping.

Looking at longer-term helping, rather than helping in emergency situations, has thus raised additional possibilities for research, including the notion of identifying a **prosocial personality**. While earlier researchers had rejected the possibility of identifying reliable personality factors to predict helping, Penner (2002) has suggested that this was due to the focus on helping in emergency situations, and a narrow focus on specific types of helping behaviours. In response, Penner and colleagues (Penner, Fritzsche, Craiger, & Freifeld, 1995) developed the Prosocial Personality Battery (PSB); see Individual Differences 10.1. Penner and Finkelstein (1998) have defined a prosocial personality orientation as 'an enduring tendency to think about the welfare and rights of other people, to feel concern, and empathy, and to act in a way that benefits them' (p. 526). The Prosocial Personality Battery comprises two factors: other-oriented empathy and helpfulness. Research has suggested that a range of behaviours correlate with one or both of these factors including speed of response in simulated emergencies, the frequency of everyday acts of helping, the frequency of helping co-workers, the willingness to mentor co-workers, and the willingness to be an organ donor (Penner, 2002). In addition, Penner (2002) suggests that his model of the prosocial personality is quite similar to Oliner and Oliner's (1992) description of the personality traits of the gentiles who rescued Jews during the Nazi Holocaust.

This consideration of longer-term helping situations has highlighted a number of dynamic models that attempt to explain why people first become involved in such sustained prosocial behaviours, how they are sustained, and what the consequences of the behaviours are for those undertaking these behaviours. While the question remains as to whether a single theory is sufficient to explain all types of helping behaviours, what many of these approaches have again highlighted is the role of identity, including the notion of collective identities, in helping behaviours of various kinds.

> **prosocial personality**
> an enduring tendency to think about the rights and welfare of others, to feel concern and empathy, and to act in a way that benefits them.

MEASURING THE PROSOCIAL PERSONALITY

Penner et al. (1995) developed the Prosocial Personality Battery (PSB) to measure people's tendency to think about the welfare and rights of other people, to feel concern and empathy for them and to act in a way that benefits them. There are two versions of the PSB: one has 56 items, the other (a short form) has 30 items. The 30-item questionnaire has very similar psychometric properties to the longer form. The PSB has two factors: other-oriented empathy and helpfulness. People scoring highly on other-oriented empathy are likely to experience empathy, and to feel concern about and responsibility for the welfare of others. People who score highly on helpfulness are more likely to report a history of helpful activities, and are also unlikely to experience self-oriented discomfort when seeing someone else in distress.

Below we present 22 items from the Prosocial Personality Battery (short form). These 22 items make up the other-oriented empathy factor. These include items measuring *social responsibility*, *empathetic concern*, *perspective taking*, *other-oriented moral reasoning* and *mutual concerns moral reasoning*. The items are all answered on a 5-point scale with the endpoints 1 (*strongly disagree*) and 5 (*strongly agree*). As you will see, some items are followed by an (R). This means that they are reverse scored when the questions are combined to make up a sub-scale.

Social responsibility

1. When people are nasty to me, I feel very little responsibility to treat them well. (R)
2. I would feel less bothered about leaving litter in a dirty park than in a clean one. (R)
3. No matter what a person has done to us, there is no excuse for taking advantage of them.
4. With the pressure for grades and the widespread cheating in school nowadays, the individual who cheats occasionally is not really as much at fault. (R)
5. It doesn't make much sense to be very concerned about how we act when we are sick and feeling miserable. (R)
6. If I broke a machine through mishandling, I would feel less guilty if it was already damaged before I used it. (R)
7. When you have a job to do, it is impossible to look out for everybody's best interest. (R)

Empathetic concern

8. When I see someone being taken advantage of, I feel kind of protective towards them.
9. Other people's misfortunes do not usually disturb me a great deal. (R)
10. When I see someone being treated unfairly, I sometimes don't feel very much pity for them. (R)
11. I am often quite touched by things that I see happen.

Perspective taking

12. I sometimes find it difficult to see things from the 'other person's' point of view. (R)
13. I sometimes try to understand my friends better by imagining how things look from their perspective.
14. If I'm sure I'm right about something, I don't waste much time listening to other people's arguments. (R)
15. I believe that there are two sides to every question and try to look at them both.
16. When I'm upset at someone, I usually try to 'put myself in their shoes' for a while.

Other-oriented moral reasoning

17. My decisions are usually based on my concern for other people.
18. I choose a course of action that maximizes the help other people receive.
19. My decisions are usually based on concern for the welfare of others.

Mutual concerns moral reasoning

20. My decisions are usually based on what is the most fair and just way to act.
21. I choose alternatives that are intended to meet everybody's needs.
22. I choose a course of action that considers the rights of all people involved.

The data from Penner et al. (1995), based on a large US sample, showed the following mean scores for each of the separate scales (after reverse-scoring items marked R): social responsibility ($M = 4.18$, SD $= 0.52$), empathetic concern ($M = 3.30$, SD $= 0.54$), perspective taking ($M = 4.28$, SD $= 0.64$), other-oriented moral reasoning ($M = 4.28$, SD $= 0.71$), and mutual concerns moral reasoning ($M = 3.84$, SD $= 0.56$). You can compare your own score with any of these mean scores, to see if you tend to score higher or lower on each scale than average.

Summary

In this section we have seen the advantages and disadvantages of laboratory research that looks at helping behaviour. The early research by Latané and Darley had the advantage of looking at real-life helping behaviours rather than self-report measures. However, it also neglected important aspects of helping situations, in particular violence and gender. Later researchers used a variety of methods – including field experiments, observational methods and analysis of court documents – to explore these absences. This research revealed that bystanders to violence might act differently than they do in other emergencies. It also showed the importance of gender – not only in violent emergencies, but also in the way researchers think about helping in general. The focus on gender led to research on longer-term sustained helping behaviours rather than short-term emergency helping. The study of long-term helping behaviours has included an interest in volunteerism and the study of the effects of volunteer behaviour on the volunteer and the person in need.

DOES EVOLUTION MAKE US SELFISH?

What is the difference between the 'coefficient of relatedness' and the 'proportion of shared genes', and which is the more important factor in whom we help most?

In considering why people do help each other, we have so far considered a number of theoretical frameworks that have arisen from social psychological research. In particular we have already seen the debates between social psychologists on the question of whether humans can be truly altruistic. This debate has been about whether humans are responding to their own discomfort and distress, or the discomfort and distress of others. However, there is another level at which the question of human altruism has been considered. Evolutionary biologists have also been concerned with the question of altruism because human cooperation is an evolutionary puzzle. Unlike other animals, humans frequently cooperate with genetically unrelated strangers, often in large groups, with people they will never meet again, and in circumstances where the reputation gains for helping are small or absent (Fehr & Gächter, 2002). The focus of this research is concerned with what Penner et al. (2005)

would call the micro-level of analysis, which they argue is underrepresented in psychological helping research.

Early research in this area of evolutionary biology suggested that what appears to be altruism – that is, personal sacrifice on behalf of others – is really just behaviour that serves self-interest in the long run. This idea was based on a gene-centred approach to understanding human behaviour. From the gene's point of view, evolutionary success depends on leaving the maximum number of copies of itself behind in the population. Richard Dawkins, in his book *The Selfish Gene* (1976, 1989), described humans as 'survival machines – robot vehicles blindly programmed to preserve the selfish molecules known as genes . . . this selfishness will usually give rise to selfishness in individual behaviour' (p. 1).

According to this view, when we help others, we must be doing so because of some other, self-interested motivation. The first explanation for why this might happen came in the form of *inclusive fitness theory* (Hamilton, 1964). Hamilton extended Charles Darwin's classic version of natural selection, which had, until this point, focused on genetic inheritance through transmission to direct offspring only. Hamilton argued that, because close relatives of an organism shared some identical genes, the idea of reproductive fitness could be extended beyond immediate offspring to include the wider network of an organism's kin. Using mathematical principles, Hamilton demonstrated that the general theory of the evolutionary emergence of genes also applies to the genes that underlie altruistic behaviour. He showed how the idea of a **coefficient of relatedness** can be used to explain how genes for altruism emerge, and what the limits of this altruistic behaviour might be. For example, assuming there is reproductive benefit to the species as a whole of the parent sacrificing their own interests to favour their own child, then a gene that causes its possessor to give parental care will leave more children survive to continue the altruism gene line. In other words, this gene for parental care comes to be naturally selected.

coefficient of relatedness (r) between two individuals can be calculated by knowing how many steps removed individuals are from a common ancestor (e.g. coefficients of relatedness between children–parents and grandchildren–grandparents are .5 and .25, respectively).

more copies than a gene which promotes child neglect. More children survive to continue the altruism gene line. In other words, this gene for parental care comes to be naturally selected.

Given the nature of genetic transfer of information (we receive half of our genome from each of our parents), the likelihood of passing on this gene to an offspring would be 50 per cent (the likelihood of a grandchild receiving this gene would then be 25 per cent, reducing to 12.5 per cent in a great grandchild, and so on). Similarly, it becomes possible to calculate this coefficient of relatedness (or r) between siblings or between cousins – in fact between any combination of family members. For example, siblings with the same mother and father share half their genetic inheritance and thus have a coefficient of relatedness of .5 (or 50 per cent). First cousins (i.e. those whose parents are siblings) will have a coefficient of relatedness of .125 (or 12.5 per cent) – while each cousin will have an *r* of .25 (or 25 per cent) in their relationship to the common grandparent. Thus, using the *coefficient of relatedness* as a mathematical principle for determining relatedness, the degree of altruism towards others can be predicted. The more distant the relatedness, the less helping will be offered. This is captured nicely in a quote attributed to the famous British geneticist and evolutionary biologist J. B. S Haldane. When asked if he would give his life to save a drowning brother, he is reputed to have said, 'No, but I would to save two brothers or eight cousins' (quoted in McElreath & Boyd, 2007, p. 82). Of course, the logic of this approach is that there is no gene-level self-interest in helping unrelated strangers, and so we are less likely to do so.

From the point of view of genetic selection, the coefficient of relatedness matters much more at the beginning of the evolutionary process, when the gene underlying kin altruism first emerges and begins to become selected. However, once these genes evolve and spread, they end up in most individuals in a species. For example, everywhere you look today, in human and animal societies, parental care seems to be the norm. However, the fact that everybody employs the same strategy does not mean that the evolutionary advantage of selectively helping kin goes away. Rather it becomes an *evolutionarily stable strategy* (Dawkins, 1979) that continues to outperform strategies of random acts of helping other unrelated strangers. In other words, **kin selection** continues to offer evolutionary advantage – which is why it does not die out.

In understanding the role of kin selection in altruism, it is important not to mistake *coefficient of relatedness* with **proportion of shared genes**. Park (2007) points out that this is a common mistake in most social psychology textbooks. Hamilton's (1964) inclusive fitness theory is *not* saying that we help others because we share a large proportion of our genes with them. After all, by some measures, humans share 99 per cent of their genes, and there is a 98 per cent genetic overlap between humans and chimpanzees. There is no easy way to divide humans by the amount of genetic material they share. In other words, it is a mistake to

kin selection (also known as *inclusive fitness theory*) proposes that we have evolved to favour people who are genetically related to us, and are more likely to help close relatives (kin) than strangers.

proportion of shared genes refers to the amount of genetic material shared by humans (and animals); humans have an almost identical proportion of shared genes with any randomly selected other human being.

characterize the idea of kin selection as something that says that we help genetically similar individuals. We are all genetically similar to each other. Hamilton's mechanism for explaining altruistic behaviour is the degree of relatedness to others specifically *in respect of the altruism gene*. All remaining genes in our bodies are completely irrelevant to the discussion.

This misunderstanding has occasionally been worked up into theories that propose differences in helping based on genetic similarity (cf. Rushton's, 1989, Genetic Similarity Theory, which argues that individuals tend to be more altruistic to individuals who are genetically similar to themselves – even if they are not kin – and less altruistic or even hostile to people less genetically similar). This attempt to stray into group-level genetic explanations has been widely criticized (Tooby & Cosmides, 1989). The idea that genes can somehow recognize similarity in other genes, and that this can be a basis for favouritism towards ingroup members and hostility towards outgroup members, is a corruption of the idea of kin selection. Kin selection says nothing about a predisposition for favouring your own group on the basis of genetic composition. As we have seen, it is a theory about the selection and transmission of genetic information – it is not a way of dividing the world up into groups who are genetically similar or dissimilar. People who use the idea of kin selection and the coefficient of relatedness to argue that humans are genetically programmed to help people in their group and to ignore or neglect outgroup members are misunderstanding and misrepresenting the science.

A second way in which self-interest is seen to shape altruism can be found in the idea of **reciprocal altruism** (Trivers, 1971). This is a theory designed to account for why we might help strangers or non-kin. Trivers suggests that altruism towards strangers could have evolved if there was a chance of being in a reverse situation in which someone who had been helped would then reciprocate the help they had received. In other words, reciprocal altruism could have evolved because it might be beneficial to incur the cost of helping (which would temporarily reduce the helper's genetic 'fitness' while promoting a stranger's 'fitness') if there is the expectation that the person who has been helped will perform an altruistic act towards the helper at a future date.

reciprocal altruism a theory designed to explain altruism towards strangers by proposing that helping non-kin may have evolved if the cost of helping another is offset by the likelihood of the return benefit.

Sharing of food is a good example. Giving food to others may mean slightly less food now (a cost) in return for the possibility of more food later (particularly when it might be especially scarce, in times of famine for instance). However, in behaving in this way, altruists are taking a risk. Since the reward for their generosity will come at some time in the future, they are relying on the goodwill of the recipient to return the favour. It is always possible for recipients to *defect* – that is, to accept the altruistically offered help but then refuse to reciprocate.

Thus, for reciprocal altruism to exist, the same individuals must come into regular contact. There must also be a large number of opportunities for exchanges that ultimately cost the altruist less than they benefit the recipient – otherwise there would be no long-term advantage in engaging in the relationships. Finally, there must be a way to detect 'cheating' or defection in order to dissuade people from doing so. Reciprocal altruism stops happening if defection occurs.

As an evolutionary biologist, Trivers (1971) was really interested in reciprocal altruism in terms of its fitness consequences for species, rather than its motivating intentions for individuals. He saw reciprocal altruism as an evolutionary mechanism rather than something that was actively adapted by interacting individuals. It is in trying to understand the psychological aspects of altruistic behaviour that researchers in behavioural economics and social psychology have begun to revisit and reframe the idea of reciprocal altruism.

When helping is not self-interested

In addition to research on kin selection and reciprocal altruism, recent experimental work has revealed a form of human cooperation between genetically unrelated individuals that cannot be explained in terms of self-interest. Using an experimental paradigm called a **public goods game**, researchers have discovered a phenomenon called *altruistic punishment* (Fehr & Gächter, 2002). In public goods games, three or more individuals interact anonymously in a game in which they can award points to themselves or allocate points to a common account which would benefit everybody; the points are translated into money at the end of the game. Purely self-interested players should always award themselves all the points and put none in the common account. However, only a tiny fraction of players ever do this. Most participants start off by sharing about half their points, and sharing less and less as time goes on.

What is particularly interesting about these experiments, however, is the fact that, when a participant sees selfish behaviour in others, they are moved to punish them. Moreover, they engage in punishment behaviour of others even when it hurts themselves. They will give up money in order to ensure the selfish player loses money – or even be prepared to pay a fine to allow them to punish a defector. Participants engage in this kind of

> **public goods game** participants are allocated tokens, and can then (secretly) decide how many to keep and how many to contribute to a public pot; contributing nothing is termed *free riding*.

behaviour even when they have no expectation of interacting with the others in the game ever again, and when nobody else would know what they had done. Fehr and Gächter argue that this kind of punishment (and the cost it entails) does not fit the principles of reciprocal altruism or reputation management.

What the punishment behaviour does is dissuade individuals in the game from behaving selfishly, and therefore contributes to the maintenance of cooperation. Thus, altruistic punishment behaviour is a form of helping. It helps the group to remain cooperative. It is a sacrifice by the individual in a way that cannot be explained in terms of self-interest. It seems to be designed to promote group interest. Gintis (2000) argues that this behaviour reveals a third principle of human altruism (in addition to kin selection and reciprocal altruism) that he calls **strong reciprocity**. Strong reciprocity is a human predisposition to cooperate with others and to punish those who defect – even when the punishment is personally costly for the punisher, and the punisher has no expectation of receiving a reward for this sacrifice at a later date.

> **strong reciprocity** a human predisposition to cooperate with others and to punish those who defect, even when this behaviour cannot be justified in terms of self-interest, extended kinship or reciprocal altruism.

Summary

Research from the perspective of evolutionary psychology has made important contributions to how we think about and understand prosocial behaviour. Recent discoveries have shown that humans do not only help those they believe to be family or kin – nor do they only act in a self-interested fashion. There is evidence for the evolutionary importance of the capacity of individuals to punish selfish behaviour in others, even when it is costly to themselves.

THE SOCIAL NEUROSCIENCE OF HELPING

What do we know about brain activation and helping behaviour?

Recent research in social neuroscience has used functional magnetic resonance imaging (fMRI) to identify brain networks involved in altruism and helping behaviour. In one such study (Sanfey, Rilling, Aronson, Nystrom, & Cohen, 2003), participants took part in public goods games while placed in a scanner. They found that different areas of the brain become activated when a participant discovers whether someone has made a fair or an unfair offer. When we see others behaving in what we think is an unfair manner, then the region of the brain known as the bilateral insula (see Figure 10.11b) is activated. This area of the brain is known to be associated with negative emotional states such as pain, hunger and distrust. The stronger the activation, the more likely people are to reject an unfair offer.

When it comes to brain activation involved in altruistic, fair and trusting behaviours, Fehr and Camerer (2007) argue that fMRI studies reveal activation in reward-related brain areas such as the striatum (see Figure 10.11a). They reviewed studies in which people could make offers to charity while inside a scanner. They point out that the areas that are commonly activated when people are engaged in giving to charity have a large degree of overlap with areas that are known to activate when people receive positive social or financial rewards. They suggest that this shows, at a neural level at least, that altruistic behaviour has its own intrinsic rewards.

Researchers have also looked at the neurobiological mechanisms underlying prosocial decisions and how they might be moderated by factors such as empathy and group membership. For example, Hein, Silani, Preuschoff, Batson, and Singer (2010) conducted a two-part experiment with football fans that used fMRI to look at brain activation when the fans were placed in a situation in which they could offer or withhold help from ingroup or outgroup members. In the first part of the experiment, participants interacted (by taking part in a quiz) with confederates of the experimenters, who pretended to be either fans of the same team as the participant (ingroup members) or fans from a local rival team (outgroup members). After this interaction the participant entered the scanner. While they were in the scanner they were either given – or watched an ingroup or an outgroup member receive – a series of electric shocks. Their brain activation was measured during this time.

In a second session of the study some time later, the same participants were scanned again. This time, however, none of the participants received shocks themselves: instead they only watched the ingroup and outgroup fan in pain. They were given the choice between three options. In the first option, they could volunteer to help the ingroup or the outgroup person by asking to be given half the shock level about to be administered. In other words, they could reduce the

FIGURE 10.11(a) and (b) *Sagittal section through the brain showing (a) the striatum and nucleus accumbens, and (b) the insula.*

pain for the other person by taking some of it upon themselves. In the second option they could simply watch a soccer video instead – thus distracting themselves while the other person was given the shocks. In the third option, they could simply watch the other person suffering the pain.

Hein et al. found that willingness to help the ingroup member was related to activation in the anterior insula (AI) region of the brain – and to post-experimental self-report measures that showed higher empathic concern. The anterior insula is one of the areas that has previously been identified as central to empathy-related brain responses (Singer & Lamm, 2009). At the same time, not helping the outgroup members was best predicted by activation in the nucleus accumbens (NAcc) region of the brain (see Figure 10.11a). NAcc activation has previously been observed in studies in which people derive pleasure from the misfortune of others (Singer et al., 2006). This suggests that watching an outgroup member receive pain could be processed in a reward-related manner.

On the basis of these results, Hein et al. suggested that this kind of fMRI study reveals the possibility of two types of motivational systems that underlie helping behaviour: activation in the AI when witnessing suffering indicates empathy-based motivation and an increased willingness to help; activation in the NAcc suggests empathy is absent and helping is withheld. Moreover, Hein et al. showed that there is an ingroup bias in empathy-related AI responses and ingroup helping. We are more likely to respond to an ingroup member's pain with an empathy-related response. However, if an outgroup member was evaluated positively then his suffering elicited AI (empathy-based) rather than NAcc (pleasure-related) activation, and he was likely to receive help despite his outgroup membership. These findings are an interesting companion to the work of Stürmer and colleagues (see the section on identity, emotion and helping). Stürmer et al. argue that the motivations for helping ingroup and outgroup members are different. Helping ingroup members is motivated by empathy, while helping outgroup members is motivated by feelings of liking or attraction (Stürmer et al., 2005; Stürmer et al., 2006).

Summary

Recent advances in technologies to study the brain have begun to reveal the neural correlates of different kinds of helping behaviour. Different areas of the brain seem to be activated when we help others, and when we refrain from helping. This activation seems to occur in centres that are associated with empathy (when we help ingroup members) and pleasure (when we fail to help outgroup members). These findings may indicate different brain activation systems for different kinds of helping behaviour. These are exciting new areas of research with the potential to transform our understanding of human prosociality.

HELPING IN THE REAL WORLD

Is it always good to help?

At first sight it might seem as though the motivation to help others must always be a good thing. In fact, in much of this chapter we have explored attempts to understand

LEADER IN THE FIELD

Arie Nadler (b. 1947) obtained his PhD from Purdue University in 1976, and is currently Professor of Social Psychology at Tel-Aviv University. He holds the Argentina Chair for Research of Psychology of Conflict and Cooperation, and was co-founder of the Tami Steinmetz Center for Peace Research at Tel-Aviv University. Nadler's work has questioned the taken-for-granted notion that helping others is universally positive. In his work, Nadler has highlighted the importance of power relations, and demonstrated how helping relations can be seen as unequal social relations, given the ability of the helper to help. Thus, those who are dependent on help may subsequently be seen as having lower status and lacking in power.

why people help in order that we might increase the likelihood that people will help. However, it turns out that not all helping behaviour has positive outcomes – and, even when intentions may be noble, some helping can harm the receivers of help.

Nadler (e.g. 2002), who has conducted extensive research in the context of the intractable Arab–Israeli conflict, points out that all helping (both interpersonal and intergroup) involves power relations. Put another way, Nadler argues that helping, almost by definition, occurs between unequals. A person or group who has superior resources directs them towards another person or group who are in need. If the helper and the recipient are in an unequal relationship, then helping can signal caring and generosity on the part of the helper, but it can also remind the recipient of their dependence and weakness. This threat to personal or group esteem can sometimes lead the recipient to resist or reject the help (Nadler & Fisher, 1986; see Leader in the Field, Arie Nadler).

For example, Nadler and Saguy (2004) show how attempts by the Israeli government to offer assistance to Palestinian groups were often rejected on the grounds that they would perpetuate Palestinians' economic, academic or cultural dependence on Israelis. Palestinians were upset when Israelis assumed they knew what kind of help was required without asking, or offered Palestinians help without asking if they needed it. Nadler refers to this kind of helping as 'assumptive' help, and demonstrates that assumptive help can be bad for the personal self-worth or collective self-esteem of the recipient (Halabi, Dovidio, & Nadler, 2008).

In addition to assuming they know what is required, powerful groups can harm those they attempt to help by offering some kinds of help and not others. As the Chinese proverb says, 'give a man a fish and he will eat for a day, teach a man to fish and he will eat for a lifetime'. Similarly, Nadler identifies two kinds of helping, *dependency-orientated help* and *autonomy orientated help*. Dependency-orientated help consists of providing the recipient with the full solution to the problem. It treats recipients as though they are unable to contribute towards solving their problems and, furthermore, reinforces their dependency on the powerful group. By contrast, autonomy-orientated help consists of providing recipients with the tools to solve the problem on their own. It treats recipients as resourceful, and assumes that, once they acquire the appropriate tools, they will be able to tackle their own difficulties.

For Nadler, the way help is offered, and the kind of help that is offered, tells us much about status relations between individuals and groups. He has developed the Intergroup Helping as Status Relations (IHSR) model (Nadler, 2002) to show how groups can use helping behaviour to preserve or challenge their status with respect to a relevant outgroup. The model makes specific predictions about the kinds of help high-status groups will offer and the kinds of help low-status groups will seek. For example, when relations between groups are perceived as stable and legitimate, then low status groups are happy to receive dependency-orientated help from high status groups (see also the summary of social identity theory in Chapter 14). However, when relations are seen as illegitimate and unstable, the politics of helping become very tense. High-status groups are motivated to withhold autonomy-orientated help and promote dependency-orientated help as a way of trying to counter the threat of the low-status group. High-status groups try to use helping to secure their own dominant social position – rather than to meet the needs of the less well-off. Nadler and colleagues refer to this as *defensive helping* (Nadler, Harpaz-Gorodeisky, & Ben-David, 2009). At the same time, the low-status group becomes less willing to receive dependency-orientated help and more motivated to seek autonomy-orientated help. When low-status groups reject offers of help they are often seen as irrational or ungrateful. However, it is usually because they perceive the kind of help on offer as being dependency-orientated and designed to undermine their ability to take control of their own destiny. Nadler's keen eye for the politics of the Israeli–Palestinian conflict has allowed him to demonstrate that groups arrange power and status relations not only through negative behaviours like discrimination and hostility, but also through seemingly positive behaviours like helping.

Do people act selfishly in life-threatening emergencies?

While, as we have seen, debates continue regarding whether human beings are essentially selfish or altruistic by nature, it is often claimed that human beings' essential

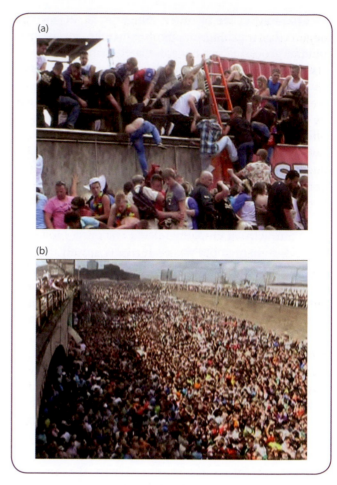

FIGURE 10.12(a) and (b) *'Loveparade 2010' in Duisburg, Germany. More than twenty people were killed and hundreds were injured in a panicked crush of partygoers in an overcrowded tunnel that served as the sole entrance to the festival.*

Source: (a) © WIEBOLD TV via APTN; (b) © BILD.DE via APTN. Both images used under licence from Press Association Images.

selfishness is revealed in emergency or life-threatening situations. Take the example of a fire in a crowded place. The common conception – fuelled by plotlines for Hollywood disaster movies – is that people try to save themselves at the expense of others. They rush to the exits, trampling others underfoot, in a single-minded attempt to save their own life (Figure 10.12). Viewed in this way, people look like selfish actors who have produced a situation of mass panic. Because everyone is looking after himself or herself, they don't cooperate, and become increasingly competitive in a way that produces irrational or aggressive behaviour. This idea of the panicked crowd has a long history. High death tolls in the Iroquois Theatre fire in Chicago in 1903 (in which 600 people died) and the Cocoanut Grove Theatre fire in Boston in 1942 (in which 492 died) have both been attributed to foolish overreactions to the fire. These events were always presented as classic cases of mass panic.

However, more recently, social psychologists have begun to change their minds about what really happens in emergencies. For example, Chertkoff and Kushigian (1999) studied the Cocoanut Grove fire in detail and discovered that physical obstructions and not mass panic were responsible for the loss of life. Deaths were caused by blocked exits and poor building design (such as doors which opened inwards rather than outwards). The club owner was found guilty of involuntary manslaughter and new fire regulations were developed to stop this happening again. However, the myth of the panicked crowd persisted.

Frey, Savage, and Torgler (2010) looked at survival rates from two of the greatest maritime disasters in history, the sinking of the Titanic and the Lusitania (see also Social Psychology Beyond the Lab 10.2). They studied passenger and survival lists from both ships and controlled for the effect of gender, age, ticket class, nationality and type of family relationship. They found that children were more likely to survive than adults on the Titanic, but more likely than adults to die on the Lusitania. Women were more likely than men to survive on the Titanic, but less likely to survive than men on the Lusitania. Frey et al. suggest that these differences in survival rates can be explained by the behaviour of the men. When there was a fair amount of time after the original shock of the emergency (as there was on the Titanic) then there was a chance for social norms to re-establish themselves. The norm of 'women and children first' became established and increased the survival rate for those categories. However, when there was no time (as in the sinking of the Lusitania) then more self-interested and selfish behaviour predominated and male survival rates were higher. This suggests that responses to emergencies can be shaped by social norms rather than panic, and that normative behaviour can become strongly established if time allows.

This idea of the response to rapidly unfolding emergencies was also studied by two fire safety researchers (Proulx & Fahy, 2003) who analysed ordinary people's responses and behaviours in the aftermath of plane strikes on the twin towers of New York City's World Trade Centre on September 11th 2001. Fires were raging on the upper floors of the 110-story towers and the only way out was down the stairwells. Based on interviews with firefighters and other emergency staff, as well as survivor testimony, Proulx and Fahy found that there was none of the mass panic that many emergency planners expect to see in a disaster. Instead, they showed that people behaved sensibly and displayed a solidarity that was a valuable asset. They knew they were in danger but they were not screaming and trampling each other. They waited in line in the packed stairwells, taking turns and

helping those that needed help. Some individuals even put themselves in greater danger to free obstructions that were preventing others from escaping. Of course, there were a few individuals who looked after themselves and ignored others in distress, but they were few and far between. Because of this orderly evacuation and these unofficial rescue efforts, most people below the impact zones managed to get out of the building alive.

In similar fashion, Drury and colleagues (Drury, Cocking, & Reicher, 2009; Drury & Reicher, 2010) showed that the response of ordinary people to the bombing of the London transport system on July 7th 2005 was also marked by a sense of togetherness and solidarity. In a coordinated terrorist attack, four bombs were detonated (three on subway trains and one on a bus) during the morning rush hour. Those on the trains were left in the dark, surrounded by the dead and injured, and in fear that there might be further explosions. In a series of interviews with survivors, including 90 people who were on the trains, Drury and colleagues found that there was no panic. People helped each other by tending to the injured, offering emotional support and sharing water. They did not flee in a frantic attempt to save themselves. In fact, most of the interviewees described a strong sense of togetherness in the face of the emergency. They talked about feelings of unity, affinity and togetherness, and contrasted this with the kinds of feelings they would normally experience in the presence of others on a crowded commuter train.

Drury suggests that emergencies produce a sense of common fate amongst the victims, and that this in turn leads to a sense of shared identity (Turner et al., 1987). Ordinary commuters sharing a train carriage on a normal workday may be physically close – but psychologically distant. In fact, the very presence of other strangers may make them think more about themselves as individuals. However, when the emergency strikes, and seems to affect everyone equally, then their identity can change to include others. People shift from thinking about 'me' to 'us'. This leads to greater mutual helping and mutual support.

Drury et al. (2009) went on to look at behaviour in a range of emergency situations, including disasters in football stadiums, music festivals and sinking ships. They showed that the same pattern applies. All the crowds seemed to display some sense of unity when the emergency began, even if they began as fragmented groups; those who reported a greater sense of common fate showed higher levels of shared identity; those with higher shared identity were more likely to talk about examples of shared helping. Based on their extensive work in this area, Drury and Reicher (2010) conclude that behaviour in emergencies is not radically different from behaviour in everyday situations. When an emergency

SOCIAL PSYCHOLOGY BEYOND THE LAB 10.2

UNDERSTANDING BEHAVIOUR IN LIFE-THREATENING EMERGENCIES

While it is possible to simulate many things in a laboratory setting, it would be impossible (for ethical and practical reasons) to create conditions in which people truly felt that their lives were in danger. And yet, when trying to answer questions about whether humans are fundamentally self-interested or whether they can behave in a truly altruistic fashion, it is how people act in these extreme situations that is of profound interest to psychologists. In the absence of evidence, there is a danger we may fall back on anecdote or prejudice. One manifestation of this is the myth of mass panic in crowd emergencies. For a long time the common-sense assumption about behaviour in life-threatening emergencies was that it was almost always marked by selfish, panic-stricken behaviour in which individuals tried to save themselves. However, recent innovative research, exploring data from real life emergencies, has begun to paint alternative pictures of how humans behave under life-threatening conditions.

For example, Frey et al. (2010) conducted a fascinating analysis of the survival rates from two of the most catastrophic marine disasters of all time – the sinking of the Titanic and the Lusitania. These were both enormous ships, built with similar designs, that sank within three years of each other with a similar loss of life (a death rate of 68.7 per cent for the Titanic and 67.3 per cent for the Lusitania). Frey et al. were able to use the sinking of these two ships as a kind of 'natural experiment'. The key difference between the two disasters was the time it took for each ship to sink. The Lusitania went under in 18 minutes, while the Titanic stayed afloat for 2 hours and 40 minutes. Frey et al. compared and contrasted survival rates, while controlling for factors such as the number of men, women and children on board each ship, the social class of the passengers, where they were likely to be located on the ship and the number and size of family groups. Some interesting differences emerged. Children were 14.8 per cent more likely to survive than adults on the Titanic, but on the Lusitania they were 5.3 per cent less likely to do so. Women were 53 per cent more likely to survive than men on the Titanic, but 1.1 per cent less likely to do so on the Lusitania. Frey et al. argue that these different survival rates suggest that – on the Titanic at least – social norms rather than self-interest seemed to govern people's behaviour. On the Titanic, compared with the Lusitania, men were more likely to help women and children into the lifeboats, and so their survival rates were higher than would be expected. On the

Lusitania, where time was scarce, individual self-interest seems to have predominated, and women and children were less likely to have survived. Frey et al. propose that, in emergencies that unfold over a longer period of time, socially determined behavioural patterns have time to re-establish themselves after the shock of the original emergency. The fact that there was time available to evacuate the ship in the case of the Titanic meant that prosocial behaviour predominated. However, in the rapidly sinking Lusitania, Frey et al. suggest that short-term flight impulses may have dominated behaviour, leading to more self-interested and selfish behaviour amongst the men and less concern for the welfare of women and children. Of course, this kind of analysis tells us very little about people's own understanding of their behaviour in these emergencies. Frey et al. did not have any data from the passengers on the ships themselves: they could only extrapolate from the patterns of survival to the kinds of behaviours which might have resulted in the different survival rates.

In a different kind of non-laboratory approach, Drury and colleagues (Drury et al., 2009; Drury & Reicher, 2010) analysed the behaviour of people in another kind of emergency, namely the aftermath of a terrorist attack. They collected evidence from survivors of the bomb attacks on the London Underground (and a London bus) on July 7th, 2005 (Figure 10.13). More specifically, they collected data from a variety of different sources, which all contained accounts of the events from the perspectives of both survivors and witnesses. These included contemporaneous newspaper accounts (from 18 newspapers) that reported a range of statements from eyewitnesses and survivors. In addition Drury et al. established a collection of 127 personal accounts that were given to official reviews, BBC websites, blogs, message boards, books and a radio documentary. Finally, they recruited primary respondents (people who had been in the bombings and were prepared to be interviewed directly). The primary respondents were recruited through newspaper advertisements – and from advertisements on the websites of support groups. Fifteen interviews were done online and 12 interviews were conducted face-to-face.

All this data from the three sources was then transcribed and prepared for analysis. The data was coded and subjected to a thematic analysis. The researchers looked for themes like 'panic' or 'helping'. Based on this analysis, Drury et al.

FIGURE 10.13(a) and (b)   *Devastation after the London terrorist attacks in July 2005.*

Source: Both images © Press Association Images.

showed that the term 'panic' was used by a few witnesses and survivors, but mostly by commentators who did not witness events directly. Descriptions from the survivors tell the opposite story. Rather than selfishness and competition, mutual helping and concern predominated. In fact, helping seemed to take place despite the fact that people felt they were in personal danger, rather than because they felt out of danger once the first bomb had gone off.

happens, people continue to observe social norms, act in terms of their social values and remember their humanity. They do not turn into savages desperate to escape. In fact, these researchers argue that 'disasters bring out the best – not the *beast* – in people' (p. 65).

Summary

Looking at the complexities of helping in the real world helps to deepen our understanding of helping behaviour. Not all helping is good – even when the motivations behind it are noble. To understand the true effects of helping, we need to ask what kind of help is being offered and who is likely to benefit. We also need to challenge prevailing myths about human nature. Research on real-life emergencies has shown that disasters do not always or necessarily bring out the selfish survivalist in humans. Rather, the evidence is that people tend to help each other – even at the potential cost of their own lives. These ideas are helping to change the way policy-makers and practitioners think about human helping behaviour in emergency situations.

CHAPTER SUMMARY

- *Why study prosocial behaviour?* The study of prosocial behaviour allows psychologists to explore basic questions about human nature. These include questions of whether humans are fundamentally selfish or selfless by nature, or whether humans are ultimately good or bad.

- *What is prosocial behaviour?* Various terms are used to define the subject matter in the area of prosocial behaviour. What is considered to be prosocial can be seen to be culturally dependent, but prosocial behaviour is essentially behaviour that is defined as beneficial to other people, but not carried out as part of an obligation.

- *What kinds of phenomena do researchers in this area study?* Research in this area covers many different kinds of behaviours, ranging from short-term helping in emergencies, everyday acts of helping, through to long-term, sustained helping where the helper may put themselves in a position of considerable danger.

- *What role does altruism play?* There is empirical support for the existence of altruistically motivated helping. Research looking at the empathy-altruism hypothesis has shown that feelings of empathy can lead to helping which has the end goal of increasing another person's welfare.

- *What determines helping in emergency situations?* Situational factors are important determinants of behaviour in emergency situations. Latané and Darley's work on the bystander effect has demonstrated the influence of the presence of others on bystander behaviour in emergencies, with a particular focus on why people do not help.

- *What role does arousal play in emergency situations?* Research that looks at why people do help has suggested that unpleasant arousal is created in an emergency situation, and that people will seek to reduce this arousal as a result of considering the costs and rewards of helping and not helping.

- *How do group processes shape helping behaviour?* Group processes have been highlighted as important across a range of helping behaviours. While these have sometimes been presented as impacting negatively on helping, a range of contemporary research has begun to highlight how our psychological connection to others can have a positive impact on helping.

- *What methods are used in helping research?* A wide range of methods has been used to study prosocial behaviours. While the use of laboratory settings has a number of advantages, research using alternative methods has provided novel insights into the factors impacting on bystander behaviour.

- *Are there gender differences in helping?* While it seems that men may help more than women, this may be a result of the kinds of helping situations that have been studied. When we study helping in long-term, close relationships, women tend to help more.

- *Why do people volunteer?* Work on the psychology of volunteerism has shown the importance of identity processes for volunteer behaviour.

- *Does evolution make us selfish?* Research from evolutionary biology has suggested that helping is not entirely selfishly motivated, and that humans will punish selfish behaviours in others.

- *What do we know about brain activation and helping behaviour?* Research from social neuroscience has helped us to identify some of the neural correlates of prosocial behaviours.

- *Is helping always good?* Prosocial behaviours are not always positive, both from the perspective of the giver and the receiver of help. Contemporary research on receiving help, for example, has demonstrated the importance of power relations in helping situations.

- *Do we behave selfishly in emergencies?* Disasters do not bring out the selfish nature of humans. Evidence from real-world disasters suggests that people in such emergencies tend to help each other, even when their own lives are in danger.

SUGGESTIONS FOR FURTHER READING

Batson, C. D. (2011). *Altruism in humans*. New York: Oxford University Press. A timely and useful overview of theory and research on the empathy-altruism hypothesis.

Bierhoff, H. W. (2002*). Prosocial behaviour*. Hove, UK: Psychology Press. Presents a wide range of research on the psychology of prosocial behaviour in its many different forms.

Dovidio, J. F., Piliavin, J. A., Schroeder, D. A., & Penner, L. A. (2006). *The social psychology of prosocial behavior*. Mahwah, N.J: Erlbaum. An authoritative overview of the field by a quartet of the leading North American scholars and researchers in this area.

Fischer, P., Krueger, J. I., Greitemeyer, T., Vogrincic, C., Kastenmüller, A., Frey, D., Heene, M., Wicher, M., & Kainbacher, M. (2011). The bystander-effect: A meta-analytic review on bystander intervention in dangerous and non-dangerous emergencies. *Psychological Bulletin, 137*, 517–537. A recent meta-analysis of the classic bystander effect, setting out the limitations of the effect in different emergency situations and pointing to different explanations of their findings.

Penner, L. A., Dovidio, J. F., Piliavin, J. A., & Schroeder, D. A. (2005). Prosocial behavior: Multilevel perspectives. *Annual Review of Psychology, 56,* 365–392. A useful review article that integrates a range of research to set out the different levels of analysis involved in a broad range of prosocial phenomena.

Piliavin, J. A., Dovidio, J. F., Gaertner, S. L., & Clark, R. D., III. (1981). *Emergency intervention.* New York: Academic Press. This book presents a wide range of research relating to the arousal: cost–reward model of intervention in emergencies, and also gives an insight into how such models are developed over time.

Stürmer, S., & Snyder, M. (Eds.). (2010). *The psychology of prosocial behavior: Group processes, intergroup relations, and helping.* Chichester, UK: Wiley-Blackwell. An edited volume that presents a range of contemporary perspectives on different forms of prosocial behaviour.

11 Affiliation, Attraction and Close Relationships

Johan C. Karremans and Catrin Finkenauer

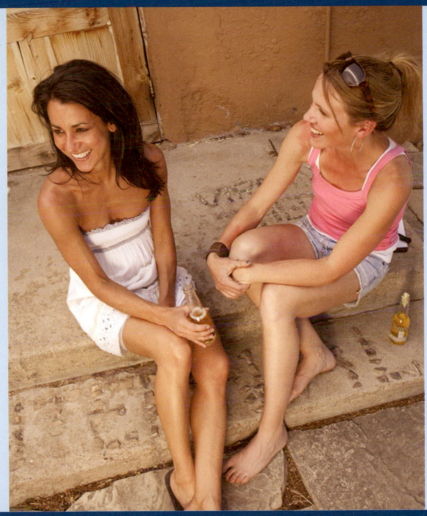

Source: © Dan Bannister. Used under licence from Shutterstock.

KEY TERMS

- attachment theory
- communal relationship
- companionate love
- derogation of alternatives
- disclosure reciprocity
- equity theory
- evolutionary psychology

- exchange relationship
- forgiveness
- investments
- mere exposure effect
- misattribution of arousal
- need to belong
- passionate love

- perceived partner responsiveness
- relationship commitment
- relationship superiority
- self-disclosure
- similarity–attraction effect
- social support
- willingness to sacrifice

CHAPTER OUTLINE

ROUTE MAP OF THE CHAPTER

It is hard to imagine a human being living in complete isolation from other people. Indeed, in our daily lives, we are almost constantly surrounded by others, ranging from strangers to people we feel very close to, like our friends or romantic partner. But why do we feel the need to be with others in the first place, and why can it be so painful to feel rejected by others? Why do we feel attracted to some people, but not to others? What determines whether some relationships are filled with happiness, whereas other relationships seem bound for disaster? This chapter addresses these questions. We begin with an explanation of the seemingly natural need of humans to connect to others. We then follow the development of a relationship, starting with a discussion of the factors that determine initial interpersonal attraction. We discuss what determines relationship satisfaction and stability, and provide an overview of the specific ingredients – the specific relationship processes – that characterize a successful, and unsuccessful, romantic relationship. We conclude with some general processes that may occur across different types of relationships.

INTRODUCTION

Perhaps even more than a transition to a higher education level, going to college is a transition to a new *social* life, a time where one meets many new people. Students are making new friends and, for many of them, college years may be the time to find a future romantic partner. For some, the prospect of meeting new people, or a romantic partner, may be a very appealing one; for others it may be a little frightening. In any case, almost all students will eventually become part of a small or large group of friends. Many of them will indeed find a romantic partner; although some may jump from one romantic partner to another, others may instantly find the love of their life. The quality of college life is surely not only a matter of whether students are successful in their studies; to a large extent it depends on the interactions and experiences students have with others, including peers, lovers, teachers, parents and old and new friends.

What are some of the main issues that have been addressed by relationship researchers? The first is a very basic one: *why do we form relationships with others in the first place? Why is it, apparently, so important for people to live their lives in proximity to others? Why do they form close bonds with others?* Once we know the answer to these questions, the next question is, *why do we form bonds with specific others, and not just with anyone?* You may think that people carefully 'choose' their friends and partner, based on the specific characteristics they like in the other person. To some extent this is true, but, as we will see in this chapter, it appears that there are also more mundane, situational factors that determine our attraction to others – factors that we may not be aware of. When we have formed a close relationship with someone – be it a friend or romantic partner – why is it that *some relationships last forever, while other relationships are less stable?* We will discuss how relationship success depends largely on the interaction patterns between two partners, but also, how differences in certain personality characteristics can explain why some people have trouble keeping their relationships intact, whereas others more easily form stable relationships. Relationship scientists have attempted to tackle these issues for a long time. A brief summary and some of the highlights of this research will be presented in this chapter. This chapter should provide you with the tools and knowledge to answer the questions highlighted above, and should broaden your understanding and insight into your own and other people's relationships.

THE IMPORTANCE OF RELATIONSHIPS

What are some of the main functions and consequences of relationships?

Relationships and psychological wellbeing

When was the last time you experienced intense joy and happiness? When was the last time you felt sad or angry? Chances are high that your answer to both these questions in some way involves other people, most likely others who are important to you. You may have experienced happiness when you were simply having a good time in a bar together with your romantic partner, your friends or family. Or you may have been feeling miserable after a conflict with someone close to you, which is perhaps still bothering you. Indeed, our emotional life greatly depends on the experiences and interactions we have with others. Studies have shown that people generally experience a more positive mood when they are around other people (for an overview, see Berscheid & Reis, 1998), especially when experiencing a certain level of closeness and intimacy with them (Diener, 1984). Being around friends and family simply makes life more pleasant. In general, a larger social network is positively related to our happiness (Kawachi & Berkman, 2001). In contrast, people generally experience the highest levels of negative affect when they are alone (Diener, 1984), and lacking contact with close others induces feelings of loneliness and depression (Cacioppo, Hughes, Waite, Hawkley, & Thisted, 2006).

Whether or not we are in a romantic relationship also contributes to our wellbeing. People who have a steady and satisfying romantic relationship are, on average, somewhat happier than their single counterparts (Easterlin, 2003). This is true for both men and women, although happiness seems more strongly associated with the *quality* of the relationship among women as compared to men. In contrast, divorce is generally related to sharp decreases in happiness (Easterlin, 2003). Of course, this does not necessarily mean that getting married will make an individual happier. People who are happier may have a higher chance of getting involved in a long-term romantic relationship than people who are less happy, because happy people are more pleasant to be with. In line with this idea, one intriguing study found that a positive emotional expression on pictures in a college yearbook predicted marriage success twenty years later (Harker & Keltner, 2001).

Still, although it is very likely that causal influences are bidirectional in this case, relationship researchers generally agree that a satisfying romantic relationship has an important impact on a person's psychological wellbeing.

Relationships and physical wellbeing

The fact that our relationships with others profoundly impact our *psychological* wellbeing may not have surprised you – surely you have experienced yourself that your mood and happiness is related to your experiences with others. Probably more impressive are the benefits of social relationships for an individual's *physical* wellbeing. Consider one striking example, a study conducted by Williams and colleagues (1992): patients with coronary heart disease had a 30 per cent higher probability of survival after five years when they were in a romantic relationship when compared to patients who were single. And among married patients, those with a happy marriage have a nearly 30 per cent higher chance of survival four years after suffering a heart attack when compared to patients with poor marriages (Coyne et al., 2001).

The beneficial effects of social relationships are not confined to people who are already ill. In a now classic study, Berkman and Syme (1979) found that in a random sample of the population, individuals who had many social ties and were socially well integrated (in terms of degree of contact with friends and relatives, romantic relationship status and being a member of informal or formal organizations) were two to three times more likely to still be alive (i.e. the mortality rate) nine years later as compared to those who lacked such social ties (Figure 11.1). The association between social ties and mortality rate was independent

of income and education level, and thus occurred across all socio-economic classes. Based on an overview of studies that reported similar beneficial health effects of social relationships, Atkins, Kaplan, and Toshima (1991) concluded that the lack of close relationships is a risk factor for cardiovascular disease at least as important as smoking!

The role of social support

What explains the important and even vital role of being part of a social network for our mental and physical health? **Social support** seems the key – in times when we need it, our close relationships are often a source of social support (Coyne & De Longis, 1986). Social support can be broadly defined as a partner's responsiveness to another's needs (Cutrona, 1996). Two different forms of support can be distinguished, namely *emotional* support and *instrumental* support. Emotional support refers to a partner's acts that are directly aimed at providing reassurance in stressful or problematic situations, whereas instrumental support refers to the practical assistance a partner may provide in dealing with a problem. Suppose an individual just heard that he failed an exam, and feels terrible about this. His partner may try to cheer him up by saying that he will surely pass the next time, or perhaps by focusing on the fact that more than 50 per cent of all students failed this exam. This is an example of emotional support. She may also offer to help him study for the next exam, for example by testing him on the material, which would be an example of instrumental support. Individuals who perceive such acts from a relationship partner as supportive do indeed experience immediate and long-term improvements in their mood and self-esteem (e.g. Collins & Feeney, 2000).

According to Cohen and Wills (1985), there are basically two ways in which social support can affect mental and physical health. First, social support may encourage people to take better care of themselves. For example, close others may try to persuade you to live a healthier life, because they care about you. Second, social support may positively affect health, because it buffers stress, and stress is directly associated with an individual's health (Baum, 1990). Consider, for example, a study by Gerin, Pieper, Levy, and Pickering (1992). Participants in this study took part in a group discussion with three other people, who in fact were not real participants, but confederates of the researchers. Two of the confederates continuously made disapproving remarks when the participant contributed to the discussion. When placing yourself in the shoes of participants, you can imagine that they experienced stress; they indeed showed increases in heart rate

> **social support** a partner's responsiveness to another's needs

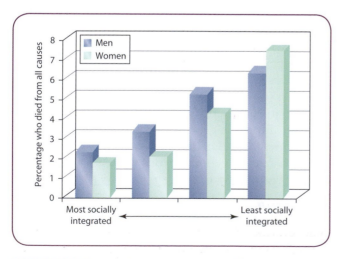

FIGURE 11.1 *The relationship between level of social integration and mortality rate.*

LENDING A HAND

RESEARCH CLOSE-UP 11.1

Coan, J. A., Schaefer, H. S., & Davidson, R. J. (2006). Lending a hand: Social regulation of the neural response to threat. *Psychological Science, 17*, 1032–1039.

Introduction

This study examined whether direct contact with others helps to alleviate distress. Specifically, the study examined whether women, who were subjected to the threat of receiving an electric shock, showed lower stress responses in the brain when they were holding their husband's hand, compared to when they were holding a stranger's hand or not holding anyone's hand.

Method and procedure

Sixteen married couples were invited to the laboratory to participate in a brain-scanning study. Both wives and husbands rated their marital quality. The wives were then tested in the brain scanner. In the scanner, they were presented, in random order, with 'threat cues' and 'safety cues' on a screen. The threat cue consisted of a red 'X', indicating that there was a 20 per cent chance of receiving an electric shock on the ankle in the next few seconds (in reality, the participants received a mild shock only twice). The safety cue was a blue 'O', indicating that no shock would follow. The brain activity of the women in response to seeing the threat and safety cues was measured. Importantly, while they were lying in the scanner, in one third of the trials the women were holding the hands of their spouses; in one third they were holding the hands of an anonymous experimenter; and in one third they did not hold anyone's hand.

Results

While holding their partner's hand, but also while holding the stranger's hand, the women showed lower activation in brain regions usually involved in the regulation of emotional and behavioural responses to threat (i.e. ventral anterior cingulate cortex, right dorsolateral prefrontal cortex, caudate, and superior colliculus), compared to when they were not holding anyone's hand. In other words, the women – or more specifically, their brains – registered less threat upon seeing an 'X' when they were holding their spouse's hand or a stranger's hand – although the effect was significantly stronger when holding their partner's hand. In addition, the more satisfied the women were with their marriage, the less activation in these threat-related brain areas they showed upon seeing a threat cue.

Conclusion

The findings indicate that merely holding a partner's hand, or even holding a stranger's hand, has direct positive consequences for how we experience stressful events – such events simply have less impact on us. The study helps to further our understanding of why relationships affect our health. For example, one particular finding of the study was that holding a partner's hand reduced activation of the hypothalamus, a structure in the brain that is known to be involved in the regulation of the immune system. So, when an individual experiences distress, at school, at work or otherwise, physical contact with a romantic partner actually *helps* to release the distress, which in turn may benefit psychological and physical health in the long run.

and blood pressure. However, when the third confederate displayed his agreement with the participant, acting as a buttress against the two other confederates, participants' stress levels reduced to normal. This study, and many others (see for another example Research Close-Up 11.1), clearly demonstrates that social support can directly buffer stress.

The immediate effects of social exclusion

Other evidence for the important role of relationships on our wellbeing comes from studies examining the immediate effects of being excluded or rejected by others. Can you recall a time when you were standing with a group of

FIGURE 11.2 *Cyberball, a computer-animated version of the ball-tossing game used in research on social exclusion. The little hand in the bottom of the screen represents the participant, the two other figures represent what the participant thinks are two anonymous other participants.*

Source: Williams, K. D., Cheung, C. K. T., & Choi, W. (2000). CyberOstracism: Effects of being ignored over the Internet. *Journal of Personality and Social Psychology, 79,* 748–762. Reprinted with permission of Professor Kipling D. Williams.

FIGURE 11.3(a) and (b) *These brain regions, which are also involved in the processing of physical pain, were activated when participants were excluded from the ball-tossing game.*

Source: From Eisenberger et al., 2003, with permission from the AAAS.

people, talking together, and one of the group members turned his back on you so that you were placed outside of the circle? Even though you may know that this happened accidentally (i.e. the person had no intention to exclude you from the group), it may still have caused immediate negative emotions, and an immediate urge to place yourself – literally – back inside the group. It is remarkable how intensely people can respond to such subtle and seemingly trivial forms of exclusion.

Williams has extensively examined the effects of social exclusion in his laboratory (Williams, 2001). In a typical study, a participant is sitting in a waiting room with two other people, who allegedly are also waiting for an upcoming study but who are, in fact, confederates. While waiting, one of these people picks up a small ball and tosses the ball to the other confederate, who then tosses the ball to the participant; the three of them start tossing the ball between them just to pass the time. However, after several throws, both confederates stop throwing the ball toward the participant, but continue throwing the ball at each other. In other words, they exclude the participant from the game. Williams's research shows that this situation causes strong immediate aversive responses, including a bad mood, lowered self-esteem, loss of control and strong physiological arousal (Williams, 2001). In fact, it appears that exclusion from this game *literally* hurts. Using a computerized version of the ball-tossing game (see Figure 11.2) called *Cyberball*, a research team in California measured participants' brain activity while they were, or were not, excluded from the game by two other anonymous participants (Eisenberger, Lieberman, & Williams, 2003). While being excluded, participants showed brain responses (i.e. activation in the dorsal anterior cingulate cortex, and right ventral prefrontal cortex; see Figure 11.3) that are typically found when people experience physical

pain! If being excluded from a virtual ball-tossing game has this powerful impact, think about the impact more meaningful forms of exclusion can have on an individual, such as a child who is bullied and rejected by his class mates.

The need to belong

Together, the research findings discussed so far indicate that having (versus lacking) relationships has important benefits for our mental and physical well-being, and that people have a strong aversion against social exclusion. Partly based on such findings, Baumeister and Leary (1995) concluded that people have a fundamental **need to belong** with other people. They argue that this fundamental need evolved in the human species as a result of natural selection. In our evolutionary past people depended heavily on others to increase their chances of survival, just as they needed water, food and warmth to stay alive. Individuals who had a natural tendency to form close relationships with others were more likely to survive and reproduce than were individuals who did not, and so, through the process of Darwinian selection, the need to belong became typical of the human species. The need to belong is reflected in people's strong responses to changes in their degree of belongingness, as discussed above – if people experience strong bonds with others, they feel good about themselves; when the need to belong is thwarted, they feel miserable. Other support for the need-to-belong hypothesis stems from the fact that humans seem to have a natural tendency to form relationships with others. Think back to the time when you entered a new school and you were surrounded by other people you had never seen before. Within days, hours or even minutes, people spontaneously seek contact with each other, and people typically form relationships very quickly in such situations. Indeed,

> **need to belong** the intrinsic motivation to affiliate with others and be socially accepted.

THEORY BOX 11.1

ATTACHMENT THEORY

Attachment theory proposes that attachment functions as a regulatory system. The figure shows this system (Hazan & Shaver, 1987, p. 3). In the diamond is the test question: is the attachment figure available (meaning: sufficiently near, attentive and responsive)? If the answer is 'yes', the child feels secure, safe, loved and confident about its worth and value. It can then be playful, smiling and engage in exploration. If the answer is 'no', two different paths are possible. The child may feel defensive and try to maintain proximity while avoiding close contact, or the child may feel fearful and anxious. Then a hierarchy of attachment behaviours is elicited. According to adult attachment theory, adults rely in a very similar way on an attachment figure – for example, the romantic partner – to regulate their feelings and emotions.

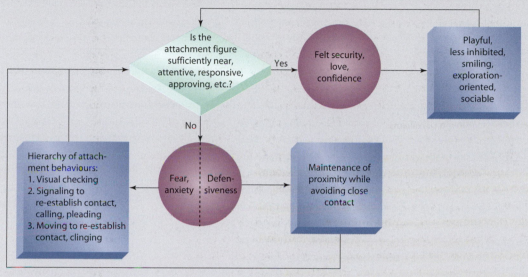

Source: From Hazan & Shaver (1987) (p. 3), with permission from Taylor and Francis.

If the attachment is available in case of threat, the child feels secure and can safely play and explore its environment. If the attachment figure is not available, the child experiences either fear or defensiveness, resulting in different behaviours.

as we will see later on in this chapter, even the mere proximity of others often results in the formation of relationships. And it appears that we have this focus on other people from the day we are born. For example, babies 30 minutes old prefer to look at human faces, compared to other equally complex stimuli (Johnson, Dziurawiec, Ellis, & Morton, 1991). It seems, indeed, that it is part of our genetic make-up to relate to other people.

Attachment

The idea that humans have evolved an innate tendency to establish close relationships with others also forms the basis of **attachment theory**, an influential theory about relationships developed by John Bowlby (1982; see Leader in the Field, John Bowlby, and Theory Box 11.1). In threatening circumstances (e.g. when there is acute danger, or when they are hungry

attachment theory the theory that proposes that the development of secure infant–caregiver attachment in childhood is the basis for the ability to maintain stable and intimate relationships in adulthood.

or thirsty), human infants have to rely on and get the attention of their caregivers – the mother often being the primary caregiver. That is why babies start crying when they are hungry, or when their temperature is not right – if they did not do this, it would lower their survival chances. According to the theory, childhood experiences with our caregivers (mother, father) shape our expectations about relationships, and how we behave in relationships, later on in life.

People form different *attachment styles* based on the interaction experiences they have with the primary caregiver. Hazan and Shaver (1987) proposed that people can generally be classified into three categories. They asked their participants to pick one of three descriptions that best described how they generally feel and behave in their relationships with others (see Figure 11.4). Individuals who presumably had caregivers in their childhood who were responsive to their needs and were available when in distress are likely to develop a secure attachment style. They generally have a positive view of themselves, and a positive view of other people as being trustworthy and

LEADER IN THE FIELD

John Bowlby (1907–1990) started his intellectual career at the University of Cambridge, where his studies included developmental psychology and, later, child psychiatry and psychoanalysis. After returning from army service in 1945, Bowlby became head of the Children's Department at the Tavistock Clinic in London. Studying maladapted children, Bowlby felt that psychoanalysis was putting far too much emphasis on the child's fantasy world and far too little on actual events. As a result, Bowlby developed attachment theory, which states that a child's actual experiences within the family have far-reaching effects on the development of his or her personality. According to Bowlby, from the first months of their relationships with both parents, children build up 'working models' of how attachment figures are likely to behave, and for the rest of their lives children's expectations are based on these models. Later, his theory became highly influential in explaining why adults form attachment bonds with others.

Question: Which of the following best describes your feelings?
SECURE
Secure: I find it relatively easy to get close to others and am comfortable depending on them and having them depend on me. I don't often worry about being abandoned or about someone getting too close to me.
INSECURE
Avoidant: I am somewhat uncomfortable being close to others; I find it difficult to trust them completely, difficult to allow myself to depend on them. I am nervous when anyone gets too close, and often love partners want to be more intimate than I feel comfortable with.
Anxious/ambivalent: I find that others are reluctant to get as close as I would like. I often worry that my partner doesn't really love me or won't want to stay with me. I want to merge completely with another person, and this desire sometimes scares people away.

FIGURE 11.4 *Measure of attachment styles used by Hazan and Shaver (1987).*

Source: Reproduced with permission of Yale University Press.

helpful. In contrast, individuals who presumably had caregivers who were unresponsive to their needs, and who did not provide support in distressing situations, are more likely to develop one of the two insecure attachment styles, avoidant or anxious/ambivalent. Individuals who develop an avoidant attachment style tend to maintain emotional distance from other people, because they view others as not being trustworthy. Individuals who develop an anxious–ambivalent style often lack confidence in themselves, tend to worry about their relationships, and compulsively seeks closeness and intimacy with other people.

It should be noted that nowadays attachment researchers view attachment styles not as three (or four; Bartholomew, 1990) discrete categories. Rather, they recognize that an individual's attachment style can be measured along two continuous dimensions (for a recent overview of attachment style, see Shaver & Mikulincer, 2009): individuals differ in the degree to which they tend to avoid intimacy with other people, and they differ in the degree to which they are anxious about being abandoned by their relationship partners (Brennan, Clark, & Shaver, 1998). Securely attached individuals score low on both dimensions, thus being low in both avoidance and anxiety; insecurely attached individuals score high on one or both of these dimensions (see Figure 11.5; also Individual Differences 11.1). Specifically, individuals scoring high on anxiety, and high on avoidance, are said to be *fearful* in their relationships with others. Individuals scoring high on anxiety but low on avoidance are termed *preoccupied*: they are uneasy in relationships and vigilant to any threats to a relationship. Finally, individuals scoring high on avoidance but low on anxiety are termed

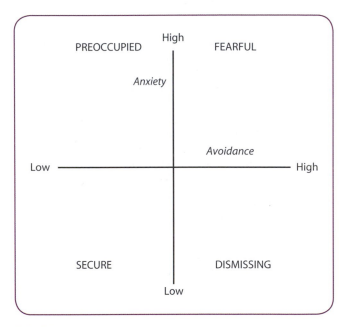

FIGURE 11.5 *The dimensional model of attachment styles.*

dismissing: they are self-reliant and largely uninterested in intimacy with others.

Although it is difficult to indicate what exactly reflects a high or low score on both dimensions, in previous samples researchers have found average scores of around 3 for the avoidance subscale, and of around 4 for the anxiety subscale (e.g. Alonso-Arbiol, Balluerka, Shaver, & Gillath, 2008; see Individual Differences 11.1). This gives you an idea of whether you are high or low in avoidance, and high or low in anxiety.

There is a great deal of evidence that differences in attachment styles do indeed have a strong impact

INDIVIDUAL DIFFERENCES 11.1

ATTACHMENT ANXIETY AND AVOIDANCE SCALE

The statements below concern how you feel in emotionally intimate relationships. We are interested in how you *generally* experience relationships, not just in what is happening in a current relationship. Respond to each statement by indicating on a scale from 1 (*strongly disagree*) to 7 (*strongly agree*) how much you agree or disagree with the statement (Fraley, Waller, & Brennan, 2000).

1. I'm afraid that I will lose my relationship partners.
2. I often worry that a relationship partner will not want to stay with me.
3. I often worry that others don't really love me.
4. I worry that others won't care about me as much as I care about them.
5. I often wish that other people's feelings for me were as strong as my feelings for him or her.
6. I worry a lot about my relationships.
7. When my partner is out of sight, I worry that he or she might become interested in someone else.
8. When I show my feelings for other people, I'm afraid they will not feel the same about me.
9. I rarely worry about my relationship partners leaving me.
10. My relationships with others makes me doubt myself.
11. I do not often worry about being abandoned.
12. I find that my partner(s) don't want to get as close as I would like.
13. Sometimes others change their feelings about me for no apparent reason.
14. My desire to be very close sometimes scares people away.
15. I'm afraid that once someone gets to know me, he or she won't like who I really am.
16. It makes me mad that I don't get the affection and support I need from others.
17. I worry that I won't measure up to other people.

18. Others only seem to notice me when I'm angry.
19. I prefer not to show another person how I feel deep down.
20. I feel comfortable sharing my private thoughts and feelings with others.
21. I find it difficult to allow myself to depend on others.
22. I am very comfortable being close to other people.
23. I don't feel comfortable opening up to other people.
24. I prefer not to be too close to others.
25. I get uncomfortable when someone wants to be very close.
26. I find it relatively easy to get close to others.
27. It's not difficult for me to get close to other people.
28. I usually discuss my problems and concerns with someone.
29. It helps to turn to close others in times of need.
30. I tell others just about everything.
31. I talk things over with others.
32. I am nervous when partners get too close to me.
33. I feel comfortable depending on other people.
34. I find it easy to depend on other people.
35. It's easy for me to be affectionate with others.
36. There are others who really understand my needs and me.

The first 18 items listed above comprise the attachment-related anxiety scale. Items 19–36 comprise the attachment-related avoidance scale. In real research, the order in which these items are presented should be randomized. To obtain your score for attachment-related *anxiety*, average your responses to items 1–18. However, because items 9 and 11 are 'reverse keyed' (i.e. high numbers represent low anxiety rather than high anxiety), you will need to reverse the answers to those questions before averaging the responses (e.g. if you answer with a 6 to item 9, you will need to re-key it as a 2 before averaging.) To obtain a score for attachment-related *avoidance*, average your responses to items 19–36. Items 20, 22, 26, 27, 28, 29, 30, 31, 33, 34, 35 and 36 will need to be reverse-keyed before you compute this average.

on people's feelings and behaviour in relationships. Secure people generally enjoy more satisfying relationships with their romantic partner, both in heterosexual (Feeney, 2002) and homosexual (Elizur & Mintzer, 2003) relationships, and with their friends (Kafetsios & Nezlek, 2002). Simpson, Rholes, and Nelligan (1992; see Leader in the Field, Jeffry A. Simpson) provided a compelling example of the effect of attachment differences in coping with stressful situations. In this study, heterosexual dating couples were unobtrusively videotaped while they were sitting in a waiting room. The couple had been told that the woman would soon participate in a task that is known to 'arouse considerable anxiety and distress in most people'. Before the experiment began, both members of the couple had completed a questionnaire, which included measures of attachment style. The ratings of the videos revealed several interesting findings. Secure women sought out more support from their partner as their level of displayed anxiety – as observed by the raters of the videos – increased. In contrast, women with an insecure attachment style (specifically, avoidant women) tended to seek *less* support from the partner as their level of anxiety increased. Put differently, secure women relied on their partners (i.e. trusted their partners) in an attempt

LEADER IN THE FIELD

Jeffry A. Simpson (b. 1958) is a professor at the University of Minnesota, studying romantic relationships. He has made important contributions in a range of relationship topics, most importantly attachment, mating, partner idealization and *emphatic accuracy*, or how accurate people are at inferring their partner's thoughts and feelings. He has received numerous honours, and is currently editor of one of the field's top journals, the *Journal of Personality and Social Psychology*. Simpson's work usually integrates relationship science with principles of evolutionary psychology.

to relieve the distress, while avoidant women did not rely on their partners, apparently not viewing their partners as what is sometimes called a *safe haven*. In addition, securely attached men provided more support when their partners displayed more signs of distress, while avoidant men were less inclined to do so. Thus, attachment style differences affect both support seeking and giving.

Summary

People have a strong and natural tendency to be around others, to form and maintain close relationships, and to prevent exclusion from others. Belongingness with others benefits both psychological and physical well-being, while being excluded from others can literally hurt. By providing social support, close others can help us to deal with stress, although individual differences in attachment styles cause individuals to rely on others to varying degrees. Overall, the important message of the chapter so far is: relationships *do* matter.

INTERPERSONAL ATTRACTION

When and why do we experience interpersonal attraction?

Now that we have established the importance of interpersonal relationships in people's lives, the remainder of the chapter will – more or less – follow the course of a relationship, starting at the beginning: with whom, and under what circumstances, do we form interpersonal relationships? What factors determine interpersonal attraction?

The benefits of physical attractiveness

In most cases, the first impression one has when meeting a new person is based on the other person's physical appearance. Does appearance matter? Probably you have heard people claim that, for them, it's only what's on the 'inside' that matters when judging another person – not the outside (perhaps you are even one of these people?). That, of course, is a noble sentiment; however, scientific evidence suggests otherwise. Consider the following research findings. Schoolteachers judge attractive pupils as more intelligent, and accordingly give them higher grades (Clifford & Walster, 1973). Attractive people raise more money for charity in their collecting boxes (Chaiken, 1979). For both men and women, each point increase on an attractiveness scale ranging from 1 to 5 is associated with an average increase in annual income of more than US $2000 (Frieze, Olson, & Russell, 1991). Judges tend to give lower sentences to attractive people (Downs & Lyons, 1991). In parallel with these findings, Kampe, Frith, Dolan, and Frith (2001) demonstrated that reward systems in the brain get activated when attractive people turn their gaze on you. This is just a selection of many other similar findings that suggest the benefits of being attractive (for an overview, see Langlois et al., 2000). One of the most remarkable, perhaps even disturbing, findings in this area is that mothers who have attractive babies (as judged by outside observers) tend to behave differently toward their child compared to mothers of unattractive babies: they are more playful and display more affectionate behaviour toward the child, both shortly after birth as well as three months later (Langlois, Ritter, Casey, & Sawin, 1995).

What is beautiful is good

There is thus little doubt that appearance does matter when judging other people (Figure 11.6). But why is attractiveness so important? Why do we even care about someone's looks? One reason is that we assume that people who are attractive also have nice personalities, as shown by Dion, Berscheid, and Walster (1972; see Leader in the Field, Ellen S. Berscheid). They asked participants to rate pictures of attractive and unattractive people on a number of personality characteristics. Attractive (as compared to unattractive) people were rated as more friendly, sociable and trustworthy, and also as more competent. The researchers called this the 'what is beautiful is good' stereotype. Later studies replicated these effects, demonstrating that both children and adults are judged as being more sociable and competent when they are more attractive. Similar effects have even been found when making personality judgements

LEADER IN THE FIELD

Ellen S. Berscheid (b. 1936) is a Regents Professor at the University of Minnesota, where she received her PhD in 1965. Berscheid has made numerous and highly influential contributions in the field of relationship science. She is particularly interested in problems associated with relationship satisfaction and stability, relationship cognition, and emotional experiences within relationships, especially love and sexual desire. In 1974, Berscheid was the centre of controversy when she was awarded a large research grant by the National Science Foundation in the US for her work on why and how people fall in love. Senator Proxmire of Wisconsin regarded this as 'wasteful federal funding of research'. The scientific community has been more positive about her work: she is the recipient of several prestigious awards, such as the Donald T. Campbell Award for Distinguished Research in Social Psychology from the Society of Personality and Social Psychology, and the Distinguished Scientist Award from the Society of Experimental Social Psychology.

FIGURE 11.6 *Although it is often said that a book should not be judged by its cover, attractiveness has an important impact on how we evaluate and behave towards others.*

Source: © Sean De Burca. Used under licence from Shutterstock.

about attractive and unattractive people when the pictures were shown for only a tenth of a second (Locher, Unger, Sociedade, & Wahl, 1993). Even within 100 milliseconds, attractive people are judged to be more friendly and skilful, illustrating the pervasiveness of the stereotype.

The important question, of course, is whether there is some truth to this: are attractive people indeed 'better' people? Do attractive and unattractive individuals behave differently? Langlois and her colleagues (Langlois et al., 2000) analysed the results of over one hundred studies that examined whether attractiveness was associated with differences in traits and behaviours. They reported that, on average, attractive people were more extraverted, had higher self-confidence, and possessed better social skills. So, yes, attractive people have, on average, somewhat more outgoing and social personalities. Langlois and colleagues concluded that, apparently, beauty is not only skin deep.

It is unlikely though that attractive people are born more sociable and friendly than unattractive people. What else explains why attractiveness tends to be correlated with social skills? Recall the study discussed above, showing that mothers behave more affectionately towards attractive than unattractive babies (Langlois et al., 1995). A little later in life, attractive children in preschool are treated significantly more favourably by their peers and their teachers than are less attractive children. This continues in adult life, when attractive individuals get more attention and receive more help and cooperation from others than do less attractive individuals (for an overview of the effects of attractiveness across the life span, see Langlois et al., 2000). No wonder attractive people become the more sociable people that most of us assume they are! It is easy to imagine how getting positive attention and responses from other people

induces a person to behave in a positive and kind manner in return. In other words, attractive people often confirm the 'what is beautiful is good' stereotype by reciprocating the favourable responses they get from others. This is another example of the self-fulfilling prophecy, as discussed in Chapter 3. Snyder, Tanke, and Berscheid (1977) provided support for this idea in a very elegant experiment, which you can read about in Research Close-Up 11.2.

Scholars in the field of **evolutionary psychology** provide another – not incompatible – explanation for the important role of attractiveness in our judgements about and behaviours toward other people. They argue that in our evolutionary past attractiveness reflected good health (Buss, 1995). Humans, who were attracted to specific features in a potential mate that were positively associated with health and chances of procreation success, were more likely to reproduce. However, although attractiveness may have marked health in

> **evolutionary psychology** an approach that explains human behaviour and preferences based on their 'reproductive value'; that is, their value in producing offspring.

HOW THE SELF-FULFILLING PROPHECY COMES ABOUT

Snyder, M., Tanke, E. D., & Berscheid, E. (1977). Social perception and interpersonal behaviour: On the self-fulfilling nature of social stereotypes. *Journal of Personality and Social Psychology, 35,* 656–666.

Introduction

The study described here examined the self-fulfilling nature of the 'what is beautiful is good' stereotype. Specifically, the authors wondered whether attractive people might live up to the stereotype because they confirm the expectations other people have about them. An individual may behave differently – more positively that is – when interacting with an attractive person compared to an unattractive person, because the individual believes (based on the stereotype) that the other attractive person is nicer. In response, the attractive person may indeed act more nicely in return, thereby behaviourally confirming the stereotype.

Method and procedure

Participants were 51 male and 51 female undergraduate students, who were scheduled to take part in mixed-sex pairs of previously unacquainted individuals. The experimenter told the participants, who did not meet in person and who were located in separate rooms, that the study involved acquaintance processes in social relationships. It was explained that the participant would engage in a telephone conversation with another student. Before the phone conversation began, the male participant received a photograph, ostensibly of the female participant with whom he would have the telephone conversation (although the photo was not of the actual conversation partner). In fact, half of the male participants were given a pre-rated photograph of an attractive female, while the other half of the male participants were given a pre-rated photograph of an unattractive female. Before the conversation took place, the male participants indicated their impression of the female, based on the photograph (e.g. 'How enthusiastic, friendly, trustworthy, intelligent, etc. do you think this person is?'). The male and the female participants then engaged in a 10-minute unstructured telephone conversation that was recorded. The women were unaware that their own photo was not used, and the men knew only about the photo they were given; thus men and women were blind to experimental condition.

Later, 22 students rated the recordings of the conversations. Half of them heard *only* the track of the tapes containing the target women's voices, and rated the impression they had of each female target. The other half heard only the male voices, and they rated the impression they had of each male perceiver.

Results

First, in line with the 'what is beautiful is good' stereotype, the males who had received the photograph of an attractive female had a much more positive initial impression of their upcoming interaction partner than did those who received the photograph of an unattractive female. Furthermore, the men who interacted with women whom they believed to be physically attractive appeared (to the observers) more sociable, sexually warm, interesting, outgoing, humorous and so on, than their counterparts in the unattractive target condition. Finally – and most interestingly – the women who were in the attractive female condition (although they were blind to this fact) were rated by the observers as more sociable, poised, sexually warm and outgoing than the women in the unattractive condition.

Conclusion

In the words of the authors, this research 'suggests that stereotypes can and do channel dyadic interaction so as to create their own social reality' (p. 663). The male perceivers only *believed* that their interaction partner was attractive, and yet they behaved very differently compared to the males who believed that their interaction partner was unattractive. In line with their expectations about the attractive female target, the men behaved in a more friendly and sociable manner in the attractive condition, and the female targets who were perceived (unbeknownst to them) to be physically attractive actually came to behave in a friendly, likable and sociable manner. In other words, they confirmed, and bolstered, the stereotype. Thus the stereotype became a self-fulfilling prophecy.

our evolutionary history, there is little evidence that attractiveness is related to health and fertility in current times, at least not in Western societies (Weeden & Sabini, 2005). In line with the 'what is beautiful is good' stereotype, however, people do *think* that attractive people are healthier, as shown in a study by Kalick, Zebrowitz,

Langlois, and Johnson (1998). Participants in this study rated the attractiveness of a number of individuals shown in photographs, and also how healthy they thought these individuals were. While participants thought that more attractive individuals were also healthier, this was in fact not the case, as revealed from their medical files.

The features that determine physical attractiveness

Before turning to the question of what *is* considered attractive, the question arises whether people agree about who is, and who is not, attractive? The answer is 'yes'. Of course, people do not always and completely agree on who is attractive, as you may have experienced when evaluating passers-by while sitting on a terrace with your friends. However, although you may give an '8' and your friend gives a '9' on a ten-point scale to a passing boy or girl, it is seldom the case that one person finds someone very attractive, while someone else finds the same person plain ugly. Indeed, research reveals that generally there is a fairly high level of consensus among people when evaluating the attractiveness of others. Even infants who are 3- and 6-months old can distinguish between faces that are rated by adults as attractive and unattractive, preferring to look at the attractive faces (Langlois, Ritter, Roggman, & Vaughn, 1991). And although there are some differences across cultures about what is considered attractive, again people from different societies generally agree on what is and what is not attractive (Cunningham, Roberts, Barbee, Druen, & Wu, 1995; see also Chapter 15).

Thus, attractiveness is not entirely 'in the eye of the beholder'. If people (including infants) largely agree on who is and who is not attractive, it should be possible to assess attractiveness objectively, at least to some extent. In other words, consensus on attractiveness suggests that attractive people possess certain objective features that differ from unattractive people. Indeed, a number of such features that contribute to attractiveness have been identified. Perhaps surprisingly at first glance, attractive people often have *average* faces. When researchers digitally create a face that is 'morphed' from a number of other faces, it is typically found that the morphed face, which is the average of the other faces, is rated as more attractive than the individual faces (Langlois, Roggman, & Musselman, 1994). Also, *symmetry* is related to attractiveness, with more symmetrical faces judged as more attractive than asymmetrical faces (e.g. Perrett et al., 1999). Researchers do not, however, agree unequivocally about the role of averageness and symmetry. For example, some have argued that the role of averageness can be fully explained in terms of symmetry, as average faces are also more symmetric; others argue that both averageness and symmetry make their own contribution to beauty (Grammer & Thornhill, 1994).

Other facial features that contribute to beauty are so-called *hormone-markers*. For example, female faces with high cheekbones and smooth skin are more attractive. These facial features tend to be associated with a high ratio of oestrogen to testosterone, and signal fertility. Women tend to be attracted by features in male faces that are associated with relatively high levels of testosterone,

FIGURE 11.7(a) and (b) *Women are generally attracted to men with large jaws, and prominent brow ridges and cheekbones. Men are generally attracted to women with high cheekbones and smooth skin. Both men and women prefer symmetrical faces.*
Source: (a) © Luna Vandoorne; (b) © Yaro. Both images used under licence from Shutterstock.

such as a large jaw, and prominent brow ridges and cheekbones (Figure 11.7).

Of course, it is not only the face that matters. The size and shape of the body also counts. As with faces, both men and women prefer symmetrical bodies (Tovée, Tasker, & Benson, 2000). Women prefer men whose torso has a narrow waist and a broad chest and shoulders – an inverted triangle (Maisey, Vale, Cornelissen, & Tovée, 1999). And there is good evidence that men have a preference for women with an hourglass shaped waist-to-hip ratio (WHR) of 0.70. Once again, this latter finding has been explained by evolutionary psychologists in terms of reproduction advantages associated with a relatively small WHR. There is indeed some evidence that a female 0.70 WHR is associated with fertility (Zaadstra et al., 1993). Hence, men who followed this preference in our evolutionary past had a higher chance of conferring their genes, including their genetic predisposition to prefer hourglass-shaped women (Figure 11.8). In sum, several features of the body and the face are reliably associated with attractiveness, suggesting that attractiveness is partly an objective phenomenon.

Contextual influences on physical attractiveness

Despite the fact that attractiveness can largely be objectively assessed, there are situational factors that influence attractiveness judgements. For example, as will be described in more detail below, people who are in a long-term heterosexual relationship tend to give lower attractiveness ratings to opposite-sex others compared

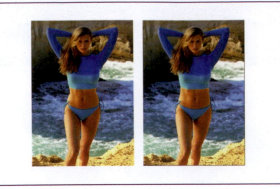

FIGURE 11.8 *Men prefer women with hourglass-shaped waist-to-hip ratios. In the picture on the left, the woman has the lowest waist-to-hip ratio – the classic hour-glass figure; the woman on the right has the highest waist-to-hip ratio.*

Source: From Streater & McBurney (2003). Waist-hip ratio and attractiveness: New evidence and a critique of a 'critical' test. *Evolution and Human Behaviour*, 24, 88–98, with permission from Elsevier.

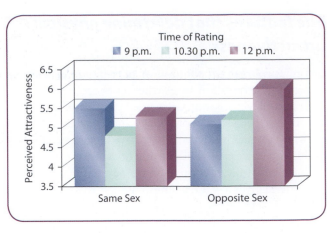

FIGURE 11.9 *The effect of getting nearer to closing time on attractiveness ratings of opposite-sex others.*

Source: Adapted from Pennebaker et al., 1979, with permission from SAGE Publications Ltd.

to people who are not in a relationship (Simpson, Gangestad, & Lerma, 1990). The time of day also influences perceptions of attractiveness, at least when in a bar. In a study by Pennebaker and colleagues (1979), researchers asked people in a bar to rate the attractiveness of other customers (on a scale from 1 to 10) at three different times in the same evening, 9 p.m., 10.30 p.m., and near closing time, at 12 p.m. Attractiveness ratings of opposite-sex customers increased more than one point at 12 p.m. (Figure 11.9). Later studies confirmed this finding, with a few qualifications of the 'closing time effect'. For example, people who are in a romantic relationship do not show the effect, or at least not as strongly as people who are not in a relationship (Madey et al., 1996).

Psychological attraction

So far, we have discussed physical attractiveness. However, it is evident that, although physical attractiveness plays an important role in how we judge and respond to others, it does not fully explain why we sometimes like some people more than others, and how sometimes this even results in love. Put simply, why do we like some people more than others? Why do we form relationships with some people and not with others?

Although people commonly think that they choose the people with whom they affiliate, often they form relationships with others without consciously thinking about it (Berscheid, 1985). When joining a sports club, when starting a new job, when moving to a new city, or when starting university, people affiliate with others. They develop relationships with people they did not know and, more often than not, with people whom they

would not have predicted that they would like, if they had been asked before meeting them. Before meeting others, people tend to consider qualities of others that they hope for, such as religion, height, weight, intelligence or profession. When meeting others, however, people experience how the other makes them feel, his or her sense of humour, and the rapport they feel with the other. As a consequence, people show a mismatch between whom they think they will like and whom they actually like.

Eastwick and Finkel (2008) showed that such processes are even at work when people establish romantic relationships. In their studies, they used a speed-dating procedure. Speed dating was invented by Rabbi Yaacov Deyo to help Jewish singles in Los Angeles to meet a suitable partner. During speed dating, single individuals go on very brief dates (three–eight minutes) with a series of potential romantic partners. Eastwick and Finkel asked individuals before they went on their speed dates to rate their preferences for a potential mate. They found, not surprisingly, that when thinking about hypothetical partners, men preferred physically attractive partners and women preferred partners with a strong earning prospect (cf. Buss, 1989; see also Social Psychology Beyond the Lab 11.1). These preferences, however, did not predict people's actual choices after a face-to-face date. Although the associations with physical attractiveness were more consistent and stronger than those of earning prospects (cf. Walster, Aronson, Abrahams, & Rottmann, 1966), both were significantly and positively related to romantic interest in actual choices. Inconsistent with the hypothesis, however, Eastwick and Finkel found no sex differences for either physical attractiveness or earning prospects: both predicted romantic interest equally for men and women. The authors concluded that people lack insight into their preferences when actually meeting potential mates. This conclusion does not only apply to

SOCIAL PSYCHOLOGY BEYOND THE LAB 11.1

DATING ADS: GENDER DIFFERENCES IN PREFERENCES FOR PHYSICAL ATTRACTIVENESS AND STATUS

Although both men and women value physical attractiveness in a potential partner, physical attractiveness is in general a more important determinant of romantic attraction for males than it is for females (Buss, 1989). Although women obviously also value physical attractiveness in a partner, women generally are more sensitive than men to signs of dominance and status when looking for a romantic partner (Buss, 1989). According to evolutionary psychologists, males have been selected to prefer women who are likely to produce healthy babies, and they are therefore sensitive to signs of youth, health and reproductive value. Women, on the other hand, had a better chance of their offspring surviving when they selected men who could provide them with the necessary resources (food, shelter, protection), which is more likely to be provided by high-status males. This gender difference in what men (physical attractiveness) and women (wealth/status) look for in finding a romantic partner has been found in more than 27 cultures across the world (Buss, 1989).

You can observe this gender difference on dating sites and in personal ads in the newspapers. Try it: visit any dating site or read the personal ads in a newspaper, and you may notice that men are more likely than women to mention that they are seeking a physically attractive partner, while women are relatively more likely than men to seek a partner with a high status. This is exactly what Greenlees and McGrew (1994) found in a study on gender differences in dating advertisements among heterosexuals. They analysed the content of a thousand 'lonely hearts' advertisements. The researchers found that 49 per cent of the men's ads explicitly indicated that the man was looking for a physically attractive partner, while only 33 per cent of the women's ads contained this information. The reverse was true with regard to status and resources. Thirty three per cent of the women's ads indicated that the woman was looking for a partner who could offer her financial security, while only 9 per cent of the men's ads indicated that the man was interested in a potential partner's wealth or status (see Figure 11.10). A study by Wiederman (1993) obtained similar findings. In addition to these gender differences in seeking attractiveness and status, this study revealed that women (more than men) were more likely to look for partners who were older than themselves, probably because older men generally have more access to resources (e.g. they have a higher income).

Not only are there gender differences in what men and women *seek* in a partner. Both men and women are smart enough to mention that they can *offer* what the other sex would be interested in. For example, Greenlees and McGrew (1994) found that 71 per cent of the women's ads referred to the woman's physical appearance, while only 50 per cent of the men's ads mentioned the man's physical appearance. Thus, women were more likely than men to 'offer' physical attractiveness. In contrast, 69 per cent of the men's ads referred to the man's status or financial security, while only 43 per cent of the women's ads contained information about the woman's financial status: the men were more likely than women to offer wealth and resources in their ads (Figure 11.10; see also Wiederman, 1993).

The research described here provides a nice example of how theory-based predictions – in this case, evolutionary driven gender differences in mate preferences – can be tested outside the laboratory, making use of data that are already out there in the real world.

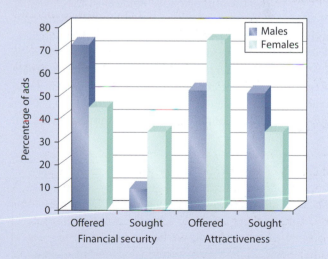

FIGURE 11.10 *An analysis of dating ads revealed that, in line with arguments from evolutionary psychology, women (relative to men) seek a partner with resources, and offer physical attractiveness. In contrast, relative to women, men seek a physically attractive partner, and offer financial resources.*

Source: From Greenlees & McGrew, 1994, with permission from Elsevier.

romantic relationships, but reflects a more general tendency showing that people are often unable to report accurately why they like another person or engage in particular behaviour (Nisbett & Wilson, 1977).

Ample research shows that physical and psychological factors that people are unaware of play a powerful role in determining who people affiliate with, and ultimately even develop close relationships with. An important but underestimated factor that reliably affects people's relationship choices and relationship development is proximity, that is, whether people are near to each other in place or time. The most important psychological factors are familiarity and similarity. These three factors – proximity, familiarity, and similarity – are closely related to one another, as we will show.

Proximity

When moving into a student house or building, many students may choose to live as far away from the elevator or stairs, kitchen or restrooms as possible. They hope that this will offer them a quieter location where they can work and sleep undisturbed. Although this consideration may have some merit, it may also reduce the likelihood of making many friends. Indeed, research shows that *proximity*, or being physically close to others (sometimes called 'propinquity'), increases the chance of becoming friends with them.

One of the most informative studies on the power of proximity is the pioneering study by Festinger, Schachter, and Back (1950). These authors examined relationship development among a sample of student couples that were assigned to apartments for graduate students in Westgate West, an apartment complex with different buildings and apartments on different floors (see Figure 11.11). Over the course of 10 months, physical proximity predicted the

FIGURE 11.11 *The Westgate West complex. Residents of the building formed more friendships with others living close to them.*

Source: Festinger, Schachter, & Back (1950). *Social pressures in informal groups: A study of human factors in housing.* New York: Harper.

development of friendships: people formed more friendships with others who lived physically close to them than with people who lived further away. For example, people were 10 times more likely to become friends with others in the same building than with people in a different building; within each building, people who lived on the same floor had more friends on the same floor than on a different floor; and people on the same floor were more likely to become friends with their next-door neighbours than with people who lived further down the aisle. It should be noted, however, that proximity did not always promote liking. In some cases, people also increasingly disliked their neighbours. After all, to like or to dislike someone, and even to love or to hate someone, one needs to know the other person. Proximity allows people to get to know others, for better and for worse.

So, rather than being due to careful selection processes, the development of friendships is, at least in part, due to chance and proximity. This is nicely illustrated in a clever, more recent study by Back, Schmukle, and Egloff (2008). The researchers followed a group of freshmen over the first year of their study. During a regular introductory session for freshmen in psychology, students were randomly assigned seat numbers. After having taken their seats, students individually introduced themselves to the group, and after each introduction, rated whether they liked each individual student and whether they would like to meet the student in the future. One year later, students were presented with photographs of all students at the introductory session and rated their friendship with each person. Findings clearly revealed a proximity effect: students in the introductory session liked students in their row and students sitting next to them much more than students sitting elsewhere. More importantly, sitting next to each other predicted friendship one year later: students had more intense friendships with those who had sat next to them than with those who had sat elsewhere. Thus, being in close physical proximity breeds liking, even if the proximity comes about by chance. Why?

Partly, the answer to this question is fairly straightforward. It is simply harder to get to meet and know people who do not live nearby, work in a different field, go to a different school or engage in very different activities. People tend to become friends with people they see frequently, with people who work in the same office, live in the same block or ride the same train every day. Conversely, it is hard and costly to maintain relationships when the physical distance is high. Students report physical separation as being a major cause for the ending of friendships (Rose, 1984) and dating relationships during the transition from high school to college (Van Horn et al., 1997).

Similarly, physical separation between husbands and wives is a predictor of marital separation (Rindfuss &

Stephen, 1990). However, information technology and new media may make the maintenance of long-distance relationships much easier: mobile phones, Skype, Facebook and e-mail allow friends or partners who are in different places to keep up with each other, and to do so more easily and cheaply. Nevertheless, face-to-face contact remains a crucial factor in maintaining close relationships. Even among long-distance relationships, those partners who have face-to-face contact are happier and more committed than partners who do not have face-to-face contact (e.g. only letters, texts, e-mail and so on; see Dainton & Aylor, 2002).

Being physically close allows people to interact more often, and consequently there are many reasons why proximity may facilitate the development of closer relationships. More frequent interactions allow people to get to know each other better, because they provide people with opportunities to share not only more, but also more intimate aspects of their lives with each other (Altman & Taylor, 1973). More frequent interactions also lead to greater interdependence between people, because the behaviour of one person increasingly affects the outcome of the other person (Berscheid, Snyder, & Omoto, 1989). Frequent interactions also allow people to become familiar with each other, and the literature overwhelmingly shows that familiarity breeds liking.

Familiarity

The finding that familiarity is linked to liking is often linked to the **mere exposure effect** (see Chapter 6) (Zajonc, 1968). Repeated, unreinforced exposure to a large variety of stimuli, ranging from Chinese symbols to abstract paintings and music (for a review, see Bornstein, 1989), increases positive affect toward the stimulus. Put differently, the more we are exposed to a stimulus, the more we like it.

This mere exposure effect holds not only for objects, but also for people. Familiarity with a new person automatically increases liking even if we do not interact with the person. To illustrate, Moreland and Beach (1992) examined mere exposure effects on liking among students. To create mere exposure conditions, four female confederates, who were similar in appearance and attractiveness, attended different numbers of lectures over the course of the semester (zero, five, 10 and 15 times respectively). The confederates did not interact with the students, but merely attended the lectures. At the end of the semester, students were given pictures of the four confederates and rated their liking for each of them and whether they thought that the confederate was similar to them. The results provided clear evidence for the mere exposure

effect in social settings: the more often the confederate had attended the lectures, the more she was liked. This effect occurred despite the fact that students had never talked to the different confederates; they merely liked them better because they recognized their faces. The fact that people like faces that they recognize has also been linked to the averageness effect for physical attractiveness, as discussed previously (Langlois et al., 1994). In this perspective, it is assumed that people are exposed to average faces more often than to faces with unusual or rare aspects. Because they are therefore more familiar with average faces, they prefer them over unusual faces. More frequent exposure also led students to perceive the confederate as more similar to themselves than they did for confederates with whom they had little or no exposure.

Similarity

Proximity and frequent interactions with others not only allow people to become familiar with others, they also allow people to discover similarities between themselves and others. Abundant research confirms that we like others who are similar to us. Byrne (1971) employed a 'bogus stranger' paradigm in his pioneering research regarding the **similarity–attraction effect**. In this paradigm, the participant completes an attitudes questionnaire

similarity–attraction effect we like others who are similar to us; others who are like us.

(e.g. I enjoy sports; I like classical music), reads an attitudes questionnaire completed by a target person with whom he or she will soon ostensibly interact, and then evaluates the likeability of that person. The attitudes endorsed by the target person are faked in such a manner as to manipulate the degree of similarity to the participant's attitudes. Contrary to the truism that opposites attract, a strong linear relationship between similarity and liking is routinely observed – similarity reliably generates attraction and liking.

Numerous empirical studies demonstrate the similarity–attraction effect for personality traits, attitudes, hobbies and ideals, and that these forms of similarity are prevalent in satisfying relationships (for a review, see Berscheid & Reis, 1998). Moreover, similarity has been shown to be important, not only in shaping initial attraction between fictitious (Byrne, 1971) and real (Byrne, Ervin & Lamberth, 1970) strangers, but also in generating the feeling that one is understood by a dating partner and spouse (Murray, Holmes, Bellavia, Griffin, & Dolderman, 2002), and in sustaining later relationship satisfaction (Klohnen & Luo, 2003). The literature also shows that people do not necessarily have to be actually similar to each other to show these effects. Rather, in happy relationships, people tend to perceive their partners as more similar to themselves than they actually are, with the same effect: the more people perceive their partner as being similar to themselves, the happier they are in their relationship (Montoya, Horton, & Kirchner, 2008; Murray et al., 2002). Perceived similarity also predicted greater proximity (i.e. the students sat closer together in the classroom), attraction, communication and friendship intensity over a period of nine weeks among previously unacquainted undergraduates (Sunnafrank & Ramirez, 2004).

Why is similarity so important for relationships? People who are similar to us are rewarding, in that they validate our beliefs and are likely to agree with us, our opinions and values (Newcomb, 1961; see Chapter 8). In this sense, similarity is reinforcing, in that it triggers positive affective reactions toward the other (Byrne, 1971). Moreover, a partner who is 'like me' is assumed to accept the self, to understand the self's needs, and therefore to be able to gratify the self's needs, whereas a partner who is 'unlike me' is assumed to be less accepting and understanding of the self (Murray et al., 2002). Similar others are also more familiar and more predictable, creating a feeling of recognition and allowing people to reduce uncertainty about the other and communicate more easily (Berger & Calabrese, 1975). Finally, similarity and liking may feed back on each other, so that detecting similarity leads to more liking, and more liking motivates people to detect more similarities (Selfhout, Denissen, Branje, & Meeus, 2009).

Is there evidence suggesting that opposites attract? The answer is *very little*. The biggest opposite that attracts is probably the fact that most women like men and most men like women. Nevertheless, researchers have tried to find exceptions to the rule that similarity attracts. Dryer and Horowitz (1997) found that, in short interactions, dominant individuals were more satisfied interacting with individuals who were instructed to play a submissive role than with individuals who were instructed to play a dominant role. Conversely, submissive individuals were more satisfied interacting with individuals who were instructed to play a dominant role than interacting with individuals who were instructed to play a submissive role. This finding makes intuitive sense, for how could a friendship endure if each friend attempted to dominate the other, or if both friends were to be submissive and no one dare to take the lead? Despite different attempts, however, the overwhelming evidence is that similarity attracts.

As can be seen from the review above, proximity, familiarity and similarity are closely related to each other and mutually reinforce each other: We are more likely to develop friendships with others who are physically near to us. We meet and interact with them more often, which allows us to become familiar with them and discover more similarities. And discovering more similarities, in turn,

motivates us to interact with the other more frequently and be closer to him or her. Thus, proximity, familiarity and similarity are powerful factors that help people to form relationships with others who are likely to like them. This *reciprocal liking* – we like people who like us – is satisfying, rewarding and boosts our self-esteem (Taylor, Gould, & Brounstein, 1981). Often it is the situation, and sometimes even chance, that determines whether we like others and whether we develop relationships with them. It seems that one needs to be, literally, in the right place at the right time to meet the right person.

Underestimating the power of the situation

That relationships develop due to powerful influences of the situation is also illustrated by research showing that people sometimes attribute arousal caused by external circumstances to attraction toward attractive others. The most famous example of research showing this **misattribution of arousal** phenomenon is the bridge study by Dutton and Aron (1974). In their study, men either crossed the Capilano suspension bridge in North Vancouver, a shaky 135 metre-long bridge 67 metres above the Capilano River, or a safer, wider bridge about 10 metres above the river not far away (Figure 11.12). At the end of either bridge an attractive female experimenter asked the men to fill out a questionnaire in which they had to describe pictures (Thematic Apperception Test, Murray,

> **misattribution of arousal** people mistakenly attribute part of their arousal to an external stimulus that is not the actual cause of their arousal.

FIGURE 11.12 *Males crossing an arousing shaky bridge may misattribute their arousal level to an attractive female standing at the end of the bridge (Dutton & Aron, 1974).*

Source: © Maxim Petrichuk. Used under licence from Shutterstock.

1943) and gave them their telephone number so that they could call her in case they had any questions. Dutton and Aron assumed that the shaky bridge would induce arousal among the men (the bridge is quite scary), who upon seeing the attractive female experimenter would attribute the arousal to their attraction toward her, rather than to their crossing the bridge.

Consistent with Dutton and Aron's predictions, men who had crossed the shaky bridge described the pictures in a more sexual way and were more likely to call the (attractive) experimenter to inquire about the fictitious experiment than were men who had crossed the safer bridge. These differences did not occur when the experimenter was male. Although this experiment took place on a shaky bridge, it has more general implications for people on first dates. When wanting a date to be attracted to you, try to be in the right (arousing) place or situation at the right time: the exit of a roller coaster, a discotheque or the finishing line of a skiing race!

Summary

The effects of physical attractiveness on how we evaluate others and how we respond to them should not be underestimated; people automatically respond more positively towards physically attractive (as opposed to less attractive) people. Rather than being entirely in the eye of the beholder, it appears that several objective features of a face and body contribute to attractiveness (e.g. symmetry, averageness, smooth skin). This section also discussed the fact that beauty is certainly not the only factor that determines our attraction to others. Although other features of a person (e.g. similarity, familiarity) may enhance why you come to like others, interpersonal attraction can often be attributed to the circumstances and the place in which two people meet each other.

ROMANTIC RELATIONSHIPS

What determines relationship stability?

Given the mental and physical health benefits of romantic relationships that we have discussed, it is not surprising that researchers have tried to understand why some relationships fail, whereas others prevail. Indeed, in the literature on relationships, romantic relationships have been most extensively investigated. What are the

specific ingredients of a satisfying and long-lasting relationship? In the past several decades, relationship researchers have been trying to answer this basic question from a number of different theoretical perspectives, which we will briefly review below. Note that when doing so, we generally refer to studies on heterosexual relationships, as by far the most research in relationship science has focused on heterosexual relationships. However, this is not to say that the same processes may not take place within homosexual relationships – there are several studies suggesting that this is indeed the case (e.g. Duffy & Rusbult, 1986; Peplau, 1982; Wienke & Hill, 2009).

Love

'Might as well face it, you're addicted to love'.

Robert Palmer

Most romantic relationships begin with two individuals falling in love with each other. In one of his songs, the singer Robert Palmer compares love with an addiction, and many others have done the same. Is this just a matter of speech? According to the results of a study by Fisher and her colleagues, not entirely (Fisher, Aron, & Brown, 2006). The researchers invited 17 participants who were madly in love to come to the lab, and asked them to bring a picture of their loved one. Participants were then placed in a brain scanner, and their brain activity was measured while they looked at their loved one. The results were quite remarkable. When the participants gazed at a photo of their beloved, regions in the brain were activated that are tightly associated with the anticipation of reward and with focused attention. This so-called dopamine system in the brain is indeed the same system that is involved in pleasure and addiction. Fisher et al. (2006) concluded that, rather than conceiving love as an emotion, 'being in love' can better be considered a strong motivation – an addictive craving to be with the other person (Figure 11.13).

Clearly, and perhaps luckily, people generally do not remain in the same intense state of being in love throughout their relationship. Berscheid and Walster (1974) called this initial, strong motivational sense of love in the early stages of a relationship **passionate love**. Consistent with the neurophysiological results described above, they defined passionate love as a state of intense longing for union with another. After some time, love generally

> **passionate love** a state of intense longing for union with another individual, usually characterized by intrusive thinking and preoccupation with the partner, idealization of the other and the desire to know the other as well as the desire to be known by the other.

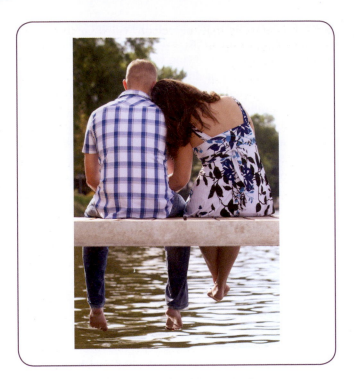

FIGURE 11.13 *Research by Helen Fisher and colleagues suggests that being in love literally means being addicted to each other.*

Source: © Andrew Jalbert. Used under licence from Shutterstock.

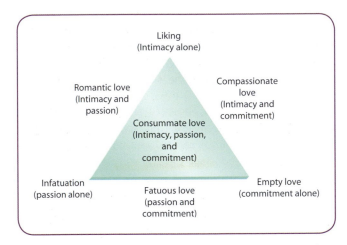

FIGURE 11.14 *The types of love as different combinations of intimacy, passion and commitment.*

Source: Based on data in Sternberg & Barnes, 1988.

companionate love refers to the feelings of intimacy and affection we feel for another person when we care deeply for the person but do not necessarily experience passion or arousal in his or her presence.

takes a somewhat different form, referred to as **companionate love**. This kind of love is defined as 'the affection and tenderness we feel for those with whom our lives are deeply intertwined' (Hatfield & Rapson, 1993, p. 9). Note that companionate love can refer to the love

you may feel for your partner, but also the love you feel for your friends and family. However, as you know, the love you feel for your partner is not exactly the same as the love you feel for a friend. What, then, distinguishes these forms of love? According to Sternberg's (1986) triangular theory of love, different forms of love consist of different combinations of three components of love, namely intimacy, passion and commitment. Intimacy encompasses feelings of closeness and connectedness; passion encompasses romance, physical attraction, and sexual consummation; commitment entails the short-term decision or realization that one loves one's partner, as well as the long-term commitment to maintain that love. Love can consist of each of these three components, combined or separately, and to varying degrees of intensity, resulting in different types of love. For example, love for a romantic partner is characterized by passion and intimacy (although passion tends to decline over the course of the relationship), while love for a friend encompasses intimacy, but not passion (see Figure 11.14).

Relationship satisfaction and stability

In contrast to what the Beatles suggested, love is not all you need. Romantic relationships do not only thrive on the basis of love: the more partners love each other, the more satisfying and stable their relationship. It is not as simple as that. In the (relatively short) history of the science of relationships, knowledge about the factors that contribute to relationship satisfaction and stability has accumulated, and we will now present a short overview.

Back in the 1950s, psychological science was dominated by behaviourism, the view that animal and human behaviour is entirely shaped by rewards and costs – how people evaluate and behave in their romantic relationship being no exception. In this tradition, **equity theory** (Adams, 1963) proposed that people are satisfied in their romantic relationships if the rewards and the costs associated with the relationship are balanced between partners – that is, if the *ratio* of rewards and costs an individual experiences is equal to the *ratio* of rewards and costs for the partner. The rewards of a relationship may be the support and love one receives, but can also consist of a nice car and a house, while the costs may be sacrifice of freedom, conflict or the burden of doing household chores. According to this perspective, a romantic relationship can be satisfying for both partners even if the rewards are not equally high. One partner

equity theory a theory that seeks to explain relationship satisfaction in terms of perceptions of fair versus unfair distributions of resources within interpersonal relationships.

may have lower rewards, but this does not really matter if the costs are also lower for this partner: as long as the *relative* rewards and costs are equal, partners perceive *equity* (i.e. the rewards and costs are distributed fairly). Although perceived equity is indeed positively related to satisfaction in the relationship, it does not predict relationship stability (Van Yperen & Buunk, 1990). In addition, other research indicates that the absolute level (rather than the ratio of rewards and costs) of rewards one perceives in a relationship is actually a better predictor of relationship satisfaction (e.g. Cate, Lloyd, Henton, & Larson, 1982).

Intuitively, this seems to make sense: the more your needs are fulfilled in a relationship, the more satisfied you are with that relationship. And yet, even if the outcomes in a relationship seem perfect – the rewards exceed the costs – does this *always* mean that an individual is satisfied? And does this *necessarily* mean that this person is motivated to continue his or her relationship? According to classic work by Kelley and Thibaut on relationships (Kelley & Thibaut, 1978), the answer to both questions is *no*, for two reasons. First, people have very different expectations about what a relationship could and should bring them. Imagine that you have been very happy and satisfied in a previous relationship. However, for some reason, the other person has broken your heart by deciding to end the relationship. The outcomes (rewards minus costs) you received in that past relationship may have formed your standard for future relationships – which Thibaut and Kelley (1959) referred to as the *comparison level* (CL). When finding a new partner, even when the rewards exceed the costs, the outcomes still may not be as high as what you expect from a relationship. Your previous relationship experiences tell you that you can do better. An individual's comparison level may not only be based on one's own prior romantic relationship experiences, but may also be influenced, for example, by what he or she has seen in other relationships, including the relationship of his or her parents.

Second, even though the outcomes of the relationship may meet your expectations, perhaps there are other attractive alternative partners that are likely to provide still better outcomes. Indeed, attractive alternatives form one of the most serious threats to the stability of a romantic relationship. As a case in point, extramarital affairs are the leading reason for divorce across 160 cultures (Betzig, 1989). Just as prior relationship experiences set a certain standard (i.e. CL), potential alternative partners also set a standard, which Thibaut and Kelley (1959) referred to as the comparison level of alternatives (CL_{alt}). As long as the outcomes an individual receives in his or her current relationship exceed the outcomes that can be received with another relationship partner – the *quality of alternatives* is

low – it is unlikely that the person will want to end the current relationship. In this case, the person is *dependent* on the relationship.

In short, according to Kelley and Thibaut's (1978, admittedly rather unromantic) analysis of a romantic relationship, a person, say Barbara, is satisfied in her relationship when the relationship provides her with the emotional and material rewards that are at least in line with, or higher than, what Barbara expects to find in a relationship. In addition, Barbara depends on the relationship to the extent that she believes that no other relationship partner can provide the same, or higher, level of outcomes for her. It is important to realize that satisfaction with and dependence on a relationship are not necessarily related. Barbara can be very satisfied with her current partner, and yet one day she meets another man who exceeds the looks and personality of her current partner, and eventually she decides to leave her relationship. In another example, if Barbara is very unsatisfied – her relationship is lower than her CL – yet feels that she has no other attractive alternative partners to turn to (i.e. her own relationship still exceeds her CL_{alt}), she is likely to remain in the relationship. Thus, the concepts CL and CL_{alt} can help us to explain why relationship dissatisfaction does not always lead to break up.

Later, Rusbult (1983, see Leader in the Field, Caryl Rusbult) argued that satisfaction and the quality of alternatives are still not sufficient to understand the stability of the relationship, and she proposed a third factor. Here, Barbara, while generally very satisfied with her relationship, meets another man she feels strongly attracted to (and who is also attracted to her). Does this mean that she will end the current relationship to start a new relationship with the attractive alternative? Not always. According to Rusbult (1983), it largely depends on the number of **investments** Barbara has already made in her relationship. She may share many mutual friends with her current partner; she has probably disclosed much of herself to her partner; part of Barbara's identity is tightly linked to her partner; they may have bought a house together, and she may even have children with her current partner. All these investments Barbara has made will be lost, at least to a large extent, when she decides to end the relationship. Thus, even in the face of an attractive alternative, prior investments in the relationship may often prevent a person from leaving the relationship.

Rusbult's *investment model*, shown in Theory Box 11.2, summarizes the factors we have discussed so far. According to the model, these three variables – satisfaction, quality of alternatives and investments – affect the level

> **investments** the level of resources (time, emotional involvement, money, self-disclosure and so on) put into a relationship, which increases the costs of withdrawing from the relationship.

THEORY BOX 11.2

THE INVESTMENT MODEL

Source: Based on Rusbult, 1983. © APA, with permission. The use of APA information does not imply endorsement by APA.

An individual's commitment to a relationship is largely determined by three factors, namely: How satisfying is the relationship? Is the relationship more – or less – rewarding than possible alternative relationships? And how much have I invested already in the relationship?

 LEADER IN THE FIELD

Caryl Rusbult (1952–2010) investigated close relationships for more than 35 years. When explaining why she got interested in long-term relationships, she blamed a persistent travelling companion on a cross-country drive from California to North Carolina. When crossing the California–Arizona boarder, her friend asked her 'Why do people stick with their partners?' Over the next two days, Caryl told him about research on proximity, similarity and physical attraction. By the time they reached Oklahoma, her friend pointed out that she had not answered his question. She had explained why people form relationships and why they like or love their partners, but she had not explained why people stay with their partners. Caryl realized that research had failed to answer this question and set out to change relationship science. As a result, she developed the *investment model* to help explain why people stick to their partners even when the relationship is not particularly satisfying. Caryl Rusbult succeeded in changing relationship science by recognizing the dynamic nature of relationships, the mutual influence relationship partners have on each other and the various levels of interdependence that make relationships work and that motivate relationship partners to stay with each other.

relationship commitment an individual's intent to maintain the relationship and to remain psychologically attached to it.

of **relationship commitment** a person experiences to the relationship: the more satisfied, the lower the quality of alternatives; and the more prior investments, the more committed a person will be to the relationship. Relationship commitment is defined here as an individual's intent to maintain the relationship and to remain psychologically attached to it (Rusbult, 1980) The investment model emphasizes that commitment is the key to relationship stability and couple well-being, because it motivates partners to act and think in the interests of the relationship. You can read more about this in Research Close-Up 11.3.

Thoughts and behaviours that enhance relationship functioning

Whether we like it or not, even (or particularly) in romantic relationships we may at times feel irritated or even hurt by our partner. Imagine Peter returning home from work, smashing the doors and shouting at his partner Barbara when she asks him something. Barbara's initial impulse may be to shout back, which is likely to make things worse, not better. Instead, she may try not to behave destructively in return, but to respond in a constructive manner. She may assume that Peter has had a bad day at the office and decide that it is better to leave him alone for a while. She may even ask Peter if there is something she can do to cheer him up. Behaving constructively in the face of a partner's destructive responses is called *accommodation*. Research has shown that highly, as compared to weakly, committed partners are more likely to accommodate when the partner behaves badly (Rusbult, Verette, Whitney, Slovik, & Lipkus, 1991).

Similarly, research on **forgiveness** – defined as a prosocial motivational change toward the offender, despite his or her hurtful behaviour (McCullough et al., 1998) – has demonstrated that responding in a forgiving rather than retaliatory manner towards a partner's hurtful acts generally promotes relationship satisfaction and longevity (Fincham, 2000; Fincham, Paleari, & Regalia, 2002; Karremans & Van Lange, 2004; Paleari, Regalia, & Fincham, 2005). Relationship commitment again is a strong predictor of whether people are willing to forgive a relationship partner (Finkel, Rusbult, Kumashiro, & Hannon, 2002; Karremans & Aarts, 2007). Forgiveness, however, not only depends on the features of the relationship with the offender, but is also determined by personality factors. Put differently, some people are simply better than others at forgiving a partner. For example, individuals who have high self-control, who have an agreeable personality and those who are low on neuroticism are more likely to forgive their relationship partners (e.g. McCullough, Bellah, Kilpatrick, & Johnson, 2001). And not only does forgiveness promote relationship functioning, it also pays off to forgive a partner at the individual level: forgiveness positively affects a person's mental and even physical health, especially when a person feels strongly committed to maintain his or her relationship with the offender (for an overview, see Karremans & Van Lange, 2008).

forgiveness forgiveness is defined as a prosocial motivational change toward the offender, despite the offender's hurtful behaviour.

Commitment also promotes **willingness to sacrifice**, defined as the tendency to forego self-interest

willingness to sacrifice the tendency to forego immediate self-interest to promote the well-being of the partner or the relationship.

WHY SOME WOMEN REMAIN IN ABUSIVE RELATIONSHIPS

RESEARCH CLOSE-UP 11.3

Rusbult, C. E., & Martz, J. M. (1995). Remaining in an abusive relationship: An investment model analysis of nonvoluntary dependence. *Personality and Social Psychology Bulletin, 21*, 558–571.

Introduction

To answer the question of why battered women some-times choose to stay with their abusive partners, this study applied Rusbult's *investment model* (e.g. Rusbult, 1980, 1983). Based on this model, the authors predicted that satisfaction would not be a reliable predictor of stay/leave behaviour, but that abused women would feel more com-mitted to their partner and would be more likely to stay in their abusive relationships when (a) they have limited or poor-quality alternatives, and (b) when they had invested more in their relationship.

Method and procedure

The participants were 100 women who sought refuge in a shelter for battered women in the US. Women were on average 29 years old and had 2.4 children. They had suf-fered relatively severe abuse, including being thrown down stairs, having a gun put in their mouth, or systematically having their fingers broken. Within 48 hours of their arrival at the shelter the women were interviewed by a staff mem-ber. During the interview several questions were asked to measure the central factors of the investment model. For example, for *commitment*, the interviewer asked whether the woman intended to separate from the partner (0 = *definitely*, 1 = *thinking about it*, 2 = *definitely not*). For *sat-isfaction*, questions like 'Do you have any positive feelings remaining for your partner?' (*yes – no*) were asked. For the *quality of alternatives*, the interviewer asked questions like 'Do you generally have transportation?' (*yes – no*), 'What is your level of education?' (*none – university degree*) and 'Are you currently employed?' (*yes – no*). Finally, to meas-ure *investments*, the interviewer asked questions like 'How many children do you have?' (*number of children*) and 'How long have you had a relationship with your partner for?' (*duration of relationship in months*). Stay/leave behaviour was assessed via telephone calls, at 3, 6, and 12 months

after departure from the shelter. Thirty-five women returned to their partner within three months, 30 returned within a year, and 32 never returned.

Results

Consistent with their hypotheses, Rusbult and Martz found that lower quality of alternatives and greater invest-ment size predicted both more commitment and less frequent leaving behaviour. Satisfaction was, as hypoth-esized, not reliably related to commitment or stay/leave behaviour, although women who returned to their part-ner tended to report somewhat more positive feelings for him and made more benign attributions for the abuse. Battered women reported stronger commitment when they had poor alternatives (e.g. less education, no means of transportation) and when they had invested more in the relationship (e.g. their relationship lasted longer, they had children with the abuser).

Discussion

Applying the investment model to women in abusive relationships allowed the researchers to explain why bat-tered women stay in such relationships. While previous research seemed to suggest that battered women 'are crazy' to stick to their relationships ('why else would a woman chose to return to a husband who nearly beats her to death?'), the investment model shed a whole new light on the reasons why battered women stay in their relationships: women who return to their partners follow-ing intense abuse do so due to structural dependence: (a) poor alternatives; and (b) high investments. These findings have major practical implications, in that they suggest that abused women may have less of a need for therapy and more of a need for alternative interventions and practical help (e.g. education, help with finding a job that can pay for a car, etc.).

---

to promote the well-being of the partner or the relation-ship (Van Lange et al., 1997). Although romantic partners often have compatible preferences or needs (i.e. they both want the same thing), sometimes the interests of both part-ners may be in conflict. Suppose Peter and Barbara visit a small village with two restaurants, one Indian, the other

Italian. They decide to have dinner, but Peter prefers the Indian, and Barbara prefers the Italian restaurant. In such situations, committed partners are more likely to make sacrifices, by foregoing their own preference for the good of the partner and relationship. This may occur in such mundane situations as deciding where to have dinner, but may also involve more serious decisions, such as deciding where to live, which job to take and so on. Partners in romantic relationships that are characterized by relatively high levels of sacrifice on the part of both partners do indeed have a higher chance of staying together (Van Lange et al., 1997).

An important reason why acts like accommodation and willingness to sacrifice promote relationship well-being and stability is that such acts *communicate* commitment to the relationship (Wieselquist, Rusbult, Foster, & Agnew, 1999). For example, when Barbara acts constructively when Peter acts nastily, Peter may infer from this, consciously or unconsciously, that Barbara must be committed to the relationship – why else would she act so nicely? After all, when Peter is acting constructively himself, he does so because he is committed to the relationship (see Chapter 5 on self-perception theory). The same may happen when Barbara sacrifices her own needs to make Peter happy; she must be committed to do so. Such acts of kindness promote Peter's trust in Barbara, fuelling his own commitment to the relationship. Wieselquist and colleagues (1999) termed this dyadic process the 'cyclical growth model' of relationships: if both partners act in ways that benefit the other partner and the relationship, this will breed trust in each other, which in turn will promote commitment in both partners, which in turn will promote acts that benefit the partner and the relationship, and so on.

Commitment not only promotes *behaviour* that benefits the relationship: committed partners also tend to *think* about their relationship and partner in a way that benefits the relationship. For example, committed partners tend to see more positive characteristics in their partner, than the partner sees in himself or herself, and they perceive their partner more positively than the typical partner (Murray, Holmes, & Griffin, 1996). Also, committed partners generally believe that their relationship has more positive features and fewer negative features than the average relationship – referred to as perceived **relationship superiority** (Buunk & Van der Eijnden, 1997). An elegant study by Rusbult, Van Lange, Wildschut, Yovetich, and Verette (2000) demonstrated that committed partners especially do so when the relationship is threatened. Participants, all college students involved in a romantic relationship, were asked to write down the positive and negative features that distinguished their relationship from the average relationship. However, before doing so, half of the participants received the following instructions: 'We are especially interested in college students' dating relationships, because previous research has demonstrated that in comparison to other types of relationships,

> **relationship superiority** the tendency of romantically involved individuals to perceive their own relationship as better than the average relationship.

college students' relationships are less likely to persist over time . . . Of course, this is not necessarily true for all college students' relationships – it is simply true on average'. In this manner, the researchers attempted to induce psychological threat to the relationship. The other half of the participants, those in the control condition, did not receive this relationship threatening information.

The results of the study showed that participants who were highly committed to their relationship listed relatively more positive, and fewer negative, features of their relationship than those who were only weakly committed. But importantly, this was especially the case among participants who had received the threat instructions. In other words, commitment induces partners to boost the positive image of their relationship, especially when the relationship is threatened. And it works: a second, longitudinal, study demonstrated that partners who perceived more relationship superiority were more likely to still be together 20 months later.

We have already discussed the potential threat of attractive alternatives. Committed partners have several efficient ways of dealing with them. First, they simply tend to pay less attention to them, and partners who are indeed inattentive to attractive alternatives are more likely to stay in their relationship (Miller, 1997). Second, committed partners tend to devalue the attractiveness of alternative partners, referred to as **derogation of alternatives**. That is, when asked to evaluate the attractiveness of attractive opposite-sex others, people in a committed heterosexual romantic relationship typically give lower attractiveness ratings than people who are not in a romantic relationship (Johnson & Rusbult, 1989; Simpson et al., 1990). Several studies indeed confirm that romantically involved individuals devalue attractive opposite-sex others, rather than singles enhancing attractive others (Lydon, Fitzsimons, & Naidoo, 2003; Ritter, Karremans, & Van Schie, 2010).

> **derogation of alternatives** the tendency of romantically involved individuals, as compared to singles, to give lower attractiveness ratings to attractive opposite-sex others.

To summarize, relationship commitment is a central factor in promoting behaviours and cognitions that not only helps partners to stay together, but also to have a well-functioning relationship. Especially when the road gets rocky – when partners experience conflict, have conflicting preferences, or when attractive alternatives present themselves – commitment helps partners to get through difficult times and helps them to protect their relationship.

Before continuing, we should briefly discuss an additional view on romantic relationship satisfaction and persistence – the *self-expansion model*. This model, developed by Aron and Aron (1986), is based on the idea that people have a fundamental motivation for self-expansion – they continuously seek psychological growth, knowledge and different perspectives. One way to fulfil this central need for self-expansion is to form relationships with others (Aron & Aron, 1986). In a romantic relationship, partners are satisfied as long as the relationship contributes to self-expansion (Aron, Aron, Tudor, & Nelson, 1991).

Moreover, when people experience self-expansion in a relationship, one could say that the identities of the two partners may become merged; the partner is 'included in the self' (Aron et al., 1991). There is some intriguing evidence that this may almost literally be the case (see Research Close-Up 11.4).

INCLUDING THE OTHER IN SELF

RESEARCH CLOSE-UP 11.4

Aron, A., Aron, E. N., Tudor, M., & Nelson, G. (1991). Close relationships as including other in the self. *Journal of Personality and Social Psychology, 60,* 241–253.

Introduction

According to the self-expansion model, when partners become involved in a relationship, their identities increasingly overlap over time. This experiment tested whether, in line with the general tenet of the self-expansion model, partners in relationships would indeed 'merge' with each other, whereby partners 'include the other in the self'. The present research set out to test whether relationship partners may sometimes literally confuse the self and the partner. Specifically, when processing information about the partner, people may sometimes process this information *as if* it were information about the self.

Method

Participants, who were all married, first completed a questionnaire in which they indicated for 90 traits (e.g. creative, introverted) to what extent each trait applied to themselves, and their partner, for each person in turn (on a 7-point scale, ranging from 1 = *extremely like me*, to 7 = *unlike me*, and 1 = *extremely like partner*, to 7 = *unlike partner*). Note that in this manner there are two categories of traits: First, there are traits that are *similar* for both the self and spouse, in that a trait is either descriptive for both (i.e. with scores < 4 for both self and spouse), or not descriptive for both (i.e. with scores > 4 for both self and spouse). Second, there are traits that are *different* for self and spouse, in that a trait is descriptive for one, but not for the other.

Later in the study the participants carried out a second task. The same 90 traits were presented in turn on a computer screen, and participants had to decide as quickly and accurately as possible whether or not the trait applied to themselves by pressing a 'me' or 'not me' button.

Results

If participants indeed 'confused' themselves with their spouse, the researchers predicted that participants in the second task would have more difficulty in responding with 'me' or 'not me' to traits that were different between self and spouse (descriptive for one, but not for the other) than to traits that were similar for both (descriptive for both, or not descriptive for both). This is exactly what the authors found: participants were significantly slower in responding either 'me' or 'not me' to traits that were different between self and partner than to traits that were similar for both (see Figure 11.15). Moreover, participants also made more 'mistakes' for traits that were different between self and partner (e.g. they responded with 'me' to a trait which they had initially indicated was not applicable to themselves, but was applicable to their partner).

Conclusion

These results strongly suggest that partners may actually 'include the other in the self'. When participants have to respond quickly to indicate whether or not a certain trait is applicable to themselves, the results suggest that the partner's traits are to some extent also taken into account, presumably because the partner is part of the self, leading to slower response times and more mistakes. Thus, a close relationship can indeed lead to confusion between self and other.

FIGURE 11.15 *Mean response times for traits on which self and spouse were 'same' versus 'different'.*

Source: Based on Aron et al., 1991. © APA, with permission. The use of APA information does not imply endorsement by APA.

Most loving relationships are perceived as self-expanding when they start: being in love is an arousing experience in itself, and not only do fresh couples often engage in novel activities: partners may inspire each other by providing, and adopting, different views and perspectives in life. However, after some time, when novelty and passion are declining, boredom may surface. According to the self-expansion model, preventing boredom is the key to a successful relationship. Consistent with this idea, a longitudinal study found that experienced boredom in a relationship predicts relationship dissatisfaction nine years later (Tsapelas, Aron, & Orbuch, 2009).

Summary

Long-lasting and well-functioning romantic relationships are characterized by both partners being strongly committed to the relationship. Strong commitment, which is based on satisfaction, investments and quality of alternatives, induces partners to behave in a pro-relationship manner, especially when the road gets rocky. Committed partners are more likely to forgive each other's mishaps, shield themselves from attractive others, and are more focused on the positive aspects of their relationship. According to the self-expansion model, the identity of two partners may even become merged.

GENERAL RELATIONSHIP PROCESSES

What are the general processes that characterize relationships?

Having focused specifically on romantic relationships, we will continue by discussing a number of processes that are common to all types of relationships, although they sometimes differ in their intensity or meaning across relationships. Below we will address two processes that have been found to affect relationship initiation, development and maintenance: what and how much information relationship partners disclose to each other, and how responsive one's partner is perceived to be. However, before discussing these processes, let us first explore the types of relationships that can be distinguished.

Types of relationships

Although people generally know quite well whether they have a relationship with another person, researchers have struggled with the definition of the term 'relationship'. What seems so obvious in everyday life is sometimes hard to capture in a scientific definition. Although researchers still have different definitions of relationships, most agree that in order to have a relationship, people need to depend on each other, that is, to be mutually *interdependent*. People are interdependent when the cognitive, affective or behavioural outcomes of one person are dependent on the other person (Kelley, 1997; Rusbult & Van Lange, 1996). For example, when Barbara helps Peter to prepare for an upcoming exam rather than going out with her friends, Peter will feel appreciated and supported. In this case Peter's feelings are interdependent with Barbara's behaviour, because what Barbara does affects Peter.

The assumption that to have a relationship people need to be interdependent sheds an interesting light on the role of anger in the deterioration of relationships. Indeed, contrary to the assumption that anger is the most important source of relationship endings, the assumption that people have relationships when they are interdependent suggests that *indifference* may be at least as bad for relationships as anger. When Barbara and Peter are angry at each other, they still are interdependent: what one partner does affects the other, even when it is in a negative way. It is when Barbara's behaviour does not make any difference for Peter any more that one may wonder whether they even have a relationship.

Although people are interdependent in all their relationships, obviously people have many different types of relationships that vary on a variety of dimensions. In the literature, researchers have identified a number of dimensions that allow us to distinguish between different types of relationships. Clark and Mills (1979) distinguished between *exchange* and *communal relationships*. In **exchange relationships** people give each other benefits only when they are likely to receive a comparable benefit in return. To illustrate, people may have an exchange relationship with a plumber: the plumber fixes their leaking pipe and the client pays the plumber the appropriate amount of money for the work done. In **communal relationships**, people exchange benefits according to each partner's needs without expecting something in return: partners are concerned with each other's welfare, rather than the deservingness of the benefits. To illustrate, a wife may cancel a party to stay at home with her sick husband because she genuinely cares about his well-being, not because she expects something in return.

exchange relationship refers to an interpersonal association between individuals who are concerned with what their partner gets and what they themselves receive to ensure equitable benefits.

communal relationship refers to an interpersonal association between individuals who are more concerned with what their partner gets rather than what they themselves receive, or relationships in which people's primary concern is being responsive to the other person's needs.

Similarly, a friend may help you to move your belongings to your new apartment on a cold, rainy Saturday morning because that's what friends are for. As can be seen from the examples, the distinction between exchange and communal relationships often covaries with intimacy and closeness. Exchange relationships are typically less close and intimate than communal relationships.

The literature also distinguishes between horizontal or reciprocal relationships and vertical or complementary relationships (Finkenauer, Engels, Branje, & Meeus, 2004; Hinde, 1979). Horizontal relationships are egalitarian and involve reciprocal exchanges of benefits, such as knowledge, care, support or disclosure. To illustrate, friendships are typical horizontal relationships: both friends receive and provide care. Vertical relationships are hierarchical and involve unequal – or complementary – exchanges of benefits. For example, in parent–child relationships the child typically receives care; the parents typically provide care.

Another important dimension is the voluntariness of the relationship. In voluntary relationships (e.g. friends, dating partners), people lack any formal bonds to maintain an intimate, stable relationship. On the contrary, in involuntary relationships (parent–child relationships, arranged marriage) formal bonds, such as biological ties or social structures, add to the persistence of the relationship.

The most important voluntary relationships throughout life are friendships (Wiseman, 1986). Friends are the first relationships children develop outside their family, and having friends is a norm even among very young children. Among adolescents, having at least one friend to confide in is often considered as a social achievement and an indicator of social competence (Hartup, 1996). Based on a review of existing friendship questionnaires, Mendelson and Aboud (1999) identified six functions of friendships: (1) stimulating companionship (e.g. doing fun activities together); (2) help (e.g. offering assistance); (3) intimacy (e.g. being open to honest disclosures of personal information); (4) reliable alliances (e.g. being loyal); (5) self-validation (e.g. allowing friends to maintain a positive self-image); and (6) emotional security (e.g. providing comfort in novel or threatening situations). Friendships thereby provide a context in which basic human needs are satisfied (Demir & Özdemir, 2010). Importantly, they provide people with opportunities to establish and reinforce social skills that are important to the development and maintenance of close relationships (Dunn, 2004). Not surprisingly, the skills that are established in friendships, including problem-solving skills, conflict resolution and empathy, are correlated with well-being and satisfaction in adulthood (Dishion & Nelson, 2007; Hartup & Stevens, 1997). Frequent contact with friends remains an important source of well-being not only in adulthood, but even in old age (Pinquart & Sörensen, 2000).

As we mentioned earlier, people also have relationships that are qualitatively different, such as homosexual relationships, or relationships between two people from different cultural backgrounds. People in these types of relationships face particular difficulties (e.g. societal pressures, prejudice) that heterosexual couples or couples from the same cultural background do not have to deal with. Without doubt these difficulties may affect relational functioning. Nevertheless, some processes characterize all relationships, as is reflected in this statement by Huston and Schwartz (1995) concerning homosexual relationships: 'The relationships formed by lesbians and gay men are in many ways very similar to heterosexual ones.' (p. 120.) Thus, despite their differences, some processes are similar in different types of relationships. In the following, we turn to two such processes, focusing on the effects of disclosure that relationship partners engage in, and the effects of partners' responsiveness to each other's needs.

Disclosure

Imagine that it is your first day at college and you are sitting next to your fellow student in the psychology introductory lecture. What do you say to each other? You probably start by telling each other where you are from and why you picked that particular university. While talking to each other you discover that you share a similar interest in psychology. Because you discover that the other is similar to you (see the section on similarity above), you tell the other student a bit more about your interests and the activities you engage in outside of the university. You then discover that you both like the same bar downtown, and agree to meet there next Friday night. This meeting may mark the beginning of a relationship, a friendship, a romantic relationship, or a companionship between two students who help each other in times of need.

Verbally revealing information about oneself to another person is called **self-disclosure** (Jourard, 1971). Self-disclosure is important in every type of interpersonal relationship, from business partnerships to love affairs, from friends to parent–child relationships, from housemates to long-distance relatives (Rubin, 1973).

> **self-disclosure** verbally revealing information about oneself to another person.

The imaginary exercise above shows how disclosure and relationships can influence and change each other. A meta-analysis of 94 studies by Collins and Miller (1994) provides convincing evidence for this suggestion. Their analysis revealed that (a) we disclose more to people we like; (b) we like people more after having disclosed to them; and (c) we like people who disclose more. Thus, once people disclose information to another person, they start liking the other more, especially if the other is responsive to their needs and values them (Reis & Shaver, 1988). Liking and intimacy, in turn, appear necessary conditions for the disclosure of more intimate personal information in relationships (e.g. Hendrick, 1981). Importantly, when one person discloses information about himself or herself, the other also likes the person more, and, in turn, discloses more information about himself or herself. In the literature this is called **disclosure reciprocity**, because people tend to match each other's level of self-disclosure, disclosing more if the other person does so and disclosing less if the other's self-disclosure declines (Cunningham, Strassberg, & Haan, 1986). As described by social penetration theory (Altman & Taylor, 1973; see Theory Box 11.3 & Figure 11.6), adults and children increase the depth and breadth of their self-disclosure to people they like (Buhrmester & Prager, 1995) and decrease the level of self-disclosure to people they do not like, which often signals the beginning of the end of a relationship (Baxter, 1987).

disclosure reciprocity
people tend to match each other's level of self-disclosure.

Mundane as well as intimate self-disclosure is important to maintain relationships. Catching up with each other at the end of a day (Sigman, 1991) by telling the other what one did, whom one saw, what rumours one heard, how the day went, or who called, signals to the relationship partner that the relationship is intact and that one is committed to it (Duck, Rutt, Hurst, & Strejc, 1991). Sharing intimate information with each other is the most frequently reported strategy to maintain relationships with friends, relatives and lovers (Canary, Stafford, Hause, &

Wallace, 1993; Parks & Floyd, 1996). Not surprisingly, sharing secrets – having a secret together and exchanging the secret information – is one of the most powerful means of creating feelings of intimacy and closeness among adult secret-keepers (Finkenauer, Kubacka, Engels, & Kerkhof, 2009) and children (Furman & Bierman, 1984). Secrets often concern intimate information that people do not want to share with others, because it makes them vulnerable to being hurt (e.g. ridicule, rejection, humiliation; e.g. Petronio 1991, 2002). Consequently, when a person wants to share a secret, he or she has to rely on the other's integrity, has to trust that person to protect it, and has to be willing to become dependent on the other.

These positive effects of self-disclosure for relationship development and maintenance emerge not only in face-to-face interactions, but also in online communications in adolescence (Valkenburg & Peter, 2009; see also Social Psychology Beyond the Lab 11.2). Because Internet communication involves fewer verbal and non-verbal cues and is thereby less complex than face-to-face communication, adolescents become *hyperpersonal* – that is, unusually intimate – in their disclosure on the Internet. However, positive effects of online disclosure only hold for adolescents who use the Internet to maintain existing relationships (Bessière, Kiesler, Kraut, & Boneva, 2008). Adolescents who use the Internet mainly to form new contacts do not show these beneficial effects of disclosure for relationship quality (Valkenburg & Peter, 2007).

How can we explain this lack of relationship-enhancing effects of disclosure for people with large groups of new friends? In the literature on disclosure and liking, researchers distinguish between generalized disclosure and dyadic disclosure (Dindia, 1994; Finkenauer et al., 2004). Generalized disclosure occurs when a person self-discloses, on average, to everyone. Dyadic disclosure

THEORY BOX 11.3

SOCIAL PENETRATION THEORY

The theory proposes that, as relationships develop, self-disclosure proceeds from superficial to more intimate topics, moving progressively further and further into a person's personality. Personality is likened to an onion, which consists of different layers, ranging from superficial qualities (e.g. weight, gender and other 'public' information) to extremely intimate qualities (e.g. beliefs, traumatic experiences and other 'private' information). As relationships develop, self-disclosure helps to 'peel' away the outer layers of personality, revealing more and more intimate information about the personality of the discloser. Progress is made along two dimensions: (1) depth – social penetration processes proceed from superficial to intimate levels of disclosure; (2) breadth – as interaction continues, disclosures spread to different areas.

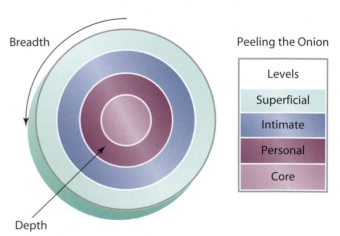

FIGURE 11.16 *Social Penetration Theory.*

Source: Scott McLean, *Business Communication for Success* (2010). Some rights reserved. Used with permission of Flat World Knowledge, Inc. www.flatworldknowledge.com

SOCIAL PSYCHOLOGY BEYOND THE LAB 11.2

ONLINE DATING

Imagine you were single and wanted to get a date, how would you go about it? You could do it the old-fashioned way: have a crush on a class-mate, wait for the right moment to ask him or her out, then pop the question, risking that he or she says no, and in that case, go through the motions with another person. Or you could do it in one of two modern ways. You could register for a speed-dating event, during which you have 10–25 dates, each of about four minutes, and hope that one of these dates reciprocates your interest and that you form a match and subsequently arrange a traditional date. Alternatively, you could engage in online dating.

Online dating is getting more and more popular: the threshold of initiating contact is extremely low (often a mouse click is sufficient) and the number of attractive alternatives is seemingly endless. Given the ease with which one can check out these alternatives, and potentially meet the love of one's life, it is almost surprising that people would prefer to go through the often nerve-wracking experience of a face-to-face interaction. But does online dating live up to its promises? Not really, it seems.

In their research, Frost, Chance, Norton, and Ariely (2008) find that using the Internet to identify a potential mate leads to inefficient and unsatisfactory dating outcomes. Many people surf the web for hours to find the 'right' one. They make lists of traits and characteristics that they think will be important for them to fall in love with a potential partner. Given all the options, and the shopping-style interface most dating sites use, it almost seems that one can choose a date in the same way as choosing a watch or dog food. People select the searchable attributes that they think are important (e.g. religion, height, weight, hair colour, age, income, hobbies). The list looks perfect, and people think that a person who has all these attributes must be the right one. But, as Frost et al. show, people are often disappointed when actually meeting the date that looked so perfect in virtual reality. In true reality there is a mismatch between what people think they want in a partner and what they experience when being with him or her (see also Norton, Frost, & Ariely, 2007, and the speed dating findings by Eastwick & Finkel, 2008). Moreover, a study by Toma, Hancock, and Ellison (2008) among online daters revealed that 80 per cent of the participants lied about at least one of the searchable attributes, especially those participants who had scores that deviated a lot from the sample mean. To give an example, the weight these participants reported in their online profiles deviated more from their observed weight than the information of people scoring closer to the sample mean. Women often lied about their weight and men about their height. Although the lies were usually not extreme, they certainly contributed to the disappointment people experienced when actually meeting the online date.

To explain people's disappointment with online dating, Frost et al. suggest that people are 'experience goods': you need to feel, see, smell and hear another person to see whether he or she feels right. You need to experience how the person makes you feel to decide whether he or she is right for you. Indeed when Frost et al. offered people a chance to go on a virtual date, where they were able to get to know the other person by exploring a virtual environment with him or her, they were much more likely to like the other person when subsequently meeting them for real than when they had met their partner through a searchable dating site. Thus, online dating sites need to provide people with opportunities to experience potential partners. Until they do, you may be better off opting for the old-fashioned way of dating.

---

occurs when people uniquely disclose information to certain relationship partners. Research suggests that in relationships between married partners and siblings generalized disclosure is not, and sometimes is even negatively, related to relationship satisfaction, while dyadic disclosure is strongly positively related to relationship satisfaction (Finkenauer et al., 2004). Eastwick and his colleagues (Eastwick, Finkel, Mochon, & Ariely, 2007) found similar effects for generalized versus dyadic liking in their speed-dating research. They found that people liked another person less when they felt that this person liked everybody, but that people liked a person more when they felt that the liking was unique to them personally. Thus, people have a need to feel special in a relationship, and they cannot feel special when a person discloses information to everybody, when the person likes everybody, or, when he or she has many 'followers' on Twitter and large groups of 'friends' on Facebook.

Perceived partner responsiveness

One cannot talk about self-disclosure without talking about **perceived partner responsiveness** (Reis & Shaver, 1988). Would you continue telling someone about how unfairly your teacher treated you in the last exam if the person checks his or her mobile while you are almost in tears? You probably would not, because the other person's behaviour clearly signals that you and your story are not important to him or her, and he or she does not care specifically about you and your need for validation.

> **perceived partner responsiveness** the perception that a relationship partner is responsive to our needs.

To disclose intimate information to another person, people need to feel that the other person understands, values and cares for the self (Reis, Clark, & Holmes, 2004). To tell another person about one's deepest thoughts and feelings, people need to feel accepted. When people feel that the other person tries to change them, or that he or she does not pay attention, they feel that the other does not accept them. This makes them feel bad about themselves (e.g. 'I do not fulfil my partner's ideals, I'm unworthy') and about the relationship (e.g. 'Why would he try to change me if he loved me?'; 'She couldn't care less about me') (Overall, Fletcher, & Simpson, 2006). Not surprisingly, people, both adults and children, disclose to people whom they trust, people who are non-judgemental, and people who are responsive to their need to be accepted as they are (e.g. Kelly & McKillop, 1996) and with whom they have good relationships (Buhrmester & Prager, 1995; Finkenauer et al., 2004). When people feel that the other does not accept them as they are and tries to change them into someone they are not, they not only stop disclosing information to them, they may even end the relationship (Overall et al., 2006). Thus, to disclose information about yourself to others, you need to feel that the other is responsive to you and your needs.

A person is responsive when he or she enacts behaviour that addresses your needs: she smiles when you reveal something funny, she validates your fears about an upcoming presentation, she shows interest when you tell her about your recent solo trip to South America, or she expresses indignation when you tell her about the fact that your ex-boyfriend broke up by sending a text message to your mobile phone. Your interpretation of her behaviour as being responsive is more important for the development of intimacy in your relationship with her than is her actual response (Laurenceau, Feldman Barrett, & Pietromonaco, 1998; Lemay, Clark, & Feeney, 2007; Reis & Shaver, 1988). So, the perception that a partner is responsive is somewhat independent of the partner's actual responsiveness, mostly because people exaggerate their partner's responsiveness: they perceive their partner as being more responsive than the partner reports themselves as being (Murray et al., 1996).

A diary study by Laurenceau, Feldman Barrett, and Rovine (2005) among 96 married couples underlines the close link between disclosure, responsiveness, and relationship maintenance. In their study they asked both husbands and wives to complete a diary every evening for six weeks. Every evening, the couples reported how much they had disclosed to their spouse during the day, whether they perceived that their partner had disclosed to them, whether they felt that their partner was responsive while they disclosed to him or her, and how close they felt to their spouse. Both self-disclosure and perceived partner disclosure predicted the intimacy people felt toward their spouse. Importantly, perceived partner responsiveness partially mediated the link between disclosure and intimacy. This means that disclosure increased intimacy both directly and indirectly through the influence of perceived partner responsiveness (see Figure 11.17): the more spouses disclosed information to their partner on one day, the more intimate they felt with their partner the next day, partly because they felt that their partner was responsive to their needs. Thus, to feel intimate, the spouse who discloses needs to perceive the listener's responses as being understanding, accepting and caring.

Attachment theory (Bowlby, 1982; see Leader in the Field, John Bowlby, earlier in this chapter) and the research it inspired (e.g. Ainsworth, Bell, & Stayton, 1974; De Wolff & Van Ijzendoorn, 1997; Landry, Smith, & Swank, 2006), underlines the fact that perceived partner responsiveness is not only important in horizontal relationships, but also in vertical relationships. Parental responsiveness – that is, a prompt, contingent and appropriate reaction to the child's needs – influences the course of children's psychosocial development (Collins, Maccoby, Steinberg, Hetherington, & Bornstein, 2000). Children whose parents were sensitive and responsive to their needs are more securely attached, have better social skills and show greater academic accomplishments. Parents' responsive reactions to children's distress (e.g. comforting, helping) are associated with children's better and more adequate regulation of negative emotions, and also with their ability to feel empathy for others and their prosocial behaviour (Davidov & Grusec, 2006).

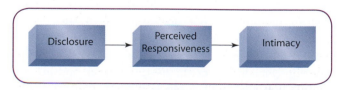

FIGURE 11.17 *A model of the mediating role of perceived responsiveness in the link between disclosure and intimacy.*

Although responsiveness and disclosure reciprocity are important in almost all relationships, their importance varies across types of relationships. Typically, you expect your friends, parents and siblings to be responsive, and you expect to disclose information to them, yet you would probably not expect the same from your children. Indeed, as we have mentioned earlier, vertical or complementary relationships involve unequal exchanges of benefits. Parents provide care and children receive care; family members of disabled people provide support and help, disabled people receive support and help (hopefully; see also Chapter 10 on the potentially unequal relationship between help-givers and help-recipients). Similarly, responsiveness and disclosure reciprocity are unequal in complementary relationships. Commonly, children disclose to their parents, but parents do not necessarily reciprocate their children's disclosure to avoid burdening them with their worries and fears (Amato & Afifi, 2006; Finkenauer et al., 2004). Also, parents typically may not expect children to be responsive to their needs, while children expect parents to be responsive to their needs, wishes and desires.

Relationship ending

As we have discussed in this and the previous section, maintenance processes, disclosure and responsiveness are at the heart of happy, harmonious and lasting relationships. It is not surprising that relationships become conflictual or even end when one of these ingredients is lacking. This is illustrated in a study by Markman (1981), who followed ninety couples from the time when they planned to get married till five and a half years later. In the initial phase of the study, couples completed a self-report questionnaire on their satisfaction with the relationship and rated the intensity of any problems they experienced in their relationship. They were also asked to discuss their major problem area by taking turns in both the discloser and the listener role. During this discussion, the couples rated their partner's responsiveness to their disclosure on a scale, ranging from 'super negative' to 'super positive'. At a one-year follow-up, initial satisfaction was positively associated with current marital adjustment, and problem intensity was negatively associated with adjustment. There was no association with the initial ratings on partner's responsiveness. However, at the later follow-ups (two and a half and five years later), only the ratings of partners' responsiveness during the communication predicted current marital adjustment. Those couples that had indicated – before getting married – that partner responsiveness was more positive were more likely to be satisfied with their marriage five years later. In contrast, those couples that

had indicated that partner responsiveness was negative became distressed over time. Thus, a simple rating of the quality of communication in the couple was able to predict marital distress five years later, suggesting that it is less important what couples argue about than how they argue and how they respond to each other.

And if a relationship ends, be it a romantic relationship, friendship or family relationship, this can have a strong impact on the partners involved. Of course, in some cases, such as the battered women in Research Close-Up 11.3, partners may be better off when they end a relationship. Still, on average, people who have been divorced suffer strong declines in their mental and physical health, both in the short and long term (Richards, Hardy, & Wadsworth, 1997). The end of a marriage not only results in the loss of economic resources, but may also involve the loss of a social network. And perhaps most importantly, the end of a marriage or a long-term (romantic) relationship is such a painful process because it often entails the end of an attachment bond. Indeed, partners often form a strong emotional attachment that cannot easily be dissolved or replaced. This is also one of the reasons why people generally find it so difficult to end a relationship. Individuals with an anxious/ambivalent attachment style especially have a hard time dealing with break-up, because it often confirms and reinforces their anxiety about being abandoned (Davis, Shaver, & Vernon, 2003). Furthermore, as we have seen in this chapter, early relationship experiences – including the dissolution of a relationship – may importantly affect our expectations about future relationships. For example, a troublesome romantic break-up may erode an individual's trust in potential future relationship partners, and it may therefore be harder to find a new partner. Most research findings suggest that the decline and dissolution of a long-term relationship is generally associated with suffering for one partner, and in most cases both partners. We can therefore only hope that the science of relationships can contribute, if only a little, to building better relationships.

Summary

People have many different relationships. In relationships people influence and affect each other, they are interdependent. In close relationships people are more interdependent than in superficial relationships: close relationship partners have a stronger and more frequent impact on each other. Disclosure and perceived partner responsiveness play a key role in the formation and maintenance of all relationships. By disclosing information about themselves and by being responsive to each other's needs, people maintain their relationships and signal that they accept and care about each other.

CHAPTER SUMMARY

- *What are the benefits of interpersonal relationships?* Our relationships with others are associated with both psychological and physical well-being, partly because partners often help us to deal more effectively with stress. In contrast, lacking relationships with others has detrimental consequences for an individual's well-being.

- *Why do we form relationships with others?* Evolutionary psychologists argue that we form relationships with others because in our evolutionary past relationships with others provided us with many survival and reproductive benefits. That's why we have an innate *need to belong*. Relatedly, attachment theory states that people have a natural tendency to form attachment bonds with others, because others help them to deal with threatening situations.

- *Do all people rely on other people to an equal extent?* It appears that, among both children and adults, differences in *attachment styles* exist. The majority of people are *securely* attached, and they are comfortable with contact and intimacy with others. However, people with an *insecure* attachment style are, for different reasons, less comfortable with intimacy and close contact. Such differences in attachment style explain to an important extent how people respond to their relationship partners – including the romantic partner.

- *Does physical attractiveness matter?* There is abundant evidence that how we evaluate and behave towards others is strongly influenced by attractiveness: we *do* judge a book by its cover. One of the reasons for this is the existence of a 'what is beautiful is good' stereotype, which entails that people tend to believe that attractive others are friendly, sociable, and competent. There seems to be some truth to this as a result of self-fulfilling prophecies: Because people assume that attractive people are friendly, they will treat attractive others positively, which in turn will elicit friendly behaviour on the part of the attractive others.

- *Is physical attractiveness entirely in the eye of the beholder?* The answer to this question is no. People generally show more consensus than disagreement about what is attractive, both within and across cultures. There are also objective physical features that determine attractiveness, such as symmetry, averageness, and so-called hormone-markers (high cheekbones, soft skin for females; large jaw and prominent eyebrows and cheekbones for males).

- *Physical attractiveness is surely not the only factor determining why we are attracted to others. What other factors are there?* First, we of course have to be in the proximity of others to even have a chance to get to like them. And we tend to like those who are physically close to us, partly because familiarity breeds liking. We also like those who are similar to us. Finally, the conditions under which we meet others can have a strong influence on attraction. In arousing situations, people may misattribute their arousal to a person they meet.

- *What is love, actually?* Brain-imaging studies show that people who are in love have a strong craving to be with the other person – comparable, at least in the brain, to an addictive craving as observed in smoking or drug addiction. However, love does not only refer to the initial stage of being madly in love. According to Sternberg's triangular theory of love, over the course of a relationship different types of love can be distinguished, consisting of a combination of different levels of passion, intimacy, and commitment.

- *What makes people strongly committed to remain in a relationship?* According to equity theory, partners are satisfied as long as there is a balance between what both partners put into (costs), and get out of (rewards), the relationship. However, relationship stability also depends on the extent to which partners perceive that there may be better alternatives for the relationship, and on how much partners have already invested in the relationship. This is summarized in the investment model, which predicts that partners are strongly committed to maintaining their relationship as long as they are highly satisfied with the relationship, the quality of alternatives is low, and they have invested much in the relationship.

- *Is relationship commitment thus directly related to the stability of the relationship?* Relationship commitment predicts relationship stability *because* relationship commitment instigates behaviours and thoughts that benefit relationship functioning, such as forgiveness, accommodation, and the derogation of alternatives. Such 'pro-relationship acts' in turn breed trust and commitment in the other partner, who in turn will be more likely to act in a pro-relationship manner.

- *What type of relationships do people have?* Relationships are characterized by the fact that relationship partners are interdependent: What one person does, affects the other person. Relationships differ on a variety of dimensions. In exchange relationships, partners ensure equitable benefits; in communal relationships, both partners' concern is to be responsive to each other. The most important voluntary relationships are friendships. They are beneficial for people's well-being throughout their life-span and have important functions in the development of social skills and competencies.

- *How do people maintain their relationships?* Disclosing information about oneself is one of the most important processes to increase intimacy and closeness in relationships, especially when the disclosure is directed at a specific relationship partner. Disclosure signals that the relationship is special and that the other person plays a unique role in the life of the discloser.

- *Why do relationships end?* Often relationships end when partners fail to be responsive to each others' needs. Not being responsive causes people to feel that the other does not care about them.

SUGGESTIONS FOR FURTHER READING

Berscheid, E., & Regan, P. C. (2005). *The psychology of interpersonal relationships*. Upper Saddle River, NJ: Prentice-Hall. A comprehensive introduction to research on relationships, for anyone interested in the basic knowledge of relationships.

Bradbury, T. N., & Karney, B. R. (2010). *Intimate relationships*. New York: Norton & Company. This book provides an excellent overview of research on intimate relationships, mostly on romantic, friends, and family relations.

Fisher, H. (2004). *Why we love: The nature and chemistry of romantic love*. New York: Henry Hold & Company. A popular-science book providing an evolutionary and neuroscientific view on love.

Fletcher, G. J. O. (2002). *The new science of intimate relationships*. Malden, MA & Oxford, UK: Blackwell. An accessible book about what science tells us about love, sex, and friendship.

Mashek, D. J., & Aron, A. (2004). *Handbook of closeness and intimacy*. Mahwah, NJ: Erlbaum. A scholarly book that summarizes the central processes in relationships, written by some of the most active and recognized relationship researchers.

Miller, R. S., & Perlman, D. (2008). *Intimate relationships*. New York: McGraw-Hill. An introductory book to the science of relationships, with many illustrations of the relevance of relationship science to the readers' everyday lives.

Regan, P. C. (2008). *The mating game*. Thousand Oaks, CA: Sage. This book offers a view on relationships from a purely evolutionary viewpoint.

Reis, H. T., & Rusbult, C. E. (2004). *Key readings on close relationships*. Washington, DC: Taylor & Francis. In this book you can read a collection of some of the 'classic' articles in the history of relationship science.

Swami, V., & Furnham, A. (2008). *The psychology of physical attraction*. New York: Routledge. Offers an overview of scholarly work on physical beauty, culture, evolution, and other aspects of human attractiveness.

Vohs, K. D., & Finkel, E. J. (Eds.). (2006). *Self and relationships: Connecting intrapersonal and interpersonal processes*. New York: Guilford Press. This book provides an overview of research that integrates people's internal worlds and their close relationships.

Williams, K. D. (2001). *Ostracism: The power of silence*. New York: Guilford. Written by one of the leading researchers in this field, this book provides a comprehensive examination of the roots and consequences of ostracism.

12 Group Dynamics

BERNARD A. NIJSTAD AND DAAN VAN KNIPPENBERG

Source: © Robert E. Daemmrich. Used under licence from Getty Images.

KEY TERMS

- cohesion
- emotional contagion
- entitativity
- expectation states theory
- group
- group commitment

- group socialization
- initiation
- interpersonal cohesion
- need to belong
- role
- role transition

- socio-emotional behaviour
- speaking hierarchy
- staffing level
- status
- task behaviour
- task cohesion
- transactive memory

CHAPTER OUTLINE

ROUTE MAP OF THE CHAPTER

Groups are pervasive in social life. In this chapter, we discuss why people form and join groups, and what types of groups can be distinguished. We further discuss three levels of analysis. At the individual level, we discuss the (changing) relations between the group and its members. At the group level, we discuss group development, group structure (status and roles) and group norms. At the intergroup level, we discuss how the (intergroup) context shapes the behaviour of group members and the structure of groups.

INTRODUCTION

Imagine you're spending a weekend in Amsterdam. You enter a subway station, which is quite crowded. From the way people are dressed – many are wearing red and white Ajax shirts – you infer that they must be Ajax fans going to support their football team (Figure 12.1). These fans show remarkable behaviour: they sing and shout in ways they would not normally do in public. Yet most of them are adults (and not all are drunk), and they only show this behaviour when there is an Ajax match. The most striking aspect of their behaviour is that the fans behave so similarly. However, many of them do not even know each other, and their behaviour is quite out of the ordinary: normally, people would not sing and shout in a subway.

The only reason these fans behave so similarly is that they share membership of a social **group**: they are all Ajax fans. In this chapter, we argue that in order to understand their behaviour and behaviour in other groups, we need to consider three *levels of analysis*: the individual level, the group level and the wider context in which groups are situated. At the individual level, all Ajax fans in the subway are individually aware of their group membership (being an Ajax fan) and of the fact that the other people in the subway are Ajax fans as well. At the group level, the fact that their behaviour is so similar indicates that it cannot be caused by idiosyncratic tendencies of individual Ajax fans, such as their individual personalities. Rather, there is something 'groupy' going on which guides their behaviour.

> **group** a group exists when two or more individuals define themselves as members of a group.

FIGURE 12.1 *These fans share membership of a social group: they are all Ajax football supporters.*

Source: © Picture Contact BV. Used under licence from Alamy.

At the broader level, one could argue that these fans only show this behaviour because of the context: there is going to be a football match in which Ajax will play against another team (also see Chapter 14 on intergroup relations). Indeed, if there had been no such match, the fans would behave quite differently.

In this chapter, we use this three-level framework to discuss some basic characteristics of groups and some basic processes in groups. We first examine the issues of what a group is, why people form or join groups and what types of groups can be distinguished. We then move on to the individual level and discuss how individuals join groups and how their group membership develops over time. We then consider the group level, as we discuss group development and group structure. Finally, we discuss the (intergroup) context in which groups exist and how this context affects processes that occur in groups.

THE PHENOMENOLOGY OF GROUPS

What types of groups can be distinguished, and what are their characteristics and functions?

Defining groups

Groups are everywhere: we see groups of friends in a bar, groups of colleagues in an organization, groups of fans in a stadium. But what exactly do we mean by the word 'group'? Many authors have suggested different components of a definition of groups. Lewin (1948) suggested that common fate is critical: people are a group to the extent that they experience similar outcomes. Sherif and Sherif (1969) proposed that some form of social structure (status or role differentiation, e.g. a leadership role) is essential, because otherwise the 'group' would just be a loose collection of individuals. Bales (1950) stressed the importance of face-to-face interaction. We suggest a broader definition of groups: following Tajfel (1981), we argue that *a group exists when two or more individuals define themselves as members of a group*.

A few things about this definition should be noted. First, many different groups would fit this definition, including religious groups (Christians), national groups (the British), organizational groups (the psychology department) and friendship groups (a student society). Second, it is subjective and does not include any 'objective' characteristics of groups, such as common fate or face-to-face interaction. Rather, it emphasizes common identity: sharing the view with others that you belong to the same group. Third, it is important to recognize that one can only talk about groups to the extent that there are people who do not belong to the group in question, although they belong to other groups. Finally, some groups are 'groupier' (or more group-like) than others, an issue we return to in our discussion of group 'entitativity' below.

Why groups?

Why do humans form, join and distinguish groups? Several theoretical perspectives can be applied to answer this question. We will discuss three: a sociobiological, a cognitive and a utilitarian perspective (also see Baron & Kerr, 2003). These three perspectives are complementary rather than mutually exclusive.

Following Darwin's theory of evolution, the *sociobiological perspective* (e.g. Bowlby, 1958) emphasizes the adaptive value of forming groups. Forming groups enables humans (and other social animals) to deal more effectively with enemies or predators, and allows cooperation in areas such as raising children, farming or hunting. Earlier in our evolutionary history, when food was often scarce and enemies and predators were dangerous, forming groups had a significant evolutionary advantage. A predisposition to form groups increased the chances of survival of the individual and, through the evolutionary principle of natural selection, this predisposition was selected and passed on to later generations. This human predisposition to form and maintain stable, strong and positive relationships with others is called the **need to belong** (see Chapter 11) (Baumeister & Leary, 1995). Baumeister and Leary argued that this human need is innate and universal. Indeed, evidence indicates that the tendency to form groups is found across all cultures and situations, suggesting that this tendency is evolutionarily 'built in'.

According to the *cognitive perspective*, groups help us to understand our world. *Social comparison theory* (Festinger, 1954; see Chapters 5 and 8) argues that people want to hold accurate views of the world. They can do this by validating their beliefs either against 'physical reality' (e.g. 'Will this glass crack if I hit it with a hammer?') or against 'social reality' (e.g. 'I like this new music; I wonder what my friends think about it?'). People turn to others especially for beliefs for which there is no physical reality (e.g. preferences). Building on these ideas, *social identity theory* (e.g. Tajfel & Turner, 1979, 1986; see Chapters 5 and 14) and *self-categorization theory* (Turner, Hogg, Oakes, Reicher & Wetherell, 1987; see Chapters 5 and 14) argue that people define themselves and others partly in terms of group

membership. These theories propose that seeing oneself and others as members of groups helps to reduce uncertainty and make sense of our world (e.g. Hogg & Abrams, 1993). Being a member of a group often provides guidelines for the way we should behave and think. If you think about the Ajax football fans we started this chapter with, their behaviour is clearly guided by their group membership and the behaviours thought to be appropriate for that group (see the later discussion of group norms). Further, seeing other people as members of specific groups helps to interpret their behaviour: knowing that the people in the subway are Ajax fans makes it much easier to understand what is going on.

A *utilitarian perspective* argues that people derive benefits from groups. *Social exchange theory* (e.g. Thibaut & Kelley, 1959; see Chapter 11; also Leader in the Field, John Walter Thibaut) argues that social relations (including those within groups) help to fulfil the individual's needs and often take the form of exchange processes. These exchanges might involve material goods (e.g. borrowing a tool, selling your car) or interpersonal helping (e.g. helping a friend move house), but also psychological 'goods' such as love, friendship or approval. Enduring exchange relations between two or more people are more effectively organized when people form a (more or less stable) group. Thus, groups exist because they facilitate mutually beneficial social exchange.

Social exchange theory argues that social relations involve costs as well as benefits, and as long as the benefits exceed the costs, the relation will yield a 'profit'. There is much evidence that people are unhappy about relations if they feel that they invest more in them (e.g. time) than they get back (e.g. approval) (e.g. Le & Agnew, 2003; see also Chapter 11). Furthermore, satisfaction with an exchange relationship depends on the degree to which there are alternative relationships that yield more profit. Thus, people join groups because they

 LEADER IN THE FIELD

John Walter Thibaut (1917–1986) was born in Marion, Ohio. He studied philosophy at the University of North Carolina. During World War II he came into contact with psychology when he was assigned to the Aviation Psychology Program. In 1946 he moved to the Massachusetts Institute of Technology to study with Kurt Lewin (see Leader in the Field, Chapter 1). After Lewin's death in 1947, Thibaut moved to the University of Michigan, where he received his PhD. His subsequent career took him to Boston University, Harvard University and back to the University of North Carolina. Thibaut is best known for his 1959 book (co-authored with Harold Kelley; see Leader in the Field, Chapter 3) *The Social Psychology of Groups*. In that book, Thibaut and Kelley laid out the foundations of social exchange theory, arguing that social relations take the form of social exchange processes.

derive benefits from their group membership. People may leave groups (if possible) when they are unhappy about the benefits relative to the costs of group membership, or when alternative groups exist that have a better cost–benefit ratio (also see Rusbult & Farrell, 1983). In general, people will leave groups when better alternatives are available, including the option of being alone.

Types of groups, entitativity and group functions

As we noted earlier, our definition of groups is relatively broad, and many types of groups may be included. However, there are different types of groups with different characteristics. Further, some groups seem more 'groupy' than other groups, a phenomenon often referred to as the **entitativity** of groups. Campbell (1958) coined the new word 'entitativity' to refer to the degree to which a collection of people is perceived as being bonded together in a coherent unit (Figure 12.2).

> **entitativity** the degree to which a collection of people is perceived as being bonded together in a coherent unit.

So, what different types of groups can we distinguish? Lickel et al. (2000) wondered whether people spontaneously distinguish between different types of groups. They provided their participants (American and Polish students) with a sample of 40 different groups, such as 'members of a family', 'black people', 'members of a jury' and 'people in line at a bank'. Participants had to rate these different groups on eight dimensions: degree of interaction among members; importance of group members to each other; common goals and common outcomes for group members; similarity among group members; duration; permeability (how easy it is to join or leave the group); and size. The groups were also rated on the degree to which the group really was a group (group entitativity). After they had done the ratings, participants were asked to sort the 40 groups into different categories using their own individual criteria, including as many or as few categories as they wanted.

Lickel et al. (2000) found that some of their 40 groups were consistently sorted into one common category, whereas other groups were consistently sorted into other categories. Further, groups that were sorted into the same category were also rated similarly on the eight dimensions. Lickel et al. identified four types of groups: intimacy groups; task groups; social categories; and loose associations. In Table 12.1 we give a summary of their findings and some examples of the different types of groups. As can be seen in the table, the types of groups differed along the different dimensions. For example, intimacy groups (e.g. a family) were rated to have high levels of interaction, were seen as important, had common goals and outcomes, had a high degree of similarity, were of long duration and low permeability and were fairly small. Social categories (e.g. women), in contrast, were rated to have low levels of interaction, were rated low on importance of members to each other, with low levels of common goals and outcomes, and low member similarity, and were rated to be of long duration, low in permeability, and large.

With regard to group entitativity, intimacy groups and task groups were seen as high in entitativity, loose associations as low in entitativity, and social categories occupied an intermediate position. Lickel et al. (2000) also considered which of their eight group characteristics best predicted group entitativity. They found that the single most important predictor was interaction among group members: higher levels of interaction were associated with higher entitativity. The other characteristics also contributed to entitativity: importance, common goals and outcomes, group member similarity and duration showed a positive relation (the higher the importance, common goals, etc., the higher the perceived entitativity), whereas group size and permeability showed a weak negative relation (larger groups and highly permeable groups were rated lower in entitativity). Note that some of the possible components of a definition of groups that we described earlier (common fate, face-to-face interaction) were positively associated with perceived group entitativity: they do indeed make groups more 'groupy' (a more extensive discussion of these issues can be found in Lickel, Hamilton, & Sherman, 2001).

FIGURE 12.2 *Intimacy groups, e.g. a family, are seen as high in entitativity.*

Source: © Juriah Mosin. Used under licence from Shutterstock.

Table 12.1 *Characteristics of different types of groups.*

Characteristic	Type of group (examples)			
	Intimacy group (family members, friends, romantic partners)	Task group (jury members, cast of a play, sports team)	Social category (women, black people, Americans)	Loose association (people at a bus stop, at the cinema, living in same area)
Interaction	High	Moderate/High	Low	Low
Importance	High	Moderate/High	Low	Low
Common goals	High	Moderate/High	Low	Low
Common outcomes	High	Moderate/High	Low	Low
Similarity	High	Moderate	Low	Low
Duration	Long	Moderate	Long	Short
Permeability	Low	Moderate	Low	High
Size	Small	Small	Large	Moderate
Entitativity	High	High	Moderate	Low

Source: Based on data reported in Lickel et al., 2000.

Earlier we noted that there are several reasons why people form, join and distinguish groups. Johnson and colleagues (2006) argued that the different group types fulfil different functions for group members. They focused on intimacy groups, task groups and social categories (ignoring the less important loose associations). Johnson et al. argued that intimacy groups mainly fulfil affiliation-related needs, such as the need to belong (cf. the sociobiological perspective). Task groups mainly have a utilitarian function and help people to satisfy achievement-related needs (such as feeling competent and achieving success; cf. the utilitarian perspective). Social categories mainly have the function of giving people a social identity (i.e. the part of one's identity that derives from one's group membership; see Chapter 14) and thus help satisfy identity-related needs (cf. the cognitive perspective). Johnson and colleagues found considerable evidence for such an association between group type and function. For example, they gave people a description of the three most important group types (intimacy groups, task groups and social categories), and asked them to which degree each type of group fulfilled certain needs (e.g. 'connectedness', 'success' or 'sense of identity'). It was found that intimacy groups scored high in satisfying needs such as connectedness, comfort and support; that task groups scored high in satisfying needs such as success, competence and mastery; and that social categories scored high in satisfying needs such as sense of identity, uniqueness and distinctiveness. Vice versa, when people were asked to name groups that they associated with the fulfilment of specific needs, people tended to list intimacy groups when asked about affiliation-related needs, task groups when asked about achievement-related needs and social categories when asked about identity-related needs.

That (certain types of) groups help satisfy one's needs also implies that when these needs are high people will be interested in membership of a group that satisfies these needs. This topic is discussed in Research Close-Up 12.1, which we suggest you read now.

Summary

Forming, joining and distinguishing groups has a number of advantages: groups help us to make sense of our world and to coordinate mutually beneficial social exchange more effectively. The tendency to form groups is probably evolutionarily built in, as groups are found everywhere. However, not every type of group is equally important or 'groupy': intimacy groups and task groups especially are seen to be important and high in entitativity, while social

PEOPLE IDENTIFY WITH ENTITATIVE GROUPS WHEN THEY ARE UNCERTAIN ABOUT THEIR IDENTITY

Hogg, M. A., Sherman, D. K., Dierselhuis, J., Maitner, A. T., & Moffitt, G. (2007). Uncertainty, entitativity, and group identification. *Journal of Experimental Social Psychology, 43*, 135–142.

Research question

Hogg and colleagues considered one of the functions of group membership: that it provides us with an identity and informs us about who we are and what we should do. The question they addressed was, under which circumstances is this identity function of groups more important? They argued that people should be especially interested in being members of a group and identify more with their group in situations that arouse uncertainty about people's self-concept. Furthermore, groups with clear boundaries, common goals and outcomes, high internal homogeneity and so on – in short, highly entitative groups – should be more attractive in these cases, because these groups provide people with a clear self-concept grounded in group membership. Hogg and colleagues thus predicted that identification with a group should be high especially when people feel uncertain about their identity, and the group is very entitative.

Design

Participants were 89 Australian students. They participated for ten Australian dollars in a two-factor experiment that manipulated self-uncertainty (low versus high) and group entitativity (low versus high) as between-subject factors, thus creating a design with four conditions.

Procedure

Participants sat in individual cubicles and were (incorrectly) told that their computers were interconnected via a chat room with other members of their group (their 'group' being those people that were present for the experiment) with whom they would later collaborate on a task. They first filled out a personality questionnaire, and subsequently received (false) feedback about the results of the questionnaires of their fellow group members. In the high entitativity condition, they learned that all group members (including the participant) had given very similar answers; in the low entitativity condition they learned that their group members gave very different answers. In addition, in the high entitativity condition, the participants were told that they would later organize themselves with a clear division of labour, clear roles and clear principles about how to approach their task. In the low entitativity condition, they were told that each person would decide individually how to approach the group task.

After this manipulation of group entitativity, self-uncertainty was manipulated. Participants were asked to describe three aspects of their life that made them feel (depending on condition) certain versus uncertain about themselves, their lives and their future. Immediately after this, participants rated identification with their group on eight items (e.g. 'this group is important to me').

Results

Figure 12.3 shows the main results: the level of identification in each of the four conditions of the experiment. As predicted, identification was high especially when self-uncertainty was aroused and the group was made highly entitative. It was lower in the other conditions. It is especially noteworthy that people do not always identify more with entitative groups; they do especially when (temporarily) feeling uncertain about themselves, but not when feeling relatively certain.

Implications

These results (and Hogg et al. report another experiment among members of a political party) clearly show that people feel drawn towards highly entitative groups, especially when self-uncertainty is high. Hogg and colleagues speculate that this might be one reason why some people are drawn towards extremist groups. Social uncertainty may lead to higher levels of self-uncertainty and thus to the greater appeal of very entitative groups, perhaps including extremist or fundamentalist groups, who clearly distinguish themselves from other groups.

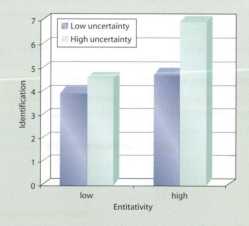

FIGURE 12.3 *Levels of identification by condition.*

Source: Adapted from Hogg, Sherman, Dierselhuis, Maitner, & Moffitt, 2007, with permission from Elsevier.

categories and loose associations are less so. Intimacy groups mainly fulfil people's need to belong, task groups help fulfil people's need for achievement, and social categories help people fulfil identity-related needs.

INDIVIDUALS IN GROUPS: THE INDIVIDUAL LEVEL OF ANALYSIS

What stages of group socialization can be distinguished and what factors determine role transitions?

In this section we consider the individual within the group: that is, we focus on the individual level of analysis. In particular, we discuss Moreland and Levine's (1982) model of group socialization, which is shown in Theory Box 12.1 (see also Leaders in the Field, John M. Levine and Richard L. Moreland). Group socialization may be

> **group socialization** the efforts of the group to assimilate new members to existing group norms and practices.

defined as the process through which the group tries to assimilate members to existing group norms and practices. As defined in Chapter 8, *norms* refer to belief systems about how (not) to behave, which guide behaviour and reflect group members' shared expectations about typical or desirable activities. In a later section of this chapter group norms are discussed more extensively. Here, the focus is on Moreland and Levine's model, which is applicable to groups that exist for comparatively long periods of time and have direct interaction between members, but which experience changes in membership. Examples would include a sports team, a team within an organization or a student society (i.e. many intimacy groups and task groups).

Moreland and Levine's model distinguishes five stages of group membership: investigation, socialization, maintenance, resocialization and remembrance. According to the model, moving from one stage to the next involves

> **role transition** a change in the relation between a group member and a group.

a **role transition**. Thus, moving from prospective member (the stage of investigation) to new member (the stage of socialization) involves the role transition of entry. Further role transitions are acceptance (from new member to full member), divergence (from full member to marginal member) and exit (from marginal member to ex-member). As can be

 LEADERS IN THE FIELD

John M. Levine (b. 1942) and **Richard L. Moreland** (b. 1951) have worked together on issues around group dynamics for more than three decades. Their collaboration started when Moreland joined the University of Pittsburgh in 1978 after receiving his PhD from the University of Michigan in that same year. Levine had worked in Pittsburgh since 1969, immediately after receiving his PhD from the University of Wisconsin. One of the first papers they wrote together was their highly influential article on group socialization that is discussed in the text. After this paper, they continued publishing on group socialization, and also worked on topics such as newcomer influence, collaboration, group composition, group commitment and group loyalty. They are also widely known for their efforts to summarize progress in the field of group dynamics in book chapters and books, such as their 1990 paper on Progress in Small Group Research that appeared in the *Annual Review of Psychology* (Levine & Moreland, 1990), their chapter on Small Groups in the *Handbook of Social Psychology* (Levine & Moreland, 1998), and a chapter on the history of small group research (Levine & Moreland, 2012). In fact, their collaboration has been so close that they have occasionally been erroneously introduced as John Moreland and Dick Levine, about which they note that 'The fact that we are flattered by such introductions says a lot about why we continue to collaborate' (Levine & Moreland, 2004, p. 170). Apart from their collaborative work, Levine is also known for his research on minority influence and newcomers, and Moreland has done important work in the area of shared cognition and transactive memory (see later in this chapter).

seen in Theory Box 12.1, the five different stages differ in the degree of **group commitment** – in other words, the degree to which a group member has a psychological bond with the group and its goals and wishes to maintain group membership. Group commitment increases gradually as people become full members, after which it decreases

> **group commitment** a psychological bond of a group member with the group and its goals including the desire to maintain group membership.

towards the point at which individuals wish to leave the group.

Role transitions occur as a result of evaluation processes in which the group and the individual evaluate one another's 'rewardingness', or the extent to which the group is rewarding for the member and to which the member is valued by the group. When the group is rewarding for members, they will try to enter the group or maintain group membership (i.e. feel group commitment). Similarly, when a group values a (prospective) member, the group will encourage the person to become or stay a member of the group (i.e. the group is committed to the member). This is related to our earlier discussion of social exchange processes and the benefits people can derive from them (e.g. to gain social approval or receive help or material goods). Indeed, according to Moreland and Levine (1982), group commitment is a function of the past, present and expected future rewardingness

THEORY BOX 12.1

THE MORELAND AND LEVINE (1982) MODEL OF GROUP SOCIALIZATION

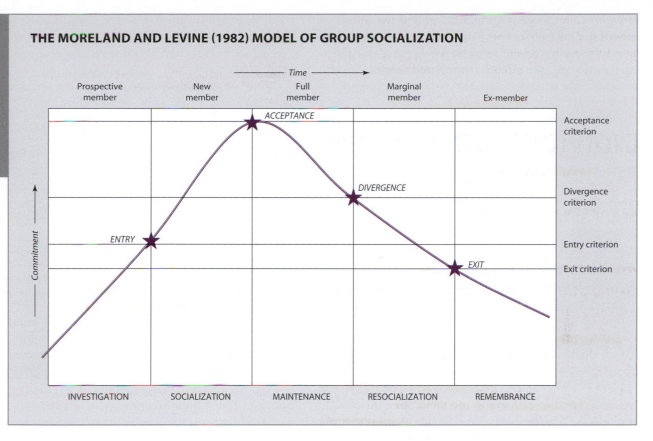

of the group, compared to the rewardingness of alternative groups. In the remainder of this section, we consider the key stages shown in Theory Box 12.1.

Joining a group and group socialization: becoming a full member

Investigation In the stage of investigation, groups look for people who might make a contribution to the attainment of group goals. Task groups will often search for people who have the required skills and abilities, whereas intimacy groups will tend to emphasize compatibility (e.g. similarity) with the existing membership. Prospective members, on the other hand, will look for groups that may potentially fulfil their needs. For example, when you have just moved to a new city to start college, you will probably try to identify specific groups that might help to fulfil your social needs. Thus, you might join a student society, hoping to find people with whom you can start a new, positive and stable relation (i.e. fulfil your need to belong). Another example of how groups fulfil members' needs is discussed in Research Close-Up 12.1.

Entry and initiation When the level of group commitment (i.e. the mutual commitment between the group and the prospective member) reaches an entry criterion, a role transition will occur: *entry*. Entry is often marked by some ritual or ceremony that makes it clear that the relation between the group and the (prospective) member has changed. In an organization, this may take the form of a welcome speech, and in social groups it may be a party. At other times the entry or **initiation** ritual can be quite unpleasant and painful for the prospective member.

> **initiation** the role transition of entry into a group, often accompanied by some ritual.

Lodewijkx and Syroit (1997) studied initiation into a Dutch sorority (a student society for female students). The novices first stay in a campsite for a week. Novices wear a shapeless, sack-like uniform, are not called by their real names and have to undergo physical hardship (hard work and lack of sleep and food). After a week they return to the city and participate in 'evening gatherings' for a further one and a half weeks. During these gatherings, which are regarded as threatening by the novices, they are often bullied and embarrassed. Then, finally, the inauguration ceremony takes place, after which they have a meal with the senior members

– the so-called 'integration party' – and the initiation is ended.

As these severe initiations take place in many different groups (e.g. the military, some sports teams, student societies), the question arises as to why groups perform these harsh rituals. Aronson and Mills (1959) suggested a classic argument that provides part of the answer. They maintained that severe initiations increase the liking for and commitment to the group. Their argument is based upon *cognitive dissonance theory* (Festinger, 1957; see Chapter 7). Suppose a prospective member has undergone harsh treatment, but it later appears that the group is not as attractive as initially believed. This would lead to cognitive dissonance: members can no longer maintain that they had good reasons to undergo the harsh treatment when they admit that the group is not so attractive after all. Thus, the member will deny that the group is unattractive and will maintain a high level of commitment to the group.

Aronson and Mills (1959) performed an experiment to test this reasoning. They offered female students the opportunity to join a discussion group about sexuality. However, some of the prospective members first had to undergo the embarrassing experience of reading sexually explicit passages aloud, while other prospective members did not have to do this. Next, the participants listened to an actual group discussion that was recorded on tape. This discussion was in fact quite boring and was about the secondary sexual behaviour of lower animals. Participants were next asked to rate the attractiveness of the group. In line with the dissonance explanation, the women who had to read the embarrassing passages rated the group as more attractive than those who did not.

Lodewijkx and Syroit (1997) did not, however, find a positive relation between severity of initiation and group liking. In their field study among the prospective members of the sorority, mentioned above, they found, in fact, that severe initiations *decreased* the liking for the group. Thus, prospective members of the sorority who rated the initiation as more severe liked the group less. The reason was that severe initiations led to loneliness and frustration, and this in turn reduced the liking for the group. What Lodewijkx and Syroit did find was that, during the initiation, positive relations developed among prospective members, and these increased liking for the group.

Thus, severe initiations do not always increase liking for the group, as they may lead to loneliness and frustration. In the Aronson and Mills study, in which the initiation was very brief, this probably did not happen. Severe initiations may also have other functions: they deter potential members who are not eager enough to join the group, and prospective members can show their interest in the group by undergoing these harsh

treatments (Moreland & Levine, 1982). Initiations also reinforce status hierarchies, and may increase conformity and dependency of new members to the group (Keating, et al., 2005).

More on initiations into student societies can be found in Social Psychology Beyond the Lab 12.1, which we suggest you read now.

Socialization After entry, the stage of socialization begins. In this stage, new members learn the *norms* of the group: the belief system about how (not) to behave, which reflects group members' shared expectations about typical or desirable activities. In addition, new members may acquire the necessary knowledge and skills to function effectively as a group member (i.e. learn their **role** in the group: the set of behaviours associated with a specific position in the group). Thus, the group tries to assimilate the member to fit the expectations of the group. However, socialization is a two-way street, and the new member may also try to influence the group in such a way that the member's needs are best met. For example, a new member may try to change the group's norms or customs (e.g. 'I think that we should meet more often'). Such newcomer influence is more likely when groups are less committed to their norms, customs and routines, for example when they have been externally imposed (rather than self-chosen), or when they have led to poor group performance in the past (see Choi & Levine, 2004). The degree to which the newcomer influences the group may also depend on newcomer characteristics, such as the newcomer's outside social status (more influence with higher status; see Levine, Choi, & Moreland, 2003, and below). Nonetheless, in general newcomers will adapt to the norms and customs of the group (rather than vice versa).

> **role** the behaviours expected of a person with a specific position in the group.

During socialization, group commitment – of the member towards the group and of the group towards the member – will generally increase, except when the new member or the group is dissatisfied. At a specific point in time (when the acceptance criterion is reached), the member will no longer be treated as somebody who needs special attention, the socialization stage is ended and the new member is accepted as a full member. The new member may gain access to information that was previously hidden, join specific informal cliques, and their behaviour is monitored less strictly. As with entry, there may be some ritual to mark the transition of acceptance as a full member. A well-known example is the Bar Mitzvah ceremony for Jewish boys at the age of 13, after which the boy is accepted as a full member of Jewish society instead of being considered a child.

SOCIAL PSYCHOLOGY BEYOND THE LAB 12.1

HAZING IN STUDENT SOCIETIES

Many new students join a student society when they enter university. Quite frequently, these student societies have initiation rituals (also called 'hazing'). Examples of behaviors that novices (or 'pledges') have to perform are asking strangers absurd questions, dressing up in embarrassing clothes and singing embarrassing songs in front of an audience (see e.g. Keating et al., 2005; Lodewijkx & Syroit, 1997).

Keating et al. (2005) argued that the precise activities that are performed during hazing are by no means random or coincidental. They found that initiation in sports teams often involved physical and painful activities, while initiations in student societies often involved having to perform embarrassing and socially deviant activities. Keating and colleagues note that these specific rituals seem quite functional: sports clubs like to distinguish themselves from other sports clubs by appearing tough and strong, while student societies might want to distinguish themselves from other groups by emphasizing that they are socially distinct (e.g. higher class; that they do not have to follow the rules of 'ordinary people').

Unfortunately, hazing activities sometimes go tragically wrong. In many countries there have been incidents in which pledges of student societies suffered injuries or even died during initiation rituals. Often, these incidents involve alcohol abuse (see e.g. Nuwer, 1999, for an overview of hazing incidents in the US). However, they need not involve alcohol. In The Netherlands, for example, a student almost died in 2005 after drinking six litres of water: each time he had lost a round during a game he had to drink a glass of water. Nobody had realized that drinking that much water within a short period of time is extremely dangerous (drinking too much water can lead to a condition known as water intoxication, and to a related problem resulting from the dilution of sodium in the body).

The question of why these rituals are performed, and why students are still interested in membership of societies that perform these harsh rituals, are of interest to social psychologists. Some answers to these questions can be found in this chapter.

---

staffing level the degree to which the actual number of group members is similar to the ideal number of group members.

Being accepted as a full member is easier in some groups than in others. In part, it depends on the **staffing level** of the group: the degree to which the actual number of group members is similar to the ideal number of group members. Groups can be overstaffed (have too many members) as well as understaffed (have too few members). One might expect that understaffed groups will be less demanding of new members (make it easier to become a full member) than overstaffed groups.

Cini, Moreland, and Levine (1993) conducted a study among 93 student groups, including fine arts clubs, social groups and political groups. They held interviews with the president of each group in which they gathered information about the staffing level of the groups and about recruitment and socialization practices. It appeared that both understaffing and overstaffing caused problems. Understaffing led to a loss of resources (e.g. too few members contributing membership fees), poorer group performance and fatigue among group members. Overstaffing led to apathy and boredom, alienation (i.e. group members felt 'lost in the crowd'), confusion

and disorganization. The solution to understaffing, not surprisingly, was to recruit new members. Consequently, the groups that were understaffed were more open: they were less selective (it was easier to become a new member), and also less demanding for new members (it was easier to become a full member). For example, new members were evaluated and expected to perform special duties less often in understaffed compared to overstaffed groups. Solutions to overstaffing, in contrast, were to restrict membership, but also to punish deviance from group norms more harshly, in the hope that deviant members would leave the group.

Being in a group: maintenance and role negotiation

After acceptance, the stage of maintenance begins. This stage is characterized by high levels of group commitment, and for both the member and the group the relation is seen as rewarding (see Theory Box 12.1, above). The major way in which groups and members try to increase the rewardingness of their relationship is through role negotiation. Thus, the member tries to occupy the role within the group that best satisfies his or her needs, whereas the group tries to assign roles to members in such a way that the group's goals can be best achieved. One of the more important roles within the group is that of group leader (see Chapter 13). However, there are often other roles that need to be fulfilled within groups, such as those of 'recruiter' (who identifies and evaluates prospective members) and 'trainer' (who has a role during the socialization of new members). The relation between the group and the member will be rewarding, and group commitment will remain high to the degree that role negotiations are successful. We examine what it means to 'be in a group' in more detail in the next section, where we discuss norms, roles and status.

Leaving a group: divergence and exit

Divergence After a time, group members may lose interest in the group, for example because they are dissatisfied with their role in the group, or because they have identified other groups that are more rewarding. On the other hand, group commitment of the group to its members may decline when members fail to live up to group expectations. For example, members may not perform well in their role, or may violate important group norms. This will lead the group to re-label these members as marginal members or deviates. The group might, for instance, no longer give marginal members full information, or other group members might exclude marginal members from informal cliques (e.g. they are no longer asked to come along for a drink after work). Often considerable pressure is exerted on deviates to realign or even to leave the group (especially if the group is overstaffed).

Schachter (1951) experimentally demonstrated the pressure that is exerted on deviates. He had groups discuss a delinquency case, in which the life history of a juvenile delinquent was provided, and groups had to decide on a punishment for a minor crime. In each of the experimental groups there were confederates playing different roles: the 'mode' who accommodated to the group's average judgement, the 'slider' who initially took an extreme position (e.g. a very harsh punishment) but then moved towards the group norm, and the 'deviate', who also took an extreme position, but maintained it throughout the discussion. Initially, the group discussion was primarily aimed at the two deviating members (the slider and the deviate) in each group, trying to change their minds. When it became apparent that the deviates would not change, the groups eventually excluded them, refusing to talk to them and ignoring their contributions (see Figure 12.4). After the discussion, deviates were also liked less than other group members.

Resocialization and exit Divergence might be followed by a period of resocialization. In this period, the group might try to persuade marginal members not to leave, or they might try to accommodate to the wishes of marginal members (e.g. give them a different role). Similarly, group members may try to convince the group not to expel them, and might try to assimilate to the group's expectations again. This might result in re-entry to the group when successful. However, when resocialization fails, group members may reach an exit criterion and leave the group. As with other role transitions, this may involve some ritual, such as a goodbye speech or a party.

According to Moreland and Levine's (1982) model of group socialization, voluntary exit from a group becomes more likely when there are alternative groups that are more attractive. An example would be a football player who leaves a club to play in a rival team because of higher earnings. However, sometimes group members will resist temptation, and remain loyal to their group despite the presence of a (perhaps) more attractive group. One factor appears to be identification: the more people identify with their group, the more positive they perceive their group to be, and the less likely they are to leave the group (even when the group has performed poorly in the past; see Van Vugt & Hart, 2004). You can measure your level of identification with a group by responding to the questions in Individual Differences 12.1.

In some cases, the group may expel a member, which can be quite a painful experience. For example, an employee might be fired or a church member might be excommunicated. Research has shown that social exclusion from groups has enormous negative effects on excluded members. Consider the following situation. You are invited to come to the psychology lab to participate in an experiment and are asked to wait in a waiting room until the experiment starts. In that room two other

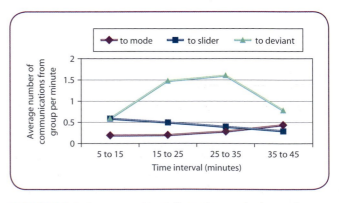

FIGURE 12.4 *Communications directed towards the mode, slider and deviant over time.*

Source: Based on Schachter, 1951. Copyright © 1951 by the American Psychological Association. Adapted with permission. The use of APA information does not imply endorsement by APA.

INDIVIDUAL DIFFERENCES 12.1

MEASURING IDENTIFICATION

Instruction

Think of a group that you are a member of. Then answer the following questions on a scale from 1 (*completely disagree*) to 4 (*neutral*) to 7 (*completely agree*) with this group in mind.

Items

1. I feel strongly affiliated with this group.
2. Other groups can learn a lot from us.
3. Belonging to this group is an important part of my identity.
4. In times of trouble, the only way to know what to do is to rely on my group's leader(s).
5. I am glad to contribute to this group.
6. Compared to other groups of this kind, this group is particularly good.
7. It is important to me that I view myself as a member of this group.
8. All group members should respect the customs, the institutions and the leaders of this group.
9. I am strongly committed to this group.
10. Relative to other groups, we are a very moral group.
11. It is important to me that others see me as a member of this group.
12. It is disloyal to criticize this group.
13. I like to help this group.
14. This group is better than other groups in all respects.
15. When I talk about the group members, I usually say 'we' rather than 'they'.
16. There is usually a good reason for every rule and regulation that the group leader(s) propose.

Source: Adapted from Roccas, Sagiv, Schwartz, Halevy, and Eidelson (2008), with permission from SAGE Publications Ltd.

Scoring

This questionnaire is taken from Roccas, Sagiv, Schwartz, Halevy, and Eidelson (2008). These authors argue that there are four basic dimensions underlying identification: *importance* ('How much do I view the group as part of who I am?'), *commitment* ('How much am I willing to benefit the group?'), *superiority* ('How much do I view my group as superior to other groups?') and *deference* ('How much do I honour, revere, and submit to the group's norms, symbols and leaders?').

Add up your answers to questions 3, 7, 11, and 15 to compute an *importance* score.

Add up your answers to questions 1, 5, 9, and 13 to compute a *commitment* score.

Add up your answers to questions 2, 6, 10, and 14 to compute a *superiority* score.

Add up your answers to questions 4, 8, 12 and 16 to compute a *deference* score.

Then divide all four scores by four (the number of items per scale) to get a minimum score of 1 and a maximum score of 7.

Norms

The test was filled out by American and Israeli university students, who were asked to report how much they identified with their nation. Based on both samples, you can interpret your scores as follows:

On *importance* a score lower than 4.3 would be low, a score of 5.4 would be average and a score higher than 6.5 would be high.

On *commitment* a score lower than 3.9 would be low, a score of 5.0 would be average and a score higher than 6.1 would be high.

On *superiority* a score lower than 2.9 would be low, a score of 4.0 would be average and a score higher than 5.1 would be high.

On *deference* a score lower than 1.9 would be low, a score of 3.0 would be average and a score higher than 4.1 would be high.

---

participants are also waiting (they are, in fact, confederates of the experimenter). One of them has brought a tennis ball and playfully throws it to the other participant. That participant joins in and throws the ball to you. For a while, the three of you play this ball-tossing game. After some time, however, the other participants no longer throw the ball to you, but only to each other, and this goes on for several minutes. How would you feel?

Williams (2001) reports extensive evidence concerning the power of social exclusion. Using the ball-tossing game (and other situations), he found that social exclusion produces severe negative moods and anger, and leads to lower ratings on belongingness and self-esteem.

Further, Eisenberger, Lieberman, and Williams (2003) found that exclusion quite literally is a form of 'social pain'. These researchers had participants play a computerized version of the ball-tossing game while lying in an fMRI (functional magnetic resonance imaging) brain scanner. Using the fMRI scanner, the researchers could identify which brain areas were active during social exclusion. Participants were led to believe that, by pushing a button, they could throw a (virtual) ball to another participant, who could then throw the ball back to them or to a third participant. In fact, there was only one real participant, and the computer was programmed in such a way that this participant received the ball nine times, after which the ball was no longer thrown to him or her. While being excluded from the game, an fMRI brain scan was made. Eisenberger et al. (2003) found that social exclusion activates an area in the brain (the anterior cingulate cortex) that is normally activated when a person is in physical pain. Furthermore, the level of activation of that brain area was correlated with participants' reports of distress.

Remembrance The last stage of the Moreland and Levine model is remembrance (see Theory Box 12.1, p. 395). In this stage, the ex-member and the group retrospectively evaluate each other. Thus, remaining group members will evaluate the ex-member's contributions to the group and will maintain some degree of commitment to the ex-member if these contributions are seen as positive. Similarly, ex-members look back on their time with the group with either fond or bitter memories. In extreme cases, ex-members may even try to destroy their former group in an act of revenge. Workplace shootings, in which employees who had been dismissed shot their boss or former colleagues, are extreme examples. One such incident happened in Kansas City, US, in 2004, where a man who had been laid off several months earlier killed five former colleagues and wounded two more before taking his own life. Such events are, of course, extreme, and occur very rarely.

Summary

Individuals move through different phases of group membership (prospective member, new member, full member, marginal member and ex-member). These stages of group membership differ in the degree of group commitment of the group and the member to each other. Moving from one stage to the next involves a role transition, and role transitions can both be extreme (e.g. severe initiation rituals) and have a large impact on members (e.g. after exit).

GROUP DEVELOPMENT AND STRUCTURE: THE GROUP LEVEL OF ANALYSIS

How do group interaction, structure, norms, status and roles develop?

In the previous section we discussed the (changing) relation of the group member with the group. In this section

we explore the group level of analysis. First, we discuss how groups themselves can also change over time. Second, groups have certain characteristics, such as norms to govern their behaviour and a group structure, in which some members have more **status** than others, or in which different members occupy different roles in the group. These issues are examined below. It should be noted that this section is mainly relevant for groups with direct (usually face-to-face) interaction.

> **status** evaluation of a role by the group in which a role is contained or defined.

Group development

Some groups are formed for a special reason and end after a given time. Examples include therapy groups, project teams and the group of students in a psychology seminar (Figure 12.5). These groups will generally develop: the interaction patterns among group members change over time. Further, there may be similarities in the way different groups develop. The basic idea is that every group faces specific challenges and has specific goals, and these challenges and goals change over time. This, in turn, has consequences for the way group members interact with each other, as well as for group performance and the rewardingness of the group to its members.

Tuckman (1965) and Tuckman and Jensen (1977) introduced a classic five-stage model of group development: forming, storming, norming, performing and adjourning (see Theory Box 12.2). In the first stage, when the group is *forming*, group members feel insecure because they do not know each other and do not know what is expected of them. As a consequence,

FIGURE 12.5 *Some groups are formed for a special reason and also end after some time, e.g. a group of students in a psychology seminar.*

Source: © Robert Kneschke. Used under licence from Shutterstock.

THEORY BOX 12.2

THE FIVE STAGES OF GROUP DEVELOPMENT

Forming	Storming	Norming	Performing	Adjourning
Group members get to know each other: high uncertainty	Group members resist influence: disagreement and high conflict	Group members share a common purpose: high friendship and cohesion	Group members work together towards their goal: performance-oriented relations	Group members leave the group: feelings of accomplishment or failure, sometimes grief or relief

Source: Based on information reported in Tuckman & Jensen, 1977.

interactions are usually polite and inhibited. In this first stage, people get to know each other and develop a shared identity as members of the same group. This might happen at the beginning of a psychology seminar: students still feel insecure, engage in polite conversation, and the atmosphere is quite subdued. Once people have got to know each other, they enter the second stage (*storming*). The challenge in the second stage is to develop a group structure. Here issues of leadership and influence are at stake, and as group members may compete about different roles in the group, there may be conflicts and disagreements. Most groups will overcome this, and when a group structure and group roles have been established, they can move on to the third stage, *norming.* In this stage, group members develop close ties, and come to agree upon the group's goals and develop norms that govern group interaction. Once this has been achieved, the group enters the *performing* stage. Because group structure and group norms have been established, the group's efforts can be directed towards achieving the group's task. Although it is probably still necessary to engage in behaviours to maintain a positive atmosphere in the group, most activities will be task-related. The final stage of group development is *adjourning.* When the task has been accomplished or is abandoned, the group will end. This might be associated either with feelings of accomplishment or with feelings of disappointment (dependent, of course, on task success).

According to the Tuckman and Jensen (1977) model, the different stages of group life should be characterized by different interaction patterns within the group. But how can we establish whether this really is true? To answer that question, it is necessary to code group interactions into specific categories and see whether certain types of behaviour are more frequent in the early or the later stages of group life. Probably the best-known coding system of group interaction is Bales's (1950) *interaction process analysis* (IPA; see also Bales & Slater, 1955;

Chapter 2; and Leader in the Field, Robert F. Bales). IPA makes the basic and important distinction between task behaviours (all behaviours directed at task completion) and socio-emotional behaviours (all behaviours directed at interpersonal relations within the group). In the socio-emotional domain it further distinguishes between positive and negative behaviours. According to Bales, task-related behaviour is necessary for task completion, but can lead to conflicts when people disagree. In order not to disturb the functioning of the group, socio-emotional behaviour is necessary to restore group harmony. The coding system of IPA is shown in Figure 12.6. As can be seen in

task behaviours behaviours during group interactions that are directed at task completion.

socio-emotional behaviours behaviours during group interactions that are directed at interpersonal relations.

LEADER IN THE FIELD

Robert F. Bales (1916–2004), a pioneer in the development of systematic methods of group observation and measurement of interaction processes, received his BA and MS degrees in Sociology from the University of Oregon. He received his PhD in sociology in 1945, and was appointed Professor of Social Relations in 1957, retiring in 1986. During the 1944–45 academic year, Bales spent a formative year as Research Associate at the Section on Alcohol Studies at Yale University. His research on the interactions in therapeutic group settings formed the basis for his first and classic book, *Interaction process analysis: A method for the study of small groups*, published in 1950. Bales hoped that by studying the interaction of many such groups he would discover recurring patterns that might help to understand and to predict the functioning of problem-solving groups. His interaction process analysis proved an extremely useful tool for studying group interaction, group member roles and group development. This research reflected his conception of social psychology as the scientific study of social interaction within the group, and group activity – rather than individual activity – as the primary unit of analysis. With this research programme Bales sought to integrate the psychological and sociological sources of social psychology.

Socio-emotional behaviour, positive	1. Shows solidarity, raises other's status, gives help, reward.
	2. Shows tension release, jokes, laughs, shows satisfaction.
	3. Agrees, shows passive acceptance, understands, concurs, complies.
Task behaviour, neutral	4. Gives suggestions, directions, implying autonomy for other.
	5. Gives opinion, evaluates, analyses, expresses feelings and wishes.
	6. Gives orientation, information, repeats, clarifies, confirms.
	7. Asks for orientation, information, repetition, confirmation.
	8. Asks for opinion, evaluation, analysis, expression of feeling.
	9. Asks for suggestion, direction, possible ways of action.
Socio-emotional behaviour, negative	10. Disagrees, shows passive rejection, formality, withholds help.
	11. Shows tension, asks for help, withdraws out of the field.
	12. Shows antagonism, deflates other's status, defends or asserts self.

FIGURE 12.6 *The coding scheme of Interaction Process Analysis.*
Source: Based on information reported in Bales (1950).

the figure, the scheme distinguishes between 12 different categories, divided into socio-emotional behaviours that are positive, task-related behaviours (which are emotionally neutral) and negative socio-emotional behaviours.

Now, according to the Tuckman and Jensen (1977) stage model, these 12 categories of behaviour should occur to differing degrees in the different stages of group life. The forming stage should be characterized by much positive socio-emotional behaviour, whereas in the storming stage more negative socio-emotional behaviour should occur. In the norming stage, there should be both positive socio-emotional behaviour and task-related behaviour, and the performing stage should be dominated by task-related behaviour. Is this what really happens? At a general level, the answer seems to be *yes*. For example, Wheelan, Davidson and Tilin (2003) found time together to be negatively related to socio-emotional behaviours (the longer the group was together, the *fewer* of these behaviours); time together was also positively related to task-related behaviours (the longer the group was together, the *more* of these behaviours). More about group development can be found in Wheelan (1994).

On the other hand, stage models such as Tuckman and Jensen's can easily be criticized as an oversimplification of reality. Some groups, for example, may never have a storming stage, whereas other groups are in conflict continuously. Further, groups may sometimes return to a previous stage instead of progressing to the next as the model would assume. Finally, it will often be impossible to establish which stage the group is in, and the assumption that the different stages are qualitatively different from each other is difficult to maintain. Rather, different activities occur in each stage, although they may vary in intensity. Most researchers would therefore argue that there are no abrupt changes in the way group members interact with each other, but rather that these changes occur gradually and that one can see this as a gradual development of groups over time.

On being similar: norms, shared cognition and cohesion

Group norms Group norms are belief systems about how (or how not) to behave, which guide behaviour but without the force of laws, and which reflect group members' shared expectations about typical or desirable activities. Some norms are prescriptive, and prescribe which attitudes, behaviour and beliefs are and are not appropriate in the context of the group; other norms are descriptive, and merely describe which behaviour is typical within the group (see Chapter 8). Norms serve as guides for attitudes and behaviour and in that way perform an important regulatory function. Group members tend to conform to group norms (i.e. think and act in accordance with group norms), either because group norms are internalized – that is, become part of the individual's belief and value system (Turner, 1991) – or because group norms are enforced by the (anticipated) reaction of other group members to normative and anti-normative behaviour (Deutsch & Gerard, 1955).

Because of this adherence to group norms, groups function more smoothly with than without norms. For instance, if everybody adheres to group norms, other group members' behaviour becomes more predictable and therefore can be anticipated. In that sense, group norms help regulate group interaction. Group norms are also an important source of information about social reality. Often, people rely on what many people see as valid and true as an accurate reflection of (social) reality. Another important function of norms is that conformity to group norms illustrates one's group commitment – it shows that one is 'a good group member' (cf. Hollander, 1958; see also Chapter 8). A particularly dramatic illustration of the power of group norms can be found in Social Psychology Beyond the Lab 12.2.

This is not to say, however, that all group members always conform to group norms. Individual group members may show deviant behaviour. If they do, however, they are likely to run into the negative responses of their fellow group members, even to the extent that they may be excluded from the group (Schachter, 1951). Because social exclusion is a highly unpleasant experience (see Williams, 2001, earlier in this chapter), such pressures to conform to group norms tend to be quite effective in many situations. Thus, groups may enforce and maintain their group norms.

As already noted in the discussion of group development, groups develop group norms relatively early in their existence (Tuckman, 1965). This is not to say that group norms do not change. Norms may change over time. This change may occur because the environment of the group changes. It may also occur because the membership of the group changes. New members tend to be socialized into the group and its norms (Moreland & Levine, 1982), but they may also introduce changes to the group. Indeed, as research on minority influence shows (see Chapter 8), if the conditions are right a deviant minority may convert a whole group towards a different way of thinking. Group norms should therefore be seen on the one hand as enforcing their own maintenance, and on the other as subject to change over time and situations. Group norms are thus both an influence on group process and an outcome of group process.

Socially shared cognition and affect An aspect of groups that has received more attention in recent years is shared cognition (Thompson, Levine, & Messick, 1999; Tindale & Kameda, 2000). Over time, groups may develop a shared understanding of different aspects of group life, such as the tasks the group performs, the role of each member in the group, and each member's particular knowledge, skills and abilities. For each individual group member, such understanding is important, but when it is shared within the group it has the added advantage of setting the stage for smooth coordination, communication and cooperation, because all group members have a similar understanding of what they are supposed to do and who does what. Socially shared cognitions, when accurately reflecting the demands faced by the group, may therefore improve group functioning and performance (Van Ginkel & Van Knippenberg, 2008).

A nice illustration of the influence of shared cognition is found in work on **transactive memory**. Transactive memory refers to shared knowledge about how information is distributed in the group. Rather than having all the information themselves, group members know who knows what and whom to ask for information about specific things (Wegner, 1987). Transactive memory makes it possible for groups to operate efficiently and adequately, because it helps locate information and 'the right person for the job' (see also Chapter 13). For an illustration of the benefits of transactive memory, see Research Close-Up 12.2.

> **transactive memory** a system of knowledge available to group members with shared awareness of each other's expertise, strengths and weaknesses.

Groups may share not only cognition but also emotions (George, 1990). Research in group emotions is still in its infancy, but there is emerging evidence that groups may come to share emotions, and that these shared emotions affect group functioning. Barsade (2002), for instance, studied **emotional contagion**, which is the transfer of moods and emotions among people in a group. Barsade had groups discuss a fictional business case, in which they had to distribute bonuses among employees. Unknown to the real participants, one of the group members was a confederate (a drama student) who was trained to show either positive or negative emotions during the exercise (through facial expressions, tone of voice and so on). Barsade found evidence for emotional contagion: group members' moods became more similar to the confederate's mood. Further, when the confederate showed positive emotions, the group discussion was more cooperative and less conflict occurred. In a similar vein, Sy, Coté, and Saavedra (2005) showed that the affect displayed by the leader of a group transferred to the members of the group and affected group performance: groups performed better when the leader displayed positive affect than when the leader displayed negative affect.

> **emotional contagion** the transfer of moods and emotions among people in a group.

THE IMPORTANCE OF KNOWING WHO KNOWS WHAT

RESEARCH CLOSE-UP 12.2

Moreland, R. L., & Myaskovsky, L. (2000). Exploring the performance benefits of group training: Transactive memory or improved communication? *Organizational Behavior and Human Decision Processes, 82*, 117–133.

Research Question

Transactive memory – shared awareness of the expertise of each of the group members – should help groups perform better. Knowing who knows what helps to locate the knowledge and expertise necessary to deal with the task at hand within the group, helps to coordinate efforts by assigning tasks to those members with most expertise for these tasks, and reduces potential problems due to disagreements. But how are these transactive memory systems formed, and do they actually benefit performance? Moreland and Myaskovsky argued that groups with members that were trained as a group for a task, rather than as separate individuals, would benefit from this because watching each other in action during training would allow the group to develop transactive memory. However, also simply telling group members (who were trained individually) which group member is good at which task should have similar beneficial effects. Only groups whose members were trained individually and who do not receive feedback about the group members' expertise should do relatively poorly.

Design

One hundred and eighty-nine students were assigned to three-person groups. These groups were assigned to three different conditions in a between-subjects design. They were assigned either to an individual training condition, a group training condition or a feedback condition in which group members learned individually about other group members' expertise (i.e. which would also allow for the formation of transactive memory).

Procedure

The group task was to assemble a radio with as few errors as possible. To that end, group members were first trained in the assembly task. Depending on condition, this training was given to the group as a whole or to individual group members. In the feedback condition, individually trained group members later learned about each other's expertise via written feedback. Subsequently, they performed the group task (i.e. assembling a radio). This group interaction was videotaped, and independent coders rated the observed behaviour on the tapes for indicators of transactive memory: *specialization*, with group members

focusing on their own expertise; *coordination* of task efforts along expertise lines; and *trust* in each other's expertise as evidenced in less argument about areas of expertise).

Results

As predicted, groups whose members were trained as a group or received feedback about other members' expertise made fewer assembly errors than groups with members that were trained individually (see Figure 12.7). This pattern of results was mirrored in the transactive memory measure (a combination of specialization, coordination and trust), and further analysis suggested that the greater transactive memory was the underlying process that brought about the better performance of group-trained and feedback groups.

Implications

This study illustrates the importance of transactive memory to group performance: groups are better able to use their expertise and engage in better-coordinated efforts the more they have a shared awareness of who knows what. The study also shows that this awareness may be achieved through a shared training experience, as well as through specific feedback about group members' areas of expertise.

FIGURE 12.7 *Number of errors as a function of training condition.*

Source: Based on Moreland & Myaskovsky, 2000, with permission from Elsevier.

SOCIAL PSYCHOLOGY BEYOND THE LAB 12.2

JONESTOWN

On 18 November 1978 more than 900 men, women and children died in a mass suicide/murder in Jonestown, a jungle encampment in Guyana, South America. Most of them drank, or were forced to drink, a fruit punch that had been laced with cyanide and tranquillizers. Parents first gave it to their children, then drank it themselves (Figure 12.8). How could this have happened? Why did a whole group of people resort to this desperate measure? Strict adherence to group norms is part of the answer.

The people of Jonestown were members of a religious cult, called the People's Temple. The cult was founded in the US by James Warren Jones and had moved to the jungle encampment in Guyana in the mid-1970s. There, the members of the cult had to work hard on the fields and lived in isolation from the outside world. Immediately before the tragedy, US Congressman Ryan had visited Jonestown with some journalists, investigating accusations that people were being held there against their will. Eighteen people indeed wanted to leave with Ryan. However, cult members attacked them at the airstrip as they were leaving, killing the congressman, three journalists and one defector, and wounding 12 others. Back in Jonestown, Jones proclaimed that the 'end had come', and

that in this extreme situation 'revolutionary suicide' was their only option. The members of the People's Temple obeyed, committing mass suicide and killing those who were unable or unwilling to kill themselves (including children and the elderly). The dramatic story of Jonestown is described in the 1980 book *Black and White* by Shiva Naipaul.

To begin to understand why they chose death, one must firstly realize that the members of the People's Temple were socialized to accept the norms of the cult. One of the more important norms was loyalty to the group, a norm that was quite strictly enforced. Moreover, the cult's leadership was extremely autocratic – whatever the cult's leader, Jones, decreed was group normative and had to be obeyed (see Hogg & Van Knippenberg, 2003, for a discussion of leaders as embodying group norms). Second, the members of the People's Temple lived in isolation from the outside world and had no contacts with relatives or others outside Jonestown. One implication of their isolation was that an end to Jonestown would imply a loss of all their current social ties. It also implied that the people of the Jonestown commune were only in contact with like-minded people. As this chapter shows, one function of groups is to provide us with knowledge of our social and physical world. In isolation, people may even begin to believe bizarre things, such as the concept of 'revolutionary suicide'. The members of the cult, for example, believed that an end to Jonestown would mean not only an end to the promised land they had believed in, but also facing torture and imprisonment by the US government. When faced with the grim prospect of losing all social ties, all hopes, everything they believed in, and of being tortured and imprisoned, several of them saw no reason to live. Those that were less inclined to go down with the cult on Jones's bidding were trapped by the strong conformity to group norms of their fellow cult members, who forced them into partaking in the mass suicide.

Although the Jonestown case is clearly extreme, and fortunately very rare, it does illustrate the power of the social group (and of an autocratic leader). It is one of social psychology's goals to understand these tragedies and hopefully prevent them in the future.

FIGURE 12.8 *Members of the People's Temple at Jonestown, Guyana, committed mass suicide in 1978. They were socialized to accept the cult's norms, especially group loyalty.*
Source: © Press Association Images.

GROUP COHESIVENESS LEADS TO BETTER PERFORMANCE WHEN THE GROUP ACCEPTS PERFORMANCE GOALS

RESEARCH CLOSE-UP 12.3

Podsakoff, P. M., MacKenzie, S. B., & Ahearne, M. (1997). Moderating effects of goal acceptance on the relationship between group cohesiveness and productivity. *Journal of Applied Psychology, 82,* 974–983.

Research question

Does group cohesion lead to better performance? Podsakoff and colleagues argued that higher cohesion does not always lead to better performance. They argued that the relationship between cohesiveness and performance should depend on the group's acceptance of performance goals. If the group accepts the performance goals of the organization, cohesiveness should be positively related to group performance. If, however, the group does not accept performance goals, then cohesiveness is expected to be unrelated (or even negatively related) to performance.

Design

The study participants were 218 members of 40 work crews at a paper mill in the US. Crews consisted of 5.25 members on average, most participants were male (96 per cent), and their average age was 39 years old. These participants responded to questions in a standardized questionnaire, and performance data was also collected from company records. The design was correlational (i.e. correlations were computed among measured variables, and no manipulations were involved), and analyses were performed at the group level.

Procedure

Two measures were obtained through a questionnaire distributed among the work crew members: group cohesiveness and acceptance of the performance goals of the company. Thus, all group members individually rated their perception of group cohesiveness and their acceptance of performance goals. Performance of each crew was obtained from company records. It consisted of the amount of paper produced as a percentage of total machine capacity.

Results

Figure 12.9 shows the results. As predicted, group cohesion and group goal acceptance interacted in predicting task performance. When groups were relatively accepting of performance goals, the relationship between group cohesion and group performance was positive. However, when groups were not accepting of performance goals, the relationship between group cohesion and performance tended to be negative.

Implications

This study illustrates that group cohesion does not necessarily motivate performance. Rather, it motivates group members to exert themselves for causes that are seen as important to the group (see Van Knippenberg & Ellemers, 2003). When group members do not accept the company's performance goals, higher cohesion will generally not improve performance.

FIGURE 12.9 *The relation between cohesion and performance for crews low and high in goal acceptance.*

Source: After Podsakoff, MacKenzie, & Ahearne, © 1997 by the American Psychological Association. Adapted with permission. The use of APA information does not imply endorsement by APA.

Group cohesion Group **cohesion** (or 'cohesiveness') is the force that binds members to the group and induces them to stay with the group (Festinger, 1950). Group cohesion is assumed to be important to group functioning, because it helps to keep the group together and motivates group members to exert themselves on behalf of the group.

> **cohesion** the force that binds members to the group.

Evidence for this proposition is mixed, however, and research suggests that it is useful to distinguish between types of cohesion. **Task cohesion** refers to the shared commitment to the group's tasks, while **interpersonal cohesion** refers to the attraction to the

> **task cohesion** cohesion based on attraction of group members to the group task.
>
> **interpersonal cohesion** cohesion based on liking of the group and its members.

group. As a meta-analysis by Mullen and Copper (1994) shows, only task cohesion is (positively) related to group performance. Further, cohesion may not always improve performance, as can be seen in Research Close-Up 12.3.

On being different: status and roles

Whereas norms make group members' behaviour more alike, there are also clear differences between group members in the way they behave and the position they have in the group. Take a football team for instance. Clearly, different players have different roles, defined by their position on the field (goalkeeper, defender, forward). Besides these formal roles, there will also be informal roles. For example, a more experienced team member (even though not formally the team captain) may have more influence on the other players than a newcomer, and another team member may always take the initiative to reconcile people after an argument.

Earlier we discussed Bales's (1950) interaction process analysis (IPA). It appears that IPA is a useful tool for looking at status and roles inside a group: it is possible to keep track of the 12 different types of behaviour (see Figure 12.6) for each group member, to see whether there are differences among group members. Research using IPA (or other coding systems) to code behaviour in freely interacting groups has revealed a number of important insights. A good overview of these insights can be found in one of the most influential books on group dynamics,

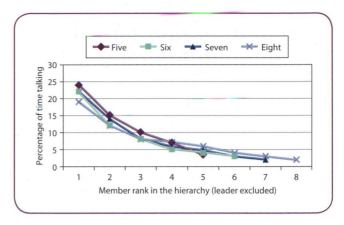

FIGURE 12.10 *Speaking hierarchy for groups of five, six, seven, and eight members. (Member rank is based on percentage of time talking.)*

Source: Taken from Stephan, 1952, with permission from SAGE publications.

McGrath's (1984) *Groups: Interaction and Performance* (see Leader in the Field, Joseph E. McGrath). We will discuss two of these findings now.

First, some group members talk more than others, and the discrepancy increases with the size of the group. Thus, groups develop a **speaking hierarchy** (Bales, 1953) in which members higher in the hierarchy talk more than those lower in the hierarchy. For example, Figure 12.10 shows the speaking hierarchy found by Stephan (1952), which depicts the percentage of time a group member was talking in different-sized groups. For example, the person talking most in an eight-person group talked about 20 per cent of the time, while the person talking least talked only about two per cent of the time. Further, people who talk more are usually seen as more influential. Later research has shown that group members do not distribute their participation evenly throughout the discussion, but rather that contributions are concentrated in periods of high activity (Dabbs & Ruback, 1987). Thus, if a person has spoken recently, he or she is more likely to speak again. Often this takes the form of a dyadic exchange, in which two group members alternate speaking turns. When this happens, we say that the group is in a *floor* position (i.e. two group members 'hold the floor'; Parker, 1988). Parker found that four-person groups were in a floor position no less than 61 per cent of their time, much more than would be expected if all group members contributed equally.

> **speaking hierarchy** hierarchy within a group based on who talks most.

Second, research using IPA has found that some people are consistently more task-oriented (i.e. they engage mostly in task-related behaviours, categories

---

LEADER IN THE FIELD

Joseph E. McGrath (1927–2007) was one of the most influential people in the field of group dynamics. This is the case not only because of his own research and writing, but also because he was an excellent mentor who supervised a number of graduate students who later became well-known researchers themselves (for example Richard Hackman, Janice Kelly, Andrea Hollingshead and Linda Argote). McGrath received his PhD from the University of Michigan in 1955, and worked at the University of Illinois from 1960 until his retirement in 1997 (after which he remained active as a researcher until his death). He has published a number of influential books, but one of his best-known is the 1984 book entitled *Groups: Interaction and Performance*. This book provides an excellent summary and integration of work on group dynamics as well as work on group performance (see Chapter 13, this volume). McGrath was especially interested in change of groups over time, and believed that research should emphasize the dynamics of groups, rather than just looking at snapshot pictures of groups in the lab. In his later work McGrath studied the differences between face-to-face versus computer-mediated communication. McGrath was also famous for the poems that he wrote on his work as a mentor and researcher, which he referred to as 'doggerels'. About mentoring of students he wrote, for example: 'So what I best could do for them/Was not to scorn nor flatter/But rather to convince them that/Their own ideas matter'.

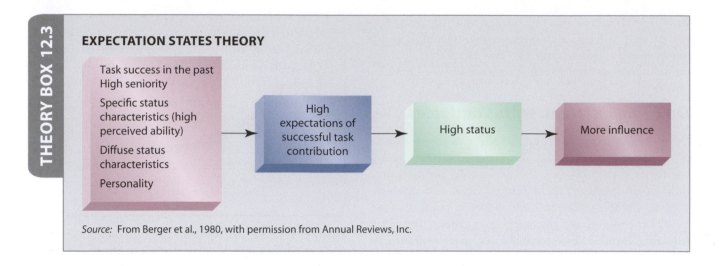

Source: From Berger et al., 1980, with permission from Annual Reviews, Inc.

4–9 in Figure 12.6), whereas others are more relationship-oriented (i.e. they engage more in socio-emotional behaviours) (Slater, 1955). The former type of person has been labelled the *task specialist* and the latter the *socio-emotional specialist*: clearly a case of (informal) role differentiation. It further appeared that these two group members interacted with each other quite frequently, and much more than would be expected according to chance (i.e. they were often in a floor position). Finally, the task specialist was seen as most influential, but he or she was liked less than the socio-emotional specialist.

Who talks most in the group and who takes which role is dependent on personality and individual abilities. For example, an extroverted person will probably talk more than an introverted person. However, this is not the whole story: there are other factors that determine who is more and who is less influential. The most comprehensive theory about status in groups is **expectation states theory** (Berger, Rosenholtz, & Zelditch, 1980). This deals with the issue of how status structures emerge in groups and how they are shaped by the outside status of group members (see Ridgeway, 2001, for an overview of the theory and the evidence for it). A simplified graphical depiction of the theory is presented in Theory Box 12.3.

Expectation states theory is applicable to groups in which members strive for a common goal or perform a common task. It assumes that several inequalities within a group, such as inequalities in participation and influence, are highly correlated because they are all derived from *performance expectations*. That is, because of specific characteristics of group members, other group members form expectations about the

expectation states theory argues that status differences within a group result from different expectations that group members have about each other.

usefulness of each group member's contributions. These expectations then serve as a self-fulfilling prophecy: the greater the expectations, the more likely a person is to speak up, offer suggestions and be evaluated positively by the others. The lower the expectations, the less likely it is that these things happen. The important question, then, is: what determines these performance expectations?

The theory assumes that performance expectations are influenced by so-called *status characteristics*. A distinction is drawn between *diffuse* status characteristics (not necessarily related to the group task), including, for example, gender, age and race, and *specific* status characteristics, such as skills and abilities (i.e. characteristics that are necessary for the group task and previous task success). These characteristics carry certain cultural expectations about competencies. For example, women have stereotypically been seen as less competent than men (especially on tasks that are more 'masculine'; e.g. Pugh & Wahrman, 1983), and more senior people may be seen as more competent (up to a certain age) than younger people (Freese & Cohen, 1973). Similarly, higher expectations are formed for people who are more experienced, have a higher status in society more generally, or have a relevant area of expertise. Obviously, these expectations may sometimes be false (e.g. a woman may in fact be more competent than a man), but they nevertheless affect people's status in the group and the amount of influence they have. The reason is that expectations need to be explicitly falsified before they lose their influence, and as long as they are not falsified, they continue to have their effect in a self-fulfilling way. There is extensive evidence supporting the theory. For example, Driskell and Mullen (1990) found that characteristics of group members affected their status and power through the expectations of other group members (for more evidence, see Ridgeway, 2001).

Summary

Groups develop over time, in the sense that their inter-action patterns change. Further, some processes cause group members to become more similar to each other, both in terms of their behaviour (as prescribed by group norms) and in terms of their cognitions and emotions. Finally, differences between group members may also emerge, for which expectation states theory offers a theoretical account. We now turn to the last level of analysis: the contextual or intergroup level.

GROUPS IN THEIR ENVIRONMENT: THE INTERGROUP LEVEL OF ANALYSIS

In what ways does the (intergroup) context affect intragroup behaviour?

Going back to our opening example of the football fans, it is clear that these people do not always behave in this way. They are also supporters of their team when the team is not playing, but it is the context of the match that draws them together and that brings out their behaviour in the subway station. Playing against another team renders these supporters' affiliation with their favourite team salient and evokes the quite uniform behaviour that clearly identifies them as a group.

What holds for these supporters holds for all groups. Groups do not live in isolation. Other groups are part of the environment in which groups function. Understanding the psychology of groups therefore requires studying the influence of the *intergroup context* on the thoughts, feelings and behaviour of group members. Part of this involves the study of intergroup relations – the way group members think, feel and act towards members of other groups (see Chapter 14). The intergroup context may, however, also affect intragroup processes, and that is the issue we focus on here.

The intergroup context and the salience of group membership

The fact that individuals are members of a specific group does not mean that this group membership is always at the forefront of their minds. Self-categorization as a group member needs to be cognitively activated, or rendered *salient*, for the group membership to exert its influence on people's self-definition (see Chapter 5). Once salient, group membership then influences group members' attitudes and behaviour via this self-definition (i.e. social identity; see Turner et al., 1987; also Chapters 8 and 14). An important influence of the intergroup context is that of rendering group membership salient. Exposure to other groups in a sense 'reminds' us of our own group memberships. Especially in the context of an intergroup confrontation of some kind, this may work to render group membership a salient influence on group members' thoughts, feelings and behaviour. Such confrontations may involve explicit competition, as in sports or in the political arena, or competition for scarce goods (e.g. customers, funding), but may also involve more implicit forms of competition, such as competition for social status (e.g. 'which is the most important department within an organization?', 'which street gang has the toughest reputation?').

These processes are well illustrated in a study by James and Greenberg (1989). They conducted two experiments in which they had students from their university work on a task solving anagrams. The task objective was to solve as many anagrams as possible, and participants' performance on the task (i.e. the number of anagrams solved) was the main dependent variable of interest. James and Greenberg argued that students would be more motivated, and therefore perform better, when their university membership was made salient in the context of a comparison between students from their university and students from another university.

James and Greenberg experimentally manipulated the extent to which students' affiliation to their university was salient. In their first experiment, they manipulated group membership salience by letting participants work in a room that was painted either white (low salience condition) or red and blue (the colours of the university: high salience condition). All participants were led to believe that the experiment was part of a larger study comparing the performance of students from their university with that of students from a 'rival' university. As expected, participants in the high group membership salience condition (red-and-blue room) solved more anagrams than did participants in the low group membership salience condition.

In their second experiment, James and Greenberg aimed to show that this effect would only be found in the presence of intergroup comparison and not in the absence of this intergroup comparison. In order to demonstrate this, they manipulated not only group membership salience but also the presence or absence of the comparison

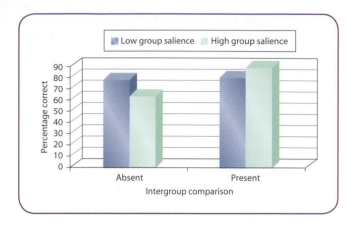

FIGURE 12.11 *Percentage of anagrams solved correctly as a function of ingroup salience and comparison condition.*

Source: Based on James & Greenberg, 1989, with permission from SAGE Publications.

with the other university. Intergroup comparison was manipulated by telling half of the participants that their performance would be compared with that of the rival university (as in the first study), whereas the other half did not receive this instruction. This time, salience was manipulated by giving participants a practice anagram that solved either as *wildcats*, which referred to their university mascot (high salience condition), or as *beavers*, which had no relevance for university membership (low salience condition). Results indicated that group salience had no effect when the intergroup comparison was absent, but that group salience led to higher (and the highest) performance when intergroup comparison was present (see Figure 12.11).

What this study shows is that group membership needs to be salient to affect behaviour, but that the context in which it is rendered salient affects whether and how group membership salience translates into behaviour (for more on this issue, see Haslam, 2004; Van Knippenberg, 2000). In the intergroup context created by James and Greenberg (1989), performing well could help establish that one's own group was superior to the comparison group. Because salient group memberships reflect on how we see ourselves, the relative standing of our group vis-à-vis other groups (i.e. are we 'better'?) reflects on how good or bad we can feel about ourselves. Obviously, then, we prefer our groups to compare favourably to other groups, and are willing

SOCIAL PSYCHOLOGY BEYOND THE LAB 12.3

THE OLD FIRM, *AND MANY, MANY MORE . . .*

Intergroup comparison and intergroup competition may invite group members to give of their best to outperform the other group. Some intergroup comparisons are more important to groups than others, however, and these comparisons in particular motivate efforts on behalf of the group to put the group in a favourable light vis-à-vis the other group.

One only needs to look around to see examples of this in everyday life. People in many countries find it easy to identify 'rival cities' – Melbourne and Sydney in Australia, Amsterdam and Rotterdam in The Netherlands, Lisbon and Porto in Portugal, etc. Sport is also full of such examples, where one opponent in particular is associated with such feelings of intergroup rivalry. As a case in point, consider Celtic and Glasgow Rangers, two football clubs from Glasgow, Scotland. Their rivalry is so intense (at least in part because it also captures antagonism between Catholics and Protestants) that a match between Celtic and Rangers even goes by a nickname – 'The Old Firm'. For both Celtic and Rangers, winning The Old Firm is perhaps the most important goal in the season, and hooliganism reaches its peak around these matches, suggesting that supporters, and especially hooligans, feel likewise (for a book on football club rivalry, see Giles Goodhead's (2004) *Us versus Them: Journeys to the World's Greatest Football Derbies*).

Such rivalries may be observed at all levels between all kinds of groups – nations, cities, organizations, universities, sport clubs, etc. What all such intergroup comparisons have in common is that they render group membership highly salient and motivate group members to outperform the other group. This may inspire great things such as superior athletic performance, but also outright undesirable behaviour such as hooliganism, as well as more silly expressions of intergroup rivalry such as an unwillingness to pronounce the other group's name (a widespread custom in the Dutch city of Rotterdam, for instance, is to not pronounce the name of Amsterdam, but rather to refer to the city simply by its telephone area code, '020').

to contribute actively to our group achieving such a favourable comparison (Tajfel & Turner, 1979). In the situation created by James and Greenberg, this led individuals for whom group membership was made salient in the context of intergroup comparison to work harder. In other situations, intergroup comparisons may have different effects: see Social Psychology Beyond the Lab 12.3 for an illustrative example.

An important influence of the intergroup context on group members is, thus, that it may render group membership salient, and may increase the likelihood that this salient self-categorization will be translated into attitudes and behaviour. The intergroup context may also affect group members' perceptions of their own group, and by doing so may affect attitudes and behaviour that are contingent on these perceptions. This is an issue that is addressed next.

The intergroup context, group perceptions and social influence

Part of what defines a group is the distinction between who is 'in' and who is 'out'. Groups exist by virtue of their members, but also by the fact that there are some people who are *not* members of the group and may indeed be members of *other* groups. Accordingly, people's perceptions of their membership groups are affected by the comparison between their own group and other groups, and group members' perceptions of their group are also contingent on what differentiates their group from other groups (Turner et al., 1987). Put differently, we ascribe characteristics to ourselves and to our groups on the basis of our perception that we possess these characteristics to a greater degree than others. For example, we will only come to the conclusion that the members of our group are intelligent if we perceive our group to be more intelligent than some other groups. Indeed, such social comparison processes for evaluating ourselves permeate social life (see Chapter 14 for further detail on intergroup social comparison). The important point for our present discussion is that if the intergroup context changes, comparison groups may change, and as a consequence our perceptions of our group may change.

Take, for instance, the case of political parties. Members of a party that is the most conservative within a country's political spectrum will probably think of their party as conservative. However, when a new party emerges that is perceived to be more conservative, the attribute 'conservative' may become less suited to distinguish the party from other parties, and party members' perceptions of their party may change to emphasize other characteristics of their party. Or consider, for example, the discussion about Turkey's prospective membership of the European Union. In contrast to the other countries of the European Union, the largest religious denomination in Turkey is Islam rather than Christianity. This fact seems to have highlighted the shared roots in Christianity of the current EU countries in the perception of many parties taking part in the discussion – an attribute that until now never really seemed at the forefront of perception within the European Union.

Changes in the intergroup context may occur because old groups disappear from the scene (e.g. a competitor goes bankrupt) or new groups emerge, or because an existing group becomes more relevant as a comparison group (as in the example of Turkey and the European Union) or less relevant as a comparison group (e.g. because a competing firm focuses more on other markets than competing directly with one's own firm in the same market). Such changes may affect which attributes of the group are salient (i.e. what differentiates the group from relevant other groups), but they may also alter our perception of a given attribute of the group. Take the example of a group of psychology students who think of themselves as intelligent. In comparison to most groups in society, this makes sense and greater intelligence may indeed be a feature distinguishing psychology students from other groups. Imagine, however, that this group finds itself in a context where comparison with a group of the proverbial rocket scientists becomes relevant. Intelligence is still a salient attribute – indeed, rocket science is invoked in everyday language to indicate levels of complexity and sophistication requiring the highest levels of intelligence and expertise – but the psychology students will find that they no longer distinguish themselves through superior intelligence. Rather, intelligence is what distinguishes rocket scientists from other groups, and psychology students may be invited to see the intelligence of their own group as modest at best.

Summary

The intergroup context may both affect the salience of group membership and inform group members' behaviour within this wider context. This context of intergroup relations can influence perceptions of group norms that may feed into attitudes and behaviour.

CHAPTER SUMMARY

- *When can we say that a group exists?* A group exists when two or more people define themselves as members of a group.

- *Why do people join groups?* The reasons why people form, join and distinguish groups are sociobiological (evolutionarily built in, for self-preservation), cognitive (to gain understanding of our world) and utilitarian (to gain benefits).

- *Are there different types of groups, and how do they differ from each other?* Different types of groups, such as task groups, intimacy groups, social categories and loose associations, differ on a number of important dimensions such as group entitativity, importance, shared objectives and which needs these groups are likely to fulfil.

- *How does group membership change over time?* Group members move through the different stages of group membership (prospective member, new member, full member, marginal member and ex-member) separated from each other by role transitions, and these different stages are characterized by different levels of commitment.

- *How can harsh initiation rituals be explained?* The role transition of entry can be marked by a harsh transition ritual. A classic explanation for these rituals is given by dissonance theory, which argues that such rituals increase commitment to the group. However, as we have seen, severe initiations often do *not* increase liking, and have other functions than increasing commitment.

- *What determines how easy it is to become a group member?* An important determinant of group openness is staffing level: it is easier to become a full member of an understaffed as compared to an overstaffed group.

- *What are the consequences of exclusion from groups?* Social exclusion from groups can lead to quite severe anger and depression.

- *How do groups change over time?* Groups develop over time, because the challenges they face and the goals they have change. Tuckman's classic theory distinguishes five stages: forming, storming, norming, performing and adjourning.

- *How can we systematically observe group interactions?* Interaction process analysis is a useful coding scheme for group interactions and makes a basic distinction between socio-emotional and task behaviours.

- *How does being in a group affect memory and emotions?* Through shared experiences, groups develop shared cognitions, such as transactive memory systems (i.e. knowing who knows what) and shared emotions.

- *What is the role of group cohesion?* Cohesion can be based on attractiveness of the group (interpersonal cohesion) or on attractiveness of the group task (task cohesion). In general, cohesion motivates group members to exert effort for causes that are important to the group.

- *How do status and role differences develop within groups?* Expectation states theory explains the emergence of a status structure in a group. It argues that certain status characteristics lead to performance expectations that subsequently lead to differences in status and influence.

- *How does the intergroup context influence intragroup behaviour?* The presence of other groups can make group membership salient. As a consequence, group members will be more strongly influenced by their group membership.

SUGGESTIONS FOR FURTHER READING

Haslam, S. A. (2004). *Psychology in organisations: The social identity approach* (2nd edn.). London: Sage. A detailed review of the influence of group norms and intergroup context on attitudes and behaviour in groups.

Hogg, M. A., & Van Knippenberg, D. (2003). Social identity and leadership processes in groups. In M. P. Zanna (Ed.), *Advances in experimental social psychology* (Vol. 35, pp. 1–52). San Diego, CA: Academic Press. An analysis of the relationship between group norms and leadership, showing how leaders may be influential by being seen to embody what is group-normative.

Lickel, B., Hamilton, D. L., & Sherman, S. J. (2001). Elements of a lay theory of groups: Types of groups, relational styles, and the perception of group entitativity. *Personality and Social Psychology Review*, *5*, 129–140. An in-depth discussion of types of groups and 'lay theories' about them (i.e. how lay people look at groups).

McGrath, J. E. (1984). *Groups: Interaction and performance.* Englewood Cliffs, NJ: Prentice Hall. Provides a very good overview of early findings in group dynamics and group performance research.

Moreland, R. L., & Levine, J. M. (1982). Socialization in small groups: Temporal changes in individual–group relations. In L. Berkowitz (Ed.), *Advances in experimental social psychology* (Vol. 15, pp. 137–192). New York: Academic Press. An extensive discussion of group socialization.

Nijstad, B. A. (2009). *Group performance*. Hove, UK: Psychology Press. Gives a more in-depth discussion of various topics dealt with in this chapter.

Peltokorpi, V. (2008). Transactive memory systems. *Review of General Psychology, 12*, 378–394. Gives a recent and comprehensive overview of the literature on transactive memory systems and other forms of shared cognition.

Ridgeway, C. L. (2001). Social status and group structure. In M. A. Hogg & R. S. Tindale (Eds.), *Blackwell handbook of social psychology: Group processes* (pp. 352–375). Oxford: Blackwell. A good summary of the research on expectation states theory.

Tindale, R. S., & Kameda, T. (2000). Social sharedness as a unifying theme for information processing in groups. *Group Processes & Intergroup Relations, 3*, 123–140. A straightforward statement of the importance and effects of the social sharedness of cognition and psychological states in groups.

Wheelan, S.A. (1994). *Group process: A developmental perspective*. Boston, MA: Allyn & Bacon. A discussion of group development that examines different stages of group life.

13 Group Performance and Leadership

STEFAN SCHULZ-HARDT AND FELIX C. BRODBECK

Source: © Mike Blank. Used under licence from Getty Images.

KEY TERMS

- brainstorming
- cognitive restriction
- cognitive stimulation
- contingency approaches
- coordination losses
- dispensability effect
- eureka effect
- group composition
- group leadership
- group learning
- group performance management
- group synchronization
- group task types
- group-to-group transfer
- group-to-individual transfer
- group-to-individual-in-group transfer
- hidden profile
- individual capability gains and losses
- individual-to-individual transfer
- Köhler effect
- laissez-faire leaders
- leader traits
- leaderless groups
- leadership behaviour
- leadership effectiveness
- leadership (in organizations)
- leadership style
- motivation losses and gains
- nominal group
- potential group performance (group potential)
- production blocking
- Ringelmann effect
- shared or team leadership
- social compensation
- social competition
- social loafing
- sucker effect
- team awareness
- transactional leaders
- transformational (charismatic) leaders

CHAPTER OUTLINE

ROUTE MAP OF THE CHAPTER

In this chapter we examine the question of how social interdependence and social interaction affect group performance. More specifically, we provide answers to the following questions: How can we identify group-level effects on performance? What are the major pitfalls and opportunities for performance when people work together in a group? What can we do to systematically optimize group performance? What makes leadership effective? Why is leadership so critical for group performance, and how can it contribute to the optimization of group performance? We answer these questions by outlining the basic underlying principles, applying them to specific group tasks, with examples, and selectively illustrating them with empirical research.

INTRODUCTION

We all often work in groups. Some of these groups are informal, for example a group of students preparing for an exam. Other groups are more or less formal; for example: a work team on the production line; a personnel selection committee; or a sports team (Figure 13.1). Thus, work in groups is an essential part of our society (for basic principles of the psychology of groups, see Chapter 12). Whereas in some cases groups are indispensable for performing a specific task (e.g. you can only play volleyball in a team), in many other cases groups are used because we expect them to raise

performance on a specific task. For example, personnel selection might also be carried out by a single person, but we often believe that a group of people will make better selection decisions. To see whether such assumptions are correct, we have to find out what determines group performance and how group performance compares with individual performance.

The comparison of group versus individual performance is a fundamental question in social psychology and actually triggered some of the earliest experiments in the field (e.g. Ringelmann, 1913; Triplett, 1898; see Chapter 1). As later research has shown, the relation between group and individual performance depends strongly on the type of task. For example, we would all

(a)

(b)

(c)

FIGURE 13.1(a), (b) and (c) *Different kinds of groups: a work team on the production line, a sports team and a personnel selection committee.*

Source: (a) © EIGHTFISH. Used under licence from Getty Images; (b) © corepics. Used under licence from Shutterstock; (c) © StockLite. Used under licence from Shutterstock.

expect that the more heads involved in solving a problem, the greater the chances of the problem being solved. However, most of us would not claim that a climbing team will climb a mountain faster the more people are involved.

In addition, simply comparing individual performance with group performance is often misleading. Imagine the following situation. You investigate weight pulling and find that individuals pull an average weight of 100 kg, whereas four-person groups pull an average weight of 105 kg. Here, group performance is superior to individual performance. Will this finding make you praise the benefits of group work? We suspect the answer is 'no'; instead, this result might make you wonder what has happened in these groups that led to their performance being only slightly above that of individuals. Thus, what is needed to determine whether group performance raises or lowers individual performance is an appropriate standard against which to compare this performance. As we will see, the appropriate baseline is again strongly dependent on the type of task. For example, you might expect the four-person group to pull four times the weight of an individual, but you wouldn't expect them to climb a mountain four times faster – or four times slower – than one person.

With that in mind, we first introduce the core concepts of actual group performance, potential group performance and different task types. In particular, we outline how potential group performance is defined for different types of tasks, and how this potential changes with group size. Next, we deal with the psychological processes that determine how groups perform against the standard of their potential performance. In particular, we describe several process losses that make groups perform below their potential, and also outline several process gains that make them surpass their potential. As we further show, the relative prevalence of process losses versus process gains in groups depends on how group performance is managed, that is, how groups are designed and how their process is being controlled. We then describe three basic principles of group performance management, namely group composition, group synchronization and group learning, which facilitate process gains rather than process losses.

The extent to which these principles are realized depends on many factors. We highlight one factor – leadership – that is particularly important in this context. Therefore, we give a brief introduction to leadership concepts and leadership research, and we outline how leadership affects group performance via the principles of *group performance management*.

SOME CORE CONCEPTS: ACTUAL GROUP PERFORMANCE, GROUP POTENTIAL AND TASK TYPE

How does group size affect performance potential for different types of task?

Actual and potential group performance

As outlined, a meaningful evaluation of group performance requires a baseline against which one can judge that performance. Naturally, group performance depends on individual performance: the better the group members are, the better – on average – group performance will be, and this also implies that what makes individual members better will – again on average – also make the group better. This individual component of group performance is, however, not what group dynamics researchers are interested in. Instead, they are interested in the group component of group performance, that is, the question of how this performance is affected by group members' awareness that common outcomes also depend on what other group members do (social interdependence) and on their interaction with these other group members (social interaction).

To determine this group-specific component, we have to know what performance would have occurred if the same members had worked independently of each other (i.e. not as a group). This latter performance will be labelled **potential group performance** or (more simply) **group potential**. The potential is contrasted with how the group actually performs, which is called *actual group performance*.

> **potential group performance (group potential)** the performance that would have occurred if the members of a group had worked independently of each other and not as a group; a common benchmark to evaluate actual group performance.

This group potential is determined in two steps. The first is to measure how the same group members or similar people perform individually. The second is to combine these individual contributions into a (hypothetical) group product. As we will see, this second step depends strongly on the type of task under investigation.

Basic types of group tasks and their implications for group potential

Dimensions of group tasks In a classic publication Steiner (1972) distinguished three dimensions underlying **group task types**. The first refers to whether the task is *unitary* or *divisible*: for unitary tasks all members have to perform the same task, whereas divisible tasks allow for the assignment of different subtasks to different members. The second dimension consists of whether the ultimate focus of task fulfilment is quantity (*maximization tasks*) or quality (*optimization tasks*). Finally, the third dimension classifies tasks by how group performance is related to the performance of each individual member. Here, Steiner made an important distinction between *additive*, *disjunctive* and *conjunctive* tasks.[1] We describe each of these tasks in some detail and show how group potential is defined for them (see the overview in Table 13.1; see Leader in the Field, Ivan D. Steiner). To further illustrate how group potential works for each task type, we also explain how group potential changes with group size.

> **group task types** group tasks are distinguished depending on whether the task is divisible between group members, whether the quality or quantity of the output is relevant, and how individual contributions are related to the group's performance.

Additive tasks Additive tasks are those in which the performance of a group is simply the sum of its members' individual performances. Additive tasks are usually maximization tasks. **Brainstorming** (i.e. generating as many ideas as possible on a given topic) is an example: the number of ideas generated by the whole group should be the sum of the ideas that the individual members generate in this situation (minus the redundant ones).

> **brainstorming** a group technique aimed at enhancing creativity in groups by means of the uninhibited generation of as many ideas as possible concerning a specified topic.

Hence, potential group performance is defined by the sum of each member's performance measured in an individual situation. As a consequence, group potential is higher than the best group member can achieve alone and – for groups consisting of members with identical individual performance – it increases linearly with group size. This means that if you double the number of members in a group, you get twice the group potential as before.

Disjunctive tasks In a disjunctive task, a group has to choose one of several judgements or proposals. A good example is problem-solving, where a group has to decide on one particular solution to a problem. Here,

LEADER IN THE FIELD

Ivan D. Steiner (1917–2001) graduated from Central Michigan University before receiving a master's degree and a doctorate from the University of Michigan. He was a PhD student of Ted Newcomb (see Leader in the Field, Chapter 1), and later also taught social psychology at the University of Illinois. He spent the last 10 years of his academic career at the University of Massachusetts (Amherst). Steiner contributed greatly to the research on group performance and became famous for his classification of group tasks. Depending on how the individual's effort contributes to the overall performance of the group, Steiner distinguished between additive, conjunctive and disjunctive tasks, each of which are affected differently by process losses and process gains.

Table 13.1 *Important types of unitary group tasks and their implications for group potential.*

Task type	Examples	Group potential
Additive	Pulling a rope; brainstorming; shovelling snow	Sum of members' individual performance
Disjunctive	Problem solving; decision-making; mathematical calculations	Best member's individual performance
Conjunctive	Mountain climbing; precision work; keeping something confidential	Weakest member's individual performance

actual group performance depends solely on the quality of the one particular judgement or proposal that is chosen by the group. Due to this restriction, disjunctive tasks are usually optimization tasks, where quality matters. Potential group performance in disjunctive tasks is determined by the best member's individual performance. As group size increases, group potential also increases, because it is more likely that at least one group member can provide the best solution or the correct answer. However, the increase in potential gained if another member is added to the group becomes smaller the larger the size of the group. If, for example, the individual chances of solving a problem are 50 per cent, a relatively large increase in potential is obtained if there are three instead of two members. In contrast, if you already have 20 members, adding another person changes very little.

FIGURE 13.2 *This group is only as fast as its slowest member.*
Source: © Kapu. Used under licence from Shutterstock.

Disjunctive tasks are often differentiated into tasks with or without a so-called **eureka effect**, which means that the correct solution, once found, is immediately recognized as being correct. A eureka effect increases the chances that a group will realize its potential. However, if the best member in the group is able to solve the problem, but the group fails to realize the correctness of that member's solution (no eureka effect), then the group might still choose a different and suboptimal option.

> **eureka effect** describes the situation when the correct solution to a problem, once it is found, is immediately recognized as being correct by group members.

Conjunctive tasks Whereas in disjunctive tasks one successful member can be enough to solve the problem, a conjunctive task requires all group members to be successful for the group to complete the task. An example is climbing a mountain as part of a roped team. Suppose that, in order to reach the peak, the climbers have to pass a difficult overhang. The climbing team will only reach the peak if all members are successful in passing the overhang. Or, if we use the speed of a climbing team as a continuous measure of performance, we can say that the group is only as fast as its slowest member (Figure 13.2). The group potential for conjunctive tasks is given by the individual performance of the group's weakest member. As a consequence, group potential *decreases* with increasing group size, because the larger the group becomes, the more likely it is to have a very weak member in the group.

Hence it can be ineffective to have large groups for conjunctive tasks. This problem is lessened if the conjunctive task is divisible and specific subtasks can be matched to group members' abilities. For example, the climbing party might decide that for difficult passages it would be useful to have the better members going ahead, fixing ropes and then helping the weaker members over these passages. In this case, potential group performance is higher than the individual performance of the weakest member.

Summary

To determine group-specific influences on the performance of groups, we have to establish what performance would have occurred in the absence of group processes. This is given by the group potential. Determining the group potential depends on the type of group task. For example, in additive tasks (e.g. brainstorming), the potential is given by the sum of the members' performances in an individual situation. The group potential in a disjunctive task (e.g. problem solving) is determined by the quality of the best proposal individually generated by a group member. In a conjunctive task (e.g. mountain climbing), the group potential is given by the weakest member's individual performance.

PROCESS LOSSES VERSUS PROCESS GAINS IN GROUP PERFORMANCE

What determines whether actual group performance remains below or surpasses potential group performance, and how does this vary across different types of task?

Types of process losses and process gains

Group potential and actual group performance often diverge. This divergence is due to *process losses* and *process gains*, both of which occur due to social interdependence and social interaction in groups. This is expressed in the following formula by Hackman and Morris (1975):

$$\text{Actual group performance} = \text{Group potential} - \text{process losses} + \text{process gains}$$

Thus, when actual group performance is below group potential, process losses must have occurred. If, in contrast, actual group performance exceeds group potential, process gains must have been present.

Different types of process losses and process gains can occur. For a group to perform, its members have to make individual contributions, and these contributions have to be coordinated. As a result, group processes can affect performance by influencing either the coordination of individual contributions, or the individual contributions themselves. With regard to individual contributions, they depend on how much the person *can* contribute and how much the person is *motivated* to contribute. Hence, group processes can influence both group members' ability and motivation to contribute to the group product. In sum, we have three types of process losses and gains, namely *coordination*, *motivation* and *individual capability*.

Coordination losses

By definition, coordination in groups can only lead to process losses, not to process gains. This is due to the fact that, as outlined, group potential is measured on the basis of an *optimal* combination of individual contributions.[2] Consequently, **coordination losses**

> **coordination losses** describe the diminished performance of a group if it fails to coordinate the contributions of its individual members in an optimal manner.

are said to occur if a group fails to coordinate the contributions of its individual members in an optimal manner. For example, in his classic investigations of group performance in physical tasks, Ringelmann (1913) found that the average weight pulled per person when performing such a task in a group decreases as the size of the group increases – the so-called **Ringelmann effect** (see Leader in the Field, Max Ringelmann). An illustration of one of his findings is shown in Figure 13.3. Later investigations showed that this process

> **Ringelmann effect** describes the finding that in physical tasks such as weight pulling, the average performance of individual group members decreases with increasing group size.

loss is due to both insufficient coordination (members fail to exert their maximal effort at the same moment) and decreased motivation (individuals work less hard when they are part of a group) (Ingham, Levinger, Graves, & Peckham, 1974). An experiment that disentangles coordination losses and motivation losses is described in Research Close-Up 13.1.

Another well-known coordination loss occurs in brainstorming. Osborn (1957) proposed that brainstorming in a group would lead to the generation of far more and better ideas than would be obtained if the same people generated ideas individually. Experiments testing this assumption contain at least two conditions. In one condition, the participants come together in a group and conduct a brainstorming session. For example, the task could be to generate as many ideas as possible concerning ways to protect the environment. The other condition determines the group potential. This is done in **nominal groups**. Nominal groups contain the same number of people as the real groups do; however,

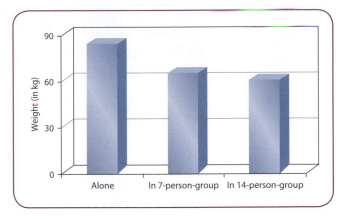

90
60
30
0

Alone   In 7-person-group   In 14-person-group

Weight (in kg)

FIGURE 13.3 *Average individual weight pulled dependent on the number of persons pulling together.*

Source: Based on data reported in Ringelmann, 1913.

LEADER IN THE FIELD

Max Ringelmann (1861–1931) was professor of agricultural engineering at the French National Institute of Agronomy. His main field of research lay in determining the efficiency of work in agricultural applications. In what may be considered one of the first experiments in social psychology, he discovered a decrease in individual performance that occurs when the individual works in a group rather than alone. He also found that each group member's individual contribution to group performance decreases as group size increases. These findings are referred to as the *Ringelmann effect*.

each person is seated in a different room and asked to generate and write down ideas individually about the topic. The experimenter collects participants' lists of ideas and collates them. Ideas that are mentioned by more than one member (redundant ideas)

> **nominal group** a number of individuals who perform a task individually and work independently of each other; nominal groups are used to determine the potential performance of groups.

are only included once, because in a real group the same idea would also be generated and counted only once.

In all of these experiments, brainstorming groups hardly ever produced as many ideas as the nominal groups generated; in most cases they were significantly below this group potential (for an overview, see Mullen, Johnson, & Salas, 1991). This deficit is not compensated by increased quality of ideas: on average, interactive brainstorming groups do not generate better (i.e. more creative or more practicable) ideas than nominal groups. As Diehl and Stroebe (1987) have shown in a series of experiments, the most important reason for this suboptimal performance in interactive brainstorming groups is a form of coordination

WHY GROUPS UNDER-PERFORM: SEPARATING COORDINATION AND MOTIVATION LOSSES

Latané, B., Williams, K., & Harkins, S. (1979, Experiment 2). Many hands make light the work: The causes and consequences of social loafing. *Journal of Personality and Social Psychology*, 37, 822–832.

Introduction

The aim of this study was to replicate Ringelmann's findings of process losses in collective work using a different task, and to demonstrate to what extent the process losses are due to insufficient coordination versus motivation losses in groups. Latané and his colleagues therefore conducted two experiments with a cheering and hand-clapping task (see below). In the first experiment, they successfully replicated the Ringelmann effect by showing that the more people there were in a group, the less noise was produced per person. To distinguish between motivation and coordination, in Experiment 2, which we examine more closely below, Latané et al. (1979) used an elegant strategy, namely the introduction of 'pseudo-groups'. In a pseudo-group, participants are led to believe they are working in a group when, in fact, they are working alone. Since no coordination losses are possible in a pseudo-group, all process losses found in pseudo-groups must be due to motivation losses, because individual capability losses are not possible with this type of task.

Method

Participants

Thirty-six male students participated in the experiment, with six participants per experimental session.

Design and procedure

The experimental design was a within-subjects design with five conditions. Each participant completed several trials: (1) alone; (2) in actual two-person groups; (3) in actual six-person groups; (4) in two-person pseudo-groups; and (5) in six-person pseudo-groups. The participants' task was to shout as loudly as possible when the experimenter gave a signal. They were blindfolded and wore headsets on which constant noise was played. This manipulation ensured that during the pseudo-group trials participants believed they were shouting with one or five other people respectively, when in fact they were shouting alone.

Results

The data were analysed with two separate analyses of variance, one comparing the individual trials with the

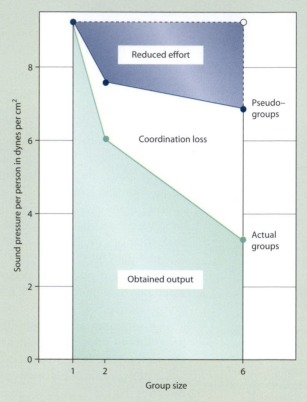

FIGURE 13.4 *Intensity of sound produced per person when cheering alone versus in actual or pseudo-groups of two or six people.*

Source: Latané et al., 1979, p. 827. Copyright © 1979 by the American Psychological Association. Adapted with permission. The use of APA information does not imply endorsement by APA.

actual two-person group and six-person group trials, the other doing the same for the pseudo-groups. Both analyses showed that the average noise produced per person decreased with the increasing number of people. People shouted less loudly in the two-person groups than when alone, and they shouted less loudly in six-person groups than in two-person groups. This was true for actual groups as well as for pseudo-groups. However, the decrement in individual performance was about twice as high in the actual groups compared with the pseudo-groups (no statistical comparisons between these conditions were made). This relationship is illustrated in Figure 13.4. The decrements in sound intensity between shouting alone and shouting in a pseudo-group can be traced back to reduced effort, since there are no differences in coordination requirements between these conditions. In contrast, the differences between pseudo-groups and actual groups can be attributed to coordination losses in the form of 'sound cancellation', whereby group members do not shout at exactly the same time, and hence there is some loss of maximum sound produced.

Discussion

The results confirm the authors' hypotheses: coordination losses are not the only source of process losses when people perform a task in a real group, compared with working individually or in a pseudo-group. Instead, reduced effort also contributes to this effect. Although one might object on the grounds that there were no direct measures of motivation and coordination losses, it has to be conceded that the arrangement of the experimental setting and conditions hardly leaves room for alternative explanations of the observed performance decrements (e.g. cognitive interference among members is implausible). In sum, the study successfully demonstrates two causal factors involved in why groups may fail to realize their full potential: motivation losses and coordination losses.

---

loss called **production blocking**: when people generate ideas in an interacting group, only one person can express her idea at any given time. During this time all other members are 'blocked' and are unable to express their own ideas.

> **production blocking** a process loss typical of brainstorming tasks in face-to-face groups; since in a group only one person can speak at a time, the other group members cannot express their own ideas at the same time.

We know that brainstorming is an additive task. Coordination losses also occur, however, in disjunctive or conjunctive tasks. For example, groups often fail to choose the best among their members' proposals, even if one member actually proposes the optimal solution. In a study by Torrance (1954), three-person groups were given several tasks, one of which was a problem-solving task with a definite answer. The participants were members of the United States Air Force; each group consisted of a pilot, a navigator and a gunner. In a military aircrew, pilots have the highest status, whereas gunners are lowest in status. Torrance's results showed that if the pilot had found the correct solution prior to discussion, the group hardly ever failed to choose this option (only in less than one out of ten cases). In contrast, when the gunner had found the correct solution, more than one-third of the groups failed to adopt this solution. Hence, the group's choice of one of their members' proposals was influenced by member status. Similarly, groups often prefer an incorrect solution proposed by the majority over a correct solution proposed by a minority (Smith, Tindale, & Steiner, 1998; see also Chapter 12). In both of these examples the individual contributions would have allowed the groups to succeed, but successful coordination among group members (choosing the right proposal) often did not occur.

Motivation losses and gains If actual group performance differs from group potential, this difference can be due to the fact that the group members' individual contributions become better or worse in a group setting compared to an individual situation. One reason for this is that working in a group can lower or increase people's motivation to contribute to task performance (**motivation losses and gains**). We will consider both motivation gains and losses, but we start with motivation losses, three of which have so far been identified in group performance research:

> **motivation losses and gains** decreases or increases in group members' motivation to contribute to group task performance.

- **Social loafing** Social loafing occurs if group members reduce their effort due to the fact that their individual contribution to the group product is not identifiable (Latané et al., 1979).

> **social loafing** a motivation loss in groups that occurs when group members reduce their effort due to the fact that individual contributions to group performance are not identifiable.

- **Dispensability effect** In the case of the dispensability effect, group members reduce their effort because their individual contribution seems to have little impact on group performance (Kerr & Bruun, 1983).[3]

> **dispensability effect** a reduction in group members' task-related effort because their individual contribution seems to have little impact on group performance.

- **Sucker effect** The sucker effect occurs if group members perceive or anticipate that other group members lower their effort. To avoid being exploited (being the 'sucker'), they reduce their effort themselves (Kerr, 1983).

> **sucker effect** a motivation loss in groups that occurs when group members perceive or anticipate that other group members will lower their effort: to avoid being exploited, they reduce their effort themselves.

Both the extent and type of motivation loss that occurs depend on task type. Additive tasks (which depend on the sum of individual performances) allow for all of the above-mentioned losses. For example, some members of the weight-pulling group could pull less hard because they believe that it is almost impossible to determine how hard each member has tried to pull (social loafing) or because they feel that – given the large number of group members – it will hardly make a difference how hard they pull (dispensability effect). At the same time, other group members might be aware of such tendencies and so reduce their effort to avoid being the 'sucker'. These losses are typically stronger the larger the group size (Latané et al., 1979). Why is this the case? The larger the group, the more difficult it is to identify individual contributions, which gives rise to more social loafing and more suspicion that others will exploit one's performance. At the same time, the relative impact of each member's individual contribution becomes smaller with increasing group size.

In disjunctive and conjunctive tasks, social loafing is less of a problem, because individual contributions in these tasks are normally visible: when a group solves a problem, it is more or less evident who came up with which proposal; when a climbing team scales a mountain, it is evident who slows down the group. However, both dispensability and sucker effects can be a problem, especially if the group contains weaker and stronger members and the members are aware of these differences.

In a disjunctive task, the group chooses one judgement or proposal: this awareness particularly pushes weak members towards reducing their effort, since they know that even if they invest a lot of effort, it is fairly unlikely that their contribution (e.g. their proposal) will be good enough to be chosen by the group (i.e. dispensability effect). In contrast, stronger members know that they are expected to take responsibility for good performance, and so are particularly prone to feel they are the 'sucker'.

In conjunctive tasks, in which all group members must successfully complete the task, the opposite happens: here the stronger members are aware that their effort is not very important for group performance, because even if they invest less effort they should be able to perform at the level of the weaker members. Hence they tend to reduce their effort, which may cause problems if, by investing more effort, they could help the weaker members to perform better (Kerr & Bruun, 1983; see Leader in the Field, Norbert Kerr). If conjunctive tasks are divisible, such problems can be avoided by matching subtasks to members' abilities. However, since this means that stronger members get more to do than weaker members, this can also induce sucker effects among the stronger members, especially if their acceptance of the division of labour is low.

LEADER IN THE FIELD

Norbert Kerr (b. 1948). Norbert Kerr received his MA and his PhD in Psychology at the University of Illinois. Since 1979 he has worked at Michigan State University, East Lansing, where he is currently a Full Professor of Psychology. In addition, he is Honorary Professor at the University of Kent (UK). His work on group decision-making and group performance has been highly influential to the field of group processes. For example, his numerous studies on jury decision-making have helped to gain insights into social influence and group dynamics in interacting groups. He has also discovered and explored basic motivation losses and motivation gains in groups.

While most social psychological research on group performance has focused on motivation losses, more recent studies have established three motivation gains in groups:

- **Social competition** If individual contributions are identifiable, group members can be more motivated during group performance compared to individual performance, because they want to outperform other members. Social competition is particularly likely if group members have relatively equal abilities and if they are rewarded for individual effort (Stroebe, Diehl, & Abakoumkin, 1996).

  > **social competition** a motivation gain in groups that occurs if the group members want to outperform each other during group tasks in which the individual contributions are identifiable.

- **Social compensation** Social compensation occurs if stronger members work harder in a group than they would do individually in order to compensate for a weaker member's suboptimal performance (Williams & Karau, 1991).

  > **social compensation** a motivation gain in groups that occurs if stronger group members increase their effort in order to compensate for weaker members' suboptimal performance.

- **Köhler effect** The Köhler effect was discovered in the 1920s but remained largely unrecognized until Witte rediscovered it in 1989. A Köhler effect is said to occur if weaker members work harder than they would do individually in order to avoid being responsible for a weak group performance (Köhler, 1926; Witte, 1989).

  > **Köhler effect** a motivation gain in groups which involves weaker group members working harder than they would do individually in order to avoid being responsible for a weak group performance.

As for motivation losses, the occurrence of motivation gains also depends on the type of task. Social competition can operate within all task types as long as individual contributions are identifiable and comparable. This is the case for most disjunctive and conjunctive tasks, but it is often not so in additive tasks. Hence, social competition is more likely to occur in disjunctive or conjunctive tasks than in additive tasks. In contrast, social compensation is mainly restricted to additive tasks, because only in additive tasks can stronger group members really compensate for another member's weak performance. Finally, the Köhler effect predominantly occurs in conjunctive tasks, since in conjunctive tasks weaker members anticipate that an inferior group performance will be attributed to them by other group members (Hertel, Kerr, & Messé, 2000). The effect is strongest if there are moderate discrepancies between group members' individual capabilities and they are aware of these differences (Messé, Hertel, Kerr, Lount, & Park, 2002): if individual capabilities are almost equal, it is less clear who is to blame for an inferior performance. If, however, the discrepancies are very large, the weaker members have almost no hope of being able to match the stronger members' performance.

In sum, within the same task type both motivation gains and motivation losses can occur. Thus, one of the challenges for group performance research is to find variables that determine whether gains or losses dominate. One key variable that has been found so far is the *importance of group goals*. Social compensation is particularly likely to occur if the common group goal is highly valued by members – otherwise motivation losses are more likely. This is well demonstrated in a series of experiments by Williams and Karau (1991). Participants performed an idea-generation task and were told that they were working with a partner (supposedly in another room) who, in fact, did not exist. The researchers manipulated whether participants expected their partner to show strong or weak performance, and whether the performance goal (generating as many ideas as possible) was relevant to them or not. In addition, for half of the participants, the task was labelled a collective task (i.e. the number of collectively generated ideas would be counted), while for the other half the task was co-active (although performed with the other person, the number of individually generated ideas would be counted).

The results are shown in Figure 13.5. When participants expected to work with a *strongly performing* partner, there was no need to compensate. In fact, those working on the collective task even engaged in a bit of social loafing: their performance was always below their potential

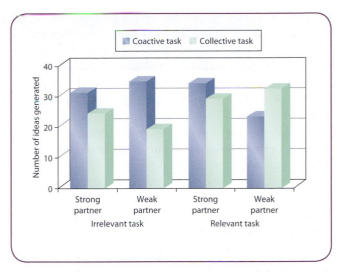

FIGURE 13.5 *Social loafing and social compensation as a function of task relevance and partner ability.*

Source: From Williams & Karau, 1991, Expt. 3. Copyright © 1991 by the American Psychological Association. Adapted with permission. The use of APA information does not imply endorsement by APA.

(i.e. less than in the co-active situation) regardless of task relevance.

In contrast, if participants worked with a *weakly performing* partner, there was a need to compensate, but only when the task was both *relevant* (i.e. the outcome was important to them) and *collective* (i.e. joint productivity would be evaluated). In this condition, performance in the collective task was actually higher than in the co-active task: participants performed beyond their potential. If, however, the group goal was irrelevant, there was a motivation loss instead of a motivation gain. When the group goal was irrelevant, however, regardless of their co-worker's ability, participants produced fewer ideas in collective conditions than in co-active conditions. Similar effects can be expected for disjunctive and conjunctive tasks. For example, a Köhler effect should only occur if the group goal is important and, thus, the weaker members do not want to feel responsible for inferior performance.

Losses and gains in individual capability If group members contribute more or less than they would do in an individual setting, this can be due to the motivation gains and losses described above. However, the same effects can be due to the fact that the group setting influences their *ability* to make such contributions. Social interaction may have a detrimental effect on group members' individual capability, for example by restricting their attention or offering role models of ineffective

SOCIAL PSYCHOLOGY BEYOND THE LAB 13.1

MOTIVATION GAINS IN THE SWIMMING POOL

Motivation losses and motivation gains do not only occur in the laboratory. Recently, Hüffmeier, and Hertel (2011) analysed the swimming competitions at the 2008 Olympics. They compared data from the semi-finals of the 100 and 200 metres free-style *individual* competition, on one hand, and the four-person relay competition on the other. They showed that the same swimmers performed better when part of a relay team than when swimming in the individual competition (Figure 13.6). This was true for all but the lead-off swimmers in the relay (those who swam the first leg). Because neither capability gains nor coordination gains are plausible for this task (particularly at the level of Olympic competitions), the authors attributed the increased performance of swimmers on the second, third or fourth leg of a relay to motivation gains. As the authors had shown in a pilot study (with competitive swimmers from local sports clubs), perceived indispensability of one's own performance for the group increases from the first to the fourth leg of a relay: in other words, as the race nears its climax, the impact of each leg of the race is seen as greater. This increasing feeling of indispensability explains the increase in motivation gains from the first leg (no motivation gains at all) to the fourth leg (strongest motivation gains in the relay). In sum, the Hüffmeier and Hertel (2011) study provides an excellent example of how motivation gains can be shown in real-world contexts.

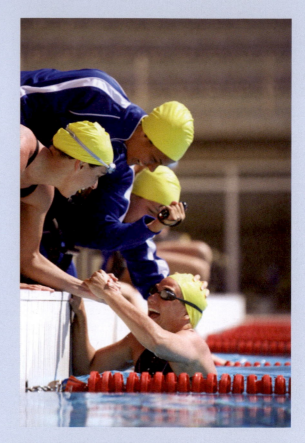

FIGURE 13.6 *Swimmers perform better when part of a relay than when swimming in individual competitions.*
Source: © Fuse. Used under licence from Getty Images.

---

strategies. However, social interaction in a group may also help members to make better contributions than they might have made individually, for example by other group members' providing intellectual stimulation or demonstrating effective strategies. Surprisingly, such **individual capability gains and losses** due to social interaction have so far been almost neglected in group performance research. As a consequence, compared to coordination

individual capability gains and losses improvements or impairments in individual group members' ability to successfully perform a task due to social interaction within the group.

and motivation losses or gains, there is a need for more research in this area.

Individual capability losses and capability gains can, however, be clearly illustrated in brainstorming tasks (e.g. Nijstad, Stroebe, & Lodewijkx, 2002). If, for example, the task is to generate as many ideas as possible for promoting environmental protection, then hearing an idea from another group member about reducing traffic can make you focus on ideas for diminishing fuel consumption, whereas in the individual situation you might also have thought about sustainable development and other issues. Hence, if you fail to come up with ideas about sustainable

FIGURE 13.7 *Computer-mediated communication allows group members to brainstorm electronically.*

Source: © Dmitriy Shironosov. Used under licence from Shutterstock.

Table 13.2 *Overview of process losses and process gains in group performance that have been documented in research so far.*

Level of process	Process losses	Process gains
Coordination	Coordination part of the Ringelmann effect Production blocking	–
Motivation	Social loafing Dispensability effect Sucker effect	Social compensation Social competition Köhler effect
Individual capability	Cognitive restriction	Cognitive stimulation

development in the group situation, this is not due to the fact that you are not trying hard enough (motivation loss); rather, due to social influence, you simply are not capable of producing these ideas at that moment. This socially determined capability loss can be termed **cognitive restriction**. On the other hand, it is also possible that you would never have thought about reducing fuel consumption, and it was only after another group member came up with the idea of reducing traffic that you generated new ideas on this issue. Again, the reason for the difference between your contribution in an individual setting and in the group is not motivational: you do not try harder in the group setting, but stimulation from other group members makes you more capable of producing diverse ideas. Thus, the corresponding socially determined capability gain can be termed **cognitive stimulation**.

Since both cognitive restriction and cognitive stimulation effects can occur, brainstorming in groups can lead either to more uniformity (Ziegler, Diehl, & Zijlstra, 2000) or to greater variety (Paulus & Yang, 2000) in idea generation. However, to demonstrate individual capability gains (stimulation), many of the well-known process losses in brainstorming – particularly production blocking – have to be eliminated first,

> **cognitive restriction** a capability loss in group tasks that involve idea generation, which occurs when an idea mentioned by another group member makes people focus on the particular category this idea belongs to, at the expense of generating ideas from other categories.

> **cognitive stimulation** a capability gain in group tasks that involve idea generation, which occurs when an idea mentioned by another group member stimulates a cognitive category one would otherwise not have thought of.

otherwise they are so strong that individual capability gains are totally submerged. Such process losses can be eliminated, for example, by using computer-mediated communication (Dennis & Valacich, 1993): instead of brainstorming in face-to-face interaction, group members are linked together via a 'chat' system (Figure 13.7). Since each member is free to type in ideas at the same time as other members, production blocking cannot occur and, hence, there are better conditions for cognitive stimulation.

For an overview of the different process losses and process gains discussed in this chapter, see Table 13.2.

Summary

If group performance is below group potential, process losses have occurred. If, instead, group performance exceeds group potential, then process gains have taken place. Process losses and gains are possible at three different theoretical levels: motivation, individual capability and coordination. Three types of motivation loss (social loafing, dispensability effect and the sucker effect) and three types of motivation gain (social competition, social compensation and the Köhler effect) have been shown so far. Far less frequently, research has demonstrated that individual capabilities can be restricted (capability loss) as well as stimulated (capability gain) in a group. With regard to coordination, studies have focused almost exclusively on coordination losses so far, due to the fact that group potential is usually defined in terms of the optimal combination of group members' individual efforts.

GROUP PERFORMANCE MANAGEMENT

How can process losses be minimized and process gains be maximized?

Three basic principles of group performance management

Over the last century, social psychological research on group performance has provided impressive evidence for process losses, but far less evidence for process gains. This might suggest that negative aspects dominate when people work together in a group. In our view this conclusion is unjustified. Social psychological experiments on group performance predominantly use randomly composed ad hoc groups, with no further means or techniques of support accompanying the group process. Furthermore, experiments are usually restricted to one, or in some cases two, task trials. While these restrictions are useful for certain types of research questions (and can be justified on pragmatic grounds), they systematically disadvantage groups in the evaluation of group performance. If you are comparing a car with a unicycle on speed or safety criteria, you would hardly use a car that had four randomly composed wheels with no means to synchronize them. In addition, you would hardly restrict your comparison to the first 10 meters. Unfortunately, this is analogous to what usually happens in group performance research.

Gaining insight into factors that put groups at a disadvantage is not only interesting for research purposes (e.g. to develop new research programmes on group performance), it also provides a key to solving the problem of how to optimize group performance. If group performance is underestimated because no systematic **group composition** and support of group functioning take place, and because the time frame is too limited, then systematically optimizing these aspects should provide a promising way to optimize group performance. Schulz-Hardt, Hertel, and Brodbeck (2007) proposed the term **group performance management** to refer to the sum of activities aimed at improving the group-specific component of group performance (i.e. maximizing process gains and minimizing process losses). They proposed three basic underlying principles:

group composition specifies how certain characteristics are distributed within a group.

group performance management the sum of activities aimed at maximizing (or improving) the group-specific component of group performance.

- Groups should be composed according to the requirements of task structure.
- Group processes during performance should be specifically synchronized in accordance with the task structure.
- Groups should be given the opportunity to perform multiple similar tasks to allow for group learning to occur.

In the following sections we explain briefly each of the three principles and give examples of how they can be applied to specific group tasks.

Group composition   Group performance depends on the kind of people who are brought together in a group. This is true in a trivial sense, in that the more capable group members are of performing the task, the better the group will perform in general. It is, however, also true in a non-trivial sense, in that certain group compositions make it more likely than others that a group will fully realize or even surpass its potential, thereby realizing process gains.

To illustrate this principle, we take a look at an important task in group decision-making research, the **hidden profile** task. Consider the following situation. A personnel selection committee consisting of group members X, Y and Z has to decide which of the two candidates, A and B, should be chosen for a sales management position. The information about the candidates (advantages and disadvantages) and the way it is distributed among the committee is illustrated in Table 13.3.

hidden profile a group decision situation in which information is distributed among group members such that no individual group member can detect the best solution based on his or her own information.

If the full information (the 'whole group' column in Table 13.3) is considered, candidate A is the better choice, with three advantages and two disadvantages, compared to candidate B (two advantages, three disadvantages). However, as becomes apparent from the first three columns, none of the committee members individually possesses this full information set. The advantages of candidate B, as well as the disadvantages of candidate A, are held by all group members prior to discussion; they are termed *shared information*. In contrast, each disadvantage of candidate B, as well as each advantage of candidate A, is held by only one group member; these items are termed *unshared information*. Due to this distribution, none of the group members can detect that A is the better choice prior to discussion – it is 'hidden' from the group members, which is why this situation is called a hidden profile. This task is particularly

Table 13.3 *Information distribution in a hidden profile task.*

	Group member X	Group member Y	Group member Z	Whole group (X + Y + Z)
Candidate A	Good analytical expertise (+)	Stays calm under pressure (+)	Works well with the team (+)	Good analytical expertise (+) Stays calm under pressure (+) Works well with the team (+)
	Lacks humour (−) **Not very creative (−)**	**Lacks humour (−)** **Not very creative (−)**	**Lacks humour (−)** **Not very creative (−)**	**Lacks humour (−)** **Not very creative (−)**
Candidate B	**Good communication skills (+)** **Known to be very reliable (+)** Tends to be short-tempered (−)	**Good communication skills (+)** **Known to be very reliable (+)** Often resentful in conflicts (−)	**Good communication skills (+)** **Known to be very reliable (+)** Refuses to do overtime (−)	**Good communication skills (+)** **Known to be very reliable (+)** Tends to be short-tempered (−) Often resentful in conflicts (−) Refuses to do overtime (−)
Implied choice	B	B	B	A

+ candidate's advantages; − candidate's disadvantages; shared information is indicated in bold.

important for group decision-making research, because it constitutes the prototype of situations in which groups can make better decisions than individual members can.

If, in contrast, the committee in our example had individual information that is representative of the overall information and so had already suggested candidate A to be the best choice (in which case it is called a *manifest profile*), making the decision in a group could hardly reveal that groups made better-quality decisions than individuals. Thus, although we do not know how often hidden profiles occur in reality (and it is impossible to determine this, because doing so would require us to have access to all relevant cognitions in the minds of the members of decision-making groups), we have to study hidden-profile situations if we want to achieve process gains in group decision-making. Recent simulations by Schultze, Faulmüller, Schmidt-Hieber, and Schulz-Hardt (2012) show that hidden profiles should occur far less frequently than manifest profiles.

However, depending on factors such as the number of decision alternatives, the relative strength of decision alternatives, and the number of group members, up to 25 per cent of all decision situations can involve hidden profiles.

Unfortunately, research has shown that most groups fail to solve hidden profiles (Stasser & Birchmeier, 2003). As Brodbeck, Kerschreiter, Mojzisch, and Schulz-Hardt (2007), as well as Mojzisch and Schulz-Hardt (2006), have outlined, this failure is caused by three different processes, summarized in Theory Box 13.1. To date, there is no solid evidence to indicate whether these processes constitute coordination losses, motivation losses or individual capability losses, so we do not categorize them as such.

- *Negotiation focus* Groups tend to negotiate the decision on the basis of their members' pre-discussion preferences rather than openly

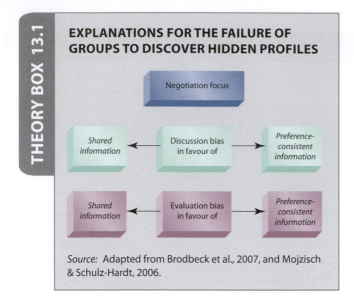

THEORY BOX 13.1

EXPLANATIONS FOR THE FAILURE OF GROUPS TO DISCOVER HIDDEN PROFILES

Source: Adapted from Brodbeck et al., 2007, and Mojzisch & Schulz-Hardt, 2006.

exchanging the relevant information (Gigone & Hastie, 1993). Because no member individually can detect the best alternative in a hidden profile prior to discussion, pre-discussion preferences are usually in favour of suboptimal alternatives (in our example, candidate B). Thus, one of the suboptimal alternatives is chosen by the group (see also Mojzisch & Schulz-Hardt, 2010).

- *Discussion bias* Even if the relevant information is exchanged in the group and, hence, a negotiation focus is avoided, this discussion is typically biased. Groups spend more time discussing shared than unshared information (Larson, Foster-Fishman, & Keys, 1994), because shared information can be introduced by more members than unshared information. Furthermore, group members predominantly introduce or repeat information that is consistent with their initial preferences (Dennis, 1996; Schulz-Hardt, Brodbeck, Mojzisch, Kerschreiter, & Frey, 2006), which can be due to a perceived 'advocacy role' (Stasser & Titus, 1985) – that is, group members believe that their primary task in a discussion is to explain why they prefer a particular alternative. However, most of the critical information for solving the hidden profile is both unshared and inconsistent with the members' initial preferences (in our example, the advantages of candidate A and the disadvantages of candidate B). As a consequence, the group does not exchange enough of this critical information to detect the best alternative.

- *Evaluation bias* The evaluation, and not just the discussion, of information in the group is also

biased in favour of information that is shared and information that is consistent with one's preferences (Mojzisch, Grouneva, & Schulz-Hardt, 2010). Group members judge shared information to be more credible and valid than unshared information, because each member individually held the shared information prior to discussion (Chernyshenko, Miner, Baumann, & Sniezek, 2003) – thus, one can be relatively sure that this information is correct – and because all group members can attest to the validity of the shared information (social validation, cf. Wittenbaum, Hubbell, & Zuckerman, 1999). Furthermore, they judge information that is consistent with their preferences to be more credible and important than information that is inconsistent with their preferences (Greitemeyer & Schulz-Hardt, 2003), because information that is consistent with one's preferences is accepted at face value, whereas information that is inconsistent with preferences is critically tested. As a consequence, even if all information is exchanged in the group, group members often undervalue the critical information and, thus, fail to detect the best alternative to choose (Greitemeyer & Schulz-Hardt, 2003; Mojzisch, Schulz-Hardt, Kerschreiter, Brodbeck, & Frey, 2008).

This description makes clear that in a hidden profile the group members' individual preferences, as well as their shared knowledge, imply the choice of suboptimal alternatives. This also negatively affects the solution of hidden profiles, and on three different theoretical levels: consensus seeking, information exchange and information evaluation.

As recent studies have demonstrated, these processes – and thus, the chances of groups solving hidden profiles – depend substantially on a particular aspect of group composition, namely, agreement versus disagreement in group members' individual pre-discussion preferences (see Brodbeck, Kerschreiter, Mojzisch, Frey, & Schulz-Hardt, 2002; Schulz-Hardt et al., 2006). The bottom line of these studies is that having a group in which members favour different alternatives prior to discussion leads to a more intensive and less biased information exchange. In consequence, it becomes more likely that a hidden profile is solved (as compared to groups where members agree on a particular suboptimal alternative right from the beginning). This facilitative effect of pre-discussion disagreement, or dissent, even occurred if none of the dissenting opinions were correct. A brief description of the Schulz-Hardt et al. (2006) study is given in Research Close-Up 13.2.

PRODUCTIVE CONFLICT IN GROUP DECISION-MAKING

RESEARCH CLOSE-UP 13.2

Schulz-Hardt, S., Brodbeck, F. C., Mojzisch, A., Kerschreiter, R., & Frey, D. (2006). Group decision making in hidden profile situations: Dissent as a facilitator for decision quality. *Journal of Personality and Social Psychology, 91*, 1080–1093.

Introduction

The idea of this study was that a conflict of initial opinions should help a group to solve hidden profiles, because this pre-discussion dissent should make it less likely that group members will prematurely agree on a suboptimal alternative, and dissent should both intensify and de-bias discussion. In order to resolve the initial conflict, more information should be exchanged compared to groups with initial consensus. Furthermore, as we know from research on minority influence (see Chapter 8), particularly dissenting minority opinions can lead to more open-mindedness and, hence, might allow for a less biased group discussion. To test these hypotheses, the authors conducted a laboratory experiment in which groups with all members favouring the same alternative prior to discussion (consent groups) were compared with different types of dissent groups.

Method

Participants

Four hundred and five female and male students comprised the final sample for this experiment, forming 135 three-person groups.

Design and procedure

The experiment had a one-factor design, with six conditions: (1) in a *manifest profile* control condition, all group members received the full information from the beginning. In the other conditions, information was distributed in a hidden-profile-manner. (2) The *homogeneity* condition consisted of groups where all three members initially favoured the same suboptimal alternative. (3) In the *minority dissent incorrect* condition[4], two members preferred the same suboptimal alternative, and the third one favoured a different suboptimal alternative. (4) In the *full diversity dissent incorrect* condition, all members favoured different suboptimal alternatives at the beginning. (5) The *minority dissent correct* condition was equal to the minority dissent incorrect condition, except that the minority member favoured the correct solution right from the beginning. (6) The *full diversity dissent correct* condition was similar to condition (4), except that one of the members favoured the correct solution right from the beginning.

The participants were first given individual information about a decision case where four candidates were applying for a vacant pilot position at an airline company. Based on the full information, one candidate was clearly superior to the others. However, in the hidden profile conditions this candidate initially seemed slightly inferior to the other three. Participants indicated their individual preferences and, based on these preferences, three-person groups of the above-mentioned compositions were formed. Participants discussed the decision case in their groups and made a collective decision regarding the chosen candidate. A reward bonus was offered to those who made the correct final choice. Discussions were videotaped and subsequently coded with regard to what pieces of information were mentioned or repeated by which of the group members.

Results

Groups with a hidden profile distribution of information made the correct choice far less often than groups with full information. However, solution rates were increased by dissent: whereas homogeneous groups hardly ever made the correct choice (only 7 per cent of the time), about a quarter of the groups with pure dissent (conditions 3 and 4) chose the right candidate. If one of the dissenting opinions was in favour of the right solution (the 'correct' conditions 5 and 6), solution rates further increased to more than 60 per cent. These findings are illustrated in Figure 13.8. Analyses

FIGURE 13.8 *Proportion of correct solutions dependent on dissent (MP = manifest profile; HP = hidden profile).*

Source: Schulz-Hardt et al. (2006). Copyright © 2006 by the American Psychological Association. Adapted with permission. The use of APA information does not imply endorsement by APA.

of the content of the group discussions showed that the beneficial effects of dissent were caused by dissent groups having a more intensive discussion (i.e. more information exchange, more discussion time) and exchanging information in a more balanced manner (i.e. more consideration of unshared information and information that was inconsistent with group members' preferences) than was the case in homogeneous groups.

Discussion

The findings support the authors' hypotheses that conflict can yield benefits for group decision making: even if all members individually prefer suboptimal alternatives at the beginning of the task, the group may find a superior alternative (and thereby realize process gains) if dissent among these individual preferences leads to a controversial discussion in the group. Hence, when forming groups that are aimed at making high-quality decisions, we should ensure that they consist of members with different opinions about the issue at hand: the more variety of opinions we can create within a group, the more likely it is that dissenting opinions will be voiced, and the more likely it is that the group will contain at least one member who proposes the correct solution.

Whereas composing groups with pre-discussion dissent facilitates performance in decision-making tasks, other tasks require other methods of group composition. For example, in a conjunctive task such as mountain climbing (all group members must successfully complete the task), it should facilitate group performance to have groups with moderate discrepancies among members' abilities, because this increases the likelihood of motivation gains among the weaker members (Messé et al., 2002) – and the weakest member determines group performance in a conjunctive task. So, if you had four climbers and had to split them into two two-person teams, teams of mixed ability should give better performance than teams of similar ability, in terms of facilitating process gains. Generally, whenever there is freedom to compose groups for particular tasks, the type of task should first be classified, and then a group composition chosen that will counteract process losses and facilitate process gains for this task type.

Group synchronization Working together in a group requires generating or modifying individual contributions (e.g. physical effort, thoughts and ideas) collaboratively and integrating these different individual contributions in a way that is functional for high performance. For many tasks, we do not 'naturally' know how to do this, or might even hold misleading preconceptions. For instance, for many people making a group decision means that everybody offers his or her preferred solution and states the arguments in its favour, and finally the group chooses the solution with the most convincing arguments. As we have seen above, a group will hardly ever solve a hidden profile in this way.

Hence, just as a vehicle with four wheels needs a differential in the axle to enable it to drive around corners (because the inner wheels have to turn more slowly than the outer wheels), groups need synchronization to perform well. By **group synchronization** we mean the sum of activities aimed at optimizing the collaborative generation, modification and integration of individual contributions in a group. Means of promoting group synchronization can vary from very simple tools (e.g. feedback about members' individual contributions) to rather complex procedures (e.g. group decision-making techniques).

> **group synchronization** the sum of activities aimed at optimizing the collaborative generation, modification and integration of individual contributions in a group.

As in the case of group composition, optimal synchronization depends on the type of task at hand. However, some means of group synchronization can be applied across a wide range of group tasks. One of these is the *continuous visibility of individual contributions*. In a physical task such as pulling a weight, this can simply mean providing group members with feedback about their own as well as other group members' individual performance. In a cognitive task such as brainstorming or making a group decision based on distributed information, this can take the form of documenting group members' ideas and informational input on a flipchart or, as often used for these and other purposes, on an information board during computer-mediated group communication. In all cases, such permanent visibility of individual contributions counteracts motivation losses like social loafing or sucker effects, and facilitates motivation gains due to social competition or Köhler effects (DeShon, Kozlowski, Schmidt, Milner, & Wiechmann, 2004; Hoeksema-Van Orden, Gaillard, & Buunk, 1998). This visibility also facilitates coordination within the group, for instance by making it easier to identify the best proposal in a disjunctive task (Henry, Strickland, Yorges, & Ladd, 1996) or by helping group members to match their own contributions to the contributions of other group members.

In contrast, some methods of group synchronization are unique for specific tasks such as group decision-making. As already outlined, our 'normal' preconceptions about how to make a decision in a group run counter to the way in which high-quality group decisions are actually made. Therefore, it can be useful to 'guide' group discussion on a decision problem by means of specific techniques. Some of these techniques are rather simple, such as dividing the decision-making process into phases, such as an information collection phase and a subsequent information evaluation/decision-making phase. Even such simple guidance for the discussion process facilitates the solution of hidden profiles (Mojzisch & Schulz-Hardt, 2010). Other techniques are more complex. For example, so-called *dialectical* techniques (i.e. techniques that formally implement debate in a group) make sure that a controversial discussion takes place, even if the group members' real opinions converge. Usually, this is achieved by dividing a decision-making group into two subgroups that are given different roles. For example, in the case of the 'devil's advocacy' procedure, a particular group member or a subgroup plays the role of the devil's advocate by criticizing all proposals made by the rest of the group. Another example is a technique called 'dialectical inquiry': in the case of this technique, the subgroup from the previous example not only criticizes the proposal, but also comes up with a counterproposal. Such dialectical techniques facilitate stimulation by including arguments or information that hardly anyone in the group would have mentioned if group members had, as they usually do, acted on their own preferences. Indeed, these techniques also raise the quality of group decisions (see Katzenstein, 1996).

Group learning   The use of groups for a particular task is an investment, and the return on this investment often takes time to be realized. At the beginning, groups have considerable costs, for example coordination losses due to the fact that group members are not used to working together on this particular task, or the effort of synchronizing the group adequately. If the group gains experience with the task over time, these costs should decrease and the chance of process gains should increase. Of course, individuals also increase their own performance if they repeatedly perform similar tasks. However, repeatedly performing similar tasks *in a group* allows for further learning processes (**group learning**) that cannot occur if people perform individually.

> **group learning** a generic term for several learning processes that can only occur if several people work interactively on the same task.

Brodbeck and Greitemeyer (2000a, b) distinguish between four different types of learning processes in groups, of which the first also occurs in individual learning settings, whereas the other three processes are bound to social interactions with other people:

1. **Individual-to-individual transfer**. This process denotes individual practice effects or the *transfer* of what an individual has learned about how to perform a task on one occasion *from* that occasion *to* the next. If individuals perform similar tasks again and again (either alone or in a group), their skills improve, and individual learning takes place, which is also beneficial for the group. For example, the performance of a group of climbers may increase simply because their members improve their skills by means of individual training.

   > **individual-to-individual transfer** individual learning processes whereby a group member's ability to perform a task on its own improves as a result of repeated individual task performance.

2. **Group-to-individual transfer**. This type of transfer occurs if social interaction in a group improves its members' skills at performing the task individually (Laughlin & Sweeney, 1977). In the climbing example mentioned above, group members may become better individual climbers because, during a group climb, other group members have shown them how to better identify grips and holes in the rock. Obviously, group-to-individual transfer is more likely when there are more opportunities to demonstrate the relevant skills and strategies.

   > **group-to-individual transfer** a group learning process whereby a group member's ability to perform a task *alone* improves as a result of social interaction between group members during repeated collective task performance.

3. **Group-to-individual-in-group transfer**. This process means that performing tasks together in a group can improve group-specific skills among their members. For example, climbing together might improve the group members' abilities to notice and correct other members' technical faults while climbing difficult overhangs. Hence, this type of transfer can only be applied in group settings, not during individual task performance.

   > **group-to-individual-in-group transfer** a group learning process whereby a group member's ability to perform a task *within groups* improves as a result of social interaction between group members during repeated collective task performance.

4. **Group-to-group transfer.** In contrast to group-to-individual transfer, group-to-group transfer means that performing a similar task several times together in *the same* group can improve its members' skills at performing well *in this particular group* (Figure 13.9). For example, by repeatedly climbing together as a group, our climbers might learn about the particular strengths and weaknesses of the members of this particular group. This might enable them to determine who should be the lead climber, who should help the weaker members during difficult passages, and so on. Such a shared knowledge of each other's expertise, strengths and weaknesses is also called *transactive memory* (Wegner, 1987; see Chapter 12).

> **group-to-group transfer** a group learning process whereby a *particular* group's capability to perform a group task improves as result of social interaction between its group members during repeated collective task performance.

Brodbeck and Greitemeyer (2000a, b) conducted experiments with so-called *rule induction tasks* (these are tasks where certain rules have to be found by systematically formulating and testing hypotheses). They provided solid evidence that, as a consequence of these four types of group learning, groups increase their potential, reduce process losses and increase the likelihood of developing process gains. Hence, facilitating group learning by having groups repeatedly perform a similar task can be an effective way to improve group performance.

So far, these group learning processes suggest that group learning facilitates individual capability gains (group-to-individual transfer) as well as improved group coordination (group-to-individual-in-group transfer; group-to-group

transfer). It is, however, plausible that the reduction of motivation losses and the development of motivation gains can also be 'learned' in groups. If the same group repeatedly performs similar tasks, group members become more familiar with each other and develop interpersonal trust. Interpersonal trust facilitates the pursuit of collective instead of individual goals (Dirks, 1999). As a consequence, group members should be less prone to social loafing or sucker effects, and should be more likely to show social compensation. Indirect evidence for this comes from a study by Erez and Somech (1996) showing that hardly any social loafing occurs in groups whose members have known each other for at least six months.

Summary

In sum, our consideration of group performance and group learning has shown that effective group performance management requires an analysis of the task structure, followed by careful group composition and choice of adequate synchronization measures. Furthermore, group learning should be facilitated by using the same group for a range of structurally similar tasks. As we have illustrated, these three basic principles affect all three categories of process losses and process gains by optimizing group coordination, as well as stimulating individual motivation and capabilities during collective work. Theory Box 13.2 summarizes these effects.

So far we have investigated basic aspects of group performance, namely task types, group process gains and losses, and principles for the management of group performance, without referring to the structure of natural

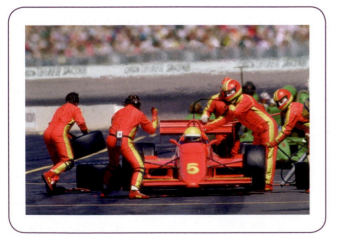

FIGURE 13.9 *A Formula 1 team of mechanics completing a fast tyre change during the race.*
Source: © David Madison. Used under licence from Getty Images.

THEORY BOX 13.2

THE THREE BASIC ELEMENTS OF GROUP PERFORMANCE MANAGEMENT AS AFFECTING ALL THREE LEVELS OF PERFORMANCE-RELATED GROUP PROCESSES

Group composition	Group synchronization	Group learning

Group-level processes:
Coordination in the group
Individual motivation in the group
Individual capability in the group

Source: Adapted from Schulz-Hardt, Hertel, & Brodbeck, 2007.

groups at work (such as work groups within organizations). We therefore turn next to a fundamental process for structuring group activity: leadership.

LEADERSHIP

What makes leadership effective?

Leadership is about *influencing others*. This admittedly very short and broad definition is the only common denominator of the many definitions that exist in the leadership literature (e.g. Bass, 2008; Yukl, 2012). We define leadership in accordance with researchers from Project GLOBE, an international research programme of some 170 scholars from more than 60 different countries, who study leadership across cultures (Chhokar, Brodbeck, & House, 2007; House, Hanges, Javidan, Dorfman, & Gupta, 2004). GLOBE researchers have developed a definition of leadership that specifies what is meant by 'influencing' others within organizational settings: **leadership (in organizations)** means *influencing, motivating or enabling others to contribute towards the effectiveness of work units and organizations.*

> **leadership (in organizations)** influencing, motivating or enabling others to contribute towards the effectiveness of work units and organizations.

The central questions that have received and continue to receive attention in leadership research are: How can we identify effective leaders? What makes leaders effective? How do leaders influence others? How are leaders perceived by others? How do leaders emerge and develop? Therefore, most leadership research focuses on at least one of the following criteria of **leadership effectiveness**: (1) the impact of leadership on the accomplishment of group and organizational objectives (e.g. high-quality decisions, solutions to problems); (2) the extent of influence on followers that can be exerted via leadership (e.g. change in behaviour, attitudes, values, motivation, well-being); (3) the perception of a person as a leader in the 'eye of the beholder'; and (4) the emergence of a person as a leader and how quickly leaders are promoted to higher ranks in an organization. Here we focus on a specific question: how can leadership help to improve group performance? This question relates mainly to the first two classes of criteria of leadership effectiveness – that is, accomplishing objectives, and influencing followers.

> **leadership effectiveness** the impact of leadership on the accomplishment of group and organizational objectives, on the behaviour, perceptions, attitudes, values, motivation or well-being of followers and peers, and on the accomplishments of those who lead.

In this section we describe approaches to the study of leadership that cover major developments in the history of leadership research. For reasons of space, only a small selection of theories and research can be described. For broader coverage, see Pierce and Newstrom (2002), and for comprehensive reviews see Bass (2008) and Yukl (2012). Thereafter, we develop a group performance perspective on leadership that integrates the research on group functioning described in the first part of this chapter with findings from leadership research.

Approaches to the study of leadership

The systematic study of leadership has been dominated by *leader-oriented approaches*, many of which were developed in the first half of the twentieth century. They focus on personality characteristics and behaviours of leaders, in order to distinguish leaders from non-leaders and to identify effective leaders in organizations. From about the 1960s, *contingency approaches* were developed, which incorporate relevant situational factors (e.g. characteristics of the organization, the task or the followers) for predicting the success of certain leader characteristics and leadership behaviours. The latest developments in leadership research emphasize the nature and dynamics of leader–follower relationships (e.g. *transformational–transactional leadership*), as well as shared leadership within work groups. For effective leadership in groups there is something to learn from all the approaches described here.

Leader-oriented approaches   The view of the leader as a 'hero' or a 'great person' has dominated leadership research for a long time, and thus the study of leadership has mainly been the study of *leaders*, that is, their characteristics, skills and behaviours on one hand, and their effects on followers, groups and organizations, on the other.

Leader traits. Since the pioneering systematic studies of leadership in the first half of the last century, a major proportion of research has focused on stable **leader traits** (e.g. personality, intelligence, motivational dispositions), on the basis of which leader emergence and leadership effectiveness may be predicted, following the idea that 'a leader is born, not made' (Figure 13.10). Today, relatively small but consistent correlations between effective or emergent leaders and the 'big five' personality characteristics are reported

> **leader traits** relatively stable personal characteristics (e.g. personality, intelligence, motivational dispositions) which are thought to predict leader emergence and leadership effectiveness.

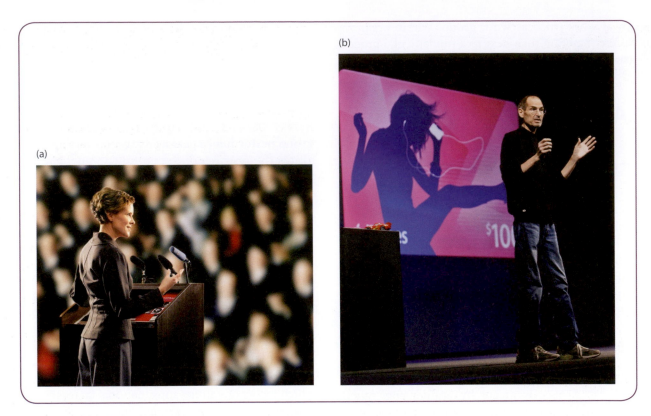

FIGURE 13.10(a) and (b) *What stable traits are characteristic of leaders?*

Source: (a) © Christoph Wilhelm. Used under licence from Getty Images; (b) © Paul Sakuma, File. Used under licence from Press Association Images.

(Judge, Bono, Ilies, & Gerhardt, 2002). For example, leaders are more likely to be effective if they score high on extraversion ($r = .31$), openness to experience ($r = .24$), and conscientiousness ($r = .28$), and low on neuroticism ($r = -.24$). The correlation in the case of the fifth personality dimension, agreeableness, is much lower ($r = .08$), but it still differs reliably from zero. Research has also found a positive correlation between intelligence and leader effectiveness ($r = .27$; Judge, Colbert & Ilies, 2004).

Only a few empirical studies have rigorously tested the assumption that personality traits have a causal impact on leader effectiveness or the emergence of an individual as a leader in an organization. Most studies on this issue have used a cross-sectional design, in which measures of leader personality and performance are taken at about the same point in time. This design is limited, because it cannot test directional causal assumptions. With such correlational designs, the possibility remains that the commonly implied causal relationship (i.e. that personality has an influence on leadership success) may work the other way around. Individuals who find themselves in leadership positions more often than others, by being pushed into them by chance, or because of their technical expertise (at school, in higher education, at work), may learn and develop the sets of skills, attitudes and behaviours necessary to succeed – or just to maintain their leadership position. By trying to satisfy respective role expectations and social norms typically applied to leaders, individuals are likely to develop or show those personal characteristics that match expectations.

A general critique of leader-trait approaches is that they do not explain in sufficient detail how the link between personal characteristics and leadership success is established: what are the variables that *mediate* this relationship?

Leadership behaviour. The search for variables that can predict leadership success better than personality traits shifted the focus of interest towards what leaders actually do – **leadership behaviour**. During the late 1940s, two research programmes in the US began to work in this area independently of each other and have shaped our understanding of leadership behaviour up to the present day. One was established at Ohio State University, the other at the University of Michigan. The two programmes identified a large number of leadership behaviours and grouped these into partially overlapping

leadership behaviour observable acts that are meant to influence, motivate or enable others to contribute towards the effectiveness of a work unit or organization.

INDIVIDUAL DIFFERENCES 13.1

You can assess your own personality using the 'big five' personality dimensions by completing a 45-item questionnaire (an abbreviated version of the original questionnaire, cf. McCrae & Costa, 1987). You can complete this test, easily and at no cost, on the 'Big Five Personality Test' website. Your scores on each dimensions are calculated automatically and you receive feedback and learn more about the five fundamental dimensions of personality whose relevance to leadership effectiveness is described above.

categorization schemes, both of which point out the difference between task-focused versus people-focused leadership behaviours.

The *Ohio Group*, while focusing on the leader as the main source of leadership behaviour, sought to classify relevant leadership aspects by assembling about 1800 leader behaviour descriptions, which were subsequently reduced to about 150 items. A preliminary questionnaire was administered to thousands of employees in civic and military organizations, who indicated the extent to which their supervisors displayed these behaviours. The final questionnaire, called the Leader Behaviour Description Questionnaire (LBDQ), is a hallmark in the history of leadership research. By using factor-analytic methods to analyse patterns of relationships among all the LBDQ items, two independent dimensions emerged: *initiating structure* (i.e. task-oriented behaviours) and *consideration* (i.e. people-oriented behaviours).

Judge, Piccolo, and Ilies (2004) conducted a meta-analysis of 200 studies, with 300 samples. They found that both consideration ($r = .49$) and initiating structure ($r = .29$) have moderately strong correlations with leadership outcomes. Consideration was more strongly related to leader effectiveness ($r = .39$), followers' motivation ($r = .40$), satisfaction with leaders ($r = .68$) and job satisfaction ($r = .40$) than was initiating structure ($r = .28$, $r = .26$, $r = .27$, $r = .19$, respectively), and both were equally strongly ($r = .23$) related to group/organizational performance (see Judge, Piccolo et al., 2004, p. 40, Table 3). The literature published prior to this meta-analysis indicated that initiating structure is more susceptible to situational differences than is consideration; for example, in some situations task orientation is positively associated with satisfaction, while in others it even has negative effects (cf. Pierce & Newstrom, 2002). This may explain why in the meta-analysis reported above, where correlations were sampled across a whole range of different situations, correlations were weaker for initiating structure than for consideration.

The *Michigan group* characterized the four overall dimensions of leadership behaviour they identified – interaction facilitation, work facilitation, goal emphasis and individual support – as the 'basic structure of what one may term *leadership*' (Bowers & Seashore, 1966, p. 247). Their understanding of 'leadership' provides the foundation for a leadership perspective that differs considerably from leader-oriented approaches. While the Ohio group's research clearly focused on the individual (formal) leader, as was described above, the Michigan group stated that effective work groups require the presence of each of the four classes of behaviours they identified, but that *anyone* in a group can provide them successfully. These behaviours need not all be shown by the same (formal) leader, as long as they are present in the work group to a sufficient extent. Because this view is of particular interest to this chapter's focus on group performance, we elaborate on it later in this section.

Cross-sectional designs are also commonly used for the empirical study of leadership behaviour, although such designs do not allow us to make causal inferences about the direction of relationship between leadership behaviour and leadership success. Again, the true causal pathways may go in the opposite direction. For example, leaders may show more consideration behaviour, because followers are already motivated and high-performing (Greene, 1975). Another threat to the correct interpretation of results from cross-sectional studies is the 'third variable problem'. For example, mutual sympathy between leader and followers, due to a match in personal values or socio-cultural backgrounds, may have a similar positive impact on both leader behaviour and follower behaviour. Equally, mutual trust can lead to more consideration on the leader's part and to higher performance on the follower's part. Thus, an apparent correlation between consideration on the part of leaders and high performance on the part of followers can be caused by a third variable (mutual sympathy or mutual trust) that makes leader behaviour and follower performance *appear to be directly* linked with each other, when in fact they are not.

Problems with correctly interpreting results from cross-sectional studies are aggravated when relying on followers' self-report measures for leader behaviours (as occurs, for example, in the LBDQ) in conjunction with followers' perceptions of leadership effectiveness (e.g. their motivation, satisfaction with the leader or job satisfaction). In the worst case all these variables are assessed by asking the same followers (*common source effect*) and by using the same questionnaire as measurement instrument (*common method effect*). Under these circumstances, the strength of the relationship between leader behaviour and leader effectiveness is likely to be overestimated.

Contingency approaches Leader-oriented approaches which focus solely on leaders' traits and behaviours have a tendency to look for simple answers to complex problems. They can account for only a limited proportion of the variance in leadership effectiveness, because the effects of leader traits and behaviours are likely to average out across different situations that may require different types of leaders or different leader behaviours. **Contingency approaches** emphasize the role of situational factors and how these qualify, or moderate, the relationship between leadership traits or behaviours and leadership effectiveness. These situational factors include *task characteristics* (e.g. task structure, task complexity), *followers' characteristics* (e.g. their level of motivation, competencies, maturity) and *characteristics of the social context* (e.g. quality of social relationships, group cohesion, group size).

> **contingency approaches** emphasize situational factors in the study of leadership (e.g. task or follower characteristics) and how these moderate the relationship between leader traits or leadership behaviours and leadership effectiveness.

Many contingency theories have been proposed, each of which stresses the importance of a particular array of situational factors and different leadership characteristics

(for reviews, see Bass, 2008; Yukl, 2012). One message contained in all contingency approaches is that leaders must be able to recognize, adapt to or change different situational circumstances, otherwise they may lose their influence on followers. To date, there is no unified theory from which we can derive the most critical situational factors that moderate relationships between leader characteristics and behaviours, on the one hand, and leadership effectiveness, on the other. One of the most widely cited contingency theories, *path–goal theory*, which has been presented by House and his colleagues (House, 1971, 1996; House & Mitchell, 1974) is shown in Theory Box 13.3.

Path–goal theory. Leaders are considered effective when their behaviour impacts on the subordinates' motivation, satisfaction and ability to perform effectively. A major concern of path–goal theory is how a leader influences the followers' perceptions of their work goals, their personal goals and the paths to goal attainment. To maximize their impact in these aspects, leaders need to master a range of leadership behaviours and use them flexibly depending on specific situational contingencies. Five classes of leadership behaviours are distinguished in newer versions of path–goal theory (House, 1996). *Clarifying behaviour* (e.g. about rewards and punishments, performance goals and means to achieve them) reduces role ambiguity and increases follower beliefs that effort in a specific direction will result in good performance, and that performance will be rewarded. *Work facilitation behaviour* (e.g. planning, scheduling, coordinating, guiding, coaching, counselling and giving feedback) eliminates roadblocks and bottlenecks, provides resources, stimulates self-development and helps to delegate authority

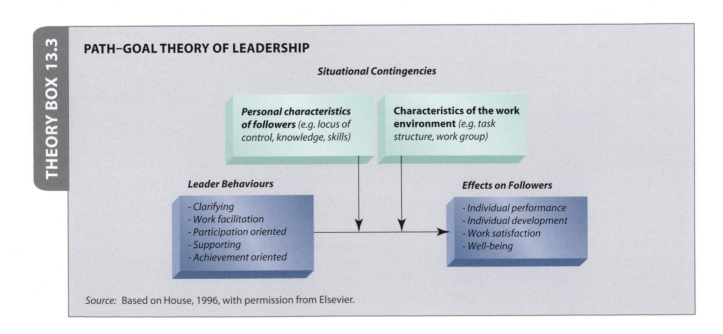

THEORY BOX 13.3

PATH–GOAL THEORY OF LEADERSHIP

Situational Contingencies

Personal characteristics of followers (e.g. locus of control, knowledge, skills)

Characteristics of the work environment (e.g. task structure, work group)

Leader Behaviours
- Clarifying
- Work facilitation
- Participation oriented
- Supporting
- Achievement oriented

Effects on Followers
- Individual performance
- Individual development
- Work satisfaction
- Well-being

Source: Based on House, 1996, with permission from Elsevier.

to subordinates. *Participative behaviour* (e.g. consulting with subordinates, incorporating subordinate opinions in decision-making) increases followers' self-confidence and the personal value of job-related effort. *Supportive behaviour* (e.g. creating a friendly and psychologically supportive environment, displaying concern for subordinates' welfare) increases the followers' involvement with the work group and both organizational and goal commitment. *Achievement-oriented behaviour* (e.g. setting high goals and seeking improvement, emphasizing excellence, showing confidence in subordinates, stressing pride in work) increases subordinate confidence and the personal value of goal-directed effort.

The extent to which the described leadership behaviours are successful depends on two classes of contingency factors: (1) *personal characteristics of the followers* (e.g. internal versus external locus of control, self-efficacy beliefs, knowledge, skills and abilities) influence the degree to which followers see the leadership behaviour as a source of satisfaction or as instrumental to future satisfaction; and (2) *characteristics of the environment* (e.g. task structure, formal authority system of the organization, primary work group), which are not within the direct control of followers, but are important to satisfy their needs or their ability to perform well. For example, followers with an internal locus of control (who believe that they, personally, control events in their life), high self-efficacy beliefs (i.e. confidence that they can carry out successfully what they wish to), or high competence in their job respond more positively to participative leadership behaviour than do followers with external locus of control (who need more work facilitation behaviour), low self-efficacy (who need more supportive behaviour) or low job competence (who need more clarifying behaviour). Examples of leadership behaviour contingencies with characteristics of the primary work group are described in detail in the next section, on group leadership.

Despite inconclusive research results and some conceptual deficiencies (e.g. House, 1996; Wofford & Liska, 1993; see Leader in the Field, Robert J. House), path–goal theory is still in use, because it provides a valuable conceptual framework for identifying situational factors relevant to leadership effectiveness. The theory's underlying idea, that certain leadership behaviours are helpful and successful under certain circumstances, has been adopted in several newer leadership theories (cf. Yukl, 2012; see Leader in the Field, Gary Yukl). Another idea that path–goal theory has infused into leadership research and practice is that the followers and their characteristics matter in the leadership process. Not only is their performance-related behaviour important, so too are their perceptions, cognitions and beliefs about work-related issues.

LEADER IN THE FIELD

Robert J. House (1932–2011) received his PhD in Management from Ohio State University in 1960. He was appointed the Joseph Frank Bernstein Endowed Chair of Organization Studies at the Wharton School at the University of Pennsylvania in 1988, and is a Fellow of the Academy of Management, the American Psychological Association and the Society of Industrial-Organizational Psychology. Dr House has published numerous articles, four of which received outstanding paper awards, and two papers are Scientific Citation Classics. His scholarly contribution to leadership research comprises two well-received theories – path–goal theory and charismatic leadership – which were both first presented in the 1970s, and a still ongoing, international research project on leadership across and within various countries (Global Leadership and Organizational Behavior Effectiveness Program, GLOBE), in which he served as principal investigator from 1993 to 2003.

Transactional, transformational and laissez-faire leadership

In the past 25 years a substantial amount of research evidence has been accumulated about what leaders and followers offer one another. **Transactional leaders** focus on the proper exchange of resources. They give followers something they want in exchange for something the leader wants (cf. Burns, 1978; Conger & Kanungo, 1998). **Transformational (charismatic) leaders**, in contrast, develop an appealing vision and focus on the alignment of the group or organizational goals with the followers' needs and aspirations, in order to influence them to make sacrifices and put the needs of the organization above their own interests. **Laissez-faire leaders** offer very little to followers ('non-leadership'); they avoid making decisions, hesitate in taking action and are often absent when needed.

Bass (1985) has refined the concept of transformational leadership into four sub-dimensions (known as the 'four I's' of transformational leadership):

> **transactional leaders** leaders who focus on the proper exchange of resources, who give followers something in exchange for something the leaders want.

> **transformational (charismatic) leaders** leaders who focus on aligning the group or organizational goals with the followers' needs and aspirations by developing an appealing vision.

> **laissez-faire leaders** leaders who engage in 'non-leadership'; that is, avoid making decisions, hesitate in taking action and are often absent when needed.

- *Idealized influence* Leaders behave in admirable ways (e.g. display conviction, display role-modelling behaviours consistent with the vision, appeal on an emotional level) so that followers tend to identify with them.

LEADER IN THE FIELD

Gary Yukl received his PhD in Industrial-Organizational Psychology from the University of California at Berkeley in 1967. He is a Professor of Management at the School of Business at the State University of New York, Albany and Fellow of the Academy of Management, the American Psychological Association, the Society of Industrial-Organizational Psychology and the American Psychological Society. Dr Yukl has written several books, including *Leadership in Organizations* (Prentice-Hall, 8th edition, 2012), a widely cited book, which is used worldwide and has been translated widely. Apart from numerous awards received for his scholarly publications about leadership and management, he has also published more than 60 articles in professional journals in psychology and management, and has consulted with and designed development programmes and projects for a variety of business and public sector organizations, as well as for various agencies of the US government.

- *Inspirational motivation* Leaders articulate a vision (e.g. provide meaning for the work task, set high standards, communicate optimism about the achievability of the vision) that is appealing and inspiring to followers.

- *Intellectual stimulation* Leaders stimulate and encourage creativity in their followers (e.g. challenge assumptions, take risks, ask followers to put into practice their own ideas).

- *Individualized consideration* Leaders attend to each follower individually (e.g. act as a mentor or coach, listen to their concerns and needs).

The concepts of transformational leadership and *charismatic leadership* (Conger & Kanungo, 1987, 1998) have much in common (Judge & Piccolo, 2004). Charismatic leaders can be described as self-confident, enthusiastic leaders able to win followers' respect and support for their vision. They also show role-modelling behaviours consistent with the vision, take personal risks and express strong confidence in their followers. On the part of the followers, charismatic leadership results in, for example, *internalization* (i.e. followers adopt the leader's ideals and goals and become inspired to attain them because they are inherently satisfying) and *social identification* (i.e. followers create a connection in their minds between their self-concepts and the shared values and identities of their group or organization). For ease of description, our use of the term 'transformational leadership' includes charismatic leadership, although we acknowledge that the different theories underlying each concept do make a clear distinction between them (e.g. Conger & Kanungo, 1998).

Transactional leadership consists of three dimensions underlying leaders' behaviour:

- *Contingent reward* Leaders set up constructive transactions or exchanges with followers (e.g. clarify expectations, establish rewards for meeting expectations).

- *Active management by exception* Leaders monitor follower behaviour, anticipate problems and take corrective action before serious difficulties occur.

- *Passive management by exception* Leaders wait until the followers' behaviour has created problems before taking action (cf. Avolio, 1999). This is not, however, to be confused with laissez-faire leadership, which represents the absence of leadership. In the case of passive management by exception, at least some leadership influence is exerted, although often after the damage is done.

The research on theories of transformational, transactional and laissez-faire leadership combines and complements the leadership-oriented and contingency approaches described above in four ways. First, it proposes that leadership is a process that is partially determined by leader traits, trainable behaviours and skills. Second, it identifies situational factors under which the different types of leadership vary in effectiveness (see Social Psychology Beyond the Lab 13.2). Third, it proposes a bidirectional influence between leader characteristics, on one hand, and attributions of followers and how they react to the leader's characteristics, on the other. Fourth, it proposes that the followers' characteristics (e.g. their needs, self-concepts, interpretations of goals and events, motivations and emotions) can moderate or mediate the relationship between leader behaviours and followers' responses.

Transformational and transactional theories of leadership have been tested with a whole variety of methods, including longitudinal studies, field studies and laboratory experiments. In a meta-analysis of 87 studies (total $N > 38{,}000$), Judge and Piccolo (2004) determined the contribution of transformational, transactional and laissez-faire leadership to the prediction of organizational criteria relevant to leadership effectiveness (follower job satisfaction, satisfaction with leader, motivation, leader job performance, effectiveness and group/organization performance). Overall, by combining the different effectiveness criteria, this analysis revealed that three leadership dimensions were positively related to outcome variables: transformational leadership ($r = .44$); transactional–contingent reward leadership ($r = .39$); and transactional–active management by exception ($r = .15$). In contrast, two of the

SOCIAL PSYCHOLOGY BEYOND THE LAB 13.2

CHARISMA IN THE US PRESIDENCY

House, Spangler, and Woycke (1991) tested a model of leader charisma and effectiveness based on a rather unusual sample, namely 34 elected US presidents, from Washington to Reagan. Among other variables, their model includes leader personality characteristics, such as motivational need for power (cf. McClelland & Burnham, 1976), situational variables, such as national crises during presidency, and behavioural charisma. The authors hypothesized that for US presidents the motivational need for power is positively related to behavioural charisma. They argue that without such a need, presidents are unlikely to have developed the persuasive skills to influence others strongly, and they are also unlikely to obtain sustained satisfaction from the leadership role. Furthermore, it was hypothesized that behavioural charisma is positively related to presidential performance, because charismatic leaders produce extraordinary performance and strong commitment to the leader and his mission in followers by arousing mission-relevant motives, shaping their basic values and increasing their self-confidence. Finally, it was hypothesized that domestic and foreign crises are positively related to charisma and presidential performance, because crises are necessary prerequisites for the emergence of behavioural charisma and provide a president with opportunities to be effective.

In terms of methods used, we can give here only a glimpse of how much care was taken to develop and apply proper operationalizations of the described variables for such an unusual sample, in which most of the individuals studied were no longer alive at the time of the study. Motivational need for power was estimated on the basis of each president's inaugural speech (Winter, 1987: construct validity ranges from .60 to .80; Winter & Stewart, 1977). On the basis of two chronological histories of America, international relations crises (13 categories), domestic and international economic crises (11 categories) and domestic unrest (23 categories) were categorized, counted and rated by eight coders on a scale from one to 10 for severity of crisis. Domestic and

international economic crises were rated 1, and for example the wars with Mexico and Korea were coded 2, World Wars I and II were coded 6, the Civil War was coded 10. A composite crises measure for each president's period was created with a reliability of .91. For presidential charisma four measures were used, two of which were taken from Simonton (1986) and two further measures were developed on the basis of sampled texts from biographies of close followers to each president (composite measure's reliability .87). Finally, five different measures of presidential performance were taken from other sources: from Winter (1987) who used indicators such as settled crises and war avoidance, and from Murray and Blessing (1983), who surveyed 517 American historians who rated the US presidents on various performance dimensions, plus three further measures which the authors developed themselves. The resulting five composite scales – direct action, subjective presidential performance, international relations performance, economic performance and social performance – had sufficient to high levels of reliability, ranging from .75 to .97.

Hypothesis tests showed that motivational need for power was significantly and positively related to behavioural charisma, and that behavioural charisma was significantly and positively related to all measures of presidential performance except for international relations. Furthermore, crises were significantly and positively related to behavioural charisma, and also to three out of five presidential performance measures. Acknowledging that their study was correlational in nature, House et al. (1991) anticipated several alternative explanations, including, for example, spuriousness of correlations due to common third variables or common source bias, and accounted for them by employing multiple methods from multiple sources, and by discussing their findings within various relevant theoretical frames. In our view they make a strong case for the validity of the hypothesized correlations found and their concluding statement about US Presidents: 'They are effective because they are charismatic' (p. 391).

leadership dimensions were negatively related to leadership outcomes: transactional–passive management by exception ($r = -.15$); and laissez-faire leadership ($r = -.37$).

Judge and Piccolo (2004) conclude that contingent reward (transactional) leadership and transformational leadership predict outcome variables to a similar extent. This is troublesome, considering that transformational–transactional leadership theory predicts that contingent reward will be reasonably effective, but not as effective as any of the transformational leadership dimensions (Bass & Avolio, 1994, p. 6). The superiority of one theory relative to the other seems to depend on the context. For example, Judge and Piccolo note that contingent reward leadership works best in business settings. Perhaps it is the resource-dependent nature of this kind of setting that is crucial – that is, business leaders are more able to reward followers tangibly (e.g. via financial incentives) in exchange for their efforts than are leaders in the other domains studied (universities/colleges, military settings, the public sector). In situations in which leaders have access to fewer or no resources, contingent reward leadership may be less effective, because it is more difficult for leaders to meet their side of the bargain. Thus, transformational leadership may be more robust in these settings than is contingent reward leadership.

Another observation from Judge and Piccolo's (2004) meta-analysis is that transformational and contingent reward leadership predicted leadership outcomes about equally strongly under weak research designs (leadership and outcomes were measured at the same time and with the same source). In contrast, under strong research designs (longitudinal designs and designs in which the leadership and the criterion were measured with different sources of data), transformational leadership predicted leadership outcomes more strongly than did contingent reward leadership.

The early tests available for measuring transformational and transactional leadership have been subject to criticism on methodological grounds. However, Rowold and Heinitz (2007) demonstrated that, although charismatic and transformational leadership overlap with each other to large extent (78 per cent common variance), both are clearly distinct from transactional leadership, and both are also superior to it in predicting outcomes (both subjective outcomes such as extra effort, effectiveness and satisfaction, and objective outcomes such as profit achieved by the work unit led by the target leader).

Summary

In this section we have reviewed various approaches to the study of leadership: leader-oriented approaches, which focus on traits; contingency approaches, which emphasize both situational factors and traits; and approaches to transactional, transformational and charismatic leadership, which combine and complement the trait and contingency approaches. This implies that leadership is inherently neither solely in people nor solely in the situational context. Instead, both categories of variables can be seen as conditions that facilitate or inhibit the expression of effective leadership processes. This is part of the reason why leadership is a complex social phenomenon and the scientific study of it is a very complex task.

Most of the approaches to the study of leadership focus on the leader as a person and less on 'leadership' as a process. For an exception, the leadership perspective taken by the Michigan group explicitly suggests that *anyone* in a work group can provide leadership functions. The more necessary leadership behaviours are effectively provided by group members, the less a (formal) leader needs to infuse them into the work group (and the less harmful are passive or laissez-faire leaders). We believe that it is in an organization's interest for their leaders to develop employees and whole work groups such that the group members facilitate each other's performance by also engaging in effective leadership behaviour. This comes very close to modern concepts of shared or team leadership, which are discussed in the next section.

LEADERSHIP IN GROUPS

How can leadership help to improve group performance?

The first researchers to turn their attention to how leadership can affect groups as a whole were Kurt Lewin and his co-workers, Lippitt and White. In a series of experiments they observed in detail how different leadership behaviours of adult leaders affected the 'social climates' of after-school clubs of 10-year-old boys (e.g. Lewin, Lippitt, & White, 1939; White & Lippitt, 1968). They implemented three different leadership styles (i.e. a repeatedly shown pattern of leadership behaviour evident across a variety of situations): *autocratic leadership* (directive, non-participative, domineering behaviours); *democratic leadership* (participative, communicative, egalitarian); and *laissez-faire leadership* ('hands-off' leadership, with few attempts made to influence others at all).

leadership style a pattern of leadership behaviour which is repeatedly shown and evident across a variety of situations.

Not surprisingly, democratic leaders were liked more than autocratic or laissez-faire leaders. They created a group-minded, friendly and task-oriented atmosphere. In contrast, autocratic leadership resulted in more frequent hostile behaviours, but also in 'apathetic' patterns of behaviour with no instances of smiling or joking. Although the quantity of work done in autocracy was somewhat greater than in democracy, there were indications that work motivation was greater in democracy. There was more 'work-minded' conversation in democratically led groups, and members continued to work hard, even when the group leader was temporarily absent. In contrast, members of autocratically led groups often stopped working when the leader left the room. Finally, there was some informal evidence that the work produced in democratically led groups showed higher levels of originality than under either of the other types of leadership. Note that the impact of a laissez-faire leader was not the same as that of a democratic leader: there was less work done, the work was poorer and students expressed less satisfaction with the laissez-faire leader. In our view, these early findings show that what leaders do has an impact on how groups function as a whole, and that an appointed leader's style of leadership has an impact on the leadership behaviours shown by the group members themselves. Under an autocratic leader the group members seem not to take responsibility for leading themselves, whereas under a democratic leader they seem to fulfil (self-)leadership functions more willingly.

Because we focus on characteristics of group functioning and how these can be facilitated by leadership, not only by an appointed leader, but also by the group members themselves, we define **group leadership** as influencing, motivating or enabling (oneself and) others to contribute towards the effectiveness and viability of work groups. This definition is meant to also comprise **leaderless groups** (e.g. self-managed work or student groups), which require **shared or team leadership**.

Bradford and Cohen (1984) argued that the predominant conception of a 'heroic leader' undermines the principally positive effects of shared responsibility for leadership functions and empowerment of followers on leadership effectiveness. The more recently developed concepts of *shared leadership* (e.g. Pearce & Sims, 2000) or *team leadership* (e.g. Sivasubramaniam, Murry, Avolio, & Jung, 2002) denote group-level leadership concepts that go beyond the commonly held concept of a single leader, in that the responsibility for leadership functions, the exercise of leadership behaviours and the perceptions of leadership roles are shared among group members. These concepts complement the view of a singular leader, who is more informed and confident than others, with the view that leadership is a mutual social influence process (e.g. Smith, 1995).

Based on the propositions about group functioning and performance described in the first part of this chapter, and the more recent developments in leadership theory and research described above, we argue that effective group leadership needs to ensure that the functions critical to (1) group and task design, (2) group synchronization and (3) group learning are taken care of (see Zaccaro, Rittman, & Marks, 2001) *with or without* a formally appointed leader.

Group and task design

According to the first principle of group performance management, group leadership requires that groups are composed in accordance with the requirements of their tasks and goals (i.e. group design), and that tasks are constantly (re)structured in accordance with the group's structure (task design).

Wageman's (2001) study of self-managed teams in the US Customer Services Division of Xerox Corporation demonstrates that effective group leadership is indeed a group design and task design activity. Across the US, all teams in this division perform basically the same task, which is to offer regular maintenance services and to respond to customer calls, for example, about machine breakdowns. Wageman measured the extent to which group leaders made sure that their work group was a 'real team', with clear membership, stability over time and group members working in close physical proximity to each other (i.e. group composition). Furthermore, she measured whether leaders infused a clear direction, with just a few, memorable objectives that focused on the ends to be achieved, rather than on the details of the means for achieving them (i.e. group goals). This study also measured to what extent leaders enabled an effective team structure, with adequate group size, sufficient skill variety (not too much heterogeneity so that coordination problems remained manageable), high task interdependence, challenging task goals, challenging performance targets and clearly articulated strategies and norms for planning and decision-making (i.e. group and task structure). Finally, she measured the degree to which

---

group leadership influencing, motivating or enabling (oneself and) others to contribute towards the effectiveness and viability of work groups.

leaderless groups groups with no appointed leader but which display effective leadership behaviours which are infused by the group members themselves (shared leadership) and/or by agents external to the group.

shared or team leadership responsibility for leadership functions, the exercise of leadership behaviour and perceptions about leadership roles are shared among group members (sometimes including agents external to the team).

organizational context factors (e.g. quality of reward and feedback systems, adequacy of training offered and availability of resources needed) supported effective group functioning. Wageman (2001) used a sample of 34 self-managed teams to test the extent to which the desired leadership activities were linked with objective group performance criteria, obtained from company records. The more leaders engaged in the task/group design activities described above, the higher was group performance and the more self-management was practised within the groups.

This is an example of how the extent to which leadership secures proper task and group design directly influences the effectiveness of group functioning.

Group synchronization

Group leadership implies the monitoring and management of ongoing group processes, for example the exchange of information, views and opinions and the social dynamics involved. The contribution of leadership to group synchronization has been most extensively demonstrated for information management during group decision-making. Via information management, effective leadership keeps the group focused on the problem at hand, facilitates communication, stimulates decision-relevant contributions and keeps them alive during discussion (e.g. Larson & Christensen, 1993; Maier, 1967). In a hidden-profile study on medical diagnostic teams, Larson, Christensen, Abbott, and Franz (1996) investigated how designated leaders (the most experienced medical doctor in each group) manage the processing of distributed information during group decision-making. They observed that leaders repeated unshared information (i.e. information held by only one group member) at a steadily increasing rate over time and raised more questions about concrete factual information than other group members. In a follow-up study, again in the domain of medical decision-making, Larson, Christensen, Franz, and Abbott (1998) replicated the above results and found positive correlations between information management behaviour and group decision quality. This is an example of how information management behaviours can counteract 'asymmetries' in the discussion and evaluation of information that were identified as a weakness of group decision-making, especially in hidden profile situations (Figure 13.11).

Larson, Foster-Fishman, and Franz (1998) also explored the effects of leadership style on group decision-making. They trained individuals to display either directive or participative leadership behaviours. Directive leadership groups outperformed participative leadership groups only when their leaders possessed sufficient information

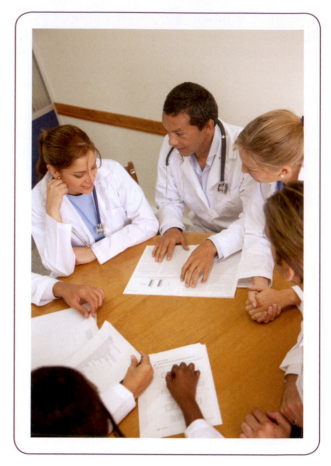

FIGURE 13.11 *How does the designated leader in a group such as this manage the processing of distributed information during group decision-making?*

Source: © Andresr. Used under licence from Shutterstock.

favouring the best decision alternative. In contrast, when directive leaders possessed information that favoured a suboptimal choice (as did the information held by other group members), group decision quality deteriorated considerably. This was not the case in groups with a participative or democratic leader who managed the group in a way that encouraged more (shared *and* unshared) information to surface. In contrast, directive leaders tend to 'sell' their opinion by emphasizing their own unshared information that is consistent with their decision preference.

Likewise, Cruz, Henningsen, and Smith (1999) concluded from their hidden profile study that the quality of the group's choice depends on the quality of a directive leader's preferred decision alternative. Overall, these findings are in line with Vroom and Jago's (1988) notion that autocratic forms of decision-making are feasible only when leaders possess sufficient information to make a high-quality decision. Considering that in situations of a hidden profile most or all group members (including the leader) are likely to hold information that does not imply the best possible decision alternative, a directive leadership style seems less functional for high-quality decision-making than does a participative leadership style. However, the study by Larson et al. (1998) also demonstrates that a participative leadership style does not guarantee high-quality decision-making under all conditions of distributed knowledge. When the leader does indeed know best, directive leadership results in better group decisions than participative leadership does. Thus, wise leaders should know when they know best and when not, and adjust their leadership style accordingly.

Group development and learning

Group leadership implies supporting group learning and development. For example, effective group leadership seeks to further the development of transactive memory systems by fostering a team learning orientation (Bunderson & Sutcliffe, 2003). This can be established by promoting mutual collaboration among group members and developing a decentralized communication structure, instead of using directive leadership, which is associated with a communication structure that centres around the leader. In a decentralized transactive memory system, a large proportion of group members hold significant parts of the group knowledge. If knowledge is distributed, not centralized, a transactive memory system is less subject to disruption when, for instance, a centrally positioned leader is overloaded with work, cannot communicate with adequate frequency and is thus not able to transmit the group's knowledge adequately.

Interdependent work in groups entails uncertainty about others' motivation, competency and behaviours: will they do the work they said they would do? Will they perform to the standards set? Will they deliver their part in time? In geographically dispersed groups especially, it is difficult to maintain the continuous communication essential for sharing group knowledge and information about individual activities related to the task. This means that members of geographically dispersed groups have to cope with particularly high levels of uncertainty. Delays in remote communication make feedback about others' activities difficult to obtain. Delayed or inaccurate feedback requires several iterations for clarification. In face-to-face groups, feedback about others' activities is more immediate and can be obtained more easily, for example by observing who attends meetings or who participates in hallway communications. In contrast,

members in distributed groups (called *virtual groups* because they mainly communicate electronically) may go for long periods without feedback about each other's activities.

Team awareness is the group members' understanding of the ongoing activities of others that provides a context for their own activity. It reduces the effort needed to coordinate tasks and resources by providing a context to interpret communications and others' actions more adequately (Weisband, 2002). Leadership can foster the development of team awareness, for example by taking actions to monitor the progress of others and to include everyone by sharing the respective information. This helps the group to cope better with individual members' work overloads. Weisband (2002) studied leadership influence on team awareness with geographically dispersed student project teams. The teams worked on a four-week project (writing a policy document on which they should all agree) via e-mail and a web-based conferencing system. The more the above-described leadership actions were *shared* (i.e. several group members engaged in the leadership activities), the more team awareness individual group members developed (i.e. they were better informed about others' activities), and the better the overall project performance. Developing team awareness among group members takes effort and time. It is an investment that becomes profitable after longer or repeated group task performance and under certain conditions, for example in distributed or virtual work teams.

> **team awareness** understanding of the ongoing activities of others which provides a context for one's own activity.

In general, leadership for group learning not only means providing the training resources for each group member to learn to perform the job better individually (individual-to-individual transfer), it also involves developing a collaborative learning orientation in which group members can discuss and improve each others' task performance strategies and behaviours (group-to-individual transfer). Furthermore, the development of transactive memory systems and team awareness benefits from encouraging group members to reflect on and constantly improve the way they collaborate and interact with each other (group-to-individual-in-group transfer), and to learn about other group members' areas of expertise, strengths and weaknesses (group-to-group transfer). The more this knowledge and awareness are developed and leadership functions are shared within the group, the more likely it is that group members can support each other, fill gaps for each other, correct and manage each other's errors, and anticipate and cope with capacity shortages on the part of particular group members before problems arise. All this improves group performance over time.

Summary

In sum, group leadership means careful composition of work groups, proactive design of task structures and active synchronization of group decision-making processes and task execution in groups. Apart from an active coaching of individual group members (e.g. via transformational leadership), leadership functions in groups also comprise the systematic development of effective transactive memory systems and team awareness among group members (which may take some time). As the Michigan group has already shown, all these leadership functions do not necessarily need to be performed by just one (formal) leader. Particularly when high task interdependence and geographically distributed virtual teamwork is involved, the shared performance of leadership functions seems to work best.

CHAPTER SUMMARY

- *What is the baseline against which we judge actual group performance?* The baseline is potential group performance, that is the performance that would have occurred if the members of the group had worked independently of each other. The potential group performance reflects the performance individuals would achieve in a group, if the group neither facilitated nor inhibited them.

- *How can we identify group-level effects on performance?* Group performance is, first and foremost, influenced by individual performance. Group members' individual performances (or abilities) constitute the basis for the definition of potential group performance. Potential group performance differs based on task type (e.g. additive, disjunctive and conjunctive tasks) because individual contributions are differently related to group performance for these different task types.

- *How are the three task types related to potential group performance?* For additive tasks the potential group performance is equal to the sum of individual inputs; for disjunctive tasks, it is equal to the performance of the best member; and for conjunctive tasks it is equal to the worst member.

- *How does social loafing differ from the dispensability effect?* Social loafing occurs when group members reduce their effort, because their individual contributions are difficult to identify for other group members. Social loafing is one of the factors contributing to the Ringelmann effect. The dispensability effect occurs when group members think that their individual effort does not contribute much to the group product.

- *How can a hidden profile result in suboptimal group performance?* A hidden profile is a group decision situation in which task-relevant information is distributed in such a way that no group member can detect the best solution based on the information he or she possesses. The correct solution can only be found if group members share their information. Because group members tend to rely on their own information, hidden profiles often lead to suboptimal group performance.

- *What are the major pitfalls and opportunities when people work together in a group?* Actual group performance diverges from potential group performance due to process losses and process gains. Process losses are coordination losses, motivation losses and individual capability losses; process gains are motivation gains and individual capability gains. These processes constitute the group-level influences on group performance.

- *What can we do to systematically optimize group performance?* Process losses can be reduced and process gains can be facilitated if three basic principles of group leadership are applied: composing groups in accordance with task requirements, synchronizing group members' efforts during collective performance, and allowing for group learning across multiple task trials.

- *What makes leadership effective?* Leadership effectiveness depends on many factors: leader traits, leadership behaviour, situational factors (e.g. task, followers, social context) and whether leader–follower relationships are transformational, transactional or non-existent (laissez-faire leadership). Note that focusing solely on the leader as the focal point of leadership limits our understanding of the complex nature of leadership, which is a mutual influence process that can also be shared among group members.

- *How can leadership help to improve group performance?* Leadership is about influencing others for the benefit of individual, group and organizational goals. Derived from the basic principles of group leadership, we identified three categories of situational contingencies that are important for high group performance: composition (e.g. align group and task structure), synchronization (e.g. manage information and activity for reducing process loss and increasing process gain), and group learning (e.g. foster individual and group development by supporting all learning processes within groups).

NOTES

1. Steiner also included a fourth task type, the 'discretionary' task, but since this has not been a focus of empirical work we will not discuss it here.
2. It is debatable whether this approach leads to an overestimation of group potential and, thus, disfavours groups in the evaluation of their actual performance. Some authors actually discuss the possibility of coordination gains on the basis of different conceptions of group potential; however, this lies outside the scope of this introductory chapter.
3. Kerr and Bruun (1983) originally termed this motivation loss as 'free riding'. However, because the everyday understanding of the term 'free riding' is almost identical to social loafing (and not with the process that is meant here), we felt that 'dispensability effect' captures the essence of the effect in a better way.
4. For ease of understanding, the condition labels have been somewhat modified compared to the original study.

SUGGESTIONS FOR FURTHER READING

Baron, R. S., & Kerr, N. (2003). *Group Process, Group Decision, Group Action* (2nd ed.). Buckingham, UK: Open University Press. One of the best and most comprehensive introductions to the diverse facets of performance and performance-related processes in groups.

Bass, B. M. (2008). *The Bass handbook of Leadership: Theory, Research, and Managerial Implications* (4th ed.). New York: Free Press. Bernhard Bass has been one of the most influential researchers in the domain of leadership. This is the most comprehensive text on leadership today, which extends far beyond the average textbook, not only in detail, but also in scope and topics covered.

Brodbeck, F. C. (2008). Leadership in organisations. In N. Chmiel (Ed.), *An introduction to work and organisational psychology: A European perspective*. (pp. 281–304). Oxford: Blackwell Publishing. A concise and up-to-date account of leadership theory and practice from a work and organizational psychology perspective. A good way quickly to catch up with what leadership theory and research is about.

Larson, J. R. Jr. (2010). *In Search of Synergy in Small Group Performance*. New York: Psychology Press. This highly informative and well-written book builds on the methodological thoroughness offered by Steiner's seminal 1972 book (see below), improves on it and brings it together with the current state of empirical research in group performance.

Nijstad, B. A. (2009). *Group Performance*. New York: Psychology Press. A comprehensive, well-written, easy-to-understand and, nevertheless, challenging and up-to-date introduction to the field of group performance processes.

Pierce, J. L., & Newstrom, J. W. (2002). *Leaders & the leadership process: Readings, self-assessments and applications*. Boston, MA: McGraw-Hill. In addition to concise descriptions of leadership theory and practice, this textbook contains many excerpts of classic theoretical and research-oriented papers, as well as self-assessments, practical applications and useful further readings in the domain of leadership.

Steiner, I. D. (1972). *Group processes and productivity*. New York: Academic Press. Steiner's book remains *the* classic and pioneering analysis of group performance on various tasks. Although 40 years old, many insights from this book are still highly relevant, and some of them still await their realization in group performance research.

Turner, M. E. (2001). *Groups at work: Theory and research*. Mahwah, NJ: Erlbaum. This book's social psychological and organizational perspectives on the fundamental topics of group performance research offer a useful tool for students and researchers who are interested in the organizational application of group performance research, and for practitioners who want to learn more about the theoretical basis of groups and group performance.

Witte, E. H., & Davis, J. H. (Eds.). (1996). *Understanding group behavior* (Vol. 1 and 2). Mahwah, NJ: Erlbaum. These two volumes contain a series of insightful papers from well-known group researchers. They are particularly valuable to readers who would like to broaden the scope from 'pure' group performance research to many other facets of intragroup and intergroup behaviour that are nevertheless relevant for group performance.

Yukl, G. (2012). *Leadership in organizations* (8th ed.). Upper Saddle River, NJ: Prentice-Hall. This classic book contains a comprehensive review of leadership theories and research. New editions appear regularly.

14 Prejudice and Intergroup Relations

RUSSELL SPEARS AND NICOLE TAUSCH

Source: © De Agostini. Used under licence from Getty Images.

KEY TERMS

- accentuation effect
- authoritarian personality
- contact hypothesis
- decategorization
- ethnocentrism
- extended contact hypothesis
- group emotions
- group identification
- illusory correlation effect
- ingroup bias

- ingroup reappraisal
- intergroup anxiety
- jigsaw classroom
- mutual differentiation
- negative interdependence
- outgroup bias
- outgroup homogeneity effect
- positive differentiation
- positive interdependence
- positive–negative asymmetry

- prejudice
- principle–implementation gap
- recategorization
- relative deprivation
- self-esteem hypothesis
- social dominance orientation
- social identity
- social reality constraints
- superordinate goals

CHAPTER OUTLINE

ROUTE MAP OF THE CHAPTER

This chapter presents a number of different explanations for prejudice and discrimination between groups. These range from individual level explanations in terms of personality and individual differences, and in terms of the cognitive mechanisms associated with social categorization and stereotyping processes, to more group level explanations focusing on the relations between groups. At the group level, behaviour that favours one's own group can be beneficial to the individual, and when realistic conflicts arise between groups, prejudice can reflect and reinforce one's group interests. However, realistic conflicts are not the only source of prejudice at the intergroup level. For example, social identity theory introduces additional psychological factors underlying ingroup bias, such as the motive to make one's group positively distinct from others. We also consider a range of additional group-level threats that can help to explain prejudice and discrimination. The trend to provide a more detailed analysis of the specific relations between groups, able to explain specific forms of prejudice, is continued by a focus on the role of different group emotions in this process. Finally we present a range of ways in which practitioners and policy makers can try to reduce prejudice (such as increasing intergroup contact) and consider the strengths and limitations of these different approaches.

INTRODUCTION

Prejudice and discrimination can take many forms, from the extreme to the almost banal. The Holocaust, the genocides in Cambodia and Rwanda (Figure 14.1), and 'ethnic cleansing' in the former Yugoslavia, are clear examples of the extreme forms. A man who leaps to the aid of a woman who seems to be having problems with her computer can also be accused of a form of prejudice, although he (or even she) might not recognize it as such. These very different examples convey the importance, but also the diversity, of prejudice, and the difficult task facing social psychologists who want to explain it, as well as propose solutions.

In many ways the study of prejudice has become more complex than it seemed in the early days of social psychology. Much of the research on prejudice back then was conducted in the US, on white people's attitudes towards black people. Overt racial prejudice was quite a clear-cut

FIGURE 14.1 *The Rwandan Genocide in 1994 was a mass murder of an estimated 800,000 people.*

Source: © Travel Ink. Used under licence from Getty Images.

issue, conforming to the classic definition of a negative or derogatory attitude towards a group. Since those days the nature of prejudice has changed, or at least expanded, but so has the nature of social psychology and the explanations we offer. The changes in prejudice are both good and bad. Although prejudice towards ethnic minorities, women, gays and lesbians (to name a few) is nowhere near as blatant as it used to be, this does not mean it has disappeared, although in many cases it does seem to have become less accepted in society. This shift is also reflected in some of the concepts in current use in social psychology: terms like 'modern' racism, 'aversive' racism, the 'new racism' (versus the old fashioned kinds) and 'subtle' or 'benevolent' prejudice (versus the blatant and hostile forms). Without getting bogged down in definitions just yet, these distinctions all convey a shift to more nuanced and less open forms of prejudice and bigotry. As Bob Dylan once sang, *The times, they are a-changin'*.

However, it would also be premature to celebrate: change is not necessarily always a sign of progress. If societal norms have rendered prejudice less acceptable, it may also have forced some forms of prejudice underground (see Chapter 4) while not always necessarily eliminating its causes. Subtle prejudices may also be more sophisticated. This may make some of the 'modern' forms of prejudice more difficult to detect and to challenge, and attempts to suppress prejudice can backfire or rebound if underlying motives remain. Moreover, some of the examples of the atrocities provided at the start of this chapter were perpetrated recently, showing that it is clearly not the case that the extreme forms of prejudice have disappeared entirely either. Despite many social changes, then, 'old fashioned' forms of prejudice and **ethnocentrism** are alas still relevant, albeit less common than they once were.

> **ethnocentrism** the tendency to judge ingroup attributes as superior to those of the outgroup and, more generally, to judge outgroups from an ingroup perspective.

Extreme forms of intergroup hostility are not always straightforward either. The Norwegian right-wing extremist who in July 2011 embarked on a 'crusade' against Muslims and multiculturalism espoused a blatant white supremacist form of prejudice that has fortunately become less common (Figure 14.2). And yet his killing spree was directed mainly at *white* Norwegians, his own ethnic ingroup who he apparently saw as part of his problem in political terms. Clearly the question of who the ingroup and outgroup are, who the 'us and them' are, is not always straightforward, but also an important *psychological* issue, and a question of ideology.

In this chapter we try to recognize and understand the diverse forms that prejudice can take, in a world that is perhaps more diverse, in Europe at least, than early social

FIGURE 14.2 *In July 2011, Norwegian right-wing extremist, Anders Behring Breivik embarked on a 'crusade' against Muslims and multiculturalism, yet his killing spree was directed mainly at white Norwegians, his own ethnic ingroup who he apparently saw as part of his problem in political terms.*

Source: © Lefteris Pitarakis. Used under licence from Press Association Images.

psychology textbooks focusing on the American context might suggest. To be sure, gender, 'race' and sexuality are important dimensions on which prejudice operates across the globe, but many others, especially those around nationality and ethnicity, are quite specific to local context, especially in a continent as diverse as Europe. Moreover, we cannot assume that prejudice around the same groups and categories will be the same everywhere. In some countries and cultures social norms against sexism and homophobia may be better developed than in others, and the same group may be a perpetrator of prejudice or a victim, depending on the local context.

While recognizing the diversity in prejudice and the importance of the normative context in which it occurs, we do not, however, think that our accounts have to be purely descriptive, or determined in each case by unique historical factors. One strength of a social psychological approach to prejudice is that it aims to provide theoretical explanations that might apply to a range of different groups and contexts at different times, while trying to do justice to the differences.

As the nature of prejudice has changed, social psychology has not stood still either. As the theories and techniques have developed, so has the very concept of prejudice itself. Consider again the classic definition of prejudice as a negative attitude towards a group. It has become clear that this is rather inadequate as a way of defining prejudice that captures all its forms. Take our example of the man who goes to help the woman with a computer problem. On the surface, such behaviour could be classified in other areas of

psychology as an example of helping or prosocial behaviour (see Chapter 10). However, socially aware readers will also detect the sensitivity in this situation: the woman might be quite competent to sort out her computer herself, and may feel patronized by the implication that she is not able to do so (a useful 'thought experiment' when considering gender equality is to consider how a man would feel if a woman offers him help in this context!). That some women might welcome such offers of help only complicates the issue further. This can be seen as an example of 'benevolent sexism' (Glick & Fiske, 1996), an ostensibly positive or helpful orientation that nevertheless reflects or reinforces less positive views of women at least on important dimensions like competence. The example of benevolent prejudice reinforces the point that the old fashioned definition of prejudice, though useful to a point, will not suffice. Instead we propose a working definition of **prejudice** as an attitude or orientation towards a group (or its members) that devalues it directly *or* indirectly, often to the benefit of the self or own group.

> **prejudice** an attitude or orientation towards a group (or its members) that devalues it directly *or indirectly*, often to the benefit of the self or own group.

Rather than getting bogged down in debates about whether men who open doors for women are really being sexist, it is perhaps more useful to see how this could reflect more general processes that might benefit one group over the other in the long run: it may be that some men are happy to open the door to the company canteen to women, but not the door to the company boardroom. In this chapter we present theoretical explanations for prejudice that try to make sense of the functions it can serve, however banal or extreme its form. When we think of more extreme examples of prejudice, such as the atrocious acts of the Norwegian extremist, Anders Breivik, it is all too easy to write off such behaviour as *evil*. Although this attribution may be an understandable way of coping with such crises, it does not explain anything. Our job as social psychologists is at least to *try* to explain such behaviour.

In order to give our journey through the field some structure we take an approach that is roughly chronological, starting with classic approaches to prejudice and finishing with more contemporary explanations that do more justice to its diversity. At the same time, and overlapping with this, we structure our treatment in terms of the *levels* of explanation that have been offered for prejudice. One important dimension distinguishing different approaches concerns the level of analysis, or whether the *individual* or *group* should form the central explanatory focus: does prejudice primarily stem from processes within individuals, or from relations between groups?

We start with the more individual-level explanations (personality-based, cognitive), moving on to more group-based explanations. Personality-based explanations arose in the heyday of psychoanalysis in the 1930s and 1940s, and saw personal needs and motives as primary. Although the psychodynamic theories went out of vogue, the interest in individual differences (and motives) has remained. With the cognitive revolution in the 1970s, explanations emphasized the cognitive mechanisms and functions of social categorization and stereotyping common to all of us that could underlie prejudice (see also Chapter 4). Although these approaches clearly differ, they both share a focus on the individual.

In contrast, group-level approaches focus on the perceiver, as well as the target, as a member of a group, with group-level needs and interests. Intergroup explanations have benefitted from the legacy of both the personality and cognitive traditions, and incorporate both motivational and cognitive processes. The group level of analysis makes the way we conceptualize prejudice more complex, but also more amenable to its diverse forms and the different contexts in which it can arise. The complex social relations between groups provide the opportunity for diverse comparisons and perceptions, which extend the negative (and positive) reactions to target groups in a number of different emotional directions (e.g. people can respond to members of different outgroups with feelings of fear, anger or even admiration) resulting in quite different feelings of prejudice and different discriminatory responses (e.g. avoidance, confrontation, paternalism). A key element that remains, in line with the modern definition, is that prejudice often serves the perceiver's interests in some way, and this is a recurring theme at all levels of explanation that indeed helps *to explain*.

All of these different levels have something to contribute to the explanation of prejudice, and although some may make more sense in some contexts than others, in many cases more than one level may be relevant. We are not saying that one level of explanation is inherently correct or superior. Take again the emotive example of the Norwegian extremist. It is hard to believe that individual-level factors such as personality did not play a central role in his case (see Chapter 5, Social Psychology beyond the Lab 5.1). Indeed, individual difference accounts may, reassuringly, help to explain why such atrocious acts remain extremely unusual – because there is something special about this individual. Nevertheless, this individual, however far from our social reality he was, clearly saw the world through a prism of 'us and them', involving very strong 'ingroup' loyalties and 'outgroup' enmities. Social categorization processes, social stereotypes and the identities and animosities of the intergroup level may all have played a crucial part here, and at the very least formed the setting in which his personal pathology played itself out (and indeed egalitarian *societal* norms against prejudice

might ironically even have *contributed* to the force of the individual-level explanation in this case, by exacerbating a personal sense of resentment). When it comes to explaining prejudice in the modern world, it is not a case of 'one size fits all'. In many cases we may need to draw on many levels of explanation to make full sense of prejudice, and also to explain how it can vary so widely between and within groups. We consider, first, the individual-level explanations that start us on this road.

PERSONALITY APPROACHES TO PREJUDICE

Is there a prejudiced personality?

People differ in terms of their attitudes towards social groups. More interestingly, it seems that attitudes towards a range of social groups are often correlated: people who have negative attitudes towards one outgroup also tend to have negative attitudes towards other outgroups (Allport, 1954b). This is most evident in the case of the outright bigot, who dislikes, for example, black people, Jews and homosexuals, three quite different groups. The generality of prejudice suggests that prejudiced beliefs may somehow be rooted within an individual's personality. So is there such a thing as a 'prejudiced personality'? In this section we introduce two facets of personality investigated by social psychologists, the authoritarian personality and social dominance orientation.

The authoritarian personality

The monstrous events that took place in Nazi Germany, in particular the Holocaust, led many scholars to believe that prejudice must be an aberration of human psychology. Surely, these actions could not have been those of *normal* men and women? Theoretical models were therefore developed that explained prejudice as a manifestation of a particular pathological personality. The most well-known of these models was proposed by Adorno, Frenkel-Brunswik, Levinson, and Sanford (1950), who suggested that individuals' social and political attitudes, and in particular their susceptibility to Fascist ideas, are expressions of deep-seated aspects of their personality that can be traced back to early childhood experiences. Their theory was heavily influenced by psychodynamic theory, which was very popular at the time. Psychodynamic theory was developed from Sigmund Freud's work on psychoanalysis. It posits that all human behaviour can be explained by the dynamic interplay of conscious and unconscious motivations. Unpleasant or unacceptable impulses are dealt with through a variety of defence mechanisms, such as the (often unconscious) displacement of negative feelings and impulses from a powerful object towards a less powerful and less threatening one (e.g. kicking your dog when you are angry at your boss).

Adorno and colleagues (1950) believed that similar processes are involved in the development of a prejudiced personality. They suggested that an overly strict upbringing, concerned with obedience to parents and conformity to conventional norms, can lead to conflicting feelings of admiration and aggression towards the parents. Rather than targeting hostile impulses directly at the parents, who are viewed as powerful and able to retaliate, these negative feelings are likely to be displaced and directed at weaker targets or 'scapegoats', such as minority groups against whom derogation and even aggression are socially sanctioned.

> **authoritarian personality** personality syndrome characterized by a simplistic cognitive style, a rigid regard for social conventions and submission to authority figures (associated with prejudice towards minority groups and susceptibility to Fascism).

Adorno et al. (1950) proposed that this personality syndrome would be reflected in a person's social attitudes, simplistic thinking (e.g. intolerance of ambiguity), a rigid regard for social conventions and deference to authority figures. Adorno and colleagues referred to this constellation of traits as the **authoritarian personality**.

To test their ideas that this personality syndrome would be linked to a variety of prejudices and was rooted in early childhood experiences, Adorno et al. (1950) constructed a personality inventory to assess the central aspects of this syndrome; it was called the 'F-scale', as it was designed to measure susceptibility to Fascist ideas. This measure contained a number of subscales, including authoritarian submission, conventionalism (the desire to adhere to ingroup norms) and authoritarian aggression (intolerance of those who violate conventional values). The scale, together with a number of other scales measuring different forms of prejudice, was then completed by a large sample (about 2000 adults) of White Californians. Lending support to the idea that personality factors are involved in prejudiced attitudes, F-scale scores were found to correlate positively with various forms of prejudice (e.g. anti-Semitism, general ethnocentrism). To provide support that this personality pattern was indeed related to strict parenting, a subset of participants who scored either very high or very low on the F-scale were then invited for in-depth clinical interviews that examined the participants' early childhood experiences. These interviews seemed to support the theory of Adorno et al. (1950), as those participants who had high scores on the F-scale (unlike low scorers) tended to idealize their parents, and indicated that their parents demanded strict obedience and imposed harsh punishments.

Although *The Authoritarian Personality* (1950) was highly influential and stimulated much empirical research, interest in the concept soon waned. This was partly due to a number of damaging methodological criticisms (the use of unrepresentative samples, potential interviewer biases in the clinical interviews and the fact that items were positively framed and open to response bias, whereby respondents tended to agree with items). More fundamentally, however, researchers started to move away from psychodynamic explanations of social phenomena (see Brown, 2010).

Research on the F-scale, and on the idea of a 'prejudiced personality', thus declined in the 1960s and 1970s. However, it was revived by Altemeyer (1981), who refined the measurement of authoritarianism and reconceptualized it as *right-wing authoritarianism*. According to Altemeyer, right-wing authoritarians tend to have highly conventional attitudes and display a high degree of submission to the established authorities in their society, such as government officials and traditional religious leaders. They also show high levels of aggression in the name of these authorities, in particular towards deviants, and are willing to help the government persecute almost any outgroup (Altemeyer, 1998). Rather than viewing the origins of right-wing authoritarianism as displaced aggression towards punitive parents, Altemeyer saw a social environment that reinforced obedience, conventionalism and aggression as a more direct determinant, and emphasized the role of social learning processes, in particular during adolescence. In short, the basis for right-wing authoritarianism lay now in attitudes and norms rather than in personality. Altemeyer (1981, 1998) developed several versions of the right-wing authoritarianism scale, which, like the original scale of authoritarianism, includes three subscales: authoritarian submission, conventionalism and authoritarian aggression. This scale has been widely used and predicts a range of social attitudes, including support for harsh punishment of lawbreakers such as the death penalty, support for aggressive military force, acceptance of the infringement of civil liberties, and prejudice towards various social groups, including homosexuals and racial and ethnic outgroups.

Prejudice and a desire for social dominance

Research on individual differences in prejudice received further attention due to the introduction of another dimension that seems to explain individual variation in prejudice, namely **social dominance orientation** (Pratto, Sidanius, Stallworth, & Malle, 1994). The concept of social dominance orientation is grounded in *social dominance theory* (Sidanius & Pratto, 1999), which proposes that forming group-based hierarchies is a universal human tendency and that most societies are therefore organized hierarchically (e.g. in terms of ethnicity, class, gender). Central to the theory is that the hierarchical social order is maintained through individual and institutional discrimination, often justified with the help of so-called 'legitimizing myths'. Legitimizing myths are consensually held values, attitudes, beliefs or cultural ideologies that provide moral and intellectual justification for group inequality, or even the oppression of some groups by others. Such legitimizing myths can include forms of prejudice such as racism and sexism (e.g. the societal dominance of white men can be justified by encouraging the belief in the intellectual inferiority of black people and women), but also ideas that seem progressive on the surface. An example of such a hierarchy-enhancing legitimizing myth is the ideology of meritocracy, which proposes that outcomes in society – such as wealth, jobs, and power – should be allocated according to merit (e.g. abilities) rather than based on irrelevant factors such as gender, ethnicity or class. Although true meritocracy should increase social justice and group equality, the belief that meritocracy exists, and that those who have power, wealth and status deserve their rewards, while those who are poor have themselves to blame, ignores the fact that people from different social backgrounds do not have the same opportunities to succeed. Thus, the belief that meritocracy exists can serve to legitimize social inequality and help to maintain the (hierarchical) status quo.

So how do we capture people's orientations towards group hierarchy versus group equality? Pratto and colleagues developed the social dominance orientation scale to assess such individual differences (Pratto et al., 1994; see Individual Differences 14.1).

If social dominance orientation assesses the degree to which people support or oppose hierarchical group relations, and if hierarchy-enhancing 'legitimizing myths' help to maintain hierarchical social systems, then the two should be closely linked. This is indeed the case. There is extensive evidence that people higher in social dominance orientation are also more sexist, racist and prejudiced towards immigrants, as well as a range of other social groups (see Pratto, Sidanius, & Levin, 2006, for a review). Moreover, there is also evidence that people high in social dominance orientation are more likely to believe

> **social dominance orientation** an individual difference variable that captures a desire for hierarchical group relations.

in the notion that people's income reflects their competence (i.e. that income allocation is meritocratic) and to oppose progressive policies to advance the cause of members of minority groups, such as affirmative action, women's rights programmes and social policies assisting the poor (Pratto et al., 1994).

Thus, like right-wing authoritarianism, social dominance orientation can explain individual differences in prejudice. But are right-wing authoritarianism and social dominance orientation related? These variables may seem similar, in that people high in right-wing authoritarianism and people high in social dominance orientation both display high levels of prejudice. But research has shown that there are a number of differences between these two dimensions that suggest that they do not have the same psychological roots (see Altemeyer, 1998). For example, unlike right-wing authoritarians, 'social dominators' do not particularly endorse submitting to authorities, nor do they value conventions or tradition (unless it serves their goals). They are also less religious, more likely to be male and more likely to be Machiavellian (manipulative of others for their personal gain) compared to people high in right-wing authoritarianism. Further evidence that these dimensions are different is that right-wing authoritarianism and social dominance orientation are only weakly correlated, and seem to explain different segments of the variance in prejudice (but together they sometimes explain over 50 per cent of the variance in prejudice against a variety of outgroups; Altemeyer, 1998).

So social dominators and right-wing authoritarians are not necessarily the same people. In combination, however, they could make a 'lethal union' (Altemeyer, 1998). According to Altemeyer, people high in social dominance orientation, who desire both intergroup hierarchy and interpersonal dominance, would make good candidates for dominant leaders who are likely to try to maximize their power even if that involves acting unethically. People high in right-wing authoritarianism, on the other hand, exemplify the submissive follower who would unquestioningly support their leader's decisions (see Son Hing, Bobocel, Zanna, & McBride, 2007).

Authoritarianism and social dominance orientation as ideologies

Although individual difference variables like right-wing authoritarianism and social dominance orientation explain a substantial amount of variation in prejudice, the question remains whether personality variables can really provide explanations for the uniformity and extent of prejudiced beliefs found in societies such as

THE SOCIAL DOMINANCE ORIENTATION SCALE (PRATTO ET AL., 1994)

Social dominance theory (Sidanius & Pratto, 1999) proposes that societies contain ideologies that each may promote or attenuate hierarchy at that time. Individual differences in the extent to which these competing ideologies are accepted are conceptualized as social dominance orientation. This scale, developed by Pratto et al. (1994), measures the extent to which individuals have a strong desire to promote or reduce intergroup hierarchies.

Instructions for completion

Below is a series of statements with which you may either agree or disagree. For each statement, please indicate the degree of your agreement/disagreement by circling the appropriate number from '1' to '7'.

		Strongly Disagree						Strongly Agree
1.	Some groups of people are just more worthy than others.	1	2	3	4	5	6	7
2.	In getting what your group wants, it is sometimes necessary to use force against other groups.	1	2	3	4	5	6	7
3.	It's OK if some groups have more of a chance in life than others.	1	2	3	4	5	6	7
4.	To get ahead in life, it is sometimes necessary to step on other groups.	1	2	3	4	5	6	7
5.	If certain groups of people stayed in their place, we would have fewer problems.	1	2	3	4	5	6	7
6.	It's probably a good thing that certain groups are at the top and other groups are at the bottom.	1	2	3	4	5	6	7
7.	Inferior groups should stay in their place.	1	2	3	4	5	6	7
8.	Sometimes other groups must be kept in their place.	1	2	3	4	5	6	7
9.	It would be good if all groups could be equal.	1	2	3	4	5	6	7
10.	Group equality should be our ideal.	1	2	3	4	5	6	7
11.	All groups should be given an equal chance in life.	1	2	3	4	5	6	7
12.	We should do what we can to equalize conditions for different groups.	1	2	3	4	5	6	7
13.	We should increase social equality.	1	2	3	4	5	6	7
14.	We would have fewer problems if we treated different groups more equally.	1	2	3	4	5	6	7
15.	We should strive to make incomes more equal.	1	2	3	4	5	6	7
16.	No one group should dominate in society.	1	2	3	4	5	6	7

Instructions for scoring

Items 9–16 (which should *not* be presented in a block, as they are shown here) should be reverse coded. How does your score compare to that of other undergraduate students? In a recent study by Jetten and Iyer (2010), first-year undergraduate students at a British university were asked to complete this scale. Their average score in the first year of their studies was quite low ($M = 2.64$, which is below the scale midpoint of 4). To find out whether your score is high or low, you can compare it to this sample. A score ≥ 3.75 (which is the mean plus one standard deviation in this sample) would be relatively high, a score ≤ 1.53 (the mean minus one standard deviation) would be relatively low.

Source: Copyright © 1994 by the American Psychological Association. Adapted with permission. Pratto et al. (1994). Social dominance orientation: A personality variable predicting social and political attitudes. *Journal of Personality and Social Psychology, 67,* 741–763. No further reproduction or distribution is permitted without written permission from the American Psychological Association.

Nazi Germany or South Africa during the Apartheid era (Figures 14.3, 14.4). Is it likely that millions of people share the same dysfunctional personality structure or specific individual orientation (Billig, 1976)? The social psychologist in you probably doubted this already. As you will already know, people's opinions and behaviours are strongly influenced by the social context, in particular the opinions and behaviours of other people around them (see Chapter 8).

Pettigrew (1958) illustrated the importance of the social context in a cross-cultural study in which he compared samples from South Africa and the southern United States (both segregated along racial lines at the time) with samples in the northern United States. He showed that, although levels of authoritarianism in the samples did not differ, racial prejudice was lower in the northern US compared to both the southern US and South Africa. This suggested that personality is not sufficient in explaining

FIGURE 14.3 *Racist sign on a bus during the apartheid in South Africa.*

Source: © DEA / A. VERGANI. Used under licence from Getty Images.

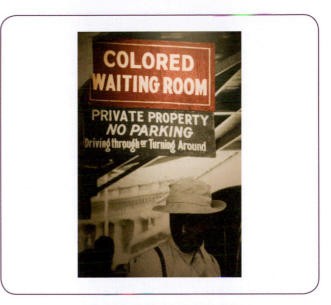

FIGURE 14.4 *A racist sign in Kansas, US at the time when racial segregation was legally enforced.*

Source: © Walter Bibikow. Used under licence from Getty Images.

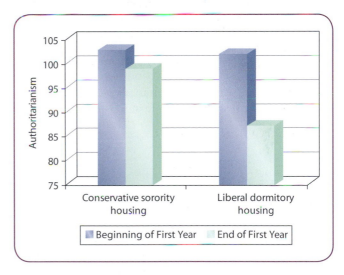

FIGURE 14.5 *Changes in authoritarianism over one year at college as a function of social norms in housing.*

Source: Adapted from Siegel & Siegel, 1957. Copyright © 1957 by the American Psychological Association. Adapted with permission. The use of APA information does not imply endorsement by APA.

racial prejudice and that social context (e.g. whether or not someone lives in a racist society) has to be taken into account. Pettigrew (1958) also measured individual differences in social conformity (e.g. 'A good group member should agree with the other members') in the South African sample. This allowed him to test more directly whether conformity to social norms played a role in prejudice. As expected, those respondents who scored high on the social conformity scale were more prejudiced than those who had low scores.

You might also wonder whether individual differences like authoritarianism and social dominance orientation really represent enduring personality characteristics, or whether these variables themselves vary as a function of social context. Siegel and Siegel (1957) assessed women college students in the United States at the beginning and end of their first year at college and compared their level of authoritarianism. The women were assigned to either sorority or dormitory housing. At this college, sororities (social organizations for female undergraduates in North America) at the time were more conservative in their attitudes, while dormitories had more liberal norms. Importantly, these housing allocations were made on a random basis, ensuring that self-selection could not account for any of the findings. The results were striking (see Figure 14.5). While the two groups did not differ in authoritarianism at the beginning of the college year, the women assigned to the more liberal housing showed a significant drop in their levels of authoritarianism at the end of the year. Thus, it seems that authoritarianism changed as a function of social context.

More recently, a study by Guimond, Dambrun, Michinov, and Duarte (2003) investigated the possibility that social dominance orientation would change due to group context. They compared junior (first-year) and senior (third- and final-year) students studying an elite subject (Law) with students who studied a less prestigious subject (Psychology). Social dominance theory suggests that people from dominant groups will show higher levels of social dominance orientation than people from subordinate or lower-status groups, because they benefit most from group hierarchy and are therefore most motivated to justify it. For example, lawyers (the group into which law students are socialized) tend to have more high-powered positions in society than do other professional groups such as psychologists. Consistent with the idea that members of dominant groups show higher levels of social dominance orientation, Guimond et al. found that the law students generally scored higher on social dominance orientation than the psychology students, even at the beginning of their studies, suggesting that levels of social dominance orientation might help to determine the subject of study and career chosen. Interestingly, these group differences were particularly pronounced among students in the senior years. This suggests that group socialization (over time) affects levels of social dominance orientation.

Research also suggests that threats in one's social environment affect these individual differences. In one study among a sample of New Zealand students, Duckitt and Fisher (2003) provided their participants with scenarios that described the future of New Zealand as either relatively stable and secure (the 'low threat' condition), or as likely to involve a rise in crime, violence and social conflict (the 'high threat' condition). They then measured right-wing authoritarianism and social dominance orientation. Results indicated that participants in the threat condition reported higher levels of right-wing authoritarianism. There was also a small increase in social dominance orientation in the threat condition.

So if variables such as authoritarianism and social dominance orientation are not entirely stable dispositions, then

what are they? A recent theoretical model reconceptualized these variables as *ideological beliefs*, determined in part by personality dimensions, but also by group relations in a given social context. Duckitt and colleagues (Duckitt, 2001, 2006; Duckitt, Wagner, Du Plessis, & Birum, 2002) proposed a dual process model (see Theory Box 14.1) in which right-wing authoritarianism and social dominance orientation represent two independent dimensions of social attitudes that express different motivational goals. Right-wing authoritarianism is generated by a view that the world is a dangerous and threatening place, and results in support for measures that establish and maintain societal control, stability and cohesion. Such a world view is brought about by the actual presence of threats in the social context (e.g. the perceived prevalence of crime, as in Duckitt & Fisher's, 2003, experiment). In addition, according to the model, individuals high on the personality dimension of social conformity are predisposed to view the world in this way. The goal motivation linked to social dominance orientation, on the other hand, is that of asserting power and group dominance, and social dominance orientation is predicted by a view that the world is a ruthlessly competitive jungle. This world view is activated in a social context characterized by high levels of inequality and competition over power and status, and is more likely to be held by individuals who are tough-minded.

Thus, the model suggests that these two world views (the world as a dangerous place, or a competitive jungle)

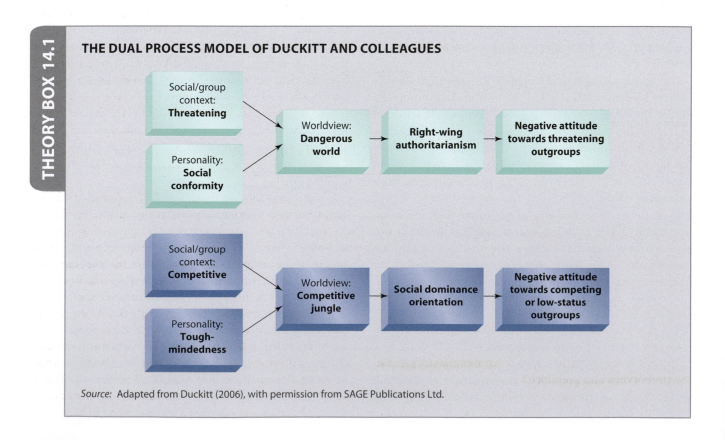

THEORY BOX 14.1

THE DUAL PROCESS MODEL OF DUCKITT AND COLLEAGUES

Source: Adapted from Duckitt (2006), with permission from SAGE Publications Ltd.

are relatively stable reflections of personality and socialization, but are also influenced by the actual social situations. The different goal motivations linked to right-wing authoritarianism and social dominance orientation further suggest that these individual differences should predict prejudice towards different kinds of groups. Because right-wing authoritarianism expresses a threat-driven motivation to establish security and maintain social order, people high in this should dislike groups that threaten these values. Social dominance orientation, on the other hand, should predict negative attitudes towards outgroups that compete for power or are subordinate, which activates the desire to establish or maintain dominance. Consistent with this view, Duckitt (2006) demonstrated that right-wing authoritarianism predicts prejudice towards groups that violate conventions (e.g. rock stars, drug dealers), while social dominance orientation predicts prejudice towards subordinate groups (e.g. disabled people).

Summary

In this section we examined personality approaches to prejudice and discussed two personality dimensions (right-wing authoritarianism and social dominance orientation) that have been linked to high levels of prejudice. We showed that these two dimensions are strong and independent predictors of prejudice and related social attitudes. We also demonstrated, however, that the view that prejudice is a stable personality dimension is not tenable. We showed that social factors play an important role in shaping individual levels of prejudice, and that these individual difference variables are themselves influenced by the social context. We gave an overview of a recent theoretical development (the dual process model) that reframed right-wing authoritarianism and social dominance orientation as ideological orientations that are determined by both personality and social context.

THE COGNITIVE APPROACH TO PREJUDICE

Can we explain prejudice purely by cognitive processes?

The cognitive approach to prejudice arose partly in reaction to the earlier psychodynamic explanations discussed previously, but also earlier socio-cultural explanations that saw stereotypes and prejudice as a product of the images we learn from our environment. In an influential volume that brought together many examples of this approach,

Hamilton (1981) explained that one aim was to see how far researchers could push the idea that the basis for prejudice was purely cognitive; just because prejudice entailed affective reactions, it did not mean that it had an affective or motivational basis. This was the era (in the 1970s and 1980s) in which research had rejected the influence of psychodynamic principles, and social psychology was increasingly influenced by theories and models in cognitive psychology and the judgement and decision-making literature. The dominant information processing models had also moved away from the idea (and ideal) that we were perfect and rational information processors, to the notion that there are limits on perception and cognition that encouraged various cognitive shortcuts or 'heuristics' and 'biases' (see Chapter 4). Within social psychology this 'meta-theory' provided a fertile ground for researchers looking to explain prejudice and stereotyping in terms of biased cognitive processes.

Tajfel's earlier work on **accentuation effects** in categorization processes (e.g. Tajfel & Wilkes, 1963) formed a basis for understanding social categorization processes, and why people might exaggerate differences between groups and similarities within them. For example, if we take a 'racial' categorization (e.g. white versus black, European versus African) we can identify skin colour as a dimension that is broadly correlated with this categorization. Having said this, there is clearly also a broad range of skin colours within these categories (i.e. the darkest European may even be darker in skin colour than the lightest-skinned African). However, the judgemental effect of this correlation between category and colour is such that people are likely to overestimate the *similarity* of skin colours *within* the categories and to overestimate the *differences* in skin colour *between* the categories (see e.g. Corneille, Huart, Becquart, & Brédart, 2004).

> **accentuation effect** when (social) categories are correlated with a continuous dimension (e.g. skin colour, eye shape) there is a judgemental tendency to overestimate *similarities within,* and *differences between* the categories on this dimension.

The accentuation explanation of categorization effects was important in showing how certain features attributed to stereotyping might occur, namely perceiving greater similarities *within* groups (group homogeneity), than *between* them. Since Allport's classic volume *The Nature of Prejudice* (1954b), one aspect of stereotyping that has been related to prejudice was 'overgeneralization', namely the tendency to see members of a category as like each other ('They are all the same'). Evidence of such accentuation or overgeneralization provides a further dimension to our conceptualization of prejudice: reduced variability within the group may be seen as a form of prejudice (or at least stereotyping), which is different from the *negative evaluation* of the group or its members. Put another way, if a

Caucasian European says 'Asians all look alike to me', this is not the same as saying 'I don't like Asians'. (Although both can be seen as a form of prejudice).

On its own the accentuation principle does not explain *negative* affective prejudice towards an outgroup (unless negativity is already correlated with group membership), nor indeed any tendency to perceive them as *more* homogeneous than the ingroup. We now consider some cognitive mechanisms that can result in prejudice towards outgroups in terms of judgements of 'them' being more homogeneous and more negative than views of 'us'.

Outgroup homogeneity, stereotyping and prejudice

One strand of the cognitive approach to stereotyping and prejudice has focused on perceptions of group variability, and specifically the idea that prejudice involves us having more homogenous perceptions of outgroups than ingroups (the **outgroup homogeneity effect**). Many different explanations for this effect have been proposed. One obvious possibility concerns 'selective exposure', the argument that we simply know more people from the ingroup, and therefore have a more variable sample to draw upon when forming impressions of the ingroup. While this may be true, it is interesting that outgroup homogeneity has also been found in the case of gender, as in a classic study by Park and Rothbart (1982). They showed evidence for more homogeneous and stereotypic perceptions of the opposite gender, yet selective exposure seems unlikely to be the process driving biased group perceptions in this case, at least for most adults, who will know many people of both genders. Park and Rothbart suggested that the way we structure and encode information about ingroups and outgroups may be important here, and subsequent research has shown that we are more likely to distinguish subgroups within the ingroup, whereas we treat the outgroup simply as 'them' (Park, Ryan, & Judd, 1992). Consider, for example, the many subgroups you recognize within your own university (e.g. the athletes, the workaholics, the Christians, the drinkers), yet when you think of a rival university, you do not think of them in this more differentiated manner.

The comparative context is important too. Haslam and Oakes (1995) pointed to an asymmetry in the way we typically see ingroup members and outgroup members that could help to explain perceptions of outgroup homogeneity. As we have seen, the social categorization process means we are likely to accentuate within-category similarities and between-category differences in

> **outgroup homogeneity effect** a tendency to see the outgroup as more homogeneous than the ingroup.

an intergroup context, which should make both ingroup and outgroup seem relatively homogeneous. However, much of the time we will interact with people from our ingroup (e.g. people from our own university, or our own country) without the outgroup being present or salient at all (i.e. an *intra*group context). In this context we would expect the tendency to accentuate within-group similarities to be weak or absent: we are more likely to see people as unique individuals (there is no outgroup to compare and contrast our group to, after all). By contrast, when we interact with outgroup members, this is very likely to make the intergroup context salient (e.g. 'We British are different from you French'). When we put these two contexts together, the asymmetry in how we normally see the ingroup versus the outgroup is likely to result in us bringing to mind more homogeneous perceptions of the outgroup than the ingroup overall.

Research also suggests that there may be circumstances in which the *ingroup* is seen as more homogenous than the outgroup, and that this is not necessarily always a bad thing (Simon, 1992; see also *The individual's relation to the group: group identification and its components*, p. 469, and Theory Box 14.2, later in this chapter). For example, if the dimension of judgement is positive (e.g. 'intelligence'), ingroup homogeneity might be good (e.g. you are happy when recruiters, for example, see students from your university as all being highly intelligent). Homogeneity of viewpoints within the group might also reflect consensus and solidarity (e.g. political conservatives share the view that liberty is a fundamental value, while socialists share the view that equality is more important). Overall, despite some early attempts to link prejudice with more homogeneous impressions of outgroups, the evidence that this always happens, and is prejudicial, is rather mixed.

Illusory correlation: a purely cognitive mechanism producing prejudice?

The classic example of a purely cognitive explanation for how prejudiced beliefs about *evaluative* group differences could be formed comes from the research on the **illusory correlation effect** by Hamilton and Gifford (1976). They identified a mechanism that could, they argued, account for how negative beliefs about ethnic minorities might develop, even in the absence of any relation between the group and negative attributes, or indeed any prior *expectations* about such group differences. Such expectations can themselves

> **illusory correlation effect** a tendency to perceive a relationship that does not actually exist (e.g. between a group and negative behaviour), or to perceive one that does exist as stronger than it actually is.

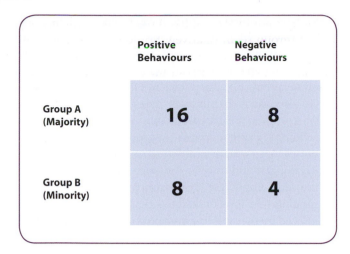

	Positive Behaviours	Negative Behaviours
Group A (Majority)	16	8
Group B (Minority)	8	4

FIGURE 14.6 *Illusory correlation paradigm.*

Source: Based on Hamilton & Gifford, 1976, with permission from Elsevier.

also lead to the perception of stereotypic differences; the extensive literature on 'schema' effects (see Chapter 4) shows how expectations can bias perception in line with established stereotypes. But how can we explain how these expectations are formed in the first place? Hamilton and Gifford presented participants with a series of slides of individual behaviours performed by members of two groups, Group A (the larger 'majority' group), and Group B (the smaller 'minority' group) – see Figure 14.6.

Behaviours differed in terms of their valence (e.g. 'M. R., a member of Group A, helped the old lady across the road'; 'R. A., a member of Group B cheated in an exam'). As you can see from Figure 14.6, there were twice as many behaviours describing Group A (the majority group) as Group B (the minority group), and the majority of behaviours for each group were positive (but, crucially, in equal proportions). This distribution reflects the fact that negative behaviours tend to be infrequent, and we also encounter minorities less frequently than the majority group. However, because the *proportion* of positive to negative behaviours is equal in both groups, there is no objective *correlation* between group membership and the valence of the behaviours. After the slide show was over, participants were presented with the behaviours again, but without group labels, and asked to remember whether they came from Group A or B. They were also asked to make ratings of members of the groups on positive and negative traits, and estimate what percentage of positive and negative behaviours came from members of Groups A and B.

On all measures participants associated Group B with the more negative behaviours or traits. Why? This finding could not be explained by a tendency to evaluate smaller

groups more negatively because, in a second experiment, where negative behaviours were now in a majority for both groups, more *positive* stereotyping of the minority group resulted. Hamilton and Gifford explained this finding in terms of the higher accessibility in memory of the most distinctive combination – infrequent behaviours in the numerically distinctive group. A distinctive combination that 'stands out', influencing memory and judgement, is an example of the 'availability heuristic', the tendency to predict the frequency of an event based on how easily it can be brought to mind (Tversky & Kahneman, 1973; see Chapter 4).

Subsequent research has considered alternative explanations for this effect, however. Some have focused on different memory mechanisms (Fiedler, 1991; Smith, 1991). Others have argued that there are real (evaluative) differences between the groups conveyed in the data that are then *accentuated* (see e.g. Klauer & Meiser, 2000; McGarty, Haslam, Turner, & Oakes, 1993). Perhaps more relevant to the rationale of the cognitive approach, however, is evidence that the illusory correlation effect is eliminated when participants are categorized as members of one of the target groups (e.g. the minority group, Group B) themselves (Schaller & Maass, 1989). It seems that motivational factors deriving from group membership can override this cognitive bias (see intergroup explanations below, p. 471).

Developments and integrations

Cognitive misers Chapter 4 goes into some of the cognitive processes underlying prejudice in more detail. Consistent with the cognitive approach, research developing the 'cognitive miser' metaphor has argued that one reason we stereotype is to simplify social perception, easing our information processing burden (we are 'cognitive misers'). A study by Macrae, Milne, and Bodenhausen (1994) provides a nice illustration of this argument. In this experiment participants were asked to form an impression of a person based on traits characteristic of them, presented on a computer (e.g. clever, caring). This was the primary task. At the same time they listened on headphones to a series of facts about a novel topic: the secondary task. When forming the impression (the primary task), participants were able to remember *more* facts about the novel topic (the secondary task), *if* the traits of the target person were also accompanied by a stereotype-consistent category label (e.g. 'Doctor' for the traits 'clever' or 'caring'). Following the cognitive miser rationale, it seems that the Doctor stereotype saved cognitive resources by helping to encode the information (Doctors tend to be caring and clever) leaving more attention free for the other task.

However, this only seems to work when the information fits the stereotype. Yzerbyt, Rocher, and Schadron (1997) showed that when information about a target person was stereotype *inconsistent* (e.g. 'Skinhead' in the case of 'caring' and 'clever'), activating the stereotype actually *impaired* performance on the secondary task. In this case *resolving* the inconsistency between target and stereotype consumed more cognitive resources. In short, it seems that activating stereotypes is not always energy-saving.

Explicit versus implicit prejudice, indirect measures and social neuroscience

As well as offering a level of explanation for prejudice, the cognitive approach has been especially innovative and influential in improving *how* we measure prejudice, with implications for how we conceptualize it. Recall that, as we wrote in the introduction to this chapter, many forms of prejudice have become more subtle and less blatant than they used to be. This does not necessarily mean that prejudice is disappearing (would that it were so!) but this is, at least in part, because social norms have changed, making expressions of prejudice less socially acceptable. However, if the underlying causes and functions of prejudice remain, people may simply become better at hiding or suppressing it. Under these conditions it is particularly important to use measures that get around this. We have already introduced implicit measures in our earlier chapter on attitudes (see Chapter 6).

The distinction between implicit and explicit bias is theoretically important, as well as for methodological reasons. Many dual-process models make a distinction between processes that tend to be efficient, automatic and less under our intentional and conscious control, and those that are more conscious and deliberative (e.g. Fazio & Olson, 2003; Fiske & Neuberg, 1990; see Chapters 4 and 6). The influential model of prejudice developed by Devine (1989) is perhaps the most well-known example of a dual process approach as applied to stereotyping and prejudice. She argued that we all have access to prejudiced stereotypes in our culture (e.g. about black people) and that these tend to be activated automatically and outside of our control, although low-prejudiced people are consciously motivated to counter this prejudice. This is discussed extensively in Chapter 4, so we will not go into further details here (see also the critique of her model by Lepore & Brown, 1997, discussed there).

The more general point to make here is that explicit and implicit measures of prejudice do not necessarily measure the same thing, and are (therefore) not always highly correlated (Amodio & Devine, 2006; Correll, Judd, Park, & Wittenbrink, 2010; Karpinski & Hilton, 2001). Because implicit measures are more suited to getting around social desirability concerns, it would be tempting to conclude as a result that implicit measures are therefore *better* than explicit measures. This conclusion would be

unwarranted, however. Some have argued also that, just because we might have certain associations (that affect our response on implicit measures), this does not necessarily mean that we endorse these associations and any prejudice based on them (e.g. Karpinski & Hilton, 2001). Amodio (2008) also warns that implicit measures have not proven to be strong or reliable predictors of explicit intergroup behaviour. In a recent review Gawronski and Payne (2010) point out that social desirability is only one dimension on which implicit and explicit measures differ, and may not be the most important. For example, we cannot explain the finding that lower-educated people tend to be more prejudiced by the simple assumption that better-educated people are more sensitive to norms of social desirability, as some have supposed. Wagner and Zick (1995) used a bogus pipeline procedure to reduce socially desirable responses. The bogus pipeline is a fake physiological procedure designed to give participants the idea that experimenters have insights into their true feelings and thoughts (rather like a polygraph or lie detector), which therefore encourages the participants to respond truthfully (Jones & Sigall, 1971). Wagner and Zick found that the education effect was just as strong when they used the bogus pipeline (i.e. when effect of social desirability should be reduced) as when they did not use it. It would therefore be premature to discard explicit measures of prejudice and always to prefer implicit ones.

Different implicit measures also differ in *what* they measure; they have their own strengths and weaknesses, and some appear to be more implicit than others. For example, Vanman, Saltz, Nathan, and Warren (2004) used activity in the facial muscles associated with smiling and frowning (electromyography, or EMG) as an implicit measure of prejudice in White Americans towards black people (i.e. more frowning, less smiling). They compared this implicit measure with another widely used measure, the Implicit Association Test or IAT (see Chapter 6), a reaction time measure. When two compatible responses (e.g. good/ingroup), are paired together, such that they require the same key press, reaction times tend to be faster than when incompatible responses are paired together (e.g. bad/ingroup, or good/outgroup; see Chapter 6 for further details). The IAT is based on the fact that response times are faster for compatible than for incompatible responses. Vanman et al. found that such EMG activity reliably predicted white participants' racial bias against black applicants, compared with white applicants, in a hiring decision. Responses on the IAT, however, did not predict this discrimination, and motivation to control prejudice was not related to facial muscle activity, whereas responses on the IAT were. In short, it seems that the white participants were more able to control their IAT responses than their facial expressions. So although implicit measures definitely add to our methodological toolkit, they need to be assessed and used on their merits. They do not necessarily provide a magic bullet, but do form an important part of our arsenal that helps to provide a more complete picture of prejudice (see Chapter 2 on research methods).

As well as distinguishing between implicit and explicit forms of prejudice, the developments in implicit measures have also allowed researchers to distinguish between prejudice and *stereotyping* at the implicit level. Various researchers had noted that stereotyping is not necessarily always prejudiced (e.g. Oakes, Haslam, & Turner, 1994). For example, we can have positive stereotypes about other groups, and also our own, and these do not have to reflect benevolent prejudice. It is therefore important to distinguish the evaluative and descriptive dimensions of stereotypes (Wittenbrink, Judd, & Park, 1997). A study by Amodio and Devine (2006) makes a good case for this point at the implicit level using the Implicit Association Test (see Chapter 6). They demonstrated both implicit evaluative bias (i.e. prejudice) towards Black Americans by White Americans, but also, independently, implicit *stereotyping* of these groups. One of the most interesting findings here, however, was that implicit stereotyping and implicit prejudice were *not* related (e.g. r = .06 in Study 1). This finding is important for evaluating the cognitive approach, and more specifically the rationale that prejudice results from cognitive biases, and that stereotyping processes explain prejudice (rather than the reverse). Ironically then, developments within social cognition research using implicit measures have tended to *weaken* the claim that prejudice results primarily from cognitive processes, and point to a stronger and relatively independent affective or emotional basis to prejudice. For example, a meta-analysis of 57 studies on racial attitudes and discrimination showed emotional prejudices to be *twice* as strongly related to discrimination than stereotypes and beliefs about these groups (Talaska, Fiske, & Chaiken, 2008). We return to a focus on emotions later in this chapter.

Another methodological innovation that follows the logic of implicit measurement even further 'upstream' concerns the developments in neuroscience that allow us to locate brain activity associated with social information processing (see also Chapter 1). This has opened up the field of 'social neuroscience' (Amodio & Frith, 2006; Blakemore, Winston, & Frith, 2004). In particular, the technique of functional magnetic resonance imaging (fMRI) allows researchers to determine the location of brain activity that can shed light on the processes, and the brain regions responsible for them, that can underlie ingroup bias and prejudice (see e.g. Amodio, 2008; Amodio & Frith, 2006, for reviews). Other techniques, such as research using event-related potentials (ERPs), are better designed to measure the time course of brain activity in the cortex than their localization in the brain (e.g. *when*

there is a specific neural response following presentation of a stimulus). Although these neuroscience measures can also be seen as indirect measures that are not under voluntary cognitive control, in some ways they provide a more *direct* window on process that is less mediated by language and self-reports. However, once again research using these techniques takes us beyond the cognitive approach, and also provides many important insights into the motivational and emotional bases of prejudice and discrimination. Moreover, as we argue shortly, just because processes relating to prejudice take place in the brain, this does not necessarily mean that they correspond to the *individual* level of analysis.

Summary

Although designed to capitalize on our cognitive limitations, the cognitive approach may also have some limitations of its own, and offers perhaps only a partial explanation of prejudice. First of all, the cognitive emphasis on social categorization and stereotyping processes as forming the basis for prejudice tends to neglect the possibility that motivation (and prejudice itself) may influence categorization and stereotyping. Moreover, we cannot assume that stereotypes are necessarily prejudiced by definition (after all, we can have stereotypes about our own groups!). The passions aroused in prejudice mean that the presence of motivation may often play a key role in *producing* as well as overriding prejudice (in contrast to Devine's approach). Although culture, cognition and personality all offer accounts of *how* prejudice might occur, it is also not always clear that they offer compelling explanations of *why* it occurs or *where* it comes from. Shifting the explanation to another level (the societal or the individual level) should not disguise this. To address this question it is now appropriate to consider the level of the phenomenon of prejudice itself: the (inter)group level.

GROUP APPROACHES TO PREJUDICE

....

Can prejudice be explained at the (inter) group level, or does it reduce to individual self-interests?

Prejudice is directed at groups. When we analyse the word prejudice, it means *pre-judging* someone, judging them before the facts are known, typically on the basis of some known group features (i.e. stereotypes). But if prejudice is about seeing and judging people *as members of groups*, it is perhaps odd that so much research on this topic views the phenomenon from the perspective of the individual's psychology and functioning. The previous sections focused on individual differences, and on the sort of cognitive processes that affect us all, as two approaches to explaining prejudice that both operate at the level of the individual. We now consider explanations at the level of the group, by focusing first on the relation of members to their own group (intragroup approaches) and then to explanations that refer more explicitly to the relation of the ingroup to the outgroup (intergroup approaches).

Intragroup processes, ingroup bias and prejudice

From a group perspective, one way to understand why people come to dislike or even hate others because of their group membership is to understand their relationship to their own group. Humans are social animals and, like other primates, we live in groups. Although we might not always recognize it, again like other primates, we derive many benefits from the group. Anthropologists, evolutionary psychologists and behavioural ecologists have emphasized the benefits of group living (see also Chapter 12). In earlier times the group provided considerable benefits in terms of security from other individuals and groups, but also in terms of cooperation within the group. Evolutionary theorists have proposed that genes that support cooperation and group living might be selected for and give the individuals (or more precisely their genes) an advantage (Dunbar, Barrett, & Lycett, 2005). Although 'group selection' (the idea that groups replicate and survive for the good of the group or species as a whole) has been discredited as a mechanism of evolution (e.g. Dawkins, 1976), 'group living' and all the traits and tendencies that contribute to that still confer many individual advantages (Dunbar et al., 2005; Sober & Wilson, 1998). Anthropologists have argued that many of the characteristics that make us uniquely human and distinguish us from other species and even other primates (e.g. large brain size, use of language and so forth) derive from our adaptation to cooperative group living in an uncertain world (Dunbar et al., 2005). Dunbar et al. suggest that there may even be an optimal group size, relating to the maximum number of people we can feasibly know and trust. Groups not only help to promote our safety, security and survival, they also help us to fulfil other needs, including esteem and respect, which are important to our position within the group. The need to be esteemed and respected by others can be seen as aspects of a general need to belong and to feel valued

by others (Baumeister & Leary, 1995). One influential account of self-esteem and its functions, the 'sociometer theory' (Leary, Tambor, Terdal, & Downs, 1995) argues that self-esteem provides us with a 'barometer' of the extent to which others accept us, and groups are one important source of this acceptance (see also Chapter 5 for sociometer model).

Returning to our focus on prejudice, what do these group benefits mean for our understanding of prejudice? If we recognize that groups can be good for individuals, is it possible to explain prejudice against outgroups merely through the benefits that the *ingroup* can provide to individuals? We might call this an 'intragroup' explanation of prejudice, because it looks inward to the benefits the ingroup provides, rather than at any threats that the outgroup may pose. A key argument is that we favour other ingroup members in our behaviour because there is an expectation of reciprocity within ingroups that we might not get from outgroups (Gaertner & Insko, 2000; Rabbie, Schot, & Visser, 1989; Yamagishi & Kiyonari, 2000; see also Chapter 10). Although expectations of greater reciprocity within the ingroup could help to explain some behaviour that favours the ingroup (and we return to this below), it does not so easily explain attitudes or behaviour that *derogate* the outgroup. To understand this we may need to move to the intergroup level, which we now consider.

Intergroup explanations of prejudice and discrimination

If prejudice occurs primarily between groups, surely it makes sense to search for 'intergroup' explanations? One typical reaction to this idea is 'Maybe, but our job as psychologists means getting inside the head, which is after all located within the individual'. While this is true, if we follow this line of reasoning too dogmatically the intergroup level of analysis might be seen as more the domain of sociology. It would be a mistake, however, to relinquish the intergroup level of analysis completely to other social sciences, and a great loss to (social) psychology. Two famous social psychologists, Donald Campbell and Muzafer Sherif (see Leader in the Field, Muzafer Sherif) realized this point, and were independently responsible, with their colleagues, for one of the first intergroup explanations of prejudice and discrimination: *realistic conflict theory*.

The key idea of realistic conflict theory is that prejudice and discrimination reflect real conflicts of interests between groups that are in competition for valued but scarce resources (like wealth, but also status and prestige). The most famous example of this explanation is the 'boys camp' study conducted by Sherif and his colleagues at Robbers Cave, Oklahoma (Sherif, Harvey, White,

LEADER IN THE FIELD

Muzafer Sherif (1906–1978) was born in Turkey and moved to the US to study at Harvard. At Yale he worked with Carl Hovland (see Leader in the Field, Chapter 1) on an influential approach to social judgement processes and how these were affected by one's own attitude and involvement in the topic, before settling at the University of Oklahoma. He also conducted pioneering research on social influence and norm formation, and developed a paradigm of influence using the autokinetic effect (see Chapter 8). However, he has perhaps become best known for his research on the Robbers Cave boys camp studies (1961), which became a cornerstone of realistic conflict theory (see also related research by Donald Campbell (see Leader in the Field, Chapter 2) and his associates). This theoretical approach remains one of the most powerful explanations of intergroup conflict.

FIGURE 14.7(a) and (b) *(a) The Rattlers compete against the Eagles in tug-of-war contest: They copy the Eagles' strategy of digging in by sitting down when the going gets tough; (b) Now they are on the same side in the tug-of-war: The Rattlers and Eagles combine their efforts to start the truck.*

Source: Photos from *The Robbers Cave Experiment* by Muzafer Sherif, et al. (Wesleyan University Press, 1988). © 1988 by Muzafer Sherif and reprinted by permission of Wesleyan University Press. www.wesleyan.edu/wespress

Hood, & Sherif, 1961), which we have already outlined in Chapter 1. For their field study, Sherif et al. capitalized on the common practice in America for parents to send their children away to camp for the summer. In this case well-adjusted white middle-class boys, around 12 years old, who did not know each other beforehand, were selected to take part, minimizing the chance that personality factors or preexisting loyalties or conflicts could play a role. In the first phase the boys formed separate groups (named the 'Eagles' and the 'Rattlers'), unaware of each other. In the second phase the experimenters introduced the groups and set up a series of competitions between them (e.g. tug-of-war, making a hut from available materials) in which only one group would win a prize (a so-called zero-sum conflict). As predicted, this led to conflict between the groups. This was only reduced in the third phase of the experiments, which gave the boys tasks that could only be achieved by the groups cooperating (e.g. to pull a truck with their food supplies out of the mud) – Figure 14.7. As we will see again later, such **superordinate goals** (goals which can *only* be achieved by the groups pooling their resources and working together) can be important in reducing prejudice and conflict between groups.

The boys camp studies clearly qualify as an intergroup explanation, because the boys' interests are bound up with their own group (just as in the intragroup explanation described earlier), but they are also negatively related to the interests of the outgroup. In other words there is a **positive interdependence** within the ingroup but a **negative interdependence** with the outgroup. When the superordinate goals, which could only be achieved together, were introduced, this negative interdependence between groups transformed into a positive interdependence between groups.

The realistic conflict explanation of prejudice, like the intragroup explanation based on reciprocity or positive

superordinate goals goals that can only be achieved by two groups working together cooperatively, to mutual benefit.

positive interdependence a situation in which there are positive bonds between individuals or groups characterized by cooperation, reciprocity and mutual benefits.

negative interdependence a situation in which bonds between individuals or groups are characterized by conflicts of interests, often leading to antagonism or *realistic conflict*.

interdependence within the group, depends to a large degree on *self-interest* resulting from tangible rewards. In other words, to the extent that one's own group benefits, individual members of the group are likely to benefit also. Although this is a powerful explanation of intergroup behaviour, one could rightly ask whether this is a truly intergroup explanation after all. That is, if group interests correspond with individual interests (just as with the intragroup explanation earlier), maybe the intergroup explanation can be *reduced* to the individual level of interest and explanation? Although engaging in conflict can also be dangerous and costly, a more persuasive example of the intergroup level of explanation would be one in which individual self-interest is ruled out. This is one key feature of the so-called *minimal group paradigm* developed by Tajfel, Billig, Bundy, and Flament (1971), which they designed to go beyond the realistic conflict approach. See Research Close-Up 14.1 to read about this paradigm, which we suggest you do now.

As we have already hinted in the section on *intra*group explanations, some researchers have argued that the findings of the minimal group studies, despite trying to rule out self-interest (by ensuring that rewards are never allocated directly to the self), did not entirely succeed in doing so. A key argument here is that people may still have *expectations* of positive interdependence and reciprocity: they expect other ingroup members to reward them, so it makes rational sense to reward others in the ingroup too (e.g. Gaertner & Insko, 2000; Rabbie et al., 1989). Indeed, research that measures perceived ingroup reciprocity, or explicitly manipulates dependence on the ingroup for rewards, confirms that these are powerful predictors of ingroup favouritism in minimal groups (Gaertner & Insko, 2000; Rabbie et al., 1989; Stroebe, Lodewijkx, & Spears, 2005).

ingroup bias behaviours or evaluations that favour the ingroup over the outgroup; ingroup favouritism treats the ingroup more positively, outgroup derogation treats the outgroup less positively.

So does this mean that evidence of minimal **ingroup bias** is not evidence of an intergroup explanation after all? Maybe not. The intragroup explanation based on interdependence and expected reciprocity could explain use of the *maximum ingroup profit* strategy in which the ingroup maximizes its benefits. However, it makes less sense for the *maximum difference* strategy (see Figure 14.8 in Research Close-Up 14.1), in which group members maximize the difference in rewards given to the ingroup versus the outgroup, even at a cost to the ingroup in terms of absolute rewards; yet, the *maximum difference* is also a strongly preferred reward strategy. *Maximum difference* looks much more like an intergroup strategy that takes into account (antagonistic) relations with the outgroup. This argument does not mean that self-interest is entirely ruled out, but use of the *maximum difference* strategy does reflect *group* interests.

So evidence for the intergroup level of explanation seems to be strengthened by the results from the minimal group paradigm as well as realistic conflict theory. Although the mechanism for the minimal ingroup bias, and specifically maximum difference, remains unclear, we go into some of the proposed explanations below. However, the first general lesson of the minimal group studies was to demonstrate that the individual level of analysis was not the whole story. This paradigm was instrumental in showing the need for a concept of self at the group level that speaks to group interests (in contrast to purely individual self-interest) to match the intergroup level of explanation. So was born the concept of *social identity*, which emerged out of the minimal group research and led later to the development of *social identity theory* (Tajfel & Turner, 1979; see below).

Now recall our question of whether explaining behaviour in psychological terms is possible when we consider intergroup behaviour (there is no psychology, at the level of the group as a whole, after all). So how is a psychology of groups possible, given that experience is always individually based? The concept of **social identity** offers one answer to this conundrum. Tajfel (1978b) defined social identity as that part of the self-concept corresponding to our knowledge of our group membership and the value and emotional significance we attach to this (see Leader in the Field, Henri Tajfel).

social identity that part of our self-concept corresponding to group memberships, and the value and emotional significance attached to these memberships.

LEADER IN THE FIELD

Henri Tajfel (1919–1982) was born to a Jewish family in Wloclawek, northern Poland and was studying in Paris when World War II broke out. Had he not concealed his Polish identity when the Nazis invaded, he would most likely have perished in the concentration camps instead of becoming a French prisoner of war. After the war he worked to resettle refugees before settling himself in Britain, where he studied Psychology as a mature student at Birkbeck College and received his PhD from London University in 1954. He moved later to the chair at Bristol University, creating an influential research group there through the 1970s. His early research on categorization and social judgement (see *accentuation* effect) formed an important foundation for social identity theory, which he developed at Bristol with John Turner (see Leader in the Field, John Turner, later in this chapter). His wartime experiences certainly coloured his understanding of intergroup relations and prejudice. Although the significance of social identity could not have been clearer from this experience, Tajfel had to create this concept in order to open up a field previously individualistic in its focus. His influence in developing social psychology in Europe both theoretically and institutionally, as one of the founding fathers of the European Journal of Social Psychology and the European Association of Social Psychology, provides a lasting legacy in Europe and beyond.

THE MINIMAL GROUP PARADIGM

Tajfel, H., Billig, M. G., Bundy, R. P., & Flament, C. (1971). Social categorization and intergroup behaviour. *European Journal of Social Psychology, 1*, 149–178.

Introduction

The purpose of these seminal experiments was to probe the minimal conditions for creating discrimination or ingroup bias. Previous research had shown that intergroup discrimination depended on realistic conflicts of interests between groups (Sherif et al., 1961) or some sense of interdependence or common fate within the group (Rabbie & Horwitz, 1969). It is not entirely clear why Tajfel and colleagues thought that stripping away such factors would reveal any evidence of bias, but it is good that they did! In the introduction they refer to the role of categorization as providing order and meaning, harking back to Tajfel's pioneering article on cognitive aspects of prejudice (Tajfel, 1969). However the important point of these studies was first to establish the minimal basis for discrimination as a phenomenon.

So what are minimal groups? Tajfel at al. spelled out the minimal criteria as including the following:

1. No face-to-face interaction (within or between groups).
2. Complete anonymity.
3. Respondents should not personally gain from their responses (to rule out self-interest).
4. A strategy designed to differentiate between groups should be in competition with rational/utilitarian principles of obtaining the maximum benefit for all, and also gaining most for the ingroup in absolute terms. In other words, for this strategy it is not important if *we get less* than we could, so long as *we get more than them*.
5. Responses should be made as important and real as possible (i.e. involve concrete rewards rather than some form of evaluation).

With these principles Tajfel et al. developed two innovative procedures relating to (a) the *social categorization process* and (b) the measurement of *reward allocations*, which are key features of the minimal group paradigm. These are highly influential and still widely used.

Method

Participants

Participants were Bristol schoolboys aged 14–15 years (*N* = 64, Experiment 1; *N* = 48, Experiment 2).

Procedure: 'mere' social categorization

Social categorization was established in two different ways. In Experiment 1 the schoolboys were categorized by means of a dot estimation procedure: they were asked to estimate the number of dots projected on a screen, presented for a fraction of a second. On the basis of 40 of these trials the boys were told that they were either in a group of *under-estimators* (i.e. a group who underestimated the number of dots) or a group of *over-estimators*. In fact, they were assigned randomly to these categories. In Experiment 2 the now-famous preference for the paintings of Klee versus Kandinsky was used. Here participants indicated their aesthetic preferences for a series of 12 paintings (six by each painter) designated as 'A' or 'B' for each paired choice (although in fact some pairs contained two by the same painter). Once again actual assignment to categories was random.

Participants then completed the reward matrices anonymously in separate cubicles.

Measures: the Tajfel matrices

Tajfel et al. developed a series of reward matrices that could be used to test for 'minimal' ingroup bias. Each matrix consisted of a row of paired numbers with (for example) the upper number of each pair corresponding to what a specific member of the ingroup would receive, if chosen, and the lower number going to a specific outgroup member. The first point to note is that Tajfel et al. therefore tried to rule out *self-interest* by requiring that rewards were allocated to a *specific* ingroup and outgroup member (and *not the groups as a whole*) so that these rewards would never get back to the allocators themselves (criterion 3). The matrices were designed to distinguish between different allocation strategies (criterion 4). These included *fairness* (equal allocation to ingroup and outgroup), *maximum joint profit* (MJP), *maximum ingroup profit* (MIP), and *maximum difference* (i.e. in favour of the ingroup; MD). See Figure 14.8 for a simplified version illustrating these different strategies (Van Leeuwen, 2000).

The design of the matrices allowed the preferences for different strategies to be tested against each other (referred to as 'pull scores'). Perhaps the most theoretically interesting strategy is the maximum difference

FIGURE 14.8 *The different response strategies on the Tajfel matrices (note: this has been adapted and simplified for illustrative purposes).*
Source: From Van Leeuwen, 2000, with permission from Dr Van Leeuwen.

strategy (see criterion 4) because, when contrasted with the maximum ingroup profit strategy, this could mean giving *fewer* rewards to the ingroup in absolute terms in order to ensure that the ingroup gets more than the outgroup.

Results

Summarizing the key findings across the studies a first point, often overlooked, is that a substantial percentage of participants opt for a fairness strategy in allocating rewards to ingroup versus outgroup (almost 20 per cent in experiment 1). Experiment 2 showed that preference for MD was stronger than MIP, which in turn was stronger than MJP. In other words, there was a preference for reward allocations that *maximized the difference* in favour of the ingroup, even at the cost in absolute terms to

the ingroup. This can also be seen as a form of *derogation* toward the outgroup.

Discussion

The results of these first minimal group studies were extremely provocative, because they seem to show that no conflict of interest, and indeed no self-interest at all, is necessary for people to discriminate on behalf of their group. In the paper Tajfel et al. proposed a 'generic' norm explanation for the discrimination, suggesting that there is a basic norm of competitiveness within Western societies that leads people to discriminate in favour of their own group. However, this explanation fell from favour, partly because a similar case can be made for a fairness norm (because there was clear evidence that this strategy was widely used too). The 'social identity' explanation would only emerge later.

Social identities refer to groups or social categories in the social world (e.g. women, Scots, overestimators, etc.) so it is clearly part of the intergroup level of social reality. However, because this identity can be an *important part of how we see ourselves*, it is also part of our own psychological make-up, and can therefore help to explain intergroup behaviour.

As Tajfel's definition makes clear, we can have strong commitment to, and identification with, these social identities. People who support 'their' football team, people who join a demonstration to protest at education cuts, against the invasion of Iraq, or in solidarity with the plight of Palestinians in Gaza, arguably all do this because of a commitment to a group and its cause and not just out of individual self-interest. The view that 'psychology

is about individuals and sociology about groups' therefore reflects a mistaken understanding of disciplinary boundaries. The idea that psychology applies only to the individual level of analysis reflects rather a *philosophical* position, sometimes called 'methodological individualism' (Schumpeter, 1908). The concept of social identity opens up a different way of thinking about intergroup relations, less focused on individual functions.

Evidence for social identity and ingroup bias from social neuroscience Quite recently research in social neuroscience has been instructive in addressing the question of whether there is a social level of self associated with the ingroup that could help to explain ingroup bias. In one study Volz, Kessler, and Von Cramon (2009) used the technique of functional magnetic resonance imaging (fMRI), which is able to localize brain activity, to address this question. The area of the brain that is associated with processing information relevant to the self is the medial prefrontal cortex (MPC), and previous research has shown that this area is especially active when the individual self-concept is implicated (see e.g. Macrae, Moran, Heatherton, Banfield, & Kelley, 2004; see Chapter 5). In their study Volz et al. categorized participants according to the minimal group procedure based on a bogus perceptual test (foreground versus background figure perceivers). While their brain activity was being monitored, participants then engaged in a number of reward distribution tasks, similar to the Tajfel matrices, designed to measure strategies of fairness and intergroup discrimination on trials that involved allocating rewards to ingroup and outgroup members (mixed trials; see also Tajfel et al., 1971).

Very similarly to the original minimal group studies, Volz et al. were able to distinguish participants who predominantly chose fairness strategies, and those who were more discriminatory in their responses. Crucially, the participants who showed more ingroup bias, also showed greater activation for those areas associated with the self and thus predicted to relate also to social identity (i.e. areas located in the medial prefrontal cortex). Those engaged in fairness, however, showed no such activation. Moreover, four participants who were found *not* to identify with their group (they scored below the midpoint of a group identification measure) also showed no such activation of the MPC, whereas four randomly selected participants who identified with their group *did*. This evidence suggests that our group self or social identity is indeed very much part of the self-concept, as Tajfel originally claimed, and just as much as is the individual self. The fact that some group identification is necessary for this social self to become activated is also evidence that a certain level of group identification is essential to social identity. Before we consider aspects of the intergroup context that might help us to explain discrimination further, it is now useful to examine in more detail the nature of group identification, as our bridge to the group, and how we conceptualize and measure this.

The individual's relation to the group: group identification and its components

What is group identification and can it explain prejudice?

Following Tajfel's definition of social identity as our psychological bridge to the group, it is possible to further

conceptualize and indeed measure **group identification** as the strength of this bridge. This may also be useful in helping to predict and explain prejudice and ingroup bias. At first sight, focusing on individual differences in group identification sounds reminiscent of other individual difference approaches to prejudice we considered earlier (e.g. right-wing authoritarianism), which we associated more with individual level explanations. An important difference here is that measures of group identification relate directly to the ingroup (and thus the group level), while allowing for individual variations in this link (helping to explain individual variation). Identification may also vary as a function of the social context in which group identities become salient. For example, even people who normally only identify weakly with their nationality may become more passionate about their country when the Olympics or the football World Cup comes round every four years (Figure 14.9). Put another way, group identification may be an outcome (or dependent variable) influenced by the social context as well as an input (or independent variable).

Recall Tajfel's definition of social identity as the knowledge of our group memberships and the value and emotional significance attached to these. This points to (at least) two different dimensions of group identification. Leach and colleagues (Leach et al., 2008) developed a scale to measure and validate the (componential) structure of group identification that fits well with Tajfel's definition. This research employed response items used in a range of previous research (in which participants

> **group identification**
> the degree to which people see themselves in terms of a group membership (group-level self-definition) and the degree of value and emotional attachment to the group (group-level self-investment).

FIGURE 14.9 *Even people who normally only identify weakly with their nationality may become more passionate about their country when the Olympics or Football World Cup comes round every four years.*

Source: © Michael Blann. Used under licence from Getty Images.

rated their agreement on 7-point Likert scales: *strongly agree* to *strongly disagree*) to test a model of the structure of group identification. The first two studies, using Dutch psychology students, examined three different group identities (as Dutch, as Europeans, as students of the University of Amsterdam). For these different group identities the same hierarchical structure for group identification was found in each case (see Theory Box 14.2). This confirmed the general distinction between a self-definition dimension of group identification and a self-investment dimension, at the upper level of the hierarchy, that in turn include further components at the lower level. The self-definition dimension comprises two components: individual self-stereotyping as a group member (e.g. 'I am similar to the average ingroup member'); and ingroup homogeneity (e.g. 'Ingroup members have a lot in common'). The self-investment dimension comprises three components: solidarity (e.g. 'I feel a bond with the group'); satisfaction (e.g. 'I feel glad to be in the group'); and centrality (e.g. 'This group is an important part of who I am'). Further studies confirmed the *construct*, *discriminant* and *predictive validity* of the scales (see Chapter 2).

Group identification is important because it makes clear that group membership is not just an objective matter, but is also *psychological* and subjective. This point

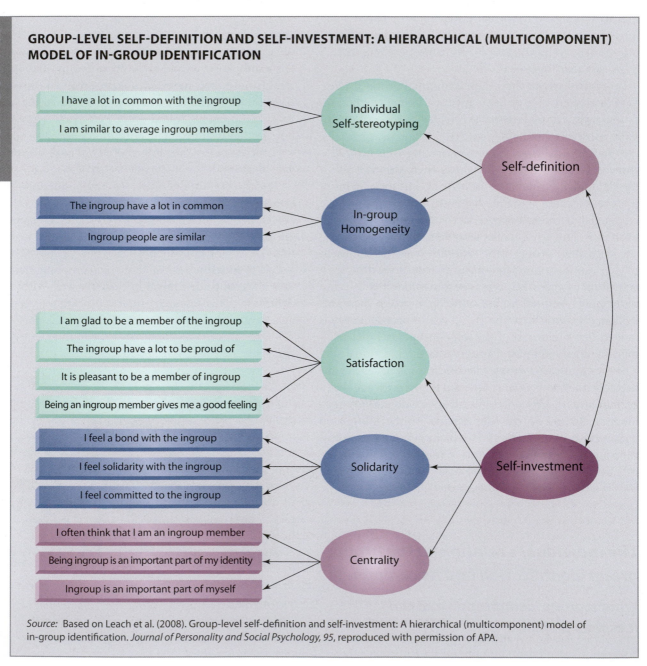

THEORY BOX 14.2

GROUP-LEVEL SELF-DEFINITION AND SELF-INVESTMENT: A HIERARCHICAL (MULTICOMPONENT) MODEL OF IN-GROUP IDENTIFICATION

I have a lot in common with the ingroup

I am similar to average ingroup members

Individual Self-stereotyping

Self-definition

The ingroup have a lot in common

Ingroup people are similar

In-group Homogeneity

I am glad to be a member of the ingroup

The ingroup have a lot to be proud of

It is pleasant to be a member of ingroup

Being an ingroup member gives me a good feeling

Satisfaction

I feel a bond with the ingroup

I feel solidarity with the ingroup

I feel committed to the ingroup

Solidarity

Self-investment

I often think that I am an ingroup member

Being ingroup is an important part of my identity

Ingroup is an important part of myself

Centrality

Source: Based on Leach et al. (2008). Group-level self-definition and self-investment: A hierarchical (multicomponent) model of in-group identification. *Journal of Personality and Social Psychology, 95*, reproduced with permission of APA.

makes groups a topic for social psychologists and not just sociologists. It can help to explain how different people might react to similar situations differently. If group identification is a measure of our relation to the group, perhaps it is an obvious candidate to help explain prejudice? And perhaps it is more relevant to the intergroup context than other individual difference variables? Whereas ideological factors such as authoritarianism and social dominance orientation are clearly *about* the intergroup context, group identification more specifically locates *us in* the intergroup context and gives us investment in our group.

So could group identification perhaps explain prejudice and ingroup bias? There is some evidence that this may indeed be the case. A series of studies by Bourhis and his collaborators has shown that high group identifiers generally show more ingroup bias in the minimal group paradigm. For example, in one study Gagnon and Bourhis (1996) showed that high group identifiers with their minimal ingroup discriminated more against the outgroup, and that group identification was actually a better predictor of discrimination in this study than expectations of ingroup-reciprocity. However some scholars have criticized this research because group identification was measured *after* discrimination, making the causal direction unclear (see Gaertner & Insko, 2000; Stroebe et al., 2005).

Some researchers have made a claim for a *general* link between ingroup identification and ingroup bias (e.g. Hinkle & Brown, 1990), but this has also been disputed (Turner, 1999). Although group identification may predict prejudice and ingroup bias under certain conditions, there are problems with seeing it as a general predictor of ingroup bias or prejudice. A first question is, how does group identification arise, what causes it (which would just defer the question of what causes prejudice and raise the problem of circularity of explanation). Moreover, does it necessarily follow that 'I like *us*, therefore I dislike *them*'? Put more graphically, Brewer (1999) has argued that 'ingroup love' is different from 'outgroup hate'; ingroup favouritism is not the same as outgroup derogation. In fact, the evidence from the minimal group paradigm shows that when the Tajfel matrices are used to distribute penalties or punishments rather than rewards, then the typical ingroup bias effect (or outgroup derogation, as implied by the punishments) tends to reduce or disappear (and it is debatable whether the maximum difference strategy is true derogation where it involves the allocation of positive rewards). Mummendey and Otten (1998) refer to this finding as the **positive–negative asymmetry**, namely the tendency to show more ingroup bias when

positive–negative asymmetry evidence that people show more ingroup bias when distributing positive rewards than punishment or penalties.

allocating positive resources (e.g. rewards) than negative ones (e.g. punishments). One explanation for this asymmetry is that punishment or outgroup derogation is *harsher* than ingroup favouritism, and less normatively accepted, especially when there is little overt justification for discrimination as in the minimal group paradigm (see *Threats to group values* later in this chapter).

Such findings tend to support Brewer's conclusion that the minimal group paradigm (despite the maximum difference effect) provides at best weak evidence for derogation of the outgroup. So, although ingroup identification (like ingroup reciprocation) can play a role in understanding prejudice, it does not easily explain more extreme forms of prejudice and discrimination on its own. However, as we shall see, the concept of identification is central to understanding social identity and the group level of explanation: we need a certain level of identification to see ourselves as group members and thus to generate minimal ingroup bias. Group identification can also be an important *moderator* variable, working in combination with other factors to explain individual differences in prejudice or discrimination. We now turn to different aspects of the intergroup context that can produce the threats that help to motivate and explain prejudice and discrimination, especially in its stronger forms.

Elaborating the intergroup level

How do threats posed by the outgroup help to explain prejudice and discrimination?

We now incorporate *relations* with the outgroup more explicitly into our theorizing. One way to think about this is to consider the outgroup posing a range of *threats* to the ingroup, with prejudice and discrimination forming ways of coping with these threats. Considering these threats also introduces some of the key intergroup theories of prejudice and discrimination.

Threats to group existence   Perhaps the most serious threat one could imagine at the intergroup level is a threat to the very existence of one's group. Fortunately examples of genocide are rare (although alas not rare enough) but milder degrees of threat (e.g. to group security) are also relevant. Although such threats can be manifest in the antagonism or aggression of the outgroup, outgroups can also pose a threat to group security for other reasons. One interesting recent evolutionary account for the emergence of xenophobia (fear of foreigners) is the threat of disease and infection they might pose (e.g. Faulkner, Schaller, Park, & Duncan, 2004). Faulkner et al. showed in four correlational studies that people who were more chronically worried about their vulnerability to disease were also more likely to show xenophobic attitudes to unfamiliar immigrant groups (i.e. those who could be seen to pose a potential disease threat). They also demonstrated this experimentally. In two experiments they presented participants with evidence for the ease with which bacteria are transmitted (or, in a control condition, evidence concerning the ease with which accidents occur). Crossed with this manipulation, the Canadian participants then either expressed their attitudes towards a familiar immigrant outgroup (e.g. Scottish, Taiwanese) or an unfamiliar immigrant outgroup (e.g. Nigerian, Mongolian). Results confirmed the prediction that attitudes to the *unfamiliar* immigrant outgroup were particularly hostile when participants were also exposed to the disease salient condition.

We now turn to a very different kind of theory, which also concerns threats to our existence. According to *terror management theory* (Greenberg, Solomon, & Pyszczynski, 1997), being reminded of our own mortality can evoke intense existential angst, causing us to seek reassurance that our lives have meaning through a retreat into familiar cultural values and groups. One of the predicted consequences is increased ingroup favouritism (Castano, Yzerbyt, Paladino, & Sacchi, 2002; Solomon, Greenberg, & Pyszczynski, 1991). Although mortality salience is a threat at the individual level, threats to the group's existence could be just as likely to evoke group-level responses, and perhaps more so. Research confirms that a sense of group continuity (i.e. that the group will still exist when you die) can be very important to group esteem (Sani, 2008) and fulfil the need to belong. Events that physically threaten the safety of some members of the group, or attacks on its icons (e.g. flag burning) could invoke potentially powerful motives and defence mechanisms. The 9/11 and subsequent suicide attacks by Al Qaida terrorists are examples that can be interpreted as threats to Western culture and values that evoke such defensive reactions (Figure 14.10).

Other more common examples of existential threat are likely to be experienced by minority groups, especially where their identity relies on group attributes that might be under threat, such as a minority language. For example, Livingstone, Spears, Manstead, and Bruder (2009) showed that the Welsh-speaking minority within Wales (where only 20 per cent of Welsh people speak their heritage language) were more likely to justify a violent campaign of arson attacks on holiday homes owned by the English in their Welsh homeland. Historically the English had tried to eradicate the Welsh language, which explains both the relatively low percentage of people who speak it today, and why Welsh speakers might feel existential threat.

FIGURE 14.10 *The 9/11 and subsequent suicide attacks by Al Qaida terrorists are examples that can be interpreted as threats to Western culture and values that evoke defensive reactions.*

Source: © Steve Winter. Used under licence from Getty Images.

Indeed this effect was strongest for Welsh speakers who felt their Welsh identity to be vulnerable (i.e. under threat) and who also perceived the relationship with England to be unfair or illegitimate. This interaction was absent for Welsh people who do not speak Welsh, who are less likely to see their Welsh identity in terms of the Welsh language, and therefore experience less existential threat.

Threats to resources: realistic and relative As we have already seen in realistic conflict theory, one of the most powerful explanations for prejudice between groups is that outgroups are seen to threaten our interests, especially when we are in conflict or competition for the same valued resources (Sherif et al., 1961; see also Esses, Jackson, Dovidio, & Hodson, 2005, for a more recent application). Clearly material factors are important in explaining intergroup conflicts. However, the minimal group studies showed that realistic threats are not necessary for discrimination, and the idea that threats are not always objective, but often more subjective, is also well made by *relative deprivation theory* (Runciman, 1966). The key idea here is that what we *have*, as groups as well as individuals, depends not just on objective circumstances, but on how we feel we are doing *compared to others*. In other words, even if we are doing quite well in objective, material terms, if we think others are doing better, we are likely to feel relatively deprived. For example, when Germany was reunified after the collapse of the former Soviet bloc, suddenly there were strong reasons for the former East Germans ('Ossis') to compare their lot with the more economically successful former West Germany ('Wessis'). The outcome of this comparison resulted in a clear feeling of **relative deprivation** for those in the East, and led to realistic conflicts over resources, such as the view that more future jobs and investment should go to East rather than West Germany (Mummendey, Kessler, Klink, & Mielke, 1999).

> **relative deprivation** a resentful feeling that the self or ingroup is worse off than the other or outgroup.

Threats to group status and esteem

If relative deprivation theory focuses on what your group lacks compared to others, social identity theory (Tajfel & Turner, 1979) emphasizes more generally how your group *is*, compared to others. A key theme in social identity theory is that people compare their own group with other groups and seek to differentiate their own group positively, thereby providing a positive social identity and sense of group worth. Making social comparisons with higher status groups on valued dimensions is therefore likely to be quite threatening, because this implies a low status and negative social identity. Social identity theory proposes that groups will strive to attain (or maintain) positive identity, and to positively differentiate their group from these outgroups. **Positive differentiation** is closely related to the concept of ingroup bias, and involves making the group positively different from a comparison outgroup on available dimensions of comparison. This could entail discrimination (as in the reward allocations of the minimal group paradigm), but it could also involve evaluative ratings that are less discriminatory (e.g. 'We are kinder than them'; 'We are more moral than them').

> **positive differentiation** involves making the group positively different from a comparison outgroup on available dimensions of comparison (e.g. by means of more positive evaluations or reward allocations) (see also *ingroup bias*).

Note that if status is seen as a valued resource, then realistic conflict theory could also explain ingroup bias. But remember that realistic conflict was more or less ruled out of the minimal group studies, and it is here that the social identity explanation has a theoretical advantage. The idea that groups are motivated to differentiate themselves positively from outgroups, to gain a positive social identity, became a cornerstone of social identity theory that was used to explain the minimal group bias effects. Positive differentiation also helps to explain why group members might choose the maximum difference strategy in the minimal group paradigm (see Research Close-Up 14.1), which is not easy to explain by ingroup reciprocity.

The idea that positive differentiation enhances esteem through a positive identity has become known as the **self-esteem hypothesis** (Abrams & Hogg, 1988; Oakes & Turner, 1980). Research has generally been supportive of this idea (Aberson, Healy, & Romero, 2000; Rubin & Hewstone, 1998), although early studies suffered from methodological problems, and often conceptualized self-esteem in individualistic or global terms, against the spirit of the group-level explanation of social identity theory.

> **self-esteem hypothesis** the prediction that ingroup bias will lead to an increase in group level self-esteem or satisfaction.

A study by Hunter, Platow, Howard, and Stringer, (1996) addressed some of these methodological shortcomings, including the criticism that much previous research had been conducted on minimal groups, where it is more difficult for a meaningful level of group identification and group-esteem to develop (see Theory Box 14.2). Hunter et al. could not have chosen more meaningful and involved groups: Catholic and Protestant school pupils in Northern Ireland in the 1990s during the height of the conflict, known as 'The Troubles'. The design of this study involved a between participants factor in which, in an experimental condition, participants had the opportunity to show ingroup bias, whereas, in a control condition, they did not. A repeated measures factor assessed self-esteem twice, three weeks apart, before and after the opportunity to show ingroup bias (i.e. for those in the experimental condition). Hunter et al. measured self-esteem relating to several distinct domains of the self-concept (13 in all, e.g. honesty; mathematical, academic, verbal, and physical ability; physical appearance; global self-esteem; religious esteem; and positive parental relations). Three weeks after the first esteem measurement session pupils in the *experimental* condition then rated the ingroup (pupils from their own school) and outgroup (pupils at a school for the opposite religion in the same town) on a subset of six of the specific domains measured for self-esteem (i.e. honesty, mathematical, academic, verbal and physical ability, and physical appearance) and overall evaluation (all from *very poor* to *very good*: 1–10). The control condition only differed from the experimental condition by excluding these ingroup and outgroup ratings (i.e. no opportunity for ingroup bias). Then pupils in both experimental and control conditions rated themselves on the 13 different domains of esteem once again (i.e. including the six domains rated in the experimental condition). This repeated measures design allowed for the assessment of *changes* in *state* self-esteem (after the opportunity for ingroup bias or not), another improvement on earlier research.

Results from the experimental condition showed that participants generally rated their ingroup higher on all dimensions (i.e. ingroup bias), although the ingroup was rated especially high on physical ability, and the outgroup lower on honesty (a clear sign of the distrust between Protestants and Catholics during The Troubles). Self-esteem increased in the experimental condition only, on honesty, academic ability, verbal ability and physical appearance, but global self-esteem was unaffected by the opportunity to discriminate. However, self-esteem was also unaffected on some other specific dimensions, as well as increasing on two domains in the experimental condition that were *not* included in the ingroup bias opportunity (religion and parental relations). Hunter et al. speculated that the specific dimensions on which self-esteem was enhanced were the ones that were the most important and relevant to pupils' identity, although they did not provide independent evidence for this. However, this research does seem to show that ingroup bias can enhance self-esteem on some key specific dimensions of group identity without necessarily improving global esteem.

If low status is threatening to our sense of esteem and undermines a positive social identity, we might expect low-status groups to be particularly likely to show ingroup bias. However, this does not always seem to be the case, as confirmed in a meta-analysis of research by Mullen, Brown, and Smith (1992). Mullen et al. found more evidence for ingroup favouritism among low-status groups outside the laboratory than those created in the laboratory. One reason for this is the role of **social reality constraints**: the point that when groups have a low status, they may feel that claiming a better position for themselves, especially on the status-defining dimension, is not justified or legitimate. This is particularly likely in laboratory studies, where status is manipulated, because there is little scope, and perhaps little motivation, to contest status feedback just received. However, this can happen in naturally occurring groups too. For example, in the study by Hunter et al. (1996) discussed above, ingroup bias was *weaker* among the *Catholic* than the *Protestant* pupils in their research, probably reflecting the lower status of this group in Northern Ireland at the time.

social reality constraints evidence that the outgroup is clearly better on a certain dimension can make ingroup bias on that dimension difficult to justify.

However, many naturally occurring groups with lower status do not always accept their lower status position (i.e. they perceive it as illegitimate). Remember that the Catholic pupils in the study carried out by Hunter et al. still showed ingroup bias (just less than the Protestants). To go back to another example, many East Germans ('Ossis') would not accept their group as being inferior, despite their economic disadvantages. Indeed esteem and group identification is often just as high (if not higher) in disadvantaged groups as those with higher status, and the threat to identity of low status can often strengthen solidarity with one's group (Ellemers, Spears, & Doosje, 2002). The issue of status legitimacy is a part of the more complete social identity theory that we discuss further below.

In many real-life intergroup comparisons groups will differ on many different dimensions, providing opportunities for groups to rate their own group as better on certain dimensions but the other group as better on others (see also Hewstone & Brown, 1986). For example, psychology students might rate themselves as more sociable but less intelligent than physics students. In this way both groups can claim a positive identity (without compromising social reality constraints). In social identity theory this is called a 'social creativity' strategy: the groups are not challenging the outgroup by means of direct competition (i.e. ingroup bias, discrimination), but are simply choosing dimensions that allow for positive differentiation. However, it is also possible to see how the use of this strategy, instead of eliminating prejudice and discrimination, could just perhaps make it more subtle. If psychology students choose to emphasize their sociability over intelligence, and physics students do the reverse, physics students may still claim they are somehow better by arguing that intelligence is a more important dimension than being sociable. Research by Mummendey and Schreiber (1984) makes exactly this point, and referred to this strategy as 'different but better'! (see Leader in the Field, Amélie Mummendey).

This example points to a problem of this social creativity strategy for low status groups: they will often find it difficult to claim superiority on the status-defining dimension (such as competence), yet this will often be the most important and valued one (Ellemers, 1993). Discriminating in terms of reward allocations may then be a more viable route to a positive identity because of social reality constraints on the status-defining dimension. Indeed, in line with relative deprivation theory, it can be easier to justify better rewards if you feel your group has been unfairly denied ('We need and deserve more resources!'). When faced with identity-based threats in terms of low status or resources, social identity theory makes similar predictions to realistic conflict and relative deprivation theories. A key difference is the motive for such behaviour. According to social identity

LEADER IN THE FIELD

Amélie Mummendey (b. 1944) was born in Bonn, where she also received her Masters in psychology, followed by her PhD from the University of Mainz in 1970. For many years Mummendey was professor at the University of Münster, building up an influential group of researchers and starting an annual series of research meetings on intergroup relations. When she moved to the chair at the University of Jena she maintained this initiative, and the Jena conference continues to this day. The group at Jena, under her leadership, became one of the most prolific centres for research on intergroup relations in Europe. She also inaugurated the International Graduate College (in collaboration with other European universities), which trained numerous social psychologists who have also become key figures in the field. Mummendey's early research focused on aggression, but her contributions to the social identity approach have been particularly notable. These include much research and theorizing on the processes underlying intergroup discrimination, but also tolerance between groups. These contributions include research on the 'different but better' differentiation strategy, the 'positive–negative asymmetry' and the ingroup projection model.

theory, discrimination would address an attempt to gain a positive identity rather than competing for material resources for their own sake.

Threats to group value(s) Other kinds of threat to identity less obviously involve esteem, but do imply a threat to values or principles central to the ingroup identity. We see this most clearly in the case of conflicting ideological or religious values. The most salient current example is perhaps the relation of radical Islam to the more secular or Christian Western world. This theme goes back to ideas of similarity – attraction (e.g. Byrne & Wong, 1962; see Chapter 11) and belief congruence (e.g. Rokeach & Rothman, 1965), which proposed that simply having different beliefs and values could be a basis for prejudice towards outgroups. This idea has re-emerged in stronger form in the *integrated threat theory* (e.g. Stephan, Diaz-Loving, & Duran, 2000); Stephan and colleagues coined the term 'symbolic threat' to refer to group values that threaten the ingroup's way of life (albeit more ideologically than physically).

Although group values different from those of the ingroup may become the target of prejudice, more optimistically group norms and values can also be a source of tolerance and reduced discrimination, to the extent that they may prescribe less prejudice and discrimination in themselves. 'Political correctness' could be seen as one such norm that, at least where values are followed, would lead to less prejudice and discrimination. Indeed such norms are not necessarily contradictory to the social identity approach, because they can become valued dimensions of identity. For example, in contrast to the Al Qaida example, many religions – including Muslim, Christian and Buddhist – are against discrimination ('Love thy neighbour...' is a theme that recurs in all three religions, as well as many others).

An influential theoretical account of group norms is provided by *self-categorization theory*, developed by John Turner and his collaborators (Turner, Hogg, Oakes, Reicher, & Wetherell, 1987; see Leader in the Field, John Turner). In this framework the concept of social identity was more explicitly distinguished from personal identity (the 'individual self'), and related to social influence processes (see Chapter 8). A key point here is that when group identities are valued (see group identification earlier in this chapter) and become salient in an intergroup context, we are likely to conform willingly to the norms associated with our group. We are also likely to see ourselves and others in terms of group attributes (e.g. stereotypes, norms), a process referred to as 'depersonalization' (see also the self-definition component of group identification earlier, and accentuation effects). Conformity to group norms that distinguish ingroup from outgroup is motivated and regulates group behaviour: what to do and what *not* to do. A good example of this is the so-called 'black sheep effect' (Marques, Yzerbyt, & Leyens, 1988) in which ingroup members who deviate from ingroup norms are judged even *more* harshly than outgroup members who show exactly the same behaviour. This is an interesting exception to ingroup favouritism: typically ingroup members would be judged more positively than outgroup members. Instead this harsher judgement of an ingroup transgression can be seen as a form of 'policing' of ingroup behaviour that might otherwise reflect badly on the ingroup image.

LEADER IN THE FIELD

John Turner (1948–2011) grew up in a working-class neighbourhood of South London and studied Psychology as an undergraduate at the University of Sussex, before moving to the University of Bristol to do his PhD under the supervision of Henri Tajfel (see Leader in the Field, this chapter). He took up a lectureship at Bristol and, after a year at the Institute for Advanced Study at Princeton, he emigrated to Australia. After a period at Macquarie University, Sydney, he moved to the chair at the Australian National University, Canberra. This group became a key centre for research on social identity processes, much as Bristol had earlier under Tajfel. Together with Tajfel, Turner developed the highly influential social identity theory of intergroup conflict (Tajfel & Turner, 1979) and went on to develop self-categorization theory, which further elaborated the distinction between social and personal identities. Whereas social identity theory is primarily a theory of intergroup relations, self-categorization theory is a more general theory of the self and the group that has been applied to a whole range of key topics in social psychology (identity salience, social influence, social stereotyping, group formation, leadership, collective behaviour, to name a few) – perhaps the closest we have today in social psychology to a 'grand theory'. His research, and especially his theoretical contributions to the field, have been immense and leave a lasting legacy to social psychology in Europe and around the world.

If there are group norms about discrimination being bad or antisocial, will discrimination harm esteem rather than enhance it? There is indeed some evidence of this (Branscombe & Wann, 1994; Scheepers, Spears, Manstead, & Doosje, 2009). Research also shows that, where the group has a norm of being fair and not discriminating, stronger identification with the group can actually increase *fairness* rather than discrimination (e.g. Jetten, Spears, & Manstead, 1997). These findings also help to explain why discrimination that actually involves derogating the outgroup is perhaps less common than examples of ingroup enhancement (see also Mummendey & Otten, 1998; Perdue, Dovidio, Gurtman, & Tyler, 1990). An explanation for this *positive–negative asymmetry* is the thought that harming others may indeed damage the ingroup image (Reynolds, Turner, & Haslam, 2000). These examples provide reassuring reminders that prejudice and discrimination are not *inevitable* consequences of group membership or group identification.

Threats to group distinctiveness If too much difference from an outgroup can be a problem, then it seems that too much similarity with an outgroup can be too! Have you ever had the experience when travelling with your friends abroad that the locals get your nationality wrong? You might be Dutch but they think you are German. You might be Italian but they think you are Spanish or French. You might be British but they think you are American. These identity confusions can be irritating (and apparently some more than others). But why? It is not that students are necessarily prejudiced towards the groups they are confused with (at least we hope not). There are actually two closely related threats to identity contained in these examples (see Ellemers et al., 2002). First, people like to be seen in terms of identities important to them (see 'centrality', a component of group-level self-definition and self-investment in Theory Box 14.2). Being seen in terms of other identities, especially erroneous ones, can evoke 'categorization threat'. But that is not the whole story. We also do not like it when another group is so similar to ours, because it undermines the very essence of what our group is that makes us different and special (i.e. not just because they miscategorize me). Hence a Dutch student may be more irritated when he or she is seen as German, rather than as French or American. In other words we tend to be most sensitive when the other group actually *is* similar to our own, in terms of attributes or stereotypes (e.g. when Swiss Germans are seen as German). Groups that are too similar to our own can therefore threaten the unique identity of the group: 'distinctiveness threat'. Some have even argued that having a distinctive group identity is even more fundamental than avoiding a negative one. For example, Mlicki and

LEADER IN THE FIELD

Naomi Ellemers (b. 1963) was born in Amsterdam and studied at the University of California, Berkeley, and the University of Groningen, where she obtained her Masters degree (1987) and PhD (1991). In 1990 she moved to a lectureship at the Free University of Amsterdam and, after becoming Senior Lecturer there (1996) she was appointed to a Chair in Social and Organizational Psychology at the University of Leiden in 1999, where she remains. She has received numerous awards for her research, including the Jos Jaspars early career award (1990) and most recently the prestigious Spinoza Prize (2010). Her doctoral research provided empirical evidence for a range of processes proposed by social identity theory, including the role of socio-structural factors (e.g. status stability, legitimacy, the permeability of group boundaries) in predicting the different coping strategies members of disadvantaged groups adopt (e.g. discrimination, social mobility). Her research addresses many issues relating to social stereotyping, discrimination, power, respect and morality in intergroup contexts. As well as many contributions to basic research within the social identity approach in particular, Ellemers has also applied her research to many work settings and in organizational contexts. Much of this research considers the role of gender (among other group identities), both in relation to discrimination and social justice, and also to diversity and productivity in workgroups.

Ellemers (1996) found that 'complaining' is an important self-stereotype of Polish identity, and though apparently negative, something that Poles will often emphasize (see Leader in the Field, Naomi Ellemers; also self-verification versus self-enhancement in relation to the personal self, Chapter 5).

Positive differentiation (also in the form of discrimination) can restore or even create group distinctiveness. Now remember the social identity explanation for the minimal ingroup bias effect, namely that people try positively to differentiate their group in order to create a *positive group distinctiveness* (and not just enhance the ingroup; see e.g. Tajfel, 1982b). This distinctiveness motive had been largely forgotten in research on minimal groups that had largely concentrated on the self-esteem hypothesis. However, because participants in the minimal group paradigm lack information about the groups (precisely because they are minimal!) this may also create distinctiveness threat (Spears, Jetten, Scheepers, & Cihangir, 2009). Spears et al. (2009) decided to put this idea to the test. In one experiment they categorized participants according to the classic procedure based on preferences for Klee or Kandinsky (see Research Close-Up 14.1). As expected, the typical ingroup bias effect was found in this condition. However, in another condition they simply added the information that people who prefer Klee tend to be extroverts, whereas those who prefer Kandinsky tend to be introverts (or vice versa to counterbalance). In this condition ingroup bias was virtually eliminated.

The explanation was that making the minimal group identities more meaningful (introvert versus extrovert) provided a distinctive group identity, making it unnecessary to create this identity by means of positive differentiation (this interpretation was supported by follow-up studies). In a meta-analysis, Jetten, Spears, and Postmes (2004) also found that high identifiers with the ingroup were particularly likely to respond to distinctiveness threat (i.e. comparison with *similar* outgroups) by differentiating more. The more invested you are in your group, the more important it is to distinguish it from similar outgroups.

Brewer (1991) developed a slightly different conception of distinctiveness threat in *optimal distinctiveness theory*. She proposed that individuals have two fundamental needs: a need to integrate or affiliate (the need to belong: Baumeister & Leary, 1995), but also a need to differentiate oneself from others; a distinctiveness motive. She argued that groups that are relatively small in size (and thus distinctive), such as numerical minorities, optimally meet these two needs.

Smaller and numerically distinctive groups may particularly value their group identity for other reasons also (it turns out that minorities often identify more strongly with their group identity than do majorities; see Leonardelli, Pickett, & Brewer, 2010). If minorities do not have power or resources, their identity may assume more importance and they may be particularly sensitive to being assimilated into the same category as the majority group, especially as this identity confusion may happen more often than the reverse (think again of the German 'Ossis'). It is no accident that the examples we chose at the start of this section tended to focus on the sensitivities of the *smaller* group of the two. Larger and more dominant groups need not worry too much about distinctiveness threat, because they will be confronted with it less often (e.g. Americans are not often called Canadians). It is also easier for them to dominate, especially in superordinate categories that contain them both.

This insight provided the inspiration for another explanation for discrimination known as the *ingroup projection model* (Mummendey & Wenzel, 1999). You will recall that emphasizing superordinate goals and interests is one method to *reduce* conflict and discrimination, according to realistic conflict theory. However, the ingroup projection model suggests that this may not always work. If one group is dominant in size and status, they will typically set the agenda for what counts as normative or 'prototypical' for the superordinate category that includes both subgroups (i.e. their norms are projected onto the superordinate group). Thus, the English may be seen as more typically British than the Welsh or Scots. In Germany, West Germans are seen as more typically German than East Germans are (especially by Wessis themselves!).

West Germans may then feel justified in discriminating more against East Germans, because they see Ossis as less typical of the German norms and ideals than Wessis (see Waldzus, Mummendey, Wenzel, & Boettcher, 2004). So although numerical group distinctiveness may provide some benefits to identity definition, it could also make your group more vulnerable to discrimination by the powerful majority.

Integrative intergroup theories

How do beliefs about our position in the social hierarchy help to explain discrimination?

The repertoire of threats groups encounter help to explain many cases of intergroup differentiation and discrimination. However, some theories cannot be reduced to a list of threats, but combine, in more complex and integrative ways, some of these explanatory principles with an analysis of the social structure (the status hierarchy, or intergroup power relations), and our beliefs and feelings about our position in this structure. In this section we consider theories that provide a more detailed analysis of how prejudice and discrimination can relate to dynamics structured by status and power between groups (see also realistic conflict theory and relative deprivation theory, already discussed).

Socio-structural theories We have already introduced social identity theory (Tajfel & Turner, 1979) in relation to a number of forms of identity threat (esteem, status, distinctiveness). These threats to identity do not occur in a 'social vacuum', but reflect the position of people in the social structure. As we saw above, groups disadvantaged by low status are likely to feel threatened. However, this threat is just a starting point: social identity theory was developed in large part to explain *how and why* low status groups cope with this situation, because (as we have already noted) discrimination and ingroup bias does not *always* result. Whether people respond to this threat with direct discrimination towards the rival group, for example, depends on whether the status relation is seen as legitimate or illegitimate and as stable or unstable (and so open to change). Tajfel and Turner (1979) referred to social comparison between groups in a status hierarchy that highlights the illegitimacy and instability of the situation as 'insecure'; insecure social comparisons encourage low status groups to imagine how things could be better (called 'cognitive alternatives to the status quo'). It is under these conditions that social identity theory predicts most intergroup conflict

FIGURE 14.11 *Although the absence of discrimination may seem like a good thing, social conflict can be important and necessary if social change is to occur, for example the 'Arab Spring' uprising in 2011.*

Source: © Alexandre Meneghini. Used under licence from Press Association Images.

(and thus discrimination). It follows that conflict and discrimination will not *always* result from status differences (an important difference from realistic conflict theory).

Although the *absence* of discrimination may seem like a good thing, social conflict can, at least sometimes, be important and necessary if social change is to occur. Take the 'Arab Spring', the wave of popular democratic uprisings that swept across many Arab countries in 2011 (Figure 14.11). Few would argue that these uprisings and mass protests reflect the operation of prejudice and discrimination (at least in the conventional pejorative sense), but they certainly reflect conflict and social change. This is why it is important to take into account power and legitimacy when thinking about prejudice and discrimination: the ingroup bias of the powerless may not be the same, or have the same aims and functions, as that of the advantaged. Whereas low-status groups may be competing to change the status quo, high-status groups may use ingroup bias to reflect and legitimize their superior position, bolstering group esteem (see Scheepers, Spears, Doosje, & Manstead, 2006a, b, for some evidence of these different functions). So as well as offering a group explanation of prejudice and discrimination, social identity theory is also a theory of social change. We will address this issue in more detail in the next section, where we show that prejudice reduction strategies can sometimes work against social change and the interests of low-status groups (Saguy, Tausch, Dovidio, & Pratto, 2009).

A second powerful factor that can contribute to the stability of the status quo is what we might call the 'ideology of individualism', or individual mobility. If social change

is not feasible, another route to a positive identity is to move into the high-status group. Of course this depends on mobility being possible (i.e. *permeable* group boundaries). Clearly this is only an option that can be tried by the few rather than the many (it is unrealistic to think of one group moving into the other en masse). In short, this is an *individual* strategy that changes nothing in the status relations between the groups. However, the ideology of individualism (the 'American dream' that anyone can make it rich, for example) is remarkably potent. Research by Wright and colleagues has shown that even very limited ('token') mobility is enough to deflect low-status group members from engaging in more group-level strategies for social change (Wright, Taylor, & Moghaddam, 1990). In one of their experiments Wright et al. showed that even a very small chance (e.g. 5 per cent) that a low-status group could gain promotion to the high-status group was sufficient to stop people in this group engaging in collective social change strategies that might give a chance for fairer outcomes for all. Intergroup strategies only became likely when no mobility at all was possible. In other words there is a tendency to think selfishly if there is a chance of promotion, however meagre, to the higher status group ('everyone for themselves'). This idea is well illustrated in Reicher and Haslam's (2006) recreation of the classic Stanford Prison Study (see Chapter 8), filmed for the BBC television in the UK. In this experiment one of the most militant and disruptive 'prisoners' became much less militant when there was the prospect of becoming one of the guards (Reicher & Haslam, 2006).

These additional dimensions to social identity theory point to the importance of ideological factors relating to beliefs about the social structure that can moderate our reactions to realistic conflicts and identity threats. Indeed Tajfel referred to an ideological continuum of beliefs about the social structure from complete individual mobility at one end (e.g. the American dream that anyone with the right effort and ability can make it to the top) to social change beliefs at the other (e.g. that 'revolution' is necessary to gain intergroup equality). If we are focused on individual mobility we are not really thinking about our group's disadvantage so much as *my* disadvantage. This is therefore a strategy associated with low identifiers and the individual level. We can now put together the various elements of social identity theory (see Theory Box 14.3).

The idea that we do not *always* discriminate or show prejudice towards outgroups is just as important as explaining discrimination itself. Any complete theory of intergroup conflict needs to be able to explain when and why it occurs, but also *when it does not*. Another approach that emphasizes the possibility that discrimination in favour of one's own group does not always occur is *system*

SOCIAL IDENTITY THEORY: HOW LOW STATUS GROUPS COPE WITH DISADVANTAGE/ IDENTITY THREAT

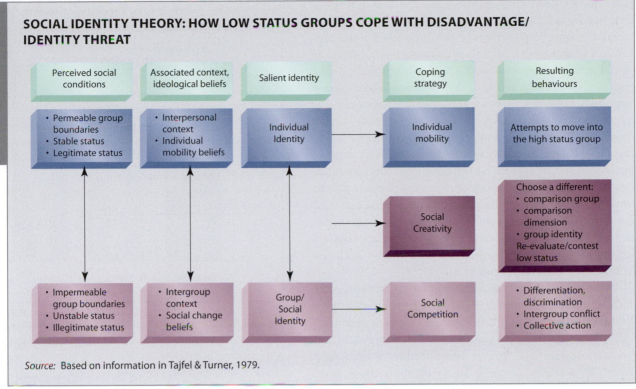

Source: Based on information in Tajfel & Turner, 1979.

justification theory (Jost & Banaji, 1994). This approach goes further than social identity theory in arguing that at least some members of low-status groups are actually *motivated* to justify the system in which differences in status and power exist. Thus, both social identity theory and system justification theory can explain <mark>outgroup</mark>

outgroup bias a tendency to favour the *outgroup* over the ingroup in terms of evaluations or reward allocations.

<mark>bias</mark> towards high-status groups: the tendency to rate the outgroup as better, typically on the status-defining dimension. However, whereas social identity theory predicts this when low status is stable and legitimate, making ingroup bias and claims to high status difficult to sustain (see social reality constraints), system justification theory argues that some low-status group members are *motivated* to defend the existing social hierarchy in the system.

These more integrative and group-level theories of intergroup relations reveal how complex prejudice and discrimination are. As we noted in the introduction, as the prevalence of blatant forms of racism, sexism and prejudice has receded, one of the growth areas of preju-dice research has focused on subtler and even benevolent forms of prejudice (e.g. Glick & Fiske, 1996). According to this view, positive views and stereotypes of outgroups can also be prejudicial, especially when they reinforce the disadvantaged positions of low-status groups. Seeing

black people as great athletes, or women as good cooks and so on, despite being apparently positive, makes such groups prisoners of stereotypes that can prevent them competing in higher-status domains. Nor do these appar-ently positive stereotypes always benefit the group any-way (have you noticed how many top TV chefs are men rather than women?).

Can emotions help to explain the variety and intensity of prejudice?

Intergroup emotion theories   In recent years emotion-based approaches have led the way in explaining the diverse forms of contemporary prejudice. Dijker (1987), who examined the different profiles of prejudice towards different ethnic minority groups in the Netherlands (e.g. Turkish, Moroccans, Surinamese) had shown that there was much to be gained in distinguishing prejudice in terms of the specific emotion reactions that specific out-groups may elicit. A number of approaches followed that used emotion theories to understand the different forms prejudice can take and the different functions it might fulfil. The first and best known is *intergroup emotion theory* (Smith, 1993). Classical emotion theories propose that emo-tions can be characterized not just by different feelings (e.g. anger, fear, contempt), but also in terms of the 'appraisals' that typically produce these states and the 'action tendencies' that follow from them. Appraisals are cognitions that assess the specific relevance of the situation for the perceiver (Lazarus, 1991). Appraisals address such questions as 'Is this person a threat to me?' (a primary appraisal); 'Can I cope with this threat in some way?' (a secondary or coping appraisal). Different appraisals can lead to distinctively different emotions. Emotions also have characteristic 'action tendencies' associated with them (Frijda, 1986). Thus, fear is likely to result in more avoidance, whereas anger is likely to result in approach behaviour (e.g. confrontation, conflict). Appraising another person as a physical threat, especially if the self is weak, may lead to feeling fear, and the action tendency to avoid the group. In contrast, a sense of being wronged by the other, along with an appraisal of strength, may lead to anger, and the action tendency of approach and confrontation.

The new insight was to argue that we could experience such emotions not as individuals but as group members: **group emotions**. Intergroup emotion theory is grounded in the social identity approach, and group identification is generally predicted to intensify these emotions (i.e. the moderation effect of group identification). Thus, if football fans of a rival team threaten me outside the football ground because I am wearing the scarf of my team, this may evoke a group-based emotion (e.g. fear or anger). However, in such cases there is always the possibility that emotions could be appraised and felt personally *or* as a group member ('Is it me, or is it *we* that feel this?'). Group emotions become perhaps more clear-cut when we experience them *vicariously*, on behalf of a fellow ingroup member. This is nicely illustrated in a study by Gordijn, Wigboldus, and Yzerbyt (2001), in which participants at one university (the University of Amsterdam) reacted to news that students at another university in the Netherlands (the University of Leiden) were angry about the plans of the authorities there to introduce stricter study requirements (e.g. higher workload, admissions exams). Only when the Amsterdam students were categorized as *students* (i.e. part of the same category as the Leiden students) did they show high levels of anger at the proposal (i.e. above the scale midpoint). Their anger was reduced when they were part of a *different* category to the victims (i.e. based on university affiliation: Amsterdam versus Leiden; see Figure 14.12). This example shows that group-based emotions are felt on behalf of fellow group members, and not personally, because these plans to change the study requirements did not affect the Amsterdam students directly.

The idea of emotional prejudice is powerful because it allows us to distinguish many different *types* of prejudice that depend on the relation between groups. Prejudices

group emotions
emotions experienced as members of social groups rather than as individuals, reflecting appraisals of events in terms of group level concerns and coping resources.

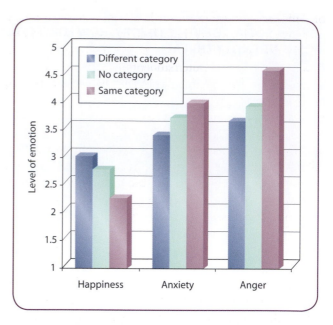

FIGURE 14.12 *Happiness, anxiety and anger experienced by Amsterdam students as a function of the categorization of the students from Leiden (different, no, or same category).*
Source: Gordijn, Wigboldus, & Yzerbyt, 2001, with permission from SAGE PUBLICATIONS LTD.

such as racism might be quite different to sexism and homophobia (try to think of the different appraisals and resulting emotions that might underlie any prejudice in these cases). Simply focusing on negative attitudes does not allow us to distinguish between these types of prejudice. Indeed, there may be many different kinds of racial prejudice, and this will not only depend on features of the target outgroup, but also aspects of the ingroup. Because the members of the ingroup may vary in their appraisals depending on their own characteristics, appraisals and emotions may even vary within the ingroup. For example, women and the elderly may experience more physical threat and therefore feel more fear towards certain groups than do young men.

A further advantage of the group emotion approach to prejudice is that it is better able to explain more extreme and intense forms of prejudice, such as outgroup derogation, than some earlier theories that focus more on explaining ingroup favouritism (Brewer's point about 'outgroup hate'). You could say group emotions put the passion into prejudice. One example of a malicious emotional prejudice is the emotion of 'intergroup *schadenfreude*' (Leach, Spears, Branscombe, & Doosje, 2003). German students will know *schadenfreude* as the pleasure people can experience when they see someone having an accident or slip up (think of those cheesy home video TV shows). However, this pleasure can turn nasty at the intergroup level. Following the writing of the philosopher Nietzsche, Leach et al., argued that experiencing group *schadenfreude* can provide a source of 'imaginary revenge' towards a bitter rival, especially when your own group is threatened by a sense of inferiority (see the discussion of status threats earlier). To test this idea, Leach et al. measured Dutch students' reactions to Germany being knocked out of the World Cup by Croatia in 1998 (a *schadenfreude* opportunity for the Dutch). The sense of inferiority was manipulated in two ways in a 2 × 2 between participants design. The Dutch students were reminded (or not) that the Netherlands had never won the World Cup before (a *chronic* inferiority threat). In a second manipulation they were reminded (or not) of the game in which Brazil had knocked the Dutch team out in this tournament (an *acute* inferiority threat). Dutch pleasure at the German loss (*schadenfreude*) was indeed significantly higher after exposure to both these threats compared to control conditions.

Although, as we noted in the introduction, blatant prejudice towards most groups has thankfully become largely unacceptable in most parts of Europe and elsewhere, there are exceptions, and the intergroup emotion approach can help to account for this. The civil war in the former Yugoslavia took place in the heart of Europe, and

witnessed many extreme forms of hostility, even between people who were previously personal friends and neighbours (Esses & Vernon, 2008). Group-based *contempt* may be particularly relevant in such cases. Contempt is a less constructive emotion than anger; with contempt there is often little hope of reconciliation (Fischer & Roseman, 2007), and it is also associated with a sense of moral superiority by the ingroup and dehumanization of the outgroup (Esses, Veenvliet, Hodson, & Mihic, 2008). Recent research confirms that contempt also predicts more violent, aggressive and extreme behaviour directed at the outgroup than does anger. For example, German students in Hessen threatened with the introduction of study fees from the local state government were more likely to support violent action, such as rioting, the more contempt they felt towards the authorities (Tausch et al., 2011).

We do not need wars or riots to find more extreme examples of prejudice in our midst, however. One group that seems to attract high levels of prejudice across Europe is the Roma people (sometimes pejoratively referred to as 'gypsies') – Figure 14.13. This is especially

(a)

(b)

(c)

FIGURE 14.13(a), (b) and (c) *One group that seems to attract high levels of prejudice across Europe is the Roma people.*

Source: (a) © Kuzma. Used under licence from Shutterstock; (b) © Paula Bronstein. Used under licence from Getty Images; (c) © Plant. Used under licence from Getty Images.

true in Romania, where prejudice and discrimination towards the Roma is blatant and even socially accepted. Why is this so? Intergroup emotion theory might help us to understand why. As we have already seen, anger and fear can underlie distinct forms of emotional prejudice. Roma people seem to attract anger because many see them as not working or contributing to the economy, but depending on state benefits (contempt is also relevant here). However, in Romania, unlike in other countries in Europe, the Roma people also represent a very sizable ethnic group, and consequently they are more likely to be seen as a source of threat (e.g. regarding street crime). This unusual but potent combination of group-based anger *and* fear helps to explain the especially blatant prejudice towards the Roma in Romania.

The intergroup-emotion approach to prejudice has spawned a rich programme of research, and many theoretical frameworks have now emerged to fill in the gaps and explain the wide variety of emotional prejudice (e.g. Cottrell & Neuberg, 2005; Iyer & Leach, 2008; Yzerbyt & Kuppens, 2009). We finally elaborate one approach that has been particularly influential in delineating different forms of prejudice. The *stereotype content model* of Fiske, Cuddy, Glick, and Xu (2002) focuses on two key appraisal dimensions of *competence* and *warmth* that are commonly used to judge others. The warmth dimension relates to how competitive the group is (cold being more competitive). Considering groups as either high or low on each of these dimensions results in four quadrants (see Theory Box 14.4). The combination of high

competence and high warmth is the most positive, and leads to positive emotions like admiration. It tends to be where we find the ingroup, but also respected outgroups (e.g. black professionals). When groups are rated low on both of these dimensions, then disgust, contempt and anger can arise and characterize what Fiske et al. call 'contemptuous prejudice'. A typical group in this cell is homeless people, and also the Roma people from our earlier example. The combination of high warmth and low competence might attract more positive emotions like sympathy and pity. However, this superficially positive reaction conceals the 'paternalistic prejudice'. Benevolent sexism falls into this category, and other examples are prejudice towards the disabled and the elderly. The combination of high competence and low warmth presents a very different kind of threat to the perceiver and one potentially more dangerous. This has been characterized as 'envious prejudice'; anti-Semitic bigotry towards Jews provides a good example of this form of prejudice (Glick, 2008). In the current financial crisis bankers are another example (although their competence could also be questioned!).

Summary

In this section we examined the value of taking a group-level approach to prejudice and discrimination. As group animals who derive many benefits from our memberships of groups there may be good reasons to trust and

---

THEORY BOX 14.4

THE STEREOTYPE CONTENT MODEL

Four types of outgroup, combinations of status and competition, and corresponding forms of prejudice as a function of perceived warmth and competence.

Warmth	Competence	
	Low	High
High	Paternalistic prejudice Low status, not competitive Pity, sympathy E.g. women (benevolent sexism)	Admiration High status, not competitive E.g. ingroup, allies
Low	Contemptuous prejudice Low status, competitive Contempt, disgust, anger E.g. homeless, Roma people	Envious prejudice High status, competitive Envy, jealousy E.g. Jews, bankers

Source: Adapted from Fiske, Cuddy, Glick, & Xu, Copyright © 2002 by the American Psychological Association. Adapted with permission. The use of APA information does not imply endorsement by APA.

favour ingroups over outgroups. Prejudice and discrimination are targeted at outgroups, so it also makes sense to explain these in intergroup terms and by analysing the threats the outgroup can pose. The concept of social identity has been particularly useful, because it refers not only to the target of prejudice, but also captures the sense of self that makes us part of the ingroup. This is not to deny a role for individual explanations of prejudice and discrimination, but they may become less relevant than intergroup factors in intergroup settings. Differences in group identification and group-relevant appraisals also help to explain variations in prejudice at the group level. However, intergroup factors also explain why group members do not always show prejudice and discrimination (e.g. social reality constraints, group norms), and tolerance and fairness can also boost group-esteem, and be strengthened by group identification when normative. With this more optimistic point in mind we now turn to the tricky but important issue of how prejudice and discrimination can be reduced.

PSYCHOLOGICAL INTERVENTIONS TO REDUCE PREJUDICE AND IMPROVE INTERGROUP RELATIONS

If social psychology can provide insights into how prejudice and conflict come about, it should have something to say about how we can reduce them. Indeed, devising interventions has been an important motivation for much of the research on prejudice and intergroup relations already discussed in this chapter, and we now address some of the main approaches. First, we introduce the classic ==contact hypothesis== and assess whether contact with outgroup members reduces prejudice. Second, we discuss the importance of levels of categorization for prejudice reduction interventions such as contact. Third, we describe the psychological processes, such as reduced anxiety and increased empathy, that are involved in prejudice reduction through contact. Fourth, we give an overview of other techniques that can influence these processes. We conclude by discussing the

contact hypothesis intergroup contact will reduce prejudice if it (1) has acquaintance potential; (2) takes place under conditions of equal status; (3) involves cooperation towards a common goal; and (4) takes place in a supportive normative climate.

wider implications of prejudice reduction interventions for intergroup equality and societal change.

The 'contact hypothesis'

How and when does intergroup contact reduce prejudice?

How can we reduce prejudice? This question was first studied in the context of race relations in the United States in the 1930s and 1940s. One of the first social psychologists to address this issue was Gordon W. Allport, whose book, *The Nature of Prejudice* (1954b), proposed that direct, face-to-face contact between members of opposing groups is likely to be the most effective way to reduce prejudice (see Leader in the Field, Gordon W. Allport). Although not the first to suggest this (e.g. Williams, 1947), he provided one of the most detailed accounts of its likely effects.

Allport was careful not to propose that simply bringing people from different groups together would be a solution to intergroup conflict and prejudice. In fact, he pointed to many situations in which proximity to outgroup members might actually intensify conflict and feelings of threat. For example, based on opinion data collected in several areas of Chicago, Allport noted that the attitudes of white Americans became more hostile the closer respondents lived to a residential area that was predominantly black. Thus, simply living close to one another does not reduce prejudice and can even increase it. He contrasted this result with findings from a number

 LEADER IN THE FIELD

Gordon W. Allport (1897–1967) was born in Montezuma, Indiana, as the youngest of four brothers. After graduating from high school second in his class in 1915 he won a scholarship to Harvard University, where one of his elder brothers, Floyd H. Allport (see Leader in the Field, Chapter 1), was already working on his PhD. Allport received his degree in Philosophy and Economics in 1919. After teaching in Istanbul for a year, Allport returned to Harvard to complete his PhD in psychology. Allport is often described as one of the founding fathers of personality psychology, and spent much of his career developing his trait theory of personality. He also made important contributions to the psychology of religion, and to the area of prejudice and intergroup relations, where his ideas inspired empirical research on prejudice reduction. His most significant books include *The Nature of Prejudice* (1954b), *Pattern and Growth in Personality* (1961) and *The Person in Psychology* (1968). Allport's work had a lasting effect on the field of social psychology and he is one of the most frequently cited psychologists. He also had a profound influence on his students, who included Stanley Milgram (see Leader in the Field, Chapter 8), Jerome Bruner, Thomas Pettigrew and Anthony Greenwald (see Leader in the Field, Chapter 7).

of studies that reported positive effects of intergroup contact. For example, in a well-known field experiment, Deutsch and Collins (1951) found that white women living in desegregated (compared to segregated) housing reported more frequent direct contact with their black neighbours, held their black neighbours in higher esteem, were less likely to express negative stereotypes of black people, and were overall much more supportive of integrated housing (75 per cent were supportive, compared to 25 per cent of women living in segregated housing).

These findings encouraged Allport (1954b), and he suggested that 'somewhere there must be a formula' (p. 250) that ensures positive effects of intergroup contact. Based on a review of the evidence available at that time, Allport proposed that contact will only be successful in reducing prejudice when it takes place under certain optimal conditions. Specifically, he suggested that intergroup contact will reduce prejudice if: (1) it has acquaintance potential; (2) it takes place under conditions of equal status; (3) it involves cooperation towards a common goal; and (4) it occurs in a supportive normative climate. We discuss each of these conditions below.

First of all, Allport (1954b) proposed that superficial contact is unlikely to reduce prejudice. Simply being exposed to outgroup members could in fact strengthen prejudice, because negative associations with the outgroup would be frequently activated and guide both perception and behaviour. Rather, Allport suggested, contact should be of sufficient frequency, duration and closeness to allow for true *acquaintance* between members of the different groups. This idea was supported in an additional housing study that examined the attitudes of residents of four other housing projects (Wilner, Walkley, & Cook, 1955). This research demonstrated that favourable racial attitudes were more likely to develop among white residents whose interactions with their black neighbours went beyond casual greetings.

Second, Allport stressed that the intergroup interactions should be structured such that the groups have *equal status* during the contact. He noted that contact between members of high- and low-status groups often takes place in conditions that confirm status hierarchies, for example in situations in which minority group members occupy low-status roles, affirming existing prejudiced views. Equal-status contact would thus ensure that negative stereotypes of the minority group as inferior would be disconfirmed. This condition is likely to have been present in Deutsch and Collins's (1951) housing study, in which black and white families came from similar economic backgrounds. Subsequent experimental studies have confirmed that equal status during contact supports prejudice reduction (e.g. Clore, Bray, Itkin, & Murphy, 1978; Cohen & Lotan, 1995).

A third condition for successful contact involves *cooperation towards a common goal* during contact. Recall the boys camp studies from Sherif et al. (1961), in which the negative attitudes that were created during the experiment were only ameliorated after the two groups worked cooperatively on a series of common goals. Laboratory studies have confirmed the effectiveness of cooperation during contact (e.g. Brown & Abrams, 1986; Ryen & Kahn, 1975), but these also indicate that equal levels of task ability need to be ensured (Cohen, 1984; Slavin, 1978) and require that the outcomes of the cooperation should be positive (Worchel, Andreoli, & Folger, 1977).

Finally, Allport emphasized the importance of the *normative climate* in which the interactions take place. As we know from Chapter 8, social norms exert powerful effects on people's attitudes and behaviour (e.g. Terry & Hogg, 1996). Also recall Pettigrew's (1958) study described above, in which he demonstrated that the social climate in which people lived (i.e. whether or not they lived in a society segregated according to race) was related to their level of racial prejudice. Several laboratory studies have also demonstrated that the amount of prejudice people express is strongly predicted by the (perceived) level of prejudice of other people in that context, especially the level of prejudice of other ingroup members (e.g. Stangor, Sechrist, & Jost, 2001). Social norms are also likely to affect people's attitudes and willingness to interact with outgroup members, and to shape the nature of intergroup interactions. This was again observed in one of the early housing studies. Wilner et al. (1955) noted that the effects of contact were reinforced when the social climate was perceived to be supportive of the contact. For example, of white residents who lived close to black people in integrated housing and reported more intimate contact with their black neighbours, 79 per cent held black people in high esteem when the social norms were viewed as supportive. This figure was reduced to 39 per cent when the social norms surrounding interracial contact were unsupportive (see Figure 14.14).

Allport suggested that a context in which contact is explicitly encouraged by institutional laws and regulations should be particularly conducive to prejudice reduction because authority support establishes norms of acceptance. Deutsch and Collins (1951) showed that the racial policy of the housing development affected perceived social norms; women in the desegregated residences expected their neighbours to approve of friendly interracial interactions, but women in the segregated housing projects expected to be ostracized for such behaviour. Further field studies in a number of different settings confirm the positive effect of institutional support (Landis, Hope, & Day, 1984; Morrison & Herlihy, 1992; Parker, 1968).

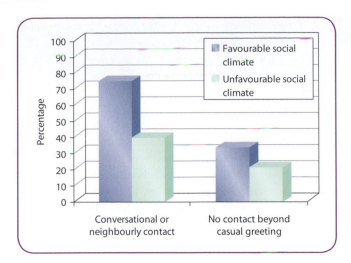

FIGURE 14.14 *Percentage of white residents living near to black residents in integrated housing who held their black neighbours in high esteem, as a function of type of interracial contact and perceived social climate (approval of contact).*

Source: Adapted from Wilner, Walkley, & Cook, 1955, with permission of University of Minnesota Press.

Allport's (1954b) contact hypothesis has been highly influential, inspiring a vast amount of empirical research, as well as the development of his initial propositions into a fully-fledged theory (see Hewstone & Swart, 2011). His ideas contributed to the US Supreme Court's decision to outlaw racially segregated schools, and have been applied widely in the 'real world' as part of interventions to improve intergroup relations. One particularly successful

jigsaw classroom a cooperative teaching method designed to reduce prejudice in diverse classrooms.

intervention is the so-called **jigsaw classroom**, a cooperative teaching method designed to reduce prejudice in diverse classrooms (e.g. Aronson & Patnoe, 1997; see Social Psychology Beyond the Lab 14.1).

So can we be confident that (appropriate) contact reduces prejudice? Early reviews (e.g. Amir, 1976; Cook, 1984) often reached conflicting conclusions. One of the most contentious issues was whether the effects of contact would actually *generalize* from the encountered outgroup members to the outgroup as a whole. This question is crucial when considering the effectiveness of intergroup contact as a tool to improve intergroup relations on a wider scale.

Furthermore, critics were also concerned about the necessity of Allport's (1954b) optimal contact conditions (see also Stephan, 1987): the long list of necessary conditions may be difficult to meet in real life, and contact under less than optimal conditions might increase prejudice. To address these concerns, and to provide a more

systematic review of the contact literature, Pettigrew and Tropp (2006) carried out a meta-analysis of over 500 studies, conducted over five decades, that had examined the relation between intergroup contact and prejudice. They found a highly significant negative relation between contact and prejudice across studies, suggesting that contact is associated with reduced prejudice. In fact, only a small percentage of studies suggested that contact is associated with increased prejudice.

Keep in mind that many of the studies included in the meta-analysis were cross-sectional, meaning that they often used questionnaires which measured levels of contact with outgroup members and attitudes towards the outgroup at the same point in time. In cross-sectional studies, it is never clear whether the negative relation between contact and prejudice indicates that contact reduces prejudice, or whether less prejudiced people simply engage in more contact. To complicate things more, a significant association between two variables can also be due to their correlation with a third, unknown (or unmeasured) variable, which causes variation in both variables. For example, if less-educated people tend to be more prejudiced as well as live in areas where contact is less likely to occur, then education could explain a negative relation between contact and prejudice. Thus, the best way of establishing a causal link between contact and prejudice is to conduct an experiment, either in the field, such as the housing experiments described earlier (Deutsch & Collins, 1951; Wilner et al., 1955) or in the laboratory (e.g. see Wilder's, 1984 study, described later). Longitudinal studies, which measure contact and prejudice at different points in time and examine the relation of contact to *changes* in prejudice, are also helpful to rule out alternative causal relations. A number of such studies have been conducted in recent years (e.g. Swart, Hewstone, Christ, & Voci, 2011; Tausch et al., 2010; Van Laar, Levin, Sinclair, & Sidanius, 2005) and tend to suggest that contact does indeed predict reductions in prejudice over time.

Let us return to the importance of Allport's (1954b) optimal contact conditions. Of the studies included in Pettigrew and Tropp's (2006) meta-analysis, some fully met Allport's optimal contact conditions, others only partially fulfilled them, and some studies did not fulfil them at all. This allowed Pettigrew and Tropp to test how important Allport's conditions are. Interestingly, the significant relation between contact and prejudice emerged irrespective of whether Allport's contact conditions were present, although studies that fulfilled the conditions showed stronger effects. The authors therefore concluded that Allport's original contact conditions are not *necessary* for positive contact effects to occur, but that they are *facilitating* conditions that are likely to make contact more effective.

SOCIAL PSYCHOLOGY BEYOND THE LAB 14.1

THE JIGSAW CLASSROOM

The jigsaw classroom is a learning technique that was developed by Aronson and his graduate students. It was first used in schools in Austin, Texas, in 1971, shortly after schools in the city were desegregated and children from different ethnic backgrounds were for the first time taught together in the same classroom. Aronson was called by a school superintendent just a few weeks after desegregation and asked to help improve the increasingly hostile interracial relations at the school (tension between groups had built up over the weeks, culminating in fights between the youngsters). After observing classes for a few days, Aronson and his students concluded that the hostility between the different ethnic groups was fuelled by a competitive climate in the classroom, where students worked individually and competed for the teacher's approval and grades. They decided that, to improve relations, this competitive climate needed to be transformed into a cooperative one. So they started to develop the jigsaw technique.

This is how it works: a class is divided into smaller task groups of six children from different ethnic backgrounds. A lesson is divided into six parts and each student is assigned one part of the material. For example, the first time the jigsaw technique was applied, fifth-graders were asked to learn about the life of Eleanor Roosevelt, and her biography was divided into six segments (e.g. her childhood, her family life, her work as First Lady and so on). Each student in a group was assigned one of these segments to prepare, and asked to report what they learned to the other members of the group, who did not have any other access to this information. In short, each group member contributed a unique piece of the jigsaw puzzle. The jigsaw process thus facilitates interaction among all students in the class, leading them to value each other as contributors to their common task. It encourages engagement with members of other ethnic groups by giving them an essential part to contribute. Note that this technique fulfils many of Allport's (1954b) conditions for optimal contact: the children work cooperatively towards a common goal, each member is vital to achieving the common task, ensuring equal status

of majority and minority children, and the interaction receives institutional support from the school.

The jigsaw technique has now been used in schools for forty years and its effectiveness has been demonstrated in a number of studies in which children were randomly assigned to either a jigsaw classroom or a traditional classroom (e.g. see Aronson & Patnoe, 1997). These studies have consistently shown that the children taught in jigsaw classrooms not only come to like each other more, but also perform better in exams and have higher self-esteem compared to children taught in traditional classrooms. Moreover, a number of studies have also shown that the children do not just come to like their outgroup classmates more, but also come to like the other ethnic groups in general more – that is, they become less prejudiced. Thus, the effects of the jigsaw classroom *generalize* from individual group members to the outgroup as a whole. We will discuss the important issue of generalization, and the conditions under which it is most likely to occur, in greater detail later in the text.

To learn more about the jigsaw classroom, visit Elliot Aronson's 'jigsaw.org' website.

FIGURE 14.15 *The 'jigsaw classroom' is a cooperative teaching method designed to reduce prejudice in diverse classrooms.*

Source: © Monkey Business Images. Used under licence from Shutterstock.

Pettigrew and Tropp (2006) were also able to address the question of whether contact effects generalize from the encountered group member to the group as a whole. They did this by comparing the effect sizes of contact obtained for ratings of individual outgroup members

with effects sizes obtained for ratings of the outgroup as a whole. Because effect sizes for outgroup ratings were not significantly smaller than effect sizes for ratings of individuals, Pettigrew and Tropp concluded that contact effects typically do generalize. But this does not yet answer the question of *when* the positive effects of contact are most likely to generalize to the outgroup as a whole.

This issue was examined in a study by Wilder (1984). In this study, female students recruited from two rival colleges (Douglas College and Rutgers College) interacted with a member of the other college (who was actually a confederate). The two groups had fairly complementary stereotypes of one another. While Rutgers women viewed Douglas women as being overly concerned with their appearance, conservative and studious, Douglas women perceived Rutgers women as liberal and interested in having fun at the expense of their studies. Moreover, pre-tests confirmed that both groups were biased in favour of the ingroup; they preferred their own college over the other college. The crucial question examined in Wilder's study was not just whether positive contact could affect views of the outgroup, but whether the effects of contact on overall outgroup attitudes would depend on the typicality of the encountered 'exemplar'.

Wilder thus varied whether the outgroup member behaved and dressed in a manner that was either typical or untypical of the outgroup. For example, for participants from Rutgers University, in the typical outgroup member condition, the confederate introduced herself as a Douglas student, was dressed neatly and wore make-up, looked at her diary to check if the experiment clashed with a meeting of her conservative political club and mentioned that she hoped the experiment would be brief because she had a lot of studying to do. She thus fulfilled the stereotypes Rutgers women had of Douglas women (neatness, conservatism and studiousness). When the confederate posed as a Rutgers woman, she wore faded jeans and a baggy T-shirt, looked at her diary to check if the experiment clashed with a meeting of her liberal political club and mentioned that she hoped the experiment would be brief because she needed to get ready for a party. In the atypical condition, the Douglas student dressed and behaved like a typical Rutgers student and vice versa. The interaction consisted of a number of problem-solving tasks during which the confederate then acted in either a positive or negative manner (she supported or rejected the participant's ideas in a number of problem-solving tasks), rendering the contact either pleasant or unpleasant. As one would expect, participants' ratings of the outgroup were more positive when the confederate behaved in a positive and cooperative manner. Importantly, however, the extent to which the contact experience generalized to evaluations of the outgroup as a whole depended on the outgroup member's typicality. Only when the encountered outgroup member was typical did the positive contact experience generalize to the outgroup as a whole (see Figure 14.16).

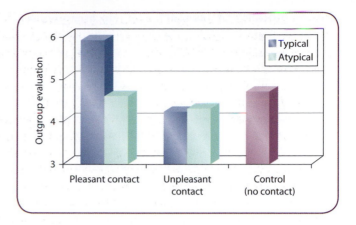

FIGURE 14.16 *Outgroup evaluation as a function of typicality of outgroup member and quality of contact.*
Source: Adapted from Wilder, 1984, with permission from Elsevier.

This finding suggested that contact effects are most likely to generalize to the outgroup when the outgroup member is viewed as representative (cf. Rothbart & John, 1985), for which there is now extensive evidence (see Brown & Hewstone, 2005). We return to the issue of generalization in the next section, where we address the role of levels of categorization in prejudice reduction.

Varying levels of categorization

Does changing the structure of categories reduce prejudice?

The question of whether to approach prejudice from an individual or group perspective also has implications for how best to implement contact as a prejudice-reduction strategy. Researchers have developed three distinct theoretical models that examine the nature of cognitive group representations during contact, and which is more effective. Although each of these models was based on the social identity/self-categorization approach (Tajfel & Turner, 1979; Turner et al., 1987), each draws quite different conclusions about how contact should be structured in order to reduce prejudice. Keep in mind that while these models were initially concerned with intergroup contact interventions, many of the ideas and questions put forward by these approaches apply more widely, in particular to the question of how relations between majority and minority groups should be managed in society. For example, is intergroup harmony in diverse societies best achieved by taking a 'colour-blind' approach and treating everyone as an individual? Or should we promote multiculturalism in which group differences are acknowledged and appreciated? As you will see, the answer is not that simple.

Three models of contact The **decategorization** approach (e.g. Brewer & Miller, 1984) recommends reducing the salience of intergroup boundaries during contact by inducing two cognitive processes: 'differentiation' (making distinctions between individual outgroup members); and 'personalization' (stressing the uniqueness of each individual outgroup member). This can be achieved by promoting opportunities to get to know each other and by encouraging the disclosure of intimate personal information during contact (e.g. Ensari & Miller, 2002). This approach is consistent with Allport's (1954b) suggestion that contact should be intimate and allow for real acquaintance with outgroup members. Brewer and Miller suggested that the attention to idiosyncratic information would result in less attention being paid to category-based stereotypical information. They believed that the repeated use of individual information would reduce the usefulness of the category in future interactions, and thereby have generalized effects (less prejudiced reactions to outgroup members in general).

> **decategorization**
> reducing the salience of intergroup boundaries through personalized contact; attention to idiosyncratic rather than category-based information about outgroup members should, over time, reduce the usefulness of the category, and reduce prejudice.

Support for the effectiveness of personalized contact comes from a series of experiments (e.g. Bettencourt, Brewer, Croak, & Miller, 1992) in which experimentally created groups were brought together to work on a cooperative task. Participants were instructed to focus either on personal characteristics (person-oriented condition) or on the task at hand (task-oriented condition). These studies demonstrated that participants in the person-oriented condition show less bias in the allocation of rewards to ingroup and outgroup members compared to participants in the task-oriented condition. This was true even when participants were asked to allocate rewards to an outgroup member whom they had not encountered before and who was presented on a video screen. This finding provided evidence that the effects of personalized contact generalize to the outgroup as a whole.

The idea that personalized contact reduces prejudice is also supported by research on intergroup friendships. Pettigrew (1997) demonstrated that people who had an outgroup friend expressed less prejudice towards the outgroup as a whole than did people who only had an outgroup neighbour or co-worker, but not a friend. Compared to other forms of contact, friendship also emerged as the strongest predictor of reduced prejudice in Pettigrew and Tropp's (2006) meta-analysis.

The decategorization approach suggests that people should interact with members of other groups as individuals and refrain from using social categories. But is this realistic? As we discussed earlier, groups fulfil important human needs, and social identities form valued parts of the self, so people might be reluctant to give up or ignore their group memberships. Rather than aiming to eliminate the use of social categories altogether, the **recategorization** approach (also referred to as the *common ingroup identity model*; Gaertner, Mann, Murrell, & Dovidio, 1989; see also Chapter 10) proposes that prejudice can be reduced by transforming cognitive group representations from two groups ('us' and 'them') to one inclusive social entity ('we').

> **recategorization**
> recommends replacing salient ingroup–outgroup distinctions at a subordinate level with a common ingroup identity at a superordinate level that includes both former ingroup and outgroup members.

Several studies have now shown that recategorization results in reduced ingroup bias (see Gaertner & Dovidio, 2000). Interestingly, a study by Gaertner et al. (1989) showed that recategorization reduces bias in a different way than decategorization (i.e. conditions that encourage participants to interact as individuals). This is shown in Figure 14.17. While decategorization and recategorization resulted in similar amounts of reduction in *bias* (see Figure 14.17a), decategorization reduced bias by making evaluations of former *ingroup* members *less* positive, while recategorization reduced bias by making evaluations of former *outgroup* members *more* positive, compared to the control condition in which participants interacted as members of different groups (see Figure 14.17b).

Although the empirical support for the benefits of recategorization is wide-ranging, many of the studies testing this model were conducted in the laboratory. This raises the question of whether a superordinate identity can overcome powerful ethnic and racial categorizations that are an important part of people's self-concepts in the 'real world'. Would you be willing to give up your national identity in favour of a broader category such as 'European'? A number of authors have suggested that there may be strong resistance to changes in category boundaries, especially when the groups are engaged in hostilities, or when they differ in size, power or status. Remember our discussion earlier about the importance of identifying with optimally distinct groups and the perils of distinctiveness threat. Minority group members may be particularly reluctant to accept a superordinate identity if it is dominated by the majority group (Simon, Aufderheide, & Kampmeier, 2001). For example, as we discussed earlier, East Germans ('Ossis') would be more reluctant to identify with Germans than would West Germans ('Wessis'). The *categorization* model (also called **mutual differentiation** model; Hewstone & Brown, 1986) presents a viewpoint that differs sharply from the decategorization and recategorization approaches. This model suggests that, rather than

> **mutual differentiation**
> (or *categorization approach to improving intergroup relations*) making group affiliations salient during contact to give members of the respective groups distinct but complementary roles.

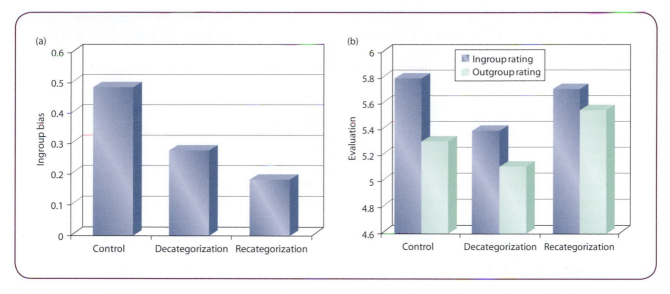

FIGURE 14.17(a) and (b)   *(a) Ingroup bias as a function of categorization; (b) Ingroup evaluation and outgroup evaluation as a function of categorization.*

Source: Adapted from Gaertner et al., 1989. Copyright © 2002 by the American Psychological Association. Adapted with permission. The use of APA information does not imply endorsement by APA.

reducing the salience of the original categories, group affiliations should be made salient during contact. This encourages the problematic relationship between the ingroup and outgroup to be addressed directly, reducing the risk that the outgroup members encountered are psychologically distanced from the outgroup, which could inhibit generalization (Rothbart & John, 1985).

But how should positive inter*group* contact be structured? Hewstone and Brown (1986) recommend that, in order to maintain social identities and positive distinctiveness, but to avoid intergroup comparisons in the interaction, the contact situation should be structured so that members of the respective groups have distinct but complementary roles to contribute towards the achievement of a common goal. Mutual strengths should be recognized and equally valued, which can be achieved by ensuring that the ingroup and the outgroup are rated on independent dimensions (Mummendey & Schreiber, 1984). Thus, this approach does not seek to change the original category structure, but aims to transform the level of interdependence between the two groups from negative to positive (i.e. from a competitive to a more cooperative relationship). Both the role of category salience in the generalization of contact effects and the advantage of letting participants work on different task dimensions have been empirically supported (Brown & Wade, 1987; Deschamps & Brown, 1983; Van Oudenhoven, Groenewoud, & Hewstone, 1996). Nonetheless, this approach also has drawbacks. Making category memberships salient could lead to biased perception and behaviour in the contact situation, and might therefore reinforce stereotypical

perceptions (Neuberg, 1996). An emphasis on group memberships may also create anxiety in the contact situation and thus risk the generalization of negative affect to the outgroup as a whole (Greenland & Brown, 1999; Islam & Hewstone, 1993a; Stephan & Stephan, 1985).

Integrative models   The three theoretical models of categorization during contact (decategorization, recategorization and mutual differentiation) make different suggestions as to how contact should be structured to be most beneficial. Each of the models is supported by empirical evidence and each has advantages and disadvantages. But which model should be applied? Rather than viewing these models as competing positions, researchers have begun to see them as complementary approaches and have started to integrate them.

For example, Pettigrew (1998) combined them into a three-stage longitudinal model. He suggested that, because initial intergroup interactions are often formal and characterized by anxiety, decategorization should optimally happen first. Personalized contact would reduce this initial anxiety and lead to interpersonal liking. The social categories should be made salient in the next step in order to achieve generalization of positive affect to the outgroup as a whole. Recategorization into a superordinate category may then happen later, leading to maximum reduction in prejudice. Pettigrew (1998) realized, however, that the final stage of recategorization may be difficult if original group memberships are not easily abandoned. In this case, group members may prefer to maintain mutual recognition as separate groups, but also to acknowledge that they share

THE BENEFITS OF DUAL CATEGORIZATION

Hornsey, M. J., & Hogg, M. A. (2000). Subgroup relations: A comparison of mutual intergroup differentiation and common ingroup identity models of prejudice reduction. *Personality and Social Psychology Bulletin, 26*, 242–256.

Introduction

In this article, Hornsey and Hogg wanted to examine what happens when naturalistic groups are asked to forsake a valued subgroup identity in favour of a superordinate identity. They were sceptical about the applicability of a common ingroup identity in the real world and hypothesized that making a superordinate category salient at the expense of a valued subgroup identity is likely to result in distinctiveness threat. This would consequently lead to greater bias towards the outgroup in order to reassert the subgroup identity. They proposed a new integrative model that suggested that dual categorization (making both the subgroup and superordinate group identity salient at the same time) would be the most effective way of reducing bias. The research was conducted in the context of different subject groups within a university in Australia.

Method

Participants

Participants were 191 undergraduate students ($N = 119$ females, $N = 72$ males) who studied either a maths/science ($N = 83$) or humanities ($N = 108$) subject. They participated individually.

Procedure and design

Participants were told that the local government was planning to build a recreational park and it was their task to choose ten out of a list of 30 objects and services that they considered to be essential for its success. In an individual condition there was no mention of any category (i.e. neither the subgroup nor the superordinate identity was salient); participants were told that the government was interested in the opinions of *ordinary individuals*. In the superordinate category condition participants were told that the government was interested in the opinions of *university students* and was planning to compare them to the opinions of town planners. A piece of cardboard with their university logo formed a visible reminder of their superordinate category. In the subordinate group condition, participants were told that the government was interested in comparing the responses of *humanities and maths/science students*. They were asked to circle their faculty area and, depending on their subject, to use either a blue or red

pen to complete the questionnaire. In a final condition, participants were given the instructions for the superordinate condition followed by the instructions for the subordinate condition, making both their subcategory and the superordinate category salient. This yielded a 2 (subgroup: salient versus not salient) $\times$ 2 (superordinate group: salient versus not salient) between-subjects design.

Measures

Participants completed a manipulation check (they indicated the extent to which their thoughts were drawn to their faculty and their university membership while completing the task to assess the salience of the two categories), a measure of their identification with their subgroup (i.e. their faculty) and a measure of ingroup bias at the subgroup level (the extent to which they would like to work with members of their own and the other faculty in an alleged subsequent task).

Results

A 2 (subgroup: salient versus not salient) $\times$ 2 (superordinate group: salient versus not salient) between-subjects analysis of variance revealed a significant interaction between subgroup salience and superordinate group salience. Figure 14.18a shows that the highest level of bias occurred in the condition in which the superordinate, but not the subordinate, group was salient. Participants also showed stronger identification with their subgroup in this condition (see Figure 14.18b). In contrast, participants in the condition in which both the superordinate and the subordinate category were salient showed relatively low levels of bias.

Discussion

Categorizing people exclusively at the superordinate group level (as recommended by the recategorization model) can threaten the distinctiveness of subgroup identities. In this example, people may not want to be seen simply as 'students', but wish to hold on to their valued identities as either maths/science or humanities students. This can result in a need to reassert the original group boundaries by increasing identification and expressing bias in favour of their subgroup. This distinctiveness threat can be avoided when the original subgroup identities are preserved within the common superordinate identity (i.e. dual categorization).

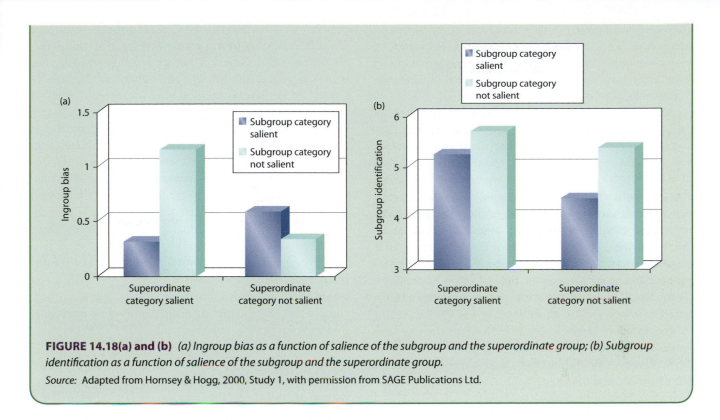

FIGURE 14.18(a) and (b) *(a) Ingroup bias as a function of salience of the subgroup and the superordinate group; (b) Subgroup identification as a function of salience of the subgroup and the superordinate group.*

Source: Adapted from Hornsey & Hogg, 2000, Study 1, with permission from SAGE Publications Ltd.

a common group identity at a superordinate level (e.g. the English, Welsh and Scots who are all also British). This has been referred to as a *dual identity* (Gaertner & Dovidio, 2000) or *dual categorization* (Hornsey & Hogg, 2000) model. A dual identity model, in which both the original subgroup identities and a superordinate identity are made salient, has now been supported in several experimental studies (see Research Close-Up 14.2). Dual identification is the most beneficial strategy for members of minority groups, resulting, for example, in less 'acculturative stress' (the stress of moving to a different culture) among immigrants (Berry, Kim, Minde, & Mok, 1987) and less ingroup bias (Gaertner, Rust, Dovidio, Bachman, & Anastasio, 1996; González & Brown, 2006). It seems to be less successful, however, in reducing prejudice among members of numerical majority groups (González & Brown, 2006). Figure 14.19 presents a schematic representation of the different models.

Psychological processes involved in intergroup contact and prejudice reduction

Which psychological processes play a role in prejudice reduction?

Understanding the psychological processes involved in prejudice reduction is important because it can enable

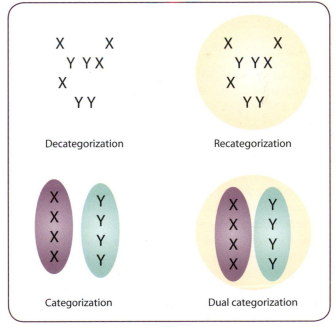

FIGURE 14.19 *Schematic representations of the decategorization, recategorization, categorization and dual categorization models.*

Source: Adapted from Brewer, 2003, with permission.

researchers to design optimal interventions that target these processes specifically. In the case of face-to-face intergroup contact, which may often be difficult to achieve in real life, such knowledge can help to identify alternative or supplementary interventions with similar psychological effects (see below). Researchers examining prejudice reduction generally, and intergroup contact specifically, have therefore paid a great deal of attention to the issue of *process* in the recent years.

Allport (1954b) did not really specify the psychological 'driving forces' of prejudice reduction through contact. He suggested, however, that negative stereotypes and attitudes towards outgroups are often due to a lack of information or erroneous information about a group, and that contact would provide an opportunity to correct these assumptions. Research on knowledge acquisition as a potential explanatory variable (or 'mediator') has found some limited support for this idea (Stephan & Stephan, 1985). While increased knowledge about the outgroup explains at least part of the reduction in prejudice (Pettigrew & Tropp, 2008), more recent work has emphasized the importance of affective processes. Contact seems to impact more strongly on affective than on cognitive variables, having a greater effect on attitudes than stereotypes (Tropp & Pettigrew, 2005), and it seems to have its effects predominantly via its impact on affective processes (Brown & Hewstone, 2005).

Much of this research has focused on **intergroup anxiety**, a negative affective state felt when anticipating or experiencing contact with an outgroup. Intergroup anxiety stems from the expectation of negative consequences for oneself during intergroup interactions, such as embarrassment or rejection, and may be exacerbated by negative outgroup stereotypes, a history of intergroup conflict or a high ratio of outgroup to ingroup members (Stephan & Stephan, 1985). Because anxiety is accompanied by a narrowed attention focus and information-processing biases, it can undermine the positive effects of contact (e.g. Wilder & Shapiro, 1989). High levels of intergroup anxiety may also lead to the avoidance of contact altogether (Plant & Devine, 2003; Shelton & Richeson, 2005) or render any interaction awkward (Shelton, 2003). Because this negative affective state is linked to outgroup members, it is strongly associated with negative outgroup attitudes. Much research has shown that successful contact helps to overcome these apprehensions; reduced anxiety is a key mediator in the negative relationship between contact and prejudice (e.g. Islam & Hewstone, 1993).

In addition to reducing negative anxiety, contact can also promote positive affective ties and increase empathy. Empathy can broadly be defined as the experience of understanding or sharing the emotional state of another

> **intergroup anxiety** a negative affective state experienced when anticipating future, or experiencing actual, contact with an outgroup member, stemming from the expectation of negative consequences for oneself during intergroup interactions.

person (see Chapter 10), and includes both emotional (empathic concern) and cognitive (perspective taking) facets (Davis, 1994). Research has shown that empathy has beneficial effects on attitudes and behaviour (Stephan & Finlay, 1999). Several studies have shown that contact positively affects both cognitive and affective components of empathy, which partially explains how contact has an effect on prejudice reduction (Harwood, Hewstone, Paolini, & Voci, 2005; Tam, Hewstone, Harwood, Voci, & Kenworthy, 2006). A meta-analysis specifically on mediators of contact effects highlighted the role of increased empathy and reduced intergroup anxiety as the key mechanisms through which intergroup contact reduces prejudice (Pettigrew & Tropp, 2008).

A final mechanism we consider here is that of **ingroup reappraisal**. Pettigrew (1997) suggested that meaningful intergroup contact can help people to realise that ingroup norms, customs and lifestyles are not inherently superior to those of outgroups. In fact, this process would be expected to reduce prejudice towards *all* outgroups, leading to a wide generalization of contact effects. Several studies support this idea. For example, Pettigrew (1997) demonstrated that respondents who had contact with members of nationally represented minority groups (e.g. Germans' contact with people of Turkish descent) were also more accepting of other national groups that are less represented in that country (e.g. Algerians; see also Van Laar et al., 2005). Pettigrew (2009) labelled this form of generalization the 'secondary transfer effect' of intergroup contact. The 'transfer' is also not confined to outgroups that are similar to each other (e.g. across national groups, in the case above). Tausch et al. (2010) showed, for example, that contact across the sectarian divide in Northern Ireland (i.e. Catholics meeting Protestants and vice versa) promoted not only more positive attitudes towards the religious outgroup, but also towards racial minorities. Tausch et al. reported secondary transfer effects across multiple intergroup contexts, and showed that they were not due to socially desirable responding (i.e. someone giving politically correct positive responses to one outgroup also giving such positive responses to other outgroups). They also provided longitudinal evidence for this secondary transfer effect, showing that contact with the other community predicted reduced racial prejudice over time.

In sum, research has successfully identified some of the key psychological processes involved in how intergroup contact reduces prejudice. As we will see next, these processes can also be set in motion by techniques other than direct face-to-face contact.

> **ingroup reappraisal** realization that ingroup norms, customs and lifestyles are not inherently superior to those of outgroups; this process is implicated in the generalization of positive contact effects to other outgroups.

Other prejudice-reduction techniques

Can prejudice be reduced by interventions other than contact?

Although face-to-face intergroup contact has been most widely researched as a prejudice-reduction intervention, actually arranging contact can involve serious practical obstacles. Different social groups often live highly segregated lives. This is particularly the case when there is a history of conflict and when there are strong social norms against intergroup interactions. Social psychologists are aware of these obstacles and have developed a number of approaches that do not require direct interaction, utilizing channels such as the Internet or other media to achieve widespread exposure (Amichai-Hamburger & McKenna, 2006).

Providing stereotype-disconfirming information about the outgroup Following Allport's (1954b) view that prejudice can result from erroneous stereotypes, research has investigated the effects of providing different types of stereotype-disconfirming information on outgroup perceptions. Several models of stereotype change have been tested: a *bookkeeping model*, whereby stereotype change happens gradually via the accumulation of stereotype-inconsistent information; a *conversion model*, which envisages radical change in response to a single piece of dramatic disconfirming information; and a *subtyping model*, whereby stereotype-inconsistent information creates a subtype and the outgroup stereotype becomes more complex (Weber & Crocker, 1983). Subtyping is also a means by which stereotypes are maintained in the face of disconfirmation, because a new subtype can be viewed as unrepresentative of the group, leaving the stereotype more or less unchanged (see Hewstone, 1994, for a review). Overall, there is some evidence that stereotypes change according to the bookkeeping model (e.g. the more interesting accountants we meet, the less we stereotype accountants as boring), and the conversion model (e.g. one really engaging accountant can sometimes change our view of the entire group), but the evidence is strongest for subtyping (e.g. if we encounter several accountants who are interesting people, but also love playing with numbers – and are therefore typical – then we are most likely to revise our prejudice that all accountants are boring; e.g. Johnston & Hewstone, 1992).

extended contact hypothesis mere knowledge that an ingroup member has a close relationship with an outgroup member can improve outgroup attitudes.

Extended contact The **extended contact hypothesis** (Wright, Aron, McLaughlin-Volpe, & Ropp, 1997) proposes that the *mere knowledge* that an ingroup member has a close relationship with an outgroup member can improve outgroup attitudes. Thus, people can experience intergroup contact indirectly (see Dovidio, Eller, & Hewstone, 2011, for a recent review). In one experimental study, Wright et al. (1997) first created negative intergroup attitudes by letting two groups in the laboratory compete with each other. They then asked *one* member from each group to engage in friendship-building exercises with the other group. The two participants believed that this exercise was part of another study. It involved disclosing increasingly personal information to each other, an exercise that was previously shown to result in high interpersonal closeness among strangers (Aron, Aron, Tudor, & Nelson, 1991). The remaining participants were asked to complete a number of unrelated questionnaires during that time. After the task was finished the groups were reunited and the experimenter encouraged participants to tell each other about the tasks they had just performed. Wright and colleagues found that outgroup attitudes improved after the friendship-building task, even among participants who themselves had *not* participated in the friendship building task. Thus, they provided evidence that extended contact can indeed improve attitudes. But *how* or *why* does extended contact reduce prejudice? Wright and colleagues suggested that one important mechanism concerns perceived group norms. As mentioned earlier, group norms do not always support intergroup interactions. Observing successful intergroup interactions, however, signals that engaging with outgroup members is acceptable to both the ingroup and the outgroup. Learning about intergroup contact would then also reduce the observers' anxiety about interacting with outgroup members in the future.

The extended contact hypothesis has now received substantial support in a variety of intergroup contexts. Evidence has also accrued about how and when it works: extended contact effects are mediated by reduced intergroup anxiety (e.g. Paolini, Hewstone, Cairns, & Voci, 2004), and by changing both ingroup and outgroup norms (e.g. Turner, Hewstone, Voci, & Vonofakou, 2008). Extended contact seems to be most effective for people who have few opportunities for direct contact (e.g. Christ et al., 2010). It has also been successfully applied in school settings: school children who learned about an intergroup friendship via a story expressed less prejudice (Cameron & Rutland, 2006). Extended contact can also happen via the media; Schiappa, Gregg, and Hewes (2005) showed that watching television programmes that portrayed intergroup contact (e.g. the American TV show *Will and Grace*, which portrays a gay man as a main character) reduced levels of prejudice towards the target groups featured.

Perspective-taking and empathy induction Interventions that attempt to promote perspective-taking and empathy typically involve role-playing and the presentation of information from the outgroup's perspective. For example, Clore and Jeffery (1972) instructed participants to assume the role of a disabled person by travelling about in a wheelchair for an hour. This exercise significantly improved attitudes toward disabled people, an effect that was still found four months later. Galinsky and Moskowitz (2000) presented their participants with a photo of an elderly person and asked them to imagine what a day in their life would be like. Compared to the two control groups, which received no further instructions or were asked to suppress the stereotype, participants in the perspective-taking condition showed reduced stereotyping of elderly people in a subsequent task (see also Finlay & Stephan, 2000).

The wider implications of prejudice reduction

Does prejudice reduction result in more equal societies?

It is important to evaluate the effects of prejudice-reduction interventions not just in terms of whether they successfully reduce prejudiced attitudes, but also in terms of whether they promote good intergroup relations more generally. An implicit assumption in much of the research we have talked about in this section has been that reducing prejudice among members of the socially dominant group would result in reduced discrimination against members of minority or disadvantaged groups, thereby increasing group equality (see Wright & Lubensky, 2009). Consequently, this research has predominantly examined the effects of interventions on members of advantaged groups, and used prejudiced beliefs and feelings as the primary outcome variables. Less is known about how these interventions affect members of minority groups. Given both that attitudes do not always predict behaviour (see Chapter 6) and that dominant groups are motivated to maintain their power (Sidanius & Pratto, 1999), we might be sceptical about the effects of contact and prejudice reduction on wider societal change. Indeed, some researchers have argued that reducing prejudice does not necessarily address or eliminate intergroup inequality (Jackman & Crane, 1986). As we have emphasized earlier in our discussion of social identity theory, members of low status groups also have an important role to play in bringing about societal change (e.g. through collective action). Thus, conflict, such as the current uprising in the Arab world, is therefore not always a bad thing and can lead to real societal change in the long run.

Recently a number of researchers have started to consider these issues. This research suggests that the link between reduced prejudice and political attitudes and actual behaviour is not clear-cut. For example, Dixon, Durrheim, and Tredoux (2007) found that while white South Africans were in favour of equality *in principle*, they tended to oppose interventions that would help to achieve this goal in practice, such as school quotas, affirmative action and land restitution. They termed this phenomenon the **principle–implementation gap.** Indeed, white South Africans' contact with black South Africans had a weaker effect on attitudes towards specific pro-black policies than it did on reducing prejudice towards black people.

> **principle–implementation gap** acceptance of racial equality in principle is accompanied by resistance to specific policies that would bring about such racial equality.

Experimental research assessing the causal effect of positive intergroup contact on attitudes and actual discriminatory behaviour also suggests that, although positive contact improves advantaged group members' attitudes towards the disadvantaged, this does not reduce discrimination (Saguy et al., 2009; see Research Close-Up 14.3). Ironically, positive contact experiences can also lead members of *dis*advantaged groups to become *less* aware of intergroup inequalities (Dixon, Tropp, Durrheim, & Tredoux, 2010; Saguy et al., 2009), to be less supportive of policies aimed at promoting equality (Dixon et al., 2007), and to be less willing to engage in collective action on behalf of their group (Wright & Lubensky, 2009).

Overall, these recent findings suggest that research on interventions to improve intergroup relations needs to go beyond using prejudice reduction as the sole indicator of the success of the intervention, and to assess more consequential outcomes, such as actual behaviour and support for policies. In other words actions (continued discrimination) speak louder than words (reduced prejudice). Moreover, interventions should also address the needs of members of disadvantaged groups to ensure that interventions do not compromise realizing their group goals.

Summary

In this section we have shown that contact between members of opposing groups is an effective tool for reducing prejudice, especially if it takes place under favourable conditions. We presented three cognitive models of intergroup contact that make different suggestions about how contact should be structured to achieve generalized prejudice reduction; recent integrations of these models seem to be particularly effective. We also demonstrated that prejudice reduction involves a number of cognitive

IRONIC CONSEQUENCES OF INTERGROUP CONTACT

RESEARCH CLOSE-UP 14.3

Saguy, T., Tausch, N., Dovidio, J. F., & Pratto, F. (2009). The irony of harmony: Intergroup contact can produce false expectations for equality. *Psychological Science, 20,* 114–121.

Introduction

The authors suggested that beyond improving attitudes toward the outgroup, positive contact can also reduce disadvantaged-group members' awareness of intergroup inequalities and raise their expectations that the advantaged group would treat them fairly. These expectations could, in turn, reduce disadvantaged group members' motivation to engage in actions aimed at achieving social change toward group equality. An experiment examined the causal effect of positive intergroup contact (i.e. that emphasized commonalities between groups rather than group differences) on (a) disadvantaged-group members' attitudes toward the outgroup, (b) attention to inequality, and (c) expectations of fair treatment by the outgroup. The researchers also measured advantaged-group members' outgroup attitudes, awareness of inequality and their actual resource allocation between groups.

Method

Participants

Participants were 210 undergraduate students (*N* = 126 females, *N* = 84 males). Each experimental session involved a mixed-gender group of six students.

Procedure and design

Participants were randomly assigned to one of two three-person groups. They were then told that there was another group and that each group would be asked to make one of two decisions: one group (the powerful, advantaged group) would be asked to decide how to distribute ten credits (a valued resource) between the groups and the other group (the disadvantaged group) would be asked to decide how to distribute 10 marbles (not valued) between the groups. Participants were then told that, before making their decisions, the two groups would have the chance to meet. To manipulate type of contact, the groups were either asked to discuss things the groups had in common in the session (e.g. 'Similar steps the groups went through in this study'; the *commonality-focused contact condition*) or aspects of the experiment on which the groups differed (e.g. 'Differences between the tasks the groups will do next'; *differences-focused*

contact condition). Thus, the study involved a 2 (group position: advantaged versus disadvantaged) × 2 (contact type: commonality-focused versus differences-focused) factorial design.

Measures

The participants then completed a number of questionnaires measuring their awareness of the intergroup inequality and their attitudes towards the other group. Participants in the disadvantaged group were also asked to estimate the number of credits they expected to receive from the advantaged group. Finally, members of the advantaged group were asked to distribute the ten credits between the two groups.

Results

As expected, both the advantaged and the disadvantaged groups were less aware of intergroup inequality in the commonality-focused contact, compared to the difference-focused contact, condition (see Figure 14.20a). In line with predictions, intergroup attitudes were more positive in the commonality-focused contact condition. Disadvantaged group members expected to receive significantly more credits from the advantaged group in the commonality-focused compared to the differences-focused condition. There was, however, no significant difference between the two contact conditions in terms of the actual distribution of credits by the advantaged group, who discriminated against the disadvantaged group in each case. Figure 14.20b shows the number of credits expected and the number of credits received.

Discussion

This study demonstrated that although positive commonality-focused contact improves intergroup attitudes this does not translate into less discrimination. Rather, commonality-focused contact made both groups *less aware* of the intergroup inequality, and raised the disadvantaged groups' hopes about the credits they would receive, an expectation that proved to be false. In fact, the advantaged group discriminated in favour of their ingroup in both contact conditions. A second, correlational study investigated whether these

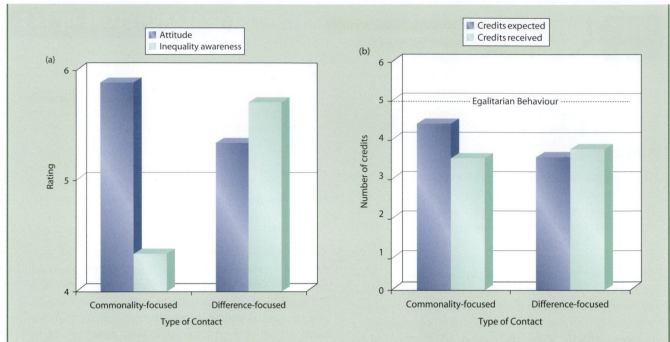

FIGURE 14.20(a) and (b) *(a) Outgroup attitudes and awareness of inequality across groups as a function of contact type; (b) Number of credits (out of 10) expected by the disadvantaged group and number of credits received from the advantaged group as a function of contact type.*

Source: Adapted from Saguy, Tausch, Dovidio, & Pratto (2009). The irony of harmony: Intergroup contact can produce false expectations for equality. *Psychological Science, 20,* 114–121. © SAGE Publications, reprinted with permission.

expectations for equal treatment have implications for disadvantaged group members' support for social change. This study surveyed Arabs in Israel (a socially disadvantaged group), and showed that more positive intergroup contact with Jews (the advantaged group) was associated with perceptions of Jews as more fair, which in turn predicted decreased support for social change. It is therefore critical to recognize that intergroup harmony per se does not necessarily translate into intergroup equality.

and affective mechanisms, such as increased knowledge, reduced intergroup anxiety, increased empathy and a reappraisal of the ingroup. We discussed how interventions other than direct intergroup contact, such as perspective-taking exercises or extended contact, can also promote these processes. We concluded this section by suggesting that interventions to improve intergroup relations need to go beyond measuring prejudice to assess the consequences of interventions for intergroup equality more generally.

CHAPTER SUMMARY

- *What is prejudice?* Prejudice is traditionally defined as a negative attitude towards an outgroup, but can also emphasize ostensibly positive aspects of a group. It typically functions to the perceiver's advantage, even when it implies a positive perception of the outgroup.

- *How do we explain prejudice?* Prejudice can be explained at both individual and group levels. At the individual level, personality and individual difference approaches help to explain variation in prejudice between people. Group-level explanations are well placed to explain the social nature of prejudice.

- *Is there a prejudiced personality?* People who are prejudiced against one outgroup are often prejudiced against others. Right-wing authoritarianism and social dominance orientation have been linked to prejudice. However, social norms play a role in shaping prejudice, and individual difference variables are themselves influenced by the social context.

- *How can cognitive processes explain prejudice?* Cognitive processes can explain how we come to see members of a social category as very like each other, and how prejudiced beliefs might form, but motivational processes can also be important in inhibiting prejudice, and also in causing it.

- *Can intragroup processes account for prejudice towards outgroups?* It may make good (evolutionary) sense to favour members of our own group, but on its own this does not provide a strong explanation of why we might actively derogate outgroups.

- *Can conflicts of interest at the intergroup level be reduced to individual self-interest?* Realistic conflicts of interest between groups provide a powerful explanation of intergroup hostility, but ingroup bias still occurs in minimal groups, and expectations of ingroup reciprocity cannot explain why people maximize the difference in reward allocations between groups.

- *What (other) threats to group identity from an outgroup can help to explain discrimination?* Threats to the ingroup include threats to its very existence, threats to group-esteem, threats to the values of the group, and threats to group distinctiveness.

- *So are prejudice and discrimination between groups inevitable?* Not at all. Intergroup factors can also help to explain the *absence* of discrimination (e.g. under conditions of legitimacy, and social reality constraints, or when it goes against group norms and threatens the image of the ingroup).

- *What do group emotions add to our understanding of prejudice?* Group emotions specify threats to the ingroup, through appraisals of how the outgroup affects it, and the appropriate response. The role of group identification in how intensely emotions are felt helps to explain variation in prejudice. Group emotions (e.g. contempt, *Schadenfreude*) can also help to explain the more extreme forms of prejudice.

- *How can prejudice be reduced?* Intergroup contact is one of the most-widely applied interventions to reduce prejudice. Contact effects are most likely to generalize to the outgroup as a whole when the encountered group members are typical of the outgroup.

- *Does changing the level of categorization reduce prejudice?* Changing group representations in different ways (through decategorization, recategorization, and mutual differentiation) has been shown to reduce prejudice, but in different ways. A dual-categorization approach (making both the original categories and a superordinate category salient) is an effective way of reducing prejudice while avoiding the pitfalls of distinctiveness threat.

- *Can prejudice be reduced by interventions other than direct contact?* Prejudice reduction can also be set in motion by other techniques, such as presenting stereotype disconfirming information, extended contact, and inducing empathy and perspective taking.

- *Does prejudice reduction result in more equal societies?* Recent findings suggest that this is not necessarily the case. Ironically, positive contact experiences can lead members of disadvantaged groups to become *less* aware of intergroup inequalities and less willing to engage in collective action on behalf of their group.

SUGGESTIONS FOR FURTHER READING

Brown, R. (2010). *Prejudice: It's social psychology* (2nd ed.). Oxford: Blackwell. A detailed overview of intergroup phenomena and their explanations.

Dovidio, J. F., Gaertner, S. L., & Saguy, T. (2009). Commonality and the complexity of 'we': Social attitudes and social change. *Personality and Social Psychology Review, 13,* 3–20. Examines the role of collective identities in the development of prejudice and inequality and in interventions to improve attitudes towards other groups and in inhibiting or facilitating social change.

Ellemers, N., Spears, R., & Doosje, B. (2002). Self and social identity. *Annual Review of Psychology, 53,* 161–186. Provides an overview of different identity threats and coping strategies that develop and extend the social identity approach.

Hewstone, M., Rubin, M., & Willis, H. (2002). Intergroup bias. *Annual Review of Psychology, 53,* 575–604. A comprehensive overview of the literature on ingroup bias.

Otten, S., Sassenberg, K., & Kessler, T. (Eds.). (2009). *Intergroup relations: The role of motivation and emotion.* New York: Psychology Press. This volume contains a number of state-of-the-art summaries of research programmes, some of which are referred to in this chapter (e.g. Yzerbyt & Kuppens on group-based emotions and prejudice, and Spears et al. on the minimal group paradigm).

Scheepers, D., Spears, R., Doosje, B., & Manstead, A. S. R. (2006b). The social functions of in-group bias: Creating, confirming, or changing social reality. In W. Stroebe & M. Hewstone (Eds.), *European review of social psychology,* (Vol. 17, pp. 359–396).

Hove, UK: Psychology Press. Provides an analysis of the different functions served by ingroup bias, contrasting low and high status groups.

Son Hing, L. S., & Zanna, M. P. (2010). Individual differences. In J. F. Dovidio, M. Hewstone, P. Glick, & V. M. Esses (Eds.), *Handbook of prejudice, stereotyping and discrimination* (pp. 163–178). London: Sage. A good overview of current thinking on the role of individual differences in prejudice.

Tausch, N., & Hewstone, M. (2010). Intergroup contact. In J. F. Dovidio, M. Hewstone, P. Glick, & V. M. Esses (Eds.), *Handbook of prejudice, stereotyping and discrimination* (pp. 544–560). London: Sage. A recent comprehensive overview of research on intergroup contact.

Tiedens, L. Z., & Leach, C. W. (Eds.). (2004). *The social life of emotions*. Cambridge, MA: Cambridge University Press. An edited collection of various perspectives on the field of intergroup emotions, also as applied to prejudice.

15 Cultural Social Psychology

PETER B. SMITH

Source: © Press Association Images.

KEY TERMS

- acculturation
- acquiescent responding
- back-translation
- better than average effect
- bicultural identity
- bicultural identity integration
- cognitive style
- cross-cultural replication
- cultural masculinity–femininity
- culture
- display rules
- eco-cultural theory
- embeddedness versus autonomy values
- hierarchy versus egalitarianism values
- individualism–collectivism
- mastery versus harmony values
- nation-level factor analysis
- power distance
- self-construal
- uncertainty avoidance

CHAPTER OUTLINE

ROUTE MAP OF THE CHAPTER

When the same social psychology study is repeated in different parts of the world it often comes up with different results. This chapter provides a model of cultural differences that can explain why this is not just a failure of experimenters' expertise. Drawing on studies that have been discussed in many of the earlier chapters in this book, it shows that cultural variations can benefit social psychologists rather than handicap them. By identifying the social behaviours that are particularly salient in different parts of the world, we can take account of causal factors that have been given insufficient attention within mainstream social psychology. We can also test which social psychological phenomena are universal and which occur only in some parts of the world.

INTRODUCTION

Wen Hua Wang's family moved to the United Kingdom when she was young. She quickly formed a bond with two other Chinese girls at school and they all did well. Wen Hua gained admission to a respected university. She finds the courses very interesting, attends all the lectures and takes copious notes. She wonders why the British students are not so committed to learning, and why some of them speak to the professor in such familiar and disrespectful ways. On group projects, she is reluctant to speak up and it seems difficult for her to find a role for herself. She would like to speak more with the professor because she is sure that he will be able to help her.

- Why is Wen Hua so strongly motivated?
- Why does she think that familiarity with the professor is disrespectful?
- Why is she reluctant to take the lead in groups?
- Why does she think the professor is the best source of help?

Wen Hua is experiencing a mild case of what has been colloquially described as 'culture shock'. In the early years of her life she has been socialized to think of herself and others around her in ways that differ from those among whom she now finds herself. Her attitudes, values and beliefs were typical of those found in Chinese societies, but now they are more unusual. She feels a strong bond between herself and those close to her, especially her family. When she attends to her studies she does so because she feels that her success will enhance the reputation of her family as much as her own reputation. She places a high value on establishing harmonious relations with others. In situations where she is unsure how to behave, she keeps to herself for fear of embarrassing others or losing face by showing ignorance or tactlessness. In the presence of those who are older or more senior than her, she feels it is important to give them respect.

This chapter will first provide some examples of what has happened when researchers have attempted to repeat social psychological studies, typically conducted originally in North America, in other parts of the world. There can be many reasons why different results are obtained in any one instance, but overall there is good reason to believe that cultural differences are involved. Psychologists have been interested in culture since the earliest beginnings of the discipline. Wilhelm Wundt established one of the world's first psychology laboratories in Leipzig, Germany in 1879. Between 1911 and 1920, he published ten volumes entitled *Völkerpsychologie* (normally translated as 'folk psychology'), which included

discussion of differing cultures around the world. More recently psychologists have discussed cultural differences in terms of variations in attitudes, values and beliefs. These variations can contribute to our understanding of the concept of culture if we take them into account. In the remainder of this chapter, we examine studies that are relevant to issues that have been discussed in preceding chapters, particularly in relation to social cognition, self-concept, personal relationships, group behaviour and intergroup relations. In each of these areas we will show how attention to cultural differences can enrich our understanding of social psychological processes.

CULTURE AND CULTURAL DIFFERENCES

What is culture and why should we study it?

The opening chapter of this book discusses some of the best-known and frequently discussed social psychology experiments. Most of these experiments were conducted in the United States and some in the United Kingdom. What would happen if they were repeated somewhere else in the world? We can answer this question, because there have been attempts at **cross-cultural replication** of all these studies, some of them many times. Consider first an early study of group dynamics that was published by Schachter (1951). In this study, Schachter set up a series of student discussion groups. Unknown to most group members, each group contained an accomplice of the experimenter. The accomplice (the 'deviate') was instructed to take up a position opposed to the views of the majority and stick to his position. Schachter predicted that the deviate would over time receive less and less attention and be rejected by the group, which is just what he found among his US respondents.

> **cross-cultural replication** a test of whether the results of a study are the same if it is repeated as exactly as possible in another cultural context.

A few years later, Schachter and seven colleagues (1954) reported on the results of a slightly different version of this study that was conducted in seven different European nations. In this case, groups of 11-year-old schoolboys were asked to decide which of several model aeroplanes to build. The results were complex and not at all as the experimenters had predicted. The groups in France did almost all reach agreement and did reject the deviate, as predicted. However, many of the groups in Belgium, West Germany (as it was then known) and the UK did not reach agreement at all, and ratings on a 7-point scale as to whether the deviate should leave the group

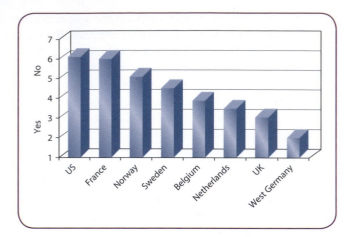

FIGURE 15.1 *Should the deviate stay in the group?*

Source: Based on Schachter et al., 1954, with permission from SAGE Publications Ltd.

varied greatly between nations, as shown in Figure 15.1. Furthermore, in a minority of the British and German groups, the deviate's viewpoint was accepted, so that he had in fact become the leader. There are many possible reasons for the variations in these particular results. For instance, the accomplices may not all have behaved in exactly the same way. The US study differed from the European ones, but even within Europe there were large differences. We need to see whether they are typical.

Figure 15.2 shows that some other classic social psychological studies have also yielded differing results when conducted in other parts of the world, while others have yielded evidence of universal effects. For instance, the studies by

Ekman and his colleagues (1987) have established that six basic emotions are conveyed by the same facial expressions in all locations that were sampled. In most cases, an effect somewhat similar to that reported in the US *is* obtained, but its magnitude varies by location. Part of the reason for this variability is that it is extremely difficult to set up exactly the same study in different parts of the world. The local context can give differing meanings to the same procedures. There may also be something unusual about these particularly famous studies. To test this possibility, two Israeli psychologists selected six lesser-known studies that had nonetheless been published in top US journals, and attempted to replicate their results in Israel (Amir & Sharon, 1987). Five of the original studies had used students and one had used school students. Amir and Sharon replicated all six studies using similar populations. In some cases the replication sample was smaller, in others it was larger. The original six US studies had yielded 37 significant effects. Amir and Sharon also found 37 significant effects, but only 25 of them replicated the US results. Twelve were new effects not found in the US. So, of the 49 results overall, only 25 were common to both nations. Clearly, there is a substantial problem, particularly bearing in mind that there are many nations in the world that are more different from the US than is Israel.

Defining culture

To understand the reasons why results vary between locations even when differences in the methods and samples used are minimized, we need a definition of

Classic study	Effect found	Replications	Effect found
Lewin, Lippitt, & White (1939) US boys clubs	Democratic leadership preferred	Meade (1985) Boys clubs in India, Hong Kong, Hawaii, US	Autocratic leaders preferred in Hong Kong and in India
Asch (1956) US students and adults	37% conformity	Studies in 16 other nations (see Bond & Smith, 1996)	From 6% conformity in France to 58% among Fijian Indians
Milgram (1963) US adults	65% fully obedient	Studies in eight other nations (see Smith & Bond, 1998)	From 16% to 95% fully obedient
Ekman (1972) Students in 5 nations	Correct identification of 6 basic emotions from US photos	Ekman et al. (1987) 14 cultural groups sampled using photos drawn from all locations	Anger, joy, sadness, disgust, surprise and fear are portrayed in the same way everywhere
Zimbardo, Maslach, & Haney (2000) US students role-playing a prison	Destructive authority achieved	Reicher & Haslam (2006) UK adults	Destructive authority overthrown

FIGURE 15.2 *Replications of some famous studies.*

Source: Based on Smith, Bond, & Kağıtçıbaşı, 2006.

culture a social system that is characterized by the shared meanings that are attributed to people and events by its members.

culture. A good definition is one that focuses on the way in which people give meaning to what goes on around them, because any particular social practice can have different meanings in different locations. For instance, if I maintain very steady eye contact with you, or come very close to you, that would be interpreted as friendly in some parts of the world and as rude or hostile in others. So if we are trying to understand social behaviours in different parts of the world, we do best to focus on the meanings attributed to events. As Rohner (1984) put it, culture is 'the totality of... learned meanings maintained by a human population, or by identifiable segments of a population, and transmitted from one generation to the next' (pp. 119–120).

As discussed in other chapters of this book, people interpret the meanings of the behaviours that they encounter. A social system can be said to have a culture when the members of that system *agree* with one another about the meaning of what is going on around them. The concept of culture can be applied to families, teams, organizations and nations. Within larger social systems we would not expect to find a total consensus on meanings, and there will typically be subcultures defined for instance by age, gender, social class, location, profession, religion and ethnicity. Despite this it can still be useful to consider nations as cultures, because there are numerous historical, political, linguistic and climatic factors that encourage a continuity of shared perspective. One of the pioneers of cultural psychology, Hofstede has an apt and more incisive definition of culture as '...the collective programming of the mind that distinguishes the members of one category of people from another' (Hofstede, 2001, p. 9). This is not a reformulation of F. Allport's (1924)

'group mind' theory (which argued for the existence of a group consciousness or a collective mind, as separate from the minds of the individuals who comprise the group; see Chapter 1); it is a statement that all of us are engaged in a continuing negotiation of meaning with those around us.

Nations as cultures

It is relatively easy to see how the actions of one person can influence the emergent culture of a newly formed small group. When we think about the cultures of larger social entities, it is clear that the majority of influence will be in the other direction; the individual will be encouraged to assign meanings to events through interactions with others who have a shared history of exposure to particular types of climate, child-rearing, educational system, political history, media exposure and employment opportunities. All of these elements may change over time, but they will not change fast because so many people are elements within the system that they comprise. The proposal that cultural variations around the world are derived from the demands imposed by differing types of physical environment is known as **eco-cultural theory**. The way in which variations in physical environment can lead to different types of subsistence, which in turn generate different types of institution, different socialization practices, and therefore different psychological attributes is summarized in broad outline in Theory Box 15.1. We examine more specific aspects of eco-cultural theories later.

eco-cultural theory a theory that proposes that different forms of culture have arisen as adaptations to differing environmental challenges to survival.

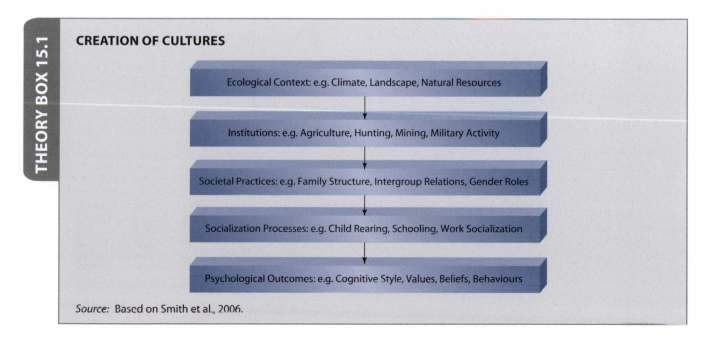

THEORY BOX 15.1

CREATION OF CULTURES

Ecological Context: e.g. Climate, Landscape, Natural Resources

↓

Institutions: e.g. Agriculture, Hunting, Mining, Military Activity

↓

Societal Practices: e.g. Family Structure, Intergroup Relations, Gender Roles

↓

Socialization Processes: e.g. Child Rearing, Schooling, Work Socialization

↓

Psychological Outcomes: e.g. Cognitive Style, Values, Beliefs, Behaviours

Source: Based on Smith et al., 2006.

Measuring culture

If culture is considered as a shared set of meanings, then we need to measure it by focusing on the ways in which we assign meanings to events. In other words, we must examine the attitudes, values and beliefs that colour our everyday interpretation of events. Hofstede (1980) pioneered the measurement of culture at the nation level (see Leader in the Field, Geert Hofstede). He reasoned that a nation's culture cannot simply be considered as the average of the attributes of those who are members of that nation. Within a nation, some individuals are more powerful than others, and differing interpretations of events may also be complementary to one another. We therefore need to know how the distribution of values and beliefs tapped by a survey relate to one another *within the nation as a whole*, not within each individual. Hofstede drew on a very large databank of opinion survey items completed by IBM employees in 50 nations, and three regions where there was insufficient data to compute separate scores for neighbouring nations. He averaged all of the responses to each individual item within each sample and then conducted a **nation-level factor analysis**. This yielded four factors that could be used to characterize the nations and regions included within his databank.

Hofstede named his dimensions of culture as **individualism–collectivism**, **power distance**, **uncertainty avoidance** and **cultural masculinity–femininity**. In individualistic nations, people are more likely to think of themselves as autonomous individuals, whereas in collectivist nations people are more likely to think of themselves in terms of their long-term group memberships. In nations high on power distance there is greater acceptance of hierarchy. In nations high on uncertainty avoidance there is low tolerance of risk and uncertainty. Cultural masculinity–femininity refers to the clarity of the distinction between gender roles: at one extreme, in nations high on cultural femininity, there is a low distinction between gender roles, whereas at the other extreme, in more masculine nations, there

nation-level factor analysis an analysis across many nations of data in which the mean response for each survey item for each nation is treated as the unit of analysis.

individualism–collectivism individualist nations are those in which people describe themselves in ways that emphasize their autonomy from others; collectivist nations are those in which people describe themselves in ways that emphasize their links with others.

power distance the extent to which hierarchy and deference are accepted within a nation.

uncertainty avoidance the extent to which a nation is averse to risk and uncertainty.

cultural masculinity–femininity the extent to which gender roles in a nation are seen as differentiated (masculinity) or similar (femininity).

is sharper distinction between what are thought of as masculine roles and feminine roles. Few people like the terms that Hofstede selected to name this last dimension, but these are the terms that he used.

The individualism–collectivism dimension has had a very strong impact on the development of cultural psychology, and it also has particular relevance to the theme of this chapter. Figure 15.3 shows the scores for individualism–collectivism assigned to nations by Hofstede (1980). US, Australia, UK, Canada and the Netherlands scored highest on individualism, whereas Guatemala, Ecuador, Panama and Venezuela scored highest on collectivism. In-between it is shown that Spain, Turkey, Greece and Portugal were found to be the four most collectivist nations from within Europe.

There are two important points to note about these scores. Firstly, the five most individualistic nations shown in Figure 15.3 are some of the nations in which most social psychological research is undertaken. Counting the first authors of papers cited in the previous edition of this textbook as an approximation, we find that 79 per cent are from the US, 7 per cent from the Netherlands, 6 per cent from the UK and 6 per cent from Germany. Studies by authors from the remaining 190 countries in the world comprise 2 per cent of the total! These figures are somewhat influenced by the fact that this textbook was produced in Europe. A US textbook would be even more focused on US studies. In whichever country you are reading this book, the majority of the material reported is still based on US research and theories, because that is where most research and theorizing on social psychology is done. Moreover, wherever they are conducted, many of the studies are based on student samples. As Henrich, Heine, and Norenzayan (2010) put it, the samples are WEIRD – that is

 LEADER IN THE FIELD

Geert Hofstede (b. 1928) graduated as a mechanical engineer from Delft Technical University in the Netherlands and worked in industry for 10 years, before completing his PhD in social psychology at the University of Groningen. He subsequently joined IBM Europe, where he founded and managed their personnel research department. After leaving the company he worked in a series of management schools during the 1970s and prepared his classic work, *Culture's Consequences*, which was published in 1980. Based on the survey responses of 117,000 IBM employees worldwide, the book provided the first empirically based classification of dimensions along which the nations of the world could be classified. More recently he has held positions at Maastricht University and Tilburg University, where he established a programme of cross-cultural training based on his cultural dimensions. His later more popular work, *Cultures and Organizations*, has been published in 16 languages. His publications have been cited by other authors more than 5000 times, a figure surpassed by very few psychologists and by none from Europe.

Most individualist				Most collectivist	
91	USA	54	Israel	26	Malaysia
90	Australia	51	Spain	25	Hong Kong
89	UK	48	India	23	Chile
80	Canada	46	Argentina	20	West African region
80	Netherlands	46	Japan	20	Singapore
79	New Zealand	41	Iran	20	Thailand
76	Italy	39	Jamaica	19	El Salvador
75	Belgium	38	Brazil	18	South Korea
74	Denmark	38	Arab region	17	Taiwan
71	Sweden	37	Turkey	16	Peru
71	France	36	Uruguay	15	Costa Rica
70	Ireland	35	Greece	14	Indonesia
69	Norway	32	Philippines	14	Pakistan
68	Switzerland	30	Mexico	13	Colombia
67	Germany	27	Yugoslavia	12	Venezuela
65	South Africa	27	Portugal	11	Panama
63	Finland	27	East African region	8	Ecuador
55	Austria			6	Guatemala

FIGURE 15.3 *Nation-level index of individualism–collectivism (Hofstede, 1980). Scores range from 0 (collectivist) to 100 (individualist).*

to say, they are often composed of people who are White and Educated who live in nations that are Industrialized, Rich and Democratic. Does this matter? It would matter if the theories and research methods used have some implicit assumptions within them that derive from the individualistic cultures of the nations in which they were formulated. The theories would be likely to fail when tested in locations where these assumptions were no longer valid.

A second important point is also clear from Figure 15.3. When people think of cultural psychology, they most often envisage a contrast between Western nations and those in some other part of the world, typically Japan or China. The table shows that within Europe there are both individualist nations and more collectivist nations. Furthermore, Japan was shown to be only moderately collectivist. China (along with other nations in which IBM was not represented at the time of Hofstede's survey) was excluded, but was later assigned a score of 20 (Hofstede, 2001). His data indicated other cultural contrasts within Europe. For instance, the Nordic nations scored further toward the 'feminine' end of his cultural masculinity–femininity dimension than any of the other nations that he sampled. This indicates a relatively strong emphasis on the *quality* of interpersonal relations (short- or long-term), but should not be confused with collectivism, which is more to do with long-term commitment to a particular group.

Hofstede's dimensions have been influential, but the actual measures that he used were limited by his reliance on a questionnaire that had been designed for other purposes and would no longer be regarded as satisfactory. His measure of individualism–collectivism comprised just four items concerning respondents' emphasis on different types of work motivation. Later researchers have been able to develop improved measures. Schwartz (1992, 1994, 2004) asked samples of students and of schoolteachers in more than 75 nations to rate how much each of a series of values is a guiding principle in their life. Each value was represented by a short phrase. He was concerned that even after translation into local languages the words used in Hofstede's survey may not have had exactly the same meaning in each culture. Schwartz therefore first did a

LEADER IN THE FIELD

Shalom H. Schwartz (b. 1936) grew up in the United States and received his PhD in social psychology from the University of Michigan in 1967, subsequently teaching in the sociology department of the University of Wisconsin. In 1979, when many of Israel's leading researchers were moving to universities in the United States, Schwartz moved in the reverse direction to the department of psychology at the Hebrew University in Jerusalem. During the 1970s and 1980s he was a pioneer of research on prosocial and altruistic behaviour. Subsequently he focused on investigating the fundamental structure of human values, testing his model in more than 70 countries. He has studied the antecedents and consequences of individual differences in value priorities and the relations of cultural dimensions of values to societal characteristics and policies. His value measures are now part of the ongoing, biannual European Social Survey.

separate individual-level study in each nation that he sampled, to determine which values consistently correlated with each other in the same way and could therefore be considered to have equivalent meanings (Schwartz, 1992; see Leader in the Field, Shalom H. Schwartz).

This approach was based on Schwartz's theoretical proposition that people everywhere will develop values relating to three basic problems, namely *survival as an individual, coordination of social interaction* and the *welfare and survival of groups*. He predicted that in all cultures people's values will cluster together in relation to these three needs, although cultures will vary in how strongly different values are endorsed. His individual-level studies confirmed

embeddedness versus autonomy values characteristic of a culture in which relations with one's long-term membership groups are prioritized, rather than emotional and intellectual separateness from others.

hierarchy versus egalitarianism values characteristic of a culture in which inequality is accepted and deference is given to one's seniors, rather than granting equality to all people.

mastery versus harmony values characteristic of a culture in which achievement is sought and esteemed, rather than harmony with nature.

that most values of individuals can be classified into the same set of clusters no matter where in the world the data are collected. Next, he conducted a nation-level analysis of his data in the same way as Hofstede had done, using only the values that he had found to have consistent meanings. Three dimensions emerged, each of which matches one of the three basic needs that he had identified. He named these as **embeddedness versus autonomy**, **hierarchy versus egalitarianism** and **mastery versus harmony**, as shown in Figure 15.4.

Finally, Schwartz (2004) used these dimensions to plot the comparative positioning of the nations that he had sampled. Examples of the nations scoring highest and lowest on each dimension are shown in Figure 15.5 (Schwartz, 2004). Schwartz's

contrast between values that he summarized as embeddedness and values summarized as autonomy parallels Hofstede's dimension of individualism–collectivism. The individualistic European nations in his sample are here shown as endorsing autonomy values. In contrast, the US scores higher on mastery. His contrast between hierarchy and egalitarianism values parallels Hofstede's dimension of power distance. Schwartz's third dimension, mastery versus harmony, is not, however, close to Hofstede's remaining dimensions. See also Social Psychology Beyond the Lab 15.1, which illustrates a practical application of value differences.

These two large-scale research projects have provided what one might consider as a provisional psychological map of the world. Each project used different methods at different times and with different respondents who were drawn from a different range of nations, but the dimensions that they identified correlate quite well with each other. They provide us with a basis from which we can begin to investigate why studies in different parts of the world can yield different results. However, we cannot treat the scores for individual nations like an independent variable in an experiment. A nation's culture is both a cause and an effect of the psychological processes that occur within it, as shown in Theory Box 15.2. We can use the scores to interpret the results of studies, but we need to return to experimental methods before we can be sure about causal relationships. Before looking at some cross-cultural studies, we must first consider some distinctive problems of research method that cross-cultural researchers have needed to overcome.

Overcoming methodological challenges

In looking at cross-cultural studies, it is useful to evaluate them in terms of how well they have overcome six key difficulties that researchers face. Firstly, we must consider the problem of language. Where respondents use

Basic need	Group survival	Social coordination	Individual survival
Dimension	Embeddedness versus autonomy	Hierarchy versus egalitarianism	Mastery versus harmony
Typical values endorsed at positive pole	Social order National security Respect tradition Honouring elders	Social power Wealth Authority	Daringness Ambition Choosing one's own goals Social recognition
Typical values endorsed at negative pole	Curiosity Enjoying life Pleasure Freedom	Honesty Equality Helpfulness Social justice	Protecting the environment Unity with nature World at peace

FIGURE 15.4 *Values defining nation-level dimensions identified by Schwartz (1994).*

Source: Based on information reported in Schwartz (1994).

Dimension	Embeddedness versus autonomy	Hierarchy versus egalitarianism	Mastery versus harmony
Highest scoring nations	Ghana Nigeria South Africa Philippines Malaysia	Uganda Zimbabwe Namibia Thailand Ghana	China Zimbabwe Korea Hong Kong USA
Lowest scoring nations	Switzerland (Francophone) Canada (Francophone) France East Germany West Germany UK Denmark Austria Netherlands	Italy Spain Sweden Norway Finland West Germany East Germany Slovenia	Italy Spain Sweden Norway Finland Estonia Slovenia West Germany

FIGURE 15.5 *Nation-level scores based on Schwartz's value survey (2004). Note: The German data were collected before reunification.*
Source: Based on data reported in Schwartz (1994).

back-translation
translation of a research questionnaire that has already been translated from one language to a second language back into the original language by a translator who has not seen the original version.

different first languages, accurate translation is essential. To be sure of adequacy, a **back-translation** of a translated questionnaire into the original language must be made by a second translator who has not seen the original. Use of local languages enhances validity. If English language versions are used with respondents for whom English is not their first language, their responses are found to become more like those obtained from respondents whose first language is English (Harzing, 2005). The use of English encourages people to respond in ways that they have learned are typical of English speakers, rather than in ways that are more typical of their own culture. This is an instance of unintended experimental priming.

Secondly, even after successful translation, measures may have different psychometric properties in different contexts, because words often have different emotional overtones in different languages. For instance, in Schwartz's studies it emerged that the meaning of 'true friendship' varies across cultures (Schwartz & Sagiv, 1995). For instance, in Japan, 'true friendship' was seen as associated with 'belonging', whereas in Western samples it was associated with 'mature love'. Thus, the Japanese associate friendship with inclusion, but Westerners link it with intimacy. A good study is one that can demonstrate the reliability and validity of its measures (see Chapter 2) in each of the cultures that is sampled.

Thirdly, respondents to questionnaires in different parts of the world differ systematically in how they use response scales. A particularly acute problem in cross-cultural studies is that in some cultures it is normative to express one's opinions by agreeing or disagreeing, while in others it is desirable to take a more neutral stance. If researchers do not control for differences in **acquiescent responding**, comparisons of mean scores from different cultures will be meaningless. Both

acquiescent responding a tendency for a respondent to agree with all items on scales measuring attitudes, beliefs or values, even those that contradict one another.

THEORY BOX 15.2

Socialization Processes

Cultural Values and Beliefs

Individual and Collective Behaviours

Source: Based on Smith et al. (2006).

SOCIAL PSYCHOLOGY BEYOND THE LAB 15.1

ADVERTISEMENTS SUSTAIN CULTURAL VALUES

Cultures are defined in terms of shared meanings. Advertisers are also interested in creating shared meanings when they seek to establish brand images for their products within particular markets. How do these two fields of interest relate to one another? Within the US, Aaker (1997) identified the types of brand images that exist by asking respondents to evaluate advertisements on rating scales representing personality dimensions. She found five types of US brand images. These could be summarized as sincerity, excitement, competence, sophistication and ruggedness. Ruggedness was defined by US raters in terms of 'outdoorness', masculinity, toughness and 'westernness'. Examples would be advertisements for Levi jeans, Harley-Davidson motorcycles and Marlboro cigarettes.

Aaker, Benet-Martínez, and Garolera (2001) replicated this study in Japan and in Spain. In Japan, four of these images were also found, but there were no products emphasizing ruggedness. Instead, there was a brand

image that focused on peacefulness. The advertisements illustrating peacefulness were characterized by Japanese raters as shy, mild mannered, peaceful, naïve, dependent and childlike (Figure 15.6a). In Spain, sincerity, excitement and sophistication were again found, but the competence and ruggedness images were replaced by a brand image focused on passion. The advertisements illustrating passion were characterized by Spanish raters as fervent, passionate and intense, but also spiritual, mystical and Bohemian (Figure 15.6b). The authors argue that there is a reciprocal relationship between culture and brand images. Exposure to particular brand images can be thought of as a series of attempts at priming by advertisers. Where the prime accords with one of the types of value preferences that Schwartz identified in different nations, the advertisement is more likely to be effective. Repeated use of brand images by advertisers will also influence the maintenance or change of cultural values.

(a)

(b)

FIGURE 15.6(a) and (b) *Cultural icons exemplifying culturally distinctive forms of advertisements: (a) The Japanese geisha, exemplifying mildness, dependence and peacefulness; and (b) Flamenco dancing, a blend of passion, intensity and spirituality.*
Source: (a) © Serika; (b) © Mad Pushup. Both images used under licence from Shutterstock.

Hofstede and Schwartz used such controls, so we can trust their mean scores. Figure 15.7 illustrates the extent of cultural variation in acquiescence along 5-point rating scales in a study that sampled 43 nations. The scores for acquiescence were created by averaging each respondent's ratings on 68 scales, where it is logically impossible for respondents to endorse all the survey items. A score above 3.0 indicates a tendency to agree with items, while one below 3.0 indicates a tendency to disagree with them. The mean scores from UK and Thailand differ by .9, which is 20 per cent of the entire scale, large enough to distort the meaning of any uncorrected comparison between nations.

A fourth priority is to be aware of the cultural subjectivity of the labels that we use for the topics that social psychologists study. For instance, in Chapters 1 and 8 we follow the usual practice of describing Asch's (1956) line judgement study as a study of conformity. Yet the phenomenon actually being studied is behavioural change in a setting in which other people have given obviously incorrect answers. Within a collectivist culture, that same behaviour might be described as tact or sensitivity in saving others from embarrassment, rather than as conformity.

Fifthly, while it is convenient to study cultural differences by sampling people from different national cultures, we need to be aware that nations differ from one another in many ways. We should be most impressed by studies that have included a check on whether the respondents in the study do actually endorse the values or other measures of cultural orientation that are typical of their nation. This is equivalent to the manipulation check that experimentalists employ. We should be even more impressed by studies that show that the differences found between two samples disappear if the measure of cultural orientation is statistically controlled. This would indicate that we can not only describe cultural differences, but that we can also explain how they bring about their effects. Several studies of this kind are discussed later in this chapter.

Finally, you will have noted in earlier chapters that psychologists try where possible to use experimental methods, so that that they can establish causal relationships between their variables. There are practical limitations on the extent to which cultural differences can be studied experimentally, but the increasing number of *bicultural* people in the world has opened up the possibility of experimental cultural studies. We can test whether the behaviour of bicultural individuals changes in the ways that our theories predict when they are primed to focus on one or the other of their alternative cultural identities. Studies of this type have high potential in testing the cultural validity of social psychological theories.

Summary

Most social psychological studies have been conducted in just a few rather distinctive nations of the world. Results from studies done elsewhere can test and improve the universal validity of social psychological theories.

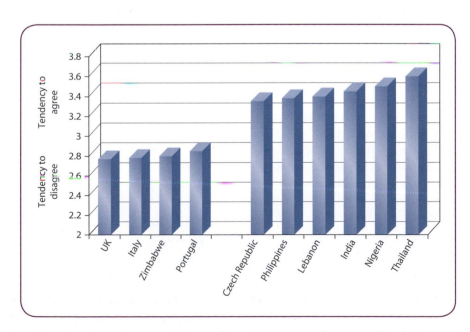

FIGURE 15.7 *Highest and lowest scoring nations on a measure of acquiescent responding to questionnaires.*
Source: Based on Smith, 2004, with permission from SAGE Publications Ltd.

Cultural differences between large-scale groupings such as nations can be mapped by examining patterns of shared values and beliefs. These maps can be used to test why the results of studies vary. Valid cross-cultural studies must overcome methodological challenges posed by differences between languages, response styles and the multiple ways in which nations differ from one another.

CULTURE AND COGNITION

What are cognitive styles and how are they related to culture?

In the preceding section we considered the contrast between individualistic cultures and collectivistic cultures. There are many factors that can contribute to the creation and maintenance of this contrast. For instance, individualistic nations are predominantly rich, whereas collectivistic nations have until recently been less so (Hofstede, 2001). In this section we focus on basic psychological processes that may also underlie this contrast. Nisbett (2003) has proposed that members of Western nations tend to process information in analytic ways, whereas members of East Asian nations tend to process information in holistic ways. What do we mean by the terms *analytic* and *holistic* in this context? Faced with some situation or problem, an analytic thinker would seek to identify a key element in the situation and focus on its effect on what goes on around it (for instance, the behaviour of a star football player). A holistic thinker would be more likely to give equal attention to each of the elements in the situation, and their interrelationships (for example, the way that the team as a whole played). A psychological experiment is a good example of the analytic perspective, because one key factor is identified and manipulated to see its effect. Nisbett reasoned that these differing **cognitive styles**

cognitive style people with an analytic style focus on the main element within information that they are processing; people with a holistic style focus on the relations between the different elements in information that they are processing.

have arisen because of the differing environments in which people have lived over past centuries. Historically, survival in some environments has been dependent upon skills in hunting, which is typically an individual activity that requires picking out targets from their background. In other environments, survival has depended on agriculture, which involves rapidly harvesting crops at particular times and then storing them for later consumption. The success of this procedure is dependent on collaborative working (Berry, 1976). As we noted earlier, theories that propose that these types of demands have

influenced the evolution of differing types of culture are known as *eco-cultural* theories.

Many studies have confirmed the existence of this type of cultural difference in information-processing styles (Nisbett, Peng, Choi, & Norenzayan, 2001). For instance, Japanese and American students were shown a series of images on a screen, each showing a line drawn within a box, as illustrated in Figure 15.8 (Kitayama, Duffy, Kawamura, & Larsen, 2003). The box at the top of the figure contains a line that is one-third of the height of the square. Respondents were next shown a new smaller or larger blank box similar to the ones shown in the lower part of the figure, but with no line drawn inside it. Without any longer being able to see the original, they were then asked to draw a line in the new box that was either in proportion to the original one in the upper box, or that was the same length as the original one (shown in the box in the upper part of the figure). The lines actually drawn in the two lower boxes show, respectively, the correct length of the line drawn proportionately (left box) and exactly (right box). This procedure is known as the 'line and frame test'. As expected, Americans were better at exact reproduction of the line, while Japanese were better at proportional reproduction of the line. Thus, the Japanese had noted the contexts of the lines, while the Americans had not. In studies of recognition and recall, Japanese and American students were shown underwater scenes and pictures of wildlife (Masuda & Nisbett, 2001). They were then shown a second set of pictures in which some changes had been made. Japanese were much better

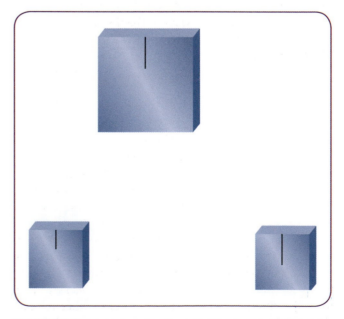

FIGURE 15.8 *Experimental task used by Kitayama et al. (2003).*

Source: Adapted from Kitayama et al. (2003). Perceiving an object and its context in different cultures: A cultural look at new look. *Psychological Science, 14*, 102–206. Adapted with permission from SAGE Publications.

at noticing changes in the animals' contexts, and also in detecting whether they had been shown a particular animal before, so long as it was in the same context as before.

Since there is evidence for a contrast in cognitive styles, it can be expected to influence the results of studies concerning social perception. As discussed in Chapter 3, many studies on causal attribution (typically using American students as participants) have yielded evidence in favour of correspondence bias. In other words, people in these experiments explain another person's behaviour more in terms of their personal traits than in terms of the circumstances in which the behaviour occurs. Norenzayan, Choi, and Nisbett (2002) gave Americans and Koreans various kinds of information about some fictitious characters and asked them to predict how these characters would behave in future. The Koreans drew more on the information concerning circumstances, whereas the Americans drew more on the characters' past behaviour. However, when no circumstantial information was provided, both Korean and US respondents were equally willing to predict future behaviour on the basis of past behaviour. Similarly, Miyamoto and Kitayama (2002) found that even when their respondents were told that an individual's behaviour had been constrained by role requirements, both Japanese and Americans did show correspondence bias.

These results are important, because they indicate that although cultural differences in cognitive styles do exist, they do not derive from differences in ability to make particular types of judgement. A change in experimental instructions can cause Asians to make judgements that are similar to Americans' judgements. It is better to think of these cultural differences as learned habits, ways of processing information that are particularly useful in a given kind of cultural context. Analytic thinking can be especially valuable, not just to hunters, but also to those living in contemporary individualistic cultures; holistic thinking can be distinctively useful, not just to rice farmers, but to those living in contemporary industrialized collectivist cultures.

Differences in cognitive style can also lead to inferences about the actions of others that have direct implications for the contrast between individualism and collectivism. Morris and Peng (1994) compared American high-school children of either European descent or Chinese descent. They were shown videos depicting images of fish of various colours swimming around. A blue fish was further to the right on the screen than the others and moved in a slightly different direction. As Figure 15.9 shows, European Americans attributed the blue fish's moves to both internal and external forces, whereas the Chinese Americans saw external forces as much more important. Americans commented more frequently that the blue fish was influencing the others. Chinese commented more frequently that the other fish were influencing the

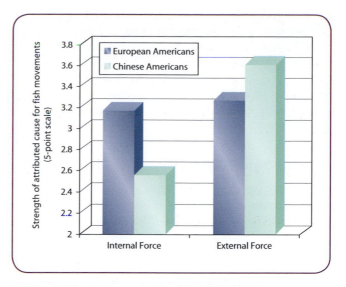

FIGURE 15.9 *What causes the blue fish to move?*

Source: Morris & Peng, 1994. © 1994 by the American Psychological Association. Reproduced with permission. The use of APA information does not imply endorsement by APA.

blue fish. This study shows how the European American children attributed individualistic motives to the blue fish, whereas the Chinese Americans saw the fish's movements in terms of response to the group.

Nisbett (2003) identified these variations as a contrast between 'Western' nations and 'East Asian' nations. Later studies show us that these labels are too global. The contrast may be more to do with individualism and collectivism than with East versus West. Kitayama, Ishii, Imada, Takemura, and Ramaswamy (2006) compared two samples from within Japan. The northern island of Hokkaido has a population descended from pioneer settlers, in contrast to the more southerly Honshu island. Kitayama et al. expected that, just as was the case in the United States, pioneers colonizing new areas would be more individualistic than those who had chosen to stay in more settled areas. They therefore predicted, and found, that their Hokkaido sample would show high correspondence bias, whereas the Honshu sample would not. Uskul, Kitayama, and Nisbett (2008) administered the line and frame test to three samples in Eastern Turkey, namely farmers, herdsmen and fishermen. They reasoned that herding and fishing are more individualistic activities than farming, which requires more collective action. Consistent with eco-cultural theory, the farmers did best at judging the relative line lengths. The herdsmen did better at judging absolute lengths.

The studies discussed in this section have made no reference to Europe. To put this right, now is a good time to look at Research Close-Up 15.1.

How do the studies in this section match up to the criteria for good cross-cultural studies that were outlined in the preceding sections? On most criteria they do very

COGNITIVE STYLES IN NORTH AMERICA, WESTERN EUROPE AND EAST ASIA

Kitayama, S., Park, H., Sevincer, A. T., Karasawa, M., & Uskul, A. K. (2009). A cultural task analysis of implicit independence: Comparing North America, Western Europe, and East Asia. *Journal of Personality and Social Psychology*, *97*, 236–255.

Research question

Over the past ten years, Kitayama and his colleagues have pioneered the study of cultural differences in cognitive styles, focusing exclusively on data from the US and from East Asia. These studies have provided increasingly detailed tests of the hypothesis originally proposed by Markus and Kitayama (1991) that cognitive styles differ in cultures characterized as independent or interdependent. These concepts are discussed in the next section of this chapter. In this study, Kitayama et al. sought to understand the distinctiveness of their earlier findings by also including European respondents. They also wanted to know whether the cognitive styles that they had postulated exist uniformly across each cultural group, or whether each style is restricted to just some members of each group.

Design and procedure

Students in Germany, UK, US and Japan completed four of the empirical tasks that had been developed in earlier studies. The design of the first task was 4 (nationalities) × 2 (vignette type). Respondents read brief vignettes in which people had engaged in socially desirable and in socially undesirable behaviours. The sequence of vignette type was reversed for half of the respondents. They were asked to rate the extent to which these people's behaviour was due to their dispositions or to the context, and whether these behaviours would have been different if the dispositions or context were different. This task is essentially the same as that used by Norenzayan, Choi, and Nisbett (2002) discussed earlier. It yields a measure of correspondence bias.

The second task was the line and frame test also described earlier, as shown in Figure 15.8. Here, the design was 4 (nations) × 2 (type of judgement required). In some trials, respondents were asked to reproduce the absolute length of lines, and in other trials they were asked to reproduce the line in proportion to the size of the box in which it was to be placed. The sequence of trials was counterbalanced. This task yields a measure of analytic versus holistic cognition.

In the third task, the students were given a list of everyday social situations. The design was 4 (nations) × 2 (situation type). Situations were either social (e.g. 'having a positive interaction with friends') or not social (e.g. 'being

caught in a traffic jam'). The participants were asked to think of the last time they were in each of these kinds of situations, and then to record which of a list of emotions they had experienced. This task gives measures of the frequency of socially engaging emotions and of socially disengaging emotions. Engaging emotions are those that necessarily do involve others, such as feeling friendly, ashamed or guilty. Disengaging emotions are these that do not necessarily involve other people, such as pride, frustration and anger.

The fourth task had a correlational design. The students from each nation rated their level of general happiness in each situation. This rating was correlated with their overall frequency of engaging and disengaging emotions to see which contributed more to overall happiness. Where happiness is more strongly correlated with engaging emotions, Kitayama et al. refer to it as *social* happiness. Where happiness is more strongly correlated with disengaging emotions, they call it *personal* happiness.

Results

Consistent with earlier results and as shown in Figure 15.10, the Americans showed more correspondence bias, more analytic cognitive style, more frequent disengaging emotions and happiness that was more personal than social. There were no significant differences between the results from Germany and those from the UK. The scores for the European students were intermediate between those from the US and Japan, but they nonetheless differed significantly from the Japanese and US results in almost all comparisons. Germans showed less correspondence bias than Americans, and both European samples showed more correspondence bias than did the Japanese. Europeans had a cognitive style that was more holistic than Americans, but more analytic than the Japanese. They reported more socially engaging emotions than Americans and more disengaging emotions than Japanese. British students gave more emphasis to social happiness than Americans did, but less than Japanese. German students gave more emphasis to social happiness than Americans did, and did not differ from the Japanese in this respect.

These results are obtained by comparing contrasts between samples on each of the separate tasks. The researchers also computed correlations between the results for the four tasks within each country's sample. The correlations found were very low. In other words, the people who scored highest on correspondence bias were not the same people who scored highest on analytic cognition or frequently experiencing personal rather than social emotions.

Implications

This important study has several implications. First of all, it confirms that we should not assume that results obtained in US studies will be replicable in Europe. In this case, the results for Europeans differed about equally from the US results and from the Japanese results. So, we should see differences in cognitive style in terms of variations along a spectrum, not as mutually exclusive.

Second, the low correlations between the different cognitive style indicators give us a new and fuller way of looking at culture. The models of culture provided by Hofstede (2001) and Schwartz (2004) suggest that cultures have a relatively homogeneous set of values and beliefs. Kitayama adds to that by proposing that a cultural context offers a range of opportunities to act and think in particular ways. These opportunities will be taken up by different types of people from within that culture. The effects obtained in a study typically will represent an interaction between the cultural context and individuals' personalities and preferences. Thus, when we look at a culture, we will find culturally distinctive phenomena, but not every individual will show all phenomena.

Study	USA	UK	Germany	Japan
Mean bias toward dispositional attribution (7-point rating scales)	1.2	1.2	1.1	.4
Mean greater accuracy on the holistic task than the relative task (in millimetres)	1.4	5.5	4.0	7.0
Mean greater frequency of disengaging emotions than engaging emotions (6-point rating scales)	.52	.24	.16	−.46
Greater personal happiness than social happiness (difference between correlation coefficients)	.16	.00	−.15	−.38

FIGURE 15.10 *Scores obtained in the four studies by Kitayama et al. (2009). The scores in each row can be compared with one another, but those obtained in each study are measured in different ways, so comparing columns is not meaningful.*

Source: Kitayama et al., 2009. © 2009 by the American Psychological Association. Reproduced with permission. The use of APA information does not imply endorsement by APA.

well. They used experimental methods, mostly with behaviours as dependent measures. However, they did not include any direct measures of cultural differences. The predictions as to what effects would be found are based on suggested differences between American and Japanese cultures that were first advanced in a classic paper by Markus and Kitayama (1991). We discuss the nature of these differences, and attempts by other researchers to measure them directly, in the next section.

Summary

Faced with the complexity of information available to them, members of individualistic cultures tend to focus on what they see as the central feature of any set of stimuli. Members of collectivistic cultures tend to take more account of the surrounding context. These differing cognitive styles affect the ways in which the behaviour of others is interpreted. Members of individualistic cultures more readily interpret the behaviours of others in

terms of fixed qualities such as personality. Members of collectivistic cultures expect less consistency of behaviour, and interpret variations in terms of contextual constraints such as roles. Cognitive styles can find expression in a variety of ways, so that there is a diversity of effects even within a single culture. Cognitive styles are habits induced by cultural socialization, and can be temporarily reversed experimentally.

CULTURE AND SELF-CONSTRUAL

Can the ways that we think about ourselves explain cultural variations in behaviour?

The paper mentioned earlier (Markus & Kitayama, 1991) was a review, which provided a further development of

LEADER IN THE FIELD

Shinobu Kitayama (b. 1957) grew up in Japan and obtained his Bachelor's and Master's degrees from the University of Kyoto. Obtaining his PhD from the University of Michigan in 1987, he taught subsequently at the University of Oregon and at Kyoto University. In 2003 he returned to the University of Michigan, where he directs the Centre for Culture and Cognition. He has been a key figure in opening up and developing studies in social cognition that contrast North America and East Asia. Jointly with Hazel Markus (see Leader in the Field, Chapter 5), he made the case for the contrasting effects of independence and interdependence. His more recent studies draw on his rich and first-hand understanding of both Japanese and US culture. He is co-editor of the *Handbook of Cultural Psychology* (2007).

Markus's earlier work on **self-construal** (see Chapter 5; also Leader in the Field, Shinobu Kitayama). Their proposal was that while people in the US tend to think of themselves as independent agents, people in Japan are more likely to think of themselves as *inter*dependent with those around them. This proposal can be seen as a special case of the differences in cognitive style considered in the preceding section, and was quickly taken as a formulation that could be applied more widely than just to the US and Japan. As illustrated in Chapter 5, Theory Box 5.3, an interdependent self is a likely consequence of being socialized within a collectivist culture.

Markus and Kitayama did not attempt to measure self-construal, but they showed that by assuming that there is a contrast between independence in the US and interdependence in Japan, they could explain a wide variety of differences in the results of studies comparing aspects of motivation, emotion and cognition in these two nations.

Numerous measures of self-construal have been created by other researchers. The best known has been that developed by Singelis (1994), which is given in full in Individual Differences 15.1. Try filling out your responses to his scale before you read any further. Subsequent studies have cited this scale more than 500 times, hence many researchers have found it useful. Some studies using the scale are discussed later.

Before going further, it is worth looking at some of the weaknesses of the Singelis self-construal scale, because these can illustrate what divides a good cross-cultural study from a poor one. All the items on the scale are positively worded, so someone who is high in acquiescent responding is likely to get high scores on both scales. This does not matter if you compare your own scores on the two scales, because your acquiescence is the same for both sets of questions. However, if the average score from one nation is compared with that from another nation, the result can be very misleading. For instance, Oyserman, Coon, and Kemmelmeier (2002)

concluded that there is no difference between the average scores from the US and Japan, which is not what we would expect on the basis of the large-scale surveys by Hofstede (1980) and Schwartz (2004). In a later analysis Schimmack, Oishi, and Diener (2005) pointed out that Oyserman et al. had taken no account of the possible presence of acquiescent responding in the studies that they reviewed. Schimmack et al. showed that when they discounted acquiescence using the techniques employed by Hofstede, the expected differences between the US, Japan and other nations were found.

A second difficulty with the Singelis scale is that many of the items tapping interdependence refer to 'your group'. As we saw in the previous section, people from collectivist cultures are much more aware of the context in which their relationships occur. When filling out the items, you may have wondered which group these items were referring to. Interdependent people would find it especially difficult to answer these items without knowing which group is being referred to. Some researchers have explored this issue more directly. English and Chen (2007) asked European American and Asian American students to rate themselves in four different situations (in class, at the gym, at a party and in the cafeteria). There was much more difference between the ways that the Chinese Americans rated their attributes in these situations than there was for the European Americans. When the test was repeated two months later, there was good consistency for self-descriptions in the same situations over time. This is important, because it shows that the Asian Americans' inconsistency across situations at the same time was not just because they did not have a clear sense of themselves. English and Chen conclude that Asian Americans have an 'if-then' view of self ('If I am in class, then I am like this'). Tafarodi, Lo, Yamaguchi, Lee, and Katsura (2004) asked students whether their 'inner self' remains the same in different situations. In the Canadian sample, 72 per cent said that it did, but only 36 per cent of Japanese and 28 per cent of Hong Kong Chinese said so. We need to consider how differences of this magnitude may affect the conclusions drawn by social psychologists from research conducted only within Western cultural groups. Let us now try to do this, by looking at attributions for success and failure.

Is self-enhancement universal?

Chapter 5 describes studies that show how we have a bias toward interpreting events around us in ways that enhance our self-image (Miller & Ross, 1975). If East Asians do not have such a strong sense of inner self, would they have less need for self-enhancement? Finding

INDEPENDENT VERSUS INTERDEPENDENT SELF-CONSTRUAL

Please indicate how much you agree or disagree with each of the statements below as a description of yourself, using the response scale presented below.

1. My personal identity, independent of others, is very important to me.
2. My relationships with those in my group are more important to me than my personal accomplishments.
3. I enjoy being unique and different from others.
4. My happiness depends on the happiness of those in my group.
5. Being able to take care of myself is a primary concern for me.
6. I am careful to maintain harmony in my group.
7. Speaking up during a class or meeting is not a problem for me.
8. I would sacrifice my self-interests for the benefit of the group.
9. Having a lively imagination is important to me.
10. I will stay in a group if they need me, even if I am not happy with the group.
11. I'd rather say 'no' directly than risk being misunderstood.
12. I should consider my parents' advice when making education or career plans.
13. I am comfortable being singled out for praise or rewards.
14. I respect decisions made by my group.
15. I am the same person at home as I am at college.
16. If my brothers or sisters fail, I feel responsible.
17. I act the same way no matter who I am with.
18. I have respect for the authority figures with whom I interact.
19. I feel comfortable using someone's first name soon after I meet him or her.
20. I would offer my seat on the bus to my professor.
21. I prefer to be direct and forthright when dealing with people that I have first met.
22. I respect people who are modest about themselves.
23. I value being in good health above everything.
24. Even when I strongly disagree with group members, I avoid an argument.

1 = Strongly disagree
2 = Disagree
3 = Slightly disagree
4 = Neutral
5 = Slightly agree
6 = Agree
7 = Strongly agree

These items comprise the self-construal scale developed by Singelis (1994). Odd-numbered items refer to independence and even-numbered items refer to interdependence. You can calculate your scores for independent and for interdependent self-construal by taking the average of your ratings on odd- and even-numbered items respectively. Higher scores indicate a stronger self-construal. Whether your scores are high or low compared to others will depend on what your nationality is. Singelis (1994) reported mean independence of 5.1 for European Americans and 4.6 for Asian Americans. He found mean interdependence of 4.4 for European Americans and 4.9 for Asian Americans. Depending upon your own degree of acquiescent responding, you may find that both your scores are above these means, or both may be below them. It can be more informative to compare on which of the two scales you scored higher.

Source: The self-construal scale: Singelis, T. M. (1994). The measurement of independent and interdependent self-construals. *Personality and Social Psychology Bulletin, 20,* 580–591. © SAGE Publications, reprinted with permission.

a satisfactory answer to this question has proved difficult, because the type of measure that is used influences the answer obtained. Heine, Lehman, Markus, and Kitayama (1999) noted that East Asians consistently score lower than North Americans on measures of self-esteem. They also show a larger gap between ratings of how they are and how they would like to be, and they react to success and failure in ways that differ from those found in North American studies. While North Americans tend to take credit for success and find excuses for failure, Japanese are more prone to attribute success to luck or help from others and take the blame for failure. These findings suggest that East Asians may have a much weaker need for self-enhancement.

Other researchers have used a different measure of self-enhancement and obtained different results. Sedikides, Gaertner, and Toguchi (2003) asked Japanese and American students to estimate the percentage of people who were better than them on various abilities. This method yields what is known as the **better than average effect** (BAE). In other words, more than 50 per cent of people think that they are better than average on most criteria. Sedikides et al. found the BAE was just as strong among Japanese as it was among Americans. They concluded that the need for self-enhancement is universal. How can this contradiction between results obtained with different methods be explained?

In the study by English and Chen (2007) it was found that, just like self-construal, self-enhancement measured by BAE varied much more between situations among Chinese Americans than among Europeans. This implies

better than average effect the finding that more than 50 per cent of participants report themselves to be better than average on a variety of criteria.

that for those with interdependent self-construal, some situations may elicit self-enhancement more than others. We may be able to understand the conflicting results if we can identify the nature of these situations. A study by Kurman (2003) focused on the role of modesty. She wanted to determine whether modesty was associated with low self-enhancement in all cultures or just in collectivist ones, where modesty norms are likely to be stronger. She first asked Singapore Chinese and urban Israeli high school students to rate how important modesty was to them. They also completed a self-construal measure. As would be expected from Hofstede's (1980) data (see Figure 15.3), the Israelis were more independent than the Singaporeans. In both samples, Kurman found that greater endorsement of modesty was associated with low self-enhancement, as measured by BAE. So, this effect may be general to all cultures, but we would expect that in cultures where modesty is more favoured, such as those in Asia, there will be fewer situations in which self-enhancement occurs.

Kurman's results help to explain how different methods give contradictory research findings, but they still leave open the question of whether the self-enhancement motive is or is not universal. Muramoto (2003) used an indirect procedure to determine whether Japanese respondents value self-enhancement, even though they express themselves modestly. She asked Japanese students to recall occasions when they had succeeded or failed. As expected, they attributed successes to others and blamed themselves for failures. However, Muramoto also asked them to rate how their friends and family would evaluate these successes and failures. Here she found that the Japanese students believed that friends and family would give them credit for successes and blame them less for failures. Further ratings showed that those people who received these kinds of support from family and friends felt that they were better understood by them. So the Japanese do wish for self-enhancement, but the cultural preference for modesty leads them to conceal this motive. This series of studies illustrates an important conclusion about the value of cross-cultural psychology. Studies may initially show contrasting results from different parts of the world, but if we investigate the reasons for these differences we can discover what is truly universal and what causes universal effects to be expressed more strongly in some locations than in others.

How many cultural differences can self-construal explain?

Self-construal is a quality of the individual. Culture is defined as a widely shared set of meanings. So, we should expect that some behaviours can be explained in terms of the ways that individuals think about themselves, while others will be more influenced by the shared cultural context. An example of the first kind of effect is shown by a cross-cultural study of embarrassment. Singelis, Bond, Sharkey, and Lai (1999) asked students in Hong Kong, Hawaii and mainland US to rate how embarrassed they would be in a series of different situations. They found that those with more interdependent self-construals expected to be more embarrassed and had lower self-esteem. Furthermore, when comparing the four samples, those samples with higher mean interdependence were the ones in which there was a higher mean expectation of being embarrassed.

In contrast, in Kurman's (2003) study, no relationship was found between self-construal and self-esteem, which is likely to be associated with self-enhancement. As already discussed, self-enhancement is explained by endorsement of modesty. The difference between these two results is likely to be because of the difference between being embarrassed, which is a private emotion, and self-enhancement, which involves public actions. Public actions will be much more affected by the shared attitudes and norms that define a culture. Matsumoto, Yoo, and Fontaine (2008) have surveyed the endorsement in 32 nations of what they call **display rules** – in other words, norms about whether emotions should be expressed in public. As expected, nations in East Asia and elsewhere that score higher on col-

> **display rules** cultural understandings as to whether emotions should be expressed openly.

lectivism score low on endorsement of display rules, and the nations that score highly on individualism, such as the US, score highly on endorsement of display rules. Figure 15.11 shows that there are also substantial variations within Europe in endorsement of emotional expression.

Self-construal over time

In Chapter 5 it was also noted that we typically see our self as having continuity through our lifespan. Consistent with this view, in this chapter we have discussed the types of self-construal that predominate in individualist and collectivist cultures. However, from Chapter 14 you will understand that through an average day we may think of ourselves in a variety of different ways, depending on our affiliations with different groups and different activities. So, can independence and interdependence vary over time? Trafimow, Triandis, and Goto (1991) were the first to show that they can (see Leader in the Field, Harry C. Triandis). They asked a group of students in the US to spend two minutes thinking of all the things that they had in common with their family (interdependent prime condition). Another group of students was asked to spend two minutes thinking of all

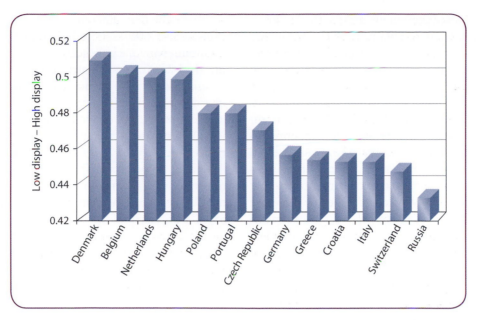

FIGURE 15.11 *Nations scoring highest and lowest on emotional display.*

Source: Based on Matsumoto et al., 2008, with permission from SAGE Publications.

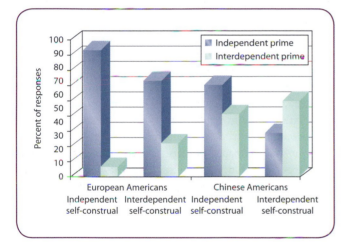

FIGURE 15.12 *Self-construals in response to priming.*

Source: Based on Trafimow et al., 1991. © 1991 by the American Psychological Association. Reproduced with permission. The use of APA information does not imply endorsement by APA.

the things that make them different from others (independent prime condition). The groups included both European Americans and Chinese Americans. Respondents were then asked to complete an open-ended measure of self-construal, in which they are asked to complete the phrase 'I am…' twenty times. Judges then coded the open-ended responses for independent and interdependent self-descriptions. Figure 15.12 shows the results. In both groups, the independent prime is associated with a higher score on independent self-construal and the interdependent prime is associated with a higher score on interdependent self-construal. However, comparing the results

on the left and right hand sides of the figure, it is clear that the European Americans remained more independent than the Chinese Americans in both conditions, and the Chinese Americans were still more interdependent in both conditions.

If scores on independence and interdependence can be changed by two minutes of experimental priming, how can these concepts be of any use in explaining cultural differences? There are two kinds of answer to this question. Firstly, we need to be aware that priming occurs not only in psychology experiments: there are many aspects of a culture that are likely to continually prime members of the culture to construe themselves in

LEADER IN THE FIELD

Harry C. Triandis (b. 1926) grew up on the Greek island of Corfu. During World War II the local schools were closed and he taught himself by reading the *Encyclopaedia Britannica*. He obtained a first degree in engineering in Canada, but transferred his interest to psychology, gaining a PhD in social psychology from Cornell University in 1958. Moving to the University of Illinois, he developed a cross-cultural perspective on the use of the semantic differential to map the meaning of concepts. His early understanding that cultural differences are best thought of as differences in assigned meanings was summarized in *The Analysis of Subjective Culture* (1972). He pioneered the development of a network of cross-cultural psychologists, was one of the first presidents of the International Association for Cross-Cultural Psychology, and was the chief editor of the *Handbook of Cross-Cultural Psychology*. More recently his many publications did much to popularize interest in individualism and collectivism. Many of his students at the University of Illinois are now leading contemporary cross-cultural psychologists.

particular ways. An ever-present example is the language that is spoken. Correct usage of most of the languages spoken in the more individualist nations of the world requires the inclusion of the pronoun 'I' when speaking about oneself. Many of the languages spoken in more collectivist nations permit one to drop the pronoun 'I' (Kashima & Kashima, 1998). Some languages, for example Arabic, do not even have a direct linguistic representation of the pronoun 'I'. So customary language use can prime self-construal of oneself as independent or interdependent. So too can adherence to cultural norms, that is to say the conventionally accepted types of response to one's behaviours typically received from other members of one's cultural group. For instance, an individual in a given culture would be aware of the local emotional display rules discussed earlier. In these ways, cultures can be constantly created and recreated through millions of interpersonal interactions, rather than having a fixed and static nature.

A second consequence of the finding that self-construal can be primed experimentally is that we can use experimental methods to investigate some aspects of cultural differences. Some examples are discussed in the final section of this chapter.

Summary

A key way in which cultures differ is in whether they encourage individuals to think of themselves as relatively independent of others or as interdependent with those to whom they are close. Independence is associated with a need to see oneself positively. Interdependence is associated with a need to maintain harmonious relations with others through publicly expressed modesty. Cultural differences are partly explained by differences in self-construal and partly by shared norms. Self-construals are changeable but are continually elicited by salient aspects of culture, such as language use and behavioural norms.

INTERPERSONAL RELATIONS

How do people relate to people whom they meet, and form relationships with them, in different cultural contexts?

In preceding sections we have seen that people from different cultures tend to have different values and to think

of themselves in different ways. We would therefore expect these differences to be reflected in how they communicate with each other. However, we cannot simply describe cultural contrasts in communication style because, as we have seen in earlier sections, people with interdependent self-construals will adapt their behaviour depending on the social context. Gudykunst et al. (1992) compared the reported communication experiences of students in Hong Kong, Japan, the US and Australia. Respondents from the US and Australia did not make any distinction between communication with members of their ingroup and their outgroup. However, those from Japan and Hong Kong did make such a distinction. When communicating with ingroup members they reported feeling more similar, having more shared networks, more questioning of each other and more feeling that they could understand one another without being explicit.

These contrasts have been further explored by Verkuyten and Masson (1996), who studied same-sex adolescent friendships among ethnic groups living in the Netherlands. Independent self-construal was higher among Dutch respondents and those from Spain, Italy and the former Yugoslavia. Interdependent self-construal was higher among Moroccan and Turkish respondents. The authors found that interdependence predicted feeling closer to one's best friend, but having a smaller number of other friends. Interdependence also predicted having more rules about how to speak to third parties about one's best friend. This study is useful because it not only identifies cultural contrasts, but also shows how self-construal measures can explain the contrasts that are found.

Prosocial behaviour with strangers

If people from collectivist nations distinguish between ingroup and outgroup relationships, it makes sense to discuss each type of relationship separately. In Chapter 10 prosocial behaviours were discussed. How do cultural differences affect the tendency to help a stranger in distress? Levine, Norenzayan, and Philbrick (2001) compared bystander helpfulness in 23 nations. They trained accomplices to create three separate situations on the streets of a major city in each nation. In the first situation, each accomplice dropped a pen while walking past a single stranger. In the second situation, as a pedestrian approached, the accomplice appeared to have hurt their leg and was struggling to pick up a pile of magazines that they had dropped. In the third situation, the accomplice was dressed as a blind person and was waiting for a green light at a pedestrian crossing. The proportion of helpful responses across these three emergencies was positively

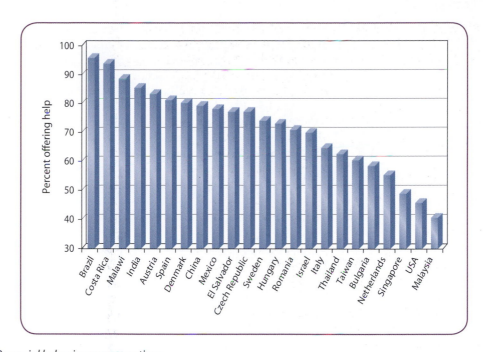

FIGURE 15.13 *Prosocial behaviour across nations.*

Source: Based on Levine et al., 2001, with permission from SAGE Publications.

correlated and was therefore combined into a single index. As Figure 15.13 shows, there was a large variation between nations.

This study provides a first indication of cultural variations in prosocial behaviour, but because few other measures were collected, it leaves many possible explanations of this effect untested. Helpfulness to strangers was unrelated to differences in individualism and collectivism, but was higher in less rich nations.

Intimate relationships

We can expect that the ways in which intimate relationships are created will reflect the prevailing cultural context. Buss (1989) asked 9500 students in 37 nations to rate the desirability of 18 qualities in a future opposite-sex romantic partner. Across the sample as a whole, men said they would prefer partners whom they perceived as young, healthy and beautiful, while women would prefer partners whom they saw as ambitious, industrious and having high earning potential (see Chapter 11 for discussion of the possible evolutionary basis for such partner choices). There were also substantial variations in preferences across nations. The greatest variability across nations was found in preference for pre-marital chastity, which was more strongly required by respondents in collectivist nations (Buss et al., 1990). In a collectivist culture, a female partner's lack of chastity would be a threat to the honour of her whole group. We discuss this in a later section. Shackelford, Schmitt, and Buss

(2005) made a further study of this dataset, using factor analysis to identify four dimensions that could be used to summarize the variation across nations. The first of these dimensions contrasted the presence of love as a precondition for a relationship, with emphasis on status and financial prospects. Figure 15.14 shows the nations scoring at either extreme of this dimension. Preference for a relationship based on love was found to be strongest in more wealthy nations, which tend to be those that are individualistic rather than collectivistic. See also Social Psychology Beyond the Lab 15.2, which gives some examples of how partner preferences are typically expressed in the UK and India.

The studies of partner preference provide an example of a field in which we find both universal and cultural variations. Gender differences are universal, but preferred partner qualities vary in strength between cultures. For a similar pattern of results, see the discussion of cultural effects on aggression in Chapter 9.

Summary

Our cultural background affects the way that we speak to others and to what extent we distinguish between relating to strangers and relating to friends. Social relationships within collectivistic cultures are more exclusive of outsiders and require less explicit communication. Choice of intimate partners is influenced not just by the personal qualities of the partners, but also by the attributes of the families from which they are drawn.

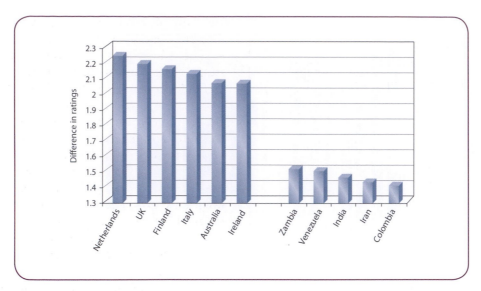

FIGURE 15.14 *Preference for love more than for status and financial prospects as a precondition for a relationship.*
Source: Based on Shackelford et al., 2005, with permission from Elsevier.

SOCIAL PSYCHOLOGY BEYOND THE LAB 15.2

THE IDEAL PARTNER FITS WITH CULTURAL NORMS

What qualities are important in seeking a partner? In the UK, personality traits and interests are emphasized. In India, caste, family status, qualifications and sometimes horoscopes are more salient. Note how in the UK individuals advertise themselves, whereas in India it is often the family rather than the individual that seeks a partner. Note also that one of the UK advertisements is for a homosexual partner.

United Kingdom	India
Lots of energy and a lust for life. Eccentric, kind-hearted female, 35, 5'9", loves singing, dancing, reading and travel; would like to meet confident pragmatic, hard-working male, 33–38, who likes a joke and a hearty laugh. **Attractive** 39yo black male speaks five languages would like to meet female, similar age for long-term relationship. Likes walking by the sea, food, cooking and travel. **New here,** looking around. I am a 32yo male seeking an honest, balanced fun female 25–34 with good sense of humour. **Tall, blonde, incredible hunk,** 27, attractive handsome young male would like to meet older non-scene, distinguished gentleman, 65+, hopefully leading to friendship and relationship.	**Smart,** very handsome Brahmin boy, 31, 180 cm, BE, MBA, own established business, monthly income six figures, send biodata and photo (must). **Delhi-based** Punjabi Khatri family seeks professionally qualified girl from educated family for IT, MBA, 29 years, 5'7" working manager in leading company. **Hindu girl,** 23, 160 cm, BTech working professional software engineer, only child, father senior bank executive, mother legal professional, seeks preferably BTech, MBA, below 28 from educated family. Caste no bar. **Beautiful** working girl in Delhi sought for handsome Uttar Pradesh Khatri boy, born 3.2.1980 / 3.15 am, 5'3", employed in a reputable company.

Sources: *The Guardian* (London), April 2010; *Sunday Times of India,* matrimonials, March 2010.

GROUP PROCESSES

How does collectivism affect group behaviours?

Asch's (1956) classic study of how groups influence the individual's behaviour has been described in Chapters 1 and 8. We might expect that the effects found would depend on the cultural context in which the study is conducted. Bond and Smith (1996) reported a meta-analysis of the 133 published replications and extensions of this study. Ninety-seven of these replications were conducted within the United States, and even within the US there was substantial variation in the level of conformity that

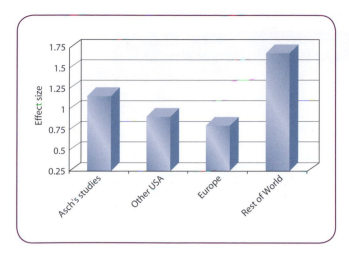

FIGURE 15.15 *Variations of effect size in the Asch conformity experiment.*

Source: Based on Bond & Smith, 1996. Culture and conformity: A meta-analysis of studies using Asch's (1952b, 1956) Line Judgment Task. *Psychological Bulletin, 119*, 111–137, with permission from APA. The use of APA information does not imply endorsement by APA.

was found. Bond and Smith were principally interested in what happened when the study was repeated elsewhere, and they found that replications had been conducted in another 16 nations. But when an experiment is repeated, it is very difficult to match exactly the ways the original study was done. To try to compare studies cross-culturally, they first studied in more detail variations across studies conducted in one country. Bond and Smith determined how much the varying results obtained within the US were associated with the differences in procedures and samples in these studies. They found the strongest variations were caused by three factors: (1) the size of the majority that gave false answers; (2) the relative lengths of the lines that were used; and (3) whether the majority were from an outgroup or not. These results were then used as statistical controls for these same sources of variation in examining the studies conducted elsewhere. The results obtained from differing regions of the world are shown in Figure 15.15. To test possible reasons for the contrasting results from different nations, Bond and Smith correlated the measures of national difference provided by Hofstede (1980) and Schwartz (2004) with the scores for conformity. They found that conformity was highest in the nations grouped in the figure as 'Rest of the World', where Hofstede's collectivism and Schwartz's embeddedness values are most strongly endorsed. Thus, conformity was highest in societies in which people emphasize their links with others and their long-term membership groups.

If members of collectivist cultures conform more frequently, then we may expect their behaviour to differ when they are in groups compared to when they are on their own. As was discussed in Chapter 13, North American researchers have identified the phenomenon of social loafing, whereby people are found to work less hard when they are in a group compared to when they are working on their own. Research Close-Up 15.2 explores why results are not the same when this type of study is conducted in other cultural contexts.

Studies of conformity and social loafing treat all members of a group as though they are equal to one another, but in real groups there are frequently differences in status that reflect formal or informal leadership processes. Since the values of some cultures emphasize hierarchy more than others, we can expect that leaders would be more powerful in some contexts than others. Milgram's (1974) well-known studies of obedience in the US are discussed in Chapter 8. Several replications of his studies in different nations have been reported, some yielding higher rates of obedience and others yielding lower rates. However, none of these replications precisely followed Milgram's procedure, so that we cannot determine the source of these variations. It is likely that variations in obedience are more affected by cultural contexts other than nationality, for instance, the contrast between military and non-military contexts.

The effects of different styles of leadership have been frequently studied by cross-cultural researchers. The classic comparison of authoritarian and democratic leadership studied by Lewin, Lippitt, and White (1939) is discussed in Chapter 13. Meade (1985) repeated this study, sampling 12- to 14-year-olds in the more hierarchical cultures of India and Hong Kong, as well as among European Americans in the US mainland and among Chinese Americans in Hawaii. Only in mainland US was democratic leadership preferred. In Hawaii, the preference was equally balanced, while in Hong Kong and India authoritarian leadership was preferred to democratic leadership. In mainland US the autocratically-led groups had low productivity and high absenteeism, whereas the democratically-led groups had high productivity and low absenteeism, thus replicating the results of Lewin et al. almost 50 years after the original study. However, in the Chinese and Indian groups the pattern of results was exactly the opposite, with authoritarian leaders achieving much higher productivity and much lower absenteeism.

More recently, House, Hanges, Javidan, Dorfman, and Gupta (2004) surveyed the leader styles preferred by business managers in 61 nations. Respondents were asked to select items from a list of traits that characterize effective leaders. The results were summarized in terms of six styles that were named as charismatic, team-oriented, participative, humane, autonomous and self-protective. Typical traits defining each of these styles are shown in Figure 15.16. Charismatic leadership is similar to the transformational/charismatic leadership discussed in Chapter 13. In general, the charismatic and team-oriented leadership styles were endorsed across the sample as a whole, while self-protective and autonomous

Leader dimension	Typical traits	Rated highest	Rated lowest
Charismatic	Visionary Inspirational Decisive Risktaker	Anglo (US, UK, Canada etc.) nations	Middle East region
Team-oriented	Group-oriented Communicative	Latin America	Middle East region
Self-protective	Status conscious Formal	Middle East region	Nordic Europe
Participative	Not autocratic A delegator	Germanic Europe	Middle East region
Humane	Modest Generous	Southern Asia	Nordic Europe
Autonomous	Individualistic Independent	Eastern Europe	Latin America

FIGURE 15.16 *Variation in desired leader qualities across regions.*

Source: Based on information reported in House et al., 2004.

leadership was rejected. However, there were also variations in the results from each of the regions from which House et al. collected data. The regions in which each style was more popular than average and less popular than average are also shown in the figure. House et al. were able to show that these variations in preferred leader styles could be predicted from measures of values that they also collected from their respondents. For instance, Latin Americans score highest on collectivism (see Figure 15.3) and they were more positive toward team-oriented leadership, while in the individualistic Anglo nations the entrepreneurial charismatic leader style was more favoured.

In the contemporary world, teams are often composed of people coming from differing cultural backgrounds. Team members are unlikely to have the same preferences for leadership or understandings about how a group should best work together. For instance, some may value assertiveness, while others expect to wait for leadership from others. This can be a problem in business, particularly in 'virtual' teams who meet only through e-mail, but also in student seminars. Earley and Mosakowski (2000) proposed that effective multicultural teams will be those that can establish a shared culture. They predicted that this would be easier to accomplish if a team comprised people from several different cultural backgrounds rather than from just two. They reasoned

that where two cultural groups are represented, each subgroup will try to impose their preferences on the other, whereas when many viewpoints are represented, the team will be forced to evolve a new culture of its own. In their first study, Earley and Mosakowski tested these ideas among teams of managers attending a business school in London. Ninety-four participants from 27 nations were assigned to four-person decision-making groups. Groups had either four people from one nation (homogeneous condition), two people from one nation and two from another (polarized condition), or four people from different nations (heterogeneous condition). The groups worked on a decision task for one hour. Two judges who were blind to the teams' composition then rated the decision quality of the teams' work on objective criteria. The homogenous groups did best and the polarized groups did worst. These findings were replicated in a second study in which group members worked with one another over a period of three months. Neither study included any measure of participants' cultural orientation additional to their nationality. We can therefore be less confident that we know whether the effects that were found are due to the reasons specified by Earley and Mosakowski. However, they confirm that cultural processes add to the challenges of establishing effective teamwork. They also indicate that heterogeneity of teams is not always detrimental: given time, very heterogenous

SOCIAL LOAFING IN CHINA, US AND ISRAEL

Earley, P. C. (1993). East meets West meets Mideast: Further explorations of collectivistic versus individualistic work groups. *Academy of Management Journal, 36,* 319–348.

Research question

Social loafing is the phenomenon in which group members work less hard when they are in a group compared to when they are on their own. It has been frequently identified in studies conducted in the US. The process is fully described in Chapter 13 (see Research Close-Up13.1). Earley tested the hypothesis that respondents' attitudes toward interdependence would affect the extent to which social loafing would occur. He predicted that those who favour interdependence (referred to as collectivists) would work hardest when working with members of their ingroup. He was also concerned to establish the extent to which social loafing occurs in real work groups as much as it does in short-term groups of students brought together for the purpose of the experiment.

Design and procedure

Participants were full-time managers who were attending training courses. The design was 3 (nationalities) × 3 (experimental conditions). The sample comprised 45 Israelis, 60 mainland Chinese and 60 Americans from the United States. All participants were given a simulated 'in-basket' of paperwork tasks on which to work. In the *individual* condition they were told that they should expect to complete 20 items within an hour. In the *ingroup collective* condition they were told that they were working in a team of ten and that the other team members were people from the same region of the country who had been selected to be similar to one another and to have many common interests. The team was expected to complete 200 items within the hour. In the *outgroup collective* condition they were told that they were working in a team of ten and that the other group members were from different regions of the country and would have little in common. They were also expected to complete 200 items within the hour. In fact, all participants were working individually. Participants also completed a questionnaire measuring their attitudes toward independence (individualism) and interdependence (collectivism). The dependent measure was the number of tasks completed per person.

Results

Scores from each nation were first standardized, so that the means for each nation were equivalent. This enables the researchers to analyse the results for the sample as a whole without reference to nationality and without distortion from other sources of difference between the samples. Earley then divided his sample between those who had endorsed independence and those who had endorsed interdependence. As Figure 15.17 shows, individualists completed significantly fewer tasks when they believed that they were working in either of the collective conditions versus individually. Collectivists completed significantly *more* tasks in the ingroup collective condition than in either of the other experimental conditions.

Pooling the results across nations ignores the fact that most of the individualists would be in the US sample and most of the collectivists would be in the Chinese sample. Therefore it is useful also to test the hypothesis separately for each nation's data. When this is done unstandardized data can be used. The results are shown in Figure 15.18, but note that the samples from each nation were quite small.

Implications

This is one of the most striking cross-cultural studies that has been conducted. The results show that social loafing is not just reduced in differing cultural contexts – it is actually

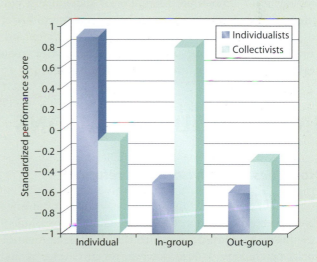

FIGURE 15.17 *Social loafing in three experimental conditions.*

Source: Republished with the permission of the Academy of Management, from Earley (1993). East meets West meets Mideast: Further explorations of collectivistic versus individualistic work groups. *Academy of Management Journal,* Vol. 36; permission conveyed through Copyright Clearance Center, Inc.

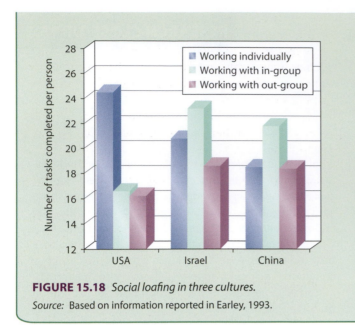

FIGURE 15.18 *Social loafing in three cultures.*

Source: Based on information reported in Earley, 1993.

reversed. Collectivists do not loaf in groups: they work harder. In an earlier study, Earley (1989) found the same result when he sampled managers who were actually at work, not in a simulated work setting. Of course there could be many reasons why a study conducted in the US, Israel and China could come up with contrasting results. By measuring participants' attitudes toward independence and interdependence directly, Earley was able to show that he could explain why the results came out as they did. If we look at these results through Western eyes, we might say that collectivists work harder in groups because of conformity pressures. However, this does not answer the question of why there might be norms favouring hard work in collectivist groups. A better explanation is to say that in collectivist cultures one's interdependent identity is inextricably linked with one's group, so that hard work enhances one's identity, just as working hard individually does for an individual.

teams can work effectively together, as has also been found by researchers who have focused on aspects of diversity unrelated to culture (e.g. Horwitz & Horwitz, 2007).

Summary

Interdependence is a central component of one's relation to groups. Consequently, members of collectivist cultures show greater conformity and work harder to contribute to group goals. They respond more positively to directive forms of leadership. Members of individualist cultures value their autonomy and therefore respond better to participative forms of leadership. These different orientations toward group processes pose difficulties when teams are composed of those from differing cultures.

INTERGROUP RELATIONS

How does collectivism affect relations with outgroups?

As has been discussed in Chapters 12 and 14, social identity theory has played a major role in the development of social psychology. It has, however, been developed and tested mostly within the predominantly more individualistic national cultures that provide the heartland of social psychology. What happens when group memberships are a more permanent and central element in one's identity, as occurs within collectivist cultures and within ethnic minority subcultures in individualistic nations? People high in interdependence may need to use different ways from

those who are more independent to maintain a positive comparison between their ingroup and relevant outgroups.

The minimal group paradigm pioneered by Tajfel, Billig, Bundy, and Flament (1971; see Research Close-Up 14.1) was first tested with 11-year-old schoolchildren. Consider the study conducted in New Zealand by Wetherell (1982). Wetherell compared the responses of three separate samples of 8-year-old children: New Zealanders of European origin, Maoris (who are indigenous to New Zealand) and Samoan immigrants to New Zealand. The European New Zealanders responded to being arbitrarily assigned to a group by maximizing the difference between ingroup rewards and outgroup rewards, just as has been repeatedly found in earlier studies based on the study carried out by Tajfel et al. However, the Samoans tried to maximize the rewards of both the ingroup and the outgroup, while the results for Maoris were intermediate between the other two samples. On the face of it, the Samoan results in particular appear contradictory to social identity theory, because the Samoans did not try to enhance the status of their own group. In trying to understand the results, Wetherell wondered whether the collectivist culture of Samoans led them to perceive fellow-Samoans, whether categorized as 'ingroup' or 'outgroup' by the experimenters, as, in fact, 'ingroup members', and the white experimenter as the outgroup. She also noted that the giving of gifts is highly esteemed in Samoan culture, so that a Samoan might achieve higher status for the ingroup by giving gifts to others. It is also possible that as young immigrants, the Samoan children did not fully understand the culturally strange procedures in which the white experimenter was asking them to participate.

In order to resolve these kinds of ambiguities, studies are required that focus on intergroup relations and also include measures of cultural relevance, such as independence and interdependence. Research Close-Up 15.3 describes some studies of this kind, which do support the cross-cultural validity of social identity theory, but which also show some culturally variable effects.

Group honour

As we have seen, many studies of individualistic and collectivistic cultures have focused on the US and East Asia. However, issues relevant to collectivism are important within intergroup relations in all parts of the world. The need to maintain the honour of one's group in relation to others is salient not just among the more collectivist immigrant communities within nations in northern Europe, but also in the more collectivist nations of southern Europe, and as we shall see, even in the southern states of the US. Rodriguez Mosquera, Manstead, and Fischer (2002a) compared understandings of the concept of honour in the Netherlands and in Spain, by comparing students' responses to Schwartz's (1992) value survey. As Schwartz had done in his earlier study, Rodriguez Mosquera et al. defined meanings of values by examining the extent to which endorsing one value was correlated with endorsing other values. In the Netherlands, honour was more strongly associated with endorsement of independent values such as *self-respect* and *achieving more than others*. In contrast, in Spain honour was more strongly associated with interdependent values such as *loyalty* and *honesty*. In a further study, Rodriguez Mosquera, Manstead, and Fischer (2002b) asked Dutch and Spanish students to imagine their response to a series of scenarios in which insults were received. The Spanish students reported feeling more threatened and more ashamed when family honour was insulted, whereas the Dutch reported more shame and anger when their autonomy and assertiveness were under threat.

Cultures in which honour is defined interdependently can be expected to show evidence of vigorous defence of the honour of one's group. For instance, Semin and Rubini (1990) compared students' reports of insults used most frequently in northern Italy with those used in southern Italy. Southern Italy has a culture that is much more collectivistic than northern Italy (Capozza, Brown, Aharpour, & Falvo, 2006). Favoured insults in northern Italy were more frequently focused on characterizing the insulted individual, for instance in terms of sexual expletives or of undesirable traits ('You're stupid'; 'You're a cretin'). In Sicily, in the south, insults were more frequently targeted at the individual's group membership, especially their family. Examples included: 'I wish a cancer on you and all your relatives'; 'Your sister is

a cow'; 'You are queer and so is your father'; 'You are a communist'; and insults based on references to incest.

Historically, the nations around the Mediterranean such as Spain, Italy and Turkey have been characterized as honour cultures, but defence of group honour is likely to be a salient value in many collectivist cultures. Even within the United States the relatively more collectivist values of the southern states are associated with acceptance of more aggressive responding to uphold the honour of one's group than in the northern US. For instance, Nisbett and Cohen (1996) mailed a job application letter to potential employers that had supposedly been written by someone convicted of a killing in an honour-related incident. Companies in the south and west of the US more often responded favourably to the application than did those in the more individualistic north of the US. Honour killings continue to be reported in the press in many nations where perceived female sexual infidelity is seen as a major threat to the honour of the group.

Negotiation

In fields such as diplomacy and business it is frequently necessary to engage in negotiation with representatives of groups whose cultures may differ from one's own. The differing values espoused within individualist and collectivist cultures make it likely that tasks of this kind will be approached in different ways. Morris et al. (1998) compared the approaches to negotiation used by business students from India, Hong Kong, the Philippines and the US. Preferred negotiation styles were characterized as either competing or avoiding conflict. The Americans were more competitive, while the Hong Kong Chinese were more avoidant. Respondents also completed Schwartz's (1992) measure of individuals' values. Morris et al. were able to show that the differences between the samples in competitiveness were associated with differences in how much respondents endorsed achievement values, while the differences in avoidance were associated with differences in how much tradition and conformity values were endorsed.

Thus, we can see that measures that are useful in defining cultural differences can help to predict some of the difficulties that will arise when people from differing cultures negotiate with one another. However, this study does not tell us how they are likely to cope with these difficulties. Successful negotiation across cultures is likely to require adaptations in one's behaviour. We can gain a better understanding of these adaptations by looking at more detailed analyses. Adair and Brett (2005) constructed a complex one-hour-long simulation of a commercial negotiation. This enabled analyses of actual negotiation behaviours over time rather than simple summaries of negotiation

SOCIAL IDENTITY IN CHINA AND THE US

RESEARCH CLOSE-UP 15.3

Chen, Y.-R., Brockner, J., & Katz, T. (1998). Toward an explanation of cultural differences in in-group favoritism: The role of individual versus collective primacy. *Journal of Personality and Social Psychology, 75,* 1490–1502.

Research question

Chen and her colleagues were interested to see how members of a team would react to adverse feedback when they were in a collectivist cultural context rather than an individualist context. If one's group identity is more fixed and salient than it is in the nations where social identity theory was first formulated, how would the different types of identity management strategies proposed by Tajfel and Turner (1986) be affected?

As discussed in Chapter 14, social identity theory specifies social mobility, social creativity and social competition as three ways in which a group member might seek to retain a positive identity, even where their group is evaluated poorly. The theory also states the circumstances in which each of these options will be employed. Where group boundaries are permeable and the group is poorly evaluated, a group member might opt for social mobility – in other words, leave the group. This option would be attractive to someone with an independent self-construal. In collectivist cultures where group boundaries are not so permeable, would respondents whose group is poorly evaluated find alternative ways to preserve their group affiliation, and would these strategies be followed especially by those who endorse interdependence? Tajfel and Turner's theory suggests that they would choose social competition or social creativity – that is to say, either comparing their group favourably with others or changing the basis of comparison with other groups. Chen et al. did not make a specific prediction as to which strategy their more collectivist respondents would employ.

Design and procedure

The design was a 2 (nation) $\times$ 2 (individual feedback) $\times$ 2 (team feedback) $\times$ 2 (success/failure) experiment. Participants were 291 students at Peking University in China and 80 students at Columbia University in the US. After filling out an attitude survey and a measure of independence/interdependence, participants were told that they had been assigned to a team whose members held similar attitudes to one another on a variety of issues. They were then given brief descriptions of ten romantic couples that were said to have been prepared by clinical psychologists. They were asked to predict whether each couple would still be together after a year, and were told that successful prediction was an indicator of intellectual and interpersonal competence. After

completing this task, participants received feedback that told them either that they had done well or poorly on the task (experimental factor 1). They were also told that their team had either done well or poorly (experimental factor 2). Finally, as dependent measures, they rated the performance of themselves, their team and other teams on various scales.

Results

Chinese respondents mostly scored higher on interdependence and US respondents mostly scored higher on independence. The findings of interest concern the ways in which respondents handled the failure feedback compared to the success feedback. Among the Americans, those who were told that they had done well individually, but their team had done poorly, gave their team much lower ratings. However, in the same situation among the Chinese there was no such decrease in ingroup ratings. Instead, they rated the performance of outgroup teams significantly more negatively. Figure 15.19 shows that the same pattern of results is obtained when the data are analysed in terms of independence–interdependence rather than in terms of nationality. Chen et al. used a 7-item measure of 'individual versus collective primacy', derived from several different measures of independent and interdependent

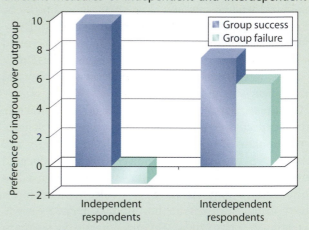

FIGURE 15.19 *Ingroup preference when receiving individual success feedback.*

Source: Based on Chen, Brockner, & Katz (1998). Toward an explanation of cultural differences in in-group favoritism: The role of individual versus collective primacy. *Journal of Personality and Social Psychology, 75,* 1490–1502, with permission from APA. The use of APA information does not imply endorsement by APA.

self-construal, including some of the items in the Singelis (1994) scales (see Individual Differences15.1). Thus, they found that of all the possible reasons why Americans and Chinese might behave differently in this experiment, the self-construal scores provide a sufficient explanation.

Implications

American respondents were clearly employing Tajfel and Turner's (1986) social mobility strategy. In effect they were saying 'If this team is no good, then I don't wish to be part of it'. For them, it was more important to preserve a positive individual identity than a positive group identity. In contrast, the Chinese response was more like 'If our team did poorly, then the others must have done

even worse'. This is consistent with Tajfel and Turner's social competition strategy. By adjusting the basis of comparison in this way, they could preserve a positive team identity. In a similar study conducted later, Chen, Brockner, and Chen (2002) showed that when outgroup teams were said to have done better than one's own team, interdependent respondents still rated their own team positively, while independent respondents did not. These studies thus give cross-cultural support to social identity theory, but show that identity strategies do vary in ways that reflect variations in individualism–collectivism. However, the results of both these studies rest on a brief and previously unknown measure of independence and interdependence that requires fuller development to ensure its validity.

style. Adair and Brett examined the extent to which intercultural negotiators modified their behaviour compared to those negotiating with others from their own culture. There were two intracultural experimental conditions and one intercultural condition. The collectivist intracultural negotiations comprised dyads drawn from Russia, Japan, Hong Kong and Thailand. The individualist intracultural negotiations comprised dyads from Germany, Israel, Sweden and the US. In all of these instances, each dyad comprised two people from the same nation. In the intercultural dyads, some US negotiators were pitted against Japanese negotiators, while others negotiated with Hong Kong Chinese. The negotiations were audiotaped, transcribed and coded into a series of predetermined categories. In order to examine the sequential development of the negotiations, the transcripts were divided into quarters.

In studies that use a complex content analysis of this kind, the numbers of dyads from each individual nation is necessarily low, so Adair and Brett analysed the results for all individualist dyads in contrast to the results for all collectivist dyads. Negotiators from the individualistic nations showed more direct exchange of information through questions (e.g. 'We could offer 40 per cent upfront') and answers (e.g. 'We couldn't possibly accept that offer'). Only during the last quarter did they make actual offers focused on a possible agreement. Negotiators from collectivistic nations used indirect information exchange more frequently. In other words, they made a mixture of offers and more generally phrased persuasive arguments (e.g. 'Everyone knows our company makes the finest products and we plan to continue introducing new ones') during the early stages, and inferred what must be the more important priorities of the other party from the relatively indirect responses (e.g. 'This deal is very important for me. I'm up for promotion and the budget is really tight') that they obtained to their offers. In the intercultural dyads, the

collectivistic negotiators were found to have adopted the more direct information exchange that is favoured by individualistic negotiators. The individualistic negotiators did not adapt their behaviour. The intercultural negotiations achieved less joint gain (measured in dollars) than both the collectivist and the individualist intracultural negotiations.

This study tells us two things. Firstly, it is consistent with expectation that the negotiators from collectivist cultures take more account of their context, and therefore it is they who adapt their behaviour more during intercultural negotiation. Secondly, this adaptation is only partially effective, because information exchange and the making of offers have different meanings in differing contexts. Early offers in collectivist cultures can serve well as an exploratory device among those who understand their purpose, but they are likely to be misunderstood by negotiators from cultures in which direct communication is favoured. Being an effective negotiator cross-culturally requires not only being willing to adapt one's behaviour, but also an awareness of how the other party will interpret those behaviours (see Social Psychology Beyond the Lab 15.3).

Summary

Members of groups within collectivist cultures give high priority to preserving their group's status. This leads them to seek harmony with ingroup members through indirect communication, and to defend their group robustly when interacting with outgroup members. These effects are broadly consistent with social psychological theories developed through sampling of members of individualist cultures, but in order to explain the particular ways in which collectivist group status is upheld in more collectivistic cultures, we need to draw on more specific concepts such as independence and interdependence.

SOCIAL PSYCHOLOGY BEYOND THE LAB 15.3

THE POLITICAL PERILS OF CROSS-CULTURAL NEGOTIATION

The costs of failing to understand the intentions of parties from other cultural contexts is nowhere more apparent than in the field of international negotiation. The US dropped the atomic bombs on Hiroshima and Nagasaki in Japan in 1945 after the Japanese had responded to a US ultimatum for unconditional surrender using the ambiguous word *mokusatsu*, which can mean 'silent contempt', 'ignore' or 'we need more time'. In this instance, it was translated as 'ignore'. However, the Japanese emperor had already agreed to surrender: conflicts within his government needed to be resolved before they were ready to respond.

More recently, it is said that the 1990 conflict in Kuwait was precipitated because US Secretary of State James Baker spoke softly to Tariq Aziz, the Iraqi foreign minister, presenting him with a letter indicating that the US would intervene militarily if Iraq did not withdraw following their invasion of Kuwait (Kimmel, 1994). Consistent with Western styles of communication, the letter was task-oriented, impersonal, definite and time-limited. An Arab understanding of threats would be that they are only meant seriously if delivered extravagantly and emphatically. Aziz would have favoured a slower-paced and less focused building up of trust between the two parties.

The United Nations Climate Change Conference held in Copenhagen in 2009 was regarded by most parties as a failure. Many factors contributed to that, but it provided numerous instances of cultural differences in negotiation style and the way in which these may have affected the outcome (Lynas, 2009). President Obama delayed his arrival at the conference until his advisers judged that there was a possibility of agreement with the Chinese. When he arrived he joined the group of predominantly Western leaders who were attempting to rescue the stalled negotiations, as shown in Figure 15.20. However, the Chinese and Indian governments sent only middle-ranking protocol officers to these meetings, thereby preventing the flexibility that might have been possible within a meeting of heads of state. Obama reacted by leaving these meetings and having two one-to-one negotiations with Chinese premier Wen Jiabao, thus illustrating his preference for direct communication. He returned from the second of these meetings announcing agreement on certain points. The Chinese responded by introducing new demands into the group discussions through their protocol officers, thus regaining control of the negotiation. Obama responded by once more seeking out the Chinese, and this time found them engaged in an alternative negotiation with a small group of key non-Western nations. Obama joined these negotiations uninvited, and a new agreement was announced. The new and rather modest deal was, in turn, much criticized by nations that had not been a party to any of these discussions, but was eventually accepted. Chinese indirectness had proved most effective in achieving the goals that they desired, but there would have been no agreement at all without the more direct initiatives of several Western leaders.

FIGURE 15.20 *Last ditch negotiations at the 2009 Copenhagen summit.*
Source: © Getty Images.

INTERCULTURAL RELATIONS

Will globalization mean the end of cultural differences?

In recent decades there have been unprecedented levels of contact between cultural groups located in different parts of the world. This has occurred through the globalization of the media, through short-term visits by tourists, students and business people and through long-term relocation by migrants and refugees. During this same period, almost all nations have become more affluent, although inequalities persist both within and between nations. Short-term population movements have most often been from individualist nations to collectivist nations, whereas the long-term population movements have mostly been in the reverse direction. The principal source of evidence as to the correlates of all this geographic mobility is provided by data collected by the World Values Survey. Initiated within a small range of nations in the early 1980s, this survey now provides information from more than 80 nations on endorsement of a wide variety of values and behaviours. The data have been collected from representative samples within each nation every few years. This makes it possible to gain a broad overview of the extent of global cultural change.

Inglehart and Baker (2000) analysed endorsement of World Values Survey items that they had found to make up a dimension of what they defined as 'post-materialist' values. Initially these authors defined a post-materialist as someone who tends to agree with survey items that can be summarized as these five statements:

- My self-expression and quality of life are more important than my economic and physical security.
- I am happy.
- Homosexuality is justifiable.
- You can trust most people.
- I have signed one or more petitions.

Subsequent research identified many additional survey items that post-materialists agree with. These items support gender equality, tolerance of minorities, recycling, state support for the needy and new technologies. When data from the 1980s was compared with that from the 1990s, a substantially increased percentage of those classified as post-materialists was found in 19 of 21 nations. The magnitude of these changes for some of these nations can be seen in Figure 15.21. The lower part of the figure shows the percentage of post-materialists *minus* the percent of materialists in each nation in 1980. The negative percentages in this part of the figure show that in 1980 there were more materialists than post-materialists in all European nations except Finland. For instance, in Italy, there were almost 40 per cent more materialists than post-materialists. The upper part of the table shows the *change* over the following decade. For instance, Italy shows a gain of post-materialists of around 45 per cent, so that by 1990 there were slightly more Italians classified as post-materialists than as materialists. Of course, respondents at these two points in time were not the same people. We do not know whether these changes have occurred through people actually changing their values, or through the replacement of populations as generations succeeded one another. Nonetheless, it appears that values that in the past were more characteristic of just a few of the most individualistic nations are becoming more widespread. These changes characterize the profile of nations as a whole, not all individuals. In each nation, there remain many individuals who would not be classified as post-materialists.

Inglehart and Oyserman (2004) explored these results and found that the nation-level scores for post-materialism correlate strongly with Hofstede's (1980) measures of individualism and Schwartz's (2004) measures of autonomy. However, they note that the profiles of nations with differing historical, religious and political systems

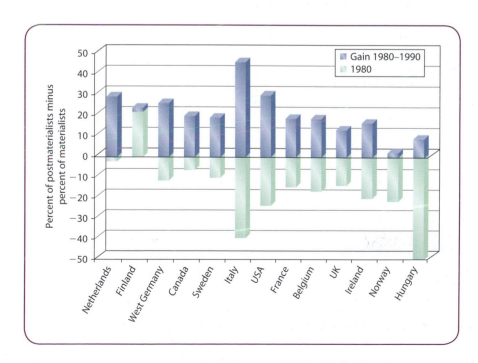

FIGURE 15.21 *Percentage of post-materialists minus percentage of materialists, 1980 and increase to 1990.*

Source: Based on data reported in Inglehart, 1997.

remain distinctive. What we are seeing is a global trend in value endorsement, not a convergence toward a single profile of 'modern' or Western values. The profiles of values endorsed for instance in East Asian nations, in the former Soviet bloc, in Islamic nations, in Latin America, in predominantly Protestant Europe, in predominantly Catholic Europe and in the Anglo nations each remain distinctive, but with rather more post-materialists in almost all nations. As Figure 15.21 also shows, the changes are happening just as much in nations that were already individualistic, such as the US, as they are in other nations that were not individualistic in time past.

Over the past several decades the great majority of nations have experienced economic growth (International Monetary Fund, 2005). The nations within which endorsement of post-materialist values has risen have been those experiencing increasing prosperity. World Values Survey data has also shown a movement *away* from post-materialist values within the much smaller number of nations that have suffered economic decline, such as the former Soviet bloc nations of Eastern Europe. Thus, future economic crises might engender a reversal of current value changes.

Migration and acculturation

One major source of cultural change is the current migration of large numbers of people from collectivist cultures in Asia, Africa and the Caribbean to more individualistic cultures in Europe, North America and Australasia. Social psychologists have a role to play in explaining the challenges that are raised by this process and in contributing to their resolution. **Acculturation** is a term that was defined some time ago as the process whereby two cultural groups that come into contact with one another cause changes in one or both parties (Redfield, Linton, & Herskovits, 1936). These changes may be in values, in behaviours

acculturation the process whereby two cultural groups that come into contact with one another cause changes in one or both parties.

and in how one feels about oneself. Although it is clear that increasing immigration does currently have a major political and social impact on the culture of individualistic nations, social psychological research has mostly been focused on the choices faced by immigrants and their descendents, leaving most of the study of changes in the nations receiving migrants to political scientists. As illustrated by Theory Box 15.3, Berry (1997) has emphasized that migrant acculturation is not simply a process whereby migrants must choose the extent to which they wish to adopt the values and behaviours of the majority culture (see Leader in the Field, John Berry). They also face choices as to how much of their culture of origin they wish to sustain. In addition, they will experience varying degrees of preference from majority culture members for each of the acculturation modes that are illustrated in Theory Box 15.3.

Most studies have shown that migrants favour the integration mode, that is to say participating in the majority culture, while also retaining the values and behaviours associated with their identity of origin (Sam & Berry, 1997). However, this preference is not always reciprocated by the majority population. For instance, Van Oudenhoven, Prins, and Buunk (1998) found that Moroccan and Turkish immigrants in the Netherlands favoured integration, but that Dutch majority respondents were more favourable to assimilation. One way in which migrants may adapt to this contrast in preferences is illustrated by Arends-Toth and Van de Vijver (2003), who found that while the Dutch majority favoured assimilation both at work and at home, Turkish migrants in the Netherlands favoured integration at work and separation at home. Look now at Individual Differences 15.2 to see how acculturation attitudes have most often been measured.

The conditions predisposing positive outcomes for intergroup contact have been discussed in Chapter 14. In relation to migration, particularly critical groups are the first and second generation children of immigrants, who experience socialization both by their family of origin and by the culture of the nation within which they have

---

THEORY BOX 15.3

BERRY'S TYPOLOGY OF ACCULTURATION MODES

Preferences	Retain original identity and group characteristics	Lose original identity and group characteristics
Valuable to join the larger society	Integration	Assimilation
Not valuable to join the larger society	Separation	Marginalization

Note: The preferences refer to the individual's preferences for him or herself.

Source: Based on Berry, 1997, with permission from John Wiley & Sons.

LEADER IN THE FIELD

John Berry (b. 1939) grew up in Canada but completed his PhD at the University of Edinburgh in the UK. His dissertation was focused on the cultural adaptations of the Inuit and Cree nations to differing environments in Northern Canada. This led to his early formulation of eco-cultural theory. He was a founding member of the International Association for Cross-Cultural Psychology and was the principal editor of the second edition of the *Handbook of Cross-Cultural Psychology*. He has also co-authored the first published textbook for the field of cross-cultural psychology as a whole. During the past three decades he has developed his model of acculturation processes, supervised the dissertations of many researchers now active in this field and assisted the Canadian government in the development of their policies relating to immigration.

been born. First-generation children arrive as migrants, while second-generation children are born within their new nation or residence. Berry, Phinney, Sam, and Vedder (2006) conducted a cross-sectional survey of more than 5000 first- and second-generation adolescents in 13 nations. Their European samples included both former colonial nations (France, Germany, Netherlands, Portugal and UK) and other nations that have recently received many migrants (Finland, Norway and Sweden). In each nation, one or more ethnic minorities were sampled, as well as a sample of non-migrants. Scores for better migrant adjustment showed a weak but positive association with the integration mode. For instance, those scoring high on integration were higher on measures of positive adjustment such as life satisfaction and self-esteem, and lower on psychological problems, poor school adjustment and behaviour problems, than those who scored lower on integration. These results were much more strongly affected by respondents' specific ethnicity than by the particular host nation within which they were living. For instance, as noted before, apart from work relations, Turkish migrants quite often favour separation rather than integration. Consequently, they score higher on adjustment in nations where there is a substantial Turkish community. Conversely, Vietnamese migrants favour integration and their adjustment is therefore less influenced by the presence or absence of other Vietnamese.

One reason why the relationship between the integration mode of adjustment and measures of adjustment is not stronger may be because the concept of integration is too broadly defined. Favouring integration implies a **bicultural identity** and there are differing ways of sustaining a bicultural identity, some of which may have better consequences than others. An immigrant or any person who is descended from more that one cultural background has two cultural identities available.

bicultural identity seeing oneself as having simultaneous membership of two culturally-distinct groups.

Bicultural identity integration is present when a person sees their alternate identities as compatible with one another. To explore this issue, look now at Research Close-Up 15.4.

bicultural identity integration present when a person sees their alternate identities as compatible with one another.

The priming study by Benet-Martínez, Leu, Lee, and Morris (2002) (see Research Close-Up 15.4) was conducted in the US, but there is no reason to expect differing results with European respondents. For instance, Verkuyten and Pouliasi (2002) compared the impact of priming on bicultural Greek children growing up in the Netherlands with control groups of monocultural Greek children living in Greece and Dutch children living in the Netherlands. The bicultural children were primed either by showing them Dutch icons (e.g. windmills, the national flag) or by showing them Greek icons (e.g. the Acropolis, the national flag). They were then presented with a series of tasks in which they had to provide reasons for events that had occurred. The first task also used the video of a fish swimming ahead of a group of other fish developed by Morris and Peng (1994), described earlier in this chapter. Later questions concerned reasons for the behaviour of hypothetical schoolchildren. For example, one question was 'One day a child is late for school. What could be the reason?' The results of these various tasks were combined to yield an index of internal versus external attribution. As Figure 15.22 shows, the researchers found that those children who had

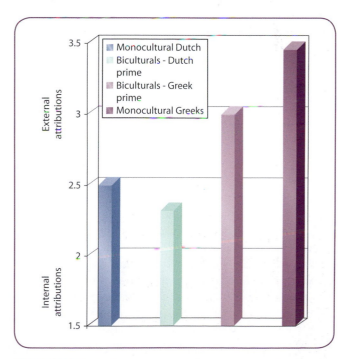

FIGURE 15.22 *Attributions made by primed and unprimed Greek and Dutch children.*

Source: Based on Verkuyten & Pouliasi, 2002, with permission from SAGE Publications.

ATTITUDES TO ACCULTURATION

Below are the items used in the research by Berry et al. (2006). You can complete them whether you are a member of an ethnic minority or a member of the majority in your nation. If you are a minority member, 'ethnic' in the items below refers to your own group. If you are a majority group member, take the phrase 'ethnic group' as referring to the most salient ethnic minorities within your nation. 'National' refers to your nation. Please indicate how much you agree or disagree with each of the statements, using the response scale presented below.

1   I feel that [ethnic group] should adapt to national cultural traditions and not maintain those of their own.
2   I would rather marry an [ethnic] than a national.
3   I feel that [ethnic group] should maintain their own cultural traditions but also adapt to those of this nation.
4   I would rather marry a national than an [ethnic].
5   I would be just as willing to marry a national as an [ethnic].
6   I feel that it is not important for [ethnic group] either to maintain their own cultural traditions or to adapt to those of this nation.
7   I feel that [ethnic group] should maintain their own cultural traditions and not adapt to those of this nation.
8   I would not like to marry either a national or an [ethnic]
9   It is more important to me to be fluent in [ethnic language] than in the national language.
10   It is more important to me to be fluent in the national language than in [ethnic language].
11   It is important to me to be fluent in both the national language and [ethnic language].
12   It is not important to me to be fluent either in [ethnic language] or the national language.

13   I prefer social activities that involve both national members and [ethnic] members.
14   I prefer to have only national friends.
15   I prefer to have only [ethnic] friends.
16   I prefer social activities that involve nationals only.
17   I prefer to have both national and [ethnic] friends.
18   I don't want to attend either national or [ethnic] activities.
19   I prefer social activities that involve [ethnic group] members only.
20   I don't want to have either national or [ethnic] friends.

1 = *Strongly disagree*
2 = *Somewhat disagree*
3 = *Not sure/neutral*
4 = *Somewhat agree*
5 = *Strongly agree*

Calculate your scores as follows: assimilation is the mean of items 1, 4, 10, 14 and 16. Integration is the mean of items 3, 5, 11, 13 and 17. Separation is the mean of items 2, 7, 9, 15 and 19. Marginalization is the mean of items 6, 8, 12, 18 and 20. In the sample of Berry et al. as a whole, mean scores for minority respondents were 2.20 for assimilation, 3.93 for integration, 2.59 for separation and 1.78 for marginalization. Means for majority members were 2.59, 3.69, 2.37 and 2.28 respectively. Thus, on average, as in other studies, all respondents favoured integration, but minority respondents did so more strongly, while majority respondents also favoured assimilation.

Source: This scale reproduced with permission of Taylor & Francis, from Berry et al. (2006). Immigrant youth in cultural transition: Acculturation, identity and adaptation across national contexts. Permission conveyed through Copyright Clearance Center, Inc.

been primed with Dutch icons made more internal attributions, while those children primed with Greek icons made more external attributions. The figure also shows the means for attributions made by the monocultural Dutch and the monocultural Greek children. The difference between the mean for the Dutch children and the bicultural people who had been primed with Dutch icons was not significant. Nor was the difference between the mean for monocultural Greek children and the bicultural people who had been primed with Greek icons. Thus, the full extent of the difference between the data from more individualistic Dutch and from the more collectivistic Greeks was reproduced through experimental priming.

Summary

Increased wealth and population mobility have been associated with global changes in values toward increased individualism and post-modern values. However, these changes are directional rather than converging on the values of any preexisting culture. Migration and intermarriage are creating increasing numbers of bicultural individuals. Bicultural identity integration appears to be associated with optimal acculturation. Experimental priming of bicultural people is creating opportunities to integrate cultural perspectives with other areas of research in social psychology.

BICULTURAL IDENTITY INTEGRATION

RESEARCH CLOSE-UP 15.4

Benet-Martínez, V. L., Leu, J., Lee, F., & Morris, M. W. (2002). Negotiating biculturalism: Cultural frame switching in biculturals with oppositional versus compatible cultural identities. *Journal of Cross-Cultural Psychology, 33*, 492–516.

Research question

Given the increasing frequency of biculturalism in many nations, Benet-Martínez and her colleagues were interested in alternate ways of handling bicultural identities. How does someone think and feel if they perceive their identities as incompatible with one another? Do compatible identities facilitate cultural integration? Can experimental methods illuminate these issues? The authors tested two main hypotheses about how individuals who are low versus high on identity integration respond when faced with an attribution task. First, because their identities are not in conflict, those who are high on identity integration were expected to respond to a US prime by making the more internal attributions that are typical of Americans, and to a Chinese prime by making the more external attributions that are typical of Chinese. Second, and in contrast, because of the identity conflict that they experience, respondents low in identity integration were expected to respond defensively, making external attributions in response to the US primes and internal attributions in response to the Chinese primes.

Design and procedure

The study used a 2 (type of identity integration) × 3 (type of prime) between-subjects design. The sample was split between those who were low or high on bicultural identity integration (BII). The primes were either American (e.g. Mickey Mouse, a cowboy, the Statue of Liberty); Chinese (e.g. the Summer Palace in Beijing, a rice farmer, the Great Wall); or control items unrelated to culture. Participants first received one of these primes, then viewed a series of videos showing a fish moving ahead of a group of other fish; this task was first used by Morris and Peng (1994), and was discussed earlier in this chapter. They were asked to rate the extent to which 'the one fish is being influenced by the group' (e.g. being chased, teased or pressured by others) and to rate the extent to which 'the one fish is influenced by some internal trait' (such as independence, personal objective or leadership). Next, each participant was asked to make a single rating of the extent to which they perceived themself as a Chinese who lives in America, rather than as a Chinese American. This provided a measure distinguishing between low and high bicultural identity integration. Finally, participants

also completed the measure of Berry's four acculturation modes (see Individual Differences 15.2).

Results

The predictions were supported. The left-hand side of Figure 15.23 indicates the results for respondents with low bicultural identity integration (BII). These data show the reverse pattern of attributions from those that were found by Morris and Peng (1994). With the Chinese prime these participants made more internal attributions, and with the American prime they made more external attributions. In contrast, the results for the respondents with high BII, shown on the right of the figure, replicate the results of Morris and Peng, as shown earlier in Figure 15.9. Despite the differing effects for high and low identity integration, both groups scored equally high on Berry's measure of integration.

Implications

This study has two important implications. Firstly, the concept of bicultural identity integration can advance our

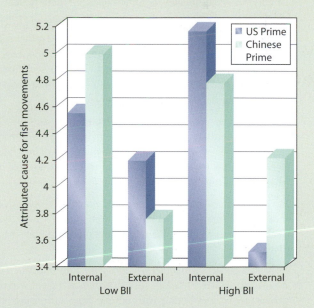

FIGURE 15.23 *Attributions made by bicultural people high and low in identity integration.*

Note: BII denotes bicultural identity integration.
Source: Based on Benet-Martínez et al., 2002, with permission from SAGE Publications.

understanding of the processes of acculturation. Berry's (1997) favoured concept of the integration mode of acculturation is broadly defined and can encompass quite different types of person. Someone with low bicultural integration is in some ways like a person who has a kind of split personality. Whichever personal identity they choose to express at a particular time, they place themselves on the outside of the other identity. The study by Benet-Martínez et al. supports the view that low BII people feel the need to compensate for that 'outsideness'. So, a low BII Chinese American responds to a Chinese prime by emphasizing their Americanness, and to an American prime by emphasizing their Chineseness. A high BII person does not feel the need to do this, and that facilitates their relations with others. For instance, in later studies by the same group, Mok, Morris, Benet-Martínez, and Karakitapoğlu-Aygün (2007) have shown that high BII Chinese Americans tend to have networks of friends of varying ethnicity, many of whom also know each other. Those with low BII have separate networks of friends who do not know each other.

A second implication of this study is that it extends the potential of experimental priming as a way of understanding cultural aspects of social psychology. Bicultural people may have more ready access to alternate identities than monocultural people, and this makes them distinctively useful to researchers. Furthermore, the effects found from priming studies with bicultural people may be parallel to those found when comparing mean differences between monocultural groups. If the effects are found to be parallel, then the prospects for establishing causal links between the various factors involved in the creation and maintenance of cultures are bright.

CHAPTER SUMMARY

- *What is culture and why should we study it?* A culture is a social system that is characterized by the shared meanings that are attributed to people and events by its members. Nations around the world have cultures that are sufficiently different that social psychological studies may yield different results in different locations.

- *What are cognitive styles and how are they related to culture?* Analytic cognitive styles are more prevalent within individualistic nations, while holistic cognitive styles are more typical in collectivist cultures. Environmental challenges and contemporary languages and norms serve to create and sustain these differences.

- *Can the ways in which we think about ourselves explain cultural variations in behaviour?* Individual-level measures of independent and interdependent self-construal provide a focused way of testing explanations for the cultural differences in social behaviour that have been found. We discussed the case of the student Wen Hua at the start of this chapter. If we were to measure her self-construal and values, we would probably find that she scores high on interdependence and endorses embeddedness, hierarchy and mastery values.

- *How do people relate to people whom they meet, and form relationships with them in different cultural contexts?* Members of collectivist cultures prioritize long-term ingroup relationships. They distinguish more sharply the ways that they behave in different types of relationship than do members of individualist cultures. In a collectivist culture, even intimate relationships between individuals are construed in terms of their relevance to group identities. Wen Hua finds it difficult to make new relationships because she is no longer in touch with her ingroup.

- *How does collectivism affect group behaviours?* In a collectivist culture, identity is derived from group memberships. To sustain that group's harmony and integrity, Wen Hua will work hard, communicate indirectly, respect status and conform more. In uncertain circumstances, Wen Hua seeks guidance from the senior figure and shows respect by working hard and not showing dissent.

- *How does collectivism affect relations with outgroups?* In a collectivist culture, group memberships are not open to change. An individual will therefore seek to enhance the esteem of his or her group by finding ways to compare it favourably with others. When interacting with people from outgroups, they will defend themselves against any threat to their group's honour.

- *Will globalization mean the end of cultural differences?* Greater prosperity and mobility have induced a global trend toward post-modern values, but differences between cultural groups are persisting. Migrant acculturation and intermarriage are creating an increasing proportion of bicultural people. Experimental priming of bicultural people provides a way in which explanation of cultural differences can directly enrich the validity of the findings of mainstream social psychology.

SUGGESTIONS FOR FURTHER READING

Chiu, C.-Y., & Hong, Y.-Y. (2006). *Social psychology of culture*. New York: Psychology Press. This text emphasizes studies that use experimental methods and make comparisons between North Americans and East Asians.

Heine, S. J. (2008). *Cultural psychology*. New York: Norton. This recent text also emphasizes comparisons between North America and East Asia.

Hofstede, G. H. (2001). *Culture's consequences: Comparing values, behaviors, institutions and organizations across nations* (2nd ed.). Thousand Oaks, CA: Sage. Detailed description of Hofstede's pioneering project.

International Association for Cross-Cultural Psychology (not dated). *Online readings in psychology and culture*. Retrieved from http://scholarworks.gvsu.edu/orpc. Free access to 87 articles discussing all areas of cross-cultural psychological research, with contributions from many of the leading figures in the field.

Kitayama, S. & Cohen, D. (Eds.). (2007). *Handbook of cultural psychology*. New York; Guilford. Interdisciplinary perspectives on the evolution of culture.

Smith, P. B., & Best, D. L. (Eds.). (2009). *Cross-cultural psychology* (four volumes). London: Sage. Seventy-three of the most influential papers in the field reprinted in full.

Smith, P. B., Bond, M. H., & Kağitiçibaşi, Ç. (2006). *Understanding social psychology across cultures: Living and working in a changing world*. London: Sage. This text develops much more fully the perspective taken in the present chapter.

Ward, C. A., Bochner, S., & Furnham, A. (2001). *The psychology of culture shock*. Hove, UK: Routledge. This is the leading textbook that addresses the issues of migration, acculturation and intercultural contact.

References

Aaker, J. L. (1997). Dimensions of brand personality. *Journal of Marketing Research, 34*, 347–356.

Aaker, J. L., Benet-Martínez, V. L., & Garolera, J. (2001). Consumption symbols as carriers of culture: A study of Japanese and Spanish brand personality constructs. *Journal of Personality and Social Psychology, 81*, 492–508.

Aarts, H., & Dijksterhuis, A. (2000). Habits as knowledge structures: Automaticity in goal-directed behavior. *Journal of Personality and Social Psychology, 78*, 53–63.

Abbey, A., Zawacki, T., Buck, P. O., Clinton, A. M., & McAuslan, P. (2004). Sexual assault and alcohol consumption: What do we know about their relationship and what types of research are still needed? *Aggression and Violent Behavior, 9*, 271–303.

Abelson, R. P. (1995). Attitude extremity. In R. E. Petty & R. E. Krosnick (Eds.), *Attitude strength: Antecedents and consequences* (pp. 25–42). Mahwah, NJ: Erlbaum.

Aberson, C. L., Healy, M., & Romero, V. (2000). Ingroup bias and self-esteem: A meta-analysis. *Personality and Social Psychology Review, 4*, 157–173.

Abrams, D., & Hogg, M. A. (1988). Comments on the motivational status of self-esteem in social identity and intergroup discrimination. *European Journal of Social Psychology, 18*, 317–334.

Abramson, L. Y., Metalsky, G. I., & Alloy, L. B. (1989). Hopelessness depression: A theory-based subtype of depression. *Psychological Review, 96*, 358–372.

Abramson, L. Y., Seligman, M. E., & Teasdale, J. D. (1978). Learned helplessness in humans: Critique and reformulation. *Journal of Abnormal and Social Psychology, 87*, 49–74.

Adair, W. L., & Brett, J. M. (2005). The negotiation dance: Time culture and behavioural sequences in negotiation. *Organizational Science, 16*, 33–51.

Adams, J. S. (1963). Towards an understanding of inequity. *Journal of Abnormal and Social Psychology, 67*, 422–436.

Adorno, T. W., Frenkel-Brunswik, E., Levinson, D. J., & Sanford, R. N. (1950). *The authoritarian personality*. New York: Harper.

Aime, F., & Van Dyne, L. (2010). Bringing social structure to both sides of an issue: How proximal and distal ties interact with minority and majority positions to affect influence in workgroups. In R. Martin & M. Hewstone (Eds.), *Minority influence and innovation: Antecedents, processes and consequences* (pp. 313–340). Hove, UK: Psychology Press.

Ainsworth, M. D. S., Bell, S. M., & Stayton, D. (1974). Infant–mother attachment and social development. In M. P. Richards (Ed.), *The integration of the child into a social world* (pp. 99–135). London: Cambridge University Press.

Ajzen, I. (1991). The theory of planned behavior. *Organizational Behavior and Human Decision Processes, 50*, 179–211.

Ajzen, I., & Fishbein, M. (1977). Attitude-behavior relations: A theoretical analysis and review of empirical research. *Psychological Bulletin, 84*, 888–918.

Ajzen, I., & Madden, T. J. (1986). Prediction of goal-directed behavior: Attitudes, intentions, and perceived behavioral control. *Journal of Experimental Social Psychology, 22*, 453–474.

Akhtar, S., & Thomson, J. A., Jr. (1982). Overview: Narcissistic personality disorder. *American Journal of Psychiatry, 139*, 12–20.

Albarracín, D., Johnson, B. T., Fishbein, M., & Muellerleile, P. A. (2001). Theories of reasoned action and planned behavior as models of condom use: A meta-analysis. *Psychological Bulletin, 127*, 142–161.

Albarracín, D., Johnson, B. T., & Zanna, M. P. (Eds.). (2005). *Handbook of attitudes*. Mahwah, NJ: Erlbaum.

Albarracín, D., & Wyer, R. S., Jr. (2000). The cognitive impact of past behavior: Influences on beliefs, attitudes, and future behavioral decisions. *Journal of Personality and Social Psychology, 79*, 5–22.

Alberts, H. J. E. M., Martijn, C., & De Vries, N. K. (2011). Fighting self-control failure: Overcoming ego depletion by increasing self-awareness. *Journal of Experimental Social Psychology, 47*, 58–62.

Aldag, R. J., & Fuller, S. R. (1993). Beyond fiasco: A reappraisal of the groupthink phenomenon and a new model of group decision processes. *Psychological Bulletin, 113*, 533–552.

Alford, C. F. (2001). *Whistleblowers: broken lives and organizational power*. Ithaca, NY and London: Cornell University Press.

Alicke, M. D. (1985). Global self-evaluation as determined by the desirability and controllability of trait adjectives. *Journal of Personality and Social Psychology, 49*, 1621–1630.

Alicke, M. D., & Govorun, O. (2005). The better-than-average effect: The self in social judgment. In M. D. Alicke, D. A. Dunning, & J. I. Krueger (Eds.), *The self in social judgment* (pp. 85–106). New York: Psychology Press.

Alicke, M. D., & Sedikides, C. (2009). Self-enhancement and self-protection: What they are and what they do. In W. Stroebe & M. Hewstone (Eds.), *European review of social psychology* (Vol. 20, pp. 1–48). Hove, UK: Psychology Press.

Allen, V. L. (1966). Situational factors in conformity. In L. Berkowitz (Ed.), *Advances in experimental social psychology* (Vol. 2, pp. 133–175). New York: Academic Press.

Allen, V. L. (1975). Social support for nonconformity. In L. Berkowitz (Ed.), *Advances in experimental social psychology* (Vol. 8, pp. 1–43). New York: Academic Press.

Allen, V. L., & Levine, J. M. (1971). Social support and conformity: The role of independent assessment of reality. *Journal of Experimental Social Psychology, 7*, 48–58.

Allport, F. H. (1919). Behavior and experiment in social psychology. *Journal of Abnormal Psychology, 14*, 297–306.

Allport, F. H. (1924). *Social psychology.* Boston, MA: Houghton Mifflin.

Allport, G. W. (1935). Attitudes. In C. Murchison (Ed.), *Handbook of social psychology* (pp. 798–844). Worcester, MA: Clark University Press.

Allport, G. W. (1954a). The historical background of modern social psychology. In G. Lindzey (Ed.), *Handbook of social psychology* (2nd ed., Vol. 1, pp. 3–56). Reading, MA: Addison-Wesley.

Allport, G. W. (1954b). *The nature of prejudice.* Reading, MA: Addison-Wesley.

Allport, G. W. (1961). *Pattern and growth in personality.* Oxford: Holt, Rinehart and Winston.

Allport, G. W. (1968). *The person in psychology: Selected essays.* Boston, MA: Beacon.

Alonso-Arbiol, I., Balluerka, N., Shaver, P. R., & Gillath, O. (2008). Psychometric properties of the Spanish and American versions of the ECR Adult Attachment Questionnaire: A comparative study. *European Journal of Psychological Assessment, 24*, 9–13.

Altemeyer, B. (1981). *Right-wing authoritarianism.* Winnipeg, Canada: University of Manitoba Press.

Altemeyer, B. (1998). The other 'authoritarian personality'. In M. P. Zanna (Ed.), *Advances in experimental social psychology* (Vol. 30, pp. 47–92). San Diego, CA: Academic Press.

Altman, I., & Taylor, D. A. (1973). *Social penetration: The development of interpersonal relationships.* New York: Holt, Rinehart and Winston.

Alvaro, E. M., & Crano, W. D. (1997). Indirect minority influence: Evidence for leniency in source evaluation and counterargumentation. *Journal of Personality and Social Psychology, 72*, 949–964.

Alwin, D. F., Cohen, R. L., & Newcomb, T. M. (1991). *Political attitudes over the life span: The Bennington women after fifty years.* Madison, WI: University of Wisconsin Press.

Amabile, T. M. (1996). *Creativity in context.* Boulder, CO: Westview.

Amato, P. R., & Afifi, T. D. (2006). Feeling caught between parents: Adult children's relations with parents and subjective well-being. *Journal of Marriage and Family, 68*, 222–235.

American Psychiatric Association. (1994). *Diagnostic and statistical manual of mental disorders* (4th ed.). Washington, DC: Author.

American Psychological Association. (2010a). *Ethical principles for psychologists and code of conduct* (2002, amended June 1, 2010).

Amichai-Hamburger, Y., & McKenna, K. Y. A. (2006). The contact hypothesis reconsidered: Interacting via the Internet. *Journal of Computer-Mediated Communication, 11*, 825–843.

Amir, Y. (1976). The role of intergroup contact in change of prejudice and intergroup relations. In P. A. Katz (Ed.), *Towards the elimination of racism* (pp. 245–308). New York: Pergamon.

Amir, Y., & Sharon, I. (1987). Are social psychological laws cross-culturally valid? *Journal of Cross-Cultural Psychology, 18*, 383–470.

Amodio, D. M. (2008). The social neuroscience of intergroup relations. In W. Stroebe & M. Hewstone (Eds.), *European review of social psychology* (Vol. 19, pp. 1–54). Hove, UK: Psychology Press.

Amodio, D. M. (2010). Can neuroscience advance social psychological theory? Social neuroscience for the behavioral social psychologist. *Social Cognition, 28*, 695–716.

Amodio, D. M., & Devine, P. G. (2006). Stereotyping and evaluation in implicit race bias: Evidence for independent constructs and unique effects on behavior. *Journal of Personality and Social Psychology, 91*, 652–661.

Amodio, D. M., Devine, P. G., & Harmon-Jones, E. (2008). Individual differences in the regulation of intergroup bias: The role of conflict monitoring and neural signals for control. *Journal of Personality and Social Psychology, 94*, 60–74.

Amodio, D. M., & Frith, C. D. (2006). Meeting of minds: The medial frontal cortex and social cognition. *Nature Reviews Neuroscience, 7*, 268–277.

Andersen, S. M., & Chen, S. (2002). The relational self: An interpersonal social-cognitive theory. *Psychological Review, 109*, 619–645.

Anderson, C. A. (1989). Temperature and aggression: Ubiquitous effects of heat on occurrence of human violence. *Psychological Bulletin, 106*, 74–96.

Anderson, C. A. (2001). Heat and violence. *Current Directions in Psychological Science, 10*, 33–38.

Anderson, C. A., Anderson, K. B., Dorr, N., DeNeve, K. M., & Flanagan, M. (2000). Temperature and aggression. In M. P. Zanna (Ed.), *Advances in experimental social psychology* (Vol. 32, pp. 63–133). New York: Academic Press.

Anderson, C. A., Berkowitz, L., Donnerstein, E., Huesmann, L. R., Johnson, J. D., Linz, D., ... & Wartella, E. (2003). The influence of media violence on youth. *Psychological Science in the Public Interest, 4*, 81–110.

Anderson, C. A., & Bushman, B. J. (1997). External validity of 'trivial' experiments: The case of laboratory aggression. *Review of General Psychology, 1*, 19–41.

Anderson, C. A., & Bushman, B. J. (2002). Media violence and the American public revisited. *American Psychologist, 57*, 448–450.

Anderson, C. A., Bushman, B. J., & Groom, R. W. (1997). Hot years and serious and deadly assault: Empirical tests of the heat hypothesis. *Journal of Personality and Social Psychology, 73*, 1213–1223.

Anderson, C. A., & Dill, K. E. (2000). Video games and aggressive thoughts, feelings, and behavior in the laboratory and in life. *Journal of Personality and Social Psychology, 78*, 772–790.

Anderson, C. A., Gentile, D. A., & Buckley, K. E. (2007). *Violent video game effects on children and adolescents*. New York: Oxford University Press.

Anderson, C. A., Shibuya, A., Ihori, N., Swing, E. L., Bushman, B. J., Sakamoto, A., … Saleem, M. (2010). Violent video game effects on aggression, empathy, and prosocial behavior in Eastern and Western countries: A meta-analytic review. *Psychological Bulletin, 136*, 151–173.

Anderson, N. B. (Ed.). (2009). Obedience – then and now [Special issue]. *American Psychologist, 64*(1).

Anderson, N. H. (1981). *Foundations of information integration theory*. New York: Academic Press.

Archer, J. (2000). Sex differences in aggression between heterosexual partners: A meta-analytic review. *Psychological Bulletin, 126*, 651–680.

Archer, J. (2004). Sex differences in aggression in real-world settings: A meta-analytic review. *Review of General Psychology, 8*, 291–322.

Archer, J., Birring, S. S., & Wu, F. C. W. (1998). The association between testosterone and aggression in young men: Empirical findings and a meta-analysis. *Aggressive Behavior, 24*, 411–420.

Archer, J., & Coyne, S. M. (2005). An integrated review of indirect, relational, and social aggression. *Personality and Social Psychology Review, 9*, 212–230.

Archer, J., & Lloyd, B. B. (2002). *Sex and gender* (3rd ed.). New York: Cambridge University Press.

Archer, J., & McDaniel, P. (1995). Violence and gender: Differences and similarities across societies. In B. R. Ruback & N. A. Weiner (Eds.), *Interpersonal violent behaviors: Social and cultural aspects* (pp. 63–87). New York: Springer.

Arends-Toth, J., & Van de Vijver, F. (2003). Multiculturalism and acculturation: Views of Dutch and Turkish Dutch. *European Journal of Social Psychology, 33*, 249–266.

Arendt, H. (1965). *Eichmann in Jerusalem: A report on the banality of evil*. New York: Viking.

Argyle, M. (1991). *Cooperation: The basis of sociability*. London: Routledge.

Armitage, C. J., & Conner, M. (2001). Efficacy of the theory of planned behaviour: A meta-analytic review. *British Journal of Social Psychology, 40*, 471–499.

Armor, D. A., & Taylor, S. E. (1998). Situated optimism: Specific outcome expectancies and self-regulation. In M. P. Zanna (Ed.), *Advances in experimental social psychology* (Vol. 30, pp. 309–379). San Diego, CA: Academic Press.

Aron, A., & Aron, E. N. (1986). *Love as the expansion of self: Understanding attraction and satisfaction*. Washington, DC: Hemisphere.

Aron, A., Aron, E. N., Tudor, M., & Nelson, G. (1991). Close relationships as including other in the self. *Journal of Personality and Social Psychology, 60*, 241–253.

Aron, A., Paris, M., & Aron, E. N. (1995). Falling in love: Prospective studies of self-concept change. *Journal of Personality and Social Psychology, 69*, 1102–1112.

Aronson, E. (1969). The theory of cognitive dissonance: A current perspective. In L. Berkowitz (Ed.), *Advances in experimental social psychology* (Vol. 4, pp. 1–34). New York: Academic Press.

Aronson, E., Ellsworth, P. C., Carlsmith, J. M., & Gonzales, M. H. (1990). *Methods of research in social psychology* (2nd ed.). New York: McGraw-Hill.

Aronson, E., & Mills, J. (1959). The effect of severity of initiation on liking for a group. *Journal of Abnormal and Social Psychology, 59*, 177–181.

Aronson, E., & Patnoe, S. (1997). *The jigsaw classroom: Building cooperation in the classroom*. New York: Longman.

Aronson, E., Wilson, T. D., & Brewer, M. B. (1998). Experimentation in social psychology. In D. T. Gilbert, S. T. Fiske, & G. Lindzey (Eds.), *Handbook of social psychology* (4th ed., Vol. 1, pp. 99–142). Boston, MA: McGraw-Hill.

Asch, S. E. (1946). Forming impressions of personality. *Journal of Abnormal and Social Psychology, 41*, 258–290.

Asch, S. E. (1951). Effects of group pressure upon the modification and distortion of judgments. In H. Guetzkow (Ed.), *Groups, leadership and men* (pp. 177–190). Pittsburgh, PA: Carnegie.

Asch, S. E. (1955). Opinions and social pressure. *Scientific American, 193*, 31–35.

Asch, S. E. (1956). Studies of independence and conformity: A minority of one against a unanimous majority. *Psychological Monographs, 70*, 70.

Asch, S. E. (1987). *Social psychology*. New York: Oxford University Press.

Atkins, C. J., Kaplan, R. M., & Toshima, M. T. (1991). Close relationships in the epidemiology of cardiovascular disease. In W. H. Jones & D. Perlman (Eds.), *Advances in personal relationships* (Vol. 3, pp. 207–231). London: Jessica Kingsley.

Averill, J. R., Malmstrom, E. J., Koriat, A., & Lazarus, R. S. (1972). Habituation to complex emotional stimuli. *Journal of Abnormal Psychology, 80*, 20–28.

Avolio, B. J. (1999). *Full leadership development: Building the vital forces in organizations.* Thousand Oaks, CA: Sage.

Back, M. D., Schmukle, S. C., & Egloff, B. (2008). Becoming friends by chance. *Psychological Science, 19*, 439–440.

Baer, J., Kaufman, J. C., & Baumeister, R. F. (2008). *Are we free?: Psychology and free will.* New York: Oxford University Press.

Bakeman, R. (2000). Behavioral observation and coding. In H. T. Reis & C. M. Judd (Eds.), *Handbook of research methods in social and personality psychology* (pp. 138–160). New York: Cambridge University Press.

Baker, S. M., & Petty, R. E. (1994). Majority and minority influence: Source-position imbalance as a determinant of message scrutiny. *Journal of Personality and Social Psychology, 67*, 5–19.

Baldwin, M. W. (1992). Relational schemas and the processing of social information. *Psychological Bulletin, 112*, 461–484.

Baldwin, M. W., Carrell, S. E., & Lopez, D. F. (1990). Priming relational schemas: My advisor and the Pope are watching me from the back of my mind. *Journal of Experimental Social Psychology, 26*, 435–454.

Baldwin, M. W., & Holmes, J. G. (1987). Salient private audiences and awareness of the self. *Journal of Personality and Social Psychology, 52*, 1087–1098.

Bales, R. F. (1950). *Interaction process analysis: A method for the study of small groups.* Cambridge, MA: Addison-Wesley.

Bales, R. F. (1953). The equilibrium problem in small groups. In T. H. Parsons, R. F. Bales, & E. A. Shils (Eds.), *Working paper in the theory of action* (pp. 111–161). New York: Free Press.

Bales, R. F., & Slater, P. E. (1955). Role differentiation in small decision-making groups. In T. Parsons & R. F. Bales (Eds.), *Family, socialization, and interaction process* (pp. 259–306). Glencoe, IL: Free Press.

Banaji, M. R., & Hardin, C. D. (1996). Automatic stereotyping. *Psychological Science, 7*, 136–141.

Bandura, A. (1977). Self-efficacy: Toward a unifying theory of behavioral change. *Psychological Review, 84*, 191–215.

Bandura, A. (1977). *Social learning theory.* Englewood Cliffs, NJ: Prentice Hall.

Bandura, A. (1983). Psychological mechanisms of aggression. In R. G. Geen & E. I. Donnerstein (Eds.), *Aggression: Theoretical and empirical reviews* (Vol. 1, pp. 1–40). New York: Academic Press.

Bandura, A. (1999). Moral disengagement in the perpetration of inhumanities. *Personality and Social Psychology Review, 3*, 193–209.

Bandura, A., Ross, D., & Ross, S. A. (1961). Transmission of aggression through imitation of aggressive models. *Journal of Abnormal and Social Psychology, 63*, 575–582.

Bandura, A., Ross, D., & Ross, S. A. (1963). Vicarious reinforcement and imitative learning. *Journal of Abnormal and Social Psychology, 67*, 601–607.

Barber, J. P., Abrams, M. J., Connolly-Gibbons, M. B., Crits-Christoph, P., Barrett, M. S., Rynn, M., & Siqueland, L. (2005). Explanatory style change in supportive-expressive dynamic therapy. *Journal of Clinical Psychology, 61*, 257–268.

Bargh, J. A. (1982). Attention and automaticity in the processing of self-relevant information. *Journal of Personality and Social Psychology, 43*, 425–436.

Bargh, J. A. (1994). The four horsemen of automaticity: Awareness, intention, efficiency, and control in social cognition. In R. S. Wyer Jr. & T. K. Srull (Eds.), *Handbook of social cognition* (2nd ed., Vol. 1, pp. 1–40). Hillsdale, NJ: Erlbaum.

Bargh, J. A. (1999). The cognitive monster: The case against the controllability of automatic stereotype effects. In S. Chaiken & Y. Trope (Eds.), *Dual-process theories in social psychology* (pp. 361–382). New York: Guilford.

Bargh, J. A. (2005). Bypassing the will: Toward demystifying the nonconscious control of social behavior. In R. R. Hassin, J. S. Uleman, & J. A. Bargh (Eds.), *The new unconscious* (pp. 37–60). New York: Oxford University Press.

Bargh, J. A., & Chartrand, T. L. (2000). The mind in the middle: A practical guide to priming and automaticity research. In H. T. Reis & C. M. Judd (Eds.), *Handbook of research methods in social and personality psychology* (pp. 253–285). New York: Cambridge University Press.

Bargh, J. A., Chen, M., & Burrows, L. (1996). Automaticity of social behavior: Direct effects of trait construct and stereotype activation on action. *Journal of Personality and Social Psychology, 71*, 230–244.

Bargh, J. A., Gollwitzer, P. M., Lee-Chai, A., Barndollar, K., & Trötschel, R. (2001). The automated will: Nonconscious activation and pursuit of behavioral goals. *Journal of Personality and Social Psychology, 81*, 1014–1027.

Bargh, J. A., & Pietromonaco, P. (1982). Automatic information processing and social perception: The influence of trait information presented outside of conscious awareness on impression formation. *Journal of Personality and Social Psychology, 43*, 437–449.

Barnett, O. W., Miller-Perrin, C. L., & Perrin, R. D. (2011). *Family violence across the lifespan* (2nd ed.). Thousand Oaks, CA: Sage.

Baron, R. A., & Richardson, D. R. (1994). *Human aggression* (2nd ed.). New York: Plenum.

Baron, R. M., & Boudreau, L. A. (1987). An ecological perspective on integrating personality and social psychology. *Journal of Personality and Social Psychology, 53*, 1222–1228.

Baron, R. M., & Kenny, D. A. (1986). The moderator-mediator variable distinction in social psychological research: Conceptual, strategic, and statistical considerations. *Journal of Personality and Social Psychology, 51*, 1173–1182.

Baron, R. S., & Kerr, N. L. (2003). *Group process, group decision, group action* (2nd ed.). Buckingham, UK: Open University Press.

Barry, C. T., Frick, P. J., Adler, K. K., & Grafeman, S. J. (2007). The predictive utility of narcissism among children and adolescents: Evidence for a distinction between adaptive and maladaptive narcissism. *Journal of Child and Family Studies, 16,* 508–521.

Barsade, S. G. (2002). The ripple effect: Emotional contagion and its influence on group behavior. *Administrative Science Quarterly, 47,* 644–675.

Bartholomew, K. (1990). Avoidance of intimacy: An attachment perspective. *Journal of Social and Personal Relationships, 7,* 147–178.

Bartholow, B. D., & Anderson, C. A. (2002). Effects of violent video games on aggressive behavior: Potential sex differences. *Journal of Experimental Social Psychology, 38,* 283–290.

Bartlett, F. C. (1932). *Remembering. A study in experimental and social psychology.* Cambridge, MA: Cambridge University Press.

Bass, B. M. (1985). *Leadership and performance beyond expectations.* New York: Free Press.

Bass, B. M. (2008). *The Bass handbook of leadership: Theory, research, and managerial applications* (4th ed.). New York: Free Press.

Bass, B. M., & Avolio, B. J. (1994). *Improving organizational effectiveness through transformational leadership.* Thousand Oaks, CA: Sage.

Bassili, J. N. (1993). Response latency versus certainty as indexes of the strength of voting intentions in a CATI survey. *Public Opinion Quarterly, 57,* 54–61.

Bassili, J. N. (1996). The 'how' and 'why' of response latency measurement in survey research. In N. Schwarz & S. Sudman (Eds.), *Answering questions: Methodology for determining cognitive and communicative processes in survey research* (pp. 319–346). San Francisco, CA: Jossey-Bass.

Bassili, J. N., & Fletcher, J. F. (1991). Response-time measurement in survey research: A method for CATI and a new look at nonattitudes. *Public Opinion Quarterly, 55,* 331–346.

Batson, C. D. (1991). *The altruism question: Toward a social-psychological answer.* Hillsdale, NJ: Erlbaum.

Batson, C. D. (1994). Why act for the public good? Four answers. *Personality and Social Psychology Bulletin, 20,* 603–610.

Batson, C. D. (2011). *Altruism in humans.* New York: Oxford University Press.

Batson, C. D., Duncan, B. D., Ackerman, P., Buckley, T., & Birch, K. (1981). Is empathic emotion a source of altruistic motivation? *Journal of Personality and Social Psychology, 40,* 290–302.

Baum, A. (1990). Stress, intrusive imagery, and chronic distress. *Health Psychology, 9,* 653–675.

Baumeister, R. F. (1984). Choking under pressure: Self-consciousness and paradoxical effects of incentives on skillful performance. *Journal of Personality and Social Psychology, 46,* 610–620.

Baumeister, R. F. (1990). Suicide as escape from self. *Psychological Review, 97,* 90–113.

Baumeister, R. F. (1991). *Escaping the self: Alcoholism, spirituality, masochism, and other flights from the burden of selfhood.* New York: Basic Books.

Baumeister, R. F., & Cairns, K. J. (1992). Repression and self-presentation: When audiences interfere with self-deceptive strategies. *Journal of Personality and Social Psychology, 62,* 851–862.

Baumeister, R. F., Campbell, J. D., Krueger, J. I., & Vohs, K. D. (2003). Does high self-esteem cause better performance, interpersonal success, happiness, or healthier lifestyles? *Psychological Science in the Public Interest, 4,* 1–44.

Baumeister, R. F., Catanese, K. R., & Wallace, H. M. (2002). Conquest by force: A narcissistic reactance theory of rape and sexual coercion. *Review of General Psychology, 6,* 92–135.

Baumeister, R. F., DeWall, C. N., Ciarocco, N. J., & Twenge, J. M. (2005). Social exclusion impairs self-regulation. *Journal of Personality and Social Psychology, 88,* 589–604.

Baumeister, R. F., & Leary, M. R. (1995). The need to belong: Desire for interpersonal attachments as a fundamental human motivation. *Psychological Bulletin, 117,* 497–529.

Baumeister, R. F., & Newman, L. S. (1994). Self-regulation of cognitive inference and decision processes. *Personality and Social Psychology Bulletin, 20,* 3–19.

Baumeister, R. F., Schmeichel, B. J., & Vohs, K. D. (2007). Self-regulation and the executive function: The self as controlling agent. In A. W. Kruglanski & E. T. Higgins (Eds.), *Social psychology: Handbook of basic principles* (2nd ed., pp. 516–539). New York: Guilford.

Baumeister, R. F., & Showers, C. J. (1986). A review of paradoxical performance effects: Choking under pressure in sports and mental tests. *European Journal of Social Psychology, 16,* 361–383.

Baumeister, R. F., Smart, L., & Boden, J. M. (1996). Relation of threatened egotism to violence and aggression: The dark side of high self-esteem. *Psychological Review, 103,* 5–33.

Baumeister, R. F., & Vohs, K. D. (2001). Narcissism as addiction to esteem. *Psychological Inquiry, 12,* 206–210.

Baumrind, D. (1964). Some thoughts on ethics of research: After reading Milgram's 'Behavioral Study of Obedience'. *American Psychologist, 19,* 421–423.

Baxter, L. A. (1987). Self-disclosure and relationship disengagement. In V. J. Derlega & J. H. Berg (Eds.), *Self-disclosure: Theory, research, and therapy* (pp. 155–174). New York: Plenum.

Beaman, A. L., Barnes, P. J., Klentz, B., & McQuirk, B. (1978). Increasing helping rates through information dissemination: Teaching pays. *Personality and Social Psychology Bulletin, 4,* 406–411.

Beaman, A. L., Cole, C. M., Preston, M., Klentz, B., & Steblay, N. M. (1983). Fifteen years of foot-in-the-door research: A meta-analysis. *Personality and Social Psychology Bulletin, 9*, 181–196.

Becker, E. (1973). *The denial of death*. New York: Free Press.

Beer, J. S. (2012). A social neuroscience perspective on the self. In M. R. Leary & J. P. Tangney (Eds.), *Handbook of self and identity* (2nd ed.). New York: Guilford.

Beer, J. S. (in press). Self-evaluation and self-knowledge. In S. T. Fiske & C. N. Macrae (Eds.), *Sage handbook of social cognition*. New York: Sage.

Beggan, J. K. (1992). On the social nature of nonsocial perception: The mere ownership effect. *Journal of Personality and Social Psychology, 62*, 229–237.

Beilock, S. L., & Carr, T. H. (2001). On the fragility of skilled performance: What governs choking under pressure? *Journal of Experimental Psychology: General, 130*, 701–725.

Belknap, J., Fisher, B. S., & Cullen, F. T. (1999). The development of a comprehensive measure of the sexual victimization of college women. *Violence Against Women, 5*, 185–214.

Bem, D. J. (1965). An experimental analysis of self-persuasion. *Journal of Experimental Social Psychology, 1*, 199–218.

Bem, D. J. (1972). Self-perception theory. In L. Berkowitz (Ed.), *Advances in experimental social psychology* (Vol. 6, pp. 1–62). New York: Academic Press.

Benet-Martínez, V. L., Leu, J., Lee, F., & Morris, M. W. (2002). Negotiating biculturalism: Cultural frame switching in biculturals with oppositional versus compatible cultural identities. *Journal of Cross-Cultural Psychology, 33*, 492–516.

Bentall, R. P., & Fernyhough, C. (2008). Social predictors of psychotic experiences: Specificity and psychological mechanisms. *Schizophrenia Bulletin, 34*, 1012–1020.

Bentall, R. P., Kinderman, P., & Kaney, S. (1994). The self, attributional processes and abnormal beliefs: Towards a model of persecutory delusions. *Behaviour Research and Therapy, 32*, 331–341.

Ben-Ze'ev, A. (2004). *Love online: Emotions on the Internet*. Cambridge, MA: Cambridge University Press.

Berger, C. R., & Calabrese, R. J. (1975). Some explorations in initial interaction and beyond: Toward a developmental theory of interpersonal communication. *Human Communication Research, 1*, 99–112.

Berger, J., Rosenholtz, S. J., & Zelditch, M. (1980). Status organizing processes. *Annual Review of Psychology, 6*, 479–508.

Berkman, L. F., & Syme, S. L. (1979). Social networks, host resistance, and mortality: A nine year follow-up study of Alameda County residents. *American Journal of Epidemiology, 109*, 186–204.

Berkowitz, L. (1993). *Aggression: Its causes, consequences, and control*. Philadelphia, PA: Temple University Press.

Berkowitz, L. (1999). Evil is more than banal: Situationism and the concept of evil. *Personality and Social Psychology Review, 3*, 246–253.

Berkowitz, L., & LePage, A. (1967). Weapons as aggression-eliciting stimuli. *Journal of Personality and Social Psychology, 7*, 202–207.

Bermeitinger, C., Goelz, R., Johr, N., Neumann, M., Ecker, U. K. H., & Doerr, R. (2009). The hidden persuaders break into the tired brain. *Journal of Experimental Social Psychology, 45*, 320–326.

Berridge, K., & Winkielman, P. (2003). What is an unconscious emotion? The case for unconscious 'liking'. *Cognition and Emotion, 17*, 181–211.

Berry, D. S., & McArthur, L. Z. (1986). Perceiving character in faces: The impact of age-related craniofacial changes on social perception. *Psychological Bulletin, 100*, 3–18.

Berry, J. W. (1976). *Human ecology and cognitive style: Comparative studies in cultural and psychological adaptation*. New York: Wiley.

Berry, J. W. (1997). Immigration, acculturation and adaptation. *Applied Psychology: An International Review, 46*, 5–34.

Berry, J. W., Kim, U., Minde, T., & Mok, D. (1987). Comparative studies of acculturative stress. *International Migration Review, 21*, 491–511.

Berry, J. W., Phinney, J. S., Sam, D. L., & Vedder, P. (2006). *Immigrant youth in cultural transition: Acculturation, identity and adaptation across national contexts*. Mahwah, NJ: Erlbaum.

Berscheid, E. (1985). Interpersonal attraction. In G. Lindzey & E. Aronson (Eds.), *Handbook of social psychology* (3rd ed., Vol. 2, pp. 413–484). New York: Random House.

Berscheid, E. (1992). A glance back at a quarter century of social psychology. *Journal of Personality and Social Psychology, 63*, 525–533.

Berscheid, E., & Regan, P. C. (2005). *The psychology of interpersonal relationships*. Upper Saddle River, NJ: Prentice Hall.

Berscheid, E., & Reis, H. T. (1998). Attraction and close relationships. In D. T. Gilbert, S. T. Fiske, & G. Lindzey (Eds.), *Handbook of social psychology* (4th ed., Vol. 2, pp. 193–281). Boston, MA: McGraw-Hill.

Berscheid, E., Snyder, M., & Omoto, A. M. (1989). The Relationship Closeness Inventory: Assessing the closeness of interpersonal relationships. *Journal of Personality and Social Psychology, 57*, 792–807.

Berscheid, E., & Walster, E. (1974). Physical attractiveness. In L. Berkowitz (Ed.), *Advances in experimental social psychology* (Vol. 7, pp. 158–215). New York: Academic Press.

Bessière, K., Kiesler, S., Kraut, R., & Boneva, B. (2008). Effects of Internet use and social resources on changes in depression. *Information, Communication & Society, 11*, 47–70.

Bettencourt, B. A., Brewer, M. B., Croak, M. R., & Miller, N. (1992). Cooperation and the reduction of intergroup bias: The role of reward structure and social orientation. *Journal of Experimental Social Psychology, 28,* 301–319.

Bettencourt, B. A., & Miller, N. (1996). Gender differences in aggression as a function of provocation: A meta-analysis. *Psychological Bulletin, 119,* 422–447.

Betzig, L. (1989). Causes of conjugal dissolution: A cross-cultural study. *Current Anthropology, 30,* 654–676.

Bickman, L., & Kamzan, M. (1973). The effect of race and need on helping behavior. *Journal of Social Psychology, 89,* 73–77.

Bieneck, S., & Krahé, B. (2011). Blaming the victim and exonerating the perpetrator in cases of rape and robbery: Is there a double standard? *Journal of Interpersonal Violence, 26,* 1–13.

Bierhoff, H. W. (2002). *Prosocial behaviour.* Hove, UK: Psychology Press.

Billig, M. (1976). *Social psychology and intergroup relations.* London: Academic Press.

Binet, A., & Henri, V. (1894). De la suggestibilité naturelle chez les enfants [The natural suggestibility of children]. *Revue Philosophique, 38,* 337–347.

Birnbaum, M. H. (2000). Introduction to psychological experiments on the Internet. In M. H. Birnbaum (Ed.), *Psychological experiments on the Internet* (pp. 3–34). San Diego, CA: Academic Press.

Björkqvist, K., Lagerspetz, K. M., & Kaukiainen, A. (1992). Do girls manipulate and boys fight? Developmental trends in regard to direct and indirect aggression. *Aggressive Behavior, 18,* 117–127.

Black, S. L., & Bevan, S. (1992). At the movies with Buss and Durkee: A natural experiment on film violence. *Aggressive Behavior, 18,* 37–45.

Blackhart, G. C., Nelson, B. C., Knowles, M. L., & Baumeister, R. F. (2009). Rejection elicits emotional reactions but neither causes immediate distress nor lowers self-esteem: A meta-analytic review of 192 studies on social exclusion. *Personality and Social Psychology Review, 13,* 269–309.

Blackwood, N. J., Bentall, R. P., ffytche, D. H., Simmons, A., Murray, R. M., & Howard, R. J. (2003). Self-responsibility and the self-serving bias: An fMRI investigation of causal attributions. *Neuroimage, 20,* 1076–1085.

Blair, I. V., & Banaji, M. R. (1996). Automatic and controlled processes in stereotype priming. *Journal of Personality and Social Psychology, 70,* 1142–1163.

Blakemore, S. J., Winston, J., & Frith, U. (2004). Social cognitive neuroscience: Where are we heading? *Trends in Cognitive Sciences, 8,* 216–222.

Blaney, P. H. (1986). Affect and memory: A review. *Psychological Bulletin, 99,* 229–246.

Blanton, H., Buunk, B. P., Gibbons, F. X., & Kuyper, H. (1999). When better-than-others compare upward: Choice of comparison and comparative evaluation as independent predictors of academic performance. *Journal of Personality and Social Psychology, 76,* 420–430.

Blascovich, J., & Tomaka, J. (1991). Measures of self-esteem. In J. P. Robinson, P. R. Shaver, & L. S. Wrightsman (Eds.), *Measures of personality and social psychological attitudes* (Vol. 1, pp. 115–160). San Diego, CA: Academic Press.

Blass, T. (1991). Understanding behavior in the Milgram obedience experiment: The role of personality, situations, and their interactions. *Journal of Personality and Social Psychology, 60,* 398–413.

Blass, T. (1992). The social psychology of Stanley Milgram. In M. P. Zanna (Ed.), *Advances in experimental social psychology* (Vol. 25, pp. 277–329). San Diego, CA: Academic Press.

Blass, T. (1999). The Milgram paradigm after 35 years: Some things we now know about obedience to authority. *Journal of Applied Social Psychology, 29,* 955–978.

Blass, T. (Ed.). (2000). *Obedience to authority: Current perspectives on the Milgram paradigm.* Mahwah, NJ: Erlbaum.

Blass, T. (2004). *The man who shocked the world: The life and legacy of Stanley Milgram.* New York: Basic Books.

Blau, P. M. (1964). *Exchange and power in social life.* New York: Wiley.

Bless, H. (2001). The consequences of mood on the processing of social information. In A. Tesser & N. Schwarz (Eds.), *Blackwell handbook of social psychology: Intraindividual processes* (pp. 391–412). Oxford: Blackwell.

Bless, H., Bohner, G., Schwarz, N., & Strack, F. (1990). Mood and persuasion: A cognitive response analysis. *Personality and Social Psychology Bulletin, 16,* 331–345.

Bless, H., Fiedler, K., & Strack, F. (2004). *Social cognition: How individuals construct social reality.* New York: Psychology Press.

Bocchiaro, P., & Zimbardo, P. G. (2010). Defying unjust authority: An exploratory study. *Current Psychology, 29,* 155–170.

Bodenhausen, G. V. (1990). Stereotypes as judgmental heuristics: Evidence of circadian variations in discrimination. *Psychological Science, 1,* 319–322.

Bodenhausen, G. V., Todd, A. R., & Richeson, J. A. (2009). Controlling prejudice and stereotyping: Antecedents, mechanisms, and contexts. In T. D. Nelson (Ed.), *Handbook of prejudice, stereotyping, and discrimination* (pp. 111–135). New York: Psychology Press.

Bohner, G., & Dickel, N. (2011). Attitudes and attitude change. *Annual Review of Psychology, 62,* 391–417.

Bohner, G., Moskowitz, G. B., & Chaiken, S. (1995). The interplay of heuristic and systematic processing of social information. In W. Stroebe & M. Hewstone (Eds.), *European review of social psychology* (Vol. 6, pp. 33–68). Chichester, UK: Psychology Press.

Bohner, G., & Wänke, M. (2002). *Attitudes and attitude change.* Hove, UK: Psychology Press.

Bolino, M. C., & Turnley, W. H. (1999). Measuring impression management in organizations: A scale development based on the Jones & Pittman Taxonomy. *Organizational Research Methods, 2,* 187–206.

Bolsin, S. N. (2003). Whistle blowing. *Medical Education, 37,* 294–296.

Bonanno, G. A., Rennicke, C., & Dekel, S. (2005). Self-enhancement among high-exposure survivors of the September 11th terrorist attack: Resilience or social maladjustment? *Journal of Personality and Social Psychology, 88,* 984–998.

Bond, C. F., & Titus, L. J. (1983). Social facilitation: A meta-analysis of 241 studies. *Psychological Bulletin, 94,* 265–292.

Bond, R., & Smith, P. B. (1996). Culture and conformity: A meta-analysis of studies using Asch's (1952b, 1956) Line Judgment Task. *Psychological Bulletin, 119,* 111–137.

Bornstein, R. F. (1989). Exposure and affect: Overview and meta-analysis of research. *Psychological Bulletin, 106,* 265–289.

Borofsky, G. L., Stollak, G. E., & Messé, L. A. (1971). Sex differences in bystander reactions to physical assault. *Journal of Experimental Social Psychology, 7,* 313–318.

Bosson, J. K., Lakey, C. E., Campbell, W. K., Zeigler-Hill, V., Jordan, C. H., & Kernis, M. H. (2008). Untangling the links between narcissism and self-esteem: A theoretical and empirical review. *Social and Personality Psychology Compass, 2,* 1415–1439.

Botvinick, M. M., Braver, T. S., Barch, D. M., Carter, C. S., & Cohen, J. D. (2001). Conflict monitoring and cognitive control. *Psychological Review, 108,* 624–652.

Bourke, J. (1999). *An intimate history of killing: Face-to-face killing in the twentieth century.* London: Granta.

Bower, G. H. (1981). Mood and memory. *American Psychologist, 36,* 129–148.

Bowers, D. G., & Seashore, S. E. (1966). Predicting organizational effectiveness with a four-factor theory of leadership. *Administrative Science Quarterly, 11,* 238–263.

Bowlby, J. (1958). The nature of the child's tie to his mother. *International Journal of Psychoanalysis, 39,* 350–373.

Bowlby, J. (1969). *Attachment and loss: Attachment* (Vol. 1). London: Hogarth.

Bowlby, J. (1982). *Attachment and loss: Attachment* (Vol. 1, 2nd ed.). New York: Basic Books.

Bowling, N., & Beehr, T. A. (2006). Workplace harassment from the victim's perspective: A theoretical model and meta-analysis. *Journal of Applied Psychology, 91,* 998–1012.

Bradbury, T. N., & Karney, B. R. (2010). *Intimate relationships.* New York: Norton.

Bradford, D. L., & Cohen, A. R. (1984). *Managing for excellence: The guide to developing high performance in contemporary organizations.* New York: Wiley.

Branscombe, N. R., Ellemers, N., Spears, R., & Doosje, B. (1999). The context and content of social identity threat. In N. Ellemers, R. Spears, & B. Doosje (Eds.), *Social identity: Context, commitment, content* (pp. 35–58). Oxford: Blackwell.

Branscombe, N. R., Schmitt, M. T., & Harvey, R. D. (1999). Perceiving pervasive discrimination among African Americans: Implications for group identification and well-being. *Journal of Personality and Social Psychology, 77,* 135–149.

Branscombe, N. R., & Wann, D. L. (1994). Collective self-esteem consequences of outgroup derogation when a valued social identity is on trial. *European Journal of Social Psychology, 24,* 641–657.

Brauer, M., & Judd, C. M. (1996). Group polarization and repeated attitude expressions: A new take on an old topic. In W. Stroebe & M. Hewstone (Eds.), *European review of social psychology* (Vol. 7, pp. 173–207). Chichester, UK: Psychology Press.

Brauer, M., Judd, C. M., & Gliner, M. D. (1995). The effects of repeated expressions on attitude polarization during group discussions. *Journal of Personality and Social Psychology, 68,* 1014–1029.

Brehm, J. W. (1956). Postdecision changes in the desirability of alternatives. *Journal of Abnormal and Social Psychology, 52,* 384–389.

Brehm, J. W. (1966). *A theory of psychological reactance.* New York: Academic Press.

Brennan, K. A., Clark, C. L., & Shaver, P. R. (1998). Self-report measurement of adult attachment. In J. A. Simpson & W. S. Rholes (Eds.), *Attachment theory and close relationships* (pp. 46–76). New York: Guilford.

Brewer, M. B. (1988). A dual process model of impression formation. In T. K. Srull & R. S. Wyer Jr. (Eds.), *Advances in social cognition* (Vol. 1, pp. 1–36). Hillsdale, NJ: Erlbaum.

Brewer, M. B. (1991). The social self: On being the same and different at the same time. *Personality and Social Psychology Bulletin, 17,* 475–482.

Brewer, M. B. (1999). The psychology of prejudice: Ingroup love or outgroup hate? *Journal of Social Issues, 55,* 429–444.

Brewer, M. B. (2000). Research design and issues of validity. In H. T. Reis & C. M. Judd (Eds.), *Handbook of research methods in social and personality psychology* (pp. 3–16). New York: Cambridge University Press.

Brewer, M. B. (2003). *Intergroup relations.* Buckingham, UK: Open University Press.

Brewer, M. B., & Miller, N. (1984). Beyond the contact hypothesis: Theoretical perspectives on desegregation. In M. B. Brewer & N. Miller (Eds.), *Groups in contact: The psychology of desegregation* (pp. 281–302). Orlando, FL: Academic Press.

Brief, A. P., Dukerich, J. M., & Doran, L. I. (1991). Resolving ethical dilemmas in management: Experimental investigations of values, accountability, and choice. *Journal of Applied Social Psychology, 21,* 380–396.

Briñol, P., & Petty, R. E. (2003). Overt head movements and persuasion: A self-validation analysis. *Journal of Personality and Social Psychology, 84,* 1123–1139.

Briñol, P., & Petty, R. E. (2008). Embodied persuasion: Fundamental processes by which bodily responses can impact attitudes. In G. R. Semin & E. R. Smith (Eds.), *Embodiment grounding: Social, cognitive, affective, and neuroscientific approaches* (pp. 184–207). Cambridge, MA: Cambridge University Press.

Briñol, P., Petty, R. E., & McCoslin, M. J. (2009). Changing attitudes on implicit versus explicit measures: What is the difference? In R. E. Petty, R. H. Fazio, & P. Briñol (Eds.), *Attitudes: Insights from the new implicit measures* (pp. 285–326). New York: Psychology Press.

Brodbeck, F. C. (2008). Leadership in organisations. In N. Chmiel (Ed.), *An introduction to work and organisational psychology: A European perspective* (2nd ed., pp. 281–304). Oxford: Blackwell.

Brodbeck, F. C., & Greitemeyer, T. (2000a). A dynamic model of group performance: Considering the group members' capacity to learn. *Group Processes & Intergroup Relations, 3,* 159–182.

Brodbeck, F. C., & Greitemeyer, T. (2000b). Effects of individual versus mixed individual and group experience in rule induction on group member learning and group performance. *Journal of Experimental Social Psychology, 36,* 621–648.

Brodbeck, F. C., Kerschreiter, R., Mojzisch, A., Frey, D., & Schulz-Hardt, S. (2002). The dissemination of critical, unshared information in decision making groups: The effects of pre-discussion dissent. *European Journal of Social Psychology, 32,* 35–56.

Brodbeck, F. C., Kerschreiter, R., Mojzisch, A., & Schulz-Hardt, S. (2007). Group decision making under conditions of distributed knowledge: The information asymmetries model. *Academy of Management Review, 32,* 459–479.

Brown, C. (1955). *My left foot.* Oxford: Simon & Schuster.

Brown, J. D. (1986). Evaluations of self and others: Self-enhancement biases in social judgments. *Social Cognition, 4,* 353–376.

Brown, J. D. (1990). Evaluating one's abilities: Shortcuts and stumbling blocks on the road to self-knowledge. *Journal of Experimental Social Psychology, 26,* 149–167.

Brown, J. D., Dutton, K. A., & Cook, K. E. (2001). From the top down: Self-esteem and self-evaluation. *Cognition and Emotion, 15,* 615–631.

Brown, J. D., & Smart, S. A. (1991). The self and social conduct: Linking self-representations to prosocial behavior. *Journal of Personality and Social Psychology, 60,* 368–375.

Brown, R. (1999). *Group processes* (2nd ed.). Oxford: Blackwell.

Brown, R. (2010). *Prejudice: It's social psychology* (2nd ed.). Chichester, UK: Wiley-Blackwell.

Brown, R., & Abrams, D. (1986). The effects of intergroup similarity and goal interdependence on intergroup attitudes and task performance. *Journal of Experimental Social Psychology, 22,* 78–92.

Brown, R., & Fish, D. (1983). The psychological causality implicit in language. *Cognition, 14,* 237–273.

Brown, R., & Hewstone, M. (2005). An integrative theory of intergroup contact. In M. P. Zanna (Ed.), *Advances in experimental social psychology* (Vol. 37, pp. 255–343). San Diego, CA: Academic Press.

Brown, R., & Kulik, J. (1977). Flashbulb memories. *Cognition, 5,* 73–99.

Brown, R., & Wade, G. (1987). Superordinate goals and intergroup behaviour: The effect of role ambiguity and status on intergroup attitudes and task performance. *European Journal of Social Psychology, 17,* 131–142.

Browning, C. R. (1992). *Ordinary men: Reserve police battalion 101 and the final solution in Poland.* New York: HarperCollins.

Brunell, A. B., Gentry, W. A., Campbell, W. K., Hoffman, B. J., Kuhnert, K. W., & DeMarree, K. G. (2008). Leader emergence: The case of the narcissistic leader. *Personality and Social Psychology Bulletin, 34,* 1663–1676.

Bruner, J. S., & Tagiuri, R. (1954). The perception of people. In G. Lindzey (Ed.), *Handbook of social psychology* (Vol. 2, pp. 634–654). Reading, MA: Addison-Wesley.

Buhrmester, D., & Prager, K. (1995). Patterns and functions of self-disclosure during childhood and adolescence. In K. J. Rotenberg (Ed.), *Disclosure processes in children and adolescents* (pp. 10–56). New York: Cambridge University Press.

Bunderson, J. S., & Sutcliffe, K. M. (2003). Management team learning orientation and business unit performance. *Journal of Applied Psychology, 88,* 552–560.

Bureau of Justice Statistics. *National Crime Victimization Survey.* Retrieved from http://bjs.ojp.usdoj.gov/content/pub/pdf/ipvus.pdf

Burger, J. M. (2009). Replicating Milgram: Would people still obey today? *American Psychologist, 64,* 1–11.

Burger, J. M., & Petty, R. E. (1981). The low-ball compliance technique: Task or person commitment? *Journal of Personality and Social Psychology, 40,* 492–500.

Burgess, M., Enzle, M. E., & Morry, M. (2000). The social psychological power of photography: Can the image-freezing machine make something of nothing? *European Journal of Social Psychology, 30,* 613–630.

Burks, V. S., Laird, R. D., Dodge, K. A., Pettit, G. S., & Bates, J. E. (1999). Knowledge structures, social information processing, and children's aggressive behavior. *Social Development, 8,* 220–236.

Burns, J. M. (1978). *Leadership.* New York: Harper & Row.

Burnstein, E., & Branigan, C. (2001). Evolutionary analyses in social psychology. In A. Tesser & N. Schwarz (Eds.), *Blackwell handbook of social psychology: Intraindividual processes* (pp. 3–21). Oxford: Blackwell.

Burnstein, E., & Vinokur, A. (1977). Persuasive argumentation and social comparison as determinants of attitude polarization. *Journal of Experimental Social Psychology, 13,* 315–332.

Burnstein, E., Vinokur, A., & Trope, Y. (1973). Interpersonal comparison versus persuasive argumentation: A more direct test of alternative explanations for group-induced shifts in individual choice. *Journal of Experimental Social Psychology, 9,* 236–245.

Bushman, B. J. (2002). Does venting anger feed or extinguish the flame? Catharsis, rumination, distraction, anger, and aggressive responding. *Personality and Social Psychology Bulletin, 28,* 724–731.

Bushman, B. J., & Baumeister, R. F. (1998). Threatened egotism, narcissism, self-esteem, and direct and displaced aggression: Does self-love or self-hate lead to violence? *Journal of Personality and Social Psychology, 75,* 219–229.

Bushman, B. J., Baumeister, R. F., & Stack, A. D. (1999). Catharsis, aggression, and persuasive influence: Self-fulfilling or self-defeating prophecies? *Journal of Personality and Social Psychology, 76,* 367–376.

Bushman, B. J., Baumeister, R. F., Thomaes, S., Ryu, E., Begeer, S., & West, S. G. (2009). Looking again, and harder, for a link between low self esteem and aggression. *Journal of Personality, 77,* 427–446.

Bushman, B. J., Bonacci, A. M., Van Dijk, M., & Baumeister, R. F. (2003). Narcissism, sexual refusal, and aggression: Testing a narcissistic reactance model of sexual coercion. *Journal of Personality and Social Psychology, 84,* 1027–1040.

Bushman, B. J., & Cooper, H. M. (1990). Effects of alcohol on human aggression: An integrative research review. *Psychological Bulletin, 107,* 341–354.

Bushman, B. J., & Geen, R. G. (1990). Role of cognitive-emotional mediators and individual differences in the effects of media violence on aggression. *Journal of Personality and Social Psychology, 58,* 156–163.

Bushman, B. J., Ridge, R. D., Das, E. H., Key, C. W., & Busath, G. L. (2007). When God sanctions killing: Effect of scriptural violence on aggression. *Psychological Science, 18,* 204–207.

Bushman, B. J., & Whitaker, J. L. (2010). Like a magnet: Catharsis beliefs attract angry people to violent video games. *Psychological Science, 21,* 790–792.

Buss, A. H., & Perry, M. (1992). The Aggression Questionnaire. *Journal of Personality and Social Psychology, 63,* 452–459.

Buss, A. H., & Warren, W. L. (2000). *The Aggression Questionnaire Manual.* Los Angeles, CA: Western Psychological Service.

Buss, D. M. (1989). Sex differences in human mate preferences: Evolutionary hypotheses tested in 37 cultures. *Behavioral and Brain Sciences, 12,* 1–49.

Buss, D. M. (1995). Evolutionary psychology: A new paradigm for psychological science. *Psychological Inquiry, 6,* 1–30.

Buss, D. M., Abbott, M., Angleitner, A., Asherian, A., Biaggio, A., Blanco-Villasenor, A., … Deraad, B. (1990). International preferences in selecting mates: A study of 37 cultures. *Journal of Cross-Cultural Psychology, 21,* 5–47.

Buss, D. M., & Chiodo, L. M. (1991). Narcissistic acts in everyday life. *Journal of Personality, 59,* 179–215.

Buss, D. M., & Kendrick, D. T. (1998). Evolutionary social psychology. In D. T. Gilbert, S. T. Fiske, & G. Lindzey (Eds.), *The handbook of social psychology* (4th ed., Vol. 2, pp. 982–1026). Boston, MA: McGraw-Hill.

Butera, F., & Levine, J. M. (Eds.). (2009). *Coping with minority status: Responses to exclusion and inclusion.* New York: Cambridge University Press.

Buunk, B. P. (2001). Perceived superiority of one's own relationship and perceived prevalence of happy and unhappy relationships. *British Journal of Social Psychology, 40,* 565–574.

Buunk, B. P., & Van der Eijnden, R. J. J. M. (1997). Perceived prevalence, perceived superiority, and relationship satisfaction: Most relationships are good, but ours is the best. *Personality and Social Psychology Bulletin, 23,* 219–228.

Byrne, D. (1971). *The attraction paradigm.* New York: Academic Press.

Byrne, D., Ervin, C. R., & Lamberth, J. (1970). Continuity between the experimental study of attraction and real-life computer dating. *Journal of Personality and Social Psychology, 16,* 157–165.

Byrne, D., & Wong, T. J. (1962). Racial prejudice, interpersonal attraction, and assumed dissimilarity of attitudes. *Journal of Abnormal and Social Psychology, 65,* 246–253.

Cacioppo, J. T., Amaral, D. G., Blanchard, J. J., Cameron, J. L., Carter, C. S., Crews, D., … Quinn, K. J. (2007). Social neuroscience: Progress and implications for mental health. *Perspectives on Psychological Science, 2,* 99–123.

Cacioppo, J. T., & Berntson, G. G. (Eds.). (2005). *Social neuroscience.* New York: Psychology Press.

Cacioppo, J. T., Gardner, W. L., & Berntson, G. G. (1997). Beyond bipolar conceptualizations and measures: The case of attitudes and evaluative space. *Personality and Social Psychology Review, 1,* 3–25.

Cacioppo, J. T., Hughes, M. E., Waite, L. J., Hawkley, L. C., & Thisted, R. A. (2006). Loneliness as a specific risk factor for depressive symptoms: Cross-sectional and longitudinal analyses. *Psychology and Aging, 21,* 140–151.

Cacioppo, J. T., Marshall-Goodell, B. S., Tassinary, L. G., & Petty, R. E. (1992). Rudimentary determinants of attitudes: Classical conditioning is more effective when prior knowledge about the attitude stimulus is low than high. *Journal of Experimental Social Psychology, 28,* 207–233.

Cacioppo, J. T., & Petty, R. E. (1979). Effects of message repetition and position on cognitive response, recall, and persuasion. *Journal of Personality and Social Psychology, 37,* 97–109.

Cacioppo, J. T., & Petty, R. E. (1982). The need for cognition. *Journal of Personality and Social Psychology, 42,* 116–131.

Cacioppo, J. T., & Petty, R. E. (1989). Effects of message repetition on argument processing, recall, and persuasion. *Basic and Applied Social Psychology, 10,* 3–12.

Cacioppo, J. T., Petty, R. E., Feinstein, J. A., & Jarvis, B. (1996). Dispositional differences in cognitive motivation: The life and times of individuals varying in need for cognition. *Psychological Bulletin, 119*, 197–253.

Cacioppo, J. T., Petty, R. E., & Kao, C. F. (1984). The efficient assessment of need for cognition. *Journal of Personality Assessment, 48*, 306–307.

Cacioppo, J. T., Priester, J. R., & Berntson, G. G. (1993). Rudimentary determinants of attitudes: Arm flexion and extension have differential effects on attitudes. *Journal of Personality and Social Psychology, 65*, 5–17.

Cai, H., Brown, J. D., Deng, C., & Oakes, M. A. (2007). Self-esteem and culture: Differences in cognitive self-evaluations or affective self-regard? *Asian Journal of Social Psychology, 10*, 162–170.

Cai, H., Sedikides, C., Gaertner, L., Wang, C., Carvallo, M., Xu, Y., … Jackson, L. E. (2011). Tactical self-enhancement in China: Is modesty at the service of self-enhancement in East Asian culture? *Social Psychological and Personality Science, 2*, 59–64.

Cairns, E., Kenworthy, J., Campbell, A., & Hewstone, M. (2006). The role of in-group identification, religious group membership and intergroup conflict in moderating in-group and out-group affect. *British Journal of Social Psychology, 45*, 701–716.

Callero, P. L., Howard, J. A., & Piliavin, J. A. (1987). Helping behavior as role behavior: Disclosing social structure and history in the analysis of prosocial action. *Social Psychology Quarterly, 50*, 247–256.

Calvert-Boyanowsky, J., & Leventhal, H. (1975). The role of information in attenuating behavioral responses to stress: A reinterpretation of the misattribution phenomenon. *Journal of Personality and Social Psychology, 32*, 214–221.

Cameron, L., & Rutland, A. (2006). Extended contact through story reading in school: Reducing children's prejudice toward the disabled. *Journal of Social Issues, 62*, 469–488.

Campbell, D. T. (1950). The indirect assessment of social attitudes. *Psychological Bulletin, 47*, 15–38.

Campbell, D. T. (1958). Common fate, similarity, and other indices of the status of aggregates of persons as social entities. *Behavioral Science, 3*, 14–25.

Campbell, D. T., & Fiske, D. W. (1959). Convergent and discriminant validation by the multitrait–multimethod matrix. *Psychological Bulletin, 56*, 81–105.

Campbell, D. T., & Stanley, J. C. (1966). *Experimental and quasi-experimental designs for research*. Chicago: Rand McNally.

Campbell, J. (1949). *The hero with a thousand faces*. New York: Pantheon.

Campbell, J., & Fehr, B. (1990). Self-esteem and perceptions of conveyed impressions: Is negative affectivity associated with greater realism? *Journal of Personality and Social Psychology, 58*, 122–133.

Campbell, W. K., & Foster, J. D. (2007). The narcissistic self: Background, an extended agency model, and ongoing controversies. In C. Sedikides & S. Spencer (Eds.), *The self* (pp. 115–138). New York: Psychology Press.

Campbell, W. K., & Sedikides, C. (1999). Self-threat magnifies the self-serving bias: A meta-analytic integration. *Review of General Psychology, 3*, 23–43.

Canary, D. J., Stafford, L., Hause, K. S., & Wallace, L. A. (1993). An inductive analysis of relational maintenance strategies: A comparison among lovers, relatives, friends, and others. *Communication Research Reports, 10*, 5–14.

Cann, A., Sherman, S. J., & Elkes, R. (1975). Effects of initial request size and timing of a second request on compliance: The foot in the door and the door in the face. *Journal of Personality and Social Psychology, 32*, 774–782.

Cannon, W. B. (1927). The James-Lange theory of emotions: A critical examination and an alternative theory. *American Journal of Psychology, 39*, 106–124.

Capozza, D., Brown, R., Aharpour, S., & Falvo, R. (2006). A comparison of motivational theories of identification. In R. Brown & D. Capozza (Eds.), *Social identities: Motivational, emotional and cultural influences* (pp. 51–72). Hove, UK: Psychology Press.

Carlson, M., Marcus-Newhall, A., & Miller, N. (1990). Effects of situational aggression cues: A quantitative review. *Journal of Personality and Social Psychology, 58*, 622–633.

Carlson, M., & Miller, N. (1987). Explanation of the relation between negative mood and helping. *Psychological Bulletin, 102*, 91–108.

Cartwright, D. (1979). Contemporary social psychology in historical perspective. *Social Psychology Quarterly, 42*, 82–93.

Carver, C. S., Blaney, P. H., & Scheier, M. F. (1979). Reassertion and giving up: The interactive role of self-directed attention and outcome expectancy. *Journal of Personality and Social Psychology, 37*, 1859–1870.

Carver, C. S., & Scheier, M. F. (1981). *Attention and self-regulation: A control-theory approach to human behavior*. New York: Springer.

Carver, C. S., & Scheier, M. F. (1998). *On the self-regulation of behavior*. New York: Cambridge University Press.

Castano, E., Yzerbyt, V., Paladino, M. P., & Sacchi, S. (2002). I belong, therefore, I exist: Ingroup identification, ingroup entitativity, and ingroup bias. *Personality and Social Psychology Bulletin, 28*, 135–143.

Cate, R. M., Lloyd, S. A., Henton, J. M., & Larson, J. H. (1982). Fairness and reward level as predictors of relationship satisfaction. *Social Psychology Quarterly, 45*, 177–181.

Chaiken, S. (1979). Communicator physical attractiveness and persuasion. *Journal of Personality and Social Psychology, 37*, 1387–1397.

Chaiken, S. (1980). Heuristic versus systematic information processing and the use of source versus message cues in persuasion. *Journal of Personality and Social Psychology, 39*, 752–766.

Chaiken, S., & Baldwin, M. W. (1981). Affective-cognitive consistency and the effect of salient behavioral information on the self-perception of attitudes. *Journal of Personality and Social Psychology, 41*, 1–12.

Chaiken, S., Lieberman, A., & Eagly, A. H. (1989). Heuristic and systematic information processing within and beyond the persuasion context. In J. S. Uleman & J. A. Bargh (Eds.), *Unintended thought* (pp. 212–252). New York: Guilford.

Chaiken, S., & Maheswaran, D. (1994). Heuristic processing can bias systematic processing: Effects of source credibility, argument ambiguity, and task importance on attitude judgment. *Journal of Personality and Social Psychology, 66,* 460–473.

Chaiken, S., & Trope, Y. (Eds.). (1999). *Dual process theories in social psychology.* New York: Guilford.

Chartrand, T. L., Van Baaren, R. B., & Bargh, J. A. (2006). Linking automatic evaluation to mood and information processing style: Consequences for experienced affect, impression formation, and stereotyping. *Journal of Experimental Psychology: General, 135,* 70–77.

Chatard, A., & Selimbegović, L. (2011). When self-destructive thoughts flash through the mind: Failure to meet standards affects the accessibility of suicide-related thoughts. *Journal of Personality and Social Psychology, 100,* 587–605.

Chen, S., & Chaiken, S. (1999). The heuristic-systematic model in its broader context. In S. Chaiken & Y. Trope (Eds.), *Dual-process theories in social psychology* (pp. 73–96). New York: Guilford.

Chen, S., Shechter, D., & Chaiken, S. (1996). Getting at the truth or getting along: Accuracy- versus impression-motivated heuristic and systematic processing. *Journal of Personality and Social Psychology, 71,* 262–275.

Chen, Y.-R., Brockner, J., & Chen, X.-P. (2002). Individual-collective primacy and in-group favouritism: Enhancement and protection effects. *Journal of Experimental Social Psychology, 38,* 482–491.

Chen, Y.-R., Brockner, J., & Katz, T. (1998). Toward an explanation of cultural differences in in-group favoritism: The role of individual versus collective primacy. *Journal of Personality and Social Psychology, 75,* 1490–1502.

Cheng, P. W. (1997). From covariation to causation: A causal power theory. *Psychological Review, 104,* 367–405.

Cheng, P. W., & Novick, L. R. (1990). A probabilistic contrast model of causal induction. *Journal of Personality and Social Psychology, 58,* 545–567.

Chernyshenko, O. S., Miner, A. G., Baumann, M. R., & Sniezek, J. A. (2003). The impact of information distribution, ownership, and discussion on group member judgment: The differential cue weighting model. *Organizational Behavior and Human Decision Processes, 91,* 12–25.

Cherry, F. E. (1995). *The 'stubborn particulars' of social psychology: Essays on the research process.* London: Routledge.

Chertkoff, J. M., & Kushigian, R. H. (1999). *Don't panic: The psychology of emergency egress and ingress.* Westport, CT: Praeger.

Chhokar, J. S., Brodbeck, F. C., & House, R. J. (2007). *Culture and leadership across the world: The GLOBE book of in-depth studies of 25 societies.* Mahwah, NJ: Erlbaum.

Chiao, J. Y., Harada, T., Komeda, H., Li, Z., Mano, Y., Saito, D., … Iidaka, T. (2009). Neural basis of individualistic and collectivistic views of self. *Human Brain Mapping, 30,* 2813–2820.

Chiu, C.-Y., & Hong, Y.-Y. (2006). *Social psychology of culture.* New York: Psychology Press.

Choi, H.-S., & Levine, J. M. (2004). Minority influence in work teams: The impact of newcomers. *Journal of Experimental Social Psychology, 40,* 273–280.

Choi, I., & Choi, Y. (2002). Culture and self-concept flexibility. *Personality and Social Psychology Bulletin, 28,* 1508–1517.

Choi, I., & Nisbett, R. E. (1998). Situational salience and cultural differences in the correspondence bias and actor-observer bias. *Personality and Social Psychology Bulletin, 24,* 949–960.

Choi, I., Nisbett, R. E., & Norenzayan, A. (1999). Causal attribution across cultures: Variation and universality. *Psychological Bulletin, 125,* 47–63.

Christ, O., Hewstone, M., Tausch, N., Wagner, U., Voci, A., Hughes, J., & Cairns, E. (2010). Direct contact as a moderator of extended contact effects: Cross-sectional and longitudinal impact on outgroup attitudes, behavioral intentions, and attitude certainty. *Personality and Social Psychology Bulletin, 36,* 1662–1674.

Christy, C. A., & Voigt, H. (1994). Bystander responses to public episodes of child abuse. *Journal of Applied Social Psychology, 24,* 824–847.

Cialdini, R. B. (2008). *Influence: Science and practice* (5th ed.). Boston, MA: Allyn & Bacon.

Cialdini, R. B., & Ascani, K. (1976). Test of a concession procedure for inducing verbal, behavioral, and further compliance with a request to give blood. *Journal of Applied Psychology, 61,* 295–300.

Cialdini, R. B., Borden, R. J., Thorne, A., Walker, M. R., Freeman, S., & Sloan, L. R. (1976). Basking in reflected glory: Three (football) field studies. *Journal of Personality and Social Psychology, 34,* 366–375.

Cialdini, R. B., Cacioppo, J. T., Bassett, R., & Miller, J. A. (1978). Low-ball procedure for producing compliance: Commitment then cost. *Journal of Personality and Social Psychology, 36,* 463–476.

Cialdini, R. B., & Fultz, J. (1990). Interpreting the negative mood-helping literature via 'mega'-analysis: A contrary view. *Psychological Bulletin, 107,* 210–214.

Cialdini, R. B., & Goldstein, N. J. (2004). Social influence: Compliance and conformity. *Annual Review of Psychology, 55,* 591–621.

Cialdini, R. B., Kallgren, C. A., & Reno, R. R. (1991). A focus theory of normative conduct: A theoretical refinement and reevaluation of the role of norms in human behavior. In M. P. Zanna (Ed.), *Advances in experimental social psychology* (Vol. 24, pp. 201–234). San Diego, CA: Academic Press.

Cialdini, R. B., Reno, R. R., & Kallgren, C. A. (1990). A focus theory of normative conduct: Recycling the concept of norms to reduce littering in public places. *Journal of Personality and Social Psychology, 58,* 1015–1026.

Cialdini, R. B., Schaller, M., Houlihan, D., Arps, K., Fultz, J., & Beaman, A. L. (1987). Empathy-based helping: Is it selflessly or selfishly motivated? *Journal of Personality and Social Psychology, 52,* 749–758.

Cialdini, R. B., & Trost, M. R. (1998). Social influence: Social norms, conformity, and compliance. In D. T. Gilbert, S. T. Fiske, & G. Lindzey (Eds.), *Handbook of social psychology* (4th ed., Vol. 2, pp. 151–192). Boston, MA: McGraw-Hill.

Cialdini, R. B., Trost, M. R., & Newsom, J. T. (1995). Preference for consistency: The development of a valid measure and the discovery of surprising behavioral implications. *Journal of Personality and Social Psychology, 69,* 318–328.

Cialdini, R. B., Vincent, J. E., Lewis, S. K., Catalan, J., Wheeler, D., & Darby, B. L. (1975). Reciprocal concessions procedure for inducing compliance: The door-in-the-face technique. *Journal of Personality and Social Psychology, 31,* 206–215.

Cini, M. A., Moreland, R. L., & Levine, J. M. (1993). Group staffing levels and responses to prospective and new members. *Journal of Personality and Social Psychology, 65,* 723–734.

Clark, M. S., & Mills, J. (1979). Interpersonal attraction in exchange and communal relationships. *Journal of Personality and Social Psychology, 37,* 12–24.

Clark, M. S., Mills, J., & Corcoran, D. M. (1989). Keeping track of needs and inputs of friends and strangers. *Personality and Social Psychology Bulletin, 15(4),* 533–542.

Claypool, H. M., Mackie, D. M., Garcia-Marques, T., McIntosh, A., & Udal, A. (2004). The effects of personal relevance and repetition on persuasive processing. *Social Cognition, 22,* 310–335.

Clifford, M. M., & Walster, E. (1973). The effect of physical attractiveness on teacher expectation. *Sociology of Education, 46,* 248–258.

Clore, G. L., Bray, R. M., Itkin, S. M., & Murphy, P. (1978). Interracial attitudes and behavior at a summer camp. *Journal of Personality and Social Psychology, 36,* 107–116.

Clore, G. L., & Jeffery, K. M. (1972). Emotional role playing, attitude change, and attraction toward a disabled person. *Journal of Personality and Social Psychology, 23,* 105–111.

Clore, G. L., Schwarz, N., & Conway, M. (1994). Cognitive causes and consequences of emotion. In R. S. Wyer & T. K. Srull (Eds.), *Handbook of social cognition* (2nd ed., Vol. 1, pp. 323–417). Hillsdale, NJ: Erlbaum.

Coan, J. A., Schaefer, H. S., & Davidson, R. J. (2006). Lending a hand: Social regulation of the neural response to threat. *Psychological Science, 17,* 1032–1039.

Coch, L., & French, J. R. P. (1948). Overcoming resistance to change. *Human Relations, 1,* 512–532.

Cohen, E. (1984). The desegregated school: Problems of status, power, and interethnic climate. In N. Miller & M. Brewer (Eds.), *Groups in contact: The psychology of desegregration* (pp. 77–96). New York: Academic Press.

Cohen, E. G., & Lotan, R. A. (1995). Producing equal-status interaction in the heterogeneous classroom. *American Educational Research Journal, 32,* 99–120.

Cohen, J. (1988). *Statistical power analysis for the behavioral sciences* (2nd ed.). Hillsdale, NJ: Erlbaum.

Cohen, L. E., & Felson, M. (1979). Social change and climate rate trends: A routine activity approach. *American Sociological Review, 44,* 588–608.

Cohen, S., & Wills, T. A. (1985). Stress, social support, and the buffering hypothesis. *Psychological Bulletin, 98,* 310–357.

Coie, J. D., & Dodge, K. A. (1998). Aggression and antisocial behavior. In W. Damon & N. Eisenberg (Eds.), *Handbook of child psychology* (5th ed., pp. 779–862). New York: Wiley.

Collins, N. L., & Feeney, B. C. (2000). A safe haven: An attachment theory perspective on support-seeking and caregiving in adult romantic relationships. *Journal of Personality and Social Psychology, 78,* 1053–1073.

Collins, N. L., & Miller, L. C. (1994). Self-disclosure and liking: A meta-analytic review. *Psychological Bulletin, 116,* 457–475.

Collins, W. A., Maccoby, E. E., Steinberg, L., Hetherington, E. M., & Bornstein, M. H. (2000). Contemporary research on parenting: The case for nature and nurture. *American Psychologist, 55,* 218–232.

Conger, J. A., & Kanungo, R. N. (1987). Toward a behavioral theory of charismatic leadership in organizational settings. *Academy of Management Review, 12,* 637–647.

Conger, J. A., & Kanungo, R. N. (1998). *Charismatic leadership in organizations.* Thousand Oaks, CA: Sage.

Converse, P. (1994). *Theodore Mead Newcomb. Biographical memoirs* (Vol. 64, pp. 322–338). Washington, DC: National Academies Press.

Converse, P. D., & DeShon, R. P. (2009). A tale of two tasks: Reversing the self-regulatory resource depletion effect. *Journal of Applied Psychology, 94,* 1318–1324.

Conway, M. A. (2005). Memory and the self. *Journal of Memory and Language, 53,* 594–628.

Conway, M. A., Singer, J. A., & Tagini, A. (2004). The self and autobiographical memory: Correspondence and coherence. *Social Cognition, 22,* 491–529.

Cook, S. W. (1984). Cooperative interaction in multiethnic contexts. In M. B. Brewer & N. Miller (Eds.), *Groups in contact: The psychology of desegregation* (pp. 155–185). Orlando, FL: Academic Press.

Cook, T. D. (1979). Meta-analysis and the integrative research review. In C. Hendrick & M. S. Clark (Eds.), *Research methods in personality and social psychology* (Vol. 11, pp. 142–163). Newbury Park, CA: Sage.

Cook, T. D., & Campbell, D. T. (1979). *Quasi-experimentation: Design and analysis issues for field settings.* Chicago: Rand McNally.

Cooley, C. H. (1902). *Human nature and the social order*. New York: Scribner.

Cooper, H. M. (1989). *Integrating research: A guide for literature reviews*. Newbury Park, CA: Sage.

Cooper, H. M., & Hedges, L. V. (Eds.). (1994). *The handbook of research synthesis*. New York: Sage.

Cooper, J., & Cooper, G. (2002). Subliminal motivation: A story revisited. *Journal of Applied Social Psychology, 32*, 2213–2227.

Cooper, J., & Worchel, S. (1970). Role of undesired consequences in arousing cognitive dissonance. *Journal of Personality and Social Psychology, 16*, 199–206.

Corneille, O., Huart, J., Becquart, E., & Brédart, S. (2004). When memory shifts toward more typical category exemplars: Accentuation effects in the recollection of ethnically ambiguous faces. *Journal of Personality and Social Psychology, 86*, 236–250.

Correll, J., Judd, C. M., Park, B., & Wittenbrink, B. (2010). Measuring prejudice, stereotypes and discrimination. In J. F. Dovidio, M. Hewstone, P. Glick, & V. M. Esses (Eds.), *Handbook of prejudice, stereotyping and discrimination* (pp. 45–62). London: Sage.

Correll, J., Park, B., Judd, C. M., & Wittenbrink, B. (2002). The police officer's dilemma: Using ethnicity to disambiguate potentially threatening individuals. *Journal of Personality and Social Psychology, 83*, 1314–1329.

Cottrell, C. A., & Neuberg, S. L. (2005). Different emotional reactions to different groups: A sociofunctional threat-based approach to 'prejudice'. *Journal of Personality and Social Psychology, 88*, 770–789.

Cottrell, N. B. (1968). Performance in the presence of other human beings: Mere presence, audience, and affiliation effects. In E. C. Simmel, R. A. Hoppe, & G. A. Milton (Eds.), *Social facilitation and imitative behavior* (pp. 91–110). Boston, MA: Allyn & Bacon.

Cottrell, N. B. (1972). Social facilitation. In C. G. McClintock (Ed.), *Experimental social psychology* (pp. 185–236). New York: Holt, Rinehart and Winston.

Covington, M. V. (2000). Goal theory, motivation, and school achievement: An integrative review. *Annual Review of Psychology, 51*, 171–200.

Coyne, J. C., & De Longis, A. (1986). Going beyond social support: The role of social relationships in adaptation. *Journal of Consulting and Clinical Psychology, 54*, 454–460.

Coyne, J. C., Rohrbaugh, M. J., Shoham, V., Sonnega, J. S., Nicklas, J. M., & Cranford, J. A. (2001). Prognostic importance of marital quality for survival of congestive heart failure. *American Journal of Cardiology, 88*, 526–529.

Craig, W., Harel-Fisch, Y., Fogel-Grinvald, H., Dostaler, S., Hetland, J., Simons-Morton, B., … Pickett, W. (2009). A cross-national profile of bullying and victimization among adolescents in 40 countries. *International Journal of Public Health, 54*, 216–224.

Craik, F. I. M., Moroz, T. M., Moscovitch, M., Stuss, D. T., Winocur, G., Tulving, E., & Kapur, S. (1999). In search of the self: A positron emission tomography study. *Psychological Science, 10*, 26–34.

Crano, W., & Prislin, R. (Eds.). (2009). *Attitudes and persuasion*. New York: Psychology Press.

Crano, W. D., & Alvaro, E. M. (1997). The context/comparison model of social influence: Mechanisms, structure, and linkages that underlie indirect attitude change. In W. Stroebe & M. Hewstone (Eds.), *European review of social psychology* (Vol. 8, pp. 175–202). Chichester, UK: Wiley.

Crano, W. D., & Chen, X. (1998). The leniency contract and persistence of majority and minority influence. *Journal of Personality and Social Psychology, 74*, 1437–1450.

Creswell, J. D., Lam, S., Stanton, A. L., Taylor, S. E., Bower, J. E., & Sherman, D. K. (2007). Does self-affirmation, cognitive processing, or discovery of meaning explain cancer-related health benefits of expressive writing? *Personality and Social Psychology Bulletin, 33*, 238–250.

Creswell, J. D., Welch, W. T., Taylor, S. E., Sherman, D. K., Gruenewald, T. L., & Mann, T. (2005). Affirmation of personal values buffers neuroendocrine and psychological stress responses. *Psychological Science, 16*, 846–851.

Crick, N. R., & Grotpeter, J. K. (1995). Relational aggression, gender, and social-psychological adjustment. *Child Development, 66*, 710–722.

Crocker, J., & Luhtanen, R. K. (2003). Level of self-esteem and contingencies of self-worth: Unique effects on academic, social, and financial problems in college students. *Personality and Social Psychology Bulletin, 29*, 701–712.

Crocker, J., & Park, L. E. (2004). The costly pursuit of self-esteem. *Psychological Bulletin, 130*, 392–414.

Crocker, J., & Schwartz, I. (1985). Prejudice and ingroup favoritism in a minimal intergroup situation: Effects of self-esteem. *Personality and Social Psychology Bulletin, 11*, 379–386.

Crocker, J., Sommers, S. R., & Luhtanen, R. K. (2002). Hopes dashed and dreams fulfilled: Contingencies of self-worth and graduate school admissions. *Personality and Social Psychology Bulletin, 28*, 1275–1286.

Crocker, J., & Wolfe, C. T. (2001). Contingencies of self-worth. *Psychological Review, 108*, 593–623.

Cross, S. E., Bacon, P. L., & Morris, M. L. (2000). The relational-interdependent self-construal and relationships. *Journal of Personality and Social Psychology, 78*, 791–808.

Cross, S. E., & Madson, L. (1997). Models of the self: Self-construals and gender. *Psychological Bulletin, 122*, 5–37.

Crutchfield, R. S. (1955). Conformity and character. *American Psychologist, 10*, 191–198.

Cruz, M. G., Henningsen, D. D., & Smith, B. A. (1999). The impact of directive leadership on group information sampling, decisions, and perceptions of the leader. *Communication Research, 26*, 349–369.

Culbertson, K. A., & Dehle, C. (2001). Impact of sexual assault as a function of perpetrator type. *Journal of Interpersonal Violence, 16*, 992–1007.

Cunningham, J. A., Strassberg, D. S., & Haan, B. (1986). Effects of intimacy and sex-role congruency on self-disclosure. *Journal of Social and Clinical Psychology, 4,* 393–401.

Cunningham, M. R., Roberts, A. R., Barbee, A. P., Druen, P. B., & Wu, C.-H. (1995). 'Their ideas of beauty are, on the whole, the same as ours': Consistency and variability in the cross-cultural perception of female facial attractiveness. *Journal of Personality and Social Psychology, 68,* 261–279.

Cunningham, S. J., Milne, A. B., & Crawford, J. R. (2007). The effects of acute alcohol intoxication on person memory: The stereotypical drunk. *Journal of Applied Social Psychology, 37,* 187–199.

Cunningham, W. A., Preacher, K. J., & Banaji, M. R. (2001). Implicit attitude measures: Consistency, stability, and convergent validity. *Psychological Science, 12,* 163–170.

Custers, R., & Aarts, H. (2005). Beyond priming effects: The role of positive affect and discrepancies in implicit processes of motivation and goal pursuit. In W. Stroebe & M. Hewstone (Eds.), *European review of social psychology* (Vol. 16, pp. 257–300). Hove, UK: Psychology Press.

Custers, R., & Aarts, H. (2005). Positive affect as implicit motivator: On the nonconscious operation of behavioral goals. *Journal of Personality and Social Psychology, 89,* 129–142.

Cutrona, C. E. (1996). *Social support in couples: Marriage as a resource in times of stress.* Thousand Oaks, CA: Sage.

Dabbs, J. M., & Ruback, B. R. (1987). Dimensions of group process: Amount and structure of vocal interaction. In L. Berkowitz (Ed.), *Advances in experimental social psychology* (Vol. 20, pp. 123–169). San Diego, CA: Academic Press.

Dainton, M., & Aylor, B. (2002). Routine and strategic maintenance efforts: Behavioral patterns, variations associated with relational length, and the prediction of relational characteristics. *Communication Monographs, 69,* 52–66.

Dana, E. R., Lalwani, N., & Duval, T. S. (1997). Objective self-awareness and focus of attention following awareness of self-standard discrepancies: Changing self or changing standards of correctness. *Journal of Social and Clinical Psychology, 16,* 359–380.

D'Argembeau, A., Comblain, C., & Van der Linden, M. (2003). Phenomenal characteristics of autobiographical memories for positive, negative, and neutral events. *Applied Cognitive Psychology, 17,* 281–294.

Darley, J. M. (1992). Social organization for the production of evil. *Psychological Inquiry, 3,* 199–218.

Darley, J. M., & Batson, C. D. (1973). 'From Jerusalem to Jericho': A study of situational and dispositional variables in helping behavior. *Journal of Personality and Social Psychology, 27,* 100–108.

Darley, J. M., & Latané, B. (1968). Bystander intervention in emergencies: Diffusion of responsibility. *Journal of Personality and Social Psychology, 8,* 377–383.

Das, E. H., De Wit, J. B. F., & Stroebe, W. (2003). Fear appeals motivate acceptance of action recommendations: Evidence for a positive bias in the processing of persuasive messages. *Personality and Social Psychology Bulletin, 29,* 650–664.

David, B., & Turner, J. C. (1996). Studies in self-categorization and minority conversion: Is being a member of the out-group an advantage? *British Journal of Social Psychology, 35,* 179–199.

David, B., & Turner, J. C. (1999). Studies in self-categorization and minority conversion: The in-group minority in intragroup and intergroup contexts. *British Journal of Social Psychology, 38,* 115–134.

Davidov, M., & Grusec, J. E. (2006). Multiple pathways to compliance: Mothers' willingness to cooperate and knowledge of their children's reactions to discipline. *Journal of Family Psychology, 20,* 705–708.

Davidson, A. R., & Jaccard, J. J. (1979). Variables that moderate the attitude-behavior relation: Results of a longitudinal survey. *Journal of Personality and Social Psychology, 37,* 1364–1376.

Davis, D., Shaver, P. R., & Vernon, M. L. (2003). Physical, emotional, and behavioral reactions to breaking up: The roles of gender, age, emotional involvement, and attachment style. *Personality and Social Psychology Bulletin, 29,* 871–884.

Davis, J. H. (1980). Group decision and procedural justice. In M. Fishbein (Ed.), *Progress in social psychology* (Vol. 1, pp. 157–229). Hillsdale, NJ: Erlbaum.

Davis, J. H., Kerr, N. L., Stasser, G., Meek, D., & Holt, R. (1977). Victim consequences, sentence severity, and decision processes in mock juries. *Organizational Behavior and Human Performance, 18,* 346–365.

Davis, M. H. (1994). *Empathy: A social psychological approach.* Boulder, CO: Westview.

Dawkins, R. (1976). *The selfish gene.* Oxford: Oxford University Press.

Dawkins, R. (1979). Twelve misunderstandings of kin selection. *Zeitschrift für Tierpsychologie, 51,* 184–200.

Dawkins, R. (1989). *The selfish gene.* New York: Oxford University Press.

De Dreu, C. K. W., & De Vries, N. K. (1993). Numerical support, information processing and attitude change. *European Journal of Social Psychology, 23,* 647–662.

De Dreu, C. K. W., & West, M. A. (2001). Minority dissent and team innovation: The importance of participation in decision making. *Journal of Applied Psychology, 86,* 1191–1201.

De Hoog, N., Stroebe, W., & De Wit, J. B. F. (2005). The impact of fear appeals on processing and acceptance of action recommendations. *Personality and Social Psychology Bulletin, 31,* 24–33.

De Vries, N. K., De Dreu, C. K. W., Gordijn, E., & Schuurman, M. (1996). Majority and minority influence: A dual role interpretation. In W. Stroebe & M. Hewstone (Eds.), *European review of social psychology* (Vol. 7, pp. 145–172). Chichester, UK: Wiley.

De Wolff, M. S., & Van Ijzendoorn, M. H. (1997). Sensitivity and attachment: A meta-analysis on parental antecedents of infant attachment. *Child Development, 68*, 571–591.

Dechesne, M., Pyszczynski, T., Arndt, J., Ransom, S., Sheldon, K. M., Van Knippenberg, A., & Janssen, J. (2003). Literal and symbolic immortality: The effect of evidence of literal immortality on self-esteem striving in response to mortality salience. *Journal of Personality and Social Psychology, 84*, 722–737.

Deci, E. L., Koestner, R., & Ryan, R. M. (1999). A meta-analytic review of experiments examining the effects of extrinsic rewards on intrinsic motivation. *Psychological Bulletin, 125*, 627–668.

Deci, E. L., & Ryan, R. M. (1985). *Intrinsic motivation and self-determination in human behavior.* New York: Plenum.

Deci, E. L., & Ryan, R. M. (1995). Human autonomy: The basis for true self-esteem. In M. H. Kernis (Ed.), *Efficacy, agency, and self-esteem* (pp. 31–49). New York: Plenum.

Deci, E. L., & Ryan, R. M. (2000). The 'what' and 'why' of goal pursuits: Human needs and the self-determination of behavior. *Psychological Inquiry, 11*, 227–268.

Demir, M., & Özdemir, M. (2010). Friendship, need satisfaction, and happiness. *Journal of Happiness Studies, 11*, 243–259.

Dennis, A. R. (1996). Information exchange and use in small group decision making. *Small Group Research, 27*, 532–550.

Dennis, A. R., & Valacich, J. S. (1993). Computer brainstorms: More heads are better than one. *Journal of Applied Psychology, 78*, 531–537.

Deschamps, J.-C., & Brown, R. (1983). Superordinate goals and intergroup conflict. *British Journal of Social Psychology, 22*, 189–195.

DeShon, R. P., Kozlowski, S. W. J., Schmidt, A. M., Milner, K. R., & Wiechmann, D. (2004). A multiple-goal, multilevel model of feedback effects on the regulation of individual and team performance. *Journal of Applied Psychology, 89*, 1035–1056.

Deutsch, M. (1968). Field theory in social psychology. In G. Lindzey & E. Aronson (Eds.), *Handbook of social psychology* (2nd ed., pp. 412–487). Reading, MA: Addison-Wesley.

Deutsch, M., & Collins, M. E. (1951). *Interracial housing: A psychological evaluation of a social experiment.* Minneapolis, MI: University of Minnesota Press.

Deutsch, M., & Gerard, H. B. (1955). A study of normative and informational social influences upon individual judgment. *Journal of Abnormal and Social Psychology, 51*, 629–636.

Devine, P. G. (1989). Stereotypes and prejudice: Their automatic and controlled components. *Journal of Personality and Social Psychology, 56*, 5–18.

Devine, P. G., Hamilton, D. L., & Ostrom, T. M. (Eds.). (1994). *Social cognition: Impact on social psychology.* San Diego, CA: Academic Press.

Devine, P. G., & Monteith, M. J. (1999). Automaticity and control in stereotyping. In S. Chaiken & Y. Trope (Eds.), *Dual-process theories in social psychology* (pp. 339–360). New York: Guilford.

Devos, T., Huynh, Q.-L., & Banaji, M. R. (2012). Implicit self and identity. In M. R. Leary & J. P. Tangney (Eds.), *Handbook of self and identity* (2nd ed., pp. 155–179). New York: Guilford.

Dewitte, S., Bruyneel, S., & Geyskens, K. (2009). Self regulating enhances self-regulation in subsequent consumer decisions involving similar response conflicts. *Journal of Consumer Research, 36*, 394–405.

Diehl, M., & Stroebe, W. (1987). Productivity loss in brainstorming groups: Toward the solution of a riddle. *Journal of Personality and Social Psychology, 53*, 497–509.

Diener, E. (1980). Deindividuation: The absence of self-awareness and self-regulation in group members. In P. B. Paulus (Ed.), *Psychology of group influence* (pp. 209–242). Hillsdale, NJ: Erlbaum.

Diener, E. (1984). Subjective well-being. *Psychological Bulletin, 95*, 542–575.

Dijker, A. J. M. (1987). Emotional reactions to ethnic minorities. *European Journal of Social Psychology, 17*, 305–325.

Dijksterhuis, A. (2004). I like myself but I don't know why: Enhancing implicit self-esteem by subliminal evaluative conditioning. *Journal of Personality and Social Psychology, 86*, 345–355.

Dijksterhuis, A., Aarts, H., Bargh, J. A., & Van Knippenberg, A. (2000). On the relation between associative strength and automatic behavior. *Journal of Experimental Social Psychology, 36*, 531–544.

Dijksterhuis, A., & Bargh, J. A. (2001). The perception-behavior expressway: Automatic effects of social perception on social behavior. In M. P. Zanna (Ed.), *Advances in experimental social psychology* (Vol. 33, pp. 1–40). San Diego, CA: Academic Press.

Dijksterhuis, A., Bargh, J. A., & Miedema, J. (2000). Of men and mackerels: Attention and automatic behavior. In H. Bless & J. P. Forgas (Eds.), *Subjective experience in social cognition and behavior* (pp. 36–51). Philadelphia, PA: Psychology Press.

Dijksterhuis, A., Bos, M. W., Nordgren, L. F., & van Baaren, R. B. (2006). On making the right choice: The deliberation-without-attention effect. *Science, 311*, 1005–1007.

Dijksterhuis, A., Chartrand, T. L., & Aarts, H. (2007). Effects of priming and perception on social behavior and goal pursuit. In J. A. Bargh (Ed.), *Social psychology and the unconscious: The automaticity of higher mental processes* (pp. 51–131). New York: Psychology Press.

Dijksterhuis, A., & Van Knippenberg, A. (1998). The relation between perception and behavior, or how to win a game of Trivial Pursuit. *Journal of Personality and Social Psychology, 74*, 865–877.

Dill, K. E., Anderson, C. A., Anderson, K. B., & Deuser, W. E. (1997). Effects of aggressive personality on social expectations and social perceptions. *Journal of Research in Personality, 31*, 272–292.

DiMaggio, P. (1997). Culture and cognition. *Annual Review of Sociology, 23*, 263–287.

Dindia, K. (1994). The intrapersonal-interpersonal dialectical process of self-disclosure. In S. Duck (Ed.), *Dynamics of relationships* (pp. 27–57). Thousand Oaks, CA: Sage.

Dion, K., Berscheid, E., & Walster, E. (1972). What is beautiful is good. *Journal of Personality and Social Psychology, 24*, 285–290.

Dirks, K. T. (1999). The effects of interpersonal trust on work group performance. *Journal of Applied Psychology, 84*, 445–455.

Dishion, T. J., & Nelson, S. E. (2007). Male adolescent friendships: Relationship dynamics that predict adult adjustment. In R. C. M. E. Engels, M. Kerr, & H. Stattin (Eds.), *Friends, lovers and groups: Key relationships in adolescence* (pp. 11–32). Chichester, UK: Wiley.

Dixon, J., & Durrheim, K. (2003). Contact and the ecology of racial division: Some varieties of informal segregation. *British Journal of Social Psychology, 42*, 1–23.

Dixon, J., Durrheim, K., & Tredoux, C. (2007). Intergroup contact and attitudes toward the principle and practice of racial equality. *Psychological Science, 18*, 867–872.

Dixon, J., Tropp, L. R., Durrheim, K., & Tredoux, C. (2010). Let them eat harmony: Prejudice-reduction strategies and attitudes of historically disadvantaged groups. *Current Directions in Psychological Science, 19*, 76–80.

Dodge, K. A. (1980). Social cognition and children's aggressive behavior. *Child Development, 51*, 162–170.

Dohmen, T. J. (2008). Do professionals choke under pressure? *Journal of Economic Behavior and Organization, 65*, 636–653.

Doise, W. (1969). Intergroup relations and polarization of individual and collective judgments. *Journal of Personality and Social Psychology, 12*, 136–143.

Dollard, J., Doob, L. W., Miller, N. E., Mowrer, O. H., & Sears, R. R. (1939). *Frustration and aggression.* New Haven, CT: Yale University Press.

Dooley, J. J., Pyzalski, J., & Cross, D. (2009). Cyberbullying versus face-to-face bullying: A theoretical and conceptual review. *Zeitschrift für Psychologie, 217*, 182–188.

Dovidio, J. F. (1995). With a little help from my friends. In G. G. Brannigan & M. R. Merrens (Eds.), *The social psychologists: Research adventures* (pp. 98–113). New York: McGraw-Hill.

Dovidio, J. F., Allen, J. L., & Schroeder, D. A. (1990). Specificity of empathy-induced helping: Evidence for altruistic motivation. *Journal of Personality and Social Psychology, 59*, 249–260.

Dovidio, J. F., Eller, A., & Hewstone, M. (2011). Improving intergroup relations through direct, extended and other forms of indirect contact. *Group Processes & Intergroup Relations, 14*, 147–160.

Dovidio, J. F., Gaertner, S. L., & Saguy, T. (2009). Commonality and the complexity of 'we': Social attitudes and social change. *Personality and Social Psychology Review, 13*, 3–20.

Dovidio, J. F., Gaertner, S. L., Validzic, A., Matoka, K., Johnson, B., & Frazier, S. (1997). Extending the benefits of recategorization: Evaluations, self-disclosure, and helping. *Journal of Experimental Social Psychology, 33*, 401–420.

Dovidio, J. F., Kawakami, K., Johnson, C., Johnson, B., & Howard, A. (1997). On the nature of prejudice: Automatic and controlled processes. *Journal of Experimental Social Psychology, 33*, 510–540.

Dovidio, J. F., Piliavin, J. A., Gaertner, S. L., Schroeder, D. A., & Clark, R. D., III. (1991). The arousal: cost-reward model and the process of intervention: A review of the evidence. In M. S. Clark (Ed.), *Prosocial behavior* (pp. 86–118). Thousand Oaks, CA: Sage.

Dovidio, J. F., Piliavin, J. A., Schroeder, D. A., & Penner, L. A. (2006). *The social psychology of prosocial behavior.* Mahwah, NJ: Erlbaum.

Downey, G., & Feldman, S. I. (1996). Implications of rejection sensitivity for intimate relationships. *Journal of Personality and Social Psychology, 70*, 1327–1343.

Downs, A. C., & Lyons, P. M. (1991). Natural observations of the links between attractiveness and initial legal judgments. *Personality and Social Psychology Bulletin, 17*, 541–547.

Driskell, J. E., & Mullen, B. (1990). Status, expectations, and behavior: A meta-analytic review and test of the theory. *Personality and Social Psychology Bulletin, 16*, 541–553.

Drury, J., Cocking, C., & Reicher, S. (2009). Everyone for themselves? A comparative study of crowd solidarity among emergency survivors. *British Journal of Social Psychology, 48*, 487–506.

Drury, J., & Reicher, S. (2010). Crowd control. *Scientific American Mind, 21*, 58–65.

Dryer, D. C., & Horowitz, L. M. (1997). When do opposites attract? Interpersonal complementarity versus similarity. *Journal of Personality and Social Psychology, 72*, 592–603.

Duck, S., Rutt, D. J., Hurst, M. H., & Strejc, H. (1991). Some evident truths about conversations in everyday relationships: All communications are not created equal. *Human Communication Research, 18*, 228–267.

Duckitt, J. (2001). A dual-process cognitive-motivational theory of ideology and prejudice. In M. P. Zanna (Ed.), *Advances in experimental social psychology* (Vol. 33, pp. 41–113). San Diego, CA: Academic Press.

Duckitt, J. (2006). Differential effects of right wing authoritarianism and social dominance orientation on outgroup attitudes and their mediation by threat from and competitiveness to outgroups. *Personality and Social Psychology Bulletin, 32*, 684–696.

Duckitt, J., & Fisher, K. (2003). The impact of social threat on worldview and ideological attitudes. *Political Psychology, 24*, 199–222.

Duckitt, J., Wagner, C., Du Plessis, I., & Birum, I. (2002). The psychological bases of ideology and prejudice: Testing a dual process model. *Journal of Personality and Social Psychology, 83,* 75–93.

Duffy, S. M., & Rusbult, C. E. (1986). Satisfaction and commitment in homosexual and heterosexual relationships. *Journal of Homosexuality, 12,* 1–23.

Dunbar, R. I. M., Barrett, L., & Lycett, J. (2005). *Evolutionary psychology: A beginner's guide.* Oxford: Oneworld.

Duncan, B. L. (1976). Differential social perception and attribution of intergroup violence: Testing the lower limits of stereotyping of Blacks. *Journal of Personality and Social Psychology, 34,* 590–598.

Dunn, J. (2004). *Children's friendships: The beginnings of intimacy.* Oxford: Wiley-Blackwell.

Dunning, D. (2005). *Self-insight: Roadblocks and detours on the path to knowing thyself.* New York: Psychology Press.

Dunning, D., & Cohen, G. L. (1992). Egocentric definitions of traits and abilities in social judgment. *Journal of Personality and Social Psychology, 63,* 341–355.

Dunning, D., & Hayes, A. F. (1996). Evidence for egocentric comparison in social judgment. *Journal of Personality and Social Psychology, 71,* 213–229.

Dunning, D., Johnson, K., Ehrlinger, J., & Kruger, J. (2003). Why people fail to recognize their own incompetence. *Current Directions in Psychological Science, 12,* 83–87.

Dunning, D., & McElwee, R. O. B. (1995). Idiosyncratic trait definitions: Implications for self-description and social judgment. *Journal of Personality and Social Psychology, 68,* 936–946.

Dunning, D., Meyerowitz, J. A., & Holzberg, A. D. (1989). Ambiguity and self-evaluation: The role of idiosyncratic trait definitions in self-serving assessments of ability. *Journal of Personality and Social Psychology, 57,* 1082–1090.

Dunning, D., Perie, M., & Story, A. L. (1991). Self-serving prototypes of social categories. *Journal of Personality and Social Psychology, 61,* 957–968.

Dunton, B. C., & Fazio, R. H. (1997). An individual difference measure of motivation to control prejudiced reactions. *Personality and Social Psychology Bulletin, 23,* 316–326.

Dutton, D. G., & Aron, A. P. (1974). Some evidence for heightened sexual attraction under conditions of high anxiety. *Journal of Personality and Social Psychology, 30,* 510–517.

Dutton, D. G., & Lake, R. A. (1973). Threat of own prejudice and reverse discrimination in interracial situations. *Journal of Personality and Social Psychology, 28,* 94–100.

Duval, S., & Wicklund, R. A. (1972). *A theory of objective self awareness.* New York: Academic Press.

Dweck, C. S. (2006). *Mindset: The new psychology of success.* New York: Random House.

Dweck, C. S., Chiu, C.-Y., & Hong, Y.-Y. (1995). Implicit theories and their role in judgments and reactions: A world from two perspectives. *Psychological Inquiry, 6,* 267–285.

Eagly, A. H., & Chaiken, S. (1993). *The psychology of attitudes.* Fort Worth, TX: Harcourt Brace Jovanovich.

Eagly, A. H., & Crowley, M. (1986). Gender and helping behavior: A meta-analytic review of the social psychological literature. *Psychological Bulletin, 100,* 283–308.

Eagly, A. H., & Steffen, V. J. (1986). Gender and aggressive behavior: A meta-analytic review of the social psychological literature. *Psychological Bulletin, 100,* 309–330.

Earley, P. C. (1989). Social loafing and collectivism: A comparison of the United States and the People's Republic of China. *Administrative Science Quarterly, 34,* 565–581.

Earley, P. C. (1993). East meets West meets Mideast: Further explorations of collectivistic versus individualistic work groups. *Academy of Management Journal, 36,* 319–348.

Earley, P. C., & Mosakowski, E. (2000). Creating hybrid team cultures: An empirical test of international team functioning. *Academy of Management Journal, 43,* 26–49.

Easterlin, R. A. (2003). Explaining happiness. *Proceedings of the National Academy of Science, 100,* 11176–11183.

Eastwick, P. W., & Finkel, E. J. (2008). Sex differences in mate preferences revisited: Do people know what they initially desire in a romantic partner? *Journal of Personality and Social Psychology, 94,* 245–264.

Eastwick, P. W., Finkel, E. J., Mochon, D., & Ariely, D. (2007). Selective vs. unselective romantic desire: Not all reciprocity is created equal. *Psychological Science, 18,* 317–319.

Eaton, J., Struthers, C. W., Shomrony, A., & Santelli, A. G. (2007). When apologies fail: The moderating effect of implicit and explicit self-esteem on apology and forgiveness. *Self and Identity, 6,* 209–222.

Eberhardt, J. S. (2005). Imaging race. *American Psychologist, 60,* 181–190.

Edwards, D., & Potter, J. (1993). Language and causation: A discursive action model of description and attribution. *Psychological Review, 100,* 23–41.

Eisenberger, N. I., Lieberman, M. D., & Williams, K. D. (2003). Does rejection hurt? An fMRI study of social exclusion. *Science, 302,* 290–292.

Eisenberger, R., & Cameron, J. (1996). Detrimental effects of reward: Reality or myth? *American Psychologist, 51,* 1153–1166.

Ekman, P. (1972). Universals and cultural differences in facial expressions of emotion. In J. Cole (Ed.), *Nebraska Symposium on Motivation* (Vol. 19, pp. 207–282). Lincoln, NE: University of Nebraska Press.

Ekman, P., Friesen, W. V., O'Sullivan, M., Chan, A., Diacoyanni-Tarlatzis, I., Heider, K., ... Ricci-Bitti, P. E. (1987). Universals and cultural differences in the judgments of facial expressions of emotion. *Journal of Personality and Social Psychology, 53*, 712–717.

Elizur, Y., & Mintzer, A. (2003). Gay males' intimate relationship quality: The roles of attachment security, gay identity, social support, and income. *Personal Relationships, 10*, 411–435.

Ellemers, N. (1993). The influence of socio-structural variables on identity management strategies. In W. Stroebe & M. Hewstone (Eds.), *European review of social psychology* (Vol. 4, pp. 27–57). Chichester, UK: Wiley.

Ellemers, N., Spears, R., & Doosje, B. (2002). Self and social identity. *Annual Review of Psychology, 53*, 161–186.

Elms, A. C., & Milgram, S. (1966). Personality characteristics associated with obedience and defiance toward authoritative command. *Journal of Experimental Research in Personality, 1*, 282–289.

Englich, B., Mussweiler, T., & Strack, F. (2006). Playing dice with criminal sentences: The influence of irrelevant anchors on experts' judicial decision making. *Personality and Social Psychology Bulletin, 32*, 188–200.

English, T., & Chen, S. (2007). Culture and self-concept stability: Consistency across and within contexts among Asian Americans and European Americans. *Journal of Personality and Social Psychology, 93*, 478–490.

Ensari, N., & Miller, N. (2002). The out-group must not be so bad after all: The effects of disclosure, typicality, and salience on intergroup bias. *Journal of Personality and Social Psychology, 83*, 313–329.

Epley, N., & Gilovich, T. (2006). The anchoring-and-adjustment heuristic. *Psychological Science, 17*, 311–318.

Epley, N., & Whitchurch, E. (2008). Mirror, mirror on the wall: Enhancement in self-recognition. *Personality and Social Psychology Bulletin, 34*, 1159–1170.

Epstein, S., & Morling, B. (1995). Is the self motivated to do more than enhance and/or verify itself? In M. H. Kernis (Ed.), *Efficacy, agency, and self-esteem* (pp. 9–29). New York: Plenum.

Erdmann, G., & Janke, W. (1978). Interaction between physiological and cognitive determinants of emotions: Experimental studies on Schachter's theory of emotions. *Biological Psychology, 6*, 61–74.

Erez, M., & Somech, A. (1996). Is group productivity loss the rule or the exception? Effects of culture and group-based motivation. *Academy of Management Journal, 39*, 1513–1537.

Esser, J. K. (1998). Alive and well after 25 years: A review of groupthink research. *Organizational Behavior and Human Decision Processes, 73*, 116–141.

Esser, J. K., & Lindoerfer, J. S. (1989). Groupthink and the space shuttle Challenger accident: Toward a quantitative case analysis. *Journal of Behavioral Decision Making, 2*, 167–177.

Esses, V. M., Haddock, G., & Zanna, M. P. (1993). Values, stereotypes, and emotions as determinants of intergroup attitudes. In D. M. Mackie & D. L. Hamilton (Eds.), *Affect, cognition, and stereotyping: Interactive processes in group perception* (pp. 137–166). San Diego, CA: Academic Press.

Esses, V. M., Jackson, L. M., Dovidio, J. F., & Hodson, G. (2005). Instrumental relations among groups: Group competition, conflict, and prejudice. In J. F. Dovidio, P. Glick, & L. A. Rudman (Eds.), *On the nature of prejudice* (pp. 225–243). Oxford: Blackwell.

Esses, V. M., Veenvliet, S., Hodson, G., & Mihic, L. (2008). Justice, morality, and the dehumanization of refugees. *Social Justice Research, 21*, 4–25.

Esses, V. M., & Vernon, R. A. (Eds.). (2008). *Explaining the breakdown of ethnic relations: Why neighbors kill*. Oxford: Blackwell.

Exum, M. L. (2006). Alcohol and aggression: An integration of findings from experimental studies. *Journal of Criminal Justice, 34*, 131–145.

Fantz, R. L. (1963). Pattern vision in newborn infants. *Science, 140*, 296–297.

Farr, R. M. (1996). *The roots of modern social psychology: 1872–1954*. Oxford: Blackwell.

Faulkner, J., Schaller, M., Park, J. H., & Duncan, L. A. (2004). Evolved disease-avoidance mechanisms and contemporary xenophobic attitudes. *Group Processes & Intergroup Relations, 7*, 333–353.

Fazio, R. H. (1990). Multiple processes by which attitudes guide behavior: The MODE model as an integrative framework. In M. P. Zanna (Ed.), *Advances in experimental social psychology* (Vol. 23, pp. 75–109). San Diego, CA: Academic Press.

Fazio, R. H. (1995). Attitudes as object-evaluation associations: Determinants, consequences, and correlates of attitude accessibility. In R. E. Petty & J. A. Krosnick (Eds.), *Attitude strength: Antecedents and consequences* (pp. 247–282). Hillsdale, NJ: Erlbaum.

Fazio, R. H. (2000). Accessible attitudes as tools for object appraisal: Their costs and benefits. In G. R. Maio & J. M. Olson (Eds.), *Why we evaluate: Functions of attitudes* (pp. 1–36). Mahwah, NJ: Erlbaum.

Fazio, R. H. (2007). Attitudes as object-evaluation associations of varying strength. *Social Cognition, 25*, 603–637.

Fazio, R. H., Chen, J. M., McDonel, E. C., & Sherman, S. J. (1982). Attitude accessibility, attitude-behavior consistency, and the strength of the object-evaluation association. *Journal of Experimental Social Psychology, 18*, 339–357.

Fazio, R. H., Jackson, J. R., Dunton, B. C., & Williams, C. J. (1995). Variability in automatic activation as an unobtrusive measure of racial attitudes: A bona fide pipeline? *Journal of Personality and Social Psychology, 69*, 1013–1027.

Fazio, R. H., & Olson, M. A. (2003). Implicit measures in social cognition research: Their meaning and use. *Annual Review of Psychology, 54,* 297–327.

Fazio, R. H., & Petty, R. E. (Eds.). (2007). *Attitudes: Structure, function, and consequences.* Hove, UK: Psychology Press.

Fazio, R. H., & Williams, C. J. (1986). Attitude accessibility as a moderator of the attitude-perception and attitude-behavior relations: An investigation of the 1984 presidential election. *Journal of Personality and Social Psychology, 51,* 505–514.

Fazio, R. H., Zanna, M. P., & Cooper, J. (1977). Dissonance and self-perception: An integrative view of each theory's proper domain of application. *Journal of Experimental Social Psychology, 13,* 464–479.

Feeney, J. A. (2002). Attachment, marital interaction, and relationship satisfaction: A diary study. *Personal Relationships, 9,* 39–55.

Fehr, E., & Camerer, C. F. (2007). Social neuroeconomics: The neural circuitry of social preferences. *Trends in Cognitive Sciences, 11,* 419–427.

Fehr, E., & Gächter, S. (2002). Altruistic punishment in humans. *Nature, 415,* 137–140.

Feinberg, T. E., & Keenan, J. P. (Eds.). (2005). *The lost self: Pathologies of the brain and identity.* New York: Oxford University Press.

Fejfar, M. C., & Hoyle, R. H. (2000). Effect of private self-awareness on negative affect and self-referent attribution: A quantitative review. *Personality and Social Psychology Review, 4,* 132–142.

Fennis, B. M. (2008). Persuasion pleasure and selling stress: The role of non-verbal communication in consumer influence settings. *Advances in Consumer Research, 35,* 797–798.

Fennis, B. M. (2010). *The psychology of advertising.* New York: Psychology Press.

Fennis, B. M., Janssen, L., & Vohs, K. D. (2009). Acts of benevolence: A limited-resource account of compliance with charitable requests. *Journal of Consumer Research, 35,* 906–924.

Fennis, B. M., & Stroebe, W. (2010). *The psychology of advertising.* Hove, UK: Psychology Press.

Ferguson, C. J. (2002). Media violence: Miscast causality. *American Psychologist, 57,* 446–447.

Ferguson, C. J. (2007). Evidence for publication bias in video game violence effects literature: A meta-analytic review. *Aggression and Violent Behavior, 12,* 470–482.

Festinger, L. (1950). Informal social communication. *Psychological Review, 57,* 271–282.

Festinger, L. (1954). A theory of social comparison processes. *Human Relations, 7,* 117–140.

Festinger, L. (1957). *A theory of cognitive dissonance.* Stanford, CA: Stanford University Press.

Festinger, L. (1980). *Retrospections on social psychology.* New York: Oxford University Press.

Festinger, L., & Carlsmith, J. M. (1959). Cognitive consequences of forced compliance. *Journal of Abnormal and Social Psychology, 58,* 203–210.

Festinger, L., & Maccoby, N. (1964). On resistance to persuasive communications. *Journal of Abnormal and Social Psychology, 68,* 359–366.

Festinger, L., Riecken, H. W., & Schachter, S. (1956). *When prophecy fails.* Minneapolis, MN: University of Minnesota Press.

Festinger, L., Schachter, S., & Back, K. (1950). *Social pressures in informal groups: A study of human factors in housing.* New York: Harper.

Fhanér, G., & Hane, M. (1979). Seat belts: Opinion effects of law-induced use. *Journal of Applied Psychology, 64,* 205–212.

Fiedler, K. (1991). The tricky nature of skewed frequency tables: An information loss account of distinctiveness-based illusory correlations. *Journal of Personality and Social Psychology, 60,* 24–36.

Fincham, F. D. (2000). The kiss of the porcupines: From attributing responsibility to forgiving. *Personal Relationships, 7,* 1–23.

Fincham, F. D., Paleari, F. G., & Regalia, C. (2002). Forgiveness in marriage: The role of relationship quality, attributions, and empathy. *Personal Relationships, 9,* 27–37.

Fine, G. A., & Elsbach, K. D. (2000). Ethnography and experiment in social psychological theory building: Tactics for integrating qualitative field data with quantitative lab data. *Journal of Experimental Social Psychology, 36,* 51–76.

Finkel, E. J., Rusbult, C. E., Kumashiro, M., & Hannon, P. A. (2002). Dealing with betrayal in close relationships: Does commitment promote forgiveness? *Journal of Personality and Social Psychology, 82,* 956–974.

Finkenauer, C., Engels, R. C. M. E., Branje, S. J. T., & Meeus, W. (2004). Disclosure and relationship satisfaction in families. *Journal of Marriage and Family, 66,* 195–209.

Finkenauer, C., Kubacka, K. E., Engels, R. C. M. E., & Kerkhof, P. (2009). Secrecy in close relationships: Investigating its intrapersonal and interpersonal effects. In T. D. Afifi & W. A. Afifi (Eds.), *Uncertainty, information management, and disclosure decisions: Theories and applications* (pp. 300–319). New York: Routledge.

Finlay, K., & Stephan, W. G. (2000). Reducing prejudice: The effects of empathy on intergroup attitudes. *Journal of Applied Social Psychology, 30,* 1720–1737.

Fischer, A. H., & Roseman, I. J. (2007). Beat them or ban them: The characteristics and social functions of anger and contempt. *Journal of Personality and Social Psychology, 93,* 103–115.

Fischer, P., & Greitemeyer, T. (2006). Music and aggression: The impact of sexual-aggressive song lyrics on aggression-related thoughts, emotions, and behavior toward the same and the opposite sex. *Personality and Social Psychology Bulletin, 32,* 1165–1176.

Fischer, P., Greitemeyer, T., Pollozek, F., & Frey, D. (2006). The unresponsive bystander: Are bystanders more responsive in dangerous emergencies? *European Journal of Social Psychology, 36,* 267–278.

Fischer, P., Krueger, J. I., Greitemeyer, T., Vogrincic, C., Kastenmüller, A., Frey, D., … & Kainbacher, M. (2011). The bystander-effect: A meta-analytic review on bystander intervention in dangerous and non-dangerous emergencies. *Psychological Bulletin, 137*, 517–537.

Fishbein, M. (1963). An investigation into the relationship between beliefs about an object and attitudes towards the object. *Human Relations, 16*, 233–240.

Fishbein, M. (1967). Attitude and the prediction of behavior. In M. Fishbein (Ed.), *Readings in attitude theory and measurement* (pp. 477–492). New York: Wiley.

Fishbein, M., & Ajzen, I. (1975). *Belief, attitude, intention, and behavior*. Reading, MA: Addison-Wesley.

Fisher, H. (2004). *Why we love: The nature and chemistry of romantic love*. New York: Holt.

Fisher, H. E., Aron, A., & Brown, L. L. (2006). Romantic love: A mammalian brain system for mate choice. *Philosophical Transactions of the Royal Society B, 361*, 2173–2186.

Fiske, S. T. (1989). Examining the role of intent: Toward understanding its role in stereotyping and prejudice. In J. S. Uleman & J. A. Bargh (Eds.), *Unintended thought* (pp. 253–283). New York: Guilford.

Fiske, S. T. (2004). *Social beings: A core motives approach to social psychology*. Chichester, UK: Wiley.

Fiske, S. T., Cuddy, A. J. C., Glick, P., & Xu, J. (2002). A model of (often mixed) stereotype content: Competence and warmth respectively follow from perceived status and competition. *Journal of Personality and Social Psychology, 82*, 878–902.

Fiske, S. T., Gilbert, D. T., & Lindzey, G. (Eds.). (2010). *Handbook of social psychology* (5th ed., Vol. 1). Hoboken, NJ: Wiley.

Fiske, S. T., Lin, M., & Neuberg, S. L. (1999). The continuum model: Ten years later. In S. Chaiken & Y. Trope (Eds.), *Dual-process theories in social psychology* (pp. 231–254). New York: Guilford.

Fiske, S. T., & Neuberg, S. L. (1990). A continuum of impression formation, from category-based to individuating processes: Influences of information and motivation on attention and interpretation. In M. P. Zanna (Ed.), *Advances in experimental social psychology* (Vol. 23, pp. 1–74). New York: Academic Press.

Fiske, S. T., & Taylor, S. E. (1991). *Social cognition* (2nd ed.). New York: McGraw-Hill.

Fiske, S. T., & Taylor, S. E. (2008). *Social cognition: From brains to culture* (3rd ed.). New York: McGraw-Hill.

Flannery, D. J., Vazsonyi, A. T., & Waldman, I. D. (Eds.). (2007). *Cambridge handbook of violent behavior and aggression*. New York: Cambridge University Press.

Fletcher, G. J. O. (2002). *The new science of intimate relationships*. Oxford: Blackwell.

Flowers, M. L. (1977). A laboratory test of some implications of Janis's groupthink hypothesis. *Journal of Personality and Social Psychology, 35*, 888–896.

Forgas, J. P., Bower, G. H., & Moylan, S. J. (1990). Praise or blame? Affective influences on attributions for achievement. *Journal of Personality and Social Psychology, 59*, 809–819.

Försterling, F. (2001). *Attribution: An introduction to theories, research, and applications*. Hove, UK: Psychology Press.

Forsyth, D. R. (1995). Norms. In A. S. R. Manstead & M. Hewstone (Eds.), *Blackwell encyclopedia of social psychology* (pp. 412–417). Oxford: Blackwell.

Fraley, R. C., Waller, N. G., & Brennan, K. A. (2000). An item response theory analysis of self-report measures of adult attachment. *Journal of Personality and Social Psychology, 78*, 350–365.

Freedman, J. L., & Fraser, S. C. (1966). Compliance without pressure: The foot-in-the-door technique. *Journal of Personality and Social Psychology, 4*, 195–202.

Freese, L., & Cohen, B. P. (1973). Eliminating status generalization. *Sociometry, 36*, 177–193.

Freud, S. (1920). *Beyond the pleasure principle*. New York: Bantam.

Frey, B. S., Savage, D. A., & Torgler, B. (2010). Interaction of natural survival instincts and internalized social norms exploring the Titanic and Lusitania disasters. *Proceedings of the National Academy of Sciences of the United States of America, 107*, 4862–4865.

Frieze, I. H. (2000). Violence in close relationships-development of a research area: Comment on Archer (2000). *Psychological Bulletin, 126*, 681–684.

Frieze, I. H., & Davis, K. E. (Eds.). (2002). *Stalking: Perspectives on victims and perpetrators*. New York: Springer.

Frieze, I. H., Olson, J. E., & Russell, J. (1991). Attractiveness and income for men and women in management. *Journal of Applied Social Psychology, 21*, 1039–1057.

Frijda, N. H. (1986). *The emotions*. Cambridge, MA: Cambridge University Press.

Frost, J. H., Chance, Z., Norton, M. I., & Ariely, D. (2008). People are experience goods: Improving online dating with virtual dates. *Journal of Interactive Marketing, 22*, 51–61.

Fujita, K., & Roberts, J. C. (2010). Promoting prospective self-control through abstraction. *Journal of Experimental Social Psychology, 46*, 1049–1054.

Fujita, K., Trope, Y., Liberman, N., & Levin-Sagi, M. (2006). Construal levels and self-control. *Journal of Personality and Social Psychology, 90*, 351–367.

Funder, D. C. (1987). Errors and mistakes: Evaluating the accuracy of social judgment. *Psychological Bulletin, 101*, 75–90.

Furman, W., & Bierman, K. L. (1984). Children's conceptions of friendship: A multimethod study of developmental changes. *Developmental Psychology, 20*, 925–931.

Gaertner, L., & Insko, C. A. (2000). Intergroup discrimination in the minimal group paradigm: Categorization, reciprocation, or fear? *Journal of Personality and Social Psychology, 79*, 77–94.

Gaertner, L., Sedikides, C., & Chang, K. (2008). On pancultural self-enhancement: Well-adjusted Taiwanese self-enhance on personally valued traits. *Journal of Cross-Cultural Psychology, 39*, 463–477.

Gaertner, S. L., & Dovidio, J. F. (2000). *Reducing intergroup bias: The common ingroup identity model*. Philadelphia, PA: Psychology Press.

Gaertner, S. L., & Dovidio, J. F. (2008). Addressing contemporary racism: The common ingroup identity model. In C. Willis-Esqueda (Ed.), *Nebraska Symposium on Motivation: Motivational aspects of prejudice and racism* (Vol. 53, pp. 111–133). New York: Springer.

Gaertner, S. L., Mann, J., Murrell, A., & Dovidio, J. F. (1989). Reducing intergroup bias: The benefits of recategorization. *Journal of Personality and Social Psychology, 57*, 239–249.

Gaertner, S. L., Rust, M. C., Dovidio, J. F., Bachman, B. A., & Anastasio, P. A. (1996). The contact hypothesis: The role of a common ingroup identity on reducing intergroup bias among majority and minority group members. In J. L. Nye & A. M. Brower (Eds.), *What's social about social cognition?* (pp. 230–260). Thousand Oaks, CA: Sage.

Gagnon, A., & Bourhis, R. Y. (1996). Discrimination in the minimal group paradigm: Social identity or self-interest? *Personality and Social Psychology Bulletin, 22*, 1289–1301.

Galinsky, A. D., & Moskowitz, G. B. (2000). Perspective-taking: Decreasing stereotype expression, stereotype accessibility, and in-group favoritism. *Journal of Personality and Social Psychology, 78*, 708–724.

Gamson, W. A., Fireman, B., & Rytina, S. (1982). *Encounters with unjust authority*. Homewood, IL: Dorsey.

Gansberg, M. (1964, March 27). 37 who saw murder didn't call the police. *New York Times* (p. 1).

Garcia, S. M., Weaver, K., Moskowitz, G. B., & Darley, J. M. (2002). Crowded minds: The implicit bystander effect. *Journal of Personality and Social Psychology, 83*, 843–853.

Gawronski, B. (2004). Theory-based bias correction in dispositional inference: The fundamental attribution error is dead, long live the correspondence bias. In W. Stroebe & M. Hewstone (Eds.), *European review of social psychology* (Vol. 15, pp. 83–217). Hove, UK: Psychology Press.

Gawronski, B., Ehrenberg, K., Banse, R., Zukova, J., & Klauer, K. C. (2003). It's in the mind of the beholder: The impact of stereotypic associations on category-based and individuating impression formation. *Journal of Experimental Social Psychology, 39*, 16–30.

Gawronski, B., & Payne, B. K. (Eds.). (2010). *Handbook of implicit social cognition: Measurement, theory, and applications*. New York: Guilford.

Geen, R. G. (2001). *Human aggression* (2nd ed.). Buckingham, UK: Open University Press.

Gentile, D. A., & Gentile, J. R. (2008). Violent video games as exemplary teachers: A conceptual analysis. *Journal of Youth and Adolescence, 37*, 127–141.

George, J. M. (1990). Personality, affect, and behavior in groups. *Journal of Applied Psychology, 75*, 107–116.

Gerard, H. B., Wilhelmy, R. A., & Conolley, E. S. (1968). Conformity and group size. *Journal of Personality and Social Psychology, 8*, 79–82.

Gergen, K. J. (1971). *The concept of self*. Oxford: Holt, Rinehart & Winston.

Gergen, K. J. (1973). Social psychology as history. *Journal of Personality and Social Psychology, 26*, 309–320.

Gergen, K. J. (1978). Experimentation in social psychology: A reappraisal. *European Journal of Social Psychology, 8*, 507–527.

Gergen, K. J. (1999). *An invitation to social construction*. London: Sage.

Gerin, W., Pieper, C., Levy, R., & Pickering, T. G. (1992). Social support in social interaction: A moderator of cardiovascular reactivity. *Psychosomatic Medicine, 54*, 324–336.

Giancola, P. R. (2003). The moderating effects of dispositional empathy on alcohol-related aggression in men and women. *Journal of Abnormal and Social Psychology, 112*, 275–281.

Giancola, P. R., & Corman, M. D. (2007). Alcohol and aggression: A test of the attention-allocation model. *Psychological Science, 18*, 649–655.

Giancola, P. R., & Parrott, D. J. (2008). Further evidence for the validity of the Taylor aggression paradigm. *Aggressive Behavior, 34*, 214–229.

Gibbons, F. X., & Buunk, B. P. (1999). Individual differences in social comparison: Development of a scale of social comparison orientation. *Journal of Personality and Social Psychology, 76*, 129–142.

Gibbons, F. X., & Wicklund, R. A. (1982). Self-focused attention and helping behavior. *Journal of Personality and Social Psychology, 43*, 462–474.

Gibson, D. C. (2005). B.T.K. Strangler versus Wichita Police Department: The significance of serial murder media relations. *Public Relations Review, 32*, 58–65.

Gibson, J. J. (1979). *The ecological approach to visual perception*. Boston, MA: Houghton Mifflin.

Gigone, D., & Hastie, R. (1993). The common knowledge effect: Information sharing and group judgment. *Journal of Personality and Social Psychology, 65*, 959–574.

Gilbert, D. (2006). *Stumbling on happiness*. New York: Knopf.

Gilbert, D. T., Fiske, S. T., & Lindzey, G. (Eds.). (1998). *Handbook of social psychology* (4th ed., Vol. 1). Boston, MA: McGraw-Hill.

Gilbert, D. T., Giesler, R. B., & Morris, K. A. (1995). When comparisons arise. *Journal of Personality and Social Psychology, 69*, 227–236.

Gilbert, D. T., & Malone, P. S. (1995). The correspondence bias. *Psychological Bulletin, 117*, 21–38.

Gilbert, D. T., Pelham, B. W., & Krull, D. S. (1988). On cognitive busyness: When person perceivers meet persons perceived. *Journal of Personality and Social Psychology, 54*, 733–740.

Gilbert, P., Price, J., & Allan, S. (1995). Social comparison, social attractiveness and evolution: How might they be related? *New Ideas in Psychology, 13*, 149–165.

Gilovich, T., & Savitsky, K. (2002). Like goes with like: The role of representativeness in erroneous and pseudo-scientific beliefs. In T. Gilovich, D. Griffin, & D. Kahneman (Eds.), *Heuristics and biases: The psychology of intuitive judgment* (pp. 617–624). New York: Cambridge University Press.

Gintis, H. (2000). Strong reciprocity and human sociality. *Journal of Theoretical Biology, 206*, 169–179.

Gladwell, M. (2005). *Blink: The power of thinking without thinking*. London: Penguin.

Glazer, M. P., & Glazer, P. M. (1989). *The whistleblowers: Exposing corruption in government and industry*. New York: Basic Books.

Glick, P. (2008). When neighbors blame neighbors: Scapegoating and the breakdown of ethnic relations. In V. M. Esses & R. A. Vernon (Eds.), *Explaining the breakdown of ethnic relations: Why neighbors kill* (pp. 121–146). Oxford: Blackwell.

Glick, P., & Fiske, S. T. (1996). The ambivalent sexism inventory: Differentiating hostile and benevolent sexism. *Journal of Personality and Social Psychology, 70*, 491–512.

Goethals, G. R., & Zanna, M. P. (1979). The role of social comparison in choice shifts. *Journal of Personality and Social Psychology, 37*, 1469–1476.

Goffman, E. (1959). *The presentation of self in everyday life*. Garden City, NY: Doubleday.

Goldie, J., Schwartz, L., McConnachie, A., & Morrison, J. (2003). Students' attitudes and potential behaviour with regard to whistle blowing as they pass through a modern medical curriculum. *Medical Education, 37*, 368–375.

Goldstein, A. P. (2002). *The psychology of group aggression*. Chichester, UK: Wiley.

Gollwitzer, P. M. (1999). Implementation intentions: Strong effects of simple plans. *American Psychologist, 54*, 493–503.

Gollwitzer, P. M., & Brandstätter, V. (1997). Implementation intentions and effective goal pursuit. *Journal of Personality and Social Psychology, 73*, 186–199.

Gollwitzer, P. M., & Sheeran, P. (2006). Implementation intentions and goal achievement: A meta-analysis of effects and processes. In M. P. Zanna (Ed.), *Advances in experimental social psychology* (Vol. 38, pp. 69–119). San Diego, CA: Academic Press.

González, R., & Brown, R. (2006). Dual identities in intergroup contact: Group status and size moderate the generalization of positive attitude change. *Journal of Experimental Social Psychology, 42*, 753–767.

Goodhead, G. (2004). *Us versus them: Journeys to the world's greatest football derbies*. London: Penguin.

Gordijn, E. H., Postmes, T., & De Vries, N. K. (2001). Devil's advocate or advocate of oneself: Effects of numerical support on pro- and counter-attitudinal self-persuasion. *Personality and Social Psychology Bulletin, 27*, 395–407.

Gordijn, E. H., Wigboldus, D., & Yzerbyt, V. (2001). Emotional consequences of categorizing victims of negative outgroup behavior as ingroup or outgroup. *Group Processes & Intergroup Relations, 4*, 317–326.

Gosling, S. D., Vazire, S., Srivastava, S., & John, O. P. (2004). Should we trust web-based studies? A comparative analysis of six preconceptions about Internet questionnaires. *American Psychologist, 59*, 93–104.

Grammer, K., & Thornhill, R. (1994). Human (Homo sapiens) facial attractiveness and sexual selection: The role of symmetry and averageness. *Journal of Comparative Psychology, 108*, 233–242.

Green, J. D., Sedikides, C., & Gregg, A. P. (2008). Forgotten but not gone: The recall and recognition of self-threatening memories. *Journal of Experimental Social Psychology, 44*, 547–561.

Greenberg, J., & Folger, R. (1988). *Controversial issues in social research methods*. New York: Springer.

Greenberg, J., Pyszczynski, T., Solomon, S., Pinel, E., Simon, L., & Jordan, K. (1993). Effects of self-esteem on vulnerability-denying defensive distortions: Further evidence of an anxiety-buffering function of self-esteem. *Journal of Experimental Social Psychology, 29*, 229–251.

Greenberg, J., Solomon, S., & Pyszczynski, T. (1997). Terror management theory of self-esteem and cultural worldviews: Empirical assessments and conceptual refinements. In M. P. Zanna (Ed.), *Advances in experimental social psychology* (Vol. 29, pp. 61–139). San Diego, CA: Academic Press.

Greenberg, K. J., & Dratel, J. L. (2005). *The torture papers: The road to Abu Ghraib*. Cambridge, MA: Cambridge University Press.

Greene, C. N. (1975). The reciprocal nature of influence between leader and subordinate. *Journal of Applied Psychology, 60*, 187–193.

Greenland, K., & Brown, R. (1999). Categorization and intergroup anxiety in contact between British and Japanese nationals. *European Journal of Social Psychology, 29*, 503–521.

Greenlees, I. A., & McGrew, W. C. (1994). Sex and age differences in preferences and tactics of mate attraction: Analysis of published advertisements. *Ethology and Sociobiology, 15*, 59–72.

Greenwald, A. G. (1968). Cognitive learning, cognitive response to persuasion, and attitude change. In A. G. Greenwald, T. C. Brock, & T. M. Ostrom (Eds.), *Psychological foundations of attitudes* (pp. 147–170). New York: Academic Press.

Greenwald, A. G. (1988). Self-knowledge and self-deception. In J. S. Lockard & D. L. Paulhus (Eds.), *Self-deception: An adaptive mechanism?* (pp. 113–131). Englewood Cliffs, NJ: Prentice Hall.

Greenwald, A. G., & Banaji, M. R. (1995). Implicit social cognition: Attitudes, self-esteem, and stereotypes. *Psychological Review, 102*, 4–27.

Greenwald, A. G., & Farnham, S. D. (2000). Using the Implicit Association Test to measure self-esteem and self-concept. *Journal of Personality and Social Psychology, 79*, 1022–1038.

Greenwald, A. G., McGhee, D. E., & Schwartz, J. L. K. (1998). Measuring individual differences in implicit cognition: The Implicit Association Test. *Journal of Personality and Social Psychology, 74*, 1464–1480.

Greenwald, A. G., Nosek, B. A., & Banaji, M. R. (2003). Understanding and using the Implicit Association Test: An improved scoring algorithm. *Journal of Personality and Social Psychology, 85*, 197–216.

Greenwald, A. G., Spangenberg, E. R., Pratkanis, A. R., & Eskenazi, J. (1991). Double-blind tests of subliminal self-help audiotapes. *Psychological Science, 2*, 119–122.

Greenwood, J. D. (1989). *Explanation and experiment in social psychological science: Realism and the social constitution of action.* New York: Springer.

Gregg, A. P., & Sedikides, C. (2010). Narcissistic fragility: Rethinking its links to explicit and implicit self-esteem. *Self and Identity, 9*, 142–161.

Greitemeyer, T., & Osswald, S. (2009). Prosocial video games reduce aggressive cognitions. *Journal of Experimental Social Psychology, 45*, 896–900.

Greitemeyer, T., & Schulz-Hardt, S. (2003). Preference-consistent evaluation of information in the hidden profile paradigm: Beyond group-level explanations for the dominance of shared information in group decisions. *Journal of Personality and Social Psychology, 84*, 322–339.

Grice, H. P. (1975). Logic and conversation. In P. Cole & J. L. Morgan (Eds.), *Syntax and semantics* (Vol. 3, pp. 41–58). New York: Academic Press.

Griffin, R. S., & Gross, A. M. (2004). Childhood bullying: Current empirical findings and future directions for research. *Aggression and Violent Behavior, 9*, 379–400.

Grove, T. (1998). *The juryman's tale.* London: Bloomsbury.

Grube, J. A., & Piliavin, J. A. (2000). Role identity, organizational experiences, and volunteer performance. *Personality and Social Psychology Bulletin, 26*, 1108–1119.

Grzelak, J., & Derlega, V. J. (1982). Cooperation and helping behavior: An introduction. In V. J. Derlega & J. Grzelak (Eds.), *Cooperation and helping behavior: Theories and research* (pp. 2–15). New York: Academic Press.

Gudykunst, W. B., Gao, G., Schmidt, K. L., Nishida, T., Bond, M. H., Leung, K., … Barraclough, R. A. (1992). The influence of individualism-collectivism, self-monitoring, and predicted-outcome value on communication in ingroup and outgroup relationships. *Journal of Cross-Cultural Psychology, 23*, 196–213.

Guerin, B. (1993). *Social facilitation.* Cambridge, MA: Cambridge University Press.

Guimond, S., Dambrun, M., Michinov, N., & Duarte, S. (2003). Does social dominance generate prejudice? Integrating individual and contextual determinants of intergroup cognitions. *Journal of Personality and Social Psychology, 84*, 697–721.

Haaland, G. A., & Venkatesan, M. (1968). Resistance to persuasive communication: An examination of the distraction hypotheses. *Journal of Personality and Social Psychology, 9*, 167–170.

Hackman, J. R., & Morris, C. G. (1975). Group tasks, group interaction process, and group performance effectiveness: A review and proposed integration. In L. Berkowitz (Ed.), *Advances in experimental social psychology* (Vol. 8, pp. 45–99). New York: Academic Press.

Haddock, G., & Carrick, R. (1999). How to make a politician more likeable and effective: Framing political judgments through the numeric values of a rating scale. *Social Cognition, 17*, 298–311.

Haddock, G., & Maio, G. R. (Eds.). (2004). *Contemporary perspectives on the psychology of attitudes.* Hove, UK: Psychology Press.

Haddock, G., Maio, G. R., Arnold, K., & Huskinson, T. (2008). Should persuasion be affective or cognitive? The moderating effects of need for affect and need for cognition. *Personality and Social Psychology Bulletin, 34*, 769–778.

Haddock, G., Rothman, A. J., Reber, R., & Schwarz, N. (1999). Forming judgments of attitude certainty, intensity, and importance: The role of subjective experiences. *Personality and Social Psychology Bulletin, 25*, 771–782.

Haddock, G., Zanna, M. P., & Esses, V. M. (1993). Assessing the structure of prejudicial attitudes: The case of attitudes toward homosexuals. *Journal of Personality and Social Psychology, 65*, 1105–1118.

Hagger, M. S., Wood, C., Stiff, C., & Chatzisarantis, N. L. D. (2010). Ego depletion and the strength model of self-control: A meta-analysis. *Psychological Bulletin, 136*, 495–525.

Haines, H., & Vaughan, G. M. (1979). Was 1898 a great date in the history of social psychology? *Journal of the History of the Behavioral Science, 15*, 323–332.

Halabi, S., Dovidio, J. F., & Nadler, A. (2008). When and how do high status group members offer help: Effects of social dominance orientation and status threat. *Political Psychology, 29*, 841–858.

Hamilton, D. L. (Ed.). (1981). *Cognitive processes in stereotyping and intergroup behavior.* Hillsdale, NJ: Erlbaum.

Hamilton, D. L., & Gifford, R. K. (1976). Illusory correlation in interpersonal perception: A cognitive basis of stereotypic judgments. *Journal of Experimental Social Psychology, 12*, 392–407.

Hamilton, V. L. (1980). Intuitive psychologist or intuitive lawyer? Alternative models of the attribution process. *Journal of Personality and Social Psychology, 39*, 767–772.

Hamilton, W. D. (1964). The genetical evolution of social behaviour. *Journal of Theoretical Biology, 7*, 1–52.

Haney, C., Banks, C., & Zimbardo, P. (1973). Interpersonal dynamics in a simulated prison. *International Journal of Criminology and Penology, 1*, 69–97.

Harari, H., Harari, O., & White, R. V. (1985). The reaction to rape by American male bystanders. *Journal of Social Psychology, 125*, 653–658.

Harari, H., Mohr, D., & Hosey, K. (1980). Faculty helpfulness to students: A comparison of compliance techniques. *Personality and Social Psychology Bulletin, 6*, 373–377.

Harker, L., & Keltner, D. (2001). Expressions of positive emotions in women's college yearbook pictures and their relationship to personality and life outcomes across adulthood. *Journal of Personality and Social Psychology, 80*, 112–124.

Harris, L. T., & Fiske, S. T. (2006). Dehumanizing the lowest of the low: Neuroimaging responses to extreme out-groups. *Psychological Science, 17*, 847–853.

Harris, L. T., Todorov, A., & Fiske, S. T. (2005). Attributions on the brain: Neuro-imaging dispositional inferences, beyond theory of mind. *Neuroimage, 28*, 763–769.

Harter, S. (1993). Causes and consequences of low self-esteem in children and adolescents. In R. F. Baumeister (Ed.), *Self-esteem: The puzzle of low self-regard* (pp. 87–116). New York: Plenum.

Harter, S. (1999). *The construction of the self: A developmental perspective.* New York: Guilford.

Hartup, W. W. (1996). The company they keep: Friendships and their developmental significance. *Child Development, 67*, 1–13.

Hartup, W. W., & Stevens, N. (1997). Friendships and adaptation in the life course. *Psychological Bulletin, 121*, 355–370.

Harwood, J., Hewstone, M., Paolini, S., & Voci, A. (2005). Grandparent-grandchild contact and attitudes toward older adults: Moderator and mediator effects. *Personality and Social Psychology Bulletin, 31*, 393–406.

Harzing, A. W. (2005). The use of English questionnaires in cross-national research: Does cultural accommodation obscure cross-national differences? *International Journal of Cross Cultural Management, 5*, 213–224.

Haslam, S. A. (2004). *Psychology in organisations: The social identity approach* (2nd ed.). London: Sage.

Haslam, S. A., & McGarty, C. (2003). *Research methods and statistics in psychology.* London: Sage.

Haslam, S. A., & Oakes, P. J. (1995). How context independent is the outgroup homogeneity effect? A response to Bartsch and Judd. *European Journal of Social Psychology, 25*, 469–475.

Haslam, S. A., & Reicher, S. D. (2007). Beyond the banality of evil: Three dynamics of an interactionist social psychology of tyranny. *Personality and Social Psychology Bulletin, 33*, 615–622.

Haslam, S. A., & Reicher, S. D. (2008). Questioning the banality of evil. *Psychologist, 21*, 16–19.

Hass, R. G., & Eisenstadt, D. (1990). The effects of self-focused attention on perspective-taking and anxiety. *Anxiety Research, 2*, 165–176.

Hassebrauck, M. (1993). Die Beurteilung der physischen Attraktivität [The evaluation of physical attractiveness]. In M. Hassebrauck & R. Niketta (Eds.), *Physische Attraktivität* (pp. 29–60). Göttingen, Germany: Hogrefe.

Hastie, R. (1993). *Inside the juror.* New York: Cambridge University Press.

Hastie, R., Penrod, S., & Pennington, N. (1983). *Inside the jury.* Cambridge, MA: Harvard University Press.

Hatfield, E., & Rapson, R. (1993). *Love, sex, and intimacy: Their psychology, biology, and history.* New York: HarperCollins.

Haugtvedt, C. P., & Petty, R. E. (1992). Personality and persuasion: Need for cognition moderates the persistence and resistance of attitude changes. *Journal of Personality and Social Psychology, 63*, 308–319.

Hawker, D. S. J., & Boulton, M. J. (2000). Twenty years' research on peer victimization and psychosocial maladjustment: A meta-analytic review of cross-sectional studies. *Journal of Child Psychology and Psychiatry, 41*, 441–455.

Hazan, C., & Shaver, P. (1987). Romantic love conceptualized as an attachment process. *Journal of Personality and Social Psychology, 52*, 511–524.

Hazan, C., & Shaver, P. R. (1994). Attachment as an organizational framework for research on close relationships. *Psychological Inquiry, 5*, 1–22.

Heatherton, T. F. (2011). Neuroscience of self and self-regulation. *Annual Review of Psychology, 62*, 363–390.

Heatherton, T. F., & Baumeister, R. F. (1991). Binge eating as escape from self-awareness. *Psychological Bulletin, 110*, 86–108.

Hechter, M., & Opp, K. D. (Eds.). (2001). *Social norms.* New York: Sage.

Hedges, L. V., & Olkin, I. (1985). *Statistical methods for meta-analysis.* New York: Academic Press.

Heffernan, M. (2011). *Wilful blindness: Why we ignore the obvious at our peril.* New York: Simon & Schuster.

Heider, F. (1944). Social perception and phenomenal causality. *Psychological Review, 51*, 358–374.

Heider, F. (1946). Attitudes and cognitive organization. *Journal of Psychology: Interdisciplinary and Applied, 21*, 107–112.

Heider, F. (1958). *The psychology of interpersonal relations.* New York: Wiley.

Heider, F., & Simmel, M. (1944). An experimental study of apparent behavior. *American Journal of Psychology, 57*, 243–259.

Hein, G., Silani, G., Preuschoff, K., Batson, C. D., & Singer, T. (2010). Neural responses to ingroup and outgroup members' suffering predict individual differences in costly helping. *Neuron, 68*, 149–160.

Heine, S. J. (2008). *Cultural psychology.* New York: Norton.

Heine, S. J., Lehman, D. R., Markus, H. R., & Kitayama, S. (1999). Is there a universal need for positive self-regard? *Psychological Review, 106*, 766–794.

Heine, S. J., Takata, T., & Lehman, D. R. (2000). Beyond self-presentation: Evidence for self-criticism among Japanese. *Personality and Social Psychology Bulletin, 26*, 71–78.

Henchy, T., & Glass, D. C. (1968). Evaluation apprehension and the social facilitation of dominant and subordinate responses. *Journal of Personality and Social Psychology, 10*, 446–454.

Henderlong, J., & Lepper, M. R. (2002). The effects of praise on children's intrinsic motivation: A review and synthesis. *Psychological Bulletin, 128*, 774–795.

Hendrick, S. S. (1981). Self-disclosure and marital satisfaction. *Journal of Personality and Social Psychology, 40*, 1150–1159.

Henrich, J., Heine, S. J., & Norenzayan, A. (2010). The weirdest people in the world? *Brain and Behavioral Science, 33*, 61–83.

Henry, R. A., Strickland, O. J., Yorges, S. L., & Ladd, D. (1996). Helping groups determine their most accurate member: The role of outcome feedback. *Journal of Applied Social Psychology, 26*, 1153–1170.

Henwood, K. L. (1996). Qualitative inquiry: Perspectives, methods and psychology. In J. T. E. Richardson (Ed.), *Handbook of qualitative research methods for psychology and the social science* (pp. 25–40). Leicester, UK: Blackwell.

Herek, G. M. (1986). The instrumentality of attitudes: Toward a neofunctional theory. *Journal of Social Issues, 42*, 99–114.

Herek, G. M., Janis, I. L., & Huth, P. (1987). Decision making during international crises: Is quality of process related to outcome? *Journal of Conflict Resolution, 31*, 203–226.

Herman, C. P., & Polivy, J. (1980). Restrained eating. In A. J. Stunkard (Ed.), *Obesity* (pp. 208–225). Philadelphia, PA: Saunders.

Hersh, S. M. (2004). *Chain of command*. London: Penguin.

Herskovits, M. (1948). *Man and his works: The science of cultural anthropology*. New York: Knopf.

Hertel, G., Kerr, N. L., & Messé, L. A. (2000). Motivation gains in performance groups: Paradigmatic and theoretical developments on the Köhler effect. *Journal of Personality and Social Psychology, 79*, 580–601.

Hewstone, M. (1989). *Causal attribution: From cognitive processes to collective beliefs*. Oxford: Blackwell.

Hewstone, M. (1994). Revision and change of stereotypic beliefs: In search of the elusive subtyping model. In W. Stroebe & M. Hewstone (Eds.), *European review of social psychology* (Vol. 5, pp. 69–109). Chichester, UK: Wiley.

Hewstone, M., & Brown, R. (1986). Contact is not enough: An intergroup perspective on the 'contact hypothesis'. In M. Hewstone & R. Brown (Eds.), *Contact and conflict in intergroup encounters* (pp. 1–44). Oxford: Blackwell.

Hewstone, M., Judd, C. M., & Sharp, M. (2011). Do observer ratings validate self-reports of intergroup contact?: A round-robin analysis. *Journal of Experimental Social Psychology, 47*, 599–609.

Hewstone, M., & Martin, R. (2010). Minority influence: From groups to attitudes and back again. In R. Martin & M. Hewstone (Eds.), *Minority influence and innovation: Antecedents, processes and consequences* (pp. 365–394). Hove, UK: Psychology Press.

Hewstone, M., Rubin, M., & Willis, H. (2002). Intergroup bias. *Annual Review of Psychology, 53*, 575–604.

Hewstone, M., & Swart, H. (2011). Fifty-odd years of inter-group contact: From hypothesis to integrated theory. *British Journal of Social Psychology, 50*, 374–386.

Higgins, E. T. (1987). Self-discrepancy: A theory relating self and affect. *Psychological Review, 94*, 319–340.

Higgins, E. T. (1996). Knowledge activation: Accessibility, applicability, and salience. In E. T. Higgins & A. W. Kruglanski (Eds.), *Social psychology: Handbook of basic principle* (pp. 133–168). New York: Guilford.

Higgins, E. T., & Bargh, J. A. (1987). Social cognition and social perception. *Annual Review of Psychology, 38*, 369–425.

Higgins, E. T., Bargh, J. A., & Lombardi, W. (1985). Nature of priming effects on categorization. *Journal of Experimental Psychology: Learning, Memory, and Cognition, 11*, 59–69.

Higgins, E. T., Bond, R. N., Klein, R., & Strauman, T. (1986). Self-discrepancies and emotional vulnerability: How magnitude, accessibility, and type of discrepancy influence affect. *Journal of Personality and Social Psychology, 51*, 5–15.

Higgins, E. T., Klein, R., & Strauman, T. (1985). Self-concept discrepancy theory: A psychological model for distinguishing among different aspects of depression and anxiety. *Social Cognition, 3*, 51–76.

Hilton, D. J. (1988). Logic and attribution. In D. J. Hilton (Ed.), *Contemporary science and natural explanation: Commonsense conceptions of causality* (pp. 33–65). Brighton, UK: Harvester.

Hilton, D. J. (1990). Conversational processes and causal explanation. *Psychological Bulletin, 107*, 65–81.

Hilton, D. J., McClure, J., & Sutton, R. M. (2010). Selecting explanations from causal chains: Do statistical principles explain preferences for voluntary causes? *European Journal of Social Psychology, 40*, 383–400.

Hilton, D. J., & Slugoski, B. R. (1986). Knowledge-based causal attribution: The abnormal conditions focus model. *Psychological Review, 93*, 75–88.

Hinde, R. A. (1979). *Towards understanding relationships*. London: Academic Press.

Hinduja, S., & Patchin, J. W. (2010). Bullying, cyberbullying and suicide. *Archives of Suicide Research, 14*, 206–221.

Hinkle, S., & Brown, R. (1990). Intergroup comparisons and social identity: Some links and lacunae. In D. Abrams & M. A. Hogg (Eds.), *Social identity theory: Constructive and critical advances* (pp. 48–70). London: Harvester Wheatsheaf.

Hirt, E. R., Deppe, R. K., & Gordon, L. J. (1991). Self-reported versus behavioral self-handicapping: Empirical evidence for a theoretical distinction. *Journal of Personality and Social Psychology, 61*, 981–991.

Hixon, J. G., & Swann, W. B., Jr. (1993). When does introspection bear fruit? Self-reflection, self-insight, and interpersonal choices. *Journal of Personality and Social Psychology, 64*, 35–43.

Hoeksema-Van Orden, C. Y. D., Gaillard, A. W. K., & Buunk, B. P. (1998). Social loafing under fatigue. *Journal of Personality and Social Psychology, 75*, 1179–1190.

Hoel, H., Rayner, C., & Cooper, C. L. (1999). Workplace bullying. In C. L. Cooper & I. T. Robertson (Eds.), *International review of industrial and organizational psychology* (pp. 195–230). New York: Wiley.

Hofling, C. K., Brotzman, E., Dalrymple, S., Graves, N., & Pierce, C. M. (1966). An experimental study in nurse-physician relationships. *Journal of Nervous and Mental Disease, 143*, 171–180.

Hofstede, G. H. (1980). *Culture's consequences: International differences in work-related values.* Beverly Hills, CA: Sage.

Hofstede, G. H. (1991). *Cultures and organizations: Software of the mind.* Maidenhead, UK: McGraw-Hill.

Hofstede, G. H. (2001). *Culture's consequences: Comparing values, behaviors, institutions and organizations across nations.* Thousand Oaks, CA: Sage.

Hogarth, R. M. (1981). Beyond discrete biases: Functional and dysfunctional aspects of judgmental heuristics. *Psychological Bulletin, 90*, 197–217.

Hogg, M. A. (2012). Social identity and the psychology of groups. In M. R. Leary & J. P. Tangney (Eds.), *Handbook of self and identity* (2nd ed., pp. 502–519). New York: Guilford.

Hogg, M. A., & Abrams, D. (1993). Towards a single process uncertainty reduction model of social motivation in groups. In M. A. Hogg & D. Abrams (Eds.), *Group motivation: Social psychological perspectives* (pp. 173–190). New York: Harvester Wheatsheaf.

Hogg, M. A., Sherman, D. K., Dierselhuis, J., Maitner, A. T., & Moffitt, G. (2007). Uncertainty, entitativity, and group identification. *Journal of Experimental Social Psychology, 43*, 135–142.

Hogg, M. A., Turner, J. C., & Davidson, B. (1990). Polarized norms and social frames of reference: A test of the self-categorization theory of group polarization. *Basic and Applied Social Psychology, 11*, 77–100.

Hogg, M. A., & Van Knippenberg, D. (2003). Social identity and leadership processes in groups. In M. P. Zanna (Ed.), *Advances in experimental social psychology* (Vol. 35, pp. 1–52). San Diego, CA: Academic Press.

Holland, R. W., Hendriks, M., & Aarts, H. (2005). Smells like clean spirit: Nonconscious effects of scent on cognition and behavior. *Psychological Science, 16*, 689–693.

Holland, R. W., Verplanken, B., & Van Knippenberg, A. (2002). On the nature of attitude-behavior relations: The strong guide, the weak follow. *European Journal of Social Psychology, 32*, 869–876.

Hollander, E. P. (1958). Conformity, status, and idiosyncrasy credit. *Psychological Review, 65*, 117–127.

Homans, G. C. (1950). *The human group.* New York: Harcourt.

Homans, G. C. (1961). *Social behavior: Its elementary forms.* New York: Harcourt.

Hong, Y.-Y., Benet-Martínez, V., Chiu, C.-Y., & Morris, M. W. (2003). Boundaries of cultural influence: Construct activation as a mechanism for cultural differences in social perception. *Journal of Cross-Cultural Psychology, 34*, 453–464.

Hood, W. R., & Sherif, M. (1962). Verbal report and judgment of an unstructured stimulus. *Journal of Psychology: Interdisciplinary and Applied, 54*, 121–130.

Hornsey, M. J. (2005). Why being right is not enough: Predicting defensiveness in the face of group criticism. In W. Stroebe & M. Hewstone (Eds.), *European review of social psychology* (Vol. 16, pp. 301–334). Hove, UK: Psychology Press.

Hornsey, M. J., & Hogg, M. A. (2000). Subgroup relations: A comparison of mutual intergroup differentiation and common ingroup identity models of prejudice reduction. *Personality and Social Psychology Bulletin, 26*, 242–256.

Hornstein, H. A. (1976). *Cruelty and kindness: A new look at aggression and altruism.* Englewood Cliffs, NJ: Prentice Hall.

Horvath, M., & Brown, J. (Eds.). (2009). *Rape: Challenging contemporary thinking.* Cullompton, UK: Willan.

Horvath, S., & Morf, C. C. (2009). Narcissistic defensiveness: Hypervigilance and avoidance of worthlessness. *Journal of Experimental Social Psychology, 45*, 1252–1258.

Horwitz, S. K., & Horwitz, I. B. (2007). The effects of team diversity on team outcomes: A meta-analytic review of team demography. *Journal of Management, 33*, 987–1015.

Houben, K., Havermans, R. C., & Wiers, R. W. (2010). Learning to dislike alcohol: Conditioning negative implicit attitudes toward alcohol and its effect on drinking behavior. *Psychopharmacology, 211*, 79–86.

House, R. J. (1971). A path goal theory of leader effectiveness. *Administrative Science Quarterly, 16*, 321–338.

House, R. J. (1996). Path-goal theory of leadership: Lessons, legacy, and a reformulated theory. *Leadership Quarterly, 7*, 323–352.

House, R. J., Hanges, P. J., Javidan, M., Dorfman, P. W., & Gupta, V. (Eds.). (2004). *Leadership, culture, and organizations: The GLOBE study of 62 societies.* Thousand Oaks, CA: Sage.

House, R. J., & Mitchell, T. R. (1974). Path-goal theory of leadership. *Journal of Contemporary Business, 3*, 81–97.

House, R. J., Spangler, W. D., & Woycke, J. (1991). Personality and charisma in the US presidency: A psychological theory of leader effectiveness. *Administrative Science Quarterly, 36*, 364–396.

Houston, D. A., & Fazio, R. H. (1989). Biased processing as a function of attitude accessibility: Making objective judgments subjectively. *Social Cognition, 7*, 51–66.

Hovland, C. I., Janis, I. L., & Kelley, H. H. (1953). *Communication and persuasion: Psychological studies of opinion change*. New Haven, CT: Yale University Press.

Hovland, C. I., Lumsdaine, A. A., & Sheffield, F. D. (1949). *Experiments on mass communication*. Princeton, NJ: Princeton University Press.

Hovland, C. I., & Weiss, W. (1951). The influence of source credibility on communication effectiveness. *Public Opinion Quarterly, 15*, 635–650.

Huesmann, L. R. (1998). The role of information processing and cognitive schema in the acquisition and maintenance of habitual aggressive behavior. In R. G. Geen & E. Donnerstein (Eds.), *Human aggression: Theories, research, and implications for policy* (pp. 73–109). New York: Academic Press.

Huesmann, L. R., & Eron, L. D. (Eds.). (1986). *Television and the aggressive child: A cross-national comparison*. Hillsdale, NJ: Erlbaum.

Huesmann, L. R., & Guerra, N. G. (1997). Children's normative beliefs about aggression and aggressive behavior. *Journal of Personality and Social Psychology, 72*, 408–419.

Huesmann, L. R., & Miller, L. S. (1994). Long-term effects of the repeated exposure to media violence in childhood. In L. R. Huesmann (Ed.), *Aggressive behavior: Current perspectives* (pp. 153–186). New York: Plenum.

Huesmann, L. R., Moise-Titus, J., Podolski, C.-L., & Eron, L. D. (2003). Longitudinal relations between children's exposure to TV violence and their aggressive and violent behavior in young adulthood. *Developmental Psychology, 39*, 201–221.

Hüffmeier, J., & Hertel, G. (2011). When the whole is more than the sum of its parts: Group motivation gains in the wild. *Journal of Experimental Social Psychology, 47*, 455–459.

Hull, J. G., Levenson, R. W., Young, R. D., & Sher, K. J. (1983). Self-awareness-reducing effects of alcohol consumption. *Journal of Personality and Social Psychology, 44*, 461–473.

Hull, J. G., & Young, R. D. (1983). The self-awareness-reducing effects of alcohol: Evidence and implications. In J. M. Suls & A. G. Greenwald (Eds.), *Psychological perspectives on the self* (Vol. 2, pp. 159–190). Hillsdale, NJ: Erlbaum.

Hunter, J. A., Platow, M. J., Howard, M. L., & Stringer, M. (1996). Social identity and intergroup evaluative bias: Realistic categories and domain specific self-esteem in a conflict setting. *European Journal of Social Psychology, 26*, 631–647.

Huskinson, T., & Haddock, G. (2004). Individual differences in attitude structure: Variance in the chronic reliance on affective and cognitive information. *Journal of Experimental Social Psychology, 40*, 82–90.

Huston, M., & Schwartz, P. (1995). The relationships of lesbians and of gay men. In J. T. Wood & S. Duck (Eds.), *Under-studied relationships: Off the beaten track* (pp. 89–121). Thousand Oaks, CA: Sage.

Huston, T. L., & Korte, C. (1976). The responsive bystander: Why he helps. In T. Lickona (Ed.), *Moral development and behavior: Theory, research, and social issues* (pp. 269–283). New York: Holt, Rinehart and Winston.

Ingham, A. G., Levinger, G., Graves, J., & Peckham, V. (1974). The Ringelmann effect: Studies of group size and group performance. *Journal of Experimental Social Psychology, 10*, 371–384.

Inglehart, R. (1997). *Modernization and postmodernization: Cultural, economic, and political change in 43 societies*. Princeton, NJ: Princeton University Press.

Inglehart, R., & Baker, W. E. (2000). Modernization, cultural change and the persistence of traditional values. *American Sociological Review, 65*, 19–51.

Inglehart, R., & Oyserman, D. (2004). Individualism, autonomy and self-expression: The human development syndrome. In H. Vinken, J. Soeters, & P. Ester (Eds.), *Comparing cultures: Dimensions of culture in a comparative perspective* (pp. 74–96). Leiden, NL: Brill.

International Association for Cross-Cultural Psychology (not dated). *Online Readings in Psychology and Culture*. Retrieved from http://scholarworks.gvsu.edu/orpc

International Monetary Fund (2005). *World economic outlook database*. Washington, DC. Retrieved from www.imf.org/external/pubs/ft/weo/2005/01/data/dbginim.cfm

Inzlicht, M., & Gutsell, J. N. (2007). Running on empty: Neural signals for self-control failure. *Psychological Science, 18*, 933–937.

Isenberg, D. J. (1986). Group polarization: A critical review and meta-analysis. *Journal of Personality and Social Psychology, 50*, 1141–1151.

Islam, M. R., & Hewstone, M. (1993a). Dimensions of contact as predictors of intergroup anxiety, perceived out-group variability, and out-group attitude: An integrative model. *Personality and Social Psychology Bulletin, 19*, 700–710.

Islam, M. R., & Hewstone, M. (1993b). Intergroup attributions and affective consequences in majority and minority groups. *Journal of Personality and Social Psychology, 64*, 936–950.

Ito, T. A., Miller, N., & Pollock, V. E. (1996). Alcohol and aggression: A meta-analysis on the moderating effects of inhibitory cues, triggering events, and self-focused attention. *Psychological Bulletin, 120*, 60–82.

Iyer, A., & Leach, C. W. (2008). Emotion in inter-group relations. In W. Stroebe & M. Hewstone (Eds.), *European review of social psychology* (Vol. 19, pp. 86–125). Hove, UK: Psychology Press.

Jackman, M. R., & Crane, M. (1986). 'Some of my best friends are black…': Interracial friendship and Whites' racial attitudes. *Public Opinion Quarterly, 50*, 459–486.

Jacobs, R. C., & Campbell, D. T. (1961). The perpetuation of an arbitrary tradition through several generations of a laboratory microculture. *Journal of Abnormal and Social Psychology, 62*, 649–658.

Jahoda, G. (2007). *A history of social psychology: From the eighteenth-century enlightenment to the Second World War*. Cambridge, UK: Cambridge University Press.

James, K., & Greenberg, J. (1989). In-group salience, intergroup comparison, and individual performance and self-esteem. *Personality and Social Psychology Bulletin, 15*, 604–616.

James, W. (1884). What is an emotion? *Mind, 9*, 188–205.

James, W. (1950). *The principles of psychology, Vol. 1, Chapter X: The consciousness of self* (pp. 291–401). New York: Dover. (Original work published 1890).

James, W. (1961). *Psychology: The briefer course, Chapter XII: The self* (pp. 159–191). Cambridge, MA: Harvard University Press. (Original work published 1892).

Janis, I. L. (1972). *Victims of groupthink: A psychological study of foreign-policy decisions and fiascoes*. Boston, MA: Houghton Mifflin.

Janis, I. L. (1982). *Groupthink* (2nd ed.). Boston, MA: Houghton Mifflin.

Jetten, J., & Iyer, A. (2010). Different meanings of the social dominance orientation concept: Predicting political attitudes over time. *British Journal of Social Psychology, 49*, 385–404.

Jetten, J., Spears, R., & Manstead, A. S. R. (1997). Strength of identification and intergroup differentiation: The influence of group norms. *European Journal of Social Psychology, 27*, 603–609.

Jetten, J., Spears, R., & Postmes, T. (2004). Intergroup distinctiveness and differentiation: A meta-analytic integration. *Journal of Personality and Social Psychology, 86*, 862–879.

Johansson, P., Hall, L., Sikström, S., & Olsson, A. (2005). Failure to detect mismatches between intention and outcome in a simple decision task. *Science, 310*, 116–119.

Johnson, A. L., Crawford, M. T., Sherman, S. J., Rutchick, A. M., Hamilton, D. L., Ferreira, M. B., & Petrocelli, J. V. (2006). A functional perspective on group memberships: Differential need fulfillment in a group typology. *Journal of Experimental Social Psychology, 42*, 707–719.

Johnson, B. T., & Eagly, A. H. (2000). Quantitative synthesis of social psychological research. In H. T. Reis & C. M. Judd (Eds.), *Handbook of research methods in social and personality psychology* (pp. 496–528). London: Cambridge University Press.

Johnson, D. J., & Rusbult, C. E. (1989). Resisting temptation: Devaluation of alternative partners as a means of maintaining commitment in close relationships. *Journal of Personality and Social Psychology, 57*, 967–980.

Johnson, E. A., & Reuband, K.-H. (2005). *What we knew: Terror, mass murder and everyday life in Nazi Germany*. New York: Basic Books.

Johnson, J. T., Jemmott, J. B., & Pettigrew, T. F. (1984). Causal attribution and dispositional inference: Evidence of inconsistent judgments. *Journal of Experimental Social Psychology, 20*, 567–585.

Johnson, M. H., Dziurawiec, S., Ellis, H., & Morton, J. (1991). Newborns' preferential tracking of face-like stimuli and its subsequent decline. *Cognition, 40*, 1–19.

Johnson, M. H., & Morton, J. (1991). *Biology and cognitive development: The case of face recognition*. Oxford: Blackwell.

Johnson, M. P., & Ferraro, K. J. (2000). Research on domestic violence in the 1990s: Making distinctions. *Journal of Marriage and Family, 62*, 948–963.

Johnson, R. D., & Downing, L. L. (1979). Deindividuation and valence of cues: Effects on prosocial and antisocial behavior. *Journal of Personality and Social Psychology, 37*, 1532–1538.

Johnson, T. J., Feigenbaum, R., & Weiby, M. (1964). Some determinants and consequences of the teacher's perception of causation. *Journal of Educational Psychology, 55*, 237–246.

Johnston, L., & Hewstone, M. (1992). Cognitive models of stereotype change: Subtyping and the perceived typicality of disconfirming group members. *Journal of Experimental Social Psychology, 28*, 360–386.

Joinson, A. N. (2003). *Understanding the psychology of Internet behaviour*. Basingstoke, UK: Palgrave Macmillan.

Jones, E. E. (1998). Major developments in five decades of social psychology. In D. T. Gilbert, S. T. Fiske, & G. Lindzey (Eds.), *Handbook of social psychology* (4th ed., Vol. 1, pp. 3–57). Boston, MA: McGraw-Hill.

Jones, E. E., & Berglas, S. (1978). Control of attributions about the self through self-handicapping strategies: The appeal of alcohol and the role of underachievement. *Personality and Social Psychology Bulletin, 4*, 200–206.

Jones, E. E., & Davis, K. E. (1965). From acts to dispositions: The attribution process in person perception. In L. Berkowitz (Ed.), *Advances in experimental social psychology* (Vol. 2, pp. 219–266). New York: Academic Press.

Jones, E. E., & Harris, V. A. (1967). The attribution of attitudes. *Journal of Experimental Social Psychology, 3*, 1–24.

Jones, E. E., & Nisbett, R. E. (1972). The actor and the observer: Divergent perceptions of the causes of behavior. In E. E. Jones, D. E. Kanouse, H. H. Kelley, R. E. Nisbett, S. Valins, & B. Weiner (Eds.), *Attribution: Perceiving the causes of behavior* (pp. 79–94). Morristown, NJ: General Learning Press.

Jones, E. E., & Pittman, T. S. (1982). Toward a general theory of strategic self-presentation. In J. M. Suls (Ed.), *Psychological perspectives on the self* (Vol. 1, pp. 231–262). Hillsdale, NJ: Erlbaum.

Jones, E. E., Rhodewalt, F., Berglas, S., & Skelton, J. A. (1981). Effects of strategic self-presentation on subsequent self-esteem. *Journal of Personality and Social Psychology, 41*, 407–421.

Jones, E. E., & Sigall, H. (1971). The bogus pipeline: A new paradigm for measuring affect and attitude. *Psychological Bulletin, 76*, 349–364.

Jordan, C. H., Spencer, S. J., & Zanna, M. P. (2005). Types of high self-esteem and prejudice: How implicit self-esteem relates to ethnic discrimination among high explicit self-esteem individuals. *Personality and Social Psychology Bulletin, 31*, 693–702.

Jordan, C. H., Spencer, S. J., Zanna, M. P., Hoshino-Browne, E., & Correll, J. (2003). Secure and defensive high self-esteem. *Journal of Personality and Social Psychology, 85*, 969–978.

Jordet, G. (2009). Why do English players fail in soccer penalty shootouts? A study of team status, self-regulation, and choking under pressure. *Journal of Sports Sciences, 27*, 97–106.

Josephs, R. A., Markus, H. R., & Tafarodi, R. W. (1992). Gender and self-esteem. *Journal of Personality and Social Psychology, 63*, 391–402.

Jost, J. T., & Banaji, M. R. (1994). The role of stereotyping in system-justification and the production of false consciousness. *British Journal of Social Psychology, 33*, 1–27.

Jostmann, N. B., & Koole, S. L. (2006). On the waxing and waning of working memory: Action orientation moderates the impact of demanding relationship primes on working memory capacity. *Personality and Social Psychology Bulletin, 32*, 1716–1728.

Jostmann, N. B., & Koole, S. L. (2007). On the regulation of cognitive control: Action orientation moderates the impact of high demands in Stroop interference tasks. *Journal of Experimental Psychology: General, 136*, 593–609.

Joule, R. V. (1987). Tabacco deprivation: The foot-in-the-door technique versus the low-ball technique. *European Journal of Social Psychology, 17*, 361–365.

Jourard, S. M. (1971). *The transparent self.* New York: Van Nostrand Reinhold.

Judd, C. M., & Kenny, D. A. (1981a). *Estimating the effects of social interventions.* London: Cambridge University Press.

Judd, C. M., & Kenny, D. A. (1981b). Process analysis: Estimating mediation in treatment evaluations. *Evaluation Review, 5*, 602–619.

Judge, T. A., Bono, J. E., Ilies, R., & Gerhardt, M. W. (2002). Personality and leadership: A qualitative and quantitative review. *Journal of Applied Psychology, 87*, 765–780.

Judge, T. A., Colbert, A. E., & Ilies, R. (2004). Intelligence and leadership: A quantitative review and test of theoretical propositions. *Journal of Applied Psychology, 89*, 542–552.

Judge, T. A., LePine, J. A., & Rich, B. L. (2006). Loving yourself abundantly: Relationship of the narcissistic personality to self- and other perceptions of workplace deviance, leadership, and task and contextual performance. *Journal of Applied Psychology, 91*, 762–776.

Judge, T. A., & Piccolo, R. F. (2004). Transformational and transactional leadership: A meta-analytic test of their relative validity. *Journal of Applied Psychology, 89*, 755–768.

Judge, T. A., Piccolo, R. F., & Ilies, R. (2004). The forgotten ones? The validity of consideration and initiating structure in leadership research. *Journal of Applied Psychology, 89*, 36–51.

Kafetsios, K., & Nezlek, J. B. (2002). Attachment styles in everyday social interaction. *European Journal of Social Psychology, 32*, 719–735.

Kahneman, D. (2011). *Thinking, fast and slow.* New York: Farrar, Straus and Giroux. A readable overview of the Nobel laureate's groundbreaking research on human decision-making, especially the use of cognitive heuristics.

Kahneman, D., & Tversky, A. (1972). Subjective probability: A judgment of representativeness. *Cognitive Psychology, 3*, 430–454.

Kalick, S. M., Zebrowitz, L. A., Langlois, J. H., & Johnson, R. M. (1998). Does human facial attractiveness honestly advertise health? Longitudinal data on an evolutionary question. *Psychological Science, 9*, 8–13.

Kalven, H., & Zeisel, H. (1966). *The American jury.* Boston, MA: Little, Brown.

Kampe, K. K. W., Frith, C. D., Dolan, R. J., & Frith, U. (2001). Reward value of attractiveness and gaze. *Nature, 413*, 589.

Kanagawa, C., Cross, S. E., & Markus, H. R. (2001). 'Who am I?' The cultural psychology of the conceptual self. *Personality and Social Psychology Bulletin, 27*, 90–103.

Kaplan, K. J. (1972). On the ambivalence-indifference problem in attitude theory and measurement: A suggested modification of the semantic differential technique. *Psychological Bulletin, 77*, 361–372.

Kaplan, M. F. (1987). The influencing process in group decision making. In C. Hendrick (Ed.), *Review of personality and social psychology* (Vol. 8, pp. 189–212). Thousand Oaks, CA: Sage.

Kaplan, M. F., & Miller, C. E. (1977). Judgments and group discussion: Effect of presentation and memory factors on polarization. *Sociometry, 40*, 337–343.

Kaplan, M. F., & Miller, C. E. (1987). Group decision making and normative versus informational influence: Effects of type of issue and assigned decision rule. *Journal of Personality and Social Psychology, 53*, 306–313.

Karpinski, A., & Hilton, J. L. (2001). Attitudes and the Implicit Association Test. *Journal of Personality and Social Psychology, 81*, 774–788.

Karremans, J. C., & Aarts, H. (2007). The role of automaticity in determining the inclination to forgive close others. *Journal of Experimental Social Psychology, 43*, 902–917.

Karremans, J. C., Stroebe, W., & Claus, J. (2006). Beyond Vicary's fantasies: The impact of subliminal priming on brand choice. *Journal of Experimental Social Psychology, 42*, 792–798.

Karremans, J. C., & Van Lange, P. A. M. (2004). Back to caring after being hurt: The role of forgiveness. *European Journal of Social Psychology, 34*, 207–227.

Karremans, J. C., & Van Lange, P. A. M. (2008). Forgiveness in personal relationships: Its malleability and powerful consequences. In W. Stroebe & M. Hewstone (Eds.), *European review of social psychology* (Vol. 19, pp. 202–241). Hove, UK: Psychology Press.

Kashima, E. S., & Kashima, Y. (1998). Culture and language: The case of cultural dimensions and personal pronoun use. *Journal of Cross-Cultural Psychology, 29*, 461–486.

Kasser, T., & Ryan, R. M. (1996). Further examining the American dream: Differential correlates of intrinsic and extrinsic goals. *Personality and Social Psychology Bulletin, 22*, 280–287.

Kassin, S. M. (1979). Consensus information, prediction, and causal attribution: A review of the literature and issues. *Journal of Personality and Social Psychology, 37*, 1966–1981.

Kassin, S. M., & Sukel, H. (1997). Coerced confessions and the jury: An experimental test of the 'harmless error' rule. *Law and Human Behavior, 21*, 27–46.

Katz, D. (1960). The functional approach to the study of attitudes. *Public Opinion Quarterly, 24*, 163–204.

Katzenstein, G. (1996). The debate on structured debate: Toward a unified theory. *Organizational Behavior and Human Decision Processes, 66*, 316–332.

Kawachi, I., & Berkman, L. F. (2001). Social ties and mental health. *Journal of Urban Health, 78*, 458–467.

Kawakami, K., Dion, K., & Dovidio, J. F. (1998). Racial prejudice and stereotype activation. *Personality and Social Psychology Bulletin, 24*, 407–416.

Kawakami, K., Dovidio, J. F., Moll, J., Hermsen, S., & Russin, A. (2000). Just say no (to stereotyping): Effects of training in the negation of stereotypic associations on stereotype activation. *Journal of Personality and Social Psychology, 78*, 871–888.

Keating, C. F., Pomerantz, J., Pommer, S. D., Ritt, S. J., Miller, L. M., & McCormick, J. (2005). Going to college and unpacking hazing: A functional approach to decrypting initiation practices among undergraduates. *Group Dynamics: Theory, Research, and Practice, 9*, 104–126.

Keenan, J. P., Wheeler, M. A., Gallup, G. G., Jr., & Pascual-Leone, A. (2000). Self-recognition and the right prefrontal cortex. *Trends in Cognitive Sciences, 4*, 338–344.

Keizer, K., Lindenberg, S., & Steg, L. (2008). The spreading of disorder. *Science, 322*, 1681–1685.

Kelley, H. H. (1950). The warm-cold variable in first impressions of persons. *Journal of Personality, 18*, 431–439.

Kelley, H. H. (1967). Attribution theory in social psychology. In D. Levine (Ed.), *Nebraska Symposium on Motivation* (Vol. 15, pp. 192–238). Lincoln, NE: University of Nebraska Press.

Kelley, H. H. (1972). Causal schemata and the attribution process. In E. E. Jones (Ed.), *Attribution: Perceiving the causes of behavior* (pp. 151–174). Morristown, NJ: General Learning Press.

Kelley, H. H. (1997). The 'stimulus field' for interpersonal phenomena: The source of language and thought about interpersonal events. *Personality and Social Psychology Review, 1*, 140–169.

Kelley, H. H., & Thibaut, J. W. (1978). *Interpersonal relations: A theory of interdependence*. New York: Wiley.

Kelley, W. M., Macrae, C. N., Wyland, C. L., Caglar, S., Inati, S., & Heatherton, T. F. (2002). Finding the self? An event-related fMRI study. *Journal of Cognitive Neuroscience, 14*, 785–794.

Kelling, G. L., & Wilson, J. Q. (1982). Broken windows. *Atlantic Monthly, 249*, 29–38.

Kelly, A. E., & McKillop, K. J. (1996). Consequences of revealing personal secrets. *Psychological Bulletin, 120*, 450–465.

Kelly, J. B., & Johnson, M. P. (2008). Differentiation among types of intimate partner violence: Research update and implications for interventions. *Family Court Review, 46*, 476–499.

Kelman, H. C., & Hamilton, V. L. (1990). *Crimes of obedience: Toward a social psychology of authority and responsibility*. New Haven, CT: Yale University Press.

Kenny, D. A., & DePaulo, B. M. (1993). Do people know how others view them? An empirical and theoretical account. *Psychological Bulletin, 114*, 145–161.

Kenny, D. A., Kashy, D. A., & Bolger, N. (1998). Data analysis in social psychology. In D. T. Gilbert, S. T. Fiske, & G. Lindzey (Eds.), *Handbook of social psychology* (4th ed., Vol. 1, pp. 233–265). Boston, MA: McGraw-Hill.

Kenworthy, J., Hewstone, M., Levine, J., Martin, R., & Willis, H. (2008). The phenomenology of minority-majority status: Effects on innovation in argument generation. *European Journal of Social Psychology, 38*, 624–636.

Kernberg, O. F. (1975). *Borderline conditions and pathological narcissism*. New York: Aronson.

Kernis, M. H. (2003). Toward a conceptualization of optimal self-esteem. *Psychological Inquiry, 14*, 1–26.

Kernis, M. H. (Ed.). (2006). *Self-esteem issues and answers: A sourcebook of current perspectives*. New York: Psychology Press.

Kernis, M. H., Cornell, D. P., Sun, C. R., Berry, A., & Harlow, T. (1993). There's more to self-esteem than whether it is high or low: The importance of stability of self-esteem. *Journal of Personality and Social Psychology, 65*, 1190–1204.

Kernis, M. H., & Goldman, B. M. (2003). Stability and variability in self-concept and self-esteem. In M. R. Leary & J. P. Tangney (Eds.), *Handbook of self and identity* (pp. 106–127). New York: Guilford.

Kernis, M. H., Grannemann, B. D., & Barclay, L. C. (1989). Stability and level of self-esteem as predictors of anger arousal and hostility. *Journal of Personality and Social Psychology, 56*, 1013–1022.

Kernis, M. H., Lakey, C. E., & Heppner, W. L. (2008). Secure versus fragile high self-esteem as a predictor of verbal defensiveness: Converging findings across three different markers. *Journal of Personality, 76*, 477–512.

Kerr, N. L. (1983). Motivation losses in small groups: A social dilemma analysis. *Journal of Personality and Social Psychology, 45*, 819–828.

Kerr, N. L. (1995). Juries. In A. S. R. Manstead & M. Hewstone (Eds.), *Blackwell encyclopedia of social psychology* (pp. 343–345). Oxford: Blackwell.

Kerr, N. L., & Bruun, S. E. (1983). Dispensability of member effort and group motivation losses: Free-rider effects. *Journal of Personality and Social Psychology, 44,* 78–94.

Kerr, N. L., & MacCoun, R. J. (1985). The effects of jury size and polling method on the process and product of jury deliberation. *Journal of Personality and Social Psychology, 48,* 349–363.

Kiesler, C. A., & Kiesler, S. B. (1969). *Conformity.* Reading, MA: Addison-Wesley.

Kihlstrom, J. F. (2010). Social neuroscience: The footprints of Phineas Gage. *Social Cognition, 28,* 757–783.

Kim, K., & Johnson, M. K. (2010). Extended self: Medial prefrontal activity during transient association of self and objects. *Social Cognitive and Affective Neuroscience, 7,* 199–207.

Kim, Y., Kasser, T., & Lee, H. (2003). Self-concept, aspirations, and well-being in South Korea and the United States. *Journal of Social Psychology, 143,* 277–290.

Kimmel, P. R. (1994). Cultural perspectives on international negotiations. *Journal of Social Issues, 50,* 179–196.

Kirsh, S. J. (1998). Seeing the world through Mortal Kombat-colored glasses: Violent video games and the development of a short-term hostile attribution bias. *Childhood: A Global Journal of Child Research, 5,* 177–184.

Kirsh, S. J. (2006). *Children, adolescents, and media violence* (1st ed.). Thousand Oaks, CA: Sage.

Kirsh, S. J. (2011). *Children, adolescents, and media violence* (2nd ed.). Thousand Oaks, CA: Sage.

Kitayama, S., & Cohen, D. (Eds.). (2007). *Handbook of cultural psychology.* New York: Guilford.

Kitayama, S., Duffy, S. M., Kawamura, T., & Larsen, J. T. (2003). Perceiving an object and its context in different cultures: A cultural look at new look. *Psychological Science, 14,* 102–206.

Kitayama, S., Ishii, K., Imada, T., Takemura, K., & Ramaswamy, J. (2006). Voluntary settlement and the spirit of independence: Evidence from Japan's 'northern frontier'. *Journal of Personality and Social Psychology, 91,* 369–384.

Kitayama, S., & Karasawa, M. (1997). Implicit self-esteem in Japan: Name letters and birthday numbers. *Personality and Social Psychology Bulletin, 23,* 736–742.

Kitayama, S., Park, H., Sevincer, A. T., Karasawa, M., & Uskul, A. K. (2009). A cultural task analysis of implicit independence: Comparing North America, Western Europe, and East Asia. *Journal of Personality and Social Psychology, 97,* 236–255.

Kitayama, S., & Uchida, Y. (2003). Explicit self-criticism and implicit self-regard: Evaluating self and friend in two cultures. *Journal of Experimental Social Psychology, 39,* 476–482.

Klandermans, B. (1997). *The social psychology of protest.* Oxford: Blackwell.

Klauer, K. C., & Meiser, T. (2000). A source-monitoring analysis of illusory correlations. *Personality and Social Psychology Bulletin, 26,* 1074–1093.

Klein, C. T. F., & Webster, D. M. (2000). Individual differences in argument scrutiny as motivated by need for cognitive closure. *Basic and Applied Social Psychology, 22,* 119–129.

Klein, O., Spears, R., & Reicher, S. (2007). Social identity performance: Extending the strategic side of SIDE. *Personality and Social Psychology Review, 11,* 28–45.

Klein, S. B. (2004). The cognitive neuroscience of knowing one's self. In M. S. Gazzaniga (Ed.), *The cognitive neurosciences* (3rd ed., pp. 1077–1089). Cambridge, MA: MIT Press.

Klein, S. B., & Kihlstrom, J. F. (1986). Elaboration, organization, and the self-reference effect in memory. *Journal of Experimental Psychology: General, 115,* 26–38.

Klein, S. B., Lax, M. L., & Gangi, C. E. (2010). A call for an inclusive approach to the social cognitive neurosciences. *Social Cognition, 28,* 748–756.

Klein, W. M. (1997). Objective standards are not enough: Affective, self-evaluative, and behavioral responses to social comparison information. *Journal of Personality and Social Psychology, 72,* 763–774.

Klinesmith, J., Kasser, T., & McAndrew, F. T. (2006). Guns, testosterone, and aggression: An experimental test of a mediational. *Psychological Science, 17,* 568–571.

Kling, K. C., Hyde, J. S., Showers, C. J., & Buswell, B. N. (1999). Gender differences in self-esteem: A meta-analysis. *Psychological Bulletin, 125,* 470–500.

Klohnen, E. C., & Luo, S. (2003). Interpersonal attraction and personality: What is attractive: Self similarity, ideal similarity, complementarity, or attachment security? *Journal of Personality and Social Psychology, 85,* 709–722.

Klomek, A. B., Sourander, A., Niemela, S., Kumpulainen, K., Piha, J., Tamminen, T., … Gould, M. S. (2009). Childhood bullying behaviors as a risk for suicide attempts and completed suicides: A population-based birth cohort study. *Journal of the American Academy of Child and Adolescent Psychiatry, 48,* 254–261.

Kobayashi, C., Glover, G. H., & Temple, E. (2006). Cultural and linguistic influence on neural bases of 'Theory of Mind': An fMRI study with Japanese bilinguals. *Brain and Language, 98,* 210–220.

Köhler, O. (1926). Kraftleistungen bei Einzel- und Gruppenarbeit [Physical performance in individual and group situations]. *Industrielle Psychotechnik, 3,* 274–282.

Koole, S. L., Dijksterhuis, A., & Van Knippenberg, A. (2001). What's in a name: Implicit self-esteem and the automatic self. *Journal of Personality and Social Psychology, 80,* 669–685.

Koole, S. L., Jostmann, N. B., & Baumann, N. (2011). Do demanding conditions help or hurt self-regulation? Manuscript submitted for publication.

Koole, S. L., & Pelham, B. W. (2003). On the nature of implicit self-esteem: The case of the name letter effect. In S. J. Spencer, S. Fein, M. P. Zanna, & J. M. Olson (Eds.), *Motivated social perception: The Ontario Symposium* (Vol. 9, pp. 93–116). Mahwah, NJ: Erlbaum.

Koss, M. P., Abbey, A., Campbell, R., Cook, S., Norris, J., Testa, M., … White, J. (2007). Revising the SES: A collaborative process to improve assessment of sexual aggression and victimization. *Psychology of Women Quarterly, 31,* 357–370.

Koss, M. P., Bailey, J. A., Yuan, N. P., Herrera, V. M., & Lichter, E. L. (2003). Depression and PTSD in survivors of male violence: Research and training initiatives to facilitate recovery. *Psychology of Women Quarterly, 27,* 130–142.

Krahé, B. (1992). *Personality and social psychology: Towards a synthesis.* London: Sage.

Krahé, B. (2001). *The social psychology of aggression* (1st ed.). Hove, UK: Psychology Press.

Krahé, B. (2012). *The social psychology of aggression* (2nd ed.). Hove, UK: Psychology Press.

Krahé, B., & Berger, A. (2005). Sex differences in relationship aggression among young adults in Germany. *Sex Roles, 52,* 829–838.

Krahé, B., & Bieneck, S. (2012). The effect of music-induced mood on aggressive affect, cognition, and behavior. *Journal of Applied Social Psychology, 42,* 271–290.

Krahé, B., Bieneck, S., & Möller, I. (2005). Understanding gender and intimate partner violence from an international perspective. *Sex Roles, 52,* 807–827.

Krahé, B., & Möller, I. (2004). Playing violent electronic games, hostile attributional style, and aggression-related norms in German adolescents. *Journal of Adolescence, 27,* 53–69.

Krahé, B., Möller, I., Huesmann, L. R., Kirwil, L., Felber, J., & Berger, A. (2011). Desensitization to media violence: Links with habitual media violence exposure, aggressive cognitions and aggressive behavior. *Journal of Personality and Social Psychology, 100,* 630–646.

Krahé, B., Schütze, S., Fritsche, I., & Waizenhöfer, E. (2000). The prevalence of sexual aggression and victimization among homosexual men. *Journal of Sex Research, 37,* 142–150.

Krahé, B., Waizenhöfer, E., & Möller, I. (2003). Women's sexual aggression against men: Prevalence and predictors. *Sex Roles, 49,* 219–232.

Kraus, S. J. (1995). Attitudes and the prediction of behavior: A meta-analysis of the empirical literature. *Personality and Social Psychology Bulletin, 21,* 58–75.

Kravitz, D. A., & Martin, B. (1986). Ringelmann rediscovered: The original article. *Journal of Personality and Social Psychology, 50,* 936–941.

Krebs, D. (1975). Empathy and altruism. *Journal of Personality and Social Psychology, 32,* 1134–1146.

Kreiner, D. S., Altis, N. A., & Voss, C. W. (2003). A test of the effect of reverse speech on priming. *Journal of Psychology: Interdisciplinary and Applied, 137,* 224–232.

Krosnick, J. A., Betz, A. L., Jussim, L. J., & Lynn, A. R. (1992). Subliminal conditioning of attitudes. *Personality and Social Psychology Bulletin, 18,* 152–162.

Krosnick, J. A., Boninger, D. S., Chuang, Y. C., Berent, M. K., & Carnot, C. G. (1993). Attitude strength: One construct or many related constructs? *Journal of Personality and Social Psychology, 65,* 1132–1151.

Krosnick, J. A., & Petty, R. E. (1995). Attitude strength: An overview. In R. E. Petty & J. A. Krosnick (Eds.), *Attitude strength: Antecedents and consequences* (pp. 1–24). Hillsdale, NJ: Erlbaum.

Krug, E. G., Dahlberg, L. L., Mercy, J. A., Zwi, A. B., & Lozano, R. (2002). World report on violence and health. Retrieved May 30, 2010, from http://whqlibdoc.who.int/hq/2002/9241545615.pdf

Kruglanski, A. W. (1989). *Lay epistemics and human knowledge: Cognitive and motivational bases.* New York: Plenum.

Kruglanski, A. W., & Freund, T. (1983). The freezing and unfreezing of lay-inferences: Effects on impressional primacy, ethnic stereotyping, and numerical anchoring. *Journal of Experimental Social Psychology, 19,* 448–468.

Kruglanski, A. W., & Stroebe, W. (Eds.). (2012). *Handbook of the history of social psychology.* New York: Psychology Press.

Kruglanski, A. W., & Webster, D. M. (1996). Motivated closing of the mind: 'Seizing' and 'freezing'. *Psychological Review, 103,* 263–283.

Kruglanski, A. W., Webster, D. M., & Klem, A. (1993). Motivated resistance and openness to persuasion in the presence or absence of prior information. *Journal of Personality and Social Psychology, 65,* 861–876.

Krull, D. S. (1993). Does the grist change the mill? The effect of the perceiver's inferential goal on the process of social inference. *Personality and Social Psychology Bulletin, 19,* 340–348.

Kuiper, N. A., & Rogers, T. B. (1979). Encoding of personal information: Self-other differences. *Journal of Personality and Social Psychology, 37,* 499–514.

Kunda, Z. (1990). The case for motivated reasoning. *Psychological Bulletin, 108,* 480–498.

Kunda, Z. (1999). *Social cognition: Making sense of people.* Cambridge, MA: MIT Press.

Kunst-Wilson, W. R., & Zajonc, R. B. (1980). Affective discrimination of stimuli that cannot be recognized. *Science, 207,* 557–558.

Kurman, J. (2003). Why is self-enhancement low in certain collectivist cultures? An investigation of two competing explanations. *Journal of Cross-Cultural Psychology, 34,* 496–510.

Lalljee, M., & Abelson, R. P. (1983). The organisation of explanations. In M. Hewstone (Ed.), *Attribution theory: Social and functional extensions* (pp. 65–80). Oxford: Blackwell.

Lalljee, M., Lamb, R., Furnham, A. F., & Jaspars, J. (1984). Explanations and information search: Inductive and hypothesis-testing approaches to arriving at an explanation. *British Journal of Social Psychology, 23,* 201–212.

Lamm, H., & Myers, D. G. (1978). Group-induced polarization of attitudes and behavior. In L. Berkowitz (Ed.), *Advances in experimental social psychology* (Vol. 11, pp. 145–195). New York: Academic Press.

Landis, D., Hope, R. O., & Day, H. R. (1984). Training for desegregation in the military. In N. Miller & M. B. Brewer (Eds.), *Groups in contact: The psychology of desegregation* (pp. 257–278). Orlando, FL: Academic Press.

Landry, S. H., Smith, K. E., & Swank, P. R. (2006). Responsive parenting: Establishing early foundations for social, communication, and independent problem-solving skills. *Developmental Psychology, 42,* 627–642.

Langer, E. J., Blank, A., & Chanowitz, B. (1978). The mindlessness of ostensibly thoughtful action: The role of 'placebic' information in interpersonal interaction. *Journal of Personality and Social Psychology, 36,* 635–642.

Langlois, J. H., Kalakanis, L., Rubenstein, A. J., Larson, A., Hallam, M., & Smoot, M. (2000). Maxims or myths of beauty? A meta-analytic and theoretical review. *Psychological Bulletin, 126,* 390–423.

Langlois, J. H., Ritter, J. M., Casey, R. J., & Sawin, D. B. (1995). Infant attractiveness predicts maternal behaviors and attitudes. *Developmental Psychology, 31,* 464–472.

Langlois, J. H., Ritter, J. M., Roggman, L. A., & Vaughn, L. S. (1991). Facial diversity and infant preferences for attractive faces. *Developmental Psychology, 27,* 79–84.

Langlois, J. H., Roggman, L. A., & Musselman, L. (1994). What is average and what is not average about attractive faces? *Psychological Science, 5,* 214–220.

LaPiere, R. T. (1934). Attitudes versus actions. *Social Forces, 13,* 230–237.

Larson, J. R., Jr. (2010). *In search of synergy in small group performance.* New York: Psychology Press.

Larson, J. R., Jr., & Christensen, C. (1993). Groups as problem-solving units: Toward a new meaning of social cognition. *British Journal of Social Psychology, 32,* 5–30.

Larson, J. R., Jr., Christensen, C., Abbott, A. S., & Franz, T. M. (1996). Diagnosing groups: Charting the flow of information in medical decision-making teams. *Journal of Personality and Social Psychology, 71,* 315–330.

Larson, J. R., Jr., Christensen, C., Franz, T. M., & Abbott, A. S. (1998). Diagnosing groups: The pooling, management, and impact of shared and unshared case information in team-based medical decision making. *Journal of Personality and Social Psychology, 75,* 93–108.

Larson, J. R., Jr., Foster-Fishman, P. G., & Franz, T. M. (1998). Leadership style and the discussion of shared and unshared information in decision-making groups. *Personality and Social Psychology Bulletin, 24,* 482–495.

Larson, J. R., Jr., Foster-Fishman, P. G., & Keys, C. B. (1994). Discussion of shared and unshared information in decision-making groups. *Journal of Personality and Social Psychology, 67,* 446–461.

Latané, B., & Darley, J. M. (1968). Group inhibition of bystander intervention in emergencies. *Journal of Personality and Social Psychology, 10,* 215–221.

Latané, B., & Darley, J. M. (1970). *The unresponsive bystander: Why doesn't he help?* New York: Appleton-Century-Crofts.

Latané, B., & Darley, J. M. (1976). Help in a crisis: Bystander response to an emergency. In J. W. Thibaut & J. T. Spence (Eds.), *Contemporary topics in social psychology* (pp. 309–332). Morristown, NJ: General Learning Press.

Latané, B., & Nida, S. (1981). Ten years of research on group size and helping. *Psychological Bulletin, 89,* 308–324.

Latané, B., Williams, K., & Harkins, S. (1979). Many hands make light the work: The causes and consequences of social loafing. *Journal of Personality and Social Psychology, 37,* 822–832.

Laughlin, P. R., & Sweeney, J. D. (1977). Individual-to-group and group-to-individual transfer in problem solving. *Journal of Experimental Psychology: Human Learning and Memory, 3,* 246–254.

Laurenceau, J.-P., Feldman Barrett, L., & Pietromonaco, P. R. (1998). Intimacy as an interpersonal process: The importance of self-disclosure, partner disclosure, and perceived partner responsiveness in interpersonal exchanges. *Journal of Personality and Social Psychology, 74,* 1238–1251.

Laurenceau, J.-P., Feldman Barrett, L., & Rovine, M. J. (2005). The interpersonal process model of intimacy in marriage: A daily-diary and multilevel modeling approach. *Journal of Family Psychology, 19,* 314–323.

Lazarus, R. S. (1991). *Emotion and adaptation.* New York: Oxford University Press.

Le, B., & Agnew, C. R. (2003). Commitment and its theorized determinants: A meta-analysis of the investment model. *Personal Relationships, 10,* 37–57.

Leach, C. W., Spears, R., Branscombe, N. R., & Doosje, B. (2003). Malicious pleasure: Schadenfreude at the suffering of another group. *Journal of Personality and Social Psychology, 84,* 932–943.

Leach, C. W., Van Zomeren, M., Zebel, S., Vliek, M. L. W., Pennekamp, S. F., Doosje, B., … Spears, R. (2008). Group-level self-definition and self-investment: A hierarchical (multicomponent) model of in-group identification. *Journal of Personality and Social Psychology, 95,* 144–165.

Leana, C. R. (1985). A partial test of Janis' groupthink model: Effects of group cohesiveness and leader behavior on defective decision making. *Journal of Management, 11*, 5–17.

Leary, M. R. (2004). *The curse of the self: Self-awareness, egotism, and the quality of human life*. New York: Oxford University Press.

Leary, M. R., & MacDonald, G. (2003). Individual differences in trait self-esteem: A theoretical integration. In M. R. Leary & J. P. Tangney (Eds.), *Handbook of self and identity* (pp. 401–418). New York: Guilford.

Leary, M. R., Tambor, E. S., Terdal, S. K., & Downs, D. L. (1995). Self-esteem as an interpersonal monitor: The sociometer hypothesis. *Journal of Personality and Social Psychology, 68*, 518–530.

LeBon, G. (1896). *The crowd: A study of the popular mind*. London: T. Fisher Unwin.

Lee, L., Piliavin, J. A., & Call, V. R. A. (1999). Giving time, money, and blood: Similarities and differences. *Social Psychology Quarterly, 62*, 276–290.

Lefkowitz, M. M., Eron, L. D., Walder, L. O., & Huesmann, L. R. (1977). *Growing up to be violent*. New York: Pergamon.

Legrand, D., & Ruby, P. (2009). What is self-specific? Theoretical investigation and critical review of neuroimaging results. *Psychological Review, 116*, 252–282.

Lemay, E. P. J., Clark, M. S., & Feeney, B. C. (2007). Projection of responsiveness to needs and the construction of satisfying communal relationships. *Journal of Personality and Social Psychology, 92*, 834–853.

Leonardelli, G. J., Pickett, C. L., & Brewer, M. B. (2010). Optimal distinctiveness theory: A framework for social identity, social cognition, and intergroup relations. In M. P. Zanna & J. M. Olson (Eds.), *Advances in experimental social psychology* (Vol. 43, pp. 63–113). San Diego, CA: Academic Press.

Lepore, L., & Brown, R. (1997). Category and stereotype activation: Is prejudice inevitable? *Journal of Personality and Social Psychology, 72*, 275–287.

Lepper, M. R., & Greene, D. (1978). *The hidden costs of reward: New perspectives on the psychology of human motivation*. Oxford: Erlbaum.

Lepper, M. R., Greene, D., & Nisbett, R. E. (1973). Undermining children's intrinsic interest with extrinsic reward: A test of the 'overjustification' hypothesis. *Journal of Personality and Social Psychology, 28*, 129–137.

Lesar, T. S., Briceland, L., & Stein, D. S. (1997). Factors related to errors in medication prescribing. *Journal of the American Medical Association, 277*, 312–317.

Levin, J., & McDevitt, J. (1993). *Hate crimes: The rising tide of bigotry and bloodshed*. New York: Plenum.

Levine, J. M. (1989). Reaction to opinion deviance in small groups. In P. B. Paulus (Ed.), *Psychology of group influence* (2nd ed., pp. 187–231). Hillsdale, NJ: Erlbaum.

Levine, J. M. (1999). Solomon Asch's legacy for group research. *Personality and Social Psychology Review, 3*, 358–364.

Levine, J. M., Choi, H.-S., & Moreland, R. L. (2003). Newcomer innovation in work teams. In P. B. Paulus & B. A. Nijstad (Eds.), *Group creativity: Innovation through collaboration* (pp. 202–224). New York: Oxford University Press.

Levine, J. M., & Moreland, R. L. (1990). Progress in small group research. *Annual Review of Psychology, 41*, 585–634.

Levine, J. M., & Moreland, R. L. (1998). Small groups. In D. T. Gilbert, S. T. Fiske, & G. Lindzey (Eds.), *Handbook of social psychology* (4th ed., Vol. 1, pp. 415–469). Boston, MA: McGraw-Hill.

Levine, J. M., & Moreland, R. L. (2004). Collaboration: The social context of theory development. *Personality and Social Psychology Review, 8*, 164–172.

Levine, J. M., & Moreland, R. L. (2012). A history of small group research. In A. W. Kruglanski & W. Stroebe (Eds.), *Handbook of the history of social psychology* (pp. 383–405). New York: Psychology Press.

Levine, J. M., & Russo, E. (1995). Impact of anticipated interaction on information acquisition. *Social Cognition, 13*, 293–317.

Levine, M. (1999). Rethinking bystander nonintervention: Social categorization and the evidence of witnesses at the James Bulger murder trial. *Human Relations, 52*, 1133–1155.

Levine, M., Cassidy, C., Brazier, G., & Reicher, S. (2002). Self-categorization and bystander non-intervention: Two experimental studies. *Journal of Applied Social Psychology, 32*, 1452–1463.

Levine, M., Cassidy, C., & Jentzsch, I. (2010). The implicit identity effect: Identity primes, group size, and helping. *British Journal of Social Psychology, 49*, 785–802.

Levine, M., & Crowther, S. (2008). The responsive bystander: How social group membership and group size can encourage as well as inhibit bystander intervention. *Journal of Personality and Social Psychology, 95*, 1429–1439.

Levine, M., Prosser, A., Evans, D., & Reicher, S. (2005). Identity and emergency intervention: How social group membership and inclusiveness of group boundaries shape helping behavior. *Personality and Social Psychology Bulletin, 31*, 443–453.

Levine, R. V., Norenzayan, A., & Philbrick, K. (2001). Cross-cultural differences in helping strangers. *Journal of Cross-Cultural Psychology, 32*, 543–560.

Levy, L. (1960). Studies in conformity behavior: A methodological note. *Journal of Psychology: Interdisciplinary and Applied, 50*, 39–41.

Lewicki, R. J. (1983). Lying and deception: A behavioral model. In M. H. Bazerman & R. J. Lewicki (Eds.), *Negotiating in organizations* (pp. 68–90). Beverly Hills, CA: Sage.

Lewin, K. (1948). *Resolving social conflicts*. New York: Harper & Row.

Lewin, K., Lippitt, R., & White, R. K. (1939). Patterns of aggressive behavior in experimentally created 'social climates'. *Journal of Social Psychology, 10*, 271–299.

Lewinsohn, P. M., Mischel, W., Chaplin, W., & Barton, R. (1980). Social competence and depression: The role of illusory self-perceptions. *Journal of Abnormal Psychology, 89*, 203–212.

Lewinsohn, P. M., Steinmetz, J., Larson, D. W., & Franklin, J. (1981). Depression-related cognitions: Antecedent or consequence? *Journal of Abnormal Psychology, 90*, 213–219.

Leyens, J. P., & Corneille, O. (1999). Asch's social psychology: Not as social as you may think. *Personality and Social Psychology Review, 3*, 345–357.

Liberman, A., & Chaiken, S. (1992). Defensive processing of personally relevant health messages. *Personality and Social Psychology Bulletin, 18*, 669–679.

Lickel, B., Hamilton, D. L., & Sherman, S. J. (2001). Elements of a lay theory of groups: Types of groups, relational styles, and the perception of group entitativity. *Personality and Social Psychology Review, 5*, 129–140.

Lickel, B., Hamilton, D. L., Wieczorkowska, G., Lewis, A., Sherman, S. J., & Uhles, A. N. (2000). Varieties of groups and the perception of group entitativity. *Journal of Personality and Social Psychology, 78*, 223–246.

Lickel, B., Miller, N., Stenstrom, D. M., Denson, T. F., & Schmader, T. (2006). Vicarious retribution: The role of collective blame in intergroup aggression. *Personality and Social Psychology Review, 10*, 372–390.

Lieberman, J. D., Solomon, S., Greenberg, J., & McGregor, H. A. (1999). A hot new way to measure aggression: Hot sauce allocation. *Aggressive Behavior, 25*, 331–348.

Liebert, R. M., & Baron, R. A. (1972). Some immediate effects of televised violence on children's behavior. *Developmental Psychology, 6*, 469–475.

Likert, R. (1932). A technique for the measurement of attitudes. *Archives of Psychology, 22*, 55.

Linder, D. E., Cooper, J., & Jones, E. E. (1967). Decision freedom as a determinant of the role of incentive magnitude in attitude change. *Journal of Personality and Social Psychology, 6*, 245–254.

Lindsay, J. J., & Anderson, C. A. (2000). From antecedent conditions to violent actions: A general affective aggression model. *Personality and Social Psychology Bulletin, 26*, 533–547.

Linville, P. W. (1987). Self-complexity as a cognitive buffer against stress-related illness and depression. *Journal of Personality and Social Psychology, 52*, 663–676.

Livingstone, A., & Haslam, S. A. (2008). The importance of social identity content in a setting of chronic social conflict: Understanding intergroup relations in Northern Ireland. *British Journal of Social Psychology, 47*, 1–21.

Livingstone, A. G., Spears, R., Manstead, A. S. R., & Bruder, M. (2009). Illegitimacy and identity threat in (inter)action: Predicting intergroup orientations among minority group members. *British Journal of Social Psychology, 48*, 755–775.

Locher, P., Unger, R., Sociedade, P., & Wahl, J. (1993). At first glance: Accessibility of the physical attractiveness stereotype. *Sex Roles, 28*, 729–743.

Lodewijkx, H. F. M., & Syroit, J. E. M. M. (1997). Severity of initiation revisited: Does severity of initiation increase the attractiveness of real groups? *European Journal of Social Psychology, 27*, 275–300.

Lord, C. G. (2004). Attitude variance: Its causes and consequences. In G. Haddock & G. R. Maio (Eds.), *Contemporary perspectives on the psychology of attitudes* (pp. 299–323). London: Psychology Press.

Lord, C. G., Ross, L., & Lepper, M. R. (1979). Biased assimilation and attitude polarization: The effects of prior theories on subsequently considered evidence. *Journal of Personality and Social Psychology, 37*, 2098–2109.

Lore, R. K., & Schultz, L. A. (1993). Control of human aggression: A comparative perspective. *American Psychologist, 48*, 16–25.

Lorenz, K. (1966). *On aggression.* London: Routledge.

Lundgren, S. R., & Prislin, R. (1998). Motivated cognitive processing and attitude change. *Personality and Social Psychology Bulletin, 24*, 715–726.

Lydon, J. E., Fitzsimons, G. M., & Naidoo, L. (2003). Devaluation versus enhancement of attractive alternatives: A critical test using the calibration paradigm. *Personality and Social Psychology Bulletin, 29*, 349–359.

Lynas, M. (2009, December 22). How do I know China wrecked the Copenhagen deal? I was in the room. *The Guardian.* Retrieved from http://www.guardian.co.uk

Maass, A., & Clark, R. D., III. (1983). Internalization versus compliance: Differential processes underlying minority influence and conformity. *European Journal of Social Psychology, 13*, 197–215.

Maass, A., & Clark, R. D., III. (1984). Hidden impact of minorities: Fifteen years of minority influence research. *Psychological Bulletin, 95*, 428–450.

Maass, A., & Volpato, C. (1994). Theoretical perspectives on minority influence: Conversion versus divergence? In S. Moscovici, A. Mucchi-Faina, & A. Maass (Eds.), *Minority influence* (pp. 135–147). Chicago, IL: Nelson-Hall.

MacBrayer, E. K., Milich, R., & Hundley, M. (2003). Attributional biases in aggressive children and their mothers. *Journal of Abnormal Psychology, 112*, 698–708.

Mackie, D., & Cooper, J. (1984). Attitude polarization: Effects of group membership. *Journal of Personality and Social Psychology, 46*, 575–585.

Mackie, D. M. (1986). Social identification effects in group polarization. *Journal of Personality and Social Psychology, 50*, 720–728.

Mackie, D. M. (1987). Systematic and nonsystematic processing of majority and minority persuasive communications. *Journal of Personality and Social Psychology, 53*, 41–52.

MacNamara, D. E. J. (1991). The victimization of whistle-blowers in the public and private sectors. In R. J. Kelly & D. E. J. MacNamara (Eds.), *Perspectives on deviance: Dominance, degradation, and denigration* (pp. 121–134). Cincinnati, OH: Anderson.

MacNeil, M. K., & Sherif, M. (1976). Norm change over subject generations as a function of arbitrariness of prescribed norms. *Journal of Personality and Social Psychology, 34*, 762–773.

Macrae, C. N., & Bodenhausen, G. V. (2000). Social cognition: Thinking categorically about others. *Annual Review of Psychology, 51*, 93–120.

Macrae, C. N., Bodenhausen, G. V., & Milne, A. B. (1998). Saying no to unwanted thoughts: Self-focus and the regulation of mental life. *Journal of Personality and Social Psychology, 74*, 578–589.

Macrae, C. N., Bodenhausen, G. V., Milne, A. B., & Jetten, J. (1994). Out of mind but back in sight: Stereotypes on the rebound. *Journal of Personality and Social Psychology, 67*, 808–817.

Macrae, C. N., Bodenhausen, G. V., Milne, A. B., Thorn, T. M. J., & Castelli, L. (1997). On the activation of social stereotypes: The moderating role of processing objectives. *Journal of Experimental Social Psychology, 33*, 471–489.

Macrae, C. N., & Johnston, L. (1998). Help, I need somebody: Automatic action and inaction. *Social Cognition, 16*, 400–417.

Macrae, C. N., Milne, A. B., & Bodenhausen, G. V. (1994). Stereotypes as energy-saving devices: A peek inside the cognitive toolbox. *Journal of Personality and Social Psychology, 66*, 37–47.

Macrae, C. N., Moran, J. M., Heatherton, T. F., Banfield, J. F., & Kelley, W. M. (2004). Medial prefrontal activity predicts memory for self. *Cerebral Cortex, 14*, 647–654.

Madey, S. F., Simo, M., Dillworth, D., Kemper, D., Toczynski, A., & Perella, A. (1996). They do get more attractive at closing time, but only when you are not in a relationship. *Basic and Applied Social Psychology, 18*, 387–393.

Maier, N. R. F. (1967). Assets and liabilities in group problem solving: The need for an integrative function. *Psychological Review, 74*, 239–249.

Maio, G. R., & Esses, V. M. (2001). The need for affect: Individual differences in the motivation to approach or avoid emotions. *Journal of Personality, 69*, 583–615.

Maio, G. R., Esses, V. M., Arnold, K., & Olson, J. M. (2004). The function-structure model of attitudes: Incorporating the need for affect. In G. Haddock & G. R. Maio (Eds.), *Contemporary perspectives on the psychology of attitudes* (pp. 9–33). London: Psychology Press.

Maio, G. R., & Haddock, G. (2010). *The psychology of attitudes and attitude change*. London: Sage.

Maio, G. R., Haddock, G., Manstead, A. S. R., & Spears, R. (2010). Attitudes and intergroup relations. In J. F. Dovidio, M. Hewstone, P. Glick, & V. M. Esses (Eds.), *Handbook of prejudice, stereotyping and discrimination* (pp. 261–275). London: Sage.

Maio, G. R., & Olson, J. M. (Eds.). (2000). *Why we evaluate: Functions of attitudes*. Mahwah, NJ: Erlbaum.

Maio, G. R., Pakizeh, A., Cheung, W., & Rees, K. J. (2009). Changing, priming, and acting on values: Effects via motivational relations in a circular model. *Journal of Personality and Social Psychology, 97*, 699–715.

Maisey, D. S., Vale, E. L. E., Cornelissen, P. L., & Tovée, M. J. (1999). Characteristics of male attractiveness for women. *Lancet, 353*, 1500.

Malle, B. F. (2006). The actor-observer asymmetry in attribution: A (surprising) meta-analysis. *Psychological Bulletin, 132*, 895–919.

Manning, R., Levine, M., & Collins, A. (2007). The Kitty Genovese murder and the social psychology of helping: The parable of the 38 witnesses. *American Psychologist, 62*, 555–562.

Mantell, D. M. (1971). The potential for violence in Germany. *Journal of Social Issues, 27*, 101–112.

Mantell, D. M., & Panzarella, R. (1976). Obedience and responsibility. *British Journal of Social and Clinical Psychology, 15*, 239–245.

Marcus-Newhall, A., Pedersen, W. C., Carlson, M., & Miller, N. (2000). Displaced aggression is alive and well: A meta-analytic review. *Journal of Personality and Social Psychology, 78*, 670–689.

Markman, H. J. (1981). Prediction of marital distress: A 5-year follow-up. *Journal of Consulting and Clinical Psychology, 49*, 760–762.

Markus, H. (1977). Self-schemata and processing information about the self. *Journal of Personality and Social Psychology, 35*, 63–78.

Markus, H. (1978). The effect of mere presence on social facilitation: An unobtrusive test. *Journal of Experimental Social Psychology, 14*, 389–397.

Markus, H., & Kitayama, S. (1991). Culture and the self: Implications for cognition, emotion, and motivation. *Psychological Review, 98*, 224–253.

Markus, H., & Kitayama, S. (1994). A collective fear of the collective: Implications for selves and theories of selves. *Personality and Social Psychology Bulletin, 20*, 568–579.

Markus, H., & Kunda, Z. (1986). Stability and malleability of the self-concept. *Journal of Personality and Social Psychology, 51*, 858–866.

Markus, H., & Nurius, P. (1986). Possible selves. *American Psychologist, 41*, 954–969.

Marques, J. M., Yzerbyt, V. Y., & Leyens, J.-P. (1988). The 'black sheep effect': Extremity of judgments towards ingroup members as a function of group identification. *European Journal of Social Psychology, 18*, 1–16.

Marrow, A. J. (1969). *The practical theorist: The life and work of Kurt Lewin*. New York: Basic Books.

Marsh, H. W. (1990). A multidimensional, hierarchical model of self-concept: Theoretical and empirical justification. *Educational Psychology Review, 2*, 77–172.

Marshall, G. D., & Zimbardo, P. G. (1979). Affective consequences of inadequately explained physiological arousal. *Journal of Personality and Social Psychology, 37*, 970–988.

Martin, R., & Hewstone, M. (2001a). Afterthoughts on afterimages: A review of the afterimage paradigm in majority and minority influence research. In C. K. W. De Dreu & N. K. De Vries (Eds.), *Group consensus and minority influence: Implications for innovation* (pp. 15–39). Oxford: Blackwell.

Martin, R., & Hewstone, M. (2001b). Conformity and independence in groups: Majorities and minorities. In M. A. Hogg & R. S. Tindale (Eds.), *Blackwell handbook of social psychology: Group processes* (pp. 209–234). Oxford: Blackwell.

Martin, R., & Hewstone, M. (2008). Majority versus minority influence, message processing and attitude change: The source-context-elaboration model. In M. P. Zanna (Ed.), *Advances in experimental social psychology* (Vol. 40, pp. 237–326). San Diego, CA: Academic Press.

Martin, R., & Hewstone, M. (Eds.). (2010). *Minority influence and innovation: Antecedents, processes and consequences*. Hove, UK: Psychology Press.

Martin, R., & Hewstone, M. (in press). Minority influence: Revisiting Moscovici's blue-green afterimage studies. In J. R. Smith & S. A. Haslam (Eds.), *Social psychology: Revisiting the classic studies*. Thousand Oaks, CA: Sage.

Martin, R., Hewstone, M., & Martin, P. Y. (2003). Resistance to persuasive messages as a function of majority and minority source status. *Journal of Experimental Social Psychology, 39*, 585–593.

Martin, R., Hewstone, M., & Martin, P. Y. (2007). Systematic and heuristic processing of majority- and minority-endorsed messages: The effects of varying outcome relevance and levels of orientation on attitude and message processing. *Personality and Social Psychology Bulletin, 33*, 43–56.

Martin, R., Hewstone, M., & Martin, P. Y. (2008). Majority versus minority influence: The role of message processing in determining resistance to counter-persuasion. *European Journal of Social Psychology, 38*, 16–34.

Martin, R., Martin, P. Y., Smith, J. R., & Hewstone, M. (2007). Majority versus minority influence and prediction of behavioral intentions and behavior. *Journal of Experimental Social Psychology, 43*, 763–771.

Mashek, D. J., & Aron, A. (2004). *Handbook of closeness and intimacy*. Mahwah, NJ: Erlbaum.

Mashek, D. J., Aron, A., & Boncimino, M. (2003). Confusions of self with close others. *Personality and Social Psychology Bulletin, 29*, 382–392.

Maslach, C. (1979). Negative emotional biasing of unexplained arousal. *Journal of Personality and Social Psychology, 37*, 953–969.

Mason, M. F., & Morris, M. W. (2010). Culture, attribution and automaticity: A social cognitive neuroscience view. *Social Cognitive and Affective Neuroscience, 5*, 292–306.

Masuda, T., & Nisbett, R. E. (2001). Attending holistically versus analytically: Comparing the context sensitivity of Japanese and Americans. *Journal of Personality and Social Psychology, 81*, 922–934.

Matsumoto, D., Yoo, S. H., & Fontaine, J. (2008). Mapping expressive differences around the world: The relationship between emotional display rules and individualism versus collectivism. *Journal of Cross-Cultural Psychology, 39*, 55–74.

Mayer, A. (1903). Über Einzel- und Gesamtleistung des Schulkindes [On the single and total performance of the schoolchild]. *Archiv für die Gesamte Psychologie, 1*, 276–416.

Mayer, N. D., & Tormala, Z. L. (2010). 'Think' versus 'feel' framing effects in persuasion. *Personality and Social Psychology Bulletin, 36*, 443–454.

Mayle, P. (1993). *Hotel Pastis*. London: Hamish Hamilton.

McAdams, D. P. (2008a). American identity: The redemptive self. *General Psychologist, 43*, 20–27.

McAdams, D. P. (2008b). Personal narratives and the life story. In O. P. John, R. W. Robins, & L. A. Pervin (Eds.), *Handbook of personality: Theory and research* (pp. 242–262). New York: Guilford.

McArthur, L. A. (1972). The how and what of why: Some determinants and consequences of causal attribution. *Journal of Personality and Social Psychology, 22*, 171–193.

McBurnett, K., Lahey, B. B., Rathouz, P. J., & Loeber, R. (2000). Low salivary cortisol and persistent aggression in boys referred for disruptive behavior. *Archives of General Psychiatry, 57*, 38–43.

McClelland, D. C., & Burnham, D. H. (1976). Power is the great motivator. *Harvard Business Review, 54*, 100–110.

McConahay, J., Hardee, B. B., & Batts, V. (1981). Has racism declined? It depends on who is asking and what is being asked. *Journal of Conflict Resolution, 25*, 563–579.

McCrae, R. R., & Costa, P. T., Jr. (1987). Validation of the five-factor model of personality across instruments and observers. *Journal of Personality and Social Psychology, 52*, 81–90.

McCrea, S. M., Hirt, E. R., & Milner, B. J. (2008). She works hard for the money: Valuing effort underlies gender differences in behavioral self-handicapping. *Journal of Experimental Social Psychology, 44*, 292–311.

McCullough, M. E., Bellah, C. G., Kilpatrick, S. D., & Johnson, J. L. (2001). Vengefulness: Relationships with forgiveness, rumination, well-being, and the Big Five. *Personality and Social Psychology Bulletin, 27*, 601–610.

McCullough, M. E., Rachal, K. C., Sandage, S. J., Worthington, E. L. J., Brown, S. W., & Hight, T. L. (1998). Interpersonal forgiving in close relationships: Theoretical elaboration and measurement. *Journal of Personality and Social Psychology, 75*, 1586–1603.

McDougall, W. (1908). *An introduction to social psychology*. London: Methuen.

McElreath, R., & Boyd, R. (2007). *Mathematical models of social evolution: A guide for the perplexed*. Chicago: University of Chicago Press.

McGarty, C., Haslam, S. A., Turner, J. C., & Oakes, P. J. (1993). Illusory correlation as accentuation of actual intercategory difference: Evidence for the effect with minimal stimulus information. *European Journal of Social Psychology, 23*, 391–410.

McGill, A. L. (1989). Context effects in judgments of causation. *Journal of Personality and Social Psychology, 57*, 189–200.

McGrath, J. E. (1984). *Groups: Interaction and performance*. Englewood Cliffs, NJ: Prentice Hall.

McGregor, I., Nail, P. R., Marigold, D. C., & Kang, S. J. (2005). Defensive pride and consensus: Strength in imaginary numbers. *Journal of Personality and Social Psychology, 89*, 978–996.

McGuire, W. J. (1969). The nature of attitudes and attitude change. In G. Lindzey & E. Aronson (Eds.), *Handbook of social psychology* (2nd ed., Vol. 3, pp. 136–314). Reading, MA: Addison-Wesley.

McGuire, W. J. (1985). Attitudes and attitude change. In G. Lindzey & E. Aronson (Eds.), *Handbook of social psychology* (3rd ed., Vol. 2, pp. 233–346). New York: Random House.

McGuire, W. J., & McGuire, C. V. (1988). Content and process in the experience of self. In L. Berkowitz (Ed.), *Advances in experimental social psychology* (Vol. 21, pp. 97–144). San Diego, CA: Academic Press.

McGuire, W. J., McGuire, C. V., & Cheever, J. (1986). The self in society: Effects of social contexts on the sense of self. *British Journal of Social Psychology, 25*, 259–270.

McLean, S. (2010). *Business Communication for Success*. Retrieved from http://catalog.flatworldknowledge.com/catalog/editions/74

Mead, G. H. (1934). *Mind, self, and society*. Chicago: University of Chicago Press.

Meade, R. D. (1985). Experimental studies of authoritarian and democratic leadership in four cultures: American, Indian, Chinese and Chinese-American. *High School Journal, 68*, 293–295.

Meeus, W. H. J., & Raaijmakers, Q. A. W. (1986). Administrative obedience: Carrying out orders to use psychological-administrative violence. *European Journal of Social Psychology, 16*, 311–324.

Meeus, W. H. J., & Raaijmakers, Q. A. W. (1995). Obedience in modern society: The Utrecht studies. *Journal of Social Issues, 51*, 155–175.

Mendelson, M. J., & Aboud, F. E. (1999). Measuring friendship quality in late adolescents and young adults: McGill Friendship Questionnaires. *Canadian Journal of Behavioural Science, 31*, 130–132.

Merrin, J., Kinderman, P., & Bentall, R. P. (2007). 'Jumping to conclusions' and attributional style in persecutory delusions. *Cognitive Therapy and Research, 31*, 741–758.

Messé, L. A., Hertel, G., Kerr, N. L., Lount, R. B., Jr., & Park, E. S. (2002). Knowledge of partner's ability as a moderator of group motivation gains: An exploration of the Köhler discrepancy effect. *Journal of Personality and Social Psychology, 82*, 935–946.

Mezulis, A. H., Abramson, L. Y., Hyde, J. S., & Hankin, B. L. (2004). Is there a universal positivity bias in attributions? A meta-analytic review of individual, developmental, and cultural differences in the self-serving attributional bias. *Psychological Bulletin, 130*, 711–747.

Miceli, M. P., & Near, J. P. (1992). *Blowing the whistle: The organizational and legal implications for companies and employees*. New York: Lexington.

Miceli, M. P., Near, J. P., & Dworkin, T. M. (2008). *Whistle-blowing in organizations*. New York: Routledge.

Michotte, A. (1963). *The perception of causality*. New York: Basic Books.

Miles, D. R., & Carey, G. (1997). Genetic and environmental architecture on human aggression. *Journal of Personality and Social Psychology, 72*, 207–217.

Milgram, S. (1963). Behavioral study of obedience. *Journal of Abnormal and Social Psychology, 67*, 371–378.

Milgram, S. (1965). Some conditions of obedience and disobedience to authority. *Human Relations, 18*, 57–76.

Milgram, S. (1974). *Obedience to authority: An experimental view*. New York: Harper & Row.

Milgram, S., Liberty, H. J., Toledo, R., & Wackenhut, J. (1986). Response to intrusion into waiting lines. *Journal of Personality and Social Psychology, 51*, 683–689.

Miller, A. G. (1986). *The obedience experiments: A case study of controversy in social science*. New York: Praeger.

Miller, A. G. (1995). Obedience. In A. S. R. Manstead & M. Hewstone (Eds.), *Blackwell encyclopedia of social psychology* (pp. 418–423). Oxford: Blackwell.

Miller, A. G. (2004). What can the Milgram obedience experiments tell us about the Holocaust? In A. G. Miller (Ed.), *The social psychology of good and evil* (pp. 193–239). New York: Guilford.

Miller, A. G., Collins, B. E., & Brief, D. E. (1995). Perspectives on obedience to authority: The legacy of the Milgram experiments. *Journal of Social Issues, 51*, 1–19.

Miller, A. G., Gordon, A. K., & Buddie, A. M. (1999). Accounting for evil and cruelty: Is to explain to condone? *Personality and Social Psychology Review, 3*, 254–268.

Miller, D. T., Downs, J. S., & Prentice, D. A. (1998). Minimal conditions for the creation of a unit relationship: The social bond between birthdaymates. *European Journal of Social Psychology, 28*, 475–481.

Miller, D. T., & Morrison, K. R. (2009). Expressing deviant opinions: Believing you are in the majority helps. *Journal of Experimental Social Psychology, 45*, 740–747.

Miller, D. T., & Ross, M. (1975). Self-serving biases in the attribution of causality: Fact or fiction? *Psychological Bulletin, 82*, 213–225.

Miller, G. A., Galanter, E., & Pribram, K. H. (1960). *Plans and the structure of behavior*. New York: Holt, Rinehart & Winston.

Miller, G. E., & Wrosch, C. (2007). You've gotta know when to fold 'em: Goal disengagement and systemic inflammation in adolescence. *Psychological Science, 18*, 773–777.

Miller, J. G. (1984). Culture and the development of everyday social explanation. *Journal of Personality and Social Psychology, 46*, 961–978.

Miller, N., Pedersen, W. C., Earleywine, M., & Pollock, V. E. (2003). A theoretical model of triggered displaced aggression. *Personality and Social Psychology Review, 7*, 75–97.

Miller, N. E. (1941). The frustration-aggression hypothesis. *Psychological Review, 48*, 337–342.

Miller, R. S. (1997). Inattentive and contented: Relationship commitment and attention to alternatives. *Journal of Personality and Social Psychology, 73*, 758–766.

Miller, R. S., & Perlman, D. (2008). *Intimate relationships*. New York: McGraw-Hill.

Miller, T. R., Cohen, M. A., & Rossman, S. B. (1993). Victim costs of violent crime and resulting injuries. *Health Affairs, 12*, 186–197.

Mischel, W. (1977). On the future of personality measurement. *American Psychologist, 32*, 246–254.

Mitchell, J. P., Banaji, M. R., & Macrae, C. N. (2005). The link between social cognition and self-referential thought in the medial prefrontal cortex. *Journal of Cognitive Neuroscience, 17*, 1306–1315.

Miyamoto, Y., & Kitayama, S. (2002). Cultural variation in correspondence bias: The critical role of attitude diagnosticity of socially constrained behavior. *Journal of Personality and Social Psychology, 83*, 1239–1248.

Mlicki, P. P., & Ellemers, N. (1996). Being different or being better? National stereotypes and identifications of Polish and Dutch students. *European Journal of Social Psychology, 26*, 97–114.

Moede, W. (1920). *Experimentelle Massenpsychologie [Experimental crowd psychology]*. Leipzig, Germany: Hirzel.

Moghaddam, F. M. (2005). The staircase to terrorism: A psychological exploration. *American Psychologist, 60*, 161–169.

Moghaddam, F. M. (2006). *From the terrorists' point of view*. Westport, CT: Praeger.

Mojzisch, A., Grouneva, L., & Schulz-Hardt, S. (2010). Biased evaluation of information during discussion: Disentangling the effects of preference consistency, social validation, and ownership of information. *European Journal of Social Psychology, 40*, 946–956.

Mojzisch, A., & Schulz-Hardt, S. (2006). Information sampling in group decision making. In K. Fiedler & P. Juslin (Eds.), *Sampling and adaptive cognition* (pp. 299–326). Cambridge, MA: Cambridge University Press.

Mojzisch, A., & Schulz-Hardt, S. (2010). Knowing others' preferences degrades the quality of group decisions. *Journal of Personality and Social Psychology, 98*, 794–808.

Mojzisch, A., Schulz-Hardt, S., Kerschreiter, R., Brodbeck, F. C., & Frey, D. (2008). Social validation in group decision-making: Differential effects on the decisional impact of preference-consistent and preference-inconsistent information. *Journal of Experimental Social Psychology, 44*, 1477–1490.

Mok, A., Morris, M. W., Benet-Martínez, V. L., & Karakitapoğlu-Aygün, Z. (2007). Embracing American culture: Structures of social identity and social networks among first-generation biculturals. *Journal of Cross-Cultural Psychology, 38*, 629–635.

Möller, I., & Krahé, B. (2009). Exposure to violent video games and aggression in German adolescents: A longitudinal analysis. *Aggressive Behavior, 35*, 75–89.

Monahan, J. L., Murphy, S. T., & Zajonc, R. B. (2000). Subliminal mere exposure: Specific, general, and diffuse effects. *Psychological Science, 11*, 462–466.

Monin, B., Sawyer, P. J., & Marquez, M. J. (2008). The rejection of moral rebels: Resenting those who do the right thing. *Journal of Personality and Social Psychology, 95*, 76–93.

Monteith, M. J. (1993). Self-regulation of prejudiced responses: Implications for progress in prejudice-reduction efforts. *Journal of Personality and Social Psychology, 65*, 469–485.

Monteith, M. J., & Mark, A. Y. (2005). Changing one's prejudiced ways: Awareness, affect, and self-regulation. In W. Stroebe & M. Hewstone (Eds.), *European review of social psychology* (Vol. 16, pp. 113–154). Hove, UK: Psychology Press.

Monteith, M. J., Sherman, J. W., & Devine, P. G. (1998). Suppression as a stereotype control strategy. *Personality and Social Psychology Review, 2*, 63–82.

Monteith, M. J., Spicer, C. V., & Tooman, G. D. (1998). Consequences of stereotype suppression: Stereotypes on AND not on the rebound. *Journal of Experimental Social Psychology, 34*, 355–377.

Montepare, J. M., & Zebrowitz-McArthur, L. (1988). Impressions of people created by age-related qualities of their gaits. *Journal of Abnormal and Social Psychology, 55*, 547–556.

Montoya, R. M., Horton, R. S., & Kirchner, J. (2008). Is actual similarity necessary for attraction? A meta-analysis of actual and perceived similarity. *Journal of Social and Personal Relationships, 25*, 889–922.

Moreland, R. L., & Beach, S. R. (1992). Exposure effects in the classroom: The development of affinity among students. *Journal of Experimental Social Psychology, 28*, 255–276.

Moreland, R. L., & Levine, J. M. (1982). Socialization in small groups: Temporal changes in individual-group relations. In L. Berkowitz (Ed.), *Advances in experimental social psychology* (Vol. 15, pp. 137–192). New York: Academic Press.

Moreland, R. L., & Myaskovsky, L. (2000). Exploring the performance benefits of group training: Transactive memory or improved communication? *Organizational Behavior and Human Decision Processes, 82*, 117–133.

Morf, C. C., Horvath, S., & Torchetti, L. (2011). Narcissistic self-enhancement: Tales of (successful?) self-portrayal. In M. D. Alicke & C. Sedikides (Eds.), *Handbook of self-enhancement and self-protection* (pp. 399–424). New York: Guilford.

Morf, C. C., Horvath, S., & Zimmermann, T. D. (2011). *In the mind of a male narcissist: Worthlessness primes aggresion*. Manuscript submitted for publication.

Morf, C. C., & Mischel, W. (2012). The self as a psycho-social dynamic processing system: Toward a converging science of self-hood. In M. R. Leary & J. P. Tangney (Eds.), *Handbook of self and identity* (2nd ed., pp. 21–49). New York: Guilford.

Morf, C. C., & Rhodewalt, F. (1993). Narcissism and self-evaluation maintenance: Explorations in object relations. *Personality and Social Psychology Bulletin, 19*, 668–676.

Morf, C. C., & Rhodewalt, F. (2001). Unraveling the paradoxes of narcissism: A dynamic self-regulatory processing model. *Psychological Inquiry, 12*, 177–196.

Morf, C. C., Torchetti, L., & Schürch, E. (2011). Narcissism from the perspective of the dynamic self-regulatory processing model. In W. K. Campbell & J. D. Miller (Eds.), *Handbook of narcissism and narcissistic personality disorder: Theoretical approaches, empirical findings, and treatments* (pp. 56–70). Hoboken, NJ: Wiley.

Mori, K., & Arai, M. (2010). No need to fake it: Reproduction of the Asch experiment without confederates. *International Journal of Psychology, 45*, 390–397.

Morris, M. W., & Peng, K. (1994). Culture and cause: American and Chinese attributions for social and physical events. *Journal of Personality and Social Psychology, 67*, 949–971.

Morris, M. W., Williams, K. Y., Leung, K., Larrick, R., Mendoza, M. T., Bhatnagar, D., … Hu, J.-C. (1998). Conflict management style: Accounting for cross-national differences. *Journal of International Business Studies, 29*, 729–748.

Morris, P. H., & Lewis, D. (2010). Tackling diving: The perception of deceptive intentions in association football (soccer). *Journal of Nonverbal Behavior, 34*, 1–13.

Morrison, E. W., & Herlihy, J. M. (1992). Becoming the best place to work: Managing diversity at American Express Travel Related Services. In S. E. Jackson (Ed.), *Diversity in the workplace: Human resources initiatives* (pp. 203–226). New York: Guilford.

Morrison, K. R., & Miller, D. T. (2008). Distinguishing between silent and vocal minorities: Not all deviants feel marginal. *Journal of Personality and Social Psychology, 94*, 871–882.

Moscovici, S. (1976). *Social influence and social change*. London: Academic Press.

Moscovici, S. (1980). Toward a theory of conversion behavior. In L. Berkowitz (Ed.), *Advances in experimental social psychology* (Vol. 13, pp. 209–239). New York: Academic Press.

Moscovici, S., Lage, E., & Naffrechoux, M. (1969). Influence of a consistent minority on the responses of a majority in a color perception task. *Sociometry, 32*, 365–380.

Moscovici, S., & Marková, I. (2006). *The making of modern social psychology: The hidden story of how an international social science was created*. Cambridge, UK: Polity.

Moscovici, S., & Personnaz, B. (1980). Studies in social influence: Minority influence and conversion behavior in a perceptual task. *Journal of Experimental Social Psychology, 16*, 270–282.

Moscovici, S., & Zavalloni, M. (1969). The group as a polarizer of attitudes. *Journal of Personality and Social Psychology, 12*, 125–135.

Moskowitz, G. B. (2005). *Social cognition: Understanding self and others*. New York: Guilford.

Moskowitz, G. B., Gollwitzer, P. M., Wasel, W., & Schaal, B. (1999). Preconscious control of stereotype activation through chronic egalitarian goals. *Journal of Personality and Social Psychology, 77*, 167–184.

Moskowitz, G. B., & Ignarri, C. (2009). Implicit volition and stereotype control. In W. Stroebe & M. Hewstone (Eds.), *European review of social psychology* (Vol. 20, pp. 97–145). Hove, UK: Psychology Press.

Mucchi-Faina, A., Maass, A., & Volpato, C. (1991). Social influence: The role of originality. *European Journal of Social Psychology, 21*, 183–197.

Mueller, C. M., & Dweck, C. S. (1998). Praise for intelligence can undermine children's motivation and performance. *Journal of Personality and Social Psychology, 75*, 33–52.

Mugny, G. (1982). *The power of minorities*. London: Academic Press.

Mugny, G., Butera, F., Sanchez-Mazas, M., & Pérez, J. A. (1995). Judgments in conflict: The conflict elaboration theory of social influence. In B. Boothe, R. Hirsig, A. Helminger, B. Meier, & R. Volkart (Eds.), *Perception, evaluation, interpretation* (pp. 160–168). Göttingen, Germany: Hogrefe and Huber.

Mugny, G., & Pérez, J. A. (1991). *The social psychology of minority influence*. Cambridge, UK: Cambridge University Press.

Mullen, B. (1986). Atrocity as a function of lynch mob composition: A self-attention perspective. *Personality and Social Psychology Bulletin, 12*, 187–197.

Mullen, B., Anthony, T., Salas, E., & Driskell, J. E. (1994). Group cohesiveness and quality of decision making. *Small Group Research, 25*, 189–204.

Mullen, B., Brown, R., & Smith, C. (1992). Ingroup bias as a function of salience, relevance, and status: An integration. *European Journal of Social Psychology, 22,* 103–122.

Mullen, B., & Copper, C. (1994). The relation between group cohesiveness and performance: An integration. *Psychological Bulletin, 115,* 210–227.

Mullen, B., Johnson, C., & Salas, E. (1991). Productivity loss in brainstorming groups: A meta-analytic integration. *Basic and Applied Social Psychology, 12,* 3–23.

Mullen, B., & Riordan, C. A. (1988). Self-serving attributions for performance in naturalistic settings: A meta-analytic review. *Journal of Applied Social Psychology, 18,* 3–22.

Mummendey, A., Kessler, T., Klink, A., & Mielke, R. (1999). Strategies to cope with negative social identity: Predictions by social identity theory and relative deprivation theory. *Journal of Personality and Social Psychology, 76,* 229–245.

Mummendey, A., & Otten, S. (1998). Positive–negative asymmetry in social discrimination. In W. Stroebe & M. Hewstone (Eds.), *European review of social psychology* (Vol. 9, pp. 107–143). Chichester, UK: Wiley.

Mummendey, A., & Schreiber, H.-J. (1984). 'Different' just means 'better': Some obvious and some hidden pathways to in-group favouritism. *British Journal of Social Psychology, 23,* 363–367.

Mummendey, A., & Wenzel, M. (1999). Social discrimination and tolerance in intergroup relations: Reactions to intergroup difference. *Personality and Social Psychology Review, 3,* 158–174.

Muramoto, Y. (2003). An indirect enhancement in relationship among Japanese. *Journal of Cross-Cultural Psychology, 34,* 552–566.

Muraven, M., & Baumeister, R. F. (2000). Self-regulation and depletion of limited resources: Does self-control resemble a muscle? *Psychological Bulletin, 126,* 247–259.

Muraven, M., Gagné, M., & Rosman, H. (2008). Helpful self-control: Autonomy support, vitality, and depletion. *Journal of Experimental Social Psychology, 44,* 573–585.

Murchison, C. (Ed.). (1935). *Handbook of social psychology.* Worchester, MA: Clark University Press.

Murdoch, D., Phil, R. O., & Ross, D. (1990). Alcohol and crimes of violence: Present issues. *International Journal of the Addictions, 25,* 1065–1081.

Murphy, S. T., & Zajonc, R. B. (1993). Affect, cognition, and awareness: Affective priming with optimal and suboptimal stimulus exposures. *Journal of Personality and Social Psychology, 64,* 723–739.

Murray, H. A. (1943). *Thematic Apperception Test Manual.* Cambridge, MA: Harvard University Press.

Murray, R. K., & Blessing, T. H. (1983). The presidential performance study: A progress report. *Journal of American History, 70,* 535–555.

Murray, S. L., Holmes, J. G., Bellavia, G., Griffin, D. W., & Dolderman, D. (2002). Kindred spirits? The benefits of egocentrism in close relationships. *Journal of Personality and Social Psychology, 82,* 563–581.

Murray, S. L., Holmes, J. G., & Griffin, D. W. (1996). The benefits of positive illusions: Idealization and the construction of satisfaction in close relationships. *Journal of Personality and Social Psychology, 70,* 79–98.

Mussweiler, T. (2006). Doing is for thinking! Stereotype activation by stereotypic movements. *Psychological Science, 17,* 17–21.

Mussweiler, T., Rüter, K., & Epstude, K. (2006). The why, who, and how of social comparison: A social cognition perspective. In S. Guimond (Ed.), *Social comparison and social psychology: Understanding cognition, intergroup relations and culture* (pp. 33–54). New York: Cambridge University Press.

Myers, D. G. (1978). Polarizing effects of social comparison. *Journal of Experimental Social Psychology, 14,* 554–563.

Myers, D. G., Bach, P. J., & Schreiber, F. B. (1974). Normative and informational effects of group interaction. *Sociometry, 37,* 275–286.

Myers, D. G., & Bishop, G. D. (1970). Discussion effects on racial attitudes. *Science, 169,* 778–779.

Myers, D. G., & Kaplan, M. F. (1976). Group-induced polarization in simulated juries. *Personality and Social Psychology Bulletin, 2,* 63–66.

Myers, D. G., & Lamm, H. (1976). The group polarization phenomenon. *Psychological Bulletin, 83,* 602–627.

Nadler, A. (2002). Inter-group helping relations as power relations: Maintaining or challenging social dominance between groups through helping. *Journal of Social Issues, 58,* 487–502.

Nadler, A., & Fisher, J. D. (1986). The role of threat to self-esteem and perceived control in recipient reaction to help: Theory development and empirical validation. In L. Berkowitz (Ed.), *Advances in experimental social psychology* (Vol. 19, pp. 81–122). Orlando, FL: Academic Press.

Nadler, A., Harpaz-Gorodeisky, G., & Ben-David, Y. (2009). Defensive helping: Threat to group identity, ingroup identification, status stability, and common group identity as determinants of intergroup help-giving. *Journal of Personality and Social Psychology, 97,* 823–834.

Nadler, A., & Saguy, T. (2004). Trust building and reconciliation between adversarial groups: A social psychological perspective. In H. J. Langholtz & C. E. Stout (Eds.), *The psychology of diplomacy* (pp. 29–46). Westport, CT: Praeger.

Naipaul, S. (1980). *Black and white.* London: Hamish Hamilton.

Near, J. P., & Miceli, M. P. (1985). Organizational dissidence: The case of whistle-blowing. *Journal of Business Ethics, 4,* 1–16.

Neely, J. H. (1977). Semantic priming and retrieval from lexical memory: Roles of inhibitionless spreading activation and limited-capacity attention. *Journal of Experimental Psychology: General, 106,* 226–254.

Nemeth, C., Mosier, K., & Chiles, C. (1992). When convergent thought improves performance: Majority versus minority influence. *Personality and Social Psychology Bulletin, 18,* 139–144.

Nemeth, C., Swedlund, M., & Kanki, B. (1974). Patterning of the minority's responses and their influence on the majority. *European Journal of Social Psychology, 4*, 53–64.

Nemeth, C. J. (1986). Differential contributions of majority and minority influence. *Psychological Review, 93*, 23–32.

Nemeth, C. J. (1995). Dissent as driving cognition, attitudes, and judgments. *Social Cognition, 13*, 273–291.

Nemeth, C. J., & Kwan, J. L. (1985). Originality of word associations as a function of majority vs. minority influence. *Social Psychology Quarterly, 48*, 277–282.

Nemeth, C. J., & Wachtler, J. (1983). Creative problem solving as a result of majority vs. minority influence. *European Journal of Social Psychology, 13*, 45–55.

Neuberg, S. L. (1996). Social motives and expectancy-tinged social interactions. In R. M. Sorrentino & E. T. Higgins (Eds.), *Handbook of motivation and cognition: The interpersonal context* (Vol. 3, pp. 225–261). New York: Guilford.

Neuberg, S. L., & Fiske, S. T. (1987). Motivational influences on impression formation: Outcome dependency, accuracy-driven attention, and individuating processes. *Journal of Personality and Social Psychology, 53*, 431–444.

Newcomb, T. M. (1943). *Personality and social change: Attitude formation in a student community.* New York: Dryden.

Newcomb, T. M. (1961). *The acquaintance process.* New York: Holt, Rinehart and Winston.

Newman, L. S., & Erber, R. (Eds.). (2002). *Understanding genocide: The social psychology of the Holocaust.* Oxford: Oxford University Press.

Nijstad, B. A. (2009). *Group performance.* Hove, UK: Psychology Press.

Nijstad, B. A., Stroebe, W., & Lodewijkx, H. F. M. (2002). Cognitive stimulation and interference in groups: Exposure effects in an idea generation task. *Journal of Experimental Social Psychology, 38*, 535–544.

Nisbett, R. E. (1993). Violence and U.S. regional culture. *American Psychologist, 48*, 441–449.

Nisbett, R. E. (2003). *The geography of thought: How Asians and Westerners think differently ... and why.* New York: Free Press.

Nisbett, R. E. (2009). *Intelligence and how to get it: Why schools and cultures count.* New York: Norton.

Nisbett, R. E., Caputo, C., Legant, P., & Marecek, J. (1973). Behavior as seen by the actor and as seen by the observer. *Journal of Personality and Social Psychology, 27*, 154–164.

Nisbett, R. E., & Cohen, D. (1996). *Culture of honor: The psychology of violence in the south.* Boulder, CO: Westview.

Nisbett, R. E., Peng, K., Choi, I., & Norenzayan, A. (2001). Culture and systems of thought: Holistic versus analytic cognition. *Psychological Review, 108*, 291–310.

Nisbett, R. E., & Ross, L. (1980). *Human inference: Strategies and shortcomings of social judgment.* Englewood Cliffs, NJ: Prentice Hall.

Nisbett, R. E., & Wilson, T. D. (1977). Telling more than we can know: Verbal reports on mental processes. *Psychological Review, 84*, 231–259.

Nissani, M. (1990). A cognitive reinterpretation of Stanley Milgram's observations on obedience to authority. *American Psychologist, 45*, 1384–1385.

Norenzayan, A., Choi, I., & Nisbett, R. E. (2002). Cultural similarities and differences in social inference: Evidence from behavioral predictions and lay theories of behavior. *Personality and Social Psychology Bulletin, 28*, 109–120.

Northcraft, G. B., & Neale, M. A. (1987). Experts, amateurs, and real estate: An anchoring-and-adjustment perspective on property pricing decisions. *Organizational Behavior and Human Decision Processes, 39*, 84–97.

Norton, M. I., Frost, J. H., & Ariely, D. (2007). Less is more: The lure of ambiguity, or why familiarity breeds contempt. *Journal of Personality and Social Psychology, 92*, 97–105.

Nosek, B. A., Banaji, M. R., & Greenwald, A. G. (2002). E-research: Ethics, security, design, and control in psychological research on the Internet. *Journal of Social Issues, 58*, 161–176.

Nosek, B. A., Greenwald, A. G., & Banaji, M. R. (2007). The Implicit Association Test at age 7: A methodological and conceptual review. In J. A. Bargh (Ed.), *Social psychology and the unconscious: The automaticity of higher mental processes* (pp. 265–292). New York: Psychology Press.

Novotny, T. E., Romano, R. A., Davis, R. M., & Mills, S. L. (1992). The public health practice of tobacco control: Lessons learned and directions for the States in the 1990s. *Annual Review of Public Health, 13*, 287–318.

Nuttin, J. M., Jr. (1985). Narcissism beyond Gestalt and awareness: The name letter effect. *European Journal of Social Psychology, 15*, 353–361.

Nuttin, J. M., Jr. (1987). Affective consequences of mere ownership: The name letter effect in twelve European languages. *European Journal of Social Psychology, 17*, 381–402.

Nuttin, J. M. (1990). In memoriam: John T. Lanzetta. *European Journal of Social Psychology, 20*, 363–367.

Nuwer, H. (1999). *Wrongs of passage: Fraternities, sororities, hazing, and binge drinking.* Bloomington, IN: Indiana University Press.

Oakes, P. J., Haslam, S. A., & Turner, J. C. (1994). *Stereotyping and social reality.* Oxford: Blackwell.

Oakes, P. J., & Turner, J. C. (1980). Social categorization and intergroup behaviour: Does minimal intergroup discrimination make social identity more positive? *European Journal of Social Psychology, 10*, 295–301.

Ochsner, K. N., Beer, J. S., Robertson, E. R., Cooper, J. C., Gabrieli, J. D. E., Kihlstrom, J. F., & D'Esposito, M. (2005). The neural correlates of direct and reflected self-knowledge. *Neuroimage, 28*, 797–814.

Ochsner, K. N., & Lieberman, M. D. (2001). The emergence of social cognitive neuroscience. *American Psychologist, 56*, 717–734.

Oliner, S. P., & Oliner, P. M. (1992). *The altruistic personality: Rescuers of Jews in Nazi Europe.* New York: Free Press.

Olson, M. A., & Fazio, R. H. (2001). Implicit attitude formation through classical conditioning. *Psychological Science, 12*, 413–417.

Olson, M. A., & Fazio, R. H. (2004). Reducing the influence of extrapersonal associations on the Implicit Association Test: Personalizing the IAT. *Journal of Personality and Social Psychology, 86*, 653–667.

Olweus, D. (1979). Stability of aggressive reaction patterns in males: A review. *Psychological Bulletin, 86*, 852–875.

Olweus, D. (1994). Bullying at school: Long-term outcomes for the victims and an effective school-based intervention program. In L. R. Huesmann (Ed.), *Aggressive behavior: Current perspectives* (pp. 97–130). New York: Plenum.

Omoto, A. M., & Snyder, M. (1993). AIDS volunteers and their motivations: Theoretical issues and practical concerns. *Nonprofit Management and Leadership, 4*, 157–176.

Omoto, A. M., & Snyder, M. (2002). Considerations of community: The context and process of volunteerism. *American Behavioral Scientist, 45*, 846–867.

Omoto, A. M., & Snyder, M. (2010). Influences of psychological sense of community on voluntary helping and prosocial action. In S. Stürmer & M. Snyder (Eds.), *The psychology of prosocial behavior: Group processes, intergroup relations, and helping* (pp. 223–243). Chichester, UK: Wiley-Blackwell.

Omoto, A. M., Snyder, M., & Martino, S. C. (2000). Volunteerism and the life course: Investigating age-related agendas for action. *Basic and Applied Social Psychology, 22*, 181–197.

Oppenheim, A. N. (1992). *Questionnaire design, interviewing and attitude measurement*. London: Pinter.

Orbell, S., Hodgkins, S., & Sheeran, P. (1997). Implementation intentions and the theory of planned behavior. *Personality and Social Psychology Bulletin, 23*, 945–954.

Orne, M. T. (1962). On the social psychology of the psychological experiment: With particular reference to demand characteristics and their implications. *American Psychologist, 17*, 776–783.

Orne, M. T. (1969). Demand characteristics and the concept of quasi-controls. In R. Rosenthal & R. Rosnow (Eds.), *Artifact in behavioral research* (pp. 143–179). New York: Academic Press.

Orobio de Castro, B., Veerman, J. W., Koops, W., Bosch, J. D., & Monshouwer, H. J. (2002). Hostile attribution of intent and aggressive behavior: A meta-analysis. *Child Development, 73*, 916–934.

Orpinas, P., & Frankowski, R. (2001). The aggression scale: A self-report measure of aggressive behavior for young adolescents. *Journal of Early Adolescence, 21*, 50–67.

Orwell, G. (1949). *Nineteen eighty-four*. London: Secker & Warburg.

Osborn, A. F. (1957). *Applied imagination*. New York: Scribner.

Osgood, C. E., Suci, G. J., & Tannenbaum, P. H. (1957). *The measurement of meaning*. Urbana, IL: University of Illinois Press.

Osterhouse, R. A., & Brock, T. C. (1970). Distraction increases yielding to propaganda by inhibiting counterarguing. *Journal of Personality and Social Psychology, 15*, 344–358.

Österman, K., Björkqvist, K., Lagerspetz, K. M., Kaukiainen, A., Landau, S. F., Fraczek, A., & Caprara, G. V. (1998). Cross-cultural evidence of female indirect aggression. *Aggressive Behavior, 24*, 1–8.

Otten, S., Sassenberg, K., & Kessler, T. (Eds.). (2009). *Intergroup relations: The role of motivation and emotion*. New York: Psychology Press.

Ouellette, J. A., & Wood, W. (1998). Habit and intention in everyday life: The multiple processes by which past behavior predicts future behavior. *Psychological Bulletin, 124*, 54–74.

Overall, N. C., Fletcher, G. J., & Simpson, J. A. (2006). Regulation processes in intimate relationships: The role of ideal standards. *Journal of Personality and Social Psychology, 91*, 662–685.

Oyserman, D., Coon, H. M., & Kemmelmeier, M. (2002). Rethinking individualism and collectivism: Evaluation of theoretical assumptions and meta-analyses. *Psychological Bulletin, 128*, 3–72.

Packer, D. J. (2008). Identifying systematic disobedience in Milgram's obedience experiments: A meta-analytic review. *Perspectives on Psychological Science, 3*, 301–304.

Paleari, F. G., Regalia, C., & Fincham, F. (2005). Marital quality, forgiveness, empathy, and rumination: A longitudinal analysis. *Personality and Social Psychology Bulletin, 31*, 368–378.

Paolini, S., Hewstone, M., Cairns, E., & Voci, A. (2004). Effects of direct and indirect cross-group friendships on judgments of Catholics and Protestants in Northern Ireland: The mediating role of an anxiety-reduction mechanism. *Personality and Social Psychology Bulletin, 30*, 770–786.

Papastamou, S. (1986). Psychologization and processes of minority and majority influence. *European Journal of Social Psychology, 16*, 165–180.

Park, B., & Rothbart, M. (1982). Perception of out-group homogeneity and levels of social categorization: Memory for the subordinate attributes of in-group and out-group members. *Journal of Personality and Social Psychology, 42*, 1051–1068.

Park, B., Ryan, C. S., & Judd, C. M. (1992). Role of meaningful subgroups in explaining differences in perceived variability for in-groups and out-groups. *Journal of Personality and Social Psychology, 63*, 553–567.

Park, G., & DeShon, R. P. (2010). A multilevel model of minority opinion expression and team decision-making effectiveness. *Journal of Applied Psychology, 95*, 824–833.

Park, J. H. (2007). Persistent misunderstandings of inclusive fitness and kin selection: Their ubiquitous appearance in social psychology textbooks. *Evolutionary Psychology, 5*, 860–873.

Parker, J. H. (1968). The interaction of Negroes and Whites in an integrated church setting. *Social Forces, 46*, 359–366.

Parker, K. C. (1988). Speaking turns in small group interaction: A context-sensitive event sequence model. *Journal of Personality and Social Psychology, 54*, 965–971.

Parker, R. N., & Auerhahn, K. (1999). Drugs, alcohol, and homicide. In M. D. Smith & M. A. Zahn (Eds.), *Homicide. A sourcebook of social research* (pp. 176–191). Thousand Oaks, CA: Sage.

Parks, M. R., & Floyd, K. (1996). Making friends in cyberspace. *Journal of Communication, 46*, 80–97.

Paulhus, D. L. (1984). Two-component models of socially desirable responding. *Journal of Personality and Social Psychology, 46*, 598–609.

Paulhus, D. L. (1991). Measurement and control of response bias. In J. P. Robinson, P. R. Shaver, & L. S. Wrightsman (Eds.), *Measures of personality and social psychological attitudes* (pp. 17–59). San Diego, CA: Academic Press.

Paulhus, D. L. (1998). Interpersonal and intrapsychic adaptiveness of trait self-enhancement: A mixed blessing? *Journal of Personality and Social Psychology, 74*, 1197–1208.

Paulhus, D. L., & John, O. P. (1998). Egoistic and moralistic biases in self-perception: The interplay of self-deceptive styles with basic traits and motives. *Journal of Personality, 66*, 1025–1060.

Paulus, P. B., & Yang, H.-C. (2000). Idea generation in groups: A basis for creativity in organizations. *Organizational Behavior and Human Decision Processes, 82*, 76–87.

Pavlova, M., Guerreschi, M., Lutzenberger, W., & Krägeloh-Mann, I. (2010). Social interaction revealed by motion: Dynamics of neuro-magnetic gamma activity. *Cerebral Cortex, 20*, 2361–2367.

Payne, B. K. (2001). Prejudice and perception: The role of automatic and controlled processes in misperceiving a weapon. *Journal of Personality and Social Psychology, 81*, 181–192.

Pearce, C. L., & Sims, H. P., Jr. (2000). Shared leadership: Toward a multi-level theory of leadership. *Advances in the Interdisciplinary Studies of Work Teams, 7*, 115–139.

Pelham, B. W., Carvallo, M., & Jones, J. T. (2005). Implicit egotism. *Current Directions in Psychological Science, 14*, 106–110.

Peltokorpi, V. (2008). Transactive memory systems. *Review of General Psychology, 12*, 378–394.

Pendry, L. (1998). When the mind is otherwise engaged: Resource depletion and social stereotyping. *European Journal of Social Psychology, 28*, 293–299.

Pendry, L., & Carrick, R. (2001). Doing what the mob do: Priming effects on conformity. *European Journal of Social Psychology, 31*, 83–92.

Pendry, L. F., & Macrae, C. N. (1994). Stereotypes and mental life: The case of the motivated but thwarted tactician. *Journal of Experimental Social Psychology, 30*, 303–325.

Pennebaker, J. W., & Chung, C. K. (in press). Expressive writing and its links to mental and physical health. In H. S. Friedman (Ed.), *Oxford handbook of health psychology*. New York: Oxford University Press.

Pennebaker, J. W., Dyer, M. A., Caulkins, R. S., Litowitz, D. L., Ackerman, P. L., Anderson, D. B., & McGraw, K. M. (1979). Don't the girls get prettier at closing time: A country and western application to psychology. *Personality and Social Psychology Bulletin, 5*, 122–125.

Penner, L. A. (2002). Dispositional and organizational influences on sustained volunteerism: An interactionist perspective. *Journal of Social Issues, 58*, 447–467.

Penner, L. A., Dovidio, J. F., Piliavin, J. A., & Schroeder, D. A. (2005). Prosocial behavior: Multilevel perspectives. *Annual Review of Psychology, 56*, 365–392.

Penner, L. A., & Finkelstein, M. A. (1998). Dispositional and structural determinants of volunteerism. *Journal of Personality and Social Psychology, 74*, 525–537.

Penner, L. A., Fritzsche, B. A., Craiger, J. P., & Freifeld, T. R. (1995). Measuring the prosocial personality. In J. Butcher & C. D. Spielberger (Eds.), *Advances in personality assessment* (Vol. 10, pp. 147–163). Hillsdale, NJ: Erlbaum.

Peplau, L. A. (1982). Research on homosexual couples: An overview. *Journal of Homosexuality, 8*, 3–8.

Perdue, C. W., Dovidio, J. F., Gurtman, M. B., & Tyler, R. B. (1990). Us and them: Social categorization and the process of intergroup bias. *Journal of Personality and Social Psychology, 59*, 475–486.

Perdue, C. W., & Gurtman, M. B. (1990). Evidence for the automaticity of ageism. *Journal of Experimental Social Psychology, 26*, 199–216.

Pérez, J. A., & Mugny, G. (1987). Paradoxical effects of categorization in minority influence: When being an outgroup is an advantage. *European Journal of Social Psychology, 17*, 157–169.

Pérez, J. A., & Mugny, G. (1996). The conflict elaboration theory of social influence. In E. H. Witte & J. H. Davis (Eds.), *Understanding group behavior: Small group processes and interpersonal relations* (Vol. 2, pp. 191–210). Mahwah, NJ: Erlbaum.

Perrett, D. I., Burt, D. M., Penton-Voak, I. S., Lee, K. J., Rowland, D. A., & Edwards, R. (1999). Symmetry and human facial attractiveness. *Evolution and Human Behavior, 20*, 295–307.

Perry, R. B. (1996). *The thought and character of William James. Briefer version*. Nashville, TN: Vanderbilt University Press. (Original work published 1948).

Peters, M. J. V., Jelicic, M., & Merckelbach, H. (2006). When stereotypes backfire: Trying to suppress stereotypes produces false recollections of a crime. *Legal and Criminological Psychology, 11,* 327–336.

Peterson, C., & Seligman, M. E. P. (1987). Explanatory style and illness. *Journal of Personality, 55,* 237–265.

Petronio, S. (1991). Communication boundary management: A theoretical model of managing disclosure of private information between marital couples. *Communication Theory, 1,* 311–335.

Petronio, S. (2002). *Boundaries of privacy: Dialectics of disclosure.* Albany, NY: State University of New York Press.

Pettigrew, T. F. (1958). Personality and sociocultural factors in intergroup attitudes: A cross-national comparison. *Journal of Conflict Resolution, 2,* 29–42.

Pettigrew, T. F. (1997). Generalized intergroup contact effects on prejudice. *Personality and Social Psychology Bulletin, 23,* 173–185.

Pettigrew, T. F. (1998). Intergroup contact theory. *Annual Review of Psychology, 49,* 65–85.

Pettigrew, T. F. (2009). Secondary transfer effect of contact: Do intergroup contact effects spread to noncontacted outgroups? *Social Psychology, 40,* 55–65.

Pettigrew, T. F., & Tropp, L. R. (2006). A meta-analytic test of intergroup contact theory. *Journal of Personality and Social Psychology, 90,* 751–783.

Pettigrew, T. F., & Tropp, L. R. (2008). How does intergroup contact reduce prejudice? Meta analytic tests of three mediators. *European Journal of Social Psychology, 38,* 922–934.

Petty, R. E., Briñol, P., & DeMarree, K. G. (2007). The Meta-Cognitive Model (MCM) of attitudes: Implications for attitude measurement, change, and strength. *Social Cognition, 25,* 657–686.

Petty, R. E., & Cacioppo, J. T. (1986a). *Communication and persuasion: Central and peripheral routes to attitude change.* New York: Springer.

Petty, R. E., & Cacioppo, J. T. (1986b). The elaboration likelihood model of persuasion. In L. Berkowitz (Ed.), *Advances in experimental social psychology* (Vol. 19, pp. 123–205). New York: Academic Press.

Petty, R. E., Cacioppo, J. T., & Goldman, R. (1981). Personal involvement as a determinant of argument-based persuasion. *Journal of Personality and Social Psychology, 41,* 847–855.

Petty, R. E., Fazio, R. H., & Briñol, P. (Eds.). (2009). *Attitudes: Insights from the new implicit measures.* New York: Psychology Press.

Petty, R. E., Haugtvedt, C. P., & Smith, S. M. (1995). Elaboration as a determinant of attitude strength: Creating attitudes that are persistent, resistant, and predictive of behavior. In R. E. Petty & J. A. Krosnick (Eds.), *Attitude strength: Antecedents and consequences* (pp. 93–130). Hillsdale, NJ: Erlbaum.

Petty, R. E., & Krosnick, J. A. (1995). *Attitude strength: Antecedents and consequences.* Hillsdale, NJ: Erlbaum.

Petty, R. E., Ostrom, T. M., & Brock, T. C. (1981). *Cognitive responses in persuasion.* Hillsdale, NJ: Erlbaum.

Petty, R. E., Schumann, D. W., Richman, S. A., & Strathman, A. J. (1993). Positive mood and persuasion: Different roles for affect under high- and low-elaboration conditions. *Journal of Personality and Social Psychology, 64,* 5–20.

Petty, R. E., & Wegener, D. T. (1998a). Attitude change: Multiple roles for persuasion variables. In D. T. Gilbert, S. T. Fiske, & G. Lindzey (Eds.), *Handbook of social psychology* (4th ed., Vol. 1, pp. 323–390). Boston, MA: McGraw-Hill.

Petty, R. E., & Wegener, D. T. (1998b). Matching versus mismatching attitude functions: Implications for scrutiny of persuasive messages. *Personality and Social Psychology Bulletin, 24,* 227–240.

Petty, R. E., & Wegener, D. T. (1999). The elaboration likelihood model: Current status and controversies. In S. Chaiken & Y. Trope (Eds.), *Dual-process theories in social psychology* (pp. 41–72). New York: Guilford.

Petty, R. E., Wells, G. L., & Brock, T. C. (1976). Distraction can enhance or reduce yielding to propaganda: Thought disruption versus effort justification. *Journal of Personality and Social Psychology, 34,* 874–884.

Pfeifer, J. H., Masten, C. L., Borofsky, L. A., Dapretto, M., Fuligni, A. J., & Lieberman, M. D. (2009). Neural correlates of direct and reflected self-appraisals in adolescents and adults: When social perspective taking informs self-perception. *Child Development, 80,* 1016–1038.

Phelps, E. A., O'Connor, K. J., Cunningham, W. A., Funayama, E. S., Gatenby, J. C., Gore, J. C., & Banaji, M. R. (2000). Performance on indirect measures of race evaluation predicts amygdala activation. *Journal of Cognitive Neuroscience, 12,* 729–738.

Phelps, E. A., & Thomas, L. A. (2003). Race, behavior, and the brain: The role of neuroimaging in understanding complex social behaviors. *Political Psychology, 24,* 747–758.

Pierce, J. L., & Newstrom, J. W. (2002). *Leaders & the leadership process: Readings, self-assessments & applications.* Boston, MA: McGraw-Hill.

Piliavin, I. M., Piliavin, J. A., & Rodin, J. (1975). Costs, diffusion, and the stigmatized victim. *Journal of Personality and Social Psychology, 32,* 429–438.

Piliavin, I. M., Rodin, J., & Piliavin, J. A. (1969). Good samaritanism: An underground phenomenon? *Journal of Personality and Social Psychology, 13,* 289–299.

Piliavin, J. A. (2009). Altruism and helping: The evolution of a field: The 2008 Cooley-Mead presentation. *Social Psychology Quarterly, 72,* 209–225.

Piliavin, J. A., Dovidio, J. F., Gaertner, S. L., & Clark, R. D., III. (1981). *Emergency intervention.* New York: Academic Press.

Pinquart, M., & Sörensen, S. (2000). Influences of socioeconomic status, social network, and competence on subjective well-being in later life: A meta-analysis. *Psychology and Aging, 15,* 187–224.

Plant, E. A., & Devine, P. G. (2003). The antecedents and implications of interracial anxiety. *Personality and Social Psychology Bulletin, 29*, 790–801.

Pliner, P., Hart, H., Kohl, J., & Saari, D. (1974). Compliance without pressure: Some further data on the foot-in-the-door technique. *Journal of Experimental Social Psychology, 10*, 17–22.

Plomin, R., Nitz, K., & Rowe, D. C. (1990). Behavior genetics and aggressive behavior in childhood. In M. Lewis & S. Miller (Eds.), *Handbook of developmental psychopathology* (pp. 119–133). New York: Plenum.

Podsakoff, P. M., MacKenzie, S. B., & Ahearne, M. (1997). Moderating effects of goal acceptance on the relationship between group cohesiveness and productivity. *Journal of Applied Psychology, 82*, 974–983.

Polizeiliche Kriminalstatistik. (2009). Retrieved February 2nd, 2011, from http://www.bka.de/pks/pks2009/download/pks-jb_2009_bka.pdf

Posner, M., & Snyder, C. R. R. (1975). Attention and cognitive control. In R. L. Solso (Ed.), *Information processing and cognition: The Loyola Symposium* (pp. 55–85). Hillsdale, NJ: Erlbaum.

Postmes, T., & Spears, R. (1998). Deindividuation and antinormative behavior: A meta-analysis. *Psychological Bulletin, 123*, 238–259.

Postmes, T., Spears, R., & Cihangir, S. (2001). Quality of decision making and group norms. *Journal of Personality and Social Psychology, 80*, 918–930.

Potter, J., & Wetherell, M. (1987). *Discourse and social psychology: Beyond attitudes and behavior.* London: Sage.

Povey, D., Coleman, K., Kaiza, P., & Roe, S. (2009). *Homicides, firearm offences and intimate violence 2007/08.* Retrieved May 29, 2010, from http://ndvf.org.uk/files/document/1346/original.pdf

Pratkanis, A. R., & Aronson, E. (2001). *Age of propaganda: The everyday use and abuse of persuasion.* New York: Freeman.

Pratto, F., Sidanius, J., & Levin, S. (2006). Social dominance theory and the dynamics of intergroup relations: Taking stock and looking forward. In W. Stroebe & M. Hewstone (Eds.), *European review of social psychology* (Vol. 17, pp. 271–320). Hove, UK: Psychology Press.

Pratto, F., Sidanius, J., Stallworth, L. M., & Malle, B. F. (1994). Social dominance orientation: A personality variable predicting social and political attitudes. *Journal of Personality and Social Psychology, 67*, 741–763.

Preacher, K. J., & Hayes, A. F. (2004). SPSS and SAS procedures for estimating indirect effects in simple mediation models. *Behavior Research Methods, Instruments & Computers, 36*, 717–731.

Prentice, D. A. (1987). Psychological correspondence of possessions, attitudes, and values. *Journal of Personality and Social Psychology, 53*, 993–1003.

Prislin, R., & Wood, W. (2005). Social influence in attitudes and attitude change. In D. Albarracín, B. T. Johnson, & M. P. Zanna (Eds.), *Handbook of attitudes* (pp. 671–705). Mahwah, NJ: Erlbaum.

Proulx, G., & Fahy, R. F. (2003, October). *Evacuation of the World Trade Center: What went right?* Paper presented at the Proceedings of the CIB-CTBUH International Conference on Tall Buildings, Malaysia.

Puce, A., & Perrett, D. (2003). Electrophysiology and brain imaging of biological motion. *Philosophical Transactions of the Royal Society B, 358*, 435–445.

Pugh, M. D., & Wahrman, R. (1983). Neutralizing sexism in mixed-sex groups: Do women have to be better than men? *American Journal of Sociology, 88*, 746–762.

Pyszczynski, T., & Greenberg, J. (1987). Toward an integration of cognitive and motivational perspectives on social inference: A biased hypothesis-testing model. In L. Berkowitz (Ed.), *Advances in experimental social psychology* (Vol. 20, pp. 297–340). San Diego, CA: Academic Press.

Pyszczynski, T., Greenberg, J., & Holt, K. (1985). Maintaining consistency between self-serving beliefs and available data: A bias in information evaluation. *Personality and Social Psychology Bulletin, 11*, 179–190.

Pyszczynski, T., Greenberg, J., & Solomon, S. (1999). A dual-process model of defense against conscious and unconscious death-related thoughts: An extension of terror management theory. *Psychological Review, 106*, 835–845.

Pyszczynski, T., Greenberg, J., Solomon, S., Arndt, J., & Schimel, J. (2004). Why do people need self-esteem? A theoretical and empirical review. *Psychological Bulletin, 130*, 435–468.

Quiamzade, A., Mugny, G., Falomir-Pichastor, J. M., & Butera, F. (2010). The complexity of majority versus minority influence processes. In R. Martin & M. Hewstone (Eds.), *Minority influence and innovation: Antecedents, processes and consequences* (pp. 21–52). Hove, UK: Psychology Press.

Rabbie, J. M., & Horwitz, M. (1969). Arousal of ingroup-outgroup bias by a chance win or loss. *Journal of Personality and Social Psychology, 13*, 269–277.

Rabbie, J. M., Schot, J. C., & Visser, L. (1989). Social identity theory: A conceptual and empirical critique from the perspective of a behavioural interaction model. *European Journal of Social Psychology, 19*, 171–202.

Rabow, J., Newcomb, M. D., Monto, M. A., & Hernandez, A. C. R. (1990). Altruism in drunk driving situations: Personal and situational factors in intervention. *Social Psychology Quarterly, 53*, 199–213.

Raine, A. (1996). Autonomic nervous system activity and violence. In D. M. Stoff & R. B. Cairns (Eds.), *Aggression and violence* (pp. 145–168). Mahwah, NJ: Erlbaum.

Randall, P. (1997). *Adult bullying: Perpetrators and victims*. London: Routledge.

Rank, S. G., & Jacobson, C. K. (1977). Hospital nurses' compliance with medication overdose orders: A failure to replicate. *Journal of Health and Social Behavior, 18*, 188–193.

Raven, B. H. (1974). The Nixon group. *Journal of Social Issues, 30*, 297–320.

Read, S. J. (1987). Constructing causal scenarios: A knowledge structure approach to causal reasoning. *Journal of Personality and Social Psychology, 52*, 288–302.

Redfield, R., Linton, R., & Herskovits, M. J. (1936). Memorandum for the study of acculturation. *American Anthropologist, 38*, 149–152.

Reeder, G. D. (2009). Mindreading: Judgments about intentionality and motives in dispositional inference. *Psychological Inquiry, 20*, 1–18.

Reeder, G. D., Kumar, S., Hesson-McInnis, M., & Trafimow, D. (2002). Inferences about the morality of an aggressor: The role of perceived motive. *Journal of Personality and Social Psychology, 83*, 789–803.

Regan, P. C. (2008). *The mating game: A primer on love, sex, and marriage*. Thousand Oaks, CA: Sage.

Reicher, S., Cassidy, C., Wolpert, I., Hopkins, N., & Levine, M. (2006). Saving Bulgaria's Jews: An analysis of social identity and the mobilisation of social solidarity. *European Journal of Social Psychology, 36*, 49–72.

Reicher, S., & Haslam, S. A. (2006). Rethinking the psychology of tyranny: The BBC prison study. *British Journal of Social Psychology, 45*, 1–40.

Reingen, P. H. (1978). On inducing compliance with requests. *Journal of Consumer Research, 5*, 96–102.

Reips, U.-D. (2002). Internet-based psychological experimenting: Five dos and five don'ts. *Social Science Computer Review, 20*, 241–249.

Reis, H. T., Clark, M. S., & Holmes, J. G. (2004). Perceived partner responsiveness as an organizing construct in the study of intimacy and closeness. In A. Aron & D. J. Mashek (Eds.), *Handbook of closeness and intimacy* (pp. 201–225). Mahwah, NJ: Erlbaum.

Reis, H. T., Earing, B., Kent, A., & Nezlek, J. (1976). The tyranny of numbers: Does group size affect petition signing? *Journal of Applied Social Psychology, 6*, 228–234.

Reis, H. T., & Judd, C. M. (Eds.). (2000). *Handbook of research methods in social and personality psychology*. New York: Cambridge University Press.

Reis, H. T., & Rusbult, C. E. (2004). *Key readings on close relationships*. Washington, DC: Taylor & Francis.

Reis, H. T., & Shaver, P. R. (1988). Intimacy as an interpersonal process. In S. Duck (Ed.), *Handbook of personal relationships: Theory, research and interventions* (pp. 367–389). London: Wiley.

Reisenzein, R. (1983). The Schachter theory of emotion: Two decades later. *Psychological Bulletin, 94*, 239–264.

Rennison, C. M., & Welchans, S. (2000). *Intimate partner violence*. Retrieved May 30, 2010, from http://bjs.ojp.usdoj.gov/content/pub/pdf/ipv.pdf

Reynolds, K. J., Turner, J. C., & Haslam, S. A. (2000). When are we better than them and they worse than us? A closer look at social discrimination in positive and negative domains. *Journal of Personality and Social Psychology, 78*, 64–80.

Rhee, S. H., & Waldman, I. D. (2002). Genetic and environmental influences on antisocial behavior: A meta-analysis of twin and adoption studies. *Psychological Bulletin, 128*, 490–529.

Rhodewalt, F., Morf, C., Hazlett, S., & Fairfield, M. (1991). Self-handicapping: The role of discounting and augmentation in the preservation of self-esteem. *Journal of Personality and Social Psychology, 61*, 122–131.

Richards, M., Hardy, R., & Wadsworth, M. (1997). The effects of divorce and separation on mental health in a national UK birth cohort. *Psychological Medicine, 27*, 1121–1128.

Ridgeway, C. L. (2001). Social status and group structure. In M. A. Hogg & R. S. Tindale (Eds.), *Blackwell handbook of social psychology: Group processes* (pp. 352–375). Oxford: Blackwell.

Rindfleisch, A., Burroughs, J. E., & Wong, N. (2009). The safety of objects: Materialism, existential insecurity, and brand connection. *Journal of Consumer Research, 36*, 1–16.

Rindfuss, R. R., & Stephen, E. H. (1990). Marital noncohabitation: Separation does not make the heart grow fonder. *Journal of Marriage and Family, 52*, 259–270.

Ring, K. (1967). Experimental social psychology: Some sober questions about some frivolous values. *Journal of Experimental Social Psychology, 3*, 113–123.

Ringelmann, M. (1913). Recherches sur les moteurs animés: Travail de l'homme [Research on animate sources of power: The work of man]. *Annales de l'Institut National Agronomique, 12*, 1–40.

Ritter, S. M., Karremans, J. C., & Van Schie, H. T. (2010). The role of self-regulation in derogating attractive alternatives. *Journal of Experimental Social Psychology, 46*, 631–637.

Rivara, F. P., Anderson, M. L., Fishman, P., Boniomi, A. E., Reid, R. J., Carrell, D., & Thompson, R. S. (2007). Healthcare utilization and costs for women with a history of intimate partner violence. *American Journal of Preventive Medicine, 32*, 89–96.

Robertson, L. S. (1986). Behavioral and environmental interventions for reducing motor vehicle trauma. *Annual Review of Public Health, 7*, 13–34.

Robins, R. W., & Beer, J. S. (2001). Positive illusions about the self: Short-term benefits and long-term costs. *Journal of Personality and Social Psychology, 80*, 340–352.

Robins, R. W., & Trzesniewski, K. H. (2005). Self-esteem development across the lifespan. *Current Directions in Psychological Science, 14,* 158–162.

Robinson, D. T., & Smith-Lovin, L. (1992). Selective interaction as a strategy for identity maintenance: An affect control model. *Social Psychology Quarterly, 55,* 12–28.

Robinson, J. P., Shaver, P., Wrightsman, L. S., & Andrews, F. M. (1991). *Measures of personality and social psychological attitudes.* San Diego, CA: Academic Press.

Robinson-Staveley, K., & Cooper, J. (1990). Mere presence, gender, and reactions to computers: Studying human-computer interaction in the social context. *Journal of Experimental Social Psychology, 26,* 168–183.

Roccas, S., Sagiv, L., Schwartz, S., Halevy, N., & Eidelson, R. (2008). Toward a unifying model of identification with groups: Integrating theoretical perspectives. *Personality and Social Psychology Review, 12,* 280–306.

Rochat, F., & Modigliani, A. (1995). The ordinary quality of resistance: From Milgram's laboratory to the village of Le Chambon. *Journal of Social Issues, 51,* 195–210.

Rochat, P., Morgan, R., & Carpenter, M. (1997). Young infants' sensitivity to movement information specifying social causality. *Cognitive Development, 12,* 441–465.

Rodriguez Mosquera, P. M., Manstead, A. S. R., & Fischer, A. H. (2002a). Honor in the Mediterranean and Northern Europe. *Journal of Cross-Cultural Psychology, 33,* 16–36.

Rodriguez Mosquera, P. M., Manstead, A. S. R., & Fischer, A. H. (2002b). The role of honour concerns in emotional reactions to offences. *Cognition and Emotion, 16,* 143–163.

Roese, N. J., & Olson, J. M. (2007). Better, stronger, faster: Self-serving judgment, affect regulation, and the optimal vigilance hypothesis. *Perspectives on Psychological Science, 2,* 124–141.

Roets, A., & Van Hiel, A. (2011). Item selection and validation of a brief, 15-item version of the need for closure scale. *Personality and Individual Differences, 50,* 90–94.

Rogers, C. R. (1951). *Client-centered therapy; its current practice, implications, and theory.* Oxford: Houghton Mifflin.

Rogers, T. B., Kuiper, N. A., & Kirker, W. S. (1977). Self-reference and the encoding of personal information. *Journal of Personality and Social Psychology, 35,* 677–688.

Rohner, R. P. (1984). Toward a conception of culture for cross-cultural psychology. *Journal of Cross-Cultural Psychology, 15,* 111–138.

Rohrer, J. H., Baron, S. H., Hoffman, E. L., & Swander, D. V. (1954). The stability of autokinetic judgments. *Journal of Abnormal and Social Psychology, 49,* 595–597.

Rokeach, M., & Rothman, G. (1965). The principle of belief congruence and the congruity principle as models of cognitive interaction. *Psychological Review, 72,* 128–142.

Rose, S. M. (1984). How friendships end: Patterns among young adults. *Journal of Social and Personal Relationships, 1,* 267–277.

Rosenberg, M. (1965). *Society and the adolescent self-image.* Princeton, NJ: Princeton University Press.

Rosenthal, A. M. (1964). *Thirty-eight witnesses: The Kitty Genovese case.* Berkeley, CA: University of California Press.

Rosenthal, R. (1966). *Experimenter effects in behavioral research.* New York: Appleton-Century-Crofts.

Rosenthal, R., & Fode, K. L. (1963). Psychology of the scientist: Three experiments in experimenter bias. *Psychological Reports, 12,* 491–511.

Rosenthal, R., & Rosnow, R. L. (1975). *The volunteer subject.* New York: Wiley.

Ross, E. A. (1908). *Social psychology.* New York: Macmillan.

Ross, L. (1977). The intuitive psychologist and his shortcomings: Distortions in the attribution process. In L. Berkowitz (Ed.), *Advances in experimental social psychology* (Vol. 10, pp. 173–220). New York: Academic Press.

Ross, L., Greene, D., & House, P. (1977). The 'false consensus effect': An egocentric bias in social perception and attribution processes. *Journal of Experimental Social Psychology, 13,* 279–301.

Ross, L., & Nisbett, R. E. (1991). *The person and the situation: Perspectives of social psychology.* New York: McGraw-Hill.

Ross, L., Rodin, J., & Zimbardo, P. G. (1969). Toward an attribution therapy: The reduction of fear through induced cognitive-emotional misattribution. *Journal of Personality and Social Psychology, 12,* 279–288.

Ross, L. D., Amabile, T. M., & Steinmetz, J. L. (1977). Social roles, social control, and biases in social-perception processes. *Journal of Personality and Social Psychology, 35,* 485–494.

Ross, M., & Sicoly, F. (1979). Egocentric biases in availability and attribution. *Journal of Personality and Social Psychology, 37,* 322–336.

Rothbart, M., & John, O. P. (1985). Social categorization and behavioral episodes: A cognitive analysis of the effects of intergroup contact. *Journal of Social Issues, 41,* 81–104.

Rowold, J., & Heinitz, K. (2007). Transformational and charismatic leadership: Assessing the convergent, divergent and criterion validity of the MLQ and the CKS. *Leadership Quarterly, 18,* 121–133.

Ruback, R. B., & Thompson, M. P. (2001). *Social and psychological consequences of violent victimization.* Thousand Oaks, CA: Sage.

Rubin, M., & Hewstone, M. (1998). Social identity theory's self-esteem hypothesis: A review and some suggestions for clarification. *Personality and Social Psychology Review, 2,* 40–62.

Rubin, Z. (1973). *Liking and loving: An invitation to social psychology.* New York: Holt, Rinehart and Winston.

Rude, S. S., Durham-Fowler, J. A., Baum, E. S., Rooney, S. B., & Maestas, K. L. (2010). Self-report and cognitive processing measures of depressive thinking predict subsequent major depressive disorder. *Cognitive Therapy and Research, 34*, 107–115.

Runciman, W. G. (1966). *Relative deprivation and social justice: A study of attitudes towards social inequality in twentieth-century England.* London: Routledge & Kegan Paul.

Rusbult, C. E. (1980). Commitment and satisfaction in romantic associations: A test of the investment model. *Journal of Experimental Social Psychology, 16*, 172–186.

Rusbult, C. E. (1983). A longitudinal test of the investment model: The development (and deterioration) of satisfaction and commitment in heterosexual involvements. *Journal of Personality and Social Psychology, 45*, 101–117.

Rusbult, C. E., & Farrell, D. (1983). A longitudinal test of the investment model: The impact on job satisfaction, job commitment, and turnover of variations in rewards, costs, alternatives, and investments. *Journal of Applied Psychology, 68*, 429–438.

Rusbult, C. E., & Martz, J. M. (1995). Remaining in an abusive relationship: An investment model analysis of nonvoluntary dependence. *Personality and Social Psychology Bulletin, 21*, 558–571.

Rusbult, C. E., & Van Lange, P. A. M. (1996). Interdependence processes. In E. T. Higgins & A. W. Kruglanski (Eds.), *Social psychology: Handbook of basic principles* (pp. 564–596). New York: Guilford.

Rusbult, C. E., Van Lange, P. A. M., Wildschut, T., Yovetich, N. A., & Verette, J. (2000). Perceived superiority in close relationships: Why it exists and persists. *Journal of Personality and Social Psychology, 79*, 521–545.

Rusbult, C. E., Verette, J., Whitney, G. A., Slovik, L. F., & Lipkus, I. (1991). Accommodation processes in close relationships: Theory and preliminary empirical evidence. *Journal of Personality and Social Psychology, 60*, 53–78.

Rushton, J. P. (1989). Genetic similarity, human altruism, and group selection. *Behavioral and Brain Sciences, 12*, 503–559.

Russell, G. W. (2004). Sport riots: A social-psychological review. *Aggression and Violent Behavior, 9*, 353–378.

Ryan, R. M., Bernstein, J. H., & Brown, K. W. (2010). Weekends, work, and well-being: Psychological need satisfactions and day of the week effects on mood, vitality, and physical symptoms. *Journal of Social and Clinical Psychology, 29*, 95–122.

Ryan, R. M., & Deci, E. L. (2008). From ego depletion to vitality: Theory and findings concerning the facilitation of energy available to the self. *Social and Personality Psychology Compass, 2*, 702–717.

Ryen, A. H., & Kahn, A. (1975). Effects of intergroup orientation on group attitudes and proxemic behavior. *Journal of Personality and Social Psychology, 31*, 302–310.

Saguy, T., Tausch, N., Dovidio, J. F., & Pratto, F. (2009). The irony of harmony: Intergroup contact can produce false expectations for equality. *Psychological Science, 20*, 114–121.

Salmivalli, C. (2010). Bullying and the peer group: A review. *Aggression and Violent Behavior, 15*, 112–120.

Sam, D. L., & Berry, J. W. (Eds.). (1997). *Cambridge handbook of acculturation psychology.* Cambridge, MA: Cambridge University Press.

Sanbonmatsu, D. M., & Fazio, R. H. (1990). The role of attitudes in memory-based decision making. *Journal of Personality and Social Psychology, 59*, 614–622.

Sanders, G. S. (1981). Driven by distraction: An integrative review of social facilitation theory and research. *Journal of Experimental Social Psychology, 17*, 227–251.

Sanders, G. S., Baron, R. S., & Moore, D. L. (1978). Distraction and social comparison as mediators of social facilitation effects. *Journal of Experimental Social Psychology, 14*, 291–303.

Sandstrom, M. J., & Jordan, R. (2008). Defensive self-esteem and aggression in childhood. *Journal of Research in Personality, 42*, 506–514.

Sanfey, A. G., Rilling, J. K., Aronson, J. A., Nystrom, L. E., & Cohen, J. D. (2003). The neural basis of economic decision-making in the ultimatum game. *Science, 300*, 1755–1758.

Sani, F. (Ed.). (2008). *Individual and collective self-continuity: Psychological perspectives.* Mahwah NJ: Erlbaum.

Sanitioso, R., Kunda, Z., & Fong, G. T. (1990). Motivated recruitment of autobiographical memories. *Journal of Personality and Social Psychology, 59*, 229–241.

Sanna, L. J. (1992). Self-efficacy theory: Implications for social facilitation and social loafing. *Journal of Personality and Social Psychology, 62*, 774–786.

Sanna, L. J., & Shotland, R. L. (1990). Valence of anticipated evaluation and social facilitation. *Journal of Experimental Social Psychology, 26*, 82–92.

Sasfy, J., & Okun, M. (1974). Form of evaluation and audience expertness as joint determinants of audience effects. *Journal of Experimental Social Psychology, 10*, 461–467.

Sassenberg, K., & Moskowitz, G. B. (2005). Don't stereotype, think different! Overcoming automatic stereotype activation by mindset priming. *Journal of Experimental Social Psychology, 41*, 506–514.

Saucier, D. A., Miller, C. T., & Doucet, N. (2005). Differences in helping Whites and Blacks: A meta-analysis. *Personality and Social Psychology Review, 9*, 2–16.

Schachter, S. (1951). Deviation, rejection, and communication. *Journal of Abnormal and Social Psychology, 46*, 190–207.

Schachter, S. (1964). The interaction of cognitive and physiological determinants of emotional state. In L. Berkowitz (Ed.), *Advances in experimental social psychology* (Vol. 1, pp. 49–80). New York: Academic Press.

Schachter, S. (1994). *Leon Festinger. Biographical memoirs* (Vol. 64). Retrieved October, 2005, from http://www.nap.edu

Schachter, S., Nuttin, J., De Monchaux, C., Maucorps, P. H., Osmer, D., Duijker, H., ... Israel, J. (1954). Cross-cultural experiments on threat and rejection. *Human Relations, 7*, 403–439.

Schachter, S., & Singer, J. (1962). Cognitive, social, and physiological determinants of emotional state. *Psychological Review, 69*, 379–399.

Schaefer, C. E., & Mattei, D. (2005). Catharsis: Effectiveness in children's aggression. *International Journal of Play Therapy, 14*, 103–109.

Schaller, M., & Maass, A. (1989). Illusory correlation and social categorization: Toward an integration of motivational and cognitive factors in stereotype formation. *Journal of Personality and Social Psychology, 56*, 709–721.

Schatzel-Murphy, E. A., Harris, D. A., Knight, R. A., & Milburn, M. A. (2009). Sexual coercion in men and women: Similar behaviors, different predictors. *Archives of Sexual Behavior, 38*, 974–986.

Scheepers, D., Spears, R., Doosje, B., & Manstead, A. S. R. (2006a). Diversity in in-group bias: Structural factors, situational features, and social functions. *Journal of Personality and Social Psychology, 90*, 944–960.

Scheepers, D., Spears, R., Doosje, B., & Manstead, A. S. R. (2006b). The social functions of in-group bias: Creating, confirming, or changing social reality. In W. Stroebe & M. Hewstone (Eds.), *European review of social psychology* (Vol. 17, pp. 359–396). Hove, UK: Psychology Press.

Scheepers, D., Spears, R., Manstead, A. S. R., & Doosje, B. (2009). The influence of discrimination and fairness on collective self-esteem. *Personality and Social Psychology Bulletin, 35*, 506–515.

Scherer, K. R., & Scherer, U. (1981). Speech behavior and personality. In J. K. Darby (Ed.), *Speech evaluation in psychiatry* (pp. 115–135). New York: Grune & Stratton.

Schiappa, E., Gregg, P. B., & Hewes, D. E. (2005). The parasocial contact hypothesis. *Communication Monographs, 72*, 92–115.

Schimmack, U., Oishi, S., & Diener, E. (2005). Individualism: A valid and important dimension of cultural differences between nations. *Personality and Social Psychology Review, 9*, 17–31.

Schlenker, B. R. (2012). Self-presentation. In M. R. Leary & J. P. Tangney (Eds.), *Handbook of self and identity* (2nd ed., pp. 542–570). New York: Guilford.

Schlenker, B. R., & Wowra, S. A. (2003). Carryover effects of feeling socially transparent or impenetrable on strategic self-presentation. *Journal of Personality and Social Psychology, 85*, 871–880.

Schmeichel, B. J., & Martens, A. (2005). Self-affirmation and mortality salience: Affirming values reduces worldview defense and death-thought accessibility. *Personality and Social Psychology Bulletin, 31*, 658–667.

Schmeichel, B. J., & Vohs, K. (2009). Self-affirmation and self-control: Affirming core values counteracts ego depletion. *Journal of Personality and Social Psychology, 96*, 770–782.

Schmitt, D. P., & Allik, J. (2005). Simultaneous administration of the Rosenberg Self-Esteem Scale in 53 nations: Exploring the universal and culture-specific features of global self-esteem. *Journal of Personality and Social Psychology, 89*, 623–642.

Schreiber, E. (1979). Bystander's intervention in situations of violence. *Psychological Reports, 45*, 243–246.

Schuette, R. A., & Fazio, R. H. (1995). Attitude accessibility and motivation as determinants of biased processing: A test of the MODE model. *Personality and Social Psychology Bulletin, 21*, 704–710.

Schultze, T., Faulmüller, N., Schmidt-Hieber, J., & Schulz-Hardt, S. (2012). *How frequent are hidden profiles? A simulation-based approach.* Unpublished manuscript, University of Goettingen.

Schulz-Hardt, S., Brodbeck, F. C., Mojzisch, A., Kerschreiter, R., & Frey, D. (2006). Group decision making in hidden profile situations: Dissent as a facilitator for decision quality. *Journal of Personality and Social Psychology, 91*, 1080–1093.

Schulz-Hardt, S., Frey, D., Lüthgens, C., & Moscovici, S. (2000). Biased information search in group decision making. *Journal of Personality and Social Psychology, 78*, 655–669.

Schulz-Hardt, S., Hertel, G., & Brodbeck, F. C. (2007). Gruppenleistung und Leistungsförderung [Group performance and its facilitation]. In H. Schuler & K.-H. Sonntag (Eds.), *Handbuch der Arbeits- und Organisationspsychologie* (pp. 698–706). Göttingen, Germany: Hogrefe.

Schumpeter, J. (1908). *Das Wesen und der Hauptinhalt der theoretischen Nationalökonomie [The Nature and Essence of Theoretical Economics].* München und Leipzig: Duncker und Humblot.

Schwartz, S. H. (1992). Universals in the content and structure of values: Theoretical advances and empirical tests in 20 countries. In M. P. Zanna (Ed.), *Advances in experimental social psychology* (Vol. 25, pp. 1–65). San Diego, CA: Academic Press.

Schwartz, S. H. (1994). Beyond individualism and collectivism: New cultural dimensions of values. In U. Kim, H. C. Triandis, Ç. Kağıtçıbaşi, S. C. Choi, & G. Yoon (Eds.), *Individualism and collectivism: Theory, method and applications* (pp. 85–119). Thousand Oaks, CA: Sage.

Schwartz, S. H. (2004). Mapping and interpreting cultural differences around the world. In H. Vinken, J. Soeters, & P. Ester (Eds.), *Comparing cultures: Dimensions of culture in a comparative perspective* (pp. 43–73). Leiden, NL: Brill.

Schwartz, S. H., & Gottlieb, A. (1976). Bystander reactions to a violent theft: Crime in Jerusalem. *Journal of Personality and Social Psychology, 34*, 1188–1199.

Schwartz, S. H., & Sagiv, L. (1995). Identifying culture-specifics in the content and structure of values. *Journal of Cross-Cultural Psychology, 26*, 92–116.

Schwarz, N. (1994). Judgment in a social context: Biases, shortcomings, and the logic of conversation. In M. P. Zanna (Ed.), *Advances in experimental social psychology* (Vol. 26, pp. 123–162). San Diego, CA: Academic Press.

Schwarz, N. (1999). Self-reports: How the questions shape the answers. *American Psychologist, 54,* 93–105.

Schwarz, N., Bless, H., Strack, F., Klumpp, G., Rittenauer-Schatka, H., & Simons, A. (1991). Ease of retrieval as information: Another look at the availability heuristic. *Journal of Personality and Social Psychology, 61,* 195–202.

Schwarz, N., & Clore, G. L. (1983). Mood, misattribution and judgments of well-being: Informative and directive functions of affective states. *Journal of Personality and Social Psychology, 45,* 513–523.

Schwarz, N., Groves, R. M., & Schuman, H. (1998). Survey methods. In D. T. Gilbert, S. T. Fiske, & G. Lindzey (Eds.), *Handbook of social psychology* (4th ed., Vol. 1, pp. 143–179). Boston, MA: McGraw-Hill.

Schwarzwald, J., Raz, M., & Zvibel, M. (1979). The application of the door-in-the-face technique when established behavioral customs exist. *Journal of Applied Social Psychology, 9,* 576–586.

Sears, D. O. (1986). College sophomores in the laboratory: Influences of a narrow data base on social psychology's view of human nature. *Journal of Personality and Social Psychology, 51,* 515–530.

Sears, D. O. (1988). Symbolic racism. In P. A. Katz & D. A. Taylor (Eds.), *Eliminating racism: Profiles in controversy* (pp. 53–84). New York: Plenum.

Sedikides, C. (1993). Assessment, enhancement, and verification determinants of the self-evaluation process. *Journal of Personality and Social Psychology, 65,* 317–338.

Sedikides, C., Campbell, W. K., Reeder, G. D., & Elliot, A. J. (1998). The self-serving bias in relational context. *Journal of Personality and Social Psychology, 74,* 378–386.

Sedikides, C., Gaertner, L., & Toguchi, Y. (2003). Pancultural self-enhancement. *Journal of Personality and Social Psychology, 84,* 60–79.

Sedikides, C., & Green, J. D. (2004). What I don't recall can't hurt me: Information negativity versus information inconsistency as determinants of memorial self-defense. *Social Cognition, 22,* 4–29.

Sedikides, C., Gregg, A. P., & Hart, C. M. (2007). The importance of being modest. In C. Sedikides & S. J. Spencer (Eds.), *The self* (pp. 163–184). New York: Psychology Press.

Sedikides, C., Rudich, E. A., Gregg, A. P., Kumashiro, M., & Rusbult, C. (2004). Are normal narcissists psychologically healthy?: Self-esteem matters. *Journal of Personality and Social Psychology, 87,* 400–416.

Sedikides, C., & Skowronski, J. J. (1997). The symbolic self in evolutionary context. *Personality and Social Psychology Review, 1,* 80–102.

Sedikides, C., & Strube, M. J. (1997). Self-evaluation: To thine own self be good, to thine own self be sure, to thine own self be true, and to thine own self be better. In M. P. Zanna (Ed.), *Advances in experimental social psychology* (Vol. 29, pp. 209–269). San Diego, CA: Academic Press.

Seidel, E.-M., Eickhoff, S. B., Kellermann, T., Schneider, F., Gur, R. C., Habel, U., & Derntl, B. (2010). Who is to blame? Neural correlates of causal attribution in social situations. *Social Neuroscience, 5,* 335–350.

Selfhout, M., Denissen, J., Branje, S. J. T., & Meeus, W. (2009). In the eye of the beholder: Perceived, actual, and peer-rated similarity in personality, communication, and friendship intensity during the acquaintanceship process. *Journal of Personality and Social Psychology, 96,* 1152–1165.

Seligman, M. E. (1975). *Helplessness: On depression, development, and death.* San Francisco, CA: Freeman.

Semin, G. R., & Rubini, M. (1990). Unfolding the concept of person by verbal abuse. *European Journal of Social Psychology, 20,* 463–474.

Shackelford, T. K., Schmitt, D. P., & Buss, D. M. (2005). Universal dimensions of human mate preferences. *Personality and Individual Differences, 39,* 447–458.

Shallice, T. (1988). *From neuropsychology to mental structure.* New York: Cambridge University Press.

Shanab, M. E., & Yahya, K. A. (1978). A cross-cultural study of obedience. *Bulletin of the Psychonomic Society, 11,* 267–269.

Shaver, P. R., & Mikulincer, M. (2009). Attachment styles. In M. R. Leary & R. H. Hoyle (Eds.), *Handbook of individual differences and social behavior* (pp. 62–81). New York: Guilford.

Shavitt, S. (1990). The role of attitude objects in attitude functions. *Journal of Experimental Social Psychology, 26,* 124–148.

Sheeran, P. (2002). Intention-behavior relations: A conceptual and empirical review. In W. Stroebe & M. Hewstone (Eds.), *European review of social psychology* (Vol. 12, pp. 1–36). Hove, UK: Psychology Press.

Sheeran, P., Milne, S., Webb, T. L., & Gollwitzer, P. M. (2005). Implementation intentions and health behaviour. In M. Conner & P. Norman (Eds.), *Predicting health behaviour: Research and practice with social cognition models* (2nd ed., pp. 276–323). Buckingham, UK: Open University Press.

Sheldon, K. M., Ryan, R., & Reis, H. T. (1996). What makes for a good day? Competence and autonomy in the day and in the person. *Personality and Social Psychology Bulletin, 22,* 1270–1279.

Shelton, J. N. (2003). Interpersonal concerns in social encounters between majority and minority group members. *Group Processes & Intergroup Relations, 6,* 171–185.

Shelton, J. N., & Richeson, J. A. (2005). Intergroup contact and pluralistic ignorance. *Journal of Personality and Social Psychology, 88,* 91–107.

Shepard, R.N. (1998). *Carl Iver Hovland: A biographical memoir.* Retrieved from http://www.nap.edu

Shepela, S. T., Cook, J., Horlitz, E., Leal, R., Luciano, S., Lutfy, E., … Worden, E. (1999). Courageous resistance: A special case of altruism. *Theory and Psychology, 9*, 787–805.

Sheridan, C. L., & King, R. G. (1972). Obedience to authority with an authentic victim. *Proceedings of the Annual Convention of the American Psychological Association, 7*, 165–166.

Sherif, M. (1935). A study of some social factors in perception. *Archives of Psychology (Columbia University), 187*, 60.

Sherif, M. (1936). *The psychology of social norms.* New York: Harper & Row.

Sherif, M. (1966). *In common predicament: Social psychology in intergroup conflict and cooperation.* Boston, MA: Houghton Mifflin.

Sherif, M. (1967). *Group conflict and co-operation.* London: Routledge & Kegan Paul.

Sherif, M., Harvey, O. J., White, B. J., Hood, W. R., & Sherif, C. W. (1961). *Intergroup cooperation and competition: The Robbers Cave experiment.* Norman, OK: University of Oklahoma.

Sherif, M., & Sherif, C. W. (1969). *Social psychology.* New York: Harper & Row.

Sherman, J. W. (2010). Social neuroscience and its contribution to social psychological theory: Introduction to the special issue. *Social Cognition, 28*, 663–666.

Shiffrin, R. M., & Schneider, W. (1977). Controlled and automatic information processing: Perceptual learning, automatic attending, and a general theory. *Psychological Review, 84*, 127–190.

Shoal, G. D., Giancola, P. R., & Kirillova, G. P. (2003). Salivary cortisol, personality, and aggressive behavior in adolescent boys: A 5-year longitudinal study. *Journal of the American Academy of Child and Adolescent Psychiatry, 42*, 1101–1107.

Shore, B. (1996). *Culture in mind: Cognition, culture, and the problem of meaning.* New York: Oxford University Press.

Shotland, R. L., & Straw, M. K. (1976). Bystander response to an assault: When a man attacks a woman. *Journal of Personality and Social Psychology, 34*, 990–999.

Shrauger, J. S., & Schoeneman, T. J. (1979). Symbolic interactionist view of self-concept: Through the looking glass darkly. *Psychological Bulletin, 86*, 549–573.

Sidanius, J., & Pratto, F. (1999). Social dominance: An integrative theory of social hierarchy and oppression. Cambridge, MA: Cambridge University Press.

Siegel, A. E., & Siegel, S. (1957). Reference groups, membership groups, and attitude change. *Journal of Abnormal and Social Psychology, 55*, 360–364.

Sigman, S. J. (1991). Handling the discontinuous aspects of continuous social relationships: Toward research on the persistence of social forms. *Communication Theory, 1*, 106–127.

Silvia, P. J., & Duval, T. S. (2001). Objective self-awareness theory: Recent progress and enduring problems. *Personality and Social Psychology Review, 5*, 230–241.

Silvia, P. J., & Eichstaedt, J. (2004). A self-novelty manipulation of self-focused attention for Internet and laboratory experiments. *Behavior Research Methods, Instruments, & Computers, 36*, 325–330.

Simon, B. (1992). The perception of ingroup and outgroup homogeneity: Reintroducing the intergroup context. In W. Stroebe & M. Hewstone (Eds.), *European review of social psychology* (Vol. 3, pp. 1–30). Chichester, UK: Wiley.

Simon, B., Aufderheide, B., & Kampmeier, C. (2001). The social psychology of minority-majority relations. In R. Brown & S. L. Gaertner (Eds.), *Blackwell handbook of social psychology: Intergroup processes* (pp. 303–323). Oxford: Blackwell.

Simonton, D. K. (1981). The library laboratory: Archival data in personality and social psychology. In L. Wheeler (Ed.), *Review of personality and social psychology* (Vol. 2, pp. 217–243). Beverly Hills, CA: Sage.

Simonton, D. K. (1986). Presidential personality: Biographical use of the Gough Adjective Check List. *Journal of Personality and Social Psychology, 51*, 149–160.

Simpson, J. A., Gangestad, S. W., & Lerma, M. (1990). Perception of physical attractiveness: Mechanisms involved in the maintenance of romantic relationships. *Journal of Personality and Social Psychology, 59*, 1192–1201.

Simpson, J. A., Rholes, W. S., & Nelligan, J. S. (1992). Support-seeking and support-giving within couple members in an anxiety-provoking situation: The role of attachment styles. *Journal of Personality and Social Psychology, 62*, 434–446.

Singelis, T. M. (1994). The measurement of independent and interdependent self-construals. *Personality and Social Psychology Bulletin, 20*, 580–591.

Singelis, T. M., Bond, M. H., Sharkey, W. F., & Lai, A. S. Y. (1999). Unpackaging culture's influence on self-esteem and embarrassability: The role of self-construals. *Journal of Cross-Cultural Psychology, 30*, 315–341.

Singer, P. (2009). *The life you can save: Acting now to end world poverty.* New York: Random House.

Singer, T., & Lamm, C. (2009). The social neuroscience of empathy. *Annals of the New York Academy of Sciences, 1156*, 81–96.

Singer, T., Seymour, B., O'Doherty, J. P., Stephan, K. E., Dolan, R. J., & Frith, C. D. (2006). Empathic neural responses are modulated by the perceived fairness of others. *Nature, 439*, 466–469.

Sivasubramaniam, N., Murry, W. D., Avolio, B. J., & Jung, D. I. (2002). A longitudinal model of the effects of team leadership and group potency on group performance. *Group & Organization Management, 27*, 66–96.

Slater, M., Antley, A., Davison, A., Swapp, D., Guger, C., Barker, C., … Sanchez-Vives, M. V. (2006). A virtual reprise of the Stanley Milgram obedience experiments. *PLoS One, 1,* 1–10.

Slater, P. E. (1955). Role differentiation in small groups. *American Sociological Review, 20,* 300–310.

Slavin, R. E. (1978). Student teams and achievement divisions. *Journal of Research and Development in Education, 12,* 39–49.

Sloman, S. A. (2005). *Causal models: How people think about the world and its alternatives.* New York: Oxford University Press.

Smith, C. M., & Tindale, R. S. (2010). Direct and indirect minority influence in groups. In R. Martin & M. Hewstone (Eds.), *Minority influence and innovation: Antecedents, processes and consequences* (pp. 263–284). Hove, UK: Psychology Press.

Smith, C. M., Tindale, R. S., & Steiner, L. (1998). Investment decisions by individuals and groups in 'sunk cost' situations: The potential impact of shared representations. *Group Processes & Intergroup Relations, 1,* 175–189.

Smith, E. R. (1991). Illusory correlation in a simulated exemplar-based memory. *Journal of Experimental Social Psychology, 27,* 107–123.

Smith, E. R. (1993). Social identity and social emotions: Toward new conceptualizations of prejudice. In D. M. Mackie & D. L. Hamilton (Eds.), *Affect, cognition, and stereotyping: Interactive processes in group perception* (pp. 297–315). San Diego, CA: Academic Press.

Smith, E. R., & Miller, F. D. (1983). Mediation among attributional inferences and comprehension processes: Initial findings and a general method. *Journal of Personality and Social Psychology, 44,* 492–505.

Smith, H. S., & Cohen, L. H. (1993). Self-complexity and reactions to a relationship breakup. *Journal of Social and Clinical Psychology, 12,* 367–384.

Smith, M. B., Bruner, J. S., & White, R. W. (1956). *Opinions and personality.* New York: Wiley.

Smith, P. B. (2004). Acquiescent response bias as an aspect of cultural communication style. *Journal of Cross-Cultural Psychology, 35,* 50–61.

Smith, P. B., & Best, D. L. (Eds.). (2009). *Cross-cultural psychology* (four volumes). London: Sage.

Smith, P. B., & Bond, M. H. (1998). *Social psychology across cultures.* London: Prentice Hall.

Smith, P. B., Bond, M. H., & Kağıtçıbaşı, Ç. (2006). *Understanding social psychology across cultures: Living and working in a changing world.* London: Sage.

Smith, P. K., Ananiadou, K., & Cowie, H. (2003). Interventions to reduce school bullying. *Canadian Journal of Psychiatry, 48,* 591–599.

Smith, P. K., Morita, Y., Junger-Tas, J., Olweus, D., Catalano, R., & Slee, P. (1999). *The nature of school bullying: A cross-national perspective.* London: Routledge.

Smith, P. K., Singer, M., Hoel, H., & Cooper, C. L. (2003). Victimization in the school and the workplace: Are there any links? *British Journal of Psychology, 94,* 175–188.

Smith, P. M. (1995). Leadership. In A. S. R. Manstead & M. Hewstone (Eds.), *Blackwell encyclopedia of social psychology* (pp. 358–362). Oxford: Blackwell.

Snyder, C. R., & Higgins, R. L. (1988). Excuses: Their effective role in the negotiation of reality. *Psychological Bulletin, 104,* 23–35.

Snyder, M. (1974). Self-monitoring of expressive behavior. *Journal of Personality and Social Psychology, 30,* 526–537.

Snyder, M. (1984). When belief creates reality. In L. Berkowitz (Ed.), *Advances in experimental social psychology* (Vol. 18, pp. 247–305). Orlando, FL: Academic Press.

Snyder, M. (1987). *Public appearances, private realities.* New York: Freeman.

Snyder, M., & Cunningham, M. R. (1975). To comply or not comply: Testing the self-perception explanation of the 'foot-in-the-door' phenomenon. *Journal of Personality and Social Psychology, 31,* 64–67.

Snyder, M., & DeBono, K. G. (1985). Appeals to image and claims about quality: Understanding the psychology of advertising. *Journal of Personality and Social Psychology, 49,* 586–597.

Snyder, M., & Kendzierski, D. (1982). Acting on one's attitudes: Procedures for linking attitude and behavior. *Journal of Experimental Social Psychology, 18,* 165–183.

Snyder, M., Tanke, E. D., & Berscheid, E. (1977). Social perception and interpersonal behavior: On the self-fulfilling nature of social stereotypes. *Journal of Personality and Social Psychology, 35,* 656–666.

Sober, E., & Wilson, D. S. (1998). *Unto others: The evolution and psychology of unselfish behavior.* Cambridge, MA: Harvard University Press.

Solomon, S., Greenberg, J., & Pyszczynski, T. (1991). A terror management theory of social behavior: The psychological functions of self-esteem and cultural worldviews. In M. P. Zanna (Ed.), *Advances in experimental social psychology* (Vol. 24, pp. 93–159). San Diego, CA: Academic Press.

Son Hing, L. S., Bobocel, D. R., Zanna, M. P., & McBride, M. V. (2007). Authoritarian dynamics and unethical decision making: High social dominance orientation leaders and high right-wing authoritarianism followers. *Journal of Personality and Social Psychology, 92,* 67–81.

Son Hing, L. S., & Zanna, M. P. (2010). Individual differences. In J. F. Dovidio, M. Hewstone, P. Glick, & V. M. Esses (Eds.), *Handbook of prejudice, stereotyping and discrimination* (pp. 163–178). London: Sage.

Sparks, G. G., & Sparks, C. W. (2002). Effects of media violence. In J. Bryant & D. Zillmann (Eds.), *Media effects: Advances in theory and research* (2nd ed., pp. 269–285). Mahwah, NJ: Erlbaum.

Spears, R., Jetten, J., Scheepers, D., & Cihangir, S. (2009). Creative distinctiveness: Explaining in-group bias in minimal groups. In S. Otten, K. Sassenberg, & T. Kessler (Eds.), *Intergroup relations: The role of motivation and emotion* (pp. 23–40). New York: Psychology Press.

Spears, R., & Smith, H. J. (2001). Experiments as politics. *Political Psychology, 22,* 309–330.

Spence, J. T., Deaux, K., & Helmreich, R. L. (1985). Sex roles in contemporary American society. In G. Lindzey & E. Aronson (Eds.), *Handbook of social psychology* (3rd ed., Vol. 2, pp. 149–178). New York: Random House.

Spence, K. W. (1956). *Behavior theory and conditioning.* New Haven, CT: Yale University Press.

Spengler, S., Von Cramon, D. Y., & Brass, M. (2009). Was it me or was it you? How the sense of agency originates from ideomotor learning revealed by fMRI. *Neuroimage, 46,* 290–298.

Spitzberg, B. H. (1999). An analysis of empirical estimates of sexual aggression victimization and perpetration. *Violence and Victims, 14,* 214–260.

Srull, T. K., & Wyer, R. S., Jr. (1980). Category accessibility and social perception: Some implications for the study of person memory and interpersonal judgments. *Journal of Personality and Social Psychology, 38,* 841–856.

Staats, A. W., & Staats, C. K. (1958). Attitudes established by classical conditioning. *Journal of Abnormal and Social Psychology, 57,* 37–40.

Stangor, C., Sechrist, G. B., & Jost, J. T. (2001). Changing racial beliefs by providing consensus information. *Personality and Social Psychology Bulletin, 27,* 486–496.

Starbuck, W. H., & Farjoun, M. (2005). *Organization at the limit: Lessons from the Columbia disaster.* Oxford: Blackwell.

Stasser, G., & Birchmeier, Z. (2003). Group creativity and collective choice. In P. B. Paulus & B. A. Nijstad (Eds.), *Group creativity* (pp. 85–109). New York: Oxford University Press.

Stasser, G., Kerr, N. L., & Bray, R. M. (1982). The social psychology of jury deliberations: Structure, process, and product. In N. L. Kerr & R. M. Bray (Eds.), *The psychology of the courtroom* (pp. 221–256). New York: Academic Press.

Stasser, G., & Titus, W. (1985). Pooling of unshared information in group decision making: Biased information sampling during discussion. *Journal of Personality and Social Psychology, 48,* 1467–1478.

Staub, E. (1989). *The roots of evil: The origins of genocide and other group violence.* Cambridge, MA: Cambridge University Press.

Steblay, N., Hosch, H. M., Culhane, S. E., & McWethy, A. (2006). The impact on juror verdicts of judicial instruction to disregard inadmissible evidence: A meta-analysis. *Law and Human Behavior, 30,* 469–492.

Steele, C. M. (1988). The psychology of self-affirmation: Sustaining the integrity of the self. In L. Berkowitz (Ed.), *Advances in experimental social psychology* (Vol. 21, pp. 261–302). San Diego, CA: Academic Press.

Steiner, I. D. (1972). *Group processes and group productivity.* New York: Academic Press.

Stephan, F. F. (1952). The relative rate of communication between members of small groups. *American Sociological Review, 17,* 482–486.

Stephan, W. G. (1987). The contact hypothesis in intergroup relations. In C. Hendrick (Ed.), *Review of personality and social psychology: Group processes and intergroup relations* (Vol. 9, pp. 13–40). Thousand Oaks, CA: Sage.

Stephan, W. G., Diaz-Loving, R., & Duran, A. (2000). Integrated threat theory and intercultural attitudes: Mexico and the United States. *Journal of Cross-Cultural Psychology, 31,* 240–249.

Stephan, W. G., & Finlay, K. (1999). The role of empathy in improving intergroup relations. *Journal of Social Issues, 55,* 729–743.

Stephan, W. G., & Stephan, C. W. (1985). Intergroup anxiety. *Journal of Social Issues, 41,* 157–175.

Sternberg, R. J. (1986). A triangular theory of love. *Psychological Review, 93,* 119–135.

Sternberg, R. J., & Barnes, M. I. (1988). *The psychology of love.* New Haven, CT: Yale University Press.

Storms, M. D. (1973). Videotape and the attribution process: Reversing actors' and observers' points of view. *Journal of Personality and Social Psychology, 27,* 165–175.

Storms, M. D., & Nisbett, R. E. (1970). Insomnia and the attribution process. *Journal of Personality and Social Psychology, 16,* 319–328.

Stotland, E. (1969). Exploratory investigations of empathy. In L. Berkowitz (Ed.), *Advances in experimental social psychology* (Vol. 4, pp. 271–314). New York: Academic Press.

Strack, F., & Deutsch, R. (2004). Reflective and impulsive determinants of social behavior. *Personality and Social Psychology Review, 8,* 220–247.

Strauman, T. J. (1992). Self-guides, autobiographical memory, and anxiety and dysphoria: Toward a cognitive model of vulnerability to emotional distress. *Journal of Abnormal Psychology, 101,* 87–95.

Strauman, T. J., & Higgins, E. T. (1988). Self-discrepancies as predictors of vulnerability to distinct syndromes of chronic emotional distress. *Journal of Personality, 56,* 685–707.

Straus, M. A. (1979). Measuring intrafamily conflict and violence: The Conflict Tactics (CT) Scales. *Journal of Marriage and the Family, 41,* 75–88.

Straus, M. A., Hamby, S. L., Boney-McCoy, S., & Sugarman, D. B. (1996). The revised Conflict Tactics Scales (CTS2): Development and preliminary psychometric data. *Journal of Family Issues, 17,* 283–316.

Streater, S. A., & McBurney, D. H. (2003). Waist-hip ratio and attractiveness: New evidence and a critique of a 'critical' test. *Evolution and Human Behaviour, 24,* 88–98.

Strickland, L. H., Aboud, F. E., & Gergen, K. J. (Eds.). (1976). *Social psychology in transition.* New York: Plenum.

Stroebe, K., Lodewijkx, H. F. M., & Spears, R. (2005). Do unto others as they do unto you: Reciprocity and social identification as determinants of ingroup favoritism. *Personality and Social Psychology Bulletin, 31,* 831–845.

Stroebe, W. (2011). *Social psychology and health* (3rd ed.). Maidenhead, UK: Open University Press.

Stroebe, W. (2012). The truth about Triplett (1898), but nobody seems to care. *Perspectives on Psychological Science, 7*, 54–57.

Stroebe, W., & Diehl, M. (1981). Conformity and counterattitudinal behavior: The effect of social support on attitude change. *Journal of Personality and Social Psychology, 41*, 876–889.

Stroebe, W., & Diehl, M. (1988). When social support fails: Supporter characteristics in compliance-induced attitude change. *Personality and Social Psychology Bulletin, 14*, 136–144.

Stroebe, W., Diehl, M., & Abakoumkin, G. (1996). Social compensation and the Köhler effect: Toward a theoretical explanation of motivation gains in group productivity. In E. H. Witte & H. Davis (Eds.), *Understanding group behaviour: Small group processes and interpersonal relations* (Vol. 2, pp. 37–65). Hillsdale, NJ: Erlbaum.

Stroebe, W., Stroebe, M. S., & Domittner, G. (1988). Individual and situational differences in recovery from bereavement: A risk group identified. *Journal of Social Issues, 44*, 143–158.

Strube, M. J. (2005). What did Triplett really find? A contemporary analysis of the first experiment in social psychology. *American Journal of Psychology, 118*, 271–286.

Strube, M. J., Lott, C. L., Lê-Xuân-Hy, G. M., Oxenberg, J., & Deichmann, A. K. (1986). Self-evaluation of abilities: Accurate self-assessment versus biased self-enhancement. *Journal of Personality and Social Psychology, 51*, 16–25.

Strube, M. J., & Roemmele, L. A. (1985). Self-enhancement, self-assessment, and self-evaluative task choice. *Journal of Personality and Social Psychology, 49*, 981–993.

Stryker, S. (1980). *Symbolic interactionism: A social structural version*. Menlo Park, CA: Benjamin Cummings.

Stryker, S., & Vryan, K. D. (2003). The symbolic interactionist frame. In J. Delamater (Ed.), *Handbook of social psychology* (pp. 3–28). New York: Kluwer Academic/Plenum.

Stürmer, S., & Snyder, M. (Eds.). (2010). *The psychology of prosocial behavior: Group processes, intergroup relations, and helping*. Chichester, UK: Wiley-Blackwell.

Stürmer, S., Snyder, M., Kropp, A., & Siem, B. (2006). Empathy-motivated helping: The moderating role of group membership. *Personality and Social Psychology Bulletin, 32*, 943–956.

Stürmer, S., Snyder, M., & Omoto, A. M. (2005). Prosocial emotions and helping: The moderating role of group membership. *Journal of Personality and Social Psychology, 88*, 532–546.

Suls, J., Martin, R., & Wheeler, L. (2002). Social comparison: Why, with whom, and with what effect? *Current Directions in Psychological Science, 11*, 159–163.

Suls, J., & Wheeler, L. (Eds.). (2000). *Handbook of social comparison: Theory and research*. New York: Kluwer Academic/Plenum.

Sumpton, R., & Gregson, M. (1981). The fundamental attribution error: An investigation of sensitivity to role-conferred advantages in self-presentation. *British Journal of Social Psychology, 20*, 7–11.

Sunnafrank, M., & Ramirez, A. J. (2004). At first sight: Persistent relational effects of get-acquainted conversations. *Journal of Social and Personal Relationships, 21*, 361–379.

Sunstein, C. R. (2009). *Going to extremes: How like minds unite and divide*. New York: Oxford University Press.

Swami, V., & Furnham, A. (2008). *The psychology of physical attraction*. New York: Routledge.

Swann, W. B., Jr. (1984). Quest for accuracy in person perception: A matter of pragmatics. *Psychological Review, 9*, 457–477.

Swann, W. B., Jr., & Bosson, J. K. (2008). Identity negotiation: A theory of self and social interaction. In O. P. John, R. W. Robins, & L. A. Pervin (Eds.), *Handbook of personality: Theory and research* (3rd ed., pp. 448–471). New York: Guilford.

Swann, W. B., Jr., & Buhrmester, M. D. (2012). Self-verification: The search for coherence. In M. R. Leary & J. P. Tangney (Eds.), *Handbook of self and identity* (2nd ed., pp. 405–424). New York: Guilford.

Swann, W. B., Jr., Hixon, J. G., Stein-Seroussi, A., & Gilbert, D. T. (1990). The fleeting gleam of praise: Cognitive processes underlying behavioral reactions to self-relevant feedback. *Journal of Personality and Social Psychology, 59*, 17–26.

Swann, W. B., Jr., Johnson, R. E., & Bosson, J. K. (2009). Identity negotiation at work. In B. Staw, & A. Brief (Eds.), *Research in Organizational Behavior, Vol 29* (pp. 81–109). Amsterdam, The Netherlands: Elsevier.

Swann, W. B., Jr., Stein-Seroussi, A., & Giesler, R. B. (1992). Why people self-verify. *Journal of Personality and Social Psychology, 62*, 392–401.

Swart, H., Hewstone, M., Christ, O., & Voci, A. (2011). Affective mediators of intergroup contact: A three-wave longitudinal study in South Africa. *Journal of Personality and Social Psychology, 101*, 1221–1238.

Swartz, M., & Watkins, S. (2003). *Power failure: The inside story of the collapse of Enron*. New York: Doubleday.

Sy, T., Coté, S., & Saavedra, R. (2005). The contagious leader: Impact of the leader's mood on the mood of group members, group affective tone, and group processes. *Journal of Applied Psychology, 90*, 295–305.

't Hart, P. (1990). *Groupthink in government: A study of small groups and policy failure*. Lisse, NL: Swets & Zeitlinger.

't Hart, P., Stern, E., & Sundelius, B. (1997). *Beyond groupthink*. Ann Arbor, MI: University of Michigan Press.

Tafarodi, R. W., Lo, C., Yamaguchi, S., Lee, W. W.-S., & Katsura, H. (2004). The inner self in three countries. *Journal of Cross-Cultural Psychology, 35*, 97–117.

Tajfel, H. (1969). Cognitive aspects of prejudice. *Journal of Social Issues, 25*, 79–97.

Tajfel, H. (1978a). *Differentiation between social groups: Studies in the social psychology of intergroup relations*. New York: Academic Press.

Tajfel, H. (1978b). Social categorization, social identity and social comparison. In H. Tajfel (Ed.), *Differentiation between social groups* (pp. 61–76). London: Academic Press.

Tajfel, H. (1981). *Human groups and social categories: Studies in social psychology*. Cambridge, MA: Cambridge University Press.

Tajfel, H. (1982a). *Social identity and intergroup identifications*. Cambridge, UK: Cambridge University Press.

Tajfel, H. (1982b). Social psychology of intergroup relations. *Annual Review of Psychology, 33*, 1–39.

Tajfel, H., Billig, M. G., Bundy, R. P., & Flament, C. (1971). Social categorization and intergroup behaviour. *European Journal of Social Psychology, 1*, 149–178.

Tajfel, H., Jaspars, J. M. F., & Fraser, C. (1984). The social dimension in European social psychology. In H. Tajfel (Ed.), *The social dimension: European developments in social psychology* (Vol. 2, pp. 1–5). New York: Cambridge University Press.

Tajfel, H., & Turner, J. C. (1979). An integrative theory of intergroup conflict. In W. G. Austin & S. Worchel (Eds.), *The social psychology of intergroup relations* (pp. 33–47). Monterey, CA: Brooks Cole.

Tajfel, H., & Turner, J. C. (1986). The social identity theory of intergroup behavior. In S. Worchel & W. G. Austin (Eds.), *Psychology of intergroup relations* (pp. 7–24). Chicago, IL: Nelson-Hall.

Tajfel, H., & Turner, J. C. (2004). The social identity theory of intergroup behavior. In J. T. Jost & J. Sidanius (Eds.), *Key readings in social psychology: Political psychology* (pp. 276–293). New York: Psychology Press.

Tajfel, H., & Wilkes, A. L. (1963). Classification and quantitative judgement. *British Journal of Psychology, 54*, 101–114.

Talaska, C. A., Fiske, S. T., & Chaiken, S. (2008). Legitimating racial discrimination: Emotions, not beliefs, best predict discrimination in a meta-analysis. *Social Justice Research, 21*, 263–296.

Tam, T., Hewstone, M., Harwood, J., Voci, A., & Kenworthy, J. (2006). Intergroup contact and grandparent–grandchild communication: The effects of self-disclosure on implicit and explicit biases against older people. *Group Processes & Intergroup Relations, 9*, 413–429.

Tangney, J. P., Baumeister, R. F., & Boone, A. L. (2004). High self-control predicts good adjustment, less pathology, better grades, and interpersonal success. *Journal of Personality, 72*, 271–324.

Taubman Ben-Ari, O. (2000). The effect of reminders of death on reckless driving: A terror management perspective. *Current Directions in Psychological Science, 9*, 196–199.

Taubman Ben-Ari, O., Florian, V., & Mikulincer, M. (1999). The impact of mortality salience on reckless driving: A test of terror management mechanisms. *Journal of Personality and Social Psychology, 76*, 35–45.

Tausch, N., Becker, J. C., Spears, R., Christ, O., Saab, R., Singh, P., & Siddiqui, R. N. (2011). Explaining radical group behavior: Developing emotion and efficacy routes to normative and nonnormative collective action. *Journal of Personality and Social Psychology, 101*, 129–148.

Tausch, N., & Hewstone, M. (2010). Intergroup contact. In J. F. Dovidio, M. Hewstone, P. Glick, & V. M. Esses (Eds.), *Handbook of prejudice, stereotyping and discrimination* (pp. 544–560). London: Sage.

Tausch, N., Hewstone, M., Kenworthy, J. B., Psaltis, C., Schmid, K., Popan, J. R., … Hughes, J. (2010). Secondary transfer effects of intergroup contact: Alternative accounts and underlying processes. *Journal of Personality and Social Psychology, 99*, 282–302.

Taylor, D. A., Gould, R. J., & Brounstein, P. J. (1981). Effects of personalistic self-disclosure. *Personality and Social Psychology Bulletin, 7*, 487–492.

Taylor, S. E., & Brown, J. D. (1988). Illusion and well-being: A social psychological perspective on mental health. *Psychological Bulletin, 103*, 193–210.

Taylor, S. E., & Fiske, S. T. (1978). Salience, attention, and attribution: Top of the head phenomena. In L. Berkowitz (Ed.), *Advances in experimental social psychology* (Vol. 11, pp. 249–288). New York: Academic Press.

Taylor, S. E., Kemeny, M. E., Aspinwall, L. G., Schneider, S. G., Rodriguez, R., & Herbert, M. (1992). Optimism, coping, psychological distress, and high-risk sexual behavior among men at risk for acquired immunodeficiency syndrome (AIDS). *Journal of Personality and Social Psychology, 63*, 460–473.

Taylor, S. E., Kemeny, M. E., Reed, G. M., Bower, J. E., & Gruenewald, T. L. (2000). Psychological resources, positive illusions, and health. *American Psychologist, 55*, 99–109.

Taylor, S. E., Lerner, J. S., Sherman, D. K., Sage, R. M., & McDowell, N. K. (2003). Portrait of the self-enhancer: Well adjusted and well liked or maladjusted and friendless? *Journal of Personality and Social Psychology, 84*, 165–176.

Taylor, S. E., & Lobel, M. (1989). Social comparison activity under threat: Downward evaluation and upward contacts. *Psychological Review, 96*, 569–575.

Taylor, S. E., Wayment, H. A., & Carrillo, M. (1996). Social comparison, self-regulation, and motivation. In R. M. Sorrentino & E. T. Higgins (Eds.), *Handbook of motivation and cognition* (Vol. 3, pp. 3–27). New York: Guilford.

Tellis, G. J. (2004). *Effective advertising: Understanding when, how, and why advertising works*. Thousand Oaks, CA: Sage.

Temkin, J., & Krahé, B. (2008). *Sexual assault and the justice gap: A question of attitude*. Oxford: Hart.

Terry, D. J., & Hogg, M. A. (1996). Group norms and the attitude-behavior relationship: A role for group identification. *Personality and Social Psychology Bulletin, 22*, 776–793.

Tesser, A. (2000). On the confluence of self-esteem maintenance mechanisms. *Personality and Social Psychology Review, 4*, 290–299.

Tesser, A., Campbell, J., & Mickler, S. (1983). The role of social pressure, attention to the stimulus, and self-doubt in conformity. *European Journal of Social Psychology, 13*, 217–233.

Tetlock, P. E. (1979). Identifying victims of groupthink from public statements of decision makers. *Journal of Personality and Social Psychology, 37*, 1314–1324.

Tetlock, P. E. (1983). Accountability and complexity of thought. *Journal of Personality and Social Psychology, 45*, 74–83.

Tetlock, P. E. (1994). Political psychology or politicized psychology: Is the road to scientific hell paved with good moral intentions? *Political Psychology, 15*, 509–529.

Tetlock, P. E. (1998). Social psychology and world politics. In D. T. Gilbert, S. T. Fiske, & G. Lindzey (Eds.), *Handbook of social psychology* (4th ed., Vol. 2, pp. 868–912). Boston, MA: McGraw-Hill.

Tetlock, P. E. (2002). Social functionalist frameworks for judgment and choice: Intuitive politicians, theologians, and prosecutors. *Psychological Review, 109*, 451–471.

Tetlock, P. E., & Levi, A. (1982). Attribution bias: On the inconclusiveness of the cognition-motivation debate. *Journal of Experimental Social Psychology, 18*, 68–88.

Thibaut, J. W., & Kelley, H. H. (1959). *The social psychology of groups*. New York: Wiley.

Thompson, L. L., Levine, J. M., & Messick, D. M. (1999). *Shared cognition in organizations: The management of knowlege*. Mahwah, NJ: Erlbaum.

Thurstone, L. L. (1928). Attitudes can be measured. *American Journal of Sociology, 33*, 529–554.

Tice, D. M. (1991). Esteem protection or enhancement? Self-handicapping motives and attributions differ by trait self-esteem. *Journal of Personality and Social Psychology, 60*, 711–725.

Tice, D. M. (1992). Self-concept change and self-presentation: The looking glass self is also a magnifying glass. *Journal of Personality and Social Psychology, 63*, 435–451.

Tice, D. M., & Baumeister, R. F. (1990). Self-esteem, self handicapping, and self-presentation: The strategy of inadequate practice. *Journal of Personality, 58*, 443–464.

Tice, D. M., Butler, J. L., Muraven, M. B., & Stillwell, A. M. (1995). When modesty prevails: Differential favorability of self-presentation to friends and strangers. *Journal of Personality and Social Psychology, 69*, 1120–1138.

Tice, D. M., & Wallace, H. M. (2003). The reflected self: Creating yourself as (you think) others see you. In M. R. Leary & J. P. Tangney (Eds.), *Handbook of self and identity* (pp. 91–105). New York: Guilford.

Tiedens, L. Z., & Leach, C. W. (Eds.). (2004). *The social life of emotions*. Cambridge, MA: Cambridge University Press.

Tindale, R. S., & Davis, J. H. (1983). Group decision making and jury verdicts. In H. H. Blumberg, A. P. Hare, V. Kent, & M. F. Davies (Eds.), *Small groups and social interaction* (Vol. 2, pp. 9–38). Chichester, UK: Wiley.

Tindale, R. S., Davis, J. H., Vollrath, D. A., Nagao, D. H., & Hinsz, V. B. (1990). Asymmetrical social influence in freely interacting groups: A test of three models. *Journal of Personality and Social Psychology, 58*, 438–449.

Tindale, R. S., & Kameda, T. (2000). Social sharedness as a unifying theme for information processing in groups. *Group Processes & Intergroup Relations, 3*, 123–140.

Toffler, B. L., & Reingold, J. (2003). *Financial accounting: Ambition, greed, and the fall of Arthur Andersen*. New York: Broadway.

Toma, C. L., Hancock, J. T., & Ellison, N. B. (2008). Separating fact from fiction: An examination of deceptive self-presentation in online dating profiles. *Personality and Social Psychology Bulletin, 34*, 1023–1036.

Tooby, J., & Cosmides, L. (1989). The innate versus the manifest: How universal does universal have to be? *Behavioral and Brain Sciences, 12*, 36–37.

Torrance, E. P. (1954). The behavior of small groups under the stress conditions of 'survival'. *American Sociological Review, 19*, 751–755.

Tovée, M. J., Tasker, K., & Benson, P. J. (2000). Is symmetry a visual cue to attractiveness in the human female body? *Evolution and Human Behavior, 21*, 191–200.

Trafimow, D., Silverman, E. S., Fan, R. M.-T., & Law, J. S. F. (1997). The effects of language and priming on the relative accessibility of the private self and the collective self. *Journal of Cross-Cultural Psychology, 28*, 107–123.

Trafimow, D., Triandis, H. C., & Goto, S. G. (1991). Some tests of the distinction between the private self and the collective self. *Journal of Personality and Social Psychology, 60*, 649–655.

Triandis, H. C. (1972). *The analysis of subjective culture*. New York: Wiley.

Triandis, H. C. (1989). The self and social behavior in differing cultural contexts. *Psychological Review, 96*, 506–520.

Triandis, H. C. (1995). *Individualism and collectivism*. Boulder, CO: Westview.

Triplett, N. D. (1898). The dynamogenic factors in pacemaking and competition. *American Journal of Psychology, 9*, 507–533.

Trivers, R. L. (1971). The evolution of reciprocal altruism. *Quarterly Review of Biology, 46*, 35–57.

Trope, Y. (1980). Self-assessment, self-enhancement, and task preference. *Journal of Experimental Social Psychology, 16*, 116–129.

Trope, Y. (1983). Self-assessment in achievement behavior. In J. M. Suls & A. G. Greenwald (Eds.), *Psychological perspectives on the self* (Vol. 2, pp. 93–121). Hillsdale, NJ: Erlbaum.

Trope, Y. (1986). Self-enhancement and self-assessment in achievement motivation. In R. M. Sorrentino & E. T. Higgins (Eds.), *Handbook of motivation and cognition: Foundations of social behavior* (Vol. 1, pp. 350–378). New York: Guilford.

Trope, Y., & Gaunt, R. (2000). Processing alternative explanations of behavior: Correction or integration? *Journal of Personality and Social Psychology, 79,* 344–354.

Tropp, L. R., & Pettigrew, T. F. (2005). Differential relationships between intergroup contact and affective and cognitive dimensions of prejudice. *Personality and Social Psychology Bulletin, 31,* 1145–1158.

Tsapelas, I., Aron, A., & Orbuch, T. (2009). Marital boredom now predicts less satisfaction 9 years later. *Psychological Science, 20,* 543–545.

Tucker, J. A., Vuchinich, R. E., & Sobell, M. B. (1981). Alcohol consumption as a self-handicapping strategy. *Journal of Abnormal Psychology, 90,* 220–230.

Tuckman, B. W. (1965). Developmental sequence in small groups. *Psychological Bulletin, 63,* 384–399.

Tuckman, B. W., & Jensen, M. A. (1977). Stages of small-group development revisited. *Group and Organization Studies, 2,* 419–427.

Turner, J. C. (1985). Social categorization and the self-concept: A social cognitive theory of group behavior. In E. J. Lawler (Ed.), *Advances in group processes: Theory and research* (Vol. 2, pp. 77–122). Greenwich, CT: JAI Press.

Turner, J. C. (1991). *Social influence.* Buckingham, UK: Open University Press.

Turner, J. C. (1999). Some current issues in research on social identity and self-categorization theories. In N. Ellemers, R. Spears, & B. Doosje (Eds.), *Social identity: Context, commitment, content* (pp. 6–34). Oxford: Blackwell.

Turner, J. C., Hogg, M. A., Oakes, P. J., Reicher, S. D., & Wetherell, M. S. (1987). *Rediscovering the social group: A self-categorization theory.* Oxford: Blackwell.

Turner, J. C., & Reynolds, K. J. (2011). Self-categorization theory. In P. A. M. Van Lange, A. Kruglanski, & E. T. Higgins (Eds.), *Handbook of theories in social psychology* (Vol. 2, pp. 399–418). London: Sage.

Turner, J. C., & Tajfel, H. (1986). The social identity theory of intergroup behavior. In S. Worchel & W. G. Austin (Eds.), *Psychology of intergroup relations* (pp. 7–24). Chicago: Nelson-Hall.

Turner, J. C., Wetherell, M. S., & Hogg, M. A. (1989). Referent informational influence and group polarization. *British Journal of Social Psychology, 28,* 135–147.

Turner, M. E. (2001). *Groups at work: Theory and research.* Mahwah, NJ: Erlbaum.

Turner, M. E., Pratkanis, A. R., Probasco, P., & Leve, C. (1992). Threat, cohesion, and group effectiveness: Testing a social identity maintenance perspective on groupthink. *Journal of Personality and Social Psychology, 63,* 781–796.

Turner, R. N., Hewstone, M., Voci, A., & Vonofakou, C. (2008). A test of the extended intergroup contact hypothesis: The mediating role of intergroup anxiety, perceived ingroup and outgroup norms, and inclusion of the outgroup in the self. *Journal of Personality and Social Psychology, 95,* 843–860.

Tversky, A., & Kahneman, D. (1973). Availability: A heuristic for judging frequency and probability. *Cognitive Psychology, 5,* 207–232.

Tversky, A., & Kahneman, D. (1974). Judgment under uncertainty: Heuristics and biases. *Science, 185,* 1124–1131.

Twenge, J. M., Baumeister, R. F., DeWall, C. N., Ciarocco, N. J., & Bartels, J. M. (2007). Social exclusion decreases prosocial behavior. *Journal of Personality and Social Psychology, 92,* 56–66.

Twenge, J. M., & Campbell, W. K. (2003). 'Isn't it fun to get the respect that we're going to deserve?' Narcissism, social rejection, and aggression. *Personality and Social Psychology Bulletin, 29,* 261–272.

Twenge, J. M., Catanese, K. R., & Baumeister, R. F. (2003). Social exclusion and the deconstructed state: Time perception, meaninglessness, lethargy, lack of emotion, and self-awareness. *Journal of Personality and Social Psychology, 85,* 409–423.

USDHEW (US Department of Health Education and Welfare). (1964). *Smoking and health: A report of the Surgeon General.* Washington, DC: US Government Printing Office.

Uskul, A. K., Kitayama, S., & Nisbett, R. E. (2008). Ecocultural basis of cognition: Farmers and fishermen are more holistic than herders. *Proceedings of the National Academy of Science, 105,* 8552–8556.

Valkenburg, P. M., & Peter, J. (2007). Preadolescents' and adolescents' online communication and their closeness to friends. *Developmental Psychology, 43,* 267–277.

Valkenburg, P. M., & Peter, J. (2009). Social consequences of the Internet for adolescents. *Current Directions in Psychological Science, 18,* 1–5.

Vallacher, R. R., & Wegner, D. M. (1987). What do people think they're doing? Action identification and human behavior. *Psychological Review, 94,* 3–15.

Van de Vliert, E., Huang, X., & Levine, R. V. (2004). National wealth and thermal climate as predictors of motives for volunteer work. *Journal of Cross-Cultural Psychology, 35,* 62–73.

Van den Bos, K., & Lind, E. A. (2002). Uncertainty management by means of fairness judgments. In M. P. Zanna (Ed.), *Advances in experimental social psychology* (Vol. 34, pp. 1–60). San Diego, CA: Academic Press.

Van Ginkel, W. P., & Van Knippenberg, D. (2008). Group information elaboration and group decision making: The role of shared task representations. *Organizational Behavior and Human Decision Processes, 105,* 82–97.

Van Goozen, S. H. M. (2005). Hormones and the developmental origins of aggression. In R. E. Tremblay, W. W. Hartup, & J. Archer (Eds.), *Developmental origins of aggression* (pp. 281–306). New York: Guilford.

Van Hiel, A., Hautman, L., Cornelis, I., & De Clercq, B. (2007). Football hooliganism: Comparing self-awareness and social identity theory explanations. *Journal of Community and Applied Social Psychology, 17*, 169–186.

Van Horn, K. R., Arnone, A., Nesbitt, K., Desilets, L., Sears, T., Griffin, M., & Brudi, R. (1997). Physical distance and interpersonal characteristics in college students' romantic relationships. *Personal Relationships, 4*, 25–34.

Van Knippenberg, D. (2000). Work motivation and performance: A social identity perspective. *Applied Psychology: An International Review, 49*, 357–371.

Van Knippenberg, D., & Ellemers, N. (2003). Social identity and group performance: Identification as the key to group-oriented efforts. In S. A. Haslam, D. Van Knippenberg, M. J. Platow, & N. Ellemers (Eds.), *Social identity at work: Developing theory for organizational practice* (pp. 29–42). New York: Psychology Press.

Van Knippenberg, D., Lossie, N., & Wilke, H. (1994). In group prototypicality and persuasion: Determinants of heuristic and systematic message processing. *British Journal of Social Psychology, 33*, 289–300.

Van Laar, C., Levin, S., Sinclair, S., & Sidanius, J. (2005). The effect of university roommate contact on ethnic attitudes and behavior. *Journal of Experimental Social Psychology, 41*, 329–345.

Van Lange, P. A. M., Rusbult, C. E., Drigotas, S. M., Arriaga, X. B., Witcher, B. S., & Cox, C. L. (1997). Willingness to sacrifice in close relationships. *Journal of Personality and Social Psychology, 72*, 1373–1395.

Van Leeuwen, E. (2000). *Unpublished lecture slides*.

Van Oudenhoven, J. P., Groenewoud, J. T., & Hewstone, M. (1996). Cooperation, ethnic salience and generalization of interethnic attitudes. *European Journal of Social Psychology, 26*, 649–661.

Van Oudenhoven, J. P., Prins, K. S., & Buunk, B. P. (1998). Attitudes of minority and majority members towards adaptation of immigrants. *European Journal of Social Psychology, 28*, 995–1013.

Van Overwalle, F. (2009). Social cognition and the brain: A meta-analysis. *Human Brain Mapping, 30*, 829–858.

Van Vugt, M., & Hart, C. M. (2004). Social identity as social glue: The origins of group loyalty. *Journal of Personality and Social Psychology, 86*, 585–598.

Van Yperen, N. W., & Buunk, B. P. (1990). A longitudinal study of equity and satisfaction in intimate relationships. *European Journal of Social Psychology, 20*, 287–309.

Vanberg, V. (1975). *Die zwei Soziologien [The two sociologies]*. Tübingen, Germany: Mohr.

Vanman, E. J., Saltz, J. L., Nathan, L. R., & Warren, J. A. (2004). Racial discrimination by low-prejudiced Whites: Facial movements as implicit measures of attitudes related to behavior. *Psychological Science, 15*, 711–714.

Vasquez, E. A., Denson, T. F., Pedersen, W. C., Stenstrom, D. M., & Miller, N. (2005). The moderating effect of trigger intensity on triggered displaced aggression. *Journal of Experimental Social Psychology, 41*, 61–67.

Vasquez, E. A., Lickel, B., & Hennigan, K. (2010). Gangs, displaced, and group-based aggression. *Aggression and Violent Behavior, 15*, 130–140.

Veltkamp, M., Aarts, H., & Custers, R. (2009). Unravelling the motivational yarn: A framework for understanding the instigation of implicitly motivated behaviour resulting from deprivation and positive affect. *European Journal of Social Psychology, 20*, 345–381.

Verkuyten, M., & Masson, K. (1996). Culture and gender differences in the perception of friendship by adolescents. *International Journal of Psychology, 31*, 207–217.

Verkuyten, M., & Pouliasi, K. (2002). Biculturalism among older children: Cultural frame switching, attributions, self-identification, and attitudes. *Journal of Cross-Cultural Psychology, 33*, 596–609.

Verona, E., & Sullivan, E. A. (2008). Emotional catharsis and aggression revisited: Heart rate reduction following aggressive responding. *Emotion, 8*, 331–340.

Verplanken, B. (2006). Beyond frequency: Habit as mental construct. *British Journal of Social Psychology, 45*, 639–656.

Verplanken, B., Aarts, H., Van Knippenberg, A., & Moonen, A. (1998). Habit versus planned behaviour: A field experiment. *British Journal of Social Psychology, 37*, 111–128.

Verplanken, B., & Orbell, S. (2003). Reflections on past behavior: A self-report index of habit strength. *Journal of Applied Social Psychology, 33*, 1313–1330.

Verwijmeren, T., Karremans, J. C., Stroebe, W., & Wigboldus, D. (2011). The working limits of subliminal advertising: The role of habits. *Journal of Consumer Psychology, 21*, 206–213.

Verwijmeren, T., Karremans, J. C., Stroebe, W., Wigboldus, D., & Van Ooijen, I. (2010). *Vicary's victory: Subliminal ads in movies affect brand choice*. Unpublished manuscript, Radboud University of Nijmegen, Netherlands.

Victoroff, J., & Kruglanski, A. W. (Eds.). (2009). *Psychology of terrorism*. New York: Psychology Press.

Vieth, A. Z., Strauman, T. J., Kolden, G. G., Woods, T. E., Michels, J. L., & Klein, M. H. (2003). Self-system therapy (SST): A theory based psychotherapy for depression. *Clinical Psychology: Science and Practice, 10*, 245–268.

Vinokur, A., & Burnstein, E. (1974). Effects of partially shared persuasive arguments on group-induced shifts: A group-problem-solving approach. *Journal of Personality and Social Psychology, 29*, 305–315.

Vinokur, A., & Burnstein, E. (1978). Novel argumentation and attitude change: The case of polarization following group discussion. *European Journal of Social Psychology, 8*, 335–348.

Visser, P. S., & Krosnick, J. A. (1998). Development of attitude strength over the life cycle: Surge and decline. *Journal of Personality and Social Psychology, 75*, 1389–1410.

Visser, P. S., Krosnick, J. A., & Lavrakas, P. (2000). Survey research. In H. T. Reis & C. M. Judd (Eds.), *Handbook of research methods in social psychology* (pp. 223–252). New York: Cambridge University Press.

Vohs, K. D., & Finkel, E. J. (Eds.). (2006). *Self and relationships: Connecting intrapersonal and interpersonal processes*. New York: Guilford.

Vohs, K. D., & Heatherton, T. F. (2000). Self-regulatory failure: A resource-depletion approach. *Psychological Science, 11*, 249–254.

Volz, K. G., Kessler, T., & Von Cramon, D. Y. (2009). In-group as part of the self: In-group favoritism is mediated by medial prefrontal cortex activation. *Social Neuroscience, 4*, 244–260.

Vonofakou, C., Hewstone, M., & Voci, A. (2007). Contact with out-group friends as a predictor of meta-attitudinal strength and accessibility of attitudes toward gay men. *Journal of Personality and Social Psychology, 92*, 804–820.

Vroom, V. H., & Jago, A. G. (1988). *The new leadership*. Englewood Cliffs, NJ: Prentice Hall.

Wageman, R. (2001). How leaders foster self-managing team effectiveness: Design choices versus hands-on coaching. *Organization Science, 12*, 559–577.

Wagner, U., & Zick, A. (1995). The relation of formal education to ethnic prejudice: Its reliability, validity and explanation. *European Journal of Social Psychology, 25*, 41–56.

Waldzus, S., Mummendey, A., Wenzel, M., & Boettcher, F. (2004). Of bikers, teachers and Germans: Groups' diverging views about their prototypicality. *British Journal of Social Psychology, 43*, 385–400.

Walker, A., Flatley, J., Kershaw, C., & Moon, D. (2009). *Crime in England and Wales 2008/09* (Vol. 1). Retrieved February 28, 2012, from http://webarchive.nationalarchives.gov.uk/20110218135832/http://rds.homeoffice.gov.uk/rds/pdfs09/hosb1109vol1.pdf

Wallace, H. M., & Baumeister, R. F. (2002). The performance of narcissists rises and falls with perceived opportunity for glory. *Journal of Personality and Social Psychology, 82*, 819–834.

Waller, B. M., Hope, L., Burrowes, N., & Morrison, E. R. (2011). Twelve (not so) angry men: Managing conversational group size increases perceived contribution by decision makers. *Group Processes & Intergroup Relations, 14*, 835–843.

Waller, J. (2002). *Becoming evil: How ordinary people commit genocide and mass murder*. Oxford: Oxford University Press.

Waller, P. F. (2002). Challenges in motor vehicle safety. *Annual Review of Public Health, 23*, 93–113.

Walster, E., Aronson, V., Abrahams, D., & Rottmann, L. (1966). Importance of physical attractiveness in dating behavior. *Journal of Personality and Social Psychology, 4*, 508–516.

Wan, E. W., & Sternthal, B. (2008). Regulating the effects of depletion through monitoring. *Personality and Social Psychology Bulletin, 34*, 32–46.

Wang, Q., & Conway, M. A. (2004). The stories we keep: Autobiographical memory in American and Chinese middle-aged adults. *Journal of Personality, 72*, 911–938.

Ward, C. A., Bochner, S., & Furnham, A. (2001). *The psychology of culture shock* (2nd ed.). Hove, UK: Routledge.

Waters, H., Hyder, A., Rajkotia, Y., Basu, S., Rehwinkel, J. A., & Butchart, A. (2004). The economic dimensions of interpersonal violence Retrieved October 29, 2010, from http://whqlibdoc.who.int/publications/2004/9241591609.pdf

Weary, G., Harvey, J. H., Schwieger, P., Olson, C. T., Perloff, R., & Pritchard, S. (1982). Self-presentation and the moderation of self-serving attributional biases. *Social Cognition, 1*, 140–159.

Webb, E. J., Campbell, D. T., Schwartz, R. D., & Sechrest, L. (2000). *Unobtrusive measures*. Thousand Oaks, CA: Sage.

Weber, R., & Crocker, J. (1983). Cognitive processes in the revision of stereotypic beliefs. *Journal of Personality and Social Psychology, 45*, 961–977.

Webster, D. M., & Kruglanski, A. W. (1994). Individual differences in need for cognitive closure. *Journal of Personality and Social Psychology, 67*, 1049–1062.

Weeden, J., & Sabini, J. (2005). Physical attractiveness and health in Western societies: A review. *Psychological Bulletin, 131*, 635–653.

Wegener, D. T., Petty, R. E., & Smith, E. R. (1995). Positive mood can increase or decrease message scrutiny: The hedonic contingency view of mood and message processing. *Journal of Personality and Social Psychology, 69*, 5–15.

Wegner, D. M. (1987). Transactive memory: A contemporary analysis of the group mind. In B. Mullen & G. R. Goethals (Eds.), *Theories of group behavior* (pp. 185–208). New York: Springer.

Wegner, D. M. (1994). Ironic processes of mental control. *Psychological Review, 101*, 34–52.

Weick, K. E. (1985). Systematic observational methods. In G. Lindzey & E. Aronson (Eds.), *Handbook of social psychology* (3rd ed., Vol. 1, pp. 567–634). New York: Random House.

Weigel, R. H., & Newman, L. S. (1976). Increasing attitude-behavior correspondence by broadening the scope of the behavioral measure. *Journal of Personality and Social Psychology, 33*, 793–802.

Weiner, B. (1979). A theory of motivation for some classroom experiences. *Journal of Educational Psychology, 71*, 3–25.

Weiner, B. (1985). An attributional theory of achievement motivation and emotion. *Psychological Review, 92*, 548–573.

Weiner, B. (1986). *An attributional theory of motivation and emotion*. New York: Springer.

Weiner, B. (2006). *Social motivation, justice, and the moral emotions: An attributional approach*. Mahwah, NJ: Erlbaum.

Weisband, S. (2002). Maintaining awareness in distributed team collaboration: Implications for leadership and performance. In P. Hinds & S. Kiesler (Eds.), *Distributed work* (pp. 311–333). Cambridge, MA: MIT Press.

Wells, G. L., & Petty, R. E. (1980). The effects of overt head movements on persuasion: Compatibility and incompatibility of responses. *Basic and Applied Social Psychology, 1*, 219–230.

Wells, S., & Graham, K. (1999). Frequency of third-party involvement in incidents of barroom aggression. *Contemporary Drug Problems, 26*, 457–480.

West, S. G., Biesanz, J. C., & Pitts, S. C. (2000). Causal inference and generalization in field settings. In H. Reis & C. M. Judd (Eds.), *Handbook of research methods in social and personality psychology* (pp. 40–84). Cambridge, UK: Cambridge University Press.

Wetherell, M. (1982). Cross-cultural studies of minimal groups: Implications for the social identity theory of intergroup relations. In H. Tajfel (Ed.), *Social identity and intergroup relations* (pp. 207–240). Cambridge, MA: Cambridge University Press.

Wetherell, M., Stiven, H., & Potter, J. (1987). Unequal egalitarianism: A preliminary study of discourses concerning gender and employment opportunities. *British Journal of Social Psychology, 26*, 59–71.

Wheelan, S. A. (1994). *Group process: A developmental perspective*. Boston, MA: Allyn & Bacon.

Wheelan, S. A., Davidson, B., & Tilin, F. (2003). Group development across time: Reality or illusion? *Small Group Research, 34*, 223–245.

White, M. J., Brockett, D. R., & Overstreet, B. G. (1993). Confirmatory bias in evaluating personality test information: Am I really that kind of person? *Journal of Counseling Psychology, 40*, 120–126.

White, P. A. (1984). A model of the layperson as pragmatist. *Personality and Social Psychology Bulletin, 10*, 333–348.

White, P. A. (1989). A theory of causal processing. *British Journal of Social Psychology, 80*, 431–454.

White, P. A. (2009). Property transmission: An explanatory account of the role of similarity information in causal inference. *Psychological Bulletin, 135*, 774–793.

White, R., & Lippitt, R. (1968). Leader behavior and member reaction in three 'social climates'. In D. Cartwright & A. Zander (Eds.), *Group dynamics: Research and theory* (3rd ed., pp. 318–335). New York: Harper & Row.

Wicker, A. W. (1969). Attitudes versus actions: The relationship of verbal and overt behavioral responses to attitude objects. *Journal of Social Issues, 25*, 41–78.

Wicklund, R. A., & Gollwitzer, P. M. (1982). *Symbolic self-completion*. Hillsdale, NJ: Erlbaum.

Wiederman, M. W. (1993). Evolved gender differences in mate preferences: Evidence from personal advertisements. *Ethology and Sociobiology, 14*, 331–351.

Wienke, C., & Hill, G. J. (2009). Does the 'marriage benefit' extend to partners in gay and lesbian relationships?: Evidence from a random sample of sexually active adults. *Journal of Family Issues, 30*, 259–289.

Wieselquist, J., Rusbult, C. E., Foster, C. A., & Agnew, C. R. (1999). Commitment, pro-relationship behavior, and trust in close relationships. *Journal of Personality and Social Psychology, 77*, 942–966.

Wiesenthal, D. L., Hennessy, D. A., & Totten, B. (2000). The influence of music on driver stress. *Journal of Applied Social Psychology, 30*, 1709–1719.

Wilder, D. A. (1977). Perception of groups, size of opposition, and social influence. *Journal of Experimental Social Psychology, 13*, 253–268.

Wilder, D. A. (1984). Intergroup contact: The typical member and the exception to the rule. *Journal of Experimental Social Psychology, 20*, 177–194.

Wilder, D. A., & Shapiro, P. N. (1989). Role of competition-induced anxiety in limiting the beneficial impact of positive behavior by an out-group member. *Journal of Personality and Social Psychology, 56*, 60–69.

Williams, H. L., Conway, M. A., & Cohen, G. (2008). Autobiographical memory. In G. Cohen & M. A. Conway (Eds.), *Memory in the real world* (pp. 21–90). New York: Psychology Press.

Williams, K. D. (2001). *Ostracism: The power of silence*. New York: Guilford.

Williams, K. D., Cheung, C. K. T., & Choi, W. (2000). CyberOstracism: Effects of being ignored over the Internet. *Journal of Personality and Social Psychology, 79*, 748–762.

Williams, K. D., & Karau, S. J. (1991). Social loafing and social compensation: The effects of expectations of co-worker performance. *Journal of Personality and Social Psychology, 61*, 570–581.

Williams, R. B., Barefoot, J. C., Califf, R, M., Haney, T. L., Saunders, W. B., Pryor, D. B., ... Mark, D. B. (1992). Prognostic importance of social and economic resources among medically treated patients with angiographically documented coronary artery disease. *Journal of the American Medical Association, 267*, 520–524.

Williams, R. M., Jr. (1947). The reduction of intergroup tensions: A survey of research on problems of ethnic, racial, and religious group relations. *Social Science Research Council Bulletin, 57*, 153.

Wilner, D. M., Walkley, R. P., & Cook, S. W. (1955). *Human relations in interracial housing*. Minneapolis, MN: University of Minnesota Press.

Wilson, A. M. (2002). Attitudes towards customer satisfaction measurement in the retail sector. *International Journal of Market Research, 44*, 213–222.

Wilson, J. (2000). Volunteering. *Annual Review of Sociology, 26,* 215–240.

Wilson, T. D. (2002). *Strangers to ourselves: Discovering the adaptive unconscious.* Cambridge, MA: Harvard University Press.

Wilson, T. D., & Brekke, N. (1994). Mental contamination and mental correction: Unwanted influences on judgments and evaluations. *Psychological Bulletin, 116,* 117–142.

Wilson, T. D., & Dunn, E. W. (2004). Self-knowledge: Its limits, value, and potential for improvement. *Annual Reviews of Psychology, 55,* 493–518.

Wilson, T. D., & Gilbert, D. T. (2003). Affective forecasting. In M. P. Zanna (Ed.), *Advances in experimental social psychology* (Vol. 35, pp. 345–411). San Diego, CA: Academic Press.

Wilson, T. D., Lindsey, S., & Schooler, T. Y. (2000). A model of dual attitudes. *Psychological Review, 107,* 101–126.

Wilson, T. D., & Nisbett, R. E. (1978). The accuracy of verbal reports about the effects of stimuli on evaluations and behavior. *Social Psychology, 41,* 118–131.

Winter, D. G. (1987). Leader appeal, leader performance, and the motives profile of leaders and followers: A study of American presidents and elections. *Journal of Personality and Social Psychology, 52,* 196–202.

Winter, D. G., & Stewart, A. J. (1977). Power motive reliability as a function of retest instructions. *Journal of Consulting and Clinical Psychology, 45,* 436–440.

Winter, L., & Uleman, J. S. (1984). When are social judgments made? Evidence for the spontaneousness of trait inferences. *Journal of Personality and Social Psychology, 47,* 237–252.

Wiseman, J. P. (1986). Friendship: Bonds and binds in a voluntary relationship. *Journal of Social and Personal Relationships, 3,* 191–211.

Witte, E. H. (1989). Köhler rediscovered: The anti-Ringelmann effect. *European Journal of Social Psychology, 19,* 147–154.

Witte, E. H., & Davis, J. H. (Eds.). (1996). *Understanding group behavior* (Vol. 1 and 2). Mahwah, NJ: Erlbaum.

Wittenbaum, G. M., Hubbell, A. P., & Zuckerman, C. (1999). Mutual enhancement: Toward an understanding of the collective preference for shared information. *Journal of Personality and Social Psychology, 77,* 967–978.

Wittenbrink, B., Judd, C. M., & Park, B. (1997). Evidence for racial prejudice at the implicit level and its relationship with questionnaire measures. *Journal of Personality and Social Psychology, 72,* 262–274.

Wittenbrink, B., & Schwarz, N. (Eds.). (2007). *Implicit measures of attitudes.* New York: Guilford.

Wofford, J. C., & Liska, L. Z. (1993). Path-goal theories of leadership: A meta-analysis. *Journal of Management, 19,* 857–876.

Wood, J. V. (1989). Theory and research concerning social comparisons of personal attributes. *Psychological Bulletin, 106,* 231–248.

Wood, W., Lundgren, S., Ouellette, J. A., Busceme, S., & Blackstone, T. (1994). Minority influence: A meta-analytic review of social influence processes. *Psychological Bulletin, 115,* 323–345.

Worchel, S., Andreoli, V. A., & Folger, R. (1977). Intergroup cooperation and intergroup attraction: The effect of previous interaction and outcome of combined effort. *Journal of Experimental Social Psychology, 13,* 131–140.

Wright, E. F., Voyer, D., Wright, R. D., & Roney, C. (1995). Supporting audiences and performance under pressure: The home-ice disadvantage in hockey championships. *Journal of Sport Behaviour, 18,* 21–28.

Wright, E. F., & Wells, G. L. (1988). Is the attitude-attribution paradigm suitable for investigating the dispositional bias? *Personality and Social Psychology Bulletin, 14,* 183–190.

Wright, S. C., Aron, A., McLaughlin-Volpe, T., & Ropp, S. A. (1997). The extended contact effect: Knowledge of cross-group friendships and prejudice. *Journal of Personality and Social Psychology, 73,* 73–90.

Wright, S. C., & Lubensky, M. E. (2009). The struggle for social equality: Collective action versus prejudice reduction. In S. Demoulin, J.-P. Leyens, & J. F. Dovidio (Eds.), *Intergroup misunderstandings: Impact of divergent social realities* (pp. 291–310). New York: Psychology Press.

Wright, S. C., Taylor, D. M., & Moghaddam, F. M. (1990). Responding to membership in a disadvantaged group: From acceptance to collective protest. *Journal of Personality and Social Psychology, 58,* 994–1003.

Wrosch, C., & Miller, G. E. (2009). Depressive symptoms can be useful: Self-regulatory and emotional benefits of dysphoric mood in adolescence. *Journal of Personality and Social Psychology, 96,* 1181–1190.

Wundt, W. (1911–1912). *Völkerpsychologie: Eine Untersuchung der Entwicklungsgesetze von Sprache, Mythus und Sitte [Ethnopsychology: An investigation into the laws of development of language, myth, and custom]* (3rd ed. Vol. 2). Leipzig, Germany: Engelmann.

Wyer, N. A. (2007). Motivational influences on compliance with and consequences of instructions to suppress stereotypes. *Journal of Experimental Social Psychology, 43,* 417–424.

Wyer, R. S., Jr., & Frey, D. (1983). The effects of feedback about self and others on the recall and judgments of feedback-relevant information. *Journal of Experimental Social Psychology, 19,* 540–559.

Yamagishi, T., & Kiyonari, T. (2000). The group as the container of generalized reciprocity. *Social Psychology Quarterly, 63,* 116–132.

Yamaguchi, S., Greenwald, A. G., Banaji, M. R., Murakami, F., Chen, D., Shiomura, K., … Krendl, A. (2007). Apparent universality of positive implicit self-esteem. *Psychological Science, 18,* 498–500.

Young, A. W., & Leafhead, K. M. (1996). Betwixt life and death: Case studies of the Cotard delusion. In P. W. Halligan & J. C. Marshall (Eds.), *Method in madness: Case studies in cognitive neuropsychiatry* (pp. 147–171). Hove, UK: Psychology Press.

Yukl, G. A. (2012). *Leadership in organizations* (8th ed.). Upper Saddle River, NJ: Prentice Hall.

Yzerbyt, V., & Kuppens, T. (2009). Group-based emotions: The social heart in the individual head. In S. Otten, K. Sassenberg, & T. Kessler (Eds.), *Intergroup relations: The role of motivation and emotion* (pp. 143–161). Hove, UK: Psychology Press.

Yzerbyt, V., Rocher, S., & Schadron, G. (1997). Stereotypes as explanations: A subjective essentialistic view of group perception. In R. Spears, P. J. Oakes, N. Ellemers, & S. A. Haslam (Eds.), *The social psychology of stereotyping and group life* (pp. 20–50). Oxford: Blackwell.

Zaadstra, B. M., Seidell, J. C., Van Noord, P. A., Te Velde, E. R., Habbema, J. D., Vrieswijk, B., & Karbaat, J. (1993). Fat and female fecundity: Prospective study of effect of body fat distribution on conception rates. *British Medical Journal, 306,* 484–487.

Zaccaro, S. J., Rittman, A. L., & Marks, M. A. (2001). Team leadership. *Leadership Quarterly, 12,* 451–483.

Zajonc, R. B. (1965). Social facilitation. *Science, 149,* 269–274.

Zajonc, R. B. (1968). Attitudinal effects of mere exposure. *Journal of Personality and Social Psychology, 9,* 1–27.

Zajonc, R. B. (1980). Compresence. In P. B. Paulus (Ed.), *Psychology of group influence* (pp. 35–60). Hillsdale, NJ: Erlbaum.

Zajonc, R. B. (1998). Emotions. In D. T. Gilbert, S. T. Fiske, & G. Lindzey (Eds.), *The handbook of social psychology* (4th ed., Vol. 2, pp. 591–632). Boston, MA: McGraw-Hill.

Zajonc, R. B., Heingartner, A., & Herman, E. M. (1969). Social enhancement and impairment of performance in the cockroach. *Journal of Personality and Social Psychology, 13,* 83–92.

Zanna, M. P., & Cooper, J. (1974). Dissonance and the pill: An attribution approach to studying the arousal properties of dissonance. *Journal of Personality and Social Psychology, 29,* 703–709.

Zanna, M. P., & Hamilton, D. L. (1972). Attribute dimensions and patterns of trait inferences. *Psychonomic Science, 27,* 353–354.

Zanna, M. P., Higgins, E. T., & Taves, P. A. (1976). Is dissonance phenomenologically aversive? *Journal of Experimental Social Psychology, 12,* 530–538.

Zanna, M. P., & Rempel, J. K. (1988). Attitudes: A new look at an old concept. In D. Bar-Tal & A. W. Kruglanski (Eds.), *The social psychology of knowledge* (pp. 315–334). Cambridge, UK: Cambridge University Press.

Zebrowitz, L. A. (1990). *Social perception.* Belmont, CA: Brooks.

Zhang, S., & Hunt, J. S. (2008). The stereotype rebound effect: Universal or culturally bounded process? *Journal of Experimental Social Psychology, 44,* 489–500.

Ziegler, R., Diehl, M., & Zijlstra, G. (2000). Idea production in nominal and virtual groups: Does computer-mediated communication improve group brainstorming? *Group Processes & Intergroup Relations, 3,* 141–158.

Zillmann, D. (1978). Attribution and misattribution of excitatory reactions. In J. H. Harvey, W. J. Ickes, & R. F. Kidd (Eds.), *New directions in attribution theory and research* (Vol. 2, pp. 335–368). Hillsdale, NJ: Erlbaum.

Zillmann, D., & Bryant, J. (1974). Effect of residual excitation on the emotional response to provocation and delayed aggressive behavior. *Journal of Personality and Social Psychology, 30,* 782–791.

Zimbardo, P. G. (1969). The human choice: Individuation, reason, and order versus deindividuation, impulse, and chaos. In W. T. Arnold & D. Levine (Eds.), *Nebraska Symposium on Motivation* (Vol. 17, pp. 237–307). Lincoln, NE: University of Nebraska Press.

Zimbardo, P. G. (2006). On rethinking the psychology of tyranny: The BBC prison study. *British Journal of Social Psychology, 45,* 47–53.

Zimbardo, P. G. (2007). *The Lucifer effect: Understanding how good people turn evil.* New York: Random House.

Zimbardo, P. G., Ebbesen, E. B., & Maslach, C. (1977). *Influencing attitudes and changing behavior* (2nd ed.). Reading, MA: Addison-Wesley.

Zimbardo, P. G., Maslach, C., & Haney, C. (2000). Reflections on the Stanford prison experiment: Genesis, transformations, consequences. In T. Blass (Ed.), *Obedience to authority: Current perspectives on the Milgram paradigm* (pp. 193–237). Mahwah, NJ: Erlbaum.

Zuckerman, M. (1979). Attribution of success and failure revisited, or: The motivational bias is alive and well in attribution theory. *Journal of Personality, 47,* 245–287.

Zuckerman, M., Kieffer, S. C., & Knee, C. R. (1998). Consequences of self-handicapping: Effects on coping, academic performance, and adjustment. *Journal of Personality and Social Psychology, 74,* 1619–1628.

Glossary

accentuation effect when (social) categories are correlated with a continuous dimension (e.g. skin colour, eye shape) there is a judgemental tendency to overestimate *similarities within*, and *differences between* the categories on this dimension.

accessibility the extent to which information is easily located and retrieved.

accountability a processing goal whereby perceivers believe they will have to justify their responses to a third party and be held responsible for their impressions; this typically leads to less stereotypical impressions.

acculturation the process whereby two cultural groups that come into contact with one another cause changes in one or both parties.

acquiescent responding a tendency for a respondent to agree with all items on scales measuring attitudes, beliefs or values, even those that contradict one another.

actor–observer difference proposed general tendency for people to explain their own behaviour in more situational terms, but other people's behaviour in more dispositional terms.

affective component of attitude the feelings or emotions associated with an attitude object.

aggression any form of behaviour intended to harm or injure another living being who is motivated to avoid such treatment.

Aggression Questionnaire (AQ) self-report instrument to measure stable individual differences in trait aggressiveness.

aggressive cues situational cues with an aggressive meaning that increase the accessibility of aggressive cognitions.

aggressive scripts cognitive representation of when and how to show aggressive behaviour.

altruism refers to behaviour carried out to benefit others without anticipation of external rewards; it is driven by exclusively empathic motivation.

analysis of non-common effects observers infer intentions behind actions by comparing the consequences of the behavioural options that were open to the actor and identifying distinctive outcomes.

anchoring/adjustment heuristic a cognitive heuristic that makes us place weight upon initial standards/schemas (anchors) and as a result means we may not always adjust sufficiently far from these anchors to provide accurate judgements.

arousal: cost–reward model suggests that observing an emergency creates a sense of arousal in the bystander, which becomes increasingly unpleasant. Bystander responds by considering costs and rewards of helping or not helping.

attachment theory the theory that proposes that the development of secure infant–caregiver attachment in childhood is the basis for the ability to maintain stable and intimate relationships in adulthood.

attitude an overall evaluation of a stimulus object.

attitude functions the psychological needs fulfilled by an attitude.

attitude–behaviour relation the degree to which an attitude predicts behaviour.

attitudinal ambivalence a state that occurs when an individual both likes and dislikes an attitude object.

attribution theories a group of theories about how individuals manage to infer the 'causes' underlying the behaviour of others, or even their own behaviour.

attributional biases systematic distortions in the sampling or processing of information about the causes of behaviour.

audience inhibition the experience of individual bystanders whose behaviour can be seen by other bystanders. In an emergency bystanders may fear embarrassment by their actions, resulting in lower likelihood of them helping.

augmenting principle the assumption that causal factors need to be stronger if an inhibitory influence on an observed effect is present. The converse of the discounting principle.

authoritarian personality a personality syndrome characterized by a simplistic cognitive style, a rigid regard for social conventions and submission to authority figures; such people are thought to be particularly prone to be prejudiced towards minority groups and receptive to Fascist ideas.

autokinetic effect perceptual illusion, whereby, in the absence of reference points, a stationary light appears to move.

automatic process a process that occurs without intention, effort or awareness and does not interfere with other concurrent cognitive processes.

availability heuristic a cognitive shortcut that allows us to draw upon information about how quickly information comes to mind about a particular event, to deduce the frequency or likelihood of that event.

averaging perceivers compute the (weighted or unweighted) mean value of pieces of information about a person; when other information is strongly positive, additional mildly positive information yields a less positive impression.

back-translation translation of a research questionnaire that has already been translated from one language to a second language back into the original language by a translator who has not seen the original version.

balance theory a cognitive consistency theory that assumes that individuals strive to maintain consistency or balance (objects or persons perceived as belonging together are evaluated similarly) in their social perceptions.

base rate information information that gives us an idea about how frequent certain categories are in the general population.

behavioural component of attitude past behaviours (also present and future anticipated behaviours) associated with an attitude object.

Bennington study a longitudinal field study of social influence on a college campus conducted by Newcomb. It maps out the way in which the political attitudes of initially conservative female students changed over time towards the liberal attitudes that were predominant on this college campus. Thus, it illustrates how individual beliefs and attitudes can be shaped by the group context.

better than average effect the finding that more than 50 per cent of participants report themselves to be better than average on a variety of criteria.

bicultural identity seeing oneself as having simultaneous membership of two culturally-distinct groups.

bicultural identity integration present when a person sees their alternate identities as compatible with one another.

brainstorming a group technique aimed at enhancing creativity in groups by means of the uninhibited generation of as many ideas as possible concerning a specified topic.

bullying (also known as *mobbing*) denotes aggressive behaviour directed at victims who cannot easily defend themselves, typically in schools and at the workplace.

bystander effect refers to the phenomenon whereby the likelihood of any one person helping in an emergency situation decreases as the number of other bystanders increases.

categorization the tendency to group objects (including people) into discrete groups based upon shared characteristics common to them.

catharsis release of aggressive tension through symbolic engagement in aggressive behaviour.

causal attribution the process whereby social perceivers arrive at conclusions about the causes of another person's behaviour.

causal power an intrinsic property of an object or event that enables it to exert influence on some other object or event.

causal schema knowledge structure shaping attributions. Causal schemas may be either abstract representations of general causal principles (e.g. multiple necessary and multiple sufficient causes schemas) or domain-specific ideas about cause and effect.

central route to persuasion a person's careful and thoughtful consideration of the arguments presented in support of a position.

central trait a dispositional characteristic viewed by social perceivers as integral to the organization of personality.

coefficient of relatedness (r) between two individuals can be calculated by knowing how many steps removed individuals are from a common ancestor (e.g. coefficients of relatedness between children–parents and grandchildren–grandparents are .5 and .25, respectively).

cognitive algebra a proposed process for averaging or summing trait information when forming impressions of other people.

cognitive component of attitude beliefs, thoughts and attributes associated with an attitude object.

cognitive dissonance an aversive state which motivates individuals to reduce it.

cognitive dissonance theory assumes that dissonance is an aversive state which motivates individuals to reduce it (e.g. by changing beliefs, attitudes or behaviour, and searching for consonant, or avoiding dissonant, information).

cognitive miser a view of people as being often limited in processing capacity and apt to take shortcuts where possible to make life simple.

cognitive neo-associationist model explains aggressive behaviour as the results of negative affect that is subjected to cognitive processing and activates a network of aggression-related thoughts and feelings.

cognitive response model assumes that attitude change is mediated by the thoughts, or 'cognitive responses', which recipients generate as they receive and reflect upon persuasive communications.

cognitive restriction a capability loss in group tasks that involve idea generation, which occurs when an idea mentioned by another group member makes people focus on the particular category this idea belongs to, at the expense of generating ideas from other categories.

cognitive stimulation a capability gain in group tasks that involve idea generation, which occurs when an idea mentioned by another group member stimulates a cognitive category one would otherwise not have thought of.

cognitive style people with an analytic style focus on the main element within information that they are processing; people with a holistic style focus on the relations between the different elements in information that they are processing.

cohesion the force that binds members to the group.

collective violence instrumental use of violence by people who identify themselves as members of a group against another group in order to achieve political, economic or social objectives.

common ingroup identity model this model seeks to reduce bias between groups by changing the nature of categorization from ingroups versus outgroups to a single, more inclusive identity. The model harnesses the forces of ingroup favouritism to reduce bias and promote helping.

communal relationship refers to an interpersonal association between individuals who are more concerned with what their partner gets rather than what they themselves receive, or relationships in which people's primary concern is being responsive to the other person's needs.

companionate love refers to the feelings of intimacy and affection we feel for another person when we care deeply for the person but do not necessarily experience passion or arousal in his or her presence.

compliance a particular kind of response whereby the target of influence acquiesces to a request from the source of influence.

The term is also used, more generally, to refer to change in public behaviour to match a norm, without corresponding change on a private level.

confederate an accomplice or assistant of the experimenter who is ostensibly another participant but who in fact plays a prescribed role in the experiment.

configural model a holistic approach to impression formation, implying that social perceivers actively construct deeper meanings out of the bits of information that they receive about other people.

Conflict Tactics Scales (CTS) instrument for measuring intimate partner violence by collecting self-reports of perpetration and/or victimization.

conformity see *majority influence*.

consensus information evidence relating to how different actors behave towards the same object.

consistency a behavioural style indicating that the same position is maintained across time; seen as central to minority influence.

consistency information evidence relating to how an actor's behaviour towards an object varies across different situations and times.

consistency theories a group of theories (see balance theory, cognitive dissonance theory) proposing that people prefer congruence or consistency among their various cognitions, especially among their beliefs, values, and attitudes.

construct an abstract theoretical concept (such as social influence).

construct validity the validity of the assumption that independent and dependent variables adequately capture the abstract variables (constructs) they are supposed to represent.

contact hypothesis intergroup contact will reduce prejudice if it (1) has acquaintance potential; (2) takes place under conditions of equal status; (3) involves cooperation towards a common goal; and (4) takes place in a supportive normative climate.

contingency approaches emphasize situational factors in the study of leadership (e.g. task or follower characteristics) and how these moderate the relationship between leader traits or leadership behaviours and leadership effectiveness.

continuum model of impression formation views impression formation as a process going from category-based evaluations at one end of the continuum to individuated responses at the other, dependent on the interplay of motivational and attentional factors.

control group a group of participants who are typically not exposed to the independent variable(s) used in experimental research.

controlled process a process that is intentional, under the individual's volitional control, effortful and entailing conscious awareness.

convergent validity established by showing that different measures of the same construct (e.g. self-report, implicit, observation) are significantly associated with each other.

conversion a change in private response after exposure to influence by others; internalized change; a change in the way one structures an aspect of reality.

coordination losses describe the diminished performance of a group if it fails to coordinate the contributions of its individual members in an optimal manner.

correspondence bias the proposed tendency to infer a personal disposition corresponding to observed behaviour even when the behaviour was determined by the situation.

correspondent inference theory proposes that observers infer correspondent intentions and dispositions for observed intentional behaviour under certain circumstances.

counterattitudinal behaviour behaviour (usually induced by monetary incentives or threats) which is inconsistent with the actor's attitude or beliefs.

covariation theory proposes that observers work out the causes of behaviour by collecting data about comparison cases. Causality is attributed to the person, entity or situation depending on which of these factors covaries with the observed effect.

cover story a false but supposedly plausible explanation of the purpose of an experiment; the intention is to limit the operation of demand characteristics.

crisis in social psychology a crisis of confidence among social psychologists that started in the late 1960s and was overcome in subsequent decades. During the crisis years, social psychologists questioned the values, the methods and the scientific status of their discipline.

cross-cultural replication a test of whether the results of a study are the same if it is repeated as exactly as possible in another cultural context.

cultural masculinity–femininity the extent to which gender roles in a nation are seen as differentiated (masculinity) or similar (femininity).

culture a social system that is characterized by the shared meanings that are attributed to people and events by its members.

cyberbullying involves the use of modern technology, such as computers, mobile phones or other electronic devices to inflict intentional harm on others.

debriefing the practice of explaining to participants the purpose of the experiment in which they have just participated, and answering any questions the participants may have.

decategorization recommends reducing the salience of intergroup boundaries through highly personalized contact; attention to idiosyncratic rather than category-based information about outgroup members should, over time, reduce the usefulness of the category, resulting in generalized prejudice reduction.

deindividuation a state in which individuals are deprived of their sense of individual identity, and are more likely to behave in an extreme manner, often antisocially and violating norms.

demand characteristics cues that are perceived as telling participants how they are expected to behave or respond in a research setting; that is, cues that 'demand' a certain sort of response.

dependent variable   the variable that is expected to change as a function of changes in the independent variable. Measured changes in the dependent variable are seen as 'dependent on' manipulated changes in the independent variable.

depressive realism   the idea that depressed people's interpretations of reality are more accurate than those of non-depressed people.

derogation of alternatives   the tendency of romantically involved individuals, as compared to singles, to give lower attractiveness ratings to attractive opposite-sex others.

desired selves   in contrast to our actual self (i.e. who we believe we are) our desired selves contain our potential (possible selves), as well as the wishes and aspirations (ideal self), and the duties and obligations (ought self) that we, or significant others, hold for us.

diffusion of responsibility   the process by which responsibility is divided between the number of bystanders present; as more people are present in an emergency, responsibility is diffused between them and each individual bystander feels increasingly less responsible than if they were alone.

direct reinforcement   experience of positive consequences of aggressive behaviour (e.g. status gain among peers) that increases the probability of future aggressive acts.

disclosure reciprocity   people tend to match each other's level of self-disclosure.

discounting principle   the presence of a causal factor working towards an observed effect implies that other potential factors are less influential. The converse of the *augmenting principle*.

discourse analysis   a family of methods for analysing talk and texts, with the goal of revealing how people make sense of their everyday worlds.

dispensability effect   a reduction in group members' task-related effort because their individual contribution seems to have little impact on group performance.

displaced aggression   tendency to respond to frustration with an aggressive response directed not at the original source of the frustration but at an unrelated, more easily accessible target.

display rules   cultural understandings as to whether emotions should be expressed openly.

dissociation model   a model that proposes that two different processes can occur independently, and that one does not inevitably follow from the other (e.g. Devine's theoretical model that proposes a dissociation between automatic and controlled processes in stereotyping).

distinctiveness information   evidence relating to how an actor responds to different objects (or 'entities') under similar circumstances.

distraction   while listening to a persuasive communication, individuals are distracted by having to perform an irrelevant activity or by experiencing sensory stimulation irrelevant to the message.

door-in-the-face technique   compliance technique in which the requester begins with an extreme request that is almost always refused, then retreats to a more moderate request, which he or she had in mind all along (also known as a 'reciprocal concessions' procedure).

dual-process theories of persuasion   theories of persuasion postulating two modes of information processing, systematic and non-systematic. Modes differ in the extent to which individuals engage in content-relevant thoughts and critical evaluation of the arguments contained in a message.

eco-cultural theory   a theory that proposes that different forms of culture have arisen as adaptations to differing environmental challenges to survival.

ego depletion   a temporary reduction of one's self-regulatory capacities due to restricted energy resources after sustained self-control efforts.

ego-defensive function   when attitudes help to protect our self-esteem.

elaboration   refers to the extent to which a person thinks about the issue-relevant arguments contained in a message.

elaboration likelihood model (ELM)   attitude change to persuasive communications is mediated by either central or peripheral processing; elaboration denotes the extent to which a person thinks about the issue-relevant arguments contained in a message.

embeddedness versus autonomy values   characteristic of a culture in which relations with one's long-term membership groups are prioritized, rather than emotional and intellectual separateness from others.

emotional contagion   the transfer of moods and emotions among people in a group.

empathic concern   an emotional state consisting of emotions such as compassion, warmth and concern for another person.

empathy   the experience of understanding or sharing the emotional state of another person.

encoding   the way in which we translate what we see into a digestible format to be stored in the mind.

entitativity   the degree to which a collection of people is perceived as being bonded together in a coherent unit.

equity theory   a theory that seeks to explain relationship satisfaction in terms of perceptions of fair versus unfair distributions of resources within interpersonal relationships.

ethnocentrism   the tendency to judge ingroup attributes as superior to those of the outgroup and, more generally, to judge outgroups from an ingroup perspective.

eureka effect   describes the situation when the correct solution to a problem, once it is found, is immediately recognized as being correct by group members.

European Association of Social Psychology   an association formed by European researchers in 1966 to further social psychology in Europe (originally named the European Association of Experimental Social Psychology).

evaluation apprehension   a learned response to the presence of others when performing a task, whereby the performer experiences arousal when anticipating evaluation by these others (can affect social facilitation, and also helping behaviour; see Chapter 10).

evaluative conditioning changes the liking for a stimulus by repeatedly pairing it with another more polarized positive or negative stimulus.

evolutionary psychology an approach that explains human behaviour and preferences based on their 'reproductive value'; that is, their value in producing offspring.

exchange relationship refers to an interpersonal association between individuals who are concerned with what their partner gets and what they themselves receive to ensure equitable benefits.

excitation transfer theory transfer of neutral physiological arousal onto arousal resulting from frustration, thus augmenting negative affect and enhancing the strength of an aggressive response.

expectation states theory argues that status differences within a group result from different expectations that group members have about each other.

experiment a method in which the researcher deliberately introduces some change into a setting to examine the consequences of that change.

experimental confound when an independent variable incorporates two or more potentially separable components it is a confounded variable. When an independent variable is confounded, the researcher's ability to draw causal inferences is seriously compromised.

experimental group a group of participants allocated to the 'experimental' condition of the experiment; that is, the condition in which participants are exposed to that level of the independent variable that is predicted to influence their thoughts, feelings or behaviour.

experimental scenario the 'package' within which an experiment is presented to participants: in field experiments it is, ideally, something that happens naturally; in laboratory experiments it is important to devise a scenario that strikes the participant as realistic and involving.

experimenter expectancy effects effects produced unintentionally by the experimenter that increase the likelihood that participants will confirm the experimenter's hypothesis.

explicit measures of attitude measures that directly ask respondents to think about and report an attitude.

extended contact hypothesis mere knowledge that an ingroup member has a close relationship with an outgroup member can improve outgroup attitudes.

external validity refers to the generalizability of research findings to settings and populations other than those involved in the research.

factorial experiment an experiment in which two or more independent variables are manipulated within the same design.

false consensus bias the assumption that other people generally share one's own personal attitudes and opinions.

field experiment a true randomized experiment conducted in a natural setting.

field theory a framework adopted by Kurt Lewin which represented the individual as an element in a larger system of social forces.

foot-in-the-door technique compliance technique in which the requester first asks for a small favour that is almost certain to be granted, then follows this up with a request for a larger, related favour.

forgiveness forgiveness is defined as a prosocial motivational change toward the offender, despite the offender's hurtful behaviour.

frustration–aggression hypothesis assumes that frustration – that is, blockage of a goal-directed activity – increases the likelihood of aggressive behaviour.

general aggression model (GAM) integrative framework explaining how personal and situational input variables lead to aggressive behaviour via cognitive appraisal and negative affective arousal.

geographic regions approach method for testing the heat hypothesis by comparing violence rates in cooler and hotter climates.

goal a positively valued behavioural end-state that encompasses the purposeful drive/motivation to engage in a behaviour/action/judgement.

goal dependent where an outcome is conditional upon a specific goal being in place (e.g. goal-dependent automatic stereotype activation).

group a group exists when two or more individuals define themselves as members of a group.

group commitment a psychological bond of a group member with the group and its goals including the desire to maintain group membership.

group composition specifies how certain characteristics are distributed within a group.

group emotions emotions experienced as members of social groups rather than as individuals, reflecting appraisals of events in terms of group level concerns and coping resources.

group identification the degree to which people see themselves in terms of a group membership (group-level self-definition) and the degree of value and emotional attachment to the group (group-level self-investment).

group leadership influencing, motivating or enabling (oneself and) others to contribute towards the effectiveness and viability of work groups.

group learning a generic term for several learning processes that can only occur if several people work interactively on the same task.

group performance management the sum of activities aimed at maximizing (or improving) the group-specific component of group performance.

group polarization tendency to make decisions that are more extreme than the average of group members' initial positions, in the direction already favoured by the group.

group socialization the efforts of the group to assimilate new members to existing group norms and practices.

group synchronization the sum of activities aimed at optimizing the collaborative generation, modification and integration of individual contributions in a group.

group task types group tasks are distinguished depending on whether the task is divisible between group members, whether the quality or quantity of the output is relevant, and how individual contributions are related to the group's performance.

groupthink a syndrome of poor group decision-making in which members of a cohesive ingroup strive for unanimity at the expense of a realistic appraisal of alternative courses of action.

group-to-group transfer a group learning process whereby a *particular* group's capability to perform a group task improves as result of social interaction between its group members during repeated collective task performance.

group-to-individual transfer a group learning process whereby a group member's ability to perform a task *alone* improves as a result of social interaction between group members during repeated collective task performance.

group-to-individual-in-group transfer a group learning process whereby a group member's ability to perform a task *within groups* improves as a result of social interaction between group members during repeated collective task performance.

habituation process whereby the ability of a stimulus to elicit arousal becomes weaker with each consecutive presentation.

heat hypothesis hypothesis that aggression increases with higher temperatures.

helping behaviour actions that are intended to provide some benefit to or improve the well-being of others.

heuristic a well-used, non-optimal rule of thumb used to arrive at a judgement that is effective in many but not all cases; stereotypes are often said to function as heuristics.

heuristic processing assessing the validity of a communication through reliance on heuristics; that is, simple rules like 'statistics don't lie', 'experts can be trusted', 'consensus implies correctness', rather than through evaluation of arguments.

heuristic–systematic model (HSM) attitude change to persuasive communications is mediated by heuristic and/or systematic processing: when motivation and ability are high, systematic processing is likely; when they are low, individuals rely on heuristic cues.

hidden profile a group decision situation in which information is distributed among group members such that no individual group member can detect the best solution based on his or her own information.

hierarchy versus egalitarianism values characteristic of a culture in which inequality is accepted and deference is given to one's seniors, rather than granting equality to all people.

hormones higher levels of testosterone and lower levels of cortisol have been linked to aggression, but they need to be considered in combination with environmental influences.

hostile aggression aggressive behaviour motivated by the desire to express anger and hostile feelings.

hostile attribution bias tendency to attribute hostile intentions to a person who has caused damage when it is unclear whether or not the damage was caused accidentally or on purpose.

hypothesis a prediction derived from a theory concerning the relationship between variables.

identity negotiation a process by which we establish who we are through mutual give-and-take interactions with others.

illusory correlation effect the tendency to perceive a relationship that does not actually exist, or to perceive one that does exist as stronger than it actually is; in group terms the erroneous tendency to associate one group more with one stereotypic or evaluative dimension than another.

implementation intentions 'if–then' plans that specify a behaviour that one will need to perform in order to achieve a goal, and the context in which the behaviour will occur.

implicit egotism nonconscious or automatic positive evaluation of self-associated objects.

implicit goal operation the process whereby a goal that enables people to regulate responses (e.g. to overcome stereotyping) is engaged without conscious awareness.

implicit measures measures of constructs such as attitudes and stereotypes that are derived from the way respondents behave (such as how long they take to make a decision or to answer a question) rather than from the content of their answers to explicit questions about these constructs. They are a class of unobtrusive measures.

implicit measures of attitude measures that assess spontaneous evaluative associations with an object, without relying on a verbal report.

implicit personality theory an integrated set of ideas held by a social perceiver about how different traits tend to be organized within a person.

implicit self-esteem the positivity of a person's automatic or nonconscious evaluation of him- or herself.

impulsive helping immediate, non-deliberative form of helping that does not appear to involve a conscious decision-making process, and in which the helper does not attend to the presence of other bystanders.

independent variable the variable that an experimenter manipulates or modifies in order to examine the effect on one or more dependent variables.

independent versus interdependent self while the independent self emphasizes autonomy and individualism and defines the self via internal attributes like traits, an interdependent self stresses the connection to others and defines the self in terms of relationships with others.

individual capability gains and losses improvements or impairments in individual group members' ability to successfully perform a task due to social interaction within the group.

individualism–collectivism individualist nations are those in which people describe themselves in ways that emphasize their autonomy from others; collectivist nations are those in which people describe themselves in ways that emphasize their links with others.

individual-to-individual transfer individual learning processes whereby a group member's ability to perform a task on their own improves as a result of repeated individual task performance.

individuating information information about a person's personal characteristics (not normally derived from a particular category membership).

informational influence influence based on accepting the information obtained from others as evidence about reality.

ingroup bias behaviours or evaluations that favour the ingroup over the outgroup; ingroup favouritism treats the ingroup more positively, outgroup derogation treats the outgroup less positively (e.g. in giving fewer rewards) or more negatively (e.g. in giving punishments).

ingroup reappraisal realization that ingroup norms, customs and lifestyles are not inherently superior to those of outgroups; this process is implicated in the generalization of positive contact effects to other outgroups.

initiation the role transition of entry into a group, often accompanied by some ritual.

innovation see *minority influence*.

instrumental aggression aggressive behaviour performed to reach a particular goal, as a means to an end.

interaction effect a term used when the combination of two (or more) independent variables in a factorial experiment yields an effect that differs from the sum of the main effects.

intergroup aggression aggressive encounters between groups or aggression based on group membership rather than individual characteristics, such as football hooliganism.

intergroup anxiety a negative affective state experienced when anticipating future, or experiencing actual, contact with an outgroup member, stemming from the expectation of negative consequences for oneself during intergroup interactions.

internal validity refers to the validity of the inference that changes in the independent variable result in changes in the dependent variable.

Internet experiment an experiment that is accessed via the Internet; participants access the experiment via the web, receive instructions and questions on their computer screen and provide responses via their keyboard or touch screen.

interpersonal aggression aggressive behaviour between individuals rather than groups.

interpersonal cohesion cohesion based on liking of the group and its members.

intimate partner violence perpetration or threat of an act of physical violence within the context of a dating or marital relationship.

intrinsic motivation behaviour is said to be intrinsically motivated if people perform it because they enjoy it. This enjoyment is sufficient to produce the behaviour and no external reward is required. In fact, external rewards (e.g. financial contributions) are likely to reduce intrinsic motivation.

introspection the process by which one observes and examines one's internal states (mental and emotional) for behaving in a certain way.

investments the level of resources (time, emotional involvement, money, self-disclosure and so on) put into a relationship, which increases the costs of withdrawing from the relationship.

jigsaw classroom a cooperative teaching method designed to reduce prejudice in diverse classrooms.

kin selection (also known as *inclusive fitness theory*) proposes that we have evolved to favour people who are genetically related to us, and are more likely to help close relatives (kin) than strangers.

Köhler effect a motivation gain in groups which involves weaker group members working harder than they would do individually in order to avoid being responsible for a weak group performance.

laboratory experiment a study, conducted in the laboratory, in which the researcher deliberately introduces some change into a setting, while holding all other factors constant, to examine the consequences of that change.

laissez-faire leaders leaders who engage in 'non-leadership'; that is, avoid making decisions, hesitate in taking action and are often absent when needed.

leader traits relatively stable personal characteristics (e.g. personality, intelligence, motivational dispositions) which are thought to predict leader emergence and leadership effectiveness.

leaderless groups groups with no appointed leader but which display effective leadership behaviours which are infused by the group members themselves (shared leadership) and/or by agents external to the group.

leadership behaviour observable acts that are meant to influence, motivate or enable others to contribute towards the effectiveness of a work unit or organization.

leadership effectiveness the impact of leadership on the accomplishment of group and organizational objectives, on the behaviour, perceptions, attitudes, values, motivation or well-being of followers and peers, and on the accomplishments of those who lead.

leadership (in organizations) influencing, motivating or enabling others to contribute towards the effectiveness of work units and organizations.

leadership style a pattern of leadership behaviour which is repeatedly shown and evident across a variety of situations.

learned helplessness theory the proposal that depression results from learning that outcomes are not contingent on one's behaviour.

lexical decision task a cognitive measure of how quickly people classify stimuli as real words or nonsense words that enables researchers to assess if some categories of words are made more accessible as a result of an experimental manipulation/processing goal. Quicker responses to certain word categories indicate increased accessibility.

lowballing technique compliance to an initial attempt is followed by a more costly and less beneficial version of the same request.

main effect a term used to refer to the separate effects of each independent variable in a factorial experiment.

majority influence (conformity) social influence resulting from exposure to the opinions of a majority, or the majority of one's group.

manipulation check a measure of the effectiveness of the independent variable.

mastery versus harmony values characteristic of a culture in which achievement is sought and esteemed, rather than harmony with nature.

media violence–aggression link hypothesis that exposure to violent media contents makes media users more aggressive.

mediating variable a variable that mediates the relation between two other variables. Assume that independent variable X and dependent variable O are related. If a third variable Z is related to both X and O, and if the X–O relation disappears when we take the role of Z into account, then Z is said to mediate the relation between X and O.

mere exposure effect increase in liking for an object as a result of being repeatedly exposed to it.

meta-analysis a set of techniques for statistically integrating the results of independent studies of a given phenomenon, with a view to establishing whether the findings exhibit a pattern of relationships that is reliable across studies.

methodological individualism the assumption that collective action must be explained by showing how it results from individual decisions and behaviour; collective behaviour is seen as essentially behaviour of the individuals who form the collective.

minimal group paradigm a set of experimental procedures designed to create groups based on essentially arbitrary criteria (with no interaction within or between them, and with no knowledge of who else belongs to each group) whose members show intergroup discrimination.

minority influence (innovation) situation in which either an individual or a group in a numerical minority can influence the majority.

misattribution of arousal people mistakenly attribute part of their arousal to an external stimulus that is not the actual cause of their arousal.

MODE model a model of attitude–behaviour relations in which motivation and opportunity are necessary to make a deliberative consideration of available information,

modelling learning by imitation, observing a model being rewarded or punished for his or her behaviour.

motivation losses and gains decreases or increases in group members' motivation to contribute to group task performance.

multicomponent model of attitude a model of attitude that conceptualizes attitudes as summary evaluations that have cognitive, affective and behavioural antecedents.

mutual differentiation (or *categorization approach to improving intergroup relations*) recommends making group affiliations salient during contact to address negative intergroup relations directly and to foster generalization from the contact experience to the outgroup as a whole; members of the respective groups should have distinct but complementary roles.

naïve scientist model a metaphor for how social information is processed that likens social perceivers to academic researchers who formulate theories and use data to test hypotheses in order to predict and control behaviour.

nation-level factor analysis an analysis across many nations of data in which the mean response for each survey item for each nation is treated as the unit of analysis.

need for cognition an individual difference variable which differentiates people according to the extent to which they enjoy thinking about arguments contained in a communication.

need for cognitive closure refers to the desire of individuals for a definite answer to a question – any answer, as opposed to uncertainty; the need reflects an individual difference variable, but can also be situationally induced.

need to belong the intrinsic motivation to affiliate with others and be socially accepted.

negative interdependence a situation in which bonds between individuals or groups are characterized by conflicts of interests, often leading to antagonism or *realistic conflict*.

negative-state-relief model this model argues that human beings have an innate drive to reduce their own negative moods; helping behaviour can elevate mood – thus in this model people help for egoistic rather than altruistic reasons.

nominal group a number of individuals who perform a task individually and work independently of each other; nominal groups are used to determine the potential performance of groups.

normative influence influence based on conforming to the positive expectations of others: people avoid behaving in ways that will lead to social punishment or disapproval.

norms belief systems about how (not) to behave, that guide behaviour but without the force of laws, and reflect group members' shared expectations about typical or desirable activities.

obedience to authority complying with orders from a person of higher social status within a defined hierarchy or chain of command.

object appraisal function when attitudes help serve as an energy-saving device.

one-dimensional perspective on attitudes a perspective that perceives positive and negative elements as stored along a single dimension.

one-shot case study a research design in which observations are made on a group after some event has occurred or some manipulation has been introduced.

operationalization the way in which a theoretical construct is turned into a measurable dependent variable or a manipulable independent variable in a particular study.

outcome dependency a motivational objective in which participants believe they will later meet a target and work together on a jointly judged task; shown to lead to less stereotypical target impressions.

outgroup bias a tendency to favour the outgroup over the ingroup in terms of evaluations or reward allocations.

outgroup homogeneity effect a tendency to see the outgroup as more homogeneous than the ingroup.

over-justification effect providing external rewards for performance of a task, which individuals previously performed because they found it enjoyable, reduces individuals' liking for, and enjoyment of, the task.

participant a person who takes part in a psychological study.

participant observation a method of observation in which the researcher studies the target group or community from within, making careful records of what he or she observes.

passionate love a state of intense longing for union with another individual, usually characterized by intrusive thinking and preoccupation with the partner, idealization of the other and the desire to know the other as well as the desire to be known by the other.

peer nominations method for measuring (aggressive) behaviour by asking other people (e.g. classmates) to rate the aggressiveness of an individual.

perceived behavioural control the notion that behavioural prediction is affected by whether people believe that they can perform the relevant behaviour.

perceived partner responsiveness the perception that a relationship partner is responsive to our needs.

peripheral route to persuasion subsumes those persuasion processes that are not based on issue-relevant thinking (e.g. evaluative conditioning, heuristic processing).

peripheral trait a trait whose perceived presence does not significantly change the overall interpretation of a person's personality.

physical aggression behaviour that is intended to inflict physical harm on the target person.

pluralistic ignorance emergency bystanders look to others in reacting to the event; as each person fails to react, they look at non-reacting bystanders, and interpret the event as not requiring a response.

positive differentiation involves making the group positively different from a comparison outgroup on available dimensions of comparison (e.g. by means of more positive evaluations or reward allocations) (see also *ingroup bias*).

positive interdependence a situation in which there are positive bonds between individuals or groups characterized by cooperation, reciprocity and mutual benefits.

positive–negative asymmetry evidence that people show more ingroup bias when distributing positive rewards than punishment or penalties.

post-experimental enquiry a technique advocated by Orne (1962) for detecting the operation of demand characteristics. The participant is carefully interviewed after participation in an experiment, the object being to assess perceptions of the purpose of the experiment.

post-test only control group design an experimental design in which participants are randomly allocated to one of two groups; one group is exposed to the independent variable, another (the control group) is not.

post-traumatic stress disorder (PTSD) characteristic patterns of symptoms observed in survivors of traumatic experiences such as rape.

potential group performance (group potential) the performance that would have occurred if the members of a group had worked independently of each other and not as a group; a common benchmark to evaluate actual group performance.

power distance the extent to which hierarchy and deference are accepted within a nation.

prejudice an attitude or orientation towards a group (or its members) that devalues it directly *or indirectly*, often to the benefit of the self or own group.

primacy effect the tendency for earlier information to be more influential in social perception and interpretation.

priming activating one stimulus (e.g. bird) facilitates the subsequent processing of another related stimulus (e.g. wing, feather).

principle–implementation gap acceptance of racial equality in principle is accompanied by resistance to specific policies that would bring about such racial equality.

probabilistic contrast comparison of the frequency of an effect in the presence of a potential cause with its frequency in the absence of that cause.

probe reaction task a simple reaction time task that assesses residual attentional capacity, that is, the amount of attention that is left over from performing the primary task. This task does not take away attention from the primary task (it is not a resource depleting task).

production blocking a process loss typical of brainstorming tasks in face-to-face groups; since in a group only one person can speak at a time, the other group members cannot express their own ideas at the same time.

proportion of shared genes refers to the amount of genetic material shared by humans (and animals); humans have an almost identical proportion of shared genes with any randomly selected other human being.

prosocial behaviour   refers to behaviour defined by society as beneficial to other people; it excludes behaviour that is motivated by professional obligations, and may be driven by more selfish (egoistic) and/or more selfless (altruistic) motivations.

prosocial personality   an enduring tendency to think about the rights and welfare of others, to feel concern and empathy, and to act in a way that benefits them.

public goods game   participants are allocated tokens, and can then (secretly) decide how many to keep and how many to contribute to a public pot; contributing nothing is termed *free riding*.

quasi-experiment   an experiment in which participants are not randomly allocated to the different experimental conditions (typically because of factors beyond the control of the researcher).

quota sample   a sample that fills certain prespecified quotas and thereby reflects certain attributes of the population (such as age and sex) that are thought to be important to the issue being researched.

random allocation   (sometimes called *random assignment*) the process of allocating participants to groups (or conditions) in such a way that each participant has an equal chance of being assigned to each group.

reactance theory   reactance is an aversive state caused by restriction of an individual's freedom of choice over important behavioural outcomes. Reactance is assumed to motivate the individual to re-establish the restricted freedom.

reactivity   a measurement procedure is reactive if it alters the nature of what is being measured (i.e. if the behaviour observed or the verbal response recorded is partly or wholly determined by the participant's awareness that some aspect of his or her behaviour is being measured).

realistic conflict theory   a theory developed by Sherif that holds that conflict and competition between groups over valued resources can create intergroup hostility and prejudice.

rebound effect   where suppression attempts fail; used here to demonstrate how a suppressed stereotype returns to have an even greater impact upon one's judgements about a person from a stereotyped group.

recategorization   recommends replacing salient ingroup–outgroup distinctions at a subordinate level with a common ingroup identity at a superordinate level that includes both former ingroup and outgroup members.

reciprocal altruism   a theory designed to explain altruism towards strangers by proposing that helping non-kin may have evolved if the cost of helping another is offset by the likelihood of the return benefit.

referent informational influence   individuals identify with a particular group and conform to a prototypical group position.

reflected appraisals   inferences regarding others' appraisals of us that we gain by observing other peoples' reactions towards us.

relational aggression   behaviour that is intended to harm the target person through damaging his or her social relationships, for example negative comments behind the person's back.

relationship commitment   an individual's intent to maintain the relationship and to remain psychologically attached to it.

relationship superiority   the tendency of romantically involved individuals to perceive their own relationship as better than the average relationship.

relative deprivation   a resentful feeling that the self or ingroup is worse off than the other or outgroup.

reliability   the degree to which a measure is free from measurement error; a measure is reliable if it yields the same result on more than one occasion or when used by different individuals.

representativeness heuristic   a mental shortcut whereby instances are assigned to categories on the basis of how similar they are to the category in general.

Ringelmann effect   describes the finding that in physical tasks such as weight pulling, the average performance of individual group members decreases with increasing group size.

role   the behaviours expected of a person with a specific position in the group.

role transition   a change in the relation between a group member and a group.

salience   attention-grabbing property of objects or events depending on perceptual features such as vividness, perceiver sensitivity or some combination of the two.

sampling   the process of selecting a subset of members of a population with a view to describing the population from which they are taken.

scapegoat theory   a theory that holds that prejudice is due to aggression that is displaced towards members of an outgroup (scapegoats), because the group or set of circumstances that was the source of frustration is not within reach.

schema   a cognitive structure or mental representation comprising pre-digested information or knowledge about objects or people from specific categories, our expectancies about objects or groups, and what defines them.

self-assessment motive   striving to reach an accurate and objective understanding of the self.

self-awareness   a psychological state in which one's attention is directed at the self.

self-categorization theory   theory explaining how the process of categorizing oneself as a group member forms social identity and brings about various forms of both group (e.g. group polarization, majority–minority influence) and intergroup (e.g. intergroup discrimination) behaviours.

self-concept   the cognitive representation of our self-knowledge consisting of a sum total of all beliefs we have about ourselves. It gives coherence and meaning to one's experience, including one's relations to other people.

self-construals   a person's views and knowledge about him- or herself is shaped through an active construal process that plays out in interaction with the social environment. This process is motivated by how one would like to see oneself.

self-determination theory   a motivational theory that accounts for people's reasons for self-regulation: if self-regulation is motivated by external pressure it is effortful and can lead to psychological conflict. However, if self-regulation is freely chosen it is much more efficient without being depleting.

self-disclosure   verbally revealing information about oneself to another person.

self-efficacy   beliefs about one's ability to carry out certain actions required to attain a specific goal (e.g. that one is capable of following a diet, or to help someone).

self-enhancement   the motivation to enhance the positivity of our self-conceptions, often over what would be objectively warranted. This is achieved by way of a variety of different strategies (e.g. self-serving attributions, basking in reflected glory, positive self-presentations).

self-esteem   the overall evaluation that we have of ourselves along a positive–negative dimension.

self-esteem hypothesis   the prediction that ingroup bias will lead to an increase in group level self-esteem or satisfaction.

self-fulfilling prophecy   when an originally false expectation leads to its own confirmation. The social perceiver's initially incorrect beliefs about a target cause that target to act in ways that objectively confirm those beliefs.

self-handicapping   the tendency to engage in self-defeating behaviours in order to provide a subsequent excuse for failure and augment ability attributions in the case of success.

self-monitoring   an individual difference variable measuring the extent to which people vary their behaviour across social situations (low self-monitors) versus behaving consistently (high self-monitors).

self-perception theory   the theory assumes that when inner states are ambiguous, people can infer these states by observing their own behaviour.

self-presentation   a range of strategies that we adopt in order to shape what others think of us.

self-reference effect   the tendency to process and remember self-related information better than other information.

self-regulation   the process of controlling and directing one's behaviour in order to achieve desired thoughts, feelings, and goals.

self-schemas   mental structures that help us organize and guide the processing of self-related information.

self-serving attributional biases   motivated distortions of attribution that function to maintain or increase self-esteem.

self-verification   motivation to affirm firmly held self-beliefs, arising from a desire for stable and coherent self-views.

self-worth contingencies   domains – both internal (e.g. virtue) and external (e.g. power) – on which we stake our self-worth.

sexual aggression   forcing another person into sexual activities through a range of coercive strategies, such as threat or use of physical force, exploitation of the victim's inability to resist, or verbal pressure.

shared or team leadership   responsibility for leadership functions, the exercise of leadership behaviour and perceptions about leadership roles are shared among group members (sometimes including agents external to the team).

similarity–attraction effect   we like others who are similar to us; others who are like us.

simple random sample   a sample in which each member of the population has an equal chance of being selected and in which the selection of every possible combination of the desired number of members is equally likely.

social adjustment function   when attitudes help us identify with liked others.

social cognition   a large topic within social psychology concerned with understanding how we think about ourselves and other people and how the processes involved impact upon our judgements and behaviour in social contexts.

social comparison   a process of comparing oneself with others in order to evaluate one's own abilities and opinions.

social compensation   a motivation gain in groups that occurs if stronger group members increase their effort in order to compensate for weaker members' suboptimal performance.

social competition   a motivation gain in groups that occurs if the group members want to outperform each other during group tasks in which the individual contributions are identifiable.

social desirability   refers to the fact that research participants are likely to want to be seen in a positive light and may therefore adjust their responses or behaviour in order to avoid being negatively evaluated.

social dominance orientation   an individual difference variable that captures a desire for hierarchical group relations.

social facilitation   an improvement in the performance of well-learned/easy tasks and a worsening of performance of poorly-learned/difficult tasks due to the presence of members of the same species.

social identity   that part of our self-concept corresponding to group memberships, and the value and emotional significance attached to these memberships.

social influence   change of attitudes, beliefs, opinions, values, and behaviour, as a result of being exposed to other individuals' attitudes, beliefs, opinions, values, and behaviour.

social loafing   a motivation loss in groups that occurs when group members reduce their effort due to the fact that individual contributions to group performance are not identifiable.

social neuroscience   an interdisciplinary field devoted to understanding how biological systems implement social processes and behaviour.

social perception   the process of collecting and interpreting information about another person's individual characteristics.

social reality constraints   evidence that the outgroup is clearly better on a certain dimension can make ingroup bias on that dimension difficult to justify.

social support   a partner's responsiveness to another's needs.

socio-emotional behaviours   behaviours during group interactions that are directed at interpersonal relations.

sociometer theory   a theory that posits that our self-esteem functions as a signal of the degree to which we feel accepted or rejected by other people.

speaking hierarchy   hierarchy within a group based on who talks most.

staffing level   the degree to which the actual number of group members is similar to the ideal number of group members.

staircase model   describes the pathway to terrorism as a succession of steps explaining why out of large numbers of disaffected people in a society only very few end up committing terrorist acts.

status   evaluation of a role by the group in which a role is contained or defined.

steam boiler model   part of Konrad Lorenz's theory of aggression, assuming that aggressive energy is produced continuously within the organism and will burst out spontaneously unless released by an external stimulus.

stereotype   a cognitive structure that contains our knowledge, beliefs and expectancies about some human social group.

stereotype suppression   the act of trying to prevent an activated stereotype from impacting upon one's judgements about a person from a stereotyped group.

strong reciprocity   a human predisposition to cooperate with others and to punish those who defect, even when this behaviour cannot be justified in terms of self-interest, extended kinship or reciprocal altruism.

subliminal advertising   advertising slogans that are presented so briefly (or faintly) that they are below the threshold of awareness.

sucker effect   a motivation loss in groups that occurs when group members perceive or anticipate that other group members will lower their effort: to avoid being exploited, they reduce their effort themselves.

summation   perceivers add together pieces of information about a person; when other information is strongly positive, additional mildly positive information yields a more positive impression.

superordinate goals   goals that can only be achieved by two groups working together cooperatively, to mutual benefit.

survey research   a research strategy that involves interviewing (or administering a questionnaire to) a sample of respondents who are selected so as to be representative of the population from which they are drawn.

systematic processing   thorough, detailed processing of information (e.g. attention to the arguments contained in a persuasive communication); this kind of processing relies on ability and effort.

task behaviours   behaviours during group interactions that are directed at task completion.

task cohesion   cohesion based on attraction of group members to the group task.

team awareness   understanding of the ongoing activities of others which provides a context for one's own activity.

terror management theory   a theory that assumes that people cope with the fear of their own death by constructing worldviews that help to preserve their self-esteem.

terrorism   politically motivated violence, intended to spread fear and terror among members of a society in order to influence the decision-making or behaviour of political agents.

theory   a set of abstract concepts (i.e. constructs) together with propositions about how those constructs are related to one another.

theory of planned behaviour   an extension to the theory of reasoned action that includes the concept of perceived behavioural control.

theory of reasoned action   a model in which behaviour is predicted by behavioural intentions, which are determined by attitudes and subjective norms.

thought-listing   a measure of cognitive responses; message recipients are asked to list all the thoughts that occurred to them while being exposed to a persuasive message.

time periods approach   method for testing the heat hypothesis by comparing violence rates in the same region during cooler and hotter periods.

trait aggressiveness   denotes stable differences between individuals in the likelihood and intensity of aggressive behaviour.

transactional leaders   leaders who focus on the proper exchange of resources, who give followers something in exchange for something the leaders want.

transactive memory   a system of knowledge available to group members with shared awareness of each other's expertise, strengths and weaknesses.

transformational (charismatic) leaders   leaders who focus on aligning the group or organizational goals with the followers' needs and aspirations by developing an appealing vision (whereby organizational needs are placed above self-interest).

triangulation   the use of multiple methods and measures to research a given issue.

true randomized experiment   an experiment in which participants are allocated to the different conditions of the experiment on a random basis.

two-dimensional perspective on attitudes   a perspective that perceives positive and negative elements as stored along separate dimensions.

uncertainty avoidance   the extent to which a nation is averse to risk and uncertainty.

unobtrusive measures   (also called *non-reactive measures*) measures that the participant is not aware of, and which therefore cannot influence his or her behaviour.

utilitarian function   when attitudes help us maximize rewards and minimise costs.

validity   a measure is valid to the extent that it measures precisely what it is supposed to measure.

value-expressive function   when attitudes help express our values.

variable   the term used to refer to the measurable representation of a construct.

violence   behaviours carried out with intention to cause serious harm that involve the use or threat of physical force.

volunteerism   when individuals give time and effort willingly without expecting rewards.

weapons effect   finding that individuals who were previously frustrated showed more aggressive behaviour in the presence of weapons than in the presence of neutral objects.

whistle blowing   a specific form of disobedience, in which people report corruption or unethical practice within an organization.

willingness to sacrifice   the tendency to forego immediate self-interest to promote the well-being of the partner or the relationship.

working self-concept   subset of relevant self-knowledge that is activated and guides our behaviour in a given situation.

Name Index

Subject Index

Wiley-Blackwell is proud to be publishing the journals of the British Psychological Society:

▶ British Journal of Clinical Psychology

▶ British Journal of Developmental Psychology

▶ British Journal of Educational Psychology

▶ British Journal of Health Psychology

▶ British Journal of Mathematical and Statistical Psychology

▶ British Journal of Psychology

▶ British Journal of Social Psychology

▶ Journal of Neuropsychology

▶ Journal of Occupational and Organizational Psychology

▶ Legal and Criminological Psychology

▶ Psychology and Psychotherapy: Theory, Research and Practice

The British Psychological Society

wileyonlinelibrary.com/journal/BPS

The only series to
be approved by the
BRITISH
PSYCHOLOGICAL
SOCIETY

BPS Student Guides in Psychology

No other series bears the BPS seal of approval

BPS Student Guides are short, accessible texts on key skills or the core elements of a degree, designed with the needs of students in mind.

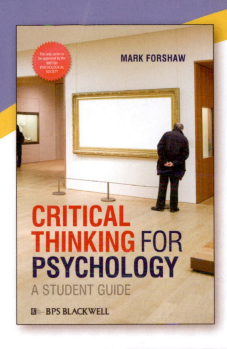

MARK FORSHAW

CRITICAL THINKING FOR PSYCHOLOGY
A STUDENT GUIDE

BPS BLACKWELL

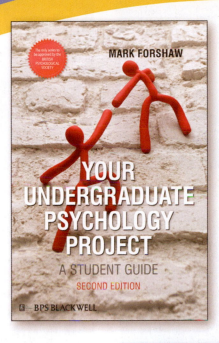

MARK FORSHAW

YOUR UNDERGRADUATE PSYCHOLOGY PROJECT
A STUDENT GUIDE
SECOND EDITION

BPS BLACKWELL

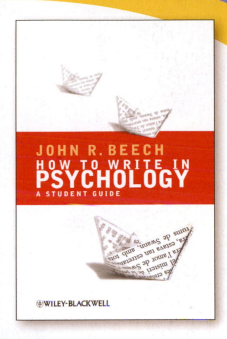

JOHN R. BEECH
HOW TO WRITE IN PSYCHOLOGY
A STUDENT GUIDE

WILEY-BLACKWELL

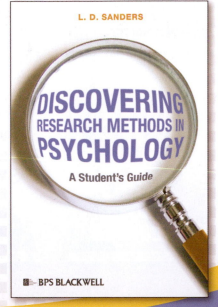

L. D. SANDERS

DISCOVERING RESEARCH METHODS IN PSYCHOLOGY
A Student's Guide

BPS BLACKWELL

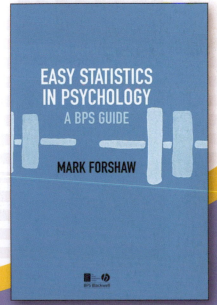

EASY STATISTICS IN PSYCHOLOGY
A BPS GUIDE
MARK FORSHAW

BPS Blackwell

For further information go to
www.wiley.com/go/bps

BPS BLACKWELL

WILEY-BLACKWELL

BPS Textbooks in Psychology

No other series bears the BPS seal of approval

Refreshingly written to consider more than Northern American research, this series is the first to give a truly international perspective. Every title fully complies with the BPS syllabus in the topic.

The only series to be approved by the BRITISH PSYCHOLOGICAL SOCIETY

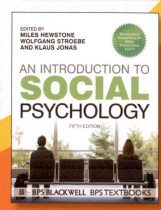

For further information go to
www.wiley.com/go/bps

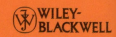